SIXTH EDITION

W9-BVC-918

Childhood and Adolescence

VOYAGES IN DEVELOPMENT

SPENCER A. RATHUS

THE COLLEGE OF NEW JERSEY

CENGAGE
Learning®

Australia • Brazil • Mexico • Singapore • United Kingdom • United States

CENGAGE
Learning·

Childhood and Adolescence: Voyages in Development, **Sixth Edition**

Spencer A. Rathus

Product Director: Jon-David Hague

Product Manager: Melissa Gena

Associate Content Developers: Sean Cronin and Adrienne McCrory

Marketing Manager: James Finlay

Senior Content Project Manager: Christy Frame

Senior Art Director: Vernon Boes

Senior Manufacturing Planner: Karen Hunt

Production and Composition: Graphic World Inc

Photo Researcher: Manojkiran Chander, Lumina Datamatics

Text Researcher: Venkatasubramanian Ramakrishnan, Lumina Datamatics

Copy Editor: Graphic World Inc

Text and Cover Designer: Lisa Delgado

Cover Image: Diego Cervo/Shutterstock

For product information and technology assistance, contact us at
Cengage Learning Customer & Sales Support, 1-800-354-9706

For permission to use material from this text or product,
submit all requests online at **www.cengage.com/permissions**
Further permissions questions can be e-mailed to
permissionrequest@cengage.com

Library of Congress Control Number: 2015957655

Student Edition:
ISBN: 978-1-305-50459-2

Loose-leaf Edition:
ISBN: 978-1-305-86188-6

Cengage Learning
20 Channel Center Street
Boston, MA 02210
USA

Cengage Learning is a leading provider of customized learning solutions with employees residing in nearly 40 different countries and sales in more than 125 countries around the world. Find your local representative at **www.cengage.com**.

Cengage Learning products are represented in Canada by Nelson Education, Ltd.

To learn more about Cengage Learning Solutions, visit **www.cengage.com**.

Purchase any of our products at your local college store or at our preferred online store **www.cengagebrain.com**.

Printed at CLDPC, USA, 03-20

To Allyn, Jordan,
Taylor, and March
(the child, not the month)

———————————————

About the Author

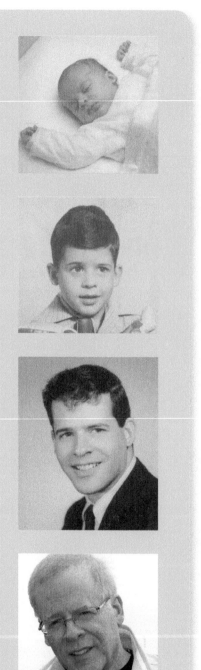

The author is shown at various stages of development in these four photgraphs

Spencer A. Rathus

Numerous personal experiences enter into Rathus's textbooks. For example, he was the first member of his family to go to college, and he found college textbooks to be cold and intimidating. Therefore, when his opportunity came to write college textbooks, he wanted them to be different—warm and encouraging, especially to students who were also the first generation in their families to be entering college. Rathus's first professional experience was in teaching high school English. Part of the task of the high school teacher is to motivate students and make learning fun. Through this experience he learned the importance of using humor and personal stories, which later became part of his textbook approach. Rathus wrote poetry and novels while he was an English teacher, and some of the poetry was published in poetry journals. The novels never saw the light of day (which is just as well, Rathus now admits in mock horror).

Rathus earned his Ph.D. in psychology and he entered clinical practice and teaching. He went on to publish research articles in journals such as *Adolescence, Behavior Therapy, Journal of Clinical Psychology, Behaviour Research and Therapy, Journal of Behavior Therapy and Experimental Psychiatry,* and *Criminology.* His research interests lie in the areas of human growth and development, psychological disorders, methods of therapy, and psychological assessment. Foremost among his research publications is the Rathus Assertiveness Schedule, which remains widely used in research and clinical practice. Rathus has since poured his energies into writing his textbooks, while teaching at Northeastern University, New York University, and currently at The College of New Jersey. His introductory psychology textbook, *Psychology: Concepts and Connections,* is soon to be in its eleventh edition.

Rathus is proud of his family. His wife, Lois, is a successful author and a professor of art at The College of New Jersey. Their daughter, Allyn, obtained her M.A. from NYU's Steinhardt School, and is teaching in New York City. Their daughter, Jordan, completed her MFA in fine arts at Columbia University and is launching her career as a video artist. Their youngest daughter, Taylor, can dance the pants off both of them. Taylor completed her BFA at NYU's Tisch program in musical theatre and is lighting up the stage. Rathus's eldest daughter, Jill, has become a psychologist and teaches at C. W. Post College of Long Island University.

Brief Contents

Contents

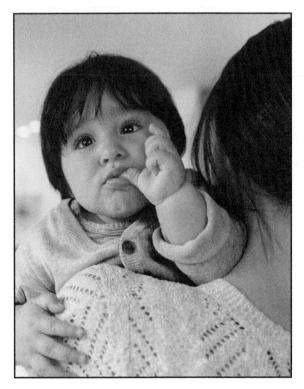

Part 2 Beginnings

2 Heredity and Conception 46

Truth or Fiction? 47

3 ## Prenatal Development 76
Truth or Fiction? 77

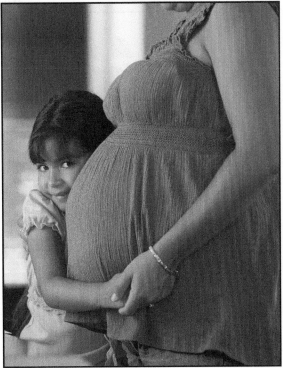

4 Birth and the Newborn Baby: In the New World 110

Truth or Fiction? **111**

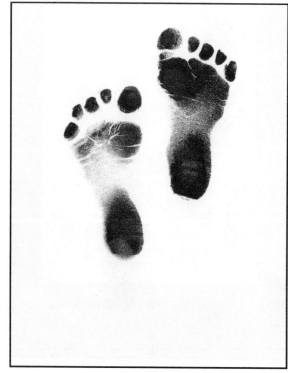

Part 3 Infancy

6   Infancy: Cognitive Development   182

7 # Infancy: Social and Emotional Development 214

Part 4 Early Childhood

Early Childhood: Physical Development   250

Truth or Fiction?   251

9 Early Childhood: Cognitive Development 276

Part 5 Middle Childhood

Part 6 Adolescence

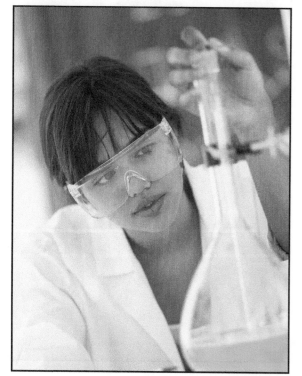

16 **Adolescence: Social and Emotional
Development   514**
Truth or Fiction?   515

My heart leaps up when I behold
A rainbow in the sky:
So was it when my life began;
So is it now I am a man;
So be it when I shall grow old,
Or let me die!
The Child is father of the Man;
And I could wish my days to be
Bound each to each by natural piety.
    William Wordsworth, 1802

Yes, the child is father of the man and, no less certainly, the mother of the woman. In our children, we have the making of ourselves. In children, parents have the most impetuous, comical, ingratiating, delightful, and—at times—infuriating versions of themselves. It is hard to believe, but true, that the babies we hold in our hands at birth may someday be larger and stronger, more talented, and more insightful than we are.

Portraying the Fascination of Children: Personal and Scientific

My goal in writing this book has been to capture the wonder of child development while portraying the field of development as the rigorous science it is. My approach is designed to help motivate students by showing them the joy of observing children. How can one hope to convey a true sense of development if one is blind to its marvels?

Childhood and Adolescence: Voyages in Development evolved from my scientific interest and research in human growth and development and also from my experiences with my own developing family. While my intention is to keep the tone of this text engaging and accessible, this book is rigorous in its reporting of research methods and science. On the other hand, the book is also "hands on"; it contains many applications, which range from preventing infant malnutrition and understanding what it is important to know about immunizations to helping children overcome enuresis and handling bullying in school.

Key Features

The sixth edition of *Childhood and Adolescence: Voyages in Development* contains the following key features:

- A thorough and rigorous update.
- **Concept Reviews:** visual presentations of complex developmental concepts.
- **A Closer Look—Diversity:** interesting and timely topics that show how culture—especially diverse cultural backgrounds—influences the many aspects of child development.

- **A Closer Look—Research:** features that offer expanded coverage of important research studies and also present research issues of great timeliness and interest.
- **A Closer Look—Real Life:** applications that allow readers to "take this book home with them" to apply what they are learning with children and adults in their own lives.

A Thorough Update

This is an exciting time to be studying child development. Every day, new research and new insights help us to better understand the mysteries and marvels of many aspects of development. Several hundred new citations refer the reader to research studies and broader documents, such as the American Academy of Pediatrics' latest recommendations on preventing sudden infant death syndrome (SIDS), the latest information on the use of C-sections, the federal government's most recent recommendations on childhood nutrition, and the most recent "Recommended Immunization Schedule for Persons Aged 0–6."

Chapter Previews

The sixth edition contains chapter preview sections that include *Major Topics, Features,* and *Truth or Fiction?* items. These previews help shape students' expectations and enhance the effectiveness of their learning by helping them create mental templates, or "advance organizers," into which they categorize the subject matter.

Chapter-by-Chapter Updates

Every chapter has undergone updating in terms of the coverage of topics and pedagogy. Following is a sampling of what is new:

What's New

Chapter 1	• Challenge to traditional views of "feminine" and "masculine" patterns of behavior, and what it means for behavior to be "gender-appropriate"
	• Revised discussion of safeguards for children in terms of education, sexual exploitation, and labor
	• Updated discussion of the psychoanalytic perspective on development
	• Discussion of the research finding that a majority of Americans believe that it is sometimes necessary to discipline children with a "good, hard spanking"
Chapter 2	• Updated discussion of the role of genetics (nature) in personal and social development
	• Updated discussions of chromosomal and genetic abnormalities and their effects
	• Updated discussion of prenatal testing for chromosomal and genetic problems
	• Updated discussion of epigenetics
	• Updated discussion of twin studies
	• Updated coverage of sex selection of fetuses in China

What's New

Chapter 3	• Revised discussion of the role of the nervous system in prenatal development • Updated discussion of the survival rate of preterm infants • Update on the use of Truvada to prevent HIV infection • Update on the (lack of) safety in maternal use of alcohol during pregnancy • Revision of effects of paternal smoking on prenatal development
Chapter 4	• Complete update of global infant and maternal mortality, as published by Save the Children • Update on the prevalence of use of C-sections • Revised section on methods of childbirth • Updated presentation of categories of postpartum mood problems, according to the fifth edition of the DSM of the American Psychiatric Association (DSM-5)
Chapter 5	• Update on the benefits and risks of breastfeeding versus bottle feeding • New coverage of wet nurses • Revised coverage of caregiver promotion of practice in development of infant locomotion • New coverage on preferential treatment of attractive infants
Chapter 6	• Updated coverage of infant-directed speech • New coverage of the emergentist theory of language development
Chapter 7	• New coverage of the "intergenerational transmission of attachment" • Revised coverage of the ethological view of attachment • Revised coverage of the effects of social deprivation on child development • Revised discussion of child abuse and neglect • Revised coverage of reasons that child abuse goes unreported • Revised coverage of sexual abuse of children • Updates on autism spectrum disorders, including problems with lack of pruning of unused synapses
Chapter 8	• Revised and updated coverage of handedness • Revised coverage of minor illness in children • Updated coverage of recommended immunizations
Chapter 9	• Revised and updated coverage of imaginary friends (virtual characters) • Updated coverage of the effects of educational television
Chapter 10	• Updated coverage of children's play • Updated coverage of prosocial behavior • Updated coverage of the effects of violent video games
Chapter 11	• Updated coverage of overweight and obesity in children: causes, effects, and weight control • Updated coverage of government guidelines for childhood nutrition: "Choose My Plate" • Updated coverage of causes and treatment of ADHD

Chapter 12	• Updated coverage of ways of stimulating children's memory • Updated coverage of children's metamemory • Updated coverage of the relationships between academic ability and creativity
Chapter 13	• Update on children's perspective-taking and the relation to social skills • Update on authoritative parenting and children's self-esteem • Update on the genetic component of self-esteem • Update on factors in children's popularity among peers • Update on the origins and treatment of conduct disorders • Update on the treatment of school phobia or school refusal
Chapter 14	• Revision of the concept that adolescence is a time of "storm and stress" • Updates on adolescent brain development • Updated coverage of adolescents and HIV • Update on anorexia nervosa and the female athlete triad • Revised section on substance use and substance use disorders, according to DSM-5 • New coverage of adolescents and "vaping"—smoking e-cigarettes
Chapter 15	• Updated coverage of the personal fable • Updated coverage of gender differences in cognitive abilities • Updated coverage of part-time adolescent employment
Chapter 16	• Updated coverage of adolescents and social networking • Revised coverage of development of sexual orientation • Updated coverage of adolescent sexual behavior • Revised coverage of changes in teenage pregnancy rates over the years, and ethnic differences in teenage pregnancy rates

What Carries Through from Edition to Edition

The sixth edition of *Childhood and Adolescence: Voyages in Development* continues to present cutting-edge topic coverage, emphasizing the latest findings and research in key areas. The text is organized chronologically. It begins with introductory theoretical material. It then traces the physical, cognitive, and social and emotional sequences that characterize development from infancy through early and middle childhood.

Concept Reviews

Concept Reviews are more than simple summaries. They take complex developmental concepts, such as theories of intelligence, and present them in dynamic layouts that readily communicate the key concepts and the relationships among concepts. Many of them include photographs and figures as well as text. Here is a sampling of the Concept Reviews found in *Childhood and Adolescence: Voyages in Development*:

- Concept Review 1.3: "Perspectives on Child Development"
- Concept Review 6.1: "The Six Substages of the Sensorimotor Stage, According to Piaget"

"A Closer Look—Diversity" Features

These features address the most challenging issues related to the way children are influenced by ethnic background, gender roles, socioeconomic status, and age in areas ranging from intellectual development to ethnic and racial identity. In many cases, cultural and ethnic factors affect the very survival of the child. This coverage helps students understand why parents of different backgrounds and genders rear their children in certain ways, why children from various backgrounds behave and think in different ways, and how the study of child development is enriched by addressing those differences. Here are some examples of such topics:

- Chapter 2: "LGBT Family Building"
- Chapter 3: "The Effects of Parents' Age on Children—Do Men Really Have All the Time in the World?"
- Chapter 4: "Maternal and Infant Mortality Around the World" (the latest information from Save the Children)

"A Closer Look—Research" Features

These research-focused features expand the book's treatment of the ways in which researchers carry out their work. Examples of topics include:

- Chapter 1: "Operant Conditioning of Vocalizations in Infants"
- Chapter 4: "Studying Visual Acuity in Neonates—How Well Can They See?"
- Chapter 5: "Strategies for Studying the Development of Shape Constancy"
- Chapter 6: "On Mirror Neurons and Really Early Childhood Imitation"

"A Closer Look—Real Life" Features

These features enable readers to "take the book home with them"—that is, to apply what they are learning to children and adults in their own lives. Examples of topics include:

- Chapter 3: "Selecting an Obstetrician"
- Chapter 8: "Ten Things You Need to Know About Childhood Immunizations"
- Chapter 9: "Helping Children Use Television Wisely" (including teaching children not to imitate the violence they observe in the media)

An Enhanced Pedagogical Package: PQ4R

PQ4R discourages students from believing that they are sponges who will automatically soak up the subject matter in the same way that sponges soak up water. The PQ4R method stimulates students to *actively* engage the subject matter. Students are encouraged to become *proactive* rather than *reactive*.

PQ4R is the acronym for *Preview, Question, Read, Reflect, Relate,* and *Review.* PQ4R is more than the standard built-in study guide. It goes well beyond the few pages of questions and exercises that are found at the ends of the chapters of many textbooks. It flows throughout every chapter. It begins and ends every chapter, and it accompanies the student page by page.

Preview

The first feature of the PQ4R method is Preview. Revised chapter previews include *Major Topics, Features,* and *Truth or Fiction?* items to help shape students' expectations. The previews enable students to create mental templates, or "advance organizers," into which they categorize the subject matter. The *Truth or Fiction?* items stimulate students to examine their own assumptions and prepare to delve into the subject matter by challenging folklore and common sense (which is often common *nonsense*). *Truth or Fiction Revisited* features throughout the chapter inform students whether they were correct in their assumptions. The *Major Topics* list outlines the material in the chapter, creating mental categories that guide students' reading.

Following is a sample of challenging *Truth or Fiction?* items from various chapters:

 You can carry the genes for a deadly illness and not become sick yourself.

 More children die from sudden infant death syndrome (SIDS) than from cancer, heart disease, pneumonia, child abuse, HIV/AIDS, cystic fibrosis, and muscular dystrophy combined.

 Infants need to have experience crawling before they develop fear of heights.

It is dangerous to awaken a sleepwalker.

Three-year-olds usually say "Daddy goed away" instead of "Daddy went away" because they *do* understand rules of grammar.

Children who watch 2–4 hours of television a day will see 8,000 murders and another 100,000 acts of violence by the time they have finished elementary school.

Question

Asking questions about the subject matter, before reading it in detail, is another feature of the PQ4R method. Reading these questions gives students goals; they attend class or read the text *in order to answer the questions*. Headings throughout the chapters are written as questions to help students use the PQ4R method most effectively. When students come to such a question, they can read the following material in order to answer it.

Read

The first R in the PQ4R method stands for Read. Although students will have to read for themselves, they are not alone. The text helps by providing:

- A *Major Topics* list that helps students organize the material in each chapter
- *Truth or Fiction?* items that stimulate students by challenging common knowledge and folklore
- Presentation of the subject matter in clear, stimulating prose
- A running glossary that defines key terms in the margin of the text, near where the terms first appear in the text
- Development of concepts in an orderly fashion so that new concepts build on previously presented concepts

I have chosen a writing style that is "personal." It speaks directly to the student and employs humor and personal anecdotes designed to motivate and stimulate students.

Reflect and Relate

Psychologists have shown that students better understand and remember subject matter when they relate it to their own lives. The "Reflect and Relate" (the second and third R in the PQ4R method) items promote that process of learning. Reflect items are also found in each Closer Look feature, guiding students to relate the content of the Closer Look feature to their own lives, and thereby aiding understanding and reinforcing remembering.

Review

The fourth R in PQ4R stands for Review. Regular reviews of the subject matter help students learn. Therefore, reviews follow all major sections in the text. These reviews contain fill-in-the-blank questions and "Reflect and Relate" items. Fill-in-the-blank exercises ask students to participate actively in the review process, not simply recognize correct answers as with multiple-choice questions. The chapter summaries provide end-of-chapter reviews in question-and-answer format, again prompting active learning.

In sum, we believe that our integrated pedagogical system gives students all the tools they need to comprehend the material and study for tests.

MindTap for Childhood and Adolescence

MindTap for Childhood and Adolescence: Voyages in Development engages and empowers students to pro-duce their best work—consistently. By seamlessly integrating course material with videos, activities, apps, and much more, MindTap creates a unique learning path that fosters increased comprehension and efficiency.

For students:

- MindTap delivers real-world relevance with activities and assignments that help students build critical thinking and analytic skills that will transfer to other courses and to their professional lives.
- MindTap helps students stay organized and efficient with a single destination that reflects what is important to the instructor, along with the tools students need to master the content.
- MindTap empowers and motivates students with information that shows where they stand at all times—both individually and compared to the highest performers in class.

Additionally, MindTap allows instructors to:

- Control what content students see and when they see it with a learning path that can be used as-is or matched to their syllabus exactly.
- Create a unique learning path of relevant readings and multimedia and activities that move students up the learning taxonomy from basic knowledge and comprehension to analysis, application, and critical thinking.
- Integrate their own content into the MindTap Reader using their own documents or pulling from sources like RSS feeds, YouTube videos, websites, Google Docs, and more.
- Use powerful analytics and reports that provide a snapshot of class progress, time in course, engagement, and completion.

In addition to the benefits of the platform, MindTap for Childhood and Adolescence: Voyages in Development includes:

- Investigate Development, a case-based simulation that enables students to observe, evaluate, and make decisions about human development and shows the implications of research on a personal level. Students interact with simulated case studies of milestones in a person's development, observing and analyzing audiovisual cues, consulting research, and making decisions. Instead of rote memorization of isolated concepts, Investigate Development compels students to think critically about research and brings human development to life.
- Formative assessments at the conclusion of each chapter.

- Interactive activities drawn from text features that foster student participation.
- Illustrative video embedded in the MindTap Reader to highlight key concepts for students.

Supplementary Materials

Online Instructor's Resource Manual

The *Instructor's Resource Manual* contains resources designed to streamline and maximize the effectiveness of course preparation. The contents include chapter overviews and outlines, learning objectives, critical thinking discussion questions, instructional goals, lecture expanders, video recommendations, and handouts.

Cengage Learning Testing Powered by Cognero

Cognero is a flexible, online system that allows you to author, edit, and manage test bank content as well as create multiple test versions in an instant. You can deliver tests from your school's learning management system, your classroom, or wherever you want. The test bank contains multiple-choice, completion, true/false, and essay questions for each chapter.

Online PowerPoint

These vibrant Microsoft® PowerPoint® lecture slides for each chapter assist you with your lecture by providing concept coverage using content directly from the textbook.

Acknowledgments

Reviewers

Many thanks to the reviewers who helped shape this book through the previous editions:

Jackie L. Adamson, *California State University–Fresno*
Laurel Anderson, *Palomar College*
Frank R. Asbury, *Valdosta State University*
Melissa Atkins, *Marshall University*
Elmida Baghdaserians, *Los Angeles Valley College*
Vivian G. Baglien, *Green River Community College*
Daniel R. Bellack, *Trident Technical College*
Pearl Susan Berman, *Indiana University of Pennsylvania*
Stephen Burgess, *Southwestern Oklahoma State University*
Kate Byerwalter, *Grand Rapids Community College*
D. Bruce Carter, *Syracuse University*
Elizabeth Cauffman, *Stanford Center on Adolescence*
Constance A. Crowley, *Union College*
Tim Croy, *Eastern Illinois University*
Kimberly Dechman, *George Mason University*
Roberta Dihoff, *Rowan University*
Rosanne Dlugosz, *Scottsdale Community College*
Ruth Doyle, *Casper College*
Adrienne K. Edlen, *Truman College*

Margaret Sutton Edmands, *University of Massachusetts–Boston*
Ann Englert, *California State Polytechnic University*
Cecilia Wharton Erlund, *University of Mary Hardin-Baylor*
JoAnn Farver, *University of Southern California*
Lawrence A. Fehr, *Widener University*
Edward Fernandes, *Barton College*
Karen Fischer, *Finger Lakes Community College*
Kim Fordham, *North Idaho College*
Lisa Fozio-Thielk, *Waubonsee Community College*
William Franklin, *California State University–Los Angeles*
Caroline Gee, *Saddleback College*
Hulda Goddy Goodson, *Palomar College*
Tresmaine R. Grimes, *Iona College*
Jill Haasch, *Elizabeth City State University*
Marissa J. Happ, *Waubonsee Community College*
Jane Hovland, *University of Minnesota–Duluth*
Cathleen Hunt, *Pennsylvania State University*
Betsy Jennings, *Chaffey College*
Patricia Kyle, *Southern Oregon University*
Charles LaBounty, *Hamline University*
Richard Langford, *California State University–Humboldt*
Sara Lawrence, *California State University–Northridge*
Karin Levine, *Creighton University*
Dennis A. Lichty, *Wayne State College*
Rebecca K. Loehrer, *Blinn College*
Frank Manis, *University of Southern California*
Jennifer Marshall, *Raymond Walters College*
Patricia M. Martin, *Onondaga Community College*
Laura Massey, *Montana State University–Bozeman*
Ashley E. Maynard, *University of Hawaii–Manoa*
Cathleen McGreal, *Michigan State University*
Julie McIntrye, *Russell Sage College*
Michael P. Meehan, *Maryville University of St. Louis*
Martha Mendez-Baldwin, *Manhattan College*
George Meyer, *Suffolk County Community College*
Ronald Mulson, *Hudson Valley Community College*
Robin Musselman, *Lehigh Carbon Community College*
Alan Y. Oda, *Azusa Pacific University*
Judy Payne, *Murray State University*
Sandra Portko, *Grand Valley State University*
John Prange, *Irvine Valley College*
Carol D. Raupp, *California State University–Bakersfield*
Mary Ann Ringquist, *University of Massachusetts–Boston*
Lee B. Ross, *Frostburg State University*
Julia Rux, *Georgia Perimeter College*
Alice A. Scharf-Matlick, *Iona College*
Debra Schwiesow, *Creighton University*
Whitney Scott, *California State University—Northridge*
Muriel Singer, *Kean University*
Linda Sperry, *Indiana State University*
Sarasue Spielman, *Oxnard College*
Lisa Swenson, *Pennsylvania State University–Hazleton*
Kimberley Taylor, *Spokane Falls Community College*
Elayne Thompson, *Harper College*
Naomi Wagner, *San Jose State University*
Shannon Welch, *University of Idaho*

Priscilla Wright, *Colorado Christian University*
Minhnoi C. Wroble Biglan, *Pennsylvania State University*
David N. Yarbrough, *University of Louisiana at Lafayette*
Glenna Zeak, *Penn State University*

With a group like this looking over your shoulder, it's difficult to make mistakes. But if any remain, I am solely responsible.

The book you hold in your hands would not be what it is without the insights and suggestions of my academic colleagues. It also owes much to the fine editorial and production team at Cengage and assembled by Cengage: Melissa Gena, Product Manager; Christy Frame, Content Project Manager; Nick Barrows, IP Project Manager; Charles Nichols, Content Digitization Project Manager; Sean Cronin and Adrienne McCrory in content development; James Finlay in marketing; and Vernon Boes, Senior Art Director.

Finally, I acknowledge the loving assistance of my family. My wife, Lois Fichner-Rathus, continues in her joint roles as supporter and critical reviewer. As shown in experiments with the visual cliff, infants will not usually go off the deep end. As a textbook author herself, and as an academic, Lois often prevents me from going off the deep end. My children I thank as the sources of stories—and stories and more stories. But mostly I thank them for being what they are: wellsprings of delight and fancy, occasional annoyances, and perpetual goads.

1

History, Theories, and Methods

TruthorFiction?

 During the Middle Ages in Europe, children were often treated as miniature adults. **p. 6**

 Children come into the world as "blank tablets"— without inborn differences in intelligence and abilities. **p. 6**

 Nail biting and smoking cigarettes are signs of conflict experienced during early childhood. **p. 9**

 Children should not be punished. **p. 16**

 Research with monkeys has helped psychologists understand the formation of attachment in humans. **p. 38**

 To learn how people develop over a lifetime, researchers have tracked some individuals for more than 50 years. **p. 39**

This book has a story to tell. An important story. A remarkable story. It is your story. It is about the remarkable journey you have already taken through childhood. It is about the unfolding of your life today. Billions have made this journey before. You have much in common with them. Yet you are unique, and things will happen to you, and because of you, that have never happened before.

Development of children is what this book is about. In a very real sense, we cannot hope to understand ourselves as adults—we cannot catch a glimpse of the journeys we have taken to arrive at this point in our lives—without understanding children.

In this chapter, we explore some of the reasons for studying development. We take a brief tour of the history of child development. It may surprise you that until relatively recent times, people were not particularly sensitive to the ways in which children differ from adults. Next, we examine some controversies in child development, such as whether there are distinct stages of development. We see how theories help illuminate our observations and how theories help point the way toward new observations. Then

PhotoDisc/First Light

3

we consider methods for the study of child development. Scientists have devised sophisticated methods for studying children, and the field of ethics helps us determine what types of research are deemed proper and what types are deemed improper.

1.1 What is Child Development? Coming to Terms With Terms

You have heard the word *child* all your life, so why bother to define it? We do so because words in common usage are frequently used inexactly. A **child** is a person experiencing the period of development from *infancy* to *puberty*—two other familiar words that are frequently used inexactly. The term **infancy** derives from Latin roots meaning "not speaking," and infancy is usually defined as the first 2 years of life, or the period of life before the development of *complex* speech. We stress the word *complex* because many children have a large vocabulary and use simple sentences before their second birthday.

Researchers commonly speak of two other periods of development that lie between infancy and adolescence: early childhood and middle childhood. Early childhood encompasses the ages from 2 to 5 years. Middle childhood generally is defined as the years from 6 to 12. In Western society, the beginning of this period usually is marked by the child's entry into first grade. To study development, we must also look further back to the origin of sperm and ova (egg cells), the process of conception, and the prenatal period. Yet we must also describe the mechanisms of heredity that give rise to traits in humans and other animals.

Development is the orderly appearance, over time, of physical structures, psychological traits, behaviors, and ways of adapting to the demands of life. The changes brought on by development are both *qualitative* and *quantitative*. Qualitative changes are changes in type or kind. Consider motor development. As we develop, we gain the abilities to lift our heads, sit up, crawl, stand, and walk. These changes are qualitative. However, within each of these qualitative changes are quantitative developments, or changes in *amount*. After babies begin to lift their heads, they lift them higher and higher. Soon after children walk, they begin to run. Then they gain the capacity to run faster.

Development occurs across many dimensions—biological, cognitive, social, emotional, and behavioral. Development is spurred by internal factors, such as genetics, and it is shaped by external factors, such as nutrition and culture.

The terms *growth* and *development* are not synonymous, although many people use them interchangeably. **Growth** is generally used to refer to changes in size or quantity, whereas development also refers to changes in quality. During the early days following conception, the fertilized egg cell develops rapidly. It divides repeatedly, and cells begin to take on specialized forms. However, it does not "grow" in that there is no gain in mass. Why? It has not yet become implanted in the uterus and is therefore without any external source of nourishment. Language development is the process by which the child's use of language becomes progressively more sophisticated and complex. Vocabulary growth, by contrast, consists of the accumulation of new words and their meanings.

Child development, then, is a field of study that tries to understand the processes that govern the appearance and growth of children's biological structures, psychological traits, behavior, understanding, and ways of adapting to the demands of life.

Professionals from many fields are interested in child development. They include psychologists, educators, anthropologists, sociologists, nurses, and medical researchers. Each brings his or her own brand of expertise to the quest for knowledge.

Motor Development This infant has just mastered the ability to pull herself up to a standing position. Soon she will be able to stand alone, and then she will begin to walk.

child A person undergoing the period of development from infancy through puberty.

infancy The period of very early childhood, characterized by lack of complex speech; the first 2 years after birth.

development The processes by which organisms unfold features and traits, grow, and become more complex and specialized in structure and function.

growth The processes by which organisms increase in size, weight, strength, and other traits as they develop.

Intellectual cross-fertilization enhances the skills of researchers in the field and enriches the lives of children.

Why Do Researchers Study Child Development?

An important motive for studying child development is curiosity—the desire to learn about children. Curiosity may be driven by the desire to answer questions about development that remain unresolved. It may also be driven by the desire to have fun. (Yes, children and the study of children can be fun.) There are other motives as well:

To Gain Insight into the Nature of Human Nature

For centuries, philosophers, scientists, and educators have argued over whether children are aggressive or loving, whether children are conscious and self-aware, whether they have a natural curiosity that demands to unravel the mysteries of the universe, or whether they merely react mechanically to environmental stimulation. The quest for answers has an impact on the lives of children, parents, educators, and others who interact with children.

To Gain Insight into the Origins of Adult Behavior

How do we explain the origins of empathy in adults? Of antisocial behavior? How do we explain the development of so-called "feminine" and "masculine" patterns of behavior? (If these patterns of behavior actually exist, do they represent the natural unfolding of genetic imperatives, societal expectations, or both?) And how do we explain the origins of special talents in writing, music, athletics, and math?

To Gain Insight into the Origins of Sex Differences and Gender Roles, and into the Effects of Culture on Development

How do gender roles—that is, culturally induced expectations for stereotypical feminine and masculine behavior—develop? Are there sex or gender differences in cognition and behavior? If so, how do they develop?

To Gain Insight into the Origins, Prevention, and Treatment of Developmental Problems

Fetal alcohol syndrome, PKU (see Chapter 2), SIDS (see Chapter 5), Down syndrome, autism, hyperactivity, dyslexia, child abuse—these are but a few of the buzzwords and terms that strike fear into parents and parents-to-be. A major focus in child development research is the search for the causes of such problems so that they can be prevented or treated.

To Optimize Conditions of Development

Most parents want to provide the best in nutrition and medical care for their children so that they will develop strong and healthy bodies. Parents want their infants to feel secure with them. They want to ensure that major transitions, such as the transition from the home to the school, will be as stress-free as possible. Researchers therefore strive to learn about issues such as:

- The effects of various foods and chemicals on the development of the embryo
- The effects of parent–infant interaction immediately following birth on bonds of attachment with children
- The effects of bottle feeding versus breastfeeding on mother–infant attachment and the baby's health

- The effects of day-care programs on parent–child bonds of attachment and on children's social and intellectual development
- The effects of various patterns of child rearing on the development of independence, competence, and social adjustment

What Views of Children Do We Find Throughout History?

In ancient times and in the Middle Ages, children often were viewed as innately evil, and discipline was harsh. Legally, medieval children in Europe were treated as property and servants. They could be sent to the monastery, married without consultation, or convicted of crimes. Children were nurtured until they were 7 years old, which was considered the "age of reason." Then they were expected to work alongside adults in the home and in the field. They ate, drank, and dressed as miniature adults.

TRUTH OR FICTION REVISITED: It is true that children were treated as miniature adults throughout most of the Middle Ages. (For example, for much of the Middle Ages, artists depicted children as small adults.) However, this meant only that more was expected of them, not that they were given more privileges.

The transition to the study of development in modern times is marked by the thinking of philosophers such as John Locke and Jean-Jacques Rousseau. The Englishman John Locke (1632–1704) believed that the child came into the world as a *tabula rasa*—a "blank tablet" or clean slate—that was written on by experience. Locke did not believe that inborn predispositions toward good or evil played an important role in the conduct of the child. Instead, he focused on the role of the environment or of experience. Locke believed that social approval and disapproval are powerful shapers of behavior. Jean-Jacques Rousseau (1712–1778), a Swiss–French philosopher, reversed Locke's stance. Rousseau argued that children are inherently good and that, if allowed to express their natural impulses, they will develop into generous and moral individuals.

TRUTH OR FICTION REVISITED: John Locke believed that children come into the world as "blank tablets"—without inborn differences in intelligence and talents. However, as we will see, there is research evidence that inborn factors—one's heredity—play a role in the development of intelligence and personality traits.

Erich Lessing/Art Resource, NY

A View of Children as Perceived in the 1600s Centuries ago, children were viewed as miniature adults. In this 17th-century painting, notice how the body proportions of the young princess (in the middle) are similar to those of her adult attendants.

During the Industrial Revolution, there was greater awareness of childhood as a special time of life. Still, children often labored in factories from dawn to dusk through the early years of the 20th century.

In the 20th century in the United States and many other developed nations, laws were passed to protect children from strenuous labor, to require that they attend school until a certain age, and to prevent them from getting married or being sexually exploited. But these safeguards are by no means universal. Nevertheless, in the United States, where children were once considered the property of parents, who could do with them as they wished, laws now protect children from the abuse and neglect of parents and other caretakers. Juvenile courts see that children who break the law receive fair and appropriate treatment in the criminal justice system.

A Young Child Laborer Children often worked long days in factories up through the early years of the 20th century. A number of cultures in the world today still use child labor.

Pioneers in the Study of Child Development

Various thoughts about child development coalesced into a field of scientific study in the 19th and early 20th centuries. Many individuals, including Charles Darwin, G. Stanley Hall, and Alfred Binet, contributed to the emerging field.

The Englishman Charles Darwin (1809–1882) is best known as the originator of the theory of evolution. But he also was one of the first observers to keep a *baby biography,* in which he described his infant son's behaviors in great detail. The American G. Stanley Hall (1844–1924) is credited with founding child development as an academic discipline. He adapted the questionnaire method for use with large groups of children so that he could study the "contents of children's minds." The Frenchman Alfred Binet (1857–1911), along with Theodore Simon (1872–1961), developed the first standardized intelligence test near the turn of the 20th century. The purpose of Binet's test was to identify public school children who were at risk of falling behind their peers in academic achievement.

By the beginning of the 20th century, child development had emerged as a scientific field of study. Within a short time, major theoretical views of the developing child had begun to emerge, proposed by such scientists as Arnold Gesell, Sigmund Freud, John B. Watson, and Jean Piaget. We next describe their theories of child development, as well as those of other theorists.

Section Review

1. A child is a person experiencing the period of development from infancy to _____.

2. _____ is the orderly appearance, over time, of structures, traits, and behaviors.

3. The word *growth* is generally used to refer to changes in size or quantity, whereas the term _____ also refers to changes in quality.

Reflect & Relate: Do you believe that children are "wild"? That children must be "tamed"? Do you see dangers (to children) in answering yes to either question? Explain.

1.2 Theories of Child Development

"Give me a dozen healthy infants, well-formed, and my own specified world to bring them up in, and I'll guarantee to train them to become any type of specialist I might suggest—doctor, lawyer, merchant, chief, and, yes, even beggar and thief, regardless of their talents, penchants, tendencies, abilities, vocations, and the race of their ancestors."

Watson, 1924, p. 82

behaviorism John B. Watson's view that a science or theory of development must study observable behavior only and investigate relationships between stimuli and responses.

John B. Watson, the founder of American **behaviorism**, viewed development in terms of learning. He generally agreed with Locke's view that children's ideas, preferences, and skills are shaped by experience. There continues to be a long-standing nature–nurture debate in the study of children. In his theoretical approach to understanding children, Watson came down on the side of nurture—the importance of the physical and social environments—found, for example, in parental training and approval. Watson's view turned upside down the history of approaches to understanding children. Nature, or the inherited, genetic characteristics of the child, had long been the more popular explanation of how children develop into who they are.

Four years after Watson sounded his call for the behavioral view, Arnold Gesell expressed the opposing idea that biological maturation was the main principle of development: "All things considered, the inevitability and surety of maturation are the most impressive characteristics of early development. It is the hereditary ballast which conserves and stabilizes growth of each individual infant" (Gesell, 1928, p. 378). Watson was talking about the behavior patterns that children develop, whereas Gesell was focusing largely on the physical aspects of growth and development. Still, the behavioral and maturational perspectives lie at opposite ends of the continuum of theories of development. Many observers fall into the trap of overemphasizing the importance of either nature or nurture; thus they risk of overlooking the ways in which nature and nurture interact. Just as a child's environments and experiences influence the development of his or her biological endowment, children often place themselves in environments that are harmonious with their personal characteristics. Children, for example, are influenced by teachers and by other students. Nevertheless, because of the traits they bring to school with them, some children may prefer to socialize with other children while other children may prefer to socialize with teachers. Still other children may prefer solitude.

What Are Theories of Child Development?

Child development is a scientific enterprise. Like other scientists, those who study development seek to describe, explain, predict, and influence the events they observe. When possible, descriptive terms and concepts are interwoven into **theories**. Theories are based on assumptions about behavior, such as Watson's assumption that training outweighs talents and abilities, or Gesell's assumption that the unfolding of maturational tendencies holds sway.

Theories enable us to derive explanations and predictions. For instance, a theory concerning the development of gender roles should allow us to predict how—and whether—children will acquire stereotypical feminine or masculine gender-typed behavior patterns. A broad theory of the development of gender roles might apply to children from different cultural and racial backgrounds and, perhaps, to children with gay male and lesbian sexual orientations as well as to children with a heterosexual orientation. If observations cannot be explained by or predicted from a theory, we may need to revise or replace the theory.

Theories also enable researchers to influence events, as in working better with parents, teachers, nurses, and children themselves to promote the welfare of children. Psychologists may summarize and interpret theory and research on the effects of day care to help day-care workers provide an optimal child-care environment. Teachers may use learning theory to help children learn to read and write. Let us consider various theoretical perspectives on child development.

What Is the Psychoanalytic Perspective on Child Development?

A number of theories fall within the psychoanalytic perspective. Each one owes its origin to Sigmund Freud and views children—and adults—as caught in conflict (Hergenhahn & Henley, 2014). Early in development, the conflict is between the child and the world outside. The expression of basic drives, such as sex and aggression, conflicts with parental expectations, social rules, moral codes, even laws.

theory A formulation of relationships underlying observed events. A theory involves assumptions and logically derived explanations and predictions.

However, the external limits—parental demands and social rules—are *internalized*; that is, they are brought inside. Once this happens, the conflict takes place between opposing *inner* forces. The child's observable behavior, thoughts, and feelings reflect the outcomes of these hidden battles.

In this section, we explore Freud's theory of **psychosexual development** and Erik Erikson's theory of psychosocial development. Each is a **stage theory** that sees children as developing through distinct periods of life. Each suggests that the child's experiences during early stages affect the child's emotional and social life then and later on.

Sigmund Freud's Theory of Psychosexual Development

Sigmund Freud (1856–1939) was a mass of contradictions. He has been both praised as the greatest thinker—or at least the greatest psychologist—of the 20th century and criticized as overrated. He preached liberal views on sexuality but was himself a model of sexual restraint. He invented a popular form of psychotherapy but experienced lifelong emotional problems, including migraine headaches, fainting under stress, hatred of the telephone, and an addiction to cigars. He smoked 20 cigars a day and could not or would not break the habit, even after he developed cancer of the jaw.

Freud focused on the emotional and social development of children and on the origins of psychological traits such as dependence, obsessive neatness, and vanity. Let us dive into Freud's theory. *Diving* is a good metaphor because Freud believed that most of the human mind lies beneath consciousness, like an iceberg. The children you observe do and say many things—cry, crawl, run, talk, build, play—but all this is the tip of the iceberg. And the tip of an iceberg is the smallest part of the iceberg. Freud theorized that people, because of their childhood experiences, are only vaguely aware of the ideas and impulses that occupy the greater depths of their minds.

Freud theorized three parts of the personality: the *id, ego,* and *superego*. The id is present at birth and is unconscious. It represents biological drives and demands instant gratification, as suggested by a baby's wailing. The ego, or the conscious sense of self, begins to develop when children learn to obtain gratification for themselves, without screaming or crying. The ego curbs the appetites of the id and makes plans that are in keeping with social conventions so that a person can find gratification yet avoid social disapproval. The superego develops throughout infancy and early childhood and brings inward the norms and morals of the child's caregivers and other members of the community. If the child misbehaves, the superego will flood him or her with guilt and shame.

According to Freud, childhood has five stages of psychosexual development: *oral, anal, phallic, latency,* and *genital.* If a child receives too little or too much gratification during a stage, the child can become *fixated* in that stage. For example, in the first stage, if the child is weaned early or breastfed too long, the child may become fixated on *oral* activities such as nail biting or smoking, or even show a "sharp tongue" or "biting wit."

Sigmund Freud Sigmund Freud is the originator of psychoanalytic theory. He proposed five stages of psychosexual development and emphasized the importance of biological factors in the development of personality.

TRUTH OR FICTION REVISITED: Sigmund Freud hypothesized that nail biting and smoking cigarettes are signs of conflict experienced during early childhood—in fact, during the so-called oral stage of development. However, there is actually no research evidence that nail biting and smoking cigarettes are signs of conflict experienced during early childhood, so we must—from a scientific perspective—consider Freud's belief to be fictional.

psychosexual development Freud's view that as children develop, they find sexual gratification through stimulating different parts of their bodies.

stage theory A theory of development characterized by hypothesizing the existence of distinct periods of life. Stages follow one another in an orderly sequence.

In the second stage, the *anal stage,* gratification is obtained through control and elimination of waste products. Excessively strict or permissive toilet training can lead to the development of so-called anal-retentive traits, such as perfectionism and neatness, or anal-expulsive traits, such as sloppiness and carelessness. In the third stage, the *phallic stage,* parent–child conflict may develop over masturbation, which many parents treat with punishment and threats. It is normal for children to develop strong sexual attachments to the parent of the other sex during the phallic stage and to begin to view the parent of the same sex as a rival.

Freud believed that by age 5 or 6, children enter a *latency stage* during which sexual feelings remain unconscious; children turn to schoolwork and typically prefer playmates of their own sex. The final stage of psychosexual development, the *genital stage,* begins with the biological changes that usher in adolescence. Adolescents

Concept Review 1.1

Comparison of Freud's and Erikson's Stages of Development

Age	Freud's Stages of Psychosexual Development	Erikson's Stages of Psychosocial Development
Birth to 1 year Photodisc/First Light	**Oral Stage.** Gratification derives from oral activities such as sucking. Fixation leads to development of oral traits such as dependence, depression, and gullibility.	**Trust versus Mistrust.** The developmental task is to come to trust the key caregivers, primarily the mother, and the environment. It is desirable for the infant to connect the environment with inner feelings of satisfaction and contentment.
About 1 to 3 years	**Anal Stage.** Gratification derives from anal activities involving elimination. Fixation leads to development of anal-retentive traits (e.g., excessive neatness) or anal-expulsive traits (e.g., sloppiness).	**Autonomy versus Shame and Doubt.** The developmental task is to gain the desire to make choices and the self-control to regulate one's behavior so that choices can be actualized.
About 3 to 6 years	**Phallic Stage.** Gratification derives from stimulation of the genital region. Fixation leads to development of phallic traits such as vanity.	**Initiative versus Guilt.** The developmental task is to add initiative—planning and attempting to achieve that which one has chosen. The preschooler is on the move and becomes proactive.
About 6 to 12 years Brand X Photography/Veer	**Latency Stage.** Sexual impulses are suppressed, allowing the child to focus on development of social and technological skills.	**Industry versus Inferiority.** The developmental task is to become absorbed in the development and implementation of skills, to master the basics of technology, and to become productive.

generally desire sexual gratification through intercourse with a member of the other sex. Freud believed that oral or anal stimulation, masturbation, and male–male or female–female sexual activity are immature forms of sexual conduct that reflect fixations at early stages of development.

Evaluation

Freud's theory has had much appeal and was a major contribution to modern thought on child development. His is a rich theory of development, explaining the childhood

Comparison of Freud's and Erikson's Stages of Development (continued)

Age	Freud's Stages of Psychosexual Development	Erikson's Stages of Psychosocial Development
Adolescence	**Genital Stage.** Sexual impulses reappear, with gratification sought through sexual relations with an adult of the other sex.	**Identity versus Role Diffusion.** The developmental task is to associate one's skills and social roles with the development of career goals. More broadly, the development of identity refers to a sense of who one is and what one believes in.
Young adulthood		**Intimacy versus Isolation.** The developmental task is to commit oneself to another person and to engage in a mature sexual love.
Middle adulthood		**Generativity versus Stagnation.** The developmental task is to appreciate the opportunity to "give back." Not only are generative people creative, but they also give encouragement and guidance to the younger generation, which may include their own children.
Late adulthood		**Ego Integrity versus Despair.** The developmental task is to achieve wisdom and dignity in the face of declining physical abilities. Ego integrity also means accepting the time and place of one's own life cycle.

Paul Hakimata/Alamy

Jon Erikson/The Image Works

origins of many traits and stimulating research on attachment, development of gender roles, and moral development. Freud's views about the anal stage have influenced child-care workers to recommend that toilet training not be started too early or handled punitively.

Yet Freud's work has been heavily criticized. For one thing, Freud developed his theory on the basis of contacts with patients (mostly women) who were experiencing emotional problems (Schultz & Schultz, 2012). He was also dealing with recollections of his patients' pasts, rather than observing children directly. Such recollections are subject to errors in memory—and to the suggestions of the person conducting the interview or the form of therapy.

Some of Freud's own disciples, including Erik Erikson and Karen Horney, believe that Freud placed too much emphasis on basic instincts and unconscious motives. They argue that people are motivated not only by drives such as sex and aggression but also by social relationships and conscious desires to achieve, to have aesthetic experiences, and to help others.

Courtesy of Renate Horney

Karen Horney

psychosocial development Erikson's theory, which emphasizes the importance of social relationships and conscious choice throughout the eight stages of development.

life crisis An internal conflict that attends each stage of psychosocial development. Positive resolution of early life crises sets the stage for positive resolution of subsequent life crises.

Erik Erikson's Theory of Psychosocial Development

Erik Erikson (1902–1994) modified and expanded Freud's theory. Erikson's theory, like Freud's, focuses on the development of the emotional life and psychological traits. But Erikson also focuses on the development of self-identity and argues that social relationships are more important than sexual or aggressive instincts. Therefore, Erikson speaks of **psychosocial development** rather than of *psychosexual development*. Furthermore, it seemed to Erikson that he had developed his own personality through a series of conscious and purposeful acts. Consequently, he places greater emphasis on the ego, or the sense of self.

Erikson (1963) extended Freud's five developmental stages to eight to include the changing concerns throughout adulthood. Rather than labeling his stages after parts of the body, Erikson labeled stages after the **life crises** that the child (and then the adult) might encounter during that stage. Erikson's stages are compared with Freud's in Concept Review 1.1 on pages 10–11.

Erikson proposed that social relationships and physical maturation give each stage its character. For example, the parent–child relationship and the infant's utter dependence and helplessness are responsible for the nature of the earliest stages of development. The 6-year-old's capacity to profit from the school setting reflects the cognitive capacities to learn to read and to understand the basics of math—along with the ability to sit still long enough to focus on schoolwork, by no means an easy task for many children, especially boys.

According to Erikson, as with Freud, early experiences affect future developments. With proper parental support early on, most children resolve early life crises productively. Successful resolution of each crisis bolsters their sense of identity—of who they are and what they stand for—and their expectation of future success.

Each stage in Erikson's theory carries a specific developmental task. Successful completion of this task depends heavily on the nature of the child's social relationships at each stage (see Concept Review 1.1).

Erikson's views, like Freud's, have influenced child rearing, early childhood education, and child therapy. For example, Erikson's views about an adolescent **identity crisis** have entered the popular culture and have affected the way many parents and teachers deal with teenagers. Some schools help students master the crisis by offering life-adjustment courses and study units on self-understanding in social studies and literature classes.

Jon Erikson/The Image Works

Erik Erikson

Evaluation

Erikson's views are appealing in that they emphasize the importance of human consciousness and choice while minimizing the role—and the threat—of dark, poorly perceived urges. They are also appealing because they portray us as prosocial and helpful, whereas Freud portrayed us as selfish and needing to be forced into compliance with social rules. There is also some empirical support for the Eriksonian view that positive outcomes of early life crises help put children on the path to positive development (Clark, 2010; Marcia, 2010). For example, infants who come to trust in their parents are more likely to achieve autonomy and ego identity later on.

What Are the Learning Perspectives on Child Development?

In this section, we first discuss two types of learning—classical conditioning and operant conditioning—that have contributed to behaviorism and the behavioral view of development. We will see how the principles of learning have been used in behavior modification to help children overcome behavior disorders or cope with adjustment problems. Then we will consider a more recent theory of learning that deals with children's cognitive processes and their overt behavior—social cognitive theory.

We begin by returning to John B. Watson's theory of behaviorism.

Behaviorism

John B. Watson argued that a scientific approach to development must focus on observable behavior only, and not on thoughts, fantasies, and other mental images.

Classical conditioning is a simple form of learning in which an originally neutral **stimulus** comes to bring forth, or elicit, the response usually brought forth by a second stimulus as a result of being paired repeatedly with the second stimulus. In the bell-and-pad treatment for bedwetting, psychologists repeatedly pair tension in the children's bladders with a stimulus that wakes them up (the bell). The children learn to respond to the bladder tension as if it was a bell—that is, they wake up (see Figure 1.1 ■).

Behaviorists argue that a good deal of emotional learning is acquired through classical conditioning. For example, touching a hot stove is painful, and one or two

Erikson saw adolescence as a stage of life during which individuals develop—or fail to develop—a sense of identity.

Before conditioning

Bladder tension (does not elicit waking up)

Bell → Waking up

After conditioning

Bladder tension

Waking up

© Cengage Learning®

Figure 1.1 ■ Schematic Representation of Classical Conditioning
Before conditioning, the bell elicits the waking up of the infant. Bladder tension, a neutral stimulus, does not wake the infant. During conditioning, bladder tension always precedes urination, which in turn causes the bell to ring. After conditioning, bladder tension wakes the infant.

identity crisis According to Erikson, an adolescent period of inner conflict during which one examines one's values and makes decisions about one's life roles.

classical conditioning A simple form of learning in which one stimulus comes to bring forth the response usually elicited by a second stimulus by being paired repeatedly with the second stimulus.

THE BELL-AND-PAD METHOD FOR TREATING BEDWETTING

During the 1930s, psychologists derived an ingenious method for helping 5- and 6-year-old children overcome bedwetting from the behavioral perspective. Most children at this age wake up and go to the bathroom when their bladders are full. But bedwetters sleep through bladder tension and reflexively urinate in bed. The psychologists' objective was to teach sleeping children with full bladders to wake up rather than wet their beds.

The psychologists placed a special pad beneath the sleeping child (Mowrer & Mowrer, 1938). When the pad was wet, an electrical circuit was closed, causing a bell to ring and the sleeping child to waken. After several repetitions, most children learned to wake up before they wet the pad. As behaviorists explain it, repeated association of bedwetting and waking due to the alarm—that is, conditioning—caused the children to wake in response to the urge to urinate.

The so-called bell-and-pad method for treating bedwetting is an exotic example of the application of learning theory in child development. Most applications of learning theory to development are found in everyday events. For example, children are not born knowing what the letters A and B sound like or how to tie their shoes. They learn these things. They are not born knowing how to do gymnastics, nor are they born understanding the meanings of abstract concepts such as big, blue, decency, and justice. All these skills and knowledge are learned.

Reflect Does this application of learning theory to a developmental problem show that we can speak of learning in terms of what a young child does as well as in terms of what a child knows? What do you think? Explain.

Nina Leen/The Life Picture Collection/Getty Images

B. F. Skinner Skinner, a behaviorist, developed principles of operant conditioning and focused on the role of reinforcement of behavior.

incidents may elicit a fear response when a child looks at a stove or considers touching it again.

In classical conditioning, children learn to associate stimuli so that a response made to one is then made in response to the other. But in **operant conditioning**, children learn to do something because of its effects. B. F. Skinner introduced the concept of **reinforcement**. Reinforcers are stimuli that increase the frequency of the behavior they follow. Most children learn to adjust their behavior to conform to social codes and rules in order to earn reinforcers, such as the approval of parents and teachers. Other children, ironically, may learn to misbehave, because misbehavior also draws attention. Any stimulus that increases the frequency of the responses preceding it serves as a reinforcer. Most of the time, food, social approval, and attention serve as reinforcers.

Skinner distinguished between positive and negative reinforcers. **Positive reinforcers** increase the frequency of behaviors when they are *applied*. Food and approval usually serve as positive reinforcers. **Negative reinforcers** increase the frequency of behaviors when they are *removed*. Fear acts as a negative reinforcer in that its removal increases the frequency of the behaviors preceding it. For example, fear of failure is removed when students study for a quiz. Figure 1.2 ■ compares positive and negative reinforcers.

Punishments are aversive events that suppress or *decrease* the frequency of the behavior they follow. (Figure 1.3 ■ compares negative reinforcers with punishments.) Punishments can be physical (such as spanking) or verbal (such as scolding or criticizing) or can consist of the removal of privileges. Surveys show that the great majority of Americans agree with the statement "It is sometimes necessary to discipline a child with a 'good, hard spanking'" (Child Trends Data Bank, 2012). It is clear that punishments can rapidly suppress undesirable behavior and may be warranted in emergencies, such as when a child

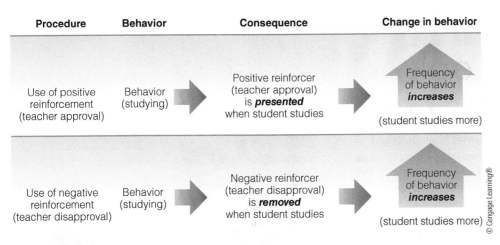

Figure 1.2 ■ Positive versus Negative Reinforcers
All reinforcers *increase* the frequency of behavior. In these examples, teacher *approval* functions as a positive reinforcer when students study harder *because* of it. Teacher *disapproval* functions as a negative reinforcer when its *removal* increases the frequency of studying.

tries to run out into traffic. Yet many learning theorists agree that punishment is usually undesirable in rearing children, for reasons such as the following (Holmes, 2014):

- Punishment does not in itself suggest an alternative, acceptable form of behavior.
- Punishment tends to suppress undesirable behavior only when its delivery is guaranteed. It does not take children long to learn that they can "get away with murder" with one parent or one teacher but not with another.
- Punished children may withdraw from the situation. Severely punished children may run away, cut class, or drop out of school.
- Punishment can create anger and hostility. After being spanked by their parents, children may hit smaller siblings or destroy objects in the home.
- Punishment may generalize too far. The child who is punished severely for bad table manners may stop eating altogether. Such overgeneralization

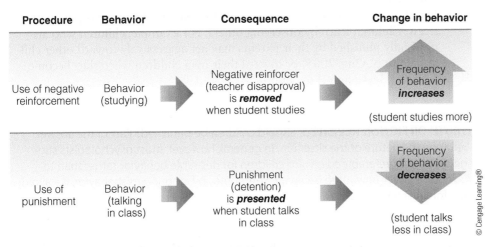

Figure 1.3 ■ Negative Reinforcers versus Punishments
Both negative reinforcers and punishments tend to be aversive stimuli. However, reinforcers increase the frequency of behavior and punishments decrease the frequency of behavior. Negative reinforcers increase the frequency of behavior when they are removed.

stimulus A change in the environment that leads to a change in behavior.

operant conditioning A simple form of learning in which an organism learns to engage in behavior that is reinforced.

reinforcement The process of providing stimuli following a behavior, which has the effect of increasing the frequency of the behavior.

positive reinforcer A reinforcer that, when applied, increases the frequency of a behavior.

negative reinforcer A reinforcer that, when removed, increases the frequency of a behavior.

punishment An unpleasant stimulus that suppresses behavior.

OPERANT CONDITIONING OF VOCALIZATIONS IN INFANTS

A classic study by psychologist Harriet Rheingold and her colleagues (1959) demonstrated how reinforcement and extinction can influence the behavior of infants—in this case, vocalization. A researcher first observed the subjects, 3-month-old infants, for about half an hour to record baseline (pre-experimental) measures of the frequency of their vocalizing. Infants averaged 13 to 15 vocalizations each. During the conditioning phase of the study, the researcher reinforced the vocalizations with social stimuli, such as encouraging sounds, smiles, and gentle touches. There was a significant increase in the frequency of vocalizing throughout this phase. By the end of an hour of conditioning spread over a 2-day period, the average incidence of vocalizations had nearly doubled to 24 to 25 within a half-hour. During the extinction phase, as during the baseline period, the researcher passively observed each infant, no longer reinforcing vocalization. After two half-hour extinction periods, average vocalizing had returned to near baseline, 13 to 16 per half-hour.

Reflect Why is it of interest that the behavior of infants can be influenced by operant conditioning? Can you think of any role this conditioning might play in attachment between parents and infants?

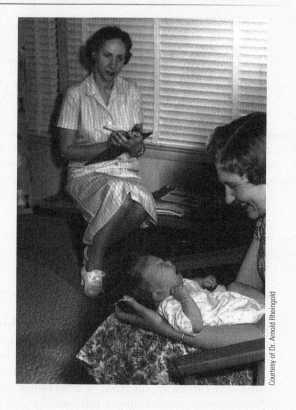

Courtesy of Dr. Arnold Rheingold

is more likely to occur when children do not know why they are being punished.

- Punishment may be imitated as a way of solving problems or coping with stress. Children learn by observing others. For example, children who are physically punished by their parents may act aggressively toward other children (Sim & Ong, 2005) or toward their own children when they become parents (Huesmann et al., 2006).

TRUTH OR FICTION REVISITED: Should children be punished? Part of the answer relies on the nature of the situation. In general, however, most psychologists suggest that it is preferable to reward children for desirable behavior rather than to punish them for unwanted behavior. Sometimes by ignoring misbehavior, we avoid reinforcing children for it.

shaping A procedure for teaching complex behavior patterns by reinforcing small steps toward the target behavior.

We can teach children complex behaviors by **shaping**, or reinforcing small steps toward the behavioral goals. In teaching a 2-year-old child to put on her own coat, it helps to first praise her for trying to stick her arm into a sleeve on a couple occasions, then to praise her for actually getting her arm into the sleeve, and so on.

Research suggests that when teachers praise and attend to appropriate behavior and ignore misbehavior, studying and classroom behavior improve while disruptive and aggressive behaviors decrease (Coffee & Kratochwill, 2013; Marchant & Anderson, 2012). Teachers frequently use **time-out** from positive reinforcement to discourage misbehavior. For example, misbehavior might be punished by having the child remain in the classroom for a few minutes before being allowed to play with other children during recess. In using time-out in the home, parents might restrict children from watching television for a specified amount of time—say, 10 minutes— if they misbehave. It is advisable to warn young children that they will have a time-out if they are misbehaving, and also to remind young children why they have been given a time-out. Otherwise, they may not reliably associate the time-out with misbehavior.

Operant conditioning is used every day in the *socialization* of young children. For example, as we will see in Chapter 10, parents and peers influence children to acquire gender-appropriate behaviors through the elaborate use of rewards and punishments. (Parenthetically, we will see that one can argue about whether a behavior is gender-appropriate, or even whether the concept of gender-appropriateness itself has any validity.) In any event, observations suggest that boys may ignore other boys when they play with dolls and housekeeping toys, but choose to play with other boys when they use transportation toys. Many children are thus encouraged to engage in behavior that is largely considered appropriate for them in their societies, even if the "appropriate" behavior in unenjoyable or unfulfilling to the children themselves.

Social Cognitive Theory

Behaviorists tend to limit their view of learning to the classical and operant conditioning of observable behavior. **Social cognitive theorists**, such as Albert Bandura (1986, 2011, 2012), have shown that much of children's learning also occurs by observing parents, teachers, other children, and characters in the media. Children may need practice to refine their skills, but they can acquire the basic know-how through observation. Children can also let these skills *lie latent*. For example, children (and adults) are not likely to imitate aggressive behavior unless they are provoked and believe that they are more likely to be rewarded than punished for aggressive behavior.

In the view of behaviorists, learning occurs by mechanical conditioning. There is no reference to thought. In social cognitive theory, cognition plays a central role: Learning alters children's mental representation of the environment and affects their belief in their ability to change the environment. Children choose whether or not to engage in the behaviors they have learned. Their values and expectations of reinforcement affect whether they will imitate the behavior they observe.

Social cognitive theorists see children as active. Children intentionally seek out or create environments in which reinforcers are available. The child with artistic ability may develop her skills by taking art lessons and by imitating her art teacher. In doing so, she creates an environment of social reinforcement in the form of praise from others. This reinforcement, in turn, influences the child's view of herself as a good artist.

Observational learning accounts for much human learning. It occurs when children observe how parents cook, clean, or repair a broken appliance. It takes place when children watch teachers solve problems on the blackboard or hear them speak a foreign language. Observational learning does not occur because of direct reinforcement. It occurs so long as children pay attention to the behavior of others.

Evaluation of Learning Theories

Learning theories have done a fine job of enabling us to describe, explain, predict, and influence many aspects of children's behavior. Psychologists and educators have

Albert Bandura Bandura and other social cognitive theorists showed that one way children learn is by observing others. Whereas behaviorists like John Watson and B. F. Skinner portrayed children as reactive to environmental stimuli, social cognitive theorists depict children as active learners who are capable of fashioning new environments.

time-out A behavior-modification technique in which a child who misbehaves is temporarily removed from positive reinforcement.

social cognitive theory A cognitively oriented learning theory that emphasizes the role of observational learning in determining behavior.

developed many applications of conditioning and social cognitive theory. The use of the bell-and-pad method for bedwetting is an example of behavior modification that probably would not have been derived from any other theoretical approach. Behavior modification has been used to help deal with autistic children, self-injurious children, and children showing temper tantrums and conduct disorders. Many of the teaching approaches used on educational TV shows are based on learning theory.

Yet learning-theory approaches to child development have been criticized. First, there is the theoretical question of whether the conditioning process in children is mechanical or whether it changes the ways in which children mentally represent the environment. Learning theorists may also underestimate the importance of maturational factors (Hergenhahn & Henley, 2014; Schultz & Schultz, 2012). Social cognitive theorists seem to be working on these issues. For example, they place more value on cognition than on conditioning and view children as being active, not as merely reacting mechanically to stimuli. Now let us turn to theories that place cognition at the heart of development.

What Is the Cognitive Perspective on Child Development?

Cognitive theorists focus on children's mental processes. They investigate the ways in which children perceive and mentally represent the world, and how they develop thinking, logic, and problem-solving ability. One cognitive perspective is **cognitive-developmental theory**, advanced by Swiss biologist Jean Piaget (1896–1980). Another is information-processing theory.

Jean Piaget's Cognitive-Developmental Theory

During adolescence, Piaget studied philosophy, logic, and mathematics, but years later he took his Ph.D. in biology. In 1920, he obtained a job at the Binet Institute in Paris, where research on intelligence tests was being conducted. Piaget tried out tests on children in various age groups. The task became boring, but then Piaget grew interested in children's *wrong* answers to test items. Someone else might have shrugged them off these "errors" and forgotten them, but Piaget realized there were methods to the children's madness. Their so-called wrong answers reflected consistent—though illogical—mental processes. Piaget looked into the patterns of thought that led to the wrong answers.

Piaget wrote dozens of books and articles on these patterns, but his work was almost unknown in English-speaking countries until the 1950s. For one thing, Piaget's writing is difficult to understand, even to native French speakers. (Piaget joked that in his scientific theorizing, he had the advantage of *not* having to read Piaget.) For another, Piaget's views differed from those of other theorists. At the time, psychology in the United Kingdom and the United States was dominated by behaviorism and psychoanalysis, and Piaget's ideas had a biological–cognitive flavor. But today Piaget's views are quite popular.

Behaviorists such as John B. Watson saw children as "blank slates" that are written upon by experience. Freud's psychoanalytic theory focused on personality and emotional development. Piaget, by contrast, was concerned with how children form concepts or mental representations of the world, and how they work with concepts to plan changes in the external world. But, like the behaviorists, he recognized that thoughts cannot be measured directly, so he tried to link his views on children's mental processes to observable behavior.

Piaget believed that cognitive development largely depends on the maturation of the brain. He regarded maturing children as natural physicists who actively intend to learn about and take intellectual charge of their worlds. In the Piagetian view, children who squish their food and laugh enthusiastically are often acting as budding scientists. In addition to enjoying a response from parents, they are studying the

Jean Piaget Piaget's cognitive-developmental theory is a stage theory that focuses on the ways children adapt to the environment by mentally representing the world and solving problems. Piaget's early training as a biologist led him to view children as mentally assimilating and accommodating aspects of their environment.

cognitive-developmental theory The stage theory that holds that the child's abilities to mentally represent the world and solve problems unfold as a result of the interaction of experience and the maturation of neurological structures.

Farrell Grehan/Historical/Corbis

texture and consistency of their food. (Parents, of course, often prefer that their children practice these experiments in the laboratory, not the dining room.)

Piaget's Basic Concepts

Piaget used the concepts of *schemes, adaptation, assimilation, accommodation,* and *equilibration* to describe and explain cognitive development. Piaget defines the **scheme** as a pattern of action or a mental structure that is involved in acquiring or organizing knowledge. Babies are said to have sucking schemes, grasping schemes, and looking schemes. (Others call these *reflexes.*) Newborn babies suck things that are placed in their mouths, grasp objects placed in their hands, and visually track moving objects. Piaget would say that infants' schemes give meaning to objects. Infants are responding to objects as "things I can suck" versus "things I can't suck" and as "things I can grasp" versus "things I can't grasp." Among older children, a scheme may be the inclusion of an object in a class. For example, the mammal class, or concept, includes a group of animals that are warm-blooded and nurse their young. The inclusion of cats, apes, whales, and people in the mammal class involves schemes that expand the child's knowledge of the natural world.

Adaptation reflects the interaction between the organism and the environment. According to Piaget, all organisms adapt to their environment; it is a natural biological tendency. Adaptation consists of assimilation and accommodation, which occur throughout life. In biology, one aspect of assimilation is the process by which food is digested and converted into the tissues that make up an animal. Cognitive **assimilation** is the process by which someone responds to new objects or events according to existing schemes or ways of organizing knowledge. Infants, for example, usually try to place new objects in their mouths to suck, feel, or explore them. Piaget would say that the child is assimilating (fitting) a new toy or object into the sucking-an-object scheme. Similarly, 2-year-olds who refer to sheep and cows as "doggies" or "bowwows" can be said to be assimilating these new animals into the doggy (or bowwow) scheme.

Sometimes, a novel object or event cannot be made to fit (that is, it cannot be assimilated into an existing scheme). In that case, the scheme may be changed or a new scheme may be created to incorporate the new event. This process is called **accommodation**. Consider the sucking reflex. Within the first month of life, infants modify sucking behavior as a result of their experience sucking various objects. The nipple on the breast or the bottle is sucked in one way, the thumb (or the big toe!) in a different way. Infants accommodate further by rejecting objects that are too large, taste bad, or have an undesirable texture or temperature.

Piaget theorized that when children can assimilate new events into existing schemes, they are in a state of cognitive harmony, or equilibrium. When something that does not fit happens along, their state of equilibrium is disturbed and they may try to accommodate. The process of restoring equilibrium is termed **equilibration**. Piaget believed that the attempt to restore equilibrium is the source of intellectual motivation and lies at the heart of the natural curiosity of the child.

Piaget's Stages of Cognitive Development

Piaget (1963) hypothesized that children's cognitive processes develop in an orderly sequence, or series, of stages. Some children may be more advanced than others at particular ages, but the developmental sequence remains the same. Piaget identified four major stages of cognitive development: *sensorimotor, preoperational, concrete operational,* and *formal operational.* These stages are described in Concept Review 1.2 and are discussed in subsequent chapters.

Because Piaget's theory focuses on cognitive development, its applications are primarily in educational settings. Teachers following Piaget's views engage the child actively in solving problems. They gear instruction to the child's developmental level and offer activities that challenge the child to advance to the next level. For example, 5-year-olds learn primarily through play and direct sensory contact with the

scheme According to Piaget, an action pattern or mental structure that is involved in the acquisition and organization of knowledge.

adaptation According to Piaget, an interaction between the organism and the environment that consists of two processes: assimilation and accommodation.

assimilation According to Piaget, the incorporation of new events or knowledge into existing schemes.

accommodation According to Piaget, the modification of existing schemes to permit the incorporation of new events or knowledge.

equilibration The creation of an equilibrium, or balance, between assimilation and accommodation as a way of incorporating new events or knowledge.

Jean Piaget's Stages of Cognitive Development

Stage	Approximate Age	Comments	
Sensorimotor	Birth–2 years	At first, the child lacks language and does not use symbols or mental representations of objects. In time, reflexive responding ends, and intentional behavior—such as making interesting stimulation last—begins. The child develops the object concept and acquires the basics of language.	*Doug Goodman/Science Source*
Preoperational	2–7 years	The child begins to represent the world mentally, but thought is egocentric. The child does not focus on two aspects of a situation at once and therefore lacks conservation. The child shows animism, artificialism, and objective responsibility for wrongdoing.	
Concrete operational	7–12 years	Logical mental actions—called operations—begin. The child develops conservation concepts, can adopt the viewpoints of others, can classify objects in series, and shows comprehension of basic relational concepts (such as one object being larger or heavier than another).	
Formal operational	12 years and older	Mature, adult thought emerges. Thinking is characterized by deductive logic, consideration of various possibilities (mental trial and error), abstract thought, and the formation and testing of hypotheses.	*Paul Hakimata/Alamy*

© 2017 Cengage Learning®

environment. Early formal instruction using workbooks and paper may be less effective in this age group (Crain, 2000).

Evaluation

Many researchers have found that Piaget may have underestimated the ages when children are capable of doing certain things. It also appears that cognitive skills may develop more gradually than Piaget thought and may not develop in distinct stages. But Piaget presented us with a view of children that is different from the psychoanalytic and behaviorist views, and he provided a strong theoretical foundation for researchers concerned with sequences in children's cognitive development. We will see more of his theory in later chapters.

Information-Processing Theory

Another face of the cognitive perspective is information processing (Brigham et al., 2011; Calvete & Orue, 2012). Psychological thought has long been influenced by the status of the physical sciences of the day. For example, Freud's psychoanalytic theory was related to the 19th century development of the steam engine—which can explode when too much steam builds up. Many of today's cognitive psychologists are influenced by computer science. Computers process information to solve problems. Information is encoded so that it can be accepted as input and then fed ("inputted") into the computer. Then it is placed in working memory (RAM) while it is manipulated. The information can be stored more permanently on a storage device, such as a hard drive. Many psychologists speak of people as also having working or short-term memory and a more permanent long-term memory (storage). If information has been placed in long-term memory, it must be retrieved before we can work on it again. To retrieve information from computer storage, we must know the code or name for the data file and the rules for retrieving data files. Psychologists note that, similarly, we need cues to retrieve information from our own long-term memories or the information may be lost to us.

Thus, many cognitive psychologists focus on information processing in people—the processes by which information is encoded (input), stored (in long-term memory), retrieved (placed in short-term memory), and manipulated (processed) to solve problems (the solutions are the output). Our strategies for solving problems are sometimes referred to as our "mental programs" or "software." In this computer metaphor, our brains are the "hardware" that runs our mental programs. Our brains—containing billions of brain cells called *neurons*—become our most "personal" computers.

When psychologists who study information processing contemplate the cognitive development of children, they are likely to speak in terms of the *size* of the child's short-term memory at a given age and of the *number of programs* a child can run simultaneously. Research suggests that these are indeed useful ways of talking about children (see Chapter 12).

The most obvious applications of information processing occur in teaching. For example, information-processing models alert teachers to the sequence of steps by which children acquire information, commit it to memory, and retrieve it to solve problems. Teachers who understand this sequence can provide experiences that give students practice with each stage.

Now that we see that the brain is a sort of biological computer, let us see what other aspects of biology can be connected with child development.

What Is the Biological Perspective on Development?

The biological perspective is directly related to physical development—to gains in height and weight, development of the brain, and developments connected with hormones, reproduction, and heredity. For example, it is clear that during prenatal development, genes and sex hormones are responsible for the biological differentiation of female and male sex organs. However, biology is also intertwined with behavior. In many species, including humans, sex hormones do apparently "masculinize" or "feminize" the embryonic brain by creating tendencies to behave in stereotypical masculine or feminine ways. Testosterone, the male sex hormone, seems to be connected with feelings of self-confidence, high activity levels, and—the negative side—aggressiveness (Hines, 2011a; Montoya et al., 2012; Rice & Sher, 2013). Here we consider one biologically oriented theory of development: *ethology*.

Ethology and Evolution: "Doing What Comes Naturally"

Ethology was heavily influenced by the 19th-century work of Charles Darwin and by the work of the 20th-century ethologists Konrad Lorenz and Niko Tinbergen (Washburn, 2007). **Ethology** is concerned with instinctive, or inborn, behavior patterns—how they help the organism adapt and how they have evolved.

The nervous systems of most, perhaps all, animals are "prewired" or "preprogrammed" to respond to some situations in specific ways. For example, birds raised

ethology The study of behaviors that are specific to a species—how these behaviors evolved, help the organism adapt, and develop during critical periods.

in isolation from other birds build nests during the mating season, even if they have never seen a nest or seen another bird building one. Nest-building could not have been learned. Birds raised in isolation also sing the songs typical of their species. Salmon spawned in particular rivers swim out into the vast oceans and then, when mature, return to the river of their origin to spawn. These behaviors are "built in," or instinctive. They are also referred to as inborn fixed action patterns (FAPs).

Evolution can work in wondrous ways. After the eggs of some species of Lake Tanganyika cichlids—mouth-brooding fish—are laid, both parents scoop them up and secure them from predators in their mouths. Fry swim out after hatching, but they often return to the mouth for protection during rest periods. Dad is under the influence of "maternal" hormones during these days. Any fry that return to his mouth after his hormone levels have returned to "normal" become just another meal (Salzburger et al., 2008). Maternal hormones create a sensitive period during which the male parent behaves in a "motherly" fashion.

In Chapter 7, we will see that Konrad Lorenz treated the first year of life as a critical period for the development of social relationships, with consequences that last a lifetime. Infant–caregiver attachment is essential to the survival and social development of children. Lorenz viewed infant–caregiver attachment as a FAP that occurs over a time period when infants are particularly sensitive to parental attention and caring. During their critical period, geese develop an attachment to the first moving object they perceive. It is as if the image of the moving object becomes "imprinted" on them, so the process is called **imprinting**. We will see that John Bowlby and Mary Ainsworth extended Lorenz's view by studying stages of attachment in humans.

Evaluation

Most theorists with an ethological perspective do not maintain that human behaviors are as mechanical as those of lower animals. Moreover, they tend to assume that instinctive behaviors can be modified through learning. But research into the ethological perspective suggests that instinct may play a number of roles in human behavior, even if the behaviors in question are not inevitable or carved in stone. The questions that researchers seek to answer are: What areas of human behavior and development, if any, involve instincts? How do inborn tendencies and experience interact as a child develops?

What Is the Ecological Systems Theory of Child Development?

Ecology is the branch of biology that deals with the relationships between living organisms and their environment. The **ecological systems theory** of child development addresses aspects of psychological, social, and emotional development as well as aspects of biological development. Ecological systems theorists explain child development in terms of the interactions between children and the settings in which they live (Bronfenbrenner & Morris, 2006).

According to Urie Bronfenbrenner (1917–2005), we need to focus on the two-way interactions between the child and the parents, not just on maturational forces (nature) or parental child-rearing approaches (nurture). For example, some parents choose to feed newborns on demand, whereas others may decide to stick to feedings that occur 4 hours apart. Some babies, however, are more accepting than others, and some never become comfortable with a strict schedule. This is the point: Parents are a key part of the child's environment and have a major influence on the child, but even babies have inborn temperaments that affect the parents.

Bronfenbrenner (Bronfenbrenner & Morris, 2006) suggested that we can view the contexts of human development as a series of systems, each embedded in the next larger system. From narrowest to widest, these are the microsystem, the mesosystem, the exosystem, the macrosystem, and the chronosystem (see Figure 1.4 ■).

imprinting The process by which some animals exhibit the fixed action pattern (FAP) of attachment in response to a releasing stimulus. The FAP occurs during a critical period and is difficult to modify.

ecology The branch of biology that deals with the relationships between living organisms and their environment.

ecological systems theory The view that explains child development in terms of the reciprocal influences between children and the settings that make up their environment.

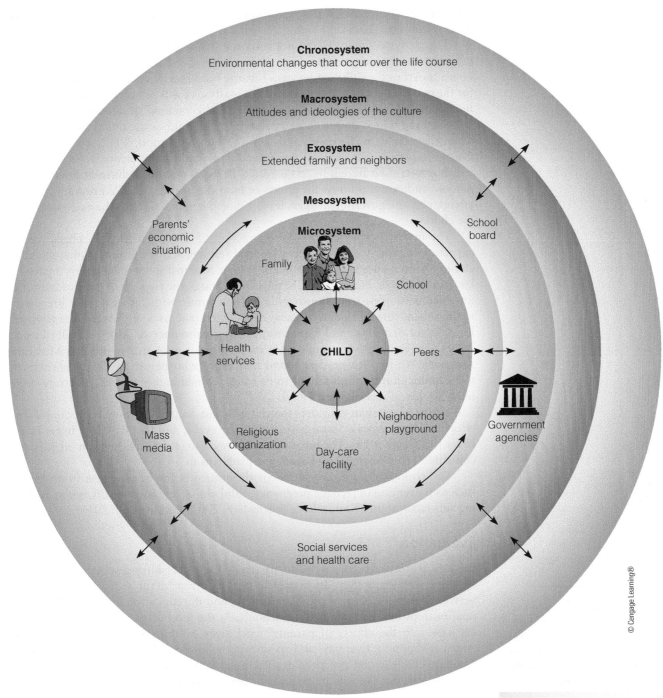

Figure 1.4 ■ The Contexts of Human Development
According to ecological systems theory, the systems within which children develop are embedded within larger systems. Children and these systems reciprocally influence each other.

© Cengage Learning®

The **microsystem** involves the interactions of the child and other people in the immediate setting, such as the home, the school, or the peer group. Initially, the microsystem is small, involving care-giving interactions with the parents or others, usually at home. As children get older, they do more, with more people, in more places.

The **mesosystem** involves the interactions of the various settings within the microsystem. For instance, the home and the school interact during parent–teacher conferences. The school and the larger community interact when children are taken

microsystem The immediate settings with which the child interacts, such as the home, the school, and the child's peers (from the Greek *mikros*, meaning "small").

mesosystem The interlocking settings that influence the child, such as the interaction of the school and the larger community when children are taken on field trips (from the Greek *mesos*, meaning "middle").

on field trips. The ecological systems approach addresses the joint effect of two or more settings on the child.

The **exosystem** involves the institutions in which the child does not directly participate but which exert an indirect influence on the child. For example, the school board is part of the child's exosystem because board members put together programs for the child's education, determine which textbooks will be acceptable, and so forth. In similar fashion, the parents' workplaces and economic situations determine the hours during which they will be available to the child, what mood they will be in when they are with the child, and so on (Hong & Eamon, 2012; Tisdale & Pitt-Catsuphes, 2012). For example, poverty and unemployment create stress in parents, which affects their parenting. As a result, children may misbehave at home and in school. Studies that address the effects of housing, health care, TV programs, church attendance, and government agencies examine the interactions of the exosystem with the child.

The **macrosystem** involves the interaction of children with the beliefs, values, expectations, and lifestyles of their cultural settings. Cross-cultural studies examine children's interactions with their macrosystem. Macrosystems exist *within* a particular culture as well. For example, in the United States, the two-wage-earner family, the low-income single-parent household, and the family with father as sole breadwinner represent three different macrosystems. Each macrosystem has its characteristic lifestyle, set of values, and expectations (Bronfenbrenner & Morris, 2006; Lustig, 2011). One issue affecting children is multiculturalism. A study with 258 Mexican-American 8th to 11th graders found that those who perceived their environment to be multicultural found school to be easier, earned higher grades, and were more likely to stay in school (Tan, 1999).

The **chronosystem** considers the changes that occur over time. For example, the effects of divorce peak about a year after the event, and then children begin to recover (see Chapter 13). The breakup has more of an effect on boys than on girls and contributes to behavioral and academic problems in boys.

The ecological approach broadens the strategies for intervention in problems, such as prevention of teenage pregnancy, child abuse, and juvenile offending, including substance abuse (Kaminski & Stormshak, 2007; Latkin et al., 2013).

Evaluation

Ecological systems theory helps focus attention on the shifting systems with which children interact as they develop. The health of the infant requires relationships between parents and the health care system, and the education of the child requires relationships between parents and schools. At the level of the exosystem, researchers look into the effects of parents' work lives, welfare agencies, transportation systems, shopping facilities, and so on. At the level of the macrosystem, we may compare child-rearing practices in the United States with those in other countries. We will consider the role of culture further in our discussion of the sociocultural perspective.

What Is the Sociocultural Perspective on Development?

The sociocultural perspective teaches that children are social beings who are affected by the cultures in which they live. Yes, we are affected by biochemical forces such as neurotransmitters and hormones. We may be biologically "prewired" to form attachments and engage in other behaviors. Perhaps there are psychological tendencies to learn in certain ways, and maybe there are ways in which the psychological past affects the present. But, as noted within the ecological perspective, we are also affected by the customs, traditions, languages, and heritages of the societies in which we live.

exosystem Community institutions and settings that indirectly influence the child, such as the school board and the parents' workplaces (from the Greek exo, meaning "outside").

macrosystem The basic institutions and ideologies that influence the child, such as the American ideals of freedom of expression and equality under the law (from the Greek makros, meaning "long" or "enlarged").

chronosystem The environmental changes that occur over time and have an impact on the child (from the Greek chronos, meaning "time").

The sociocultural perspective overlaps other perspectives on child development, but theorists use the term *sociocultural* in a couple of different ways. One way refers quite specifically to the *sociocultural theory* of the Russian psychologist Lev Semenovich Vygotsky (1896–1934). The other way broadly addresses the effect on children of human diversity, including such factors as ethnicity and gender.

Vygotsky's Sociocultural Theory

Whereas genetics is concerned with the biological transmission of traits from generation to generation, Vygotsky's (1978) theory is concerned with the transmission of information and cognitive skills from generation to generation. The transmission of skills involves teaching and learning, but Vygotsky does not view learning in terms of the conditioning of behavior. Rather, he focuses on how the child's social interaction with adults, largely in the home, organizes a child's learning experiences in such a way that the child can obtain cognitive skills—such as computation or reading skills—and use them to acquire information. Like Piaget, Vygotsky sees the child's functioning as adaptive, and the child adapts to his or her social and cultural interactions.

The key concepts in Vygotsky's theory include the *zone of proximal development* and *scaffolding*. The word *proximal* means "nearby" or "close," as in the words *approximate* and *proximity*. The **zone of proximal development (ZPD)** is a range of tasks that a child can carry out with the help of someone who is more skilled. It is similar to an apprenticeship. Many researchers find that observing how a child learns when working with others provides more information about that child's cognitive abilities than does a simple inventory of knowledge. When learning with other people, the child tends to internalize—or bring inward—the conversations and explanations that help him or her gain the necessary skills (Vygotsky, 1962; Poehner, 2012; Wass et al., 2011). In other words, children not only learn the meanings of words from teachers but also learn ways of talking to themselves about solving problems within a cultural context. Outer speech becomes inner speech. What was the teacher's becomes the child's. What was a social and cultural context becomes embedded within the child.

A *scaffold* is a temporary skeletal structure that enables workers to fabricate a building, bridge, or other more permanent structure. In Vygotsky's theory, teachers and parents provide children with problem-solving methods that serve as cognitive **scaffolding** while the child gains the ability to function independently. For example, a child's instructors may offer advice on sounding out letters and words that provide a temporary support until reading "clicks" and the child no longer needs the device. Children may be offered scaffolding that enables them to use their fingers or their toes to do simple calculations. Eventually, the scaffolding is removed and the cognitive structures stand alone. A Puerto Rican study found that students also use scaffolding when they are explaining to one another how they can improve school projects, such as essay assignments (Guerrero & Villamil, 2000). The authors show that scaffolding can be mutual, not just unidirectional.

Evaluation

A good deal of research evidence supports Vygotsky's view that the presence of skilled adults helps children master tasks (Norton & D'Ambrosio, 2008). More-skilled children also play effective roles in teaching children (John-Steiner, 2007). Private speech appears to help children plan ways to carry out tasks and see them through. Among 5-, 7-, and 9-year-olds who are given tasks with medium and high levels of difficulty, private speech facilitates task performance (Montero & De Dios, 2006). However, many teachers are unaware of the role of private speech in task performance, and some report that they discourage it when it distracts them—the teachers—or other children (Deniz, 2004).

zone of proximal development (ZPD) Vygotsky's term for the range of tasks that a child can carry out with the help of someone who is more skilled, frequently an adult who represents the culture in which the child develops.

scaffolding Vygotsky's term for temporary cognitive structures or methods of solving problems that help the child as he or she learns to function independently.

Brand X Pictures/Jupiterimages

Len Rubenstein/Photolibrary/Getty Images

The Sociocultural Perspective and Human Diversity

The field of child development focuses mainly on individuals and is committed to the dignity of the individual child. The sociocultural perspective asserts that we cannot understand individual children without awareness of the richness of their diversity (Pickren et al., 2012; Russo et al., 2012). For example, children diverge or differ in their ethnicity, gender, and socioeconomic status.

Children's **ethnic groups** involve their cultural heritage, their race, their language, and their common history. The numbers of African Americans and Latino and Latina Americans (who may be White, Black, or Native American in racial origin) are growing more rapidly than those of European Americans (U.S. Bureau of the Census, 2012). The cultural heritages, languages, and histories of ethnic minority groups are thus likely to have an increasing effect on the cultural life of the United States. Yet the dominant culture in the United States has often disparaged the traditions and languages of people from ethnic minority groups. For example, it has been considered harmful to rear children bilingually, even though research suggests that bilingualism broadens children's knowledge, as we will see in Chapter 12.

ethnic groups Groups of people distinguished by their cultural heritage, race, language, and common history.

Studying diversity is also important in helping ensure that children have appropriate educational experiences. Educators need to understand children's family values and cultural expectations in order to teach them and guide their learning. Many professionals—teachers, psychologists, social workers, psychiatrists, and others—are called on to help children and families who are having problems in school or in the community. Professionals may need special training to identify the problems of children and families from ethnic minority groups and to treat them in culturally sensitive ways (Murry, 2014).

Throughout this text, we consider many issues that affect children from various ethnic groups. A few examples of these issues are bilingualism, ethnic differences in intelligence test scores, the prevalence of suicide among members of different ethnic minority groups, and patterns of child rearing among parents of various ethnic minority groups.

Gender is another aspect of human diversity. Gender is the psychological state of being male or being female, as influenced by cultural concepts of gender-appropriate behavior. Unfortunately, females and males are often polarized by cultural expectations. (In an effort to diminish the polarization of males and females, in this textbook we use terms such as "the other sex" rather than "the opposite sex.") Female–male differences may be exaggerated, as in the case of intellectual abilities. Males may very well differ from females in some respects, but history has created more burdens for women than for men as a result. Gender-role expectations affect children's self-esteem and shackle their hopes and dreams for the future.

Historically, females have traditionally been discouraged from pursuing careers in the sciences, politics, and business. Women today are making inroads into academic and vocational spheres—such as medicine, law, science, math, engineering, and the military—that were traditionally male preserves. Today, a majority of college students in the United States are female, but girls were not considered qualified for education until relatively recent times. Women were not admitted to college in the United States until 1833, the year Oberlin College opened its doors to women. Yet there remain many parts of the world, such as parts of the Middle East, where few if any women obtain an education. Opportunities for women are crucial to the development of girls. Opportunities for adults give children their sense of what is possible for them. Just as many children from ethnic minority groups wonder whether they can experience the rewards and opportunities they see in the dominant culture, so do girls wonder whether the career and social roles they admire are available to them.

A child's **socioeconomic status (SES)** is his or her position in society based mainly on economic considerations. A child's SES is largely connected with his or her level of education (wealthier families generally keep their children in school longer and have more resources to determine the quality of their education), eventual occupation (children in wealthier families are more likely to find their way into positions with high prestige, power, and income), and health (children with wealthier parents are more likely to receive all their vaccinations, to eat healthful diets, and to be tended to when they are ill). SES is therefore associated with opportunity, and children in poverty clearly have unequal opportunity to obtain society's rewards (Haushofer & Fehr, 2014; Shaw & Shelleby, 2014).

In this book, the focus on human diversity extends beyond ethnicity, gender, and socioeconomic status to include children with various sexual orientations and disabilities. This approach broadens our understanding of all children as they experience the developmental changes brought about by quite different influences of heredity and experience.

Concept Review 1.3 summarizes similarities and differences among the perspectives on child development.

socioeconomic status (SES)
Social position as determined mainly by level of income.

Perspectives on Child Development

Perspective or Theory	Core Concepts	Is Nature or Nurture More Important?	Is Development Viewed as Continuous or Discontinuous?	Is the Child Viewed as Active or Passive?
The Psychoanalytic Perspective				
Theory of psychosexual development (Sigmund Freud) *Hulton Archive/Stringer/ Archive Photos/Getty Images*	Social codes channel primitive impulses, resulting in unconscious conflict.	Interaction of nature and nurture: Maturation sets the stage for reacting to social influences.	Discontinuous: There are five stages of development, which express or repress sexual impulses in certain ways.	Passive: The child is largely at the mercy of older people and cultural modes of conduct.
Theory of psychosocial development (Erik Erikson) *Jon Erikson/The Image Works*	Children undergo life crises that are largely based on social relationships, opportunities, and expectations.	Interaction of nature and nurture: Maturation sets the stage for reacting to social influences and opportunities.	Discontinuous: There are eight stages of development, each of which involves a particular kind of life crisis.	Active: The child (or adult) makes conscious decisions about the formation of his or her own personality and behavior.
The Learning Perspective: Behavioral and Social Cognitive Theories				
Behaviorism (John B. Watson) *Nina Leen/The Life Picture Collection/Getty Images*	Behavior is learned by association, as in classical and operant conditioning.	Nurture: Children are seen almost as blank tablets.	Continuous: Behavior reflects the summation of conditioned responses.	Passive: Responses are learned by association and maintained by reinforcement.
Social cognitive theory (Albert Bandura and others) *Jon Brenneis/Life Magazine/ The Life Images Collection/Getty Images*	Conditioning occurs but children also learn by observing others, and they choose whether to display learned responses.	Emphasizes nurture but allows for the expression of natural tendencies.	Continuous.	Active: Children influence the environment even as the environment influences them.

Perspectives on Child Development (continued)

Perspective or Theory	Core Concepts	Is Nature or Nurture More Important?	Is Development Viewed as Continuous or Discontinuous?	Is the Child Viewed as Active or Passive?
The Cognitive Perspective				
Cognitive-Developmental theory (Jean Piaget)	Children adapt to the environment by assimilating new events to existing mental structures and accommodating those structures.	Emphasizes nature but allows for influences of experience.	Discontinuous: Cognitive development follows an invariant sequence of four stages.	Active: Children are budding scientists who seek to understand and manipulate their worlds.
Information-Processing theory (numerous theorists)	Children's cognitive functioning is compared to that of computers—how they input, manipulate, store, and output information.	Interaction of nature and nurture.	Continuous: The child's capacity for storing information and his or her ability to run multiple "programs" at once develop continuously.	Active: Children seek to obtain and manipulate information.
The Biological Perspective				
Ethology and evolution (Charles Darwin, Konrad Lorenz, Niko Tinbergen)	Organisms are biologically "prewired" to develop certain adaptive responses during sensitive periods.	Emphasizes nature, but experience is also critical; e.g., imprinting occurs during a sensitive period but experience determines the object of imprinting.	Discontinuous: Certain kinds of learning are said to occur during *critical periods*, which are biologically determined.	Not indicated, although organisms respond automatically to FAPs.
The Ecological Perspective				
Ecological systems theory (Urie Bronfenbrenner)	Children's development occurs within interlocking systems, and development is enhanced by intervening in these systems.	Interaction of nature and nurture: Children's personalities and skills contribute to their development.	Not specifically indicated.	Active: Influences are bidirectional; systems influence the child, and vice versa.

Farrell Grehan/Historical/Corbis

Perspectives on Child Development (continued)

Perspective or Theory	Core Concepts	Is Nature or Nurture More Important?	Is Development Viewed as Continuous or Discontinuous?	Is the Child Viewed as Active or Passive?
The Sociocultural Perspective				
Sociocultural theory (Lev Vygotsky)	Children internalize sociocultural dialogues in developing problem-solving skills.	Interaction of nature and nurture: Nurture is discussed in social and cultural terms.	Continuous: Children learn in the "zone" with experienced members of a culture, thereby accumulating knowledge and skills.	Both: Children seek to develop problem-solving abilities by internalizing cultural dialogues, but the dialogues originate externally.
Sociocultural perspective and human diversity (numerous theorists)	Children's development is influenced by sociocultural factors, such as ethnicity, gender, and SES.	Nurture.	Not specifically indicated.	Not indicated.

© 2017 Cengage Learning®

Section Review

4. _____ are intended to enable us to explain, predict, and control events.

5. _____ hypothesized five stages of psychosexual development.

6. Erikson extended Freud's five stages of development to _____.

7. Behaviorism sees children's learning as mechanical and relies on classical and _____ conditioning.

8. According to _____, children assimilate new events to existing schemes or accommodate schemes to incorporate novel events.

9. Information-_____ theory focuses on the processes by which information is encoded, stored, retrieved, and manipulated.

10. The _____ systems theory explains child development in terms of the interaction between children and the settings in which they live.

11. Vygotsky's _____ theory is concerned with the transmission of information and cognitive skills from generation to generation.

Reflect & Relate: How have your ethnic background and your sex influenced your development? Consider factors such as race, country of origin, language, nutrition, values, and the dominant culture's reaction to people of your background.

Controversies in Child Development

The discussion of theories of development reveals that students of human development can see things in very different ways. Let us consider how they react to three of the most important debates in the field.

Which Exerts the Greater Influence on Children: Nature or Nurture?

Think about your friends for a moment. Some may be tall and lanky, others short and stocky. Some are outgoing and sociable; others are more reserved and quiet. One may be a good athlete, another a fine musician. What made them this way? How much does inheritance have to do with it, and how much of a role does the environment play?

Researchers are continually trying to sort out the extent to which human behavior is the result of **nature** (heredity) and of **nurture** (environmental influences). What aspects of behavior originate in our **genes** and are biologically programmed to unfold in the child and adolescent as time goes on, so long as minimal nutrition and social experiences are provided? What aspects of behavior can be traced largely to such environmental influences as nutrition and learning?

Scientists seek the natural causes of development in children's genetic heritage, the functioning of the nervous system, and maturation. Scientists seek the environmental causes of development in children's nutrition, social and cultural backgrounds, and opportunities to learn about the world, including cognitive stimulation during early childhood, and formal education.

Some theorists lean heavily toward natural explanations of development (e.g., cognitive-developmental and biological theorists), whereas others lean heavily toward environmental explanations (e.g., learning theorists). But today nearly all researchers would agree that nature and nurture play important roles in nearly every aspect of development. Consider language development. Language is based in structures found in certain areas of the brain. Thus, biology (nature) plays a vital role in language development. But children also come to speak the languages spoken in their homes and in their nations. Parent–child similarities in accent and vocabulary provide additional evidence for the role of learning (nurture) in language development.

Mark Richards/PhotoEdit

Stages of Physical Development Certain aspects of physical development seem to occur in stages. Girls usually spurt in growth before boys. The girl and boy who are dancing are the same age.

Is Development Continuous or Discontinuous?

Do developmental changes occur gradually (continuously), the way a seedling becomes a tree? Or do changes occur in major qualitative leaps (discontinuously) that dramatically alter our bodies and behavior, the way a caterpillar turns into a butterfly?

Some theorists view human development as a continuous process in which the effects of learning mount gradually, with no major sudden qualitative changes. In contrast, other theorists believe that a number of rapid qualitative changes usher in new stages of development. Maturational theorists point out that the environment, even when enriched, profits us little until we are ready, or mature enough, to develop in a certain way. For example, newborn babies will not imitate their parents' speech, even when parents speak clearly and deliberately. Nor does aided practice in "walking" during the first few months after birth significantly accelerate the emergence of independent walking. Newborns are not biologically ready to do these things.

nature The processes within an organism that guide that organism to develop according to its genetic code.

nurture The processes external to an organism that nourish it as it develops according to its genetic code or that cause it to swerve from its genetically programmed course. Environmental factors that influence development.

genes The basic building blocks of heredity.

Stage theorists such as Sigmund Freud and Jean Piaget saw development as discontinuous. They saw biological changes as providing the potential for psychological changes. Freud focused on the ways in which biological developments might provide the basis for personality development. Piaget believed maturation of the nervous system allowed cognitive development.

Certain aspects of physical development do occur in stages. For example, from the age of 2 years to the onset of puberty, children gradually grow larger. Then the adolescent growth spurt occurs as rushes of hormones cause rapid biological changes in structure and function (as in the development of the sex organs) and in size. Psychologists disagree on whether developments in cognition occur in stages.

Are Children Active (Prewired to Act on the World) or Passive (Shaped by Experience)?

Broadly speaking, all animals are active. But in the field of child development, the issue has a more specific meaning. Historical views of children as willful and unruly suggest that people have generally seen children as active—even if mischievous (at best) or evil (at worst). John Locke introduced a view of children as passive beings (blank tablets); experience "wrote" features of personality and moral virtue on them.

At one extreme, educators who view children as passive may assume that they must be motivated to learn by their instructors. Such educators are likely to provide a traditional curriculum with rigorous exercises in spelling, music, and math to promote absorption of the subject matter. They are also likely to apply a powerful system of rewards and punishments to keep children on the straight and narrow.

At the other extreme, educators who view children as active may assume that they have a natural love of learning. Such educators are likely to argue for open education and encourage children to explore an environment rich with learning materials. These educators are likely to listen to the children to learn about their unique likes and talents, and then to support the children as they pursue their own agendas.

These are extremes. Most educators would probably agree that children show individual differences and that some require more guidance and external motivation than others. In addition, children can be active in some subjects and passive in others. Whether children who do not actively seek to master certain subjects are coerced tends to depend on how important the subject is for functioning in today's society, the age of the child, the attitudes of the parents, and many other factors.

Urie Bronfenbrenner (Bronfenbrenner & Morris, 2006) argued that we miss the point when we assume that children are either entirely active or passive. Children are influenced by the environment, but children also influence the environment. The challenge is to observe the ways in which children interact with their settings. Albert Bandura (2006a, 2006b) also refers to the two-way influences between children and the environment.

These debates are theoretical. Scientists value theory for its ability to tie together observations and suggest new areas of investigation, but they also follow an **empirical** approach. That is, they engage in research methods such as those described in the following section to find evidence for or against various theoretical positions.

empirical Based on observation and experimentation.

Section Review

12. Researchers in child development try to sort out the effects of _____ (heredity) and nurture (environmental influences).

13. Learning theorists tend to see development as continuous, whereas stage theorists see development as _____.

Reflect & Relate: Consider the active–passive controversy. Do you see yourself as being active or passive? Explain.

1.4 How Do We Study Child Development?

What is the relationship between children's intelligence and their achievement? What are the effects of maternal use of aspirin and alcohol on the fetus? How can you rear children to become competent and independent? What are the effects of parental divorce on children? We all may have expressed opinions on questions such as these at one time or another. But scientists insist that such questions be answered by research. Strong arguments or references to authority figures are not evidence. Scientific evidence is obtained only by the scientific method.

American Images Inc/Digital Vision/Getty Images

How Can We Use the Scientific Method to Explain This Boy's Aggression? What is the cause of this boy's aggression? Would he behave differently if the other child reacted to him with anger instead of fear? How does the scientific method help us answer this type of question?

What Is the Scientific Method?

The scientific method is a systematic way of forming and answering research questions. It enables scientists to test the theories discussed in the previous section. Many researchers describe the scientific method as consisting of five steps:

Step 1: Forming a Research Question

Daily experiences, theory, and even folklore help generate questions for research. Daily experience in using day-care centers may stimulate us to wonder whether day care affects children's intellectual or social development or the bonds of attachment between children and parents. Reading about observational learning may prompt research into the effects of TV violence.

Step 2: Developing a Hypothesis

The second step is the development of a hypothesis. A **hypothesis** is a specific statement about behavior that is tested through research. One hypothesis about day care might be that preschool children placed in day care will acquire greater skill in getting along with other children than will preschoolers who are cared for in the home. A hypothesis about TV violence might be that elementary school children who watch more violent TV shows will behave more aggressively toward other children.

Step 3: Testing the Hypothesis

The third step is testing the hypothesis. Psychologists test the hypothesis through carefully controlled information-gathering techniques and research methods, such as **naturalistic observation,** the case study, correlation, and the experiment.

For example, we could introduce two groups of children—children who are in day care and children who are not in day care—to a new child in a college child-research center and see how each group acts toward the new child. Concerning the effects of TV violence, we could have parents help us tally which TV shows their children watch and rate the shows for violent content. Then we could ask the children's teachers to report how aggressively the children act toward classmates. We could do some math to determine whether more aggressive children also watch more violence on television. We will describe research methods such as these later in the chapter.

hypothesis A specific statement about behavior that is tested by research.

naturalistic observation A method of scientific observation in which children (and others) are observed in their natural environments.

Step 4: Drawing Conclusions

Scholars of development then draw conclusions from their research results. Those results may confirm a hypothesis or disconfirm a hypothesis.

Step 5: Publishing Findings

Scientists publish their research findings in professional journals and thus make their data available to scientists and the public at large for scrutiny. This gives other scientists the opportunity to review the data and conclusions to help determine their accuracy.

Now let us consider the information-gathering techniques and the methods used by researchers. Then we will discuss ethical issues concerning research in child development.

What Methods of Observation Do Researchers Use to Gather Information About Children?

Researchers use various methods to gather information. For example, they may ask children to keep diaries of their behavior, ask teachers or parents to report on the behavior of their children, or use interviews or questionnaires with children themselves. There are significant problems in asking children to report their behavior or their experiences. For example, in court cases involving actual or suspected child sexual abuse, the testimony of children—the victims—has been challenged because of questions about children's memory and suggestibility. The concern is that, in the course of being prepared to testify, some children may have inaccurate memories or judgments implanted, either deliberately or inadvertently, through the power of suggestion (Jack & Zajac, 2014). When possible, researchers directly observe children in the laboratory ("structured observations") or in the natural setting ("naturalistic observations"). Let us discuss two ways of gathering information: the naturalistic observation method and the case study method.

Naturalistic Observation

Naturalistic observation studies of children are conducted in "the field"—that is, in the natural, or real-life, settings in which they happen. In field studies, investigators observe the natural behavior of children in settings such as homes, playgrounds, and classrooms and try not to interfere. Interference could affect, or "bias", the results. Researchers may try to "blend into the woodwork" by sitting quietly in the back of a classroom or may observe the class through a one-way mirror.

William H. Brown and his colleagues (2009) used naturalistic observation to study the activity levels of 3- to 5-year-olds in preschools. They found that the children spend 89% of their days in sedentary activity, 8% in light activity, and 3% in moderate to vigorous physical activity.

Naturalistic observation studies have been done with children of different cultures. For example, researchers have observed the motor behavior of Native American Hopi children who are strapped to cradle boards during their first year of life. They have observed language development in the United States, Mexico, Turkey, Kenya, and China—seeking universals that might suggest a major role for maturation in the acquisition of language skills. They have also observed the ways in which children are socialized in Russia, Israel, Japan, and other nations in an effort to determine what patterns of child rearing are associated with the development of behaviors such as attachment and independence.

The Case Study

Another way of gathering information about children is the case study method. The **case study** is a carefully drawn account of the behavior of an individual. Parents who keep diaries of their children's activities are involved in informal case studies. Case studies themselves often use a number of different kinds of information about children. In addition to direct observation, case studies may include questionnaires,

case study A carefully drawn biography of the life of an individual.

standardized tests, and interviews with the child and his or her parents, teachers, and friends. Information gleaned from school and other records may be included. Scientists who use the case study method take great pains to record all relevant factors in a child's behavior, and they are cautious in drawing conclusions about what leads to what.

Jean Piaget used the case study method in carefully observing and recording the behavior of children, including his own children (see Chapter 6). Sigmund Freud developed his psychoanalytic theory largely on the basis of case studies. Freud studied his patients in great depth and followed some of them for many years.

The Survey

Researchers conduct surveys to learn about behavior and mental processes that cannot be observed in the natural setting or studied experimentally. They may employ questionnaires, as they did in the nearby feature on high school students' attitudes toward living together without being married. When it comes to children, they may survey parents and teachers rather than the children themselves. They may personally interview people rather than distributing questionnaires. Researchers may also examine records, such as hospital records, to determine factors such as the birth weight of children in different parts of the country or of children of different ethnic backgrounds.

Correlation: What Does It Mean to Correlate Information?

Correlation is a mathematical method that researchers use to determine whether one behavior or trait being studied is related to, or correlated with, another. Consider, for example, the **variables** of intelligence and achievement. These variables are assigned numbers such as intelligence test scores or academic grade averages. Then the numbers or scores are mathematically related and expressed as a correlation coefficient. A **correlation coefficient** is a number that varies between +1.00 and −1.00.

Numerous studies report **positive correlations** between intelligence and achievement. In general, the higher children score on intelligence tests, the better their academic performance is likely to be. The scores attained on intelligence tests are positively correlated (about +0.60 to +0.70) with overall academic achievement.[1]

There is a **negative correlation** between children's school grades and their commission of delinquent acts. The higher a child's grades are in school, the less likely the child is to engage in criminal behavior. Figure 1.6 ■ illustrates positive and negative correlations.

Steve Debenport/E+/Getty Images

standardized test A test of some ability or trait in which an individual's score is compared to the scores of a group of similar individuals.

correlation A relationship between variables in which one variable increases as a second variable also increases (a positive correlation) or decreases (a negative correlation).

variables Quantities that can vary from child to child or from occasion to occasion, such as height, weight, intelligence, and attention span.

correlation coefficient A number ranging from +1.00 to −1.00 that expresses the direction (positive or negative) and strength of the relationship between two variables.

positive correlation A relationship between two variables in which one variable increases as the other variable increases.

What Is the Relationship between Intelligence and Achievement? Does the correlational method allow us to say that intelligence causes or is responsible for academic achievement? Why or why not?

Limitations of Correlational Information

Correlational information can reveal relationships between variables, but it does not show cause and effect. For example, children who watch TV shows or play video games with a lot of violence are more likely to engage in aggressive behavior at home and in school. Thus, it may seem logical to assume that exposure to violence

SURVEYING HIGH SCHOOL SENIORS' ATTITUDES TOWARD LIVING TOGETHER BEFORE GETTING MARRIED

Living together with a partner without being married—cohabitation—was called "living in sin" a couple generations ago. Yet more than half of today's marriages are preceded by the couple living together (Wilcox & Marquardt, 2011). The number of households consisting of an unmarried adult male and female living together in the United States has increased more than tenfold since 1960, from fewer than half a million couples to about 7.9 million couples today (U. S. Bureau of the Census, 2014). More than half a million additional households consist of cohabiting same-sex couples. Most social scientists today view cohabitation as a new stage of courtship.

The University of Michigan's "Monitoring the Future" research group has been surveying some 6,000 students a year for nearly 40 years, and over those years, high school seniors' approval of cohabitation has changed markedly from a minority to a solid majority. As you can see in Figure 1.5 ■, nearly 70 percent of today's high school seniors believe that it is a good idea for couples to live together before getting married to test their compatibility, and the percentage continues to be on the rise.

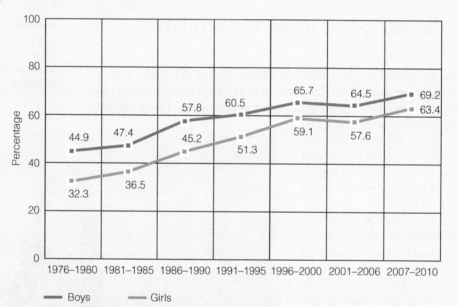

Figure 1.5 ■ Percentage of High School Seniors Approving of Couples' Living Together Before Marriage, by Period
Source: Bachman, J. G., Johnston, L. D., & O'Malley, P. M. (2014). *Monitoring the future: Questionnaire responses from the nation's high school seniors 2012.* Survey Research Center. Institute for Social Research. Ann Arbor, MI: The University of Michigan.

negative correlation A relationship between two variables in which one variable decreases as the other variable increases.

in the media makes children more aggressive. But it could also be that children who are more aggressive to begin with prefer violent TV shows and video games. In this case, another type of investigation has clarified the picture: Psychologists note that hundreds of *experiments* show that viewing violence increases aggressive behavior (Hasan et al., 2013; Robertson et al., 2013).

Similarly, studies in locations as far flung as the United States and China report that children (especially boys) in divorced families sometimes have more adjustment

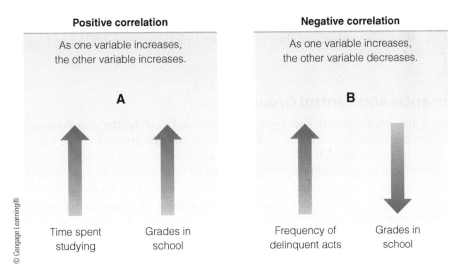

Positive correlation

As one variable increases,
the other variable increases.

A

Time spent
studying

Grades in
school

Negative correlation

As one variable increases,
the other variable decreases.

B

Frequency of
delinquent acts

Grades in
school

© Cengage Learning®

Figure 1.6 ■ Examples of Positive and Negative Correlations
When two variables are correlated positively, one increases as the other increases. There is a positive correlation between the amount of time spent studying and grades, as shown in Part A. When two variables are correlated negatively, one increases as the other decreases. There is a negative correlation between the frequency of a child's delinquent acts and his or her grades, as shown in Part B. As delinquent behavior increases, grades tend to decline.

problems than children in intact families (Potter, 2010; Vélez et al., 2011). However, these studies do not show that divorce causes these adjustment problems. It could be that the same factors that led to divorce (such as parental disorganization or conflict) also led to adjustment problems among the children. Or, having a child with adjustment problems might put a strain on the parents' marriage and ultimately be a factor contributing to divorce.

When we study patterns of child rearing, we must also ask why parents choose to rear their children in certain ways. It is possible that the factors that lead parents to make these choices, such as the cultural environment, also influence the behavior of the children. Thus, correlational research does not enable us to place clear "cause" and "effect" labels on variables. To investigate cause and effect, researchers turn to the experimental method.

What Is an Experiment? What Are an Experiment's Advantages Over Correlation?

The experiment is the preferred method for investigating questions of cause and effect. An **experiment** is a research method in which a group of subjects receives a **treatment** while another group does not. All subjects are then observed to determine whether the treatment makes a difference in their behavior.

Experiments are used when possible because they enable researchers to control the experiences of children and other subjects to determine the outcomes of a treatment. Experiments, like other research methods, are usually undertaken to test a hypothesis. For example, a researcher might hypothesize that exposure to TV violence causes aggressive behavior in children. To test this hypothesis, she might devise an experiment in which some children are purposely exposed to TV violence and others are not. Remember that it is not enough to demonstrate that children who choose to watch more violent shows behave more aggressively; such evidence is only correlational. We review this research—correlational and experimental—in Chapter 10.

Independent and Dependent Variables

In an experiment to determine whether TV violence causes aggressive behavior, subjects in the experimental group would be shown a TV program containing violence, and its effects on behavior would be measured. TV violence would be considered an **independent variable**, a variable whose presence is manipulated by the experimenters

experiment A method of scientific investigation that seeks to discover cause-and-effect relationships by introducing independent variables and observing their effects on dependent variables.

treatment In an experiment, a condition received by subjects so that its effects may be observed.

independent variable In a scientific study, the condition that is manipulated (changed) so that its effects can be observed.

so that its effects can be determined. The measured result (in this case, the child's behavior) is called a **dependent variable**. Its presence or level presumably depends on the independent variable.

Experimental and Control Groups

Experiments use experimental and control groups. Subjects in the **experimental group** receive the treatment, whereas subjects in the **control group** do not. Every effort is made to ensure that all other conditions are held constant for both groups of subjects. Holding other conditions constant gives us confidence that experimental outcomes reflect the treatments and not chance factors. In a study on the effects of TV violence on children's behavior, children in the experimental group would be shown TV programs containing violence, and children in the control group would be shown programs that do not contain violence.

Random Assignment

Subjects should be assigned to experimental or control groups on a chance or random basis. We could not conclude much from an experiment on the effects of TV violence if the children were allowed to choose whether they would be in a group that watched a lot of TV violence or in a group that watched TV shows without violence. Children who chose to watch TV violence might have more aggressive tendencies to begin with! In an experiment on the effects of TV violence, we would therefore have to assign children randomly to view TV shows with or without violence, regardless of their personal preferences. As you can imagine, this would be difficult, if not impossible, to do in the child's own home. But such studies can be performed in laboratory settings, as we will see in Chapter 10.

Ethical and practical considerations also prevent researchers from doing experiments on the effects of many significant life circumstances, such as divorce and different patterns of child rearing. We cannot randomly assign some families divorce or conflict and assign other families "bliss." Nor can we randomly assign authoritarian parents to raise their children in a permissive manner, or vice versa. In some areas of investigation, we must be relatively satisfied with correlational evidence.

When experiments cannot ethically be performed on humans, researchers sometimes carry out experiments with animals and then generalize the findings to humans. For example, no researcher would separate human infants from their parents to study the effects of isolation on development. But experimenters have deprived monkeys of early social experience. Such research has helped psychologists investigate the formation of parent–child bonds of attachment (see Chapter 7).

dependent variable In a scientific study, a measure of an assumed effect of an independent variable.

experimental group A group made up of subjects who receive a treatment in an experiment.

control group A group made up of subjects in an experiment who do not receive the treatment, but for whom all other conditions are comparable to those of subjects in the experimental group.

TRUTH OR FICTION REVISITED: It is true that research with monkeys has helped psychologists understand the formation of attachment in humans. Why monkeys? The reason is that ethical considerations prevent investigators from carrying out experimental research on this issue with humans.

How Do Researchers Study Developments That Take Place Over the Years?

The processes of development occur over time, and researchers have devised different strategies for comparing children of one age to children (or adults) of other ages.

In **longitudinal research**, the same children are observed repeatedly over time, and changes in development (such as gains in height or changes in approach to problem solving) are recorded. In **cross-sectional research**, children of different ages are observed and compared. It is assumed that when a large number of children are chosen at random, the differences found in the older age groups are a reflection of how the younger children will develop, given time.

Longitudinal Studies

Some ambitious longitudinal studies have followed the development of children and adults for more than half a century. One, the Fels Longitudinal Study, began in 1929. Children were observed twice a year in their homes and twice a year in the Fels Institute nursery school. From time to time, younger investigators dipped into the Fels pool of subjects, further testing, interviewing, and observing these individuals as they grew into adults. In this way, researchers have been able to observe the development of intelligence and of patterns of independence and dependence. They found, for example, that intelligence test scores at ages 3 and 18 were significantly related to intellectual and occupational status after the age of 26 (McCall, 1977). But the correlations were not high enough to allow long-term prediction for individual children.

The Terman Study of the Gifted, also begun in the 1920s, tracked children with high IQ scores for more than half a century. Male subjects, but not female subjects, who obtained high IQ scores went on to high achievements in the professional world. Why the difference? Contemporary studies of women show that those with high intelligence generally match the achievements of men; these findings suggest that women of the earlier era were held back by traditional gender-role expectations.

TRUTH OR FICTION REVISITED: It is true that researchers have followed some subjects in developmental research for more than 50 years. This is an example of longitudinal research. Could cross-sectional research have been used for this study? Would cross-sectional research have been advantageous or disadvantageous? In what ways?

Most longitudinal studies span months or a few years, not decades. In Chapter 13, for example, we will see that briefer longitudinal studies have found that the children of divorced parents undergo the most severe adjustment problems within a few months of the divorce. By 2 or 3 years afterward, many children regain their equilibrium, as indicated by improved academic performance, social behavior, and other measures (Hetherington, 2006; Moon, 2011).

Longitudinal studies have drawbacks. For example, it can be difficult to enlist volunteers to participate in a study that will last a lifetime. Many subjects fall out of touch as the years pass; others die. Also, those who remain in the study tend to be more motivated than those who drop out. The researchers must be patient. To compare 3-year-olds with 6-year-olds, they must wait 3 years. In the early stages of such a study, the idea of comparing 3-year-olds with 21-year-olds remains a distant dream. When the researchers themselves are middle-aged or older, they must hope that the candle of yearning for knowledge will be kept lit by a new generation of researchers.

Cross-Sectional Studies

Because of the drawbacks of longitudinal studies, most research that compares children of different ages is cross-sectional. In other words, most investigators

longitudinal research The study of developmental processes by taking repeated measures of the same group of children at various stages of development.

cross-sectional research The study of developmental processes by taking measures of children of different age groups at the same time.

Lynn Koenig/Moment/Getty Images

Is Growing Up Using an iPad an Example of the Cohort Effect? Children and adults of different ages experience cultural and technological events specific to their age groups. Therefore, drawing conclusions based on cross-sectional research may be limited by the cohort effect.

cohort effect Similarities in behavior among a group of peers that stem from the fact that group members are approximately the same age.

cross-sequential research An approach that combines the longitudinal and cross-sectional methods by following individuals of different ages for abbreviated periods of time.

Figure 1.7 ■ Example of Cross-Sequential Research Cross-sequential research combines three methods: cross-sectional, longitudinal, and time-lag. The child's age at the time of testing appears in the boxes. Vertical columns represent cross-sectional comparisons. Horizontal rows represent longitudinal comparisons. Diagonals represent time-lag comparisons.

gather data on what the "typical" 6-month-old is doing by finding children who are 6 months old today. When they expand their research to the behavior of typical 12-month-olds, they seek another group of children, and so on.

A major challenge to cross-sectional research is the **cohort effect**. A cohort is a group of people born at about the same time. As a result, they experience cultural and other events unique to their age group. In other words, children and adults of different ages are not likely to have shared similar cultural backgrounds. People who are 70 years old today, for example, grew up largely without television. (Really, there was a time when television did not exist!) People who are 60 years old today grew up before people landed on the Moon. Today's 50-year-olds did not spend their earliest years with *Sesame Street*. And today's children are growing up taking iPods and the Internet for granted. In fact, for today's children, Jennifer Lopez is an older woman.

Children of past generations also grew up with different expectations about gender roles and appropriate social behavior. Women in the Terman study generally chose motherhood over careers because of the expectations during those times. Today, girls are growing up with female role models who are astronauts, government officials, and athletes. Moreover, today the great majority of mothers are in the workforce, and their attitudes about women's roles have changed.

In other words, today's 80-year-olds are not today's 5-year-olds as seen 75 years later. Today's 80-year-olds did not grow up with the Internet, cell phones, television, rock 'n' roll, or hip-hop. The times change, and their influence on children changes also. In longitudinal studies, we know that we have the same individuals as they developed over 5, 25, even 50 years or more. In cross-sectional research, we can only hope that the individuals will be comparable.

Cross-Sequential Research

Cross-sequential research combines the longitudinal and cross-sectional methods so that many of their individual drawbacks are overcome. In the cross-sequential study, the full span of the ideal longitudinal study is broken up into convenient segments (see Figure 1.7 ■). Assume that we wish to follow the attitudes of children toward gender roles from the age of 4 through the age of 12. The typical longitudinal study would take 8 years. However, we can divide this 8-year span in half by studying two samples

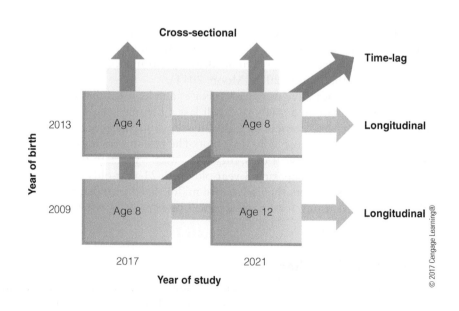

© 2017 Cengage Learning®

of children (a cross-section) instead of one: 4-year-olds and 8-year-olds. We would then interview, test, and observe each group at the beginning of the study (2017) and 4 years later (2021). By the time of the second observation period, the 4-year-olds would have become 8 years old, and the 8-year-olds would have turned 12.

An obvious advantage to this collapsed method is that the study is completed in 4 years rather than 8 years. Still, the testing and retesting of samples provide some of the continuity of the longitudinal study. By observing both samples at the age of 8 (this is called a **time-lag comparison**), we can also determine whether they are, in fact, comparable or whether the 4-year difference in their birthdate is associated with a cohort effect—that is, cultural and other environmental changes that lead to different attitudes.

Concept Review 1.4 summarizes the major features of cross-sectional, longitudinal, and cross-sequential research.

time-lag comparison The study of developmental processes by taking measures of children of the same age group at different times.

Comparison of Cross-Sectional, Longitudinal, and Cross-Sequential Research

	Cross-Sectional Research	Longitudinal Research	Cross-Sequential Research
Description	Studies children of different ages at the same point in time.	Studies the same children repeatedly over time.	Breaks the span of a longitudinal study into convenient segments to study children beginning at different ages.
Advantages	Can be completed in a short period of time. No dropouts or practice effects.	Allows researchers to follow development over time. Studies relationships between behavior at earlier and later ages.	Can be completed in a shorter period of time than a longitudinal study but retains some of its continuity. Allows some comparison of behavior at earlier and later ages.
Disadvantages	Does not study development across time. Cannot study the relationship between behavior displayed at earlier and later ages. Is prey to the cohort effect (subjects from different age groups may not be comparable).	Expensive. Takes a long time to complete. Subjects drop out, and dropouts may differ systematically from remaining subjects. Practice effects may occur.	More expensive than cross-sectional research. Not completely longitudinal. Some dropout effect (not as much as in longitudinal research). Some cohort effect (less than in cross-sectional research). Some practice effects.

© 2017 Cengage Learning®

Researchers adhere to ethical standards that are intended to promote the dignity of the individual, foster human welfare, and maintain scientific integrity. These standards also ensure that researchers do not use methods or treatments that harm subjects.

Various professional groups—such as the American Psychological Association and the Society for Research in Child Development—and government review boards have proposed guidelines for research with children. The overriding purpose of these guidelines is to protect children from harm. These guidelines include the following:

Researchers are not to use methods that may do physical or psychological harm (Axelin & Salanterä, 2008; Bersoff, 2008). In practice, this sort of issue boils down to exactly how much harm is being proposed and, sometimes, whether the value of the study outweighs the possible harm. For example, in using Mary Ainsworth's "Strange Situation" to study attachment between infants and caregivers, researchers separate infants from their caregivers for brief periods of time, often causing some distress. How much distress is too much? In Chapter 7, we will see that researchers have performed distressful or possibly distressful experiments with monkeys that they would not undertake with children.

Children and their parents must be informed about the purposes of the research and about the research methods (Boccia et al., 2009; Salas et al., 2008). This allows participants to provide *informed consent* to the study. In most cases, it is the parent who becomes informed, and the child goes along with the parent's wishes. Is such a situation ethical?

Children and their parents must provide voluntary consent to participate in the study (Boccia et al., 2009). Here we must consider what happens if the parent

A Closer Look   Research

THE CONDITIONING OF "LITTLE ALBERT": A CASE STUDY IN ETHICS

In 1920, the behaviorist John B. Watson and his future wife, Rosalie Rayner, published a report (Watson & Rayner, 1920) of their demonstration that emotional reactions can be acquired through classical conditioning. The subject of their demonstration was an 11-month-old lad who has become known as "Little Albert." Albert was a phlegmatic fellow; he wasn't given to ready displays of emotion. But he did enjoy playing with a laboratory rat. Using a method that many psychologists subsequently criticized as being unethical, Watson startled Little Albert by clanging steel bars behind his head whenever the infant played with the rat. After repeated pairings, Albert showed fear of the rat even when the clanging was halted. Albert's fear also generalized to objects that were similar in appearance to the rat, such as a rabbit and the fur collar on

a woman's coat. This study has become a hallmark in psychology, although Watson has also been criticized for not counterconditioning Albert's fear.

In counterconditioning, an object or situation that evokes a response opposed to a conditioned response is repeatedly associated with the feared object. A few years after the experiment with Little Albert, Mary Cover Jones, a protégé of Watson, carried out a mini-experiment in counterconditioning with a boy named Peter. Peter feared rabbits but enjoyed cookies. Unfortunately, these findings didn't do Albert any good. Albert's mother, distraught at the events that had occurred, removed her son from the laboratory.

Reflect Do you think Watson's experiment with Little Albert was ethical? Why or why not?

"volunteers" the child but the child seems unwilling. Eliminating reluctant children from a sample may systematically exclude certain kinds of children and lead to results that cannot be generalized to all children. Yet how much cajoling should a researcher do? And if parental consent is legally sufficient, should the researcher proceed with the child?

Children and their parents may withdraw from the study at any time, for any reason (Bersoff, 2008). What should the researcher do if the child becomes tired or bored and starts crying or screeching, "I want to go home!"?

Children and their parents should be offered information about the results of the study (Bersoff, 2008). Informing participants about the results is known as *debriefing*. The child, of course, may not be mature or experienced enough to understand the outcomes of the study, but the parent should be.

The identities of the children participating in a study are to remain *confidential* (Bersoff, 2014; Miller et al., 2008). Sometimes conflicts of interest or conflicts between principles arise. What, for example, should researchers do if they acquire information from children that suggests they have been subjected to abuse? Whom do they inform, if anyone (Donner et al., 2008; Gorin et al., 2008)?

Researchers should present their research plans to a committee of their colleagues and obtain the committee's approval before proceeding (Bersoff, 2008).

These guidelines present researchers with a number of hurdles to overcome, before proceeding with and while conducting research. But because they protect the welfare of children, the guidelines are valuable.

Section Review

14. The steps of the scientific method include formulating a research question, developing a _____, testing the hypothesis, drawing conclusions, and publishing results.

15. _____-observation studies are conducted in the real-life setting.

16. The _____ study is a carefully drawn account or biography of an individual child.

17. A correlational study describes relationships but does not reveal _____ and effect.

18. In an experiment, members of an experimental group receive a treatment, whereas members of a _____ group do not.

19. _____ research observes the same children repeatedly over time.

20. In cross-_____ research, children of different ages are observed and compared.

Reflect & Relate: How do you gather information about the behavior and mental processes of other people? Which of the methods described in this section come closest to your own? Are your methods adequately scientific? Explain.

Chapter Review

1.1 What Is Child Development? Coming to Terms with Terms

The field of child development attempts to advance knowledge of the processes that govern the development of children's physical structures, traits, behaviors, and cognitions. *Growth* consists of changes in size or quantity, whereas *development* also includes changes in quality. Researchers study child development to gain insight into human nature, the origins of adult behavior, the origins of developmental problems, ways of optimizing development, and the effects of culture on development. Locke focused on the role of the environment, or experience, in development. Rousseau argued that children are good by nature, and if allowed to express their natural impulses, they will develop into moral and giving people. Darwin originated the modern theory of evolution and was one of the first observers to keep a baby biography. Hall founded child development as an academic discipline. Binet developed the first modern standardized intelligence test.

1.2 What Are the Various Theories of Child Development?

Theories are related sets of statements about events. Theories of development help us describe, explain, and predict development, and they enable researchers to influence development through education of caregivers and teachers. Freud viewed children as caught in conflict. He believed that people undergo *oral, anal, phallic, latency,* and *genital* stages of psychosexual development. Too little or too much gratification in a stage can lead to fixation. Erikson's psychosocial theory views social relationships as more important than sexual or aggressive impulses. Erikson extended Freud's five developmental stages to eight (to include adulthood) and named stages after life crises. Watson argued that scientists must address observable behavior only, not mental activity. Behaviorism relies on two types of learning: classical conditioning and operant conditioning. In classical conditioning, one stimulus comes to elicit the same response as another by being paired repeatedly with it. In operant conditioning, children learn to engage in or to discontinue behavior because of its effects (reinforcement or lack of reinforcement). Social cognitive theorists, such as Bandura, argue that much learning occurs by observing models and that children choose whether or not to engage in behaviors they have learned. Piaget saw children as actors on the environment, not reactors. He studied how children form mental representations of the world and manipulate them. Piaget's theory relies on the concepts of *schemes, adaptation, assimilation, accommodation,* and *equilibration.* He hypothesized that children's cognitive processes develop in an invariant series of stages: *sensorimotor, preoperational, concrete operational,* and *formal operational.* Information-processing theory deals with the ways in which children encode information, transfer it to working memory (short-term memory), manipulate it, place information in storage (long-term memory), and retrieve it from storage.

The biological perspective focuses on heredity and on developments such as the formation of sperm and ova, gains in height and weight, maturation of the nervous system, and the way hormones spur the changes of puberty. Ethology involves instinctive, or inborn, behavior patterns, termed *fixed action patterns (FAPs).* Many FAPs, such as those involved in attachment, occur during a *critical period* of life.

Bronfenbrenner's ecological theory explains development in terms of the *reciprocal interaction* between children and the settings in which development occurs. These settings are the *microsystem, mesosystem, exosystem, macrosystem,* and *chronosystem.* The sociocultural perspective emphasizes that children are social beings who are influenced by their cultural backgrounds. Vygotsky introduced the sociocultural concepts of *scaffolding* and the *zone of proximal development (ZPD).* Children internalize conversations and explanations that help them gain skills. Children learn ways of solving problems within a cultural context. The sociocultural perspective also addresses the richness of children's diversity, including their ethnicity and sex. Understanding the cultural heritages and historical problems of children from various ethnic groups is necessary for effective education and psychological intervention.

1.3 What Controversies Surround the Issue of Nature versus Nurture in Child Development?

Development would appear to reflect the interaction of nature (genetics) and nurture (nutrition, cultural and family backgrounds, and opportunities to learn about the world). Maturational, psychoanalytic, and cognitive-developmental theorists see development as discontinuous (occurring in stages). Aspects of physical development, such as the adolescent growth spurt, do occur in stages. Learning theorists tend to see development as more continuous. Bronfenbrenner and Bandura do not see children as entirely active or entirely passive. They believe that children are influenced by the environment but that the influence is reciprocal.

1.4 How Do We Study Child Development?

The scientific method is a systematic way of formulating and answering research questions that includes developing a hypothesis, testing the hypothesis, drawing conclusions, and publishing results. Researchers use naturalistic observation, the case study, and the survey. Naturalistic observation is conducted in "the field"—in the actual settings in which children develop. The case study is a carefully drawn account or biography of the behavior of a child. Information may be derived from diaries, observation, questionnaires, standardized tests, interviews, and public records. Surveys can be used to learn about behavior and mental processes that cannot be observed in the natural setting or studied experimentally. Correlation enables researchers to determine whether one behavior or trait is related to another. A correlation coefficient can vary between +1.00 and −1.00. Correlational studies can reveal relationships but not cause and effect. In an experiment, an experimental group receives a treatment (the independent variable) while another group (a control group) does not. Subjects are observed to determine whether the treatment has an effect. Longitudinal research studies the same children repeatedly over time. Cross-sectional research observes and compares children of different ages. A drawback to cross-sectional research is the cohort effect. Cross-sequential research combines the longitudinal and cross-sectional methods by breaking down the span of the ideal longitudinal study into convenient segments.

1.5 What Ethical Considerations Influence the Kinds of Research That May Be Conducted with Children?

Ethical standards are established to promote the dignity of the individual, foster human welfare, and maintain scientific integrity. Researchers are not to use treatments that may do harm. Subjects must participate voluntarily.

Key Terms

child 4
infancy 4
development 4
growth 4
behaviorism 7
theory 8
psychosexual development 9
stage theory 9
psychosocial development 12
life crisis 12
identity crisis 12
classical conditioning 13
stimulus 13
operant conditioning 14
reinforcement 14
positive reinforcer 14
negative reinforcer 14
punishment 14
shaping 16
time-out 17
social cognitive theory 17
cognitive-developmental theory 18

scheme 19
adaptation 19
assimilation 19
accommodation 19
equilibration 19
ethology 21
imprinting 22
ecology 22
ecological systems theory 22
microsystem 23
mesosystem 23
exosystem 24
macrosystem 24
chronosystem 24
zone of proximal development (ZPD) 25
scaffolding 25
ethnic groups 26
socioeconomic status (SES) 27
nature 31
nurture 31
genes 31

empirical 32
hypothesis 33
naturalistic observation 33
case study 34
standardized test 35
correlation 35
variables 35
correlation coefficient 35
positive correlation 35
negative correlation 35
experiment 37
treatment 37
independent variable 37
dependent variable 38
experimental group 38
control group 38
longitudinal research 39
cross-sectional research 39
cohort effect 40
cross-sequential research 40
time-lag comparison 41

2

Heredity and
Conception

Major Topics

Features

TruthorFiction?

 Your father determined whether you are female or male. **p. 50**

 Brown eyes are dominant over blue eyes. **p. 51**

 You can carry the genes for a deadly illness and not become sick yourself. **p. 52**

 Girls are born with all the egg cells they will ever have. **p. 66**

About 120–150 boys are conceived for every 100 girls. **p. 66**

Sperm travel about at random inside a woman's reproductive tract, so which one reaches the ovum first is a matter of luck. **p. 66**

Extensive athletic activity may contribute to infertility in the male. **p. 69**

"Test-tube" babies are grown in a laboratory dish throughout their 9-month gestation period. **p. 71**

You can select the sex of your child. **p. 72**

Let's talk about the facts of life. Here are a few of them:

- People cannot breathe underwater (without special equipment).
- People cannot fly (without special equipment).
- Fish cannot learn to speak French or dance an Irish jig, even if you raise them in enriched environments and send them to finishing school.

We cannot breathe underwater or fly because we have not inherited gills or wings. Fish are similarly limited by their heredity. In this chapter, we explore heredity and conception. We learn that development begins long before conception. Development involves the origins of the genetic structures that determine that human embryos will grow arms rather than wings, lungs rather than gills, and hair rather than scales. Our discussion thus begins with an examination of the building blocks of heredity: genes and chromosomes. Then we describe the process of conception and find that the odds against any specific sperm uniting with an ovum are quite literally astronomical.

Rubberball/Brand X Pictures/Getty Images

2.1 The Influence of Heredity on Development: The Nature of Nature

Heredity defines one's nature, which is based on the biological transmission of traits and characteristics from one generation to another. Because of their heredity, fish cannot speak French or do a jig.

Heredity makes possible all things human. The structures we inherit make our behavior possible *and* impose limits on it. The field within the science of biology that studies heredity is called **genetics**.

Genetic (inherited) influences are fundamental in the transmission of physical traits, such as height, hair texture, and eye color. Genetics also appears to play a role in intelligence and in traits such as activity level, sociability, shyness, anxiety, empathy, effectiveness as a parent, happiness, and even interest in arts and crafts (Gregory et al., 2009; Ebstein et al., 2010; Sirgy, 2012). Genetic factors are also involved in psychological problems such as schizophrenia, depression, and dependence on nicotine, alcohol, and some other substances (Kendler et al., 2012; Tansey et al., 2014; Voineskos, 2015).

What Are Chromosomes and Genes?

The fundamental units of heredity are microscopic structures called chromosomes and genes. **Chromosomes** are rod-shaped structures found in cells. A normal human cell contains 46 chromosomes organized into 23 pairs. Each chromosome contains thousands of segments called genes. **Genes** are the biochemical materials that regulate the development of traits. Some traits, such as blood type, appear to be transmitted by a single pair of genes that is made up of one gene from each parent. Other traits, referred to as **polygenic**, are determined by combinations of pairs of genes.

We have 20,000 to 25,000 genes in every cell of our bodies (Gonzaga-Jaurequi et al., 2012). Genes are segments of large strands of **deoxyribonucleic acid (DNA)**. DNA takes the form of a double spiral, or helix, similar in appearance to a twisting ladder (see Figure 2.1 ■). In all living things, from one-celled animals to fish to

heredity The transmission of traits and characteristics from parent to child by means of genes.

genetics The branch of biology that studies heredity.

chromosomes Rod-shaped structures that are composed of genes and found within the nuclei of cells.

gene The basic unit of heredity. Genes are composed of deoxyribonucleic acid (DNA).

polygenic Resulting from many genes.

deoxyribonucleic acid (DNA) Genetic material that takes the form of a double helix made up of phosphates, sugars, and bases.

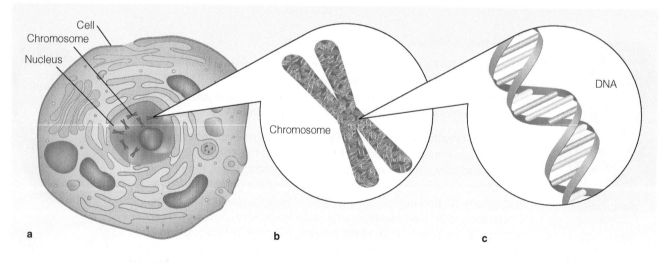

a   b   c

Figure 2.1 ■ The Double Helix of DNA
DNA consists of phosphate, sugar, and a number of bases. It takes the form of a double spiral, or helix.
© Cengage Learning®

people, the sides of the "ladder" consist of alternating segments of phosphate and simple sugar. The "rungs" of the ladder are attached to the sugars and consist of one of two pairs of bases, either adenine with thymine (A with T) or cytosine with guanine (C with G). The sequence of the rungs is the genetic code that will cause the developing organism to grow arms or wings, skin or scales.

What Are Mitosis and Meiosis?

We begin life as a single cell, or **zygote**, that divides again and again. There are two types of cell division: mitosis and meiosis. **Mitosis** is the cell division process by which growth occurs and tissues are replaced. Through mitosis, our genetic code is carried into new cells in our bodies. In mitosis, strands of DNA break apart, or "unzip" (see Figure 2.2 ■). The double helix then duplicates. The DNA forms two camps on either side of the cell, and then the cell divides. Each incomplete rung combines with the appropriate "partner" element (that is, G combines with C, and A with T) to form a new complete ladder. The two resulting identical copies of the DNA strand move apart when the cell divides, each becoming a member of one of the newly formed cells. As a consequence, the genetic code is identical in new cells unless **mutations** occur due to radiation or other environmental influences. Mutations are also believed to occur by chance, but rarely.

Sperm and ova are produced through **meiosis**, or *reduction division*. In meiosis, the 46 chromosomes within the cell nucleus first line up into 23 pairs. The DNA ladders then unzip, leaving unpaired chromosome halves. When the cell divides, one member of each pair goes to each newly formed cell. As a consequence, each new cell nucleus contains only 23 chromosomes, not 46. Thus, a cell that results from meiosis has half the genetic material of a cell that results from mitosis.

During fertilization we receive 23 chromosomes from our father's sperm cell and 23 chromosomes from our mother's ovum, and the combined chromosomes form 23 pairs (see Figure 2.3 ■). Twenty-two of the pairs are **autosomes**—pairs that look alike and possess genetic information concerning the same set of traits. The 23rd pair consists of the **sex chromosomes**, which look different from other chromosomes and determine our sex. We all receive an X sex chromosome (so called because of its X shape) from our mother.

zygote A new cell formed from the union of a sperm and an ovum (egg cell); a fertilized egg.

mitosis The form of cell division in which each chromosome splits lengthwise to double in number. Half of each chromosome combines with chemicals to retake its original form and then moves to the new cell.

mutation A sudden variation in a heritable characteristic, caused by an accident that affects the composition of genes.

meiosis The form of cell division in which each pair of chromosomes splits and one member of each pair moves to the new cell. As a result, each new cell has 23 chromosomes.

autosome A member of a pair of chromosomes (with the exception of sex chromosomes).

sex chromosome A chromosome in the shape of a Y (male) or an X (female) that determines the sex of the child.

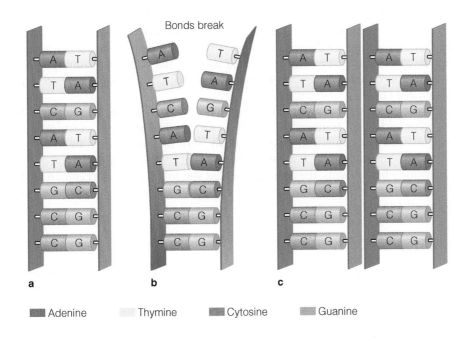

Bonds break

a　　　　b　　　　c

■ Adenine　　■ Thymine　　■ Cytosine　　■ Guanine

Figure 2.2 ■ Mitosis
(a) A segment of a strand of DNA before mitosis. (b) During mitosis, chromosomal strands of DNA "unzip." (c) The double helix is rebuilt in the cell as each incomplete "rung" combines with appropriate molecules. The resulting identical copies of the DNA strand move apart when the cell divides, each joining one of the new cells.
© Cengage Learning®

Figure 2.3 ■ The 23 Pairs of Human Chromosomes
People normally have 23 pairs of chromosomes. Females have two X chromosomes, whereas males have an X and a Y sex chromosome.

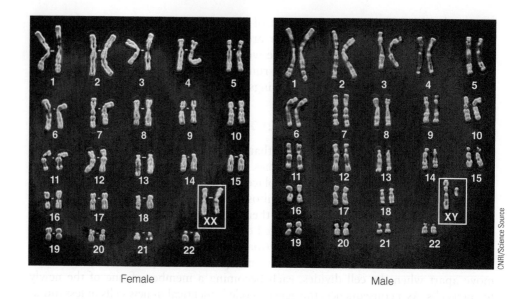

Female   Male

CNRI/Science Source

TRUTH OR FICTION REVISITED: It is true that your father determined whether you are a female or a male. The mother's ova have only X chromosomes. If the father's sperm cell supplies another X sex chromosome, the baby will be female. If the father's sperm cell supplies a Y sex chromosome (named after its Y shape), the baby will be male.

What Are Identical and Fraternal Twins?

Now and then, a zygote divides into two cells that separate so that each subsequently develops into an individual, and those two individuals have the same genetic makeup. Such individuals are known as identical twins, or **monozygotic (MZ) twins.** If the woman produces two ova in the same month and each is fertilized by a different sperm cell, they develop into fraternal twins, or **dizygotic (DZ) twins.**

Twinning rates have been increasing in developed countries for two main reasons: increasing age of mothers and the use of assisted reproductive technologies (Davies et al., 2012; Kurosawa et al., 2012). As women reach the end of their childbearing years, **ovulation** becomes less regular, resulting in a number of months when more than one ovum is released. Thus, the chances of twins increase with parental age (Hediger, 2011). Fertility drugs also increase the chances of multiple births by causing more than one ovum to ripen and be released during a woman's cycle (Hediger, 2011).

About two-thirds of twin pregnancies are DZ twins (Fellman, 2013). While MZ twins occur with equal frequency in all ethnic groups, DZ twins are most frequently born to African Americans and least frequently born to Asian Americans.

DZ twins run in families. If a woman is a twin, if her mother was a twin, or if she has previously borne twins, the chances rise that she will bear twins (Fellman, 2013). Similarly, women who have borne several children have an increased likelihood of twins in subsequent pregnancies.

What Are Dominant and Recessive Traits?

Traits are determined by pairs of genes. Each member of a pair of genes is referred to as an **allele.** When both of the alleles for a trait, such as hair color, are the same, the person is said to be **homozygous** for that trait. (*Homo,* in this usage, derives from the Greek root meaning "same," not from the Latin root meaning "man.") When the alleles for a trait differ, the person is **heterozygous** for that trait.

monozygotic (MZ) twins Twins that derive from a single zygote that has split into two; identical twins. Each MZ twin carries the same genetic code.

dizygotic (DZ) twins Twins that derive from two zygotes; fraternal twins.

ovulation The release of an ovum from an ovary.

allele A member of a pair of genes.

homozygous Having two identical alleles.

heterozygous Having two different alleles.

Gregor Mendel (1822–1884), an Austrian monk, established a number of laws of heredity through his work with pea plants. Mendel realized that some traits result from an "averaging" of the genetic instructions carried by the parents. When the effects of both alleles are shown, there is said to be incomplete dominance or codominance.

Mendel also discovered the "law of dominance." When a *dominant* allele is paired with a *recessive* allele, the trait determined by the dominant allele appears in the offspring. For example, the offspring from the crossing of purebred tall peas and purebred dwarf peas were tall, suggesting that tallness is dominant over dwarfism. We now know that many genes determine **dominant traits** or **recessive traits**. For example, the offspring of Mendel's crossing of purebred tall and purebred dwarf peas carried recessive genes for dwarfism.

TRUTH OR FICTION REVISITED: It is true that brown eyes are dominant over blue eyes. If one parent carries genes for only brown eyes and the other parent carries genes for only blue eyes, the children will have brown eyes. But brown-eyed parents can also carry recessive genes for blue eyes so that if both brown-eyed parents have recessive genes for blue eyes, their children have a one in four chance of having blue-eyes.

If the recessive gene from one parent combines with the recessive gene from the other parent, the recessive trait will be shown. As suggested by Figure 2.4 ■, approximately 25% of the offspring of brown-eyed parents who carry recessive genes for blue eye color will have blue eyes. Mendel found that 25% of the offspring of parent peas that carried recessive dwarfism were dwarfs. Table 2.1 ● lists several other examples of dominant and recessive traits in humans.

dominant trait A trait that is expressed.

recessive trait A trait that is not expressed when the gene or genes involved have been paired with dominant genes. Recessive traits are transmitted to future generations and expressed if they are paired with other recessive genes.

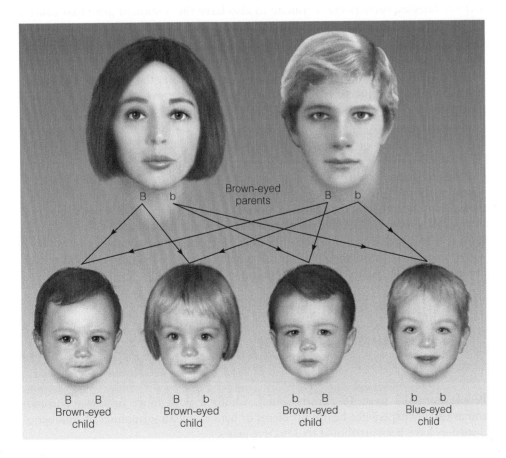

Figure 2.4 ■ Transmission of Dominant and Recessive Traits
Each of these two brown-eyed parents carries a gene for blue eyes. Their children have an equal chance of receiving a gene for brown eyes or a gene for blue eyes from each parent.
© Cengage Learning®

● TABLE 2.1

Examples of Dominant and Recessive Traits

Dominant Trait	Recessive Trait
Dark hair	Blonde hair
Dark hair	Red hair
Curly hair	Straight hair
Normal color vision	Red–green color blindness
Normal vision	Myopia (nearsightedness)
Farsightedness	Normal vision
Normal pigmentation	Deficiency of pigmentation in skin, hair, and retina (albinism)
Normal sensitivity to touch	Extremely fragile skin
Normal hearing	Some forms of deafness
Dimples	Lack of dimpling
Type A blood	Type O blood
Type B blood	Type O blood
Tolerance of lactose	Lactose intolerance

© 2017 Cengage Learning®

People who bear one dominant gene and one recessive gene for a trait are said to be **carriers** of the recessive gene. In the cases where recessive genes give rise to serious illnesses, carriers are fortunate to also have the dominant gene that cancels the recessive gene's effects.

TRUTH OR FICTION REVISITED: It is true that you can carry the genes for a deadly illness and not become sick yourself. This occurs when genes for the illness are recessive, and dominant genes cancel their effects.

Chromosomal or genetic abnormalities can cause health problems. Some chromosomal disorders (such as Down syndrome) reflect abnormalities in the 22 pairs of autosomes; others (such as XYY syndrome) reflect abnormalities in the 23rd pair—the sex chromosomes. Some genetic abnormalities, such as cystic fibrosis, are caused by a single pair of genes; others are caused by combinations of genes. Diabetes mellitus, epilepsy, and peptic ulcers are **multifactorial problems**; that is, they reflect both a genetic predisposition *and* environmental contributors. Chromosomal and genetic abnormalities are discussed in the following sections.

carrier A person who carries and transmits characteristics but does not exhibit them.

multifactorial problems Problems that stem from the interaction of heredity and environmental factors.

2.2 Chromosomal and Genetic Abnormalities

People normally have 46 chromosomes. Children with more or fewer chromosomes usually experience health problems or behavioral abnormalities. A number of disorders have been attributed to defective genes.

Risk of Giving Birth to an Infant with Down Syndrome, According to the Age of the Mother

Age of the Mother	Probability of Down Syndrome in the Child
20	1 in 1,667
30	1 in 953
40	1 in 106
49	1 in 11

Sources: American Fertility Association (2014).

What Kinds of Problems Are Caused by Chromosomal Abnormalities?

Chromosomal abnormalities occur when children do not have the normal complement of 46 chromosomes. The risk of chromosomal abnormalities rises with the age of the parents (Desai et al., 2013; Sandin et al., 2012). Although we commonly consider the age of the mother, the age of the father apparently plays a role as well. For example, men who are 40 years of age and older are five to six times as likely as men below the age of 30 to have children with autistic disorders (Park et al., 2010; Powrie et al., 2010). Here we consider Down syndrome and sex-linked chromosomal abnormalities.

Down Syndrome

Down syndrome is usually caused by an extra chromosome on the 21st pair, resulting in 47 chromosomes. The probability of having a child with Down syndrome varies positively with the age of the parents: Older parents are more likely to bear children with the syndrome (see Table 2.2 ●).

A syndrome is a group of symptoms that characterize a disorder. Children with Down syndrome typically have a rounded face, a protruding tongue, a broad, flat nose, and a sloping fold of skin over the inner corners of the eyes (see Figure 2.5 ■). Some parents arrange for cosmetic surgery to alter the appearance of the eyes of children with Down syndrome to discourage stereotyping by others. People with Down syndrome usually die from cardiovascular problems by middle age, although modern medicine has extended their lives appreciably. Children with the syndrome show deficits in cognitive development, language development, and motor development (van Gameren-Oosterom et al., 2013). They encounter frequent disorders of the ear, nose, and throat, which also contribute to academic problems (Virji-Babul et al., 2006). Even so, Down syndrome varies widely in its expression.

Children with Down syndrome often have adjustment problems in school and in the community at large. Other children are not always sensitive to their needs and feelings and may poke fun at them. Children with Down syndrome and other problems also tend to need more attention from their parents. Parental response is variable; some parents are overwhelmed and a few are abusive, but many parents report that helping to meet the special needs of their children has contributed to their own self-esteem and self-worth (Gowers & Bryan, 2005).

George Doyle/Stockbyte/Getty Images

Figure 2.5 ■ Down Syndrome
The development and adjustment of children with Down syndrome are related to their acceptance by their families. Children with Down syndrome who are reared at home develop more rapidly and achieve higher levels of functioning than those who are reared in institutions.

Down syndrome A chromosomal abnormality characterized by intellectual disability and caused by an extra chromosome in the 21st pair.

Sex-Linked Chromosomal Abnormalities

Several disorders stem from an abnormal number of sex chromosomes and are therefore said to be **sex-linked chromosomal abnormalities**. Most individuals with an abnormal number of sex chromosomes are infertile. Beyond that commonality there are many differences, some of them associated with "maleness" or "femaleness" (Frühmesser & Kotzot, 2011; Heard & Turner, 2011).

Approximately 1 male in 700–1,000 has an extra Y chromosome. The Y chromosome is associated with maleness, and the extra Y sex chromosome apparently heightens male secondary sex characteristics. For example, XYY males are somewhat taller than average and develop heavier beards. Because of characteristics such as these, males with XYY sex chromosomal structure were once referred to as "supermales." But the prefix *super* often implies superior, and it turns out that XYY males tend to have more problems than XY males. For example, they are often mildly delayed, particularly in language development. As part of their "excessive maleness," it was once thought that XYY males were given to aggressive criminal behavior. When we examine prison populations, we find that the number of XYY males is "overrepresented" relative to their number in the general population. However, it may be that the number of XYY males in prisons reflects their level of intelligence rather than aggressiveness.

About 1 male in 500 has **Klinefelter syndrome**, which is caused by an extra X sex chromosome (an XXY sex-chromosomal pattern). XXY males produce less of the male sex hormone **testosterone** than normal males. As a result, male primary and secondary sex characteristics, such as the testes, deepening of the voice, musculature, and the male pattern of body hair, do not develop properly. XXY males usually have enlarged breasts *(gynecomastia)* and usually exhibit mild intellectual disability, particularly in language skills (Frühmesser & Kotzot, 2011). XXY males are typically treated with testosterone replacement therapy, which can foster growth of sex characteristics and elevate mood, but the therapy does not reverse infertility.

About 1 female in 2,500 has a single X sex chromosome and as a result develops what is called **Turner syndrome**. The external genitals of girls with Turner syndrome are normal, but their ovaries are poorly developed and they produce little of the female sex hormone **estrogen**. Girls with this problem are shorter than average and infertile. Because of low estrogen production, they do not develop breasts or menstruate. Researchers have connected a specific pattern of cognitive deficits with low estrogen levels: problems in visual–spatial skills, mathematics, and nonverbal memory (Bray et al., 2011; Hong et al., 2011). Some studies find these girls to be more extroverted and more interested in seeking novel stimulation than other girls (e.g., Boman et al., 2006).

About 1 female in 1,000 has an XXX sex chromosomal structure, or *triple X syndrome*. Such girls are normal in appearance; however, they tend to have lower-than-average language skills and poorer short-term memory. Development of external sexual organs appears normal enough, although there is increased incidence of infertility (N. R. Lee et al., 2011).

Our discussion of chromosomal and genetic abnormalities is summarized in Table 2.3 ●.

What Kinds of Problems Are Caused by Genetic Abnormalities?

We will discuss several such problems, beginning with phenylketonuria.

Phenylketonuria

The enzyme disorder **phenylketonuria (PKU)** is transmitted by a recessive gene and affects about 1 child in 8,000. Therefore, if both parents possess the gene, PKU will

sex-linked chromosomal abnormalities Abnormalities that are transmitted from generation to generation, carried by a sex chromosome, usually an X sex chromosome.

Klinefelter syndrome A chromosomal disorder found among males that is caused by an extra X sex chromosome and is characterized by infertility and mild intellectual disability.

testosterone A male sex hormone produced mainly by the testes.

Turner syndrome A chromosomal disorder found among females that is caused by having a single X sex chromosome and is characterized by infertility.

estrogen A female sex hormone produced mainly by the ovaries.

phenylketonuria (PKU) A genetic abnormality in which phenylalanine builds up and causes intellectual disability.

Chromosomal and Genetic Disorders

Health Problem	Incidence	Comments	Treatment
CHROMOSOMAL DISORDERS			
Down syndrome	1 birth in 700–800 overall; risk increases with parental age.	A condition characterized by a third chromosome on the 21st pair. A child with Down syndrome has characteristic folds of skin over the corners of the eyes and intellectual disability.	No treatment, but educational programs are effective; syndrome is usually fatal, as a result of complications, by middle age.
Klinefelter syndrome	1 male in 500–900	A disorder that affects males, characterized by an extra X sex chromosome and connected with underdeveloped male secondary sex characteristics and gynecomastia.	Hormone (testosterone) replacement therapy; special education.
Turner syndrome	1 female in 2,500	A disorder that affects females, characterized by a single X sex chromosome and associated with infertility and problems in visual–spatial skills and mathematics.	Hormone (estrogen) replacement therapy; special education.
XXX syndrome	1 female in 1,000	A sex-chromosomal disorder that affects females and is connected with mild intellectual disability.	Special education.
XYY syndrome	1 male in 700–1,000	A sex-chromosomal disorder that affects males and is connected with heavy beards, tallness, and mild intellectual disability.	None.
GENETIC DISORDERS			
Cystic fibrosis	1 birth in 2,000 among European Americans; 1 birth in 16,000 among African Americans.	A genetic disease caused by a recessive gene in which the pancreas and lungs become clogged with mucus, impairing respiration and digestion.	Physical therapy to loosen mucus and prompt bronchial drainage; antibiotics for infections of respiratory tract; management of diet.
Duchenne muscular dystrophy	1 male birth in 3,000–5,000	A fatal sex-linked degenerative muscle disease caused by a recessive gene, usually found in males and characterized by loss of the ability to walk during middle childhood or early adolescence.	None; usually fatal by adolescence because of respiratory infection or cardiovascular damage.
Hemophilia	1 male in 4,000–10,000	A sex-linked disorder in which blood does not clot properly.	Transfusion of blood to introduce clotting factors.
Huntington disease (HD)	1 birth in 18,000	A fatal neurological disorder caused by a dominant gene; onset is in adulthood.	None; usually fatal within 20 years of onset of symptoms.
Neural tube defects	1 birth in 1,000	Disorders of the brain or spine in which part of the brain is missing, and spina bifida, in which part of the spine is exposed or missing.	None for anencephaly, which is fatal; surgery to close spinal canal in spina bifida.
Phenylketonuria (PKU)	1 birth in 8,000–10,000	A disorder caused by a recessive gene in which children cannot metabolize the amino acid phenylalanine, which builds up in the form of phenylpyruvic acid and causes intellectual disability. PKU is diagnosable at birth.	Controlled by special diet, which can prevent intellectual disability.
Sickle-cell anemia	1 African American in 500	A blood disorder caused by a recessive gene that mostly afflicts African Americans; deformed blood cells obstruct small blood vessels, decreasing their capacity to carry oxygen.	Transfusions to treat anemia and prevent strokes; antibiotics for infections; anesthetics; fatal before adulthood to about half of those with the disorder.
Tay-Sachs disease	1 Jewish American of Eastern European origin in 3,000–3,600	A fatal neurological disorder caused by a recessive gene that primarily afflicts Jews of Eastern European origin.	None; usually fatal by age 3–4.

be transmitted to one child in four (as in Figure 2.4). Two children in four will possess the gene but will not develop the disorder. These two, like their parents, will be carriers of the disease. One child in four will not receive the recessive gene. Therefore, he or she will not be a carrier.

Children with PKU cannot metabolize an amino acid called phenylalanine. As a consequence, the substance builds up in their bodies and impairs the functioning of the central nervous system. The results are serious: intellectual disability, psychological disorders, and physical problems. We have no cure for PKU, but it can be detected in newborn children through analysis of the blood or urine. Children with PKU who are placed on diets low in phenylalanine within 3 to 6 weeks after birth develop normally. The diet prohibits all meat, poultry, fish, dairy products, beans, and nuts. Fruits, vegetables, and some starchy foods are allowed (Casey, 2013; Dawson et al., 2011). Pediatricians recommend staying on the diet at least until adolescence, and some encourage staying on it for life.

Huntington Disease

Huntington disease (HD) is a fatal, progressive, degenerative disorder and is a dominant trait. Physical symptoms include uncontrollable muscle movements. Psychological symptoms include personality change and loss of intellectual functioning (van Dujin et al., 2014). Because the onset of HD is delayed until middle adulthood, many individuals with the defect have borne children, only to discover years later that they and possibly half of their offspring will inevitably develop it. Fortunately, the disorder is rare—affecting about 1 American in 18,000. Medicines are helpful in treating some of the symptoms of HD, but they do not cure it.

Sickle-Cell Anemia

Sickle-cell anemia is caused by a recessive gene. Sickle-cell anemia is most common among African Americans but also occurs in people from Central and South America, the Caribbean, Mediterranean countries, and the Middle East. Nearly 1 African American in 10 and about 1 Latin American in 20 are carriers. In sickle-cell anemia, red blood cells take on the shape of a sickle and clump together, obstructing small blood vessels and decreasing the oxygen supply. The lessened oxygen supply can impair cognitive skills and academic performance (Smith et al., 2013). Physical problems include painful and swollen joints, jaundice, and potentially fatal conditions such as pneumonia, stroke, and heart and kidney failure.

Tay-Sachs Disease

Tay-Sachs disease is also caused by a recessive gene. It causes the central nervous system to degenerate, resulting in death. The disorder is most commonly found among children in Jewish families of Eastern European background. About 1 in 30 Jewish Americans from this background carries the recessive gene for Tay-Sachs. Children with the disorder progressively lose control over their muscles. They experience visual and auditory sensory losses, develop intellectual disability, become paralyzed, and die toward the end of early childhood, by about the age of 5.

Cystic Fibrosis

Cystic fibrosis, also caused by a recessive gene, is the most common fatal hereditary disease among European Americans. About 30,000 Americans have the disorder, but another 10 million (1 in every 31 people) are carriers (Cystic Fibrosis Foundation, 2014). Children with the disease suffer from excessive production of thick mucus that clogs the pancreas and lungs. Most victims die of respiratory infections in their 20s.

Huntington disease (HD) A fatal genetic neurological disorder whose onset is in middle age.

sickle-cell anemia A genetic disorder that decreases the blood's capacity to carry oxygen.

Tay-Sachs disease A fatal genetic neurological disorder in which nerve cells in the brain and spinal cord are progressively destroyed

cystic fibrosis A fatal genetic disorder in which mucus obstructs the lungs and pancreas.

Sex-Linked Genetic Abnormalities

Some genetic defects, such as **hemophilia**, are carried on only the X sex chromosome. For this reason, they are referred to as **sex-linked genetic abnormalities**. These defects also involve recessive genes. Females, who have two X sex chromosomes, are less likely than males to show sex-linked disorders, because the genes that cause the disorder would have to be present on both of a female's sex chromosomes for the disorder to be expressed. Sex-linked diseases are more likely to afflict sons of female carriers because males have only one X sex chromosome, which they inherit from their mothers.

One form of **muscular dystrophy**, Duchenne muscular dystrophy, is sex-linked. Muscular dystrophy is characterized by a weakening of the muscles, which can lead to wasting away, inability to walk, and sometimes death. Other sex-linked abnormalities include diabetes, color blindness, and some types of night blindness.

How Do Health Professionals Determine Whether Children Will Have Genetic or Chromosomal Abnormalities?

It is now possible to detect the genetic abnormalities that are responsible for hundreds of diseases. In an effort to help parents avert these predictable tragedies, **genetic counseling** is widely used. Genetic counselors compile information about a couple's genetic heritage to explore whether their children might develop genetic abnormalities. Couples who face a high risk of passing along genetic defects to their children sometimes decide to adopt children rather than conceive their own.

In addition, **prenatal** testing can indicate whether the embryo or fetus is carrying genetic abnormalities. Prenatal testing includes amniocentesis, chorionic villus sampling (CVS), ultrasound, and blood tests.

Although we will discuss amniocentesis and CVS, it should be noted that their use tends to be declining because blood tests and ultrasound are becoming more sophisticated and used more frequently. By the time an amniocentesis is normally scheduled, a woman today may have had several blood tests and ultrasounds, which provide evidence of chromosomal as well as genetic abnormalities, and also provide reasonably clear pictures of the embryo and fetus.

Amniocentesis

Amniocentesis is usually performed on the mother at about 14–16 weeks after conception, although many physicians perform the procedure earlier ("early amniocentesis"). In this procedure, the health professional uses a syringe (needle) to withdraw fluid from the amniotic sac (see Figure 2.6 ■). The fluid contains cells that are sloughed off by the fetus. The cells are separated from the amniotic fluid, grown in a culture, and then examined microscopically for genetic and chromosomal abnormalities.

Amniocentesis was once routinely recommended for women who become pregnant after the age of 35, because the chances of Down syndrome increase dramatically as women—or their mates!—approach or pass the age of 40. But

Marka/press/Alamy

The actor Richard Burton was diagnosed with hemophilia. Here we see him with Elizabeth Taylor, who starred with him in the film *Cleopatra*.

hemophilia A genetic disorder in which blood does not clot properly.

sex-linked genetic abnormalities Abnormalities resulting from genes that are found on the X sex chromosome.

muscular dystrophy A chronic disease characterized by a progressive wasting away of the muscles.

genetic counseling Advice concerning the probabilities that a couple's children will show genetic abnormalities.

prenatal Before birth.

amniocentesis A procedure for drawing out and examining fetal cells sloughed off into amniotic fluid to determine whether various disorders are present.

Figure 2.6 ■ Amniocentesis
Amniocentesis allows prenatal identification of certain genetic and chromosomal disorders via the examination of genetic material sloughed off by the fetus into the amniotic fluid. Amniocentesis also enables parents to learn the sex of their unborn child. Would you want to know?
© Cengage Learning®

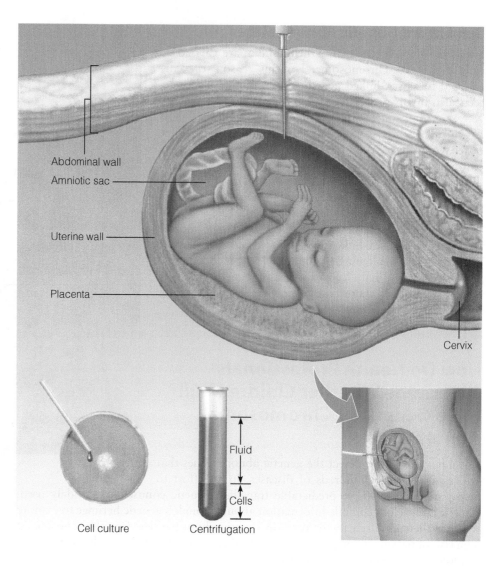

Abdominal wall

Amniotic sac

Uterine wall

Placenta

Cervix

Fluid

Cells

Cell culture   Centrifugation

women younger than 35 who are carrying the children of aging fathers may also desire prenatal screening. Amniocentesis can detect the presence of well more than 100 chromosomal and genetic abnormalities in the fetus, including sickle-cell anemia, Tay-Sachs disease, **spina bifida**, muscular dystrophy, and Rh incompatibility. Women (or their partners) who carry or have a family history of any of these disorders are advised to have amniocentesis performed. If the test reveals the presence of a serious disorder, the parents may decide to abort the fetus, or they may decide to continue the pregnancy and prepare themselves to raise a child who has special needs.

Amniocentesis also permits parents to learn the sex of their unborn child through examination of the sex chromosomes, but most parents learn the sex of their baby earlier by means of ultrasound. Amniocentesis carries some risk of miscarriage (about 1 woman in 100 who undergo the procedure will miscarry), so health professionals do not conduct it to learn the sex of the child.

Chorionic Villus Sampling

Chorionic villus sampling (CVS) is similar to amniocentesis but offers the advantage of diagnosing fetal abnormalities earlier in pregnancy. CVS is carried out between the 9th and 12th weeks of pregnancy. A small syringe is inserted through the vagina

spina bifida A neural tube defect that causes abnormalities of the brain and spine.

chorionic villus sampling (CVS) A method for the prenatal detection of genetic abnormalities that samples the membrane enveloping the amniotic sac and fetus.

into the **uterus**. The syringe gently sucks out a few of the threadlike projections (villi) from the outer membrane that envelops the amniotic sac and fetus. Results are available within days of the procedure. CVS has not been used as frequently as amniocentesis because many studies have shown that CVS carries a slightly greater risk of spontaneous abortion.

The relative risks of amniocentesis and CVS are highly controversial. Some studies have suggested that the risks of the procedures are about equivalent. However, there are two types of amniocentesis: "late" and "early." And there are also different types of CVS. Yet some health professionals assert that the risks of these procedures have been exaggerated (Akolekar et al., 2014; Ogilvie & Akolekar, 2013). Another factor to consider, sad to say, is that some practitioners are better at carrying out these procedures than others. If you are considering having CVS or amniocentesis, ask your doctor for the latest information about the risks of each procedure. Also ask around to make sure that your doctor is the right doctor to carry out the procedure.

Ultrasound

For more than half a century, the military has been using sonar to locate enemy submarines. Sonar sends high-frequency sound waves into the depths of the ocean, and the waves bounce back from objects such as submarines (and whales and schools of fish and the ocean floor) to reveal their presence. Within the past generation, health professionals have also introduced the use of (very!) high-frequency sound waves to obtain information about the fetus. The sounds waves are too high in frequency to be heard by the human ear and are referred to as **ultrasound**. However, they are reflected by the fetus, and a computer can use the information to generate a visual picture of the fetus. The picture is referred to as a **sonogram**, a term derived from roots meaning "written with sound" (see Figure 2.7 ■). In the fourth and fifth months, ultrasound is usually used to perform complete anatomical scans of the fetus.

uterus The hollow organ within females in which the embryo and fetus develop.

ultrasound Sound waves too high in pitch to be sensed by the human ear.

sonogram A procedure for using ultrasonic sound waves to create a picture of an embryo or fetus.

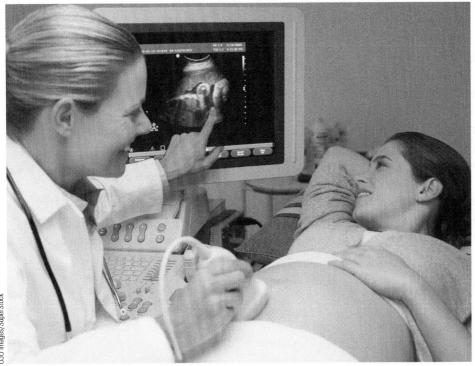

Figure 2.7 ■ Sonogram of a 5-Month-Old Fetus
In the ultrasound technique, sound waves are bounced off the fetus and provide a picture, called a sonogram, that enables professionals to detect various abnormalities.

Ultrasound is used in amniocentesis and CVS to better determine the position of the fetus. It helps the physician to make sure that the needle enters the sac surrounding the fetus and not the fetus itself—although a mistake will *not* be lethal to the fetus. Ultrasound is also used to locate fetal structures when intrauterine transfusions are necessary for the survival of a fetus with Rh disease.

Ultrasound is used to track the growth of the fetus, to determine fetal age and sex, and to detect multiple pregnancies and structural abnormalities. Although ultrasound is beneficial for pregnant women whose fetuses are at risk of serious medical problems, it may not improve birth outcomes for women with low-risk pregnancies.

Blood Tests

Parental blood tests can reveal the presence of recessive genes for a variety of disorders, such as sickle-cell anemia, Tay-Sachs disease, and cystic fibrosis. When both parents carry genes for these disorders, the disorders can be detected in the fetus by means of amniocentesis or CVS.

Another kind of blood test, the **alpha-fetoprotein (AFP) assay**, is used to detect neural tube defects such as spina bifida and certain chromosomal abnormalities. Neural tube defects cause an elevation in the AFP level in the mother's blood. Elevated AFP levels also are associated with increased risk of fetal death. However, the mother's AFP level varies with other factors. For this reason, the diagnosis of a neural tube defect is confirmed by other methods of observation, such as amniocentesis or ultrasound.

A blood test administered as early as seven weeks into pregnancy can determine the sex of the fetus (Devaney et al., 2011). Health professionals examine fetal DNA found in the blood for the characteristic male or female chromosomal structure.

In the next section, we will see that our development is affected not only by genes but also by environmental influences.

alpha-fetoprotein (AFP) assay A blood test that assesses the mother's blood level of alphafetoprotein, a substance that is linked to fetal neural tube defects.

Section Review

1. A normal human cell contains 46 _____, which are organized into 23 pairs.

2. Each chromosome contains thousands of genes, segments of _____ acid (DNA), which takes the form of a twisting ladder.

3. _____ is the cell-division process by which growth occurs and tissues are replaced.

4. Sperm and ova are produced through _____.

5. When a zygote divides into two cells that separate so that each develops into an individual, _____ (MZ) twins result.

6. When two ova are fertilized by different sperm cells, they develop into _____ (DZ) twins.

7. People who bear one dominant gene and one recessive gene for a trait are said to be _____ of the recessive gene.

8. In persons with _____, the 21st pair of chromosomes has an extra, or third, chromosome.

9. Phenylketonuria (PKU) is transmitted by a _____ (dominant or recessive?) gene.

10. _____ anemia is caused by a recessive gene and is most common among African Americans.

11. In the prenatal testing method of _____, fetal cells found in amniotic fluid are examined for genetic abnormalities.

12. The use of _____ can form a picture ("sonogram") of the fetus.

Reflect & Relate: Many methods of prenatal testing, including amniocentesis, some blood tests, and ultrasound, can enable parents to learn the sex of their fetus. If you were having such testing, would you want to know the sex of your fetus, or would you prefer to wait? Explain

2.3 Heredity and the Environment: Nature versus Nurture

Now that we have studied heredity, we know why we have arms rather than wings and hairy skin rather than feathers. Well, perhaps not so hairy for many of us. But none of us is the result of heredity alone.

Reaction Range: What Is the Difference Between Our Genotypes and Our Phenotypes?

Heredity provides the biological basis for a **reaction range** in the expression of traits. Our inherited traits can vary in expression, depending on environmental conditions. In addition to inheritance, the development of our traits is influenced by nutrition, learning, exercise, and—unfortunately—accident and illness. A potential Shakespeare who is reared in poverty, seldom leaves his hometown, and is never taught to read or write will not create a *Hamlet*. Our traits and behaviors represent the interaction of heredity and environment. The sets of traits that we inherit from our parents are referred to as our **genotypes**. Our actual sets of traits are called our **phenotypes**. Our phenotypes develop because of both genetic and environmental influences.

What Is Canalization?

Our genotypes lead to **canalization** of the development of various traits, both physical and—to some degree—psychological (Roy et al., 2014). Environmental restrictions, such as scarcity of food, may prevent children from reaching heights within their reaction ranges. However, if food becomes more readily available, there is a tendency to "snap back" into the genetically determined "canal" (Blair & Raver, 2012). Infant motor development is canalized in that the sequence of development is invariant: rolling over, sitting up, crawling, creeping, and so on. Similarly, the sequence of development of types of two-word utterances is invariant. The development of personality and intelligence is apparently less canalized, with the environment playing stronger roles.

What Is Meant by Genetic–Environmental Correlation?

There is also genetic–environmental correlation. One of the problems in sorting out the influences of heredity and environment, or nature and nurture, is that genes in part determine the environments to which people are exposed. Developmental psychologist Sandra Scarr (1998) described three types of correlations between genetic and environmental influences, and they are related to the age of the individual.

Passive Correlation

Not only do biological parents contribute genes to their offspring, but they also intentionally and unintentionally place their offspring in certain kinds of environments. Just as artistically oriented parents are likely to transmit genes that predispose their children to having an interest in the arts, they are also likely to expose their children to artistic activities, such as visits to museums and piano lessons. Athletic parents may enroll their children in soccer lessons and sports camps. These parents might also ridicule the interests of the other group, purposefully contributing to the development of their children's attitudes. This type of correlation is termed a **passive genetic–environmental correlation** because the children have no choice in the matter.

reaction range The variability in the expression of inherited traits as they are influenced by environmental factors.

genotype The genetic form, or constitution, of a person as determined by heredity.

phenotype The actual form, or constitution, of a person as determined by heredity and environmental factors.

canalization The tendency of growth rates to return to genetically determined patterns after undergoing environmentally induced change.

passive genetic–environmental correlation The correlation between the genetic endowment parents give their children and the environments in which they place their children.

Evocative Correlation

An **evocative genetic–environmental correlation** exists because the child's genotype is connected with behaviors that evoke, or elicit, certain kinds of responses from others. These responses, in turn, become part of the social environment of the child. A sociable, active, even-tempered infant is likely to receive more positive social stimulation from caregivers and other people than a passive, socially withdrawn infant. A good-looking infant and child is likely to evoke more attentive and playful responses from others, including his or her mother, and possibly develop more skillful social behavior as a result (Principe & Langlois, 2012). Teachers are more likely to befriend and smile at children who are interested in their subjects, pay attention, and avoid misbehavior.

Active Correlation

As we mature, we are more likely to take an active, conscious role in choosing or creating our environments. This attitude is called an **active genetic–environmental correlation**. The intelligent, highly motivated child may ask to be placed in honors classes. The strong, coordinated, aggressive child may join athletic teams. The child or adolescent with less academic or athletic talent may choose to be a "loner" or join a deviant peer group in which friends reinforce his or her behaviors. At some point, children may ask caregivers to help them attend activities that enable them to pursue genetically inspired interests. Adolescents may also select after-school activities that are connected with their academic, artistic, or athletic interests. Choosing environments that allow us to develop inherited preferences is termed **niche-picking** (Groothuis & Trillmich, 2011).

Genetic–Environmental Correlation Both of these girls are athletic, but the one on the left immediately felt at home during a ballet class and chose to continue. The one on the right was not at all tempted by dance, but she enjoyed soccer and was competitive, so she joined her school's soccer team.

Brand X Photography/Veer

RubberBall Photography/Veer

evocative genetic–environmental correlation The correlation between the child's genetic endowment and the responses the child elicits from other people.

active genetic–environmental correlation The correlation between the child's genetic endowment and the choices the child makes about which environments they will seek.

niche-picking Choosing environmental conditions that foster one's genetically transmitted abilities and interests.

epigenesis The view that development reflects continual bidirectional exchanges between one's genotype and one's environmental conditions.

The Epigenetic Framework

The relationship between genetic and environmental influences is not a one-way street. Instead, it is bidirectional. Even though our genes affect the development of our traits and behaviors, our traits and behaviors also prompt certain kinds of responses from other people and lead us to place ourselves in certain environments. These environments—specialized schools, after-school activities, museums, the theater, certain films and TV programs—all affect the manner in which genes are expressed. According to what researchers call **epigenesis**, or the *epigenetic framework*, our development reflects continuing bidirectional exchanges between our genetic heritages and the environments in which we find or place ourselves (Lerner & Benson, 2013).

Although the relationship between nature and nurture is complex, researchers have developed a number of strategies to help sort out the effects of heredity and the environment on development.

How Do Researchers Sort Out the Effects of Genetics and Environmental Influences on Development? (Are the Traits of Relatives Related?)

To help sort out the effects of genetics and environmental influences on development, researchers study the distribution of a particular behavior pattern among relatives who differ in degree of genetic closeness. This type of research is known as a kinship study. The more closely people are related, the more genes they have in common. Parents and children have a 50% overlap in their genetic endowments, and so do siblings (brothers and sisters), on average. Aunts and uncles have a 25% overlap with nieces and nephews, and so do grandparents with their grandchildren. First cousins share 12.5% of their genetic endowment. Thus, if genes are implicated in a physical trait or behavior pattern, people who are more closely related should be more likely to share the pattern. You probably look more like a parent or brother or sister than like a cousin, and you probably look very little like a stranger.

Twin Studies: Looking in the Genetic Mirror

Monozygotic (MZ) twins share 100% of their genes, whereas dizygotic (DZ) twins have a 50% overlap, just as other siblings do. If MZ twins show greater similarity on some trait or behavior than DZ twins, a genetic basis for the trait or behavior is indicated.

MZ twins resemble each other more closely than DZ twins in physical and psychological traits. MZ twins are more likely than DZ twins to look alike, to be similar in height, and even to have similar cholesterol levels (Dubois et al., 2012; Plomin et al., 2013a). This finding holds even when the MZ twins are reared apart and the DZ twins are reared together (Bouchard & Loehlin, 2001). Other physical similarities between pairs of MZ twins may be more subtle, but they are also strong. For example, research shows that MZ twin sisters begin to menstruate about 1 to 2 months apart, whereas DZ twins begin to menstruate about 1 year apart.

MZ twins are more alike than DZ twins in their blood pressure, brain wave patterns, speech patterns, gestures, and mannerisms (Bouchard & Loehlin, 2001; Plomin et al., 2013a). Heredity even has an effect on their preference for coffee or tea (Luciano et al., 2005).

MZ twins resemble one another more strongly than DZ twins in intelligence; in personality traits such as sociability, anxiety, friendliness, conformity, and even happiness; and in the tendency to choose marriage over the single life (Hur, 2005; Johnson et al., 2004; Trzaskowski et al., 2013). David Lykken and Mike Csikszentmihalyi (2001) suggest that we inherit a tendency to have a certain level of happiness. Despite the ups and downs of life, we tend to drift back to our usual levels of cheerfulness or irritability. It seems that our bank accounts, our levels of education, and our marital status are less influential than genes as contributors to happiness. Heredity is also a key contributor to psychological developmental factors such as cognitive functioning and early signs of attachment (such as smiling, cuddling, and expressing fear of strangers) (Plomin et al., 2013). Twin studies show that at least half of the variation in the tendency to develop obesity is genetic (Hebebrand & Hinney, 2009). MZ twins are more likely than DZ twins to share psychological disorders such as **autism**, depression, schizophrenia, and even vulnerability to alcoholism (Lundstrom et al., 2012; Plomin et al., 2013; Slane et al., 2012).

Of course, twin studies are not perfect. MZ twins may resemble each other more closely than DZ twins partly because they are treated more similarly. MZ twins frequently are dressed identically, and parents themselves sometimes have difficulty telling them apart.

One way to get around this problem is to find and compare MZ twins who were reared in different homes. Any similarities between MZ twins reared apart cannot be explained by a shared home environment and would appear to be largely a result of heredity. In the fascinating Minnesota Study of Twins Reared Apart (McGue & Christensen, 2013), researchers have been measuring the physiological and psychological characteristics of 56 sets of MZ adult twins who were separated in infancy and reared in different homes. The MZ twins reared apart are about as similar as MZ twins reared together on a variety of measures of intelligence, personality, temperament, occupational and leisure-time interests, and social attitudes. These traits thus appear to have a genetic underpinning.

Adoption Studies

Adoption studies in which children are separated from their natural parents at an early age and reared by adoptive parents provide special opportunities for sorting out nature and nurture. As we will see in discussions of the origins of intelligence (see Chapter 12) and of various psychological problems (see Chapters 10 and 13), psychologists look for the similarities between children and their adoptive and natural parents. When children who are reared by adoptive parents are nonetheless more similar to their natural parents in a trait, that is a powerful argument for a genetic role in the appearance of that trait.

Traits are determined by pairs of genes. One member of each pair comes from each parent, and they are joined in the process called *conception*. In the following section, we will talk about the birds and the bees and the microscope to understand how conception works.

Section Review

13. The sets of traits that we inherit are referred to as our _____ (genotypes or phenotypes?).

14. The actual traits that we display at any point in time are the product of genetic and environmental influences and are called our _____ (genotypes or phenotypes?).

15. Parents and children have a _____ % overlap in their genetic endowments.

16. _____ (MZ) twins share 100% of their genes.

17. _____ (DZ) twins have a 50% overlap, as do other siblings.

Reflect & Relate: Do you know any sets of twins? Are they monozygotic or dizygotic? How are they alike? How do they differ?

2.4 Conception: Against All Odds

autism A developmental disorder characterized by failure to relate to others, communication problems, intolerance of change, and ritualistic behavior (see Chapter 6).

On a balmy day in October, Marta and her partner Jorge rush to catch the train to their jobs in the city. Marta's workday is outwardly the same as any other. Within her body, however, a remarkable drama is unfolding. Yesterday, hormones caused an ovarian follicle to rupture, releasing its egg cell, or ovum. Like all women, Marta was born with nearly all the ova she would ever have, each encased in a follicle. How this particular follicle was selected to ripen and release its ovum this month remains a mystery. But for the next day or so, Marta will be capable of conceiving.

Yesterday morning, Marta used her ovulation timing kit, which showed that she was about to ovulate. That night, Marta and Jorge made love, hoping that Marta would conceive. Jorge ejaculated hundreds of millions of sperm—a normal amount. Only a few thousand survived the journey through the cervix and uterus to the fallopian tube that contained the ovum, released just hours earlier. Of these, a few hundred remained to bombard the ovum. One succeeded in penetrating the ovum's covering, resulting in conception. From a single cell formed by the union of sperm and ovum, a new life began to form. The zygote is only 1/175th of an inch across—a tiny beginning for the drama about to take place.

Marta is 37 years old. She is followed closely with prenatal testing to check for the presence of chromosomal abnormalities, such as Down syndrome. (Down syndrome is more common among children born to women in their late 30s and older.) The tests also indicate the sex of the fetus. Many parents prefer to know the sex of their baby before it is born. "Why," they say, "should the doctor know and we don't know?" But Marta and Jorge ask their doctor not to inform them. "Why ruin the surprise?" Jorge tells his friends. So Marta and Jorge are left to debate boys' names *and* girls' names for the next few months.

The process that brings together the genes from both parents is called **conception**—the union of an ovum and a sperm cell. Conception, from one perspective, is the beginning of a new human life. But conception is also the end of a fantastic voyage in which a single ovum of the several hundred thousand produced by the woman unites with one of the hundreds of millions of sperm produced by the man in the average ejaculate.

Ova

Although females are born with hundreds of thousands of ova, they are immature in form. In addition to ova, the ovaries also produce the female hormones estrogen and progesterone. At puberty, in response to hormonal command, some ova begin to mature. Each month, an egg (occasionally more than one) is released from its ovarian follicle about midway through the menstrual cycle and enters a nearby **fallopian tube** (see Figure 2.8 ■). It might take 3 to 4 days for an egg to be propelled by small, hairlike structures called cilia and, perhaps, by contractions in the wall of the tube, along the few inches of the fallopian tube to the uterus. Unlike sperm, eggs do not propel themselves.

conception The union of a sperm cell and an ovum that occurs when the chromosomes of each of these cells combine to form 23 new pairs.

fallopian tube A tube through which ova travel from an ovary to the uterus.

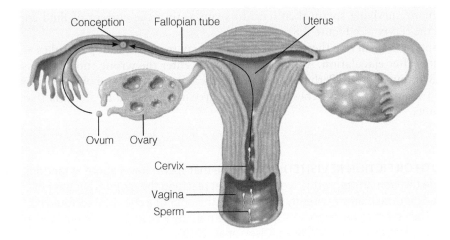

Figure 2.8 ■ Female Reproductive Organs
Conception is something of an obstacle course. Sperm must survive the pull of gravity and vaginal acidity, risk winding up in the wrong fallopian tube, and surmount other hurdles before they reach the ovum.
© Cengage Learning®

If the egg is not fertilized, it is discharged through the uterus and the vagina, along with the **endometrium** that formed to support an embryo, in the menstrual flow. During a woman's reproductive years, only about 400 ova (that is, 1 in 1,000) will ripen and be released.

In an early stage of development, egg cells contain 46 chromosomes. Each developing egg cell contains two X sex chromosomes. After meiosis, each ovum contains 23 chromosomes, one of which is an X sex chromosome.

Ova are much larger than sperm. Both the chicken egg and the 6-inch ostrich egg are just one cell, although the sperm of these birds are microscopic. Human ova are barely visible to the eye, but their bulk is thousands of times greater than that of sperm cells.

Sperm Cells

Sperm cells develop through several stages. Like ova, in one early stage, each sperm cell contains 46 chromosomes, including one X and one Y sex chromosome. After meiosis, each sperm has 23 chromosomes. Half have X sex chromosomes and half have Y sex chromosomes. Each sperm cell is about 1/500 of an inch long, one of the smallest types of cells in the body. Sperm with Y sex chromosomes appear to swim faster than sperm with X sex chromosomes.

The 200–400 million sperm in the ejaculate may seem to be a wasteful investment because only one sperm can fertilize an ovum. But only 1 in 1,000 sperm will ever approach an ovum. Millions of sperm deposited in the vagina flow out of the woman's body because of gravity. Normal vaginal acidity kills many more sperm. The many surviving sperm then have to swim against the current of fluid coming from the cervix (see Figure 2.8).

Sperm that survive these initial obstacles may reach the fallopian tubes 60–90 minutes after ejaculation. About half the sperm enter the wrong tube—that is, the tube without the egg. Perhaps 2,000 enter the correct tube, and even fewer manage to swim the final 2 inches against the currents generated by the cilia that line the tube.

endometrium The inner lining of the uterus.

spontaneous abortion Unplanned, accidental abortion; also called *miscarriage*.

A Closer Look

WHERE ARE THE MISSING CHINESE GIRLS?

In some nations in which boys are strongly preferred over girls, such as India and China, "sex selection" means the selective abortion of female fetuses. In China, where most couples have only been allowed to have one child, this preference led to a scarcity of female adults (Jian, 2013).

Beginning in 1979, China attempted to gain control of its mushrooming population by permitting only one child per family in urban areas, although a second child was usually permitted in rural areas. As shown in Table 2.4 ●, the desirability of having small families has generally caught on in the Chinese population. The great majority of women interviewed in a recent survey expressed the desire to have either one or two children. However, there were some differences according to the woman's age, her area of residence, and her level of education. How would you account for them?

Because more boys than girls die in infancy, a "normal" ratio of boys to girls is about 106 to 100, which characterized China in the 1970s. The ratio changed to about 108.5 boys to 100 girls in the early 80s, then 111 to 100 in 1990, and 117 to 100 in 2000. It is now at least 120 boys for every 100 girls, and some estimates put it as high as 123 to 100 (Jian, 2013).

Therefore, a great shortage of Chinese women is being created, which may not be much of a problem for parents today but will certainly be a problem for men seeking mates in future years. Chinese officials are concerned that the shortfall means that millions of men will have no prospect of getting married and settling down when they are of age. Thus, there will be an increased likelihood of social unrest, which can manifest itself as political dissent as well as ordinary crime (Trent, 2011).

While some men go without mates, others find mates from nearby Asian countries, such as Vietnam. In recognition

Chinese people show a preference for boys and, because they usually have just one chance to have a child, often use sex-selection techniques to guarantee having a child of the preferred sex.

of these problems, and the desires of city-dwellers to have more children, China has begun to relax the one-child-per-family rule (Buckley, 2013).

Reflect

- Do you think there are any circumstances under which a government, such as China's, has the right to limit family size? Why or why not?
- How would you explain the relationship between the number of children a Chinese woman desires and her age? Her area of residence (urban or rural)? Her level of education?
- What sources of error might distort the results in Table 2.4?
- Do you have a preference for boys or girls? What lengths would you go to in order to have a baby of your preferred sex?

● TABLE 2.4

Preferred Number of Children Among Chinese Women (Percent Expressing Preference)

Age of Woman	Preferred Number of Children			
	0	1	2	3 or more
15–19	2.1	49	45	1.9
20–29	1.3	47	48	2.1
30–39	0.8	32	60	6.1
40–49	1.0	27	62	11.0
Area of Residence				
Urban	3.1	52	43	1.5
Rural	0.4	30	61	7.5
Level of Education				
Illiterate or semiliterate	0.4	17	67	14.0
Primary school	0.3	25	65	8.5
Secondary school	2.1	46	47	2.5
College	4.0	49	44	2.2

Source: National Family Planning and Reproductive Health Survey. Ding & Hesketh (2006).
Note: Number of women interviewed: 39,344.

CHAPTER 2 HEREDITY AND CONCEPTION **67**

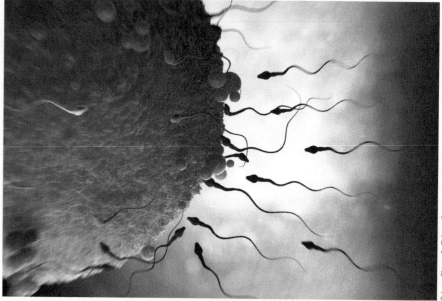

Figure 2.9 ■ Human Sperm Swarming Around an Ovum in a Fallopian Tube
Fertilization normally occurs in a fallopian tube, not in the uterus. Thousands of sperm may wind up in the vicinity of an ovum, but only one fertilizes it. How this sperm cell is "selected" remains one of the mysteries of nature.

Of all the sperm swarming around the egg, only one enters (see Figure 2.9 ■). Ova are surrounded by a gelatinous layer that must be penetrated if fertilization is to occur. Many of the sperm that have completed their journey to the ovum secrete an enzyme that briefly thins the layer, but it still enables only one sperm to penetrate. Once a sperm cell has entered, the layer thickens, locking other sperm out. How this one sperm cell is "selected" is another biological mystery. Nevertheless, other sperm are unable to enter.

The chromosomes from the sperm cell line up across from the corresponding chromosomes in the egg cell. Conception finally occurs as the chromosomes combine to form 23 new pairs with a unique set of genetic instructions.

For couples who want children, few problems are more frustrating than the inability to conceive. Physicians often recommend that couples try to conceive on their own for 6 months before seeking medical assistance. The term *infertility* usually is not applied until the couple has failed to conceive for a year. We will consider the problem of infertility next.

2.5 Infertility and Assisted Reproductive Technology

About one American couple in six or seven has fertility problems (American Fertility Association, 2014). Infertility was once viewed as a problem of the woman, but it turns out that the problem lies with the man in about 40% of cases.

What Are the Causes of Infertility?

The following fertility problems are found in men (American Fertility Association, 2014):

- Low sperm count
- Deformed sperm
- Poor ability of the sperm to swim to the ovum ("low sperm motility")
- Infectious diseases, such as sexually transmitted infections
- Chronic diseases, such as diabetes
- Injury of the testes
- An "autoimmune" response, in which the man's body attacks his own sperm as foreign agents

A low sperm count—or lack of sperm—is the most common infertility problem found in men. Men's fertility problems have a variety of causes: genetic factors, environmental poisons, diabetes, sexually transmitted infections (STIs), overheating of the testes (which happens now and then among athletes, such as long-distance runners), pressure (which can be caused by certain bicycle seats—have your doctor recommend a comfortable, safe seat), aging, and certain prescription and illicit drugs (American Fertility Association, 2014).

TRUTH OR FICTION REVISITED: Yes, extensive athletic activity can contribute to infertility in the male. Sometimes the sperm count is adequate, but other factors (such as prostate or hormonal problems) can deform sperm or deprive them of their **motility** (their ability to move actively). Motility can also be impaired by the scar tissue from infections, such as STIs.

Women encounter the following major fertility problems (American Fertility Association, 2014):

- Irregular ovulation, including failure to ovulate
- Declining hormone levels of estrogen and progesterone that occur with aging and may prevent the ovum from becoming fertilized or from remaining implanted in the uterus
- Inflammation of the tissue that is sloughed off during menstruation ("endometriosis")
- Obstructions or malfunctions of the reproductive tract, which are often caused by infections or diseases involving the reproductive tract

The most common problem in women is irregular ovulation or lack of ovulation. This problem can have many causes, including irregularities among the hormones that govern ovulation, stress, and malnutrition. So-called fertility drugs (such as *Clomiphene* and *Pergonal*) are made up of hormones that cause women to ovulate. These drugs may cause multiple births by stimulating more than one ovum to ripen during a month (Chehab et al., 2015).

Infections may scar the fallopian tubes and other organs, impeding the passage of sperm or ova. Such infections include **pelvic inflammatory disease (PID)**. PID can result from any of a number of bacterial or viral infections, including the STIs gonorrhea and chlamydia. Antibiotics are usually helpful in treating bacterial infections, but infertility can be irreversible if the infection has gone without treatment for too long.

Endometriosis can obstruct the fallopian tubes, where conception normally takes place. This problem is clear enough. But endometriosis is also believed to somehow dampen the "climate" for conception; the mechanisms involved in this effect are not as well understood. Endometriosis has become a fairly frequent cause of infertility today because so many women are delaying childbearing to further their educations and to establish careers. What apparently happens is this: Each month, tissue develops to line the uterus in case the woman conceives. This tissue, called the endometrium, is then normally sloughed off during menstruation. However, some of it may back up into the abdomen through the same fallopian tubes that would provide a duct for an ovum. Endometrial tissue then collects in the abdomen, where it can cause abdominal pain and reduce the chances of conception. Physicians may treat endometriosis with hormones that temporarily prevent menstruation or through surgery.

How Are Couples with Fertility Problems Assisted in Becoming Parents?

Let us now consider some of the methods that have been developed in recent years to help infertile couples bear children.

motility Self-propulsion.

pelvic inflammatory disease (PID) An infection of the abdominal region that may have various causes and may impair fertility.

endometriosis Inflammation of endometrial tissue sloughed off into the abdominal cavity rather than out of the body during menstruation; the condition is characterized by abdominal pain and sometimes by infertility.

Artificial Insemination

artificial insemination Injection of sperm into the uterus to fertilize an ovum.

Multiple ejaculations of men with low sperm counts can be collected and quick-frozen. The sperm can then be injected into the woman's uterus at the time of ovulation. This is one **artificial insemination** procedure. Sperm from men with low sperm motility can also be injected into their partners' uteruses, so that the sperm can begin their journey closer to the fallopian tubes. When a man has no sperm or an extremely

A Closer Look

Diversity

LGBT FAMILY BUILDING

Heterosexual couples are not the only ones who want children. Heterosexual (and gay and lesbian) singles do, too. And so do couples who belong to the gay, lesbian, bisexual, and transgendered community.

Some gay and lesbian couples have children from previous marriages or other kinds of relationships. But if they don't, and if they want children, they have to decide who these children will be and how to make it happen. Transgendered individuals who have had genital surgery are also sterile, so they cannot father or bear offspring.

Lesbians, of course, can conceive through sexual intercourse with a friend or confidant, but many prefer not to do so. The American Fertility Association (2012b) notes that lesbians can also conceive through assisted productive technologies such as at-home insemination, intrauterine insemination (IUI), in vitro fertilization (IVF), and reciprocal in vitro fertilization (RIVF). All these methods require obtaining donor sperm from either a known or an anonymous source. IUI, known better perhaps as artificial insemination, is a low-technology method in which washed sperm are inserted directly into the uterus through a catheter. If IUI does not work, a woman may consider IVF. When both members of a lesbian couple are fertile, they sometimes choose to harvest the eggs from one partner, have them fertilized with donor sperm, and then insert the resulting embryos in the other partner, who may become pregnant through this process. The other partner may do the same. That's why this method is called *reciprocal* IVF. It permits both partners to play a role in bearing the child.

Gay males need a surrogate mother who will become impregnated by their sperm and carry the embryo and fetus to term. The two potential fathers' sperm are analyzed, and either the sperm with the strongest likelihood to impregnate the surrogate are selected or the sperm may be mixed so that the fathers do not know which partner actually fathered the child. Of course, actual fatherhood usually becomes clear enough in terms of the child's appearance and behavior as time goes on.

DNA testing can also be used to make the determination. But both men played a role in the process, and as long as their relationship remains stable, they usually make no effort to precisely determine paternity.

They've got each other. How do they go about building a family?

The American Fertility Association (www.theafa.org) invites all individuals—heterosexual couples; would-be single parents; lesbian, gay, bisexual, and transgendered couples—who have fertility questions or issues to contact them.

Reflect

- If you were receiving artificial insemination, would you want to know the identity of the sperm donor? Why or why not?

- How would you choose a sperm donor?

- If you were a partner in a gay male couple, would you consider mixing your sperm before attempting to impregnate a surrogate? Why or why not?

- If you were a partner in a lesbian couple, would you be interested in reciprocal IVF? Why or why not?

low sperm count, his partner can be artificially inseminated with the sperm of a donor who resembles the man in physical traits. Women who want a baby but do not have a partner may also opt for artificial insemination. So may lesbian couples. The child then bears the genes of one of the parents—the mother.

In Vitro Fertilization

Have you heard the expression "test-tube baby"? Does it sound as though a baby develops in a test tube? Not so. In this method, the mother's ova are fertilized in a laboratory dish. Then one or more embryos are injected into the mother's uterus to become implanted and develop.

> **TRUTH OR FICTION REVISITED:** It is not true that test-tube babies are grown in a test tube—but close. In this method, more technically known as **in vitro fertilization (IVF)**, ripened ova are removed surgically from the mother and placed in a laboratory dish. The father's sperm are also placed in the dish. One or more ova are fertilized and then injected into the mother's uterus to become implanted.

In vitro fertilization may be appropriate when the fallopian tubes are blocked, because the ova need not travel through them. If the father's sperm are low in motility, they are sometimes injected directly into the ovum.

Donor IVF

Donor IVF is used when a woman does not produce ova of her own but her uterus is apparently capable of providing an adequate environment to bring a baby to term. An ovum is harvested from another woman—the donor. It is fertilized in vitro, often by sperm from the partner of the recipient. Then, as in other cases of IVF, the fertilized ovum is placed directly into the uterus of the recipient. The embryo becomes implanted and undergoes the remainder of prenatal development in the recipient's uterus. This procedure is known as an **embryonic transplant**.

Because only a minority of attempts lead to births, it can take several attempts to achieve a pregnancy. Several embryos may be injected into the uterus at once, heightening the odds that one of the embryos will become implanted. IVF remains costly but is otherwise routine, and some clinics guarantee a pregnancy.

Surrogate Mothers

In recent years, stories about **surrogate mothers** have filled the headlines. Surrogate mothers bring babies to term for other women who are infertile. (The word *surrogate* means "substitute.") Surrogate mothers may be artificially inseminated by the partners of infertile women, in which case the baby carries the genes of the father. But sometimes—as with 53-year-old singer–songwriter James Taylor and his 47-year-old wife—ova are surgically extracted from the biological mother, fertilized in vitro by the biological father, and then implanted in another woman's uterus, where the baby is carried to term.

There is also a growing number of cases in which gay male couples artificially inseminate surrogate mothers. In one case, the gay men mixed their sperm so that it would not be clear who the biological father was. However, as the child matured, his similarity to one of the men became unmistakable.

Surrogate mothers are usually paid fees and asked to sign agreements to surrender the baby. These contracts have been annulled in some states, however, so that surrogate mothers cannot be forced to hand over their babies (Lewin, 2014). In the

in vitro fertilization (IVF) Fertilization of an ovum in a laboratory dish.

donor IVF The transfer of a donor's ovum, fertilized in a laboratory dish, to the uterus of another woman.

embryonic transplant The transfer of an embryo from the uterus of one woman to that of another.

surrogate mother A woman who is artificially inseminated and carries to term a child who is then given to another woman, typically the spouse of the sperm donor.

SELECTING THE SEX OF YOUR CHILD: FANTASY OR REALITY?

Folklore is replete with methods—and nonmethods—of sex selection. Some cultures advised coitus under the full moon to conceive boys. The Greek philosopher Aristotle suggested making love during a north wind to beget sons; a south wind would produce daughters. Sour foods were once suggested for parents desirous of having boys. Those who wanted girls were advised to consume sweets. Husbands who yearned to have boys might be advised to wear their boots to bed. It goes without saying that none of these methods worked (but we will say it anyhow).

These methods, or nonmethods, would supposedly lead to the conception of children of the desired sex. Methods applied after conception have also been used, such as the abortion of fetuses because of their sex.

TRUTH OR FICTION REVISITED: Today, there is a reliable method for selecting the sex of your child prior to implantation: preimplantation genetic diagnosis (PGD). PGD was developed to detect genetic disorders, but it also enables health professionals to learn the sex of the embryo.

In preimplantation genetic diagnosis, ova are fertilized in vitro, leading to conception of perhaps six to eight embryos. After a few days of cell division, a cell is extracted from each. The sex chromosomal structure of the cell is examined microscopically to determine whether the embryo is female or male. Embryos of the desired sex are implanted in the woman's uterus, where one or more can grow to term. PGD is medically invasive and expensive, and implantation cannot be guaranteed. Yet when implantation does occurs, the sex of the embryo is known.

Reflect Would you want to select the sex of your child? Explain.

---

case of Taylor and his wife, the surrogate mother was a friend of the family, and she delivered twins.

Biologically, surrogate motherhood might seem the mirror image of the more common artificial insemination technique in which a fertile woman is artificially inseminated with sperm from a donor. But the methods are psychologically very different. For example, sperm donors usually do not know the identity of the women who have received their sperm, nor do they follow the child's prenatal development. Surrogate mothers, however, are involved throughout the course of prenatal development.

Ethical and legal dilemmas revolve around the fact that artificially inseminated surrogate mothers have a genetic link to their babies. If they change their minds and do not want to hand the babies over to the contractual parents, there can be legal struggles.

Adoption

Adoption is another way for people to obtain children. Despite occasional conflicts that pit adoptive parents against biological parents who change their minds about giving up their children, most adoptions result in the formation of loving families.

Many Americans find it easier to adopt infants from other countries or infants with special needs. Until the past generation, most adopted children were European-American babies adopted within a few days of birth. But the more widespread use of contraception and the decisions of many unwed mothers to keep their babies has contributed to a scarcity of European-American babies. Today, greater numbers of adopted children are older, have spent some time in foster care, are of other races, have special needs, and/or were born in other countries (Gauthier et al., 2011; Priest et al., 2014). Similarly, a generation or so ago, most adoptive parents were infertile married European-American couples of secure socioeconomic status. Today, however, many adoption agencies allow more diversity in their pool of adoptive parents; for example, they consider applications from older people and single people.

Although most adopted children and adoptive parents fare well, everything is relative. Adopted children are apparently less likely to be secure with their caregivers than biological children are (Pace et al., 2014; Gilmore, 2008). Everything else being equal, the younger the child at the time of adoption, the more smoothly the adoption seems to go (Klahr et al., 2011). Although adoptive parents of children from other races and ethnic backgrounds may make strong efforts to "expose" their adoptive children to their cultures of origin, children adopted at younger ages acquire the language and customs of their adoptive parents more readily (Gauthier et al., 2011). Insecurities and anxiety are most likely to emerge in middle childhood, if they do emerge at all, because of increased understanding of what adoption means. One cause of problems for adopted children is that they often feel they were inexplicably rejected by their birth mother, which has detrimental effects on the development of a child's self-esteem (Klahr et al., 2011). Institutionalization prior to adoption, which can be a form of social deprivation, can heighten problems. Post-institutionalized children are at still greater risk of being insecure with the adoptive parents, and the insecurity can be found early (Chatham, 2008). One study found that such children had higher levels of cortisol (a stress hormone) than noninstitutionalized children in the presence of their mothers (Wismer Fries et al., 2008).

An aspect of adoption that is not often considered is its effects on the relinquishing mother (Aloi, 2009). These mothers frequently experience loss and guilt, along with wondering how their child is developing and adjusting.

In most of the next chapter, we will deal with issues on a smaller scale, beginning with the division of the single cell formed by the union of sperm cell and ovum into two cells, then four, and so on.

STR/AFP/Getty Images

Film actors Angelina Jolie and Brad Pitt derive satisfaction from adopting children even though they are fertile.

Section Review

18. The union of an ovum and a sperm cell is called _____.

19. Each month, an ovum is released from its follicle and enters a nearby _____ tube.

20. Low _____ count is the most common infertility problem in the male.

21. Failure to _____ is the most frequent infertility problem in women.

Reflect & Relate: What methods do people use to try to select the sex of their children? Do you believe it is acceptable to attempt to select the sex of one's child? Support your point of view.

Chapter Review

2.1 What Are the Influences of Heredity on Development?

Heredity defines one's nature, as determined by the biological transmission of traits and characteristics from one generation to another. Heredity is fundamental in the transmission of physical traits and is also involved in psychological traits, including psychological disorders. Chromosomes are rod-shaped structures found in cell nuclei. People normally have 46 chromosomes organized into 23 pairs. Each chromosome contains thousands of genes—the biochemical materials that regulate the development of traits. Genes are segments of strands of DNA, which takes the form of a twisting ladder. In mitosis, strands of DNA break apart and are rebuilt in the new cell. Sperm and ova are produced by meiosis—or reduction division—and have 23 rather than 46 chromosomes. If a zygote divides into two cells that separate and each develops into an individual, the result is monozygotic (MZ) twins, which are identical. If two ova are fertilized by different sperm cells, they develop into dizygotic (DZ) twins, which are fraternal. DZ twins run in families. Traits are determined by pairs of genes. Mendel established laws of heredity and realized that some traits result from an "averaging" of the genetic instructions carried by the parents. However, genes can also be dominant (as in the case of brown eyes) or recessive (blue eyes). When recessive genes from both parents combine, the recessive trait is shown. People who bear one dominant gene and one recessive gene for a trait are carriers of the recessive gene. Some genetic abnormalities are caused by a single pair of genes; others are caused by combinations of genes.

2.2 What Are Some Chromosomal and Genetic Abnormalities?

Chromosomal abnormalities become more likely as parents age. Intellectual disability is common in many such disorders. Down syndrome is caused by an extra chromosome on the 21st pair. Children with Down syndrome have characteristic facial features, including a downward-sloping fold of skin at the inner corners of the eyes, and various physical health problems. Disorders that arise from abnormal numbers of sex chromosomes are called sex-linked. These include XYY males and girls with a single X sex chromosome. Phenylketonuria (PKU) is a metabolic disorder transmitted by a recessive gene. Huntington disease (HD) is a fatal progressive degenerative disorder and a dominant trait. Sickle-cell anemia is caused by a recessive gene and is most common among African Americans. Tay-Sachs disease is a fatal disease of the nervous system that is caused by a recessive gene and is most common among children in Jewish families of Eastern European origin. Cystic fibrosis is caused by a recessive gene and is the most common fatal hereditary disease among European Americans. Sex-linked genetic abnormalities are carried on only the X sex chromosome and include hemophilia, Duchenne muscular dystrophy, diabetes, and color blindness. Prenatal testing procedures can determine the presence of various genetic and chromosomal abnormalities. Such tests include amniocentesis, chorionic villus sampling (CVS), ultrasound, and parental blood tests.

2.3 How Do Heredity and the Environment Interact to Influence Development?

Our genotypes are the sets of traits that we inherit. However, inherited traits vary in expression, depending on environmental conditions. One's actual set of traits at a given point in time is one's phenotype. Researchers can study the distribution of a trait among relatives who differ in degree of genetic closeness. Parents and children have a 50% overlap in genes, as do brothers and sisters, with the exception of MZ twins, who have 100% overlap. MZ twins resemble each other more closely than DZ twins on physical and psychological traits, even when reared apart. If adopted children are closer to their natural parents than to their adoptive parents on a physical or psychological trait, that trait is likely to have a strong genetic basis.

2.4 What Happens during Conception?

The process of a sperm uniting with an ovum is conception. Fertilization normally occurs in a fallopian tube. If the egg is not fertilized, it is discharged. Men typically ejaculate hundreds of millions of sperm. More boys are conceived than girls, but male fetuses have a higher rate of spontaneous abortion. Chromosomes from the sperm cell align with chromosomes in the egg cell, combining to form 23 new pairs.

2.5 What Are Some of the Causes of Infertility, and How Does Reproductive Technology Help People Become Parents?

Male fertility problems include low sperm count and motility, infections, and trauma to the testes. Female fertility problems include failure to ovulate, infections, endometriosis, and obstructions. Fertility drugs stimulate ovulation. Artificial insemination can be done with the sperm from multiple ejaculations of a man with a low sperm count or with the sperm of a donor. In vitro fertilization (IVF) can be used when the fallopian tubes are blocked. An embryo can also be transferred into a host uterus when the mother cannot produce ova.

Key Terms

heredity 48
genetics 48
chromosomes 48
gene 48
polygenic 48
deoxyribonucleic acid (DNA) 48
zygote 49
mitosis 49
mutation 49
meiosis 49
autosome 49
sex chromosome 49
monozygotic (MZ) twins 50
dizygotic (DZ) twins 50
ovulation 50
allele 50
homozygous 50
heterozygous 50
dominant trait 51
recessive trait 51
carrier 52
multifactorial problems 52
Down syndrome 53
sex-linked chromosomal abnormality 54

Klinefelter syndrome 54
testosterone 54
Turner syndrome 54
estrogen 54
phenylketonuria (PKU) 54
Huntington disease (HD) 56
sickle-cell anemia 56
Tay-Sachs disease 56
cystic fibrosis 56
hemophilia 57
sex-linked genetic abnormalities 57
muscular dystrophy 57
genetic counseling 57
prenatal 57
amniocentesis 57
spina bifida 58
chorionic villus sampling (CVS) 58
uterus 59
ultrasound 59
sonogram 59
alpha-fetoprotein (AFP) assay 60
reaction range 61
genotype 61

phenotype 61
canalization 61
passive genetic–environmental correlation 61
evocative genetic–environmental correlation 62
active genetic–environmental correlation 62
niche-picking 62
epigenesis 62
autism 64
conception 65
fallopian tube 65
endometrium 66
spontaneous abortion 66
motility 69
pelvic inflammatory disease (PID) 69
endometriosis 69
artificial insemination 70
in vitro fertilization (IVF) 71
donor IVF 71
embryonic transplant 71
surrogate mother 71

3

Prenatal
Development

TruthorFiction?

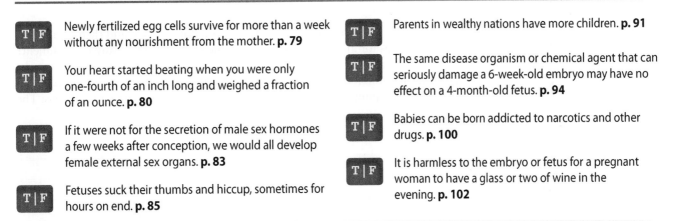

| T | F | Newly fertilized egg cells survive for more than a week without any nourishment from the mother. **p. 79**

| T | F | Your heart started beating when you were only one-fourth of an inch long and weighed a fraction of an ounce. **p. 80**

| T | F | If it were not for the secretion of male sex hormones a few weeks after conception, we would all develop female external sex organs. **p. 83**

| T | F | Fetuses suck their thumbs and hiccup, sometimes for hours on end. **p. 85**

| T | F | Parents in wealthy nations have more children. **p. 91**

| T | F | The same disease organism or chemical agent that can seriously damage a 6-week-old embryo may have no effect on a 4-month-old fetus. **p. 94**

| T | F | Babies can be born addicted to narcotics and other drugs. **p. 100**

| T | F | It is harmless to the embryo or fetus for a pregnant woman to have a glass or two of wine in the evening. **p. 102**

The most rapid and dramatic human developments are literally "out of sight." They take place in the uterus. Within 9 months, a child develops from a nearly microscopic cell into a newborn about 20 inches long. Its weight increases a billionfold.

We can date pregnancy from the onset of the last menstrual period before conception, which makes the normal gestation period 280 days. We can also date pregnancy from the assumed date of fertilization, which normally occurs 2 weeks after the beginning of the woman's last menstrual cycle. With this accounting method, the gestation period is 266 days.

Soon after conception, the single cell formed by the union of sperm and egg begins to multiply—becoming two cells, then four, then eight, and so on. During the weeks and months that follow, tissues, organs, and structures begin to form, and the fetus gradually takes on the unmistakable shape of a human being. By the time a fetus is born, it consists of hundreds of billions of cells—more cells than there are stars in the Milky Way galaxy. Prenatal development is divided into three periods: the germinal stage (approximately the first 2 weeks), the embryonic stage (the third through the eighth weeks), and the fetal stage (the third month through birth). Health professionals also commonly speak of prenatal development in terms of three trimesters of 3 months each.

Diego Cervo/Image Source Salsa/Alamy

3.1 The Germinal Stage: Wanderings

germinal stage The period of development between conception and the implantation of the embryo.

blastocyst A stage within the germinal period of prenatal development in which the zygote has the form of a sphere of cells surrounding a cavity of fluid.

embryonic disk The platelike inner part of the blastocyst that differentiates into the ectoderm, mesoderm, and endoderm of the embryo.

trophoblast The outer part of the blastocyst from which the amniotic sac, placenta, and umbilical cord develop.

umbilical cord A tube that connects the fetus to the placenta.

placenta An organ connected to the uterine wall and to the fetus by the umbilical cord. The placenta serves as a relay station between mother and fetus for the exchange of nutrients and wastes.

Within 36 hours after conception, the zygote divides into two cells. It then divides repeatedly as it proceeds on its journey to the uterus. Within another 36 hours, it has become 32 cells. It takes the zygote 3 to 4 days to reach the uterus. The mass of dividing cells wanders about the uterus for another 3 to 4 days before it begins implanting in the uterine wall. Implantation takes another week or so. The period from conception to implantation is called the **germinal stage** (see Figure 3.1 ■).

A few days into the germinal stage, the dividing cell mass takes the form of a fluid-filled ball called a **blastocyst**. A blastocyst already shows cell differentiation. Cells begin to separate into groups that will eventually become different structures. The inner part of the blastocyst has two distinct layers of cells that form a thickened mass of cells called the **embryonic disk**. These cells will develop into the embryo and, later, the fetus.

The outer part of the blastocyst, the **trophoblast**, at first consists of a single layer of cells. However, it rapidly differentiates into four membranes that will protect and nourish the embryo. One membrane produces blood cells until the embryo's liver develops and takes on this function. Then the membrane disappears. Another membrane develops into the **umbilical cord** and the blood vessels of the **placenta**. A third membrane develops into the amniotic sac, and the fourth becomes the chorion, which will line the placenta.

Without Visible Means of Support?

Now, the dividing mass of cells moves through a fallopian tube and then "wanders" through the uterus for another few days; how, then, does it obtain any nourishment? Although people are not chickens, the dividing cluster of cells that will become the embryo and then the fetus is at first nourished only by the yolk of the egg cell, just like a chick developing in an egg. Therefore, the cluster makes no gain in mass. The

Figure 3.1 ■ The Ovarian Cycle, Conception, and the Early Days of the Germinal Stage
The zygote first divides about 36 hours after conception. Continuing division creates the hollow sphere of cells termed the blastocyst. The blastocyst normally becomes implanted in the wall of the uterus.
© Cengage Learning®

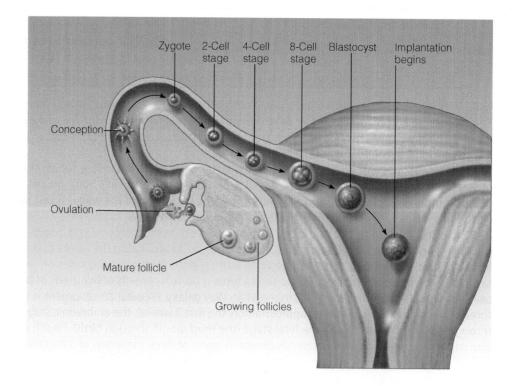

blastocyst gains mass only when it receives nourishment from the outside. In order for that to happen, it must be implanted in the wall of the uterus. Implantation may be accompanied by some bleeding, which is usually normal and results from the rupturing of small blood vessels that line the uterus.

TRUTH OR FICTION REVISITED: It is true that newly fertilized egg cells survive without any nourishment from the mother for more than a week. They are nourished by the yolk of the ovum until they become implanted in the wall of the uterus.

Bleeding can also be a sign of miscarriage (also called "spontaneous abortion"). However, most women who experience implantation bleeding do not miscarry but go on to have normal pregnancies and normal babies. Miscarriage usually results from abnormalities in the developmental process, such as chromosomal problems, substance use, exposure to environmental toxins, hormonal problems, infections, and chronic illnesses such as diabetes. Miscarriage is higher among women past the age of 30, with the probability of miscarriage increasing with age. It is also more common among women who have had previous miscarriages. Many women miscarry early in pregnancy, but their menstrual flow appears about on schedule, so they may not even realize they had conceived. Nearly one-third of all pregnancies result in miscarriage, most of them occurring in the first 3 months (MedlinePlus, 2014). Women who have recurrent miscarriages tend to experience a good deal of anxiety and are at higher risk of their relationships ending than women who have not had miscarriages (Sugiura-Ogasawara et al., 2013).

Section Review

1. A few days into the germinal stage, the dividing cell mass becomes a fluid-filled ball of cells that is called a _____.

2. The outer part of the blastocyst—called the _____—differentiates into membranes that will protect and nourish the embryo.

3. The dividing cluster of cells is nourished by the yolk of the ovum before _____.

Reflect & Relate: Nearly all of us have known—or have been—pregnant women. What early signs made the women suspect that they were pregnant? How do these signs fit with what was happening in their bodies?

3.2 The Embryonic Stage

The **embryonic stage** begins with implantation and covers the first 2 months, during which the major organ systems differentiate. Development follows two general trends: **cephalocaudal** (Latin for "head to tail") and **proximodistal** ("near to far"). The apparently oversized heads of embryos and fetuses at various stages of prenatal development show that growth of the head takes precedence over growth of the lower parts of the body (see Figure 3.2 ■). You can also think of the body as containing a central axis that coincides with the spinal cord. Organ systems in close proximity to this axis develop sooner than the extremities, which are farther from the axis. Relatively early maturation of the brain and organ systems that lie near the central axis enables these organs to play important roles in the subsequent development of the embryo and fetus.

embryonic stage The stage of prenatal development that lasts from implantation through the eighth week of pregnancy. It is characterized by the development of the major organ systems.

cephalocaudal From head to tail.

proximodistal From the inner part (or axis) of the body outward.

Figure 3.2 ■ Human Embryos and Fetuses at Various Stages of Development
Development proceeds in cephalocaudal and proximodistal directions. Development of the head takes precedence over development of the lower parts of the body, enabling the brain to participate in subsequent developments.
© Cengage Learning®

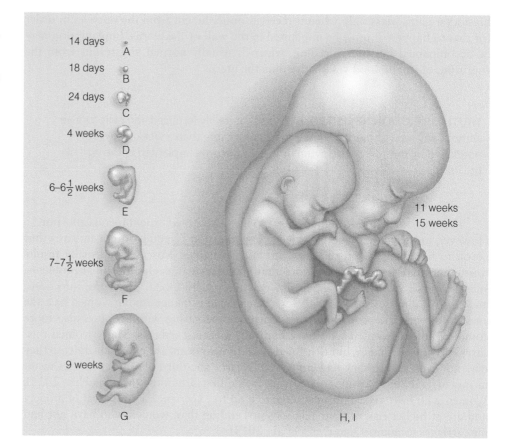

14 days — A
18 days — B
24 days — C
4 weeks — D
6–6½ weeks — E
7–7½ weeks — F
9 weeks — G
11 weeks / 15 weeks — H, I

During the embryonic stage, the embryonic disk's outer layer of cells, or **ectoderm**, develops into the nervous system, sensory organs, nails, hair, and teeth, and the outer layer of skin. At about 21 days, two ridges appear in the embryo and fold to make up the **neural tube**, which develops into the brain and spinal cord. The embryonic disk's inner layer, or **endoderm**, forms the digestive and respiratory systems, the liver, and the pancreas. A bit later in the embryonic stage, the **mesoderm**, or middle layer of cells, becomes differentiated. The mesoderm develops into the excretory, reproductive, and circulatory systems, as well as the muscles, the skeleton, and the inner layer of the skin.

During the third week after conception, the head and blood vessels begin to form. Arm buds and leg buds begin to appear toward the end of the first month. Eyes, ears, nose, and mouth begin to take shape. By this time, the nervous system, including the brain, has also begun to develop. In accordance with the principle of proximodistal development, the upper arms and legs develop before the forearms and lower legs. Next come hands and feet, followed in 6–8 weeks by webbed fingers and toes. By the end of the second month, the limbs have separated and are elongating. The webbing is gone. By this time, the embryo is looking quite human. The head has the lovely round shape of your own, and the facial features have become quite distinct. Bear in mind that all this detail is inscribed on an embryo that is only about 1 inch long and weighs only about 1/30th of an ounce.

ectoderm The outermost cell layer of the newly formed embryo from which the skin and nervous system develop.

neural tube A hollowed-out area in the blastocyst from which the nervous system develops.

endoderm The inner layer of the embryo from which the lungs and digestive system develop.

mesoderm The central layer of the embryo from which the bones and muscles develop.

TRUTH OR FICTION REVISITED: It is true that your heart started beating when you were only one-fourth of an inch long and weighed a fraction of an ounce. The major organ systems develop within the first 2 months of pregnancy. The heart will continue to beat without rest every minute of every day for perhaps 80 or 90 years, or more.

A Closer Look

Real LIFE

SELECTING AN OBSTETRICIAN

A healthy pregnancy can make the difference between a joyous experience and a lifetime of regrets. One way to help ensure a healthy pregnancy is to obtain adequate prenatal health care. The physician who provides prenatal care is called an obstetrician.

Many women learn about obstetricians from friends and relatives. Others, especially women in a new locale, rely on the phone book. In either case, there are things you will want to know about the obstetrician and questions you will need to ask. Many questions concern the degree to which the obstetrician will enable you to be in control of your own childbirth experience. Here are some ideas:

1. As when consulting any helping professional, inquire about the individual's academic credentials and experience. Degrees, licenses, and certificates about residencies should be displayed. If they are not, you might want to ask why.

2. Ask questions. You're going to be bursting with questions over the next several months. If the obstetrician does not handle them well now, you may not be comfortable later on.

3. Ask what kinds of problems the obstetrician runs into most often. How does she or he handle them? This is an indirect way of inquiring about the frequency of cesarean sections (C-sections), for example. Then, too, you never know what "bombshells" will be dropped when you ask an open-ended question.

4. Follow up with questions such as "What percentage of your deliveries are cesareans?" Today, the typical number in the United Sates is one in three, although in some countries, the percentage is as high as 60%

(Visser, 2015). If you lean in the direction of not wanting a C-section unless absolutely necessary, you can say something such as "I've been reading that too many cesareans are done these days. What do you think?"

5. Ask questions about medication during childbirth. For example, "What are your-attitudes toward medication?" You'll quickly get a sense of whether the obstetrician is open-minded about medication and willing to follow your lead.

6. Ask whether the physician routinely performs an episiotomy. This practice is on the wane, and you may want to avoid it unless absolutely necessary.

7. Ask about the obstetrician's beliefs concerning routine testing, weight gains, vitamin supplements, use of amniocentesis or ultrasound, and a whole range of issues. You will also want to learn about the physician's usual scheduling of visits early and late in pregnancy. Each answer will provide you with specific information and will also give you an opportunity to determine how the obstetrician is relating to you as a person.

8. See how the obstetrician handles you during the initial physical exam. You should have the feeling that you are being handled gently, respectfully, and competently. If you're not sure, do some comparison shopping. It's your body and your child. You have the right to gather enough information to make you feel confident that you are making the best choice.

The physician may have the expertise, but you are in charge. You know how your body feels and how you respond to health problems and discomfort. You want an obstetrician who is open, helpful, and competent. Be assertive in making your choice.

PhotoDisc/Getty Images

The rapid development of the nervous system enables it to participate in further developments. Before the end of the first month of embryonic development, the neural tube is producing about 400 million nerve cells, called *neurons,* per day. Neurons transmit information to other neurons, muscles, and glands. Once they have been produced, neurons migrate to various parts of the brain, where they will develop to function as different brain structures. In the fifth week, neurons form the cerebral hemispheres; the outer "bark" of the hemispheres is the cerebral cortex—the crowning glory of the brain—which the child will eventually use to perceive the itch from a mosquito bite, compose a concerto, or solve an algebraic equation. During the second month of embryonic development, the cells in the nervous system actually begin to "fire"—that is, to transmit messages. They do so by releasing countless chemicals called *neurotransmitters* into the fluid between neurons, muscles, and glands. These neurotransmitters are then taken up by receiving cells via structures which have miniature "docks." But at the beginning, much firing is probably random; much of the "content" of messages transmitted from neuron to neuron is anybody's guess. (No, the embryo isn't contemplating the NFL playoffs or Albert Einstein.)

By the end of the embryonic period, teeth buds have formed. The sensory organs—eyes, ears, and nose—are all taking shape. The embryo's kidneys are filtering acid from the blood, and its liver is producing red blood cells.

Sexual Differentiation: How Do Some Babies Develop into Girls and Others into Boys?

By 5 to 6 weeks, the embryo is only one-quarter to one-half inch long. Nevertheless, nondescript sex organs already have formed, including the internal and external genital organs. Figure 3.3 ■ shows changes in the internal organs. Both female and male embryos possess a pair of sexually undifferentiated gonads and two sets of primitive duct structures, the so-called Müllerian (female) ducts and Wolffian (male) ducts. At this stage of development, both the internal and the external genitals resemble primitive female structures.

By about the seventh week, the genetic code (XY or XX) begins to assert itself, causing sex organs to differentiate. Genetic activity on the Y sex chromosome causes the testes to begin to differentiate. Ovaries begin to differentiate if the Y chromosome is *absent*. By about 4 months after conception, males and females show distinct external genital structures.

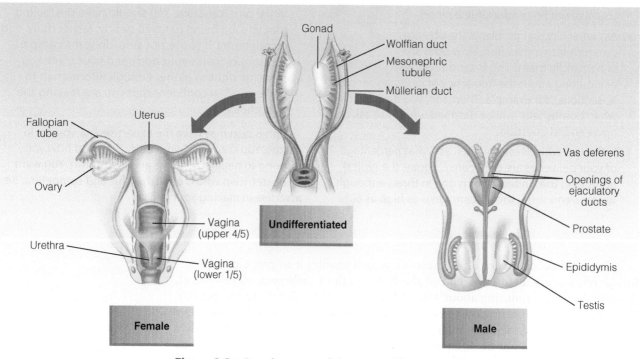

Figure 3.3 ■ Development of the Internal Genital Organs from the Age of 5–6 Weeks after Conception.
© Cengage Learning®

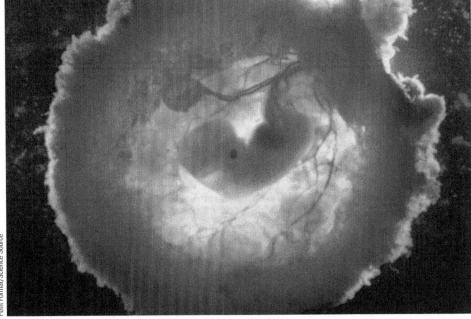

A Human Embryo at 7 Weeks
At this late point in the embryonic stage, the major organ systems except for the sex organs have already become differentiated.

Petit Format/Science Source

Sex Hormones and Sexual Differentiation

Prenatal sexual differentiation requires hormonal influences as well as genetic influences. Male sex hormones—**androgens**—are critical in the development of male genital organs. Once testes have developed in the embryo, they begin to produce androgens. The most important of these is **testosterone**. Testosterone spurs the differentiation of the male (Wolffian) duct system (see Figure 3.3) and remains involved in sexual development and activity for a lifetime. Each Wolffian duct develops into a complex maze of ducts and storage facilities for sperm. At about the eighth week of prenatal development, another androgen—dihydrotestosterone (DHT)—spurs the formation of the external male genital organs, including the penis. Yet another testicular hormone, secreted somewhat later, prevents the Müllerian ducts from developing into the female duct system. That hormone is called Müllerian inhibiting substance (MIS).

TRUTH OR FICTION REVISITED: It is true that without male sex hormones (androgens), all people—whether genetically female or male—would develop female external sex organs. However, apparent "females" who have a male XY sex chromosomal structure are infertile (Reichman et al., 2014).

Female embryos and fetuses do produce small amounts of androgens, but not normally enough to cause sexual differentiation along male lines. However, they do play important roles in the development of some secondary sexual characteristics in adolescence, such as the appearance of pubic and underarm hair. Androgens are also important in the sex drives of females throughout their lives (Davis, 2013). But in the female embryo and fetus, low levels of androgens are connected with degeneration of the Wolffian ducts and further development of female sexual organs. The Müllerian ducts develop into fallopian tubes, the uterus, and the inner part of the vagina. The presence of the female sex hormones is not necessary for these developments to occur, although female sex hormones will become crucial in puberty.

androgens Male sex hormones.

testosterone A male sex hormone produced by the testes that promotes the development of male sexual characteristics and sperm.

Why Is the Amniotic Sac Called a "Shock Absorber"?

The embryo and fetus develop within a protective **amniotic sac** in the uterus. The sac is surrounded by a clear membrane and contains **amniotic fluid**. The fluid serves as a kind of natural air bag, allowing the embryo and fetus to move around without injury. It also helps to maintain an even temperature.

What Are the Functions of the Placenta?

How does the embryo get nourishment from its mother? How does it eliminate waste products? The answers involve the placenta and the umbilical cord. The placenta is a mass of tissue that permits the embryo (and, later on, the fetus) to exchange nutrients and wastes with the mother. The placenta is unique in origin. It grows from material supplied by both the mother and the embryo. The fetus is connected to the placenta by the umbilical cord. The mother is connected to the placenta by the system of blood vessels in the uterine wall.

In one of the more fascinating feats of prenatal engineering, it turns out that the mother and baby have separate circulatory systems. Her bloodstream is hers, and the embryo's bloodstream is the embryo's. The pancake-shaped placenta contains a membrane that acts as a filter; only certain substances can pass through it. The membrane permits oxygen and nutrients to reach the embryo from the mother. It also permits carbon dioxide (which is the gas that you breathe out and plants "breathe" in) and waste products to pass to the mother from the child. Once the mother has these waste products, she eliminates them through her own lungs and kidneys. This is the good part. The bad part is that a number of harmful substances can sneak through the placenta. They include various "germs" (microscopic disease-causing organisms), such as the ones that cause syphilis (a bacterium called *Treponema pallidum*) and German measles (Delorme-Axford et al., 2014). Yet even here there is a silver lining: most pregnant women who are infected with HIV (the virus that causes AIDS) do not transmit it to the baby through the placenta during prenatal development (Delorme-Axford et al., 2014). HIV is more likely to be transmitted during childbirth, when the placenta can break down and the bloodstreams of mother and baby can mix (Lynch et al., 2011). But some drugs—aspirin, narcotics, alcohol, tranquilizers, and others—do cross the placenta and can affect the baby in various ways.

The placenta also secretes hormones that preserve the pregnancy, prepare the breasts for nursing, and stimulate the uterine contractions that prompt childbirth. Ultimately, the placenta passes from the woman's body after the child is delivered. For this reason, it is also called the afterbirth.

amniotic sac The sac containing the fetus.

amniotic fluid Fluid within the amniotic sac that suspends and protects the fetus.

Section Review

4. The embryo and fetus develop within an _____ sac, which functions as a shock absorber, among other things.

5. Development follows two general trends: cephalocaudal and _____.

6. The _____ (inner or outer?) layer of cells of the ectoderm develops into the nervous system, the sensory organs, and the outer layer of skin.

7. Without sex hormones, all embryos would develop the appearance of _____ (males or females?).

8. The _____ permits the embryo to exchange nutrients and wastes with the mother.

9. The embryo and fetus are connected to the placenta by the _____.

Reflect & Relate: Are you surprised at how early the heart begins to beat and at the size of the embryo when it happens? Explain.

3.3 The Fetal Stage

The **fetal stage** lasts from the beginning of the third month until birth. The fetus begins to turn and respond to external stimulation at about the 9th or 10th week. By the end of the first trimester, all the major organ systems have formed. The fingers and toes are fully formed. The eyes can be clearly distinguished, and the sex of the fetus can be determined visually.

The second trimester is characterized by further maturation of fetal organ systems and dramatic gains in size. The brain continues to mature, contributing to the fetus's ability to regulate its own basic body functions. During the second trimester, the fetus advances from 1 ounce to 2 pounds in weight and increases four to five times over in length, from about 3 inches to 14 inches. Soft, downy hair grows above the eyes and on the scalp. The skin turns ruddy because of blood vessels that show through the surface. (During the third trimester, fatty layers will give the skin a pinkish hue.)

By the end of the second trimester, the fetus opens and shuts its eyes, sucks its thumb, alternates between periods of wakefulness and sleep, and perceives light and sounds.

TRUTH OR FICTION REVISITED: It is true that sharp spasms of the diaphragm, or fetal hiccups, may last for hours. If you have any doubts, check with a weary pregnant woman.

About 50% to 60% of babies who are born at 22–25 weeks of gestation survive, but the survival rate is related to the quality of care they receive (Kyser et al., 2013). There is significant hospital-to-hospital variation in the survival rate for these extremely preterm infants (Rysavy et al., 2015).

fetal stage The stage of development that lasts from the beginning of the ninth week of pregnancy through birth.

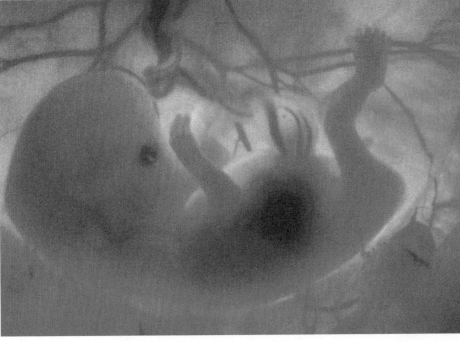

Claude Edelmann/Science Source

A Human Fetus at 12 Weeks By the end of the first trimester, the formation of all major organ systems is complete. Fingers and toes are fully formed, and the sex of the fetus can be determined visually.

A Human Fetus at 4½ Months
At this midway point between conception and birth, the fetus is covered with fine, downy hair called lanugo.

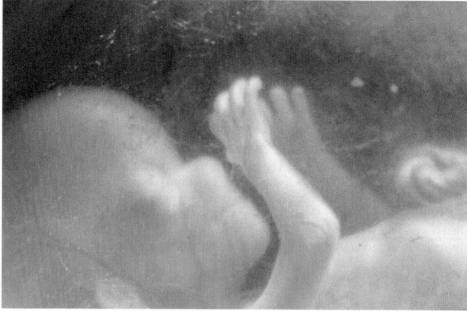

Petit Format/Science Source

During the third trimester, the organ systems of the fetus continue to mature. The heart and lungs become increasingly capable of sustaining independent life. The fetus gains about 5½ pounds and doubles in length. Newborn boys average about 7½ pounds, and newborn girls average about 7 pounds.

During the seventh month, the fetus normally turns upside down in the uterus so that delivery will be head first. By the end of the seventh month, the fetus will have almost doubled in weight, gaining another 1 pound, 12 ounces, and will have increased another 2 inches in length. If the baby is born now, the chances of survival are nearly 90%. If the baby is born at the end of the eighth month, the odds are overwhelmingly in favor of survival.

The Hands of a Human Fetus at 5 Months By 5 months of age, the hands have been fully formed for a month or so. The fetus may occasionally suck its thumb.

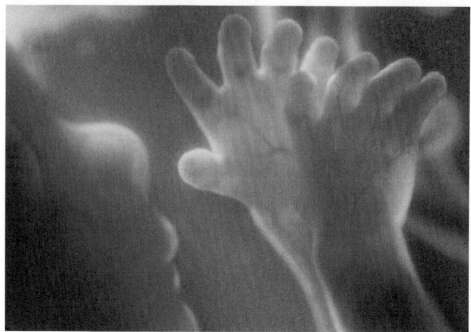

Petit Format/Nestle/Science Source

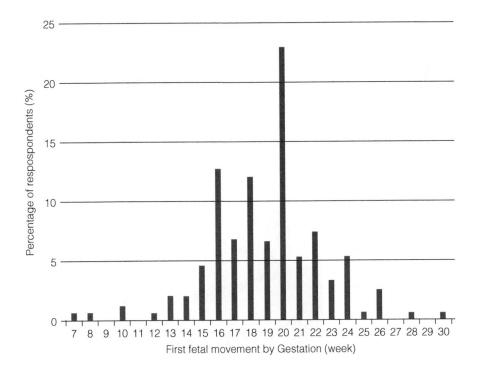

Figure 3.4 ■ Maternal Perception of First Fetal Movements by Week of Gestation About 75% of mothers report feeling movements of the baby by about 20 weeks of gestation, with the 20th week being the most common week that fetal movements are first reported. Raynes-Greenough, C. H., Gordon, A., Li, Q., & Hyett, J. A. (2013).

The first fetal movements frequently occur during the fourth or fifth month and are often described by the mother as being "light as a feather" (Adolph & Berger, 2005; Raynes-Greenough et al., 2013; see Figure 3.4 ■). By 29–30 weeks, the mother gets her kicks; that is, the fetus moves its limbs so vigorously that the mother may complain of being kicked—often at 4 a.m. (Raynes-Greenough et al., 2013). The fetus also turns somersaults, which the mother clearly feels.

Fetuses show different patterns of prenatal activity (de Vries & Hopkins, 2005). Slow squirming movements begin at about 5 or 6 months. Sharp jabbing or kicking movements begin at about the same time and increase in intensity until shortly before birth. As the fetus grows, it becomes cramped in the uterus, and movement is constricted. Many women become concerned that their fetuses are markedly less active during the ninth month than earlier, but most of the time this change is normal.

There are individual differences in level of fetal activity, but a Dutch study found no sex differences in fetal movement (de Medina et al., 2003). On the other hand, prenatal activity predicts activity levels after birth. For instance, highly active fetuses show more advanced motor development after birth than their more lethargic counterparts (de Vries & Hopkins, 2005).

Section Review

10. The fetal stage is characterized by _____ of organ systems and gains in size and weight.

11. Fetuses apparently discriminate sounds of different pitches during the _____ trimester of pregnancy.

12. Mothers usually detect fetal movements during the _____ month.

Reflect & Relate: During the fourth month, when the baby's movements can be detected, many women have the feeling that their babies are "alive." What is your view on when the baby is alive? What standard or standards are you using to form your opinion?

ON FETAL PERCEPTION—BACH AT BREAKFAST AND BEETHOVEN AT BRUNCH?

When I was a beginning graduate student and knew everything, I was astounded by what I thought was the naïveté of parents-to-be who listened to Bach or Beethoven or read Shakespeare aloud to promote the cultural development of their fetuses. But in more recent years, I admit that my wife and I made more of an effort to expose our fetuses to good music as well. Part of the reason is based on research from 1938. Sontag and Richards reported the results of a study in which they stimulated pregnant woman by such means as ringing a bell, and then measured the effect on the heart rate of the fetus, as assessed by an instrument on the mother's abdomen. Many of the mothers smoked, and the researchers also assessed the effects of smoking on the fetal heart rate. And they got the fetus all shook up by placing a vibrator against the mother's abdomen.

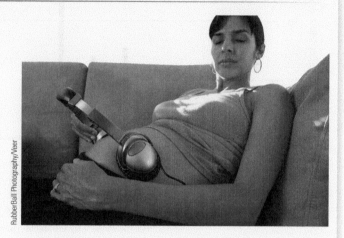

RubberBall Photography/Veer

Sontag and Richards found that powerful vibrations usually induced faster heart rates in the fetus, but maternal smoking had less predictable effects. Cigarette smoke contains the stimulant nicotine but also reduces the supply of oxygen in the bloodstream, and oxygen is needed to fuel bursts of activity. These researchers spent their time assessing the effects of maternal smoking on the fetus rather than warning the mothers about the harmful effects of smoking because this was 1938, and much less was known about the effects of smoking.

Sontag and Richards also discovered that fetuses are sensitive to sound waves during the last months of pregnancy. This has led to a wave of more recent research, including studies investigating whether neonates are "loyal" and prefer their mothers' voices to those of strangers, and whether listening to classical music during pregnancy rather than heavy metal has measurable effects. During the third trimester, fetuses also respond to sounds of different frequencies through a variety of movements and changes in heart rate, suggesting that by this time they can discriminate pitch (Partanen et al., 2013; Ullal-Gupta et al., 2013).

A classic experiment by DeCasper and Fifer (1980) is even more intriguing. In this study, women read the Dr. Seuss book *The Cat in the Hat* out loud twice daily during the final month and a half of pregnancy. After birth, their babies were given special pacifiers: Sucking on them in one way would activate recordings of their mothers reading *The Cat in the Hat*. Sucking on them in another way would activate their mothers' reading of another book—*The King, the Mice, and the Cheese*—which was written in very different rhythms. The newborns "chose" to hear *The Cat in the Hat*. Using similar research methods, DeCasper and his colleagues found that newborns prefer the mother's voice to that of their father or that of an unfamiliar woman (DeCasper & Prescott, 1984; DeCasper & Spence, 1986, 1991). Fetal learning may be one basis for the development of attachment to the mother (Yee & Kisilevsky, 2014).

Highlights of Prenatal Development

First Trimester

Period of the Ovum

First 2 weeks	• Dividing cluster of cells enters and moves around the uterus, living off the yolk of the egg cell. • Blastocyst becomes implanted in the wall of the uterus, possibly accompanied by implantation bleeding.	 David M. Phillips/Science Source

Embryonic Stage

3 weeks	• Head and blood vessels form. • Brain begins to develop.	
4 weeks	• Heart begins to beat and pump blood. • Arm buds and leg buds appear. • Eyes, ears, nose, and mouth form. • Nerves begin to develop. • Umbilical cord is functional. • Embryo weighs a fraction of an ounce and is one-half inch long.	 Petit Format/Science Source
5–8 weeks	• Hands and feet develop with webbed fingers and toes. • Undifferentiated sex organs appear. • Teeth buds develop. • Kidneys filter uric acid from the blood; liver produces blood cells. • Bone cells appear. • Head is half the length of the entire body. • Embryo weighs about 1/13 of an ounce and is 1 inch long.	

Fetal Stage

9–12 weeks	• All major organ systems are formed. • Fingers and toes are fully formed. • Eyes can be clearly distinguished. • Sex of fetus can be determined visually (e.g., by ultrasound). • Mouth opens and closes; fetus swallows. • Fetus responds to external stimulation. • Fetus weighs 1 ounce and is 3 inches long.	 Petit Format/Science Source

(continued on page 90)

Highlights of Prenatal Development (continued)

Second Trimester

13–16 weeks	• Mother detects fetal movement. • Many reflexes are present. • Fingernails and toenails form. • Head is about one-fourth the length of the body.	 Petit Format/Nestle/Science Source
17–20 weeks	• Hair develops on head. • Fine, downy hair (lanugo) covers body. • Fetus sucks its thumb and hiccups. • Heartbeat can be heard when listener presses head against-mother's abdomen.	
21–24 weeks	• Eyes open and shut. • Light and sounds can be perceived. • Fetus alternates between periods of wakefulness and sleep. • Skin looks ruddy because blood vessels show through the surface. • Survival rate is low if fetus is born. • Fetus weighs about 2 pounds and is 14 inches long; growth rate is slowing down.	

Third Trimester

25–28 weeks	• Organ systems continue to mature. • Fatty layer begins to develop beneath the skin. • Fetus turns head down in the uterus. • Fetus cries, swallows, and sucks its thumb. • Chances of survival are good if born now. • Fetus weighs 3–4 pounds and is 16 inches long.	
29 to 38 weeks	• Organ systems function well. • Fatty layer continues to develop. • Fetal activity level decreases in the weeks before birth as a result of crowding. • Weight increases to an average of 7–7½ pounds; boys are about half a pound heavier than girls; length increases to about 20 inches.	 Ansell Horn/Phototake

© Cengage Learning®

BIRTH RATES AROUND THE WORLD

Let's have a look at some history and some pre-history—that is, some guesstimates of events that might have occurred before records were made. According to the U.S. Census Bureau, which was *not* distributing questionnaires at the time, some 5 million humans walked the Earth about 10,000 years ago. It took another 5,000 years for that number to expand to 14 million. Skipping ahead 2,000 years to the year 1, humans gained a stronger foothold on the planet, and the number increased tenfold, to some 170 million. By 1900, the population increased tenfold again, to about 1.7 billion. In 1950, estimates placed the number at about 2.5 billion, and today—with increases in the food supply, sanitary water supplies, and vaccinations—the number is estimated to be close to 7 billion.

Therefore, we are in the middle of a population explosion, are we not? The answer depends on where you look (Table 3.1). Parents need to have slightly more than two children to "reproduce themselves," because some children are lost to illness, accidents, or violence. Some children will also be infertile. Others will decide not to have children of their own.

TRUTH OR FICTION REVISITED: It is not true that parents in wealthy nations have more children. Table 3.1 shows that in developed countries such as Spain,

Greece, Italy, Japan, Canada, Russia, and the United Kingdom, parents are not reproducing themselves at levels adequate to maintain their populations. (Reproduction rates change from time to time, and immigration is also related to a country's population growth or decline.)

Reflect

- How do the birth rates of countries where 30% or fewer of the population use modern means of contraception compare with those where 60% or more use modern means? What are the relationships between literacy and birth rate? Between education and birth rate?

- How would you judge whether a particular birth rate in a particular nation is a good thing or a bad thing? If it is a bad thing, what can be done about it? Explain your views.

- Why do parents in wealthier nations tend to have fewer children? What are your feelings about this? Explain your views.

- Does the information in Table 3.2 show cause and effect? Why or why not?

[1]U.S. Census Bureau. Historical estimates of world population. http://www.census.gov/ipc/www/worldhis.html. Accessed July 31, 2015.

3.4 Environmental Influences on Prenatal Development

Yes, the fetus develops in a protective "bubble"—the amniotic sac. Nevertheless, the developing fetus is subject to many environmental hazards. Scientific advances have made us keenly aware of the types of things that can go wrong and what we can do to prevent these problems. In this section, we will consider some of the environmental factors that have an effect on prenatal development.

How Does Maternal Nutrition Affect Prenatal Development?

We quickly bring nutrition inside, but nutrition originates outside. Therefore, nutrition is one of the environmental factors that influence prenatal (and subsequent) development.

Fertility Rates and Related Factors Around the World

Nation	Fertility Rates	Rate of Usage of Modern Methods of Contraception (%)	Literacy Rates (%)		Years of Education	
			Men	Women	Men	Women
Afghanistan	5.97	15	**	**	10	6
Brazil	1.80	77	90	90	14	14
Canada	1.69	72	**	**	15	16
China	1.56	84	97	91	11	12
Congo	4.44	13	**	**	11	10
Cuba	1.45	72	100	100	15	17
France	1.99	75	**	**	16	16
Germany	1.46	66	**	**	**	**
Greece	1.54	46	98	96	16	16
India	2.54	49	75	51	11	10
Iran	1.59	59	89	81	13	13
Iraq	4.54	33	86	70	11	9
Israel	2.91	52	**	**	15	16
Italy	1.48	41	99	99	16	17
Jamaica	2.26	66	81	91	13	14
Japan	1.42	44	**	**	15	15
Kenya	4.62	39	91	84	11	11
Mexico	2.23	67	95	92	13	14
Pakistan	3.20	19	69	40	8	6
Philippines	3.05	34	95	96	11	12
Russia	1.53	65	100	99	14	15
Saudi Arabia	2.64	**	90	81	15	14
Spain	1.50	62	98	97	16	17
United Kingdom	1.87	84	**	**	16	17
U.S.A.	2.08	73	**	**	16	17

Source: United Nations. (2012). Department of Economic and Social Affairs. Economic and Social Development. Social Indicators. http://unstats.un.org/unsd/demographic/products/socind/childbearing.htm#tech Table 2d, Contraceptive preference; Table 4a, Literacy; Table 4e, School life expectancy.
**Missing information

It is a common misconception that fetuses "take what they need" from their mothers. If this were true, pregnant women would not have to be highly concerned about their diets. But malnutrition in the mother, especially during the last trimester when the fetus should be making rapid gains in weight, has been linked to low birth weight, prematurity, stunted growth, retardation of brain development, cognitive deficiencies, behavioral problems, and even cardiovascular disease (Monk et al., 2013; de Souza et al., 2011).

Fortunately, the effects of fetal malnutrition can sometimes be overcome by a supportive caregiving environment. Experiments with children who suffered from fetal malnutrition show that enriched day-care programs enhance intellectual and social skills by 5 years of age (Ramey et al., 1999). Supplementing the diets of pregnant women who might otherwise be deficient in their intake of calories and protein also shows modest positive effects on the motor development of the women's infants (Morton, 2006).

On the other hand, maternal obesity is linked with a higher risk of **stillbirth** (Crane et al., 2013; Tennant et al., 2011). Obesity during pregnancy also increases the likelihood of neural tube defects. In a study reported in *The Journal of the American Medical Association* women who weighed 176–195 pounds before pregnancy were about twice as likely as women who weighed 100–130 pounds to bear children with neural tube defects; women who weighed 242 pounds or more were four times more likely to have children with neural tube defects (Shaw et al., 1996). In the Shaw study, folic acid supplements did not appear to prevent neural tube defects in the babies of women who weighed more than 154 pounds.

What Should a Pregnant Woman Eat?

Pregnant women need the following food elements to maintain their health and to give birth to healthy babies: protein, which is heavily concentrated in red meat, fish, poultry, eggs, beans, milk, and cheese; vitamin A, which is found in milk and vegetables; vitamin B, which is found in wheat germ, whole grain breads, and liver; vitamin C, which is found in citrus fruits; vitamin D, which is derived from sunshine, fish liver oil, and vitamin D–fortified milk; vitamin E, which is found in whole grains, some vegetables, eggs, and peanuts; iron, which is concentrated heavily in meat (especially liver), egg yolks, fish, and raisins; the trace minerals zinc and cobalt, which are found in seafood; calcium, which is found in dairy products; and, yes, calories. Research also demonstrates the importance of consuming folic acid, which is found in leafy green vegetables. Women who eat a well-rounded diet do not require food supplements, but most doctors recommend them, to be safe (de Souza et al., 2011). Pregnant women who take folic acid supplements reduce the risk of giving birth to babies with neural tube defects, which can cause paralysis and death (Giussani, 2011).

How Much Weight Should a Pregnant Woman Gain?

Malnutrition in the mother can adversely affect fetal development. Women who are too slender risk having preterm deliveries and low-birthweight babies (Ricketts et al., 2014). Pregnant women who are adequately nourished are more likely to deliver babies who are average or above-average in size. Their infants are also less likely to develop colds and more serious respiratory disorders.

The slimmer a woman is before pregnancy, the more weight she is advised to gain during pregnancy. For example, a woman with a body mass index (BMI)[1] below 18.5 is typically advised to gain 28–40 pounds (Rasmussen et al., 2009; see Table 3.2 ● on page 95). Women of normal weight, those with a BMI of 18.5–24.9, are usually advised to gain 25–35 pounds. However, 55% of pregnant women in the United States are overweight or obese (Parker-Pope, 2009). Women who are overweight, with a BMI of 25.0–29.9, are advised to gain 15–25 pounds. And obese women, those with a BMI above 30.0, are advised to limit their weight gain to 11–20 pounds. Gaining weight gradually is most desirable.

stillbirth The birth of a dead fetus.

● TABLE 3.2

Body Mass Index (BMI) and Weight Status

BMI	Weight Status
Below 18.5	Underweight
18.5–24.9	Normal weight
25.0–29.9	Overweight
30.0 and above	Obese

Source: NIH Publication no. 98-4083. *Clinical Guidelines on the Identification, Evaluation, and Treatment of Overweight and Obesity in Adults: The Evidence Report.* NHLBI (National Heart, Lung, and Blood Institute); 1998.

What Are Teratogens? Does It Matter When, During Pregnancy, a Woman Is Exposed to Them?

Most of what the mother does for the embryo is not only remarkable but also healthful. There are exceptions, however. Consider the case of teratogens. **Teratogens** (the word derives from frightening roots meaning "giving birth to monsters") are environmental agents that can harm the embryo or fetus. Teratogens include drugs that the mother ingests, such as thalidomide (connected with birth deformities) and alcohol, and substances that the mother's body produces, such as Rh-positive antibodies. Another class of teratogens is the heavy metals, such as lead and mercury, which are toxic to the embryo. Hormones are healthful in countless ways; for example, they help maintain pregnancy. However, excessive amounts of hormones are harmful to the embryo. If the mother is exposed to radiation, that radiation can harm the embryo. Then, of course, disease-causing organisms—also called pathogens—such as bacteria and viruses are also teratogens. When it comes to pathogens, bigger is better for the embryo; that is, larger pathogens are less likely to pass through the placenta and affect the embryo. But smaller pathogens sneak through, including those that cause mumps, syphilis, measles, and chicken pox. Some disorders, such as toxemia, are not transmitted to the embryo or fetus but adversely affect the environment in which it develops.

What Are the Critical Periods of Vulnerability?

Exposure to particular teratogens is most harmful during **critical periods** that correspond to the times when organs are developing (Figure 3.5 ■). For example, the heart develops rapidly during the third to fifth weeks after conception. Therefore, the heart is most vulnerable to certain teratogens at this time. The arms and legs, which develop later, are most vulnerable during the fourth to eighth weeks.

TRUTH OR FICTION REVISITED: It is true that the same disease organism or chemical agent that can do serious damage to a 6-week-old embryo may have no effect on a 4-month-old fetus. Because the major organ systems differentiate during the embryonic stage, the embryo is generally more vulnerable to teratogens than the fetus. But many teratogens are harmful throughout the entire course of prenatal development.

teratogens Environmental influences or agents that can damage the embryo or fetus.

critical period In this context, a period during which an embryo is particularly vulnerable to a certain teratogen.

Let us consider the effects of various health problems of the mother, beginning with sexually transmitted infections (STIs).

ADVICE FOR EXPECTANT FATHERS

I got hungry while we were waiting for the contractions to get more frequent, and I made the mistake of bringing a tuna sandwich into the birthing room. My wife gave me a horrible look and threatened to throw up on me—and much worse—if I didn't get it out of there immediately.
—A former expectant father, now a father

First piece of advice: Unless your will is made out and you've grown weary of your journey through this world, do *not* bring a tuna sandwich into the delivery room.

It's women who get pregnant, but these days it's often politically correct to say things like "We're pregnant"—especially when a father doesn't want to be left out of the process. But expectant fathers may not feel as though they are also pregnant, and they can indeed feel left out of the process. They can also have concerns about the pregnancy, and some fears. Following are some concerns expressed by expectant fathers, and some thoughts about responding to them:

1. *Will I be a good father? How will I know what to do? Women seem to take to motherhood naturally, but is fatherhood "natural"?* One might counter, of course, that we can wonder whether motherhood is really so natural for women when they have typically been thrust into caregiving roles with dolls and with other people's children since early childhood. Think of parenting as a skill that can be learned, and if the father is motivated, he can acquire that skill.

2. *What if I die when they need me?* "I realized I was no longer the kid," said one expectant father. "I was going to have one. Suddenly my life didn't seem as open-ended." It's always good to think about our responsibilities toward others. Expectant fathers may be exaggerating the threats in their lives, but taking out an insurance policy is a good idea. A young father may find that a term life insurance policy fits into his financial picture quite well.

3. *Will she love the baby more than she loves me?* Perhaps, but that doesn't mean she'll love the father less. Having a baby creates a totally new configuration of attachments and emotions in a family. At the very least, it expands the potential for feelings of love. Many new fathers say things such as "I never knew I had that much love in me." Your baby will form an attachment to you as well as to his or her mother, and the sum total of positive feelings you will be experiencing will most likely increase. Remember that your partner may

also be wondering whether you will prefer the baby to her, especially if it's a daughter.

4. *How can I help during the pregnancy when I don't particularly understand women's medical issues?* A vast knowledge gap can emerge as the mother becomes well educated about pregnancy, childbirth, and parenting, and the father feels left out. The father can support the mother by trying to remain involved. For example, he can attend as many clinical visits as he can fit into his schedule, but he should not, perhaps, blow things out of proportion if he must miss some. He can also generally help by listening when his partner expresses her concerns, trying to understand them, and offering to help.

5. *Will I do what I'm supposed to do at the birth? Does she even really want me at the birth, or is she just being "politically correct" by including me?* Back to the tuna fish: You may have attended clinical visits and childbirth lessons with your partner, but you won't be the only person there to assist.

6. *But I don't even particularly like kids, so how am I going to feel about this one?* Because "this one" is, as the expression goes, "your own flesh and blood," you'll probably have rather positive feelings. Does that mean you'll never be annoyed when the baby cries at night or when your partner dotes on the baby? Not at all, but you'll be able to put these concerns into perspective.

7. *What do I do if it's a girl? What do I do if it's a boy?* Many fathers worry that they won't provide a masculine enough role model for sons and that they won't have any idea what to do if it's a girl. "The fact of the matter is that I wanted a boy because I didn't know what I would do with a girl. But even so, I wasn't sure I wanted to have to toss around a football or a baseball with a boy. I never threw a football all that well, in truth. When we had a girl, I bonded with her immediately—she was very cute—and I found myself prepared to hug her. And I learned quickly enough that a large part of fatherhood is really about changing diapers, no matter how bad the smell."

Reflect Which of these concerns might you or a partner experience? Have you had—or has a partner had—any of these concerns? Why do you think many people, female and male, say things such as "*We're* expecting a baby" these days?

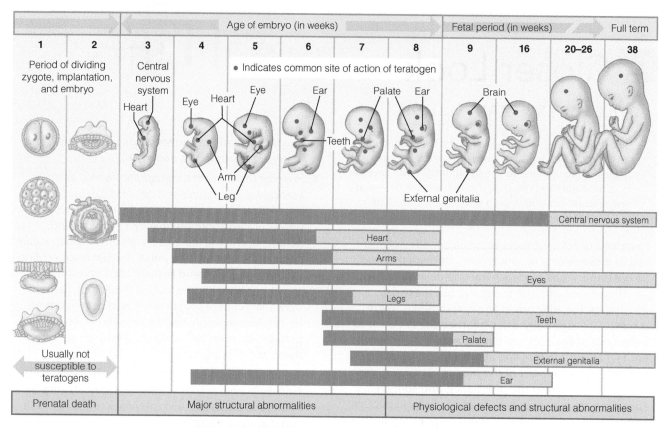

Figure 3.5 ■ Critical Periods in Prenatal Development
Knowledge of the sequence of prenatal development allows one to understand why specific teratogens are most harmful during certain periods of prenatal development. Major structural abnormalities are most likely to occur when teratogens strike during the embryonic period.
National Institutes of Health. National Institute on Alcohol Abuse and Alcoholism. Pubs.niaaa.nih.gov (Accessed December 8, 2012)

Sexually Transmitted Infections

The **syphilis** bacterium can cause miscarriage, stillbirth, or **congenital** syphilis. Routine blood tests early in pregnancy can diagnose syphilis. The syphilis bacterium is vulnerable to antibiotics, and rates of syphilis are currently low in Western nations. Also, the bacterium does not readily cross the placental membrane early in pregnancy. The fetus will probably not contract syphilis if an infected mother is treated with antibiotics before the fourth month of pregnancy. However, an infected woman has about a 40% chance of having a child who is stillborn or dies shortly after birth (Centers for Disease Control and Prevention, 2013). If the mother is not treated, the baby has a 40% to 70% chance of being infected in utero and of developing congenital syphilis. About 12% of those infected die.

Infected babies may show no symptoms when they are born, but they may develop symptoms within a few weeks if they go untreated. The symptoms of congenital syphilis include skin sores, a runny nose, which is sometimes bloody (and infectious), slimy patches in the mouth, inflamed bones in the arms and legs, swollen liver, jaundice, anemia, and a small head. Congenital syphilis can impair vision and hearing, damage the liver, and deform the bones and teeth. Untreated babies may develop intellectual disability or have seizures.

HIV/AIDS (human immunodeficiency virus/acquired immunodeficiency syndrome) disables the body's immune system, leaving victims prey to a variety of fatal illnesses, including respiratory disorders and cancer. HIV/AIDS is lethal unless treated with a combination of antiviral drugs. Even then, the drugs do not work for everyone, and the eventual outcome remains in doubt (Rathus et al., 2014).

syphilis A sexually transmitted infection that can attack major organ systems.

congenital Present at birth; resulting from the prenatal environment.

HIV/AIDS HIV stands for human immunodeficiency virus, which cripples the body's immune system. AIDS stands for acquired immunodeficiency syndrome—the body's state when the immune system is weakened to the point where it is vulnerable to diseases that would otherwise be fought off.

HIV can be transmitted through sexual relations, blood transfusions, sharing hypodermic needles while shooting up drugs, childbirth, and breastfeeding. About one-fourth of babies born to HIV-infected mothers become infected themselves (Coovadia, 2004). During childbirth, blood vessels in the mother and baby rupture, allowing an exchange of blood and transmission of HIV. HIV is also found in breast milk. An African study found that the probability of transmission of HIV through breast milk was about 1 in 6 (16.2%) (Nduati et al., 2000). It appears that women can decrease the risk of becoming infected with HIV by regular use of antiviral drugs such as Truvada (Callahan et al., 2015).

Children from ethnic and racial minority groups are at greater risk of being infected with HIV. African Americans account for approximately half of the pediatric cases of HIV/AIDS, and Latin Americans (especially those of Puerto Rican origin) account for almost one-fourth of such cases (Bangs & Davis, 2015; Office of Minority Health & Health Disparities [OMHD], 2010). Inner-city neighborhoods, where there is widespread intravenous drug use, are especially hard hit (OMHD, 2010). Death rates resulting from AIDS are higher among African American and Puerto Rican children than among European American children (OMHD, 2010), apparently because African Americans and Puerto Ricans have less access to health care. Research evidence suggests that highly active antiretroviral therapy (HAART), which has extended the lives of many adults with HIV/AIDS, may also have benefits for infected children (Ajulo et al., 2014).

The Flu

Although influenza ("the flu") primarily infects the mother's respiratory system, it has been suspected that the flu may play a causal role in the development of fetal brain abnormalities and lead to problems such as autism and schizophrenia (Wilson et al., 2014). Yet Limin Shi and Patterson (2005) studied the maternal and fetal tissues of laboratory animals for influenza virus and found that it appears to only rarely be transmitted to the fetuses of infected mothers. It may be that the effects of the flu on the fetus are most likely to involve the mother's inflammatory response to the virus—for example, her secretion of high levels of substances such as corticosteroids and interleukin-6 (Limin Shi & Patterson, 2005).

Rubella

Rubella (German measles) is a viral infection. Women who are infected during the first 20 weeks of pregnancy stand at least a 20% chance of bearing children with birth defects such as deafness, intellectual disability, heart disease, or eye problems, including blindness (Food and Drug Administration, 2004; Rubella, 2009).

Many adult women had rubella as children and became immune in this way. Women who are not immune are best vaccinated before they become pregnant, although they can be inoculated during pregnancy, if necessary. Inoculation has led to a dramatic decline in the number of American children born with defects caused by rubella, from about 2,000 cases in 1964–1965 to 21 in 2001 (Thompson et al., 2014).

Pre-Eclampsia

Pre-eclampsia (also known as *toxemia*) is a life-threatening disease, characterized by high blood pressure, that may afflict women late in the second or early in the third trimester (Bangal et al., 2012). Affected women often have **premature** or undersized babies. Pre-eclampsia is also a cause of pregnancy-related maternal deaths (Bangal et al., 2012). Pre-eclampsia appears to be linked to malnutrition, but the causes are unclear. Pregnant women who do not receive prenatal care are more likely than others to die from pre-eclampsia (Verlohren et al., 2012).

rubella A viral infection that can cause retardation and heart disease in the embryo. Also called German measles.

pre-eclampsia A life-threatening disease that can afflict pregnant women. It is characterized by high blood pressure.

premature Born before the full term of gestation. (Also referred to as preterm.)

PREVENTING ONE'S BABY FROM BEING INFECTED WITH HIV

Pregnant women who are infected with HIV or other STIs should discuss these conditions with their physicians. Measures can be taken that will help prevent their babies from being infected. The current recommendations concerning transmission of HIV from mother to baby include HAART, cesarean section (C-section), and formula feeding. HAART stands for highly active antiretroviral therapy—a combination of three drugs that reduce the amount of HIV in the bloodstream. C-sections help to prevent transmission of HIV to the baby because the baby is not exposed to the mother's blood to the extent that it is during vaginal delivery, when blood vessels rupture. HIV is also found in breast milk; hence the recommendation for formula feeding. All in all, the combination of HAART, C-section, and formula feeding has reduced mother-to-infant transmission of HIV from about 25% to 1–2% (Coovadia, 2004).

For up-to-date information on HIV/AIDS, call the National AIDS Hotline at 1-800-342-AIDS. If you want to receive information in Spanish, call 1-800-344-SIDA. You can also log on to the website of the Centers for Disease Control and Prevention: www.cdc.gov (accessed July 31, 2015). Once there, search the site for the phrases "Diseases & Conditions" and then search for "HIV/AIDS."

Reflect What have you done—or what will you do—to try to protect your babies from being infected with HIV or with any other disease organism?

Rh Incompatibility

In **Rh incompatibility**, antibodies produced by the mother are transmitted to a fetus or newborn infant and cause brain damage or death. Rh is a blood protein that is found in the red blood cells of some individuals. Rh incompatibility occurs when a woman who does not have this factor—and is thus Rh negative—is carrying an Rh-positive fetus, which can happen if the father is Rh positive. The negative–positive combination occurs in about 10% of American couples and becomes a problem in some pregnancies. Rh incompatibility does not affect a first child, because women will not have formed Rh antibodies. The chances of an exchange of blood are greatest during childbirth. If an exchange occurs, the mother produces Rh-positive antibodies to the baby's Rh-positive blood. These antibodies can enter the fetal bloodstream during subsequent deliveries, causing anemia, mental deficiency, or death.

If an Rh-negative mother is injected with Rh immunoglobulin within 72 hours after delivery of an Rh-positive baby, she will not develop the antibodies. A fetus or newborn child at risk of Rh disease may receive a blood transfusion to remove the mother's antibodies.

What Are the Effects of Drugs Taken by the Mother on Prenatal Development?

Rh antibodies can be lethal to children, but many other substances can have harmful effects. In this section, we discuss the effects of various drugs on the unborn child—prescription drugs, over-the-counter drugs, and illegal drugs. Even commonly used medications, such as aspirin, can be harmful to the fetus. If a woman is pregnant or thinks she may be, it is advisable for her to consult her obstetrician before taking any drugs, not just prescription medications. A physician usually can recommend a safe and effective substitute for a drug that can potentially harm a developing fetus.

Rh incompatibility A condition in which antibodies produced by the mother are transmitted to the child, possibly causing brain damage or death.

Accutane

Accutane (generic name: isotretinoin) is derived from vitamin A and is prescribed for difficult cases of acne that do not respond to other forms of treatment. It works by reducing the size of the oil glands in the skin, thus also reducing the amount of acne-causing bacteria present. It also helps prevent pores from clogging and has anti-inflammatory properties. However, Accutane is associated with numerous abnormalities during the first trimester of pregnancy, affecting the eyes and ears, brain, heart, and immune system (Fisher et al., 2008; Peterka et al., 2007). To avoid these outcomes, women are required to demonstrate via a pregnancy test that they are not pregnant when they begin or continue the drug, and it is recommended that they use two types of birth control during treatment. Not all women follow these precautions.

Thalidomide

Thalidomide was marketed in the 1960s as a treatment for insomnia and nausea—not specifically for pregnant women. It was available in Germany and England without prescription. Within a few years, more than 10,000 babies with missing or stunted limbs were born in these countries and elsewhere, as a result of their mothers using thalidomide during pregnancy (Kawamura et al., 2014). Thalidomide is considered safe for people who are not pregnant and is used to treat disorders as varied as dermatological problems and Kaposi's sarcoma, a form of cancer that affects many people with HIV/AIDS.

Thalidomide provides a dramatic example of critical periods of vulnerability to various teratogens. The extremities undergo rapid development during the second month of pregnancy (see Figure 3.4). Thalidomide taken during this period almost invariably causes birth defects.

Antibiotics

Several antibiotics may be harmful to the fetus. Tetracycline, which is frequently prescribed for bacterial infections, can lead to yellowed teeth and bone abnormalities (Vennila et al., 2014). Other antibiotics, including aminoglycosides such as streptomycin, are strongly implicated in hearing loss (Cannizzaro et al., 2014). Prenatal use of antibiotics also appears to increase the risk of childhood asthma (Murk et al., 2011).

Hormones

Women at risk for miscarriages have been prescribed hormones such as progestin and DES to help maintain their pregnancies. **Progestin** is chemically similar to male sex hormones and can masculinize the external sex organs of female embryos. Prenatal progestin has also been linked to aggressive behavior and masculine-typed behaviors in females (Hines, 2011b).

DES (diethylstilbestrol), a powerful estrogen, was given to many women during the 1940s and 1950s to help prevent miscarriage (Gee et al., 2014), but it has caused cervical and testicular cancer in some of their offspring. Among daughters of DES users, about 1 in 1,000 will develop cancer in the reproductive tract. Daughters are also more likely to have babies who are premature or have low birth weight. Daughters and sons of mothers who took DES have high rates of infertility and immune system disorders (Gee et al., 2014).

Vitamins

Although pregnant women are often prescribed multivitamins to maintain their own health and to promote the development of their fetuses, too much of a good thing can be dangerous. High doses of vitamins A and D have been associated with central nervous system damage, small head size, and heart defects (Gilbert-Barness et al., 2014; Wagner et al., 2014).

thalidomide A sedative linked to birth defects, especially deformed or absent limbs.

progestin A hormone that is used to maintain pregnancy and can also cause masculinization of the fetus.

DES Abbreviation for diethylstilbestrol, an estrogen that has been linked to cancer in the reproductive organs of children of women who used it when pregnant.

Heroin and Methadone

Maternal addiction to heroin or methadone is linked to low birth weight, prematurity, and toxemia. These narcotics readily cross the placental membrane, and the fetuses of women who use them regularly can become addicted (Hudak & Tan, 2012).

> **TRUTH OR FICTION REVISITED:** It is true that babies can be born addicted to narcotics and other substances used regularly by their mothers. They are usually weaned off the substance through gradual tapering of doses.

Addicted newborns may be given the narcotic or a substitute shortly after birth so that they will not suffer serious withdrawal symptoms. The drug is then withdrawn gradually. There are also behavioral effects. For example, infants exposed to heroin in utero show delays in motor and language development at the age of 12 months (Beckwith & Burke, 2014).

Marijuana (Cannabis)

Smoking marijuana during pregnancy apparently poses a number of risks for the fetus, including slower fetal growth and low birth weight (Hayatbakhsh et al., 2012). The risks are all proportional to the amount of marijuana smoked; that is, women who smoke more, or who inhale more secondary smoke (smoke from others who are smoking), place their fetuses at relatively greater risk. The babies of women who regularly used marijuana show increased tremors and startling, suggesting immature development of the nervous system (Minnes et al., 2011).

Research into the cognitive effects of maternal prenatal use of marijuana has yielded mixed results. Some studies suggest that there may be no impairment, but others suggest that cognitive skills, including learning and memory, may be impaired (Giussani, 2011; Huizink, 2013). One study assessed the behavior of 10-year-olds who had been exposed prenatally to maternal use of marijuana (Goldschmidt et al., 2000). The study included the children of 635 mothers, aged 18–42. Prenatal use of marijuana was significantly related to increased hyperactivity, impulsivity, and problems in paying attention (as measured by the Swanson, Noland, and Pelham checklist), increased delinquency (as measured by the Child Behavior Checklist), and increased delinquency and aggressive behavior (as measured by teacher report). The researchers hypothesized that the pathway between prenatal marijuana exposure and delinquency involves the effects of marijuana on attention, impairing the abilities to learn in school and to conform to social rules and norms. Fetal exposure to marijuana may impair systems in the brain that regulate emotional behavior (Dvorak & Day, 2014; Wang et al., 2004).

Researchers have found that maternal use of marijuana predisposes offspring to dependence on opiates (narcotics derived from the opium poppy). The fetal brain, like the adult brain, has cannabinoid receptors—called CB-1-receptors—and other structures that are altered by exposure to marijuana. The alterations make the individual more sensitive to the reinforcing properties of opiates, even in adulthood (Hurd et al., 2014). In any event, longitudinal research with 763 women recruited in the fourth month of pregnancy found that prenatal exposure to maternal marijuana smoking is a reasonably good predictor of whether the child will smoke marijuana at the age of 14 (Day et al., 2006).

Cocaine

There is little doubt that prenatal exposure to cocaine can harm the child. Pregnant women who abuse cocaine increase the risk of stillbirth, low birth weight, and birth defects (Stillbirth Collaborative Research Network Writing Group, 2011). The infants are often excitable and irritable, or lethargic. The more heavily exposed to cocaine they are in utero, the more problems they have with jitteriness, concentration, and sleep (Richardson et al., 2013). Lewis and colleagues (2004) compared 189 4-year-olds who had been exposed to cocaine in utero with 185 4-year-olds who had not, on the Clinical Evaluation of Language Fundamentals–Preschool (CELF-P) test. Children exposed to cocaine had much lower expressive language scores and somewhat lower receptive language scores. That is, their relative ability to express themselves was affected more than their ability to understand language. The study controlled for prenatal exposure to cigarette smoke, alcohol, and marijuana. There are suggestions that delays in cognitive development persist at 10 years of age (Lewis et al., 2011).

A study of 473 6-year-olds by Delaney-Black and colleagues (2004) compared children who were exposed to cocaine in utero (204) with those who were not. The study found effects for the amount of cocaine used by the mother and the sex of the child. Boys were more likely to be affected than girls. According to teacher reports, boys whose mothers used cocaine regularly were likely to be rated as hyperactive, to be indifferent to their environment, and to show deficits in cognitive skills. The study controlled for maternal use of alcohol and illegal drugs other than cocaine while pregnant.

The studies with humans are correlational. That is, mothers are not randomly assigned to use cocaine; instead, they make the choice themselves. This problem is technically termed a selection factor. Thus, it may be that the same factors that lead mothers to use cocaine also affect their children. To overcome the selection factor, numerous experiments have been conducted with laboratory animals. In one study, randomly selected pregnant rats were given cocaine during days 12–21 of gestation, whereas control rats received no cocaine (Huber et al., 2001). The rat pups were then exposed to stressors such as cold-water swimming and tail flicks. The pups exposed to cocaine showed less tolerance of the stressors—as measured by behaviors such as tail twitches and convulsions—than control subjects. Another study found that such group differences in response to stressors endure into rat adulthood—that is, 90–120 days of age (J. O. Campbell et al., 2000).

Alcohol

No drug has meant so much to so many people as alcohol. Alcohol is our dinnertime relaxant, our bedtime sedative, our cocktail-party social lubricant. We use alcohol to celebrate holy days, applaud our accomplishments, and express joyous wishes. Millions of adolescents assert their maturity with alcohol. Alcohol is used at least occasionally by the majority of high school and college students (L. D. Johnston et al., 2014, 2015). Alcohol even kills germs on surface wounds.

However, because alcohol passes through the placenta, drinking by a pregnant woman poses risks for the embryo and fetus. Heavy drinking can be lethal to the fetus and neonate. It is also connected with deficiencies and deformities in growth. Some children of heavy drinkers develop **fetal alcohol syndrome (FAS)** (Kooistra et al., 2010; O'Leary et al., 2010). Babies with FAS are often smaller than normal, and so are their brains. They may have distinct facial features: widely spaced eyes, an underdeveloped upper jaw, a flattened nose. There may be malformation of the limbs, poor coordination, and cardiovascular problems. A number of psychological characteristics are connected with FAS and appear to reflect dysfunction of the brain: intellectual disability, hyperactivity, distractibility, lessened verbal fluency, and learning disabilities (Kooistra et al., 2010). There can be deficits in speech and hearing, practical reasoning, and visual–motor coordination.

Small head
Flat face
Thin upper lip
Small eye openings
Short nose
Low nasal bridge
Underdeveloped jaw

An Infant with Fetal Alcohol Syndrome (FAS)

Gwen Shockey/Science Source

fetal alcohol syndrome (FAS) A cluster of symptoms shown by children of women who drank during pregnancy, including characteristic facial features and intellectual disability.

The facial deformities of FAS diminish as the child moves into adolescence, and most children catch up in height and weight. But the intellectual, academic, and behavioral deficits of individuals with FAS persist. Academic and intellectual problems relative to peers range from verbal difficulties to deficiency in spatial memory (Guerrini et al., 2007). Studies find that the average academic functioning of adolescents and young adults with FAS is at the second- to fourth-grade level. Maladaptive behaviors such as poor judgment, distractibility, and difficulty perceiving social cues are common (Schonfeld et al., 2005).

FAS is part of a broader group of fetal alcohol–related problems referred to as fetal alcohol spectrum disorders (P. D. Connor et al., 2006). Pregnant women who have as few as one or two drinks a day may be more likely to miscarry or have growth-delayed babies than pregnant women who do not drink (American Pregnancy Association, 2011).

TRUTH OR FICTION REVISITED: It is not true that it is safe for a pregnant woman to drink a glass of wine a day. Although some health professionals "allow" pregnant women to drink a glass of wine with dinner, research suggests that even moderate drinkers place their offspring at increased risk for a less severe set of effects known as fetal alcohol effect (FAE). Here is the key takeaway: *There is no guaranteed safe minimum amount of drinking during pregnancy* (Kelly et al., 2013)

Image Source/Getty Images

The reported effects of maternal drinking, like the effects of maternal use of cocaine, are based on correlational evidence. No researcher would randomly assign some pregnant women to drink and others to abstain. However, researchers have randomly assigned experimental animals to intake alcohol, and the results support the correlational evidence with humans. For example, research with animals reveals that exposure to alcohol during gestation is connected with retarded growth, facial malformations, characteristic of FAS, deficiencies in the immune system, and structural and chemical differences in the central nervous system (O'Leary et al., 2010).

Caffeine

Many pregnant women consume caffeine in the form of coffee, tea, soft drinks, chocolate, and nonprescription drugs. The findings from research on caffeine's effects on the developing fetus have been inconsistent (Minnes et al., 2011). Some studies report no adverse findings, but others have found that pregnant women who take in a good deal of caffeine are more likely than nonusers to have a miscarriage or a low birth weight baby (Bakker et al., 2010; Sengpiel et al., 2013). Because of such findings, many obstetricians recommend that pregnant women avoid caffeine. The attitude is: When in doubt, why not avoid a risk?

Cigarettes

Cigarette smoke contains many ingredients, including the stimulant nicotine, the gas carbon monoxide, and hydrocarbons ("tars"), which are carcinogens. Fortunately, only the first two of these, nicotine and carbon monoxide, pass through the placenta and reach the fetus. That's the end of the fortunate news. Nicotine stimulates the fetus, but its long-term effects are uncertain. Carbon monoxide is toxic; it decreases the amount of oxygen available to the fetus. Oxygen deprivation is connected with cognitive and behavioral problems, including impaired motor development (Giussani, 2011). The cognitive difficulties include academic delays, learning disabilities, and intellectual disability. Not all children of smokers develop these problems, but many

fetal alcohol effect (FAE) A cluster of symptoms, less severe than those of fetal alcohol syndrome, shown by children of women who drank moderately during pregnancy.

do not function as well as they would have if they had not been exposed to maternal smoking.

Pregnant women who smoke are likely to deliver smaller babies than nonsmokers (Anblagan et al., 2013). In addition, their babies are more likely to be stillborn or to die soon after birth (Stillbirth Collaborative Research Network Writing Group, 2011). Babies of fathers who smoke have higher rates of birth defects, infant mortality, lower birth weights, and cardiovascular problems (Misra et al., 2010).

Maternal smoking may also have long-term negative effects on development. Children whose mothers smoke during pregnancy are more likely to show short attention spans, hyperactivity, lower cognitive and language scores, and poor grades (Kuja-Halkola et al., 2014).

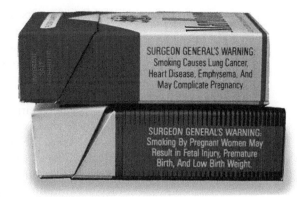

Okay—smoking during pregnancy poses significant threats to the fetus. So why do pregnant women do it? Are they ignorant of the risks to their children? Perhaps. Despite decades of public education efforts, there remain some women who are unaware that smoking will hurt the fetus. But most American women are aware of the threat. Even so, they may say that they can't quit or that they can't suspend smoking until the baby is born. Why? Some claim they are under too much stress to stop smoking, although cigarette smoking actually contributes to stress; smoking is not a one-way ticket to relaxation. Others smoke to fight feelings of depression (nicotine is a stimulant and depression is, well, depressing), because "everybody" around them smokes (often "everybody" translates into "the partner"), or because they just don't have the willpower (or perhaps I should say the "won't power") to deal with the withdrawal symptoms of quitting. Some parents simply deny that their smoking is likely to harm their children, despite knowledge to the contrary.

The problems connected with smoking may also be caused by fathers. Men who smoke are more likely to produce abnormal sperm. Babies of fathers who smoke have higher rates of birth defects and infant mortality, lower birth weights, and cardiovascular problems. Also keep in mind that if the father or anyone else smokes in the household of a pregnant woman, the woman is being exposed to "second-hand smoke." Second-hand smoking, like maternal smoking, is harmful to the fetus, and generally in the same ways (Evlampidou et al., 2015; Niu et al., 2015).

What Are the Effects of Environmental Hazards During Pregnancy?

Mothers know when they are ingesting drugs, but there are many (many!) other substances in the environment that they may take in unknowingly. These are environmental hazards to which we are all exposed, and we refer to them collectively as pollution.

Prenatal exposure to heavy metals such as lead, mercury, cadmium, selenium, and zinc threatens the development of children (Chen et al., 2014; Gorini et al., 2014). Longitudinal research finds that newborns who have mildly elevated levels of lead in their umbilical cord blood show delayed mental development at 1 and 2 years of age (Heindel & Lawler, 2006). However, their cognitive functioning can improve if they are no longer exposed to lead in the home.

One study of the effects of prenatal exposure to lead recruited 442 children in Yugoslavia (Wasserman et al., 2000). Some of the children lived in a town with a smelter; the others did not. (Smelting—the melting of lead-bearing scrap metal into metallic lead—is a major source of lead fume emissions.) The children received intelligence testing at the ages of 3, 4, 5, and 7, using Wechsler and other scales. The researchers found that the children from the town with the smelter obtained somewhat lower intelligence test scores. It is conceivable, of course, that people who choose to live in a town without a smelter differ from those who are willing to cozy up to one.

Experiments with rodents support the correlational findings with humans. For example, mice exposed to lead in utero do not form memories as well as those that are free of prenatal exposure to lead (de Oliveira et al., 2001). Research with rats has found that prenatal exposure to lead decreases the levels of neurotransmitters (the chemical messengers of the brain) in all areas of the brain, but especially in the hippocampus. The hippocampus is involved in memory formation.

The devastating effects of mercury on the fetus were first recognized among the Japanese who lived around Minamata Bay. Industrial waste containing mercury was dumped into the bay and accumulated in the fish that were a major food source for local residents. Children born to women who had eaten the fish during pregnancy were often profoundly intellectually disabled and neurologically damaged—a cluster of symptoms that have become known as Minamata Disease (Mayes & Ward, 2003). Prenatal exposure to even small amounts of mercury and other heavy metals such as cadmium and chromium can produce subtle deficits in cognitive functioning and physical health (Heindel & Lawler, 2006).

Polychlorinated biphenyls (PCBs) are used in many industrial products. Like mercury, they accumulate in fish that feed in polluted waters. Newborns whose mothers had consumed PCB-contaminated fish from Lake Michigan were smaller and showed poorer motor functioning and less responsiveness than newborns whose mothers had not eaten these fish. Furthermore, even those PCB-exposed infants who appeared normal at birth showed deficits in memory at 7 months and at 4 years of age (Jacobson et al., 1992).

An unfortunate natural experiment in the effects of prenatal exposure to PCBs took place in Taiwan during the late 1970s, when a group of people accidentally ingested contaminated rice. Children born to mothers who ate the rice had characteristic signs of PCB poisoning, including hyperpigmented skin. The researchers (Lai et al., 2001) had the opportunity to compare the cognitive development of 118 children born to exposed mothers with other children in the community. The children were all followed through the age of 12 and were tested with instruments including the Bayley Scales of Infant Development, the Chinese version of the Stanford–Binet Intelligence Scale, and two nonverbal intelligence tests. The children of mothers who ate the contaminated rice scored lower than the control children on each of these measures throughout the observation period. It appears that prenatal exposure to PCBs has long-term harmful effects on cognitive development.

Experiments with mice show that fetal exposure to radiation in high doses can cause defects in a number of organs, including the eyes, central nervous system, and skeleton (e.g., Hossain et al., 2005). Pregnant women who were exposed to atomic radiation during the bombing of Hiroshima and Nagasaki in World War II gave birth to babies who were more likely to be intellectually disabled in addition to being physically deformed (Sadler, 2005). Pregnant women are advised to avoid unnecessary exposure to X-rays. (Ultrasound, which is not an X-ray, has not been shown to be harmful to the fetus [Park, 2008].)

The risks to the embryo and fetus from radiation and other environmental agents are summarized in Concept Review 3.2.

What Are the Apparent Effects of Maternal Stress on the Child?

Although pregnancy can be a time of immense gratification for women, it can also be a time of stress. The baby might be unplanned and unwanted. Parents might not have the financial resources or the room for the child. The mother might be experiencing physical discomforts because of the pregnancy.

How does a mother's emotional state affect her fetus? Emotions such as stress and anxiety are psychological feeling states, but they also have physiological components. For example, they are linked to the secretion of "stress hormones" such as adrenaline and corticosteroids. Adrenaline stimulates the mother's heart rate, respiratory rate,

THE EFFECTS OF PARENTS' AGE ON CHILDREN—DO MEN REALLY HAVE ALL THE TIME IN THE WORLD?

What if 30-year-old women started looking at 50-year-old men as damaged goods, what with their washed-up sperm, meaning those 50-year-olds might actually have to date (gasp!) women their own age? What if men, as the years passed, began to look with new eyes at Ms. Almost Right?

—Lisa Belkin

The artist Pablo Picasso, shown here, fathered children in his 70s. Former Senator Strom Thurmond fathered a child in his 90s. It has been widely known that women's chances of conceiving children decline as they age. As noted by Belkin (2009), the traditional message has been "Women, you'd better hurry up. Men, you have all the time in the world."

Private Collection/Roger-Viollet, Paris/The Bridgeman Art Library

Not so, apparently. True: From a biological vantage point, the 20s may be the ideal age for women to bear children. Teenage mothers in the United States, especially those who are disadvantaged, have a higher incidence of infant mortality and children with low birth weight (Madkour et al., 2014).

What about women older than 30? Women's fertility declines gradually until the mid-t30s, after which it declines more rapidly. Women beyond their middle 30s may have passed the point at which their reproductive systems function most efficiently. Women possess nearly all their ova in immature form at birth. Over 30 years,

these cells are exposed to the slings and arrows of an outrageous environment of toxic wastes, chemical pollutants, and radiation, thus increasing the risk of chromosomal abnormalities such as Down syndrome (Behrman et al., 2000). Women who wait until their 30s or 40s to have children also increase the likelihood of having stillborn or preterm babies (Berg et al., 2003). But with adequate prenatal care, the risk of bearing a premature or unhealthy baby still is relatively small, even for older first-time mothers (Berg et al., 2003). This news should be encouraging for women who have delayed, or plan to delay, bearing children until their 30s or 40s.

Older fathers are more likely to produce abnormal sperm, leading to fertility problems (Belkin, 2009). But that's only the tip of the iceberg. University of Queensland researchers analyzed data from some 33,000 U.S. children and found that the older the father is at conception, the lower a child's score tends to be on tests of reading skills, reasoning, memory, and concentration. The ages of 29 and 30 are something of a turning point for men, because children conceived past these ages are at greater risk for the psychological disorders of schizophrenia and bipolar disorder (Perrin et al., 2007). Children born to men past 40 also have a greater risk of autism (Reichenberg et al., 2006).

RISKY BUSINESS?

Chance of autism spectrum disorder among 132,271 subjects, by paternal age:

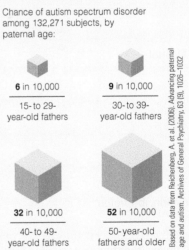

Based on data from Reichenberg, A. et al. (2006). Advancing paternal age and autism. Archives of General Psychiatry, 63 (9), 1026–1032

These findings do not mean that the majority of children born to men past their reproductive "prime" will develop these problems, but it does mean that men's age, like women's age, is related to risks for their children. As noted by one of the researchers studying schizophrenia, "It turns out the optimal age for being a mother is the same as the optimal age for being a father" (Malaspina, 2009).

Risks of Various Agents to the Embryo and Fetus

Agent	Risks
Prescription Drugs*	
Accutane (used to treat acne; repeated blood tests are required to show that one is not pregnant or encountering drug-related problems)	Stillbirth, malformation of limbs and organs. Do not use during pregnancy.
Bendectin	Cleft palate, malformation of the heart. Do not use.
Carbamazepine (and other anticonvulsant drugs)	Spina bifida. Do not use during pregnancy.
Diethylstilbestrol (DES; once used to help maintain pregnancy)	Cancer of the cervix or testes in offspring. (No longer available.)
Strong general anesthesia during labor (sedation that goes beyond normal medical practice)	Anoxia, asphyxiation, brain damage. Can request local anesthesia instead.
Progestin (a synthetic version of the natural hormone progesterone, which is sometimes used to help maintain pregnancy)	Masculinization of the sex organs of female embryos, possible development of "masculine" aggressiveness. Ask obstetrician.
Streptomycin (an antibiotic)	Deafness. Ask obstetrician about alternatives.
Tetracycline (an antibiotic)	Malformed bones, yellow teeth. Ask obstetrician about alternatives.
Thalidomide (several uses, including sedation)	Malformed or missing limbs. Do not use during pregnancy.
Other Drugs	
Alcohol	Fetal death, low birth weight, addiction, academic and intellectual problems, hyperactivity, distractibility, fetal alcohol syndrome (FAS) including characteristic facial features. Best not to drink alcohol during pregnancy.
Aspirin, ibuprofen	Bleeding, respiratory problems. Ask obstetrician about alternatives.
Caffeine (the stimulant found in coffee, tea, colas, chocolate)	Stimulates fetus (not necessarily a problem in itself); miscarriage and low birth weight are suspected. Ask obstetrician about latest information.

Corbis Photography/Veer

Small head
Flat face
Small eye openings
Short nose
Low nasal bridge
Underdeveloped jaw
Thin upper lip
Gwen Shockey/Science Source
An Infant with Fetal Alcohol Syndrome (FAS)

Image Source/Getty Images

Risks of Various Agents to the Embryo and Fetus (continued)

Agent	Risks
Cigarette smoke (the stimulant nicotine and carbon monoxide are transmitted through the placenta)	Stimulates fetus (not necessarily a problem in itself), premature birth, low birth weight, fetal death, academic problems, hyperactivity, short attention span. Best not to smoke during pregnancy.
Opiates—heroin, morphine, others	Low birth weight, premature birth, addiction, toxemia (preeclampsia). Avoid during pregnancy.
Marijuana	Tremors, startling, premature birth, birth defects, neurological problems. Avoid during pregnancy.
Vitamins[†]	
Vitamin A (high doses)	Cleft palate, damage to the eyes.
Vitamin D (high doses)	Intellectual deficiency.
Pathogens (disease-causing agents)	
HIV (the virus that causes AIDS)	Physical deformity and intellectual deficiency. Check with obstetrician about avoiding transmission to fetus and neonate.
Rubella (German measles)	Neurological impairment involving sensation and perception (vision, hearing), intellectual disability, heart problems, cataracts.
Syphilis (a sexually transmitted infection caused by the *Treponema pallidum* bacterium)	Infant mortality, seizures, intellectual disability, sensory impairment (vision, hearing), liver damage, malformation of bones and teeth. Possible to treat during pregnancy; ask obstetrician.
Environmental Hazards	
Heavy metals (lead, mercury, zinc)	Intellectual deficiency, hyperactivity, stillbirth, problems in memory formation. Remain alert to your environment and adjust, if possible.
Paint fumes (heavy exposure)	Intellectual deficiency. Remain alert to your environment and adjust, if possible.
PCBs (polychlorinated biphenyls), dioxin, other insecticides and herbicides	Stillbirth, low birth weight, cognitive impairment, motor impairment. Remain alert to your environment and adjust, if possible.
X-rays	Deformation of organs. Ask obstetrician before having X-rays.
Biochemical Incompatibility With Mother	
Rh antibodies	Infant mortality, brain damage. Mother can receive Rh immunoglobulin after delivery. Neonate may receive blood transfusion.

*Normally healthful, even life-saving drugs can be harmful to the embryo and fetus. Women should inform their physicians when they are pregnant, may be pregnant, or are planning to become pregnant.

†Adequate intake of vitamins is essential to the well-being of the mother and the embryo and fetus. Most obstetricians advise pregnant women to take vitamin supplements. However, too much of a good thing can be harmful. In brief, don't do "megavitamins." And when in doubt, ask your obstetrician.

© Cengage Learning®

and other bodily functions. Hormones pass through the placenta and also have an effect on the fetus. For example, corticosteroids appear to decrease the growth of the placenta (Elfayomy & Almasry, 2014; Subramaniam et al., 2013). Extremes of anxiety, which are correlated with secretion of corticosteroids, have been shown to heighten the probabilities of low birth weight, prematurity, and miscarriage (James, 2014; Van den Bergh et al., 2005). However, injections of corticosteroids may help prevent certain types of brain injury in premature infants (Liu et al., 2008).

Section Review

13. Mothers who ingest folic acid reduce their risk of giving birth to babies with _____ tube defects.

14. _____ are environmental agents that can harm the developing embryo or fetus.

15. Women _____ (can or cannot?) be successfully treated for syphilis during pregnancy.

16. Toxemia is mainly characterized by high _____ pressure.

17. In _____ incompatibility, antibodies produced by the mother are transmitted to a fetus or newborn infant and cause brain damage or death.

18. _____ was once prescribed to help women maintain their pregnancies, but it caused cervical and testicular cancer in some of their children.

19. The babies of women who regularly used _____ during pregnancy have been found to show increased tremors and startling.

20. Heavy maternal use of alcohol is linked to _____ alcohol syndrome (FAS).

21. Women who smoke during pregnancy deprive their fetuses of _____, sometimes resulting in stillbirth or persistent academic problems.

22. Fetal exposure to the heavy metals lead and mercury can _____ (slow or accelerate?) mental development.

Reflect & Relate: How will your knowledge of critical periods of prenatal development enable you to predict—and possibly prevent—the effects of various agents on the embryo and fetus? How difficult do you think it would be for you or someone you know to give up drinking alcohol or smoking during pregnancy? Would looking upon the "sacrifice" as temporary make it easier?

Chapter Review

3.1 What Happens During the Germinal Stage of Prenatal Development?

During the germinal stage, the zygote divides repeatedly but does not gain in mass. It travels through a fallopian tube to the uterus, where it implants. It then takes the form of a blastocyst. Layers of cells form within the embryonic disk. The outer part of the blastocyst differentiates into membranes that will protect and nourish the embryo. Before implantation, the dividing cluster of cells is nourished by the yolk of the original egg cell. Once implanted in the uterine wall, it obtains nourishment from the mother.

3.2 What Happens During the Embryonic Stage of Prenatal Development?

The embryonic stage lasts from implantation until the eighth week of development, during which the major organ systems differentiate. Development follows cephalocaudal and proximodistal trends. The outer layer of the embryonic disk develops into the nervous system, sensory organs, nails, hair, teeth, and skin. Two ridges form the neural tube, from which the nervous system develops. The inner layer of the embryonic disk forms the digestive and respiratory systems, the liver, and the pancreas. The middle layer becomes the excretory, reproductive, and circulatory systems, as well as the muscles, the skeleton, and the inner layer of the skin. The heart begins to beat during the fourth week. Toward the end of the first month, arm and leg buds appear and the face takes shape. The nervous system has also begun to develop. By the end of the second month, limbs are elongating, facial features are becoming distinct, teeth buds have formed, the kidneys are working, and the liver is producing red blood cells. By 5 to 6 weeks, the embryo has undifferentiated sex organs that resemble female structures. Testes produce male sex hormones that spur development of male genital organs and the male duct system. The embryo and fetus exchange nutrients and wastes with the mother through a mass of tissue called the placenta. The umbilical cord connects the fetus to the placenta. The germs that cause syphilis and rubella can pass through the placenta. Some drugs also pass through, including aspirin, narcotics, and alcohol.

3.3 What Happens During the Fetal Stage of Prenatal Development?

The fetal stage lasts from the end of the embryonic stage until birth. The fetus begins to turn at the 9th or 10th week. The second trimester is characterized by maturation of organs and gains in size. By the end of the second trimester, the fetus opens and shuts its eyes, sucks its thumb, alternates between wakefulness and sleep, and responds to light and sounds. During the third trimester, the heart and lungs become increasingly capable of sustaining independent life. The mother usually detects fetal movements during the fourth month. By the end of the second trimester, the fetus turns somersaults.

3.4 How Do Environmental Factors Affect Prenatal Development?

Malnutrition in the mother has been linked to low birth weight, prematurity, stunted growth, retardation of brain development, cognitive deficiencies, and behavioral problems. Folic acid reduces the risk of neural tube defects. Teratogens are environmental agents that can harm the embryo and fetus. Exposure to particular teratogens is most harmful during critical periods—the times when certain organs are developing. The embryo is generally more vulnerable than the fetus because the major organ systems are differentiating. Women who contract rubella may bear children who suffer from deafness, intellectual disability, heart disease, or cataracts. Syphilis can cause miscarriage, stillbirth, or congenital syphilis. Babies can be infected with HIV in utero, during childbirth, or through breastfeeding. Toxemia is characterized by high blood pressure and is connected with preterm and/or undersized babies. In Rh incompatibility, antibodies produced by the mother are transmitted to a fetus or newborn infant and cause brain damage or death. Maternal use of Accutane is connected with numerous abnormalities in the embryo. Thalidomide causes missing or stunted limbs in babies. Tetracycline can cause yellowed teeth and bone problems. DES leads to high risk of cervical and testicular cancer. High doses of vitamins A and D are associated with nervous system damage and heart defects. Maternal addiction to narcotics is linked to low birth weight, prematurity, and toxemia, and fetuses can be born addicted themselves. Marijuana may cause tremors and startling in babies. Cocaine increases the risk of stillbirth, low birth weight, and birth defects. Maternal use of alcohol is linked to death of the fetus and neonate, malformations, growth deficiencies, and fetal alcohol syndrome (FAS). Caffeine is associated with miscarriage and low birth weight. Maternal cigarette smoking is linked to low birth weight, stillbirth, and intellectual disability. Prenatal exposure to heavy metals threatens cognitive development. Prenatal exposure to mercury is connected with neurological damage. Prenatal exposure to PCBs is associated with babies that are smaller, less responsive, and more likely to develop cognitive deficits. Fetal exposure to radiation can cause neural and skeletal problems. Maternal stress is linked to the secretion of hormones such as adrenaline, which pass through the placenta and affect the baby. Maternal stress may be connected with complications during pregnancy and labor, preterm or low birth weight babies, and irritable babies.

Key Terms

4

Birth and the Newborn Baby: In the New World

TruthorFiction?

T | F The fetus signals its mother when it is ready to be born. **p. 112**

T | F After birth, babies are held upside down and slapped on the buttocks to stimulate independent breathing. **p. 115**

T | F The way that the umbilical cord is cut determines whether the baby's "belly button" will be an "innie" or an "outie." **p. 115**

T | F Women who give birth according to the Lamaze method do not experience pain. **p. 118**

T | F In the United States, nearly 1 of every 3 births is by cesarean section. **p. 119**

T | F It is abnormal to feel depressed following childbirth. **p. 127**

T | F Parents must have extended early contact with their newborn children if adequate bonding is to take place. **p. 130**

T | F More children die from sudden infant death syndrome (SIDS) than from cancer, heart disease, pneumonia, child abuse, HIV/AIDS, cystic fibrosis, and muscular dystrophy combined. **p. 144**

During the last few weeks before she gave birth, Michele explained: "I couldn't get my mind off the pregnancy—what it was going to be like when I finally delivered Lisa. I'd had the amniocentesis, so I knew it was a girl. I'd had the ultrasounds, so all her fingers and toes had been counted, but I was still hoping and praying that everything would turn out all right. To be honest, I was also worried about the delivery. I had always been an A student, and I guess I wanted to earn an A in childbirth as well. Matt was understanding, and he was even helpful, but, you know, it wasn't him.

"My obstetrician was bending over backwards (she could bend—I couldn't) being politically correct and kept on talking about how *we* had gotten pregnant and about how *we* were going to have the baby. Toward the end there, I would have been thrilled if it had really been *we*. Or I would even have allowed Matt to do it all by himself. But the fact is it was *me*. And I was worrying about how I could even reach the steering wheel of the car in those days, much less deliver a perfect, healthy child. On television, of course, they do it without even disturbing their mascara, but I was living in the real world. And waiting, waiting, waiting. And, oh yes, did I mention waiting?"

Nearly all first-time mothers struggle through the last weeks of pregnancy and worry about the mechanics of delivery. Childbirth is a natural function, of course, but so many mothers have gone to classes to learn how to do what comes naturally! They worry about whether they'll get to the hospital or birthing center on time ("Is there gas in the car?" "Is the Uber APP working?" "Is it snowing?"). They worry about whether the baby will start breathing on its own properly. They may wonder if they'll do it on their

Mehmed Zelkovic/Moment Select/Getty Images

111

own or need a C-section. And they may worry about whether it will hurt, and how much, and when they should ask for anesthetics, and, well, how to earn that A.

Close to full **term**, Michele and other women are sort of front-loaded, and they feel bent out of shape. Guess what? They are. The weight of the fetus may also be causing backaches. Will they deliver the baby, or will the baby, by being born, deliver them—from discomfort? "Hanging in and having Lisa was a wonderful experience," Michele said. "I think Matt should have had it."

4.1 Countdown...

Early in the last month of pregnancy, the head of the fetus settles in the pelvis. This is called dropping or lightening. Because lightening decreases pressure on the diaphragm, the mother may, in fact, feel lighter.

The first uterine contractions are called **Braxton-Hicks contractions** or false labor contractions. They are relatively painless and may be experienced as early as the sixth month of pregnancy. They tend to increase in frequency as the pregnancy progresses and may serve to tone the muscles that will be used in delivery. Although they may be confused with actual labor contractions, real labor contractions are more painful and regular and are also usually intensified by walking.

A day or so before labor begins, increased pelvic pressure from the fetus may rupture superficial blood vessels in the birth canal so that blood appears in vaginal secretions. The mucous tissue that plugged the cervix and protected the uterus from infection becomes dislodged. At about this time, 1 woman in 10 has a rush of warm liquid from the vagina. (Women tend to say their "water has broken.") This liquid is amniotic fluid, and its discharge means that the amniotic sac has burst. The amniotic sac usually does not burst until the end of the first stage of childbirth, as described later. Indigestion, diarrhea, an ache in the small of the back, and abdominal cramps are also common signs that labor is beginning.

> **TRUTH OR FICTION REVISITED:** The fetus may actually signal the mother when it is "ready" to be born—that is, when it is mature enough to sustain life outside the uterus. The adrenal and pituitary glands of the fetus may participate in timing of labor by hormone signaling (Snegovskikh et al., 2006; Swaggart et al., 2015).

Fetal hormones stimulate the placenta (which is a gland as well as a relay station for nutrition and wastes between mother and fetus) and the uterus to secrete **prostaglandins** (Plunkett et al., 2011; Snegovskikh et al., 2011). Prostaglandins are the main culprits when women experience uncomfortable cramping before or during menstruation; they also serve the function of exciting the muscles of the uterus to engage in labor contractions. As labor progresses, the pituitary gland releases **oxytocin**, another hormone. Oxytocin stimulates contractions that are powerful enough to expel the baby.

In this chapter, we discuss the events of childbirth and the characteristics of the **neonate**. Arriving in the new world may be a bit more complex than you had thought, and neonates may be able to do a bit more than you had imagined.

term The typical period of time between conception and the birth of a baby.

Braxton-Hicks contractions The first (usually painless) contractions of childbirth.

prostaglandins Hormones that stimulate uterine contractions.

oxytocin A pituitary hormone that stimulates labor contractions.

neonate A newborn child.

4.2 The Stages of Childbirth

Regular uterine contractions signal the beginning of childbirth. Researchers speak of childbirth as occurring in three stages.

What Happens During the First Stage of Childbirth?

During the first stage of childbirth, uterine contractions **efface** and **dilate** the cervix. This passageway needs to widen to about 4 inches (10 centimeters) to allow the baby to pass. Dilation of the cervix is responsible for most of the discomfort during childbirth. If the cervix dilates rapidly and easily, there may be less discomfort.

The first stage is the long stage. Among women undergoing their first deliveries, it may last from a few hours to more than a day. Half a day to a day is about average, but the first stage sometimes is much briefer and sometimes lasts up to a couple of days. Subsequent pregnancies take less time and may be surprisingly rapid—sometimes between 1 and 2 hours. The first contractions are not usually all that uncomfortable and are spaced 10–20 minutes apart. They may last from 20 to 40 seconds each.

As the process continues, the contractions become more powerful, frequent, and regular. Women are usually advised to go to the hospital or birthing center when the contractions are 4 to 5 minutes apart. Until the end of the first stage of labor, the mother is frequently in a labor room with her partner or another companion.

If the woman is to be "prepped"—that is, if her pubic hair is to be shaved—it takes place now. The prep is intended to reduce the chances of infection during delivery and to facilitate the performance of an **episiotomy**, which will be described later. A woman may be given an enema to prevent an involuntary bowel movement during labor. However, many women find prepping and enemas degrading and prefer obstetricians who do not routinely perform them.

During the first stage of childbirth, fetal monitoring may be used. One kind of monitoring is an electronic sensing device strapped around the woman's abdomen. It can measure the fetal heart rate as well as the frequency, strength, and duration of the mother's contractions. An abnormal heart rate alerts the medical staff to possible fetal distress so that appropriate steps can be taken, such as speeding up the delivery by such means as forceps or the vacuum extraction tube. The forceps is a curved instrument that fits around the baby's head and makes it possible to pull the baby out of the mother's body. The vacuum extraction tube relies on suction to pull the baby through the birth canal.

When the cervix is almost fully dilated, the head of the fetus begins to move into the vagina, or birth canal. This process is called **transition**. During transition, which lasts about 30 minutes or less, contractions are usually frequent and strong.

What Happens During the Second Stage of Childbirth?

The second stage of childbirth follows transition. This stage begins when the baby appears at the opening of the vagina (now referred to as the birth canal; see Figure 4.1 ■). The second stage is briefer than the first stage. It may last minutes or a few hours and culminates in the birth of the baby. The woman may be taken to a delivery room for the second stage of childbirth.

The contractions of the second stage stretch the skin surrounding the birth canal farther and propel the baby farther along. The baby's head is said to have crowned when it begins to emerge from the birth canal. Once crowning has occurred, the baby normally emerges completely within minutes.

The physician, nurse, or midwife may perform an episiotomy once crowning takes place. The purpose of the episiotomy is to prevent random tearing when the area between the birth canal and the anus becomes severely stretched. Women are unlikely to feel the incision because the pressure of the crowning head tends to numb the region between the vagina and the anus. Like prepping and the enema, the episiotomy is somewhat controversial, and the research evidence appears to

efface To thin.

dilate To widen or enlarge.

episiotomy A surgical incision in the area between the birth canal and the anus that widens the vaginal opening, preventing random tearing during childbirth.

transition The initial movement of the head of the fetus into the birth canal.

Figure 4.1 ■ The Stages of Childbirth

In the first stage, uterine contractions efface and dilate the cervix to about 4 inches so that the baby may pass. The second stage begins with movement of the baby into the birth canal and ends with the birth of the baby. During the third stage, the placenta separates from the uterine wall and is expelled through the birth canal.

© Cengage Learning®

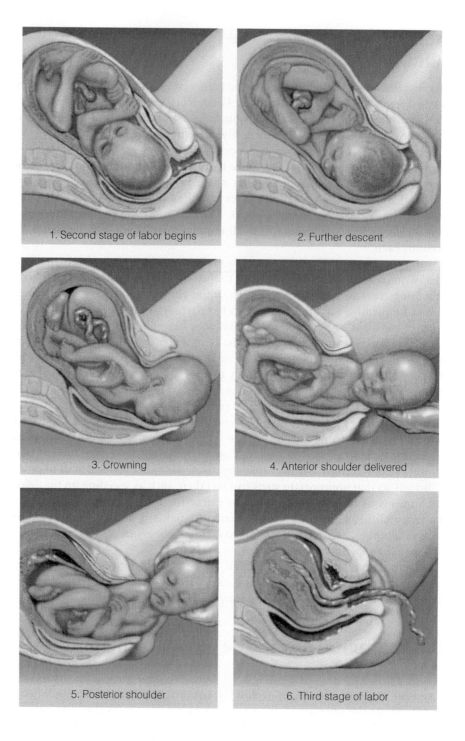

1. Second stage of labor begins

2. Further descent

3. Crowning

4. Anterior shoulder delivered

5. Posterior shoulder

6. Third stage of labor

be mixed as to whether it is desirable. Nevertheless, a European study did find a significant reduction in the incidence of anal tears with episiotomy (Frethelm et al., 2013).

The incision may cause itching and discomfort—sometimes intense pain—as it heals (Rezaei et al., 2014). Many health professionals believe that an episiotomy is warranted when the baby's shoulders are wide or the baby's heart rate declines for a long period of time. But the strongest predictor of whether a practitioner will choose to use episiotomy is not the condition of the mother or the baby, but rather whether the physician usually performs an episiotomy.

Whether or not the physician performs an episiotomy, the passageway into the world outside is a tight fit, and the baby squeezes through. Mothers may be alarmed at the visual results of the tight fit. Sometimes the baby's head and facial features are quite bent out of shape. The baby's head can wind up elongated, its nose can be flattened or pushed to the side, and the ears can be contorted—as though this little thing got caught up in a prizefight! My wife and I sometimes joke that our second child was born with her nose apparently coming out the side of her cheek. (It wasn't.) Parents understandably wonder whether their baby's features will "pop up" properly or return to a more normal shape. They do—most of the time.

Don't wait for the baby to be held upside down and slapped on the buttocks to spur breathing on its own. That happens in old movies but not in today's hospitals and birthing centers. Today, mucus is suctioned from the baby's mouth as soon as the head emerges from the birth canal, to clear any obstructions from the passageway for breathing. The procedure may be repeated when the baby has fully emerged.

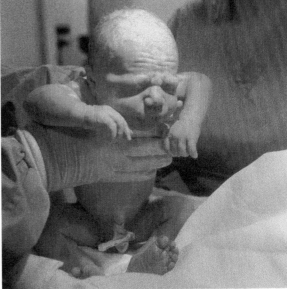

Owen Franken/Stone/Getty Images

Figure 4.2 ■ A Clamped and Severed Umbilical Cord
The stump of the cord dries and falls off in about 10 days.

TRUTH OR FICTION REVISITED: Despite the content of an old movie or two, it is not true that newborn babies are held upside down and slapped on the buttocks to stimulate independent breathing. However, mucus is usually suctioned from the baby's mouth.

When the baby is breathing adequately on its own, the umbilical cord is clamped and severed about 3 inches from the baby's body (see Figure 4.2 ■). At about 266 days after conception, mother and infant have finally become separate beings. The stump of the umbilical cord will dry and fall off on its own in about 7–10 days. There are exceptions. My daughter Allyn, nearly 2 at the time, yanked the umbilical cord off of her newborn sister Jordan, causing a crisis in the family but no enduring harm to Jordan.

TRUTH OR FICTION REVISITED: It is not true that the way the umbilical cord is cut determines whether the baby's "belly button" will be an "innie" or an "outie." Your belly-button status—whether you have an outie or an innie—is unrelated to the methods of your obstetrician.

You might think it would be nice for mother and baby to hang out for a while at this juncture, but the baby is frequently whisked away by a nurse, who performs various procedures: footprinting the baby, supplying an ID bracelet, putting antibiotic ointment (erythromycin) or drops of silver nitrate into the baby's eyes to prevent bacterial infections, and giving the baby a vitamin K injection to help its blood clot properly if it bleeds (newborn babies do not manufacture vitamin K). While this goes on, the mother is in the third stage of labor.

What Happens During the Third Stage of Childbirth?

The third stage of labor is also referred to as the *placental stage*. It can last from a few minutes to an hour or more. During this stage, the placenta separates from the wall of the uterus and is expelled through the birth canal along with fetal membranes. Bleeding is normal at this time. The uterus begins to shrink, although it will take some time for it to return to its approximate pre-pregnancy size. The obstetrician now sews the episiotomy, if one has been performed.

Section Review

1. The first uterine contractions are "false" and are called _____ contractions.

2. A day or so before delivery, about 1 woman in 10 has a rush of _____ fluid from the vagina.

3. In the first stage of childbirth, uterine contractions cause the cervix to become effaced and _____.

4. _____ occurs when the cervix is almost fully dilated and the head of the fetus begins to move into the birth canal.

5. When the baby is breathing adequately, the _____ cord is clamped and severed.

6. During the third stage, the _____ separates from the uterine wall and is expelled.

Reflect & Relate: How do you feel about the routine performance of "prepping" and episiotomy? Why are these controversial and personal issues?

Methods of Childbirth

What methods of childbirth are in use today? What are their effects?

Think of old movies in which a woman is giving birth in her home on the prairie, and a neighbor emerges heralding the good news to the anxious father and members of the community. Perhaps prairies have not hosted the majority of childbirths over the millennia, but childbirth was once a more intimate procedure that usually took place in the woman's home and involved her, perhaps a **midwife**, and her family. This pattern is followed in many less developed nations today, but only rarely in the United States and other developed nations. Contemporary American childbirths usually take place in hospitals, where they are overseen by physicians who use sophisticated instruments and anesthetics to protect mother and child from complications and discomfort. There is no question that modern medicine has saved lives, but childbearing has also become more impersonal. Some argue that modern methods wrest from women control over their own bodies. They even argue that anesthetics have denied many women the experience of giving birth, although many or most women admit that they appreciate having the experience "muted." Before going any further, let us note strongly that the extent to which anesthetics are used should be the choice of the mother. But now let us consider methods for facilitating childbirth.

midwife An individual who helps women in childbirth.

anesthesia A method that produces partial or total loss of the sense of pain.

How Is Anesthesia Used in Childbirth?

Painful childbirth has historically been seen as the standard for women (a "woman's lot"). But the development of modern medicine and **anesthesia** has led many people to believe that women need not experience discomfort during childbirth. Today, at least some anesthesia is used in most American deliveries.

General anesthesia achieves its anesthetic effect by putting the woman to sleep, typically by means of a barbiturate that is injected into a vein in the hand or arm. Other drugs in common use are tranquilizers, oral barbiturates, and narcotics. These drugs are not anesthetics per se, but they may reduce anxiety and the perception of pain without causing sleep.

General anesthesia can have negative effects on the infant, including abnormal patterns of sleep and wakefulness and decreased attention and social responsiveness shortly after birth. The higher the dose, the greater the effect. But there is mixed evidence about whether these anesthetics have long-term effects on the child (Eger et al., 2014). Some of the variability has to do with how different physicians administer the drugs, rather than with the drugs themselves.

An Epidural Anesthesia Kit
An epidural "block" enables the woman giving birth to stay awake but feel no sensation in the pelvis or below.

Regional or local anesthetics deaden pain without putting the mother to sleep. In the pudendal block, the mother's external genitals are numbed by local injection. In the epidural block and the spinal block, anesthesia is injected into the spinal canal or spinal cord, temporarily numbing the body below the waist. Local anesthesia has minor depressive effects on the strength and activity levels of neonates shortly after birth, but when the drugs are administered properly, the effects are short-lived (Eger et al., 2014). The epidural has gained significantly in popularity over the past few decades (Tulp & Paech, 2014).

In contrast to the use of anesthesia, there is a trend toward **natural childbirth**. The term simply means that the woman does not use anesthesia. Today, instead, a woman is likely to be educated about the biological aspects of reproduction and delivery, encouraged to maintain physical fitness, and taught relaxation and breathing exercises.

What About Hypnosis and Biofeedback?

Hypnosis has been used to help clients stick to diets, quit smoking, and undergo dental treatments with less discomfort. It has also been used with some success as an alternative to anesthesia during childbirth (Camann, 2014; Landolt & Milling, 2011). Mothers who use "HypnoBirthing" do not listen to someone telling them to sleep, or stare at someone waving a watch on a cord in front of their eyes. Rather, they are encouraged to focus on relaxing scenes and to decrease their muscle tension. HypnoBirthing does not fully eliminate pain, but, like some other contemporary psychological methods of childbirth, it puts the mother in charge and gives her "something to do" while she is delivering her baby.

Biofeedback is a method that provides the woman in labor with continuous information about what is happening with various bodily functions. Muscle tension and blood pressure are among the functions that can be targeted. Studies suggest that helping women reduce muscle tension can have some positive effects on coping with discomfort during labor (Chaillet et al., 2014).

What Is Meant by Prepared Childbirth?

Most women who are pregnant for the first time expect pain and discomfort during childbirth. Certainly the popular media image of childbirth is one in which the woman

natural childbirth A method of childbirth in which women use no anesthesia and are educated about childbirth and strategies for coping with discomfort.

Masterfile

An Exercise Class for Pregnant Women Years ago, the rule of thumb was that pregnant women were not to exert themselves. Today, it is recognized that exercise is healthful for pregnant women because it promotes cardiovascular fitness and increases muscle strength. Fitness and strength are assets during childbirth as well as at other times.

sweats profusely and screams and thrashes in pain. When the French obstetrician Fernand Lamaze visited Russia, he discovered that many Russian women bore babies without anesthetics or notable pain. He studied their relaxation techniques and brought these to Western Europe and the United States, where they became known as the **Lamaze method**, also called *prepared childbirth*. Lamaze (1981) contended that women could engage in breathing and relaxation exercises that would lessen fear and pain; giving them something to do could distract them from discomfort.

In the Lamaze method, women do not go it alone. The mother-to-be attends Lamaze classes with a "coach"—most often her partner—who will aid her in the delivery room by massaging her, timing contractions, offering social support, and coaching her in patterns of breathing and relaxation. The woman is taught to breathe in a specific way during contractions. As in HypnoBirthing and biofeedback, she is taught how to contract specific muscles in her body while the rest of her body remains generally relaxed. The idea is that she will be able to transfer this training to the process of childbirth by remaining generally at ease while her uterine muscles contract. The procedure tones muscles that will be helpful in childbirth (such as leg muscles) and enables her to minimize tension, conserve energy, and experience less anxiety. Again, childbirth becomes the mother's agenda, not the agenda of helping professionals.

The woman is also educated about the process of childbirth. The father-to-be or another coach is integrated into the process. The woman receives more social support as a result.

> **TRUTH OR FICTION REVISITED:** It is not true that women who give birth according to the Lamaze method do not experience pain. But they apparently report less pain and ask for less medication when others, such as their partners, are present (Camann, 2014).

Lamaze method A method of childbirth in which women are educated about childbirth, learn to relax and breathe in patterns that conserve energy and lessen pain, and have a coach (usually the father) present during childbirth. Also termed *prepared childbirth*.

Social support during labor can be provided by individuals other than the father or a woman's partner. A mother, sibling, or friend can serve as a coach. Studies also demonstrate the benefit of continuous emotional support during labor by an experienced but nonprofessional female companion known as a doula. Women with doulas appear to have shorter labors than women without doulas (Hartocollis, 2015). Dr. Jacques Moritz, an obstetrician at New York's Mount Sinai Roosevelt hospital, notes that "A doula is like a personal trainer. Not that you can't do it yourself; it's just nicer if you have a personal coach for it"

Partner in the Delivery Room
Today, the woman's partner is usually integrated into the process of childbirth. In this case, the father and mother take pride in "their" accomplishments of childbirth.

Harriet Gans/The Image Works

(cited in Hartocollis, 2015). Many medical insurance programs now offer some payment for doulas.

Why Are Cesarean Sections Used So Widely? What Are Their Pluses and Minuses?

Many controversies surround the **cesarean section**. The first that comes to my mind involves its proper spelling. Years ago the term was spelled *Caesarean* section, after the Roman emperor Julius Caesar, who was once thought to have been delivered in this manner. Now, however, the more common spelling is *cesarean*. In any event, the term is usually abbreviated *C-section*.

In a C-section, the physician delivers the baby by abdominal surgery. She or he cuts through the abdomen and the uterus and physically removes the baby. The incisions are then sewn up. Most health professionals encourage the mother to get up and walk around on the same day as the surgery, but make no mistake about it: Doing so is usually painful. When the C-section first came into common practice, it left visible scars on the abdomen. However, physicians usually perform C-sections today in such a way that the incision is more or less hidden by the upper edge of the woman's pubic hair. This method is called the "bikini cut," referring to the shape of the swimsuit bottom.

> **TRUTH OR FICTION REVISITED:** It is true that nearly 1 in every 3 births in the United States is currently by C-section. The figure is close to 33%.

C-sections accounted for about 21% of births in 1996 (Figure 4.3 ■), and now, about 20 years later, they account for about one-third of births in the United States (Osterman & Martin, 2013). Why the upsurge?

Physicians prefer a C-section to vaginal delivery when they believe that normal delivery may threaten the mother or child or may simply be more difficult than desired. Typical indications for the C-section are a small pelvis in the mother, maternal weakness or fatigue (brought about, for example, by prolonged labor), or a baby that is too large or in apparent distress. C-sections are also performed when the physician wants to prevent the circulatory systems of the mother and baby from mixing, as might occur when there is bleeding during vaginal delivery. C-sections in such cases help prevent transmission of genital herpes or HIV, the virus that causes

cesarean section A method of childbirth in which the neonate is delivered through a surgical incision in the abdomen. (Also spelled *Caesarean*.)

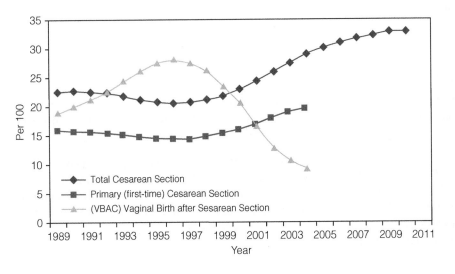

Figure 4.3 ■
Since 1996, the percentage of American women undergoing C-sections has mushroomed from 21% to 32.7%. The percentage of women having a vaginal delivery after a C-section has declined, owing largely to fear that the healed uterine incision for the earlier C-section might rupture. Source: U.S. National Center for Health Statistics. (2014). Rates for total cesarean section, primary caesarean section, and vaginal birth after caesarean (VBAC), United States. Retrieved from http://www.cdc.gov/nchs/fastats/delivery.htm (Accessed 2015, February 25).

AIDS. The combination of anti-HIV drugs and C-section cuts the chance that an HIV-infected mother will transmit HIV to her baby from about 1 in 100 for women who use the drugs alone to 1 in 400 (Townsend et al., 2014). The physician may also perform a C-section when it appears that the baby is facing in the wrong direction. It is normal, and safest, for babies to be born head first. A C-section is indicated if the baby is going to be born sideways or "backwards"—that is, feet first. One of the risks of a baby's facing the wrong direction is hypoxia—restriction of the baby's air supply—upon delivery. C-sections have been shown to reduce the risk of hypoxia (Roberts et al., 2015).

Some women simply ask for C-sections. Some want to avoid the pain of vaginal delivery; others want to control exactly when the baby will be born. (We know of a woman who chose to deliver on a certain day so as not to interfere with her husband's trip to the Super Bowl. No comment.) All in all, however, the strongest predictor of whether a woman will have a C-section is whether she has already had a C-section (Witt et al., 2014).

As you can see from Figure 4.3, the percentage of vaginal births among women who have previously had a C-section has also been declining, mainly because health professionals fear that the uterine incision made during the C-section may rupture during a subsequent vaginal delivery (Begum et al., 2014). Is "Once a C-section, always a C-section" the medical standard today?

Is Home Birth Too Risky, or Is It Something to Consider?

The overwhelming majority of U.S. women give birth in hospitals. In the United States, there is about 1 maternal death for every 2,400 births. In developing countries, where medical resources are scarce, as many as 1 woman in 15 will die in childbirth (State of the World's Mothers, 2014). Although the difference may be partly explained by women giving birth in hospitals, home delivery can actually be a reasonably safe option for healthy women who are believed to have little risk of complications, especially if they have given birth before. A certified nurse midwife can assess a woman's risk for complications and her proximity to emergency medical care, and will usually do so before agreeing to assist with a home birth.

Home birth generally represents an effort by the mother to recapture childbirth as a warm family experience. It challenges the "obstetric view" of birth, which tends to medicalize the experience by making health professionals, rather than the mother, the primary actors in the drama. Some women also choose home birth because it decreases the cost of maternity care for women who have uncomplicated pregnancies and deliveries.

Section Review

7. _____ anesthesia achieves its anesthetic effect during childbirth by putting the woman to sleep.

8. In a(n) _____ block, anesthesia is injected into the spine, numbing the body below the waist.

9. _____ argued that women can learn to dissociate uterine contractions from pain and fear through breathing exercises and muscle-relaxation techniques.

10. A _____ is performed for various reasons, including when a baby is too large to pass through the woman's pelvis, when the mother or baby is in distress, and when there is a need to try to prevent transmission of genital herpes or HIV.

Reflect & Relate: If you were delivering a child, would you want to use anesthetic medication? Would you use the Lamaze method? Why or why not? If you were a prospective father, what would your thoughts be? What are the pros and cons of both methods?

4.4 Birth Problems

Although every delivery is remarkable from the parents' point of view, most deliveries are unremarkable from a medical standpoint. Still, a number of problems can and do occur. In this section, we will discuss the effects of oxygen deprivation and the problems of preterm and low birth weight neonates.

What Are the Effects of Oxygen Deprivation at Birth?

Researchers use two terms to discuss oxygen deprivation: *anoxia* and *hypoxia*. **Anoxia** derives from roots meaning "without oxygen." **Hypoxia** derives from roots meaning "under" and "oxygen," the point again being that the baby does not receive enough oxygen throughout pregnancy to develop properly. Prenatal oxygen deprivation can impair the development of the central nervous system, leading to a host of problems, including cognitive and motor problems, cerebral palsy, and even psychological disorders (Herrera-Marschitz et al., 2014). Much research has focused on the effects of oxygen deprivation on the hippocampus, a brain structure that is vital in memory formation. Children who were deprived of oxygen at birth often show the predicted problems in learning and memory, and also problems in motor development and spatial relations (Thaler et al., 2013).

Prolonged cutoff of the baby's oxygen supply during delivery can also increase the risk of psychological and physical health problems, such as early-onset **schizophrenia** and cerebral palsy (Kotlicka-Antczak et al., 2014). Most researchers now consider schizophrenia a disease of the brain, and oxygen deprivation is believed to impair the development of neural connections in the brain. And, of course, severe, prolonged oxygen deprivation is lethal.

Oxygen deprivation can be caused by maternal disorders (such as diabetes), by immaturity of the baby's respiratory system, and by accidents, some of which involve pressure against the umbilical cord during birth. The fetus and emerging baby receive oxygen through the umbilical cord. Passage through the birth canal is tight, and the umbilical cord is usually squeezed during the process. If the squeezing is temporary, the effect is like holding one's breath for a moment, and no problems are likely to ensue. (In fact, slight oxygen deprivation at birth is not unusual, because the transition from receiving oxygen through the umbilical cord to breathing on its own may not take place immediately after the baby is born.) But if constriction of the umbilical cord is prolonged, developmental problems can result. Prolonged constriction is more likely during a **breech presentation**, or bottom-first presentation, when the baby's body may press the umbilical cord against the birth canal.

Fetal monitoring can help detect anoxia before it causes damage. A C-section can be performed if the fetus seems to be in distress.

What Are the Risks in Being Born Preterm or Low in Birth Weight?

Because the fetus makes dramatic gains in weight during the last weeks of pregnancy, prematurity and low birth weight usually go hand in hand. A baby is considered premature, or **preterm**, when birth occurs at or before 37 weeks of gestation, compared with the normal 40 weeks. A baby is considered to have a low birth weight when it weighs less than 5½ pounds (about 2,500 grams). When a baby's birth weight is low, even though it is born at full term, it is referred to as being **small for dates**. Mothers who smoke, use other drugs, or fail to receive proper nutrition place their babies at greater risk of being small for dates. Small-for-dates babies tend to remain shorter

anoxia A condition characterized by lack of oxygen.

hypoxia A condition characterized by less oxygen than is required.

schizophrenia A severe psychological disorder that is characterized by disturbances in thought and language, perception and attention, motor activity, and mood, and by withdrawal and absorption into daydreams or fantasy.

breech presentation A position in which the fetus enters the birth canal buttocks first.

preterm Born at or before completion of 37 weeks of gestation.

small for dates A description of neonates who are unusually small for their age.

and lighter than their age-mates and show slight delays in learning and problems in attention as compared to age-mates (Heinonen et al., 2011). Preterm babies who survive are more likely than small-for-dates babies to achieve normal heights and weights.

About 7% of children are premature, although the incidence varies in different racial and ethnic groups. However, among multiple births, even twins, the risk of having a preterm child rises to at least 50% (Kurosawa et al., 2012; Shiozaki et al., 2014).

Neonates weighing between 3¼ and 5½ pounds are seven times more likely to die than infants of normal birth weight, whereas those weighing less than 3⅓ pounds are nearly 100 times as likely to die (Save the Children, 2013; Strunk et al., 2012). But physical survival is only one issue connected with prematurity and low birth weight.

By and large, the lower a child's birth weight, the more poorly he or she fares on measures of neurological development and cognitive functioning throughout the school years (Clark et al., 2013; Edwards et al., 2011). Children whose birth weight was less than 750 grams fare less well at middle school age than children whose birth weight was 750–1,499 grams (Taylor et al., 2004). Both low birth weight groups perform more poorly than children whose birth weight was normal. There also seem to be sex differences. The cognitive functioning and school achievement of girls with low birth weight seem to improve more rapidly than those of boys with low birth weight (Edwards et al., 2011; Munck et al., 2010).

There are also risks for delayed motor development. One study compared 96 children with very low birth weight (VLBW) with normal-term children at 6, 9, 12, and 18 months, correcting for age according to the expected date of delivery (Jeng et al., 2000). The median age at which the full-term infants began to walk was 12 months, compared with 14 months for the VLBW infants. By 18 months of age, all full-term infants were walking, whereas 11% of the VLBW infants had not yet begun to walk.

The outcomes for low birth weight children are variable. One research group followed a group of 1,338 Dutch individuals who were born in 1983 with either a gestational age of less than 32 weeks or a birth weight of less than 3⅓ pounds (Walther et al., 2000). The children were assessed at the age of 2 years by their pediatricians, and at the ages of 5 and 9–14 years by teams of investigators, including teachers and parents. All in all, only 10% of the group could be characterized as having a severe disability at ages 9–14. However, many more children appeared to have mild to moderate problems in learning or behavior.

Preschool experience appears to foster the cognitive and social development of VLBW children. Hoy and McClure (2000) compared a group of VLBW children who attended preschool with a group who did not and also with a group of normal birth weight children of the same age. The VLBW children who attended preschool outperformed the VLBW children who did not on measures of cognitive functioning and teacher ratings. They earned higher grades, worked harder, were more likely to participate in social interactions, and were more likely to be rated as "learns a lot." However, their performance on all measures was still exceeded somewhat by the normal birth weight children.

Signs of Prematurity

Preterm babies show characteristic signs of immaturity. They are relatively thin because they have not yet formed the layer of fat that gives so many full-term children their round, robust appearance. They often have fine, downy hair, referred to as **lanugo**, and an oily white substance on the skin known as **vernix**. Lanugo

lanugo Fine, downy hair that covers much of the body of neonates, especially preterm babies.

vernix An oily, white substance that coats the skin of neonates, especially preterm babies.

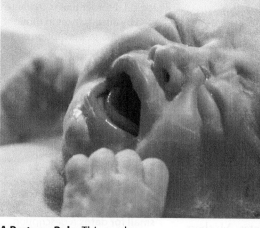

Color Day Production/The Image Bank/Getty Images

A Preterm Baby This newborn shows lanugo and vernix, both characteristics of prematurity.

and vernix disappear within a few days or weeks. If the babies are born 6 weeks or more before full term, their nipples have not yet emerged. The testicles of boys born this early have not yet descended into the scrotum. After birth, however, the nipples develop further and the testes descend.

The muscles of preterm babies are immature. As a result, the babies' vital sucking and breathing reflexes are weak. The muscles of preterm babies may not be mature enough to sustain independent breathing. Also, the walls of the tiny air sacs in their lungs may tend to stick together because they do not yet secrete substances (*surfactants*) that lubricate the walls of the sacs. As a result, babies born more than a month before full term may breathe irregularly or suddenly stop breathing, evidence of a cluster of problems known as **respiratory distress syndrome**. About 1 baby in 7 who is born 1 month early has the syndrome. It is found more frequently among infants born still earlier. Respiratory distress syndrome causes a large percentage of U.S. neonatal deaths. Preterm infants with severe respiratory stress syndrome show poorer development in cognitive, language, and motor skills and more persistent neurological abnormalities over the first 2 years of development than infants with less severe respiratory distress and full-term infants. Injecting pregnant women at risk for delivering preterm babies with corticosteroids increases the babies' chances of survival (Murphy et al., 2011). These babies are less likely to have respiratory distress syndrome or severe lung disease. They are less likely to need treatment with oxygen or mechanical help breathing.

Major strides have been made in helping low birth weight children survive. Techniques include increased prenatal use of steroids, decreased use of postnatal steroids, and C-section (Griffin et al., 2015). Still, low birth weight children who survive often have problems, including below-average achievement in language arts and mathematics and various physical, motor, perceptual, neurological, and behavioral impairments—even social shyness and timidity (Burnett et al., 2014; Williamson & Jakobson, 2014).

Preterm infants with very low birth weights (under 3¹⁄₃ pounds) are likely to show the greatest cognitive deficits and developmental delays. Still, medical advances in recent years have reduced the severity and incidence of handicaps among babies with very low birth weights.

Alexis Hutchinson, 5, left, with her sister, Joslyn, 9, at their home in Iowa. Alexis was born premature at 22 weeks, and 1.1 pounds, but she received excellent care at the hospital in which she was born and now shows no apparent ill effects from the circumstances of her birth.

Treatment of Preterm Babies

Because of their physical frailty, preterm infants usually remain in the hospital and are placed in **incubators**, which maintain a temperature-controlled environment and afford some protection from disease. The infants may be given oxygen, although excessive oxygen can cause permanent eye injury.

One might assume that parents would be more concerned about preterm babies than babies who have gone to full term, and thus would treat them better. Ironically, this is not the case. Parents often do not treat preterm neonates as well as they treat full-term neonates. For one thing, preterm neonates are less physically attractive than full-term babies. Preterm infants usually do not have the robust, appealing appearance of many full-term babies. Their cries are higher pitched and grating, and they are more irritable (Kaye & Shah, 2015). The demands of caring for preterm babies can be stressful and depressing to mothers (Habersaat et al., 2014; Shaw et al., 2014). Mothers of preterm babies frequently report that they feel alienated

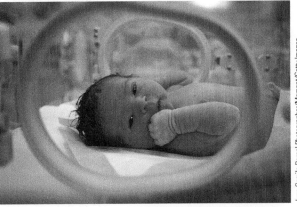

Incubator Premature newborns typically spend a couple of days in an incubator at the hospital before they go home.

respiratory distress syndrome A cluster of breathing problems, including weak and irregular breathing, to which preterm babies are particularly prone.

incubator A heated, protective container in which premature infants are kept.

from their babies and harbor feelings of failure, guilt, and low self-esteem (Baum et al., 2012; Vigod et al., 2010). They respond less sensitively to their infants' behavior than mothers of full-term babies (Bugental et al., 2013). Mothers of preterm infants also touch and talk to their infants less and hold them at a greater distance during feeding. Fear of hurting preterm babies can further discourage parents from handling them, but encouraging mothers to massage their preterm infants can help them cope with fear of handling their babies and with feelings of helplessness and hopelessness (Holditch-Davis et al., 2014).

After they come home from the hospital, preterm infants remain more passive and less sociable than full-term infants (Korja et al., 2011), so they demand less interaction with parents. However, when parents do interact with them during the first year, they are more likely to poke at, caress, and talk to them, perhaps in an effort to prod them out of their passivity. Mothers of preterm babies report feeling overprotective toward them. This may in part explain why 1-year-old preterm infants explore less and stay closer to their mothers than do full-term babies of the same age.

Preterm infants (as all infants!) fare better when they have responsive and caring parents. Preterm children who are reared in attentive and responsive environments attain higher intelligence test scores, have higher self-esteem, display more positive social skills, and have fewer behavioral and emotional problems in childhood than do preterm children reared in less responsive homes (Bugental et al., 2013).

Intervention Programs

A couple of generations ago, preterm babies were left as undisturbed as possible. For one thing, concern was aroused by the prospect of handling such a tiny, frail creature. For another, preterm babies would not normally experience interpersonal contact or other sources of external stimulation until full term. However, experiments carried out over the past two decades suggest that preterm infants profit from early stimulation just as full-term babies do. Preterm babies benefit from being cuddled, rocked, talked to, and sung to; from being exposed to recordings of their mothers' voices; and from having mobiles placed within view. Recent studies have shown the value of live and recorded music in the preterm infant's environment (Nordhov et al., 2012). Other effective forms of stimulation include massage and "kangaroo care" (Athanasopoulou & Fox; 2014; Feldman et al., 2014), in which the baby spends several hours a day lying skin to skin, chest to chest, with one of its parents, usually the mother. Kangaroo care provides olfactory sensations as well as tactile stimulation. It has been shown to decrease stress and pain in preterm infants, as measured, for example, by more rapid recovery from the "heel stick," a hospital procedure in which blood is drawn from the heel with a syringe (C.C. Johnston et al., 2011). In the long term, preterm infants exposed to stimulation tend to gain weight more rapidly, show fewer respiratory problems, and make greater advances in motor, intellectual, and neurological development than control preemies (Santos et al., 2015).

Other intervention programs help parents adjust to the birth and care of low birth weight infants. One such program involved 92 preterm infants at three sites (Als et al., 2003). The following factors contributed to superior cognitive and motor development in the infants and better adjustment in the parents: early discontinuation of intravenous feeding, hospitalization with intensive care for digestive and other problems, and individualized counseling to foster appreciation of the infant.

As you can see in the nearby "A Closer Look—Diversity" feature, maternal and infant mortality remains a serious problem in many parts of the world.

MATERNAL AND INFANT MORTALITY AROUND THE WORLD

Belinda Images/SuperStock

Why are maternal and infant mortality so low in Europe?

Modern medicine has made vast strides in decreasing the rates of maternal and infant mortality, but the advances are not equally spread throughout the world. Save the Children, a nonprofit relief and development organization, tracks the likelihood that a woman will die in childbirth and that an infant will die during its first year. The likelihood of maternal and infant mortality is connected with what Save the Children (2014) terms the "mother's index," which includes factors such as the lifetime risk of maternal death during pregnancy and delivery, the under-5 mortality rate for children, the years of formal schooling of mothers, economic status (as measured by national income per person), and participation of women in national government—a measure of the extent to which a society empowers women. Figure 4.4 ■ shows the various reasons why children die, according to a recent edition of *State of the World's Mothers* (Save the Children, 2014).

Number 1 on the mother's index in 2014 was Finland, where the chances of the woman dying are about 1 in 12,200, and where only 3 infants in 1,000 die during the first five years (see Table 4.1 ●). Women receive an

Figure 4.4 ■ Why Do Young Children Die?
Estimates show that pneumonia, diarrhea, and malaria remain the leading killers of children under 5 worldwide. Together they account for 41 percent of child deaths. More than 40 percent of all under-5 deaths occur in the first month of life. Most of these children could be saved by increasing coverage for known, affordable, and effective interventions. Ensuring proper nutrition is a critical aspect of prevention, because malnutrition contributes to more than a third of all child deaths. Data from Save the Children, 2011

Pneumonia 18%
Malaria 8%
Injury 3%
AIDS 2%
Measles 1%
Other 17%
Neonatal causes 41%
15% Diarrhea

average of 17 years of formal schooling (the same as in the United States), per capita income is $46,490 (about the same as the United States), and 42% to 43% of national government seats are held by women (as compared to only about 19% in the United States). In the United States, 1 in 2,400 women stands a lifetime risk of dying during pregnancy or childbirth (46th in the world), and a child has a 7.1 in 1,000 chance of dying under the age of 5 (41st in the world). Half the countries in the world have a higher percentage of females in national government than the United States. The performance of the United States in the rankings is related to the large number of "nations within the nation." For example, there is great disparity in wealth, and richer Americans fare better in the rankings than poorer Americans. High-quality medical intervention is more available in some parts of the country than others. Many mobile Americans base their residence, in part, on the availability of good medicine.

Reflect: How can you make certain that you—or those you care about—receive the health care needed during pregnancy and childbirth?

Maternal and Child Mortality in Selected Countries as Related to Income Level and Empowerment of Women

Country	Lifetime Risk of Maternal Mortality (1 in number shown)	Under-5 mortality rate (per 1,000 live births)	Average years of formal schooling for women	National income per person (in U.S. dollars)	Participation of women in national government (percentage of seats held by women)
Finland	12,200	2.9	16.9	$46,490	42.5
Ireland	8,100	4.0	18.7	$39,930	19.0
Italy	20,300	3.7	16.1	$35,290	20.6
France	6,200	4.1	16.3	$42,420	25.1
Germany	10,600	4.0	16.4	$44,270	32.4
Poland	14,400	5.8	15.4	$12,480	21.8
Japan	13,100	3.4	15.3	$44,900	11.3
Mexico	790	15.7	13.7	$9,420	11
Sweden	14,100	2.8	16.0	$53,150	44.7
Canada	5,200	5.6	15.1	$45,560	28.0
United Kingdom	4,600	5.1	16.7	$37,840	22.6
United States	2,400	7.1	16.8	$48,620	18.9
Russia	2,000	11.9	14.3	$10,730	12.1
China	1,700	14.6	11.9	$4,940	21.3
Cuba	1,000	5.8	15.4	$5,460	45.2
Israel	5,100	4.3	15.7	$28,930	21.7
Nigeria	29	124.1	9.0	$1,280	6.6
India	170	61.3	10.7	$1,410	10.9
Afghanistan	32	101.1	8.8	$470	27.6

Readers may wonder why the United States is not at the top of the list. One answer is that states with above-average poverty rates, large rural populations, and less-than-average levels of education have the highest maternal and infant mortality rates. According to a report by the Centers for Disease Control and Prevention's National Center for Health Statistics (http://www.cdc.gov/nchs/linked.htm), African American women have the highest infant mortality rate at 13.60 per 1,000 live births, as compared to 4.55 per 1,000 births for the group with the lowest mortality rate: Cuban Americans. European American women had 5.66 infant deaths per 1,000 births, as compared with 8.45 for Native Americans, 7.82 for Puerto Ricans, 5.47 for Mexican Americans, 4.67 for Asian Americans, and 4.65 for Central and South Americans. How do you explain these ethnic differences?
Sources: Save the Children (2013, 2014).

Section Review

11. Prenatal _____ deprivation can impair the development of the central nervous system, leading to cognitive and motor problems and even psychological disorders.

12. A baby is considered _____ when birth occurs at or before 37 weeks of gestation.

13. A baby has a low _____ when it weighs less than 5½ pounds (about 2,500 grams).

14. Research suggests that it is _____ (helpful or harmful?) to stimulate preterm infants.

Reflect & Relate: If you had a preterm infant, do you think you would want to handle him or her as much as possible, or would you tend to leave him or her alone? Explain.

4.5 The Postpartum Period

The term *postpartum* derives from roots meaning "after" and "birth." The **postpartum period** consists of the weeks following delivery, but there is no specific time limit. "Parting is such sweet sorrow," Shakespeare has Juliet tell Romeo. The "parting" from the baby is also frequently a bittersweet experience. The family's long wait is over, concerns about pregnancy and labor are over, fingers and toes have been counted, and, despite some local discomfort, the mother's "load" has been lightened—most literally. However, according to the American Psychiatric Association (2013), about 70% of new mothers have periods of tearfulness, sadness, and irritability that the Association refers to as the "baby blues" (p. 423). In this section, we will discuss two issues of the postpartum period: maternal depression and bonding.

What Kinds of Psychological Problems Do Women Encounter During the Postpartum Period?

These problems include the baby blues, postpartum anxiety, and more serious mood disorders, which occasionally include "psychotic features" (American Psychiatric Association, 2013).

> **TRUTH OR FICTION REVISITED:** Actually, it is normal to feel depressed following childbirth. The so-called "baby blues" actually affect the majority of women in the weeks after delivery (American Psychiatric Association, 2013, 2014). Baby blues and some other postpartum mood problems are so common that they are statistically normal (American Psychiatric Association, 2013).

These problems are not limited to the United States or even to developed nations. They are far-flung, and researchers find them occurring in China, Turkey, Guyana, Australia, and South Africa with similar frequency (American Psychiatric Association, 2013, 2014). Researchers believe that the baby blues are this universally common because of the hormonal changes that follow delivery. Table 4.2 ● shows the kinds of psychological problems, including depression, that mothers might experience before or after delivery.

The baby blues last about 10 days and are generally not severe enough to impair the mother's functioning. Don't misunderstand; the baby blues are seriously discomforting and not to be ignored, as in "Oh, you're just experiencing what most women go through." The point is that most women can handle the baby blues, even though they are pretty awful at times, partly because the women know that they are transient.

A minority of women, but perhaps as many as one in seven, encounter the more serious mood disorder frequently referred to as major depression with the specifier "with perinatal onset" (previously termed **postpartum depression, or PPD**). *Perinatal onset* refers to the period just before or after birth. The disorder most often begins about a month after delivery and may linger for weeks, even months. Like other major depressive disorders, it is characterized by serious sadness, feelings of hopelessness and helplessness, feelings of worthlessness, difficulty concentrating, and major changes in appetite (usually loss of appetite) and sleep patterns (frequently

postpartum period The time that immediately follows childbirth.

postpartum depression (PPD) Severe, prolonged depression that afflicts 10–20% of women after delivery and that is characterized by sadness, apathy, and feelings of worthlessness.

Kinds of Maternal Psychological Problems That Can Occur Before or After Delivery

Type of Problem	Incidence	Symptoms	Comments
Baby blues	About 7 new mothers in 10	• Feeling let down • Crying for no apparent reason • Impatience, irritability, restlessness, anxiety	Occurs in first weeks and disappears on its own No treatment is necessary
Major depression with perinatal onset (previously termed *postpartum depression*); there is now increased recognition that such depressive episodes can occur prior to as well as after childbirth	About 1 new mother or mother-to-be in 7 or 8	• Frequent sadness, crying, helplessness, despair, possible thoughts of suicide, anxiety, panic, feelings of inadequacy, guilt, shame • Changes in appetite • Trouble getting to sleep or staying asleep, or getting too much sleep; fatigue; lack of feeling for the baby or excessive concern for the baby • Irritability • Difficulty concentrating • Frightening feelings, thoughts, images • Loss of interest in sex	Occurs prior to delivery or within about four weeks following delivery May persist for months Treatable with medication or psychotherapy
Postpartum anxiety	Possibly more common than postpartum depression	• Excessive, irrational fears • Rapid heart rate, elevated blood pressure • Dizziness • Excessive concern about coping with baby and other life changes • Intrusive images, thoughts, and impulses	Likely to be short-lived No treatment may be necessary If persistent, can be treated with medication or psychotherapy
Postpartum psychosis	About 1 new mother in 1,000	• Hallucinations • Severe insomnia • Agitation • Bizarre feelings or behavior	Occurs within a few weeks after delivery An emergency that requires professional help

insomnia). There can also be severe fluctuations in mood, with women sometimes feeling elated. Some women show obsessive concern with the well-being of their babies at this time. PPD can also interfere with the mother–baby relationship in the short term.

Many researchers have suggested that major depression with perinatal onset is caused by the interaction of psychological factors and physiological (mainly hormonal) factors, including a sudden drop in estrogen (O'Hara & McCabe, 2013). Feelings of depression before getting pregnant are a risk factor for the postpartum problem, as are concerns about all the life changes that motherhood creates, marital problems, and having a sick or unwanted baby. In addition to these psychological factors, there is much focus today on the contribution of physiological factors: There are major changes in body chemistry during and after pregnancy, and women around the world seem to experience similar disturbances in mood, even when their life experiences and support systems are radically different (O'Hara & McCabe, 2013). But it is clear that stress can heighten the risk of developing postpartum depression (Hillerer et al., 2014).

According to the American Psychiatric Association (2013), postpartum mood episodes are accompanied by "psychotic features" in about 1 woman in 1,000. A psychotic feature may mean a break with reality. Mothers with these features may have delusional thoughts about the infant that place the infant at risk of injury or death. Some women experience delusions that the infant is possessed by the devil, and some have "command hallucinations" to kill the infant; they experience a command to kill the infant as though it is coming from outside themselves—perhaps from a commanding person or some kind of divine or evil spirit—even though the idea originates within. But they may not be able to tell the difference, and the infant may be in serious jeopardy. Women with postpartum psychosis frequently have a history of psychological disorders and/or substance abuse (Comtois et al., 2008). Remember, too, that psychotic features are rare, and when they occur, they do not always place the baby at risk.

Women who experience milder mood disorders in the periods before and after birth usually profit from social support and a history of high self-esteem. They may benefit from counseling, even if counseling does little more than explain that many women encounter baby blues and get over it. Drugs that increase estrogen levels or act as antidepressants may help, but most women get over the problem on their own. At the very least, women should know that the problem does not necessarily mean that there is something wrong with them or that they are failing to live up to their obligations.

How Critical Is Parental Interaction with Neonates in the Formation of Bonds of Attachment?

Bonding—that is, the formation of bonds of attachment between parents and their children—is essential to the survival and well-being of children. Since the publication of controversial research by Marshall Klaus and John Kennell in 1978, many have wondered about the answer to this question.

Klaus and Kennell argued that the first hours postpartum provided a special— even a necessary—opportunity for bonding between parents and neonates. They labeled these hours a "maternal-sensitive" period during which the mother is particularly disposed, largely because of hormone levels, to form a bond with the neonate. In their study, one group of mothers was randomly assigned to standard hospital procedure, in which their babies were whisked away to the nursery shortly after birth. Throughout the remainder of the hospital stay, the babies visited their mothers during feedings. The other group of mothers spent 5 hours a day with their infants during the hospital stay. The hospital staff encouraged and reassured the group of mothers who had extended contact. Follow-ups over 2 years suggested that extended contact benefited both the mothers and their children. Mothers with extended contact were more likely than control mothers to cuddle their babies, soothe them when they cried, and interact with them.

Critics note that the Klaus and Kennell studies are fraught with methodological problems. For example, we cannot separate the benefits of extended contact from benefits attributable to parents' knowledge that they were in a special group and from the extra attention the hospital staff gave them. In short, the evidence that the hours after birth are critical is tainted. Consider, too, the millions of solid adoptive parent–child relationships, in which parents did not have early access to their children.

Parent–child bonding has been shown to be a complex process involving parental desire to have the child; parent–child familiarity with one another's sounds, odors, and tastes; and parental caring. Serious maternal depression can delay bonding with newborns (Klier, 2006), but even so, a Dutch study found that mother–infant attachment appears to be normal by the age of 14 months (Tharner et al., 2012). A history of rejection by her parents can interfere with a woman's bonding with her own children (Brockington, 2011).

Kelvin Murray/Stone/Getty Images

Are the first hours postpartum a special "maternal-sensitive" period for mother–baby bonding?

bonding The process of forming bonds of attachment between parent and child.

HAVE WE FOUND THE DADDY HORMONES?

Are oxytocin and vasopressin the "Daddy hormones"? Perhaps so, at least in prairie voles, which are a kind of tailless mouse, and sheep. These hormones are connected with the creation of mother–infant bonds in sheep, pair bonds in monogamous voles, and bonds of attachment between vole fathers and their young. Experimental research clearly shows that increasing vasopressin levels transform an indifferent male into a caring, monogamous, and protective mate and father (Keebaugh et al., 2015; Young, 2015).

Oxytocin and vasopressin are secreted by the pituitary gland, which secretes many hormones that are involved in reproduction and the nurturing of young. For example, prolactin regulates maternal behavior in lower mammals and stimulates the production of milk in women. Oxytocin stimulates labor but is also involved in social recognition and bonding. Vasopressin enables the body to conserve water by inhibiting urine production when fluid levels are low; however, it is also connected with paternal behavior patterns in

A Vole Surveying the Environment before Leaving the Nest The hormones oxytocin and vasopressin stimulate the formation of bonds of attachment in voles. Do they play a similar role in humans?

Arndt Sven-Erik/Arterra Picture Library/Alamy

some mammals. For example, male prairie voles form pair bonds with female prairie voles after mating with them (Keebaugh et al., 2015). Mating stimulates the secretion of vasopressin, and vasopressin causes the previously promiscuous male to sing "I only have eyes for you."

After learning about their effects on voles, we may wonder how oxytocin and vasopressin may be connected with the formation of bonds between men and women and between men and children. And will perfume makers soon be lacing new scents with the stuff?

Reflect In your own experience, and in the portrayals of males and females you see in the media, what are the apparent sex differences in "cuddling," parenting, and tendencies toward monogamy? To what extent do you think these differences result from cultural influences and to what extent from chemistry—that is, chemicals such as oxytocin and vasopressin? Explain.

TRUTH OR FICTION REVISITED: Despite the Klaus and Kennell studies, which made a brief splash a generation ago, it is not true that parents must have extended early contact with their newborn children if adequate bonding is to take place. Researchers now view the hours after birth as one element—and not even an essential element—in a complex and prolonged bonding process.

Some Notes on Father–Newborn Bonding

An Australian study found that professionally employed new fathers are quite interested in seeking information about father–newborn bonding (Fletcher et al., 2008). The Internet surfing behavior of a sample of 253 professionals revealed that the two parenting-related online topics that most interested them were baby games and father–infant bonding. They were significantly less interested in topics such as resuming sex after the delivery and breastfeeding.

A Swedish study of 10 fathers who were interviewed about a year after their children were born found that it was typical for fathers to feel overwhelmed at first, but that they were motivated to master parenting and to find a new "completeness" in their lives (Premberg et al., 2008). The fathers tended to bond with their babies by assigning them primary importance and spending time alone with them. The fathers reported that newborns generally provided feelings of happiness and warmth in the home, and they experienced a deeper relationship with their partner as a result. Can these findings be generalized to the United States? Perhaps not; Sweden is an upper-middle-class country, with many affluent individuals, and the sample was not chosen entirely at random.

Research suggests that father–newborn bonding is affected by the father's relationship with the mother as well as by the father's own psychological well-being (Condon, 2006). As an example, many new mothers experience postpartum depression, which can compound the stress in a home that is already changed by the addition of a needy newborn. This stress can interfere with father–newborn bonding as well as introduce its own challenges.

Section Review

15. Research suggests that the _____ (majority or minority?) of new mothers experience periods of depression.

16. Postpartum depression has been connected with a precipitous decline in the hormone _____.

17. Research _____ (does or does not?) show that early parental interaction with neonates is critical in the formation of bonds of attachment.

Reflect & Relate: Pretend for a minute that you are visiting a friend who has just had a baby. She is weepy and listless and worries that she doesn't have the "right" feelings as a new mother. What would you say to her? Why?

4.6 Characteristics of Neonates

Many neonates come into the world looking a bit fuzzy, but even though they are utterly dependent on others, they are probably more aware of their surroundings than you had imagined. Neonates make rapid adaptations to the world around them. In this section, we will see how health professionals assess the health of and describe the characteristics of neonates.

How Do Health Professionals Assess the Health of Neonates?

The neonate's overall level of health is usually evaluated at birth according to the **Apgar scale,** developed by Virginia Apgar in 1953. Apgar scores are based on five signs of health, as shown in Table 4.3 ●. The neonate can receive a score of 0, 1, or 2 on each sign. The total Apgar score, therefore, can vary from 0 to 10. A score of 7 or higher usually indicates that the baby is not in danger. A score below 4 suggests that the baby is in critical condition and requires medical attention. By 1 minute after birth, most normal babies attain scores of 8–9 (Clayton & Crosby, 2006).

The acronym APGAR is commonly used as an aid in remembering the five criteria of the Apgar scale: A—the general appearance or color of the neonate, P—the pulse or heart rate, G—grimace (a 1-point indicator of reflex irritability), A—general activity level or muscle tone, and R—respiratory effort, or rate of breathing.

The Brazelton Neonatal Behavioral Assessment Scale (**NBAS**), developed by pediatrician T. Berry Brazelton, measures neonates' reflexes and other behavior patterns (Brazelton & Nugent, 2011). The test screens neonates for behavioral

Apgar scale A measure of a newborn's health that assesses appearance, pulse, grimace, activity level, and respiratory effort.

NBAS Brazelton Neonatal Behavioral Assessment Scale.

● TABLE 4.3

The Apgar Scale

Points	0	1	2
Appearance: Color	Blue, pale	Body pink, extremities blue	Entirely pink
Pulse: Heart rate	Absent (not detectable)	Slow—below 100 beats/minute	Rapid—100–140 beats/ minute
Grimace: Reflex irritability	No response	Grimace	Crying, coughing, sneezing
Activity level: Muscle tone	Completely flaccid, limp	Weak, inactive	Flexed arms and legs; resists extension
Respiratory effort: Breathing	Absent (infant is apneic)	Shallow, irregular, slow	Regular breathing; lusty crying

Source: Adapted from Boukydis & Lester (2008).

and neurological problems by assessing several areas of behavior: motor behavior, including muscle tone and most reflexes; response to people; response to stress; adaptive behavior; and physiological control. A low score on the NBAS may suggest neurological problems such as brain damage.

The NBAS was constructed to assess normal infants. Brazelton developed the Neonatal Intensive Care Unit Network Neurobehavioral Scale (**NNNS**) in collaboration with Barry Lester and Edward Tronick (2004) to help assess and consult with the parents of infants at risk—especially infants who have been exposed to parental substance abuse (Table 4.4 ●). Substances include but are not limited to cocaine, heroin, alcohol, methamphetamine, and polydrug abuse. The NNNS is administered

● TABLE 4.4

Infant Responses Assessed by the Neonatal Intensive Care Unit Network Neurobehavioral Scale (NNNS)

- Describe what events, handling, and movements caused the infant to change emotional states.
- Describe circumstances under which the infant cried or fussed during assessment.
- Describe how the consultant soothed the infant.
- Summarize ways in which the infant soothed himself or herself during the consultation.
- Describe how the infant responded to a bell or rattle.
- Describe how the infant responded to being cuddled.
- Describe signs of stress such as startles shown by the infant.
- Describe the causes or antecedents of these signs of stress.
- Describe the infant's quality of movement.
- Describe reflexes shown by the infant, especially those that were inadequate.
- Describe the infant's quality of sucking.

NNNS Neonatal Intensive Care Unit Network Neurobehavioral Scale.

Source: Adapted from Boukydis & Lester (2008).

in the presence of a parent and assesses the infant's relative stability or instability in emotional states, overall irritability, signs of stress, response to various handling techniques, response to soothing efforts, response to auditory and visual stimulation, and ability to soothe himself or herself (Boukydis & Lester, 2008). While the scale is being administered, the consultant has the opportunity to observe parent–infant interactions and suggest more effective child-rearing behavior.

What Are Reflexes? What Reflexes Are Shown by Newborns?

If soon after birth you had been held for a few moments with your face down in comfortably warm water, you would not have drowned. Instead of breathing the water in, you would have exhaled slowly through the mouth and engaged in swimming motions. (We urge readers not to test babies for this reflex. The hazards are obvious.) This swimming response is "prewired"—innate or inborn—and it is just one of the many reflexes shown by neonates.

Reflexes are simple, unlearned, stereotypical responses that are elicited by certain types of stimulation. They do not require higher brain functions; they occur automatically, without thinking. Reflexes are the most complicated motor activities displayed by neonates. Neonates cannot roll over, sit up, reach for an object that they see, or raise their heads.

Let us return to our early venture into the water. If you had been placed into the water not a few moments but several months after birth, the results might have been very different—and disastrous. After a few months, the swimming reflex, like many others, ceases to exist. However, at 6–12 months of age, infants can learn how to swim voluntarily. In fact, the transition from reflexive swimming to learned swimming can be reasonably smooth with careful guided practice.

Many reflexes have survival value. Adults and neonates, for example, reflexively close their eyes when assaulted with a puff of air or sudden bright light. Other reflexes seem to reflect interesting facets of the evolution of the nervous system. The swimming reflex seems to suggest that there was a time when our ancestors profited from being born able to swim.

Pediatricians learn a good deal about the adequacy of neonates' **neural** functioning by testing their reflexes. The absence or weakness of a reflex may indicate immaturity (as in prematurity), slowed responsiveness (which can result from anesthetics used during childbirth), brain injury, or intellectual disability. Let us examine some of the reflexes shown by neonates.

The rooting and sucking reflexes are basic to survival. In the **rooting reflex**, the baby turns the head and mouth toward a stimulus that strokes the cheek, chin, or corner of the mouth. The rooting reflex facilitates finding the mother's nipple in preparation for sucking. Babies will suck almost any object that touches their lips. The sucking reflex grows stronger during the first days after birth and can be lost if not stimulated. As the months go on, reflexive sucking becomes replaced by voluntary sucking.

In the startle or **Moro reflex**, the back arches and the legs and arms are flung out and then brought back toward the chest, with the arms in a hugging motion. The Moro reflex occurs when a baby's position is suddenly changed or support for the head and neck is suddenly lost. It can also be elicited by making loud noises, by bumping the baby's crib, or by jerking the baby's blanket. In terms of our evolutionary history, the Moro reflex would probably have enhanced the survival of infants clinging to parents that regularly climbed trees. The Moro reflex is usually lost by 6–7 months after birth (although similar movements can be found in adults who suddenly lose support). Absence of the Moro reflex can indicate immaturity or brain damage.

During the first few weeks following birth, babies show an increasing tendency to reflexively grasp fingers or other objects pressed against the palms of their hands. In this **grasping reflex**, or palmar reflex, they use four fingers only (the thumbs are not included). The grasping reflex is stronger when babies are startled. Most babies

reflex An unlearned, stereotypical response to a stimulus.

neural Of the nervous system.

rooting reflex A reflex in which infants turn their mouths and heads in the direction of a stroking of the cheek or corner of the mouth.

Moro reflex A reflex in which infants arch their back, fling out their arms and legs, and draw them back toward the chest in response to a sudden change in position.

grasping reflex A reflex in which infants grasp objects that cause pressure against their palms.

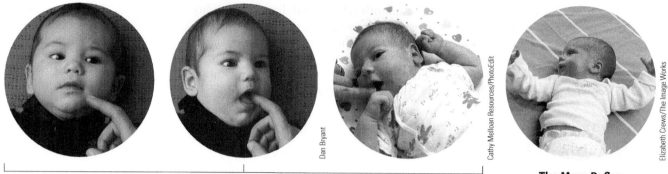

The Rooting Reflex

The Moro Reflex

Dan Bryant

Cathy Melloan Resources/PhotoEdit

Elizabeth Crews/The Image Works

can support their own weight in this way. They can be lifted into the air as they reflexively cling with two hands. Some babies can actually support their weight with just one hand. (Please do not try this!) Absence of the grasping reflex may indicate depressed activity of the nervous system, which can stem from use of anesthetics during childbirth. The grasping reflex is usually lost by 3–4 months of age, and babies generally show voluntary grasping by 5–6 months.

One or 2 days after birth, babies show a reflex that mimics walking. When held under the arms and tilted forward so that the feet press against a solid surface, a baby will show a **stepping reflex** in which the feet advance one after the other. A full-term baby "walks" heel to toe, whereas a preterm infant is more likely to remain on tiptoe. The stepping reflex usually disappears by 3 or 4 months of age.

In the **Babinski reflex**, the neonate fans or spreads the toes in response to stroking of the foot from heel to toes. The Babinski reflex normally disappears toward the end of the first year, to be replaced by curling downward of the toes. Persistence of the Babinski reflex may suggest defects of the lower spinal cord, lagging development of nerve cells, or other disorders.

The **tonic-neck reflex** is observed when the baby is lying on its back and turns its head to one side. The arm and leg on that side extend, while the limbs on the opposite side flex. You can see why this reflex sometimes is known as the "fencing position."

Some reflexes, such as breathing and blinking the eye in response to a puff of air, remain with us for life. Others, such as the sucking and grasping reflexes, are gradually replaced by voluntary sucking and grasping after a number of months. Still others, such as the Moro and Babinski reflexes, disappear, indicating that the nervous system is maturing on schedule.

How Well Do Neonates Sense the World Around Them?

In 1890, William James, one of the founders of modern psychology, wrote that the neonate must sense the world "as one great blooming, buzzing confusion." The neonate emerges from being literally suspended in a temperature-controlled environment to being—again, in James's words—"assailed by eyes, ears, nose, skin, and entrails at once." Let us describe the sensory capabilities of neonates. We will see that James, for all his eloquence, probably exaggerated their disorganization.

Vision

Neonates can see, but they do not possess great sharpness of vision, or **visual acuity**. Visual acuity is expressed in numbers such as 20/20 and 20/200. The ideal is 20/20, meaning that you can see objects clearly at a distance of 20 feet. Investigators estimate that neonates are nearsighted, with visual acuity in the neighborhood of 20/600 (Kellman & Arterberry, 2006). Neonates can best see objects that are about

stepping reflex A reflex in which infants take steps when held under the arms by leaning forward so that their feet press against the ground.

Babinski reflex A reflex in which infants fan their toes when the undersides of their feet are stroked.

tonic-neck reflex A reflex in which infants turn their head to one side, extend the arm and leg on that side, and flex the limbs on the opposite side. Also known as the fencing position.

visual acuity Keenness or sharpness of vision.

The Grasping Reflex

The Stepping Reflex

The Tonic-Neck Reflex

A Closer Look · Research

STUDYING VISUAL ACUITY IN NEONATES—HOW WELL CAN THEY SEE?

How do psychologists determine the visual acuity of neonates? Naturally, they cannot ask babies to report how well they see, but psychologists can determine what babies are looking at and draw conclusions from this information.

One method of observing what a baby is looking at is by using a "looking chamber" of the sort employed in research by Robert Fantz and his colleagues (1975). In this chamber, the baby lies on its back, with two panels above. Each panel contains a visual stimulus. The researcher observes the baby's eye movements and records how much time is spent looking at each panel. A similar strategy can be carried out in the baby's natural environment. Filtered lights and a movie or TV camera can be trained on the baby's eyes. Reflections from objects in the environment can then be recorded to show what the baby is looking at.

Neonates will stare at almost any nearby object for minutes—golf balls, wheels, checkerboards, bull's-eyes, circles, triangles, even lines (Maurer & Maurer, 1976). But babies have their preferences, as measured by the amount of time they spend fixating on (looking at) certain objects. For example, they will spend more time looking at black and white stripes than at gray blobs. This fact suggests one strategy for measuring visual acuity in the neonate. As black and white stripes become narrower, they eventually take on the appearance of that dull gray blob. And, as the stripes are progressively narrowed, we can assume that babies continue to discriminate them as stripes only so long as they spend more time looking at them than at blobs.

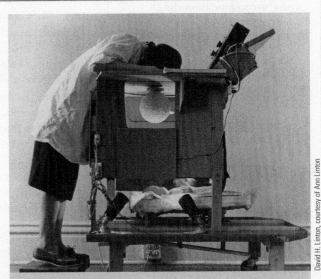

The Looking Chamber This chamber makes it easier for the researcher to observe the baby's eye movements and to record how much time the baby spends looking at a visual stimulus.

Studies such as these suggest that neonates are very nearsighted. But we should remember that they, unlike older children and adults, are not motivated to "perform" in such experiments. If they were, they might show somewhat greater acuity.

Reflect What are the problems in studying the "preferences" of newborn children? How do researchers "get around" these problems? Are you confident that they are studying the preferences of newborns? Explain.

7 to 9 inches away from their eyes (Braddick & Atkinson, 2011). Neonates also see best through the centers of their eyes. They do not have the peripheral vision of older children (Candy et al., 1998). To learn how psychologists measure the visual acuity of infants, see the nearby "A Closer Look—Research" feature.

Neonates can visually detect movement, and many neonates can track movement the first day after birth. In fact, they appear to prefer (that is, they spend more time looking at) moving objects, rather than stationary ones (Kellman & Arterberry, 2006).

Visual accommodation consists of the self-adjustments made by the lens of the eye to bring objects into focus. If you hold your finger at arm's length and bring it gradually nearer, you will feel tension in your eyes as your lenses automatically foreshorten and thicken in an effort to keep the image in focus. When you move the finger away, the lens accommodates by lengthening and flattening to keep the finger in focus. Neonates show little or no visual accommodation; they see as if through a fixed-focus camera. Objects placed about 7–9 inches away are in clearest focus for most neonates, although this range can be somewhat expanded when lighting conditions are bright. Interestingly, this is about the distance of the face of an adult who is cradling a neonate in his or her arms. It has been speculated that this sensory capacity for gazing into others' eyes may promote attachment between neonates and caregivers. Visual accommodation improves dramatically during the first 2 months (Kavšek et al., 2012; Kellman & Arterberry, 2006).

Now bring your finger toward your eyes, trying to maintain a single image of the approaching finger. If you do so, it is because your eyes turn inward, or converge, on the finger, resulting in a crossed-eyed look and feelings of tension in the eye muscles (see Figure 4.5 ■). **Convergence** is made possible by coordination of the eye muscles. Neonates do not have the muscular control to converge their eyes on an object that is close to them. For this reason, one eye may be staring off to the side while the other fixates on an object straight ahead. Convergence does not occur until 7–8 weeks of age for near objects, although neonates show some convergence for objects at intermediate distances (Kellman & Arterberry, 2006).

The degree to which neonates perceive color remains an open question. The research problem is that colors vary in **intensity** (brightness), **saturation** (richness), and **hue**. For this reason, when babies appear to show preference for one color over another, we cannot be certain that they are responding to the hue. They may be responding to the difference in brightness or saturation. So, you say, simply change hues and keep intensity and saturation constant. A marvelous idea—but easier said than done, unfortunately.

visual accommodation The automatic adjustments made by the lenses of the eyes to bring objects into focus.

convergence The inward movement of the eyes as they focus on an object that is drawing nearer.

intensity Brightness.

saturation Richness or purity of a color.

hue Color.

Figure 4.5 ■ Convergence of the Eyes
Neonates do not have the muscular control to converge their eyes on an object that is close to them. However, they do show some convergence for objects at intermediate viewing distances.

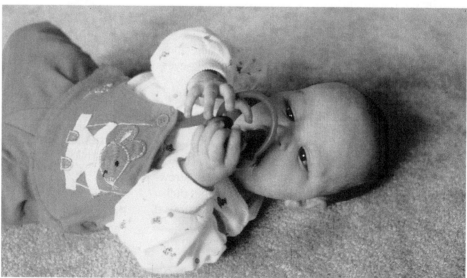

© Elizabeth Crews Photography

Physiological observations also cast doubt on the capacity of neonates to have highly developed color vision. There are two types of cells in the retina of the eye that are sensitive to light: rods and cones. **Rods** transmit sensations of light and dark. **Cones** transmit sensations of color. At birth, the cones are less well developed than the rods in structure.

Infants younger than 1 month of age do not show the ability to discriminate stimuli that differ in color. Two-month-olds can do so, but they require large color differences. By 4 months, infants can see most, if not all, of the colors of the visible spectrum (Kimura et al., 2010).

Even at birth, babies do not just passively respond to visual stimuli. Babies placed in the dark open their eyes wide and actively search the visual field (Braddick & Atkinson, 2011).

Hearing

Fetuses respond to sound months before they are born. Although myelination of the auditory pathways is not complete before birth, fetuses' middle and inner ears normally reach their mature shape and size before they are born. Normal neonates hear well, unless their middle ears are clogged with amniotic fluid (Zhiqi et al., 2010). Most neonates turn their heads toward unusual sounds, such as the shaking of a rattle.

Neonates have the capacity to respond to sounds of different **amplitude** and **pitch**. They are more likely to respond to high-pitched sounds than to low-pitched sounds (Homae et al., 2011). By contrast, speaking or singing to infants softly, in a relatively low-pitched voice, can have a soothing effect (Conrad et al., 2011; Volkova et al., 2006). This may explain the widespread practice in many cultures of singing lullabies to infants to promote sleep (Volkova et al., 2006).

The sense of hearing may play a role in the formation of affectional bonds between neonates and their mothers that goes well beyond the soothing potential of the mothers' voices. Research indicates that neonates prefer their mothers' voices to those of other women, but they do not show similar preferences for the voices of their fathers (DeCasper & Prescott, 1984; Freeman et al., 1993). It may be tempting to conclude that the human nervous system is prewired to respond positively to the voice of one's biological mother. However, neonates have already had several months of experience in the uterus, and for a good part of this time, they have been capable of sensing sounds. Because they are predominantly exposed to prenatal sounds produced by their mothers, learning appears to play a role in neonatal preferences.

There is fascinating evidence that neonates are particularly responsive to the sounds and rhythms of speech, although they do not show preferences for specific languages. Neonates can discriminate between different speech sounds, and they can discriminate between new sounds of speech and those that they have heard before (Gervain et al., 2012).

Smell: The Nose Knows—Early

Neonates can definitely discriminate distinct odors, such as those of onions and anise (licorice). They show more rapid breathing patterns and increased bodily movement in response to powerful odors. They also turn away from unpleasant odors, such as ammonia and vinegar, as early as the first day after birth (Werner & Bernstein, 2001).

The nasal preferences of neonates are quite similar to those of older children and adults (Werner & Bernstein, 2001). When a cotton swab saturated with the odor of rotten eggs was passed beneath their noses, neonate infants spat, stuck out their tongues, wrinkled their noses, and blinked their eyes. However, they showed smiles and licking motions when presented with the odors of chocolate, strawberry, vanilla, butter, bananas, and honey.

rods In the eye, rod-shaped receptors of light that are sensitive to intensity only. Rods permit black-and-white vision.

cones In the eye, cone-shaped receptors of light that transmit sensations of color.

amplitude The maximum vibration of a sound wave. The higher the amplitude of sound waves, the louder they are.

pitch The highness or lowness of a sound, as determined by the frequency of sound waves.

Classic research by Aidan Macfarlane (1975, 1977) and others suggests that the sense of smell, like hearing, may provide a vehicle for mother–infant recognition and attachment. Macfarlane suspected that neonates may be sensitive to the smell of milk because, when held by the mother, they tend to turn toward her nipple before they have had a chance to see or touch it. In one experiment, Macfarlane placed nursing pads above and to the sides of neonates' heads. One pad had absorbed milk from the mother, and the other was clean. Neonates less than a week old spent more time turning to look at their mothers' pads than at the new pads.

Neonates also turn toward preferred odors. In the second phase of this research, Macfarlane suspended pads with milk from the neonates' mothers and from strangers to the sides of babies' heads. For the first few days following birth, the infants did not turn toward their mothers' pads. However, by the time they were 1 week old, they turned toward their mothers' pads and spent more time looking at them than at the strangers' pads. It appears that they learned to respond positively to the odor of their mothers' milk during the first few days. Afterward, a source of this odor received preferential treatment even when the infants were not nursing.

Breastfed 15-day-old infants also prefer their mothers' axillary (underarm) odor to odors produced by other lactating women and by nonlactating women. Bottle-fed infants do not show this preference (Cernoch & Porter, 1985; Porter et al., 1992). The investigators explain this difference by suggesting that breastfed infants may be more likely than bottle-fed infants to be exposed to their mothers' axillary odor; that is, mothers of bottle-fed infants usually remain clothed. Axillary odor, along with odors from breast secretions, might contribute to the early development of recognition and attachment (A. C. Lee et al., 2011).

Taste—Do Neonates Have Taste?

The short answer is yes, they do. The somewhat longer answer is that neonates are sensitive to different tastes, and their preferences, as suggested by their facial expressions in response to various fluids, appear to be similar to those of adults (Beauchamp & Mennella, 2011; Werner & Bernstein, 2001). Neonates swallow without showing any facial expression suggestive of a positive or negative response when distilled water is placed on their tongues. Sweet solutions are met with smiles, licking, and eager sucking, as shown in Figure 4.6a ■ (Rosenstein & Oster, 1988). Neonates discriminate among solutions with salty, sour, and bitter tastes, as suggested by reactions in the lower part of the face (Rosenstein & Oster, 1988). Sour fluids (see Figure 4.6b) elicit pursing of the lips, nose wrinkling, and eye blinking. Bitter solutions (see Figure 4.6c) stimulate spitting, gagging, and sticking out the tongue.

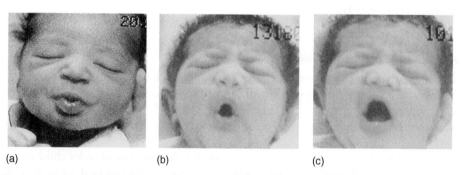

(a)   (b)   (c)

Figure 4.6 ■ Facial Expressions Elicited by Sweet, Sour, and Bitter Solutions
Neonates are sensitive to different tastes, as shown by their facial expressions when tasting (a) sweet, (b) sour, and (c) bitter solutions.
Rosenstein, D.S. & Oster, H. (1988). Differential facial responses to four basic tastes in newborns. *Child Development, 59,* 1555–1568.

Sweet solutions have a calming effect on neonates (Fernandes et al., 2011). One study found that sweeter solutions increase the heart rate, suggesting heightened arousal, but also slow down the rate of sucking (Crook & Lipsitt, 1976). The researchers interpret this finding to suggest an effort to savor the sweeter solution—to make the flavor last. Although we do not know why infants ingest sweet foods more slowly, this difference could be adaptive in the sense of preventing overeating. Sweet foods tend to be high in calories; eating them slowly gives infants' brains more time to respond to bodily signals that they have eaten enough and thus should stop eating. Ah, to have the wisdom of a neonate!

Touch and Pain

The sense of touch is an extremely important avenue of learning and communication for babies. Not only do the skin senses provide information about the external world, but the sensations of skin against skin also appear to provide feelings of comfort and security that may be major factors in the formation of bonds of attachment between infants and their caregivers, as we will see in Chapter 7.

Neonates are sensitive to touch. Many reflexes—including the rooting, sucking, Babinski, and grasping reflexes—are activated by pressure against the skin.

It was once widely believed that neonates are not as sensitive to pain as older babies are. Considering the squeezing that takes place during childbirth, relative insensitivity to pain would seem to be adaptive. However, this belief has been challenged by health professionals (Cong et al., 2013; Goskan et al., 2015). What would appear to be accurate enough is that neonates are not cognitively equipped to fret about pain that may be coming or to ruminate about pain they have experienced. But they are certainly conditionable. In other words, if they perceive themselves to be in a situation that has brought them pain in the past, we should not be surprised if they shriek—and shriek and shriek. Health professionals now recommend that neonates and older infants be given anesthetics if they are going to undergo uncomfortable procedures, such as circumcision.

On Really Early Childhood "Education"—Can Neonates Learn?

The somewhat limited sensory capabilities of neonates suggest that they may not learn as rapidly as older children do. After all, we must sense clearly those things we are to learn about. However, neonates seem capable of at least two basic forms of learning: classical conditioning and operant conditioning.

Classical Conditioning of Neonates

In classical conditioning of neonates, involuntary responses are conditioned to new stimuli. In a typical study (Lipsitt, 2002), neonates were taught to blink in response to a tone. Blinking (the unconditioned response) was elicited by a puff of air directed toward the infant's eye (the unconditioned stimulus). A tone was sounded (the conditioned stimulus) as the puff of air was delivered. After repeated pairings, sounding the tone caused the neonate to blink (the conditioned response). Thus neonates are equipped to learn that events peculiar to their own environments (touches or other conditioned stimuli) may mean that a meal is at hand—or, more accurately, at mouth. One neonate may learn that a light switched on overhead precedes a meal. Another may learn that feeding is preceded by the rustling of a carpet of thatched leaves. The conditioned stimuli are culture-specific; the capacity to learn is universal.

Operant Conditioning of Neonates

Operant conditioning, like classical conditioning, can take place in neonates. In Chapter 3, we described an experiment in which neonates learned to suck on a

Figure 4.7 ■ A Neonate
Sucking to Hear Her Mother's
Voice

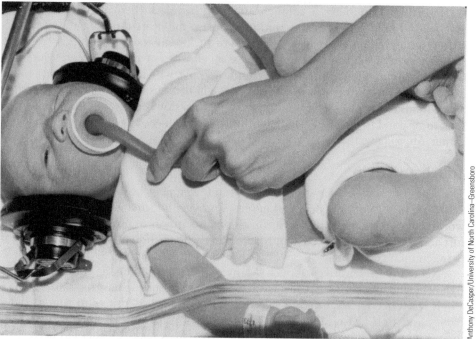

Anthony DeCasper/University of North Carolina–Greensboro

pacifier in such a way as to activate a recording of their mothers reading *The Cat in the Hat* (DeCasper & Fifer, 1980; DeCasper & Spence, 1991) (see Figure 4.7 ■). The mothers had read this story aloud during the final weeks of pregnancy. In this example, the infants' sucking reflexes were modified through the reinforcement of hearing their mothers read a familiar story.

The younger the child, the more important it is that reinforcers be administered rapidly. Among neonates, it seems that reinforcers must be administered within 1 second after the desired behavior is performed if learning is to occur. Infants aged 6–8 months can learn if the reinforcer is delayed by 2 seconds, but if the delay is 3 seconds or more, learning does not take place (Millar, 1990). Although there are individual differences in conditionability in neonates, these differences do not correspond to differences in the complex cognitive abilities we refer to as intelligence later on.

What Patterns of Sleep and Waking Are Found Among Neonates?

As adults, we spend about one-third of our time sleeping. Neonates greatly outdo us, spending two-thirds of their time, or about 16 hours per day, in sleep. And in one of life's basic challenges to parents, neonates do not sleep their 16 hours consecutively. A number of different states of sleep and wakefulness have been identified in neonates and infants, as shown in Table 4.5 ●. Although individual babies differ in the amount of time they spend in each of these states, sleep clearly predominates over wakefulness in the early days and weeks of life.

Different infants require different amounts of sleep and follow different patterns of sleep, but virtually all infants distribute their sleeping throughout the day and night in a series of naps. The typical infant exhibits about six cycles of waking and sleeping in a 24-hour period. The longest nap typically approaches 4½ hours, and the neonate is usually awake for a little more than 1 hour during each cycle.

This pattern of waking and sleeping changes rapidly and dramatically over the course of the years. Even after a month or so, the infant has fewer but longer sleep periods and usually takes longer naps during the night. Parents whose babies do

TABLE 4.5

States of Sleep and Wakefulness in Infancy

Quiet sleep (non-REM)	Regular breathing, eyes closed, no movement
Active sleep (REM)	Irregular breathing, eyes closed, rapid eye movement, muscle twitches
Drowsiness	Regular or irregular breathing, eyes open or closed, little movement
Alert inactivity	Regular breathing, eyes open, looking around, little body movement
Alert activity	Irregular breathing, eyes open, active body movement
Crying	Irregular breathing, eyes open or closed, thrashing of arms and legs, crying

not know the difference between night and day usually teach them the difference by playing with them during daytime hours, once feeding and caretaking chores have been carried out, and by putting them back to sleep as soon as possible when they awaken hungry during the night. Most parents do not require professional instruction in this method. At 3 a.m., parents are not likely to feel playful.

By the ages of about 6 months to a year, many infants begin to sleep through the night. Some infants start sleeping through the night even earlier (Salzarulo & Ficca, 2002). A number of infants begin to sleep through the night for a week or so and then revert to their wakeful ways again for a while.

REM and Non-REM Sleep

Sleep is not a consistent state. It can be divided into **rapid eye movement (REM) sleep** and **non–rapid eye movement (non-REM) sleep** (see Figure 4.8 ■). Studies with the **electroencephalograph (EEG)** show that we can subdivide non-REM sleep into four additional stages of sleep, each with its characteristic brain waves, but our discussion will be limited to REM and non-REM sleep. REM sleep is characterized by rapid eye movements that can be observed beneath closed lids. The EEG patterns produced during REM sleep resemble those of the waking state. For this reason, REM sleep is also called paradoxical sleep. However, we are difficult to awaken during REM sleep. About 80% of the time, adults who are roused during REM sleep report that they have been dreaming. Is the same true of neonates?

rapid eye movement (REM) sleep Periods of sleep during which we are likely to dream, as indicated by rapid eye movements.

non–rapid eye movement (non-REM) sleep Periods of sleep during which we are unlikely to dream.

electroencephalograph (EEG) An instrument that measures electrical activity of the brain.

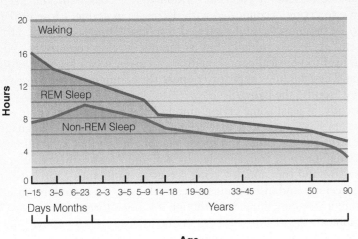

Figure 4.8 ■ REM Sleep and Non-REM Sleep
Neonates spend nearly 50% of their time sleeping in rapid eye movement (REM) sleep. The percentage of time spent in REM sleep drops off to 20–25% for 2-to 3-year-olds.
Source: Roffwarg et al. (1966).

Note from Figure 4.8 that neonates spend about half their sleeping time in REM sleep. As they develop, the percentage of sleeping time spent in REM sleep declines. By 6 months or so, REM sleep accounts for only about 30% of the baby's sleep. By 2–3 years, REM sleep drops off to about 20–25% (Salzarulo & Ficca, 2002). There is a dramatic falling off in the total number of hours spent in sleep as we develop (Blumberg & Seelke, 2010). Figure 4.8 shows that most of the drop-off can be attributed to less REM sleep.

What is the function of REM sleep in neonates? Research with humans and other animals, including kittens and rat pups, suggests that the brain requires a certain amount of activity for the creation of proteins that are involved in the development of neurons and synapses (Blumberg & Seelke, 2010). Brain activity can be stimulated by internal or external sources. In older children and adults, external sources of stimulation are provided by activity, by a vast and shifting array of sensory impressions, and, perhaps, by thought processes during the waking state. The neonate, however, spends its brief waking periods largely isolated from the kaleidoscope of events of the world outside and is not likely to be lost in deep thought. Thus, in the waking state, the brain may not be provided with the needed stimulation. Perhaps the neonate compensates by spending relatively more time in REM sleep, which most closely parallels the waking state in terms of brain waves. While infants are in REM sleep, internal stimulation spurs the brain on to appropriate development. Preterm babies spend an even greater proportion of their time in REM sleep than full-term babies, perhaps—goes the argument—because they require relatively greater stimulation of the brain.

Why Do Babies Cry? What Can Be Done to Soothe Them?

No discussion of the sleeping and waking states of the neonate would be complete without mentioning crying—a comment that parents will view as an understatement. I have known first-time parents who have attempted to follow an imaginary 11th commandment: "The baby shall not cry." Guess what? They fail.

The main reason babies cry seems to be simple enough. Studies suggest a one-word answer: pain (Out et al., 2010).

Some parents have entered into conflict with hospital nurses who tell them not to worry when their babies are crying on the other side of the nursery's glass partition. Nurses often tell the parents that their babies must cry because crying helps clear their respiratory systems of fluids that linger from the amniotic sac and also stimulates the circulatory system.

On the other hand, let us consider some classic longitudinal research conducted by Silvia Bell and Mary Ainsworth (1972). These researchers followed the interactions of 26 mother–infant pairs and found that a consistent and prompt maternal response to crying is connected with decreases in crying. Close physical contact appears to be the most helpful maternal response (Douglas & Hill, 2011). Crying is apparently expressive initially, but as infants develop cognitively and learn that crying can lead to physical contact with a caregiver, it can become a form of communication. These findings appear to oppose the common view that responding to a crying baby "spoils" the baby.

Apparently, at least some crying among babies is universal (Barr et al., 2015). Some scholars have suggested that crying may be a primitive language, but it is not. Languages contain units and groupings of sounds that symbolize objects and events. Crying does not. Still, as noted by Bell and Ainsworth, crying appears to be both expressive and functional. Crying serves as an infant's expressive response to unpleasant feelings and also stimulates caretakers to do something to help. Crying thus communicates something, even though it is not a form of language. Crying may also communicate the identity of the crier across distance. Cries have multiple markers of individuality, and they may signal to parents and other caretakers the location of their infant in a group.

Before parenthood, many people wonder whether they will be able to recognize the meaning of their babies' cries, but it usually does not take them long. Parents typically learn to distinguish cries that signify hunger, anger, and pain. A sudden, loud, insistent cry associated with flexing and kicking of the legs may indicate colic—that is, pain resulting from gas or other sources of distress in the digestive tract. The baby may seem to hold its breath for a few moments, then gasp and begin to cry again. Crying from colic can be severe and persistent—lasting for hours, although cries generally seem to settle into a pattern after a while (Barr et al., 2005; Gudmundsson, 2010). Much to the relief of parents, colic tends to disappear by the third to sixth month, as a baby's digestive system matures.

Parents and other people, including children, have similar bodily responses to infant crying: increases in heart rate, blood pressure, and sweating (Reijneveld et al., 2004). Infant crying makes them feel irritated and anxious and motivates them to run to the baby to try to relieve the distress. The pitch of an infant's cries appears to provide information (Zeifman, 2004). Adults perceive high-pitched crying as more urgent, distressing, and sick sounding than low-pitched crying (Out et al., 2010).

Certain high-pitched cries, when prolonged, may signify health problems. For example, the cries of chronically distressed infants differ from those of normal infants in both rhythm and pitch. Patterns of crying may be indicative of such problems as chromosomal abnormalities, infections, fetal malnutrition, and exposure to narcotics (Douglas & Hill, 2011). A striking example of the link between crying and a health problem is the syndrome called cri du chat, French for "cry of the cat." This is a genetic disorder that produces abnormalities in the brain, atypical facial features, and a high-pitched, squeaky cry.

There are certain patterns of crying. For example, peaks of crying appear to be concentrated in the late afternoon and early evening (McGlaughlin & Grayson, 2001). Although some cries may seem extreme and random at first, they tend to settle into a pattern that is recognizable to most parents. Infants seem to produce about the same number of crying bouts during the first 9 months or so, but the duration of the bouts grows briefer, by half, during this period (IJzendoorn & Hubbard, 2000).

Soothing

Now that you are an expert on the causes and patterns of crying, you might be able to develop some ideas about how to soothe infants who are crying. Skin-to-skin physical contact with the infant is soothing (Hane et al., 2015). Sucking also seems to function as a built-in tranquilizer. Sucking on a pacifier decreases crying and agitated movement in neonates who have not yet had the opportunity to feed (Moon et al., 2011). Therefore, the soothing function of sucking need not be learned through experience. However, sucking (drinking) a sweet solution also appears to have a soothing effect (Stevens et al., 2005). Can it be that even babies are programmed to enjoy "comfort food"?

Parents find many other ways to soothe infants: patting, caressing and rocking, swaddling, and speaking to them in a soft voice. Parents then usually try to find the specific cause of the distress by offering a bottle or pacifier or checking the diaper. These responses to a crying infant are shown by parents in many cultures, such as those of the United States, France, and Japan.

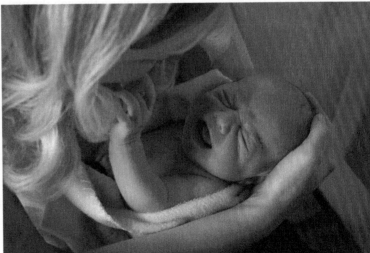

Misty Bedwell/Design Pics Inc/Alamy

Soothing How can a crying baby be soothed? Picking the baby up, talking to it quietly, patting, stroking, and rocking all seem to have calming effects.

Learning occurs quickly during the soothing process. Parents learn by trial and error what types of embraces and movements are likely to soothe their infants. And infants learn quickly that crying is followed by being picked up or other forms of intervention. Parents sometimes worry that if they pick up the crying baby quickly, they are reinforcing the baby's crying. In this way, they believe, the child may become spoiled and find it progressively more difficult to engage in self-soothing to get to sleep.

Fortunately, as infants mature and learn, crying tends to be replaced by less upsetting verbal requests for intervention. Among adults, of course, soothing techniques take very different forms, including presenting a bouquet of flowers or admitting that one started the argument.

4.7 Sudden Infant Death Syndrome (SIDS)

What is SIDS? What are the risk factors for SIDS? **Sudden infant death syndrome (SIDS)**—also known as crib death—is a disorder of infancy that apparently strikes while the baby is sleeping. In the typical case, a baby goes to sleep, apparently in perfect health, and is found dead the next morning. There is no sign that the baby struggled or was in pain.

> **TRUTH OR FICTION REVISITED:** It is true that more children die from sudden infant death syndrome (SIDS) than die from cancer, heart disease, pneumonia, child abuse, HIV/AIDS, cystic fibrosis, and muscular dystrophy combined (Lipsitt, 2003).

The incidence of SIDS has been declining, in part because some cases of SIDS have been reattributed to accidental suffocation. Even so, some 2,000–3,000 infants in the United States still die each year of SIDS. It is the most common cause of death during the first year, and most of these deaths occur between 2 and 5 months of age (Käll & Lagercrantz, 2012). New parents frequently live in dread of SIDS and check regularly through the night to see whether their babies are breathing. It is not abnormal, by the way, for babies occasionally to suspend breathing for a moment.

SIDS is more common among the following:

- Babies aged 2–4 months
- Babies who are put to sleep on their stomachs or their sides (sleeping prone decreases the oxygen supply to the brain [Wong et al., 2011])
- Premature and low birth weight infants
- Male babies
- Babies in families of lower socioeconomic status
- Bottle-fed babies (Hauck et al., 2011)
- African American babies
- Babies of teenage mothers
- Babies whose mothers smoked during or after pregnancy or whose mothers used narcotics during pregnancy

sudden infant death syndrome (SIDS) The death, while sleeping, of apparently healthy babies who stop breathing for unknown medical reasons. Also called crib death.

The Children's Hospital Boston Study

Perhaps the most compelling study to date was led by health professionals at the Children's Hospital Boston and published in *The Journal of the American*

Medical Association (Paterson et al., 2006). This study focused on an area in the brainstem called the **medulla** (see Figure 4.9 ■), which is involved in basic functions such as breathing and the sleep-wake cycle. Among other things, the medulla causes us to breathe if we are in need of oxygen. The researchers compared the medullas of babies who died from SIDS with those of babies who died at the same age from other causes. They found that the medullas of the babies who died from SIDS were less sensitive to the brain chemical **serotonin**, a chemical that helps keep the medulla responsive. The problem was particularly striking in the brains of boys, which could account for the sex difference in the incidence of SIDS.

What precautions should you take to guard against SIDS if you are a new parent? Following are some suggestions from the American Academy of Pediatrics (2012):

- Place your baby to sleep on his back for every sleep.
- Place your baby to sleep on a firm sleep surface. To learn more about crib safety, visit the Consumer Product Safety Commission website at www.cpsc.gov.
- Keep soft objects, loose bedding, and any objects that could increase the risk of entrapment, suffocation, or strangulation out of the crib.
- Place your baby to sleep in the same room where you sleep but not in the same bed.
- Breastfeed as much and for as long as you can.
- Schedule and go to all well-child visits.
- Keep your baby away from smokers and places where people smoke.
- Do not let your baby get too hot.
- Offer a pacifier at nap time and bedtime.
- Do not use home cardiorespiratory monitors to help reduce the risk of SIDS.
- Do not use products that claim to reduce the risk of SIDS.

Perhaps within a few years we will have a screening test for SIDS and a method for preventing or controlling it. In the next chapter, we will continue to follow physical development over the first 2 years.

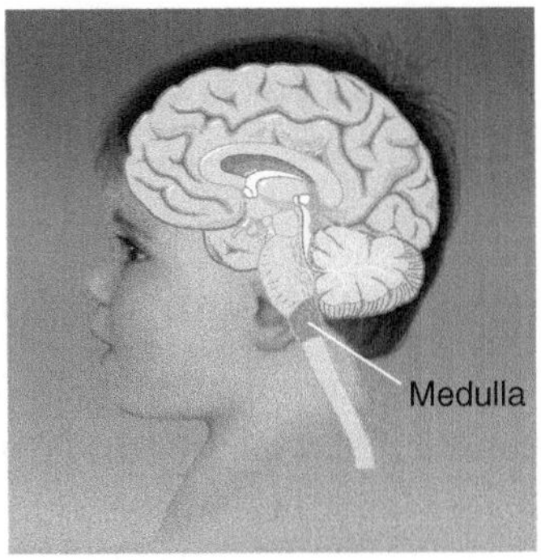

Figure 4.9 ■ The Medulla
Research by a team at the Children's Hospital Boston suggests that sudden infant death syndrome (SIDS) may be caused by a relatively low level of sensitivity of the medulla to the brain chemical serotonin.
© Cengage Learning®

medulla A part of the brain stem that regulates vital and automatic functions such as breathing and the sleep–wake cycle.

serotonin A neurotransmitter that is involved in the responsiveness of the medulla, emotional responses such as depression, and motivational responses such as hunger.

Section Review

18. In the United States today, the neonate's overall level of health is usually evaluated at birth according to the _____ scale.

19. In the _____ reflex, the baby turns the head and mouth toward a stimulus that strokes the cheek, chin, or corner of the mouth.

20. Neonates are rather _____ (nearsighted or farsighted?).

21. Neonates _____ (do or do not?) prefer their mothers' voices to those of other women.

22. As babies mature, they spend a _____ (greater or smaller?) percentage of their time sleeping in REM sleep.

23. _____ is the most common cause of death in infants between the ages of 1 month and 1 year.

Reflect & Relate: Have you or a family member had to adjust to the waking and sleeping patterns of a baby? Do you think it is normal to occasionally resent being awakened repeatedly throughout the night? Explain.

Chapter Review

How Is Labor Initiated?

The first uterine contractions are called Braxton-Hicks contractions or false labor contractions. A day or so before labor begins, some blood spotting can occur in vaginal secretions. At about this time, 1 woman in 10 has a rush of amniotic fluid from the vagina. The initiation of labor may be triggered by secretion of hormones by the fetus. Maternal hormones stimulate contractions strong enough to expel the baby.

4.2 **What Are the Stages of Childbirth?**

Childbirth begins with the onset of regular contractions of the uterus, which cause the cervix to become effaced and dilated. The first stage may last from a few hours to more than a day. During transition, the cervix is almost fully dilated and the head of the fetus moves into the birth canal. The second stage begins when the baby appears at the opening of the birth canal. It ends with the birth of the baby. Once the baby's head emerges from the mother's body, mucus is suctioned from its mouth so that breathing is not obstructed. When the baby is breathing on its own, the umbilical cord is clamped and severed. During this stage, the placenta separates from the uterine wall and is expelled along with fetal membranes.

4.3 **What Methods of Childbirth Are in Use Today?**

General anesthesia puts the woman to sleep, but it decreases the strength of uterine contractions and lowers the responsiveness of the neonate. Regional or local anesthetics deaden pain in parts of the body without putting the mother to sleep. HypnoBirthing teaches mothers how to relax during childbirth and encourages focusing on pleasant imagery. Biofeedback provides a woman with information about what is happening in her body. Prepared childbirth teaches women to dissociate uterine contractions from pain and fear by associating other responses, such as relaxation, with contractions. A coach aids the mother in the delivery room. In a C-section, the baby is delivered surgically through the abdomen. C-sections are most likely to be recommended if the baby is large or in distress or if the mother's pelvis is small or she is tired or weak. Herpes and HIV infections in the birth canal can be avoided by C-section. Home birth is generally safe for healthy women who have already borne children.

4.4 **What Kinds of Birth Problems Are There?**

Prenatal oxygen deprivation can be fatal if prolonged; it can also impair development of the nervous system, leading to cognitive and motor problems. A baby is preterm when birth occurs at or before 37 weeks of gestation. A baby has a low birth weight when it weighs less than 5½ pounds (about 2,500 grams). A baby who is low in birth weight but born at full term is said to be small for dates. The chances of having preterm babies rise with multiple births, such as twins. The risks associated with prematurity include infant mortality and delayed neurological and motor development. Preterm babies are relatively thin and often have vernix on the skin and lanugo. Sucking and breathing reflexes may be weak. The walls of air sacs in the lungs may stick together, leading to respiratory distress. Preterm babies usually remain in the hospital in incubators. Preterm infants profit from early stimulation just as full-term babies do. Parents often do not treat preterm neonates as well as they treat full-term neonates, perhaps because preterm infants are less attractive and have irritating, high-pitched cries.

4.5 **What Do We Know about the Postpartum Period?**

Women may encounter the baby blues, postpartum depression, and—very rarely—postpartum psychosis during the postpartum period. These problems are found around the world and probably reflect hormonal changes following birth, although stress can play a role. High self-esteem and social support help women manage these adjustment problems. Early research by Klaus and Kennell suggested that the first few hours after birth present a "maternal-sensitive" period during which women's hormone levels particularly dispose them to "bond" with their neonates. However, the study confounded the effects of extra time with their babies with the effects of special attention from health professionals.

4.6 What Are the Characteristics of Neonates? How Do We Assess Their Health?

The neonate's overall health is usually evaluated with the Apgar scale. The Brazelton Neonatal Behavioral Assessment Scale also screens neonates for behavioral and neurological problems. The rooting and sucking reflexes are basic to survival. Other key reflexes include the startle reflex, the grasping reflex, the stepping reflex, the Babinski reflex, and the tonic-neck reflex. Most reflexes disappear or are replaced by voluntary behavior within months. Neonates are nearsighted. Neonates visually detect movement, and many track movement. Fetuses respond to sound months before they are born. Neonates are particularly responsive to the sounds and rhythms of speech. The nasal preferences of neonates are similar to those of older children and adults. Neonates prefer sweet solutions and find them soothing. The sensations of skin against skin are also soothing and may contribute to the formation of bonds of attachment. Neonates are capable of classical and operant conditioning. For example, they can be conditioned to blink their eyes in response to a tone. Neonates spend two-thirds of their time sleeping. Nearly all neonates distribute sleep through naps. Neonates spend about half their time sleeping in REM sleep, but as time goes on, REM sleep accounts for less of their sleep. REM sleep may be connected with brain development. Babies cry mainly because of pain and discomfort. Crying may communicate the identity of the crier across distance, as well as hunger, anger, pain, and the presence of health problems. Pacifiers help because sucking is soothing. Parents also try picking babies up, patting, caressing and rocking them, and speaking to them in a low voice.

4.7 What Is Sudden Infant Death Syndrome (SIDS)? How Can We Prevent It?

SIDS is a disorder of infancy that apparently strikes while the baby is sleeping. SIDS is the most common cause of death in infants between the ages of 1 month and 1 year. SIDS is more common among babies who are put to sleep in the prone position, preterm and low birth weight infants, male infants, and infants whose mothers smoked during or after pregnancy or whose mothers used narcotics during pregnancy.

Key Terms

term   112
Braxton-Hicks contractions   112
prostaglandins   112
oxytocin   112
neonate   112
efface   113
dilate   113
episiotomy   113
transition   113
midwife   116
anesthesia   116
natural childbirth   117
Lamaze method   118
cesarean section   119
anoxia   121
hypoxia   121
schizophrenia   121
breech presentation   121
preterm   121

small for dates   121
lanugo   122
vernix   122
respiratory distress syndrome   123
incubator   123
postpartum period   127
postpartum depression (PPD)   127
bonding   129
Apgar scale   131
NBAS   131
NNNS   132
reflex   133
neural   133
rooting reflex   133
Moro reflex   133
grasping reflex   133
stepping reflex   134
Babinski reflex   134
tonic-neck reflex   134

visual acuity   134
visual accommodation   136
convergence   136
intensity   136
saturation   136
hue   136
rods   137
cones   137
amplitude   137
pitch   137
rapid eye movement (REM) sleep   141
non–rapid eye movement (non-REM)
   sleep   141
electroencephalograph (EEG)   141
sudden infant death syndrome
   (SIDS)   144
medulla   145
serotonin   145

5

Infancy: Physical Development

TruthorFiction?

T | F The head of the newborn child doubles in length by adulthood, but the legs increase in length by about five times. **p. 150**

T | F Infants triple their birth weight within a year. **p. 152**

T | F Breastfeeding helps prevent obesity later in life. **p. 158**

T | F A newborn's brain weighs about 25% of its adult weight, but grows to some 70% of its adult weight by the child's first birthday. **p. 164**

T | F The cerebral cortex—the outer layer of the brain that is vital to human thought and reasoning—is only one-eighth of an inch thick. **p. 165**

T | F Native American Hopi infants spend the first year of life strapped to a board, yet they begin to walk at about the same time as children who are reared in other cultures. **p. 169**

T | F Infants need to have experience crawling before they develop a fear of heights. **p. 174**

I am a keen observer of children—of my own, that is. From my experiences, I have derived the following basic principles of physical development:

- Just when you think your child has finally begun to make regular gains in weight, she or he will begin to lose weight or go for months without gaining an ounce.
- No matter how early your child sits up or starts to walk, your neighbor's child will do it earlier.
- Children first roll over when one parent is watching but will steadfastly refuse to repeat it when the other parent is called in.
- Children begin to get into everything before you get childproof latches on the cabinets.
- Every advance in locomotor ability provides your child with new ways to get hurt.
- Children display their most exciting developmental milestones when you don't have the camera or can't get the video function of the cell phone to work.

More seriously, in this chapter, we discuss various aspects of physical development during the first 2 years. We examine changes in physical growth, the development of the brain and the nervous system, motor development, and the development and coordination of sensory and perceptual capabilities, such as vision and hearing.

Tetra Images/Getty Images

5.1 Physical Growth and Development

What a fascinating creature the newborn is: tiny, seemingly helpless, apparently oblivious to its surroundings, yet perfectly formed and fully capable of letting its caregivers know when it is hungry, thirsty, or uncomfortable. And what a fascinating creature is this same child 2 years later: running, climbing, playing, talking, hugging, and kissing.

It is hard to believe that only 2 short years can bring about such remarkable changes. It seems that nearly every day brings a new accomplishment. Yet, as we will see, not all infants share equally in the explosion of positive developments. Therefore, we will also be mentioning some developmental problems and what can be done about them.

What Are the Sequences of Physical Development? Head First?

During the first 2 years, children make enormous strides in physical growth and development. In this section, we will explore sequences of physical development, changes in height and weight, and nutrition. Three key sequences of physical development are cephalocaudal development, proximodistal development, and differentiation (see Concept Review 5.1).

Cephalocaudal Development

Development proceeds from the head to the lower parts of the body. When we consider the central role of the brain, which is contained within the skull, the cephalocaudal sequence appears quite logical. The brain regulates essential functions, such as heartbeat. Through the secretion of hormones, the brain also regulates the growth and development of the body and influences basic drives, such as hunger and thirst.

The head develops more rapidly than the rest of the body during the embryonic stage. By 8 weeks after conception, the head makes up half the length of the embryo. The brain develops more rapidly than the spinal cord. Arm buds form before leg buds. Most newborn babies have a strong, well-defined sucking reflex, although their legs are spindly and their limbs move back and forth only in diffuse excitement or agitation. Infants can hold up their heads before they gain control over their arms, their torsos, and, finally, their legs. They can sit up before they can crawl and walk. When they first walk, they use their hands to hold onto a person or object for support.

Because they get off to a later start, the lower parts of the body must do relatively more growing to reach adult size.

TRUTH OR FICTION REVISITED: The head does double in length between birth and maturity, but the torso triples in length. The arms increase their length by about four times, but the legs and feet increase by about five times.

Proximodistal Development

Growth and development also proceed from the trunk outward—from the body's central axis toward the periphery. The proximodistal principle also makes sense.

Sequences of Physical Development

Cephalocaudal Development

Cephalocaudal means that development proceeds from the "head" to the "tail" or, in the case of humans, to the lower parts of the body. Cephalocaudal development gives the brain an opportunity to participate more fully in subsequent developments.

This photo shows that infants gain control over their hands and upper body before they gain control over their lower body.

Felix St. Clair Renard/Riser/Getty Images

Proximodistal Development

Proximodistal means that development proceeds from the trunk or central axis of the body outward. The brain and spine make up the central nervous system along the central axis of the body and are functional before the infant can control the arms and legs.

In this photo, you can see that the infant's arm is only slightly longer than her head. Compare this to the length of your own head and arm.

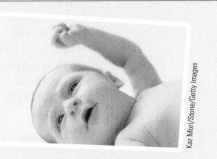

Kaz Mori/Stone/Getty Images

Differentiation

As children mature, physical reactions become less global and more specific. This infant engages in diffuse motor activity. Within a few months, he will be grasping for objects and holding onto them with a more and more sophisticated kind of grasp.

This photo shows that infants engage in diffuse motion before they begin to reach and grasp.

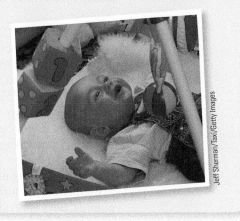

Jeff Sherman/Taxi/Getty Images

The brain and spinal cord follow a central axis down through the body, and it is essential that the nerves be developing before the infant can gain control over the arms and legs. Also, the life functions of the newborn baby—heartbeat, respiration, digestion, and elimination of wastes—are all carried out by organ systems close to the central axis. These must be in operation or ready to operate when the child is born.

In terms of motor development, infants gain control over their trunks and their shoulders before they can control their arms, hands, and fingers. They make clumsy swipes at objects with their arms before they can voluntarily grasp them with their hands. Infants can grab large objects before picking up tiny things with their fingers. Similarly, infants gain control over their hips and upper legs before they can direct their lower legs, feet, and toes.

Differentiation

As children mature, their behaviors become less loose and diffuse and more specific and distinct, a tendency called **differentiation**. If a neonate's finger is pricked or burned, he or she may withdraw the finger but also thrash about, cry, and show general signs of distress. Toddlers may also cry, show distress, and withdraw the finger, but they are less likely to thrash about wildly. Thus, the response to pain has become more specific. An older child or adult is also likely to withdraw the finger but is relatively less likely to wail and show general distress.

What Patterns of Growth Occur in Infancy?

The most dramatic gains in height and weight occur during prenatal development. Within a span of 9 months, children develop from a zygote that is about 1/175th of an inch long to a neonate that is about 20 inches in length. Weight increases by a factor of billions.

During the first year after birth, gains in height and weight are also dramatic, although not by the standards of prenatal gains. Infants usually double their birth weight in about 5 months and triple it by the first birthday (World Health Organization, 2010a, 2010b). Their height increases by about 50% in the first year, so a child whose length at birth was 20 inches is likely to be about 30 inches tall at 12 months.

> **TRUTH OR FICTION REVISITED:** It is true that infants triple their birth weight within a year. They usually double their birth weight in only 5 months.

Growth in infancy has long been viewed as a slow and steady process. Growth charts in pediatricians' offices resemble the smooth, continuous curves shown in Figure 5.1 ■. But research suggests that infants actually grow in spurts. It turns out that about 90% to 95% of the time, they are not growing at all. One study measured the heights of infants throughout their first 21 months (Lampl, 2012). The infants remained the same size for 2 to 63 days and then shot up in length from one-fifth of an inch (0.5 centimeter) to a full inch (2.5 centimeters) in less than 24 hours. Parents who swear that their infants sometimes consume enormous amounts of food and grow overnight may not be exaggerating.

Infants grow another 4 to 6 inches during the second year and gain another 4 to 7 pounds. Boys generally reach half their adult height by their second birthday. Girls, however, mature more quickly than boys and are likely to reach half their adult height at the age of 18 months (World Health Organization, 2010a, 2010b). The growth rates of taller-than-average infants, as a group, tend to slow down. Those of shorter-than-average infants, as a group, tend to speed up. This is not to suggest that there is no relationship between infant and adult heights or that we all wind up in an average range. Tall infants, as a group, wind up taller than short infants, but (in most cases) not by as much as seemed likely during infancy.

Changes in Body Proportions

In rendering the human form, Greek classical sculptors followed the "golden section" rule: The length of the head equals one-eighth the height of the body (including the head). This may be the ideal of human beauty, but the reality is that among adults,

differentiation The process by which behaviors and physical structures become more specialized.

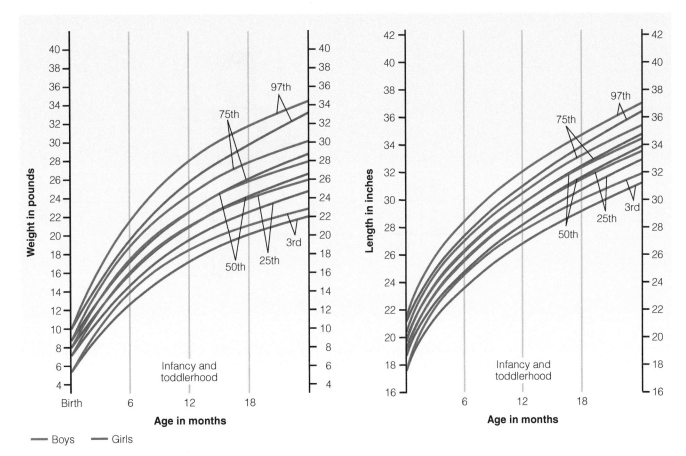

— Boys   — Girls

Figure 5.1 ■ Growth Curves for Weight and Height (Length) from Birth to Age 2 Years
The curves indicate the percentiles for weight and length at different ages. Lines labeled 97th
show the height and weight of children who are taller and heavier than 97% of children of a
particular age. Lines marked 50th indicate the height and weight of the average child of a given
age: Half their agemates are shorter and lighter, and half are heavier and taller. Lines labeled
3rd designate children who are taller and heavier than only 3% of children their age, and so on.
Source: Kuczmarski et al. (2000, Figures 1-4).

the length of the head actually varies from about one-eighth to one-tenth of the
body's height. Among children, the head is proportionately larger (see Figure 5.2 ■).

Development proceeds in a cephalocaudal manner. A few weeks after conception, an embryo is almost all head. At the beginning of the fetal stage, the head is
about half the length of the fetus. In the neonate, the head is about one-fourth the

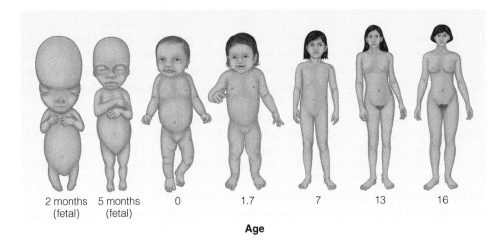

2 months   5 months   0   1.7   7   13   16
(fetal)   (fetal)

Age

**Figure 5.2 ■ Changes in the
Proportions of the Body**
Development proceeds in a
cephalocaudal sequence. The
head is proportionately larger
among younger children.
© Cengage Learning®

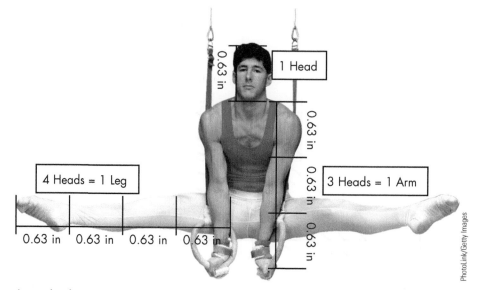

As we develop, our body proportions change.

length of the body. The head gradually diminishes in relation to the rest of the body, even though it doubles in size by adulthood.

Among adults, the arms are nearly three times the length of the head. The legs are about four times as long—nearly half the length of the body. Among neonates, the arms and legs are about equal in length. Each is only about one and a half times the length of the head. By the first birthday, the neck has begun to lengthen visibly, as have the arms and legs. The arms grow more rapidly than the legs do at first (an example of the cephalocaudal trend), and by the second birthday, the arms are actually longer than the legs. The legs then grow more rapidly, soon catching up with and surpassing the arms in length.

We have described typical growth patterns. Most infants follow these patterns and thrive. Some, however, do not.

Failure to Thrive

Haley is 4 months old. Her mother is breastfeeding her, as she puts it, "all the time," because Haley is not gaining weight. Not gaining weight for a while is normal enough, but Haley is also irritable and she feeds fitfully, sometimes refusing the breast entirely. Her pediatrician is evaluating her for a syndrome called **failure to thrive (FTT)**.

We live in one of the world's most bountiful nations. Few have trouble accessing food. Nevertheless, a number of infants, such as Haley, show FTT, which is a serious disorder that impairs growth in infancy and early childhood (Olsen et al., 2007). FTT is sometimes a fuzzy diagnosis. Olsen and his colleagues (2007) identify seven criteria for diagnosing FTT, including low weight for age and low body mass index (BMI). They found that 27% of infants meet one or more of these criteria during the first year of life, but this percentage is probably misleadingly high because most infants meet only one of the standards.

Historically, researchers have spoken of biologically based ("organic") FTT versus nonbiologically based ("nonorganic") FTT. The idea is that in organic FTT, an underlying health problem accounts for the failure to obtain or make use of adequate nutrition. Nonorganic FTT (abbreviated NOFTT in the research literature) apparently has psychological roots, social roots, or both (Jaffe, 2011). In either case, the infant does not make normal gains in weight and size.

Regardless of the cause or causes, feeding problems are central to FTT. Research has shown that infants with FTT tend to be introduced to solid and finger foods

failure to thrive (FTT) A disorder of impaired growth in infancy and early childhood characterized by failure to gain weight within normal limits.

later than other children. As in Haley's case, they are more likely to be described as variable eaters and less often as being hungry (Llewellyn, 2011). Infants with FTT tend to show feeding problems, including slow feeding and weak sucking (Hollen et al., 2014). FTT is linked not only to slow physical growth but also to cognitive, behavioral, and emotional problems (Jaffe, 2011). For example, at the age of 2 to 12 months, infants with FTT express more negative feelings, vocalize less, and often refuse to make eye contact with adults (Steward, 2001). Another study found that at the age of 8½, children who had been diagnosed with FTT at the median age of 20 months remained smaller, were less cognitively advanced, and were more emotionally and behaviorally disturbed than typical children (Dykman et al., 2001). They wind up shorter and lighter than their peers at the ages of 8 and 12 (Black et al., 2007; Drewett et al., 2006).

Many investigators believe that deficiencies in caregiver–child interaction play a key role in FTT (Fleisher, 2014), leading to *reactive-attachment disorder*. For example, compared with mothers of healthy infants, mothers of infants with FTT show fewer adaptive social interactions (they are less likely to "go with the flow") and fewer positive feelings toward their infants. The mothers also terminate feedings more arbitrarily (Robinson et al., 2001). Perhaps as a consequence, children with FTT are less likely than other children to be securely attached to their mothers (Benoit & Coolbear, 2004). Why are the mothers of children with FTT less likely to help their children feel secure? Many have a large number of children, an unstable home environment, or psychological problems of their own (Mackner et al., 2003).

Because FTT often results from a combination of factors, treatment may not be easy. Children with FTT need both nutritional support and attention to possible adjustment problems (Simonelli et al., 2005). It turns out that Haley's parents will profit from both personal counseling and advice on relating to Haley.

The condition **marasmus** is a form of FTT that is characterized by wasting away due to a diet low in essential nutrients. It typically appears in the first year of life. In some cases, a mother who is breastfeeding does not produce enough milk. Bottle feeding may also be inadequate. In any event, marasmus is life-threatening.

Catch-Up Growth

A child's growth can be slowed from its genetically predetermined course by many organic factors, including illness and dietary deficiency. However, once the problem is alleviated, the child's rate of growth frequently accelerates and returns to approximate the normal course from which it had been deflected (Parsons et al., 2011). The tendency to return to one's genetically determined pattern of growth is referred to as **canalization**. Once Haley's parents receive counseling and once Haley's FTT is overcome, Haley will put on weight rapidly and catch up to the norms for her age.

Nutrition: Fueling Development

The overall nutritional status of children in the United States is good compared with that of children in most other countries (Save the Children, 2014). The nutritional status of poor U.S. children has improved through federal programs such as the Food Stamp Program; the Supplemental Nutrition Program for Women, Infants, and Children (WIC); the Child and Adult Care Food Program; and the National School Lunch and School Breakfast programs. Even so, infants and young children from low-income families are more likely than other children to display signs of poor nutrition, such as anemia and FTT (Bucholz et al., 2011; National Center for Children in Poverty, 2012).

marasmus A wasted, potentially lethal body condition caused by inadequate nutrition and characterized by painful thinness.

canalization The tendency of growth rates to return to genetically determined patterns after undergoing environmentally induced change.

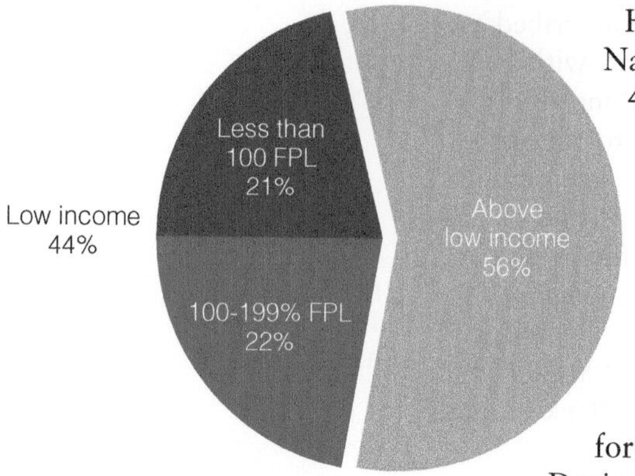

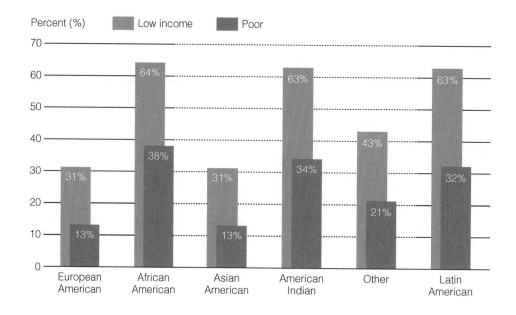

Figure 5.3 ■ Percentage of U.S. Children Living in Families with Low Income Levels, Including Those Who Live Below the Federal Poverty Level (FPL)[1]

Source: National Center for Children in Poverty. (2012). *Basic Facts about Low-Income Children, 2010.* http://www.nccp .org/publications/pub_1049.html. Accessed May 17, 2015.

Figure 5.4 ■ Percentage of Children in Low-Income and Poor Families by Race/Ethnicity

Source: National Center for Children in Poverty (www.nccp.org). http://www.nccp.org/publications/pub_1049.html. Accessed May 17, 2015.

How many children live in low-income families? According to the National Center for Children in Poverty (Addy & Wight, 2012), almost 44% of children live either below the federal poverty level (21%) or between the federal poverty level and twice the federal poverty level (22%) (see Figure 5.3 ■). Children make up 24% of the U.S. population, but they make up 34% of all people living in poverty.

According to the National Center for Children in Poverty (2012), the numbers include *the majority* of African American children, Latin American children, and Native American children (see Figure 5.4 ■).

From birth, infants should be fed either breast milk or an iron-fortified infant formula. Solid foods are often introduced at 4–6 months. During the first 4 months, the tongue-thrust reflex protects the infant from choking by pushing out solid substances. But between 4 and 6 months, the reflex diminishes gradually, giving solids a chance of being swallowed (Sears, 2009). At 4–6 months, the infant can also indicate hunger by leaning forward, and indicate fullness by turning away from food. Nevertheless, the American Academy of Pediatrics (2012) recommends that infants be fed breast milk throughout the first year and longer, if possible. (For more information, visit the American Academy of Pediatrics at www.aap.org.) The first solid food is usually iron-enriched cereal, followed by strained fruits, then vegetables, and finally meats, poultry, and fish. Finger foods such as teething biscuits are introduced in the latter part of the first year.

---

[1] What was the federal poverty level (FPL) in 2011?

- $22,350 for a family of four
- $18,530 for a family of three
- $14,710 for a family of two

Is a poverty-level income enough to support a family?
Research suggests that on average, families need an income equal to about two times the federal poverty level to meet their most basic needs. Families with incomes below this level are referred to as low income:

- $44,700 for a family of four
- $37,060 for a family of three
- $29,420 for a family of two

FOOD TIMELINE FOR THE FIRST TWO YEARS[2]

All babies are unique individuals. Talk to your doctor or a registered dietitian about the nutrient-rich foods your baby needs and when to introduce them. The following are typical (but not required!) age ranges for moving infants from breast milk to table foods:

- Birth to 6 Months: Babies obtain all the nutrients they need from breast milk for the first 6 months. Infant formula is an acceptable alternative when mothers decide to decrease or discontinue breastfeeding. You should not give your baby cow's milk until after the first birthday.

- By 4 to 6 Months: Even though most babies are ready to eat solid foods now, they will continue to obtain most of their calories, protein, vitamins, and minerals from breast milk or infant formula. Parents can introduce iron-fortified infant cereal such as rice or barley mixed with breast milk or formula. Infants can also eat "Number 1" fruits and vegetables (check the product packaging for the number). Introduce one vegetable or fruit at a time so that the cause of a potential negative reaction is discernible.

- By 6 to 8 Months: This is another appropriate time to begin puréed or mashed fruits and vegetables, and also meats. Infants can now eat "Number 2" foods (check the packaging). Again, gradually introduce single-item foods one at a time. Watch carefully for any reactions such as diarrhea, vomiting, or unusual rashes.

- By 7 to 10 Months: Babies are usually ready to begin feeding themselves with finger foods, such as dry cereal or teething biscuits. Some infants can begin to use a cup for water, but expect spills.

- By 8 to 12 Months: At this stage, most infants are ready for soft or cooked table foods. We had been feeding our first daughter Allyn nothing but breast milk, but at the age of 9 months we went to a delicatessen, where she suddenly grabbed a pickle and wouldn't put it down despite our urgings. She had no negative reaction, and (needless to say?) she began eating foods other than breast milk at that time.

- From 1 to 2 Years: Babies continue developing eating skills. They feed themselves and enjoy the same foods as the rest of the family. Choking on firm, round foods is a risk, so cut these foods into smaller, ¼-inch squares.

When in doubt, parents should check with their pediatrician. What is good for adults is not always good for infants. Parents who are on low-fat, high-fiber diets to ward off cardiovascular problems, cancer, and other health problems should not assume that the same diet is most healthful for infants.

What Are the Pros and Cons of Breastfeeding vs. Bottle Feeding?

In many developing nations, women have no choice: If their infants are going to be nourished, they will have to breastfeed. Yet even in developed nations, where formula is readily available, breast milk today is considered by most health professionals to be the "medical gold standard" and by many—perhaps most—mothers to be the "moral gold standard" (Walker, 2010).

Breastfeeding is, of course, the "natural" way to nourish a baby. Infant formulas were developed in the 1930s. Over the next several decades, the incidence of breastfeeding declined because women were entering the workforce, bottle feeding was seen as "scientific," and the women's movement encouraged women to become liberated from traditional roles. Thus, breastfeeding has political and social aspects as well as nutritional aspects (Bakalar, 2014). Much of the decision whether to breastfeed involves domestic and occupational arrangements, day care, social support, reactions to public breastfeeding, and beliefs about mother–infant bonding.

---

[2] Adapted from Academy of Nutrition and Dietetics. (2012). *Getting Started on Eating Right.* http://www.eatright.org/Public/content.aspx?id58044. Accessed February 17, 2012.

SelectStock/Getty Images

African American women are less likely than European American women to breastfeed, which may be connected with higher rates of infant mortality, asthma, diabetes, and obesity among black children (Black Breast-Feeding, 2015). In fact, breastfeeding appears to be associated with lower rates of obesity when the children reach 35 years of age (Fergusson et al., 2014). A survey of 35 African American and Latin American mothers or pregnant adolescents (ages 12 to 19) found that those who recognized the benefits of breastfeeding were more likely to do it (Hannon et al., 2000). They reported benefits such as promoting mother–infant bonding and the infant's health. A survey of 349 Latin American mothers found that younger mothers and mothers born in the United States were more likely to breastfeed (Newton, 2009). Barriers to breastfeeding include fear of pain, embarrassment by public exposure, and unease with the act itself. However, an influential person—such as the woman's partner or mother—often encourages the mother to breastfeed (Hunter & Cattelona, 2014). Community support through volunteer workers ("Birth Sisters"), visiting nurses, and community clinics also encourages women to breastfeed. Better-educated women are more likely to breastfeed, even among low-income women (Sloan et al., 2006).

TRUTH OR FICTION REVISITED: Drinking breast milk is related to a better chance of avoiding obesity later in life. Perhaps this is because breast milk is lower in fat than whole milk.

In any event, breastfeeding has become more popular during the past generation, largely because of increased knowledge of its health benefits, even among women at the lower end of the socioeconomic spectrum. Most American mothers—more than 70%—breastfeed their children, at least for a while, although there are significant differences state by state, with Oregon and Vermont being among the highest breastfeeding rates and Louisiana, Mississippi, and West Virginia being among the lowest (Breastfeeding Report Card, 2014). However, only about 2 women in 5 continue to breastfeed after 6 months, and only 1 in 5 is still breastfeeding at 1 year (Breastfeeding, 2006). The American Academy of Pediatrics (2012), as noted, recommends that women breastfeed for a year or longer.

Many women bottle feed because they return to work after childbirth and are therefore unavailable (Mirkovic et al., 2014). Their partners, extended families, nannies, or child-care workers give their children bottles during the day. Some mothers pump their milk and bottle it for their children's use when they are away. Some parents bottle feed because doing so enables both parents to share in feeding around the clock. The father may not be equipped to breastfeed, but he can bottle feed. Even though bottle feeding requires preparing formulas, many women find it to be less troublesome.

Colostrum is an early form of breast milk that is produced late in pregnancy and following childbirth. It is high in proteins and carbohydrates but low in fat, thus packing a high level of nutrients into a low volume. It also carries many of the mother's antibodies, boosting the early functioning of the baby's immune system. Infants who are nourished by breast milk are less likely to develop obesity later in life.

kwashiorkor A form of protein–energy malnutrition in which the body may break down its own reserves of protein, resulting in enlargement of the stomach, swollen feet, and other symptoms.

WASTING AWAY FROM HUNGER

One in every 8 or 9 people in the world goes hungry (see Figure. 5.5 ■). Protein–energy malnutrition (PEM) is the most severe form of malnutrition. Protein is essential for growth, and food energy translates into calories. Here are a few facts about children and hunger (World Hunger Organization, 2012):

- In the developing world (largely in Africa and Asia), about 1 child in 3 under age 5 has stunted growth, and more than 90% of the world's hungry children live on one of these two continents.

- Children who are "wasting" have a markedly increased risk of death. About 13% of children under age 5 in the developing world are wasted, with 5% extremely wasted—some 26 million children.

- The main cause of hunger for children is poverty.

- Children may suffer from PEM before birth if their mother is malnourished.

- Malnutrition, also known as "the silent emergency," has contributed to about 60% of the 11 million deaths of children each year.

- Children with PEM suffer up to 160 days of illness per year.

In the condition known as **kwashiorkor**, the child may eat enough calories from starchy foods but does not take in enough protein. As a result, the body may metabolize its own reserves of protein, leading to enlargement of the stomach, swollen feet, a rash, and loss of hair (Ndekha, 2008). Irritability and lack of energy may follow.

The World Health Organization (2011) has issued step-by-step guidelines on the treatment of children with PEM in the clinical setting. These guidelines are being promoted for use worldwide by physicians, nurses, and all other frontline health workers. The guidelines for instruction include:

- Educating health workers on the extent and severity of PEM.

- Identifying children with severe malnutrition. Symptoms include hypoglycemia (shakiness resulting from low blood sugar levels), hypothermia, shock, dehydration, and severe anemia.

- Preparing appropriate feeding formulas and food supplements.

- Using antibiotics and other medicines to treat disease.

- Monitoring the child's intake of food and the child's waste products; preparing and using a weight chart.

- Monitoring the child's vital signs—pulse, respiration rate, and temperature—and being aware of signs of danger.

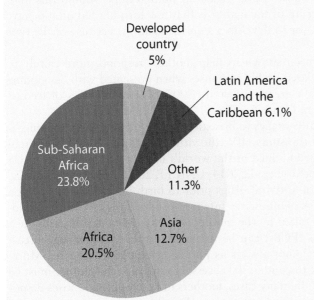

Developed country 5%

Latin America and the Caribbean 6.1%

Sub-Saharan Africa 23.8%

Other 11.3%

Africa 20.5%

Asia 12.7%

Figure 5.5 ■ Prevalence (%) of Undernourishment Around the World, 2012–2014
Source: http://www.worldhunger.org/articles/Learn/world%20 hunger%20facts%202002.htm#Number_of_hungry_people_in_ the_world. Accessed May 17, 2015.

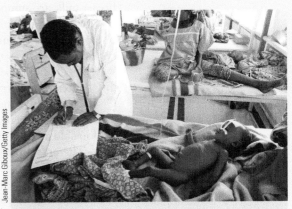

Jean-Marc Giboux/Getty Images

Kwashiorkor
In kwashiorkor, the enlargement of the stomach and other symptoms result from failure to take in adequate protein.

(continued on page 160)

- Bathing the child.
- Involving mothers in care so that they can continue care at home, including feeding and play activities (for purposes of stimulation); providing mothers with comprehensive instructions at discharge.

The mortality rate of children with PEM can be as high as 50%, but with adequate care, the rates can be reduced to less than 5%. For more information, contact the Department of Nutrition for Health and Development, World Health Organization, 1211 Geneva 27, Switzerland (phone: 141 22 791 2624/4342; fax: 141 22 791 4156).

Reflect: What can you do to help alleviate PEM in developing nations?

Breastfeeding also has health benefits for the mother: It reduces the risk of early breast cancer and ovarian cancer, and it builds the strength of bones, which can reduce the likelihood of the hip fractures that result from osteoporosis following menopause. Breastfeeding also helps shrink the uterus and lessens weight retention after delivery (American Academy of Pediatrics, 2015).

Human newborns prefer human milk to formula. An interesting study recruited breastfed and bottle-fed 4-day-old infants as subjects and presented them with the odors of human milk and formula (Marlier & Schaal, 2005). Those who were breastfed were presented with the odors of unfamiliar human milk—that is, milk from strangers. Preference was measured in terms of the direction in which the infants turned their heads and the intensity of their sucking movements. Although the responses of the infants were somewhat more complex than I am presenting here, both groups generally showed preference for human milk. Should this finding influence parents? The truth of the matter is that few formula-fed infants have been shown to refuse to eat (or to develop a sour disposition) because of the type of food.

Breastfeeding has also been shown to help mothers respond more calmly to stress, as defined by stress-related bodily responses when presented with demanding mental arithmetic problems (Mezzacappa et al., 2005). The advantages of feeding breast milk are summarized in Figure 5.6 ■.

There are also some disadvantages to breastfeeding. For example, breast milk is one of the bodily fluids that transmits HIV (the virus that causes AIDS). Researchers estimate that as many as one-third of the world's infants who have HIV/AIDS were infected in this manner (Rose et al., 2014; UNICEF, 2012). (However, as noted in Chapter 4, maternal use of antiviral drugs prior to birth in combination with a C-section vastly reduce the risk of mother-to-infant transmission of HIV during childbirth.) Alcohol, many drugs taken by the mother, and environmental hazards such as polychlorinated biphenyls (PCBs) can be transmitted to infants through breast milk. Therefore, breast milk is not always as pure as it would seem to be. Moreover, in order for breast milk to contain the necessary nutrients, the mother must be adequately nourished herself. In many cases, mothers in developing countries do not eat well enough to pass along proper nutrition to their infants.

Another disadvantage is that in breastfeeding, the mother assumes sole responsibility for nighttime feedings. She also must weather the physical demands of producing and expelling milk, a tendency for soreness in the breasts, and the inconvenience of being continuously available to meet the infant's feeding needs.

Breast milk remains the ideal food for a baby, even if the mother smokes (Breastfeeding, 2006). Although nicotine may be present in breast milk, harmful effects on the infant have not been noted.

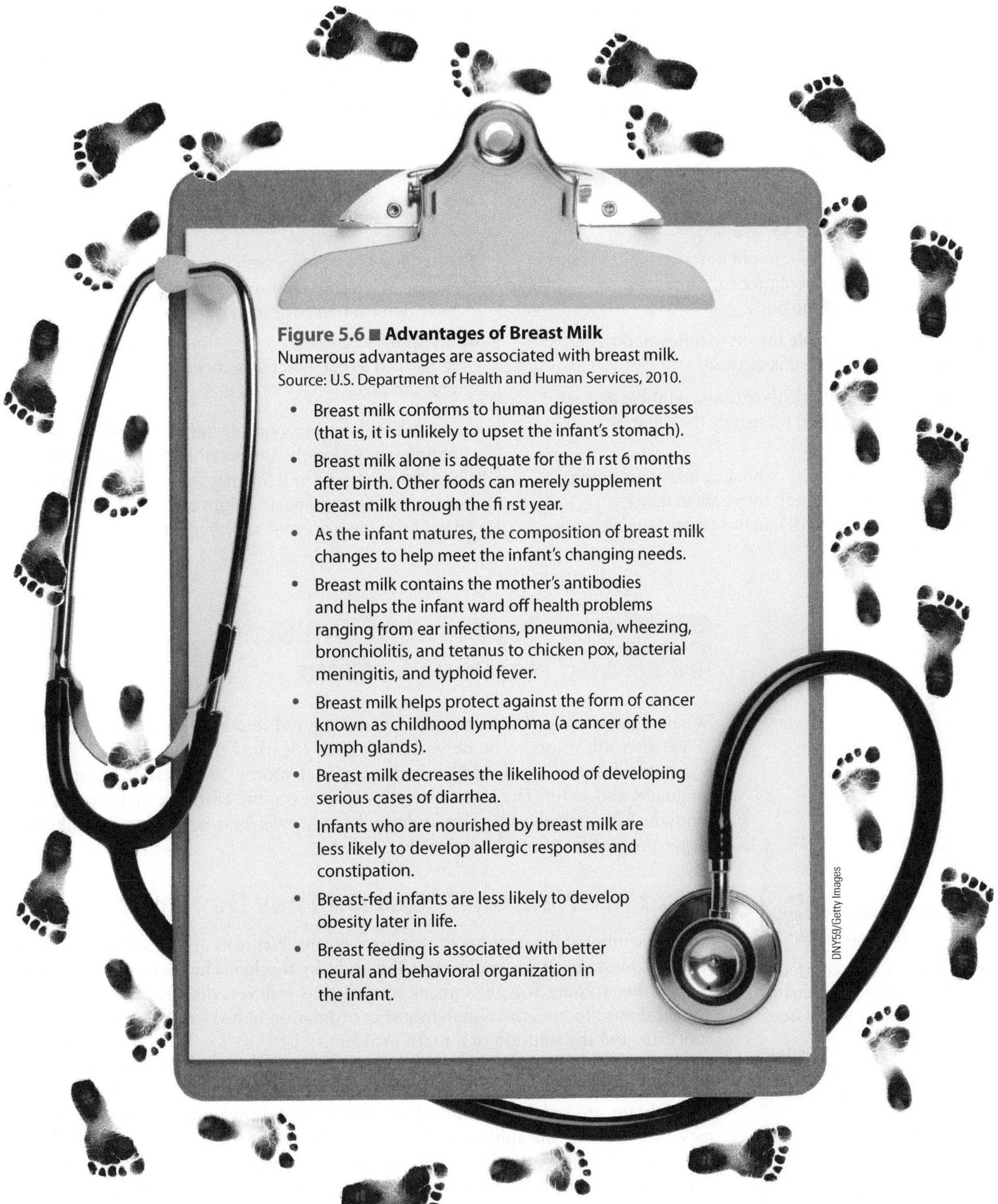

Figure 5.6 ■ Advantages of Breast Milk

Numerous advantages are associated with breast milk.

Source: U.S. Department of Health and Human Services, 2010.

- Breast milk conforms to human digestion processes (that is, it is unlikely to upset the infant's stomach).

- Breast milk alone is adequate for the first 6 months after birth. Other foods can merely supplement breast milk through the first year.

- As the infant matures, the composition of breast milk changes to help meet the infant's changing needs.

- Breast milk contains the mother's antibodies and helps the infant ward off health problems ranging from ear infections, pneumonia, wheezing, bronchiolitis, and tetanus to chicken pox, bacterial meningitis, and typhoid fever.

- Breast milk helps protect against the form of cancer known as childhood lymphoma (a cancer of the lymph glands).

- Breast milk decreases the likelihood of developing serious cases of diarrhea.

- Infants who are nourished by breast milk are less likely to develop allergic responses and constipation.

- Breast-fed infants are less likely to develop obesity later in life.

- Breast feeding is associated with better neural and behavioral organization in the infant.

DNY59/Getty Images

Steven Davidi/Getty Images

The hormones prolactin and oxytocin are involved in breastfeeding. The word *prolactin* means in favor of ("pro") producing milk. By a few days after delivery, prolactin stimulates the mammary glands to produce milk. Oxytocin is secreted in response to suckling and stimulates the breasts to eject milk. The baby need not be the mother's biological child; so-called "wet nurses" were employed by affluent women during recent centuries so that the mothers need not participate directly in the process. When breastfeeding is discontinued, prolactin and oxytocin are no longer secreted, and lactation ends—for wet nurses as well as the biological mothers of infants.

Women who have questions about breastfeeding can speak with lactation consultants at hospitals and consult La Leche League International (www.llli.org).

Section Review

1. Cephalocaudal development describes the processes by which development proceeds from the _____ to the lower parts of the body.

2. The _____ principle means that development proceeds from the trunk outward.

3. Infants usually double their birth weight in about _____ months and triple it by their first birthday.

4. Compared to mothers of healthy infants, mothers of infants with failure to thrive show fewer _____ (positive or negative?) feelings toward their infants.

5. After illness or dietary deficiency, children show _____, which is a tendency to return to their genetically determined pattern of growth.

6. Breast milk contains _____ that can prevent problems such as ear infections, meningitis, tetanus, and chicken pox.

Reflect & Relate: How closely did your parents pay attention to your height and weight? Did they chart it? When did you begin to think that you were average (or above or below average) in height and weight? What effect did your size have on your self-concept and self-esteem?

5.3 Development of the Brain and Nervous System

When I was a child, I did not think it was a good idea to have a nervous system. Who, after all, wants to be nervous? But then I learned that the nervous system is a system of **nerves** involved in heartbeat, visual–motor coordination, thought and language, and so on. The human nervous system is more complex than that of other animals. Although elephants and whales have heavier brains, our brains make up a larger proportion of our body weight.

What Are Neurons? How Do They Develop?

nerves Bundles of axons from many neurons.

neurons Nerve cells; cells found in the nervous system that transmit messages.

dendrites The rootlike parts of a neuron that receive impulses from other neurons.

axon A long, thin part of a neuron that transmits impulses to other neurons through small branching structures called axon terminals.

neurotransmitter A chemical substance that makes possible the transmission of neural impulses from one neuron to another.

The basic units of the nervous system are neurons. **Neurons** are cells that receive and transmit messages from one part of the body to another. The messages transmitted by neurons account for phenomena as varied as reflexes, the perception of an itch from a mosquito bite, the visual–motor coordination of a skier, the composition of a concerto, and the solution of a math problem.

People are born with about 100 billion neurons, most of which are in the brain. Neurons vary according to their functions and locations in the body. Some neurons in the brain are only a fraction of an inch in length, whereas neurons that carry messages between the spine and the toes can be several feet in length. Each neuron possesses a cell body, dendrites, and an axon (see Figure 5.7 ■). **Dendrites** are short fibers that extend from the cell body and receive incoming messages from thousands of adjoining transmitting neurons. The **axon** extends trunklike from the cell body and accounts for much of the difference in length among neurons. It is the axons that can grow to several feet in length. Messages are released from axon terminals in the form of chemicals called **neurotransmitters**. These messages are then received by the dendrites of adjoining neurons, muscles, or glands. As the child matures, the axons of neurons grow in length, and the dendrites and axon terminals proliferate, creating vast interconnected networks for the transmission of complex messages.

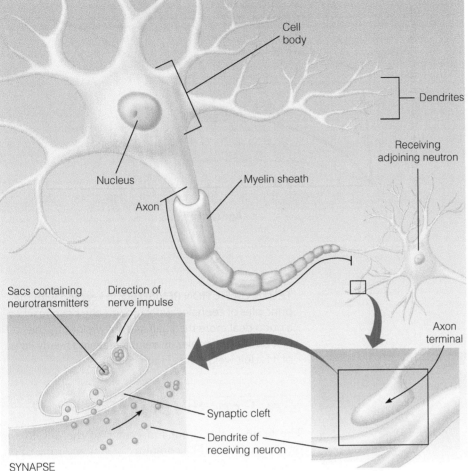

Figure 5.7 ■ Anatomy of a Neuron
"Messages" enter neurons through dendrites, are transmitted along the axon, and then are sent through axon terminals to muscles, glands, and other neurons. Neurons develop by means of proliferation of dendrites and axon terminals and through myelination.
© Cengage Learning®

Labels in figure: Cell body; Dendrites; Nucleus; Myelin sheath; Axon; Receiving adjoining neutron; Sacs containing neurotransmitters; Direction of nerve impulse; Axon terminal; Synaptic cleft; Dendrite of receiving neuron; SYNAPSE

Myelin

Many neurons are tightly wrapped with white, fatty **myelin sheaths** that give them the appearance of a string of white sausages. The high fat content of the myelin sheath insulates the neuron from electrically charged atoms in the fluids that encase the nervous system. In this way, leakage of the electric current being carried along the axon is minimized, and messages are conducted more efficiently.

The term **myelination** refers to the process by which axons become coated with myelin. Myelination is not complete at birth. Myelination is part of the maturation process that leads to the abilities to crawl and walk during the first year after birth. Incomplete myelination accounts for some of the helplessness of neonates. Myelination of the prefrontal matter of the brain continues into the second decade of life and is connected with advances in working memory and language ability (Kalat, 2015). Breakdown of myelin is believed to be associated with Alzheimer's disease, a source of cognitive decline that usually begins in middle or late adulthood.

In the disease **multiple sclerosis**, myelin is replaced by a hard, fibrous tissue that disrupts the timing of neural transmission, thus interfering with muscle control (Sanchez-Gomez et al., 2014). The disorder phenylketonuria (PKU) leads to intellectual disability by inhibiting the formation of myelin in the brain (Velumian & Samoilova, 2014). Congenital infection with HIV has been shown to be connected with abnormalities in the formation of myelin and with cognitive and motor impairment, as measured by the Bayley Scales of Infant Development (Blanchette et al., 2001).

myelin sheath A fatty, white substance that encases and insulates neurons, permitting more rapid transmission of neural impulses.

myelination The process by which axons are coated with myelin.

multiple sclerosis A disorder in which myelin is replaced by hard, fibrous tissue that impedes neural transmission.

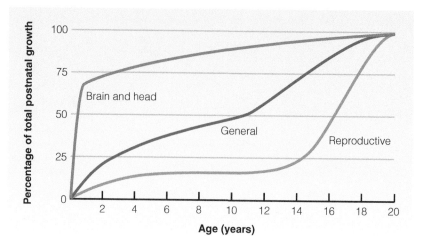

medulla An oblong area of the hindbrain involved in heartbeat and respiration.

cerebellum The part of the hindbrain involved in muscle coordination and balance.

cerebrum The large mass of the forebrain, which consists of two hemispheres.

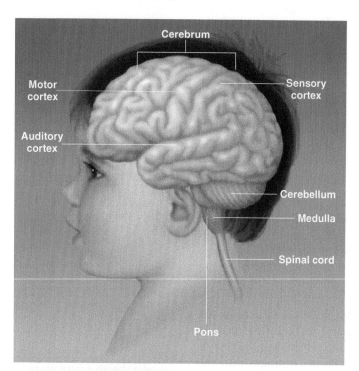

Figure 5.9 ■ Structures of the Brain
The convolutions of the cortex increase its surface area and, apparently, its intellectual capacity. (In this case, wrinkles are good.) The medulla is involved in vital functions such as respiration and heartbeat; the cerebellum is involved in balance and coordination.
© Cengage Learning®

TRUTH OR FICTION REVISITED: In keeping with the principles of cephalocaudal growth, the brain reaches a good deal more than half its adult weight by the first birthday. It triples in weight, reaching nearly 70% of its adult weight (see Figure 5.8 ■).

How Does the Brain Develop?

The brain is the command center of the developing organism. (If you like computer analogies, think of the brain as the central processing unit.) It contains neurons and provides the basis for physical, cognitive, and personal and social development.

The brain of the neonate weighs a little less than a pound—nearly one-fourth of its adult weight. Let us look at the brain, as shown in Figure 5.9 ■, and discuss the development of the structures within.

Structures of the Brain

Many nerves that connect the spinal cord to higher levels of the brain pass through the **medulla** and the pons. The medulla is vital in the control of basic functions, such as heartbeat and respiration. The medulla is part of an area called the brain stem, which may be implicated in sudden infant death syndrome (SIDS; see Chapter 4).

Above the medulla lies the **cerebellum**, which is Latin for "little brain." The cerebellum helps the child maintain balance, control motor behavior, and coordinate hand and eye movements with bodily sensations.

The **cerebrum** is the crowning glory of the brain. It makes possible the breadth and depth of human learning, thought, memory, and language. Only in human beings does the cerebrum constitute such a large proportion of the brain. The surface of the cerebrum consists of two hemispheres—left and right—that become increasingly wrinkled as the child develops, coming to show ridges and valleys called fissures. This surface is the cerebral cortex. The wrinkles allow a great deal of surface area to be packed into the brain.

Neonate

Six months   **Two years**

Growth Spurts of the Brain

The brain makes gains in size and weight in different ways. One way is through the formation of neurons, a process completed by birth. The first major growth spurt of the brain occurs during the fourth and fifth months of prenatal development, when neurons proliferate. A second growth spurt in the brain occurs between the 25th week of prenatal development and the end of the second year after birth. Whereas the first growth spurt of the brain is due to the formation of neurons, the second growth spurt is due primarily to the proliferation of dendrites and axon terminals—that is, growth of the connections between neurons (see Figure 5.10 ■).

Figure 5.10 ■ Increase in Neural Connections in the Brain
A major growth spurt in the brain occurs between the 25th week of prenatal development and the end of the second year after birth. This growth spurt is due primarily to the proliferation of dendrites and axon terminals.
Source: Conel (1959).

Brain Development in Infancy

There is a clear link between what infants can do and the myelination of areas within the brain. At birth, the parts of the brain involved in heartbeat and respiration, sleeping and arousal, and reflex activity are fairly well myelinated and functional.

Myelination of motor pathways allows neonates to show stereotyped reflexes, but otherwise neonates' physical activity tends to be random and badly organized. Myelination of the motor area of the cerebral cortex begins at about the fourth month of prenatal development. Myelin develops rapidly along the major motor pathways from the cerebral cortex during the last month of pregnancy and continues after birth. The development of intentional physical activity coincides with myelination as the unorganized movements of the neonate come under increasing control. Myelination of the nerves to muscles is largely developed by the age of 2 years, although research using magnetic resonance imaging (MRI) suggests that myelination continues into early adulthood and beyond (Silk & Wood, 2011).

Although neonates respond to touch and can see and hear quite well, the areas of the cortex that are involved in vision, hearing, and the skin senses are less well myelinated at birth. As myelination progresses and the interconnections between the various areas of the cortex thicken, children become increasingly capable of complex and integrated sensorimotor activities (Bartzokis et al., 2010).

Neonates whose mothers read *The Cat in the Hat* aloud during the last few weeks of pregnancy show a preference for this story (see Chapter 3). It turns out that myelination of the neurons involved in the sense of hearing begins at about the sixth month of pregnancy—coinciding with the period in which fetuses begin to respond to sound. Myelination of these pathways is developing rapidly at term and continues until about the age of 4 years.

Although the fetus shows some response to light during the third trimester, it is hard to imagine what use the fetus could have for vision. It turns out that the neurons involved in vision begin to myelinate only shortly before full term, but then they complete the process of myelination rapidly. Within a short 5 to 6 months after birth, vision has become the dominant sense.

How Do Nature and Nurture Interact to Affect the Development of the Brain?

Development of the areas of the brain that control sensation and movement begins as a result of maturation, but sensory stimulation and physical activity during early infancy also spur their development (Posner et al., 2013). Sensory stimulation does not mean computer programs for infants, Baby Mozart, and electronic toys; it can consist of social interaction with caregivers, being held and spoken to, and the like. Therefore, experience interacts with the unfolding of the genetic code to produce the brain—and intellectual functioning—as seen by a snapshot at a given point in time (Posner et al., 2013; Syed et al, 2010).

Research with animals shows how sensory stimulation sparks growth of the cortex. Researchers have provided complex environmental exposure—in some cases, rat "amusement parks" with toys such as ladders, platforms, and boxes—to demonstrate the effects of enriched environments. In these studies, rats exposed to more complex environments develop heavier brains than control animals. The weight differences in part reflect more synapses per neuron than in other rats (B. J. Anderson, 2011). On the other hand, animals reared in darkness show shrinkage of the visual cortex, impaired vision, and impaired visual–motor coordination (B. J. Anderson, 2011; Talaei & Salami, 2013). If they can't use it, they lose it.

Human brains also are affected by experience. Infants actually have more connections among neurons than adults do. Connections that are activated by experience survive; the others do not (Lewis, 2011).

The great adaptability of the brain appears to be a double-edged sword. Adaptability enables us to develop different patterns of neural connections to meet the demands of different environments. However, lack of stimulation—especially during critical early periods of development (as we will see later)—can impair adaptability.

Brain nourishment, like early experience, plays a role in the brain's achieving what is permitted by the child's genes. Inadequate fetal nutrition, especially during the prenatal growth spurt of the brain, has several negative effects. These include smallness in the overall size of the brain, the formation of fewer neurons, and less myelination (Guerrini & Dobyns, 2014; Massaro et al., 2014).

Section Review

7. _____ are the basic units of the nervous system.

8. Each neuron possesses a cell body, dendrites, and a(n) _____.

9. The brain reaches nearly _____% of its adult weight by the first birthday.

10. The wrinkled part of the brain, called the _____, enables the child to maintain balance and to control physical behavior.

Reflect & Relate: Are you surprised that there is such a close connection between experience and development of the brain? How does the information presented in this section fit with the adage "Use it or lose it"?

Motor Development: How Moving

"Zoe crawled so fast it seemed she was on high-octane fuel!" "Anthony was walking forward and backward by the age of 13 months."

These are the types of comments parents make about their children's motor development. Motor development involves the activity of muscles, leading to changes in posture, movement, and coordination of movement with the infant's developing sensory apparatus. Motor development includes some of the most fascinating changes in infants, in part because so much seems to happen so fast, and so much of it during the first year.

Like physical development, motor development follows cephalocaudal and proximodistal patterns and differentiation. Infants gain control of their heads and upper torsos before they can effectively use their arms. This trend illustrates cephalocaudal development. Infants also can control their trunks and shoulders before they can use their hands and fingers, demonstrating the proximodistal trend.

Lifting and Holding the Torso and Head: Heads Up?

Neonates can move their heads slightly to the side. They can thus avoid suffocation if they are lying face down and their noses or mouths are obstructed by bedding. At about 1 month, infants can raise their heads. By about 2 months, they can also lift their chests while lying on their stomachs.

When neonates are held, their heads must be supported. But by 3 to 6 months of age, infants generally manage to hold their heads quite well, so that supporting the head is no longer necessary. Unfortunately, infants who can normally support their heads cannot do so when they are lifted or moved about in a jerky manner; thus infants who are handled carelessly can sustain neck injuries.

Control of the Hands: Getting a Grip on Things?

The development of hand skills is a clear example of proximodistal development. Infants track (follow) slowly moving objects with their eyes shortly after birth, but they do not generally reach for them. They show a grasp reflex but do not reliably reach for the objects that appear to interest them. Voluntary reaching and grasping require visual–motor coordination. By about the age of 3 months, infants make clumsy swipes at objects, failing to grasp them, because their aim is poor or because they close their hands too soon or too late.

Between the ages of 4 and 6 months, infants become more successful at grasping objects (Daum et al., 2013). However, they may not know how to let go of an object and may hold it indefinitely, until their attention is diverted and the hand opens accidentally. Four to 6 months is a good age for giving children rattles, large plastic spoons, mobiles, and other brightly colored hanging toys that can be grasped but are harmless when they wind up in the mouth.

Grasping is reflexive at first. Voluntary grasping (holding) replaces reflexive grasping by the age of 3–4 months. Infants first use an **ulnar grasp**, in which they hold objects clumsily between their fingers and their palm. By 4 to 6 months, they can transfer objects back and forth between hands. The oppositional thumb comes into play at about the age of 9–12 months. Use of the thumb gives infants the ability to pick up tiny objects in a **pincer grasp** (see Figure 5.11 ■). By about 11 months of age, infants can hold objects in each hand and inspect them in turn.

Between the ages of 5 and 11 months, infants adjust their hands in anticipation of grasping moving targets. They also gather information from the objects' movements to predict their future location and catch them (Keitel et al., 2014). Think of the complex concepts required to explain this behavior, and then think of how well infants perform it—without any explanation at all! Of course, I am not suggesting that infants solve problems in geometry and physics to grasp moving objects; that interpretation, as developmental-psychologist Marshall M. Haith (1998) would describe it, would put a "cog in infant cognition."

Another aspect of visual–motor coordination is stacking blocks. On average, children can stack two blocks at 15 months, three blocks at 18 months, and five blocks at 24 months (Keitel et al., 2014). At about 24 months of age, children can also copy horizontal and vertical lines.

JS Photo/Alamy

Figure 5.11 ■ Pincer Grasp
Infants first hold objects between their fingers and palm. Once the oppositional thumb comes into play at about 9 to 12 months of age, infants are able to pick up tiny objects using what is termed a pincer grasp.

ulnar grasp A method of grasping objects in which the fingers close somewhat clumsily against the palm.

pincer grasp The use of the opposing thumb to grasp objects between the thumb and other fingers.

Locomotion: Getting a Move On?

Locomotion is movement from one place to another. Children gain the capacity to move their bodies through a sequence of activities that includes rolling over, sitting up, creeping, crawling, walking, and running. There is much variation in the ages at which infants first engage in these activities. Although the sequence mostly remains the same, some children skip a step. For example, an infant may crawl without ever having creeped.

Most infants can roll over, from back to stomach and from stomach to back, by about the age of 6 months. They can also sit (and support their upper bodies, necks, and heads) for extended periods if they are aided by a person or placed in a seat with a strap, such as a high chair. By about 7 months of age, infants usually begin to sit up by themselves.

At about 8–9 months, most infants begin to creep, a motor activity in which they lie prone and use their arms to pull themselves along, dragging their bellies and feet behind. Crawling, a more sophisticated form of locomotion in which infants move themselves along up on their hands and knees, requires a good deal more coordination and usually appears a month or so after creeping (see Figure 5.12 ■).

There are fascinating varieties. Some infants travel from one place to another by rolling over and over. Some lift themselves and swing their arms while in a sitting position, in effect dragging along on their buttocks. Still others do a "bear walk" in which they move on their hands and feet, without allowing their elbows and knees to touch the floor. And some creep until they are ready to stand and walk from place to place while holding onto chairs, other objects, and people.

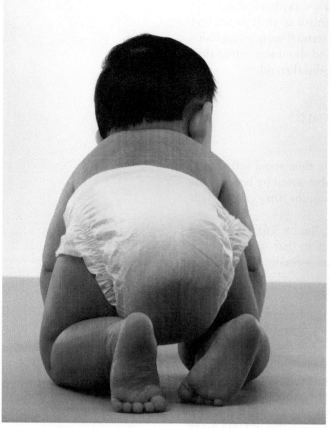

Figure 5.12 ■ Crawling
Crawling requires lifting the body off the floor and coordinating of arm and leg movements.

Standing overlaps with creeping and crawling. Most infants can remain in a standing position by holding on to something at the age of 8 or 9 months. At this age, they may also be able to walk a bit when supported by adults. Such walking is voluntary and does not have the stereotyped appearance of the walking reflex described in Chapter 4. About 2 months later, they can pull themselves to a standing position by holding on to the sides of their cribs or other objects and can stand briefly without holding on. Soon afterward, they walk about unsteadily while holding on. By 12–15 months or so, they walk by themselves (Adolph & Tamis-LeMonda, 2014), earning them the name **toddler** (see Figure 5.13 ■). Attempts to master these new motor skills are often accompanied by signs of pleasure such as smiling, laughing, and babbling.

Toddlers soon run about, supporting their relatively heavy heads and torsos by spreading their legs in bow-legged fashion. Because they are top-heavy and inexperienced, they fall frequently. Some toddlers require consoling when they fall. Others spring right up and run on again with barely an interruption. Many toddlers are skillful at navigating steep and shallow slopes (Adolph & Tamis-LeMonda, 2014). They walk down shallow slopes but prudently elect to slide or crawl down steep ones. Walking lends children new freedom. It enables them to get about rapidly and to grasp objects that were formerly out of reach. Give toddlers a large ball to toss and run after; it is about the least expensive and most enjoyable toy they can be given.

As children mature, their muscle strength, the density of their bones, and their balance and coordination improve. By the age of 2 years, they can climb steps one at a time, placing both feet on each step. They can run well, walk backward, kick a large ball, and jump several inches.

locomotion Movement from one place to another.

toddler A child who walks with short, uncertain steps. Toddlerhood lasts from about 12 months to 30 months of age, thereby bridging infancy and early childhood.

Black African and African American infants generally reach such motor milestones as sitting, walking, and running before European and European American infants do (Haywood & Getchell, 2014). Although genetic factors may be involved in the earlier motor development of Black African and African American infants, environmental factors also appear to play a role. African infants excel in areas of motor development in which they have received considerable stimulation and practice. For example, parents in Africa and in cultures of African origin, such as Jamaica, stress the development of sitting and walking and provide infants, from birth, with experiences (including stretching and massage) that stimulate the development of these behaviors. From the second or third months, other activities are added, such as propping infants in a sitting position, bouncing them on their feet, and exercising the stepping reflex.

How Do Nature and Nurture Interact to Affect Motor Development?

Research with humans and other species leaves little doubt that both maturation (nature) and experience (nurture) are involved in motor development (Haywood & Getchell, 2014). Certain voluntary motor activities are not possible until the brain has matured in terms of myelination and the differentiation of the motor areas of the cortex. Although the neonate shows stepping and swimming reflexes, these behaviors are controlled by more primitive parts of the brain. They disappear when cortical development inhibits some functions of the lower parts of the brain, and when they reappear, they differ in quality.

Infants also need some opportunity to experiment before they can engage in milestones such as sitting up and walking. Even so, many of these advances can apparently be attributed to maturation. In classic research, Wayne and Marsena Dennis (1940) reported on the motor development of Native American Hopi children who spent their first year strapped to a cradle board (see Figure 5.14 ■). Although denied a full year of experience in locomotion, the Hopi infants gained the capacity to walk early in their second year, at about the same time as other children. Classic cross-cultural research (Hindley et al., 1966) reported that infants in five European cities began to walk at about the same time (generally, between 12 and 15 months), despite cultural differences in encouragement to walk.

TRUTH OR FICTION REVISITED: It is true that Native American Hopi infants spend their first year strapped to a board but begin to walk at about the same time as children who are reared in other cultures. Put it this way: they apparently begin to walk when they are biologically ready, despite lack of experience in many aspects of locomotion that may be gained prior to walking.

MBI/Stockbroker/Alamy

Figure 5.13 ■ Walking
By 12 to 15 months or so, babies walk by themselves, earning them the name toddler.

On the other hand, evidence is mixed on whether specific training can accelerate the appearance of motor skills. For example, in a classic study with identical twins, Arnold Gesell (1929) gave one twin extensive training in hand coordination, block building, and stair climbing from early infancy. The other twin was allowed to develop on his own. At first, the trained twin had better skills, but as time passed, the untrained twin became just as skilled.

Figure 5.14 ■ A Native American Hopi Infant Strapped to a Cradle Board Researchers have studied Hopi children who are strapped to cradle boards during their first year to see whether their motor development is significantly delayed. Once released from their boards, Hopi children advance rapidly in their motor development, suggesting the important role of maturation in motor development.

Although the appearance of motor skills can be accelerated by training (Zelazo & Müller, 2010), the effect seems slight. Practice in the absence of neural readiness has limited results. There is also little evidence that training leads to eventual superior motor skills. Caution: we are *not* suggesting that caregivers ignore opportunities to encourage or help infants with various aspects of locomotion. We are merely pointing out that infants may require less practice than caregivers might imagine.

Although being strapped to a cradle board did not delay the motor development of Hopi infants, Wayne Dennis (1960) reported that infants in an Iranian orphanage were significantly retarded in their motor development. In contrast to the Hopi infants, the institutionalized infants experienced extreme social and physical deprivation. Under these conditions, they grew apathetic, and all aspects of development suffered. But there is also a bright side to this tale of deprivation. The motor development of similar infants in a Lebanese orphanage accelerated dramatically in response to such minimal intervention as being propped up in their cribs and being given a few colorful toys (Sayegh & Dennis, 1965).

Nature apparently provides the limits—the "reaction range"—for the expression of inherited traits. Nurture determines whether the child will develop skills that reach the upper limits of the range. Even a fundamental skill such as locomotion is determined by a complex interplay of maturational and environmental factors (Haywood & Getchell, 2014). There may be little purpose in trying to train children to enhance their motor skills before they are ready. Once children are ready, however, teaching and practice do make a difference. One does not become an Olympic athlete without "good genes." But one also usually does not become an Olympic athlete without high-quality training. And because motor skills are important to the self-concepts of children, good teaching is all the more valuable.

Section Review

11. Infants can first raise their heads at about the age of _____ month(s).

12. Infants first use a(n) _____ (ulnar or pincer?) grasp for holding objects.

13. Researchers assess infants' ability to stack blocks as a measure of their _____ motor coordination.

14. Infants _____ (sit up or crawl?) before they _____ (sit up or crawl?).

15. As children mature, their bones _____ (increase or decrease?) in density.

16. Research reveals that both maturation and _____ play indispensable roles in motor development.

17. Arnold Gesell _____ (did or did not?) find that extensive training in hand coordination, block building, and stair climbing gave infants enduring advantages over untrained infants in these skills.

Reflect & Relate: "When did your baby first sit up?" "When did he walk?" Why are people so concerned about when infants do what? Imagine that you are speaking to a parent who is concerned that her child is not yet walking at 14 months. What would you say to the parent? When should there be cause for concern?

Sensory and Perceptual Development: Taking In the World

What a world we live in—green hills and reddish skies; rumbling trucks, murmuring brooks, and voices; the sweet and the sour; the acrid and the perfumed; the metallic and the fuzzy. What an ever-changing display of sights, sounds, tastes, smells, and touches! The pleasures of the world, and its miseries, are known to us through sensory impressions and the organization of these impressions into personal inner maps of reality. Our eyes, our ears, the sensory receptors in our noses and our mouths, our skin senses—these are our tickets of admission to the world.

In Chapter 4, we examined the sensory capabilities of the neonate. In this section, we will see how infants develop the ability to integrate disjointed **sensations** into meaningful patterns of events termed **perceptions**. We will see what captures the attention of infants, and we will see how young children develop into purposeful seekers of information—selecting the sensory impressions they choose to capture. We will focus on the development of vision and hearing because most of the research on sensory and perceptual development in infancy has been done in these areas.

We will see that many things that are obvious to us are not so obvious to infants. *You* may know that a coffee cup is the same whether you see it from above or from the side, but make no such assumptions about the infant's understanding. *You* may know that an infant's mother is the same size whether she is standing next to the infant or approaching from two blocks away, but do not assume that the infant agrees with you.

We cannot ask infants to explain why they look at some things and not at others. Nor can we ask them if their mother appears to be the same size whether she is standing close to them or far away. But investigators of childhood sensation and perception have devised clever methods to investigate these questions, and their findings provide us with fascinating insights into the perceptual processes of even the neonate. They reveal that many basic perceptual competencies are present early in life.

Development of Vision: The Better to See You With

Development of vision involves development of visual acuity or sharpness, development of peripheral vision (seeing things off to the sides while looking straight ahead), visual preferences, depth perception, and perceptual constancies (for example, knowing that an object remains the same object even though it may look different when seen from a different angle—you knew that, didn't you?).

Development of Visual Acuity and Peripheral Vision

Newborns are extremely nearsighted, with vision beginning at about 20/600. The most dramatic gains in visual acuity are made between birth and 6 months of age, with acuity reaching about 20/50 (Fulton et al., 2014). Gains in visual acuity then become more gradual, approximating adult levels (20/20 in the best cases) by about 3–5 years of age.

Neonates also have poor peripheral vision (Fulton et al., 2014). Adults can perceive objects that are nearly 90 degrees off to the side (i.e., directly to the left or right), although objects at these extremes are unclear. Neonates cannot perceive visual stimuli that are off to the side by an angle of more than 30 degrees, but their peripheral vision expands to an angle of about 45 degrees by the age of 7 weeks. By 6 months of age, their peripheral vision is about equal to that of an adult.

Let us now consider the development of visual perception. In so doing, we will see that infants frequently prefer the strange to the familiar and will avoid going off the deep end—sometimes.

sensation The stimulation of sensory organs, such as the eyes, ears, and skin, and the transmission of sensory information to the brain.

perception The process by which sensations are organized into a mental map of the world.

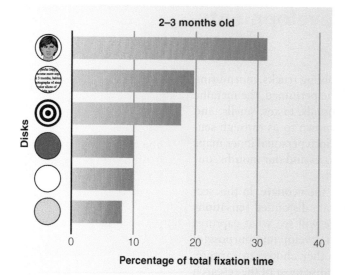

2–3 months old

Disks

Percentage of total fixation time

Figure 5.15 ■ Preferences for Visual Stimuli in 2-Month-Olds

Infants appear to prefer complex to simple visual stimuli. By the time they are 2 months old, they also tend to show preference for the human face. Researchers continue to debate whether the face draws attention because of its content (i.e., being a face) or because of its stimulus characteristics (complexity, arrangement, etc.).
© Cengage Learning®

Visual Preferences: How Do You Capture an Infant's Attention?

Neonates look at stripes longer than at blobs. This finding has been used in much of the research on visual acuity. Classic research found that by the age of 8–12 weeks, most infants also show distinct preferences for curved lines over straight lines (Fantz et al., 1975).

Robert Fantz (1961) wondered whether there was something intrinsically interesting about the human face that drew the attention of infants. To investigate this question, he showed 2-month-old infants the six disks illustrated in Figure 5.15 ■. One disk contained a caricature of human features, another contained newsprint, and still another contained a bull's-eye. The remaining three disks were featureless but were colored red, white, and yellow. In this study, the infants fixated significantly longer on the human face.

Some studies suggest that the infants in Fantz's (1961) study may have preferred the human face because it had a complex, intriguing pattern of dots (eyes) within an outline and not because it was a face. But other theorists, such as Michelle de Haan and Margrite Groen (2006), assert that "reading" faces is particularly important to infants because they do not understand verbal information as communicated through language. Thus, it would make evolutionary sense for them to orient toward the human face and perceive the differences between some facial expressions at very early ages.

Researchers therefore continue to investigate infants' preferences for the human face. They ask whether humans come into the world "prewired" to prefer human stimuli to other stimuli that are just as complex, and, if so, just what it is about human stimuli that draws attention. Some researchers—unlike de Haan and Groen—argue that neonates do not "prefer" faces because they are faces per se but because of the structure of their immature visual systems (Simion et al., 2001). A supportive study of 34 neonates found that the longer fixations on facelike stimuli resulted from a larger number of brief fixations (looks) rather than from a few prolonged fixations (Cassia et al., 2001). The infants' gaze, then, was sort of bouncing around from feature to feature rather than "staring" at the face in general. The researchers interpreted this finding to show that the stimulus properties of the visual object are more important than the fact that it represents a human face. Even so, of course, the "immature visual system" would be providing some "prewired" basis for attending to the face.

Learning clearly plays a role. Neonates can discriminate their mother's face from a stranger's after 8 hours of mother–infant contact spread over 4 days (Bushnell, 2001). By 3–5 months of age, infants respond differently to happy, surprised, and sad faces (Muir & Hains, 1993). Moreover, infants as young as 2 months prefer attractive faces to unattractive faces (Ramsey et al., 2004). This preference is more deeply ingrained by 6 months of age (Ramsey et al., 2004). Do standards of attractiveness have an inborn component, or are they learned (very!) early?

Neonates appear to direct their attention to the edges of objects. This pattern persists for the first several weeks (S. P. Johnson, 2011). When they are given the opportunity to look at human faces, 1-month-old infants tend to pay most attention to the "edges"—that is, the chin, an ear, or the hairline. Two-month-old infants move in from the edge, as shown in Figure 5.16 ■. They focus particularly on the eyes, although they also inspect other inner features, such as the mouth and nose (Aslin, 2012). (Similarly, adults prefer attractive infant faces and, everything else being equal, may give attractive infants preferential treatment [Schein & Langlois, 2015].)

Some researchers (e.g., Haith, 1979) explain infants' tendencies to scan from the edges of objects inward by noting that for the first several weeks of life, infants seem to be essentially concerned with where things are. Their attention is captured by movement and sharp contrasts in brightness and shape, such as those that are found where the edges of objects stand out against their backgrounds. But by about 2 months of age, infants tend to focus on the *what* of things. They may locate objects by looking at their edges, but now they scan systematically within the boundaries of objects (Aslin, 2012).

Development of Depth Perception: On Not Going Off the Deep End?

Infants generally respond to cues for depth by the time they are able to crawl (6–8 months of age or so), and most have the good sense to avoid "going off the deep end"—that is, crawling off ledges and tabletops into open space (Campos et al., 1978).

In a classic study on depth perception, Eleanor Gibson and Richard Walk (1960) placed infants of various ages on a fabric-covered runway that ran across the center of a clever device called a visual cliff. The visual cliff consists of a sheet of Plexiglas that covers a cloth with a high-contrast checkerboard pattern (Figure 5.17 ■). On one side, the cloth is placed immediately beneath the Plexiglas, and on the other, it is dropped about 4 feet below. Because the Plexiglas alone would easily support the infant, this is a visual cliff rather than an actual cliff. In the Gibson and Walk study, 8 out of 10 infants who had begun to crawl refused to venture onto the seemingly unsupported surface, even when their mothers beckoned encouragingly from the other side.

Psychologists can assess infants' emotional responses to the visual cliff long before infants can crawl. For example, Joseph Campos and his colleagues (1970) found that 1-month-old infants showed no change in heart rate when placed face down on the "cliff." They apparently did not perceive the depth of the cliff. At 2 months, infants showed decreases in heart rate when so placed, which psychologists interpret as a sign of interest. But the heart rates of 9-month-olds accelerated on the cliff, which is interpreted as a fear response. The study appears to suggest that infants profit from some experience crawling about (and, perhaps, accumulating some bumps) before they develop fear of heights. The 9-month-olds, but not the 2-month-olds, had had such experience. Other studies support the view that infants usually do not develop fear of heights until they can move around (Sorce et al., 2000; Witherington et al., 2010). Newly walking infants are highly reluctant to venture out onto the visual cliff, even when their mothers signal them to do so (Sorce et al., 2000; Witherington et al., 2010).

Infants' tendencies to avoid falling off a cliff are apparently connected with their body positions at the time (Franchak & Adolph, 2012). Infants generally sit before they crawl, and by 9 months of age, we can think of most of them as experienced sitters. Crawling enters the picture at about 9 months. Karen Adolph examined the

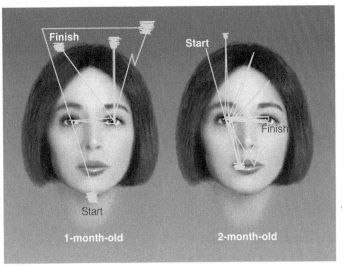

Figure 5.16 ■ Eye Movements of 1- and 2-Month-Olds
One-month-olds direct their attention to the edges of objects. Two-month-olds "move in from the edge." When looking at a face, for example, they focus on the eyes and other inner features. How do researchers explain this change?
Source: Salapatek (1975).

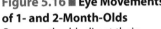

Figure 5.17 ■ The Visual Cliff
This young explorer has the good sense not to crawl out onto an apparently unsupported surface, even when his mother beckons from the other side.
© Cengage Learning®

behavior of nineteen 9-month-old infants who were on the edge of crawling as well as on the edge of a visual cliff. The infants were placed in a sitting or crawling position and enticed to reach out for an object over the cliff. The infants were more likely to avoid the cliff when they were sitting. This suggests that different postures involve the brain in different ways and that infants' avoidance of the cliff is connected with their posture. Adolph's findings bring into question the view that avoidance of the cliff depends on general knowledge, such as fear of heights, associations between perceived depth and falling, or awareness that the body cannot be supported in empty space.

TRUTH OR FICTION REVISITED: Evidence is mixed on whether infants need to have experience crawling before they develop fear of heights. Some who develop fear of heights do not have such experience. This would appear to be a case in which survival might be enhanced by *not* having to learn from experience.

Development of Perceptual Constancies

It may not surprise you that a 12-inch ruler is the same length whether it is 2 feet or 6 feet away or that a door across the room is a rectangle whether it is closed or ajar. Awareness of these facts depends not on sensation alone but on the development of perceptual constancies. **Perceptual constancy** is the tendency to perceive an object to be the same, even though the sensations produced by the object may differ under various conditions.

Consider again the example of the ruler. When it is 2 feet away, its image, as focused on the retina, is a certain length. This length is the image's "retinal size." From 6 feet away, the 12-inch ruler is only one-third as long in terms of retinal size, but we perceive it as being the same size because of size constancy. **Size constancy** is the tendency to perceive the same objects as being the same size even though their retinal sizes vary as a function of their distance. From 6 feet away, a 36-inch yardstick casts an image equal in retinal size to that of the 12-inch ruler at 2 feet, but—if recognized as a yardstick—it is perceived as longer, again because of size constancy.

In a classic study of the development of size constancy, Thomas Bower (1974) conditioned 2½- to 3-month-old infants to turn their heads to the left when shown a 12-inch cube from a distance of 3 feet. He then presented them with three experimental stimuli: (1) a 12-inch cube 9 feet away, whose retinal size was smaller than that of the original cube; (2) a 36-inch cube 3 feet away, whose retinal size was larger than that of the original cube; and (3) a 36-inch cube 9 feet away, whose retinal size was the same as that of the original cube. The infants turned their heads most frequently in response to the first experimental cube, even though its retinal image was only one-third the length of that to which they had been conditioned; this suggests that they had achieved size constancy. Later studies have confirmed Bower's finding that size constancy is present in early infancy. Some research suggests that even neonates possess rudimentary size constancy (Slater et al., 2010).

Shape constancy is the tendency to perceive an object as having the same shape even though, when the object is perceived from another angle, the shape projected onto the retina may change dramatically. When the top of a cup or a glass is seen from above, the visual sensations are in the shape of a circle. When the cup is seen from a slight angle, the sensations are elliptical, and when it is seen from the side, the retinal image is the same as that of a straight line. However, we still perceive the rim of the cup or glass as being a circle because of our familiarity with the object. In the first few months after birth, infants see the features of their caregivers, bottles, cribs, and toys from all different angles, so by the time they are 4 or 5 months old, a broad grasp of shape constancy seems to be established, at least under certain conditions

perceptual constancy The tendency to perceive objects as the same even though the sensations produced by them may differ when, for example, they differ in position or distance.

size constancy The tendency to perceive objects as being the same size even though the sizes of their images on the retina may differ as a result of distance.

shape constancy The tendency to perceive objects as being the same shape even though the shapes of their images on the retina may differ when the objects are viewed from different positions.

A Closer Look · Research

STRATEGIES FOR STUDYING THE DEVELOPMENT OF SHAPE CONSTANCY

People are said to show shape constancy when they perceive objects as having the same shape even though, when viewed from another angle, the shape projected onto the retina may be very different. We can determine whether infants have developed shape constancy through the process of *habituation,* which involves paying less attention to a repeated stimulus.

Neonates tend to show a preference for familiar objects (Barrile et al., 1999). But once they are a few months old, infants show a preference for novel objects. They have become habituated to familiar objects, and—if we can take the liberty of describing their responses in adult terms—they are apparently bored by them. Certain bodily responses indicate interest in an object, including a slower heart rate (as with 2-month-old infants placed face down on a visual cliff) and concentrated gazing. Therefore, when infants have become habituated to an object, their heart rates speed up moderately and they no longer show concentrated gazing.

Here, then, is the research strategy. Show an infant stimulus A for a prolonged period of time. At first, the heart rate will slow and the infant will focus on the object. But as time goes on, the heart rate will again rise to prestimulated levels and the infant's gaze will wander. Now show the infant stimulus B. If the heart rate again slows and the gaze again becomes concentrated, we can infer that stimulus B is perceived as a novel (different) object. But if the heart rate and pattern of gazing do not change, we can infer that the

infant does not perceive a difference between stimuli A and B.

If stimuli A and B are actually the same object seen from different angles, what does it mean when the infant's heart rate and pattern of gazing do not change? We can assume this lack of change means that the infant perceives stimuli A and B to be the same—in this case, the same object. Therefore, we can conclude that the infant has developed shape constancy.

Using a strategy similar to that just described, Caron and his colleagues (1979) first habituated 3-month-old infants to a square shown at different angles. The infants then were presented with one of two test stimuli: (1) the identical square, shown at an entirely new angle, or (2) a novel figure (a trapezoid), shown at the new angle. The two test stimuli projected identical trapezoidal images on the retina, even though their real shapes were different. Infants who were shown the square at the new angle showed little change in response. However, infants shown the trapezoid did show different responses. Therefore, it seems that infants perceived the trapezoid as novel, even though it cast the same retinal image as the square. But the infants were able to recognize the "real" shape of the square despite the fact that it cast a trapezoidal image on the retina. In other words, they showed shape constancy.

Reflect Can you think of examples of habituation in your own life?

(Slater et al., 2010). Strategies for studying the development of shape constancy are described in the nearby "A Closer Look—Research" feature.

Development of Hearing: The Better to Hear You With?

Neonates can crudely orient their heads in the direction of a sound (Burnham & Matlock, 2010). By 18 months of age, the accuracy of their sound-localizing ability approaches that of adults. Sensitivity to sounds increases in the first few months of life (Burnham & Mattock, 2010). As infants mature, the range of the pitch of the sounds they can sense gradually expands to include the adult's range of 20–20,000 cycles per second. The ability to detect differences in the pitch and loudness of sounds improves considerably throughout the preschool years. Auditory acuity also improves gradually over the first several years (Burnham & Mattock, 2010), although infants' hearing can be acute; many parents complain their napping infants

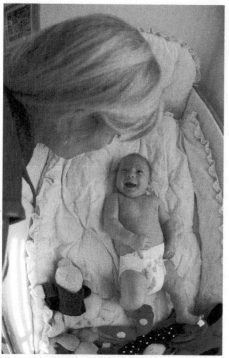

Delighted! Infants typically prefer the sound of their mother's voice and can discriminate the sounds of their parents' voices by the age of 3½ months.

awaken at the slightest sound. This is especially true if parents have been overprotective in attempting to keep their rooms as silent as possible. Infants who are normally exposed to a backdrop of moderate noise levels become habituated to them and are not likely to awaken unless there is a sudden, sharp noise.

By the age of 1 month, infants perceive differences between speech sounds that are highly similar. In a classic study relying on the **habituation** method, infants of this age could activate a recording of "bah" by sucking on a nipple (Eimas et al., 1971). As time went on, habituation occurred, as shown by decreased sucking in order to hear the "bah" sound. Then the researchers switched from "bah" to "pah." If the sounds had seemed the same to the infants, their lethargic sucking patterns would have continued. But the infants immediately sucked harder, suggesting that they perceived the difference. Other researchers have found that within another month or two, infants reliably discriminate between three-syllable words such as *marana* and *malana* (Kuhl et al., 2006).

Infants can discriminate the sounds of their parent's voices by 3½ months of age. In classic research, infants of this age were oriented toward their parents as they reclined in infant seats. The experimenters played recordings of the mother's or father's voice while the parents themselves remained inactive (Brower & Wilcox, 2012; Spelke & Owsley, 1979). The infants reliably looked at the parent whose voice was being played.

Young infants are capable of perceiving most of the speech sounds present in the world's languages. But after exposure to their native language, infants gradually lose the capacity to discriminate those sounds that are not found in the native tongue (Werker et al., 2007). Before 6 months of age, for example, infants reared in an English-speaking environment could discriminate sounds found in Hindi (a language of India) and Salish (a Native American language). But by 10–12 months of age, they had lost the ability to do so, as shown in Figure 5.18 ■ (Werker, 1989).

Infants also learn at an early age to ignore small, meaningless variations in the sounds of their native language. Adults do this routinely. For example, if someone speaking your language has a head cold or a slight accent, you ignore the minor variations in the person's pronunciation and hear these variations as the same sound. But when you hear slight variations in the sounds of a foreign language, you might assume that each variation carries a different meaning, and so you hear the sounds as different.

Infants can screen out meaningless sounds as early as 6 months of age (Kuhl et al., 2006). Patricia Kuhl and her colleagues (1997) presented American and Swedish infants with pairs of sounds in either their own language or the other language. The infants were trained to look over their shoulder when they heard a difference in the sounds and to ignore sound pairs that seemed to be the same. The infants routinely ignored variations in sounds that were part of their language, because they apparently perceived these variations as the same sound. But they noticed slight variations in the sounds of the other language. Another study demonstrated the same ability in infants as young as 2 months (Marean et al., 1992). By their first birthday, many infants understand many words, and some may even say a word or two of their own.

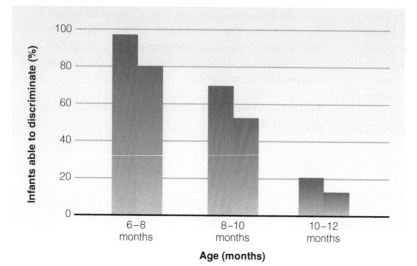

Figure 5.18 ■ Declining Ability to Discriminate the Sounds of Foreign Languages
Infants show a decline in the ability to discriminate sounds not found in their native language. Before 6 months of age, infants from English-speaking families could discriminate sounds found in Hindi (red bars) and Salish, a Native American language (blue bars). By 10-12 months of age, they could no longer do so.
Source: Werker (1989).

Development of Coordination of the Senses: If I See It, Can I Touch It?

Neonates crudely orient their heads toward sounds and pleasant odors. In this way, they increase the probability that the sources of the sounds and odors will also be sensed through visual scanning. Young infants can also recognize that objects experienced by one sense (e.g., vision) are the same as those experienced through another sense (e.g., touch). This ability has been demonstrated in infants as young as 1 month (Bushnell, 1993). One experiment demonstrating such understanding in 5-month-olds takes advantage of the fact that infants of this age tend to look longer at novel than at familiar sources of stimulation. Julie Féron and her colleagues (2006) first allowed 5-month-old infants to handle (become manually familiar with) groups of either two or three objects, presented one by one, to their right hand. They were then shown visual displays of either two or three objects. The infants looked significantly longer at the group of objects that differed from the one with which they had become manually familiar, showing a transfer of information from the sense of touch to the sense of vision.

Do Children Play an Active or a Passive Role in Perceptual Development?

Newborn children may have more sophisticated sensory capabilities than you expected. Still, their ways of perceiving the world are largely mechanical, or passive. The description of a stimulus capturing an infant's attention seems quite appropriate. Neonates seem to be generally at the mercy of external stimuli. When a bright light strikes, they attend to it. If the light moves slowly across the plane of their vision, they track it.

As time passes, broad changes occur in the perceptual processes of children, and the child's role in perception appears to become decidedly more active. Developmental psychologist Eleanor Gibson (1969, 1991) noted a number of these changes:

1. Intentional action replaces "capture" (automatic responses to stimulation). As infants mature and gain experience, purposeful scanning and exploration of the environment take the place of mechanical movements and passive responses to potent stimulation.

   Consider the scanning "strategies" of neonates. In a lighted room, neonates move their eyes mostly from left to right and back again. Mechanically, they sweep a horizontal plane. If they encounter an object that contrasts sharply with the background, their eye movements bounce back and forth against the edges. However, even when neonates awaken in a dark room, they show the stereotypical horizontal scanning pattern, with about two eye movements per second (Haith, 1990).

   The stereotypical quality of these initial scanning movements suggests that they are inborn. They provide strong evidence that the neonate is neurologically prewired to gather and seek visual information. They do not reflect what we would consider a purposeful, or intentional, effort to learn about the environment.

2. Systematic search replaces unsystematic search. Over the first few years of life, children become more active as they develop systematic ways of exploring the environment. They come to pay progressively more attention to details of objects and people and to make finer and finer discriminations.

3. Attention becomes selective. Older children become capable of selecting the information they need from the welter of confusion in the environment. For example, when older children are separated from their parents in a department store, they have the capacity to systematically scan for people of their parents' height, hair color, vocal characteristics, and so on. They are also more

habituation A process in which one becomes used to a repeated stimulus and therefore pays less attention to it.

EFFECTS OF EARLY EXPOSURE TO GARLIC, ALCOHOL, AND—GULP—VEGGIES

Research shows that infants begin to learn about the flavors found in their cultures through breast milk, and possibly even through amniotic fluid (Mennella et al., 2005). For example, psychologist Julie Mennella (2014) of the Monell Chemical Senses Center found that when women eat garlic, their infants suckle longer. It is not necessarily the case that the infants ingest more milk. It is also possible that they are spending at least some of the extra time in analyzing what they are tasting. They keep the milk in their mouths, pause, and perceive the flavors. Vanilla flavoring has a similar effect on suckling—increasing the duration.

Infants ingest amniotic fluid while they are still in the womb, and this fluid also acquires a distinct smell after a woman eats garlic, according to Mennella. It would appear that the fetus detects this change in its environment.

No Direct Road to Alcohol Abuse Does exposure to alcohol in the breast milk of mothers who drink create a disposition toward alcohol abuse in the infant? Mennella's research suggests that the truth may lie in the opposite direction. First of all, infants appear not to like the taste of alcohol in breast milk. Mennella (2001, 2014) found that infants aged 2–5 months drink less breast milk when the mother has recently drunk alcohol. In fact, they ingest more breast milk once the alcohol is out of the mother's system, apparently to compensate for the lessened calorie intake at the previous feeding.

A study by Mennella and Garcia (2000) showed that early exposure to the odor of alcohol may also be something of a turnoff to infants. In this study, Mennella and Garcia compared the preferences of children who had been exposed to alcohol around the house during infancy with those of children who had not. All the children were about 4–6 years old at the time of testing. Children who had been exposed to alcohol early were significantly more likely than the other children to dislike the odor of a bottle containing alcohol.

I would not suggest that parents drink alcohol to discourage their children from drinking later on. But the findings do seem to contradict what one might have expected.

And What About Encouraging Children to Eat Their Veggies During Infancy? Many parents in the United States understand the benefits of eating vegetables and bring out the jars of vegetable baby food when they are feeding their infants. Does early exposure to these foods encourage or discourage eating them?

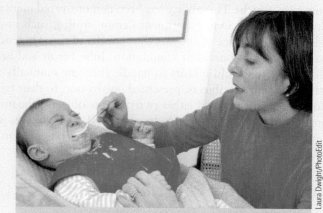

Laura Dwight/PhotoEdit

How Do You Encourage Children to Eat Their Veggies? Do you want to talk about cruel experimental treatments that skirt the edges of the ethical limits of the researchers? Try this one on for size: Leann Birch and her colleagues repeatedly exposed 4- to 7-month-old infants to baby food consisting of vegetables. Actually, the "treatment" apparently had the effect of teaching the infants to like vegetables. In terms of what the experimenters measured, they found that the infants exposed to vegetables ate more of them during test trials.

Early exposure generally seems to have a positive effect on children's appetites for vegetables (Mennella, 2014). Consider a study of 4- to 7-month-old infants by Leann Birch and her colleagues (1998). The investigators repeatedly exposed infants to vegetables such as peas and green beans in the form of baby food to see whether the infants would subsequently eat more or less of them. Thirty-nine infants were fed the target foods once a day for 10 consecutive days. During that period, their consumption of the vegetables doubled from an average of 35 grams to an average of 72 grams. Moreover, the infants became more likely to eat similar foods—that is, other vegetables. Mennella and her colleagues have also found that the infants of mothers who eat more diverse diets are more willing to eat a variety of foods (Menella, 2014). Moreover, studies of rodents, pigs, and sheep show that once they are weaned, young animals prefer the flavors to which they were exposed through their mothers' milk. Early exposure to the foods that are traditional within a culture may be a key to shaping an infant's food preferences (Mennella, 2014).

Reflect: Do you like vegetables? Can you trace your food preferences to early experiences in the home?

capable of discriminating the spot where the parent was last seen. A younger child is more likely to be confused by the welter of voices and faces and aisles and to be unable to extract essential information from this backdrop.

4. Irrelevant information becomes ignored. Older children gain the capacity to screen out, or deploy their attention away from, stimuli that are irrelevant to the task at hand. This might mean shutting out the noise of cars in the street or radios in the neighborhood in order to focus on a book.

In short, children develop from passive, mechanical reactors to the world about them into active, purposeful seekers and organizers of sensory information. They develop from beings whose attention is diffuse and "captured" into people who make decisions about what they will attend to. This is a process that, like so many others, appears to depend on both maturation and experience.

Let us now screen out distractions and turn our attention to considering the importance of maturation (the development of nature) and experience (nurture) in perceptual development.

What Is the Evidence for the Roles of Nature and Nurture in Perceptual Development?

Compelling evidence supports the idea that our inborn sensory capacities play a crucial role in our perceptual development. For one thing, neonates come into the world with a good number of perceptual skills. They can see nearby objects quite well, and their hearing is usually fine. They are also born with tendencies to track moving objects, to systematically scan the horizon, and to prefer certain kinds of stimuli. Preferences for different kinds of visual stimuli appear to unfold on schedule as the first months wear on. Sensory changes, like motor changes, appear to be linked to maturation of the nervous system.

For these reasons, it seems clear that we do have certain inborn ways of responding to sensory input—certain "categories" and built-in limits—that enable us to perceive certain aspects of the world of physical reality.

Evidence that experience plays a crucial role in perceptual development is also compelling. We could use any of hundreds of studies with children and other species to make the point, but let us limit our discussion to a couple of examples of research with kittens and human infants.

Children and lower animals have critical periods in their perceptual development. Failure to receive adequate sensory stimulation during these critical periods can result in permanent sensory deficits (Cascio, 2010; Werker & Hensch, 2015). For example, newborn kittens raised with a patch over one eye wind up with few or no cells in the visual area of the cerebral cortex that would normally be stimulated by light entering that eye. In effect, that eye becomes blind, even though sensory receptors in the eye itself may fire in response to light. On the other hand, when the eye of an adult cat is patched for the same amount of time, the animal does not lose vision in that eye. The critical period apparently has passed. Similarly, if health problems require that a child's eye must be patched for an extensive period of time during the first year, the child's visual acuity in that eye may be impaired.

Consider a study of visual acuity among 28 human infants who had been deprived of all patterned visual input by cataracts in one or both eyes until they were treated at 1 week to 9 months of age (Maurer et al., 1999). Immediately following treatment, their visual acuity was no better than that of normal neonates, suggesting that their lack of visual experience had impaired their visual development. However, their visual acuity improved rapidly over the month following treatment. They showed some improvement in as little as 1 hour after visual input.

And so, with perceptual development, just as with other dimensions of development, nature and nurture play indispensable roles. Today, few theorists would subscribe to either extreme. Most agree that nature and nurture interact to shape perceptual development. Nature continues to guide the unfolding of the child's physical systems. Yet nurture continues to interact with nature in the development of these systems. We know that inborn physical structures, such as the nature of the cortex of the brain, place limits on our abilities to respond to the world. But we also know that experience continues to help shape our most basic physical structures. For example, sensorimotor experiences thicken the cortex of the brain. Sensory experiences are linked to the very development of neurons in the cortex, causing dendrites to proliferate and affecting myelination.

In the next chapter, we will see how nature and nurture influence the development of thought and language in infants.

Section Review

18. At 2 months of age, infants tend to fixate longer on a _____ (scrambled or real?) face.

19. Neonates direct their attention to the _____ (center or edges?) of objects.

20. Researchers have studied depth perception in infants through the use of the visual _____.

21. Research suggests that infants have developed size constancy by about _____ months.

22. As infants develop, they have _____ (greater or less?) ability to screen out meaningless sounds in their native languages.

23. As time passes during infancy, one change in perceptual development is that intentional action replaces _____, or automatic responses to stimulation.

24. Research shows that both nature and _____ are essential to perceptual development.

Reflect & Relate: What do you think it would mean if infants came into the world "prewired" to prefer the human face to other, equally complex visual stimulation? Can you explain the evolutionary advantage that such prewiring would provide?

Chapter Review

5.1 What Are the Sequences of Physical Growth and Development During Infancy?

Three key sequences of physical development are cephalocaudal development, proximodistal development, and differentiation. Infants usually double their birth weight in 5 months and triple it by the first birthday. Height increases by about half in the first year. Infants grow another 4–6 inches in the second year and gain another 4–7 pounds. The head gradually diminishes in proportion to the rest of the body. Failure to thrive (FTT) is a serious disorder that impairs growth in infancy and early childhood. FTT can have organic or nonorganic causes. Deficiencies in caregiver–child interaction may play a major role in FTT.

5.2 What Are the Nutritional Needs of Infants?

Infants require breast milk or an iron-fortified infant formula. Introduction of solid foods is recommended at

4–6 months. Caregivers are advised to gradually build up the baby's diet to include a variety of foods. Breast milk is tailored to human digestion, contains essential nutrients, provides the mothers' antibodies, helps protect against infant diarrhea, and is less likely than formula to cause allergies. However, some environmental toxins are found in breast milk.

5.3 How Do the Brain and Nervous System Develop During Infancy?

Neurons are cells that receive and transmit messages in the form of chemicals called neurotransmitters. As the child matures, axons grow in length, dendrites and axon terminals proliferate, and many neurons become wrapped in myelin, enabling them to function more efficiently. The brain is the command center of the developing organism. The brain triples in weight by the first birthday, reaching nearly 70% of its adult weight. There are two major prenatal growth spurts. Neurons proliferate during the first growth spurt; the second spurt is due mainly to the proliferation of dendrites and axon terminals. Sensory and motor areas of the brain begin to develop because of maturation, but sensory stimulation and motor activity also spur development. Rats raised in enriched environments develop more dendrites and axon terminals. Malnutrition is related to a small brain, fewer neurons, and less myelination.

5.4 How Does Motor Activity Develop During Infancy?

Motor development consists of developments in the activity of muscles and is connected with changes in posture, movement, and coordination. Children gain the ability to move their bodies through a sequence of activities that includes rolling over, sitting up, crawling, creeping, walking, and running. The sequence remains stable, but some children skip a step. Both maturation (nature) and experience (nurture) play indispensable roles in motor development. Infants need some opportunity for experimentation before they can engage in milestones such as sitting up and walking. Development of motor skills can be accelerated by training, but the effect is generally slight.

5.5 How Do Sensation and Perception Develop During Infancy?

Neonates are nearsighted and have poor peripheral vision. Acuity and peripheral vision approximate adult levels by the age of 6 months. Neonates attend longer to stripes than to blobs, and by 8–12 weeks of age they prefer curved lines to straight lines. Two-month-old infants fixate longer on the human face than on other stimuli. Some researchers argue that neonates prefer faces not because they are faces but because they are complex images. Infants can discriminate their mother's face from a stranger's after about 8 hours of contact. Neonates direct their attention to the edges of objects, but 2-month-olds scan from the edges inward. Researchers study the development of depth perception by means such as the classic visual cliff apparatus. Most infants refuse to venture out over the visual cliff by the time they can crawl. Researchers have speculated that infants may need some experience crawling before they can develop fear of heights. Perceptual constancy is a tendency to perceive an object to be the same, even though it produces different sensations under different conditions. Size constancy appears to be present by 2½–3 months of age; shape-constancy develops by age 4–5 months. Neonates reflexively orient their heads toward a sound. By 18 months of age, infants locate sounds about as well as adults. Infants discriminate caregivers' voices by 3½ months of age. Early infants can perceive most of the speech sounds throughout the languages of the world, but by 10–12 months of age, this ability lessens. Neonates seem to be at the mercy of external stimuli, but later on, intentional action replaces capture. Systematic search replaces unsystematic search, attention becomes selective, and irrelevant information gets ignored. Evidence shows that sensory changes are linked to maturation of the nervous system (nature) but that experience also plays a crucial role in perceptual development (nurture). For one thing, there are critical periods in the perceptual development of children and lower animals, such that sensory experience is required to optimize—or maintain—sensory capacities.

Key Terms

differentiation   152
failure to thrive (FTT)   154
marasmus   155
canalization   155
kwashiorkor   158
nerves   162
neurons   162
dendrites   162
axon   162

neurotransmitter   162
myelin sheath   163
myelination   163
multiple sclerosis   163
medulla   164
cerebellum   164
cerebrum   164
ulnar grasp   167
pincer grasp   167

locomotion   168
toddler   168
sensation   171
perception   171
perceptual constancy   174
size constancy   174
shape constancy   174
habituation   177

Infancy: Cognitive Development

Major Topics

Features

TruthorFiction?

 For 2-month-old infants, "out of sight" is "out of mind." **p. 187**

 A 1-hour-old infant may imitate an adult who sticks his or her tongue out. **p. 193**

 Psychologists can begin to measure intelligence in infancy. **p. 196**

Infant crying is a primitive form of language. **p. 198**

 You can advance children's development of pronunciation by correcting their errors. **p. 205**

Children are "prewired" to listen to language in such a way that they come to understand words and rules of grammar. **p. 211**

Laurent resumes his experiments of the day before. He grabs in succession a celluloid swan, a box, etc., stretches out his arm and lets them fall. He distinctly varies the position of the fall. Sometimes he stretches out his arm vertically, sometimes he holds it obliquely, in front of or behind his eyes, etc. When the object falls in a new position, he lets it fall two or three times more on the same place, as though to study the spatial relation; then he modifies the situation.

—Jean Piaget (1963 [1936])

Is this the description of a scientist at work? In a way, it is. Although Swiss psychologist Jean Piaget was describing his 11-month-old son Laurent, children of this age frequently act like scientists, performing what Piaget called "experiments in order to see."

In this chapter, we chronicle the developing thought processes of infants and toddlers—that is, their cognitive development. First we focus on the sensorimotor stage of cognitive development hypothesized by Piaget. Then we examine infant memory and imitation. We next explore individual differences in infant intelligence. Finally, we turn our attention to a singularly human and most remarkable aspect of cognitive development: language.

Rubberball

183

6.1 Cognitive Development: Jean Piaget

Cognitive development focuses on the development of children's ways of perceiving and mentally representing the world. Piaget labeled children's concepts of the world **schemes**. He hypothesized that children try to use **assimilation** to absorb new events into existing schemes; and when assimilation does not enable them to make sense of novel events, children try to modify existing schemes through **accommodation**.

Piaget (1963 [1936]) hypothesized that children's cognitive processes develop in an orderly sequence, or series, of stages. As with motor and perceptual development, some children may be more advanced than others at particular ages, but the developmental sequence does not normally vary (Barrouillet, 2015). Piaget identified four major stages of cognitive development: sensorimotor, preoperational, concrete operational, and formal operational. In this chapter, we will discuss the sensorimotor stage.

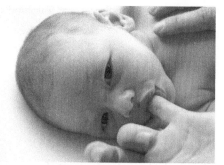

Simple Reflexes At birth, neonates assimilate objects into reflexive responses. But even within hours after birth, neonates begin to modify reflexes as a result of experience. For example, they adapt sucking patterns to the shape of the nipple. (But don't be too impressed; porpoises are born swimming and "know" to rise to the surface of the ocean to breathe.)

scheme According to Piaget, an action pattern (such as a reflex) or mental structure that is involved in the acquisition or organization of knowledge.

assimilation According to Piaget, the incorporation of new events or knowledge into existing schemes.

accommodation According to Piaget, the modification of existing schemes in order to incorporate new events or knowledge.

What Is the Sensorimotor Stage of Cognitive Development?

Piaget referred to the first 2 years of cognitive development as the sensorimotor stage, a time when children demonstrate these developments by means of sensory and motor activity. Although it may be difficult for us to imagine how we can develop and use cognitive processes in the absence of language, children do so in many ways.

During the sensorimotor stage, infants progress from responding to events with reflexes, or ready-made schemes, to goal-directed behavior that reveals awareness of past events. During this stage, they come to form mental representations of objects and events, to hold complex pictures of past events in mind, and to solve problems by mental trial and error.

Piaget divided the sensorimotor stage into six substages, each of which is characterized by more complex behavior than the preceding substage. But there is also continuity from substage to substage. Each substage can be characterized as a variation on a theme in which earlier forms of behavior are repeated, varied, and coordinated.

Substage 1: Simple Reflexes

The first substage covers the first month after birth. It is dominated by the assimilation of sources of stimulation into inborn reflexes such as grasping, visual tracking, crying, sucking, and crudely turning the head toward a sound.

At birth, reflexes have a stereotypical, inflexible quality. But even within the first few hours, neonates begin to modify reflexes as a result of experience. For example, infants adapt (accommodate) patterns of sucking to the shape of the nipple and the rate of flow of fluid.

During the first month or so, infants apparently do not connect stimulation perceived through different sensory modalities. For example, they make no attempt to grasp objects that they visually track. Crude turning toward sources of sounds and smells has a mechanical look such that it cannot be considered purposeful searching.

Substage 2: Primary Circular Reactions

The second substage, primary circular reactions, lasts from about 1 to 4 months of age and is characterized by the beginnings of the ability to coordinate various sensorimotor schemes. In this substage, infants tend to repeat stimulating actions that first occurred by chance. For example, they may lift their arm repeatedly to bring it into view. A circular reaction is a behavior that is repeated. **Primary circular reactions** focus on the infant's own body rather than on the external environment. Piaget noticed the following primary circular reaction in his son, Laurent:

> At 2 months 4 days, Laurent by chance discovers his right index finger and looks at it briefly. At 2 months 11 days, he inspects for a moment his open right hand, perceived by chance. At 2 months 17 days, he follows its spontaneous movement for a moment, then examines it several times while it searches for his nose or rubs his eye.
>
> At 2 months 21 days, he holds his two fists in the air and looks at the left one, after which he slowly brings it toward his face and rubs his nose with it, then his eye. A moment later the left hand again approaches his face; he looks at it and touches his nose. He recommences and laughs five or six times in succession while moving the left hand to his face.... He laughs beforehand but begins to smile again on seeing the hand.
>
> —Piaget (1963 [1936], pp. 96–97)

Thus, Laurent, early in the third month, visually tracks the behavior of his hand, but his visual observations do not seem to influence their movement. At about 2 months 21 days, Laurent can apparently exert some control over his hands, because he seems to know when a hand is about to move (and entertain him). But the link between looking at and moving the hands remains weak. A few days later, however, his looking "acts" on the hands, causing them to remain in his field of vision. It thus appears that some sensorimotor coordination has been achieved. An action is repeated because it stimulates the infant.

In terms of assimilation and accommodation, we can say that the child is attempting to assimilate the motor scheme (moving the hand) into the sensory scheme (looking at it). But the schemes do not automatically fit. Several days of apparent trial and error pass, during which the infant seems to be trying to make accommodations so that the schemes will fit.

Goal-directed behavior makes significant advances during the second substage. During the month after birth, infants visually track objects that contrast with their backgrounds, especially moving objects. But this ready-made behavior is largely automatic, so that the infant is "looking and seeing." By the third month, infants may examine objects repeatedly and intensely, as Laurent did. It seems that the infant is no longer simply looking and seeing but is now "looking in order to see." And by the end of the third month, Laurent seems to be moving his hands in order to look at them.

Because Laurent (and other infants) repeat actions that enable them to see, cognitive-developmental psychologists consider sensorimotor coordination self-reinforcing. Laurent does not seem to be looking or moving his hands because these acts allow him to satisfy a more basic drive such as hunger or thirst; however, the desire to prolong stimulation may be just as "basic."

Substage 3: Secondary Circular Reactions

The third substage lasts from about 4 to 8 months and is characterized by **secondary circular reactions**, in which patterns of activity are repeated because of their effect on the environment. In the second substage (primary circular reactions), infants are focused on their own bodies, as Piaget described in Laurent. In the third substage (secondary circular reactions), the focus shifts to objects and environmental events. Infants may now learn to pull strings in order to make a plastic face appear or to shake an object in order to hear it rattle.

Although infants in the third substage track the trajectory of moving objects, they abandon the search when the object disappears from view. As we will see, concepts about objects are quite limited at these ages, especially when the third substage begins.

Primary Circular Reactions In the substage of primary circular reactions, infants repeat actions that involve their bodies. The 3-month-old in this picture is also beginning to coordinate visual and sensorimotor schemes; that is, looking at the hand is becoming coordinated with holding it in the field of vision.

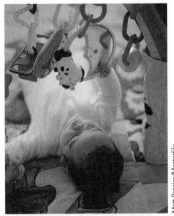

Secondary Circular Reactions In the substage of secondary circular reactions, patterns of activity are repeated because of their effect on the environment. This infant shakes a rattle to produce an interesting sound.

primary circular reactions The repetition of actions that first occurred by chance and that focus on the infant's own body.

secondary circular reactions The repetition of actions that produce an effect on the environment.

Coordination of Secondary Schemes During this substage, infants coordinate their behaviors to attain specific goals. This infant is looking under a couch to retrieve a toy.

Substage 4: Coordination of Secondary Schemes

In the fourth substage, infants no longer act simply to prolong interesting occurrences. Now they can coordinate schemes to attain specific goals. Infants begin to show intentional, goal-directed behavior in which they differentiate between the means of achieving a goal and the goal or end in itself. For example, they may lift a piece of cloth in order to reach a toy that they had seen a parent place under the cloth. In this example, the scheme of picking up the cloth (the means) is coordinated with the scheme of reaching for the toy (the goal or end).

This example indicates that the infant has *mentally represented* the toy placed under the cloth. Consider another example. At the age of 5 months, one of Piaget's daughters, Lucienne, was reaching across her crib for a toy. As she did so, Piaget obscured the toy with his hand. Lucienne pushed her father's hand aside but, in doing so, became distracted and began to play with the hand. A few months later, Lucienne did not allow her father's hand to distract her from the goal of reaching the toy. She moved the hand firmly to the side and then grabbed the toy. The mental representation of the object appears to have become more persistent. The intention of reaching the object was also maintained; therefore, Lucienne perceived the hand as a barrier and not just as another interesting stimulus.

During the fourth substage, infants also gain the capacity to copy actions that are not in their own repertoires. Infants can now imitate many gestures and sounds that they had previously ignored. The imitation of a new facial gesture implies that infants have mentally represented their own faces and can tell what parts of their faces they are moving through feedback from facial muscles. For example, when a girl imitates her mother sticking out her tongue, it would appear that she has coordinated moving her own tongue with feedback from muscles in the tongue and mouth. In this way, imitation suggests a great deal about the child's emerging self-concept.

Substage 5: Tertiary Circular Reactions

In the fifth substage, which lasts from about 12 to 18 months of age, Piaget looked on the behavior of infants as characteristic of budding scientists. Infants now engage in **tertiary circular reactions**, or purposeful adaptations of established schemes to specific situations. Behavior takes on a new experimental quality, and infants may vary their actions dozens of times in a deliberate trial-and-error fashion in order to learn how things work.

Piaget reported an example of tertiary circular reactions by his daughter Jacqueline. The episode was an experiment in which Piaget placed a stick outside Jacqueline's playpen, which had wooden bars (Piaget, 1963 [1936]). At first, Jacqueline grasped the stick and tried to pull it sideways into the playpen. The stick was too long and did not fit through the bars. Over a number of days of trial and error, however, Jacqueline discovered that she could bring the stick between the bars by turning it upright. In future presentations, she would immediately turn the stick upright and bring it in.

Jacqueline's eventual success with the stick was the result of overt trial and error. In the sixth substage, described next, the solution to problems is often more sudden, suggesting that children have manipulated the elements of the problems in their minds and engaged in mental trial and error before displaying the correct overt response.

Tertiary Circular Reactions In this substage, infants vary their actions in a trial-and-error fashion to learn how things work. This child is fascinated by the results of pulling on the end of a roll of toilet paper.

tertiary circular reactions The purposeful adaptation of established schemes to new situations.

Substage 6: Invention of New Means Through Mental Combinations

The sixth substage lasts from about 18 to 24 months of age. It serves as a transition between sensorimotor development and the development of symbolic thought. External exploration is replaced by mental exploration.

Recall Jacqueline's trials with the stick. Piaget waited until his other children, Lucienne and Laurent, were 18 months old, and then he presented them with the playpen and stick problem. By waiting until 18 months, he could attribute differences in their performance to the age change instead of a possible warm-up effect from earlier tests. Rather than engaging in overt trial and error, the 18-month-old children sat and studied the situation for a few moments. Then they grasped the stick, turned it upright, and brought it into the playpen with little overt effort.

Jacqueline had at first failed with the stick. She then turned it every which way, happening on a solution almost by chance. Lucienne and Laurent solved the problem fairly rapidly, suggesting that they mentally represented the stick and the bars of the playpen and perceived that the stick would not fit through as it was. They must then have rotated the mental image of the stick until they perceived a position that would allow the stick to pass between the bars.

At about 18 months, children may also use imitation to symbolize, or stand for, a plan of action. Consider how Lucienne goes about retrieving a watch chain her father placed in a matchbox. It seems that symbolic imitation serves her as a way of thinking out loud:

> I put the chain back into the box and reduce the opening. [Lucienne] is not aware of [how to open and close] the match box. [She] possesses two preceding schemes: turning the box over in order to empty it of its contents, and sliding her fingers into the slit to make the chain come out. [She] puts her finger inside and gropes to reach the chain, but fails. A pause follows during which Lucienne manifests a very curious reaction....
>
> She looks at the slit with great attention. Then, several times in succession, she opens and shuts her mouth, at first slightly, then wider and wider! Apparently Lucienne understands the existence of a cavity.... [Lucienne then] puts her finger in the slit, and, instead of trying as before to reach the chain, she pulls so as to enlarge the opening. She succeeds and grasps the chain.
>
> —Piaget (1963 [1936], pp. 337–338)

What Is Object Permanence? How Does It Develop?

Object permanence is the recognition that an object or person continues to exist when out of sight. Your child development textbook continues to exist when you accidentally leave it in the library after studying for the big test, and an infant's mother continues to exist even when she is in another room. Your realization that your book exists, although out of view, is an example of object permanence. If an infant acts as though its mother no longer exists when she is out of sight, the infant does not have the concept of object permanence. The development of object permanence is tied into the development of infants' working memory and reasoning ability (Kibbe & Leslie, 2013; Yermolayeva & Rakison, 2014).

Neonates show no tendency to respond to objects that are not within their immediate sensory grasp. By the age of 2 months, infants may show some surprise if an object (such as a toy duck) is placed behind a screen and then taken away so that when the screen is lifted, it is absent. However, they make no effort to search for the missing object. Through the first 6 months or so, when the screen is placed between the object and the infant, the infant behaves as though the object is no longer there (see Figure 6.1 ■).

TRUTH OR FICTION REVISITED: It is true that "out of sight" is "out of mind" for 2-month-old infants. Apparently, they do not yet reliably mentally represent objects they see.

object permanence Recognition that objects continue to exist even when they are not seen.

Figure 6.1 ■ Development of Object Permanence
To the infant who is in the early part of the sensorimotor stage, out of sight is truly out of mind. Once a sheet of paper is placed between the infant and a toy, the infant loses all interest in the toy. From evidence of this sort, Piaget concluded that the toy is not mentally represented. On the right we see a child in a later part of the sensorimotor stage. This child does mentally represent objects and lifts the cloth to reach a toy that has been screened from sight.

Doug Goodman / Science Source

There are some interesting advances in the development of the object concept by about the sixth month (Piaget's substage 3). For example, an infant at this age will tend to look for an object that has been dropped, behavior that suggests some form of object permanence. There is also reason to believe that by this age, the infant perceives a mental representation (image) of an object, such as a favorite toy, in response to sensory impressions of part of the object. This is shown by the infant's reaching for an object that is partly hidden.

By 8–12 months of age (Piaget's substage 4), infants will seek to retrieve objects that have been completely hidden. But in observing his own children, Piaget (1963 [1936]) noted an interesting error known as the A-not-B error. Piaget repeatedly hid a toy behind a screen (A), and each time, his infant removed the screen and retrieved the toy. Then, as the infant watched, Piaget hid the toy behind another screen (B) in a different place. Still, the infant tried to recover the toy by pushing aside the first screen (A). It is as though the child had learned that a certain motor activity would reinstate the missing toy. The child's concept of the object did not, at this age, extend to recognition that objects usually remain in the place where they have been most recently mentally represented.

But under certain conditions, 9- to 10-month-old infants do not show the A-not-B error. They apparently need a certain degree of maturation of the front lobes of the cerebral cortex, which fosters the development of working memory and attention (Johansson et al., 2014). Also, if infants are allowed to search for the object immediately after seeing it hidden, the error often does not occur. But if they are forced to wait 5 or more seconds before looking, they are likely to commit the A-not-B error (Wellman et al., 1986).

Most children develop object permanence before they develop emotional bonds to specific caregivers. It seems logical that infants must have permanent representations of their mothers before they show distress at being separated from them. But wait, you say. Don't even 3- or 4-month-old infants cry when mother leaves and then stop crying when she returns and picks them up? Doesn't this behavior pattern show object permanence? Not necessarily. Infants appear to appreciate the comforts provided by their mothers and to express displeasure when these comforts end (such as when their mothers depart). The expression of displeasure frequently results in the reinstatement of pleasure (being held, fed, and spoken to). Therefore, infants may learn to engage in these protests when their mothers leave because of the positive consequences of protesting, —not because they have developed object permanence.

Nevertheless, studies by Renee Baillargeon and her colleagues (Aguiar & Baillargeon, 1999; Wang et al., 2005) show that some rudimentary knowledge of object permanence may be present as early as 2½–3½ months. In one study, Baillargeon

(1987) first showed 3½- and 4½-month-olds the event illustrated in the top part of Figure 6.2 ▪. A screen rotated back and forth through a 180-degree arc like a drawbridge. After several trials, the infants showed habituation; that is, they spent less time looking at the screen. Next, a box was placed in the path of the screen, as shown in the middle drawing of Figure 6.2. The infant could see the box at the beginning of each trial but could no longer see it when the screen reached the box. In one condition, labeled the "possible event," the screen stopped when it reached the box. In another condition, labeled the "impossible event," the screen rotated through a full 180-degree arc, as though the box were no longer behind it. (How could this happen? Unknown to the infant, a trapdoor was released, causing the box to drop out of the way.) The infants looked longer at the "impossible event" than at the "possible" one. (Infants look longer at unexpected events.) So it seems they were surprised that the screen did not stop when it reached the box. Therefore, children as young as 3½ months of age realized that the box continued to exist when it was hidden. But why, then, do infants not actively look for hidden objects until about 8 months of age? Perhaps, as Piaget suggested, *coordination of acts* (such as removing a barrier in order to reach a toy) does not occur until the later age.

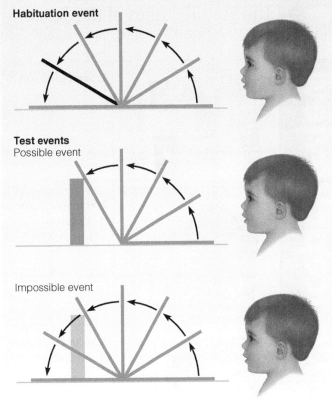

Figure 6.2 ▪ Object-Permanence before 4 Months of Age?
Renee Baillargeon (1987) used the technique shown here to demonstrate that knowledge of object permanence may exist before 4 months of age. She first showed infants a screen rotated back and forth like a drawbridge (top drawing). After infants showed habituation, a box was placed in the path of the screen. The middle drawing shows a possible event—the screen stops when it reaches the box. The bottom drawing shows an impossible event—the screen rotates through a full 180-degree arc as though the box were no longer behind it. (The experimenter had removed it, unknown to the infant.) Infants looked longer at the impossible event, suggesting they realized the box still existed even when hidden behind the screen.

© Cengage Learning®

What Are the Strengths and Limitations of Piaget's Theory of Sensorimotor Development?

Piaget's theory remains a comprehensive model of infant cognition. Many of his observations of his own infants have been confirmed by others. The pattern and sequence of events he described have been observed among American, European, African, and Asian infants (Werner, 1988). Still, research has raised questions about the validity of many of Piaget's claims (Reed, 2013).

First, most researchers now agree that cognitive development is not as tied to discrete stages as Piaget suggested (Fuller, 2012; Reed, 2013). A stage theory requires that changes be discontinuous. In Piaget's theory, children's developing cognitive responses to the world would have to change relatively suddenly. Although later developments do seem to build on earlier ones, the process appears to be more gradual than discontinuous.

Second, Piaget emphasized the role of maturation, almost to the point of excluding adult and peer influences on cognitive development. However, these interpersonal influences have been shown to play roles in cognitive development (Chen & Hancock, 2011; Reed, 2013).

Third, Piaget appears to have underestimated infants' competence (Reed, 2013). For example, infants display object permanence earlier than he believed (Wang et al., 2005).

Another example of early infant competence is provided by studies on **deferred imitation,** which is imitation of an action that may have occurred hours, days, or even weeks earlier. The presence of deferred imitation suggests that children have mentally represented behavior patterns. Piaget believed that deferred imitation appears at about 18 months, but others have found that infants show deferred imitation as early as 9 months. In one study, 9-month-old infants watched an adult perform behaviors such as pushing a button to produce a beep (Meltzoff et al., 2013). When

deferred imitation The imitation of people and events that were encountered or experienced hours, days, or weeks in the past.

The Six Substages of the Sensorimotor Stage, According to Piaget

	Substage	Comments
© Praefice/G&J/iStockphoto/Black Star	**1.** Simple reflexes (0–1 month)	Assimilation of new objects into reflexive responses. Infants "look and see." Inborn reflexes can be modified by experience.
Picture Partners/Alamy	**2.** Primary circular reactions (1–4 months)	Repetition of actions that may have initially occurred by chance but that have satisfying or interesting results. Infants "look in order to see." The focus is on the infant's body. Infants do not yet distinguish between themselves and the external world.
Matt Brasier/Masterfile	**3.** Secondary circular reactions (4–8 months)	Repetition of schemes that have interesting effects on the environment. The focus shifts to external objects and events. There is initial cognitive awareness that schemes influence the external world.
Heleen Sitter/The Image Bank/Getty Images	**4.** Coordination of secondary schemes (8–12 months)	Coordination of secondary schemes, such as looking and grasping to attain specific goals. There is the beginning of intentionality and means–end differentiation. We find imitation of actions not already in infants' repertoires.
David Mendelsohn/Masterfile	**5.** Tertiary circular reactions (12–18 months)	Purposeful adaptation of established schemes to specific situations. Behavior takes on an experimental quality. There is overt trial and error in problem solving.
Photo by Stephen Ausmus/Courtesy of the USDA	**6.** Invention of new means through mental combinations (18–24 months)	Mental trial and error in problem solving. Infants take "mental detours" based on cognitive maps. Infants engage in deferred imitation and symbolic play. Infants' cognitive advances are made possible by mental representations of objects and events and the beginnings of symbolic thought.

A Closer Look | Research

ORANGUTANS, CHIMPS, MAGPIES, AND OBJECT PERMANENCE

Let us not limit our discussion of the development of object permanence to humans. Comparative psychologists have also studied the development of object permanence in nonhuman species, including dogs and cats, primates, and even magpies. Animal boosters will be intrigued by the findings reported in these articles:

- "Object Permanence in Orangutans (*Pongo pygmaeus*), Chimpanzees (*Pan troglodytes*), and Children (*Homo sapiens*)" (Call, 2001)

- "Tracking the Displacement of Objects: A Series of Tasks with Great Apes (*Pan troglodytes, Pan paniscus, Gorilla gorilla,* and *Pongo pygmaeus*) and Young Children (*Homo sapiens*)" (Barth & Call, 2006)

Most researchers conclude that primates such as chimpanzees and gorillas do not make use of language—even sign language—in the sophisticated way that humans do, but Call (2001) found that three species—orangutan, chimp, and human—performed at the same intellectual level in tasks used to assess object permanence. The caveat is that orangutans and chimpanzees mature more rapidly than humans, and Call was comparing juvenile and adult orangutans with 19- to 26-month-old human infants.

Now, the magpies. Magpies are notorious thieves in the bird world, and they also hide their food to protect it from other animals—especially other magpies. Bettina Pollock and her colleagues (2000) found that magpies develop object permanence before they begin to hide food. Think about it: Magpies would not profit from hiding their food if "out of sight" meant "out of existence."

Reflect Why do you think that scientists study the development of object permanence in nonhuman species? Can you provide at least two possible reasons?

---

given a chance to play with the same objects a day later, many infants imitated the actions they had witnessed.

Let me mention one final example of infant competence that occurs much earlier than Piaget predicted. Five-month-old infants may be able to grasp some basic computational concepts: more and less (see the nearby "A Closer Look—Research" feature). In Piaget's view, this ability does not emerge until approximately 2 years of age.

Psychologists Andrew Meltzoff and M. Keith Moore (2002) assert bluntly that "the sensorimotor theory of infancy has been overthrown," but they admit that "there is little consensus on a replacement." Perhaps Piaget is not so readily replaced.

Section Review

1. Piaget labeled children's concepts of the world as _____.

2. Children try to _____ new events into existing schemes.

3. Piaget's _____ stage spans the first 2 years of cognitive development.

4. Primary _____ reactions are characterized by repeating stimulating actions that occur by chance.

5. In _____ circular reactions, activity is repeated because of its effect on the environment.

6. _____ circular reactions are purposeful adaptations of established schemes to specific situations.

7. Object _____ is recognition that an object or person continues to exist when out of sight.

Reflect & Relate: How might an outside observer gather evidence that you and a friend or family member have mentally represented each other? How are you asked to demonstrate that you have mentally represented the subject matter in this textbook and in this course?

6.2 Information Processing

The information-processing approach to cognitive development focuses on how children manipulate or process information coming in from the environment or already stored in the minds (Reed, 2013).

What Is the Capacity of the Memory of Infants?

Many of the cognitive capabilities of infants—recognizing the faces of familiar people, developing object permanence, and, in fact, learning in any form—depend on one critical aspect of cognitive development: memory (Kibbe & Leslie, 2014). Even neonates demonstrate memory for stimuli to which they have been exposed previously. As mentioned earlier, neonates adjust their rate of sucking to hear a recording of their mother reading a story she had read aloud during the last weeks of pregnancy (DeCasper & Fifer, 1980; DeCasper et al., 2011). Remember, too, that neonates who are breastfed are able to remember and show recognition of their mother's unique odor (Cernoch & Porter, 1985).

Memory improves dramatically between 2 and 6 months of age and then again by 12 months (Pelphrey et al., 2004; Rose et al., 2011). The improvement may indicate that older infants are more capable than younger ones of encoding (i.e., storing) information, retrieving information already stored, or both (Patel et al., 2013).

A series of studies by Carolyn Rovee-Collier and her colleagues (Giles & Rovee-Collier, 2011; Rovee-Collier, 1993) illustrates some of these developmental changes in infant memory (see Figure 6.3 ■). One end of a ribbon was tied to a brightly colored mobile suspended above the infant's crib. The other end was tied to the infant's ankle, so that when the infant kicked, the mobile moved. Infants quickly learned to increase their rate of kicking. To measure memory, the infant's ankle was again fastened to the mobile after a period of 1 or more days had elapsed. Research shows that 2-month-olds remember how to make the mobile move after delays of up to 3 days, and 3-month-olds remember for more than a week (Barr et al., 2014).

Infant memory can be improved if infants receive a reminder before they are given the memory test (Bearce & Rovee-Collier, 2006). In one study that used a reminder ("priming"), infants were shown the moving mobile on the day before the memory test, but they were not allowed to activate it. Under these conditions, 3-month-olds remembered how to move the mobile after a 28-day delay (Rovee-Collier, 1993).

Imitation: Infant See, Infant Do

Imitation is the basis for much of human learning. Deferred imitation—that is, the imitation of actions after a time delay—occurs as early as 6 months of age (Campanella & Rovee-Collier, 2005; Schneider, 2015). To help them remember the imitated act, infants are usually permitted to practice it when they learn it. But in one study, 12-month-old infants were prevented from practicing the behavior they imitated. Even so, they were able to demonstrate it 4 weeks later, suggesting that they had mentally represented the act (Klein & Meltzoff, 1999).

But why might newborns possess a kind of imitation "reflex" after birth? This form of imitation is apparently inborn and contributes to the formation of caregiver–infant bonds; therefore, it enhances the likelihood of survival of the newborn (Meltzoff et al., 2013). This early form of imitation is apparently made possible by brain structures that researchers call "mirror neurons" (Rizzolatti & Fabbri-Destro, 2011; see the nearby "A Closer Look—Research" feature).

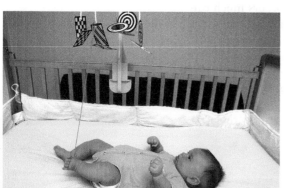

Figure 6.3 ■ Investigating Infant Memory
In this technique, developed by Carolyn Rovee-Collier, the infant's ankle is connected to a mobile by a ribbon. Infants quickly learn to kick to make the mobile move. Two- and 3-month-olds remember how to perform this feat after a delay of a few days. If they are given a reminder by simply viewing the mobile, their memory lasts for 2–4 weeks.

Michael Newman/PhotoEdit

A Closer Look

ON MIRROR NEURONS AND REALLY EARLY CHILDHOOD IMITATION

Infants engage in deferred imitation as early as 6 months of age. But it turns out that infants can often imitate behavior less than 1 hour after birth! Neonates only 0.7–71 hours old have been found to imitate adults who open their mouths or stick out their tongues (Fogassi & Rizzolatti, 2013; Meltzoff et al., 2013; see Figure 6.4 ■).

Some studies have not found imitation in early infancy (Abravanel & DeYong, 1991; Subiaul et al., 2012), and one key factor may be the infants' age. The studies that find imitation generally have been done with very young infants—up to 2 weeks old—whereas the studies that do not find imitation have tended to use older infants. Therefore, the imitation of neonates is likely to be reflexive and made possible by "mirror neurons." Thus, this early form of imitation disappears when reflexes are "dropping out" and re-emerges when it has a firmer cognitive footing.

> **TRUTH OR FICTION REVISITED:** It is true that a 1-hour-old infant may imitate an adult who sticks out his or her tongue. But such imitation is reflexive. That is, the infant is not observing the adult and then deciding to stick out his or her tongue.

Many researchers believe that social organization and human culture, as we know them, are made possible by certain kinds of neurons—*mirror neurons*—that are present at birth (Cozolino, 2014; Fogassi & Rizzolatti, 2013). And these neurons, like so many other important psychological discoveries, were found by accident.

A research team in Parma, Italy, headed by Vittorio Gallese and including Giacomo Rizzolatti (Gallese et al., 1996), was recording the activity of individual neurons in monkeys' brains as the animals reached for objects. One of the researchers reached for an object that had been handled by a monkey, and quite to his surprise, a neuron in the monkey's brain fired in the same way it had fired when the animal had picked up the object. The research team followed up the phenomenon and discovered many such neurons in the frontal lobes of their monkeys, just before the motor cortex, which they then dubbed *mirror neurons*. Mirror neurons in monkeys, and in humans, are activated by performing a motor act or by observing another monkey or human engage in the same act (Cattaneo et al., 2010; see Figure 6.5 ■).

Mirror neurons in humans are also connected with emotions. Certain regions of the

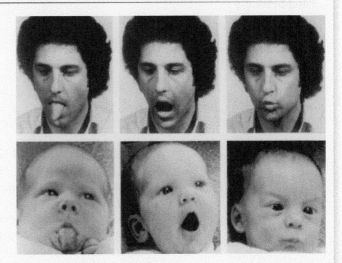

Figure 6.4 ■ Imitation in Infants
These 2- to 3-week-old infants are imitating the facial gestures of an adult experimenter. How are we to interpret these findings? Can we say that the infants "knew" what the experimenter was doing and "chose" to imitate the behavior, or is there an alternative explanation?
From A. N. Meltzoff & M.K. Moore, "Imitation of facial and manual gestures by human neonates," Science, 198 (1977), 75–78. Used by permission of Andrew N. Meltzoff, Ph.D.

brain—particularly in the frontal lobe—are active when people experience emotions such as disgust, happiness, or pain, and also when they observe another person experiencing an emotion (Rizzolatti & Fabbri-Destro, 2011). It thus appears that there is a neural basis for empathy—the identification or vicarious experiencing of feelings in others based on the observation of visual and other cues. Mirror neurons are also apparently connected with gender differences in empathy and the instinctive human capacity to acquire language (Arbib, 2015; Brucker et al., 2015).

Figure 6.5 ■ A Newborn Rhesus Monkey Imitates Protrusion of the Tongue, a Feat Made Possible by Mirror Neurons, Not by Learning
Evolution of Neonatal Imitation. Gross L, PLoS Biology Vol. 4/9/2006, e311 http://dx.doi.org/10.1371/journal.pbio.0040311

Section Review

8. The _____-processing approach to cognitive development focuses on how children manipulate or process information.

9. _____ improves dramatically between the ages of 2 and 6 months.

10. The imitation of actions after a time delay is called _____ imitation.

Reflect & Relate: Why do adolescents and adults stick their tongues out at infants? (Why not ask a few adolescents and adults?)

6.3 Social Influences on Early Cognitive Development

Vygotsky's sociocultural theory talks about the transmission of skills from adults and older children to young children through teaching and learning. When we hear of teaching and learning, we may think of school, but Vygotsky also focused on infants' social interaction with adults, which at first normally takes place largely in the home. Vygotsky emphasized that children's cognitive development involves internalizing skilled strategies from joint problem solving with partners who are more skilled. These partners bring the intellectual tools of their society within the grasp of children in what Vygotsky called the *zone of proximal development*. During infancy, caregivers may provide such a zone by helping children play with blocks and picture books. We will see that children's receptive vocabulary exceeds their expressive vocabulary—that is, they can understand more than they can say—and adults who name objects in the environment and in picture books enhance infants' ability to think about these objects before they can talk about them (Daniels et al., 2007).

Adults frequently provide a learning situation in which they encourage their infants to try new things with their help. Then, as the infants show increasing ability to master tasks for themselves, the adults tend to permit the infants to do things by themselves, although they may continue to offer encouragement "from the sidelines." Adults may show a 16-month-old infant how to place blocks on top of one another to make a tower, but once the infant successfully copies the task, the adult typically allows the infant to do it by herself.

Julia Robinson and her colleagues (2008) studied the relationship between maternal *scaffolding* in low-income families and their preschoolers' ability to regulate their attention in a task that involved parent–child interaction. The maternal scaffolding differed largely according to the children's ability to remain task-oriented. Mothers of children who showed poor attention regulation were more likely to engage their children verbally, asking more strategic questions and providing hints and prompts. The children then engaged in a second task without their mothers' help. Those children whose mothers provided the highest amount of scaffolding performed best in the second, "child-alone" task.

Section Review

11. According to Vygotsky, children's cognitive development involves their _____ skilled approaches from joint problem solving with more skilled partners.

Reflect & Relate: Have you used scaffolding in playing with 12- to 24-month-olds? What did you do? What did the infant do?

6.4 Individual Differences in Cognitive Functioning Among Infants

Cognitive development does not proceed in the same way or at the same pace for all infants (Rose et al., 2011). Efforts to understand the differences in cognitive development have relied on so-called scales of infant development or infant intelligence.

Measuring cognition or intelligence in infants is quite different from measuring it in adults. Infants cannot, of course, be assessed by asking them to explain the meanings of words, the similarity between concepts, or the rationales for social rules. One of the most important tests of intellectual development among infants contains very different kinds of items. It is the Bayley Scales of Infant Development (BSID), which was constructed in 1933 by psychologist Nancy Bayley and has since been revised.

The Bayley test currently consists of 178 mental scale items and 111 motor scale items. The mental scale assesses verbal communication, perceptual skills, learning and memory, and problem-solving skills. The motor scale assesses gross motor skills, such as standing, walking, and climbing, and fine motor skills, as shown by the ability to manipulate the hands and fingers. A behavior rating scale based on examiner observation of the child during the test is also used. The behavior rating scale assesses attention span, goal directedness, persistence, and aspects of social and emotional development. Table 6.1 ● contains sample items from the mental and motor scales and shows the ages at which 50% of the infants taking the test passed the items.

● TABLE 6.1

Items from the Bayley Scales of Infant Development (BSID–II)

Age	Mental Scale Items	Motor Scale Items
1 month	The infant quiets when picked up.	The infant makes a postural adjustment when put to the examiner's shoulder.
2 months	When the examiner presents two objects (bell and rattle) above the infant in a crib, the infant glances back and forth from one to the other.	The infant holds his or her head steady when being carried about in a vertical position.
5 months	The infant is observed to transfer an object from one hand to the other during play.	When seated at a feeding-type table and presented with a sugar pill that is out of reach, the infant attempts to pick it up.
8 months	When an object (toy) in plain view of the infant (i.e., on a table) is covered by a cup, the infant removes the cup in order to retrieve the object.	The infant raises herself or himself into a sitting position.
12 months	The infant imitates words that are spoken by the examiner.	When requested by the examiner, the infant stands up from a position in which she or he had been lying on her or his back on the floor.
14–16 months	The infant builds a tower with two cubes (blocks) after the examiner demonstrates the behavior.	The infant walks alone with good coordination.

Source: Adapted from N. Bayley, *Scales of Infant and Toddler Development*, Third Edition. http://www.pearsonassessments.com/HAIWEB/Cultures/en-us/Productdetail.htm?Pid=015-8027-23X (Accessed December 8, 2012.)

The Bayley Scales of Infant Development The Bayley scales measure the infant's mental and motor development.

Testing Infants: Why and with What?

As you can imagine, it is no easy matter to test an infant. Items must be administered on a one-to-one basis by a patient tester, and it can be difficult to judge whether the infant is showing the targeted response. Why, then, do we test infants?

One reason is to screen infants for handicaps. A highly trained tester may be able to detect early signs of sensory or neurological problems, as suggested by development of visual–motor coordination. In addition to the Bayley scales, a number of tests have been developed to screen infants for such difficulties, including the Brazelton Neonatal Behavioral Assessment Scale (NBAS) and the Neonatal Intensive Care Unit Network Neurobehavioral Scale (NNNS) (see Chapter 4).

How Well Do Infant Scales Predict Later Intellectual Performance?

Researchers have also tried to use infant scales to predict development, but this effort has been less than successful. The answer is somewhat less than clear. One study found that scores obtained during the first year of life correlated only moderately with scores obtained a year later (Harris et al., 2005). Certain items on the Bayley scales appear to predict related intellectual skills later in childhood. For example, Bayley items measuring infant motor skills predict subsequent fine motor and visual–spatial skills at 6–8 years of age (Siegel, 1992). Bayley language items also predict language skills at the same age (Siegel, 1992).

One study found that the Bayley scales and socioeconomic status were able to predict cognitive development among low birth weight children from 18 months to 4 years of age (Dezoete et al., 2003). But overall or global scores on the Bayley and other infant scales apparently do not predict school grades or IQ scores among schoolchildren very well (Bornstein & Colombo, 2012). Predictability of teenage and adult intelligence test scores becomes stronger once children reach the ages of 6 or 7 (Bornstein & Colombo, 2012). Perhaps the sensorimotor test items used during infancy are not that strongly related to the verbal and symbolic items used to assess intelligence at later ages.

The overall conclusion seems to be that the Bayley scales can identify gross lags in development and relative strengths and weaknesses. However, they are only moderate predictors of intelligence scores even 1 year later, and they are still poorer predictors of scores taken beyond longer stretches of time.

What Is Visual Recognition Memory? How Is It Used to Enhance Predictability of Infant Intelligence?

visual recognition memory The kind of memory shown in an infant's ability to discriminate previously seen objects from novel objects.

In a continuing effort to find aspects of intelligence and cognition that might remain consistent from infancy through later childhood, a number of researchers have recently focused on visual recognition memory (Rose et al., 2012). **Visual recognition memory** is the ability to discriminate previously seen objects from novel objects. This procedure is based on habituation, as are many of the methods for assessing perceptual development (see Chapter 5).

Let us consider longitudinal studies of this type. Susan Rose and her colleagues (1992) showed 7-month-old infants pictures of two identical faces. After 20 seconds, the pictures were replaced with one picture of a new face and a second picture of the familiar face. The amount of time the infants spent looking at each of the faces in the second set of pictures was recorded. Some infants spent more time looking at the new face than at the older face, suggesting that they had better memory for visual stimulation. The children were given standard IQ tests yearly from ages 1 through 6. It was found that the children with greater visual recognition memory later attained higher IQ scores.

Rose and her colleagues (2001) also showed that, from age to age, individual differences in capacity for visual recognition memory are stable. This finding is important because intelligence—the quality that many researchers seek to predict from visual recognition memory—is also theorized to be a reasonably stable trait. Similarly, items on intelligence tests are age graded; that is, older children perform better than younger children, even as developing intelligence remains constant. So, too, with visual recognition memory. Capacity for visual recognition memory increases over the first year after birth (Rose et al., 2012).

A number of other studies have examined the relationship between either infant visual recognition memory or infant preference for novel stimulation (which is a related measure) and later IQ scores. In general, they show good predictive validity for broad cognitive abilities throughout childhood, including measures of intelligence and language ability (Heimann et al., 2006; Rose et al., 2012).

In sum, scales of infant development appear to provide useful data as screening devices, research instruments, or ways to describe the things that infants do and do not do. But for researchers and lay people who want to be able to predict the intellectual capacities of infants in years to come, results have so far been disappointing. Tests of visual recognition may hold better promise as predictors of what we would consider to be intelligent behavior at later ages.

Many parents today spend a good deal of time trying to teach their children skills that will enhance their intelligence testing scores. Any number of commercial products prey on parents' fears that their children might not measure up, and these products are found on the shelves of such stores as Toys "R"Us and on the virtual shelves of online stores. Although these products in themselves probably do no harm, parents might better advised to spend their time reading to children, playing with them, and taking them on stimulating excursions. Even a supermarket provides ample opportunities for parents to talk with their infants about shapes, colors, temperatures, and kinds of foods.

Now let us turn our attention to a fascinating aspect of cognitive development: the development of language. Language development boosts cognitive development, perhaps immeasurably, by enabling humans to learn about, and talk about, things that have happened outside their immediate experience.

Section Review

12. The Bayley Scales of Infant Development contain mental scale items and _____ scale items.

13. The Brazelton Neonatal Behavioral Assessment Scale is used to screen for sensory or _____ problems.

14. _____ recognition memory consists of an infant's ability to discriminate previously seen objects from novel objects.

Reflect & Relate: When you have observed infants, what kinds of behaviors have led you to think that one is "brilliant" or another one "dull"? How do your "methods" correspond to those used by researchers who attempt to assess intellectual functioning among infants?

6.5 Language Development

"The time has come," the Walrus said,
"To talk of many things
Of shoes—and ships—and sealing wax—
Of cabbages—and kings—
And why the sea is boiling hot—
And whether pigs have wings."

—Lewis Carroll, *Through the Looking Glass*

Lewis Carroll wasn't quite telling the truth in his well-known children's book. The sea is not boiling hot—at least not in most places or at most times. Nor do walruses speak. At the risk of alienating walrus aficionados, I will assert that walruses neither speak nor use other forms of language to communicate. But children do. Children come "to talk of many things"—perhaps only rarely of sealing wax and cabbages, but certainly about things more closely connected with their environments and their needs. Children may be unlikely to debate "whether pigs have wings," but they do develop the language skills that will eventually enable them to do just that. Lewis Carroll enjoyed playing with language, and we will see that children join in that game. In physical development, the most dramatic developments come early, fast, and furious, long before the child is born. Language does not come so early, and its development may not seem quite so fast and furious. Nevertheless, during the years of infancy, most children develop from creatures without language to little people who understand nearly all the things that are said to them and who relentlessly sputter words and simple sentences for all the world to hear. Though much of the world might think they have little of value to say, most parents find their utterances just priceless.

In this section, we will trace language development from early crying and cooing through the production of two-word sentences. We will then consider theoretical views of language development.

What Are Prelinguistic Vocalizations?

Children develop language according to an invariant sequence of steps, or stages, as outlined in Table 6.2 ●. We begin with the **prelinguistic** vocalizations. True words are symbols of objects and events. Prelinguistic vocalizations, such as cooing and babbling, do not represent objects or events.

Newborn children, as parents are well aware, have an unlearned but highly effective form of verbal expression: crying and more crying. Crying is accomplished by blowing air through the vocal tract. There are no distinct well-formed sounds. Crying is about the only sound that infants make during the first month.

TRUTH OR FICTION REVISITED: Actually, infant crying is not a primitive form of language. Cries do not contain symbols, or represent objects or events.

During the second month, infants begin **cooing**. Infants use their tongues when they coo. For this reason, coos are more articulated than cries. Coos are often vowel-like and may resemble extended "oohs" and "ahs." Cooing appears to be linked to feelings of pleasure or positive excitement. Infants tend not to coo when they are hungry, tired, or in pain.

Cries and coos are innate but can be modified by experience (Volterra et al., 2004). When parents respond positively to cooing by talking to their infants, smiling

prelinguistic Referring to vocalizations made by the infant before the development of language. (In language, words symbolize objects and events.)

cooing Prelinguistic, articulated vowel-like sounds that appear to reflect feelings of positive excitement.

Milestones in Language Development in Infancy

Approximate Age	Vocalization and Language
Birth	• Cries.
12 weeks	• Cries less. • Smiles when talked to and nodded at. • Engages in squealing and gurgling sounds (cooing). • Sustains cooing for 15–20 seconds.
16 weeks	• Responds to human sounds more definitely. • Turns head, searching for the speaker. • Chuckles occasionally.
20 weeks	• Cooing becomes interspersed with consonant-like sounds. • Vocalizations differ from the sounds of mature language.
6 months	• Cooing changes to single-syllable babbling. • Neither vowels nor consonants have a fixed pattern of recurrence. • Common utterances sound somewhat like *ma, mu, da,* or *di.*
8 months	• Continuous repetition (reduplication) enters into babbling. • Patterns of intonation become distinct. • Utterances can signal emphasis and emotion.
10 months	• Vocalizations mixed with sound play—gurgling, bubble blowing. • Makes effort to imitate sounds made by older people, with mixed success.
12 months	• Identical sound sequences replicated more often. • Words (e.g., *mamma, dadda*) emerge. • Many words and requests understood (e.g., "Show me your eyes").
18 months	• Repertoire of 3–50 words. • Explosive vocabulary growth. • Babbling consists of several syllables with intricate intonation. • Little effort to communicate information. • Occasional joining of words into spontaneous two-word utterances. • Understands nearly everything spoken.
24 months	• Vocabulary more than 50 words, naming everything in the environment. • Spontaneous creation of two-word sentences. • Clear efforts to communicate.

Source: Table items adapted from Lenneberg (1967, pp. 128–130).

Note: Ages are approximations. Slower development does not necessarily indicate language problems. Albert Einstein did not talk until the age of 3.

at them, and imitating them, cooing increases. Early parent–child "conversations," in which parents respond to coos and then pause as the infant coos, may foster infant awareness of taking turns as a way of verbally relating to other people.

By about 8 months of age, cooing decreases markedly. Somewhere between 6 and 9 months, children begin to babble. **Babbling** is the first vocalizing that sounds like human speech. In babbling, infants frequently combine consonants and vowels, as in *ba, ga,* and sometimes the much-valued *dada* (McCardle et al., 2009). At first,

babbling The child's first vocalizations that have the sounds of speech.

dada is purely coincidental (sorry, you dads), despite the family's jubilation over its appearance.

In verbal interactions between infants and adults, the adults frequently repeat the syllables produced by their infants. They are likely to say *dadada* or *bababa* instead of simply *da* or *ba*. Such redundancy apparently helps infants discriminate these sounds from others and further encourages them to imitate their parents (Elkind, 2007; Fagan, 2015; Tamis-LeMonda et al., 2006).

After infants have been babbling for a few months, parents often believe that their children are having conversations with themselves. At 10–12 months, infants tend to repeat syllables, showing what linguists refer to as **echolalia**. Parents overhear them going on and on, repeating consonant–vowel combinations (*ah-bah-bah-bah-bah*), pausing, and then switching to other combinations.

Toward the end of the first year, infants are also using patterns of rising and falling **intonation** that resemble the sounds of adult speech. It may sound as though the infant is trying to speak the parents' language. Parents may think that their children are babbling in English or in whatever tongue is spoken in the home.

How Does the Child Develop Vocabulary?

Vocabulary development consists of the child's learning the meanings of words. In general, children's **receptive vocabulary** development outpaces their **expressive vocabulary** development (Klee & Stokes, 2011). This means that at any given time, they can understand more words than they can use. One study, for example, found that 12-month-olds could speak an average of 13 words but could comprehend the meanings of 84 words (Tamis-LeMonda et al., 2006). Infants usually understand much of what others are saying well before they themselves utter any words at all. Their ability to segment speech sounds into meaningful units—or words—before 12 months is a good predictor of their vocabulary at 24 months (Newman et al., 2006).

The Child's First Words

Ah, that long-awaited first word! What a milestone! Sad to say, many parents miss it. They are not quite sure when their infants utter their first word, often because the first word is not pronounced clearly or because pronunciation varies from usage to usage.

The first word—which represents *linguistic* speech—is typically spoken between 11 and 13 months, but a range of 8–18 months is normal (Klee & Stokes, 2011). First words tend to be brief, consisting of one or two syllables. Each syllable is likely to consist of a consonant followed by a vowel. Vocabulary acquisition is slow at first. It may take children 3 or 4 months to achieve a vocabulary of 10–30 words after the first word is spoken (de Villiers & de-Villiers, 1999).

By about 18 months of age, children may be producing up to 50 words. Many of them are quite familiar, such as *no, cookie, mama, hi,* and *eat.* Others, such as *all gone* and *bye-bye,* may not be found in the dictionary, but they function as words; that is, they are used consistently to symbolize the same meaning.

More than half (65%) of children's first words make up "general nominals" and "specific nominals" (Hoff, 2014; Tamis-LeMonda et al., 2014a). General nominals are similar to nouns in that they include the names of classes of objects (*car, ball*), animals (*doggy, cat*), and people (*boy, girl*). They also include both personal and relative pronouns (*she, that*). Specific nominals are proper nouns, such as *Daddy* and *Rover.* The attention of infants seems to be captured by movement. Words expressing movement are frequently found in early speech. Of children's first 50 words, the most common are names for people, animals, and objects that move (*Mommy, car, doggy*) or that can be moved (*dolly, milky*), action words (*bye-bye*), a number of modifiers (*big, hot*), and expressive words (*no, hi, oh*) (Tamis-LeMonda et al., 2014a).

echolalia The automatic repetition of sounds or words.

intonation The use of pitches of varying levels to help communicate meaning.

receptive vocabulary The sum total of the words whose meanings one understands.

expressive vocabulary The sum total of the words that one can use in the production of language.

BABBLING HERE, THERE, AND EVERYWHERE

Babbling, like crying and cooing, appears to be inborn. Children from different cultures, where languages sound very different, all seem to babble the same sounds, including many they could not have heard (Elman, 2009). Deaf children whose parents use sign language babble with their hands and fingers, using repetitive gestures that resemble the vocal babbling of infants who can hear (Bloom, 1998; Koopmans-van Beinum et al., 2001).

Despite the fact that babbling is innate, it is readily modified by the child's language environment. One study followed infants growing up in French-, Chinese-, and Arabic-speaking households (Boysson-Bardies & Halle, 1994). At 4–7 months of age, the infants began to use more of the sounds in their language environment; foreign phonemes began to drop out. The role that experience plays in language development is further indicated by the fact that the babbling of deaf infants never begins to approximate the sounds of the parents' language.

Reflect: We say that babbling is innate. Yet as infants develop through the first year, they begin to babble sounds heard in the home, and foreign sounds begin to drop out. Why?

At about 18–22 months of age, there is a rapid burst in vocabulary acquisition (Tamis-LeMonda et al., 2014a). The child's expressive vocabulary may increase from 50 to more than 300 words in just a few months. This vocabulary spurt could also be called a naming explosion, because almost 75% of the words added during this time are nouns. The rapid pace of vocabulary growth continues through the preschool years, with children acquiring an average of nine new words per day (Hoff, 2014).

Referential and Expressive Styles in Language Development

Some children prefer a referential approach in their language development, whereas others take a more expressive approach (Hoff, 2014; Tamis-LeMonda et al., 2014a). Children who exhibit the **referential language style** use language primarily to label objects in their environments. Their early vocabularies consist mainly of nominals. Children who adopt an **expressive language style** use language primarily as a means for engaging in social interactions. Children with an expressive style use more pronouns and many words involved in social routines, such as *stop*, *more*, and *all gone*. More children employ an expressive style than a referential style (Tamis-LeMonda et al., 2014a), but most use a combination of the styles.

Why do some children prefer a referential style and others an expressive style? It may be that some children are naturally oriented toward objects, whereas others are primarily interested in social relationships. Nelson also found that the parents' ways of teaching children play a role. Some parents focus on labeling objects for children as soon as they notice their vocabularies expanding. Others are more oriented toward social interactions themselves, teaching their children to say *hi*, *please*, and *thank you*.

referential language style Use of language primarily as a means for labeling objects.

expressive language style Use of language primarily as a means for engaging in social interaction.

Overextension

Young children try to talk about more objects than they have words for (not so surprising—so do adults, now and then). To accomplish their linguistic feats, children often extend the meaning of one word to refer to things and actions for which they do not have words (Mayor & Plunkett, 2010). This process is called **overextension**. In classic research, Eve Clark (1973, 1975) studied diaries of infants' language development and found that overextensions are generally based on perceived similarities

overextension Use of words in situations in which their meanings become extended or inappropriate.

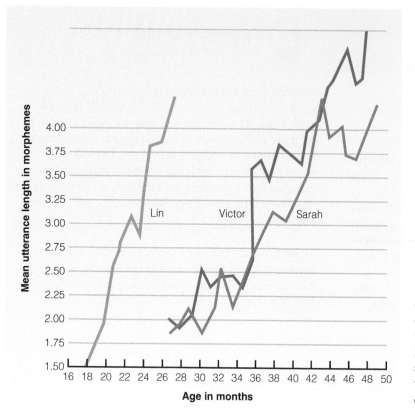

Figure 6.6 ■ **Mean Length of Utterance for Three Children** Some children begin speaking earlier than others. However, the mean length of utterance (MLU) increases rapidly once speech begins.
Source: Roger Brown (1973).

in function or form between the original object or action and the new one to which the first word is being extended. She provides the example of the word *mooi*, which one child originally used to designate the moon. The child then overextended *mooi* to designate all round objects, including the letter *o* and cookies and cakes.

Overextensions gradually pull back to their proper references as the child's vocabulary and ability to classify objects develop (Cohen & Brunt, 2009; Mayor & Plunkett, 2010). Consider the example of a child who first refers to a dog as a "bowwow." The word *bowwow* then becomes overextended to refer to horses, cats, and cows as well. In effect, *bowwow* comes to mean something akin to *familiar animal*. Next, the child learns to use the word *moo* to refer to cows. But *bowwow* still remains extended to horses and cats. As the child's vocabulary develops, she acquires the word *doggy*, so dogs and cats may now be referred to with either *bowwow* or *doggy*. Eventually, each animal has one or more correct names.

How Do Infants Create Sentences? On Telegraphing Ideas

The infant's first sentences are typically one-word utterances, but these utterances appear to express complete ideas and therefore can be thought of as sentences. Roger Brown (1973) called brief expressions that have the meanings of sentences **telegraphic speech**. When we write text messages, we use principles of syntax to cut out all the unnecessary words. "Home Tuesday" might stand for "I expect to be home on Tuesday." Similarly, only the essential words are used in children's telegraphic speech—in particular, nouns, verbs, and some modifiers.

Mean Length of Utterance

The **mean length of utterance (MLU)** is the average number of **morphemes** that communicators use in their sentences. Morphemes are the smallest units of meaning in a language. A morpheme may be a whole word or part of a word, such as a prefix or suffix. For example, the word *walked* consists of two morphemes: the verb *walk* and the suffix-*ed*, which changes the verb to the past tense. In Figure 6.6 ■, we see the relationship between chronological age and MLU for three children tracked by Roger Brown (1973, 1977): Lin, Victor, and Sarah.

The patterns of growth in MLU are similar for each child, showing swift upward movement broken by intermittent and brief regressions. Figure 6.7 also shows us something about individual differences. Lin was precocious compared to Victor and Sarah, extending her MLU at much earlier ages. However, as suggested earlier, the receptive language of all three children would have exceeded their expressive language at any given time. Also, Lin's earlier extension of MLU does not guarantee that she will show more complex expressive language than Victor and Sarah at maturity.

Let us now consider the features of two types of telegraphic speech: the holophrase and two-word sentences.

telegraphic speech Type of speech in which only the essential words are used.

mean length of utterance (MLU) The average number of morphemes used in an utterance.

morpheme The smallest unit of meaning in a language.

Holophrases

Holophrases are single words that are used to express complex meanings. For example, *Mama* may be used by the child to signify meanings as varied as "There goes Mama," "Come here, Mama," and "You are Mama." Most children readily teach their parents what they intend by augmenting their holophrases with gestures, intonations, and reinforcers; that is, they act delighted when parents do as requested and howl when they do not.

Infants are likely to combine single words with gestures as they undertake the transition from holophrases to two-word utterances (Tamis-LeMonda et al., 2006). For example, pointing can signify "there" before the word is used.

Two-Word Sentences

When the child's vocabulary consists of 50–100 words (usually somewhere between 18 and 24 months of age), telegraphic two-word sentences begin to appear (Saffran, 2009; Tamis-LeMonda et al., 2006). In the sentence "That ball," the words *is* and *a* are implied.

Two-word sentences, although brief and telegraphic, show understanding of **syntax** (Saffran, 2009; Slobin, 2001). The child will say "Sit chair," not "Chair sit," to tell a parent to sit in a chair. The child will say "My shoe," not "Shoe my," to show possession. "Mommy go" means Mommy is leaving, whereas "Go Mommy" expresses the wish for Mommy to go away.

6.6 Theories of Language Development: Can You Make a Houseplant Talk?

Since all normal humans talk but no house pets or house plants do, no matter how pampered, heredity must be involved in language. But since a child growing up in Japan speaks Japanese whereas the same child brought up in California would speak English, the environment is also crucial. Thus, there is no question about whether heredity or environment is involved in language, or even whether one or the other is "more important." Instead, . . . our best hope [might be] finding out how they interact.

—Steven Pinker (2007)

Countless billions of children have learned the languages spoken by their parents and have passed them down, with minor changes, from generation to generation. But how do they do so? In discussing this question—and so many others—we refer to the possible roles of nature and nurture. Learning theorists have come down on the side of nurture, and those who point to a basic role for nature are said to hold a nativist view.

How Do Learning Theorists Account for Language Development?

Learning plays an obvious role in language development. Children who are reared in English-speaking homes learn English, not Japanese or Russian. Learning theorists usually explain language development in terms of imitation and reinforcement.

The Role of Imitation

From a social cognitive perspective, parents serve as **models**. Children learn language, at least in part, by observation and imitation. It seems likely that many

holophrase A single word that is used to express complex meanings.

syntax The rules in a language for placing words in the proper order to form meaningful sentences.

models In learning theory, those whose behaviors are imitated by others.

TWO-WORD SENTENCES HERE, THERE, AND . . .

Two-word sentences appear at about the same time in the development of all languages (Slobin, 2001). Also, the sequence of emergence of the types of two-word utterances—for example, first subject–verb ("Mommy go"), then verb–object ("Hit ball"), location ("Ball here"), and possession ("My ball")—is the same in languages as diverse as English, Luo (an African tongue), German, Russian, and Turkish. This is an example of the point that language develops in a series of steps that appear to be invariant. Dan Slobin interprets his findings to mean that the construction of sentences serves specific functions of communication in various languages. Slobin does not argue that there is an innate linguistic structure but rather that basic human processes of cognition, communication, and information processing are found across cultures (Slobin, 2001).

Reflect: Which theory of language do Slobin's findings appear to support?

vocabulary words, especially nouns and verbs (including irregular verbs), are learned by imitation.

But imitative learning does not explain why children spontaneously utter phrases and sentences that they have not heard (Tamis-LeMonda et al., 2006). Parents, for example, are unlikely to model utterances such as "Bye-bye sock" and "All gone Daddy," but children do say them.

And children sometimes steadfastly avoid imitating certain language forms suggested by adults, even when the adults are insistent. Note the following exchange between 2-year-old Ben and a (very frustrated) adult (Kuczaj, 1982, p. 48):

Ben:	*I like these candy. I like they.*
Adult:	*You like them?*
Ben:	*Yes, I like they.*
Adult:	*Say them.*
Ben:	*Them.*
Adult:	*Say "I like them."*
Ben:	*I like them.*
Adult:	*Good.*
Ben:	*I'm good. These candy good too.*
Adult:	*Are they good?*
Ben:	*Yes. I like they. You like they?*

Ben is not resisting the adult because of obstinacy. He does repeat "I like them" when asked to do so. But when given the opportunity afterward to construct the object *them*, he reverts to using the subjective form *they*. Ben is likely at this period in his development to use his (erroneous) understanding of syntax spontaneously to actively produce his own language, rather than just imitating a model.

The Role of Reinforcement

B. F. Skinner (1957) conceded that prelinguistic vocalizations such as cooing and babbling may be inborn. But parents reinforce children for babbling that approximates the form of real words, such as *da*, which, in English, resembles *dog* or *daddy* (Tamis-LeMonda et al., 2014a). Children, in fact, do increase their babbling when it results in adults smiling at them, stroking them, and talking in response to their vocalizations. We have seen that as the first year progresses, children babble the sounds of their native tongues with increasing frequency, while foreign sounds tend to drop out. The behaviorist explains this pattern of changing frequencies in terms of reinforcement (of the sounds of the adults' language) and **extinction** (of foreign sounds). An alternative, nonbehavioral explanation is that children actively attend to the sounds in their linguistic environments and are intrinsically motivated to utter them.

From Skinner's perspective, children acquire their early vocabularies through **shaping**. That is, parents require that children's utterances be progressively closer to actual words before they are reinforced. In support of Skinner's position, research has shown that reinforcement accelerates the growth of vocabulary in children, especially children with learning disabilities (August et al., 2005; Kroeger & Nelson, 2006). Skinner viewed multiword utterances as complex stimulus–response chains that are also taught by shaping. As children's utterances increase in length, parents foster correct word order by uttering sentences to their children and reinforcing imitation. As with Ben, when children make grammatical errors, parents recast their utterances correctly. They reinforce the children for repeating them.

But recall Ben's refusal to be shaped into correct syntax. If the reinforcement explanation of language development were sufficient, parents' reinforcement would facilitate children's learning of syntax and pronunciation. We do not have such evidence. For one thing, parents are more likely to reinforce their children for the accuracy, or "truth value," of their utterances than for grammatical correctness (Tamis-LeMonda et al., 2014a). Parents, in other words, generally accept the syntax of their children's vocal efforts. The child who points down and says "The grass is purple" is not likely to be reinforced, despite correct syntax. But the enthusiastic child who shows her empty plate and blurts out "I eated it all up" is likely to be reinforced, despite the grammatical incorrectness of *eated*. Research confirms that most parents do not overtly correct their children's errors (Morgenstern et al., 2013).

Also, selective reinforcement of children's pronunciation can backfire. Children whose parents reward proper pronunciation but correct poor pronunciation develop vocabulary more slowly than children whose parents are more tolerant about pronunciation (Nelson, 1973).

Fostering Language Development Language growth in young children is enhanced when parents and caregivers, such as this mother, engage infants "in conversation" about activities and objects in their environment, such as this picture book.

> **TRUTH OR FICTION REVISITED:** Actually, the evidence suggests that correcting children's pronunciation may slow their vocabulary development.

Learning theory also cannot account for the invariant sequences of language development and for children's spurts in acquisition. Even the types of two-word utterances emerge in a consistent pattern in diverse cultures. Although timing differs from child to child, the types of questions used, passive versus active sentences, and so on all emerge in the same order. It is unlikely that parents around the world teach language skills in the same sequence.

On the other hand, there is ample evidence that aspects of the child's language environment influence the development of language. Much of the research in this area has focused on the ways in which adults—especially mothers—interact with their children.

extinction The decrease and eventual disappearance of a response in the absence of reinforcement.

shaping In learning theory, the gradual building of complex behavior patterns through reinforcement of successive approximations of the target behavior.

INFANT-DIRECTED SPEECH—OF "YUMMY YUMMY" AND "KITTY CATS"

One fascinating way that adults attempt to prompt the language development of young children is through the use of baby talk or infant-directed speech, sometimes referred to as "motherese" (Meltzoff et al., 2013; Singh et al., 2009). "Motherese" is actually a limiting term because grandparents, fathers, siblings, and unrelated people, including older children, also use varieties of infant-directed speech when talking to infants. Moreover, at least one study found that women (but not men) often talk to their pets as though they were infants (Xu et al., 2013). Infant-directed speech is used in languages as diverse as Arabic, English, Comanche, Italian, French, German, Xhosa (an African tongue), Japanese, Mandarin Chinese, and even a Thai sign language (Lee & Davis, 2010).

Researchers have found that infant-directed speech has the following characteristics (Kim & Johnson, 2014; McMurray et al., 2013):

- Infant-directed speech is spoken more slowly than speech addressed to adults. It is spoken at a higher pitch, and there are distinct pauses between ideas.

- Sentences are brief, and adults make the effort to speak in a grammatically correct manner.

- Sentences are simple in syntax. The focus is on nouns, verbs, and just a few modifiers.

- Key words are put at the ends of sentences and are spoken in a higher and louder voice.

- Facial expression is encouraging.

Infant-Directed Speech Mothers and others tend to speak slowly to infants, with careful enunciation. They also frequently use high-pitched speech and repetition.

- The diminutive morpheme *y* is frequently added to nouns. *Dad* becomes *Daddy*, and *horse* becomes *horsey*.

- Adults repeat sentences several times, sometimes using minor variations, as in "Show me your nose." "Where is your nose?" "Can you touch your nose?" Adults also repeat children's utterances, often rephrasing them in an effort to expand children's awareness of their expressive opportunities. If the child says, "Baby shoe," the mother may reply, "Yes, that's your shoe. Shall Mommy put the shoe on baby's foot?"

- Infant-directed speech includes a type of repetition called reduplication. *Yummy* becomes *yummy yummy*. *Daddy* may alternate with *Da-da*.

- Much infant-directed speech focuses on naming objects. Vocabulary is concrete, referring to objects in the immediate environment. For example, stuffed lions may be called "kitties." Purposeful overextension is intended to avoid confusing the child by adding too many new labels.

- Objects may be overdescribed by being given compound labels. Rabbits may become "bunny rabbits," and cats may become "kitty cats." In this way parents may try to be sure that they are connecting with the child by using at least one label that the child will recognize.

- Parents speak for the children, as in "Is baby tired?" "Oh, we're so tired." "We want to take our nap now, don't we?" This parent is pretending to have a two-way conversation with the child. In this way, parents seem to be trying to help their children express themselves by offering models of sentences they can use later on.

- Users of infant-directed speech stay a step ahead of the child. As children's vocabularies grow and their syntax develops, adults step up their own language levels, remaining just ahead of the child. In this way, adults seem to be encouraging the child to continue to play catch-up.

Thus, adults and older children use a variety of strategies to communicate with young children and to draw them out. Does it work? Does infant-directed speech foster language development? Research supports its use.

Infants as young as 5 months old prefer "baby talk," or infant-directed speech, over adult talk (Schachner & Hannon, 2011). The short, simple sentences and high pitch are more likely to produce a response from the child and to enhance vocabulary development than are complex sentences and those spoken in a lower pitch.

Children who hear their utterances repeated and recast do seem to learn from the adults who are modeling the new expressions (Trevarthen, 2003). Repetition of children's vocalizations also appears to be one method of reinforcing vocalizing.

How Can Adults Enhance Language Development in Children?

Studies show that language growth in young children is enhanced when mothers and other adults do the following things (Tamis-LeMonda et al., 2014a):

- Use a simplified form of speech known as "infant-directed speech."
- Use questions that engage the child in conversation.
- Respond to the child's expressive language efforts in a way that is "attuned." For example, they relate their speech to the child's utterance by saying, "Yes, your doll is pretty" in response to the child's statement "My doll."
- Join the child in paying attention to a particular activity or toy.
- Gesture to help the child understand what they are saying.
- Describe aspects of the environment occupying the infant's current focus of attention.
- Read to the child.
- Talk to the child a great deal.

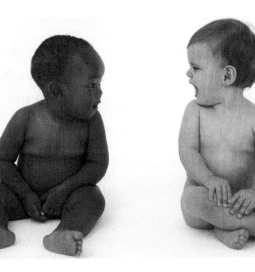

Pixland/Masterfile

Do Infants Have an Inborn "Language Acquisition Device"? According to Noam Chomsky's psycholinguistic theory, humans have an inborn language acquisition device that leads to commonalities in language development in all cultures. Babbling, for example, emerges at about the same time everywhere, and at about the same time, infants begin to sound as if they are babbling the sounds that occur in the language spoken in the home. Chomsky also hypothesizes that all languages have a universal grammar, regardless of how different they might seem.

How Does Psycholinguistic Theory Explain Language Development?

The nativist view holds that innate or inborn factors cause children to attend to and acquire language in certain ways. From this perspective, children bring an inborn tendency in the form of neurological "prewiring" to language learning (Hoff, 2014).

According to Steven Pinker and Ray Jackendoff (2005), the structures that enable humans to perceive and produce language evolved in bits and pieces. The individuals who possessed these "bits" and "pieces" were more likely to reach maturity and transmit their genes from generation to generation, because communication ability increased their chances of survival.

According to **psycholinguistic theory**, language acquisition involves an interaction between environmental influences—such as exposure to parental speech and reinforcement—and an inborn tendency to acquire language (Clancy & Finlay, 2001; Tamis-LeMonda et al., 2014b). Noam Chomsky (1988, 1990) and some others labeled this innate tendency a **language acquisition device (LAD)**. Evidence for

psycholinguistic theory The view that language learning involves an interaction between environmental influences and an inborn tendency to acquire language. The emphasis is on the inborn tendency.

an inborn tendency is found in the universality of human language abilities; in the regularity of the early production of sounds, even among deaf children; and in the invariant sequences of language development, regardless of which language the child is learning (Pinker, 2007).

The inborn tendency primes the nervous system to learn grammar. On the surface, languages differ a great deal in their vocabulary and grammar. Chomsky refers to these elements as the **surface structure** of language. However, the LAD serves children all over the world because languages share what Chomsky refers to as a "universal grammar"—an underlying **deep structure** or set of rules for transforming ideas into sentences. From Chomsky's perspective, children are genetically prewired to attend to language and to deduce the rules for constructing sentences from ideas. Consider an analogy with computers: According to psycholinguistic theory, the universal grammar that resides in the LAD is the basic operating system of the computer, and the particular language that a child learns to use is the word-processing program.

The Sensitive Period for Language Learning

Numerous researchers have suggested that language learning occurs during one or more **sensitive periods**, which begin at about 18–24 months of age and last until puberty (Bedny et al., 2012; Uylings, 2006). During these sensitive periods, neural development (as in the differentiating of brain structures) provides plasticity that facilitates language learning (Bates, 2001). Experience with language also alters the structure of the brain, although the exact relationships have not been discovered (Uylings, 2006).

Evidence for a sensitive period is found in recovery from brain injuries in some people. Injuries to the hemisphere that controls language (usually the left hemisphere) can impair or destroy the ability to speak (Wright et al., 2012). But before puberty, children suffering left-hemisphere injuries frequently recover a good deal of speaking ability. Lenneberg (1967) suggested that in young children, left-hemisphere damage may encourage the development of language functions in the right hemisphere. But adaptation ability wanes in adolescence, when brain tissue has reached adult levels of differentiation.

The best way to determine whether people are capable of acquiring language once they have passed puberty would be to run an experiment in which one or more children were reared in such severe isolation that they were not exposed to language until puberty. Of course, such an experiment could not be run because of ethical and legal barriers.

However, the disturbing case history of Genie offers insights into the issue of whether there is a sensitive period for language development (Siegal & Surian, 2012). Genie's father locked her in a small room at the age of 20 months and kept her there until she was 13. Her social contacts during this period were limited to her mother, who entered the room only to feed Genie, and to beatings by her father. When Genie was rescued, she weighed only about 60 pounds, did not speak, was not toilet trained, and could barely stand. Genie was placed in a foster home, where she was exposed to English for the first time in nearly 12 years. Her language development followed the normal sequence of much younger children in a number of ways, but she never acquired the proficiency of children reared under normal circumstances. Five years after her liberation, Genie's language remained largely telegraphic. She still showed significant problems with syntax; for example, failing to reverse subjects and verbs to phrase spontaneous questions. She showed confusion concerning the use of the past tense (adding *ed* to words) and had difficulty using negative helping verbs such as *isn't* and *haven't*.

Genie's language development provides some support for the sensitive-period hypothesis, although her language problems might also be partly attributed to

language acquisition device (LAD) In psycholinguistic theory, neural "prewiring" that facilitates the child's learning of grammar.

surface structure The superficial grammatical construction of a sentence.

deep structure The underlying meaning of a sentence.

sensitive period In linguistic theory, the period from about 18 months to puberty when the brain is thought to be especially capable of learning language because of its plasticity.

BRAIN STRUCTURES INVOLVED IN LANGUAGE

Many parts of the brain are involved in language development; however, some of the key biological structures appear to be based in the left hemisphere of the cerebral cortex for nearly all right-handed people and for two out of three left-handed people (Hoff, 2014). The sounds of speech elicit greater electrical activity in the left hemisphere of newborns than in the right hemisphere, as indicated by the activity of brain waves. In the left hemisphere of the cortex, the two areas most involved in speech are Broca's area and Wernicke's area (Figure 6.7 ■). Even in the human fetus, Wernicke's area is usually larger in the left hemisphere than in the right. Damage to either area is likely to cause an **aphasia**— a disruption in the ability to understand or produce language (Hoff, 2014).

Broca's area is located near the section of the motor cortex that controls the muscles of the tongue, throat, and other areas of the face that are used when speaking. When Broca's area is damaged, people speak slowly and laboriously, with simple sentences—a pattern known as **Broca's aphasia**. Their ability to understand the speech of others is relatively unaffected, however. Wernicke's area lies near the auditory cortex and is connected to Broca's area by nerve fibers. People with damage to Wernicke's area may show **Wernicke's aphasia**. Although they usually speak freely and with proper syntax, their abilities to comprehend other people's speech and to think of the words to express their own thoughts are impaired. Thus, Wernicke's area seems to be essential to understanding the relationships between words and their meanings.

A part of the brain called the angular gyrus lies between the visual cortex and Wernicke's area. The angular gyrus "translates" visual information, such as written words, into auditory information (sounds) and

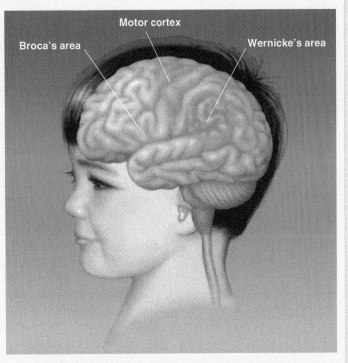

Figure 6.7 ■ Broca's and Wernicke's Areas of the Cerebral Cortex
Broca's area and Wernicke's area of (usually) the left hemisphere are most involved in speech. Damage to either area can produce an aphasia—an impairment in the ability to understand or produce language.
© Cengage Learning®

sends it on to Wernicke's area. It appears that problems in the angular gyrus can give rise to dyslexia, or serious impairment in reading, because it becomes difficult for the reader to segment words into sounds.

---

her years of malnutrition and abuse. She may have been mentally retarded to begin with. Her efforts to acquire English after puberty were clearly laborious, and the results were substandard compared even to the language of many 2- and 3-year-olds.

Further evidence for the sensitive-period hypothesis is provided by a study of a deaf boy named Simon, who was observed from the ages of 2½–9 years (Newport, 1992). Researchers reported that Simon signed in **American Sign Language (ASL)** with correct grammar, even though he had been exposed to only grammatically

American Sign Language (ASL)
The communication of meaning through the use of symbols that are formed by moving the hands and arms; the language used by some deaf people.

incorrect ASL by his parents and their friends, who also were deaf. Simon's parents and their friends had not learned to sign until they were teenagers. At that age, people often learn languages imperfectly. But Simon showed early mastery of grammatical rules that his parents used incorrectly or not at all. Simon's deduction of these rules on his own supports the view that the tendency to acquire language is inborn, and it also provides evidence that such learning occurs most readily during a sensitive period early in life.

What Is the Emergentist Theory of Language Development?

The **emergentist theory of language development** focuses on the interactions between the biological structures that make language acquisition possible and the cognitive and social processes that lead language to "emerge."

What does it mean for something to "emerge" from something else? Synonyms for "emerge from" include "coming out of" and "arising from." Think of cooking. (Why not?) Chocolate cake with chocolate frosting emerges from ingredients such as flour, sugar, cocoa powder, baking soda, salt, buttermilk, vegetable oil, eggs, vanilla extract, semisweet chocolate, butter, and—yes—coffee. There are also processes involved: heating an oven, buttering cake pans, mixing the ingredients, and baking them. The frosting also requires mixing, but not baking. From these "simple" ingredients and processes, the "complex" chocolate cake emerges. Think of chemistry: Water emerges from the combination of hydrogen and oxygen.

The emergentist theory of language development proposes that the child's complex abilities to understand and produce language *emerge* naturally from simpler biological, cognitive, and social processes (Hollich et al., 2000; MacWhinney, 1998; MacWhinney & O'Grady, 2015).

What are the "ingredients" in the emergence of language? These include:

- Genetics (the actions of genes make certain behaviors and mental processes possible)
- Neurons
- Sensory systems (hearing is usually the main method, but deaf children can learn to use sign language)
- The auditory area of the brain, which eventually translates written words into the sounds that are processed by the brain
- Wernicke's area of the brain (see Fig. 6.8), which makes it possible to understand the relationships between words and their meanings
- Broca's area of the brain (see Fig. 6.8), which is crucial in the production of speech
- A section of the motor cortex that is close to Broca's area and controls the muscles used in speech
- Ability to learn by association
- Attention
- Cognitive "pressure" to make sense of the environment
- Social interaction

According to emergentist theory, these are some of the elements that go into the "cake" of language development (MacWhinney & O'Grady, 2015). But there are also the processes, which include:

- The formation of neural networks that make language acquisition possible
- The infant's interaction with parents and other users of language
- The infant's linkage of auditory (the auditory area of the brain) with articulatory (speech) and conceptual systems (cognitive understanding)

aphasia A disruption in the ability to understand or produce language.

Broca's aphasia A form of aphasia caused by damage to Broca's area and characterized by slow, laborious speech.

Wernicke's aphasia A form of aphasia caused by damage to Wernicke's area and characterized by impaired comprehension of speech and difficulty in attempting to produce the right word.

emergentist theory of language development The view that the child's complex abilities to understand and produce language emerge from simpler processes that are biological, cognitive, and social in nature.

- The infant's development of strategies for learning the names of things and the meanings of words
- The infant's searching for regularities in the ways that words are used

All of these processes are "species-specific" or instinctive in humans. Although they are highly complex, language "emerges" automatically, which is quite fortunate because even the most intelligent and well-educated adults have some difficulty in understanding the "ingredients" and processes involved in language development.

TRUTH OR FICTION REVISITED: When we consider the evidence from psycholinguistic theory and emergentist theory, it becomes apparently true that children are "prewired" to listen to language in such a way that they come to understand words and rules of grammar.

In sum, the development of language in infancy represents the interaction of environmental and biological factors. The child brings a built-in readiness to the task of language acquisition, whereas houseplants and other organisms do not. The child must also have the opportunity to hear spoken language and to interact verbally with others. In the next chapter, we will see how interaction with others affects the social development of the infant.

Section Review

15. _____ is the first vocalizing that sounds like human speech.

16. Children with a(n) _____ language style use language mainly to label objects.

17. Children try to talk about more objects than they have words for, which often results in _____ of the meanings of words.

18. _____ are single words that are used to express complex meanings.

19. The sequence of emergence of the different types of two-word utterances is _____ (the same or different?) in diverse languages.

20. _____ theorists explain language development in terms of imitation and reinforcement.

21. According to _____ theory, language acquisition involves an interaction between environmental influences and an inborn tendency to acquire language.

22. Chomsky refers to this inborn tendency as a language _____ device (LAD).

23. Key biological structures that provide a basis for language are based in the _____ (left or right?) hemisphere of the cerebral cortex for most people.

24. The brain areas most involved in speech are Broca's area and _____ area.

Reflect & Relate: Why are so many parents concerned with exactly when their children learn to talk?

Chapter Review

6.1 How Does Cognitive Development Proceed During Infancy, According to Piaget?

Piaget's sensorimotor stage is the first 2 years of cognitive development, during which changes are shown by means of sensory and motor activity. The first substage is dominated by the assimilation of stimulation into reflexes. In the second substage, primary circular reactions, infants repeat stimulating actions that occur by chance. In the third substage, secondary circular reactions, patterns of activity are repeated because of their effects. In the fourth substage, infants intentionally coordinate schemes to attain goals. In the fifth substage, tertiary circular reactions, infants purposefully adapt established schemes to specific situations. In the sixth substage, external exploration is replaced by mental exploration. Object permanence is recognition that an object or person continues to exist when out of sight. Through the first 6 months or so, when a screen is placed between an object and an infant, the infant behaves as though the object is no longer there. Evidence supports the pattern and sequence of events described by Piaget. However, cognitive development may not be tied to discrete stages as Piaget believed. Piaget also appears to have been incorrect about the ages at which infants develop various concepts.

6.2 What Is the Information-Processing View of Cognitive Development During Infancy?

Two means of doing so are memory and imitation. Older infants are more capable of encoding and retrieving information. Neonates reflexively imitate certain behaviors, such as sticking out the tongue. Infants later show deferred imitation, suggesting that they have mentally represented actions.

6.3 How Do We Apply Vygotsky's Sociocultural Theory to the Cognitive Development of Infants?

Vygotsky stressed that cognitive development involves children's internalizing skilled strategies learned during joint problem solving with more skilled people—a *zone of proximal development*. During infancy, caregivers may provide such a zone by helping children gain skills with age-appropriate materials such as blocks and picture books.

6.4 What Individual Differences in Cognitive Functioning Do We Find Among Infants?

Some infants develop cognitive functioning more rapidly than others. The Bayley Scales of Infant Development (BSID) have mental scale and motor scale items that can suggest early signs of sensory or neurological problems. Certain BSID items predict intellectual skills later in childhood, but overall scores on such scales do not predict school grades accurately. Visual recognition memory is the ability to discriminate previously seen objects from novel objects. It moderately predicts IQ scores in later childhood.

6.5 How Does Language Develop During Infancy?

Prelinguistic vocalizations do not represent objects or events; they include crying, cooing, and babbling. Children from different cultures initially babble the same sounds. Receptive vocabulary development outpaces expressive vocabulary. The first word typically is spoken between 11 and 13 months of age. It may take another 3–4 months to achieve a vocabulary of 10–30 words. Children's first words are mostly nominals. Children with a referential language style use language mainly to label objects. Those with an expressive language style mainly seek social interactions. Infants often extend the meaning of a word to refer to things and actions for which they do not have words. Infants' early sentences are telegraphic. Two-word sentences show an understanding of syntax. The kinds of two-word sentences are the same among children from diverse linguistic environments.

6.6 What Are the Various Theories of Language Development: Can You Make a Houseplant Talk?

Learning theorists explain language development in terms of imitation and reinforcement. But children do not imitate sentences that are inconsistent with their grasp of grammar. The nativist view holds that innate "prewiring" causes children to attend to and acquire language in certain ways. Chomsky asserts that learning language involves the interaction between experience and prewiring. For most people, key biological structures are based in the left hemisphere: Broca's area and Wernicke's area. Damage to either area may cause a characteristic aphasia. Lenneberg proposed that plasticity of the brain provides a sensitive period for learning language that begins at about 18–24 months and lasts until puberty.

Key Terms

scheme   184
assimilation   184
accommodation   184
primary circular reactions   185
secondary circular reactions   185
tertiary circular reactions   186
object permanence   187
deferred imitation   189
visual recognition memory   196
prelinguistic   198
cooing   198
babbling   199
echolalia   200

intonation   200
receptive vocabulary   200
expressive vocabulary   200
referential language style   201
expressive language style   201
overextension   201
telegraphic speech   202
mean length of utterance (MLU)   202
morpheme   202
holophrase   203
syntax   203
models   203
extinction   205

shaping   205
psycholinguistic theory   207
language acquisition device (LAD)   208
surface structure   208
deep structure   208
sensitive period   208
American Sign Language (ASL)   209
aphasia   210
Broca's aphasia   210
Wernicke's aphasia   210
emergentist theory of language development   210

7

Infancy: Social and Emotional Development

TruthorFiction?

 Infants who are securely attached to their mothers do not like to stray from them. **p. 217**

 You can predict how strongly infants are attached to their fathers if you know how many diapers per week their fathers change. **p. 218**

 Fear of strangers is abnormal among infants. **p. 219**

T | F Fathers maltreat children twice as often as mothers do. **p. 228**

T | F Child abusers have frequently been the victims of child abuse themselves. **p. 231**

T | F Autism is caused by the mercury in the measles-mumps-rubella vaccine. **p. 235**

T | F Autistic children may respond to people as though they are pieces of furniture. **p. 235**

T | F All children are born with the same temperament. Treatment by caregivers determines whether they are difficult or easygoing. **p. 244**

T | F Girls prefer dolls and toy animals, and boys prefer toy trucks and sports equipment, only after they have become aware of the gender roles assigned to them by society. **p. 246**

When she was 2 years old, my daughter almost succeeded in preventing the publication of a book on which I was working. When I locked myself into my study, she positioned herself outside the door and called, "Daddy, oh Daddy." At other times she would bang on the door or cry. When I would give in (several times a day) and open the door, she would run in and say, "I want you to pick up me," and hold out her arms or climb into my lap. How would I ever finish the book? Being a psychologist, I found solutions easily. For example, I could write away from home. But this solution had the drawback of distancing me from my family. Another solution was to ignore my daughter and let her cry. If I refused to reinforce crying, crying might become extinguished. There was only one problem with this solution: I didn't *want* to extinguish her efforts to get to me. Attachment, you see, is a two-way street.

Attachment is one of the key issues in the social and personality development of the infant. If this chapter had been written by the poet John Donne, it might have begun "No children are islands unto themselves." Children come into this world fully dependent on others for their survival and well-being.

This chapter is about some of the consequences of that absolute dependency. It is about the social relationships between infants and caregivers and about the development of the bonds of attachment that usually—but not always—bind them. It is about the behaviors of infants that prompt social and emotional responses from adults and about the behaviors of adults that prompt social and emotional responses from infants. It is also about infants' unique and different ways of reacting socially and emotionally.

Voisin/Phanie/SuperStock

Let us first consider the issue of attachment and the factors that contribute to its development. Next we examine some circumstances that interfere with the development of attachment: social deprivation, child abuse, and autism. Then we turn to a discussion of day care. Finally, we look at the development of emotions and personality in infancy, including the self-concept, temperament, and gender differences.

7.1 Attachment: Bonds That Endure

Attachment is what most people refer to as affection or love. Mary Ainsworth (1989), one of the preeminent researchers on attachment, defined attachment as an emotional tie formed between one animal or person and another specific individual. Attachment keeps organisms together and tends to endure. John Bowlby believed that attachment is essential to the very survival of the infant (Ainsworth & Bowlby, 1991; Bowlby, 1988). He argued that babies are born with behaviors—crying, smiling, clinging—that elicit caregiving from parents.

Babies and children try to maintain contact with caregivers to whom they are attached. They engage in eye contact, pull and tug at them, and ask to be picked up. When they cannot maintain contact, infants show behaviors suggestive of **separation anxiety**. They may thrash about, fuss, cry, screech, or whine. Parents who are seeking a few minutes to attend to their own needs sometimes see these behaviors as manipulative, and in a sense, they are; children learn that the behaviors achieve their desired ends. But what is wrong with "manipulating" a loved one to end distress?

Patterns of Attachment: What Does It Mean for a Child to Be "Secure" or "Insecure"?

Mary Ainsworth and her colleagues (1978) identified various patterns of attachment. Broadly, infants show either **secure attachment** or insecure attachment. Ainsworth and other investigators have found that most infants, older children, and adults in the United States are securely attached (Beebe et al., 2010; Zeanah et al., 2011).

Think of security in terms of what infants do. Ainsworth developed the strange-situation method as a way of measuring attachment. In this method, an infant is exposed to a series of separations and reunions with a caregiver (usually the mother) and a stranger who is a confederate of the researchers. In the strange situation, securely attached infants mildly protest their mothers' departure, seek interaction upon reunion, and are readily comforted by them.

Hold on! This is science, and in the science of development we speak of insecurity as "insecure attachment." The two major types of insecure attachment are **avoidant attachment** and **ambivalent/resistant attachment**. Babies who show avoidant attachment are least distressed by their mothers' departure. They play without fuss when alone and ignore their mothers upon reunion. Ambivalent/resistant babies are the most emotional. They show severe signs of distress when their mothers leave and show ambivalence upon reunion by alternately clinging to their mothers and pushing them away. Additional categories of insecure attachment have been proposed, including **disorganized–disoriented attachment**. Babies exhibiting this pattern appear dazed, confused, or disoriented. They may show contradictory behaviors, such as moving toward the mother while looking away from her.

attachment An affectional bond between individuals characterized by a seeking of closeness or contact and a show of distress upon separation.

separation anxiety Fear of being separated from a target of attachment, usually a primary caregiver.

secure attachment A type of attachment characterized by showing mild distress at leave-takings, seeking nearness to an attachment figure, and being readily soothed by this figure.

avoidant attachment A type of insecure attachment characterized by apparent indifference to the leave-takings of, and reunions with, an attachment figure.

Research indicates that securely attached infants and toddlers are happier, more sociable with unfamiliar adults, and more cooperative with parents; get along better with peers; and are better adjusted in school than insecurely attached children (Borelli et al., 2010; George et al., 2010). Insecure attachment in infancy predicts psychological disorders during adolescence (Lee & Hankin, 2009; Steele, 2005). Infants use the mother as a secure base from which to venture out and explore the environment (Belsky, 2006a). Secure attachment is also related to experiencing fewer negative emotions toward unfamiliar people (Mikulincer & Shaver, 2001), and it encourages children to explore interactions with new people.

> **TRUTH OR FICTION REVISITED:** Infants who are securely attached to their mothers are actually likely to "stray" from their mothers, but the reason is apparently that the security provided by attachment makes their mothers into secures base for exploration of the environment.

Researchers have found evidence for the "intergenerational transmission of attachment" (Berzenski et al., 2014; Miljkovitch et al., 2012). The children of secure mothers show the most secure patterns of attachment themselves (Cicchetti et al., 2006). Siblings may form quite different attachment relationships with their mother (O'Connor et al., 2011). Siblings of the same gender are more likely than girl–boy pairs to form similar attachment relationships with their mother.

Security is also connected with the infant's temperament (Lickenbrock et al., 2013; Solmeyer & Feinberg, 2011). The mothers of "difficult" children are less responsive to them and report feeling more distant from them (Bates & Pettit, 2015; Lickenbrock et al., 2013).

Securely attached toddlers also have longer attention spans, are less impulsive, and are better at solving problems (Granot & Mayseless, 2001; Vando et al., 2008). At ages 5 and 6, securely attached children are better liked by peers and teachers, are more competent, are less aggressive, and have fewer behavior problems than insecurely attached children (Belsky, 2006a; Coleman, 2003).

What Are the Roles of the Caregivers in the Formation of Bonds of Attachment?

Attachment can be used as a measure of the quality of care that infants receive (Belsky, 2006a; Sullivan et al., 2011). The parents of securely attached infants are more affectionate, cooperative, and predictable in their caregiving. They respond more sensitively to their infants' smiles, cries, and other social behaviors (Bigelow et al., 2010; Xue et al., 2010).

Providing economically stressed families with support services can enhance their involvement with their infants and increase secure attachment. In one study, low-income women received child-care information and social support from home visitors during pregnancy and through the child's third year (Spieker et al., 2005). The visitors first worked with the mothers on how they conceptualized their fetuses. Following childbirth, the home visitors helped the mothers accurately interpret their babies' cues and respond to them. They also encouraged mother–infant interaction and play, which by and large resulted in appropriate maternal responsiveness and secure attachment between infant and mother.

ambivalent/resistant attachment A type of insecure attachment characterized by severe distress at the leave-takings of, and ambivalent behavior at reunions with, an attachment figure.

disorganized–disoriented attachment A type of insecure attachment characterized by dazed and contradictory behaviors toward an attachment figure.

Insecure attachment occurs more often among infants whose mothers are mentally ill or abusive (Cicchetti et al., 2006; McCartney et al., 2004). It is found more often among infants whose mothers are slow to meet their needs or meet them coldly (Steele et al., 2003).

Siblings tend to develop similar attachment relationships with their mother (IJzendoorn et al., 2000; O'Connor et al., 2011). The IJzendoorn study pooled data on sibling attachment from research groups in the United States, the Netherlands, and Canada to form 138 pairs of siblings. Children's security of attachment was assessed with the strange-situation procedure at 12–14 months. Maternal sensitivity to infants' needs was also observed. Broad sibling attachment relationships with the mother were found to be significantly alike (secure or insecure, but not necessarily the same kinds of insecurity). It was also found that siblings of the same gender are more likely to form similar attachment relationships with their mother than are girl–boy pairs. Mothers, that is, may behave differently with daughters and sons.

Although it is tempting to seek the sources of attachment in caregivers' behavior and personalities, that is not the whole story. Security is also connected with the baby's temperament (Belsky, 2006a; Solmeyer & Feinberg, 2011). Babies who are more active and irritable and who display more negative emotions are also more likely to develop insecure attachment. Such babies may elicit parental behaviors that are not conducive to the development of secure attachment. For example, mothers of "difficult" children are less responsive to their children and report that they feel less emotionally close to them (Alink et al., 2008; Morrell & Steele, 2003).

Caregivers respond to babies' behavior, just as babies respond to caregivers' behavior. The processes of attachment are a two-way street.

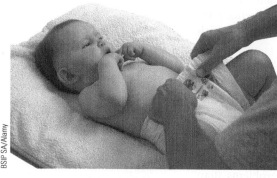

Fathers and Attachment: The "Diaper Index" The number of diapers a father changes reflects his involvement in child rearing. Children develop strong attachments to fathers as well as mothers, especially if the father interacts positively and affectionately with the child.

Involvement of Fathers

How involved is the average father with his children? The brief answer in developed nations is they are more involved now than in the past. Gender roles are blurring to some degree, and fathers, like mothers, can rear infants competently and sensitively (Grossmann et al., 2002). But studies of parents in the United States show that father–child interactions differ qualitatively and quantitatively from mother–child interactions (Lucassen et al., 2011). Mothers engage in far more interactions with their infants. Most fathers spend much less time on basic child-care tasks, such as feeding and diaper changing, than mothers do. Fathers are more likely to play with their children than to feed or clean them (Lucassen et al., 2011). Fathers more often than mothers engage in physical rough-and-tumble play, such as tossing their babies into the air and poking them (Fagan et al., 2014). Mothers are more likely to play games such as patty-cake and peekaboo and to play games involving toys (Lucassen et al., 2011).

TRUTH OR FICTION REVISITED: It is true that you can predict how strongly babies are attached to their fathers if you know how many diapers the fathers change each week. Research shows that the more diapers the father changes, the stronger the attachment (Fillo et al., 2015; Ross et al., 1975). However, there is no magical connection between diapers and love. It would appear to be the case, rather, that the number of diapers the father changes roughly reflects his involvement in child rearing.

How strongly, then, do infants become attached to their fathers? The answer depends on the quality of the time that the father spends with the baby. The more affectionate the interaction between father and infant, the stronger the attachment (Lucassen et al., 2011). Infants under stress still seek out their mothers more than their fathers (Frenkel & Fox, 2015). But when observed at their natural activities in the home and other familiar settings, they seek proximity and contact with their fathers about as often as with their mothers.

How Stable Are Bonds of Attachment?

Patterns of attachment tend to persist when caregiving conditions remain consistent (Beebe et al., 2010; Stupica et al., 2011). But attachment patterns can change when child care changes. Egeland and Sroufe (1981) followed a number of infants who were severely neglected and others who received high-quality care from 12 to 18 months of age. Attachment patterns remained stable (secure) for infants who received fine care. However, many neglected infants changed from insecurely to securely attached over the 6-month period, sometimes because of a relationship with a supportive family member or because home life grew less tense. Children can also become less securely attached to caregivers when the quality of home life deteriorates (Levendosky et al., 2011).

Children adopted at various ages can become securely attached to adoptive parents (Niemann & Weiss, 2011; Raby et al., 2013; Schoenmaker et al., 2014). Children show resilience in their social and emotional development. Early insecurities can be overcome.

Early attachment patterns tend to endure into middle childhood, adolescence, and even adulthood (Ammaniti et al., 2005; Schoenmaker et al., 2015). As Erik Erikson (1963) argued in *Childhood and Society*, positive relationships with caregivers may set the stage for positive relationships throughout life.

Are There Stages of Attachment? What Are They?

Cross-cultural studies by Mary Ainsworth (1967) and others have led to a theory of stages of attachment. In one study, Ainsworth tracked the attachment behaviors of Ugandan infants. Over a 9-month period, she noted their efforts to maintain contact with the mother, their protests when separated, and their use of the mother as a base for exploring the environment. At first, the Ugandan infants showed **indiscriminate attachment**; that is, they showed no particular preferences for the mother or another familiar caregiver. Specific attachment to the mother, as evidenced by separation anxiety and other behaviors, began to develop at about 4 months of age and grew to be intense by about 7 months. Fear of strangers developed 1 or 2 months later.

In another study, shown in Figure 7.1 ■, Scottish infants showed indiscriminate attachment during the first 6 months or so after birth (Schaffer & Emerson, 1964). Then indiscriminate attachment waned. Specific attachments to the mother and other familiar caregivers intensified, as demonstrated by the appearance of separation anxiety, and remained at high levels through the age of 18 months. Fear of strangers, which is a normal part of the development of attachment, occurred a month or so after the intensity of specific attachments began to mushroom. Thus, in both this and the Ugandan study, fear of strangers followed separation anxiety and the development of specific attachments by a number of weeks.

TRUTH OR FICTION REVISITED: Fear of strangers is not abnormal at all. It may not be universal, but it is quite common. Moreover, when it occurs, it tends to begin and end within certain age ranges.

indiscriminate attachment The display of attachment behaviors toward any person.

Figure 7.1 ■ The Development of Attachment
During the first 6 months, infants tend to show indiscriminate attachment. Indiscriminate attachment then wanes while specific attachments grow intense and remain at high levels. Fear of strangers develops a month or so after the intensity of specific attachments begins to blossom.
Adapted from Schaffer & Emerson (1964).
© Cengage Learning®

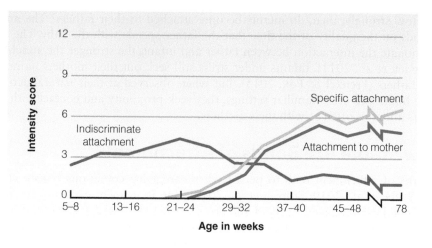

From studies such as these, Ainsworth and her colleagues (1978) identified the following three phases of attachment:

1. The **initial pre-attachment phase** lasts from birth to about 3 months and is characterized by indiscriminate attachment.
2. The **attachment-in-the-making phase** occurs at about 3 or 4 months and is characterized by preference for familiar figures.
3. The **clear-cut attachment phase** occurs at about 6 or 7 months and is characterized by intensified dependence on the primary caregiver, usually the mother.

Most infants have more than one adult caregiver, however, and are likely to form multiple attachments—to the father, day-care providers, grandparents, and other caregivers, as well as to the mother. In most cultures, single attachments are the exception, not the rule.

What Are the Various Theories of Attachment? How Does Each Emphasize Nature or Nurture in Its Explanation of the Development of Attachment?

Attachment, like so many other behavior patterns, seems to develop as a result of the interaction of nature and nurture.

Cognitive View of Attachment: Is the Caregiver Mentally Represented?

The cognitive view of attachment focuses on the contention that an infant must have developed some concept of object permanence before specific attachment becomes possible. In other words, if caregivers are to be missed when absent, the infant must perceive that they continue to exist. We have seen that infants tend to develop specific attachments at about the age of 6–7 months. In support of the cognitive view, recall that rudimentary object permanence concerning physical objects develops somewhat earlier (see Chapter 6).

initial pre-attachment phase The first phase in the formation of bonds of attachment, lasting from birth to about 3 months of age and characterized by indiscriminate attachment.

attachment-in-the-making phase The second phase in the development of attachment, occurring at 3 or 4 months of age and characterized by preference for familiar figures.

clear-cut attachment phase The third phase in the development of attachment, occurring at 6 or 7 months of age and characterized by intensified dependence on the primary caregiver.

Behavioral View of Attachment: Is the Caregiver a Reinforcer?

Early in the 20th century, behaviorists argued that attachment behaviors are learned through conditioning. Caregivers feed their infants and tend to their other physiological needs. Thus, infants associate their caregivers with gratification and learn to approach them to meet their needs. From this perspective, a caregiver becomes a conditioned reinforcer.

Psychoanalytic Views of Attachment: Is the Caregiver a Love Object?

Psychoanalytic theorists view the development of attachment somewhat differently from behaviorists. The caregiver, usually the mother, becomes not just a "reinforcer" but also a love object who forms the basis for all later attachments.

In both the psychoanalytic and behaviorist views, the caregiver's role in gratifying the child's needs is crucial. Freud emphasized the importance of oral activities, such as eating, in the first year. Freud believed that the infant becomes emotionally attached to the mother during this time because she is the primary satisfier of the infant's needs for food and sucking.

Erik Erikson believed that the first year is critical for developing a sense of trust in the mother, which fosters attachment. Erikson wrote that the mother's general sensitivity to the child's needs, not just the need for food, fosters the development of trust and attachment.

The Harlows' View of Attachment: Is the Caregiver a Source of Contact Comfort?

Harry and Margaret Harlow (1966) conducted a series of classic experiments to demonstrate that feeding is not as critical to the attachment process as Freud suggested. In one study, the Harlows placed rhesus monkey infants in cages with two surrogate mothers (see Figure 7.2 ■). One "mother" was made from wire mesh, from

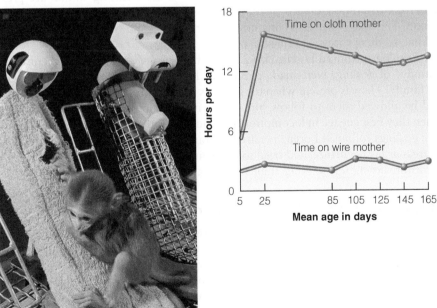

Figure 7.2 ■ Attachment in Infant Monkeys
Although this rhesus monkey infant is fed by the wire "mother," it spends most of its time clinging to the soft, cuddly, terry cloth "mother." It knows where to get a meal, but contact comfort is apparently more important than food in the development of attachment in infant monkeys (and perhaps infant humans).
Adapted from Harlow & Harlow (1966).

With permission of the Harlow Primate Laboratory

which a baby bottle was extended. The other surrogate mother was made of soft, cuddly terry cloth. Infant monkeys spent most of their time clinging to the cloth mother, even though she did not offer food. The Harlows concluded that monkeys—and perhaps humans—have a need for **contact comfort** that is as basic as the need for food.

Harlow and Zimmerman (1959) found that a surrogate mother made of cloth could also serve as a comforting base from which an infant monkey could explore its environment (see Figure 7.3 ■). Toys such as stuffed bears were placed in cages with infant rhesus monkeys and their surrogate mothers. When the infants were alone or had wire surrogate mothers for companions, they cowered in fear as long as the "bear monster" was present. But when the cloth mothers were present, the infants clung to them for a while and then explored the intruding "monster." With human infants, too, the bonds of mother–infant attachment appear to provide a secure base from which infants feel encouraged to explore their environments.

Figure 7.3 ■ Security
With its terry cloth surrogate mother nearby, this infant rhesus monkey apparently feels secure enough to explore the "bear monster" placed in its cage. But infants with wire surrogate mothers or no mother all cower in a corner when such "monsters" are introduced.

The Ethological View of Attachment: Evolution, Attachment, and Survival

Ethologists note that for many animals, attachment is species-specific or instinctive. Attachment, like other species-specific responses, is theorized to occur in the presence of a species-specific releasing stimulus. According to John Bowlby, one component of attachment in humans—and its releasing stimulus—is a baby's smile in response to a human voice or face (Ainsworth & Bowlby, 1991; Bowlby, 1988). Bowlby proposed that the baby's smile helps ensure survival by eliciting affection from caregivers. By 2–3 months of age, the human face begins to elicit a **social smile** in infants (Emde et al., 1976). Instinctive behaviour should be universal among the members of a species, and the development of smiling seems to follow the same sequence throughout the world (Labouvie-Vief, 2015).

In many nonhuman animals, attachment apparently occurs during a critical period of life. If it does not occur then, it may never do so. During this period, young animals can form an attachment to caregivers if the releasing stimuli are present. Waterfowl become attached to the first moving object they encounter during this period. The image of the moving object seems to become "imprinted" on the young animal, so this process is termed *imprinting*.

Ethologist Konrad Lorenz (1962, 1981) became well known when pictures of his "family" of goslings were made public (see Figure 7.4 ■). How did Lorenz acquire his family? He was present when the goslings hatched and during their critical period, and he allowed them to follow him. The critical period for geese and ducks begins when they first engage in locomotion and ends when they develop a fear of strangers. The goslings followed Lorenz persistently, ran to him when frightened, honked with distress at his departure, and tried to overcome barriers placed between them. If you substitute crying for honking, it all sounds rather human.

Ethology, Ainsworth, and Bowlby

Now let us return full circle to Mary Ainsworth and John Bowlby (1991). At the beginning of a major retrospective article, they wrote that "the distinguishing characteristic of the theory of attachment that we have jointly developed is that it is an ethological approach to personality development." The theoretical aspects of their work developed almost by accident and have a broad base in the psychological and biological perspectives of their day.

Bowlby intended his contribution as an up-to-date version of psychoanalytic object-relations theory [developed largely by Margaret Mahler],

contact comfort The pleasure derived from physical contact with another; a hypothesized need or drive for physical contact with another.

social smile A smile that occurs in response to a human voice or face.

Figure 7.4 ■ Imprinting: A Source of Attachment in Ethological Theory
Konrad Lorenz may not look like Mommy to you, but these goslings became attached to him because he was the first moving object they perceived and followed. This type of attachment process is referred to as imprinting.

compatible with contemporary ethology [e.g., Lorenz] and evolution theory [e.g., Charles Darwin], supported by research, and helpful to clinicians in understanding and treating child and adult patients. Nevertheless, it was developmental psychologists rather than clinicians who first adopted attachment theory.

—Ainsworth & Bowlby (1991)

Yet theirs is not the attachment theory of Konrad Lorenz. True, there are what Bowlby believed to be "releasing stimuli," such as the human face and the crying, smiling, and clinging of infants. But caregiving in humans is largely learned, not inborn. Their ethological perspective is also informed by Bowlby's observations of rhesus monkeys (Suomi, 2005). Children and infants of many other species also try to maintain contact with caregivers to whom they have grown attached. When they cannot maintain contact, they show signs of distress: honking and flapping about in geese, whining and barking in dogs, crying and fussing in children.

Ainsworth and Bowlby (1991) wrote that the critical period for attachment in humans is extended for months or years (Upton & Sullivan, 2010). It involves learning and perceptual and cognitive processes. The type of attachment that develops is related to the quality of the caregiver–infant relationship. Caregiving itself and infant responsiveness, such as infant smiling, appear to spur the development of attachment. Theories of attachment are reviewed in Concept Review 7.1.

Section Review

1. Ainsworth defines_____ as an affectional tie that is formed between one animal or person and another specific individual.

2. One of Ainsworth's contributions to the field of child development is the _____ method of measuring attachment.

3. Broadly, infants have either secure attachment or _____ attachment.

4. Securely attached infants use the caregiver as a secure base from which to _____ the environment.

5. Ainsworth's study of Ugandan infants found that they at first show _____ attachment.

6. From the _____ perspective, a caregiver becomes a conditioned reinforcer.

7. The Harlows' research with monkeys suggests that _____ comfort is a key source of attachment.

8. Lorenz believed that attachment is a species-_____ action pattern.

Reflect & Relate: To which caregiver are you most attached? Why?

Theories of Attachment

Theory	Characteristics
Cognitive theory (proponent: Alan Sroufe)	• Emotional development is connected with and relies on cognitive development. • Infant must develop object permanence before attachment to a specific other becomes possible. • Infant must be able to discriminate familiar people from strangers to develop fear of strangers.
Behaviorism (proponent: John B. Watson)	• Caregiver is a conditioned reinforcer; attachment behaviors are learned through conditioning. • Caregivers meet infants' physiological needs; thus, infants associate caregivers with gratification. • Feelings of gratification associated with meeting needs generalize into feelings of security when the caregiver is present.
Psychoanalytic theory (proponents: Sigmund Freud, Erik Erikson, Margaret Mahler)	• Caregiver is a love object who forms the basis for future attachments. • Infant becomes attached to the mother during infancy because she primarily satisfies the infant's needs for food and sucking (Freud). • First year is critical in developing a sense of trust in the mother, which, in turn, fosters feelings of attachment (Erikson).
Contact comfort (proponents: Harry and Margaret Harlow) Nina Leen/Time & Life Pictures/Getty Images	• Caregiver is a source of contact comfort. • Experiments with rhesus monkeys suggest that contact comfort is more crucial to attachment than feeding is. • Attachment is an inborn fixed action pattern (FAP) that occurs in the presence of a species-specific releasing stimulus during a critical period of development (Lorenz).
Ethological theory (proponents: Konrad Lorenz, Mary Ainsworth, John Bowlby) Nina Leen/The LIFE Picture Collection/Getty Images	• Waterfowl become attached to the first moving object they encounter (Lorenz). • The image of the moving object becomes "imprinted" on the young animal (Lorenz). • Caregiving in humans is elicited by infants' cries of distress (Bowlby). • The human face is a releasing stimulus that elicits a baby's smile (Bowlby). • Smiling helps ensure survival by eliciting caregiving and feelings of affection (Bowlby). • Attachment in humans is a complex process that continues for months or years (Ainsworth). • The quality of attachment is related to the quality of the caregiver–infant relationship (Ainsworth). • Attachment in humans occurs in stages or phases (Ainsworth): 1. The initial pre-attachment phase: birth to about 3 months; indiscriminate attachment. 2. The attachment-in-the-making phase: 3 or 4 months; preference for familiar figures. 3. The clear-cut attachment phase: 6 or 7 months; intensified dependence on the primary caregiver.

7.2 When Attachment Fails

What happens when children are reared in group settings, such as some orphanages, where they have little or no contact with parents or other caregivers? What happens when parents neglect or abuse their children? In both cases, children's attachments may be impaired. Attachment may also fail in some children because of the development of autism spectrum disorders (ASDs). In this section, we consider the effect of social deprivation, child abuse, and ASDs on the development of attachment.

What Are the Effects of Social Deprivation on Child Development?

Children who are reared in institutions where they receive little social stimulation from caregivers exhibit various problems and delays in their physical, intellectual, social, and emotional development. But why? Is the cause of the problems the insufficient social stimulation, or is it the family factors that led to the children's placement in institutions? We know that the children's problems are correlated or connected with their institutional residency, but without experimentation, it is difficult to know why.

Ethical considerations prevent us from conducting experiments in which we would randomly assign children to social stimulation or to social deprivation. However, experiments of this kind have been undertaken with rhesus monkeys, and the results are consistent with those of the correlational studies of children. Let us first examine these animal experiments and then turn to the correlational research involving children.

Experiments with Monkeys

The Harlows and their colleagues conducted studies of rhesus monkeys that were "reared by" wire mesh and terry cloth surrogate mothers. In later studies, rhesus monkeys were reared without even this questionable "social" support. They were reared without seeing any other animal, whether monkey or human.

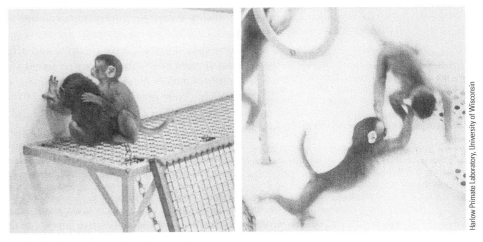

Figure 7.5 ■ Monkey Therapists
In the left-hand photo, a 3- to 4-month-old rhesus monkey "therapist" tries to soothe a monkey that was reared in social isolation. The deprived monkey remains withdrawn. She clutches herself into a ball and rocks back and forth. The right-hand photo was taken several weeks later and shows that deprived monkeys given young "therapists" can learn to play and adjust to community life. Socially withdrawn preschoolers have similarly profited from exposure to peers.

The Harlows (Harlow et al., 1971) found that rhesus infants reared in this most solitary confinement later avoided contact with other monkeys. They did not engage in the characteristic playful chasing and romping. Instead, they cowered in the presence of others and failed to respond to them. Nor did they attempt to fend off attacks by other monkeys. Rather, they sat in the corner, clutching themselves and rocking back and forth. Females who later bore children tended to ignore or abuse them.

Can the damage done by social deprivation be overcome? When monkeys deprived for 6 months or longer are placed with younger, 3- to 4-month-old females for a couple of hours a day, the younger monkeys make efforts to initiate social interaction with their deprived elders (see Figure 7.5 ■). Many of the deprived monkeys begin to play with the youngsters after a few weeks, and many of them eventually expand their social contacts to other rhesus monkeys of various ages (Suomi et al., 1972). Perhaps of greater interest is the related finding that socially withdrawn 4- and

5-year-old children make gains in their social and emotional development when they are provided with younger playmates (Furman et al., 1979; Rubin & Coplan, 2010).

Studies with Children

Again, we cannot run the sorts of experiments we have run with monkeys on children. Take a moment to consider why this is so. What practical problems would prevent running such studies? What ethical issues would stand in the way? Putting those questions aside for the moment, would you want to run such studies with children? Why or why not?

Studies with children have therefore been run with "found" participants—without random assignment to the home life or the institutional life. Institutionalized children whose material needs are met but who receive little social stimulation from caregivers exhibit problems in their physical, intellectual, social, and emotional development (Esposito & Gunnar, 2014; Koss et al., 2014). Spitz (1965) noted that many institutionalized children appear to develop a syndrome characterized by withdrawal and depression. They show progressively less interest in their world and become increasingly inactive. Some of them die.

In one institution, infants were maintained in separate cubicles for most of their first year to ward off infectious diseases (Provence & Lipton, 1962). Adults tended to them only to feed and change their diapers. As a rule, baby bottles were propped up in the infants' cribs. Attendants rarely responded to the babies' cries, and the infants were rarely played with or spoken to. By the age of 4 months, the infants in this institution showed little interest in adults. They rarely tried to gain their attention, even when in distress. A few months later, some of them sat withdrawn in their cribs and rocked back and forth, almost like the Harlows' monkeys. Language deficiencies were striking. As the first year progressed, little babbling was heard within the infants' cubicles. None were speaking even one word at 12 months.

Why do children whose material needs are met show such dramatic deficiencies? Is it because they do not receive the love and affection of a human? Or is it because they do not receive adequate sensory or social stimulation?

The answer may depend, in part, on the age of the child. Classic studies by Leon Yarrow and his colleagues (Yarrow et al., 1971; Yarrow & Goodwin, 1973) suggest that deficiencies in sensory stimulation and social interaction may cause more problems than lack of love in infants who are too young to have developed specific attachments. However, once infants have developed specific attachments, separation from their primary caregivers can lead to problems.

In the first study, the development of 53 adopted children was followed over a 10-year period (Yarrow et al., 1971). The researchers compared the development of three subgroups: (1) children who were transferred to their permanent adoptive homes almost immediately after birth, (2) children who were given temporary foster mothers and then transferred to permanent adoptive homes before they were 6 months old, and (3) children who were transferred from temporary foster mothers to their permanent adoptive homes after they were 6 months old. At the age of 10, children in the first two groups showed no differences in social and emotional development. However, children in the third group showed significantly less ability to relate to other people. Perhaps their deficits resulted from being separated from their initial foster mothers after they had become attached to them.

In the second study, Yarrow and Goodwin (1973) followed the development of 70 adopted children who were separated from temporary foster parents between birth and the age of 16 months. The researchers found strong correlations between the age at which the children were separated and later feeding and sleeping problems, decreased social responsiveness, and extremes in attachment behaviors (see Figure 7.6 ■). Disturbed attachment behaviors included excessive clinging to the new mother and violent rejection of her. None of the children who were separated from their initial foster mothers before the age of 3 months showed moderate or severe disturbances. All the children who were separated at 9 months or older did show such disturbances. Forty to 90% of the children separated between the ages of 3 and 9 months showed moderate to severe disturbances. The incidence of problems increased as the age advanced.

The Yarrow studies suggest that babies in institutions, at least up to the age of 3 months or so, may require general sensory and social stimulation more than a specific relationship with a primary caregiver. After the age of 3 months, some disturbance is likely if there is instability in the caregiving staff. By the ages of 6–9 months, disturbance seems to be guaranteed if there is instability in the position of primary caregiver. Fortunately, there is also evidence that children show some capacity to recover from early social deprivation.

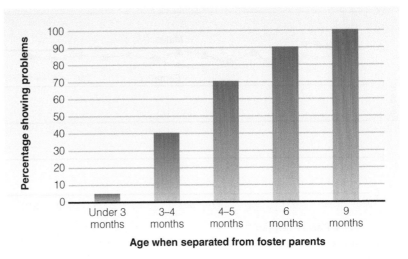

Figure 7.6 ■ The Development of Adopted Children Separated from Temporary Foster Parents
The older the child at the time of separation, the more likely it is that behavioral disturbances will occur.
Source: Data from Yarrow & Goodwin (1973)

The Capacity to Recover from Social Deprivation

Studies with animals and children show that early social deprivation is linked to developmental deficits. However, other studies suggest that infants also have powerful capacities to recover from deprivation.

Kagan and Klein (1973) reported that many children may be able to recover fully from 13 or 14 months of deprivation. The natives in an isolated Guatemalan village believe that fresh air and sunshine will make children ill. Thus, children are kept in windowless huts until they can walk. They are played with infrequently. During their isolation, the infants behave apathetically; they are physically and socially deficient when they start to walk. But by 11 years of age, they are alert, active, and as intellectually able as American children of the same age.

A classic longitudinal study of children reared in orphanages also offers evidence of the ability of children to recover from social deprivation (Skeels, 1966). In this study, a group of 19-month-old, apparently intellectually deficient children were placed in the care of older institutionalized girls. The girls spent a great deal of time playing with, talking to, and nurturing them. Four years after being placed with the girls, the "intellectually deficient" children made dramatic gains in intelligence test scores, whereas children who remained in the orphanage showed declines in IQ.

The children placed in the care of the older girls also appeared to be generally well adjusted. By the time Skeels reported on their progress in 1966, most were married and were rearing children of their own who showed no intellectual or social deficits. Unfortunately, many of the children who had been left in the orphanage were still in some type of institutional setting. Few of them showed normal social and emotional development. Few were functioning as independent adults.

The good news is that many children who have been exposed to early social deprivation can catch up in their social and emotional development and lead normal adult lives if they receive individual attention and environmental stimulation (Rutter, 2006). On the other hand, persistent social deprivation may be associated with lasting hormonal changes indicative of stress (Koss et al., 2014).

How Common Are Child Abuse and Neglect? What Are Their Effects?

We have considered the results of rearing children in settings in which contact with parents is reduced or absent. But living with one's parents does not guarantee that a

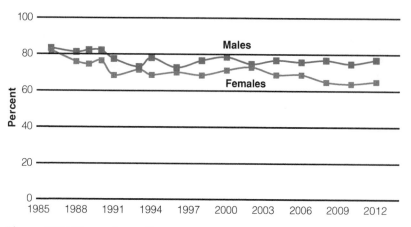

Figure 7.7 ■ Percentage of Males and Females Ages 18 to 65 Who Agree or Strongly Agree That It Is Sometimes Necessary to Discipline a Child with a "Good, Hard Spanking," Selected Years, 1986–2012.
Source: Child Trends Data Bank. (2012). Attitudes toward spanking. http://www.childtrends.org/wp -content/uploads/2012/10/51_ Attitudes_Toward_Spanking.pdf

child will receive tender loving care. Sadly, there's no place like home—for violence, that is.

Some Facts About the Incidence of Child Abuse and Neglect

Child abuse has recently become a hot topic due to the publicity surrounding child abuse by professional sports stars (e.g., Eder & Vorzi, 2014). Consider the following statistics from national surveys (U.S. Department of Health and Human Services [USDHHS], 2013): By the time a child is 2 years of age, 9 in 10 parents have engaged in some sort of psychological or emotional abuse; more than half of parents have slapped or spanked their children; and one-third of parents have pushed, grabbed, or shoved their children.

One of the problems is the widespread belief in spanking as an appropriate form of discipline or punishment for child misbehavior. As shown in Figure 7.7 ■, survey research shows that over the past 30 years there has been some decline in the percentage of adults who say that a "good, hard spanking" is sometimes necessary. However, in a recent year, more than three-quarters of males (77%) and nearly 2 women in 3 (65%) continue to agree with this point of view. Also, many people do not know where to draw the line between discipline and severe punishment, or child abuse (Dyson, 2014). There is no perfect way to distinguish the two, but sociologist Michael Eric Dyson (2014) notes that the word "discipline" derives from the Latin "discipuli," which refers to a student or a disciple, suggestive of a teacher–pupil relationship. The word "punishment," however, derives from the Greek "poine," and refers to revenge and is the root of the word "pain."

Also consider the relationship between the abuser and the victim. Four-fifths of victims (81%) were maltreated by a parent (see Figure 7.8 ■). More than one-third of victims were maltreated by the mother acting alone (37%). One child in 5 (19%) was maltreated by the father acting alone. Nearly one-fifth (19%) were maltreated by the parents acting together; only 13% of victims were maltreated by a perpetrator other than a parent.

TRUTH OR FICTION REVISITED: Actually, despite the fact that men are usually more aggressive than women, about twice as many children are maltreated by their mothers acting alone as by their fathers acting alone. Why do you think this is so? (Hint: with whom do most children tend to spend more time?)

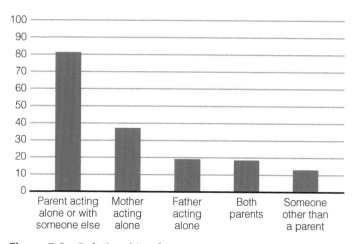

Figure 7.8 ■ Relationship of Perpetrator to Victim
Four out of five children who are maltreated are maltreated by parents.
Source: Data from Child Maltreatment (2010).

Younger children suffer the highest rates of victimization. More than one-third of victims (34%) were under the age of 4 (see Figure 7.9 ■). About a quarter (23%) were aged 4–7 years. Girls are slightly more likely than boys to be maltreated: 51.5% versus 48.5%. You might expect that older children would be more likely than younger children to be maltreated because they are more capable of "getting into trouble." Perhaps the results are based on facts that younger children, especially those under the age of 1, are most likely to cry—which can irritate some parents—and least capable of reporting the maltreatment to anyone else. And when we compare them to 16- or 17-year-olds, we can also note that the younger children are less capable of defending themselves or leaving home as a result of maltreatment.

Types of maltreatment are shown in Figure 7.10 ■. Note that neglect is many times more common than abuse. Neglect is, in effect, passive, whereas abuse is active. And nearly 1 child in 10 is sexually abused.

Nearly 3 million American children are neglected or abused each year by their parents or caregivers (Finkelhor et al., 2013). About 1 in 6 of these children experiences serious injury. Thousands die. More than 150,000 of the 3 million are sexually abused. But researchers believe that 50–60% of cases of child abuse and neglect go unreported, so the number of actual incidents is a good deal higher (USDHHS, 2013). One reason so many cases go unreported is that, as noted, it can be difficult, especially for abusers, to draw the line between "normal discipline" and abuse. Other reasons include fear of embarrassing a family; fear of legal consequences; and, sometimes, a mother's fear that she will be victimized by the abuser if she reports the crime. In any event, child neglect is responsible for more injuries and deaths than child abuse (USDHHS, 2013).

The U.S. Department of Health and Human Services recognizes six types of maltreatment of children (USDHHS, 2013):

- Physical abuse: actions causing pain and physical injury.
- Sexual abuse: sexual molestation, exploitation, and intercourse.
- Emotional abuse: actions that impair the child's emotional, social, or intellectual functioning.
- Physical neglect: failure to provide adequate food, shelter, clothing, or medical care.
- Emotional neglect: failure to provide adequate nurturance and emotional support.
- Educational neglect: permitting or forcing the child to be truant.

Although blatant abuse is more horrifying, more injuries, illnesses, and deaths result from neglect (USDHHS, 2013).

Table 7.1 ● shows examples of the three types of neglect.

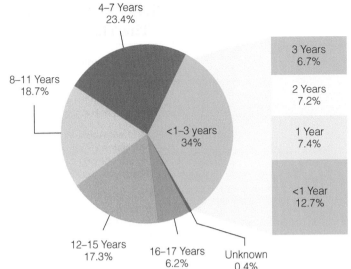

Figure 7.9 ■ Rates of Victimization, by Age
Younger children are the most likely to be maltreated.
Source: Data from Child Maltreatment (2010).

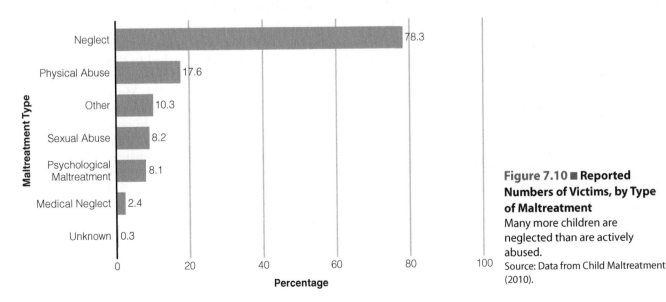

Figure 7.10 ■ Reported Numbers of Victims, by Type of Maltreatment
Many more children are neglected than are actively abused.
Source: Data from Child Maltreatment (2010).

The Three Forms of Child Neglect—Examples

Physical Neglect	Educational Neglect	Emotional Neglect
A 2-year-old who was found wandering in the street late at night, naked and alone	An 11-year-old and a 13-year-old who were chronically truant	Siblings who were subjected to repeated incidents of family violence between their mother and father
An infant who had to be hospitalized for near-drowning after being left alone in a bathtub	A 12-year-old whose parents permitted him to decide whether to go to school, how long to stay there, and in which activities to participate	A 12-year-old whose parents permitted him to drink and use drugs
Children who were living in a home contaminated with animal feces and rotting food	A special education student whose mother refused to believe he needed help in school	A child whose mother helped him shoot out the windows of a neighbor's house

Sexual Abuse of Children

No one knows how many children are sexually abused (Finkelhor et al., 2013). Although most sexually abused children are girls, one-quarter to one-third are boys (USDHHS, 2013). When we sample the population at large rather than rely on cases of abuse that are reported to authorities, it appears that the prevalence of sexual abuse among children is about 2% each year, but the rate for girls aged 14 to 17 is above 10% in a given year (Finkelhor et al., 2013). This chapter is about infants, but many boys in middle childhood and adolescence have been sexually abused by religious leaders and by athletic coaches—as made all too clear in news reports in recent years.

Sexual abuse of children ranges from exhibitionism, kissing, fondling, and sexual touching to oral sex and anal intercourse and, with girls, vaginal intercourse. Acts such as touching children's sexual organs while changing or bathing them, sleeping with children, and appearing nude before them are open to interpretation and are often innocent.

Effects of Child Abuse and Neglect

Maltreated children show a high incidence of personal and social problems and psychological disorders (Sousa et al., 2011). In general, maltreated children are less securely attached to their parents. They are less intimate with their peers and are more aggressive, angry, and noncompliant than other children (Blow, 2014; Moylan et al., 2010). They rarely express positive emotions, have lower self-esteem, and show impaired cognitive functioning, leading to poorer performance in school (Sousa et al., 2011). When they reach adulthood, they are more likely to act aggressively toward their intimate partners (Gomez, 2011). As they mature, maltreated children are at greater risk for delinquency, academic failure, and substance abuse (Sousa et al., 2011; Sperry & Widom, 2013).

A protester carries a sign indicating that saying one is sorry is not a sufficient response for people who are guilty of child abuse, including the killers of the boy on the sign.

Causes of Child Abuse and Neglect

A number of factors contribute to the probability that parents will abuse their children. They include situational stress, a history of child abuse in at least one of the parents' families of origin, lack of adequate coping and problem-solving skills, deficiency in child-rearing skills, unrealistic expectations of what a child should be able to do at a given developmental level, and substance abuse (Wolfe, 2011).

Stress has many sources, including such life changes as parental conflict and divorce or separation, the loss of a job, moving, and the birth of a new family member (Douglas & Mohn, 2014). Unemployment seems to be a particularly predisposing life change for child abuse (Douglas & Mohn, 2014).

Stress is created by crying infants themselves. Consequently, infants who are already in pain of some kind and relatively difficult to soothe may be more likely to be abused (Stupica et al., 2011). Abusive parents may find the cries of their infants particularly aversive, so the infants' crying may precipitate abusive behavior (Schuetze et al., 2003). Ironically, mothers who are deeply depressed or using cocaine may neglect crying infants because they perceive the cries to be less aversive (Schuetze et al., 2003). Children who act disobediently, inappropriately, or unresponsively are at greater risk of abuse (Wolfe, 2011). Why? Parents tend to become frustrated and irritated when their children show prolonged signs of distress or misbehavior. Abusive mothers are more likely than nonabusive mothers to assume that their children's misbehavior is intentional, even when it is not. Within our culture, intentional misconduct is seen as more deserving of punishment than incidental misconduct. Abusive mothers also tend to believe that they have little control over their child's misbehavior.

TRUTH OR FICTION REVISITED: It is true that child abusers have frequently been the victims of child abuse themselves. Why does child abuse run in families?

There are probably a number of reasons that child abuse tends to run in families (Dyson, 2014). One is that parents serve as role models for their children. As noted by Murray Straus (1995), "Spanking teaches kids that when someone is doing something you don't like and they won't stop doing it, you hit them." If children grow up observing their parents using violence as a means of coping with stress and feelings of anger, they are less likely to learn to diffuse their anger through techniques such as humor, verbal expression of feelings, reasoning, or even counting to 10 to let the anger pass.

Exposure to violence in their own homes may lead some children to accept family violence as a norm (Dyson, 2014). They may see nothing wrong with it. Certainly, parents can find any number of "justifications" for violence—if they seek them. One is the adage "Spare the rod, spoil the child." Another is the belief that they are hurting their children "for their own good"—to discourage behavior that is likely to get them into trouble.

Still another "justification" of child abuse is the sometimes cloudy distinction between the occasional swat on the rear end and spanking. Child abusers may argue that all parents hit their children (which is not true), and they may claim not to understand why outsiders are making such a fuss about private family behavior. Child abusers who were subjected to abuse also may harbor the (incorrect) belief that "everyone does it."

The patterns of attachment of the perpetrators of child abuse have also been studied. One study, for example, found that nonfamilial perpetrators of sexual child abuse were significantly less likely to have a secure attachment style in their relationships (Jamieson & Marshall, 2000).

In any event, child abuse must be conceptualized and dealt with as a crime of violence. Whether or not child abusers happen to be victims of abuse themselves, child abusers are criminals, and children must be protected from them.

PREVENTION OF SEXUAL ABUSE OF CHILDREN

Many of us were taught by our parents never to accept a ride or an offer of candy from a stranger. However, many instances of sexual abuse are perpetrated by a familiar adult, often a family member or friend (Finkelhor et al., 2014). Prevention programs help children understand what sexual abuse is and how they can avoid it. In addition to learning to avoid strangers, children need to recognize the differences between acceptable touching, such as an affectionate embrace or pat on the head, and unacceptable or "bad" touching. Even elementary school children can learn the distinction between "good touching" and "bad touching." School-based programs can help prepare children to handle an actual encounter with a molester. Children who receive training are more likely to use strategies such as running away, yelling, or saying no when they are threatened by an abuser (Finkelhor et al., 2013). They are also more likely to report incidents to adults.

Researchers recognize that children can easily be intimidated or overpowered by adults or older children. Children may be unable to say no in a sexually abusive situation, even though they want to and know it is the right thing to do. Although children may not always be able to prevent abuse, they can be encouraged to tell someone about it. Most prevention programs emphasize teaching children messages such as "It's not your fault," "Never keep a bad or scary secret," and "Always tell your parents about this, especially if someone says you shouldn't tell them" (Finkelhor et al., 2013).

Children also need to be alerted to the types of threats they might receive for disclosing abuse. They are more likely to resist threats if they are reassured that they will be believed when they report the abuse, that their parents will continue to love them, and that they and their families will be protected from the molester.

In most states, teachers and helping professionals are required to report suspected abuse to authorities. Tighter controls and better screening are needed to monitor the hiring of day-care employees. Administrators and teachers in preschool and day-care facilities also need to be educated to recognize the signs of sexual abuse and to report suspected cases.

Reflect How would you attempt to teach a child the difference between "good touching" and "bad touching"?

What to Do About Child Abuse and Neglect

Dealing with child abuse is a frustrating task. Social agencies and the courts can find it difficult to distinguish between spanking and abuse, as many abusers do. Because of the belief in this country that parents have the right to rear their children as they wish, police and the courts have historically tried to avoid involvement in domestic quarrels and family disputes. However, the alarming incidence of child abuse has spawned new efforts at detection and prevention. Many states require helping professionals such as psychologists and physicians to report any suspicion of child abuse. Many states legally require anyone who suspects child abuse to report it to authorities.

A number of techniques have been developed to help prevent child abuse. One approach focuses on strengthening parenting skills among the general population (Bugental et al., 2010). Parent education classes in high school are an example of this approach.

Another approach targets groups at high risk for abuse, such as poor, single teen mothers (Joshi et al., 2006). In some programs, for example, home visitors help new parents develop skills in caregiving and home management (Duggan et al., 2004).

A third technique focuses on presenting information about abuse and providing support to families. For instance, many locales have child abuse hotlines. Private citizens who suspect child abuse may call for advice. Parents who are having difficulty controlling aggressive impulses toward their children are encouraged to call. Some hotlines are serviced by groups such as Parents Anonymous, whose members have had similar difficulties and can help callers diffuse feelings of anger in less harmful ways.

Characteristics of Autism Spectrum Disorders

Key Indicators	Other Indicators
• Does not babble, point, or make meaningful gestures by 1 year of age • Does not speak one word by 16 months • Does not combine two words by age 2 • Does not respond to name • Loses language or social skills	• Has poor eye contact • Does not seem to know how to play with toys • Excessively lines up toys or other objects • Is attached to one particular toy or object • Does not smile • At times seems to be hearing impaired

Source: Adapted from Strock (2004).

Another helpful measure is increased publicity about the magnitude of the child abuse problem. The public may also need more education about where an occasional swat on the behind ends and child abuse begins. Perhaps the format for such education could be something like this: "If you are doing such and such, make no mistake about it—you are abusing your child."

What Are Autism Spectrum Disorders? On Being Alone Among the Crowd

Autism spectrum disorders (ASDs) are characterized by impaired communication skills, poor social interactions, and repetitive, stereotyped behavior (American Psychiatric Association, 2013; see Table 7.2 ●). They tend to become evident by the age of 3 years and sometimes before the end of the first year. A CDC study of 407,578 children from 14 different areas in the United States found that about 1 in every 152 children was identified as having an ASD (Rice, 2007). Other researchers place the number as high as 1 in 68 children (Bhat et al., 2014; Moyal et al., 2013). There are several variations of ASDs, but autism is the major type and will be our focus here. Other forms of ASDs include:

- Asperger's disorder: an ASD characterized by social deficits and stereotyped behavior but without the significant cognitive or language delays associated with autism.
- Rett's disorder: an ASD characterized by a range of physical, behavioral, motor, and cognitive abnormalities that begin after a few months of apparently normal development.
- Childhood disintegrative disorder: an ASD involving abnormal functioning and loss of previously acquired skills that begins after about 2 years of apparently normal development.

Autism

Peter nursed eagerly, sat and walked at the expected ages. Yet some of his behavior made us vaguely uneasy. He never put anything in his mouth. Not his fingers nor his toys—nothing....

More troubling was the fact that Peter didn't look at us, or smile, and wouldn't play the games that seemed as much a part of babyhood as diapers. He rarely laughed, and when he did, it was at things that didn't seem funny to us. He didn't cuddle, but sat upright in my lap, even when I rocked him. But children differ and we were content to let Peter be himself. We thought it hilarious when my brother, visiting us when Peter was 8 months old, observed, "That kid has no social instincts, whatsoever." Although Peter

autism spectrum disorders (ASDs) Developmental disorders—including autism, Asperger's syndrome, Rett's disorder, and childhood disintegrative disorder—that are characterized by impaired communication skills, poor social interactions, and repetitive, stereotyped behavior.

was a first child, he was not isolated. I frequently put him in his playpen in front of the house, where the schoolchildren stopped to play with him as they passed. He ignored them, too.

It was Kitty, a personality kid, born two years later, whose responsiveness emphasized the degree of Peter's difference. When I went into her room for the late feeding, her little head bobbed up and she greeted me with a smile that reached from her head to her toes. And the realization of that difference chilled me more than the wintry bedroom.

Peter's babbling had not turned into speech by the time he was 3. His play was solitary and repetitious. He tore paper into long thin strips, bushel baskets of it every day. He spun the lids from my canning jars and became upset if we tried to divert him. Only rarely could I catch his eye, and then saw his focus change from me to the reflection in my glasses....

[Peter's] adventures into our suburban neighborhood had been unhappy. He had disregarded the universal rule that sand is to be kept in sandboxes, and the children themselves had punished him. He walked around a sad and solitary figure, always carrying a toy airplane, a toy he never played with. At that time, I had not heard the word that was to dominate our lives, to hover over every conversation, to sit through every meal beside us. That word was autism.[1]

Peter, the boy with "no social instincts," was autistic. The word *autism* derives from the Greek *autos*, meaning "self." (An automobile is a self-driven method of moving from place to place.) **Autism** is four to five times more common among boys than girls. But females with autism show relatively greater social communication impairment, lower cognitive abilities, and more conduct disorders or "acting out" (Frazier et al., 2014). Perhaps the most poignant feature of autism among both females and males is the child's utter aloneness (American Psychiatric Association, 2013). Autistic children do not show interest in social interaction and may avoid eye contact. Attachment to others is weak or absent.

Other features of autism include communication problems, intolerance of change, and ritualistic or stereotypical behavior (American Psychiatric Association, 2013). Parents of autistic children frequently report that they were "good babies." This usually means that they made few demands. However, as autistic children develop, they tend to shun affectionate contacts such as hugging, cuddling, and kissing.

Development of speech lags (Bennett et al., 2014). There is little babbling or communicative gesturing during the first year. Autistic children may show **mutism**, **echolalia**, and pronoun reversal, referring to themselves as "you" or "he." About half use language by middle childhood, but their speech is unusual and troubled (Zimmerman, 2008).

Autistic children become bound by ritual (Estes et al., 2011). Even slight changes in routines or the environment may cause distress. The teacher of a 5-year-old autistic girl would greet her each morning with "Good morning, Lily, I am very, very glad to see you." Lily would ignore the greeting, but she would shriek if the teacher omitted even one of the *very*'s. This feature of autism is termed "preservation of sameness." When familiar objects are moved from their usual places, children with autism may throw tantrums or cry until the objects are restored. They may insist on eating the same food every day. Autistic children show deficits in peer play, imaginative play, imitation, and emotional expression. Many sleep less than their agemates (Georgiades et al., 2010).

Some autistic children mutilate themselves, even as they cry out in pain. They may bang their heads, slap their faces, bite their hands and shoulders, or pull out their hair.

autism An autism spectrum disorder characterized by extreme aloneness, communication problems, intolerance of change, and ritualistic behavior.

mutism Inability or refusal to speak.

echolalia The automatic repetition of sounds or words.

---

[1] Adapted from Eberhardy (1967).

Causes of Autism Spectrum Disorders

Some theorists have argued that children develop ASDs in response to parental rejection. From this viewpoint, autistic behavior shuts out the cold outside world. But research evidence shows that the parents of autistic children are not deficient in child rearing (Landrigan, 2010).

Various lines of evidence suggest a key role for biological factors in autism (Bhat et al., 2014; Chmielewski & Beste, 2015). For example, very low birth weight and advanced maternal age may heighten the risk of autism (Schieve et al., 2015). A role for genetic mechanisms is suggested by kinship studies (Vorstman & Burbach, 2014). For example, the concordance (agreement) rates for ASDs are about 60% among pairs of identical (monozygotic) twins, who fully share their genetic heritage, compared with about 10% for pairs of fraternal (dizygotic) twins, whose genetic codes overlap by only 50% (Kendler, 2010; Plomin et al., 1994). Twin status appears to increase susceptibility to the symptoms of autism, especially among males. Researchers suspect that multiple genes are involved in ASDs and interact with other factors, environmental and/or biological.

Investigation of biological factors has suggested neurological involvement. Many children with ASDs have abnormal brain wave patterns or seizures (Chonchaiya et al., 2012). Other researchers note unusual activity in the motor region of the cerebral cortex, and less activity in some other areas of the brain, including the frontal and temporal lobes and the limbic system (Fournier et al., 2010). Yet other researchers find that autistic children may be less likely than other children to "prune" unused synapses, possibly causing their brains to be overloaded with stimulation (Tang et al., 2014). Perhaps the relative lack of pruning contributes to abnormal brain sensitivities to neurotransmitters such as serotonin, dopamine, acetylcholine, and norepinephrine (Bauman et al., 2006). Still other researchers link autism to disorders of the immune system, which they believe originate during prenatal development (Zimmerman, 2008).

Autism The most poignant feature of autism is the child's utter aloneness. Other symptoms include communication problems, intolerance of any change, and ritualistic or stereotypical behaviour.

> **TRUTH OR FICTION REVISITED:** While we are discussing biological factors in causation, let us delete one such possible factor. It has been widely believed—it has almost achieved folklore status—that vaccines or the mercury preservative used in a number of vaccines, such as the measles-mumps-rubella (MMR) vaccine, can cause autism. We should note, rather strongly, that there is *no* scientific evidence for this view, regardless of whether or not it is widely held (Archer, 2014; Dixon & Clarke, 2013; Uno et al., 2015).

All in all, it seems clear that we can consider autism a disease of the brain and that parents of children with autism should not blame themselves. Although it appears that heredity creates a vulnerability to autism, the conditions that interact with heredity to produce autistic behavior remain unknown.

Treatment of Autism Spectrum Disorders

Treatment for ASDs is based largely on principles of learning, although investigation of biological approaches is also under way (Strock, 2004). Behavior modification has been used to increase the child's ability to attend to others, to play with other children, and to discourage self-mutilation (Sigafoos et al., 2009).

> **TRUTH OR FICTION REVISITED:** Many autistic children do respond to people—or fail to respond to them—as though they are furniture. They run around them rather than relating to them as people.

Because children with ASDs show behavioral deficits, behavior modification is used to help them develop new behavior. For example, many autistic children who respond to people as if they are furniture can be taught to accept people as reinforcers—for example, by pairing praise with food treats (Drasgow et al., 2001). Praise can then be used to encourage speech and social play. The most effective treatment programs focus on individualized instruction to correct behavioral, educational, and communication deficits. In a classic study conducted by O. Ivar Lovaas at UCLA (Lovaas et al., 1989), autistic children received more than 40 hours of one-to-one behavior modification a week for at least 2 years. Significant intellectual and educational gains were reported for 9 of the 19 children (47%) in the program. The children who improved achieved normal scores on intelligence tests and succeeded in first grade. Only 2% of an untreated control group achieved similar gains. Somewhat less intensive educational programs have also yielded positive results with many autistic toddlers (Stahmer et al., 2004).

Biological approaches for the treatment of ASDs are under study. Drugs that enhance serotonin activity (selective serotonin reuptake inhibitors [SSRIs]), such as those used to treat depression, can help prevent self-injury, aggressive outbursts, depression and anxiety, and repetitive behavior (Reiersen & Handen, 2011). Drugs that are usually used to treat schizophrenia—the "major tranquilizers"—are helpful with stereotyped behavior, hyperactivity, and self-injury, but not with cognitive and language problems (Reiersen & Handen, 2011).

Autistic behavior generally continues into adulthood to one degree or another. Yet some children with autism go on to earn college degrees and function independently (Moyal et al., 2014). Others need continuous treatment, which may include institutionalized care.

We have been examining the development of attachment and some of the circumstances that may interfere with its development. In recent years, a lively debate has sprung up concerning the effects of day care on children's attachment and on their social and cognitive development. Let us turn now to a consideration of these issues.

Section Review

9. The Harlows found that rhesus infants reared in isolation later _____ (sought or avoided?) contact with other monkeys.

10. Spitz noted that many institutionalized children appear to develop a syndrome characterized by _____ and depression.

11. Relatively more deaths occur from _____ (physical abuse or neglect?).

12. Children with _____ do not show interest in social interaction, have communication problems, are intolerant of change, and display repetitive behavior.

Reflect & Relate: What would you do if you learned that the child of a neighbor was being abused? What would you do if you were a teacher and learned that a child in your class was being abused?

7.3 Day Care

Seeking a phrase that can strike fear into the hearts of millions of American parents? Try *day care*. Only a relatively small percentage of American families still fit the conventional model where the father works and the mother stays at home and cares for the children. Most American parents, including mothers with infants,

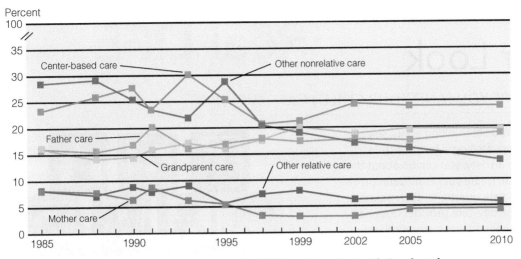

Figure 7.11 ■ Primary Care Arrangements for Children Ages 0–4 with Employed Mothers, United States
Source: Data from Child Care (2011).

are in the workforce, including 64% of mothers with children under the age of 6, and 57% of mothers with infants (O'Brien et al., 2014). According to the U.S. Government's Forum on Child and Family Statistics (Child Care, 2011), 48% of children aged 0–4 years whose mothers work outside the home are primarily cared for by a relative—their father, a grandparent, a sibling, or another relative (see Figure 7.11 ■). Nearly 1 in 4 (24%) spend most of their time in center-based care, such as a day-care center, a nursery school, a preschool program, or Head Start (O'Brien et al., 2014). Most of the remaining children have a babysitter or a nanny. Clearly, infants were not placed in nursery schools, preschool programs, or Head Start, because these are usually intended for children over the age of 2.

Because so many families rely on day care, parents, psychologists, educators, and other professionals are vitally concerned about the effects of day care. Let us examine some research findings:

- *Attachment.* Some studies find that infants placed in day care are more likely to be insecure, but most infants, whether cared for in the home or in day care, are securely attached (O'Brien et al., 2014).
- *Social, emotional, and cognitive development.* Infants with day-care experience are more peer oriented and play at higher developmental levels. They are more independent, self-confident, outgoing, affectionate, and cooperative (Bekkhus et al., 2011; O'Brien et al., 2014). High-quality day care—usually defined by the richness of the learning environment and the ratio of caregivers to children—is associated with greater language and cognitive skills (Belsky, 2009; Thompson, 2008).
- *Aggression.* About 17% of children placed in day care are rated as moderately more aggressive toward peers and adults than children reared at home by their mother (Belsky, 2001). Might the difference in part reflect competition for limited resources?

In any case, reality intrudes. Millions of parents do not have the option of deciding whether to place their children in day care; their only choice is where. And some parents, given their financial and geographic circumstances, might not even have that choice.

A Closer Look   Real LIFE

FINDING CHILD CARE YOU (AND YOUR CHILD) CAN LIVE WITH

It is normal to be anxious. You are thinking about selecting a day-care center or a private home for your child, and there are risks. Despite anxiety, you can go about the task with a checklist that can guide your considerations. Above all: Don't be afraid to ask questions, even pointed, challenging questions. If the day-care provider does not like questions or if the provider does not answer them satisfactorily, you want your child someplace else. So much for the preamble. Here's the checklist:

RubberBall/SuperStock

1. Does the day-care center have a license?

2. How many children are cared for at the center? How many caregivers are there? It is important for caregivers not to be overburdened by too many children, especially infants.

3. How were the caregivers hired? How were they trained? Did the center check references? What were the minimum educational credentials? Do the caregivers have any education or training in the behavior and needs of children? Do the caregivers attempt to engage the children in activities and educational experiences, or are they inactive unless a child cries or screams?

4. Is the environment childproof and secure? Can children stick their fingers in electric sockets? Are toys and outdoor equipment in good condition? Are sharp objects within children's reach? Can anybody walk in off the street? What is the history of children being injured or otherwise victimized in this day-care center? When are meals served? Snacks? What do they consist of? Will your child find them appetizing or go hungry?

5. Is it possible for you to meet the caregivers who will be taking care of your child? If not, why not?

6. Does the center seem to have an enriching environment? Do you see books, toys, games, and educational objects strewn about?

7. Are there facilities and objects such as swings and tricycles that will enhance your child's physical and motor development? Are children supervised when they play with these things or left on their own?

8. Does the center's schedule coincide with your needs?

9. Is the center located conveniently for you? Does it appear to be in a safe location or to have adequate security arrangements?

10. Are parents permitted to visit unannounced?

11. Do you like the overall environment and feel of the center or home? Listen to your "gut."

Reflect Which of the considerations in selecting a day-care center are most important to you? Why?

Section Review

13. The _____ (minority or majority?) of mothers in the United States work outside the home.

14. Infants with day-care experience play at _____ (higher or lower?) developmental levels than do home-reared babies.

15. Belsky and his colleagues found that once children are in school, those who had spent more time in day care were rated by teachers, caregivers, and mothers as being _____ (more or less?) aggressive toward other children.

Reflect & Relate: What are your concerns about placing children in day care? How do your concerns fit with the evidence on the effects of day care?

7.4 Emotional Development

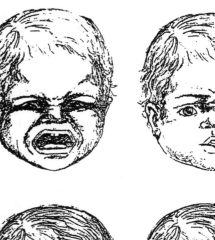

Emotions color our lives. We are green with envy, red with anger, blue with sorrow. We may experience purple passion or yellow cowardice. Positive emotions such as love can fill our days with pleasure. Negative emotions such as fear, depression, and anger can fill us with dread and make each day a chore.

An **emotion** is a state of feeling that has physiological, situational, and cognitive components. Physiologically, when emotions are strong, our hearts may beat more rapidly and our muscles may tense up. Situationally, we may feel fear in the presence of a threat and experience joy or relief in the presence of a loved one. Cognitively, fear is accompanied by the idea that we are in danger.

It is unclear how many emotions babies have, and they cannot tell us what they are feeling. We can only observe how they behave, including their facial expressions. Facial expressions appear to be universal in that they are recognized in different cultures around the world, so they are considered a reliable index of emotion.

Infants' initial emotional expressions appear to reflect two basic states of emotional arousal: a positive attraction to pleasant stimulation, such as the caregiver's voice or being held, and withdrawal from aversive stimulation, such as a sudden loud noise (Lagercrantz, 2010). By the age of 2–3 months, social smiling has replaced reflexive smiling. Social smiling is usually highly endearing to caregivers. At 3–5 months, infants laugh at active stimuli, such as repetitively touching their bellies or playing "Ah, boop!"

Carroll Izard's (2004; Izard et al., 2006) **differential emotions theory** proposes that infants are born with discrete emotional states. However, the timing of their appearance is linked to the child's cognitive development and social experiences. For example, Izard & Malatesta (1987) reported that 2-month-old babies receiving inoculations showed distress, whereas older infants showed anger.

Izard claimed to have found many discrete emotions at the age of 1 month by using his Maximally Discriminative Facial Movement Scoring System. Figure 7.12 ■ shows four infant facial expressions that Izard believes are associated with the basic emotions of anger/rage, enjoyment/joy, fear/terror, and interest/excitement. Izard and his colleagues reported that facial expressions indicating interest, disgust, and pain are present at birth. They and others have observed expressions of anger and sadness at 2 months of age, expressions of surprise at 4 months, and expressions of fear at 7 months (Izard & Malatesta, 1987). However, some researchers have suggested that this type of research is fraught with problems. First, observers cannot always accurately identify the emotions shown in slides or drawings of infant facial expressions. Second, we cannot know the exact relationship between a facial expression and an infant's inner feelings, which, of course, are private events. Even if the drawings accurately represent young infants' facial expressions, we cannot be certain that they express the specific emotions they would suggest if they were exhibited by older children and adults.

Figure 7.12 ■ Illustrations from Izard's Maximally Discriminative Facial Movement Scoring System
What emotion do you think each of these infants is experiencing?
Source: Izard (1983).

Is Emotional Development Linked to Patterns of Attachment?

Emotional development has been linked with various histories of attachment. In a longitudinal study of 112 children at ages 9, 14, 22, and 33 months, Kochanska

emotion A state of feeling that has physiological, situational, and cognitive components.

differential emotions theory Izard's view that the major emotions are distinct at birth but emerge gradually in accord with maturation and the child's developing needs.

(2001) studied the development of fear, anger, and joy using laboratory situations designed to evoke these emotions. Patterns of attachment were assessed using the strange-situation method. Differences in emotional development could first be related to attachment at the age of 14 months. Resistant children were most fearful and least joyful. Fear was their most powerful emotion. They frequently responded with distress even in episodes designed to evoke joy. When they were assessed repeatedly over time, it became apparent that securely attached children were becoming significantly less angry. By contrast, the negative emotions of insecurely attached children rose: Avoidant children grew more fearful, and resistant children became less joyful. At 33 months of age, securely attached children were less likely to show fear and anger, even when they were exposed to situations designed to elicit these emotions.

Enough disagreement. Let us focus on fear, an emotion that we can all agree is little fun. We will focus on a common fear of infants: the fear of strangers.

What is Meant by Fear of Strangers? Is It Something to Worry About?

When my daughter Jordan was 1 year old, her mother and I decided we had to get a nanny for a few hours a day so that we could teach, write, breathe, and engage in other life activities. We hired a graduate student in social work who had a mild, engaging way about her. She nurtured Jordan and played with her for about 4 months, during which time Jordan came to somewhat grudgingly accept her—most of the time. Still, Jordan was never completely comfortable with her and frequently let out a yowl as if buildings were collapsing around her, although the nanny did nothing except attempt to soothe her in a calm, consistent manner.

Stranger anxiety—also called fear of strangers—tends to emerge at about 6–9 months of age. It is common but not universal.

Jordan had a nanny *and* she had fear of strangers. Unfortunately, she met the nanny during the period when she had developed fear of strangers. The fear was eventually to subside, as these fears do, but during her entire encounter with the nanny, the nanny wondered what she was doing wrong. The answer, of course, was simple: She was existing, within sight of Jordan. Worse yet, Jordan's parents were not there to protect her from this vicious foe.

Was Jordan's response to her nanny "normal"? The answer is yes. Development of fear of strangers—sometimes termed **stranger anxiety**—is normal. Stranger anxiety appears at about 6–9 months of age in many different cultures, including those of the United States, Great Britain, Guatemala, and Zambia (Brooker et al., 2013). By 4 or 5 months of age, infants smile more in response to their mothers than in response to strangers. At this age, infants may compare the faces of strangers and their mothers, looking back and forth. Somewhat older infants show marked distress by crying, whimpering, gazing fearfully, and crawling away. Fear of strangers may begin at about 5–7 months, peak between 9 and 12 months, and decline in the second year or reach a second peak between 18 and 24 months and then decline in the third year.

Children who have developed fear of strangers show less distress in response to strangers when their mothers are present (Rapee, 2012). Babies are less likely to show fear of strangers when they are held by their mothers than when they are placed a few feet away. Children also are less likely to show fear of strangers when they are in familiar surroundings, such as their homes, than when they are in the laboratory (Brooker et al., 2013).

Social Referencing: What Should I Do Now?

Social referencing is the seeking out of another person's perception of a situation to help us form our own view of it. Leslie Carver and Brenda Vaccaro (2007) suggest that social referencing requires three components: (1) looking at another, usually

stranger anxiety A fear of unfamiliar people that emerges between 6 and 9 months of age. Also called *fear of strangers*.

social referencing Using another person's reaction to a situation to form one's own assessment of it.

older individual in a novel, ambiguous situation; (2) associating that individual's emotional response with the unfamiliar situation; and (3) regulating one's own emotional response in accord with the response of the older individual. In an experiment, Carver and Vaccaro (2007) found that 12-month-old infants were quicker to mold their responses to those of an adult who displayed a negative emotion than to model their responses after those of an adult who exhibited a neutral or a positive emotion. Perhaps we are wired to respond to danger first and pleasure later.

Infants display social referencing as early as 6 months of age. They use a caregiver's facial expression or tone of voice as a clue on how to respond (Schmitow & Stenberg, 2013). In one study, 8-month-old infants were friendlier to a stranger when their mothers exhibited a friendly facial expression in the stranger's presence than when she looked worried (Boccia & Campos, 1989).

How Do Infants Regulate Their Emotions?

Emotional regulation consists of the ways in which young children control their own emotions. For example, infants use emotional signals from an adult to help them cope with uncertainty. Emotional regulation is another important feature of early emotional development. Even young infants display certain behaviors to control unpleasant emotional states. They may look away from a disturbing event or suck their thumbs (Lewis, 2013; Rothbart & Sheese, 2007). Caregivers play an important role in helping infants learn to regulate their emotions. Early in life, a two-way communication system develops in which the infant signals the caregiver that help is needed, and the caregiver responds. Claire Kopp (1989, p. 347) gave an example of how this interaction works:

> A 13-month-old, playing with a large plastic bottle, attempted to unscrew the cover, but could not. Fretting for a short time, she initiated eye contact with her mother and held out the jar. As her mother took it to unscrew the cover, the infant ceased fretting.

Research evidence suggests that the children of secure mothers are likely not only to be securely attached themselves but also to regulate their own emotions in a positive manner (Lewis, 2013; Thompson & Meyer, 2007). A German longitudinal study (Zimmermann et al., 2001) related emotional regulation in adolescence with patterns of attachment during infancy, as assessed using the strange-situation method. Forty-one adolescents, aged 16 and 17 years, were placed in complex problem-solving situations with friends. It turned out that those adolescents who were secure as infants were most capable of regulating their emotions to interact cooperatively with their friends. Yet another study (Volling, 2001) addressed the relationship between attachment in infancy and emotional regulation in an interaction with a distressed sibling at the age of 4. Of 45 preschoolers in the study, those who had an insecure-resistant infant–mother attachment at the age of 1 year engaged in more conflict with their siblings and showed greater hostility at the age of 4.

emotional regulation
Techniques for controlling one's emotional states.

Section Review

16. The _____ (majority or minority?) of infants develop fear of strangers.

17. Social _____ is the seeking out of another person's perception of a situation to help us form our own view of it.

18. Emotional _____ consists of the ways in which young children control their own emotions.

Reflect & Relate: Have you ever found yourself in a novel situation and been uncertain what to do? How about when you entered adolescence or began your first college class? Did you observe other people's reactions to the situation in an effort to determine what to do? This behavior is termed social referencing. At what age do humans begin to use social referencing?

7.5 Personality Development

An individual's **personality** is his or her distinctive ways of responding to people and events. In this section, we will examine important aspects of personality development in the infant years. First, we will look at the emergence of the self-concept. We will then turn to a discussion of temperament. Finally, we will consider gender differences in behavior.

What Is the Self-Concept? How Does It Develop?

The **self-concept** is the sense of self. It appears to emerge gradually during infancy. At some point, infants understand that the hand they are moving in and out of sight is "their" hand. At some point, they understand that their own bodies extend only so far and that at a certain point, external objects and the bodies of others begin.

At birth, we may find the world to be a confusing blur of sights, sounds, and inner sensations. Yet, the "we" may be missing, at least for a while. When our hands first come into view, there is little evidence that we realize those hands "belong" to us and that we are somehow separate and distinct from the world outside.

personality An individual's distinctive ways of responding to people and events.

self-concept One's impression of oneself; self-awareness.

temperament Individual differences in styles of reaction that are present early in life.

Development of the Self-Concept

Psychologists have devised ingenious methods to assess the development of the self-concept among infants. One of these is the mirror technique. This technique involves the use of a mirror and a dot of rouge. Before the experiment begins, the researcher observes the infant for baseline data on how frequently the infant touches his or her nose. Then the mother places rouge on the infant's nose, and the infant is placed before a mirror. Not until about the age of 18 months do infants begin to touch their own noses when they look in the mirror (Keller et al., 2005; Taumoepeau & Reese, 2014).

Nose touching suggests that children recognize themselves and that they have a mental picture of themselves that enables them to perceive that the dot of rouge is an abnormality. Most 2-year-olds can point to pictures of themselves, and they begin to use "I" or their own name spontaneously (Smiley & Johnson, 2006).

Self-awareness affects the infant's social and emotional development (Foley, 2006). Knowledge of the self permits the child to develop notions of sharing and cooperation. Self-awareness also makes possible the development of "self-conscious" emotions, such as embarrassment, envy, empathy, pride, guilt, and shame (Foley, 2006). One illustration of the development of these "self-conscious" emotions comes from a study by Deborah Stipek and her colleagues (1992). They found that children older than 21 months often seek their mothers' attention and approval when they have successfully completed a task, whereas younger toddlers do not.

Temperament: Easy, Difficult, or Slow to Warm Up

Each child has a characteristic way of reacting and adapting to the world. The term **temperament** refers to stable individual differences in styles of reaction that are present early in life. Many researchers believe that temperament forms the basic core of personality and that there is a strong genetic component to temperament (Shiner & DeYoung, 2013; Zuckerman, 2011).

Self-Awareness In about the middle of the second year, infants begin to develop self-awareness, which has a powerful effect on social and emotional development.

The child's temperament includes many aspects of behavior. Alexander Thomas and Stella Chess, in their well-known New York Longitudinal Study, followed the development of temperament in 133 girls and boys from birth to young adulthood (Chess & Thomas, 1991; Thomas & Chess, 1989). They identified nine characteristics of temperament. Other researchers have identified additional characteristics (e.g., Gartstein et al, 2003). These include:

1. Activity level
2. Smiling/laughter
3. Regularity in child's biological functions, such as eating and sleeping
4. Approach or withdrawal from new situations and people
5. Adaptability to new situations
6. Sensitivity to sensory stimulation
7. Intensity of responsiveness
8. Quality of mood—generally cheerful or unpleasant
9. Distractibility
10. Attention span and persistence
11. Soothability
12. Distress shown when limitations occur

Types of Temperament

Thomas and Chess (1989) found that from the first days of life, many of the children in their study could be classified into one of three types of temperament: "easy" (40% of their sample), "difficult" (10%), and "slow to warm up" (15%). Only 65% of the children studied by Chess and Thomas fit into one of the three types of temperament. Some of the differences among these three types of children are shown in Table 7.3 ●. As you can see, the easy child has regular sleep and feeding schedules, approaches new situations (such as a new food, a new school, or a stranger) with enthusiasm and adapts easily to them, and is generally cheerful. It is obvious why such a child is relatively easy for parents to raise. Some children are more inconsistent and show a mixture of temperament traits. For example, a toddler may have a pleasant disposition but be frightened of new situations.

The difficult child, on the other hand, has irregular sleep and feeding schedules, is slow to accept new people and situations, takes a long time to adjust to new routines, and responds to frustrations with tantrums and loud crying. Parents

● TABLE 7.3

Types of Temperament

	Temperament Category		
	Easy	**Difficult**	**Slow to warm up**
Regularity of biological functioning	Regular	Irregular	Somewhat irregular
Response to new stimuli	Positive approach	Negative withdrawal	Negative withdrawal
Adaptability to new situations	Adapts readily	Adapts slowly or not at all	Adapts slowly
Intensity of reaction	Mild or moderate	Intense	Mild
Quality of mood	Positive	Negative	Initially negative; gradually more positive

Source: Based on Thomas, A., & Chess, S. (1989).

find this type of child more difficult to deal with. The slow-to-warm-up child falls somewhere between the other two. These children have somewhat irregular sleep and feeding patterns and do not react as strongly as difficult children. They initially respond negatively to new experiences and adapt slowly, only after repeated exposure.

TRUTH OR FICTION REVISITED: Children are not all born with the same temperament. Thomas and Chess found that many children have one of three kinds of temperament from the first days of life: easy, difficult, or slow to warm up.

Stability of Temperament

How stable is temperament? Evidence indicates that there is at least moderate consistency in the development of temperament from infancy onward (Shiner, 2012; Zuckerman, 2011). The infant who is highly active and cries in novel situations often becomes a fearful toddler. An anxious, unhappy toddler tends to become an anxious, unhappy adolescent. The child who refuses to accept new foods during infancy may scream when getting the first haircut, refuse to leave a parent's side during the first day of kindergarten, and have difficulty adjusting to college as a young adult. Difficult children in general are at greater risk for developing psychological disorders and adjustment problems later in life (Bales et al., 2013; Sayal et al., 2013). A longitudinal study tracked the progress of infants with a difficult temperament from 1½ through 12 years of age (Guerin et al., 1997). Temperament during infancy was assessed by the mother. Behavior patterns were assessed by both parents during the third year through the age of 12 and by teachers from the ages of 6 to 11. A difficult temperament correlated significantly with parental reports of behavioral problems from ages 3 to 12, including problems with attention span and aggression. Teachers concurred that children who had shown difficult temperaments during infancy were more likely to be aggressive later on and to have shorter attention spans.

Differences in Temperament Differences in temperament emerge in early infancy. The photo on the left shows the positive reactions of a 5-month-old girl being fed a new food for the first time. The photo on the right shows the very different response of another girl of about the same age when she is introduced to a new food.

Goodness of Fit: The Role of the Environment in Development of Temperament

Our daughter was a difficult infant, but we weathered the storm. At the age of 15, she was climbing out the second-story bedroom window at 2 a.m. to be with friends. When we discovered it, she sarcastically asked if we disapproved. "Yes," we said. "Use the front door; you're less likely to get hurt." She graduated college with honors. She has occasional outbursts, but that's her boyfriend's problem. And they love her on the job. She's a hard worker and the most creative thing they've ever seen.

—The Author's Files

The environment also affects the development of temperament. An initial biological predisposition toward a certain temperament may be strengthened or weakened by the parents' reaction to the child. Consider the following: Parents may react to a difficult child by becoming less available and less responsive. They may insist on imposing rigid care-giving schedules, which in turn can cause the child to become even more difficult to handle (Laxman et al., 2013). This example illustrates a discrepancy, or poor fit, between the child's behavior style and the parents' expectations and behaviors.

On the other hand, parents may respond in such a way as to modify a child's initial temperament in a more positive direction. Take the case of Carl, who in early life was one of the most difficult children in the New York Longitudinal Study:

Whether it was the first solid foods in infancy, the beginning of nursery and elementary school, first birthday parties, or the first shopping trip, each experience evoked stormy responses, with loud crying and struggling to get away. However, his parents learned to anticipate Carl's reactions, knew that if they were patient, presented only one or a few new situations at a time, and gave him the opportunity for repeated exposure, Carl would finally adapt positively. Furthermore, once he adapted, his intensity of responses gave him a zestful enthusiastic involvement, just as it gave his initial negative reactions a loud and stormy character. His parents became fully aware that the difficulties in raising Carl were due to his temperament and not to their being "bad parents." The father even looked on his son's shrieking and turmoil as a sign of lustiness. As a result of this positive parent–child interaction, Carl never became a behavior problem.

—Chess & Thomas (1984, p. 263)

This example demonstrates **goodness of fit** between the behaviors of child and parent. A key factor is the parents' realization that their youngster's behavior does not mean that the child is weak or deliberately disobedient, or that they are bad parents. This realization helps parents modify their attitudes and behaviors toward the child, whose behavior may in turn change in the desired direction (Brook et al., 2009; Laxman et al., 2013).

7.6 Gender Differences

All cultures make a distinction between females and males and have beliefs and expectations about how they ought to behave. For this reason, a child's gender is a key factor in shaping her or his personality and other aspects of development.

goodness of fit Agreement between the parents' expectations of, or demands on, the child and the child's temperamental characteristics.

What Are the Differences in Behavior Between Infant Girls and Boys?

Girls tend to advance more rapidly in their motor development in infancy: They sit, crawl, and walk earlier than boys do (Hines, 2013; Zelazo, 2013). However, female and male infants are quite similar in their responses to sights, sounds, tastes, smells, and touch. Although a few studies have found that infant boys are more active and irritable than girls, others have not (Hines, 2013; Zelazo, 2013). Girls and boys also are similar in their social behaviors. They are equally likely to smile at people's faces, for example, and do not differ in their dependency on adults (Maccoby & Jacklin, 1974). One area in which girls and boys begin to differ early in life is their preference for certain toys and play activities. By 12–18 months of age, girls prefer to play with dolls, doll furniture, dishes, and toy animals, whereas boys prefer transportation toys (trucks, cars, airplanes, and the like), tools, and sports equipment as early as 9–18 month of age (Berenbaum et al., 2008; Leaper & Bigler, 2011). Conversely, gender differences that appear to show up later, such as differences in spatial relations skills, are not necessarily evident in infancy (Örnkloo & von Hofsten, 2007). By 24 months, both girls and boys appear to be quite aware of which behaviors are considered gender-consistent and which gender-inconsistent, as measured in terms of time spent looking at the "novel" (in this case, "gender-inconsistent," as dictated by cultural stereotypes) behavior (Hill & Flom, 2007).

TRUTH OR FICTION REVISITED: It appears to be fiction that children play with gender-typed toys only after they have become aware of the gender roles assigned to them by society. It may well be the case that (most) girls prefer dolls and toy animals and that (most) boys prefer toy trucks and sports equipment before they have been socialized—even before they fully understand whether they themselves are female or male. Researchers continue to try to sort out the effects of nature and nurture in children's gender-related preferences.

Do Adults Behave Differently in Their Interactions with Infant Girls and Boys?

Adults respond differently to girls and boys. For example, in some studies, adults are presented with an unfamiliar infant who is dressed in boy's clothes and has a boy's name, whereas other adults are introduced to a baby who is dressed in girl's clothing and has a girl's name. (In reality, it is the same baby who simply is given different names and clothing.) When adults believe they are playing with a girl, they are more likely to offer "her" a doll; when they think the child is a boy, they are more likely to offer a football or a hammer. "Boys" also are encouraged to engage in more physical activity than are "girls" (Worell & Goodheart, 2006). Perhaps it is no wonder that infants labeled as "girls" are perceived as littler and softer (as well as nicer and more beautiful) than infants labeled as "boys."

Do Parents Treat Their Infant Sons and Daughters Differently?

Yes, like the adults with the unfamiliar babies, parents are more likely to encourage rough-and-tumble play in their sons than in their daughters. Fathers are especially likely to do so (John et al., 2013; Paquette & Dumont, 2013). Further, parents talk more to infant daughters than to infant sons. They smile more at daughters, are more emotionally expressive toward them, and focus more on feelings when talking to them (Blakemore & Hill, 2008).

Thinkstock Images/Getty Images

Adults Treat Infant Girls and Boys Differently Is it just as easy to imagine the mother in this picture as the father? Why or why not?

Perhaps the most obvious way in which parents treat their baby girls and boys differently is in their choice of clothing, room furnishings, and toys. Infant girls are likely to be decked out in a pink or yellow dress embellished with ruffles and lace, whereas infant boys wear blue or red (Wong & Hines, 2015). Parents also provide baby girls and boys with different bedroom decorations and toys. Examination of the contents of rooms of children found that boys' rooms were often decorated with animal themes and with blue bedding and curtains. Girls' rooms featured flowers, lace, ruffles, and pastel colors. Given the preferences of the adults in their lives, it is not surprising that girls and boys show tendencies to prefer gender-typed colors by the ages of 2 to 3 (Wong & Hines, 2015). Ironically, about 100 years ago, pink was generally viewed as stronger and more masculine, whereas blue was seen as more dainty and delicate (Wong & Hines, 2015).

Other studies find that parents react favorably when their preschool daughters play with "toys for girls" and their sons play with "toys for boys." Parents and other adults show more negative reactions when girls play with toys for boys and when boys play with toys for girls (Goble et al., 2012; Worell & Goodheart, 2006). In general, fathers are more concerned than mothers that their children engage in activities viewed as "appropriate" for their gender.

Parents thus attempt to influence their children's behavior during infancy and lay the foundation for development in early childhood. It is to that period of life that we will turn next, in Chapter 8.

Section Review

19. Psychologists devised the mirror technique to assess development of the self-_____.

20. The child's _____ consists of the stable individual differences in styles of reaction that are present very early in life.

21. The three basic types of temperament are easy, difficult, and _____ to warm up.

22. Girls prefer to play with dolls, whereas boys show a preference for playing with transportation toys, as early as _____ months of age.

Reflect & Relate: Have you known infants who were easygoing or difficult? How did their temperaments affect their relationships with their parents?

Chapter Review

7.1 What Is Attachment? What Kinds of Attachment Do Infants Develop?

An attachment is an enduring emotional tie between one animal or person and another specific individual. Children try to maintain contact with persons to whom they are attached. Most infants in the United States are securely attached. In the strange situation, a securely attached infant mildly protests the mother's departure and is readily comforted by her. The two major types of insecure attachment are avoidant attachment and ambivalent/resistant attachment. Infants with avoidant attachment are least distressed by their mothers' departure. Infants with ambivalent/resistant attachment show severe distress when their mothers leave but are ambivalent upon reunion. Securely attached infants are happier, more sociable, and more cooperative. They use the mother as a secure base from which to explore the environment. At ages 5 and 6, securely attached children are preferred by peers and teachers and are more competent. High-quality care contributes to security. Parents of securely attached infants are more likely to be affectionate and sensitive to their needs. Security of attachment is related to the infant's temperament as well as to caregivers' behavior. The initial pre-attachment phase lasts from birth to about 3 months and is characterized by indiscriminate attachment. The attachment-in-the-making phase occurs at about 3 or 4 months and is characterized by preference for familiar figures. The clear-cut attachment phase occurs at about 6 or 7 months and is characterized by dependence on the primary caregiver. Cognitive theorists suggest that an infant must develop object permanence before specific attachment is possible. Behaviorists suggest that infants become attached to caregivers because caregivers meet their physiological needs. Psychoanalysts suggest that the primary caregiver becomes a love object. The Harlows' experiments with monkeys suggest that contact comfort is a key to attachment. Ethologists view attachment as an inborn fixed action pattern (FAP), which occurs during a critical period in response to a releasing stimulus.

7.2 What Happens When Attachment Fails?

The Harlows found that rhesus infants reared in isolated confinement later avoided contact with other monkeys. Females who later had offspring tended to ignore or abuse them. Institutionalized children who receive little social stimulation encounter problems in development. Many exhibit withdrawal and depression. Deficiencies in sensory stimulation and social interaction may cause more problems than lack of love per se. Infants have considerable capacity to recover from deprivation. Nearly 3 million American children are neglected or abused each year, and neglect results in more serious harm than does abuse. About 150,000 children are sexually abused each year. Maltreated children are less intimate with peers and are more aggressive, angry, and noncompliant than other children. Child abuse and neglect may run in families because abusive parents serve as role models. Exposure to violence in the home may lead children to accept family violence as the norm. Some parents rationalize that they are hurting their children "for their own good"—to discourage problem behavior. Autism spectrum disorders (ASDs) are characterized by impairment in communication skills and social interactions, and by repetitive, stereotyped behavior. The most striking feature of autism is the child's aloneness. Other features include communication problems, intolerance of change, stereotypical behavior, mutism, echolalia, and self-mutilation. Evidence suggests a role for biological factors in autism. Genetic studies find higher concordance rates for autism among monozygotic than among dizygotic twins. Researchers also suspect neurological involvement. Behavior modification has been used to increase the child's attention to others and social play and to decrease self-mutilation. Aversive stimulation has been used to curtail self-injury. Researchers are studying the use of SSRIs and major tranquilizers.

7.3 What Are the Effects of Day Care?

Infants with day-care experience are more independent, self-confident, outgoing, affectionate, and cooperative with peers and adults. Children in high-quality day care outperform children who remain in the home in cognitive skills. Children in day care are also more aggressive, but some aggression may indicate independence, not maladjustment.

7.4 How Do Emotional Responses Develop During Infancy?

Emotions are states of feeling that have physiological, situational, and cognitive components. Izard proposed that infants are born with several emotional states but that their appearance is linked to cognitive development and social experiences. Fear of strangers is normal in that most infants develop it at about the age of 6–9 months. Infants display social referencing as early as 6 months of age, when they use caregivers' facial expressions or tones of voice for information on how to respond in novel situations. Emotional regulation is emotional self-control. Caregivers help infants learn to regulate their emotions. The children of secure mothers are more likely to regulate their emotions positively.

7.5 How Do Children's Personalities Develop During Infancy?

The self-concept is the sense of self. Findings using the mirror technique suggest that the self-concept develops by about 18 months of age. Self-awareness enables the child to develop concepts of sharing and cooperation and "self-conscious" emotions such as embarrassment, envy, empathy, pride, guilt, and shame. The term *temperament* refers to stable individual differences in styles of reaction to the world that are present early in life. These reactions include activity level, regularity, approach or withdrawal, adaptability, response threshold, response intensity, quality of mood, distractibility, attention span, and persistence. Thomas and Chess found that most infants can be classified as having an easy, difficult, or slow-to-warm-up temperament. Temperament remains moderately consistent from infancy through young adulthood.

7.6 What Gender Differences Do We Find During Infancy?

Female infants sit, crawl, and walk earlier than boys do. By 12–18 months of age, girls prefer to play with dolls and similar toys, whereas boys prefer transportation toys and gear.

Key Terms

attachment 216
separation anxiety 216
secure attachment 216
avoidant attachment 216
ambivalent/resistant attachment 217
disorganized–disoriented
    attachment 217
indiscriminate attachment 219
initial pre-attachment phase 220

attachment-in-the-making phase 220
clear-cut attachment phase 220
contact comfort 222
social smile 222
autism spectrum disorders
    (ASDs) 233
autism 234
mutism 234
echolalia 234

emotion 239
differential emotions theory 239
stranger anxiety 240
social referencing 240
emotional regulation 241
personality 242
self-concept 242
temperament 242
goodness of fit 245

8

Early Childhood:
Physical Development

Major Topics

Features

TruthorFiction?

 Some children are left-brained and others are right-brained. **p. 253**

 Sedentary parents are more likely to have "couch potatoes" for children. **p. 256**

 Julius Caesar, Michelangelo, Tom Cruise, and Oprah have something in common. (Hint: They don't all have book clubs.) **p. 258**

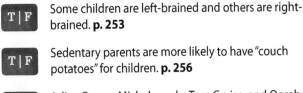 Some diseases are normal. **p. 262**

T | F Infections are the most common cause of death among children in the United States. **p. 266**

T | F It is dangerous to awaken a sleepwalker. **p. 270**

T | F Competent parents toilet train their children by their second birthday. **p. 271**

Two-year-old Mark is having lunch in his high chair. He is not without ambition. He begins by shoving fistfuls of hamburger into his mouth. He picks up his cup with both hands and drinks milk. Then he starts banging his spoon on his tray and his cup. He kicks his feet against the chair. He throws hamburger on the floor.

Compare Mark's behavior with that of Larry, age 3½, who is getting ready for bed. Larry carefully pulls his plastic train track apart and places each piece in the box. Then he walks to the bathroom, brings his stool over to the sink, and stands on it. He takes down his toothbrush and toothpaste, opens the cap, squeezes toothpaste on the brush, and begins to brush his teeth.

Mark and Larry are in early childhood, the years from 2 to 6. These years are sometimes called the play years, and they include the preschool period, which usually ends at about age 5, when most children enter kindergarten. During early childhood, physical growth is slower than it was in infancy. Children become taller and leaner, and by the end of early childhood they look more like adults than like infants. There is an explosion in motor skills; children become stronger, faster, and better coordinated.

Language improves enormously, and children can carry on conversations with others. As cognitive skills develop, a new world of make-believe or "pretend" play emerges. Curiosity and eagerness to learn are hallmarks of early childhood.

Physical and cognitive developments enable the child to emerge from total dependence on parents and caregivers to become part of the broader world outside the family. Peers take on an increasingly important role. Children develop a sense of their own abilities and shortcomings.

We learn about all these developments of early-childhood—physical, cognitive, social, and emotional—in Chapters 8, 9, and 10.

Ronald Greer/Alamy

8.1 Growth Patterns

In early childhood, physical and motor development proceeds by leaps and bounds—literally! While toddlers like Mark are occupied with grasping, banging, and throwing things, 3-year-olds like Larry are busy manipulating objects and exercising their newly developing fine motor skills.

What Changes Occur in Height and Weight During Early Childhood?

Following the dramatic gains in height of the first 2 years, the growth rate slows (Kuczmarski et al., 2000). Girls and boys tend to gain about 2–3 inches in height per year throughout early childhood. Weight gains also remain fairly even, at about 4–6 pounds per year (see Figure 8.1 ■). Children become increasingly slender as they gain in height and lose some "baby fat." Boys as a group are only slightly taller and heavier than girls in early childhood (see Figure 8.1). Noticeable variations in growth patterns also occur from child to child.

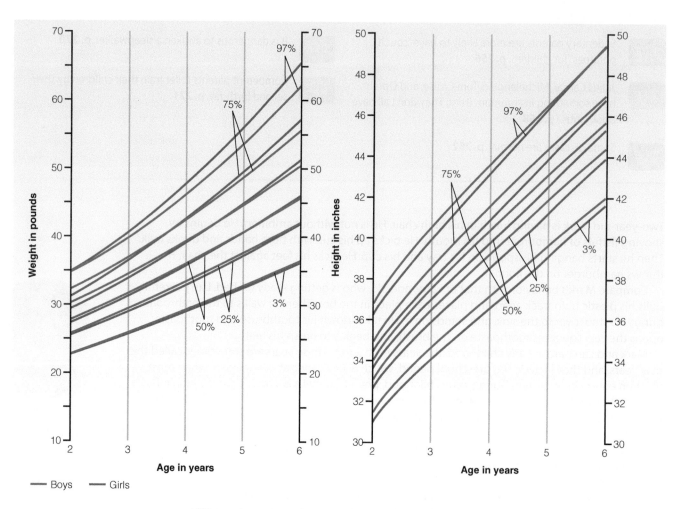

Figure 8.1 ■ Growth Curves for Height and Weight, Ages 2 to 6 Years
The growth rate slows down during early childhood. As in infancy, boys are only slightly taller and heavier than girls. Variations in growth patterns from child to child are evident.
Source: Kuczmarski et al. (2000, Figures 9–12).

How Does the Brain Develop During Early Childhood?

The brain develops more quickly than any other organ in early childhood. At 2 years of age, for example, the brain already has attained 75% of its adult weight. By the age of 5, the brain has reached 90% of its adult weight, even though the total body weight of the 5-year-old is barely one-third of what it will be as an adult (Tanner, 1989).

The increase in brain size is due in part to the continuing process of myelination of nerve fibers (see Chapter 5). Completion of the myelination of the neural pathways that link the cerebellum to the cerebral cortex facilitates the development of fine motor skills (Allen et al., 2011; Fletcher, 2011). The cerebellum is involved in balance and coordination, and the young child's balancing abilities increase dramatically as myelination of these pathways nears completion.

Brain Development and Visual Skills

Brain development is also linked to improvements in the ability to attend to and process visual information (Seiler et al., 2011). These skills are critical in learning to read. The parts of the brain that enable the child to sustain attention and screen out distractions become increasingly myelinated between the ages of about 4 and 7 (Nelson & Luciana, 2001). As a result, most children are ready to focus on schoolwork at these ages.

The speed with which children process visual information improves throughout childhood, reaching adult levels at the beginning of adolescence (Scherf et al., 2009; Seiler et al., 2011). The child's ability to scan visual material systematically also improves in early childhood. For example, researchers in one classic study presented children with pairs of pictures of similar-looking houses and asked the children whether or not the houses were identical (Vurpillot, 1968). Four-year-olds almost never showed thorough, systematic visual scanning of the features of the houses, but 9-year-olds often did so.

Are Some Children Right-Brained and Others Left-Brained?

It has become popular to speak of people as being "right-brained" or "left-brained." We have even heard it said that some instructional methods are aimed at the right brain (they are presented in an emotionally laden, aesthetic way), whereas others are aimed at the left brain (they are presented in a logical and straightforward manner).

The notion is that the hemispheres of the brain are involved in different kinds of intellectual and emotional functions and responses. Research does suggest that in right-handed individuals, the left hemisphere is relatively more involved in intellectual undertakings that require logical analysis and problem solving, language, and mathematical computation (Scull, 2010). The other hemisphere (usually the right hemisphere) is generally superior in visual–spatial functions (it is better at putting puzzles together), recognition of faces, discrimination of colors, aesthetic and emotional responses, understanding metaphors, and creative mathematical reasoning.

TRUTH OR FICTION REVISITED: Actually, it is not true that some children are left-brained and others are right-brained. Brain functions are not split up so precisely, as has been popularly believed.

The functions of the left and right hemispheres overlap to some degree, and the hemispheres also tend to respond simultaneously when we focus our attention on one thing or another. They are aided in "cooperation" by the myelination of the **corpus callosum**—a thick bundle of nerve fibers that connects the hemispheres (Luders et al., 2010). Myelination of the corpus callosum proceeds rapidly during early and middle childhood and is largely complete by the age of 8. By that time, children can better integrate logical and emotional functioning.

What Is Meant by Plasticity of the Brain?

Many parts of the brain have specialized functions. Specialization enables our behavior to be more complex. But specialization also means that injuries to certain parts of the brain can result in loss of these functions.

Fortunately, the brain also shows **plasticity** (M. V. Johnston et al., 2009). *Plasticity* means that the brain frequently can compensate for injuries to particular areas. This compensatory ability is greatest at about 1–2 years of age and then gradually declines, although it may not be completely gone, even in adulthood (Kolb & Gibb, 2007; Nelson et al., 2006). When we suffer damage to the areas of the brain that control language, we may lose the ability to speak or understand language. However, other areas of the brain may take over these functions in young children who suffer such damage. As a result, the children may dramatically regain the ability to speak or comprehend language (Nelson et al., 2006). In adolescence and adulthood, regaining such functions is much more difficult and may be all but impossible.

Two factors are involved in the brain's plasticity (Gauthier et al., 2009; Nelson et al., 2006). The first is "sprouting," or the growth of new dendrites. To some degree, new dendrites can allow for the rearrangement of neural circuits. The second factor is the redundancy of neural connections. In some cases, similar functions are found at two or more sites in the brain, although they are developed to different degrees. If one site is damaged, the other may be able to develop to perform the function.

Section Review

1. Children gain about _____ inches in height per year throughout early childhood.

2. Weight gains average about _____ pounds per year.

3. The _____ develops more rapidly than any other organ in early childhood.

4. _____ of the neural pathways that link the cerebellum to the cerebral cortex facilitates the development of fine motor skills.

5. The _____ is involved in balance and coordination.

6. Research suggests that in _____ handed individuals, the left hemisphere is relatively more involved in

logical analysis and problem solving, language, and mathematical computation.

7. The _____ hemisphere of the cerebral cortex is usually superior in visual–spatial functions and emotional responses.

8. Because of its _____, the brain can often compensate for injuries to particular areas.

Reflect & Relate: Have you ever compared the growth of a child to the norms on a growth chart? What were you looking for? What were your concerns?

corpus callosum The thick bundle of nerve fibers that connects the hemispheres of the brain.

plasticity The tendency of new parts of the brain to take up the functions of injured parts.

gross motor skills Skills that employ the large muscles used in locomotion.

 Motor Development

There is an explosion of motor skills in early childhood. As children's nervous systems mature, their movements become more precise and coordinated.

How Do Gross Motor Skills Develop in Early Childhood?

During ages 2–6, children make great strides in the development of **gross motor skills**, which involve the large muscles used in locomotion (see Table 8.1 ●). At

Development of Gross Motor Skills in Early Childhood

2 Years (24–35 Months)	3 Years (36–47 Months)	4 Years (48–59 Months)	5 Years (60–71 Months)
• Runs well straight ahead • Walks up stairs, two feet to a step • Kicks a large ball • Jumps a distance of 4–14 inches • Throws a small ball without falling • Pushes and pulls large toys • Hops on one foot, two or more hops • Tries to stand on one foot • Climbs on furniture to look out of window	• Goes around obstacles while running • Walks up stairs, one foot to a step • Kicks a large ball easily • Jumps from the bottom step • Catches a bounced ball, using torso and arms to form a basket • Goes around obstacles while pushing and pulling toys • Hops on one foot, up to three hops • Stands on one foot • Climbs nursery-school apparatus	• Turns sharp corners while running • Walks down stairs, one foot to a step • Kicks or catches a ball? • Jumps from a height of 12 inches • Throws a ball overhand • Turns sharp corners while pushing and pulling toys • Hops on one foot, four to six hops • Stands on one foot for 3–8 seconds • Climbs ladders • Rides a tricycle well	• Runs lightly on toes • Jumps a distance of 3 feet • Catches a small ball, using hands only • Hops 2–3 yards forward on each foot • Stands on one foot for 8–10 seconds • Climbs actively and skillfully • Skips on alternate feet • Rides a bicycle with training wheels

Note: The ages are averages; there are individual variations.

about the age of 3, children can balance on one foot. By age 3 or 4, they can walk up stairs as adults do, by placing a foot on each step. By age 4 or 5, they can skip and pedal a tricycle (Allen et al., 2011). They are better able to coordinate two tasks, such as singing and running at the same time, than are toddlers (Haywood & Getchell, 2008). In early childhood, children appear to acquire motor skills by teaching themselves and observing the behavior of other children. The opportunity to play with other children seems more important than adult instruction at this age.

Throughout early childhood, girls and boys are not far apart in their motor skills. Girls are somewhat better at tasks requiring balance and precision of movement. Boys, on the other hand, show some advantage in throwing and kicking (Moreno-Briseño et al., 2010; Tzuriel & Egozi, 2010).

Individual differences are more impressive than sex differences throughout early and middle childhood. Some children develop motor skills earlier than others. Some are genetically predisposed to developing better coordination or more strength than others. Motivation and practice also are important in children's acquisition of motor skills. Motor experiences in infancy may affect the development of motor skills in early childhood. For example, children who have early crawling experience perform better than those who do not on tests of motor skills in early childhood (Haywood & Getchell, 2008).

Physical Activity

Children spend quite a bit of time in physical activity in early childhood. One study found that they spend an average of more than 25 hours a week in large-muscle activity (D. W. Campbell et al., 2002). Two- to 4-year-olds are more likely than 4- to 6-year-olds to engage in physically oriented play, such as grasping, banging, and mouthing objects (D. W. Campbell et al., 2002). Consequently, they need more space and less furniture in a preschool or day-care setting.

The level of motor activity begins to decline after 2 or 3 years of age. Children become less restless and are able to sit still longer (D. W. Campbell et al., 2002; Eaton et al., 2001). Between the ages of 2 and 4, children in free play show an increase in sustained, focused attention.

Horizon International Images Limited/Alamy

Rough-and-Tumble Play Play fighting and chasing activities—known as rough-and-tumble play—are found among young children in societies around the world.

Rough-and-Tumble Play

Rough-and-tumble play consists of running, chasing, fleeing, wrestling, hitting with an open hand, laughing, and making faces. Rough-and-tumble play is not the same as aggressive behavior. Aggression involves hitting with fists, pushing, taking, grabbing, and angry looks. Unlike aggression, rough-and-tumble play helps develop both physical and social skills in children (Cillessen &-Bellmore, 2010; Pellis & Pellis, 2007).

Play fighting and chasing activities are found during early childhood in societies around the world (Whiting & Edwards, 1988). But the particular form that rough-and-tumble play takes is influenced by culture and environment. For example, rough-and-tumble play among girls is quite common among the Pilaga Indians and the !Kung of Botswana but less common among girls in the United States. In the United States, rough-and-tumble play usually occurs in groups made up of the same sex. However, !Kung girls and boys engage in rough-and-tumble play together. And among the Pilaga, girls often are matched against the boys.

Individual Differences in Activity Level

Children differ widely in their activity levels. Some children are much more active than others. In a study of 4- to 7-year-olds (Moore et al., 1991), children of active mothers were twice as likely to be active as children of inactive mothers. Children of active fathers were 3.5 times as likely to be active as children of inactive fathers.

TRUTH OR FICTION REVISITED: Sedentary parents are more likely to have "couch potatoes" for children. Physically active children are more likely to have physically active parents.

Several reasons may explain these relationships. First, active parents may serve as role models for activity. Second, sharing of activities by family members may play a role. Parents who are avid tennis players may involve their children in games of tennis from an early age. By the same token, couch-potato parents who prefer to view tennis on television rather than play it may be more likely to share this sedentary activity with their children. Third, active parents may encourage and support their child's participation in physical activity. Finally, a tendency to be active or inactive may be transmitted genetically, as shown by evidence from kinship studies (see Chapter 2) (Saudino, 2012; Wood et al., 2008). Genetic and environmental factors apparently interact to determine a child's activity level.

GENDER DIFFERENCES IN MOTOR ACTIVITY

During early childhood, boys tend to be more active than girls, at least in some settings (Haywood & Getchell, 2014). Boys spend more time than girls in large-muscle activities. Boys tend to be more fidgety and distractible than girls and to spend less time focusing on tasks.

Why are boys more active and restless than girls? One theory is that boys of a given age are less mature physically than girls of the same age. Children tend to become less active as they develop. Therefore, the gender difference in activity level may be a maturational difference (Haywood & Getchell, 2014). However, parental encouragement and reward of motor activity in boys and discouragement of such behavior in girls may be involved as well.

Boys also are more likely than girls to engage in rough-and-tumble play (Haywood & Getchell, 2014). What might account for this gender difference? Some psychologists suggest that the reasons are largely based in biology, especially having to do with the sex hormone testosterone. Others argue that the socializing influences of the family and culture at large promote play differences among girls and boys.

Reflect: Why is it useful to know about gender differences in motor activity?

How Do Fine Motor Skills Develop in Early Childhood?

Fine motor skills develop gradually and lag gross motor skills (Fletcher, 2011). This is yet another example of the proximodistal trend in development (see Chapters 3 and 5). Fine motor skills involve the small muscles used in manipulation and co-ordination. Control over the wrists and fingers enables children to hold a pencil properly, dress themselves, and stack blocks (see Table 8.2 ●). Young children can labor endlessly in attempting to tie their shoelaces and get their jackets zipped.

fine motor skills Skills that employ the small muscles used in manipulation, such as those in the fingers.

● TABLE 8.2

Development of Fine Motor Skills in Early Childhood

2 Years (24–35 Months)	3 Years (36–47 Months)	4 Years (48–59 Months)	5 Years (60–71 Months)
• Builds a tower of 6 cubes • Copies vertical and horizontal lines • Imitates folding of paper • Prints on an easel with a brush • Places simple shapes in correct holes	• Builds a tower of 9 cubes • Copies circle and cross • Copies letters • Holds crayons with fingers, not fist • Strings 4 beads using a large needle	• Builds a tower of 10 or more cubes • Copies square • Prints simple words • Imitates folding paper three times • Uses pencil with correct hand grip • Strings 10 beads	• Builds 3 steps from 6 blocks, using a model • Copies triangle and star • Prints first name and numbers • Imitates folding of square paper into a triangle • Traces around a diamond drawn on paper • Laces shoes

Note: The ages are averages; there are individual variations.

There are terribly frustrating (and funny) scenes of children alternating between steadfastly refusing to allow a parent to intervene and requesting the caregiver's help.

Children's Drawings

The development of drawing in young children is closely linked to the development of motor and cognitive skills. Children first begin to scribble during the second year. Initially, they seem to make marks for the sheer joy of it, and parents sometimes confuse their drawings with "messiness" (Jolley, 2010). Yet there is a method to these drawings.

Rhoda Kellogg (1959, 1970) studied more than 1 million drawings made by children. She found a meaningful pattern in the scribbles and identified 20 basic scribbles that she considered the building blocks of all art. These basic scribbles include vertical, horizontal, diagonal, circular, curving, waving or zigzagging lines, and dots.

Children go through four stages as they progress from making scribbles to drawing pictures: the *placement, shape, design,* and *pictorial stages.* Two-year-olds place their scribbles in various locations on the page (for example, in the middle of the page or near one of the borders). By age 3, children are starting to draw basic shapes: circles, squares, triangles, crosses, Xs, and odd shapes. As soon as they can draw shapes, children begin to combine them in the design stage. Between ages 4 and 5, the child reaches the pictorial stage, in which designs begin to resemble recognizable objects.

Children's early drawings tend to be symbolic of a broad category rather than specific. For example, a child might draw the same simple building whether she is asked to draw a school or a house (Tallandini & Valentini, 1991). Children between 3 and 5 years old usually do not set out to draw a particular thing. They are more likely to first see what they have drawn and then name it. As motor and cognitive skills improve beyond the age of 5, children improve at copying figures and become able to draw an object they have in mind (Dağlioğlu et al., 2010; Rübeling et al., 2011).

When Does Handedness Emerge? Are There Any Advantages or Disadvantages to Being Left-Handed?

Handedness emerges during infancy. By the age of 2–3 months, a rattle placed in the infant's hand is held longer with the right hand than with the left (Fitzgerald et al., 1991). By 4 months of age, most infants show a clear-cut right-hand preference in exploring objects using the sense of touch (Streri, 2002). Preference for grasping with the right or left hand increases markedly between the ages of 6 and 14 months (Ferre et al., 2010). Handedness becomes more strongly established during the early childhood years. Most people are right-handed, although studies vary as to how many are left-handed. Some people are ambidextrous—they can use their right and left hands and arms equally effectively. Many professional baseball players have batted either "righty" or "lefty."

TRUTH OR FICTION REVISITED: Julius Caesar, Michelangelo, Tom Cruise, and Oprah do have something in common: They are all left-handed.

Left-Handedness: Is It Gauche to Be Left-Handed? Myths and Realities

Being a "lefty" has been commonly regarded as a deficiency or liability. The language still swarms with slurs on lefties. We speak of "left-handed compliments," of having

Fine Motor Skills Control over the wrists and fingers enables children to hold a pencil, play a musical instrument, and, as shown in this photograph, work with modeling clay.

Robert Brenner/PhotoEdit

"two left feet," and of strange events as "coming out of left field." The word *sinister* means "left-hand or unlucky side" in Latin. *Gauche* is a French word that literally means "left," although in English it is used to mean awkward or ill-mannered. The English word *adroit*, meaning "skillful," derives from the French *à droit*, literally translated as "to the right." Also consider positive usages such as "being righteous" or "being on one's right side."

Although being "gauche" may be defined as being awkward, the literature is mixed as to whether there are advantages or disadvantages to being right-handed or left-handed. For example, there is little evidence that children who are left-handed are more likely than right-handed children to be prone to injury (Johnston et al., 2013). Nor did this study find differences in the likelihood of illness or conduct disorders. However, except in the case of reading achievement, it seems that left-handed children may have lower scores in tests of cognitive development (Johnston et al., 2013; Somers et al., 2015). A study of 237 right-handed and 199 left-handed healthy adults found small effects for handedness overall, but there appeared to be some advantage in motor skills for right-handed individuals (Mellet et al., 2014).

Left-Handed Is left-handedness or right-handedness connected with any advantages or disadvantages?

Then there is the realm of mental health. A study of 692 children aged 4–18 who were referred for psychiatric evaluation found that the percentage of left-handed children who were referred was significantly greater than their percentage of the overall population (Logue et al., 2014). This study also found evidence for greater incidences of oppositional defiant disorder among left-handed children. Yet a study of 47 right-handers and 50 left-handers found some advantages for left-handed individuals in mental flexibility, ability to control impulses, and working memory (Beratis et al., 2013).

It is difficult to know what to take away from research in this area, but it is likely that overall differences in the correlates of handedness are small. Putting it another way: If your child is gifted or deficient in cognitive or motor skills, it is unlikely to be due to handedness per se. Then, too, there is more variation in cognitive and motor skills *within* the groups of left-handed and right-handed people than there is *between* them. If we study thousands of individuals, we may find that right-handed people have somewhat greater motor skills. However, think of all the left-handed pitchers and batters in Major League Baseball. They do not exactly show deficiencies in motor skills.

Theories of Handedness

Handedness runs in families to some degree (Medland et al., 2009). Left-handed members of the English royal family include the Queen Mother, Queen Elizabeth II, Prince Charles, and Prince William (Lundborg, 2014).

On the other hand, identical (monozygotic [MZ]) twins frequently differ in handedness (Sommer et al., 2002). Are MZ twins sometimes "mirror opposites" (Sommer et al., 2002)? If so, the disagreement on handedness among MZ twins would not contradict a role for genetics in handedness.

There also appears to be a relationship between prenatal testosterone and handedness. Girls developing in the uterus with male co-twins are less likely than girls developing in the uterus alone or with female co-twins to be left-handed, suggesting the possibility of "prenatal testosterone transfer" from the male co-twin to the female co-twin (Vuoksimaa et al., 2010).

In any case, handedness develops early. Ultrasound studies reveal that about 95% of fetuses suck their right thumbs rather than their left (Vuoksimaa et al., 2010).

Interestingly, handedness is also found in species other than humans; for example, chimpanzees, parrots, and crustaceans, which include crabs (yes, crabs) (Versace & Vallortigara, 2015). It appears that hand preferences in chimpanzees are heritable but that environmental factors can modify inborn preferences.

Section Review

9. _____ (Girls or Boys?) are somewhat better at tasks requiring balance and precision of movement.

10. _____ (Girls or Boys?) show some advantage in throwing and kicking.

11. Motor activity begins to _____ (increase or decrease?) after 2 or 3 years of age.

12. During early childhood, _____ (girls or boys?) tend to be more active.

13. Left-handed people have a _____ (higher or lower?) incidence of language problems and psychological disorders than right-handed people.

Reflect & Relate: Think of left-handed people you know (perhaps including yourself). Do they seem to be awkward in any activities? Explain. Do you know anyone who was "changed" from a lefty to a righty? Why was the change made? How was it done? Was it successful? Explain.

8.3 Nutrition

As children move from infancy into early childhood, their nutritional needs change.

Sean Siah/Alamy

Ah yes—what is she to do about all those vegetables? (Her parents would be happy if she ate them, of course.)

What Are Children's Nutritional Needs in Early Childhood?

During early childhood, children still need to consume the basic foodstuffs: proteins, fats, carbohydrates, minerals, and vitamins. But more calories are required as children get older. For example, the average 4- to 5-year-old needs 1,400–1,600 calories, compared with about 1,000–1,300 calories for the average 1- to 3-year-old (**United States Department of Agriculture**, 2015). However, they grow at a slower rate than infants. This means that in early childhood, children need fewer calories per pound of body weight.

What Are Children's Patterns of Eating?

During the second and third years, a child's appetite typically decreases and becomes erratic, which often worries parents. But because the child is growing more slowly now, he or she needs fewer calories. Also, young children who eat less at one meal typically compensate by eating more at another. Children may develop strong (and strange) preferences for certain foods (Remington et al., 2012). At one time during her third year, my daughter Allyn wanted to eat nothing but SpaghettiOs®.

Many children (and adults) consume excessive amounts of sugar and salt, which can be harmful to their health. Infants seem to be born liking the taste of sugar, although they are fairly indifferent to salty tastes. Girls like fruits and vegetables more than boys do (Remington et al., 2012). Boys prefer fatty and sugary foods, meat, and eggs. Preference for both sweet and salty foods increases if children are repeatedly exposed to them during childhood (Remington et al., 2012). Parents also serve as role models in the development of food preferences. If a parent—especially the parent who usually prepares meals—displays an obvious dislike for vegetables, children may develop a similar dislike (Hannon et al., 2003). The message to parents is clear: The eating habits you help create will probably last.

My Daily Food Plan

Based on the information you provided, this is your daily recommended amount for each food group.

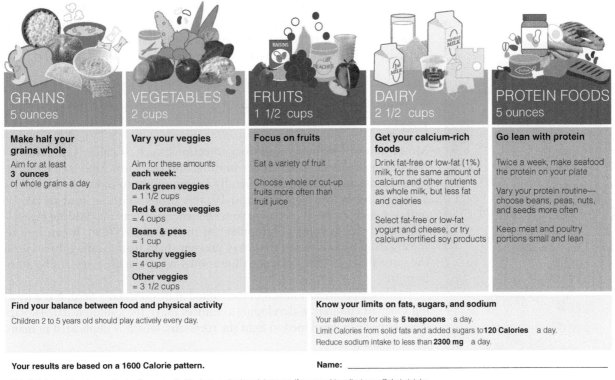

GRAINS 5 ounces	VEGETABLES 2 cups	FRUITS 1 1/2 cups	DAIRY 2 1/2 cups	PROTEIN FOODS 5 ounces
Make half your grains whole Aim for at least **3 ounces** of whole grains a day	**Vary your veggies** Aim for these amounts each week: **Dark green veggies** = 1 1/2 cups **Red & orange veggies** = 4 cups **Beans & peas** = 1 cup **Starchy veggies** = 4 cups **Other veggies** = 3 1/2 cups	**Focus on fruits** Eat a variety of fruit Choose whole or cut-up fruits more often than fruit juice	**Get your calcium-rich foods** Drink fat-free or low-fat (1%) milk, for the same amount of calcium and other nutrients as whole milk, but less fat and calories Select fat-free or low-fat yogurt and cheese, or try calcium-fortified soy products	**Go lean with protein** Twice a week, make seafood the protein on your plate Vary your protein routine—choose beans, peas, nuts, and seeds more often Keep meat and poultry portions small and lean

Find your balance between food and physical activity

Children 2 to 5 years old should play actively every day.

Know your limits on fats, sugars, and sodium

Your allowance for oils is **5 teaspoons** a day.
Limit Calories from solid fats and added sugars to **120 Calories** a day.
Reduce sodium intake to less than **2300 mg** a day.

Your results are based on a 1600 Calorie pattern.   Name: _____

This Calorie level is only an estimate of your needs. Monitor your body weight to see if you need to adjust your Calorie intake.

Figure 8.2 ■ Government-Recommended Daily Food Plan For 4– to 5-Year-Olds Eating 1600 Calories Per Day

Source: http://www.choosemyplate.gov/food-groups/downloads/results/MyDailyFoodPlan_1600_4and5yr.pdf

What is the best way to get children to eat their green peas or spinach or other healthful foods they may dislike? (Notice that it is rarely dessert that the child refuses to eat.) One method is to encourage the child to taste tiny amounts of the food 8 or 10 times within a period of a few weeks so that it becomes more familiar. Familiarity with food may breed content, not contempt. Figure 8.2 ■ shows a healthful diet for 4- to 5-year-olds (United States Department of Agriculture, 2015). It contains foods from all of the food groups but is low in fat. Potatoes are allowed and even encouraged, but not in the form of French fries, which are deep fried in fat. There is emphasis on fruits, vegetables, and whole grains.

Section Review

14. During the second and third years, a child's appetite typically _____ (increases or decreases?).

Reflect & Relate: Did you ever try to convince a 2- or 3-year-old to eat something? What did you do? What were the consequences?

Blend Images/Superstock

8.4 Health and Illness

Nearly all children get ill now and then. Some seem to be ill every other week or so. Most of these illnesses are minor, and children seem to eventually outgrow many of them, including ear infections. However, some illnesses are more serious. Fortunately, we have ways of preventing or curing a great many of them.

What Minor Illnesses Do Children Develop in Early Childhood?

Minor illnesses include respiratory infections, such as colds, and gastrointestinal upsets, such as nausea, vomiting, and diarrhea. American children between the ages of 1 and 3 generally average eight to nine minor illnesses a year. Between the ages of 4 and 10, this drops to about four to six illnesses a year. Being ill can have some beneficial effects on children's development in that it spurs development of the immune system. It can lead to the creation of antibodies that may prevent them from coming down with the same illnesses later—say, in adulthood—when the illnesses can be more harmful.

Although diarrheal illness in the United States is usually mild, it is a leading killer of children in developing countries (Save the Children, 2014). Vaccines have been developed to fight the rotavirus, which is implicated in many cases of diarrhea.

TRUTH OR FICTION REVISITED: Respiratory infections, nausea, vomiting, and diarrhea during early childhood are all normal, statistically speaking. And most of the time, they are mild.

What Major Illnesses Do Children Encounter?

Let us travel around the world and consider some facts about illnesses that afflict children (Save the Children, 2014).

- Pneumonia kills more children under the age of 5 than AIDS, malaria, and measles combined—as many as 3 million children a year. This amounts to 1 under-5 death in every 3 children. Antibiotics that vanquish bacterial pneumonia cost less than 30 cents a dose, but only 20% of children with pneumonia receive them.
- Diarrhea kills almost 2 million under-5 children each year. The treatment to prevent children from dying from diarrhea is **oral rehydration therapy** with salts that cost less than 50 cents a dose. But only 38% of children with diarrhea receive this therapy.
- Malaria, which is transmitted to people by mosquitoes, kills some 800,000 under-5 children in sub-Saharan Africa annually. One in every six childhood deaths in that part of the world is caused by malaria.
- Measles kills some 240,000 children each year. It is one of the world's leading causes of death that is preventable by vaccination.
- Malnutrition is connected with half of the deaths of children under the age of 5. Poorly nourished children have lower resistance to infection and are thus more vulnerable to illnesses such as diarrhea and pneumonia.

oral rehydration therapy
A treatment involving the administration of a salt and sugar solution to a child who is dehydrated from diarrhea.

TEN THINGS YOU NEED TO KNOW ABOUT CHILDHOOD IMMUNIZATIONS

1. Why your child should be vaccinated
Children need immunizations (shots) to protect them from dangerous childhood diseases. These diseases can have serious complications and can even kill children.

2. Diseases that childhood vaccines prevent
- Diphtheria
- Haemophilus influenzae type b (Hib disease, a major cause of bacterial meningitis)
- Hepatitis A
- Hepatitis B
- Human papillomavirus (HPV)
- Influenza
- Measles
- Meningococcal disease
- Mumps
- Pertussis (whooping cough)
- Pneumococcal disease (causes bacterial meningitis and blood infections)
- Polio
- Rotavirus
- Rubella (German measles)
- Tetanus (lockjaw)
- Varicella (chickenpox)

3. Number of doses your child needs
The following vaccinations are recommended by age 2 and can be given over five visits to a doctor or clinic:
- 4 doses of diphtheria, tetanus, and pertussis vaccine (DTaP)
- 3–4 doses of Hib vaccine (depending on the brand used)
- 4 doses of pneumococcal vaccine
- 3 doses of polio vaccine
- 2 doses of hepatitis A vaccine
- 3 doses of hepatitis B vaccine
- 1 dose of measles, mumps, and rubella vaccine (MMR)
- 2–3 doses of rotavirus vaccine (depending on the brand used)
- 1 dose of varicella vaccine
- 1 or 2 annual doses of influenza vaccine (number of doses depends on influenza vaccine history)

4. Like any medicine, vaccines can cause minor side effects.
Side effects can occur with any medicine, including vaccines. Depending on the vaccine, these can include: slight fever, rash, or soreness at the site of injection. Slight discomfort is normal and should not be a cause for alarm. Your health-care provider can give you additional information.

5. It's extremely rare, but vaccines can cause serious reactions—weigh the risks!
Serious reactions to vaccines are extremely rare. The risk of serious complications from a disease that could have been prevented by vaccination is far greater than the risk of a serious reaction to a vaccine.

6. What to do if your child has a serious reaction
If you think your child is experiencing a persistent or severe reaction, call your doctor or get the child to a doctor right away. Write down what happened and the date and time it happened. Ask your doctor, nurse, or health department to file a Vaccine Adverse Event Reporting System (VAERS) report or go to www.vaers.hhs.gov to file this form yourself electronically.

7. Why you should not wait to vaccinate Children under 5 are especially susceptible to disease because their immune systems have not built up the necessary defenses to fight infection. By immunizing on time (by age 2), you can protect your child from disease and also protect others at school or day care.

8. Be sure to track your shots via a health record A vaccination health record helps you and your health-care provider keep your child's vaccinations on schedule. If you move or change providers, having an accurate record might prevent your child from repeating vaccinations he or she has already had. A shot record should be started when your child receives his or her first vaccination and should be updated with each vaccination visit.

9. Some children are eligible for free vaccinations
A federal program called Vaccines for Children provides free vaccines to eligible children, including those without health insurance coverage, those enrolled in Medicaid, American Indians and Alaskan Natives, and those whose health insurance does not cover vaccines.

(continued)

Continued from page 263

10. **More information is available**

- General immunization questions can be answered by the CDC Contact Center at 1-800-CDC-INFO (1-800-232-4636) English and Español.
- Questions about vaccines and vaccine-preventable diseases frequently asked by people calling the TTY Service Hotline at 1-888-232-6348 (TTY hotline)

Reflect

- Are you unclear about any of the diseases these vaccinations protect against?

- Do you know whether the children in your life have had every recommended vaccine?
- Do you know what to do if a child has missed a vaccination?
- Do you know what to do if you are unsure of the answer to any of these questions?

Source: Centers for Disease Control and Prevention. (2014). U.S. Department of Health and Human Services. *10 Things You Need to Know about Childhood Immunizations*. http://www.cdc.gov/vaccines/vac-gen/10-shouldknow.htm. Accessed March 26, 2015.

Advances in immunization, along with the development of antibiotics and other medications, have dramatically reduced the incidence of serious and potentially fatal childhood diseases in the United States. Because most preschoolers and schoolchildren have been inoculated against major childhood illnesses such as rubella (German measles), measles, tetanus, mumps, whooping cough, diphtheria, and polio, these diseases no longer pose the threat they once did. Still, as you can see in Table 8.3 ●, immunization in the United States is not universal. The recommended immunization schedule of the American Academy of Pediatrics is shown in Figure 8.3 ■.

Nearly one-third of the children in the United States younger than 18 years of age—about 20 million children—suffer from a chronic illness (Agency for Healthcare Research and Quality, 2004). The illnesses include such major disorders as arthritis, diabetes, cerebral palsy, and cystic fibrosis. Other chronic medical problems such as asthma and migraine headaches are less serious but still require extensive health care.

● TABLE 8.3

Coverage Estimates for School Entry Vaccinations (U.S. National Estimate)

Vaccine	% Kindergarten Children Vaccinated
Polio	95.84%
Diphtheria	95.28%
Tetanus	95.08%
Pertussis	95.07%
Measles, mumps, rubella	94.82%
Hepatitis B	96.49%
Varicella	93.65%
Influenza	67.78%

Source: Centers for Disease Control and Prevention. (2011). Coverage Estimates for School Entry Vaccinations: 2009–2010 School Year. National Center for Immunization and Respiratory Diseases. http://www2.cdc.gov/nip/schoolsurv/nationalavg.asp. Accessed August 4, 2012.

Vaccines	Birth	1 mo	2 mos	4 mos	6 mos	9 mos	12 mos	15 mos	18 mos	19-23 mos	2-3 yrs	4-6 yrs	7-10 yrs	11-12 yrs	13-15 yrs	16-18 yrs
Hepatitis B[1] (HepB)	1st dose	←----2nd dose----→			←--------------------3rd dose--------------------→											
Rotavirus[2] (RV) RV1 (2-dose series); RV5 (3-dose series)			1st dose	2nd dose	See footnote 2											
Diphtheria, tetanus, & acellular pertussis[3] (DTaP: <7 yrs)			1st dose	2nd dose	3rd dose			←----- 4th dose -----→				5th dose				
Tetanus, diphtheria, & acellular pertussis[4] (Tdap: ≥7 yrs)														(Tdap)		
Haemophilus influenzae type b[5] (Hib)			1st dose	2nd dose	See footnote 5		3rd or 4th dose, See footnote 5									
Pneumococcal conjugate[6] (PCV13)			1st dose	2nd dose	3rd dose		←----- 4th dose -----→									
Pneumococcal polysaccharide[6] (PPSV23)																
Inactivated Poliovirus[7] (IPV) (<18 yrs)			1st dose	2nd dose	←--------------------3rd dose--------------------→							4th dose				
Influenza[8] (IIV; LAIV) 2 doses for some; See footnote 8					Annual vaccination (IIV only)							Annual vaccination (IIV or LAIV)				
Measles, mumps, rubella[9] (MMR)							←-----1st dose ------→					2nd dose				
Varicella[10] (VAR)							←-----1st dose------→					2nd dose				
Hepatitis A[11] (HepA)							←--------- 2-dose series, See footnote 11 ---------→									
Human papillomavirus[12] (HPV2: females only; HPV4: males and females)														(3-dose series)		
Meningococcal[13] (Hib-Men-CY ≥6 weeks; MenACWy-D ≥9 mos; MenACWY-CRM ≥2 mos)				See footnote 13										1st dose		Booster

Range of recommended ages for all children

Range of recommended ages for catch-up immunization

Range of recommended ages for certain high-risk groups

Range of recommended ages during which catch-up is encouraged and for certain high-risk groups

Not routinely recommended

This schedule includes recommendations in effect as of January 1, 2014. Any dose not administered at the recommended age should be administered at a subsequent visit, when indicated and feasible. The use of a combination vaccine generally is preferred over separate injections of its equivalent component vaccines. Vaccination providers should consult the relevant Advisory Committee on Immunization Practices (ACIP) statement for detailed recommendations, available online at www.cdc.gov. Clinically significant adverse events that follow vaccination should be reported to the Vaccine Adverse Event Reporting System (VAERS) online (www.vaers.hhs.gov) or by telephone (800-822-7967). Suspected cases of vaccine-preventable diseases should be reported to the state or local health department. Additional information, including precautions and contraindications for vaccination, is available from CDC online (www.cdc.gov) or by telephone (800-CDC-INFO [800-232-4636]).

This schedule is approved by the Advisory Committee on Immunization Practices (www.cdc.gov), the American Academy of Pediatrics (www.aap.org), the American Academy of Family Physicians (www.aafp.org), and the American College of Obstetricians and Gynecologists (www.acog.org).

Figure 8.3 ■ Recommended Immunization Schedule for Children Aged 0 Through 18 years—2014
This schedule includes recommendations endorsed by the federal government and the American Academy of Pediatrics (*Pediatrics, 133*[2], 357–363, and http://pediatrics.aappublications.org/content/133/2/357.full.pdf+html).
Source: American Academy of Pediatrics (*Pediatrics,* 133[2], 357–363, and http://pediatrics.aappublications.org/content/133/2/357.full.pdf+html).

Although many major childhood diseases have been largely eradicated in the United States and other industrialized nations, they remain fearsome killers of children in developing countries. Around the world, more than 13 million children die each year. Two-thirds of these children die of just six diseases: pneumonia, diarrhea, measles, tetanus, whooping cough, and tuberculosis (Save the Children, 2014). Air pollution from the combustion of fossil fuels for heating and cooking gives rise to many respiratory infections, which are responsible for nearly 1 death in 5 among children who are younger than 5 years of age (Save the Children, 2014). Diarrheal diseases are almost completely related to unsafe drinking water and a general lack of sanitation and hygiene. Children's immune systems and detoxification mechanisms are not as strong as those of adults, so they are more vulnerable to chemical, physical, and biological hazards in the water, soil, and air.

Lead is a particularly harmful pollutant. Many youngsters are exposed to lead in early childhood, often by eating chips of lead paint from their homes or by breathing in dust from the paint. Infants who are fed formula made with tap water also are at risk of lead poisoning, because the pipes that carry water into homes sometimes contain lead. Lead causes neurological damage and may result in lowered cognitive functioning and other developmental delays in early childhood. To help you assess

TABLE 8.4

Leading Causes of Death, United States: Ages 1–4 and 5–14, All Races, Female and Male Combined

Ages 1–4	Ages 5–14
Accidents	Accidents
Congenital malformations, deformations, and chromosomal abnormalities with which the child is born	Cancer
Homicide	Congenital malformations, deformations, and chromosomal abnormalities with which the child is born
Cancer	Homicide
Heart disease	Suicide
Influenza and pneumonia	Influenza and pneumonia
Septicemia; blood poisoning	Heart disease
Chronic respiratory disease	Chronic respiratory disease
Conditions originating in the perinatal period	Tumors that are not ordinarily lethal
Tumors that are not ordinarily lethal	Cerebrovascular diseases (stroke)

Source: Kochanek et al. (2011, Table 7).

and minimize the risks of lead poisoning in children younger than 6 years of age, see the nearby "A Closer Look—Real Life" feature.

Low-cost measures such as vaccines, antibiotics, and oral rehydration therapy could prevent most of these deaths. In oral rehydration therapy, a simple homemade salt and sugar solution is given to a child who is dehydrated from diarrhea. One promising finding is that most children in developing countries are now immunized against tuberculosis, measles, polio, diphtheria, tetanus, and whooping cough (Save the Children, 2014).

What Is the Role of Accidents as a Cause of Death in Early Childhood?

If you were to go back to the year 1900, you would certainly be correct if you believed infections were the leading cause of death in early adulthood. In 1900,[1] the five leading causes of death for children aged 1–4 were pneumonia (bacterial pneumonia is now usually treated successfully with antibiotics, and the symptoms of viral pneumonia are most often treated successfully), diarrhea (which is most often readily treated in developed countries today, although it remains deadly elsewhere), diphtheria (which is now prevented by vaccination), tuberculosis, and measles (also now prevented by vaccination).

TRUTH OR FICTION REVISITED: Infections are not the most common cause of death in early childhood in the United States (see Table 8.4 ●). Accidents are.

---

[1] As reported by Esther B. Clark. (1950). Leading causes of childhood death. Palo Alto, CA: The Palo Alto Clinic, Department of Pediatrics. http://www.ncbi.nlm.nih.gov/pmc/articles/PMC1520569/pdf/califmed00241-0024.pdf. Accessed August 4, 2012.

A Closer Look

Real LIFE

PROTECTING CHILDREN FROM LEAD POISONING

People can get lead in their body if they put their hands or other objects covered with lead dust in their mouths, eat paint chips or soil that contains lead, or breathe in lead dust (especially during renovations that disturb painted surfaces). If the condition is not detected early, children with high levels of lead in their bodies can suffer from damage to the brain and nervous system, behavioral and learning problems (such as hyperactivity), delayed growth, hearing problems, and headaches.

Lead is found mainly in paint. Many homes built before 1978 have lead-based paint. The federal government banned lead-based paint from housing in 1978. Some states stopped its use even earlier. Lead can be found in homes in the city, country, and suburbs, in apartments and single-family homes, in both private and public housing, in soil around a home, in household dust, and in drinking water. Your home might have plumbing with lead or lead solder. Call your local health department or water supplier to find out about testing your water. Use only cold water for drinking and cooking, and run water for 15 to 30 seconds before drinking it, especially if you have not used it for a few hours. Lead is also found on some job sites, on old painted toys and furniture, on food and liquids stored in lead crystal or lead-glazed pottery or porcelain, and near lead smelters or other industries that release lead into the air.

Peeling, chipping, chalking, or cracking lead-based paint is a hazard and needs immediate attention. Lead-based paint may also be a hazard when found on surfaces that children can chew or that get a lot of wear and tear. However, lead-based paint that is in good condition is usually not a hazard.

Consult your doctor for advice on testing your children. A simple blood test can detect high levels of lead. You can get your home checked in one of two ways: (1) a paint inspection tells you the lead content of every different type of painted surface in your home or (2) a risk assessment tells you whether there are any sources of serious lead exposure (such as peeling paint and lead dust). It also tells you what actions to take to address these hazards. Have qualified professionals do the work.

Contact the National Lead Information Center for more information (phone: 1-800-424-LEAD [5323]), or go online: www.epa.gov.

Reflect Have you checked your residence for the risk of lead poisoning? If not, why not? (Will you now do so? When?)

Source: Abridged from Lead Poisoning Prevention. (2015). http://www.epa.gov/region07/citizens/lead.htm. (Accessed March 26, 2015).

Today, none of these causes of death remains in the top five, although pneumonia (along with influenza) occupies sixth place. Accidents now cause more deaths in early childhood than the next six most frequent causes combined (Johnson et al., 2014). Motor vehicle accidents are the single most common cause of death in early childhood, followed by drowning and fires.

Accidents also are the major killer of children in most other countries of the world, except for those developing nations still racked by high rates of malnutrition and disease. Injuries are responsible for nearly half the deaths of children 2–6 years of age and for more than half the deaths of children through the age of 14. Boys are more likely than girls to incur accidental injuries at all ages and in all socioeconomic groups.

Accidental injuries occur most often among low-income children. Poor children are five times as likely to die from fires and more than twice as likely to die in motor vehicle accidents (Kochanek et al., 2011). The high accident rate of low-income children may result partly from their living in dangerous housing and neighborhoods. Poor parents also are less likely than higher-income parents to take such preventive measures as using infant safety seats, fastening children's seat belts, installing smoke detectors, and having at hand the telephone number of a poison control center. The

Automobile Safety Automobile accidents are the most common cause of death in young children in the United States. All 50 states now require child restraint seats in automobiles. These laws have contributed to a reduction in child deaths and injuries.

families of children who are injured frequently may be more disorganized and under more stress than other families. Injuries often occur when family members are distracted and children have minimal supervision.

Prevention of Accidental Injury

Legislation has helped to reduce certain injuries in children. All 50 states require child safety seats in automobiles, and their use has decreased deaths from automobile injuries. Most large cities in the United States also require the installation of window guards in high-rise apartment buildings. In a number of countries, the risks of injury to children have been reduced because of legislation requiring manufacturers to meet safety standards for such items as toys and flammable clothing.

Section Review

15. The most frequent cause of death of children in the United States is _____.

16. Many children are exposed to _____ by eating chips of paint.

Reflect & Relate: What pollutants in your area are harmful to children? What can you do about them?

Sleep

Children in the early years do not need as much sleep as infants. Most young children sleep 10–11 hours in a 24-hour period (National Sleep Foundation, 2012a; see Table 8.5 ●). A common pattern is 9–10 hours at night and a nap of 1–2 hours. In the United States, the young child's bedtime routine typically includes putting on pajamas, brushing teeth, and being read a story. Many young children also take a so-called-**transitional object**—such as a favored blanket or a stuffed animal—to bed with them (Chamness, 2008). Children who sleep in bed with their parents are unlikely to use a transitional object (Goldberg & Keller, 2007).

But we're not ending the discussion here, because putting a child to bed sounds much too easy. As so many parents know, getting children to sleep can be a major challenge of parenthood. Many children resist going to bed or going to sleep. Getting to

● TABLE 8.5

How Much Sleep Do You Really Need?

Age	Sleep Needs
Newborns (0–2 months)	12–18 hours
Infants (3–11 months)	14–15 hours
Toddlers (1–3 years)	12–14 hours
Preschoolers (3–5 years)	11–13 hours
School-age children (5–10 years)	10–11 hours
Teens (10–17 years)	8.5–9.25 hours
Adults	7–9 hours

Source: National Sleep Foundation (2015a).

transitional object A soft, cuddly object often carried to bed by a child to ease the separation from parents.

sleep late can be a problem because preschoolers tend not to make up fully for lost sleep (Kohyama et al., 2002). In the next section, we will focus on sleep disorders.

What Sleep Disorders Affect Children?

In this section, we will focus on the sleep disorders of sleep terrors, nightmares, and sleepwalking.

Sleep Terrors and Nightmares

First, a few words about terms. **Sleep terrors** are more severe than the anxiety dreams we refer to as nightmares (National Sleep Foundation, 2015a). For one thing, sleep terrors usually occur during deep sleep. **Nightmares** take place during lighter rapid eye movement (REM) sleep, when about 80% of normal dreams occur. In fact, nightmares sort of qualify as "normal" dreams—because of their frequency, not because of desirability!

Deep sleep alternates with lighter, REM sleep. Sleep terrors tend to occur early during the night, when periods of deep sleep are longest. Nightmares tend to occur more often in the morning hours, when periods of REM sleep tend to lengthen (National Sleep Foundation, 2014). Children have several periods of REM sleep a night and may dream in each one of them. Don't be confused by the fact that sleep terrors are sometimes referred to as night terrors. The term *night terrors* always refers to sleep terrors, never to nightmares.

Sleep terrors usually begin in childhood or early adolescence and are outgrown by late adolescence. They are often (but not always) associated with stress, such as moving to a new neighborhood, attending school for the first time, adjusting to parental divorce, or being caught up in a war zone (National Sleep Foundation, 2015a). (Children are also more likely to have nightmares under stress.) Children with sleep terrors may wake suddenly with a surge in heart and respiration rates, talk incoherently, and thrash about. Children are not completely awake during sleep terrors and may fall back into more restful sleep. Fortunately, the incidence of sleep terrors wanes as children develop and spend less time in deep sleep. They are all but absent among adults.

Children who have frequent nightmares or sleep terrors may come to fear going to sleep. They may show distress at bedtime, refuse to get into their pajamas, and insist that the lights be kept on during the night. As a result, they can develop **insomnia**. Children with frequent nightmares or sleep terrors need their parents' understanding and affection. They also profit from a regular routine in which they are expected to get to sleep at the same time each night. Yelling at them about their "immature" refusal to have the lights out and return to sleep will not relieve their anxieties.

Sleepwalking

Sleepwalking, or **somnambulism**, is much more common among children than among adults. Like sleep terrors, sleepwalking tends to occur during deep sleep. Onset is usually between the ages of 3 and 8.

During medieval times, people believed that sleepwalking was a sign of possession by evil spirits. Psychoanalytic theory suggests that sleepwalking gives people the chance to express feelings and impulses they would inhibit while awake. But children who sleepwalk have not been shown to have any more trouble controlling impulses than other children do. Moreover, what children do when they sleepwalk is usually too boring to suggest exotic motivation. They may rearrange toys, go to the bathroom, or go to the refrigerator and have a glass of milk. Then they return to their rooms and go back to bed. Their lack of recall in the morning is consistent with sleep terrors, which also occur during deep sleep. Sleepwalking episodes are brief; most tend to last no longer than half an hour.

sleep terrors Frightening dreamlike experiences that occur during the deepest stage of non-REM sleep, shortly after the child has gone to sleep.

nightmares Frightening dreams that occur during REM sleep, often in the morning hours.

insomnia A sleep disorder characterized by difficulty falling asleep, difficulty remaining asleep during the night, and waking early.

somnambulism Sleepwalking.

There are some myths about sleepwalking; for example, that sleepwalkers' eyes are closed, that they will avoid harm, and that they will become violently agitated if they are awakened during an episode. All of these notions are false. Sleepwalkers' eyes are usually open, although they may not respond to onlooking parents. Children may incur injury when sleepwalking, just as they may when awake.

> **TRUTH OR FICTION REVISITED:** It is not true that it is dangerous to awaken a sleepwalker. Children may be difficult to rouse when they are sleepwalking, just as during sleep terrors. But if they are awakened, they are more likely to show confusion and disorientation (again, as during sleep terrors) than violence.

Today, sleepwalking in children is assumed to reflect immaturity of the nervous system, not any acting out of dreams or psychological conflicts. As with sleep terrors, the incidence of sleepwalking drops as children develop. Parents may find it helpful to discuss persistent sleep terrors or sleepwalking with a health professional.

A Closer Look — Research

CROSS-CULTURAL DIFFERENCES IN SLEEPING ARRANGEMENTS

The commonly accepted practice in middle-class American families is for infants and children to sleep in separate beds and, when finances permit, in separate rooms from their parents. Child-care experts in the United States have generally endorsed this practice. Sleeping in the same room, they have sometimes warned, can lead to problems such as the development of overdependence, difficulty of breaking the habit when the child gets older, and even accidental sexual stimulation of the child (National Sleep Foundation, 2015b).

Nevertheless, bed sharing has been promoted as a means for facilitating breastfeeding. In fact, co-sleeping or bed sharing is the most common sleeping arrangement throughout the world for mothers who are breastfeeding (Young, 2006). Some health professionals are concerned that bed sharing can be dangerous for infants, because parents may roll onto them and crush or suffocate them (Weber et al., 2011).

In many other cultures, children commonly sleep with their mothers for the first few years of life, often in the same bed. The practice is found among 79% of preschool children in China (Huang et al., 2010). Co-sleeping occurs in cultures that are technologically advanced, such as Austria (Rothrauff et al., 2004) and Japan (Takahashi, 1990), as well as in those that are less technologically sophisticated, such as among the indigenous Sami people of Norway (Javo et al., 2004).

Surveys find that resistance to going to bed occurs regularly in 20–40% of American infants and preschoolers (National Sleep Foundation, 2015a), but it seldom occurs in cultures that practice co-sleeping. Some

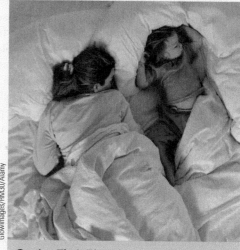

Getting Their Z's In the United States, most parents believe that it is harmful or at least inappropriate for parents to sleep with their children. Parents in many other cultures are more relaxed about sleeping arrangements.

psychologists believe that the resistance shown by some young American children at bedtime is caused by the stress of separating from parents. This view is supported by the finding that young children who sleep with or near their parents are less likely to use transitional objects or to suck their thumbs at night than are children who sleep alone (Goldberg & Keller, 2007).

Reflect Would you (or do you) allow your child to share your bed with you? Why or why not?

Section Review

17. Most 2- to 3-year-olds sleep about _____ hours at night and also have one nap during the day.

18. _____ (Nightmares or Sleep terrors?) usually occur during deep sleep.

19. _____ is also referred to as somnambulism.

Reflect & Relate: Critical thinkers insist on evidence before they will accept beliefs, even widely held cultural beliefs. What are your attitudes toward children sleeping with their parents? Are your attitudes supported by research evidence? Explain.

8.6 Elimination Disorders

The elimination of waste products occurs reflexively in neonates. As children develop, their task is to learn to inhibit the reflexes that govern urination and bowel movements. The process by which parents teach their children to inhibit these reflexes is referred to as toilet training. The inhibition of eliminatory reflexes makes polite conversation possible.

> **TRUTH OR FICTION REVISITED:** It is not true that competent parents toilet train their children by their second birthday. Most American children are toilet trained between the ages of 3 and 4, although they normally have some "accidents" beyond those ages.

enuresis Failure to control the bladder (urination) after the normal age for control has been reached.

bedwetting Failure to control the bladder during the night.

In toilet training, as in so many other areas of physical growth and development, maturation plays a crucial role. During the first year, only an exceptional child can be toilet trained, even when parents devote a great deal of time and energy to the task. If parents wait until the third year to begin toilet training, the process usually runs smoothly.

An end to diaper changing is not the only reason parents are motivated to toilet train their children. Parents often experience pressure from grandparents, other relatives, and friends who point out that so-and-so's children were all toilet trained before the age of ___. (You fill in the blank. Choose a number that will make most of us feel like inadequate parents!) Parents, in turn, may pressure their children to become toilet trained. And so toilet training can become a major arena for parent–child conflict. Children who do not become toilet trained within reasonable time frames are said to have enuresis, encopresis, or both.

What Is Enuresis?

Give it a name like *enuresis* (en-you-REE-sis), and suddenly it seems like a serious medical problem rather than a bit of an annoyance. **Enuresis** is the failure to control the bladder (urination) once the "normal" age for achieving control of the bladder has been reached. Conceptions of the normal age vary. The American Psychiatric Association (2013) is reasonably lenient on the issue and places the cutoff age at 5 years. The frequency of "accidents" is also an issue. The American Psychiatric Association (2013) does not consider such accidents enuresis unless the incidents occur at least twice a month for 5- and 6-year-olds or once a month for children who are older.

A nighttime "accident" is referred to as **bedwetting**. Nighttime control is more difficult to achieve than daytime control. At night, children must first wake up when their bladders are full. Only then can they go to the bathroom.

Toilet Training If parents wait until the third year to begin toilet training, the process usually goes relatively rapidly and smoothly.

Piotr Powietrzynski/Photolibrary/Getty Images

About 10% of children wet their beds. The problem is equally common among boys and girls until about the age of 5, when it becomes twice as common among boys (Tasman et al., 2015). The incidence drops as age increases. A study of 3,344 Chinese children found that these children appeared to attain control a bit earlier: 7.7% obtained nocturnal urinary control by the age of 2, 53% by the age of 3, and 93% by the age of 5 (Liu et al., 2000b). Just as in American studies, girls achieved control earlier than boys.

Causes of Enuresis

Enuresis usually has organic causes, such as infections of the urinary tract, kidney problems, or immaturity in development of the motor cortex of the brain (Tasman et al., 2015). Thus, cases with different causes might clear up at different rates or profit from different kinds of treatment. In the case of immaturity of parts of the brain, administering no treatment at all might be in order.

Numerous psychological explanations of enuresis have also been advanced. Psychoanalytic theory suggests that enuresis is a way of expressing hostility toward parents (because of their harshness in toilet training) or a form of symbolic masturbation. These views are largely unsubstantiated. Learning theorists point out that enuresis is most common among children whose parents attempted to train them early. Early failures might have conditioned anxiety over attempts to control the bladder. Conditioned anxiety, then, prompts rather than inhibits urination.

Situational stresses seem to play a role. Children are more likely to wet their beds when they are entering school for the first time, when a sibling is born, and when they are ill. There may also be a genetic component; there is a strong family history in the majority of cases (Robson, 2009).

It has also been noted that bedwetting tends to occur during the deepest stage of sleep. This is also the stage when sleep terrors and sleepwalking take place. For this reason, bedwetting could be considered a sleep disorder. Like sleepwalking, bedwetting could reflect immaturity of certain parts of the nervous system (Goessaert et al., 2015). Just as children outgrow sleep terrors and sleepwalking, they tend to outgrow bedwetting (Goessaert et al., 2015). In most cases, bedwetting resolves itself by adolescence and usually by the age of 8.

What Is Encopresis?

"Soiling," or **encopresis**, is lack of control over the bowels. Soiling, unlike enuresis, is more common among boys (Tasman et al., 2015). However, the overall incidence of soiling is lower than that of enuresis. By 7 or 8, only a few children have continuing problems controlling their bowels (Tasman et al., 2015).

Soiling, in contrast to enuresis, is more likely to occur during the day. Thus, it can be acutely embarrassing to the child, especially in school.

Encopresis stems from both physical causes, such as constipation, and psychological factors. Risk factors for encopresis are shown in Table 8.6 ●. Soiling may follow harsh punishment of toileting accidents, especially in children who are already anxious or under stress. Punishment may cause the child to tense up on the toilet, when moving one's bowels requires that one relax the anal sphincter muscles. Harsh punishment also focuses the child's attention on soiling. The child then begins to ruminate about soiling, so that soiling, punishment, and worrying about future soiling become a vicious cycle.

We now leave our exploration of physical development in early childhood and begin, in the next chapter, an examination of cognitive development.

encopresis Failure to control the bowels after the normal age for bowel control has been reached. Also called *soiling*.

WHAT TO DO ABOUT BEDWETTING

Parents are understandably disturbed when their children continue to wet their beds long after most children stay dry through the night. Cleaning up is a hassle, and parents also often wonder what their child's bedwetting "means"—what it means about the child and what it means about their own adequacy as parents.

Bedwetting may "mean" only that the child is slower than most children to keep his or her bed dry through the night. Bedwetting may mean nothing at all about the child's intelligence or personality or about the parents' capabilities. Certainly a number of devices (alarms) can be used to teach the child to awaken in response to bladder pressure (Perrin et al., 2015). Medications also can be used to help the child retain fluids through the night (Perrin et al., 2015). Before turning to these methods, however, parents may wish to consider the following suggestions:

- **Limit fluid intake late in the day.** Less pressure on the bladder makes it easier to control urinating, but do not risk depriving the child of liquids. On the other hand, it makes sense to limit fluid intake in the evening, especially at bedtime. Drinks with caffeine, such as colas, coffee, and tea, act as diuretics, making it more difficult to control urination, so it is helpful to cut down on them after lunch.

- **Wake the child during the night.** Waking the child at midnight or 1 A.M. may make it possible for him or her to go to the bathroom and urinate. Children may complain and say that they don't have to go, but often they will. Praise the child for making the effort.

- **Try a night-light.** Many children fear getting up in the dark and trying to find their way to the bathroom. A night-light can make the difference. If the bathroom is far from the child's bedroom, it may be helpful to place a chamber pot in the bedroom. The child can empty the pot in the morning.

- **Maintain a consistent schedule so that the child can form helpful bedtime and nighttime habits.** Having a regular bedtime not only helps ensure that your child gets enough sleep, but also enables the child to get into a routine of urinating before going to bed and keeps the child's internal clock in sync with the clock on the wall. Habits can be made to work for the child rather than against the child.

- **Use a "sandwich" bed.** This is simply a plastic sheet, covered with a cloth sheet, covered with yet another plastic sheet, and then still another cloth sheet. If the child wets his or her bed, the top wet sheet and plastic sheet can be pulled off, and the child can get back into a comfortable, dry bed. In this way, the child develops the habit of sleeping in a dry bed. Moreover, the child learns how to handle his or her "own mess" by removing the wet sheets.

- **Have the child help clean up.** The child can throw the sheets into the wash and, perhaps, operate the washing machine. The child can make the bed, or at least participate. These behaviors are not punishments; they help connect the child to the reality of what is going on and what needs to be done to clean things up.

- **Reward the child's successes.** Parents risk becoming overly punitive when they pay attention only to the child's failures. Ignoring successes also causes them to go unreinforced. When the child has a dry night, or half of a dry night, make a note of it. Track successes on a calendar. Connect them with small treats, such as more TV time or time with you. Make a "fuss"—that is, a positive fuss. Also consider rewarding partial successes, such as the child's getting up after beginning to urinate so that there is less urine in the bed.

- **Show a positive attitude.** "Accentuate the positive." Talk with your child about "staying dry" rather than "not wetting." Communicate the idea that you have confidence that things will get better. (They almost always do.)

Reflect

- Why do so many parents "take it personally" when their children wet their beds?

- What do we mean when we say that children "outgrow" bedwetting?

- How do you feel about giving a preschool child medicine to help curb bedwetting? Explain.

● TABLE 8.6

Risk Factors for Developing Encopresis

- Eating diets high in fat and sugar (junk food) and low in fiber.
- Not drinking enough water.
- Not exercising.
- Refusing to use the bathroom, especially public bathrooms.
- Having a history of constipation or painful experience during toilet training (ulcerative colitis or anal fissures). Note: Many children with encopresis have a history of painful defecation before 36 months of age.
- Having cognitive delays such as autism or intellectual deficiency.
- Having attention deficit disorders or difficulty focusing.
- Having conduct or oppositional disorders.
- Having obsessive compulsive disorders.
- Having a poor ability to identify physical sensations or symptoms.
- Having a chaotic, unpredictable life.

Source: Coelho. (2011).

Section Review

20. In toilet training, maturation _____ (does or does not?) play a crucial role.

21. Bedwetting is more common among _____ (girls or boys?).

22. A common physical cause of encopresis is _____.

Reflect & Relate: Why do you think so many parents become upset when their children are a bit behind others in toilet training? Do you think it is bad if it takes 3 or 4 years for a child to learn to use the toilet reliably? If so, why?

Chapter Review

8.1 Growth Patterns

Children gain about 2–3 inches in height and 4–6 pounds in weight per year in early childhood. The brain develops more quickly than any other organ in early childhood, in part because of myelination. Myelination enhances children's ability to attend to and process visual information, enabling them to read and to screen out distractions.

8.2 Motor Development

In the preschool years, children make great strides in the development of gross motor skills, which involve the large muscles. Girls are somewhat better at tasks requiring balance and precision; boys have some advantage in throwing and kicking. Fine motor skills develop gradually. After 2 or 3 years of age, children become less restless and are more able to sustain attention during play. Boys are more fidgety and distractible, perhaps because they are less mature physically. Kellogg identified 20 "scribbles" that she considers the building blocks of art. By 6 months, most infants show clear-cut hand preferences, which become still more established during early childhood. Being left-handed is apparently connected with language problems, some health problems, and some psychological disorders. But a high number of "math whizzes," athletes, and artists are left-handed.

8.3 Nutrition

The typical 4- to 6-year-old needs 1,800 calories a day, compared with 1,300 for the average 1- to 3-year-old.

8.4 Health and Illness

The incidence of minor illnesses, such as colds, nausea and vomiting, and diarrhea, is high. Although diarrheal illness is usually mild in the United States, it is a leading killer of children in developing countries. Immunization and antibiotics reduce the incidence of serious childhood diseases.

8.5 Sleep

Most 2- and 3-year-olds sleep about 10 hours at night and nap during the day. Sleep terrors are more severe than nightmares. Sleep terrors and sleepwalking usually occur during deep sleep.

8.6 Elimination Disorders

Most American children are toilet trained by about age 3 or 4 but continue to have "accidents" at night for another year or so. Enuresis is the failure to control the bladder once a child has reached the "normal" age for doing so; the American Psychiatric Association places that age at 5 years. Encopresis (soiling) is lack of control over the bowels.

Key Terms

corpus callosum   254
plasticity   254
gross motor skills   254
fine motor skills   257
oral rehydration therapy   262

transitional object   268
sleep terrors   269
nightmares   269
insomnia   269

somnambulism   269
enuresis   271
bedwetting   271
encopresis   272

9

Early Childhood:
Cognitive Development

Major Topics

Features

TruthorFiction?

T | F Having imaginary playmates is a sign of loneliness or psychological problems. **p. 279**

T | F Two-year-olds tend to assume that their parents are aware of everything that is happening to them, even when their parents are not present. **p. 280**

T | F "Because Mommy wants me to" may be a perfectly good explanation—for a 3-year-old. **p. 280**

T | F Children's levels of intelligence—not just their knowledge—are influenced by early learning experiences. **p. 289**

T | F An academic preschool education provides children with advantages in school later on. **p. 291**

T | F One- and 2-year-olds are too young to remember past events. **p. 297**

T | F During her third year, a girl explained that she and her mother had finished singing a song by saying, "We singed it all up." **p. 303**

T | F Three-year-olds usually say "Daddy goed away" instead of "Daddy went away" because they *do* understand rules of grammar. **p. 303**

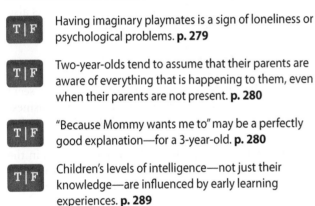

I was confused when my daughter, Allyn, at the age of 2½, insisted that I continue to play "Billy Joel" on the stereo. Put aside the question of her taste in music. My problem stemmed from the fact that when she asked for Billy Joel, the name of the singer, she could be satisfied only by my playing the song "Moving Out." When "Moving Out" had ended and the next song, "The Stranger," had begun to play, she would insist that I play "Billy Joel" again. "That is Billy Joel," I would protest. "No, no," she would insist, "I want Billy Joel!"

Finally, it dawned on me that for Allyn, the words *Billy Joel* symbolized the song "Moving Out," not the name of the singer. Of course my insistence that the second song was also "Billy Joel" could not satisfy her! She was conceptualizing Billy Joel as a property of a particular song, not as the name of a person who could sing many songs.

Children between the ages of 2 and 4 tend to show confusion between symbols and the objects they represent. They do not yet recognize that words are arbitrary symbols for objects and events and that people can use different words. They tend to think of words as inherent properties of objects and events.

In this chapter, we discuss cognitive development during early childhood. First, we examine Piaget's preoperational stage of cognitive development. Piaget viewed cognitive development largely in terms of maturation; however,

Masterfile

in the section on Vygotsky's views on cognitive development, we will see that social and other factors foster cognitive development by placing children in "the zone," as Vygotsky might have put it. Next, we consider other factors in cognitive development, such as how children acquire a "theory of mind" and develop memory. Finally, we continue our exploration of language development.

Jean Piaget's Preoperational Stage

According to Piaget, the **preoperational stage** of cognitive development lasts from about age 2 to age 7. Be warned: Any resemblance between the logic of a preschooler and your own may be purely coincidental!

How Do Children in the Preoperational Stage Think and Behave?

preoperational stage The second stage in Piaget's scheme, characterized by inflexible and irreversible mental manipulation of symbols.

symbolic play Play in which children make believe that objects and toys are other than what they are. Also termed *pretend play*.

Preoperational thought is characterized by the use of symbols to represent objects and relationships among them. Perhaps the most important symbolic activity of young children is language. But we will see that children's early use of language leaves something to be desired in the realm of logic.

Children begin to scribble and draw pictures in the early years. These drawings are symbols of objects, people, and events in children's lives. Symbolism is also expressed as symbolic or pretend play, which emerges during early childhood.

What Is Symbolic or Pretend Play?

Children's **symbolic play**—the "let's pretend" type of play—may seem immature to busy adults meeting the realistic demands of the business world, but it requires cognitive sophistication (Hoff, 2013; Taylor, 2013).

Piaget (1962 [1946]) wrote that pretend play usually begins in the second year, when the child begins to symbolize objects. The ability to engage in pretend play is based on the use and recollection of symbols; that is, on mental representations of things children have experienced or heard about. At 19 months, my daughter picked up a pine cone and looked it over. Her babysitter said, "That's a pine cone." My daughter pretended to lick it, as if it were an ice cream cone. Children first engage in pretend play at about 12 or 13 months of age. They make believe that they are performing familiar activities, such as sleeping or feeding themselves. By age 15–20 months, they can shift their focus from themselves to others. A child may thus pretend to feed her doll. By 30 months, she or he can make believe that the other object takes an active role. The child may now pretend that the doll is feeding itself (Fehr & Russ, 2014; Hoffmann & Russ, 2012).

Symbolic Play Symbolic play—also called pretend play—usually begins in the second year, when the child starts to form mental representations of objects. This 2½-year-old may engage in a sequence of play acts such as having a doll sit down at the table and offering it a make-believe cup of tea.

The quality of preschoolers' pretend play has implications for subsequent development. For example, preschoolers who engage in violent pretend play are less empathic, less likely to help other children, and more likely to engage in antisocial behavior later on (Hoff, 2013; Taylor, 2013). Preschoolers who engage in more elaborate pretend play are more likely to do well in school later on (Hoffman & Russ, 2012). Solitary pretend play on the playground—when other children are available—may be suggestive of social maladjustment and low peer acceptance (Nelson et al., 2008). The quality of pretend play is also connected with preschoolers' creativity and their ability to relate to peers (Taylor, 2013).

Imaginary friends—also known as *virtual characters* (Aguiar & Taylor, 2015)—are one example of pretend play. At age 2, Allyn acquired an imaginary playmate named Loveliness. He told Allyn to do lots of things: move things from here to there, get food for him, and so on. At times, Allyn was overheard talking to Loveliness in her room. It is estimated that between 10% and 50% of preschoolers have imaginary companions (Davis et al., 2013). Imaginary companions are most commonly found among firstborn and only children (Gleason, 2013; Hoff, 2013). Having an imaginary playmate does not mean that the child has problems with real relationships (Gleason, 2013; Hoff, 2005). In fact, children with imaginary companions are less aggressive, more cooperative, and more creative than other children (Gleason, 2013; Hoff, 2013). They have more real friends, show greater ability to concentrate, and are more advanced in language development (Taylor, 2013).

TRUTH OR FICTION REVISITED: It is not true that having imaginary playmates is a sign of loneliness or psychological problems. Research points to positive traits in children with imaginary friends, such as less aggressiveness and more creativity (Gleason, 2013).

As long as we are talking about play, let us note that some toys are called Transformers. In the following section, we will see that the mental processes of children are also "transformers."

What Are "Operations"?

Operations are mental acts (or schemes) in which objects are changed or *transformed* and then can be returned to their original states. Mental operations are flexible and reversible.

Consider the example of planning a move in checkers. A move requires knowledge of the rules of the game. The child who plays the game well (as opposed to just making moves) is able to picture the results of the move—how, in its new position, the piece will support or be threatened by other pieces and how other pieces might be left undefended by the move. Playing checkers well requires that the child be able to picture, or focus on, different parts of the board and relationships between pieces at the same time. By considering several moves, the child shows flexibility. By picturing the board as it would be after a move, and then picturing it as it is, the child shows reversibility.

Having said all this, let us return to the fact that this section is about preoperational children—children who cannot yet engage in flexible and reversible mental operations. Young children's logic reflects the fact that their ability to perform operations is "under construction." The preoperational stage is thus characterized by features such as egocentrism, immature notions about what causes what, confusion between mental and physical events, and the ability to focus on only one dimension at a time.

Egocentrism: Why Do Young Children Think "It's All About Me"?

Sometimes the attitude "It's all about me" is a sign of early childhood, not of selfishness. One consequence of one-dimensional thinking is egocentrism. **Egocentrism,** in Piaget's use of the term, does not mean that preoperational children are selfish

operations Flexible, reversible mental manipulations of objects, in which objects can be mentally transformed and then returned to their original states.

egocentrism Putting oneself at the center of things such that one is unable to perceive the world from another person's point of view. Egocentrism is normal in early childhood, but is a matter of choice, and rather intolerable, in adults. (Okay, I sneaked an editorial comment into a definition. No apologies.)

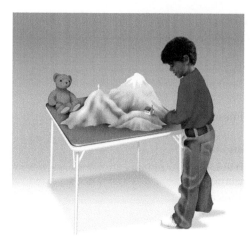

Figure 9.1 ■ The Three-Mountains Test
Piaget used the three-mountains test to learn whether children at certain ages are egocentric or can take the viewpoints of others.
© Cengage Learning®

(although, of course, they may be). It means that they do not understand that other people may have different perspectives on the world. When I asked Allyn—still at the age of 2½—to tell me about a trip to the store with her mother, she answered, "You tell me." It did not occur to her that I could not see the world through her eyes.

TRUTH OR FICTION REVISITED: It is true that 2-year-olds may assume that their parents are aware of everything that is happening to them, even though their parents are not present. They may believe the words from Shakespeare: "All the world's a stage." They may see the world as a stage that has been erected to meet their needs and entertain them.

Piaget used the "three-mountains test" (see Figure 9.1 ■) to show that egocentrism literally prevents young children from taking the viewpoints of others. In this demonstration, the child sits at a table before a model of three mountains. The mountains differ in color. One has a house on it, and another a cross at the summit.

Piaget then placed a doll elsewhere on the table and asked the child what the doll sees. The language abilities of very young children do not permit them to provide verbal descriptions of what can be seen from where the doll is situated, so they can answer in one of two ways. They can select a photograph taken from the proper vantage point, or they can construct another model of the mountains, as the doll would see them. The results of a classic experiment with the three-mountains test suggest that 5- and 6-year-olds usually select photos or build models that correspond to their own viewpoints (Laurendeau & Pinard, 1970).

Causality: Why? Because!

Preoperational children's responses to questions such as "Why does the sun shine?" show other facets of egocentrism. At the age of 2 or so, children may answer that they do not know or change the subject. Three-year-olds may think that the sun shines because it wants to shine or because someone (or something) else wants it to shine. In this case, the sun's behavior is thought of as being caused by will—perhaps the sun's wish to bathe the child in its rays or the child's wish to remain warm. In either case, the answer puts the child at the center of the conceptual universe. The sun becomes an instrument similar to a lightbulb.

TRUTH OR FICTION REVISITED: It is true that "Because Mommy wants me to" may be a perfectly good explanation—for a 3-year-old. This line of "reasoning" is another reflection of early childhood egocentrism.

precausal A type of thought in which natural cause-and-effect relationships are attributed to will and other preoperational concepts, as in thinking that the sun sets because it is tired.

transductive reasoning Reasoning from the specific to the specific. (In deductive reasoning, one reasons from the general to the specific; in inductive reasoning, one reasons from the specific to the general.)

Piaget labels this type of structuring of cause and effect **precausal**. Preoperational children believe that things happen for reasons and not by accident (Sobel & Legare, 2014). However, unless preoperational children know the natural causes of an event, their reasons are likely to have an egocentric flavor and not be based on science. Consider the question "Why does it get dark outside?" The preoperational child usually does not have knowledge of the earth's rotation and is likely to answer something like "So I can go to sleep."

Another example of precausal thinking is **transductive reasoning**. In transductive reasoning, children reason by going from one specific isolated event to another (Anastasiou et al., 2015; Sobel & Legare, 2014). For example, a 3-year-old may argue that she should go on her swings in the backyard because it is light outside or that she should go to sleep because it is dark outside. Separate, specific events, daylight (or being awake) and going on the swings, are thought of as having cause-and-effect relationships.

Preoperational children also show **animism** and **artificialism** in their attributions of causality. In animistic thinking, they attribute life and intentions to inanimate objects, such as the sun and the moon. ("Why is the moon gone during the day?" "It is afraid of the sun.") Artificialism assumes that environmental features such as rain and thunder have been designed and made by people (Baillargeon et al., 2010). In *Six Psychological Studies,* Piaget (1967 [1964]) wrote that "Mountains 'grow' because stones have been manufactured and then planted. Lakes have been hollowed out, and for a long time the child believes that cities are built [before] the lakes adjacent to them" (p. 28). Table 9.1 ● lists other examples of egocentrism, animism, and artificialism.

How Do Young Children Confuse Mental and Physical Events? On "Galaprocks" and Dreams That Are Real

What would you do if someone asked you to pretend you were a galaprock? Chances are you might inquire what a galaprock is and how it behaves. So might a 5-year-old child. But a 3-year-old might not think that such information is necessary

animism The attribution of life and intentionality to inanimate objects.

artificialism The belief that environmental features were made by people.

● **TABLE 9.1**

Kinds of Preoperational Thought

Type of Thought	Sample Questions	Typical Answers
Egocentrism (placing oneself at the center of things such that one is unable to perceive the world from another's point of view)	Why does it get dark out?	So I can go to sleep.
	Why does the sun shine?	To keep me warm.
	Why is there snow?	For me to play in.
	Why is grass green?	Because that's my favorite color.
	What are TV sets for?	To watch my favorite shows and cartoons.
Animism (attributing life and consciousness to physical objects)	Why do trees have leaves?	To keep them warm.
	Why do stars twinkle?	Because they're happy and cheerful.
	Why does the sun move in the sky?	To follow children and hear what they say.
	Where do boats go at night?	They sleep like we do.
Artificialism (assuming that environmental events are human inventions)	What makes it rain?	Someone emptying a watering can.
	Why is the sky blue?	Somebody painted it.
	What is the wind?	A man blowing.
	What causes thunder?	A man grumbling.
	How does a baby get in Mommy's tummy?	Just make it first. (How?) You put some eyes on it, then put on the head.

(Gottfried et al., 2003). Have you seen horror movies in which people's dreams become real? It could be said that preoperational children tend to live in such worlds, although, for them, that world is normal and not horrible.

Young children can pretend to be galaprocks without knowing what they are because, according to Piaget, the preoperational child has difficulty making distinctions between mental and physical phenomena. Children between the ages of 2 and 4 show confusion between symbols and the things that they represent. Egocentrism contributes to the assumption that their thoughts exactly reflect external reality. They do not recognize that words are arbitrary and that people can use different words to refer to things. In *Play, Dreams, and Imitation in Childhood,* Piaget (1962 [1946]) asked a 4-year-old child, "Could you call this table a cup and that cup a table?" "No," the child responded. "Why not?" "Because," explained the child, "you can't drink out of a table!"

Another example of the preoperational child's confusion of the mental and the physical is the tendency to believe that dreams are real. Dreams are cognitive events that originate within the dreamer but seem to be perceived through the dreamer's senses. These facts are understood by 7-year-olds, but many 4-year-olds believe that dreams are real (Honig & Nealls, 2011). They think that their dreams are visible to others and that dreams come from the outside. It is as though they were watching a movie.

How Many Dimensions of a Problem Do Young Children Focus on at Once? On Mental Blinders

To gain further insight into preoperational thinking, consider two problems. First, imagine that you pour water from a low, wide glass into a tall, thin glass, as in Figure 9.2(b). Now, does the tall, thin glass contain more than, less than, or the same amount of water as the low, wide glass? We won't keep you in suspense. If you said the same (with possible minor exceptions for spillage and evaporation), you are correct.

Now that you're on a roll, here's the second problem. If you flatten a ball of clay into a pancake, do you wind up with more, less, or the same amount of clay? If you said the same, you are correct once more.

What Is Meant By Conservation? (Hint: We're Not Talking About the Environment)

conservation In cognitive psychology, the principle that properties of substances, such as weight and mass, remain the same (are conserved) when superficial characteristics such as their shapes or arrangement are changed.

To arrive at the correct answers to these questions, you must understand the law of **conservation**, which holds that properties of substances, such as volume, mass, and number, remain the same—that is, they are conserved—even if you change their shape or arrangement. Now, preoperational children are not conservationists. I don't mean that they throw out half-eaten meals (although they do so often enough). I mean that they tend to focus on *only one* aspect of a problem at a time.

Conservation requires the ability to focus on two aspects of a situation at once, such as height and width. The preoperational boy in Figure 9.2 ■ focuses, or centers,

Figure 9.2 ■ Conservation
(a) The boy in this illustration agreed that the amounts of water in two identical containers are equal. (b) He then watched as water from one container was poured into a tall, thin container. (c) When asked whether the amounts of water in the two containers are now the same, he says no.
© Cengage Learning®

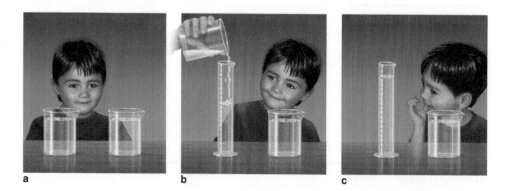

a   b   c

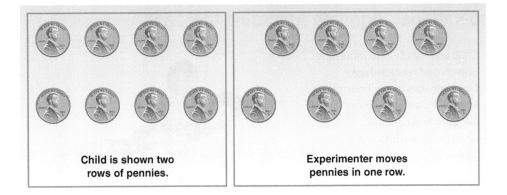

Child is shown two rows of pennies.

Experimenter moves pennies in one row.

on only one dimension at a time, a characteristic of thought that Piaget called **centration**. First, the boy is shown two low, wide glasses of water and agrees that they contain the same amount of water. Then, as he watches, water is poured from one of the low, wide glasses into a tall, thin glass. Asked which glass has more water, the boy points to the tall glass. Why? When he looks at the glasses, he is swayed by the fact that the water level in the tall glass is higher.

The preoperational child's failure to show conservation also comes about because of a characteristic of thought known as **irreversibility**. The child does not realize that pouring water from the tall glass to the low, wide glass can be reversed, restoring things to their original condition. If all this sounds rather illogical, that is because it is illogical—or, to be precise, preoperational. But if you have any doubts concerning its accuracy, borrow a 3-year-old and try the water experiment for yourself.

After you have tried the experiment with the water, try the following experiment on conservation of number. Make two rows with four pennies in each, the pennies located about half an inch apart. As the 3-year-old child is watching, increase the space between the pennies in the second row until they are about an inch apart, as shown in Figure 9.3 ■. Then ask the child which row has more pennies. What do you think the child will say? Why?

centration Focusing on one dimension of a situation while ignoring others.

irreversibility Lack of recognition that actions can be reversed.

class inclusion The principle that one category or class of things can include several subclasses.

What Do Young Children Put in Their Classes? On Class Inclusion

The term **class inclusion**, as we are using it here, does not refer to whether a class is open to children from diverse backgrounds. We are talking about an aspect of conceptual thinking that you most likely take for granted: including new objects or categories in broader mental classes or categories.

Class inclusion also requires children to focus on two aspects of a situation at once (Quinn, 2010). Class inclusion means that one category or class of things includes other subclasses. For example, the class "animals" includes the subclasses of dogs and cats.

In one of Piaget's class-inclusion tasks, the child is shown several objects from two subclasses of a larger class (see Figure 9.4 ■). For example, a 4-year-old child is shown pictures of four cats and six dogs. She is asked whether there are more dogs or more animals. Now, she knows what dogs and cats are. She also knows that they are both animals. What do you think she will

Figure 9.4 ■ Class Inclusion
Do you see more dogs or animals? A typical 4-year-old will say there are more dogs than animals in the example. Why?
© Cengage Learning®

Features of Preoperational Cognition According to Piaget

Symbolic thought	• Child uses symbols to represent objects and relationships. • Child engages in symbolic play. • Symbolic play grows more frequent and complex. • Child may have imaginary friend(s). • Mental operations are inflexible and irreversible.	Elizabeth Crews
Egocentrism	• Child does not take viewpoint of others. • Child may lack empathy for others. • Piaget used the three-mountains test to assess egocentrism.	© Cengage Learning®
Precausal thinking	• Child believes things happen for a reason. • Child engages in transductive reasoning ("I should sleep because it's dark outside"). • Child shows animism (attributes life and will to inanimate objects). • Child shows artificialism (assumes environmental features are made by people).	
Confusion of mental and physical events	• Child assumes thoughts reflect external reality. • Child believes dreams are real.	© Cengage Learning®
Focus on one dimension at a time	• Child does not understand law of conservation. • Child focuses on one dimension at a time. • Child does not show appropriate class inclusion (may not include dogs as animals).	Child is shown two rows of pennies. Experimenter moves pennies in one row. © Cengage Learning®

A Closer Look

Diversity

DEVELOPMENT OF CONCEPTS OF ETHNICITY AND RACE

Americans are encouraged to be "colorblind" in matters of employment, housing, and other areas in which discrimination has historically occurred. However, children, like adults, are not literally colorblind. Therefore, it is fascinating to see how children's concepts of race and ethnicity develop. Research on the connection between cognitive development and the development of concepts about people from different ethnic and racial backgrounds suggests when it might be most useful to intervene to help children develop open attitudes toward people from different backgrounds (Quintana et al., 2006; Wilson & Leaper, 2015).

From interviews of 500 African American, Asian American, Latin American, and Native American children,

If You Are Born White, Do You Remain White as You Grow Up? If You Are Born Asian, Do You Remain Asian? If You Are Born . . . According to research by Quintana, children between the ages of 3 and 6 tend to think about racial differences in physical terms. They do not necessarily see race as a fixed or stable attribute. They may think that people can change their race by means of surgery or sun tanning.

Bonnie Kamin/PhotoEdit

psychologists Stephen Quintana (1998, 2011) and Lisa Rabasca (2000) concluded that children undergo several levels of understanding of ethnicity and race. Between the ages of 3 and 6, children generally think about racial differences in physical terms. They do not necessarily see race as a fixed or stable attribute. They may think that a person could change his or her race by means of surgery or tanning in the sun.

From the ages of 6 to 10, children generally understand that race is a matter of ancestry that affects not only physical appearance but also one's language, diet, and leisure activities. But understanding at this stage is literal, or concrete. For example, children believe that being Mexican American means that one speaks Spanish and eats Mexican-style food. Interethnic friendships are likely to develop among children of this age group.

From the ages of about 10 to 14, children tend to link ethnicity with social class. They become aware of connections between race and income, race and neighborhood, and race and affirmative action. During adolescence, many individuals begin to take pride in their ethnic heritage and experience a sense of belonging to their ethnic group. They are less open to intergroup relationships than younger children are.

Quintana's research found that middle childhood and early adolescence (ages 6–14) are probably the best times to fend off the development of prejudice by teaching children about people from different cultural backgrounds. "That's when [children are] able to go beyond the literal meaning of the words and address their own observations about race and ethnicity," he noted (cited in Rabasca, 2000). Children at these ages also tend to be more open to forming relationships with children from different backgrounds (Quintana, 2011).

Reflect: Why does Quintana suggest that early childhood might be too soon to try to prevent the development of prejudice? Do you agree? Explain.

---

say? Preoperational children typically answer that there are more dogs than animals (Piaget, 1963 [1936]). That is, they do not show class inclusion.

Why do children make this error? According to Piaget, the preoperational child cannot think about the two subclasses and the larger class at the same time. Therefore, he or she cannot easily compare them. The child views dogs as dogs, or as animals, but finds it difficult to see them as both dogs and animals at once (Muller et al., 2015).

How Accurately Do Piaget's Views Represent Cognitive Development in Early Childhood?

Piaget was an astute observer of the cognitive processes of young children. But more recent research questions the accuracy of his age estimates concerning children's failures (or apparent failures) to display certain cognitive skills. For example, the difficulty young children have with the three-mountains test may not be due to egocentrism (Miller, 2010). One can attribute much of the difficulty to the demands that this method makes on the child. The three-mountains test presents a lifeless scene, one devoid of people and human motives. By contrast, when children are asked to place a boy doll behind tabletop screens so that it cannot be "seen" by police dolls, 3½-year-olds succeed most of the time.

Language development may also play a role in tests of children's egocentrism and other aspects of cognitive development. Young children may not quite understand what is being asked of them in the three-mountains test, even though they may proceed to select the (wrong) photograph rather quickly (Miller, 2010). Let me give you an example. I was interested in knowing whether my daughter, at age 2 years 9 months, thought that her mother could see her from another room. "Can Mommy see you now?" I asked. "Sure," said my daughter, "if she wants to." She thought I was asking whether her mother could have permission to see her, not whether her mother had the capacity to see her from behind a wall.

Newer studies indicate that the young child's understanding of causality is somewhat more sophisticated than Piaget believed (Meltzoff, 2010). Again, much depends on how the task is presented. When 4- to 7-year-olds are asked the kind of open-ended questions that Piaget used, such as "Where did the ocean come from?", they give artificialistic responses, such as "The ocean comes from sinks." But when asked direct questions, such as "Do you think people made the oceans?", most will correctly respond that people do not make natural things such as oceans or flowers, but they do make objects such as cups and televisions (Meltzoff, 2010; Miller, 2010).

The demands of the standard conservation task may also present a misleading picture of the child's knowledge. Piaget and other experimenters filled identical beakers with the same amount of water and then poured water from one of the beakers into a beaker of another shape. Before pouring the water, the experimenter typically asked the child whether both beakers have the same amount of water and instructed the child to watch the pouring carefully. In doing so, perhaps the experimenter is "leading the witness"—that is, leading the child to expect a change.

Section Review

1. According to Piaget, _____ play is based on the use of symbols.

2. _____ are mental acts in which objects are changed or transformed and can then be returned to their original states.

3. Piaget used the three-mountains test to show that preoperational children are _____.

4. The type of thinking in which children attribute will to inanimate objects is termed _____ thinking.

5. In _____ reasoning, children reason from one specific event to another.

6. The law of _____ holds that properties of substances, such as volume, mass, and number, remain the same even when their shape or arrangement changes.

7. Preoperational children focus on _____ (how many?) dimension(s) of a problem at once.

Reflect & Relate: Preoperational children focus on one dimension of a problem at a time. Do we as adults sometimes focus on one dimension of a situation at a time? If you injure someone in an accident, should you be held responsible? (Note the two elements: the injury and the fact that it is accidental.) Most people would probably say, "An accident is an accident." But what if a utility injures 8 million people in a nuclear accident? Should it be held responsible? (That is, does the enormity of the damage affect responsibility?)

9.2 Vygotsky's Views on Early Childhood Cognitive Development

According to Vygotsky, one of the most important factors in cognitive development is scaffolding. Scaffolding refers to Vygotsky's concept of social supports, as we will see in this section. Other factors, as we will see in the following section, are familial and social: the home environment, preschool education, and television.

What Are Scaffolding and the Zone of Proximal Development?

Parental responsiveness and interaction with the child are key ingredients in the child's cognitive development. One component of this social interaction is scaffolding (see Chapter 1). A scaffold is a temporary structure used for holding workers

A Closer Look · Research

EFFECTS OF SCAFFOLDING ON CHILDREN'S ABILITIES TO RECALL AND RETELL STORIES

According to Vygotsky, children's cognitive development is promoted by scaffolding; that is, by interaction with older, more knowledgeable people, often their caregivers, who teach and guide them. Researchers have studied the relationships between such interactions in children and adults and the children's ability to retell and remember stories.

In an experiment by K. Alison Clarke-Stewart and Robert Beck (1999), thirty-one 5-year-olds observed a videotaped film segment with their mothers, talked about it with their mothers, and then retold the story to a researcher. Clarke-Stewart and Beck found that the quality of the stories, as retold by the children, was related to the scaffolding strategies their mothers had used. Children whose mothers focused their attention on the tape, asked them to talk about it, and discussed the feelings of the characters told better stories than children whose mothers did not use such scaffolding strategies and children in a control group who did not discuss the story at all. Children's understanding of the characters' emotional states was most strongly connected with the number of questions the mother asked and her correction of their misunderstandings of what they saw.

In a longitudinal study, Catherine Haden and her colleagues (2001) observed 21 mother–child pairs as they engaged in specially constructed tasks when the children were 30, 36, and 42 months of age. They analyzed the children's recall of their performance 1 day and 3 weeks afterward at all three ages. It turned out that the children best recalled those aspects of the tasks they had both worked on and discussed with their mothers. Recall under these circumstances exceeded recall when the activities were (1) handled jointly but talked about only by the mother or (2) handled jointly but not discussed.

In sum, scaffolding within a zone of proximal development promotes children's learning and memory.

Reflect Did your caregivers ever watch television with you and discuss what you saw? What types of things did they say or ask? Did any of your teachers in elementary school use scaffolding after you watched a film or video in class? What did they do?

Picture Partners/Alamy

Scaffolding Children's cognitive development is promoted by scaffolding;, that is, their interaction with older, more knowledgeable people. Research shows that children better recall and retell stories when their caregivers focus their attention on them, prod children to talk about them, and discuss the feelings of the characters.

during building construction. Similarly, cognitive scaffolding is temporary support provided by a parent or teacher to a learning child. The guidance provided by the adult decreases as the child gains skill and becomes capable of carrying out the task on her or his own (Clark, 2014; Daniels, 2010).

A related concept is Vygotsky's zone of proximal development (ZPD). Adults or older children can best guide the child through this zone by gearing their assistance to the child's capabilities. Human neurobiology underlies cognitive development in early childhood, but key forms of children's cognitive activities develop through interaction with older, more experienced individuals who teach and guide them within appropriate learning environments such as schools and shops (Clark, 2014).

9.3 Other Factors in Early Childhood Cognitive Development: The Home Environment, Preschool, and Television

There are many factors in cognitive development in early childhood. Some of them reflect the views of Piaget or Vygotsky, but they have developed as topics of their own.

How Does the Home Environment Affect the Cognitive Development of Children?

Bettye Caldwell and her colleagues (e.g., Bradley et al., 2003) developed a measure for evaluating children's home environments labeled, appropriately enough, HOME—an acronym for Home Observation for Measurement of the Environment. With this method, researchers directly observe parent–child interaction in the home. The HOME inventory contains six scales, as shown in Table 9.2 ●. The HOME inventory items are better predictors of young children's later IQ scores

The Home Environment The home environment of the young child is linked to intellectual development and later academic achievement. Key aspects of the home environment include the parents' involvement and encouragement of the child, the availability of toys and learning materials, and the variety of experiences to which the child is exposed.

Syd Johnson/The Image Works

Scales of the HOME Inventory

Scale	Sample Items
Parental emotional and verbal responsiveness	• The parent spontaneously vocalizes to the child during the visit. • The parent responds to the child's vocalizations with vocal or other verbal responses.
Avoidance of restriction and punishment	• The parent does not shout at the child. • The parent does not interfere with the child's actions or restrict the child's movements more than three times during the visit.
Organization of the physical environment	• The child's play environment seems to be safe and free from hazards.
Provision of appropriate play materials	• The child has a push or a pull toy. • The child has one or more toys or pieces of equipment that promote muscle activity. • The family provides appropriate equipment to foster learning.
Parental involvement with child	• The parent structures the child's play periods. • The parent tends to keep the child within her or his visual range and looks at the child frequently.
Opportunities for variety in daily stimulation	• The child gets out of the house at least four times a week. • The parent reads stories to the child at least three times a week.

© Cengage Learning®

than is social class, mother's IQ, or infant IQ scores (Bradley, 2006). Longitudinal research shows that the home environment is also related to occupational success as an adult (Huesmann et al., 2006) and academic success as a student. For example, harsh home environments have been linked with poor academic outcomes in school (Schwartz et al., 2013).

In a longitudinal study, Caldwell and her colleagues observed children from poor and working-class families over a period of years, starting at 6 months of age. The HOME inventory was used at the early ages, and standard IQ tests were given at ages 3 and 4. The children of mothers who were emotionally and verbally responsive, who were involved with their children, and who provided appropriate play materials and a variety of daily experiences during the early years showed advanced social and language development even at 6 months of age (Parks & Bradley, 1991). These children also attained higher IQ scores at ages 3 and 4 and higher achievement test scores at age 7. Other studies support the view that being responsive to preschoolers, stimulating them, and encouraging independence are connected with higher IQ scores and greater school achievement later on (Bradley, 2006; Bradley & Corwyn, 2006). Molfese and her colleagues (1997) found that the home environment was the single most important predictor of scores on IQ tests among children ages 3–8.

TRUTH OR FICTION REVISITED: Longitudinal research by Caldwell and others confirms that early learning experiences affect children's levels of intellectual functioning. Stimulating home environments play especially powerful roles.

How Do Preschool Educational Programs Affect Children's Cognitive Development?

What kinds of preschools are available? Why do parents choose them? How important are academic experiences in early childhood? Do they facilitate cognitive development? Research suggests that preschool education enables children to get an early start on achievement in school (Bridges et al., 2012; Lamy, 2012).

Affluent parents may fret about whether their youngsters will gain admittance to the most prestigious and challenging preschools—such as the Dalton School or the Spence School in Manhattan—because these preschools open the doorways to their elementary schools and secondary schools and then, often, to the most competitive colleges and universities. These schools typically offer *academic programs,* in which teachers structure learning experiences and the curricula take children, step by step, through learning letters, numbers, shapes and colors, and other academic competencies. The intention is to give children a running start for achievement in a challenging kindergarten and a challenging elementary school.

Other preschools are more *child-centered.* In these settings, teachers provide a variety of activities. Children are permitted to choose those that interest them the most. Although academic-type learning may occur, the child is more likely to set the pace and acquire whatever academic skills are available through play. The input of parents tends to be more accepted and even desired in child-centered programs, whereas parental views may be seen as counterproductive in more structured academic programs (Burgess & Fleet, 2009).

Preschool Education for Economically Disadvantaged Children

The parents of children reared in poverty typically do not have the means to send their children to private schools. Therefore, their preschoolers may receive no academic-type education at all unless public programs are available for them. Whereas the often skilled and academically aware children of affluent parents can enhance their competencies through formal instruction at the ages of 3 and 4, the children of poor parents generally perform less well on standardized intelligence tests, and they are at greater risk for school failure (Lamy, 2012; Robbins et al., 2012).

In an effort to correct some of these social imbalances, public preschool programs attempt to enhance the cognitive development and academic skills of poor children and thus increase their readiness for elementary school. Some, such as the federally funded Head Start program, also provide health care to children and social services to their families. Children in these programs typically are exposed to letters and words, numbers, books, exercises in drawing, pegs and pegboards, puzzles, and toy animals and dolls, in addition to other materials and activities that middle-class children can usually take for granted. Many programs encourage parental involvement in the program itself.

Head Start Preschoolers enrolled in Head Start programs have made dramatic increases in readiness for elementary school and in intelligence test scores. Head Start and similar programs also can have long-term effects on educational and employment outcomes.

Studies of Head Start show that environmental enrichment can enhance the cognitive development of economically disadvantaged children (Bierman et al., 2014; Zhai et al., 2011). The initial effects can be dramatic. In the Milwaukee Project, poor children of low-IQ mothers were provided with enriched day care from the age of 6 months. By the late preschool years, their IQ scores averaged about 121, compared with an average of 95 for children from similar backgrounds who did not receive day care (Garber, 1988). In addition to positively influencing IQ scores, Head Start and other programs also lead to gains in school readiness tests and achievement tests (Fuhs & Day, 2011). Programs that involve and educate parents are particularly beneficial (Stipek & Hakuta, 2007).

> **TRUTH OR FICTION REVISITED:** Studies of the effects of Head Start and other methods of providing young children with enriched learning environments show that these programs can provide children with advantages in school. Their IQ scores also tend to rise.

Preschool intervention programs can have long-term effects on life outcomes for poor children (Reynolds et al., 2011). During the elementary and high school years, graduates of preschool programs are less likely to have been left back or placed in classes for slow learners. They are more likely to graduate from high school, go on to college, and earn higher incomes. They are also less likely to become involved in substance abuse or other areas of delinquent behavior, or to be unemployed or on welfare in adulthood (Reynolds et al., 2011).

A contributor to the cycle of poverty is the incidence of pregnancy among single teenage girls. Pregnancy in these cases usually means that formal education comes to an end, so these children are destined to be reared by poorly educated mothers. Some researchers have found that girls from preschool education programs are less likely to become single mothers (Doyle et al., 2009). Girls who attended preschool intervention programs became pregnant as frequently as matched controls, but they were more likely to return to school after giving birth.

Educators recognize that academic environments in the preschool years benefit advantaged as well as disadvantaged children (Pianta, 2012). On the other hand, excessive pressure to achieve during the preschool years, especially on the part of middle-class parents, may impair children's learning and social–emotional development.

Is Television a Window on the World for Young Children, or a Prison within a False World?

American children spend more time watching television than they do in school. By the age of 3, the average child already watches 2–3 hours of television a day (Palmer, 2003). Television has great potential for teaching a variety of cognitive skills, social behaviors, and attitudes. In Chapter 10, we will explore the effects of television on children's social behaviors and attitudes (uh-oh). Here, we will focus on television's effect on cognitive development in early childhood. In many ways, television provides children with an important window on the outside world and on the cognitive skills required to succeed in that world (Mares & Pan, 2013).

What Are the Effects of Educational Television on Cognitive Development?

Television, in general, has been shown to have mixed effects on children's development. For example, no relationship has been found between general viewing and language development in children under the age of 2 (Zimmerman et al., 2007). However, educational television might have superior effects.

The Children's Television Act requires that networks devote a number of hours per week to educational television. Many, but not all, of the resultant programs have been shown to have mild to moderate positive effects on preschoolers' cognitive development, and more so with girls than with boys (Mares & Pan, 2013). *Sesame Street* is the most successful children's educational TV program. Begun in

"Street" Smart? *Sesame Street* is viewed regularly by an estimated 50–60% of children in the United States between the ages of 2 and 3. Research shows that regular viewing of the program improves children's cognitive and language skills.

1969, *Sesame Street* had the goal of promoting the intellectual growth of preschoolers, particularly those of lower socioeconomic status. Large-scale evaluations of the effects of the program have concluded that regular viewing increases children's learning of numbers, letters, and cognitive skills such as sorting and classification (Mares & Pan, 2013). These effects are found for African American and European American children, for girls and boys, and for children in urban, suburban, and rural settings.

What about the effects of watching television on other aspects of cognitive behavior in the young child? Characters on *Sesame Street* talk out differences and do not fight with one another. Therefore, it is not surprising that most research indicates that exposure to such educational programs as *Sesame Street* may increase impulse control and concentration among preschoolers (Cole et al., 2003). In fact, a joint project by Israelis and Palestinians is under way to bring a Middle Eastern version of *Sesame Street* to the region, in the hope that it may contribute to a more peaceful interaction between the groups (Lampel & Honig, 2006).

We can argue about just how much good a program like *Sesame Street* does, but few would argue that it does any harm. Researchers conclude that educational television can have positive benefits (Schmidt & Anderson, 2007; Schmidt et al., 2009) but that "entertainment television" can be harmful (Lillard et al., 2015). Suggested guidelines for helping children use television wisely are presented in the nearby "A Closer Look—Real Life" feature.

And What About Commercials?

Critics are concerned that the cognitive limitations of young children make them particularly susceptible to commercials, which can be misleading and even harmful. Preschoolers do not understand the selling intent of advertising, and they often are unable to tell the difference between commercials and program content (Chambers et al., 2015; Lillard et al., 2015). Exposure to commercials does not make the child a sophisticated consumer. In fact, children who are heavy TV viewers are more likely than light viewers to believe commercial claims.

Commercials that encourage children to choose nutritionally inadequate foods— such as sugared breakfast cereals, candy, and fast foods—are harmful to children's nutritional beliefs and diets. Young children do not understand that sugary foods are detrimental to health, nor do they understand disclaimers in ads that, for example, caution that sugared cereals should be part of a balanced breakfast (Chambers et al., 2015; Lillard et al., 2015).

What Is the Couch-Potato Effect?

Watching television, of course, is a sedentary activity. Parents might prefer that their children spend more time exercising, but television also functions as an engrossing babysitter. However, research in the United States, England, and even China shows that preschool children who watch more television are more likely to be overweight than peers who watch less television (Borghese et al., 2015). The number of hours watching television is a stronger predictor of being overweight than diet (Borghese et al., 2015; Chen & Wang, 2015)!

HELPING CHILDREN USE TELEVISION WISELY

Overall, television appears to have some positive effects on cognitive development. But there is more to life than television. Let me share some ideas on how parents can help their children reap the benefits of television without allowing it to take over their lives.

General Suggestions

- Encourage children to watch educational programming.
- Help children choose among cartoon shows. Not all are filled with violence.
- Encourage your children to sit with you when you are watching educational programming.
- If your child is spending too much time in front of the tube, make a chart together of his or her total activities, including television, homework, and play with friends. Discuss what to eliminate and what to substitute.
- Set a weekly viewing limit.
- Rule out television at certain times, such as before breakfast and on school nights.
- Make a list of alternative activities—riding a bicycle, reading a book, working on a hobby.
- Encourage the entire family to choose a program before turning the TV set on. Turn the set off when the show is over.

Coping with Violence

- Watch at least one episode of programs the child watches to see how violent they are.
- When viewing television together, discuss the violence with the child. Talk about why the violence happened and how painful it is. Discuss how conflict can be resolved without violence.
- Explain to the child how violence on TV shows is faked.
- Encourage children to watch programs with characters who cooperate with, help, and care for each other. Such programs can influence children in a positive way.

Applying Television to Real Life

- Ask children to compare what they see on the screen with people, places, and events they know firsthand, have read about, or have studied in school.
- Tell children what is real and what is make-believe on television, including the use of stunt people, dream sequences, and animation.
- Explain to the child your values with regard to sex, alcohol, and drugs.

Understanding Advertising

- Explain to children that the purpose of advertising is to sell products.
- On shopping trips, let children see that toys that look big, fast, and exciting on the screen are disappointingly small and slow close up.
- Talk to the child about nutrition. If the child can read package labels, allow her or him to choose a breakfast cereal from those in which sugar levels are low.

Reflect Do you know parents who use television as a babysitter? What risks do they run?

KidStock/Blend Images/Getty Images

TV, TV Everywhere—How Do We Teach Children to Stop to Think? Parents can have a positive effect on children's cognitive processing of the information they glean from TV programs and commercials.

This research is correlational, to be sure; that is, children choose (or are allowed) to watch more or less television. They are not randomly assigned to view various amounts of television. Thus, it may be that the same factors that lead them to choose more television also lead them to put on more body fat. Nevertheless, there may be little harm (and much good!) in encouraging children to spend more time in physical activity.

Section Review

8. Cognitive _____ is temporary support provided by a parent or teacher to a child who is learning to perform a task.

9. Caldwell and her colleagues found that the children of parents who are emotionally and verbally _____ show advanced social and language development.

10. Molfese and her colleagues found that the _____ was the single most important predictor of scores on IQ tests among children.

11. Head Start programs _____ (can or cannot?) significantly enhance the cognitive development of economically disadvantaged children.

12. During the elementary and high school years, graduates of preschool programs are _____ (more or less?) likely to have been left back or placed in classes for slow learners.

13. American children spend _____ (more or less?) time watching television than they do in school.

Reflect & Relate: What was your early home environment like? How do you think it would have appeared in terms of the factors listed in Table 9.2? How can you use the information in this section to create a home environment for your own children? How much television did you watch as a child? Can you think of things you learned by watching television? Can you imagine developing in a world without television? Explain.

9.4 Theory of Mind: What Is the Mind? How Does It Work?

Adults appear to have a common sense understanding of how the mind works. This understanding, known as a **theory of mind**, allows us to explain and predict behavior by referring to mental processes. For example, we understand that we can acquire knowledge through our senses or through hearsay. We understand the distinction between external and mental events, and between how things appear and how they really are. By observing other people, we are able to infer their perceptions, thoughts, and feelings. We understand that people's mental states affect their behavior.

What Are Young Children's Ideas About How the Mind Works?

Piaget might have predicted that preoperational children are too egocentric and too focused on misleading external appearances to have a theory of mind. But research has shown that even preschool-age children can accurately predict and explain human action and emotion in terms of mental states. They are beginning to understand where knowledge comes from, and they have a rudimentary ability to distinguish appearance from reality (Lecce et al., 2015; Marcovitch et al., 2015). Let us consider these developments.

On False Beliefs: Just Where Did Those Crayons Go?

One important indication of the young child's understanding that mental states affect behavior is the ability to understand false beliefs. This concept involves children's ability to separate their beliefs from those of another person who has false knowledge of a situation. It is illustrated in a study of 3-year-olds by Louis Moses and John Flavell (1990). The children were shown a videotape in which a girl named Cathy found some crayons in a bag. When Cathy left the room briefly, a clown entered the room. The clown removed the crayons from the bag, hid them in a drawer, and put rocks in the bag instead. When Cathy returned, the children were asked whether Cathy thought there were going to be rocks or crayons in the bag. Most of the 3-year-olds incorrectly answered "rocks," demonstrating their difficulty in understanding that the other person's belief would be different from their own

theory of mind A common sense understanding of how the mind works.

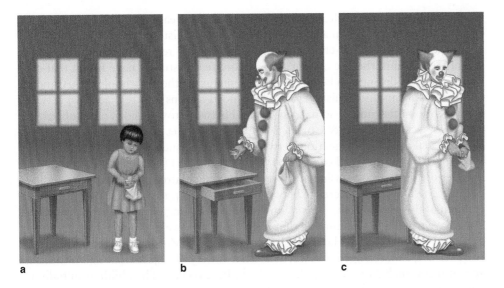

Figure 9.5 ■ False Beliefs
John Flavell and his colleagues showed preschoolers a videotape in which a girl named Cathy found crayons in a bag (a). When Cathy left the room, a clown entered, removed the crayons from the bag, hid them in a drawer (b), and filled the bag with rocks (c). When asked whether Cathy thought there would be rocks or crayons in the bag, most 3-year-olds said "rocks." Most 4-year-olds correctly answered "crayons," showing the ability to separate their own beliefs from someone who has false beliefs about a situation.
© Cengage Learning®

(see Figure 9.5 ■). But by the age of 4–5 years, children do not have trouble with this concept and correctly answer "crayons" (Flavell, 1993). By the ages of 4 and 5, children in the United States and China are also starting to understand that beliefs may be held with differing degrees of certainty (Marcovitch et al., 2015).

Another intriguing demonstration of the false-belief concept comes from studies of children's ability to deceive others. For example, Sodian and her colleagues (1991) asked children to hide a toy truck driver in one of five cups in a sandbox so that another person could not find it. The child was given the opportunity to deceive the other person by removing real trails in the sand and creating false ones. Once again, 4-year-olds acted in ways that were likely to mislead the other person. Younger children did not.

The ability to understand false beliefs is related to the development of executive functioning, including working memory, ability to pay sustained attention to problems, and self-control (Marcovitch et al., 2015).

On the Origins of Knowledge: Where Does It Come From?

Another aspect of theory of mind is how we acquire knowledge. By age 3, most children begin to realize that people gain knowledge about a thing by looking at it (Lecce et al., 2015). By age 4, children understand that particular senses provide information about certain qualities of an object; that is, they recognize that we come to know an object's color through our eyes, but its weight by feeling it (O'Neill & Chong, 2001). In one study, 3-, 4-, and 5-year-olds learned about the contents of a toy tunnel in three different ways (O'Neill & Gopnik, 1991). They saw the contents, were told about them, or felt them. The children then were asked what was in the tunnel and how they knew. Although 4- and 5-year-olds had no trouble identifying the sources of their knowledge, the 3-year-olds struggled. For example, after feeling but not seeing a ball in the tunnel, a number of 3-year-olds told the experimenter that they could tell it was a blue ball. They did not realize that it was impossible to discover the ball's color just by feeling it.

The Appearance–Reality Distinction: Are Appearances at Some Ages More Deceiving Than at Others?

One of the most important things children must acquire in developing a theory of mind is a clear understanding of the difference between real events and mental events, fantasies, and misleading appearances (Corriveau & Harris, 2015; Lecce et al., 2015). This is known as the **appearance–reality distinction**.

Piaget's view was that children do not differentiate reality from appearances or mental events until the age of 7 or 8. But more recent studies have found that children's ability to distinguish between the two emerges in the preschool years. Children as young as 3 can distinguish between pretended actions and real actions, between pictures of objects and the actual objects, and between toy versions of an object and the real object (Callaghan & Corbit, 2015; Marcovitch et al., 2015). By the age of 4, children make a clear distinction between real items (such as a cup) and imagined items (such as an imagined cup or an imagined monster) (Leerkes et al., 2008).

Despite these accomplishments, preoperational children still show some difficulties in recognizing the difference between reality and appearances, perhaps because children of this age still have only a limited understanding of **mental representations**. They have trouble understanding that a real object or event can take many forms in our minds (Corriveau & Harris, 2015). In a study by Marjorie Taylor and Barbara Hort (1990), children aged 3–5 were shown a variety of objects that had misleading appearances, such as an eraser that looked like a cookie. The children initially reported that the eraser looked like a cookie. But once they learned that it was actually an eraser, they tended to report that it looked like an eraser, ignoring its cookie-like appearance. Apparently, the children could not mentally represent the eraser as both being an eraser and looking like a cookie.

Three-year-olds also apparently cannot understand changes in their mental states. In one study (Gopnik & Slaughter, 1991), 3-year-olds were shown a crayon box. They consistently said they thought crayons were inside. The box was opened, revealing birthday candles, not crayons. When the children were asked what they had thought was in the box before it was opened, they now said "candles."

Children aged 2½–3 also find it difficult to understand the relationship between a scale model and the larger object or space that it represents (Walker & Murachver, 2012). Perhaps this is because the child cannot conceive that the model can be two things at once: both a representation of something else and an object in its own right.

Section Review

14. Moses and Flavell used crayons and a clown to learn whether preschoolers can understand _____ beliefs.

15. By age 3, most children begin to realize that people gain knowledge about things through the _____.

Reflect & Relate: Think of research on the origins of knowledge—on where knowledge comes from. Can you relate this area of research to arguments we might find among adults about sources of knowledge, such as experience versus revelation?

9.5 ## Development of Memory: Creating Documents, Storing Them, Retrieving Them

appearance–reality distinction The difference between real events and mental events, fantasies, and misleading appearances.

mental representations The mental forms that a real object or event can take.

Even newborns have some memory skills, and memory improves substantially throughout the first 2 years of life.

What Memory Skills Do Children Have in Early Childhood? How Do We Know?

Two of the basic tasks used in the study of memory are *recognition* and *recall*. Recognition is the easiest type of memory task. For this reason, multiple-choice tests are easier than fill-in-the-blank or essay tests. In a recognition test, one simply indicates whether a presented item has been seen before or which of a number of items is paired with a stimulus (as in a multiple-choice test). Children are capable of simple recognition during early infancy; they recognize their mother's nursing pads, her voice, and her face. To test recognition memory in a preschooler, you might show the child some objects and then present those objects along with some new ones. The child is then asked which objects you showed her the first time.

Recall is more difficult than recognition. In a recall task, children must reproduce material from memory without having it in front of them. If I ask you to name the capital of Wyoming, that is a test of recall. A recall task for a preschooler might consist of showing her some objects, taking them away, and asking her to name the objects from memory.

When preschoolers are presented with objects, words, or TV shows, they typically recognize more, later on, than they can recall (Schneider, 2010). In fact, younger preschoolers are almost as good as older ones at recognizing objects they have seen. But they are not nearly as good at recall (Schneider, 2010). In Figure 9.6 ■, compare the abilities of 3- and 4½-year-olds to recognize and recall various objects from a life-size playhouse (Jones et al., 1988). (We will discuss the "activities" part of this figure later.)

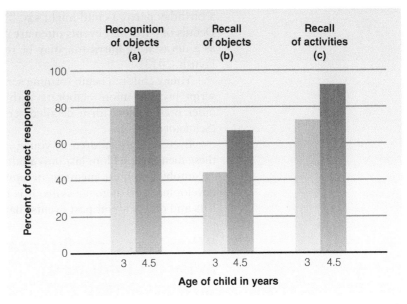

Figure 9.6 ■ Recognition and Recall Memory
Preschoolers can recognize previously seen objects (a) better than they can recall them (b). They are also better at recalling their activities (c) than at recalling objects (b). Older preschoolers have better memories than younger ones.
Source: Jones et al. (1988).

How Competent Are Young Children's Memories?

Until recently, most studies of children's memory were conducted in laboratory settings. The tasks had little meaning for the children. The results appeared to show that the memories of young children are deficient relative to those of older children. But parents often tell you that their children have excellent memories for events. It turns out that they are right. Children, like adults, frequently remember what they *want* to remember (Crisp & Turner, 2011). More recently, psychologists have focused their research on children's memory for meaningful events and activities.

TRUTH OR FICTION REVISITED: It is not true that 1- and 2-year-olds are too young to remember past events. Children as young as 11½ months can remember organized sequences of events they have just experienced (Schneider, 2010). Even after a delay of 6 weeks, 16-month-old children can re-enact a sequence of events they experienced only one time, such as placing a ball in a cup, covering it with another cup, and shaking the resulting "rattle" (Schneider, 2010). By the age of 4, children can remember events that occurred at least 1½ years earlier (Bauer & Fivush, 2010, 2013; Schneider, 2010).

Catherine Nelson and Robyn Fivush (2004) report the results of studies in which children aged 2–5 are interviewed to study their memory for recurring events in their lives, such as having dinner, playing with friends, and going to birthday parties. Even 3-year-olds can present coherent, orderly accounts of familiar events. Furthermore, young children seem to form **scripts**, which are abstract, generalized accounts of these repeated events. For example, in describing what happens during

scripts Abstract generalized accounts of familiar repeated events.

a birthday party, a child might say, "You play games, open presents, and eat cake." Details of particular events often are omitted. However, an unusual experience, such as a devastating hurricane, may be remembered in detail for many years (Bauer & Fivush, 2013).

Young children begin forming scripts after experiencing an event only once. The script becomes more elaborate with repeated experiences. As might be expected, older preschoolers form detailed scripts more quickly than younger preschoolers (Schneider, 2010).

Even though children as young as 1 and 2 years clearly can remember events, these memories seldom last into adulthood. This memory of specific events—known as **autobiographical memory** or *episodic memory*—appears to be linked to the development of language skills. It is facilitated by children's talking with their parents and others about past events (Bauer & Fivush, 2013).

What Factors Influence Memory Skills in Early Childhood?

The factors that affect memory include what the child is asked to remember, the interest level of the child, the availability of retrieval cues or reminders, and what memory measure we are using. Let us discuss each of these in turn.

Types of Memory

Preschoolers' memories for activities are better than their memories for objects. Return to Figure 9.6 once again. Compare children's accuracy in recalling the activities they engaged in while in the playhouse with their accuracy in recalling the objects they used. Children are better at recalling their activities, such as washing a shirt and chopping ice, than at recalling specific objects, such as shirts and ice picks (Schneider, 2010).

Children also find it easier to remember events that follow a logical order than events that do not occur in a particular order. For instance, 3- and 5-year-olds have a better memory for the activities involved in making pretend cookies out of Play-Doh (you put the ingredients in the bowl, then mix the ingredients, then roll out the dough, and so on) than for the activities involved in sand play, which can occur in any order (Bauer & Fivush, 2010).

Interest Level

There is nothing new about the idea that we pay more attention to the things that interest us. The world is abuzz with signals, and we tend to remember those to which we pay attention. Attention opens the door to memory.

Interest level and motivation also contribute to memory among young children (Schneider, 2010). Research consistently shows that (most) preschool boys are more interested in playing with toys such as cars and weapons, whereas (most) preschool girls are more interested in playing with dolls, dishes, and teddy bears. Later, the children typically show better recognition and recall for the toys in which they had an interest (Goble et al., 2012; Martin & Ruble, 2004).

Retrieval Cues

To retrieve information (a file) from your computer's storage, you have to remember its name or some part of it. Then you can use a Find routine. The name is the retrieval cue. In the same way, we need retrieval cues to find things in our own memories.

Andres Rodriguez / Alamy

Childhood Memory Young children's memories of events, like ours, are enhanced by the use of retrieval cues, such as photographs.

autobiographical memory The memory of specific episodes or events.

Although young children can remember a great deal, they depend more than older children do on cues provided by adults to help them retrieve their memories. Consider the following interchange between a mother and her 2-year-old child (Hudson, 1990, p. 186).

Mother: What did we look for in the grass and in the bushes?
Child: Easter bunny.
Mother: Did we hide candy eggs outside in the grass?
Child: (nods)
Mother: Remember looking for them? Who found two? Your brother?
Child: Yes, brother.

Preschoolers whose parents elaborate on the child's experiences and ask questions that encourage the child to contribute information to the narrative remember an episode better than children whose parents simply provide reminders (Nelson & Fivush, 2004). Parental assistance is more important under some conditions than others. For example, when 4-year-olds are internally motivated to remember items needed to prepare their own sack lunches, they do equally well with or without parental coaching. But when the task is simply to recall a series of items, they do better with parental assistance (Schneider, 2010).

Types of Measurement

What we find is in part determined by how we measure it. Children's memory is often measured or assessed by asking them to say what they remember. But verbal reports, especially from preschoolers, appear to underestimate children's memory (Schneider, 2010). In one longitudinal study, children's memory for certain events was tested at age 2½ and again at age 4. Most of the information recalled at age 4 had not been mentioned at age 2½, which indicates that when they were younger, the children remembered much more than they reported (Fivush & Hammond, 1990).

What measures might be more accurate than a verbal report? When preschoolers are allowed to use dolls to re-enact an event, their recall exceeds that exhibited when they give a verbal report of the event (Schneider, 2010).

rehearsal Repetition—mental, behavioral, or both.

Memory Strategies: How Do Children Remember to Remember?

When adults and older children are trying to remember things, they use strategies to help their memory. One common strategy is mental repetition, or **rehearsal**. If you are trying to remember a new friend's phone number, for example, you might repeat it several times. Another strategy is to organize things to be remembered into categories. Many students outline textbook chapters to prepare for an exam. Organizing information in a meaningful way makes it easier to learn and remember. Similarly, if you are going to buy some things at the grocery store, you might mentally group together items that belong to the same category: dairy items, produce, household cleaners, and so on.

Helping Young Children Remember Memory functioning in early childhood—and at other ages—is aided when adults provide cues to help children remember. Adults can help by elaborating on the child's experiences and asking questions that encourage the child to contribute information.

But preschool children generally do not appear to use memory strategies on their own initiative. Most young children do not spontaneously engage in rehearsal until about 5 years of age (Bebko et al., 2014). They also rarely group objects into related categories to help them remember. By about age 5, many children have learned to verbalize information silently to themselves, counting mentally rather than aloud.

Even very young children use some simple and concrete memory aids to help them remember. They look, point, and touch when trying to remember. For example, in a study by Judith DeLoache and her colleagues (1985), 18- to 24-month-old children observed as the experimenter hid a Big Bird doll under a pillow. Then they were given attractive toys to play with and, after a short period of time, were asked to find the hidden object. During the play interval, the children frequently looked or pointed at the hiding place or repeated the name of the hidden object. These behaviors suggest the beginning of the use of strategies to prompt the memory.

Young children also can be taught to successfully use strategies they might not use on their own. Six-year-old children who are trained to rehearse show improvement in their ability to recall items on a memory test (Schneider, 2010). Similarly, having preschoolers sort objects into categories enhances memory (Bauer & Fivush, 2013). Even 3- and 4-year-olds will use rehearsal and labeling if they are instructed to try to remember something (Schneider, 2010).

The preschooler's use of memory strategies is not nearly as sophisticated as that of the school-age child. Children's use of memory strategies and understanding of how memory works advance greatly in middle childhood.

Section Review

16. Children are capable of simple _____ (recognition or recall?) during infancy.

17. Memory for events in one's life is referred to as _____ memory.

18. Preschoolers' memories for activities are _____ (better or worse?) than their memories for objects.

19. Interest level is _____ (positively or negatively?) connected with ability to remember.

20. Using mental repetition to remember is termed _____.

Reflect & Relate: How do you prepare for a test? For example, how do you remember lists of new vocabulary words? What strategies does your textbook author (that's me!) use to help you remember the subject matter in this course?

9.6 Language Development: Why "Daddy Goed Away"

Children's language skills develop dramatically during the preschool years. By the fourth year, children are asking adults and each other questions, taking turns talking, and engaging in lengthy conversations (Hoover et al., 2011). Some milestones of language development that occur during early childhood are listed in Table 9.3 ●. Let us consider a number of them.

Words, Words, and More Words—How Does Vocabulary Develop in Early Childhood?

The development of vocabulary proceeds at an extraordinary pace during early childhood. Preschoolers learn an average of nine new words per day (Tamis-LeMonda et al., 2014a; Tomasello, 2010). But how can this be possible when each new word has so many potential meanings? Consider the following example. A toddler observes a small black dog running through the park. His older sister points to the animal and says "doggy." The word *doggy* could mean this particular dog, or all dogs, or all animals. It could refer to one part of the dog (such as its tail) or to its behavior (running, barking) or to its characteristics (small, black) (Waxman & Goswami, 2012). Does the child consider all these possibilities before determining what *doggy* actually means?

Studies have generally shown that word learning, in fact, does not occur gradually but is better characterized as a **fast-mapping** process, in which the child quickly

fast mapping A process of quickly determining a word's meaning, which facilitates children's vocabulary development.

● TABLE 9.3

Development of Language Skills in Early Childhood

Age	Characteristics	Typical Sentences
2½ years	• There is a rapid increase in vocabulary, with new additions each day. • There is no babbling. • Intelligibility is still not very good. • Child uses two or three words in sentences. • Child uses plurals. • Child uses possessives. • Child uses past tense. • Child uses some prepositions.	Two cups. Sarah's car. It broke. Keisha in bed.
3 years	• Child has vocabulary of some 1,000 words. • Speech nears 100% intelligibility. • Articulation of *l* and *r* is frequently faulty. • Child uses three or four words in sentences. • Child uses yes–no questions. • Child uses *wh* questions. • Child uses negatives. • Child embeds one sentence within another.	Will I go? Where is the doggy? I not eat yucky peas. That's the book Mommy buyed me.
4 years	• Child has vocabulary of 1,500–1,600 words. • Speech is fluent. • Articulation is good except for *sh, z, ch,* and *j* sounds. • Child uses five or six words in sentences. • Child coordinates two sentences.	I went to Allie's and I had cookies.

© Cengage Learning®

attaches a new word to its appropriate concept (Holland et al., 2015; Tomasello, 2010). The key to fast mapping seems to be that children are equipped with early cognitive biases, or constraints, that lead them to prefer certain meanings over others (Waxman & Goswami, 2012).

One bias that children have is assuming that words refer to whole objects and not to their component parts or their characteristics, such as color, size, or texture (Tomasello, 2010). This inclination is known as the **whole-object assumption**. In the example given at the beginning of the section, this bias would lead the young child to assume that "doggy" refers to the dog rather than to its tail, its color, or its barking.

Children also seem to hold the bias that objects have only one label. Therefore, novel terms must refer to unfamiliar objects and not to familiar objects that already have labels. This is the **contrast assumption**, which is also known as the mutual exclusivity assumption (Waxman & Goswami, 2012). How might this bias help children figure out the meaning of a new word? Suppose that a child is shown two objects, one of which has a known label ("doggy") and one of which is an unknown object. Let us further suppose that an adult now says, "Look at the lemur." If the child assumes that "doggy" and "lemur" each can refer to only one object, the child will correctly figure out that "lemur" refers to the other object and is not just another name for "doggy." This bias facilitates children's learning of words (Waxman & Goswami, 2012).

Putting Words Together—How Does Grammar Develop in Early Childhood?

Somewhat similar to the naming explosion in the second year is a "grammar explosion" that occurs during the third year (Tamis-LeMonda et al., 2014a).

whole-object assumption The assumption that words refer to whole objects and not to their component parts or characteristics.

contrast assumption The assumption that objects have only one label. Also known as the mutual exclusivity assumption (if a word means one thing, then it cannot mean another).

● TABLE 9.4
Examples of Allyn's Speech During the Third Year

- Objecting to something said to her: "No, that is not a good talk to say. I don't like that."
- Describing her younger sister: "Jordan is very laughy today."
- On the second floor of her home: "This is not home. This is upstairs."
- Objecting to her father's departure: "Stay here for a couple of whiles."
- Directing her father to turn up the stereo: "Make it a big louder, not a small louder."
- Use of the plural number: "I see two policemans."
- Requesting a nickel: "Give me another money."
- Explaining that she and her mother are finished singing a song: "We singed it all up."
- Requesting an empty cup: "Give me that. I need it to drink nothing."
- Use of the possessive case: "That car is blue, just like us's."
- When she wants her father to hold her: "I want you to pick up me."
- Refusing to answer a question: "I don't want you to ask that to me."
- Confessing what she did with several coins: "I taked those money and put it on the shelf."

© Cengage Learning®

Tymonko Galyna/Shutterstock.com

Vocabulary Development When this adult points to the goat and says "goat," the child assumes that "goat" refers to the whole animal, rather than to its horns, fur, size, or color. This bias, known as the whole-object assumption, helps children acquire a large vocabulary in a relatively short period of time.

overregularization The application of regular grammatical rules (e.g., to create past tense and plurals) to irregular verbs and nouns.

Children's sentence structure expands to include the words missing in telegraphic speech. During the third year, children usually add to their vocabulary an impressive array of articles (*a, an, the*), conjunctions (*and, but, or*), possessive adjectives (*your, her*), pronouns (*she, him, one*), and prepositions (*in, on, over, around, under, through*). Usually between the ages of 3 and 4, children show knowledge of rules for combining phrases and clauses into complex sentences. An early example of a complex sentence is "You goed and Mommy goed, too." Table 9.4 ● lists some interesting examples of one child's use of language during the third year. (All right! I'm prejudiced. It's my child.)

Overregularization—Why We Sitted Down

One of the more intriguing language developments—**overregularization**—is apparently based on the simple fact that children acquire grammatical rules as they learn language. At young ages, they tend to apply these rules rather strictly, even in cases that call for exceptions (Ambridge et al., 2013). Consider the formation of the past tense and plurals in English. We add -*d* or -*ed* to regular verbs and -*s* to regular nouns. Thus, *walk* becomes *walked* and *doggy* becomes *doggies*. But then there are irregular verbs and irregular nouns. For example, *sit* becomes *sat* and *go* becomes *went*. *Sheep* remains *sheep* (plural) but *child* becomes *children*.

At first, children learn a small number of these irregular constructions by imitating their parents. Two-year-olds tend to form them correctly temporarily. Then they become aware of the syntactic rules for forming the past tense and plurals in English. As a result, they tend to make charming errors (Tomasello, 2010).

Some parents recognize that their children were forming the past tense of irregular verbs correctly early on, and then, some time later, they began to make errors. And some of these parents become concerned that their children are "slipping" in their language development and attempt to correct them. However, overregularization reflects accurate knowledge of grammar, not faulty language development. (Really.) In another year or two, *mouses* will be boringly transformed into *mice,* and Mommy will no longer have "sitted down." I recommend that parents enjoy overregularization while they can.

In a classic experiment designed to show that preschool children are not just clever mimics in their formation of plurals but have actually grasped rules of grammar, Berko (1958) showed children pictures of nonexistent animals. She first showed them a single animal and said, "This is a wug." Then she showed them a picture of two animals and said, "Now there are two of them. There are two ___," asking the children to finish the sentence. Ninety-one percent of the children said "wugs," providing the proper plural of the bogus word.

Asking Questions—Not as Easy as You Might Think

Children's first questions are telegraphic and characterized by a rising pitch (which signifies a question mark in English) at the end. "More milky?" for example, can be translated into "May I have more milk?" or "Would you like more milk?" or "Is there more milk?" depending on the context. It is usually toward the latter part of the third year that the *wh* questions appear. Consistent with the child's general cognitive development, certain *wh* questions (*what, who,* and *where*) appear earlier than others (*why, when, which,* and *how*) (Tamis-LeMonda et al., 2014a). *Why* is usually too philosophical for a 2-year-old, and *how* is too involved. Two-year-olds are also likely to be now-oriented, so *when* is of less than immediate concern. By the fourth year, most children are spontaneously producing *why, when,* and *how* questions. These *wh* words are initially tacked on to the beginnings of sentences. "Where Mommy go?" can stand for "Where is Mommy going?" or "Where did Mommy go?" or "Where will Mommy go?", and its meaning must be derived from context. Later on, the child will add the auxiliary verbs *is, did,* and *will* to indicate whether the question concerns the present, past, or future.

Passive Sentences—The Food Was Eaten by the Dog?

Passive sentences, such as "The food was eaten by the dog," are difficult for 2- and 3-year-olds to understand, so young preschoolers almost never produce them (even when the dog has in fact eaten the food). In a fascinating study of children's comprehension (Strohner & Nelson, 1974), 2- to 5-year-olds used puppets and toys to act out a number of sentences that were read to them. Two- and 3-year-olds in the study made errors in acting out passive sentences (e.g., "The car was hit by the truck") 70% of the time. Older children had less difficulty interpreting the meanings of passive sentences correctly. However, most children usually do not produce passive sentences spontaneously even at the ages of 5 and 6.

Pragmatics: Can Preschoolers Be Practical?

Pragmatics in language development consists of the practical aspects of communication. Children are showing pragmatism when they adjust their speech to fit the social situation (Nelson, 2006). For example, children show greater formality in their choice of words and syntax when they are role-playing high-status figures, such as teachers or physicians, in their games. They also say "please" more often when making requests of high-status people. Children also show pragmatism in their adoption of infant-directed speech when they address a younger child.

Pragmatism provides another example of the ways in which cognitive and language development are intertwined. Preschoolers tend to be egocentric; therefore, a 2-year-old telling another child "Gimme my book," without specifying which book, may be assuming that the other child knows what she herself knows. She is also probably overestimating the clearness of her communication and how well she is understood. Once children can perceive the world through the eyes of others, however, they advance in their abilities to make themselves understood to others. Now the child recognizes that the other child will require a description of the book or of its location to carry out the request. Between the ages of 3 and 5, egocentric speech gradually disappears and there is rapid development of pragmatic skills. The child's conversation shows increasing sensitivity to the listener; for example, he or she takes turns talking and listening.

What Are the Connections Between Language and Cognition? Which Comes First: The Concept or the Word?

Language and cognitive development are strongly interwoven (Waxman & Goswami, 2012). For example, the child gradually gains the capacity to discriminate between animals on the basis of distinct features, such as size, patterns of movement, and the sounds they make. At the same time, the child also is acquiring words that represent broader categories, such as *mammal* and *animal*.

But it's chicken-and-egg time. Which comes first? Does the child first develop concepts and then acquire the language to describe them, or does the child's increasing language ability lead to the development of new concepts?

Does Cognitive Development Precede Language Development?

Piaget (1976) believed that cognitive development precedes language development. He argued that children must first understand concepts before they can use words that describe the concepts. Object permanence emerges toward the end of the first year. Piaget believed that words that relate to the disappearance and appearance of people and objects (such as *all gone* and *bye-bye*) are used only after the emergence of object permanence.

From Piaget's perspective, children learn words in order to describe classes or categories that they have already created. Children can learn the word *doggy* because they have perceived the characteristics that distinguish dogs from other things.

Some studies support the notion that cognitive concepts may precede language. For example, the vocabulary explosion that occurs at about 18 months of age is related to the child's ability to group a set of objects into categories, such as "dolls" and "cars" (Quinn, 2010). Young children may need to experience an action themselves or by observation in order to learn the meaning of a verb (Pulverman et al., 2006).

pragmatics The practical aspects of communication, such as adaptation of language to fit the social situation.

Does Language Development Precede Cognitive Development?

Although many theorists argue that cognitive development precedes language development, others reverse the causal relationship and claim that children create cognitive classes in order to understand things that are labeled by words (Dodd & Crosbie, 2010; Horst et al., 2009). When children hear the word *dog*, they try to understand it by searching for characteristics that separate dogs from other things. Research with 4½-year-olds shows that descriptions of events can prompt children to create categories in which to classify occurrences (Nazzi & Gopnik, 2000).

The Interactionist View: On Outer Speech and Private (Inner) Speech

Today, most developmentalists find something of value in each of these cognitive views (Waxman & Goswami, 2012). In the early stages of language development, concepts often precede words, so that many of the infant's words describe classes that have already developed. Later, however, language is not merely the servant of thought; language influences thought.

Vygotsky also made key contributions to our understanding of the relationships between concepts and words. Vygotsky believed that during most of the first year, vocalizations and thought are separate. But during the second year, thought and speech—cognition and language—usually combine forces. "Speech begins to serve intellect and thoughts begin to be spoken" (Vygotsky, 1962, p. 43). Usually during the second year, children discover that objects have labels. Learning labels becomes more active, more self-directed (Geraghty et al., 2014). At some point, children ask what new words mean. Learning new words clearly fosters the creation of new categories and classes. An interaction develops in which classes are filled with labels for new things, and labels nourish the blossoming of new classes.

Vygotsky's concept of **private speech** (also called *inner speech*) is a key feature of his position. At first, according to Vygotsky, children's thoughts are spoken aloud. You can overhear the 3-year-old giving herself instructions as she plays with toys. At this age, her vocalizations may serve to regulate her behavior. But language gradually becomes internalized. What was spoken aloud at ages 4 and 5 becomes an internal dialogue by age 6 or 7. This internal dialogue, or private speech, is the ultimate binding of language and thought. Private speech is involved in the development of planning and self-regulation, and facilitates learning. Vygotsky's ideas about the self-regulative function of language have inspired psychological treatment approaches for children with problems in self-control. For example, hyperactive children can be taught to use self-directed speech to increase their self-control (Crain, 2000).

Language is thus connected not only with thought but also with the social and emotional development of the young child. We will turn to these areas of development in Chapter 10.

private speech Vygotsky's concept of the ultimate binding of language and thought. Private speech originates in vocalizations that may regulate the child's behavior and become internalized by age 6 or 7.

Section Review

21. Word learning does not occur gradually but is better characterized as a fast _____ process.

22. The _____ object assumption refers to the fact that young children assume that words refer to whole objects and not to their component parts or to their characteristics, such as color or texture.

23. Young children tend to assume that objects have _____ (how many?) label(s).

24. Young children have the _____ assumption, which holds that novel terms must refer to unfamiliar objects and not to familiar objects that already have labels.

25. Vygotsky's concept of _____ speech refers to the fact that what was spoken aloud at ages 4 and 5 becomes an internal dialogue by age 6 or 7.

Reflect & Relate: What are some of the new words you are learning by reading this book? Do the words you chose to list have a single meaning or multiple meanings? How does their number of meanings affect your acquisition of these words? (Consider the examples *conservation, scaffold,* and *mapping.*)

Chapter Review

9.1 How Does Jean Piaget Describe Cognitive Development During Early Childhood? (What Is the Preoperational Stage?)

Piaget's preoperational stage lasts from about age 2 to age 7 and is characterized by the use of symbols to represent objects and relationships. Pretend play is based on the use and recollection of symbols or on mental representations of things. By 30 months, children can pretend that objects are active. Preoperational thinking is characterized by egocentrism, precausal thinking, confusion between mental and physical events, and ability to focus on only one dimension at a time. Young children's thinking about causality is egocentric, animistic, and artificialistic. In transductive reasoning, children reason by going from one instance of an event to another. Preoperational children have difficulty distinguishing between mental and physical events. Egocentrism contributes to their belief that their thoughts reflect reality. The law of conservation holds that properties of substances, such as volume, mass, and number, stay the same (are conserved) even if their shape or arrangement changes. Conservation requires focusing on two aspects of a situation at once.

9.2 What Are Vygotsky's Views on Cognitive Development During Early Childhood?

Scaffolding and the zone of proximal development, as envisioned by Vygotsky, are among the most important factors in cognitive development. Others include social and family factors such as family income, parents' educational level, family size, and the presence of stressful family events such as divorce, job loss, or illness. The children of responsive parents who provide appropriate play materials and stimulating experiences show gains in social and language development. Head Start programs enhance economically disadvantaged children's cognitive development, academic skills, and readiness for school.

9.3 What Are the Influences of the Home Environment, Preschool, and Television on Cognitive Development During Early Childhood?

Factors such as parental responsiveness, avoidance of restriction and punishment, organization of the physical environment, and provision of proper play materials and opportunities for variety all promote cognitive development. Preschool programs, especially Head Start, not only increase readiness for school but also decrease the likelihood of future juvenile delinquency and teenage pregnancy. TV programs such as *Sesame Street* can enhance children's cognitive development, but children need to be made aware of the pitfalls of attachment to violent shows and of commercials.

9.4 What Is Meant by a Child's "Theory of Mind"? How Does It Develop During Early Childhood?

As children's theory of mind develops, children come to understand that there are distinctions between external and mental events and between appearances and realities. By age 3, most children begin to realize that people gain knowledge through the senses. By age 4, children understand which sense is needed to provide information about qualities such as color (vision) and weight (touch). Although Piaget believed that children do not differentiate reality from appearances or mental events until the age of 7 or 8, research reveals that preschoolers can do so.

9.5 How Does the Memory Develop in Early Childhood?

Preschoolers recognize more items than they can recall. Autobiographical memory is linked to language skills. By the age of 4, children can remember events that occurred 1½ years earlier. Young children seem to form scripts, which are abstract, generalized accounts of events. Factors affecting memory include what the child is asked to remember, interest level and motivation, the availability of retrieval cues, and the memory measure being used. Preschoolers engage in behaviors such as looking, pointing, and touching when trying to remember. Preschoolers can be taught to use strategies such as rehearsal and grouping of items, which they might not use on their own.

9.6 How Does Language Develop in Early Childhood?

Preschoolers acquire about nine new words per day. Word learning often occurs rapidly through fast mapping. During the third year, children usually add articles, conjunctions, possessive adjectives, pronouns, and prepositions. Between the ages of 3 and 4, children combine phrases and clauses into complex sentences. Preschoolers tend to overregularize irregular verbs and noun forms as they acquire rules of grammar. Piaget believed that children learn words in order to describe classes or categories they have created. Other theorists argue that children create classes to understand things that are labeled by words. Vygotsky believed that during most of the first year, vocalizations and thought are separate. But usually during the second year, cognition and language combine forces. To Vygotsky, private speech is the ultimate binding of language and thought.

Key Terms

preoperational stage 278
symbolic play 278
operations 279
egocentrism 279
precausal 280
transductive reasoning 280
animism 281
artificialism 281

conservation 282
centration 283
irreversibility 283
class inclusion 283
theory of mind 294
appearance–reality distinction 296
mental representations 296
scripts 297

autobiographical memory 298
rehearsal 299
fast mapping 300
whole-object assumption 301
contrast assumption 301
overregularization 302
pragmatics 304
private speech 305

10

Early Childhood: Social and Emotional Development

TruthorFiction?

| T \| F | Parents who are restrictive and demand mature behavior wind up with rebellious children, not mature children. **p. 311** |

| T \| F | There is no point in trying to reason with a 4-year-old. **p. 311** |

| T \| F | Firstborn children are more highly motivated to achieve than later-born children. **p. 318** |

| T \| F | Children who are physically punished are more likely to be aggressive. **p. 328** |

| T \| F | Children who watch 2–4 hours of television a day will see 8,000 murders and another 100,000 acts of violence by the time they have finished elementary school. **p. 329** |

| T \| F | Children mechanically imitate the aggressive behavior they view in the media. **p. 330** |

| T \| F | The most common fear among preschoolers is fear of social disapproval. **p. 334** |

| T \| F | A 2½-year-old may know that she is a girl but still think that she can grow up to be a daddy. **p. 340** |

Jeremy and Jessica are both 2½ years old. They are standing at the water table in the preschool classroom. Jessica is filling a plastic container with water and spilling it out. She watches the water splash down the drain. Jeremy watches and then goes to get another container. He, too, fills his container with water and spills it out. The children stand side by side. They empty and refill their plastic pails; they glance at each other and exchange a few words. They continue playing like this for several minutes, until Jessica drops her pail and runs off to ride the tricycle. Soon after, Jeremy also loses interest and finds something else to do.

Meanwhile, 4½-year-olds Melissa and Mike are building in the block corner, making a huge rambling structure that they have decided is a spaceship. They talk animatedly as they work, negotiating who should be captain of the ship and who should be the space alien. Mike and Melissa take turns adding blocks. They continue to build, working together and talking as they play.

These observations illustrate some of the changes that occur in social development during early childhood. Toddlers often spend time watching and imitating each other, but they do not interact very much. Older preschoolers are more likely to take turns, work cooperatively toward a goal, and share. They often engage in fantasy play that involves adopting adult roles.

In this chapter, we explore social and emotional development in early childhood. We consider the roles played by parents, siblings, and peers. We examine child's play, helping and sharing, and aggression. Then we look at personality and emotional development. We begin with the development of the self-concept, move on to Erikson's stage of initiative versus guilt, and explore the changing nature of children's fears. Finally, we discuss the development of gender roles and gender differences in behavior.

Philip James Corwin/Corbis

309

10.1 Influences on Development: Parents, Siblings, and Peers

Young children usually spend most of their time within the family. Most parents attempt to foster certain behaviors in their children (Laible et al., 2015). They want them to develop a sense of responsibility and conform to family routines. They want them to develop into well-adjusted individuals. They want them to acquire social skills. In other words, they want to ensure healthy social and emotional development. How do parents go about trying to achieve these goals? What part do siblings play? How do children's peers influence social and emotional development?

What Are the Dimensions of Child Rearing?

Parents have different approaches to rearing their children. Investigators of parental patterns of child rearing have found it useful to classify them according to two broad dimensions: warmth–coldness and restrictiveness–permissiveness (Baumrind, 1989, 2013). Warm parents and cold parents can be either restrictive or permissive.

Warmth–Coldness

Warm parents are affectionate toward their children. They tend to hug and kiss them and smile at them frequently. They are caring and supportive and generally behave in ways that communicate their enjoyment of their children.

Cold parents may not enjoy being with their children and may have few feelings of affection for them. They are likely to complain about their children's behavior, saying that they are naughty or have "minds of their own." Warm parents may also say that their children have "minds of their own," but they are frequently proud of and entertained by their children's stubborn behavior. Even when they are irked by it, they usually focus on attempting to change it instead of rejecting the children. Warm parents are also less likely than cold parents to use physical discipline (Holden et al., 2011).

It requires no stretch of the imagination to conclude that it is better to be warm than cold toward children. The children of parents who are warm and accepting are more likely to develop internalized standards of conduct—a moral sense or conscience (Gauvain, 2013). Parental warmth also is related to the child's social and emotional well-being (Holden et al., 2011).

Where does parental warmth come from? Some of it reflects parental beliefs about how to best rear children, and some of it reflects parents' tendencies to imitate the behavior of their own parents. But research by E. Mavis Hetherington and her colleagues (Feinberg et al., 2001) suggests that genetic factors may be involved as well.

Restrictiveness–Permissiveness

Parents must generally decide how restrictive they will be. How will they respond when children make excessive noise, play with dangerous objects, damage property, mess up their rooms, hurt others, go nude, or masturbate? Parents who are restrictive tend to impose rules and to watch their children closely.

Consistent control combined with support and affection is termed the **authoritative** style of parenting (Baumrind, 2013). On the other hand, if "restrictiveness" means physical punishment, interference, or intrusiveness, it can have negative effects, such as disobedience, rebelliousness, and lower levels of cognitive development (Grusec & Davidov, 2015; Larzelere et al., 2013).

authoritative A child-rearing style in which parents are restrictive and demanding, yet communicative and warm.

Permissive parents impose few, if any, rules and supervise their children less closely. They allow their children to do what is "natural"—make noise, treat toys carelessly (although they may also extensively childproof their homes to protect their children and the furniture), and experiment with their own bodies. They may also allow their children to show some aggression, intervening only when another child is in danger. Parents may be permissive for different reasons. Some parents believe that children need the freedom to express their natural urges. Others may simply be uninterested and uninvolved.

Cross-cultural research suggests that the permissive parenting style is connected with higher self-esteem and adjustment, compared with other parenting styles, in Spain and Brazil (Martínez et al., 2003). The investigators suggested that these cultures may be somewhat more "laid back" than "Anglo-Saxon" cultures and that there is a better fit between indulgence of children and their adjustment in Spanish and Latin American cultures.

How Do Parents Enforce Restrictions?

Regardless of their general approaches to child rearing, most (if not all) parents are restrictive now and then, even if only when they are teaching their children not to run into the street or touch a hot stove. Parents tend to use the methods of induction, power assertion, and withdrawal of love.

Inductive Techniques

Inductive methods aim to impart knowledge that will enable children to produce desirable behavior in similar situations. The main inductive technique is "reasoning," or explaining why one kind of behavior is good and another is not. Reasoning with a 1- or 2-year-old can be basic. "Don't do that—it hurts!" qualifies as reasoning with toddlers. "It hurts!" is an explanation, although a brief one (Grusec, 2014).

Inductive Reasoning Inductive methods for enforcing restrictions attempt to teach children the principles they should use in guiding their own behavior. This mother is using the inductive technique of reasoning.

inductive Characteristic of disciplinary methods, such as reasoning, that try to teach an understanding of the principles behind parental demands.

Power-Assertive Methods

Power-assertive methods include physical punishment and denial of privileges. Parents often justify physical punishment with sayings such as "Spare the rod, spoil the child." Parents may insist that power assertion is necessary because their children are noncompliant. And let us not forget that the majority of American parents believe that spanking is sometimes necessary (Child Trends Data Bank, 2012). However, the use of power-assertive methods is related to parental authoritarianism as well as to children's behavior (Grusec & Davidov, 2015; Larzelere et al., 2013). Parental power-assertion is associated with lower acceptance by peers, poorer grades, and higher rates of antisocial behavior in children. The more parents use power-assertive techniques, the less children appear to develop internal standards of moral conduct. Parental punishment and rejection are often linked with aggression and delinquency (Grusec & Davidov, 2015).

Withdrawal of Love

Some parents control children by threatening them with withdrawal of love. They isolate or ignore misbehaving children. Because most children need parental approval and contact, loss of love can be more threatening than physical punishment. Withdrawal of love may foster compliance, but it may also instill guilt and anxiety (Grusec, 2014; Grusec & Davidov, 2015).

Preschoolers more readily comply when asked to do something than when asked to stop doing something (Kochanska et al., 2001). One way to manage children who are doing something wrong or bad is to involve them in something else.

What Parenting Styles Are Involved in the Transmission of Values and Standards?

Traditional views of the ways in which children acquire values and standards for behavior focus on parenting styles. Psychologist Diana Baumrind (1989, 2013) studied the relationship between parenting styles and the development of competent behavior in young children. She used the dimensions of warmth–coldness and restrictiveness–permissiveness. She developed a grid of four parenting styles based on whether parents are high or low on each of the two dimensions, as seen in Table 10.1 ●.

Authoritative Parents

The parents of the most capable children are rated as high in both parental behavior patterns listed in Table 10.1. They make strong efforts to control their children (i.e., they are highly restrictive), and they make strong demands for maturity. However, they also reason with their children and show them strong support and feelings of love. Baumrind (2013), as noted, applies the label *authoritative* to these parents to

● TABLE 10.1

Baumrind's Patterns of Parenting

Parental Style	Parental Behavior Patterns	
	Restrictiveness and Control	Warmth and Responsiveness
Authoritative	High	High
Authoritarian	High	Low
Permissive–Indulgent	Low	High
Rejecting–Neglecting	Low	Low

Source: Based on Baumrind, D. (1989). Rearing competent children. In W. Damon (Ed.). Child development today and tomorrow (pp. 349–378). San Francisco: Jossey-Bass.

suggest that they have a clear vision of what they want their children to do but they also respect their children and provide them with warmth.

Compared to other children, the children of authoritative parents tend to show self-reliance and independence, high self-esteem, high levels of activity and exploratory behavior, and social competence. They are highly motivated to achieve and do well in school (Grusec, 2014; Grusec & Davidov, 2015).

Authoritarian Parents: "Because I Say So"

We noted that "Because I say so" may be a perfectly fine explanation as to why a 3-year-old should or should not do something. However, "Because I say so" could also be conceptualized as the motto of parents whom Baumrind labels as **authoritarian**. Authoritarian parents consider obedience to be a virtue, almost regardless of the demands being made on the child (or adult). Authoritarian parents believe in strict guidelines for determining right and wrong. They demand that their children accept these guidelines without question. Like authoritative parents, they are controlling. Unlike authoritative parents, however, their enforcement methods rely on coercion. Moreover, authoritarian parents do not communicate well with their children. They do not show respect for their children's viewpoints, and most researchers find them to be generally cold and rejecting. However, among some ethnic groups, authoritarianism reflects cultural values, and these authoritarian parents are also warm and reasonably flexible (Grusec, 2014). When families immigrate to societies with different values, they tend to bring their traditional values with them. In one specific example, Arabic speaking parents tend to bring authoritarian attitudes to Australia (Renzaho et al., 2011).

In Baumrind's research, the sons of authoritarian parents were relatively hostile and defiant, and the daughters were low in independence and dominance (Baumrind, 2013). Other researchers have found that children of authoritarian parents are less competent socially and academically than children of authoritative parents. Children of authoritarian parents also tend to be conflicted, anxious, and irritable. They are less friendly and spontaneous in their social interactions (Grusec & Davidov, 2015; Shuster et al., 2012). As adolescents, they may be conforming and obedient or, on the other hand, aggressive (Shuster et al., 2012). Some may be both: conforming and also demanding, aggressively, that their peers be conforming as well.

Permissive Parents

Baumrind found two types of parents who are permissive, as opposed to restrictive. One type is labeled permissive–indulgent, and the other is labeled rejecting–neglecting. **Permissive–indulgent** parents are rated low in their attempts to control their children and in their demands for mature behavior. They are easygoing and unconventional. Their brand of permissiveness is accompanied by high nurturance (warmth and responsiveness).

Rejecting–neglecting parents also are rated low in their demands for mature behavior and in their attempts to control their children. But unlike indulgent parents, they are low in warmth and responsiveness.

The neglectful parenting style is associated with poor outcomes for children. By and large, the children of neglectful parents are the least competent,

authoritarian A child-rearing style in which parents demand submission and obedience from their children but are not very communicative and warm.

permissive–indulgent A child-rearing style in which parents are not controlling and restrictive but are warm.

rejecting–neglecting A child-rearing style in which parents are neither restrictive and controlling nor supportive and responsive.

Zoey/Image Source

A Permissive Parent Some parents are considered permissive and demand little of their children in terms of mature behavior or control. Permissive-indulgent parents still provide plenty of warmth and support for their children, whereas rejecting-neglecting parents tend to neglect or ignore their children.

responsible, and mature and the most prone to problem behaviors. Children of permissive–indulgent parents, like those of neglectful parents, show less competence in school and more deviant behavior (such as misconduct and substance abuse) than children of more restrictive, controlling parents. But children from permissive–indulgent homes, unlike those from neglectful homes, are fairly high in social competence and self-confidence (Baumrind, 2013; Grusec & Davidov, 2015).

How Do the Situation and the Child, Herself, Influence Parenting Styles?

Parenting styles are not just a one-way street from parent to child. Parenting styles also depend partly on the situation and partly on the characteristics of the child (Grusec, 2006; Grusec & Davidov, 2015).

One example of how the situation affects the parenting style is that parents are more likely to use power-assertive techniques for dealing with aggressive behavior than for dealing with social withdrawal (Lipman et al., 2006; Sengsavang & Krettenauer, 2015). Parents prefer power assertion over induction when they believe that children understand the rules they have violated, are capable of acting appropriately, and are responsible for their bad behavior. Stressful life events, marital discord, and emotional problems all contribute to parental use of power assertion.

Baumrind's research suggests that we can make an effort to avoid some of the pitfalls of being authoritarian or overly permissive. Some recommended techniques that parents can use to help control and guide their children's behavior are listed in Table 10.2 ●.

How Do Siblings Influence Social and Emotional Development in Early Childhood?

Our neighbor—who will deny this story (but don't believe her)—admits that when she was 5, she would carefully walk her younger sister, then 2, into the middle of the street. And leave her there! Fortunately, both survived. They are quite close now. They literally lived to laugh about it.

Despite our neighbor's tale, children make tremendous advances in social skills and behavior during early childhood. Their play increasingly involves other children.

● TABLE 10.2

Advice for Parents in Guiding Young Children's Behavior

Do...	Don't...
• Reward good behavior with praises, smiles, and hugs.	• Pay attention only to a child's misbehavior.
• Give clear, simple, realistic rules appropriate to the child's age.	• Issue too many rules or enforce them haphazardly.
• Enforce rules with reasonable consequences.	• Try to control behavior solely in the child's domain (such as thumb sucking), which can lead to frustrating power struggles.
• Ignore annoying behavior such as whining and tantrums.	• Nag, lecture, shame, or induce guilt.
• Childproof the house, putting dangerous and breakable items out of reach. Then establish limits.	• Yell or spank.
• Be consistent.	• Be overly permissive.

They learn how to share, cooperate, and comfort others. But young children, like adults, can be aggressive as well as loving and helpful.

In many cases, children spend more time with their siblings in the early years than they spend with their parents. Siblings make a unique contribution to one another's social, emotional, and cognitive development (Dunn, 2015). They serve many functions, including giving physical care, providing emotional support and nurturance, offering advice and direction, serving as role models, providing social interaction that helps develop social skills, and making demands and imposing restrictions (Dunn, 2015). They also advance each other's cognitive development, as shown in research concerning false beliefs and the theory of mind (which were discussed in the previous chapter).

In early childhood, when siblings spend a great deal of time together, their interactions are often emotionally loaded and marked by both positive aspects (cooperation, teaching, nurturance) and negative aspects (conflict, control, competition) (Dunn, 2015). By and large, older siblings are more nurturant, but also more dominating, than younger siblings. Younger siblings are more likely to imitate older siblings and to accept their direction.

However, older siblings may also imitate younger siblings, especially when parents remark "how cute" the baby is being in front of the older child. At the age of 2 years 5 months, my daughter Allyn would pretend that she could not talk every once in a while, just like her 5-month-old sister Jordan.

In many cultures (including this one, laments my wife, a firstborn child), older girls are given the chore of caring for younger siblings (Underwood & Rosen, 2011). Younger siblings frequently turn to older sisters when the mother is unavailable. ("They still do," notes my wife.)

Parents often urge their children to stop fighting among themselves, and there are times when these conflicts look deadly (and occasionally they are). It is important to note, however, that garden-variety conflict among siblings can have positive outcomes. (Really!) It appears that conflict between siblings enhances their social competence, their development of self-identity (who they are and what they stand for), and their ability to rear their own children in a healthful manner (Ross et al., 2006). When adults look back on their childhood conflicts with their siblings, their memories of them are often positive. Nevertheless, severe sibling conflict sometimes leads to adjustment problems later on, such as engaging in risky behavior during adolescence, especially in brother–brother pairs (Solmeyer et al., 2014).

As siblings move from early childhood through middle childhood and into adolescence, their relationships change in at least two ways (Underwood & Rosen, 2011). First, as siblings grow more competent and their developmental statuses become similar, their relationship becomes more egalitarian. In other words, as later-born siblings grow older and become more self-sufficient, they need and accept less nurturance and direction from older siblings. Second, sibling relationships become less intense as children grow older. The exercise of power and the amount of conflict decline. The extent of warmth and closeness diminishes somewhat as well, although the attachment between siblings remains fairly strong throughout adolescence.

Other factors also affect the development of sibling relationships. For example, there is more conflict between siblings in families in which the parents treat the children differently (Dunn, 2015). Conflict between siblings also is greater when the relationships between the parents or between the parents and children are troubled (Dunn, 2015).

Adjusting to the Birth of a Sibling

The birth of a sister or brother is often a source of stress for young children because of changes in family relationships and the environment. When a new baby comes

Siblings Siblings make a unique contribution to one another's social, emotional, and cognitive development.

INDIVIDUALISM, COLLECTIVISM, AND PATTERNS OF CHILD REARING

Much of the research on parenting styles has been done with middle-class European American families. But parenting styles must be viewed within the context of particular cultures (Renzaho et al., 2011; Shuster et al., 2012). Socialization methods that appear authoritarian or punitive by middle-class standards may be used more frequently among poor families from ethnic minority groups to prepare children to cope with the hazards of daily life. Placing a high value on unquestioned obedience might be considered overly restrictive in a quiet middle-class neighborhood, but unquestioned obedience might well be warranted now and then in a more dangerous, inner-city environment. Poor families in other countries also tend to use authoritarian child-rearing styles.

A study by Kobayashi-Winata and Power (1989) compared the child-rearing practices of middle-class Japanese and American parents whose children ranged in age from 4 to 7. In both groups of families, the most compliant children had parents who provided opportunities for appropriate behavior and who used relatively little punishment. But American parents were more likely to rely on external punishments such as sending children to their rooms, whereas Japanese parents more often used verbal commands, reprimands, and explanations (see Table 10.3 ●).

These differences in disciplinary practices apparently reflect cultural differences. Cross-cultural research reveals that people in the United States and many northern European nations tend to be individualistic (Becker et al., 2012). In contrast, many people from cultures in Africa, Asia, and Central and South America tend to be collectivistic (Becker et al., 2012).

Individualists tend to define themselves in terms of their personal identities and to give priority to their personal goals (Hartung et al., 2010; Triandis, 2005). When asked to complete the statement "I am...," they are likely to respond in terms of their personality traits ("I am outgoing," "I am artistic") or their occupations ("I am a nurse," "I am a systems analyst"). In contrast,

● TABLE 10.3

Cultural Values and Child-Rearing Techniques in the United States and Japan

Culture	Parental Values	Child-Rearing Practices
United States middle class	• Early socialization • Independence • Individualism	• Expect child to follow more rules • Listen to child's opinion • Use external punishment (e.g., send child to his or her room)
Japanese middle class	• Group harmony • Dependence on others • Conformity	• Make fewer demands • Be more indulgent • Use verbal commands • Use reprimands and explanations

regression A return to behaviors characteristic of earlier stages of development.

individualist A person who defines herself or himself in terms of personal traits and gives priority to her or his own goals.

into the home, the mother pays relatively more attention to it and spends much less time in playful activities with the older child. No wonder the child may feel displaced and resentful of the affection lavished on the newborn. These feelings are reflected, for example, in the comments of a 3-year-old who worried that his new sister would take all his mother's love and not leave enough for him.

Children show a mixture of negative and positive reactions to the birth of a sibling. These include **regression** to babyish behaviors, such as increased clinging, crying, and toilet accidents. Anger and naughtiness may increase as well. But the same children often show increased independence and maturity, insisting on feeding or dressing themselves and helping to care for the baby (Underwood & Rosen, 2011).

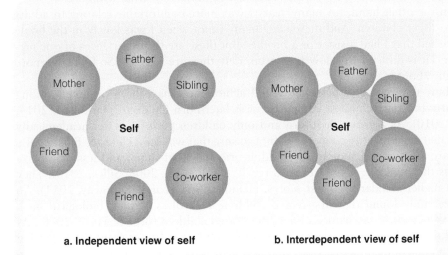

Figure 10.1 ■ The Self in Relation to Others from the Perspectives of Individualists and Collectivists
(a) To an individualist, the self is separate from other people. (b) To a collectivist, the self is complete only in terms of relationships to other people. Are there differences in the ways in which people in individualistic and collectivistic cultures rear their children?
Source: Based on Markus & Kitayama (1991).

a. Independent view of self

b. Interdependent view of self

collectivists tend to define themselves in terms of the groups to which they belong and to give priority to the group's goals (Berry & Triandis, 2006; Triandis, 2005). They feel complete in terms of their relationships with others (see Figure 10.1 ■). They are more likely than individualists to conform to group norms and judgments (Berry & Triandis, 2006; Hartung et al, 2010). When asked to complete the statement "I am…," they are more likely to respond in terms of their families, gender, or nation ("I am a father," "I am a Buddhist," "I am Japanese").

It must be noted, however, that individuals from within the same country can belong to different "cultures" in terms of individualistic and collectivistic tendencies. In Lebanon, for example, Ayyash-Abdo (2001) found that college students who spoke French or English were more likely to be individualistic than those who spoke mainly Arabic. Traditional Islamic values were connected with collectivism.

Other studies reveal additional differences in the child-rearing techniques of American and Far Eastern parents that appear to foster the American emphasis on early socialization and independence and the Chinese focus on group harmony and dependence on others (Chen & Eisenberg, 2012).

Reflect
- Do you think it is better to raise a child to be individualistic or collectivistic? Explain.
- We all belong to subcultures within the United States. Would you characterize your subculture as mainly individualistic or collectivistic? Explain.
- The culture of the United States is said to value "rugged individualism." Is that always true? Explain.
- Can you make the case that a culture or subculture is individualistic in some ways but collectivistic in others? Explain.

What can parents do to help a young child cope with the arrival of a new baby? For one thing, they can prepare the child by explaining in advance what is to come. For example, one item on the agenda of those who run sibling preparation classes in many locales is to reduce **sibling rivalry** when a new child is born into a family (Stanford University School of Medicine, 2012). Parental support is extremely important as well. Children show less distress following the birth of a sibling when the parents spend time with them, give them encouragement, and praise them (Kavcic & Zupancic, 2005).

Birth Order: Just Where Is the Child in the Family?

Let me confess at the beginning of this section that I am an only child. As I was developing, I experienced what I imagine are most of the advantages and, yes, drawbacks

collectivist A person who defines herself or himself in terms of relationships to other people and groups and gives priority to group goals.

sibling rivalry Jealousy or rivalry among brothers and sisters.

of being an only child. First and perhaps foremost, I was the little king in my household in the Bronx. A petty tyrant at best, and at worst. I enjoyed all the resources my family had to offer: a relatively good allowance (with which I bought a comic book a day—Superman did nothing that escaped my attention) and lots of parental attention. I never knew that we were poor because I got most of what I wanted.

On the other hand, for many years I was more comfortable relating to adults than to other children. And there were many times when I was lonely in the home and wished that I had a sister or a brother. But these are the experiences of one person, and it is difficult to know how accurately they are recalled. So let us be more scientific about it.

Many differences in personality and achievement have been observed among firstborn and only children compared with later-born children (Harkonen, 2014; Silles, 2010). As a group, firstborn and only children perform better academically (that's me) and are more cooperative (not so sure that was me) (Healy & Ellis, 2007). They are also helpful (not so sure), adult-oriented (that's me), and less aggressive (I guess that was me; it's not easy to recall) (Beck et al., 2006; Silles, 2010). They obtain higher standardized test scores, including SAT scores (Sulloway, 2011). An adoptee study found that first-reared children, regardless of their biological birth order, were more conscientious than later-reared children (Beer & Horn, 2000). As part of their achievement orientation, firstborn children also see themselves as being more in control of their successes (Phillips & Phillips, 2000). On the negative side, firstborn and only children show greater anxiety (that's me) and are less self-reliant (hmmm—I wonder).

TRUTH OR FICTION REVISITED: It is true that firstborn children, as a group, are more highly motivated to achieve than later-born children. But keep in mind that there are many (many!) exceptions to the rule. The research also remains unclear as to *why* firstborns are often more highly motivated.

Interviews with the parents of 478 children ranging in age from 3 to 9 years found that firstborn children are more likely than later-born children to have imaginary playmates (Bouldin & Pratt, 1999). It is Allyn, our firstborn, who had the imaginary playmate Loveliness. Our second-born (Jordan) and our third-born (Taylor) may have been too busy coping with older siblings to have imaginary playmates.

Later-born children may learn to act aggressively to compete for the attention of their parents and older siblings (Silles, 2010). They also contend with the fact that they do not come first. Perhaps for that reason, their self-concepts tend to be lower than those of firstborn or only children. But the social skills they acquire from dealing with their family position seem to translate into greater popularity with peers. They tend to be more rebellious, liberal, and agreeable than firstborn children—factors that may all be connected with their popularity (Barni et al., 2014).

Differences in personality and achievement among firstborn and later-born children may be linked to contrasting styles in parenting. Firstborn children start life as only children. For a year or more, they receive the full attention of parents. Even after other children come along, parents still tend to relate more often to the first child. Parents continue to speak at levels appropriate for the firstborn. Parents impose tougher restrictions on firstborn children and make greater demands of them. Parents are more highly involved in their activities. Firstborn children are often recruited to help teach younger siblings (Zajonc, 2001). As I can testify, being asked to teach something (often) prompts one to learn something about it.

By and large, parents are more relaxed and flexible with later-born children. Children are aware of the greater permissiveness often given to later-born children and may complain about it. (Endlessly.) Why are parents more indulgent with later-born children? They have probably gained some self-confidence in child rearing.

They see that the firstborn child is turning out just fine. (All right, the firstborn child usually turns out to be just fine, and sometimes "just fine" needs to be qualified as "just fine much of the time.") Parents may therefore assume that later-born children will also turn out, well, just fine. In any event, my wife and I were more relaxed with Jordan and with Taylor than we were with Allyn.

There is also a more negative interpretation of parents' relative "relaxation" in rearing later-born children. Parents have just so many resources, in terms of time, energy, and, yes, money. As new children come along, they dilute the resources, so not as much can be devoted to each of them.

How Do Peers Influence Social and Emotional Development in Early Childhood?

The importance of **peers** in the development of the young child is widely recognized. As children move into the preschool years, they spend more time in the company of other children. Peer interactions serve many functions. Children learn social skills in the peer group: sharing, helping, taking turns, dealing with conflict. They learn how to lead and how to follow. Physical and cognitive skills develop through peer interactions. Peers also provide emotional support (Bukowski et al., 2015).

Infants first show positive interest in one another at about 6 months of age. If they are placed on the floor facing one another, they will smile, occasionally imitate one another, and often touch one another. Social interaction increases over the next few months, but during the first year, contacts between infants tend to be brief. In the second year, children show more interest in each other and interact by playing with each other's toys. But they still show relatively little social interaction (Bukowski et al., 2015). By about 2 years of age, however, children imitate one another's play and engage in social games such as follow the leader (Bukowski et al., 2015; Underwood & Rosen, 2011). By the age of 2, children have preferences for a few particular playmates.

The preference of toddlers for certain other children is an early sign of friendship (Bukowski et al., 2015). Friendship extends beyond casual interactions. It is characterized by shared positive experiences and feelings of attachment (Gleason & Hohmann, 2006). Even early friendships can be fairly stable. One- to 6-year-olds tend to maintain their friendships from one year to the next, some for as long as 3 years (Rubin et al., 2006). On the other hand, parental conflict can spill over into peer conflict. Children of fighting parents are less tolerant of the bumps and bruises of peer relationships (Du Rocher Schudlich et al., 2004).

Preschool children behave somewhat differently toward their friends than toward ordinary playmates. Friends, compared with other children, show higher levels of interaction, helpful behavior, and smiling and laughing and more frequent cooperation and collaboration (Rubin et al., 2006). Conflicts between young friends are less intense and are resolved more readily than other conflicts.

What are children's conceptions of friendships? When preschoolers are asked what they like about their friends, they typically mention the toys and activities they share (Gleason & Hohmann, 2006). Children in early elementary school usually report that their friends are the children with whom they do things and have fun (Gleason & Hohmann, 2006). Not until late childhood and adolescence do friends' traits and notions of trust, communication, and intimacy become key aspects of friendship.

IS386/Image Source Plus/Alamy

Friendship Friendship takes on different meanings as children develop. Preschoolers focus on sharing toys and activities. Five- to 7-year-olds report that friends are children with whom they have fun. Sharing confidences becomes important in late childhood and adolescence.

peers Children of the same age. (More generally, people of similar background and social standing.)

Section Review

1. Investigators of child rearing find it useful to classify parents according to two dimensions: warmth–coldness and _____.

2. _____ methods of enforcing restrictions attempt to give children knowledge that will enable them to generate desirable behavior patterns in similar situations.

3. _____ parents are both warm and restrictive.

4. _____ parents believe that obedience is a virtue for its own sake.

5. _____-born children tend to be the most highly motivated to achieve.

Reflect & Relate: Where do you fit into your family of origin? Are you a firstborn or only child? Were you born later? How does your own development and personality compare to the stereotypes discussed in this section?

10.2 Social Behavior: In the World, Among Others

During the early childhood years, children make tremendous strides in the development of social skills and behavior. Their play activities increasingly involve other children. They learn how to share, cooperate, and comfort others. But young children, like adults, are complex beings. They can be aggressive at times, as well as loving and helpful. We will turn now to the development of social behavior in the early years.

What Are the Characteristics of Play? How Does Play Affect Children's Development?

While children play, researchers work to understand just how they do so. They have found that play has many characteristics. It is meaningful, pleasurable, voluntary, and internally motivated. Play is fun! But play also serves many important functions in the life of the young child. Play helps children develop cognitive skills, motor skills, and coordination (Burghardt, 2015). It contributes to social development because children learn to share play materials, take turns, and try on new roles through **dramatic play**. It supports the development of such cognitive qualities as curiosity, exploration, symbolic thinking, and problem solving (Bergen, 2015; Christie & Roskos, 2015). Play may even help children learn to control impulses (Bergen, 2015).

Play and Cognitive Development

Play contributes to and expresses milestones in cognitive development. Jean Piaget identified four kinds of play, each characterized by increasing cognitive complexity (De Lisi, 2015):

- *Functional play.* Beginning in the sensorimotor stage, the first kind of play involves repetitive motor activity, such as rolling a ball or running and laughing.
- *Symbolic play.* Also called pretend play, imaginative play, or dramatic play, symbolic play emerges toward the end of the sensorimotor stage and increases during early childhood. In symbolic play, children create settings, characters, and scripts (Mottweiler & Taylor, 2014).
- *Constructive play.* Constructive play is common in early childhood. Children use objects or materials to draw something or make something, such as a tower of blocks.
- *Formal games.* The most complex form of play, according to Piaget, involves formal games with rules. These include board games, which are sometimes

dramatic play Play in which children enact social roles; made possible by the attainment of symbolic thought. A form of pretend play.

Symbolic Play These 5-year-old girls are pretending that they are riding on a train composed of a row of chairs that they have put together.

enhanced or invented by children, and games involving motor skills, such as marbles and hopscotch, ball games involving sides or teams, and video games. Such games may involve social interaction as well as physical activity and rules. People play such games for a lifetime.

Other researchers have focused on the social dimensions of play.

Theories of Play

Psychologists and sociologists have been studying categories of play for the better part of a century. Mildred Parten (Dyson, 2015; Henricks, 2015), for example, observed the development of six categories of play among 2- to 5-year-old nursery school children: unoccupied play, solitary play, onlooker play, parallel play, associative play, and cooperative play (see Table 10.4 ●). Unoccupied play, solitary play, and onlooker play are considered types of **nonsocial play**—play in which children do not interact socially. Nonsocial play occurs more often in 2- and 3-year-olds than in older preschoolers. Parallel play, associative play, and cooperative play are considered **social play**. In each type of social play, children are influenced by other children as they play. Parten found that associative play and cooperative play become common by age 5. They are more likely to be found among older and more experienced preschoolers (Bukowski et al., 2015). Girls are somewhat more likely than boys to engage in social play (Underwood & Rosen, 2011).

But there are exceptions to these age trends in social play. Nonsocial play can involve educational activities that foster cognitive development. In fact, many 4- and 5-year-olds spend a good deal of time in parallel constructive play. For instance, they may work on puzzles or build with blocks near other children. Parallel constructive players are frequently perceived by teachers to be socially skillful and are popular with their peers. Some toddlers are also more capable of social play than one might expect, given their age. Two-year-olds who have older siblings or a great deal of group experience may engage in advanced forms of social play (Dunn, 2015).

Gender Differences in Play

One of the key gender differences in play concerns choice of toys. Lisa Serbin and her colleagues (2001) explored infants' visual preferences for gender-stereotyped

nonsocial play Forms of play (solitary play or onlooker play) in which play is not influenced by the play of nearby children.

social play Play in which children interact with others and are influenced by their play. Examples include parallel play, associative play, and cooperative play.

Categories of Play, According to Parten

Category	Nonsocial or Social?	Description
Unoccupied play	Nonsocial	Children do not appear to be playing. They may engage in random movements that seem to be without a goal. Unoccupied play appears to be the least frequent kind of play in nursery schools.
Solitary play	Nonsocial	Children play with toys by themselves, independently of the children around them. Solitary players do not appear to be influenced by children around them. They make no effort to approach them.
Onlooker play	Nonsocial	Children observe other children who are at play. Onlookers frequently talk to the children they are observing and may make suggestions, but they do not overtly join in.
Parallel play	Social	Children play with toys similar to those of surrounding children. However, they treat the toys as they choose and do not directly interact with other children.
Associative play	Social	Children interact and share toys. However, they do not seem to share group goals. Although they interact, individuals still treat toys as they choose. The association with the other children appears to be more important than the nature of the activity. They seem to enjoy each other's company.
Cooperative play	Social	Children interact to achieve common group goals. The play of each child is subordinated to the purposes of the group. One or two group members direct the activities of others. There is also a division of labor, with different children taking different roles. Children may pretend to be members of a family, animals, space monsters, and all sorts of creatures.

Associative Play or Cooperative Play? In associative play, children share toys but do not share common goals. In cooperative play the activities of each child are subordinated to the goals of the group.

Capable97/Shutterstock.com

toys using the assumption that infants spend more time looking at objects that are of greater interest. They found that both girls and boys showed significant preferences for gender-stereotyped toys by 18 months of age. Other research reveals that infants show visual preferences for gender-stereotyped toys as early as 3–8 months of age (Alexander et al., 2009). Although preferences for gender-typed toys are well developed by the ages of 15–36 months, girls are more likely to stray from the stereotypes (Bussey & Bandura, 1999; Underwood & Rosen, 2011). Girls ask for and play with "boys' toys" such as cars and trucks more often than boys choose dolls and other "girls' toys." "Cross-role" activities may reflect the greater prestige of "masculine" activities and traits in American culture. Therefore, a boy playing with "girls' toys" might be seen as taking on an inferior role. A girl playing with "boys' toys" might be considered to have a desire for power or esteem.

Girls and boys differ not only in toy preferences but also in their choice of play environments and activities. During the preschool and early elementary school years, boys prefer vigorous physical outdoor activities such as climbing, playing with large vehicles, and rough-and-tumble play (Underwood & Rosen, 2011). In middle childhood, boys spend more time than girls in play groups of five or more children and in competitive play. Girls are more likely than boys to engage in arts and crafts and domestic play. Girls' activities are more closely directed and structured by adults (A. Campbell et al., 2002).

Why do children show these early preferences for gender-stereotyped toys and activities? Biological factors may play a role; for example, boys' slightly greater strength and activity levels and girls' slightly greater physical maturity and coordination. But also, adults treat girls and boys differently. They provide gender-stereotyped toys and room furnishings and encourage gender typing in play and household chores (Leaper, 2011). Children are active participants in the process, however. They tend to seek out information on which kinds of toys and play are considered to be "masculine" or "feminine" and then to conform their preferences and behavior to the label (Martin & Dinella, 2012; Martin & Ruble, 2004).

Some studies find that children who "cross the line" by showing interest in toys or activities considered appropriate for the other gender are often teased, ridiculed, rejected, or ignored by their parents, teachers, other adults, and peers. Boys are more likely than girls to be criticized (Zosuls et al., 2011).

Another well-documented finding is that children begin to prefer playmates of the same gender by the age of 2. Girls develop this preference somewhat earlier than boys (Hay et al., 2004). The tendency strengthens during middle childhood.

Two factors may be involved in the choice of the gender of playmates in early childhood. One is that boys' play is more oriented toward dominance, aggression, and rough play (Hines, 2011b). The second is that boys are not very responsive to girls' polite suggestions.

Philip James Corwin/Corbis

A Girl Enjoying a Game of Baseball Although preferences for gender-typed toys are well established by the age of 3, girls are more likely to stray from the stereotypes, as in this photograph of a girl playing the masculine-typed game of baseball.

What Is Prosocial Behavior? How Does It Develop?

My wife recalls always trying to help others in early childhood. She remembers sharing her toys, often at her own expense. She had many sad times when toys or favors she gave were not returned or when toys were broken by others.

Prosocial behavior, sometimes known as *altruism*, is behavior intended to benefit another without expectation of reward. Prosocial behavior includes helping and comforting others in distress, sharing, and cooperating.

Even in the first year of life, children begin to share. They spontaneously offer food and objects to others (Markova & Legerstee, 2006). In the second year, children continue to share objects, and they also begin to comfort distressed companions and help others with tasks and chores (Israel et al., 2015).

prosocial behavior Behavior intended to benefit another without expectation of reward.

By the preschool and early school years, children frequently engage in prosocial behavior. Some types of prosocial behavior occur more often than others. One study observed 4- and 7-year-olds at home and found that helping occurred more often than sharing, affection, and reassuring (Grusec, 1991). Research suggests that the development of prosocial behavior is linked to the development of other capabilities in the young child, such as empathy and taking the perspective of others (Grusec & Hastings, 2015).

Empathy: "I Feel Your Pain"

Empathy is sensitivity to the feelings of others. It is the ability to understand and share another person's feelings and is connected with sharing and cooperation. A survey of American and Japanese mothers of preschoolers found that both groups reported that cooperativeness and interpersonal sensitivity were the most desirable characteristics in young children (Olson et al., 2001).

From infancy, children respond emotionally when others are in distress (Roberts et al., 2014). Infants frequently begin to cry when they hear other children crying, although this early agitated response may be largely reflexive. Even so, crying might signal an early development in empathy.

Empathy appears to promote prosocial behavior and to decrease aggressive behavior, and these links are evident by the second year (Grusec & Hastings, 2015; Roberts et al., 2014). During the second year, many children approach other children and adults who are in distress and try to help them. They may hug a crying child or tell the child not to cry. Toddlers who are rated as emotionally unresponsive to the feelings of others are more likely to behave aggressively throughout the school years (Olson et al., 2000).

Girls, as a group, show more empathy than boys (Roberts et al., 2014). It is unclear whether this gender difference reflects socialization of girls to be attuned to the emotions of others or genetic factors, although some researchers argue that exposure to testosterone has a suppressive effect on empathy (Durdiakova et al., 2015; Zilioli et al., 2014).

Perspective-Taking: Standing in Someone Else's Shoes

According to Piaget, children in the preoperational stage tend to be egocentric; that is, they tend not to be able to see things from the vantage points of others. Various cognitive abilities, such as being able to take another person's perspective, are related to knowing when someone is in need or distress. Perspective-taking skills improve with age, and so do prosocial skills. Among children of the same age, those with better developed perspective-taking ability also show more prosocial behavior and less aggressive behavior (Grusec & Hastings, 2015).

Influences on Prosocial Behavior

Yes, altruistic behavior is usually defined as prosocial behavior that occurs in the absence of rewards or the expectation of rewards. Nevertheless, prosocial behavior is influenced by rewards and punishments. Observations of nursery school children show that the peers of children who are cooperative, friendly, and generous respond more positively to them than they do to children whose behavior is self-centered (Grusec & Davidov, 2015; Grusec & Hastings, 2015). Children who are rewarded in this way for acting prosocially are likely to continue these behaviors (Grusec & Davidov, 2015).

Some children at early ages are made responsible for doing household chores and caring for younger siblings. They are taught helping and nurturance skills, and their performances are selectively reinforced by other children and adults. Children

empathy Ability to share another person's feelings.

who are given such tasks are more likely to show prosocial behavior than children who do not have such responsibilities (Bremner et al., 2010).

There is evidence that children can acquire sharing behavior by observing models who help and share. In one experiment in sharing, 29- to 36-month-olds were more likely to share toys with playmates who first shared toys with them (Levitt et al., 1985). The children appeared to model—and reciprocate—the sharing behavior of their peers.

It seems that children's prosocial behavior is influenced by the kinds of interactions they have with their parents. For example, prosocial behavior and empathy are enhanced in children who are securely attached to their parents and in children whose mothers show a high degree of empathy (Roberts et al., 2014).

Parenting styles also affect the development of prosocial behavior. Prosocial behavior is fostered when parents use inductive techniques such as explaining how behavior affects others ("You made Josh cry. It's not nice to hit"). Parents of prosocial children are more likely to expect mature behavior from their children. They are less likely to use power-assertive techniques of discipline (Roberts et al., 2014).

Aggression—The Dark Side of Social Interaction: How Does It Develop?

Children, like adults, are complex beings. Not only can they be loving and altruistic, but they can also be aggressive. Some children, of course, are more aggressive than others. Aggression consists of behavior intended to cause pain or hurt to another person.

Aggressive behaviors, like other social behaviors, seem to follow developmental patterns. For one thing, the aggression of preschoolers is frequently instrumental or possession-oriented (Persson, 2005). That is, young children tend to use aggression to obtain the toys and things they want, such as a favored seat at the table or in the car. But older preschoolers are more likely to resolve their conflicts over toys by sharing than by fighting (Caplan et al., 1991). Anger and aggressive behavior in preschoolers usually lead other preschoolers to reject them (Gower et al., 2014; Morine et al., 2011).

By age 6 or 7, aggression tends to become hostile and person-oriented. Children taunt and criticize each other and call each other names; they also attack one another physically.

Aggressive behavior appears to be generally stable and predictive of a wide variety of social and emotional difficulties in adulthood (Mesman et al., 2001; Nagin & Tremblay, 2001). Boys are more likely than girls to show aggression from childhood through adulthood, a finding that has been documented in many cultures (Frieze & Li, 2010). Olson and her colleagues (2000) found that toddlers who were perceived as difficult and defiant were more likely to behave aggressively throughout the school years. A longitudinal study of more than 600 children found that aggressive 8-year-olds tended to remain more aggressive than their peers 22 years later, at age 30 (Eron et al., 1991). Aggressive children of both genders were more likely to have criminal convictions as adults, to abuse their spouses, and to drive while drunk. Tendencies toward aggressiveness remain remarkably stable from childhood to adulthood (Kokko et al., 2014).

What Are the Causes of Aggression in Children?

Why are some children more aggressive than others? Aggression in childhood appears to result from a complex interplay of biological factors and environmental factors such as reinforcement and modeling.

DO YOU HAVE TO BE TAUGHT TO HATE?

In the musical *South Pacific,* Lieutenant Cable sings, "You've got to be taught [to] hate . . . people whose skin is a diff'rent shade. You've got to be taught before you are six or seven or eight [to] hate all the people your relatives hate!"

It is widely assumed that children learn racial prejudices at home, but the evidence has been less than clear. No clear, consistent relationship has been found between the expressed, or explicit, racial attitudes of European American parents and the racial attitudes of their children (Castelli et al., 2009). Yet in early childhood, children show preferences for playing with members of their own ethnic group and are more likely to ascribe positive traits to their own ethnic group (Castelli et al., 2007). The attitudes of children and their parents' attitudes toward people of other races can differ, although there is apparently some overlap when the children strongly identify with their parents (Sinclair et al., 2005).

Because of the inconsistency of findings with expressed or explicit attitudes, some recent research has turned to the assessment of implicit attitudes, as shown, for example, in body language in the presence of the other persons: body posture, eye contact, and the like (Hofmann et al., 2008). Are young children sensitive to these nonverbal behaviors and their implications? Research suggests that preschoolers accurately interpret what it means for adults of different races to lean toward one another or back away when they

are interacting, and to maintain or avoid eye contact (Castelli et al., 2008).

In a recent study, Luigi Castelli and his colleagues (2009) recruited 72 middle-class Italian families living in northern Italy. Confidentiality was guaranteed. In each family, the mother, the father, and a biological child (36 girls and 36 boys with a mean age of 58 months) participated.

Children were assessed individually in their kindergartens. They were shown two drawings, one of a white preschooler and one of a black preschooler, and they were asked which of the two they would prefer to play with. Two out of three children (67%) said they would prefer the white playmate. Then the children were given eight cards, one at a time, with a single trait written on each. Four were positive (*nice, happy, clean, likable*); four were negative (*ugly, sad, dirty, bad*). The experimenter asked the child to assign each card to either the white child or the black child. As a result, each pictured child could obtain a score between 0 and 4 on positive traits, and the same on negative traits. As shown in Figure 10.2 ■, positive traits were more likely to be attributed to the white child and negative traits to the black child.

The parents were tested on scales of explicit (intentional) and implicit (unconscious) prejudice. Results on the explicit scale (the Blatant-Subtle Prejudice Scale) showed that the parents tended to express

Evolutionary Theory

Is aggression "natural"? According to evolutionary theory, more individuals are produced than can find food and survive into adulthood. Therefore, there is a struggle for survival. Individuals who possess characteristics that give them an advantage in this struggle are more likely to reach reproductive maturity and contribute their genes to the next generation. In many species, then, whatever genes are linked to aggressive behavior are more likely to be transmitted to new generations (Ray, 2012).

Biological Factors

Evidence suggests that genetic factors may be involved in aggressive behavior, including criminal and antisocial behavior (Bezdjian et al., 2011). Jasmine Tehrani and Sarnoff Mednick (2000) report that there is a greater concordance (agreement) rate for criminal behavior between monozygotic (MZ) twins, who fully share their genetic code, than between dizygotic (DZ) twins, who, like other brothers and sisters, share only half of their genetic code.

If genetics is involved in aggression, genes may do their work at least in part through the male sex hormone testosterone. Testosterone is apparently connected with feelings nonprejudiced—even quite egalitarian—attitudes toward black people. However, results on the implicit scale found that fathers and mothers both showed a good deal of implicit prejudice.

Statistical techniques revealed that there was a statistically significant association between children's choices and their mothers' implicit racial attitudes. There was no connection with the mothers' explicit attitudes. There was no relationship between children's behaviors and their fathers' explicit or implicit attitudes. In terms of assigning positive or negative traits to the white and black children, the greater the mothers' implicit prejudice, the fewer positive traits and the more negative traits their children attributed to the black child. We should note, however, that although the correlations between the mothers' implicit attitudes and their children's choices were too high to be due to chance, they were only of the magnitudes 0.29, 0.339, and 0.352 (see Table 1 in the article). Positive correlations, as noted in Chapter 1, can range from 0.00 to 1.00. The correlations found in the present study must be considered mild, not even moderate.

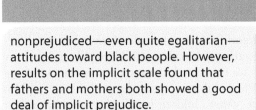

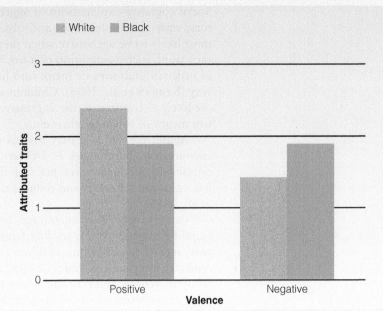

Figure 10.2 ■

Mean number of positive and negative traits attributed to the white child and to the black child.

Source: Castelli et al. (2009).

Reflect What can we conclude from this study? Is there a relationship between young children's racial attitudes and the implicit racial attitudes of their mothers? How strong is that relationship? Can you think of other factors in the development of racial preferences?

of self-confidence, high activity levels, and—the negative side—aggressiveness (Carre & Olmstead, 2015; Platje et al., 2015). Males are more aggressive than females, and males have higher levels of testosterone than females (Portnoy et al., 2014). Studies show, for example, that 9- to 11-year-old boys with conduct disorders are likely to have higher testosterone levels than their less aggressive peers (Booth et al., 2003; Chance et al., 2000). Research with same-gender female DZ twins and opposite-gender DZ twins suggests that fetal exposure to male sex hormones (in this case, from intrauterine exposure to a male fraternal twin) may heighten aggressiveness (Cohen-Bendahan et al., 2005).

Cognitive Factors

Aggressive boys are more likely than nonaggressive boys to incorrectly interpret the behavior of other children as potentially harmful (Dodge et al., 2002; Yaros et al., 2014). This bias may make the aggressive child quick to respond aggressively in social situations. Research with primary schoolchildren finds that children who believe in the legitimacy of aggression are more likely to behave aggressively when they are presented with social provocations (Gini et al., 2014; Underwood & Rosen, 2011).

Aggressive children are also often found to be lacking in empathy and in the ability to see things from the perspective of other people (Grusec & Hastings, 2015).

They fail to conceptualize the experiences of their victims, so they are less likely to inhibit their aggressive impulses.

Social Cognitive Theory

Social cognitive explanations of aggression focus on the role of environmental factors, such as reinforcement and observational learning. Children, like adults, are most likely to be aggressive when they are frustrated in attempts to gain something they want, such as attention or a toy. When children repeatedly push, shove, and hit in order to grab toys or break into line, other children usually let them have their way (Kempes et al., 2005). Children who are thus rewarded for acting aggressively are likely to continue to use aggressive means, especially if they do not have alternative means of achieving their ends.

Aggressive children may associate with peers who value their aggression and encourage it (Stauffacher & DeHart, 2006). Aggressive children have often been rejected by less aggressive peers, a fact that decreases their motivation to please less aggressive children and reduces their opportunity to learn social skills (Morine et al., 2011).

Parents may also encourage aggressive behavior, sometimes inadvertently. Gerald Patterson (2005) studied families in which parents use coercion as the primary means for controlling children's behavior. In a typical pattern, parents threaten, criticize, and punish a "difficult" or "impossible" child. The child then responds by whining, yelling, and refusing to comply until the parents give in. Both parents and child are relieved when the cycle ends. Thus, when the child misbehaves again, the parents become yet more coercive and the child yet more defiant, until parents or child gives in. A study with 407 5-year-olds found that the Patterson model predicts aggressive behavior in both genders (Eddy et al., 2001).

Children learn not only from the effects of their own behavior but also from observing the behavior of others. They may model the aggressive behavior of their peers, their parents, or their communities at large (Underwood, 2011). Children are more apt to imitate what their parents do than to heed what they say. If adults say they disapprove of aggression but smash furniture or hit each other when frustrated, children are likely to develop the notion that this is the way to handle frustration.

> **TRUTH OR FICTION REVISITED:** It is true that children who are physically punished are more likely to be aggressive themselves. Perhaps physically aggressive parents serve as models for aggression and also stoke their children's anger.

Media Influences

Real people are not the only models of aggressive behavior in children's lives. A classic study by Albert Bandura and his colleagues (1963) suggested that televised models had a powerful influence on children's aggressive behavior. One group of preschool children observed a film of an adult model hitting and kicking an inflated Bobo doll, whereas a control group saw an aggression-free film. The experimental and control children were then left alone in a room with the same doll as hidden observers recorded their behavior. The children who had observed the aggressive model showed significantly more aggressive behavior toward the doll themselves (see Figure 10.3 ■). Many children imitated bizarre attack behaviors devised for the model in this experiment—behaviors that they would not have thought up themselves.

The children exposed to the aggressive model also showed aggressive behavior patterns that had not been modeled. Therefore, observing the model not only led to imitation of modeled behavior patterns but also apparently **disinhibited** previously

disinhibit To stimulate a response that has been suppressed (inhibited) by showing a model engaging in that response without aversive consequences.

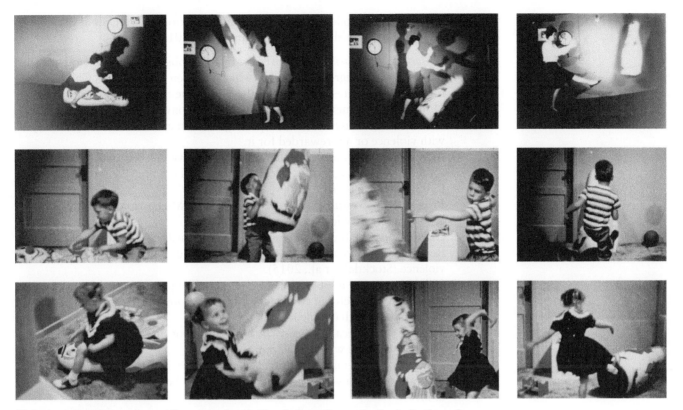

Figure 10.3 ■ Photos from Albert Bandura's Classic Experiment in the Imitation of Aggressive Models
Research by Albert Bandura and his colleagues showed that children frequently imitate the aggressive behavior they observe. In the top row, an adult model strikes a clown doll. The second and third rows show a boy and a girl imitating the aggressive behavior.
Albert Bandura/Department of Psychology, Stanford University

learned aggressive responses. The results were similar whether children observed human or cartoon models on film.

The Bandura study was a setup—an experimental setup, to be sure, but still a setup. It turns out that television is one of children's major sources of informal observational learning. It also turns out that television is a fertile source of aggressive models throughout much of the world (Huesmann et al., 2003, 2013). Children are routinely exposed to scenes of murder, beating, and sexual assault, just by turning on the TV set. Are children less likely to be exposed to violence when their watching is restricted to G-rated movies? No. Virtually all G-rated animated films have scenes of violence. Other media that contain violence include movies, rock music and music videos, advertising, video games, and the Internet.

> **TRUTH OR FICTION REVISITED:** It is true that children who watch 2–4 hours of television a day will see some 8,000 murders and another 100,000 acts of violence by the time they have finished elementary school (Huesmann et al., 2003). Perhaps it is remarkable that so many children—exposed to all this—are not more violent in their own lives.

In any event, most organizations of health professionals agree that media violence does contribute to aggression (Huesmann et al., 2013). This relationship has been found for girls and boys of different ages, social classes, ethnic groups, and cultures. Consider the following ways in which depictions of violence contribute to aggression (Anderson et al., 2010; Huesmann et al., 2013).

- *Observational learning.* Children learn from observation. TV violence supplies models of aggressive "skills," which children may acquire. Children tend to imitate the aggressive behavior they see in the media (see Figure 10.3).
- *Disinhibition.* Punishment inhibits behavior. Conversely, media violence may disinhibit aggressive behavior, especially when media characters "get away" with violence or are rewarded for it.
- *Increased arousal.* Media violence and aggressive video games increase viewers' level of arousal; that is, television "works them up." We are more likely to be aggressive under high levels of arousal.
- *Priming of aggressive thoughts and memories.* Media violence "primes" or arouses aggressive ideas and memories.
- *Habituation.* We become "habituated to," or used to, repeated stimuli. Repeated exposure to TV violence may decrease viewers' sensitivity to real violence (Stockdale et al., 2015).
- Children who see a lot of violence are more likely to view violence as an effective way of settling conflicts. Children exposed to violence are more likely to assume that violence is acceptable.
- Viewing violence can decrease the likelihood that one will take action on behalf of a victim when violence occurs.
- Viewing violence may lead to real-life violence. Children exposed to violent programming at a young age are more likely to be violent themselves later in life.

Even so, there is no simple one-to-one connection between observing media violence and behaving aggressively in real life.

TRUTH OR FICTION REVISITED: It is not true that children mechanically imitate the aggressive behavior they view in the media. Nevertheless, exposure to violence in the media increases the probability of violence by viewers.

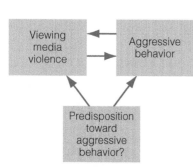

Figure 10.4 ■ Violence in the Media and Aggressive Behavior
What are the connections between viewing media violence and engaging in aggressive behavior? Does exposure to media violence cause aggressive behavior? Do aggressive children prefer to tune in to violent shows or play violent video games? Or do other factors, such as personality traits, predispose some children both to seek out media violence and to behave aggressively?
© Cengage Learning®

Violent video games may create the greatest risk of violence because they require audience participation (De Lisi et al., 2013; Lin, 2013). Players don't just watch; they join in (Dubow et al., 2010). Playing violent video games increases aggressive thoughts and behavior in the laboratory (Anderson et al., 2010). However, males are more likely than females to act aggressively after playing violent video games and are more likely to see the world as a hostile place. Students who obtain higher grades are less likely to behave aggressively following exposure to violent video games. Thus, cultural stereotyping of males and females, possible biological gender differences, and moderating variables such as academic achievement figure into the effects of media violence.

There is apparently a circular relationship between exposure to media violence and aggressive behavior (Anderson et al., 2010; Bushman & Anderson, 2009; see Figure 10.4 ■). Yes, TV violence and violent video games contribute to aggressive behavior, but aggressive youngsters are also more likely to seek out this kind of "entertainment."

The family constellation also affects the likelihood that children will imitate the violence they see on television. Studies find that parental substance abuse, physical punishments, and father absence contribute to the likelihood of aggression in early childhood (Boisvert, 2014; Braun & Champagne, 2014). Parental rejection further increases the likelihood of aggression in children (Casselman & McKenzie, 2015; Hoffman & Edwards, 2004). These family factors suggest that the parents of aggressive children are absent or unlikely to help young children understand that the kinds of socially inappropriate behaviors they see in the media are not for them. A harsh home life may also confirm the TV viewer's vision of the world as a violent place and further encourage reliance on television for companionship. In Chapter 9, we saw how parents can help children understand that the violence they view in the media is not real and is not to be imitated.

Section Review

6. In _____ play, children play with toys by themselves.

7. In _____ play, children interact and share toys.

8. Preschoolers tend to prefer to play with children of the _____ (other or same?) gender.

9. _____ is another term for prosocial behavior.

10. Preschoolers tend to _____ (admire or reject?) aggressive peers.

11. Aggressive behavior is linked with the hormone _____.

12. _____ theorists explain aggressive behavior in terms of reinforcement and observational learning.

13. Observing aggression in the media tends to _____ (inhibit or disinhibit?) aggressive behavior in children.

Reflect & Relate: Do you believe that violence in the media causes aggression? (What does the word *cause* mean?) Media violence is everywhere—not only in R-rated films but also in G-rated films and in video games. There are connections between media violence and aggression, but not everyone who witnesses media violence behaves aggressively. How, then, do we explain the connections between violence in the media and aggression?

10.3 Personality and Emotional Development

In the early childhood years, children's personalities start becoming more defined. Their sense of self—who they are and how they feel about themselves—continues to develop and becomes more complex. They begin to acquire a sense of their own abilities and their increasing mastery of the environment. As they move out into the world, they also face new experiences that may cause them to feel fearful and anxious. Let us explore some of these facets of personality and emotional development.

How Does the Self Develop During Early Childhood?

The sense of self, or the self-concept, emerges gradually during infancy. Infants and toddlers visually begin to recognize themselves and differentiate themselves from other individuals, such as their parents.

In the preschool years, children continue to develop their sense of self. Almost as soon as they begin to speak, they describe themselves in terms of certain categories, such as age groupings (baby, child, adult) and gender (girl, boy). These self-definitions that refer to concrete external traits have been called the **categorical self**.

Children as young as 3 years are able to describe themselves in terms of behaviors and stable or recurrent emotions (Rosen & Patterson, 2011). For example, in response to the question "How do you feel when you're scared?" young children frequently respond, "Usually like running away" (Eder, 1989). Or, in answer to the question "How do you usually act around grown-ups?" a typical response might be "I mostly been good with grown-ups." Thus, even preschoolers seem to understand that they have stable, enduring traits.

One aspect of the self-concept is self-esteem, the value or worth that people attach to themselves. Children who have a good opinion of themselves during the

categorical self Definitions of the self that refer to concrete external traits.

preschool years are more likely to show secure attachment and have parents who are attentive to their needs (Roisman & Groh, 2011). They also are more likely to engage in prosocial behavior (Grusec & Davidov, 2015).

Preschool children begin to make evaluative judgments about two different aspects of themselves by the age of 4 (Underwood & Rosen, 2011). The first aspect is their cognitive and physical competence (e.g., being good at puzzles, counting, swinging, tying shoes), and the second is their social acceptance by peers and parents (e.g., having lots of friends, being read to by Mom) (Piek et al., 2006). But preschoolers do not yet make a clear distinction between different areas of competence. For example, a child of this age is not likely to report being good in school but poor in physical skills. Either one is "good at doing things" or one is not (Harter, 2012).

Children also become increasingly capable of self-regulation in early childhood. They become more and more capable of controlling their eliminatory processes, of controlling aggressive behavior, of engaging in play with other children, and of focusing on cognitive tasks such as learning to count and to sound out letters. Self-regulatory abilities are connected with maturation of the brain and the rearing practices of caregivers.

During middle childhood, personality traits become increasingly important in children's self-definitions. Children then are also able to make judgments about their self-worth in many different areas of competence, behavioral conduct, appearance, and social relations.

Initiative versus Guilt

As preschool children continue to develop a separate sense of themselves, they increasingly move out into the world and take the initiative in learning new skills. Erik Erikson refers to these early childhood years as the stage of initiative versus guilt.

Children in this stage strive to achieve independence from their parents and master adult behaviors. They are curious, try new things, and test themselves. These qualities are illustrated in the following account of a day in the life of a 5-year-old:

> In a single day, he decided to see how high he could build his blocks, invented a game that consisted of seeing who could jump the highest on his parents' bed, and led the family to a new movie containing a great deal of action and violence (Crain, 2000).

During these years, children learn that not all of their plans, dreams, and fantasies can be realized. Adults prohibit children from doing certain things, and children begin to internalize these adult rules. Fear of violating the rules may cause the child to feel guilty and may curtail efforts to master new skills. Parents can help children develop and maintain a healthy sense of initiative by encouraging their attempts to learn and explore and by not being unduly critical and punitive.

The Horrors of Early Childhood: What Sorts of Fears Do Children Have During the Preschool Years?

In Erikson's view, fear of violating parental prohibitions can be a powerful force in the life of a young child. Both the frequency and the content of fears change as children move from infancy into the preschool years. The number of fears seems to follow a predictable course, peaking between 2½ and 4 years of age and then tapering off (Muris & Field, 2011).

HELPING CHILDREN COPE WITH FEARS

A number of methods have been developed to help children cope with fears. Professionals who work with children today are most likely to use such behavior-modification methods as desensitization, operant conditioning, and participant modeling (Gordon et al., 2007). Each method is based on principles of learning.

Desensitization

Desensitization exposes children gradually to the sources of their fears while they are engaging in behavior that is incompatible with fear (Gordon et al., 2007). Fear includes bodily responses such as rapid heart rate and respiration rate. Thus, doing things that reduce the heart and respiration rates is incompatible with fear.

In a classic study, Mary Cover Jones (1924) used a form of desensitization along with counterconditioning to eliminate a fear of rabbits in a 2-year-old boy named Peter. Desensitization consisted of bringing a rabbit gradually closer to Peter. Fear was counterconditioned in that as the rabbit was being brought closer, the boy was experiencing pleasure from munching away merrily on candy and cookies. Peter cast a wary eye in the rabbit's direction, but he continued to eat. Jones suspected that if she brought the rabbit too close too quickly, the cookies left on Peter's plate and those already eaten might have decorated the walls. But gradually the animal could be brought nearer without upsetting the boy. Eventually, Peter could eat and touch the rabbit at the same time. Jones gave the child a treat. Having the child play with a game or favorite toy or asking the child to talk about a favorite book or TV hero is another way of relaxing the child.

Operant Conditioning

In operant conditioning, children are guided to desirable behaviors and then reinforced for engaging in them. When behavior modification is used in the classroom, good behavior is reinforced and misbehavior is ignored.

Parents and other adults use operant techniques all the time. They may teach children how to draw letters of the alphabet by guiding their hand and saying "Good!"

when the desired result is obtained. When children fear touching a dog, parents frequently take their hands and guide them physically in petting the animal. Then they say something reinforcing, such as "Look at that big girl/boy petting that doggy!" or "Isn't the puppy nice and soft?" (Ollendick & Seligman, 2006).

Participant Modeling

In participant modeling, children first observe live models or filmed or taped models (ideally, children similar in age) engaging in the behavior that evokes fear. Then they imitate the behavior of the models. In an often-cited experiment on participant modeling, Bandura and his colleagues (1969) found that participant modeling helped people who were afraid of snakes. Figure 10.5 ■ shows children and adults in the Bandura study who imitated unafraid models.

Reflect   How can you apply the methods discussed in this feature to a "grown-up" fear you might have?

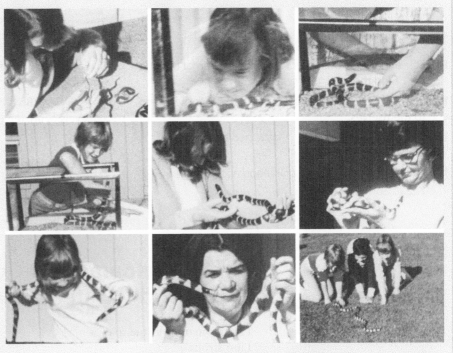

Figure 10.5 ■ Participant Modeling
Participant modeling helps children overcome fears through principles of observational learning. In these photos, children with a fear of snakes observe and then imitate models who are unafraid. As another example, parents often try to convince children that something tastes good by eating it in front of them and saying "Mmm!"
Albert Bandura/Department of Psychology, Stanford University

The preschool period is marked by a decline in fears of loud noises, falling, sudden movement, and strangers. The fantasies of young children frequently involve stories they are told and media imagery. Frightening images of imaginary creatures can persist. Many young children are reluctant to have the lights turned off at night for fear that these creatures may harm them in the dark. Imaginary creatures also threaten personal safety.

TRUTH OR FICTION REVISITED: It is not true that fear of social disapproval is the most common fear among preschoolers. Preschoolers are most likely to have fears that revolve around animals, imaginary creatures, the dark, and themes involving personal physical safety (Muris & Field, 2011).

But real objects and situations also cause many children to fear for their personal safety, such as lightning, thunder and other loud noises, the dark, high places, sharp objects and being cut, blood, unfamiliar people, strange people, stinging and crawling insects, and other animals.

During middle childhood, children's fears become more realistic. They grow less fearful of imaginary creatures, but fears of bodily harm and injury remain fairly common. Children become more fearful of failure and criticism in school and in social relationships (Underwood & Rosen, 2011).

Girls report more fears and higher levels of anxiety than boys (Muris & Field, 2011). Whether these findings reflect actual differences in fears and anxieties or differences in the willingness of girls and boys to report "weaknesses" is a matter of debate.

Section Review

14. Self-definitions that refer to concrete external traits are called the _____ self.

15. Self-_____ is the value or worth that people attach to themselves.

16. Children who are _____ attached tend to have high self-esteem.

17. Erikson referred to early childhood as the stage of _____ versus guilt.

18. Early childhood fears tend to revolve around personal _____.

19. _____ (Boys or Girls?) report more fears and higher levels of anxiety.

Reflect & Relate: Do you remember any fears you had during early childhood? Have they faded over the years?

10.4 Development of Gender Roles and Gender Differences

I am woman, hear me roar . . .
I am strong
I am invincible
I am woman

These lyrics are from the song "I Am Woman" by Helen Reddy and Ray Burton. They capture our attention because they run counter to the stereotype of the woman as vulnerable and in need of a man's protection. The stereotype of the vulnerable woman, like all stereotypes, is a fixed, oversimplified, and often distorted idea about a group of people—in this case, women. The idea of the chivalrous, protective man is also a stereotype.

What Are Stereotypes and Gender Roles? How Do They Develop?

Cultural stereotypes of males and females involve broad expectations of behavior that we call **gender roles** (Leaper & Farkas, 2015). Researchers who investigate people's perceptions of gender differences in personality tend to find groups of "masculine" and "feminine" traits such as those listed in Table 10.5 ●.

Gender-role stereotypes appear to develop through a series of stages. First, children learn to label the genders. At about 2–2½ years of age, children can distinguish between pictures of girls and boys (Alexander et al., 2009). By age 3, they display knowledge of gender stereotypes for toys, clothing, work, and activities (Campbell et al., 2004). Children of this age generally agree that boys play with cars and trucks,

gender role A complex cluster of traits and behaviors that are considered stereotypical of females or of males.

● TABLE 10.5
Cultural Stereotypes of "Masculine" and "Feminine" Traits—Are They Accurate?

Masculine	Feminine
Adventurous	Affectionate
Aggressive	Agreeable
Assertive	Appreciative
Capable	Artistic
Coarse	Cautious
Confident	Dependent
Courageous	Emotional
Determined	Fearful
Disorderly	Fickle
Enterprising	Gentle
Hardheaded	Kind
Independent	Nurturant
Intelligent	Patient
Pleasure-seeking	Prudish
Quick	Sensitive
Rational	Sentimental
Realistic	Shy
Reckless	Softhearted
Sensation-seeking	Submissive
Scientific	Suggestible
Stern	Talkative
Tough	Unambitious

Sources: Amanatullah & Morris, 2010; Guzzetti, 2010; Schmitt et al., 2012; Zhenget al., 2011.

help their fathers, and tend to hit others. They also agree that girls play with dolls, help their mothers, and do not hit others (Cherney et al., 2006).

Showing distress apparently becomes gender-typed so that preschoolers judge it to be acceptable for girls. One study found that preschool boys but not girls were rejected by their peers when they showed distress (Walter & LaFreniere, 2000).

Children become increasingly traditional in their stereotyping of activities, occupational roles, and personality traits between the ages of 3 and 9 or 10 (Hilliard & Liben, 2010). Traits such as "cruel" and "repairs broken things" are viewed as masculine, and traits such as "often is afraid" and "cooks and bakes" are seen as feminine. A study of 55 middle-class, primarily European American children, ages 39–84 months, found that they considered men to be more competent in traditionally masculine-typed occupations (such as occupations in science and transportation) and women to be more competent in traditionally feminine-typed occupations (such as nursing and teaching) (Levy et al., 2000). The children equated competence with income: They believed that men earned more money in the masculine-typed jobs but that women earned more in the feminine-typed jobs.

A study of 229 African American, Mexican American, and Dominican American children found them to be rigid in their gender-role stereotyping during early childhood, with their dress-up play and choice of toys, and with sex segregation increasing between the ages of 3 and 5 (Halim et al., 2013). Another study confirmed the nearly universal insistence of 3- to 6-year-old girls to wear dresses, often pink, and the similarly strong refusal of boys of the same age to wear anything "with a hint of femininity" (Halim et al., 2014). Older children and adolescents become somewhat more flexible in their perceptions of males and females (Halim et al., 2013). They retain the broad stereotypes but also perceive similarities between the genders and recognize that there are individual differences. They are more capable of recognizing the arbitrary aspects of gender categories and more willing to try behaviors that typify the other gender. But even though American children appear to be used to the idea that both mothers and fathers "belong" in the workplace, they find it less acceptable for fathers to remain in the home (Sinno & Killen, 2009).

Children and adolescents show some chauvinism by perceiving their own gender in a somewhat better light (Zosuls et al., 2011). For example, girls perceive other girls as nicer, more hardworking, and less selfish than boys. Boys, on the other hand, think that they are nicer, more hardworking, and less selfish than girls (Hilliard & Liben, 2010; Martin & Dinella, 2011).

Gender Differences: How Do Females and Males Differ in Their Cognitive, Social, and Emotional Development?

Clearly, females and males are anatomically different. If they weren't, none of us would be here. But according to the gender-role stereotypes we have just examined, people believe that they also differ in their behaviors, personality characteristics, and abilities.

Gender differences in infancy are small and rather inconsistent. In this chapter, we have reviewed gender differences during early childhood. Young girls and boys display some differences in their choices of toys and play activities, even by 13 months of age (van de Beek et al., 2009). Boys engage in more rough-and-tumble play and also are more aggressive. Girls tend to show more empathy and to report more fears. Girls show greater verbal ability than boys, whereas boys show greater visual–spatial ability than girls.

Gender Stereotyping? Does this woman fit the feminine stereotype? Why or why not?

PhotoStock–Israel/Alamy

What Are the Origins of Gender Differences?

Like mother, like daughter; like father, like son—at least often, if not always (Maccoby, 2015). Why is it that little girls (often) grow up to behave according to the cultural stereotypes of what it means to be female? Why is it that little boys (often) grow up to behave like male stereotypes? Let us have a look at various explanations of the development of gender differences.

The Roles of Evolution and Heredity

According to evolutionary psychologists, gender differences were fashioned by natural selection in response to problems in adaptation that were repeatedly encountered by humans over thousands of generations (Bugental et al., 2015). The story of the survival of our ancient ancestors is recorded in our genes. Genes that bestow attributes that increase an organism's chances of surviving to produce viable offspring are most likely to be transmitted to future generations. We thus possess the genetic codes for traits that helped our ancestors survive and reproduce. These traits include structural gender differences, such as those found in the brain, and differences in body chemistry, such as hormones.

Consider a gender difference. Males tend to place relatively more emphasis on physical appearance in mate selection than females do, whereas females tend to place relatively more emphasis on personal factors such as intelligence, stability, and financial status (Bugental et al., 2015). Why? Evolutionary psychologists believe that evolutionary forces favor the survival of women who seek status in their mates and the survival of men who seek physical allure, because these preferences provide reproductive advantages.

Evolution has also led to the development of the human brain. As we will see in the next section, the organization of the brain apparently plays a role in gender typing.

Organization of the Brain

The organization of the brain is largely genetically determined, and one thing that affects it is prenatal exposure to sex hormones (Avinum & Knafo-Noam, 2015). The hemispheres of the brain are specialized to perform certain functions. In most people, the left hemisphere is more involved in language skills, whereas the right hemisphere is specialized to carry out visual–spatial tasks.

Both males and females have a left hemisphere and a right hemisphere. They also share other structures in the brain, but the question is whether they use them in quite the same way. Consider the hippocampus, a brain structure that is involved in the formation of memories and in relaying incoming sensory information to other parts of the brain (Ohnishi et al., 2006). Matthias Riepe and his colleagues (Grön et al., 2000) have studied the ways in which humans and rats use the hippocampus when they are navigating mazes. Males use the hippocampus in both hemispheres when they are navigating (Grön et al., 2000). Females, however, rely on the hippocampus in the right hemisphere in concert with the right prefrontal cortex—an area of the brain that evaluates information and makes plans. Researchers have also found that females, as a group, rely more than men do on landmarks when they are finding their way ("Go a block past Ollie's Noodle Shop, turn left, and go to the corner past Café Lalo") (Andersen et al., 2012). Men tend to rely more on geometry, as in finding one's position in terms of coordinates or on a map ("You're on the corner of Eleventh Avenue and 57th Street, and you want to get to Seventh Avenue and 55th Street, so...") (Andersen et al., 2012).

Some psychological activities, such as the understanding and production of language, are regulated by structures in the left hemisphere, particularly Broca's area and Wernicke's area. But emotional and aesthetic responses, along with some other psychological activities, are more or less regulated in the right hemisphere. Brain-imaging research suggests that the left and right hemispheres of males may be more specialized than those of females (Shaywitz & Shaywitz, 2003). If the brain hemispheres of women "get along better" than those of men—that is, if they better share the regulation of various cognitive activities—we may have an explanation why women frequently outperform men in language tasks that involve some spatial organization, such as spelling, reading, and enunciation. Yet men, with more specialized spatial relations skills, could be expected to generally outperform women at visualizing objects in space and reading maps.

Sex Hormones

Researchers suggest that the development of gender differences in personality, along with the development of anatomical gender differences, may be related to prenatal levels of sex hormones. Although results of many studies that tried to correlate prenatal sex hormone levels with subsequent gender-typed play have been mixed, a study of 212 pregnant women conducted by Bonnie Auyeung and her colleagues (2009) found that fetal testosterone was related to masculine- or feminine-typed play at the age of 8½ years. Other studies show that children display gender-typed preferences—with boys preferring transportation toys and girls preferring dolls—as early as the age of 13 months (Knickmeyer et al., 2005). Another study investigated the gender-typed visual preferences of 30 human infants at the early ages of 3–8 months (Alexander et al., 2009). The researchers assessed interest in a toy truck and in a doll by using eye-tracking technology to indicate the direction of visual attention. Girls showed a visual preference for the doll over the truck (that is, they made a greater number of visual fixations on the doll), and boys showed a visual preference for the truck.

The gender differences in activity preferences of children are also found in rhesus monkeys. For example, male rhesus juveniles and boys are more likely than female rhesus juveniles and girls to engage in rough-and-tumble play (Wallen & Hassett, 2009). Researchers also introduced wheeled toys and plush toys into a 135-member rhesus monkey troop and found that male monkeys, like boys, showed consistent, strong preferences for the wheeled toys, whereas female monkeys, like girls, showed greater flexibility in preferences, sometimes playing with the plush toy and sometimes playing with the wheeled toy (Hassett et al., 2008). Do these cross-species findings suggest that such preferences in humans can develop without human gender-typed socialization experiences?

Let us also consider psychological views of the development of gender differences.

Social Cognitive Theory

Social cognitive theorists pay attention both to the roles of rewards and punishments (reinforcement) in gender typing and to the ways in which children learn from observing others and then decide what behaviors are appropriate for them. Children learn much about what society considers "masculine" or "feminine" by observing and imitating models of the same gender. These models may be their parents, other adults, children, and even TV characters.

The importance of observational learning was shown in a classic experiment conducted by Kay Bussey and Albert Bandura (1984). In this study, children obtained information on how society categorizes behavior patterns by observing how often they were performed either by men or by women. While children of ages 2–5 observed them, female and male adult role models exhibited different behavior patterns, such as choosing a blue or a green hat, marching or walking across a room, and repeating different words. Then the children were given a chance to imitate the models. Girls were twice as likely to imitate the woman's behavior as the man's, and boys were twice as likely to imitate the man's behaviors as the woman's.

Socialization also plays a role in gender typing. Parents, teachers, other adults—even other children—provide children with information about the gender-typed behaviors they are expected to display (Leaper, 2013). Boys are encouraged to be

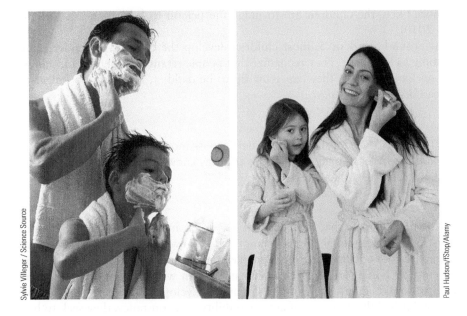

Acquiring Gender Roles What psychological factors contribute to the acquisition of gender roles? Psychoanalytic theory focuses on the concept of identification. Social cognitive theory focuses on imitation of the behavior patterns of same-sex adults and reinforcement by parents and peers.

independent, whereas girls are more likely to be restricted and given help. Boys are allowed to roam farther from home at an earlier age and are more likely to be left unsupervised after school (Leaper, 2013).

Fathers are more likely than mothers to communicate norms for gender-typed behaviors to their children (Leaper, 2013). Mothers are usually less demanding. Fathers tend to encourage their sons to develop instrumental behavior (behavior that gets things done or accomplishes something) and their daughters to develop warm, nurturant behavior. Fathers are likely to cuddle daughters. By contrast, they are likely to toss their sons into the air and use hearty language with them, such as "How're yuh doin', Tiger?" and "Hey you, get your keister over here." Being a nontraditionalist, I would toss my young daughters into the air, which raised objections from relatives who criticized me for being too rough. This, of course, led me to modify my behavior. I learned to toss my daughters into the air when the relatives were not around!

Maternal employment is associated with somewhat less polarized gender-role concepts for girls and boys (Goldberg et al., 2012; Greene et al., 2013). The daughters of employed women also have higher educational and career aspirations than the daughters of unemployed women, and they are more likely to choose careers that are nontraditional for women (Greene et al., 2013).

Let us now consider two cognitive approaches to gender typing: cognitive-developmental theory and gender-schema theory.

Cognitive-Developmental Theory

Lawrence Kohlberg (1966) proposed a cognitive-developmental view of gender typing. According to this perspective, children play an active role in gender typing (Martin & Ruble, 2004). They form concepts about gender and then fit their behavior to the concepts. These developments occur in stages and are entwined with general cognitive development.

According to Kohlberg, gender typing involves the emergence of three concepts: gender identity, gender stability, and gender constancy. The first step in gender typing is attaining **gender identity**. Gender identity is the knowledge that one is male or female. At 2 years, most children can say whether they are boys or girls. By the age of 3, many children can discriminate anatomical gender differences (Bem, 1989; Campbell et al., 2004). By 5 or 6, children can identify the gender of adults based on waist-to-hip ratios—the more similar the girth of the waist and that of the hips,

gender identity Knowledge that one is female or male. Also, the name of the first stage in Kohlberg's cognitive-developmental theory of the assumption of gender roles.

the more likely the children are to judge the person to be a man (K. L. Johnson et al., 2010).

At around age 4 or 5, most children develop the concept of **gender stability**, according to Kohlberg. They recognize that people retain their gender for a lifetime. Girls no longer believe they can grow up to be daddies, and boys no longer think they can become mommies.

> **TRUTH OR FICTION REVISITED:** It's true! Because most 2½-year-olds have not developed gender stability, a girl of this age may know that she is a girl but still think she can grow up to be a daddy.

Kohlberg believes that by the age of 5–7 years, most children develop the more sophisticated concept of **gender constancy**. Children with gender constancy recognize that gender does not change, even if people modify their dress or behavior. A woman who cuts her hair short remains a woman. A man who dons an apron and cooks dinner remains a man. According to cognitive-developmental theory, once children have established the concepts of gender stability and constancy, they seek to behave in ways that are consistent with their gender (Halim et al., 2014; Liben et al., 2014).

Cross-cultural studies have found that the concepts of gender identity, gender stability, and gender constancy emerge in the order predicted by Kohlberg (Zosuls et al., 2011). But children may achieve gender constancy earlier than Kohlberg stated. More important, Kohlberg's theory cannot account for the age at which gender-typed preferences for toys emerges. Girls show preferences for dolls and soft toys, and boys for hard transportation toys, as early as 3–8 months of age (Alexander et al., 2009)!

Gender-Schema Theory

Sandra Bem's **gender-schema theory** proposes that children use gender as one way of organizing their perceptions of the world (Golden & McHugh, 2015; Martin & Dinella, 2012). A gender schema is a cluster of concepts about male and female physical traits, behaviors, and personality traits. For example, consider the dimension of strength–weakness. Children learn that strength is linked to the male gender-role stereotype and weakness to the female stereotype. They also learn that some dimensions, such as strength–weakness, are more relevant to one gender than to the other—in this case, to males. A boy will learn that the strength he displays in weight training or wrestling affects the way others perceive him. But most girls do not find this trait to be important to others, unless they are competing in gymnastics, tennis, swimming, or other sports. A girl is likely to find that gentleness and neatness are more important in the eyes of others than strength.

From the viewpoint of gender-schema theory, gender identity alone can inspire "gender-appropriate" behavior. As soon as children understand the labels "girl" and "boy," they seek information concerning gender-typed traits and try to live up to them (Halim et al., 2014; Wong & Hines, 2015). A boy may fight back when provoked because boys are expected to do so. A girl may be gentle and kind because that is expected of girls. Both boys' and girls' self-esteem will depend on how they measure up to the gender schema.

Studies indicate that children do possess information according to a gender schema. For example, boys show better memory for "masculine" toys, activities, and occupations, whereas girls show better memory for "feminine" toys, activities, and occupations. However, gender-schema theory does not answer the question of whether biological forces also play a role in gender typing.

This and the previous two chapters lay the groundwork for the next major period in development: the middle childhood years. We will explore those years in the next three chapters, beginning with physical development in Chapter 11.

gender stability The concept that one's gender is a permanent feature.

gender constancy The concept that one's gender remains the same despite superficial changes in appearance or behavior.

gender-schema theory The view that one's knowledge of the gender schema in one's society (the behavior patterns that are considered appropriate for men and women) guides one's assumption of gender-typed preferences and behavior patterns.

Theories of the Development of Gender Differences

Nature and Gender Typing

Deals with the roles of evolution, heredity, and biology in gender typing.

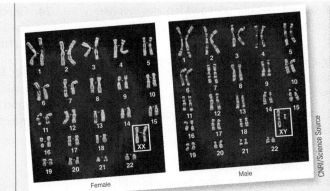

Female   Male

CNRI/Science Source

Perspective	Key Points	Comments
Evolution and heredity	Psychological gender differences were fashioned by natural selection in response to challenges that humans faced repeatedly over thousands of generations.	Evolutionary theorists believe that gender differences in aggression are natural. They suggest that a woman's allure is strongly connected with her age and health, which are markers of reproductive capacity, but the value of men as reproducers is also connected with factors that create a stable environment for child rearing.
Sex hormones	Sex hormones may prenatally "masculinize" or "feminize" the brain by creating predispositions consistent with gender roles.	Male rats are generally superior to females in maze-learning ability, a task that requires spatial skills. Aggressiveness appears to be connected with testosterone.

Nurture and Gender Typing

Deals with theories in psychology—for example, learning theory and cognitive theory—and related research.

Sylvie Villeger/Science Source

Paul Hudson/fStop/Alamy

Perspective	Key Points	Comments
Social cognitive theory	Children learn what is "masculine" and what is "feminine" by observational learning	Parents and others tend to reinforce children for gender-appropriate behavior
Cognitive-developmental theory	Gender typing is connected with the development of the concepts of gender identity, gender stability, and gender constancy.	Research evidence shows that children develop gender-typed preferences and behaviors before the development of gender stability and gender constancy.
Gender-schema theory	Cultures tend to organize social life around polarized gender roles. Children accept these scripts and try to behave in accord with them.	Research evidence suggests that polarized female–male scripts pervade our culture. For example, children tend to distort their memories to conform to the gender schema.

Section Review

20. Cultural stereotypes of males and females involve broad expectations for behavior that are called gender _____.

21. Brain imaging suggests that the hemispheres of the brain are more specialized in _____ (males or females?).

22. _____ (Mothers or Fathers?) are more likely to communicate norms for gender-typed behaviors to children.

23. Kohlberg proposes that the emergence of three concepts guides gender typing: gender identity, gender stability, and gender _____.

24. Gender-_____ theory proposes that children blend their self-concepts with the gender schema of their culture.

Reflect & Relate: Do you see yourself as being traditionally feminine or traditionally masculine? Have the gender roles and stereotypes of our culture created opportunities or conflicts for you? Or both? Explain.

Chapter Review

10.1 What Are the Influences of Parents, Siblings, and Peers on Development?

Parental approaches to child rearing can be classified according to the independent dimensions of warmth–coldness and restrictiveness–permissiveness. Consistent control and firm enforcement of rules can have positive consequences for the child. Parents tend to use inductive methods, power assertion, and withdrawal of love to enforce rules. Inductive methods rely on "reasoning," or explaining why one sort of behavior is good and another is not. The main methods are authoritative, authoritarian, and permissive. Authoritative parents are restrictive but warm and tend to have the most competent and achievement-oriented children. Authoritarian parents are restrictive and cold. The sons of authoritarian parents tend to be hostile and defiant; daughters are low in independence. Children of neglectful parents show the least competence and maturity. Parents tend to prefer power-assertive techniques when they believe that children understand the rules they have violated and are capable of acting appropriately. Stress contributes to the use of power assertion. Siblings provide caregiving, emotional support, advice, role models, social interaction, restrictions, and cognitive stimulation (Dunn, 2015). However, they are also sources of conflict, control, and competition. Younger siblings usually imitate older siblings. Firstborn and only children are generally more highly motivated to achieve, more cooperative, more helpful, more adult-oriented, and less aggressive. Later-born children tend to be more aggressive, to have lower self-esteem, and to have greater social skills with peers. Children learn social skills from peers: sharing, helping, taking turns, and coping with conflict. Peers foster the development of physical and cognitive skills and provide emotional support. Preschoolers' friendships are characterized by shared activities and feelings of attachment.

10.2 How Does Social Behavior Develop During Early Childhood?

Play is meaningful, pleasurable, and internally motivated and develops motor, social, and cognitive skills. It may help children deal with conflict and anxiety. Parten followed the development of six categories of play among 2- to 5-year-olds: unoccupied play, solitary play, onlooker play, parallel play, associative play, and cooperative play. Children show preferences for gender-stereotyped toys by 15–30 months of age. Boys' toys commonly include transportation toys (cars and trucks) and weapons; girls' toys more often include dolls. Boys in early childhood prefer vigorous outdoor activities and rough-and-tumble play. Girls are more likely to engage in arts and crafts. Preferences for toys may involve the interaction of biological factors and socialization. Prosocial behavior—altruism—begins to develop in the first year, when children begin to share.

Development of prosocial behavior is linked to the development of empathy and perspective-taking. Girls show more empathy than boys do. The aggression of preschoolers is frequently instrumental or possession-oriented. By age 6 or 7, aggression becomes hostile and person-oriented. Aggressive behavior appears to be generally stable and predictive of problems in adulthood. Genetic factors may be involved in aggressive behavior. Genes may be expressed in part through the male sex hormone testosterone. Aggressive boys are more likely than nonaggressive boys to incorrectly assume that other children mean them ill. Social cognitive theory suggests that children become aggressive as a result of frustration, reinforcement, and observational learning. Aggressive children are often rejected by less aggressive peers. Children who are physically punished are more likely to behave aggressively. Observing aggressive behavior teaches aggressive skills, disinhibits the child, and habituates children to violence.

10.3 How Do the Self, Self-Esteem, and Various Fears Develop During Middle Childhood?

Self-definitions that refer to concrete external traits are called the categorical self. Children as young as 3 years can describe themselves in terms of characteristic behaviors and internal states. Secure attachment and competence contribute to the development of self-esteem. Preschoolers are most likely to fear animals, imaginary creatures, and the dark; the theme involves threats to personal safety. Girls report more fears than boys do.

10.4 How Do Gender Roles and Gender Differences Develop During Early Childhood?

A stereotype is a fixed conventional idea about a group. Females are stereotyped as dependent, gentle, and home-oriented. Males are stereotyped as aggressive, self-confident, and independent. Cultural expectations of females and males are called gender roles. Males tend to excel in spatial relations skills, whereas girls tend to excel in verbal skills. Stereotypical gender preferences for toys and play activities are in evidence at an early age. Males are more aggressive than females. The magnitude and origins of all these gender differences are under debate. Male sex hormones are connected with greater maze-learning ability in rats and with aggressiveness. Social cognitive theorists explain the development of gender-typed behavior in terms of observational learning and socialization. According to Kohlberg's cognitive-developmental theory, gender typing involves the emergence of three concepts: gender identity, gender stability, and gender constancy. According to gender-schema theory, preschoolers attempt to conform to the cultural gender schema.

Key Terms

authoritative   310
inductive   311
authoritarian   313
permissive–indulgent   313
rejecting–neglecting   313
individualist   316
regression   316
collectivist   317

sibling rivalry   317
peers   319
dramatic play   320
nonsocial play   321
social play   321
prosocial behavior   323
empathy   324

disinhibit   328
categorical self   331
gender role   335
gender identity   339
gender stability   340
gender constancy   340
gender-schema theory   340

11

Middle Childhood
Physical Development

TruthorFiction?

T | F Children outgrow "baby fat." **p. 349**

T | F The typical American child is exposed to about 10,000 food commercials each year. **p. 351**

T | F Most American children are physically fit. **p. 357**

T | F Hyperactivity is caused by chemical food additives. **p. 360**

T | F Stimulants are often used to treat children who are hyperactive. **p. 361**

T | F Some children who are intelligent and are provided with enriched home environments cannot learn how to read or do simple math problems. **p. 363**

It is 6-year-old Jessica's first day of school. During recess, she runs to the climbing apparatus in the schoolyard and climbs to the top. As she reaches the top, she announces to the other children, "I'm coming down." She then walks to the parallel bars, goes halfway across, lets go, and tries again.

Steve and Mike are 8-year-olds. They are riding their bikes up and down the street. Steve tries riding with no hands on the handlebars. Mike starts riding fast, standing up on the pedals. Steve shouts, "Boy, you're going to break your neck!"

Middle childhood is a time for learning many new motor skills. Success in both gross and fine motor skills reflects children's increasing physical maturity, their opportunities to learn, and personality factors such as their persistence and self-confidence. Competence in motor skills enhances children's self-esteem and their acceptance by their peers.

In this chapter, we examine physical and motor development during middle childhood. We also discuss children with certain disorders.

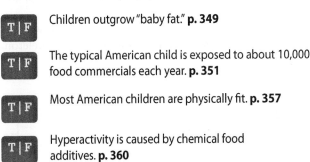

RubberBall/SuperStock

11.1 Growth Patterns

Gains in height and weight are fairly steady throughout middle childhood. But notable variations in growth patterns also occur from child to child.

What Patterns of Growth Occur in Middle Childhood?

Following the growth trends begun in early childhood, boys and girls continue to gain a little over 2 inches in height per year during the middle childhood years. This pattern of gradual gains does not vary significantly until children reach the adolescent **growth spurt** (see Figure 11.1 ■). The average gain in weight between the ages of 6 and 12 is about 5–7 pounds a year. During these years, children continue to become less stocky and more slender (Kuczmarski et al., 2000).

Most deviations from these average height and weight figures are quite normal. Individual differences are more marked in middle childhood than they were earlier. For example, most 3-year-olds are within 8–10 pounds and 4 inches of one another. But by the age of 10, children's weights may vary by as much as 30–35 pounds, and their heights may vary by as much as 6 inches.

As bones lengthen and broaden and muscles strengthen, many children want to engage in more exercise. Because their muscles are adjusting to a growing skeleton,

growth spurt A period during which growth advances at a dramatically rapid rate compared with other periods.

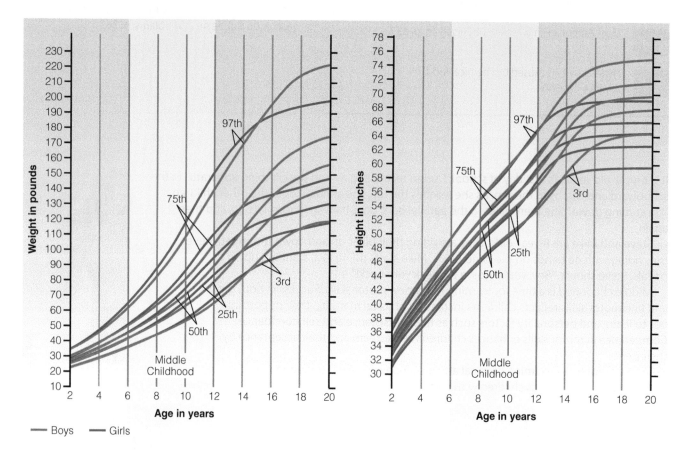

Figure 11.1 ■ Growth Curves for Height and Weight
Gains in height and weight are fairly steady during middle childhood. Boys continue to be slightly heavier and taller than girls through 9 or 10 years of age. Girls then begin their adolescent growth spurt and surpass boys in height and weight until about age 13 or 14.
Source: Kuczmarski et al. (2000, Figures 9–12).

children may experience aches and stiffness that have been dubbed "growing pains," especially in the legs (Baxter-Jones & Faulkner, 2012).

Between the ages of 6 and 12, children lose their primary teeth, and the permanent teeth grow in. Because the permanent teeth grow in at full size, they may at first seem too large for the child's face, but the facial bones "catch up," widening and lengthening the face so that the teeth and face once again come "into proportion."

How Does the Brain Develop in Middle Childhood?

The brain undergoes its most dramatic growth during prenatal development and infancy. Myelination of axons continues to occur during middle childhood and, apparently, into young adulthood. Growth of the volume and weight of the brain decelerates, although there are overall gains in size and weight. The frontal part of the brain is most highly involved in the so-called "executive functions" of planning and self-regulation. And it is here that dramatic developments take place in middle childhood (Hackman et al., 2015; Lagattuta et al., 2015). We can think of executive functioning as having several aspects: deployment of attention, cognitive flexibility, goal setting, and information processing. Information processing is connected with "fluid reasoning," or the ability to think logically and solve problems in novel situations. Neuroscientific research suggests that the child's gaining of control over his or her attentional processes emerges in infancy and develops rapidly in early childhood. However, cognitive flexibility, goal setting, and information processing (fluid reasoning) appear to undergo an important period of development during the ages of 7–9 and to be relatively mature by about the age of 12, thus setting the stage for the cognitive advances of adolescence (Anderson, 2002; Ferrer et al., 2009).

What Are the Connections Between Nutrition and Growth in Middle Childhood?

In middle childhood, average body weight doubles. Children also expend a good deal of energy as they engage in physical activity and play. To fuel this growth and activity, children need to eat more than they did in the preschool years. The average 4- to 6-year-old needs 1,400–1,800 calories per day, but the average 7- to 10-year-old requires 2,000 calories a day (Gidding et al., 2006).

Nutrition involves much more than calories, as we will see in the section on overweight children. The federal government has a food pyramid that suggests it is healthful to eat fruits and vegetables, fish, poultry (without skin), and whole grains and to limit intake of fats, sugar, and starches. However, the food offered to children in school and elsewhere tends to be heavy on sugar, animal fats, and salt (Bray & Bouchard, 2014). In addition, food portions have grown over the past couple of decades, particularly for salty snacks, desserts, soft drinks, fruit drinks, French fries, hamburgers, cheeseburgers, and Mexican food (Bray & Bouchard, 2014).

Fast-food restaurants offer the largest portions and the most fattening foods. The National Bureau of Economic Research (NBER) found that for ninth-graders, having a fast-food restaurant within 0.1 mile of their school is connected with a 5.2% increase in their obesity rate (Currie et al., 2009). The NBER found no association between fast-food restaurants and obesity rate when the restaurant is 0.25 or 0.5 mile away.

Nutrition and social class are also connected (Turrell & Vandevijvere, 2015). Consider two studies with African American mothers and daughters. Daughters living at the poverty line were likely to be fed diets high in fats and fast foods (Miklos et al., 2004). Middle-class mothers, however, were concerned about the weight of their daughters and encouraged physical activity as a means of weight control. Middle-class mothers also tended to limit their daughters' consumption of snack foods and sugar-laden carbonated beverages. Instead, they encouraged their daughters to drink water (V. J. Thompson et al., 2003).

What Are the Gender Similarities and Differences in Physical Growth During Middle Childhood?

Figure 11.1 reveals that boys continue to be slightly heavier and taller than girls through the age of 9 or 10. Girls then begin their adolescent growth spurt and surpass boys in height and weight until about age 13 or 14. At that time, boys are approaching the peak of their adolescent growth spurt, and they become taller and heavier than girls (De Leonibus et al., 2014).

The steady gain in height and weight during middle childhood is accompanied by an increase in muscular strength for both girls and boys (Boyden et al., 2015). The relative proportion of muscle and fatty tissue is about the same for boys and girls in early middle childhood. But this begins to change at about age 11, as males develop relatively more muscle tissue and females develop more fatty tissue.

How Do Vision and Hearing Develop During Middle Childhood?

In middle childhood, some 25% of children in the United States are myopic, or nearsighted. Myopia is readily treated with corrective lenses. The incidence of myopia tends to increase into young adulthood, when some 60% of the population has difficulty bringing distant objects into focus. Laser surgery is typically reserved for more serious vision problems with children, and there can be complications (Daoud et al., 2009). An experiment found some psychological benefits for children who wear contact lenses. In the study, 237 children 8–11 years old were assigned at random to wear glasses, and 237 were assigned to wear soft contact lenses (Walline et al., 2009). The study lasted for 3 years. At the end of the experiment, there were no differences in children's global self-worth; however, the children who wore the contact lenses rated their physical appearance, athletic competence, and social acceptance significantly higher.

Children 6–12 years old are not as likely as younger children to come down with ear infections, because the Eustachian tube, which runs down from the inner ear to the throat, elongates and narrows as children grow. As a result, bacteria and infected fluids cannot move so readily from the throat to the ear. Children with frequent ear infections are more likely to experience headaches—including migraines—hay fever, and asthma (Krueger et al., 2015). Ear infections can also lead to hearing loss and difficulty acquiring language (Dalla-Bona et al., 2015; Li et al., 2015).

Overweight Children

The problems of being overweight or obese frequently begin during childhood.

How Many Children in the United States Are Overweight? Why Are They Overweight?

Between 16% and 25% of children and adolescents in the United States are overweight or obese (see Figure 11.2 ■). Consider some facts about childhood overweight and obesity (Bray & Bouchard, 2014):

- Over the past 20 years, the prevalence of obesity among children has doubled.
- Latin American boys are significantly more likely than European American boys to be overweight.

- African American girls are significantly more likely than European American girls to be overweight.
- Children who are obese are more likely to have high blood pressure and high cholesterol (not only once they reach adulthood, but even as children!).
- Children who are obese are more likely to develop diabetes.
- Obese children are more likely to have respiratory problems, including asthma; joint problems; fatty liver disease; gallstones; and acid reflux—all in childhood.

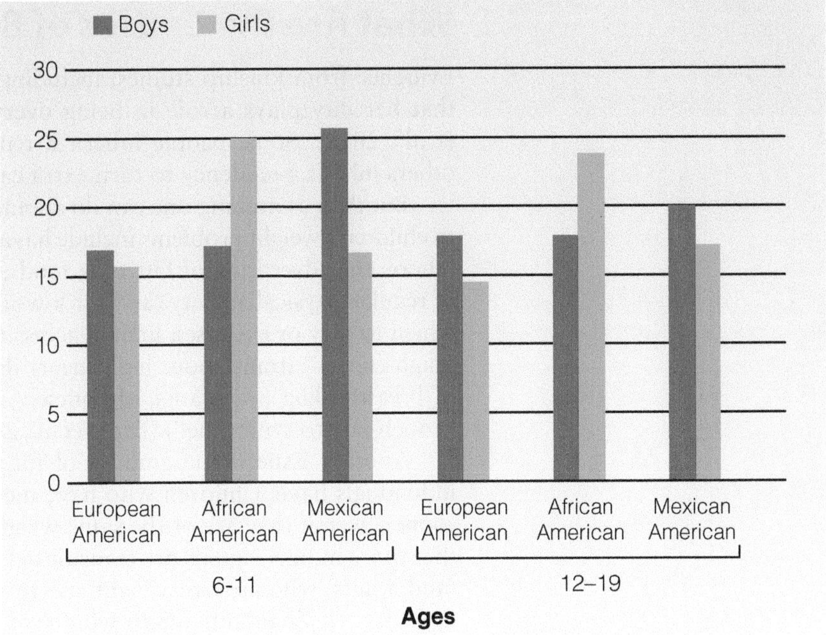

In the United States, the majority of overweight children become overweight adults (Bray & Bouchard, 2014). By contrast, only about 40% of normal-weight boys and 20% of normal-weight girls become overweight adults. However, similar samples of overweight Japanese and Swiss children apparently did not mostly become overweight adults (Funatogawa et al., 2008; Junod, 2008). Perhaps there is greater social pressure to slim down as one develops in those cultures. Or perhaps widespread dietary habits in those countries lead to some weight loss as individuals develop.

> **TRUTH OR FICTION REVISITED:** Although parents often assume that heavy children will "outgrow" their "baby fat," most overweight children actually become overweight adults. But biology isn't necessarily destiny; we will see that caregivers can help children manage their weight.

Figure 11.2 ■ Percentages of Children (Ages 6–11) and Adolescents (Ages 12–19) Who Are Overweight
In arriving at these figures, the American Heart Association considered both body weight and body composition (amount of muscle and fat tissue).
Source: American Heart Association (2009).

Overweight children, despite the stereotype, are usually far from jolly. Research suggests that heavy children are often rejected by their peers or are the objects of derision (Bray & Bouchard, 2014; Williams et al., 2013). They usually perform poorly in sports, which can bestow prestige on slimmer children (Salvy et al., 2008). As overweight children approach adolescence, they become even less popular because they are less likely to be found sexually attractive. It is no surprise, then, that overweight children have poorer body images than children of normal weight (Quick et al., 2014). A study of 244 children aged 8 to 17 found that overweight children and adolescents are also more likely to be depressed and anxious than peers whose weight is normal (Morrison et al., 2015).

Children who are overweight are at greater risk for a number of physical health problems in childhood and later in life (Bray & Bouchard, 2014). These include high blood pressure, hardening of the arteries (atherosclerosis), type 2 diabetes, fatty liver disease, ovarian disorders, and abnormal breathing patterns during sleep. Being overweight in childhood can accelerate the development of heart disease, which can lead to heart attacks or strokes in adulthood. The dramatically increased prevalence of overweight in childhood might even reverse the contemporary increase in life expectancy, such that overweight youth have less healthy and shorter lives than their parents. As Daniels (2006) notes, this would be the first reversal of the steady increase in life expectancy to occur in modern life.

What Are the Causes of Being Overweight?

Evidence from kinship studies, including twin studies, and adoption studies shows that heredity plays a role in being overweight (den Hoed & Loos, 2014; Perusse et al., 2014). Some people inherit a tendency to burn up extra calories, whereas others inherit a tendency to turn extra calories into fat.

But there is nothing one can do about one's heredity. Other factors that contribute to children's weight problems include having high-sugar drinks and unhealthful food at school; the advertising of fattening foods; variation in diets at child-care centers; lack of regular physical activity (and for low-income children, lack of community places in which to play or exercise); limited access to healthful, affordable foods; availability of "high-energy" (translation: high-sugar) drinks; large portion sizes (supersizing); lack of breastfeeding (as infants, of course); and television and other media (that is, the "couch-potato syndrome") (Berge et al., 2015; Leech et al., 2014).

Another issue is the amount of fat cells—also known as adipose tissue—that individuals have. Children who have more fat cells than other children feel hungry sooner, even if they are of the same weight. Perhaps possessing more fat cells means that more hunger signals are transmitted to the hypothalamus in the brain. Children (and adults) who are overweight and those who were once overweight usually have more fat cells than individuals who have weighed less. This "abundance" is no blessing. Having been overweight in childhood may cause adolescent or adult dieters to feel persistent hunger, even after they have leveled off at a weight that is more healthful (Guerdjikova et al., 2007).

Evidence that genetic and physiological factors are involved in one's body weight does not mean that the environment is without influence. Family, peers, and other environmental factors also play roles in children's eating habits—and the results of those habits (Overweight and obesity, 2011). Overweight parents, for example, may be models of poor exercise habits. Overweight parents may also encourage overeating and keep foods that are high in sugar and fat content in the home for snacks (Farrow et al., 2015).

The amount of TV watching also affects children's weight (Schumacher & Queen, 2007). Children who watch television extensively during the middle childhood years are more likely to become overweight as adolescents (Schumacher & Queen, 2007). The influence of TV watching is at least threefold (Stephenson & Banet-Weiser, 2007). First, children tend to consume snacks while watching. Second, television bombards children with commercials for fattening foods, such as candy and potato chips. Third, watching television is a sedentary activity. We burn fewer calories sitting than engaging in physical activity. Children who are heavy TV viewers are less physically active overall.

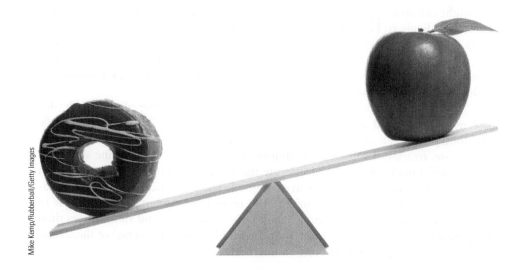

Mike Kemp/Rubberball/Getty Images

TRUTH OR FICTION REVISITED: It is true that American children are exposed to about 10,000 food commercials per year, the bulk of them for fast foods (such as those sold at Burger King and Pizza Hut), highly sweetened cereals, soft drinks, and candy bars (Ohri-Vachaspati et al., 2015; Overweight and obesity, 2011). Caregivers are advised to discuss the problems created by fast-food commercials with children, just as they are encouraged to discuss the effects of media violence.

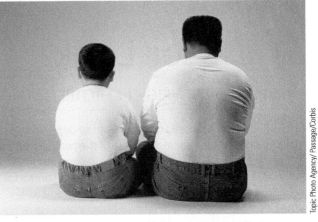

We know that being overweight runs in families, but we don't know exactly why. Heredity plays a role, but so do environmental factors, such as eating fast foods and spending too much time watching television.

Stressors and emotional reactions can also prompt children to eat (Michels et al., 2015). Overeating may occur in response to severe stresses, such as those inflicted by bickering in the home, parental divorce, or the birth of a sibling. Family celebrations and arguments are quite different, but both can lead to overeating or breaking a diet. Efforts to curb food intake also may be hampered by negative feeling states, such as anxiety and depression (Overweight and obesity, 2011). The self-defeating rule of thumb here seems to be something like this: If life is awful, try chocolate (or French fries, or pizza, or whatever).

For some suggestions on how parents can help their children (and themselves) lose weight, see the nearby "A Closer Look—Real Life" feature.

Section Review

1. Gains in height and weight are generally _____ (abrupt or steady?) throughout middle childhood.

2. Children gain a little over _____ inches in height per year during middle childhood.

3. Children gain about _____ pounds a year during middle childhood.

4. _____ (Boys or Girls?) are slightly heavier and taller through the age of 9 or 10.

5. Boys begin to become more muscular than girls at about the age of _____.

6. About _____% of American children are overweight.

7. Children _____ (do or do not?) tend to outgrow "baby fat."

8. Being overweight _____ (does or does not?) run in families.

Reflect & Relate: What were your gains in height and weight like in middle childhood? Were they "average" or below or above average? Think of people you know who were overweight as children: Did they "outgrow" it?

11.3 Childhood Asthma

Asthma is an allergy-type respiratory disorder characterized by spasms in the lungs, difficulty breathing, wheezing, often coughing (dry hacking), and a feeling of tightness in the chest that prevents the sufferer from getting enough air (NHLBI, 2011). The wheezing can be severe enough to disturb sleep and speech.

What Is the Prevalence of Asthma?

A study of more than a million children reported by more than 300 health centers around the world found that the prevalence of wheezing ranged from 2.4% in Jodhpur,

HELPING OVERWEIGHT CHILDREN MANAGE THEIR WEIGHT

Health-conscious parents not only want to be slimmer themselves but also are more aware of the health benefits their children gain by avoiding being overweight. However, losing weight is a difficult problem in self-control for children and adults alike. Nevertheless, childhood is the best time to prevent or reverse obesity because it is easiest to promote a lifetime pattern of healthful behaviors during childhood (Childhood obesity facts, 2011).

Methods such as improving nutritional knowledge, reducing calories, introducing exercise, and modifying behavior show promise for helping children lose excess weight (Strategies and solutions, 2011).

Behavioral methods involve tracking the child's calorie intake and weight, keeping the child away from temptations, setting a good example, and systematically using praise and other rewards. The most successful weight-loss programs for children combine exercise, decreased caloric intake, behavior modification, and emotional support from parents. Here are some suggestions:

- Teach children about nutrition: calories, protein, vitamins, minerals, fiber, food groups, and so on. Indicate which foods may be eaten without concern (such as green vegetables) and which foods should be eaten only sparingly (cakes, cookies, soft drinks sweetened with sugar, and so on). Check out the U.S. Department of Agriculture tip sheet "Choose MyPlate" on page xxx.

- Do not insist that the entire family sit down at the same time for a large meal.

- Allow children to eat only when they are hungry.

- Allow children to stop eating when they feel full.

- Prepare low-calorie snacks for your child to eat throughout the day. Children who feel deprived may binge.

- Do not cook, eat, or display fattening foods when the child is at home. The sight and aroma of such foods can be tantalizing.

- Involve the child in more activities. When children are busy, they are less likely to think about food. (And physical activity burns calories.)

- If you take your child food shopping, try to avoid the market aisles with ice cream, cake, and candy.

- Ask relatives and friends not to offer fattening treats when you visit.

- Do not allow snacking while sitting in front of the TV set or while playing, reading, or engaging in any other activity. Allowing children to snack while watching television makes eating a mindless habit.

- Involve the child in exercise, such as swimming or prolonged bicycle riding. Exercise will burn calories, increase the child's feelings of competence and self-esteem, improve cardiovascular condition, and possibly promote lifetime exercise habits.

- Reward the child for steps in the right direction, such as eating less or exercising more. Praise is a powerful reward, but children also respond to tangible rewards such as a new toy.

- Do not assume that it is a catastrophe if the child slips and goes on a binge. Talk with the child about what triggered the binge to avert similar problems in the future.

- Remind the child that tomorrow is a new day and a new start.

- If you and your children are overweight, consider losing weight together. It is more effective for overweight children and their parents to diet and exercise together than for children to go it alone.

RubberBall/SuperStock

Reflect

- You believe that a friend's or relative's child is dangerously obese, but the parent thinks the weight is normal or just "baby fat." What do you do?

- Imagine yourself about to visit a relative or friend whose self-esteem is wrapped up in spreading appealing but fattening food around during visits. How can you prevent your children from overeating? Must you stay home or go somewhere else?

You are concerned about your child's weight, and you learn that he or she has been sneaking "forbidden" foods. What do you do?

choose MyPlate

10 **tips** to a great plate

ChooseMyPlate.gov

Making food choices for a healthy lifestyle can be as simple as using these 10 Tips.
Use the ideas in this list to *balance your child's calories*, to choose foods to *eat more often*, and to cut back on foods to *eat less often*.

1 balance calories
Find out how many calories your child needs for a day as a first step in managing your child's weight. Go to www.ChooseMyPlate.gov to find your child's calorie level. Being physically active also helps your child balance calories.

2 enjoy your food, but eat less
Have your child take the time to fully enjoy her or his meal. Eating too fast or when attention is elsewhere may lead to eating too many calories. Pay attention to your child's hunger and fullness cues before, during, and after meals. Use them to recognize when your child needs to eat and when your child has eaten enough.

3 avoid oversized portions
Use a smaller plate, bowl, and glass. Portion out foods before your child eats. When eating out, choose a smaller size option, share a dish, or take home part of your meal.

4 foods to eat more often
Eat more vegetables, fruits, whole grains, and fat-free or 1% milk and dairy products. These foods have the nutrients you need for health—including potassium, calcium, vitamin D, and fiber. Make them the basis for meals and snacks.

5 make half your plate fruits and vegetables
Choose red, orange, and dark-green vegetables like tomatoes, sweet potatoes, and broccoli, along with other vegetables for your child's meals. Add fruit to meals as part of main or side dishes or as dessert.

6 switch to fat-free or low-fat (1%) milk
They have the same amount of calcium and other essential nutrients as whole milk, but fewer calories and less saturated fat.

7 make half your grains whole grains
To eat more whole grains, substitute a whole-grain product for a refined product—such as eating whole-wheat bread instead of white bread or eating brown rice instead of white rice.

8 foods to eat less often
Cut back on foods high in solid fats, added sugars, and salt. They include cakes, cookies, ice cream, candies, sweetened drinks, pizza, and fatty meats like ribs, sausages, bacon, and hot dogs. Use these foods as occasional treats, not everyday foods.

9 compare sodium in foods
Use the Nutrition Facts label to choose lower sodium versions of foods like soup, bread, and frozen meals. Select canned foods labeled "low-sodium," "reduced sodium," or "no salt added."

10 drink water instead of sugary drinks
Cut calories by drinking water or unsweetened beverages. Soda, energy drinks, and sports drinks are a major source of added sugar, and calories, in American diets.

United States
Department of Agriculture
Center for Nutrition
Policy and Promotion

DG TipSheet No. 1
June 2011
USDA is an equal opportunity provider and employer.

www.choosemyplate.gov

Go to www.ChooseMyPlate.gov for more information.

India, to 37.6% in Costa Rica for 6- to 7-year-olds, and from 0.8% in Tibet to 32.6% in Wellington, New Zealand, for 13- to 14-year-olds (Lai et al., 2009). The researchers found that, by and large, childhood asthma is more likely to be found in more affluent nations. However, the problem tended to be more serious in poorer nations.

Some children die from severe attacks of asthma, as do some adults. Just as asthma tends to be more severe in poor nations, it is more likely to be lethal among poorer Americans.

What Factors Increase the Risk of Developing Asthma?

A Canadian study mailed questionnaires to the mothers of more than 26,000 children to find the answers (Martel et al., 2008). Children who had previously had respiratory infections and skin irritations (dermatitis) were at higher risk of developing asthma. Other determinants of asthma included male gender, administration of oxygen after birth, prescription of antibiotics during the first 6 months, asthma in the father or in siblings, maternal asthma during pregnancy, use of antibiotics during pregnancy, and maternal receipt of public assistance. Protective factors included the use of nasal steroids during pregnancy, breastfeeding, day-care attendance, and, surprisingly, having pets in the home. In sum, risk factors seem to be previous respiratory or allergy problems, a family history of asthma, and lower socioeconomic status (SES). It is doubtful that pets in the home actually protect children from asthma. It is more likely that parents with fewer allergies are more likely to have pets.

How Is Asthma Treated?

The National Institutes of Health lists medicines for treating asthma (NHLBI, 2011). Nasal corticosteroids block reaction to allergens and reduce airway constriction. Other medicines include cromolyn sodium and nedocromil, immunomodulators, leukotriene modifiers, and long-acting beta-agonist (LABA) bronchodilators (NHLBI, 2011). Parents are also typically advised to try to remove dust, dander, mites, and other sources of respiratory irritation from the home as much as possible. Some children "outgrow" asthma, meaning that symptoms tend to improve in some children when they reach adolescence and young adulthood (Sozener et al., 2015). For some, the symptoms do not return; for others, they may return after some years have passed.

11.4 Motor Development

The school years are marked by increases in the child's speed, strength, agility, and balance (Kopp, 2011). These developments, in turn, lead to more skillful performance of motor activities, such as skipping.

How Do Gross Motor Skills Develop During Middle Childhood?

Throughout middle childhood, children show steady improvement in their ability to perform various gross motor skills (Kopp, 2011). School-age children are usually eager to participate in group games and athletic activities that require the movement of large muscles, such as catching and throwing balls. As seen in Concept Review 11.1, children are hopping, jumping, and climbing by age 6 or so, and by age 6 or 7, they are usually capable of pedaling and balancing on a bicycle. By the ages of 8–10, children are showing the balance, coordination, and strength that allow them to engage in gymnastics and team sports.

During these years, the muscles are growing stronger, and the pathways that connect the cerebellum to the cortex are becoming increasingly myelinated. Experience also plays an indispensable role in refining many sensorimotor abilities, especially at championship levels, but individual differences that seem inborn are also present. Some people, for example, have better visual acuity or better depth perception than others. For reasons such as these, they will have an edge in playing in the outfield or hitting a golf ball.

One of the most important factors in athletic performance is **reaction time**, or the amount of time required to respond to a stimulus. Reaction time is basic to the child's timing of a swing of the bat to meet the ball. Reaction time is basic to adjusting to a fly ball or hitting a tennis ball. Reaction time is also involved in children's responses to cars and other (sometimes deadly) obstacles when they are riding their bicycles or running down the street.

Reaction time gradually improves (i.e., decreases) from early childhood to about age 18 (Kopp, 2011). However, individual differences can be large (Largo et al., 2001). Reaction time begins to increase again in the adult years. Even so, 75-year-olds still outperform children. Baseball and volleyball may be "child's play," but, everything else being equal, adults respond to the ball more quickly.

How Do Fine Motor Skills Develop During Middle Childhood?

By the age of 6–7 years, children can usually tie their shoelaces and hold their pencils as adults do (see Concept Review 11.1). Their abilities to fasten buttons, zip zippers, brush their teeth, wash themselves, coordinate a knife and fork, and use chopsticks all develop in the early school years and improve during childhood (Abdelaziz et al., 2001; Beilei et al., 2002).

What Are the Gender Similarities and Differences in Motor Development During Middle Childhood?

Throughout middle childhood, boys and girls perform similarly in most motor activities. Boys show slightly greater overall strength and, in particular, more forearm strength, which aids them in swinging a bat or throwing a ball (Butterfield & Loovis, 1993).

Girls, on the other hand, show somewhat greater limb coordination and overall flexibility, which is valuable in dancing, balancing, and gymnastics (Abdelaziz et al., 2001; Cratty, 1986). Girls with a certain type of physique seem particularly well suited to gymnastics. Those who are short, lean, and small-boned make the best gymnasts, according to Olympic coaches, because they displace gravity most effectively. This may explain why female gymnasts are considered old for the sport by the time they reach their late teens. By then, they have often grown taller and their body contours have filled out (Erlandson et al., 2008).

At puberty, gender differences in motor performance favoring boys become progressively greater (Dorfberger et al., 2009). What factors might account for the development of gender differences in physical performance? The slight gender differences in motor performance prior to puberty are not large enough to be attributed to biological variables. (The one exception may be throwing, a skill in which boys excel from an early age.) Boys are more likely than girls to receive encouragement, support, and opportunities for participation in sports (Martin & Dinella, 2012). Even during the preschool years, parents emphasize physical activity in boys more than in girls. By middle childhood, boys are involved in competitive games and in games

reaction time The amount of time required to respond to a stimulus.

Development of Motor Skills During Middle Childhood

Age	Skills	
Gross Motor Skills		
6 years	• Hops, jumps, climbs	
7 years	• Balances on and pedals a bicycle	
8 years	• Has good body balance	
9 years	• Engages in vigorous bodily activities, especially team sports such as baseball, football, volleyball, and basketball	
10 years	• Balances on one foot for 15 seconds; catches a fly ball	
12 years	• Displays some awkwardness as a result of asynchronous bone and muscle development	
Fine Motor Skills		
6–7 years	• Ties shoelaces • Throws a ball by using wrist and finger release • Holds a pencil with fingertips • Follows simple mazes • May be able to hit a ball with a bat	
8–9 years	• Spaces words when writing • Writes and prints accurately and neatly • Copies a diamond shape correctly • Swings a hammer well • Sews and knits • Shows good hand–eye coordination	

of longer duration. They also engage in more vigorous activity on average than girls (Barnett et al., 2014).

At puberty, when boys begin to excel in such areas as running, the long jump, sit-ups, and grip strength, boys' greater size and strength confer a biological advantage. But some environmental factors that operated in middle childhood may assume even greater importance in puberty. "Tomboy" behavior in girls is less socially accepted in adolescence than it was in middle childhood. Therefore, girls may become less interested in participating in athletic activities and may be less motivated to do well in the ones they do pursue (Martin & Dinella, 2012). By the ages of 12 and 13, girls are less likely than boys to perceive themselves as competent (Barnett et al., 2014), and self-perception of competence predicts the extent of participation in sports (Barnett et al., 2014).

In any event, physical activity decreases with age between middle childhood and adolescence in both genders (R. A. Thompson et al., 2003). Physical activities become increasingly stereotyped by children as being masculine (e.g., football) or feminine (e.g., dance) (Barnett et al., 2014).

Are Children in the United States Physically Fit? If Not, Why Not?

The health benefits of exercise for both adults and children are well known. Exercise reduces the risk of heart disease, stroke, diabetes, and certain forms of cancer (Erwin et al., 2012; Singh et al., 2012). Exercise confers psychological benefits as well. Physically active children and adolescents have a better self-image and better coping skills than those who are inactive (Babic et al., 2014; Physical activity and health, 2011).

TRUTH OR FICTION REVISITED: Although American adults are becoming more conscientious about exercising and staying fit, most children in the United States are not physically fit. Two out of three American children do not meet the standards set by the President's Council on Fitness, Sports & Nutrition (2015).

What are some possible reasons for this decline in fitness? Again, one obvious culprit is watching television. Students who watch relatively little television have less body fat and are more physically fit than those who watch for several hours per day (Lindsay et al., 2014).

Cardiac and muscular fitness, in both childhood and adulthood, is developed by participation in continuous exercise, such as running, walking quickly, swimming laps, bicycling, or jumping rope for intervals of several minutes at a time. However, schools and parents tend to focus on sports such as baseball and football, which are less apt to promote fitness (Schumacher & Queen, 2007).

What Can Be Done During Middle Childhood to Improve Physical Fitness?

Children with high levels of physical activity are more likely to have school officials and parents who encourage them to exercise and who actively exercise themselves (Physical activity and health, 2011). How, then, can more children be motivated to engage in regular physical activity? Here are some ideas for parents:

- Engage in family outdoor activities that promote fitness: walking, swimming, bicycling, skating.
- Reduce the amount of time spent watching television.
- Encourage outdoor play during daylight hours after school.
- Do not assume that your child gets sufficient exercise by participating in a team sport. Many team sports involve long periods of inactivity.

Organized sports for children are enormously popular, but many children lose their enthusiasm and drop out. Participation in sports declines as middle childhood progresses (Schumacher & Queen, 2007). Why? Sometimes parents or coaches push children too hard, too early, or too quickly. If competition is stressed, children may feel frustrated or inferior; sometimes they get injured. Parents are advised not to place excessive demands for performance on their children. Let them progress at their own pace. Encourage them to focus on the fun and health benefits of physical activity and sports, not on winning.

Section Review

9. During middle childhood, children show _____ (abrupt or steady?) improvement in gross motor skills.

10. By the age of about _____, children show the balance, coordination, and strength that allow them to engage in gymnastics and team sports.

11. Reaction time gradually _____ (increases or decreases?) from early childhood to about age 18.

12. _____ (Boys or Girls?) tend to show greater overall strength.

13. _____ (Boys or Girls?) show somewhat greater coordination and flexibility.

14. Most children in the United States tend to be physically _____ (fit or unfit?).

Reflect & Relate: When did you become "good" at things such as riding a bicycle, skating, or team sports? Did these activities provide you with an opportunity for fulfillment and social approval, or were they a source of anxiety? Did you approach these activities with pleasure or shy away from them? Explain.

 11.5 Disorders That Affect Learning

Certain disorders are most apt to be noticed in the middle childhood years, when the child enters school. The school setting requires that a child sit still, pay attention, and master a number of academic skills. But some children have difficulty with one or more of these demands. Table 11.1 ● lists several disorders that can affect a child's learning, especially in school. We will consider attention-deficit/hyperactivity disorder, learning disabilities, and communication disorders in greater depth.

What Is Attention-Deficit/Hyperactivity Disorder (ADHD)?

Nine-year-old Eddie is a problem in class. His teacher complains that he is so restless and fidgety that the rest of the class cannot concentrate on their work. He hardly ever sits still. He is in constant motion, roaming the classroom

---

● **TABLE 11.1**

Types of Disorders That Affect Learning

Overall intellectual functioning	• Intellectual deficiency (Chapter 12)
Learning disabilities	• Reading disability (dyslexia) (this chapter) • Mathematics disability (dyscalculia) (this chapter) • Disorder of written expression (this chapter)
Speech disorders	• Articulation disorders (this chapter) • Voice disorders (this chapter) • Fluency disorders (this chapter)
Physical disabilities	• Visual impairment (this chapter) • Hearing impairment (this chapter) • Paralysis
Social and emotional disorders	• Attention-deficit/hyperactivity disorder (this chapter) • Autism spectrum disorders (Chapter 7) • Conduct disorders (Chapter 13) • Childhood depression (Chapter 13) • Childhood anxiety (Chapter 13)

© Cengage Learning®

Behaviors Connected with Attention-Deficit/Hyperactivity Disorder (ADHD)

Category	Behavior
Inattention	• Easily distracted from tasks and activities • Doesn't pay attention to instructions and details • Does not complete work in class or homework • Does not organize tasks and activities • Loses pencils, books, and homework assignments
Hyperactivity	• Fidgets in seat in class • Walks around or leaves classroom suddenly during assignments and activities • Sleeps restlessly • Runs around persistently, "like a motor" • Has difficulty playing quietly • Talks excessively
Impulsiveness	• Acts first, thinks second • Goes from one thing to another without completing assignments or activities • "Calls out" in class • Does not wait his or her turn

Source: Adapted from American Psychological Association. http://www.apa.org/topics/adhd/index.aspx (Accessed December 6, 2012).

and talking to other children while they are working. He has been suspended repeatedly for outrageous behavior, most recently swinging from a fluorescent light fixture, from which he was unable to get himself down. His mother reports that Eddie has been a problem since he was a toddler. By the age of 3 he had become unbearably restless and demanding. He has never needed much sleep and always awakened before anyone else in the family, making his way downstairs and wrecking things in the living room and kitchen. Once, at the age of 4, he unlocked the front door and wandered into traffic; thankfully, he was rescued by a passer-by.

Psychological testing shows Eddie to be average in academic ability, but to have a "virtually non-existent" attention span. He shows no interest in television or in games or toys that require some concentration. He is unpopular with peers and prefers to ride his bike alone or to play with his dog. He has become disobedient at home and at school and has stolen small amounts of money from his parents and classmates.

Eddie has been treated with methylphenidate (Ritalin), but it was discontinued because it had no effect on his disobedience and stealing. However, it did seem to reduce his restlessness and increase his attention span at school.

—Adapted from Spitzer et al. (2002)

How Does Run-of-the-Mill Failure (or Refusal!) to "Listen" to Adults Differ from Attention-Deficit/Hyperactivity Disorder?

Many parents think that their children do not pay enough attention to them—that they tend to run around as the whim strikes and to do things in their own way. Some inattention, especially at early ages, is to be expected. In **attention-deficit/hyperactivity disorder (ADHD)**, however, the child shows developmentally inappropriate or excessive inattention, impulsivity, and **hyperactivity** (Bruchmüller et al., 2012). A more thorough list of symptoms is given in Table 11.2 ●. The degree of hyperactive behavior is crucial, because many normal children are labeled overactive and fidgety

attention-deficit/hyperactivity disorder (ADHD) A behavior disorder characterized by excessive inattention, impulsiveness, and hyperactivity.

hyperactivity Excessive restlessness and overactivity; one of the primary characteristics of attention-deficit/hyperactivity disorder (ADHD). Not to be confused with misbehavior or with high activity levels that are normal during childhood.

from time to time. In fact, if talking too much were the sole criterion for ADHD, the label would have applied to many of us as children.

The onset of ADHD occurs by age 7. According to the American Psychiatric Association (2013), the behavior pattern must have persisted for at least 6 months for the diagnosis to be made. The hyperactivity and restlessness of children with ADHD impair their ability to function in school. They simply cannot sit still. They also have difficulty getting along with others. Their disruptive and noncompliant behavior often elicits punishment from parents. ADHD is quite common. According to the Centers for Disease Control and Prevention, it is diagnosed in about 11% of school-age children and about twice as often in boys as girls (Schwartz & Cohen, 2013). There was a 50% rise in the incidence of diagnoses for ADHD between 2003 and 2013, and two of three children diagnosed with the disorder are placed on stimulants such as Ritalin and Adderall.

Is ADHD Overdiagnosed?

"Those are astronomical numbers," remarked Yale University pediatrician William Graf (cited in Schwartz & Cohen, 2013). "I'm floored. Mild symptoms are being diagnosed so readily." Many psychologists and educators agree that ADHD is overdiagnosed. Many children who do not toe the line in school tend to be diagnosed with ADHD and are medicated to encourage more acceptable behavior.

Thomas R. Frieden (2013), director of the Centers for Disease Control and Prevention, expresses concern about the common prescription of the stimulants: "The right medications for ADHD, given to the right people, can make a huge difference. Unfortunately, misuse appears to be growing at an alarming rate."

What Are the Causes of ADHD?

Because ADHD is characterized in part by excessive motor activity, many theorists focus on possible physical causes. For one thing, ADHD tends to run in families for both girls and boys with the disorder (Martel et al., 2011). Some researchers suggest that there may be a genetic component to the disorder (Martel et al., 2011). If so, at least one genetic component might involve the manner in which children process the brain messengers dopamine and serotonin (Groenman et al., 2015; Tong et al., 2015).

ADHD is also found to coexist with other psychological disorders and problems, ranging most commonly from oppositional defiant disorder and anxiety disorders to mood disorders and tics (Maric et al., 2015; Melegari et al., 2015). Brain-imaging studies have found that the brain chemistry of children who have ADHD differs in certain respects from that of children who have ADHD plus other disorders, such as serious mood disorders. This raises the prospect that different causes and treatments will be discovered for various groups of children with ADHD.

In the 1970s, it was widely believed—because of the arguments and anecdotes of Benjamin Feingold—that artificial food colorings and (benzoate) food preservatives were largely responsible for hyperactivity. Feingold then introduced what was dubbed the "Feingold diet," which removed all such chemicals from foods and, according to Feingold and other researchers, had a small but measurable effect in reducing hyperactivity in children (Stevenson et al., 2014).

TRUTH OR FICTION REVISITED: Today, researchers generally agree that research attempting to connect food coloring and preservatives with the epidemic of ADHD is at best inconclusive (Nigg & Holton, 2014; Rytter et al., 2015); that is, studies of the use of the Feingold diet have yielded conflicting results. On the other hand, reviews of the research suggest that eliminating food colorings may have a small beneficial effect.

On a neurological level, researchers suggest that ADHD is connected with failure to exercise adequate inhibitory processes; that is, children with ADHD do not inhibit, or control, impulses that most children are capable of controlling (Davies et al., 2014). But *inhibition* is defined in somewhat different ways by different theorists. We may distinguish between inhibition that is under the executive control of the brain (a sort of cognitive–neurological inhibition) and inhibition that is normally motivated by emotions such as anxiety and fear (for example, anxiety about disappointing a teacher or fear of getting poor grades). ADHD probably does not reflect failure to respond to feelings of anxiety or fear. The disorder is more likely to result from a lack of executive control, but the precise nature of this control—its possible neurological aspects, for example—remains poorly understood.

How Do Health Professionals Treat ADHD? How Can It Be Possible That Children with ADHD Are Commonly Treated with Stimulants?

Stimulants such as Ritalin increase the activity of the nervous system, and are often used to treat hyperactive children. In fact, they are the most widespread treatment for ADHD. It may seem ironic that stimulants are used for children who are already overly active. The rationale is that the activity of the hyperactive child stems from the inability of the cerebral cortex to inhibit more primitive areas of the brain (Friedman & Rapoport, 2015). The drugs block the reuptake (reabsorption) of two neurotransmitters in the brain: dopamine and noradrenaline. Keeping more of these neurotransmitters active has the effect of stimulating the cerebral cortex and facilitating cortical control of primitive areas of the brain.

TRUTH OR FICTION REVISITED: It is true that stimulants are often used to treat children with ADHD—children who are already overactive. Although this treatment approach may at first seem to be self-defeating, it happens that the stimulants apparently stimulate the cerebral cortex to inhibit the activity of the more primitive areas of the brain, which are often responsible for ADHD.

Children with ADHD who are given stimulants show increased attention span, improved cognitive and academic performance, and a reduction in disruptive, annoying, and aggressive behaviors (Friedman & Rapoport, 2015). The use of stimulants is controversial, however. Some critics argue that stimulants suppress gains in height and weight, do not contribute to academic gains, and lose effectiveness over time. Another concern is that stimulants are overused or misused in an attempt to control high activity levels that are normal of children at home or in the classroom.

Supporters of stimulant treatment argue that many children who have ADHD are helped by medication. They counter that the suppression of growth appears to be related to the dosage of the drug and that low doses seem to be about as effective as large doses (Evans et al., 2001).

Cognitive behavioral therapy also shows promise in treating children with ADHD (Maric et al., 2015; Pfiffner, 2014). This approach attempts to increase the child's self-control and problem-solving abilities through modeling, role-playing, and self-instruction. A Spanish study found that it was possible to teach many children with ADHD to "stop and think" before giving in to angry impulses and behaving in an aggressive manner (Miranda & Presentacion, 2000). However, the Multimodal Treatment Study sponsored by the National Institute of Mental Health found that stimulant medication was more effective than cognitive behavioral therapy (Greene & Ablon, 2001; Whalen, 2001). Waxmonsky (2005) suggests that children may fare better with medication, whereas adolescents and adults with ADHD may be able to profit more from cognitive behavioral therapy.

stimulants Drugs that increase the activity of the nervous system.

AFRICAN AMERICAN YOUTH AND ADHD

The diagnosis and treatment of attention-deficit/hyperactivity disorder (ADHD) have come under scrutiny in the media and in medical circles, but as is often the case with medical concerns that become public issues, the focus has been almost exclusively on European American middle-class children (Zuckerman et al., 2014).

African American children, like other children, can suffer from ADHD, but according to many researchers, cultural issues make diagnosis and treatment of the disorder challenging in these children (Zuckerman et al., 2014). Although African American children respond to treatment as well as European American children (Hervey-Jumper et al., 2006), European American children who display comparable symptoms receive medications for ADHD at twice the rate of African American children.

Mattox emphasized that a lack of "culturally competent providers" is one obstacle preventing African American children from getting optimal care for ADHD. Another challenge is poverty. Moreover, a substantial number of such children are in the juvenile justice or child welfare systems, where the personnel change often and "inadequate medical care and diagnoses" are facts of life.

Teachers are more likely to believe that African American children may be hyperactive than European American children when they display essentially the same behavior (Garland et al., 2015). African American parents may also be less well-informed about ADHD than their European American counterparts and more likely to attribute ADHD symptoms to other causes, such as sugar intake. In addition, school officials are more likely to assign African American children to special-education classes than European American children, and class placement is "the only educational resource used" to address many African American children's ADHD (Bailey & Owens, 2005; McAweeney et al., 2010). But proper treatment might enable them to remain in their regular classes. Special-education placements often go unchallenged by African American parents, because they may be less aware of their rights regarding school decisions and because they face limited access to other potentially useful services in their communities.

Table 11.3 ● reveals the results of a Harris poll on barriers that prevent Latino and Latina American, African American, and European American children from getting treatment for ADHD.

Reflect: Check out Table 11.3. How would you say the three groups are alike in the barriers they face? How do they seem to differ?

● TABLE 11.3

Barriers That Prevent Parents from Obtaining Treatment for ADHD for Their Children

Barrier	Latin Americans (%)	African Americans (%)	European Americans (%)
Concern that the child will be "labeled"	51	57	52
Lack of information about ADHD	57	58	51
Concern that treatment will be based on the child's racial or ethnic background	19	36	13
Language barriers between parent or child and health-care professional	32	28	23
Cost of treatment	53	52	47

[1]Adapted from Rowen (1973).

Some children "outgrow" ADHD, but longitudinal studies have found that at least two-thirds of children with ADHD continue to exhibit one or more of the core symptoms in adolescence and adulthood (Shaw et al., 2014). Problems in attention, conduct, hyperactivity, and learning frequently continue.

What Are Learning Disabilities?

Nelson Rockefeller served as vice president of the United States under President Gerald Ford. He was intelligent and well-educated, extremely well-spoken. And yet, despite the best of tutors, he could never master reading. Rockefeller suffered from **dyslexia**.

> **TRUTH OR FICTION REVISITED:** It is true that some children who are intelligent and who are provided with enriched home environments cannot learn how to read or do simple math problems (Armstrong et al., 2013). Many such children have learning disorders, which have traditionally been referred to as learning *disabilities*.

Dyslexia is one type of **learning disability**. The term *learning disabilities* refers to a group of disorders characterized by inadequate development of specific academic, language, and speech skills (see Concept Review 11.2). Children with learning

dyslexia A reading disorder characterized by problems such as letter reversals, mirror reading, slow reading, and reduced comprehension (from the Greek roots *dys*, meaning "bad," and *lexikon*, meaning "of words").

learning disabilities A group of disorders characterized by inadequate development of specific academic, language, and speech skills.

Kinds of Learning Disabilities

		Concept Review 11.2
Dyslexia (difficulty reading)	• Reading ability is substantially less than what one would expect considering the individual's age, level of intelligence, and educational background. • The difficulty in reading interferes with the individual's scholastic achievement or daily living. • If there is also a sensory or perceptual defect, the reading problems are worse with it than one would expect.	
Disorder of written expression	• Makes mistakes in spelling that exceed what one would expect considering the individual's age, level of intelligence, and educational experiences. • Makes errors in grammar and punctuation; shows difficulty organizing paragraphs. • Shows anxiety and frustration when attempting to write; for example, breaking pencils and tearing up assignments. • Typically concurrent with dyslexia.	
Dyscalculia (difficulty in mathematics)	• Mathematical ability is substantially less than what one would expect considering the individual's age, level of intelligence, and educational background. • The math problems interfere with the individual's scholastic achievement or daily living. • If there is also a sensory or perceptual defect, the problems in mathematics are worse with it than one would expect.	

disabilities may have problems in math, writing, or reading. Some have difficulty in articulating sounds of speech or in understanding spoken language. Others have problems in motor coordination. Children are usually considered to have a learning disability when they are performing below the level expected for their age and level of intelligence and when there is no evidence of other handicaps such as vision or hearing problems, intellectual disability, or socioeconomic disadvantage (Armstrong et al., 2013). However, some psychologists and educators, such as Frank Vellutino (Vellutino et al., 2004), argue that too much emphasis is placed on the discrepancy between intelligence and reading achievement.

Children with learning disabilities frequently display other problems as well. They are more likely than other children to have ADHD (Plourde et al., 2015), and as they mature, they are more likely to develop schizophrenia as adolescents or adults (Pallanti & Salerno, 2015). They do not communicate as well with their peers, have poorer social skills, show more behavior problems in the classroom, and are more likely to experience emotional problems (Frith, 2001; Lyon et al., 2003).

For most children who have learning disabilities, the problems persist through life. But with early recognition and appropriate remediation, many individuals can learn to overcome or compensate for their learning disability (Vellutino et al., 2004).

Dyslexia

It has been estimated that dyslexia affects anywhere from 5% to 17.5% of American children (Shaywitz & Shaywitz, 2013). Most studies show that dyslexia is much more common in boys than in girls. Figure 11.3 ■ is a writing sample from a dyslexic child.

In childhood, treatment of dyslexia focuses on remediation (Bakker, 2006; Tijms, 2007). Children are given highly structured exercises to help them become aware of how to blend sounds to form words, such as identifying word pairs that rhyme and pairs that do not rhyme. Later in life, the focus tends to be on accommodation rather than on remediation. For example, college students with dyslexia may be given extra time to do the reading involved in taking tests. Interestingly, college students with dyslexia are frequently excellent at word recognition. Even so, they continue to show problems in decoding new words.

Figure 11.3 ■ A Writing Sample from a Dyslexic Child
Dyslexic children have trouble perceiving letters in their correct orientation. They may perceive letters upside down (confusing *w* with *m*) or reversed (confusing *b* with *d*). This perceptual difficulty may lead to rotations or reversals in their writing, as shown in the sample.

Will & Deni McIntyre/Science Source

Origins of Dyslexia

Current views of dyslexia focus on the ways in which sensory and neurological problems may contribute to reading problems we find in dyslexic individuals, but first let us note that genetic factors appear to be involved in dyslexia. Dyslexia runs in families. It has been estimated that 25–65% of children who have one dyslexic parent are dyslexic themselves (Plomin et al., 2013). About 40% of the siblings of children with dyslexia are also dyslexic.

Genetic factors may give rise to neurological problems. The problems can involve "faulty wiring" or circulation problems in the left hemisphere of the brain, which is usually involved in language functions (Shaywitz & Shaywitz, 2013). The circulation problems result in less oxygen than is desirable. A part of the brain called the angular gyrus lies in the left hemisphere between the visual cortex and Wernicke's area. The angular gyrus "translates" visual information, such as written words, into auditory information (sounds) and sends it on to Wernicke's area. Problems in the angular gyrus may give rise to reading problems by making it difficult for the reader to associate letters with sounds (Shaywitz & Shaywitz, 2013). Other researchers find evidence that brain abnormalities that pose a risk for schizophrenia also pose a risk for dyslexia, suggesting an overall vulnerability to cognitive deficits (Finn et al., 2014).

Some researchers report evidence that dyslexic children have difficulty controlling their eye movements (Boden & Giaschi, 2007), but most researchers today focus on dyslexic individuals' "phonological processing"— the ways in which they make, or do not make, sense of sounds. It was once thought that dyslexic children hear as well as other children, but now it seems that they may not discriminate sounds as accurately as other children (Shaywitz & Shaywitz, 2013). As a result, *b*'s and *d*'s and *p*'s, for example, may be hard to tell apart at times, creating confusion that impairs reading ability (Shaywitz & Shaywitz, 2013).

We also have the **double-deficit hypothesis** of dyslexia, which suggests that dyslexic children have neurologically based deficits both in *phonological processing* and in *naming speed* (Finn et al., 2014). Therefore, not only do they have difficulty sounding out a *b* as a *b*, but it also takes them longer than other children to name or identify a *b* when they attempt to do so.

Other Learning Disabilities

Other learning disabilities include mathematics disorder and disorder of written expression. *Mathematics disorder* is diagnosed in children who have severe deficiencies in arithmetic skills. They may have problems understanding basic mathematical terms or operations, such as addition and subtraction; decoding mathematical symbols such as + and =; or learning multiplication tables. The problem may become apparent during the first grade but often is not recognized until about the second or third grade. Children with *disorder of written expression* have grossly deficient writing skills. The deficiency may be characterized by errors in spelling, grammar, or punctuation, or by difficulty in composing sentences and paragraphs. Severe writing difficulties generally become apparent by age 7 (second grade), although milder cases may not be recognized until the age of 10 (fifth grade) or later.

Communication Disorders

Communication disorders are persistent problems in understanding or producing language. They include expressive language disorder, mixed receptive/expressive language disorder, phonological disorder, and stuttering. Each of these disorders interferes with academic or occupational functioning or ability to communicate socially.

Expressive language disorder is impairment in the use of spoken language, such as slow vocabulary development, errors in tense, difficulty recalling words,

double-deficit hypothesis The theory of dyslexia that suggests that dyslexic children have biological deficits in two areas: *phonological processing* (interpreting sounds) and *naming speed* (for example, identifying letters, such as *b* versus *d*, or *w* versus *m*).

communication disorders Persistent problems in understanding or producing language.

and problems producing sentences of appropriate length and complexity for the individual's age. Children who are affected may also have a phonological (articulation) disorder, compounding their speech problems.

Mixed receptive/expressive language disorder is characterized by difficulties both understanding and producing speech. There may be difficulty understanding words or sentences. In some cases, children have trouble understanding certain word types (such as words expressing differences in quantity—*large, big,* or *huge*), spatial terms (such as *near* or *far*), or sentence types (such as sentences that begin with the word *unlike*). Other cases are marked by difficulty understanding simple words or sentences.

Phonological disorder is a persistent difficulty articulating the sounds of speech in the absence of defects in the oral speech mechanism or neurological impairment. Children with the disorder may omit, substitute, or mispronounce certain sounds, especially *ch, f, l, r, sh,* and *th,* which most children articulate properly by the time they reach the early school years. It may sound as if they are uttering "baby talk." Children with more severe cases have problems articulating sounds usually mastered during the preschool years: *b, m, t, d, n,* and *h.* Speech therapy is often helpful, and mild cases often resolve themselves by about the age of 8.

Stuttering is a disturbance in the ability to speak fluently with appropriate timing of speech sounds. The lack of normal fluency must be inappropriate for the person's age in order to justify the diagnosis. Stuttering usually begins between 2 and 7 years of age and affects about 1 child in 100. It is characterized by one or more of the following: (a) repetitions of sounds and syllables; (b) prolongations of certain sounds; (c) interjections of inappropriate sounds; (d) broken words, such as pauses occurring within a spoken word; (e) blocking of speech; (f) circumlocutions (substitutions of alternative words to avoid problematic words); (g) an excess of physical tension when emitting words; and (h) repetitions of monosyllabic whole words (for example, "I-I-I-I am glad to meet you"). Stuttering occurs in three times as many males as females. Most children who stutter—upwards of 80%—overcome the problem without any treatment, typically before age 16.

What causes stuttering? Although the question is still unresolved, most researchers believe that genetic and environmental influences interact in producing stuttering (Grigorenko, 2009). Brain scans reveal abnormal patterns of neural activity in the basal ganglia of the brain (Etchell et al., 2014). Stuttering also appears to have an emotional component. Children who stutter tend to be more emotionally reactive than nonstutterers; when faced with stressful or challenging situations, they become more upset or excited (Alm, 2014). Social anxiety, or overconcern with how others see them, may also contribute to the problem (Alm, 2014).

Treatment of communication disorders is generally approached with specialized speech therapy or fluency training and with psychological counseling for anxiety or other emotional problems.

mainstreaming Placing children with disabilities in classrooms of children without disabilities. Today, most students with mild disabilities spend at least part of their school day in regular classrooms. The goals of mainstreaming include providing broader educational opportunities for students with disabilities and fostering interactions with children without disabilities.

Should Children with Learning Disabilities Be Placed in Regular Classrooms (That Is, Should They Be "Mainstreamed")?

Special educational programs have been created to meet the needs of schoolchildren who have mild to moderate disorders. These include learning disabilities, communication disorders, emotional disturbance, mild intellectual deficiency, and physical disabilities such as blindness, deafness, or paralysis. Evidence is mixed on whether placing children with disabilities in separate classes can also stigmatize them and segregate them from other children. Special-needs classes also negatively influence teacher expectations. Both the teacher and the students themselves come to expect very little. This negative expectation becomes a self-fulfilling prophecy, and the exceptional students' achievements suffer.

Mainstreaming is intended to counter the negative effects of special-needs classes. In mainstreaming, children with various disorders are placed in regular classrooms that have been adapted to their needs. Most students with mild learning disabilities spend most of their school day in regular classrooms (Soan & Tod, 2006). Although the goals of mainstreaming are laudable, observations of the results are mixed. Some studies indicate that children with disabilities may achieve more when they are mainstreamed (e.g., Fergusson, 2007). But other studies suggest that many children with disabilities do not fare well in regular classrooms (Frostad & Pijl, 2007). Rather than inspiring them to greater achievements, regular classrooms can be overwhelming for many students with disabilities (Silverman, 2007).

Our discussion of problems in learning and communication leads us into an investigation of cognitive development in middle childhood and the conditions that influence it. We will address this topic in Chapter 12.

Section Review

15. Children with _____ (ADHD) show developmentally inappropriate or excessive inattention, impulsivity, and hyperactivity.

16. ADHD is more common among _____ (boys or girls?).

17. ADHD _____ (does or does not?) tend to run in families.

18. Children with ADHD are likely to be treated with _____ (stimulants or tranquilizers?).

19. Learning _____ are a group of disorders characterized by inadequate development of specific academic, language, and speech skills.

20. Difficulty learning to read is called _____.

21. Current views of dyslexia focus on the ways in which _____ problems contribute to the perceptual problems we find in dyslexic children.

22. Stuttering _____ (does or does not?) tend to run in families.

Reflect & Relate: Did you know any children with disabilities who were "mainstreamed" in your classes? How were they treated by other students? How were they treated by teachers? Do you believe that mainstreaming was helpful for them?

Chapter Review

11.1 What Growth Patterns Occur During Middle Childhood?

Children tend to gain a little over 2 inches in height and 5–7 pounds in weight per year during middle childhood. Children become more slender. Boys are slightly heavier and taller than girls through the age of 9 or 10, when girls begin the adolescent growth spurt. At around age 11, boys develop relatively more muscle tissue, and females develop more fatty tissue.

11.2 How Many Children Are Overweight or Obese? Why?

About one-sixth of American children are overweight, and the prevalence of being overweight has been increasing. Overweight children usually do not "outgrow" their "baby fat." During childhood, heavy children are often rejected by their peers. Heredity plays a role in being overweight. Children with high numbers of fat cells feel food-deprived sooner than other children. Overweight parents may encourage overeating by keeping fattening foods in the home. Sedentary habits also foster being overweight.

11.3 What Are the Causes and Treatment of Childhood Asthma?

Asthma is an allergy-type respiratory disorder characterized by spasms in the lungs, difficulty breathing, wheezing, often coughing (dry hacking), and a feeling of tightness in the chest that prevents the sufferer from getting enough air. Treatments for asthma include nasal steroids and bronchodilators.

11.4 How Does Motor Development Proceed During Middle Childhood?

Middle childhood is marked by increases in speed, strength, agility, and balance. Children show regular improvement in gross motor skills and are often eager to participate in athletic activities, such as ball games that require movement of large muscles. Muscles grow stronger, and pathways that connect the cerebellum to the cortex become more myelinated. Reaction time gradually decreases. Fine motor skills also improve; most 6- to 7-year-olds tie their shoelaces and hold pencils as adults do. Boys have slightly greater overall strength, whereas girls have better coordination and flexibility, which are valuable in dancing, balancing, and gymnastics. Boys generally receive more encouragement than girls to excel in athletics. Most children in the United States are not physically fit. One reason is the amount of time they spend watching television.

11.5 What Are Causes and Treatments of Learning Disorders?

Attention-deficit/hyperactivity disorder (ADHD) involves lack of attention, impulsivity, and hyperactivity. ADHD impairs children's ability to function in school. ADHD tends to be overdiagnosed and overmedicated. ADHD runs in families and often coexists with other problems. Children with ADHD do not inhibit impulses that most children control, suggesting poor executive control in the brain. Stimulants are used to stimulate the cerebral cortex to inhibit more primitive areas of the brain. Stimulants increase the attention span and academic performance of children with ADHD, but there are side effects, and the medications may be used too often. Cognitive behavioral therapy can also help teach children self-control. Learning disabilities are characterized by inadequate development of specific academic, language, and speech skills. Children may be diagnosed with a learning disability when their performance is below that expected for their age and level of intelligence. Current views of dyslexia focus on the ways in which neurological problems may contribute to perceptual problems. Genetic factors appear to be involved because dyslexia runs in families. The double-deficit hypothesis suggests that dyslexic children have neurologically based deficits in phonological processing and in naming speed. Communication disorders are persistent problems in understanding or producing language. They include expressive language disorder, mixed receptive/expressive language disorder, phonological disorder, and stuttering.

Key Terms

12

Middle Childhood: Cognitive Development

TruthorFiction?

Did you hear the one about the judge who pounded her gavel and yelled, "Order! Order in the court!"? "A hamburger and French fries, Your Honor," responded the defendant. Or how about this one? "I saw a man-eating lion at the zoo." "Big deal! I saw a man eating snails at a restaurant." Or how about, "Make me a glass of chocolate milk!"? "Poof! You're a glass of chocolate milk." These children's jokes are based on ambiguities in the meanings of words and phrases. Most 7-year-olds find the joke about order in the court funny and can recognize that the word *order* has more than one meaning. The jokes about the man-eating lion and chocolate milk strike most children as funny at about the age of 11, when they can understand ambiguities in grammatical structure.

Children make enormous strides in their cognitive development during the middle childhood years. Their thought processes and language become more logical and more complex. In this chapter, we follow the course of cognitive development in middle childhood. First, we continue our discussion of Piaget's cognitive-developmental view from Chapter 9, also reflecting on cognitive-developmental views of moral development. We then consider the information-processing approach that has been stimulated by our experience with the computer. We next explore the development of intelligence, ways of measuring it, and the roles of heredity and environment in shaping it. Finally, we turn to the development of language.

Fancy Photography/Veer

According to Piaget, the typical child is entering the stage of **concrete operations** by the age of 7.

What Is Meant by the Stage of Concrete Operations?

In the stage of concrete operations, which lasts until about the age of 12, children show the beginnings of the capacity for adult logic. However, their thought processes, or operations, generally involve tangible objects rather than abstract ideas. This is why we refer to their thinking as "concrete."

The thinking of the concrete-operational child is characterized by **reversibility** and flexibility. Consider adding the numbers 2 and 3 to get 5. Adding is an operation. The operation is reversible in that the child can then subtract 2 from 5 to get 3. There is flexibility in that the child can also subtract 3 from 5 to get the number 2. To the concrete-operational child, adding and subtracting are not just rote activities. The concrete-operational child recognizes that there are relationships among numbers—that operations can be carried out according to rules. This understanding lends concrete-operational thought flexibility and reversibility.

Concrete-operational children are less egocentric than preoperational children. Their abilities to take on the roles of others and to view the world and themselves from other peoples' perspectives are greatly expanded. They recognize that people see things in different ways because of different situations and different sets of values.

Compared with preoperational children, who can focus on only one dimension of a problem at a time, concrete-operational children can engage in **decentration**; that is, they can focus on multiple parts of a problem at once. Decentration has implications for conservation and other intellectual undertakings.

Conservation

Concrete-operational children show understanding of the laws of conservation. The 7-year-old girl in Figure 12.1 ■ would say that the flattened ball still has the same amount of clay. If asked why, she might reply, "Because you can roll it up again like the other one." This answer shows reversibility.

concrete operations The third stage in Piaget's cognitive-developmental theory of moral development, characterized by flexible, reversible thought concerning tangible objects and events.

reversibility According to Piaget, recognition that processes can be undone, leaving things as they were before. Reversibility is a factor in conservation of the properties of substances.

decentration Simultaneous focusing (centering) on more than one aspect or dimension of a problem or situation.

Figure 12.1 ■ Conservation of Mass
This girl is in the concrete-operational stage of cognitive development. She has rolled two clay balls. In the photo on the left, she agrees that both have the same amount (mass) of clay. In the photo on the right, she (gleefully) flattens one clay ball. When asked whether the two pieces still have the same amount of clay, she says yes.

© Judy Allen

The concrete-operational girl knows that objects can have several properties or dimensions. Things that are tall can also be heavy or light. Things that are red can also be round or square, or thick or thin. Knowledge of this principle enables the girl to decenter and to avoid focusing on only the diameter of the clay pancake. By attending to both the height and the width of the clay, she recognizes that the loss in height compensates for the gain in width.

Children do not necessarily develop conservation in all kinds of tasks simultaneously. Conservation of mass usually develops first, followed by conservation of weight and conservation of volume. Piaget theorized that the gains of the concrete-operational stage are so tied to specific events that achievement in one area does not necessarily transfer to achievement in another.

Transitivity

Question of the day: If your parents are older than you are and you are older than your children, are your parents older than your children? (How do you know?)

We have posed some tough questions in this book, but this one about your parents is a real ogre. The answer, of course, is yes. But how did you arrive at this answer? If you said yes simply on the basis of knowing that your parents are older than your children (e.g., 58 and 56 compared with 5 and 3), your answer did not require concrete-operational thought. One aspect of concrete-operational thought is the principle of **transitivity**: If A exceeds B in some property (say, age or height) and if B exceeds C, then A must also exceed C.

Researchers can assess whether or not children understand the principle of transitivity by asking them to place objects in a series, or order, according to some property or trait, such as lining up one's family members according to age, height, or weight. Placing objects in a series is termed **seriation**.

Piaget frequently assessed children's abilities at seriation by asking them to place 10 sticks in a row, in the order of their size. Children who are 4 or 5 years of age usually place the sticks in a random sequence or in small groups, as in small, medium, or large. Six- to 7-year-old children, who are in transition between the preoperational and concrete-operational stages, may place the sticks in the proper sequence. However, they usually do so by trial and error, rearranging their series a number of times. In other words, they are capable of comparing two sticks and deciding that one is longer than the other, but their overall perspective seems limited to the pair they are comparing at the time rather than encompassing the entire array.

But consider the approach of 7- and 8-year-olds who are capable of concrete operations. They go about the task systematically, usually without error. They look over the array of 10 sticks and then select either the longest or the shortest and place it at the point from which they will build their series. Then they select the next longest (or next shortest) and continue in this fashion until the task is complete.

Knowledge of the principle of transitivity enables concrete-operational children to go about their task unerringly. They realize that if stick A is longer than stick B and stick B is longer than stick C, then stick A is also longer than stick C. After putting stick C in place, they need not double-check to make sure it will be shorter than stick A; they know it will be.

Concrete-operational children also have the decentration capacity that enables them to seriate in two dimensions at once. Consider a seriation task used by Piaget and his longtime colleague, Barbel Inhelder (Inhelder & Piaget, 1959). In this test, children are given 49 leaves and asked to classify them according to size and brightness (from small to large and from dark to light) (see Figure 12.2 ■). As the grid is completed from left to right, the leaves become lighter. As it is filled in from top to bottom, the leaves become larger. Preoperational 6-year-olds can usually order the leaves according to size or brightness, but not both simultaneously. But concrete-operational children of age 7 or 8 can work with both dimensions at once and fill in the grid properly.

transitivity The principle that if A is greater than B in a property and B is greater than C, then A is greater than C.

seriation Placing objects in an order or series according to a property or trait.

Figure 12.2 ■ A Grid for Demonstrating the Development of Seriation
To classify these 49 leaves, children must be able to focus on two dimensions at once: the size of the leaves and their relative lightness. They must also recognize that if quantity A of a particular property exceeds quantity B and quantity B exceeds quantity C, then quantity A must also exceed quantity C. This relationship is referred to as the *principle of transitivity*.
© Cengage Learning®

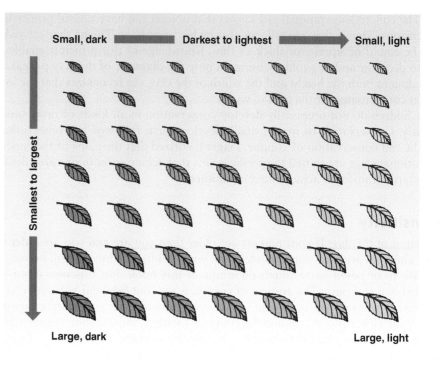

A number of researchers have argued that children can seriate earlier than Piaget believed and that Piaget's results reflected the demand characteristics of his experiments (De Leeuw et al., 2004; Siegler & Alibali, 2005). This may be so, but the sequence of developments in seriation and transitivity seems to have been captured fairly well by Piaget.

Class Inclusion

Another example of an operation is **class inclusion,** which we learned about in Chapter 9. In the example in Chapter 9 (p. 289), a 4-year-old was shown pictures of four cats and six dogs. When asked whether there were more dogs or more animals, she said more dogs. This preoperational child apparently could not focus on the two subclasses (dogs and cats) and the larger class (animals) at the same time. But concrete-operational children can focus on two dimensions (in this case, classes and subclasses) at the same time. Therefore, they are more likely to answer the question about the dogs and the animals correctly (Chapman & McBride, 1992; Deneault & Ricard, 2006). Their thought still remains concrete in that they will give you the correct answer if you ask them about dogs and animals (or daffodils and flowers), but not if you attempt to phrase the question in terms of abstract symbols, such as A, B$_1$, and B$_2$. As with other areas of cognitive development, researchers have taken issue with Piaget's views of the ages at which class-inclusion skills develop. They have argued that language continues to pose hazards for the children being tested. Aspects of concrete-operational thinking are summarized in Concept Review 12.1.

Can We Apply Piaget's Theory of Cognitive Development to Educational Practices?

It seems that we can (Crain, 2000; Mayer, 2008). Piaget pointed out some applications himself. First, Piaget believed that learning involves active discovery. Therefore, teachers should not simply try to impose knowledge on the child but, rather, should find interesting and stimulating materials. Second, instruction should be geared to

class inclusion The principle that one category or class of things can include several subclasses.

Aspects of Concrete-Operational Thinking

Conservation

Concrete-operational children show conservation of mass and number.

The girl on the right shows conservation of the mass of the clay. Refer to Figure 9.3 (p. 283), showing the experiment using pennies to test conservation of number. A concrete-operational child will conserve number and say that both panels have the same number of pennies. Preoperational children will say that the wider row has "more."

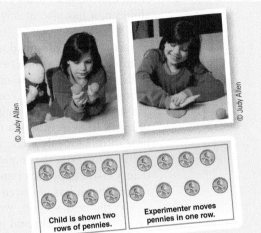

Child is shown two rows of pennies.

Experimenter moves pennies in one row.

Seriation

A concrete-operational child understands the principle of transitivity (if A > B and B > C, then A > C). Therefore, the child can place the sticks in order from longest to shortest.

Class Inclusion

Here are 10 animals, including 6 dogs. When asked whether there are more dogs or more animals, the preoperational child, focusing on one aspect of the problem at a time, may see that there are more dogs than cats and say "dogs." The concrete-operational child is more likely to recognize that the class "animals" includes both "dogs" and "cats" and thus will answer "animals."

the child's level of development. When teaching a concrete-operational child about fractions, for example, the teacher should not just lecture but should allow the child to divide concrete objects into parts. Third, Piaget believed that learning to take into account the perspectives of others is a key ingredient in the development of both cognition and morality. Accordingly, he thought that teachers should promote group discussions and interactions among their students.

Evaluation of Piaget's Theory

Although Piaget's theory has led many psychologists to recast their concepts of children, it has also met with criticism on several grounds. As noted in Chapters 6 and 9, some researchers have shown that Piaget underestimated children's abilities at various ages. Modified task demands suggest that children are capable of conservation and other concrete-operational tasks earlier than Piaget believed. Cognitive skills may develop more independently and continuously than Piaget thought—not in stages. For example, conservation does not arrive all at once. Children develop conservation for mass, weight, and volume at different ages. The onset of conservation can be seen in terms of the gradual accumulation of problem-solving abilities instead of suddenly changing cognitive structures (Barrouillet, 2015; Flavell et al., 2002). However, the sequences of development—which are at the core of Piaget's theory—still appear to remain the same. In sum, Piaget's theoretical edifice has been rocked, but it has not been dashed to rubble.

In the next section, we will revisit Piaget and examine his views on children's decisions about right and wrong. Then we will consider Lawrence Kohlberg's views on the same topic.

Section Review

1. Concrete-operational children are _____ (more or less?) egocentric than preoperational children.

2. The principle of _____ holds that if A exceeds B and B exceeds C, then A must exceed C.

3. Class _____ involves the ability to recognize that one class of things (A) can include subclasses (B₁ and B₂).

Reflect & Relate: George becomes angry that Delores wants to break off their relationship and beats her so badly that she must remain in the hospital for 6 months. Gus makes a mistake at the nuclear energy plant where he works, causing a nuclear accident in which a great deal of radiation is released, killing 300 people within a week and shortening the lives of more than a million people because of cancer. Which person has done something naughtier: George or Gus? Explain your viewpoint. (Now you are ready to read the next section.)

12.2 Moral Development: The Child as Judge

Moral development is a complex issue with both cognitive and behavioral aspects. On a cognitive level, moral development concerns the basis on which children make judgments that an act is right or wrong. In this section, we examine the contributions of Piaget and Kohlberg to our understanding of children's moral development.

Piaget and Kohlberg argued that moral reasoning exhibits the same cognitive-developmental pattern around the world. The moral considerations that children weigh at a given age are likely to reflect the values of the social and cultural settings in which they are being reared. However, moral reasoning is also theorized to reflect the orderly unfolding of cognitive processes (Nucci et al., 2014). Moral reasoning is related to the child's overall cognitive development.

How Does Piaget View the Development of Moral Reasoning?

For years, Piaget observed children playing games such as marbles and making judgments on the seriousness of the wrongdoing of characters in stories. On the basis of these observations, Piaget (1932) concluded that children's moral judgments develop in two major overlapping stages: moral realism and autonomous morality.

The Stage of Moral Realism

The first stage is usually referred to as the stage of **moral realism**, also termed **objective morality**. During this stage, which emerges at about the age of 5, children consider behavior to be correct when it conforms to authority or to the rules of the game. When asked why something should be done in a certain way, the 5-year-old may answer, "Because that's the way to do it" or "Because my Mommy says so."

At about the age of 5, children perceive rules as embedded in the structure of things. Rules, to them, reflect ultimate reality—hence the term *moral realism*. Rules and right and wrong are seen as absolute. They are not seen as deriving from people's efforts to meet social needs.

Another consequence of viewing rules as embedded in the fabric of the world is the belief in **immanent justice,** or automatic retribution. Immanent justice reasoning consists of thinking that negative experiences are punishment for prior misdeeds, even when realistic causal links are absent (Callan et al., 2014). Five- or 6-year-old children who lie or steal usually believe that they will be found out or at least punished for their acts. If they trip and scrape their knees, they may assume that this accident represents punishment for a transgression.

Children in the stage of moral realism are tough judges indeed. They do not excuse the person who harms by accident. As an illustration, consider children's responses to Piaget's story about broken cups. Piaget told children a story in which one child breaks 15 cups accidentally and another child breaks one cup deliberately. Which child is naughtier? Which should be punished more? Children in the stage of moral realism typically say that the child who did the most damage is naughtier and should be punished more. The amount of damage is more important than the wrongdoer's intentions (Piaget, 1932).

Mina Chapman/Corbis Super RF / Alamy

Moral Realism It looks bad, but Mom asked her to find the car keys. If the girl breaks things or drops them on the floor in the effort, is she being "bad"? Children in the stage of moral realism might well say, "Yes, she's being bad" because they focus on one dimension of the situation: the amount of damage done and not the intentions of the "wrongdoer."

> **TRUTH OR FICTION REVISITED:** It is true that you are guilty for having done something "wrong" in the eyes of a 5-year-old, even when your behavior was an accident. Preoperational children tend to focus on only one dimension at a time. Therefore, they tend to judge the wrongness of an act in terms of the amount of damage done, rather than considering both the damage done *and* the intentions of the wrongdoer.

The Stage of Autonomous Morality

Piaget found that when children reach the ages of 9–11, they begin to show **autonomous morality**. Their moral judgments tend to become more self-governed. Children come to view social rules as arbitrary agreements that can be changed. Children no longer automatically view obedience to authority figures as right. They realize that circumstances can require the breaking of rules.

Children who show autonomous morality are capable of flexible operational thought. They can focus simultaneously on multiple dimensions, so they consider not only social rules but also the motives of the wrongdoer.

Children in this stage also show a greater capacity to take the point of view of others—to empathize with them. Decentration and increased empathy prompt children to weigh the intentions of the wrongdoer more heavily than the amount of damage done. The child who broke one cup deliberately may be seen as more deserving of punishment than the child who broke 15 cups accidentally. Children become capable of considering mitigating circumstances. Accidents are less likely to be considered crimes.

Piaget assumed that autonomous morality usually develops as a result of cooperative peer relationships. But he also believed that parents could help foster

moral realism The first stage in Piaget's cognitive-developmental theory of moral development. In this stage, children judge acts as moral when they conform to authority or to the rules of the game. Morality is perceived as embedded in the structure of the universe.

objective morality The perception of morality as objective, or as existing outside the cognitive functioning of people; a characteristic of Piaget's stage of moral realism.

autonomous morality by creating egalitarian relationships with their children and explaining the reasons for social rules. As we will see in the next section, knowledge of social rules is also a key factor in Kohlberg's theory of moral development.

How Does Kohlberg View the Development of Moral Reasoning?

Kohlberg (1981, 1985) advanced the cognitive-developmental theory of moral development by elaborating on the kinds of information children use and on the complexities of moral reasoning. Before we discuss Kohlberg's views, read the following tale, which Kohlberg used in his research, and answer the questions that follow.

> In Europe, a woman was near death from a special kind of cancer. There was one drug that the doctors thought might save her. It was a form of radium that a druggist in the same town had recently discovered. The drug was expensive to make, but the druggist was charging 10 times what the drug cost him to make. He paid $200 for the radium and charged $2,000 for a small dose of the drug. The sick woman's husband, Heinz, went to everyone he knew to borrow the money, but he could only get together about $1,000, which was half of what it cost. He told the druggist that his wife was dying and asked him to sell it cheaper or let him pay later. But the druggist said: "No, I discovered the drug and I'm going to make money from it." So Heinz got desperate and broke into the man's store to steal the drug for his wife.
> —Kohlberg (1969)

Kohlberg emphasized the importance of being able to view the moral world from the perspective of another person (Krebs, 2013; Lapsley & Carlo, 2014). Look at this situation from Heinz's perspective. What do you think? Should Heinz have tried to steal the drug? Was he right or wrong? As you can see from Table 12.1 ●, the issue is more complicated than a simple yes or no. Heinz is caught in a moral dilemma in which legal or social rules (in this case, laws against stealing) are pitted against a strong human need (Heinz's desire to save his wife). According to Kohlberg's theory, children and adults arrive at yes or no answers for different reasons. These reasons can be classified according to the level of moral development they reflect.

Children (and adults) are faced with many moral dilemmas. Consider cheating in school: When children fear failing a test, they may be tempted to cheat. Different children may decide not to cheat for different reasons. One child may simply fear getting caught. A second child may decide that it is more important to live up to her moral principles than to get the highest possible grade. In each case, the child's decision is not to cheat. However, the cognitive processes behind each decision reflect different levels of reasoning.

As a stage theorist, Kohlberg argued that the developmental stages of moral reasoning follow the same sequence in all children. Children progress at different rates, and not all children (or adults) reach the highest stage. But children must experience Stage 1 before they enter Stage 2, and so on. According to Kohlberg, there are three levels of moral development and two stages within each level.

Let us return to Heinz and see how responses to the questions we have posed can reflect different levels and stages of moral development.

The Preconventional Level of Moral Development

At the **preconventional level**, children base their moral judgments on the consequences of their behavior. For instance, Stage 1 is oriented toward obedience and punishment. Good behavior means being obedient, which enables one to avoid punishment. According to Stage 1 reasoning, Heinz could be urged to steal the drug

immanent justice The view that a negative experience is a direct consequence of wrongdoing, reflecting the belief that morality is embedded within the structure of the universe.

autonomous morality The second stage in Piaget's cognitive-developmental theory of moral development. In this stage, children base moral judgments on the intentions of the wrongdoer more so than on the amount of damage done. Social rules are viewed as agreements that can be changed.

preconventional level According to Kohlberg, a period during which moral judgments are based largely on expectations of rewards or punishments.

Kohlberg's Levels and Stages of Moral Development

Stage of Development	Examples of Moral Reasoning That Support Heinz's Stealing the Drug	Examples of Moral Reasoning That Oppose Heinz's Stealing the Drug
Level I: Preconventional—Typically Begins in Early Childhood[a]		
Stage 1: Judgments guided by obedience and the prospect of punishment (the consequences of the behavior)	It is not wrong to take the drug. Heinz did try to pay the druggist for it, and it is only worth $200, not $2,000.	Taking things without paying is wrong because it is against the law. Heinz will get caught and go to jail.
Stage 2: Naively egoistic, instrumental orientation (things are right when they satisfy people's needs)	Heinz ought to take the drug because his wife really needs it. He can always pay the druggist back.	Heinz should not take the drug. If he gets caught and winds up in jail, it won't do his wife any good.
Level II: Conventional—Typically Begins in Middle Childhood		
Stage 3: Good-boy/good-girl orientation (moral behavior helps others and is socially approved)	Stealing is a crime, so it is bad, but Heinz should take the drug to save his wife or else people would blame him for letting her die.	Stealing is a crime. Heinz should not take the drug because his family will be dishonored and they will blame him.
Stage 4: Law-and-order orientation (moral behavior is doing one's duty and showing respect for authority)	Heinz must take the drug to do his duty to save his wife. Eventually, however, he has to pay the druggist for it.	If we all took the law into our own hands, civilization would fall apart, so Heinz should not steal the drug.
Level III: Postconventional—Typically Begins in Adolescence[b]		
Stage 5: Contractual, legalistic orientation (one must weigh pressing human needs against society's need to maintain social order)	This thing is complicated because society has a right to maintain law and order, but Heinz has to take the drug to save his wife.	I can see why Heinz feels he has to take the drug, but laws exist for the benefit of society as a whole and cannot simply be cast aside.
Stage 6: Universal ethical principles orientation (people must follow universal ethical principles and their own conscience, even if it means breaking the law)	In this case, the law comes into conflict with the principle of the sanctity of human life. Heinz must take the drug because his wife's life is more important than the law.	If Heinz truly believes that stealing the drug is worse than letting his wife die, he should not take it. People have to make sacrifices to do what they think is right.

[a] Tends to be used less often in middle childhood.
[b] May not develop at all.
© Cengage Learning®

because he did ask to pay for it first. But he could also be urged not to steal the drug so that he will not be sent to jail (see Table 12.1).

In Stage 2, good behavior allows people to satisfy their own needs and, perhaps, the needs of others. A Stage 2 reason for stealing the drug is that Heinz's wife needs it. Therefore, stealing the drug—the only way of attaining it—is not wrong. A Stage 2 reason for not stealing the drug is that Heinz's wife might die even if he does so. Thus, he might wind up in jail needlessly.

In a study of U.S. children aged 7 through 16, Kohlberg (1963) found that Stage 1 and Stage 2 types of moral judgments were offered most frequently by 7- and 10-year-olds. There was a steep falling off of Stage 1 and 2 judgments after age 10.

The Conventional Level of Moral Development

At the **conventional level** of moral reasoning, right and wrong are judged by conformity to conventional (family, religious, societal) standards of right and wrong. According to the Stage 3 "good-boy/good-girl" orientation, it is good to meet the needs and expectations of others. Moral behavior is what is "normal"—what the majority does. From the Stage 3 perspective, Heinz should steal the drug because that is what a "good husband" would do. It is "natural" or "normal" to try to help

conventional level According to Kohlberg, a period during which moral judgments largely reflect social rules and conventions.

one's wife. Or Heinz should not steal the drug because "good people do not steal." Stage 3 judgments also focus on the role of sympathy—on the importance of doing what will make someone else feel good or better.

In Stage 4, moral judgments are based on rules that maintain the social order. Showing respect for authority and duty is valued highly. From this perspective, one could argue that Heinz must steal the drug because it is his duty to save his wife. He would pay the druggist when he could. Or one could argue that Heinz should not steal the drug because he would be breaking the law. He might also be contributing to the breakdown of the social order. Many people do not develop beyond the conventional level.

Kohlberg (1963) found that Stage 3 and Stage 4 types of judgments emerge during middle childhood. They are all but absent among 7-year-olds. However, they are reported by about 20% of 10-year-olds (and by higher percentages of adolescents).

The Postconventional Level of Moral Development

At the **postconventional level**, moral reasoning is based on the person's own moral standards (Snarey & Samuelson, 2014). If this level of reasoning develops at all, it is found among adolescents and adults (see Table 12.1).

In Chapter 15, we will discuss the postconventional level in depth. We will include Carol Gilligan's research showing that although girls' moral judgments have frequently been considered inferior to boys', girls actually consider more factors in arriving at their judgments of right and wrong. We will also evaluate Kohlberg's theory and see that other theorists are proposing major modifications.

Section Review

4. Piaget believed that children's moral judgments develop in two stages: moral realism and _____ morality.

5. Preoperational children judge the wrongness of an act in terms of the _____ (amount of damage done or intentions of the wrongdoer?).

6. In Kohlberg's _____ level, children base their moral judgments on the consequences of their behavior.

7. At the _____ level, right and wrong are judged by conformity to conventional _____ (family, religious, societal) standards of right and wrong.

Reflect & Relate: Do you believe that Heinz should have taken the drug without paying? Why or why not? What does your reasoning suggest about your level of moral development?

postconventional level According to Kohlberg, a period during which moral judgments are derived from moral principles and people look to themselves to set moral standards.

information processing The view in which cognitive processes are compared to the functions of computers. The theory deals with the input, storage, retrieval, manipulation, and output of information. The focus is on the development of children's strategies for solving problems— their "mental programs."

12.3 Information Processing: Learning, Remembering, Problem Solving

Whereas Piaget looked on children as budding scientists, psychologists who view cognitive development in terms of **information processing** see children (and adults) as akin to computer systems. Sort of. Children, like computers, obtain information (input) from the environment, store it, retrieve it, manipulate it, and then respond to it overtly (output). One goal of the information-processing approach is to learn how children store, retrieve, and manipulate information—how their "mental programs" develop. Information-processing theorists also study the development of children's strategies for processing information (Cowan, 2014; Howe, 2015).

Although something may be gained from thinking of children as computers, children, of course, are not computers. Children are self-aware and capable of creativity and intuition.

In the following sections, we will discuss these key elements of information processing:

- *Development of selective attention*—Development of children's abilities to focus on the elements of a problem and find solutions.
- *Development of the capacity for storage and retrieval of information*—Development of the capacity of memory and of children's understanding of the processes of memory and how to strengthen and use memory.
- *Development of strategies for processing information*—Development of the ability to solve problems; for example, finding the correct formula and applying it.

How Do Children Develop Selective Attention?

A key cognitive process is the ability to pay attention to relevant features of a task. The ability to focus one's attention and screen out distractions advances steadily through middle childhood (Lim et al., 2015). Preoperational children who are engaged in problem solving tend to focus (or center) their attention on one element of the problem at a time—a major reason why they lack conservation. Concrete-operational children, by contrast, can attend to multiple aspects of the problem at once, which enables them to conserve number, volume, and so on.

An experiment by Strutt and colleagues (1975) illustrates how selective attention and the ability to ignore distraction develop during middle childhood. The researchers asked children between 6 and 12 years of age to sort a deck of cards as quickly as possible on the basis of the figures depicted on each card (e.g., circle versus square). In one condition, only the relevant dimension (form) was shown on each card. In a second condition, a dimension not relevant to the sorting also was present (e.g., a horizontal or vertical line in the figure). In a third condition, two irrelevant dimensions were present (e.g., a star above or below the figure, in addition to a horizontal or vertical line in the figure). As seen in Figure 12.3 ■, the irrelevant information interfered with sorting ability for all age groups, but older children were much less affected than younger children. In the next section, we will learn more about how children gain the ability to store and retrieve information.

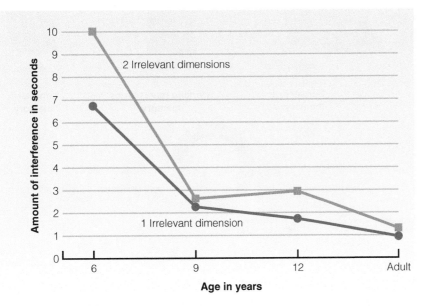

Figure 12.3 ■ Development of the Ability to Ignore Distractions
Strutt and his colleagues demonstrated how the ability to ignore distractions develops during middle childhood. The effect of irrelevant dimensions on sorting speed was determined by subtracting the speed of the sort in the no-irrelevant-dimension condition from the speed in the other two conditions. As shown here, irrelevant information interfered with sorting ability for all age groups, but older children were less affected than younger ones.
Source: Strutt et al. (1975).

What Developments Occur in the Storage and Retrieval of Information During Middle Childhood?

The storage and retrieval of information involves what we generally refer to as **memory**. But keep in mind that the word *memory* is not a scientific term, even though psychologists and other scientists may use it for the sake of convenience. Psychologists usually use the term to refer to the processes of storing and retrieving information. Many, but not all, psychologists divide memory functioning into three major processes or structures: sensory memory, working memory (short-term memory), and long-term memory (see Figure 12.4 ■).

Sensory Memory

When we look at an object and then blink our eyes, the visual impression of the object lasts for a fraction of a second in what is called **sensory memory** or the **sensory register**. Then the "trace" of the stimulus decays. The concept of sensory memory applies to all the senses. For example, when we are introduced to somebody, the trace of the sound of the name also decays, but as we will see in the next section, we can maintain the name in memory by focusing on it.

Working Memory (Short-Term Memory)

When children focus their attention on a stimulus in the sensory register, it tends to be retained in **working memory** (also called *short-term memory*) for up

memory The processes by which we store and retrieve information.

sensory memory The structure of memory that is first encountered by sensory input. Information is maintained in sensory memory for only a fraction of a second.

sensory register Another term for sensory memory.

working memory The structure of memory that can hold a sensory stimulus for up to 30 seconds after the trace decays. Also called short-term memory.

Figure 12.4 ■ The Structure of Memory
Many psychologists divide memory into three processes, or "structures." Sensory information enters the registers of sensory memory, where memory traces are held briefly before decaying. If we attend to the information, much of it is transferred to working memory (also called short-term memory), where it may decay or be displaced if it is not transferred to long-term memory. We usually use rehearsal (repetition) or elaborative strategies to transfer memories to long-term memory. Once in long-term memory, memories can be retrieved through appropriate search strategies. But if information is organized poorly or if we cannot find cues to retrieve it, it may be "lost" for all practical purposes.
© Cengage Learning®

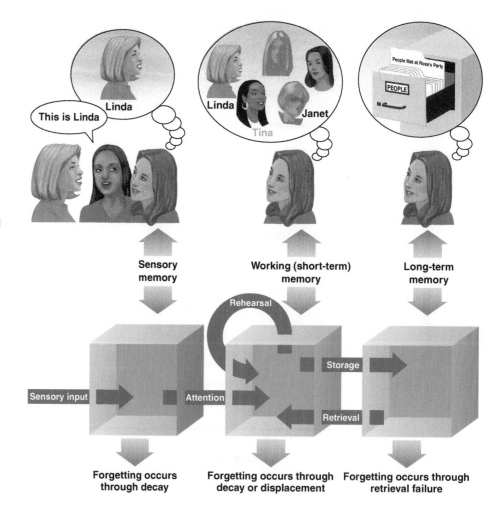

to 30 seconds after the trace of the stimulus decays. The ability to maintain information in short-term memory depends on cognitive strategies and on the basic capacity to continue to perceive a vanished stimulus. Memory function in middle childhood seems largely adultlike in organization and strategies and shows only gradual improvement in a quantitative sense through early adolescence (Howe, 2015).

Auditory stimuli can be maintained longer in short-term memory than can visual stimuli. For this reason, one strategy for promoting memory is to **encode** visual stimuli as sounds, or auditory stimulation. Then the sounds can be repeated out loud or mentally. For example, in Figure 12.4, mentally repeating the sound of Linda's name helps the other girl remember it; that is, the sounds can be **rehearsed**.

Capacity of Short-Term Memory

The basic capacity of short-term memory can be described in terms of the number of "bits" or chunks of information that can be kept in memory at once. To remember a new phone number, for example, one must keep seven chunks of information in short-term memory simultaneously; that is, one must rehearse them consecutively.

Classic research shows that the typical adult can keep about seven chunks of information—plus or minus two—in short-term memory at a time (Cowan, 2015; Miller, 1956). As measured by the ability to recall digits, the typical 5- to 6-year-old can work on two chunks of information at a time. The ability to recall a series of digits improves throughout middle childhood, and adolescents, like adults, can keep about seven chunks of information in short-term memory at the same time (Gignac & Weiss, 2015; Silva et al., 2012).

The information-processing view focuses on children's capacity for memory and their use of cognitive strategies, such as the way in which they focus their attention (Swanson & Alloway, 2012). Certain Piagetian tasks require several cognitive strategies instead of one. Young children often fail at such tasks because they cannot simultaneously hold many pieces of information in their short-term memories. Put another way, preschoolers can solve problems that have only one or two steps, whereas older children can retain information from earlier steps as they proceed to subsequent steps.

But how do young children remember the alphabet, which is 26 chunks of information? Children usually learn the alphabet by **rote learning**—simple associative learning based on repetition. After the alphabet is repeated many, many times, M triggers the letter N, N triggers O, and so on. The typical 3-year-old who has learned the alphabet by rote will not be able to answer the question "What letter comes after N?" However, if you recite "H, I, J, K, L, M, N" with the child and then pause, the child is likely to say, "O, P." The 3-year-old probably will not realize that he or she can find the answer by using the cognitive strategy of reciting the alphabet, but many 5- or 6-year-olds will.

TRUTH OR FICTION REVISITED: It is not true that learning the alphabet requires keeping 26 chunks of information in mind at once. Instead, children typically learn the alphabet by rote repetition. They also often use "alphabet songs," which underscore the location of a letter in relation to other letters and to music.

encode To transform sensory input into a form that is more readily processed.

rehearse Repeat.

rote learning A memorization technique based on repetition.

Children are also helped to learn the alphabet by singing the "alphabet song," especially in a group setting. There is thus social reinforcement—fun!—in learning and producing the song correctly. Moreover, the groupings of letters trigger subse-

THE LONG-TERM EFFECTS OF GOOD TEACHING

Just the title of this Closer Look—"The Long-Term Effects of Good Teaching"—will stimulate arguments. Who, some readers will want to know, can say what makes a good teacher? We all have memories of teachers we would consider "good" and of teachers we would think of as not so good. But what do we look at when we make our judgments? Do we look at how likeable the teacher was? How helpful and empathic? Or do we ask ourselves whether we learned something? And what else do we consider?

Many psychologists and educators believe that it is difficult to measure "good teaching" objectively (Lowrey, 2012). Yet a team of economists—not educators—tried to do precisely that, and one of the outcomes they looked at was admittedly financial: what students earned over the years. But they didn't just decide that students who went on to earn more had better teachers in elementary and high school. Rather, for the sake of the study, they defined good teachers as those who raised students' scores on standardized achievement tests. Economist Raj Chetty and his colleagues (2012) tracked elementary and high school students over a period of 20 years and found that "good teachers" not

only raise test scores but also contribute to lasting academic and financial gains for the students. They labeled such teaching "value-added" teaching, and, as Figure 12.5 ■ shows, there is a strong correlation between value-added teaching and financial outcome at age 28. (The relatively low dollar amounts reflect the times during which data were gathered.) Value-added teaching even lowered the risk of unwanted teenage pregnancy. One commentator summarized the data as showing that "having a good fourth-grade teacher" increases the likelihood that a student will go on to college by 25%, lowers the risk of teen pregnancy by 25%, and boosts the student's lifetime income by an average of $25,000 (Kristof, 2012a).

Some readers also object to the notion of "teaching for the test." If we are talking about tests that are given to a particular class, or to a particular grade in a single school district, that objection is perfectly understandable. But if we are talking about standardized achievement tests, does the objection carry a bit less weight? After all, if those tests measure achievement, isn't it a good thing if teachers' students show greater achievement on those tests?

In any event, the association between "good teaching" and life outcomes seems clear enough: Not only do students who have "value-added" teachers score better on those tests, but they are also likely to make more money throughout their lifetimes.

The authors of the study did not claim that value-added teachers were the most likeable teachers. A next step would seem to be to study the behavior of value-added teachers to discover what types of things they are doing and whether there are principles of effective teaching that might be applied more widely.

Reflect Looking back to grades four through eight, how would you describe your favorite teachers? Which teachers helped you learn the most? How did they do so?

Juice Images242/Alamy

Good Teaching Research shows that good teaching can raise students' earnings—for a lifetime.

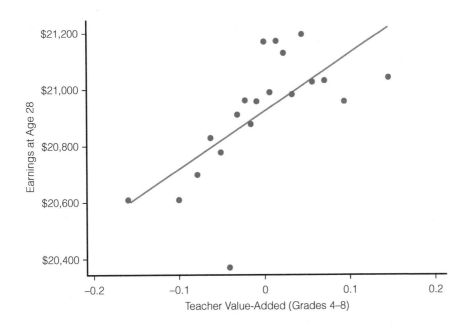

Figure 12.5 ■ The Long-Term Impact of Teachers
Teaching that raises students' standardized achievement test scores also raises their lifetime incomes and lowers the risk of teenage pregnancy.
Source: Chetty et al. (2012).

Y-axis: Earnings at Age 28
X-axis: Teacher Value-Added (Grades 4–8)

quent groupings. In the song, "A-B" triggers "C-D," which in turn triggers "E-F-G." "H-I-J-K," sung slowly, triggers the run "L-M-N-O-P," and so on.

The educational TV program *Sesame Street* has had fun with the alphabet by presenting it as a single word: "Ab-k-defky-jekyl-mnop-qr-stoov-wuk-siz" (sort of). All these approaches reinforce one another so that the alphabet becomes automatic for most English speakers.

Long-Term Memory

Think of your **long-term memory** as a vast storehouse of information containing names, dates, places, what Johnny did to you in second grade, and what Alyssa said about you when you were 12. Long-term memories may last days, years, or, for practical purposes, a lifetime.

Your computer may be able to store many terabytes of information, but there is no known limit to the amount of information that can be stored in your long-term memory (Howe, 2015). From time to time, it may seem that we have forgotten, or lost, a long-term memory, such as the names of elementary or high school classmates. But it is more likely that we simply cannot find the proper cues to help us retrieve the information. It is "lost" in the same way we misplace an object but know that it is still in the house. It remains there somewhere for the finding.

How is information transferred from short-term memory to long-term memory? Rehearsal is one method. Older children are more likely than younger children to use rehearsal (Cowan, 2014; Silva et al., 2012). But pure rehearsal, with no attempt to make information meaningful by linking it to past learning, is no guarantee that the information will be stored permanently.

A more effective method than simple rehearsal is to purposefully relate new material to well-known information. Relating new material to well-known material is an **elaborative strategy**. For example, English teachers encourage children to use new vocabulary words in sentences to help them remember them. In this way, children are building extended **semantic codes** that will help them retrieve the words' meanings in the future.

long-term memory The memory structure capable of relatively permanent storage of information.

elaborative strategy A method for increasing retention of new information by relating it to well-known information.

semantic code A code based on the meaning of information.

Before we proceed to the next section, here's a question for you: Which of the following words is spelled correctly: *retreival* or *retrieval*? The spellings sound alike, so an acoustic code for reconstructing the correct spelling would not be any help. But a semantic code, such as the spelling rule "i before e except after c," would enable you to reconstruct the correct spelling: retrieval. This is why children are taught rules and principles. Of course, whether these rules are retrieved in the appropriate situation is another issue.

Organization in Long-Term Memory

As children's knowledge of concepts advances, the storehouse of their long-term memory becomes gradually organized according to categories. Preschoolers tend to organize their memories by grouping objects that share the same function (Cowan et al., 2010). "Toast" may be grouped with "peanut butter sandwich" because both are edible. Only during the early elementary school years are toast and peanut butter likely to be joined under the concept of food.

When items are correctly categorized in long-term memory, children are more likely to recall accurate information about them (Figure 12.6 ■). For instance, do you "remember" whether whales breathe underwater? If you did not know that whales are mammals or if you knew nothing about mammals, a correct answer might depend on some remote instance of rote learning. If children have incorrectly classified whales as fish, they might search their "memories" and construct the incorrect answer that whales breathe underwater. Correct categorization, in sum, expands children's knowledge and enables them to retrieve information more readily.

But it has also been shown that when the knowledge of children in a particular area surpasses that of adults, the children have a superior capacity to store and retrieve related information. For example, children who are chess experts are superior to adult amateurs at remembering where chess pieces have been placed on the board (Gelman, 2010).

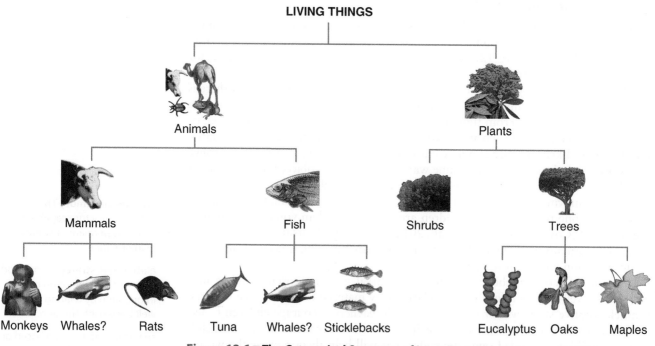

Figure 12.6 ■ The Categorical Structure of Long-Term Memory
Where are whales filed in the cabinets of children's memory? Do whales breathe underwater? Are they warm-blooded? Do they nurse their young? A child's classification of the whale concept will provide answers to these questions.
© Cengage Learning

EARLY MATH MATTERS: DOES A CHILD'S EDUCATION IN MATH NEED TO BEGIN PRIOR TO KINDERGARTEN?

We might like to think that children will do just fine in math if they begin acquiring math competencies in kindergarten. However, many children encounter difficulties in math in elementary school because they are weak in basic whole-number skills when they *enter* kindergarten. Whole-number skills include comprehending what numbers mean and relationships between numbers (National Mathematics Advisory Panel, 2008). Children with adequate whole-number skills can grasp the value of small quantities quickly, such as recognizing that a group of dogs consists of four or six dogs; they can make judgments about the magnitude of numbers (e.g., that 5 is closer to 6 than to 2); they understand counting principles (e.g., the final number when counting a group of chairs equals the total number of chairs); and they are capable of simple addition and subtraction (e.g., 2 and 3 make 5; 5 take away 3 is 2). Such number skills permit children to learn more complex mathematical principles and relationships as the elementary grades proceed (Bull et al., 2011).

One longitudinal study assessed elementary schoolchildren's number competencies at six different times, from the start of kindergarten to the end of third grade, and related them to achievement in math (Jordan et al., 2009). The relationship between number competencies at the outset and achievement in math was strong and consistent throughout the course of the study. Children from low-income homes progressed in math more slowly than their more affluent counterparts, and their math achievement was lower. However, their slower pace of progress was apparently attributable to their poorer whole-number skills at the outset of the study, not to their socioeconomic status per se. Children enter kindergarten at different ages, and those who were older at entry outperformed their younger counterparts in math. They

How Early Is Early Enough? Research shows that children are better prepared for math when they have acquired "whole-number skills" before entering kindergarten. Learning not only provides facts and skills, but also changes the brain, in effect making children "smarter."

had apparently had more time to develop number competencies.

The study suggests that children who do not develop basic whole-number skills prior to entering kindergarten will be at a disadvantage for achievement in math (Ramani & Siegler, 2008). Parents who can afford to send their children to preschool during early childhood, or who can take advantage of Head Start programs, apparently place their children in better "starting positions."

Reflect Does it seem "fair" that children apparently need to acquire basic number competencies before they begin kindergarten? Explain. Do you have any advice for people of lower socioeconomic status who might not be able to provide a nursery school experience for their children?

Development of Recall Memory

Recall memory involves retrieval of information from memory. As children develop, their capacity for recalling information increases (Cowan, 2014; Gathercole & Alloway, 2008). Improvement in memory is linked to their ability to quickly process (i.e., scan and categorize) information. Children's memory is a good overall indicator of their cognitive ability (Alloway & Alloway, 2013; Cowan, 2014; Gignac & Weiss, 2015).

In an experiment on categorization and memory, researchers placed objects that fell into four categories (furniture, clothing, tools, fruit) on a table before second- and fourth-graders (Hasselhorn, 1992). The children were allowed 3 minutes to arrange the pictures as they wished and to remember as many as they could. Fourth-graders were more likely to categorize and recall the pictures than second-graders.

Research also reveals that children are more likely to accurately recall information when they are strongly motivated to do so (Baltazar et al., 2012; Roebers et al., 2014). Fear of poor grades can encourage recall even in middle childhood. The promise of rewards also helps.

What Do Children Understand About the Functioning of Their Cognitive Processes and, More Particularly, Their Memory?

Children's knowledge and control of their cognitive abilities is termed **metacognition**. The development of metacognition is shown by having the ability to formulate problems, being aware of the processes required to solve a problem, activating cognitive strategies, maintaining focus on the problem, and checking answers.

When a sixth-grader decides which homework assignments to do first, memorizes the state capitals for tomorrow's test, and then tests herself to see which ones she needs to study more, she is displaying metacognition. Teaching students metacognitive skills improves their performance in reading and other areas of education (Flavell et al., 2002; Roebers et al., 2014).

Metamemory is one aspect of metacognition. It more specifically refers to children's awareness of the functioning of their memory. Older children show greater insight into how memory works (Towse et al., 2008). For example, young elementary school students frequently announce that they have memorized educational materials before they have actually done so. Older students are more likely to assess their knowledge accurately (Cowan et al., 2010; Daugherty & Ofen, 2015). As a result, older children store and retrieve information more effectively than younger children (Daugherty & Ofen, 2015; Silva et al., 2012).

Older children also show more knowledge of strategies that can be used to facilitate memory. Preschoolers generally use rehearsal if someone else suggests it, but not until about the age of 6 or 7 do children use rehearsal on their own (Flavell et al., 2002; Lecce et al., 2014). Older elementary schoolchildren also become better at adapting their memory strategies to fit the characteristics of the task at hand (Cowan et al., 2010; Daugherty & Ofen, 2015).

As children develop, they also are more likely to use selective rehearsal to remember important information that is, they exclude the meaningless mass of perceptions milling about them by confining rehearsal to what they are trying to remember. Selectivity in rehearsal is found more often among adults than among 10-year-olds (Camos & Barrouillet, 2011).

If you are trying to remember a new phone number, you know that you should rehearse it several times or write it down before setting out to do math problems. However, 5-year-olds, when asked whether it would make a difference if they jotted the number down before or after doing the math problems, do not reliably report that doing the problems first would matter. Ten-year-olds, however, are aware that new mental activities (the math problems) can interfere with old ones (memorizing the telephone number) and usually suggest jotting the number down before doing the math problems.

Your metamemory is, of course, advanced to the point where you recognize that it would be poor judgment to read this book while watching *Bachelor in Paradise* or fantasizing about your next vacation. Isn't it?

metacognition Awareness of and control of one's cognitive abilities, as shown by the intentional use of cognitive strategies in solving problems.

metamemory Knowledge of the functions and processes involved in one's storage and retrieval of information (memory), as shown by the use of cognitive strategies to retain information.

CHILDREN'S EYEWITNESS TESTIMONY

Jean Piaget distinctly "remembered" an attempt to kidnap him from his baby carriage as he was being wheeled along the Champs Élysées. He recalled the excited throng, the abrasions on the face of the nurse who rescued him, the police officer's white baton, and the flight of the assailant. Although they were graphic, Piaget's memories were false. Years later, the nurse admitted that she had made up the tale.

Children are often called on to testify about events they have seen or experienced, often involving child abuse. But how reliable is children's testimony?

Even preschoolers can recall and describe personally experienced events, although the accounts may be sketchy (Goodman et al., 2011; Klemfuss & Ceci, 2012). However, there are many individual differences. Consequently, the child witness is typically asked questions to prompt information. But such questions may be "leading"; that is, they may suggest an answer. For example, "What happened at school?" is not a leading question, but "Did your teacher touch you?" is.

Can children's testimony be distorted by leading questions? It appears that by the age of 10 or 11, children are no more suggestible than adults, but younger children are more prone to being misled (Bruck et al., 2006; Goodman et al., 2011).

One hotly debated question is whether children can be led into making false reports of abuse. There is no simple answer to this question, as illustrated by a study carried out by Gail Goodman and her colleagues (Goodman et al., 2011; Goodman & Clarke-Stewart, 1991). They interviewed 5- and 7-year-old girls following a routine medical checkup that included genital and anal exams for half the girls. Most of the children

Glowimages/Alamy

How Reliable Is Children's Eyewitness Testimony? This question remains hotly debated. By age 10 or 11, children may be no more suggestible than adults. The findings for younger children, however, are inconsistent.

who experienced genital and anal touching failed to mention it when simply asked what happened during the exam. But when asked specific leading questions ("Did the doctor touch you there?"), 31 of 36 girls mentioned the experience. Of the 36 girls who did not have genital and anal exams, none reported any such experience when asked what happened during the exam. When asked the leading questions, however, 3 girls falsely reported being touched in these areas. This illustrates the dilemma faced by investigators of sexual abuse: Children may not reveal genital contact until specifically asked, but asking may influence some children to give a false report.

Research indicates that repeated questioning may lead children to make up events that never happened to them (Goodman et al., 2011). In one study, preschoolers were questioned each week for 11 weeks about events that either had or had not happened to them (Ceci, 1993). By the 11th week, 58% of the children reported at least one false event as true.

What, then, are investigators to do when the only witnesses to criminal events are children? Maggie Bruck and her colleagues (2006) recommended that interviewers avoid leading or suggestive questions to minimize influencing the child's response. It might also be useful to ask the child whether he or she actually saw what happened or merely heard about it. Young children do not always make this distinction by themselves.

Reflect There are problems in children's eyewitness testimony. What would be lost if we did not allow children's eyewitness testimony? Give examples.

Section Review

8. The ability to screen out distractions _____ (increases or decreases?) through middle childhood.

9. When children focus on stimuli, they can keep them in _____ memory for up to 30 seconds.

10. Children can remember visual stimuli longer when they _____ it as sounds.

11. Repetition of sounds or other stimuli is known as _____ learning.

12. _____ rehearsal consists of relating new information to things that are already known.

13. _____ is awareness of the functioning of one's own memory processes.

Reflect & Relate: How is information transferred from short-term memory to long-term memory? How is the process analogous to placing information in a computer's "memory" or into a computer's "storage" device? What happens if you forget to "save" information in the computer's memory?

12.4 Intellectual Development, Creativity, and Achievement

At an early age, we gain impressions of how intelligent we are compared to other family members and schoolmates. We think of some people as having more **intelligence** than others. We associate intelligence with academic success, advancement on the job, and appropriate social behavior (Strenze, 2015).

What Is Intelligence?

"Intelligence does not exist," writes Tulio Otero (2015). Really? His point is this: Despite our sense of familiarity with the concept of intelligence, intelligence cannot be seen, touched, or measured physically. For this reason, intelligence is subject to various interpretations. Theories about intelligence—and what it is—are some of the most controversial issues in psychology today. They are particularly controversial because of the obsession with how much intelligence this person or that person has, and how he or she got it.

Psychologists generally distinguish between achievement and intelligence. **Achievement** is what a child has learned, the knowledge and skills that have been gained by experience. Achievement involves specific content areas, such as English, history, and math. Educators and psychologists use achievement tests to measure what children have learned in academic areas. The strong relationship between achievement and experience seems obvious. We are not surprised to find that a student who has taken Spanish but not French does better on a Spanish achievement test than on a French achievement test.

The meaning of intelligence is more difficult to pin down (Nisbett, 2009; 2013). Most psychologists would agree that intelligence provides the cognitive basis for academic achievement. Intelligence is usually perceived as a child's underlying competence or learning ability, whereas achievement involves a child's acquired competencies or performance. Most psychologists also would agree that many of the competencies underlying intelligence manifest themselves during middle childhood, when most children are first exposed to formal schooling. Psychologists disagree, however, about the nature and origins of a child's underlying competence or learning ability.

Let us consider some theoretical approaches to intelligence. Then we will see how researchers and practitioners actually assess intellectual functioning.

intelligence A complex and controversial concept, defined by David Wechsler as "[the] capacity . . . to understand the world [and the] resourcefulness to cope with its challenges." Intelligence implies the capacity to make adaptive choices (from the Latin *inter*, meaning "among," and *legere*, meaning "to choose").

achievement That which is attained by one's efforts and presumed to be made possible by one's abilities.

What Are the Various Factor Theories of Intelligence?

Many investigators have viewed intelligence as consisting of one or more major mental abilities, or **factors.** In 1904, the British psychologist Charles Spearman suggested that the various behaviors that we consider intelligent have a common, underlying factor: *g*, or "general intelligence." He thought that *g* represented broad reasoning and problem-solving abilities. He supported this view by noting that people who excel in one area generally show the capacity to excel in others. But he also noted that even the most capable people seem more capable in some areas—perhaps in music or business or poetry—than in others. For this reason, he also suggested that *s*, or "specific capacities," accounts for a number of individual abilities.

This view seems to make sense. Most of us know children who are good at math but poor in English, or vice versa. Nonetheless, some link—*g*—seems to connect different mental abilities. Few, if any, people surpass 99% of the population in one mental ability yet are surpassed by 80% or 90% of the population in other abilities.

To test his views, Spearman developed **factor analysis,** a statistical technique that enables researchers to determine which items on tests seem to be measuring the same things. Researchers continue to find a key role for *g* in performance on many intelligence tests. Jackson and Rushton (2006) claim that *g* underlies scores on the verbal and quantitative parts of the SAT, although we can also note that it would be absurd to argue that education has nothing to do with SAT scores. A number of researchers (S. B. Kaufman et al., 2012) connect *g* with academic achievement and *working memory*—the ability to keep various elements of a problem in mind at once. Many contemporary psychologists continue to speak of the extent to which a particular test of intellectual ability measures *g* (S. B. Kaufman et al., 2012).

The American psychologist Louis Thurstone (1938) used factor analysis and concluded that intelligence consists of several specific factors, which he termed *primary mental abilities,* including visual–spatial abilities, perceptual speed, numerical ability, ability to learn the meanings of words, ability to bring to mind the right word rapidly, and ability to reason. Thurstone suggested, for example, that an individual might be able to rapidly develop lists of words that rhyme but might not be particularly able to solve math problems.

What Is Sternberg's Triarchic Theory of Intelligence?

Psychologist Robert Sternberg (2015) constructed a three-pronged, or **triarchic,** theory of intelligence, which is similar to a view proposed by the Greek philosopher Aristotle. The three prongs of Sternberg's theory are analytical intelligence, creative intelligence, and practical intelligence (see Figure 12.7 ■).

factor A condition or quality that brings about a result—in this case, "intelligent" behavior. A cluster of related items, such as those found on an intelligence or personality test.

factor analysis A statistical technique that enables researchers to determine the relationships among a large number of items, such as test items.

triarchic Governed by three. Descriptive of Sternberg's view that intellectual functioning has three aspects: analytical intelligence, creative intelligence, and practical intelligence.

Figure 12.7 ■ Sternberg's Triarchic Theory of Intelligence
Robert Sternberg views intelligence as three-pronged—as having analytical, creative, and practical aspects.
© Cengage Learning

Analytical intelligence
(academic ability)
Abilities to solve problems, compare and contrast, judge, evaluate, and criticize

Creative intelligence
(creativity and insight)
Abilities to invent, discover, suppose, and theorize

Practical intelligence
("street smarts")
Abilities to adapt to the demands of one's environment and apply knowledge in practical situations

Analytical intelligence is academic ability. It enables us to solve problems and acquire new knowledge. Creative intelligence is defined by the abilities to cope with novel situations and to profit from experience. Creativity enables us to relate novel situations to familiar situations (that is, to perceive similarities and differences) and fosters adaptation. Both Aristotle and Sternberg speak of practical intelligence, or "street smarts." Practical intelligence enables people to adapt to the demands of their environment, including the social environment. Psychologists who believe that creativity is separate from analytical intelligence (academic ability) find moderate relationships between academic ability and creativity (Simonton, 2014). However, to Sternberg, creativity is a basic facet of intelligence.

What Is the Theory of Multiple Intelligences?

Psychologist Howard Gardner (1983; Sternberg, 2015), like Sternberg, believes that intelligence—or intelligences—reflects more than academic ability. Gardner refers to each kind of intelligence in his theory as "an intelligence" because they differ in quality (see Figure 12.8 ■). He also believes that the various intelligences are based in different areas of the brain, although there are overlaps.

Three of Gardner's intelligences are familiar enough: verbal ability, logical–mathematical reasoning, and spatial intelligence (visual–spatial skills). But Gardner also includes bodily–kinesthetic intelligence (as shown by dancers and gymnasts), musical intelligence, interpersonal intelligence (as shown in empathy and ability to relate to others), and personal knowledge (self-insight). Occasionally, individuals show great "intelligence" in one area—such as the genius of young Mozart with the piano or that of the island girl who can navigate her small boat to hundreds of islands by observing the changing patterns of the stars—without notable abilities in other areas. Naturalist intelligence refers to the ability to look at natural events, such as various kinds of animals and plants or the stars above, and develop insights into

Figure 12.8 ■ Gardner's Theory of Multiple Intelligences

Howard Gardner argued that there are many intelligences, not just one, including bodily talents as expressed through dancing or gymnastics. Each "intelligence" is presumed to have its neurological base in a different part of the brain. Each is an inborn talent that must be developed through educational experiences if it is to be expressed.
© Cengage Learning®

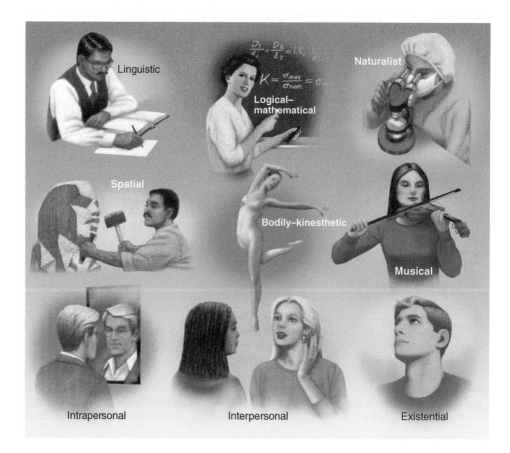

their nature and the laws that govern their behavior. Existential intelligence involves dealing with the larger philosophical issues of life. According to Gardner, one can compose symphonies or advance mathematical theory yet be average in, say, language and personal skills. (Aren't some academic "geniuses" foolish or cumbersome in their personal lives?)

Critics of Gardner's view agree that people function more intelligently in some areas of life than others. They also agree that many people have special talents, such as bodily–kinesthetic talents, even if their overall intelligence is average. But they question whether such special talents are "intelligences" (Neisser et al., 1996). Language skills, reasoning ability, and the ability to solve math problems seem to be more closely related than musical or gymnastic talent to what most people mean by intelligence.

As we consider this critique of Gardner, keep in mind that there is no clear consensus among psychologists and educators as to exactly what intelligence *is*. The lack of consensus doesn't mean that one person's view of intelligence is as useful as that of another person, but it does mean that the continuing effort to define intelligence can be considered a "work in progress."

The various theories of intelligence are reviewed in Concept Review 12.2. We do not yet have the final word on the nature of intelligence, but I would like to share with you David Wechsler's definition of intelligence. Wechsler is the originator of the most widely used series of contemporary intelligence tests, and he defined intelligence as "[the] capacity of an individual to understand the world [and the] resourcefulness to cope with its challenges" (Wechsler, 1975, p. 139). To Wechsler, intelligence involves accurate representation of the world and effective problem solving (adapting to one's environment, profiting from experience, selecting the appropriate formulas and strategies, and so on).

What Is Meant by Emotional Intelligence and Social Intelligence?

Psychologists Peter Salovey and John Mayer developed the theory of emotional intelligence, which holds that social and emotional skills are a form of intelligence, just as academic skills are (Boyatzis et al., 2015; Stein & Deonarine, 2015). Emotional intelligence and social intelligence bear a resemblance to two of Gardner's intelligences: awareness of one's inner feelings and sensitivity to the feelings of others. It also involves control or regulation of one's emotions.

The theory suggests that self-awareness and social awareness are best learned during childhood. Failure to develop emotional intelligence is connected with childhood depression and aggression. Moreover, childhood experiences may help mold the brain's emotional responses to the challenges of life.

To illustrate social intelligence, Goleman (2006) described how an American commander prevented a confrontation between his troops and an Iraqi mob by ordering the troops to point their rifles at the ground and smile. Although there was a language barrier, the aiming of the weapons downward and the smiles were a form of universal communication that was understood by the Iraqis, who then smiled back. Conflict was avoided. According to Goleman, the commander had shown social intelligence—the ability to read the Iraqis' social concerns and solve the social problem by coming up with a useful social response. Like emotional intelligence, social intelligence corresponds to one of Gardner's intelligences, and critics question whether it brings anything new to the table.

How Do We Measure Intellectual Development?

There may be disagreements about the nature of intelligence, but thousands of intelligence tests are administered by psychologists and educators every day.

Theories of Intelligence

Theory	Basic Information	Comments
General versus specific factors (main proponent: Charles Spearman)	• Spearman created factor analysis to study intelligence. • There is strong evidence for the general factor (g) in intelligence. • s factors are specific abilities, skills, and talents.	• The concept of g remains in use today—a century later.
Primary mental abilities (proponent: Louis Thurstone)	• Thurstone used factor analysis. • There are many "primary" abilities. • All abilities and factors are academically oriented.	• Other researchers (e.g., Guilford) claim to have found hundreds of factors. • The more factors that are claimed, the more they overlap.
Triarchic theory (proponent: Robert Sternberg)	• Intelligence is three-pronged, with analytical, creative, and practical components. • Analytical intelligence is analogous to academic ability.	• The theory coincides with the views of Aristotle. • Critics do not view creativity as a component of intelligence.
Multiple intelligences (proponent: Howard Gardner)	• Gardner theorized distinct "intelligences." • Intelligences include academic intelligences, personal and social intelligences, talents, and philosophical intelligences. • The theory posits different bases in the brain for different intelligences.	• Proponents continue to expand the number of "intelligences." • Critics see little value in theorizing "intelligences" rather than aspects of *intelligence*. • Most critics consider musical and bodily skills to be special talents, not "intelligences."

George Skadding/Getty Images

Robert Sternberg/Tufts University

intelligence quotient (IQ)
Originally, a ratio obtained by dividing a child's score (or "mental age") on an intelligence test by his or her chronological age. In general, a score on an intelligence test.

The Stanford–Binet Intelligence Scale (SBIS) and the Wechsler scales for preschool children, school-age children, and adults are the most widely used and respected intelligence tests. The SBIS and Wechsler scales yield scores called **intelligence quotients**. The SBIS and Wechsler scales have been carefully developed and revised over the years. They have been used to make vital educational decisions about children. In many cases, children whose test scores fall below or above certain scores are placed in special classes for intellectually deficient or gifted children.

TRUTH OR FICTION REVISITED: Despite the public's tendency to speak of a person's "IQ" or "intelligence" as being pretty much the same thing, the concepts are actually significantly different in meaning. The term *IQ* refers to a score obtained on an intelligence test on a given testing occasion—that is, a number. But the term *intelligence* is abstract; it refers to something that cannot be directly seen or measured, even though we might point to behaviors that we believe represent intelligent functioning (or not). In fact, the definition of intelligence has been a continual source of controversy among psychologists and educators because of questions about what it is, how it develops, whether some groups have "more" of it than others, and what these questions mean for the dignity of the individual (Greenwood, 2015; Nisbett, 2013; Otero, 2015).

It must be noted just as emphatically that each test has been accused of discriminating against ethnic minorities (such as African American children and Latin American children), the foreign-born, and the children of the socially and economically disadvantaged (Nisbett, 2013). Because of the controversy surrounding IQ tests, no single test should be used to make important decisions about a child. Decisions about children should be made only after a battery of tests is administered by a qualified psychologist, in consultation with parents and teachers.

The Stanford–Binet Intelligence Scale

The SBIS originated in the work of Alfred Binet and Theodore Simon in France about a century ago. The French public school system sought an instrument to identify children who were unlikely to profit from the regular classroom so that they could receive special attention. The Binet–Simon scale came into use in 1905. Since then, it has undergone revision and refinement.

Binet assumed that intelligence increased with age and, therefore, older children should get more items right. Thus, Binet arranged a series of questions in order of difficulty, from easier to harder. Items that were answered correctly by about 60% of the children at a given age level were considered to reflect average intellectual functioning at that age. It was also required that the questions be answered correctly by fewer children who were a year younger and by a greater number of children who were a year older.

The Binet–Simon scale yielded a score called a **mental age (MA)**. The MA shows the intellectual level at which a child is functioning. A child with an MA of 6 is functioning, intellectually, like the average 6-year-old child. In taking the test, children earned months of credit for each correct answer. Their MA was determined by adding the months of credit they attained.

Lewis Terman adapted the Binet–Simon scale for use with American children. Because Terman carried out his work at Stanford University, he renamed the test the Stanford–Binet Intelligence Scale. The first version of the SBIS was published in 1916. The SBIS yielded an intelligence quotient, or IQ, rather than an MA. The SBIS today can be used with children from the age of 2 onward up to adults. Table 12.2 ● shows the kinds of items that define typical performance at various ages.

The IQ indicates the relationship between a child's mental age and his or her actual or **chronological age (CA)** . The ratio reflects the fact that the same MA score has different meanings for children of different ages; that is, an MA of 8 is an above-average score for a 6-year-old but a below-average score for a 10-year-old.

mental age (MA) The accumulated months of credit that a person earns on the Stanford–Binet Intelligence Scale.

chronological age (CA) A person's age.

Items Similar to Those on the Stanford-Binet Intelligence Scale

Age	Item
2 years	1. Children show knowledge of basic vocabulary words by identifying parts of a doll, such as the mouth, ears, and hair. 2. Children show counting and spatial skills along with visual–motor coordination by building a tower of four blocks to match a model.
4 years	1. Children show word fluency and categorical thinking by filling in the missing words when they are asked questions such as "Father is a man; mother is a ___?" "Hamburgers are hot; ice cream is ___?" 2. Children show comprehension by answering correctly when they are asked questions such as "Why do people have automobiles?" and "Why do people have medicine?"
9 years	1. Children can point out verbal absurdities, as in this question: "In an old cemetery, scientists unearthed a skull that they think was that of George Washington when he was only 5 years of age. What is silly about that?" 2. Children display fluency with words, as shown by answering these questions: "Can you tell me a number that rhymes with snore?" and "Can you tell me a color that rhymes with glue?"
Adult	1. Adults show knowledge of the meanings of words and conceptual thinking by correctly explaining the differences between word pairs, such as "sickness and misery," "house and home," and "integrity and prestige." 2. Adults show spatial skills by correctly answering questions such as "If a car turned to the right to head north, in what direction was it heading before it turned?"

© Cengage Learning®

The IQ is computed by the formula IQ = (Mental Age/Chronological Age) × 100, or

$$\text{IQ} = \frac{\text{Mental Age (MA)}}{\text{Chronological Age (CA)}} \times 100$$

According to this formula, a child with an MA of 6 and a CA of 6 has an IQ of 100. An 8-year-old who does as well on the SBIS as the average 10-year-old will have an IQ of 125. Children who do not answer as many items correctly as other children of their age will have MAs that are lower than their CAs. Their IQ scores will be below 100.

TRUTH OR FICTION REVISITED: It is true that two children can answer exactly the same items on an intelligence test correctly, yet one can be above average in intelligence and the other below average. The children would have different ages, and the younger of the two would obtain a higher IQ score.

Today, IQ scores on the SBIS are derived by comparing children's and adults' performances with those of other people of the same age. People who get more items correct than average receive IQ scores above 100, and people who answer fewer items correctly receive below 100.

The Wechsler Scales

Wechsler (1975) developed a series of scales for use with school-age children (Wechsler Intelligence Scale for Children; WISC), younger children (Wechsler Preschool and Primary Scale of Intelligence; WPPSI), and adults (Wechsler Adult Intelligence Scale; WAIS). These tests have been repeatedly revised. They are available in Spanish and English.

The Wechsler scales group test questions into subtests (such as those shown in Table 12.3 ●). Each subtest measures a different intellectual task. For this reason, the test compares a person's performance on one type of task (such as defining words) with her or his performance on another (such as using blocks to construct geometric designs). The Wechsler scales thus suggest children's strengths and weaknesses and provide overall measures of intellectual functioning.

Wechsler described some subtests as measuring verbal tasks and others as assessing performance tasks. In general, verbal subtests require knowledge of verbal concepts, whereas performance subtests require familiarity with spatial-relations concepts (see Figure 12.9 ■). Wechsler's scales make it possible to compute verbal and performance IQs. Non-technically oriented college students often obtain higher verbal than performance IQ scores.

Figure 12.10 ■ indicates the labels that Wechsler assigned to various IQ scores and the approximate percentages of the population who attain IQ scores at those levels. As you can see, most children's IQ scores cluster around the average. Only about 5% of the population obtain IQ scores above 130 or below 70.

Why Do So Many Psychologists and Educators Consider Standard Intelligence Tests to Be Culturally Biased?

I was almost one of the testing casualties. At 15 I earned an IQ test score of 82, three points above the track of the special education class. Based on this score, my counselor suggested that I take up bricklaying because I was "good with my hands." My low IQ, however, did not allow me to see that as desirable.

—Robert Williams (1974, p. 32)

● TABLE 12.3

Kinds of Items Found on the Wechsler Intelligence Scales

Verbal Items	Nonverbal Performance Items
Information: "What is the capital of the United States?" "Who was Shakespeare?" Comprehension: "Why do we have ZIP codes?" "What does 'A stitch in time saves 9' mean?" Arithmetic: "If 3 candy bars cost 25 cents, how much will 18 candy bars cost?" Similarities: "How are good and bad alike?" "How are peanut butter and jelly alike?" Vocabulary: "What does *canal* mean?" Digit span: Repeating a series of numbers, presented by the examiner, forward and backward.	Picture completion: Pointing to the missing part of a picture. Picture arrangement: Arranging cartoon pictures in sequence so that they tell a meaningful story. Block design: Copying pictures of geometric designs using multicolored blocks. Object assembly: Putting pieces of a puzzle together so that they form a meaningful object. Coding: Rapid scanning and drawing of symbols that are associated with numbers. Mazes: Using a pencil to trace the correct route from a starting point to home.

Note: The items for verbal subtests are similar but not identical to actual test items on the Wechsler intelligence scales.
© Cengage Learning®

Picture arrangement

These pictures tell a story, but they are in the wrong order. Put them in the right order so that they tell a story.

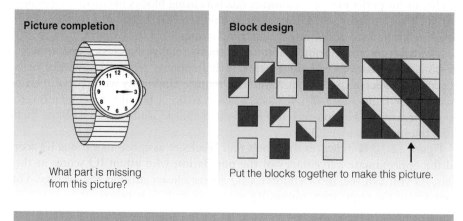

Picture completion

What part is missing from this picture?

Block design

Put the blocks together to make this picture.

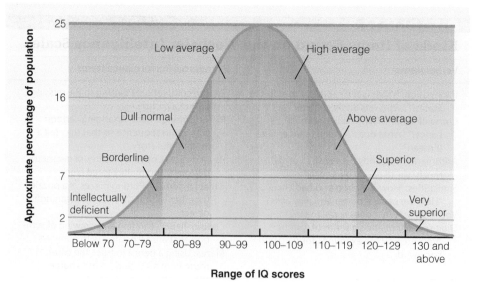

Object assembly

Put the pieces together as quickly as you can.

Figure 12.10 ■ **Variations in IQ Scores**
IQ scores vary according to a bell-shaped, or "normal," curve. Scores tend to cluster around the central score (100) and then to decrease in frequency as they move upward and downward.
© Cengage Learning®

Approximate percentage of population

Low average   High average

Dull normal   Above average

Borderline   Superior

Intellectually deficient   Very superior

Below 70   70–79   80–89   90–99   100–109   110–119   120–129   130 and above

Range of IQ scores

This testimony, offered by African American psychologist Robert Williams, echoes the sentiments of many psychologists. Most psychologists and educational specialists consider intelligence tests to be at least somewhat biased against African Americans and members of lower social classes (Daley & Onwuegbuzie, 2011; Saklofske et al., 2015). To fill in a bit more historical background, let us note that during the 1920s, intelligence tests were used to prevent many Europeans and others from immigrating to the United States. For example, testing pioneer H. H. Goddard assessed 178 newly arrived immigrants at Ellis Island and claimed that most of the Hungarians, Italians, and Russians were "feeble-minded." It was apparently of little concern to Goddard that these immigrants, by and large, did not understand English—the language in which the tests were administered! Because of a history of abuse of intelligence testing, some states have outlawed the use of IQ tests as the sole standard for placing children in special-education classes.

On the other hand, supporters of standard intelligence tests point out that they appear to do a decent job of measuring the cognitive skills that are valued in modern high-tech societies (Maynard et al., 2005). The vocabulary and arithmetic subtests on the Wechsler scales, for example, clearly reflect achievement in language arts and computational ability. Although the broad types of achievement measured by these tests reflect intelligence, they might also, of course, reflect cultural familiarity with the concepts required to answer questions correctly. In particular, the tests seem to reflect middle-class European American culture in the United States (Saklofske et al., 2015).

If scoring well on intelligence tests requires a certain type of cultural experience, the tests are said to have a **cultural bias**. Children reared in African American neighborhoods could be at a disadvantage, not because of differences in intelligence but because of cultural differences (Nisbett, 2013; Nisbett et al., 2012). For this reason, psychologists have tried to construct **culture-free** or culture-fair intelligence tests.

Some tests do not rely on expressive language at all. For example, Cattell's (1949) Culture-Fair Intelligence Test evaluates reasoning ability through the child's comprehension of the rules that govern a progression of geometric designs, as shown in Figure 12.11 ■.

Culture-free tests have not lived up to their promise. First, middle-class children still outperform lower-class children on them (Saklofske et al., 2015). Middle-class children, for example, are more likely to have basic familiarity with materials such as blocks and pencils and paper. They are more likely than disadvantaged children to have arranged blocks into various designs (practice relevant to the Cattell test). Second, culture-free tests do not predict academic success as well as other intelligence tests, and scholastic aptitude remains the central concern of educators.

Might there be no such thing as a culture-free intelligence test? Motivation to do well, for example, might be a cultural factor. Because of lifestyle differences, some children from low-income families in the United States might not share the motivation of middle-class children to succeed on tests (Daley & Onwuegbuzie, 2011; Suzuki et al., 2011).

cultural bias A factor hypothesized to be present in intelligence tests that bestows an advantage on test takers from certain cultural or ethnic backgrounds but that does not reflect true intelligence.

culture-free Descriptive of a test in which cultural biases have been removed. On such a test, test takers from different cultural backgrounds would have an equal opportunity to earn scores that reflect their true abilities.

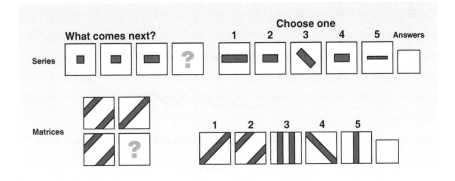

Figure 12.11 ■ Sample Items from Cattell's Culture-Fair Intelligence Test
Culture-fair tests attempt to exclude items that discriminate on the basis of cultural background rather than intelligence.
© Cengage Learning®

What Are the Various Patterns of Intellectual Development?

Sometimes you have to run rapidly to stay in the same place—at least in terms of taking intelligence tests. The "average" taker of an intelligence test obtains an IQ score of 100. However, that person must answer more questions correctly as childhood progresses in order to obtain the same score. Even though his or her intelligence is "developing" at a typical pace, he or she continues to obtain the same score.

Rapid advances in intellectual functioning occur during childhood. Within a few years, children gain the ability to symbolize experiences and manipulate symbols to solve increasingly complex problems. Their vocabularies leap, and their sentences become more complex. Their thought processes become increasingly logical and abstract, and they gain the capacity to focus on two or more aspects of a problem at once.

Intellectual growth seems to occur in at least two major spurts. The first growth spurt occurs at about the age of 6. This spurt coincides with entry into a school system and also with the shift from preoperational to concrete-operational thought (Rose & Fischer, 2011). The school experience may begin to help crystallize intellectual functioning at this time. The second spurt occurs at about age 10 or 11.

Once they reach middle childhood, however, children appear to undergo relatively more stable patterns of gains in intellectual functioning, although there are still spurts (Deary et al., 2004). As a result, intelligence tests gain greater predictive power. In a classic study by Marjorie Honzik and colleagues (1948), intelligence test scores at the age of 9 correlated strongly (+0.90) with scores at the age of 10 and more moderately (+0.76) with scores at the age of 18. Scores at age 11 even show a moderate to high relationship with scores at the age of 77 (Deary et al., 2004).

Despite the increased predictive power of intelligence tests during middle childhood, individual differences exist. In the classic Fels Longitudinal Study (see Figure 12.12 ■), two groups of children (Groups 1 and 3) made reasonably consistent gains in intelligence test scores between the ages of 10 and 17, whereas three groups showed declines. Group 4, children who had shown the most intellectual promise at age 10, went on to show the most precipitous decline, although they still wound up in the highest 2–3% of the population (McCall et al., 1973). Many factors influence changes in intelligence test scores, including changes in the child's home environment, social and economic circumstances, educational experiences, and even intake of B vitamins such as folic acid (Deary et al., 2004).

Figure 12.12 ■ Five Patterns of Change in IQ Scores for Children in the Fels Longitudinal Study
In the Fels Longitudinal Study, IQ scores remained stable between the ages of 2 ½ and 17 for only one of the five groups—Group 1.
Source: McCall et al. (1973).

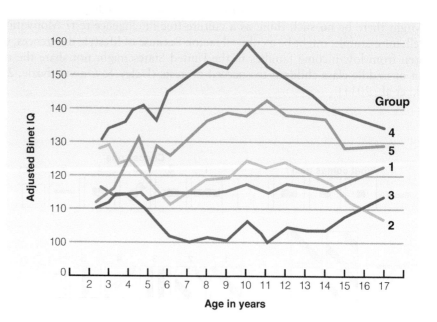

Although intelligence test scores change throughout childhood, many children show reasonably consistent patterns of below-average or above-average performance. In the next section, we will discuss children who show consistent patterns of extreme scores—low and high.

How Do Children Differ in Their Intellectual Development?

The average IQ score in the United States is close to 100. About half the children in the United States obtain IQ scores in the broad average range from 90 to 110 (see Figure 12.10). Nearly 95% score between 70 and 130. But what of the other 5%? Children who obtain IQ scores below 70 are generally labeled "intellectually disabled." Children who score 130 and above are usually labeled "gifted." These labels—verbal markers of extreme individual differences—lead to certain expectations of children. Ironically, the labels can place heavy burdens on both children and parents.

Intellectual Disability

According to the American Association on Intellectual and Developmental Disabilities (AAIDD, 2015), "Intellectual disability is . . . characterized by significant limitations both in intellectual functioning and in adaptive behavior, which covers a range of everyday social and practical skills. This disability originates before the age of 18." In terms of numbers, intellectual disability involves an IQ score of no higher than 70–75.

Most of the children (more than 80%) who are intellectually disabled are mildly disabled. Mildly disabled children, as the term implies, are the most capable of adjusting to the demands of educational institutions and, eventually, to society at large (Hodapp et al., 2011). Many mildly disabled children are mainstreamed in regular classrooms, as opposed to being placed in special-needs classes.

Children with Down syndrome are most likely to fall within the moderately disabled range. Moderately disabled children can learn to speak; to dress, feed, and clean themselves; and, eventually, to engage in useful work under supportive conditions, as in a sheltered workshop. However, they usually do not acquire skills in reading and arithmetic. Severely and profoundly disabled children may not acquire speech and self-help skills and may remain highly dependent on others for survival throughout their lives.

Some causes of intellectual disability are biological (Carlier & Roubertoux, 2014). Disability, for example, can stem from chromosomal abnormalities, such as Down syndrome; genetic disorders, such as phenylketonuria (PKU); or brain damage (Haier, 2011; Hodapp et al., 2011). Brain damage can have many origins, including accidents during childhood and problems during pregnancy. For example, maternal alcohol abuse, malnutrition, and diseases during pregnancy can lead to intellectual disability in the fetus.

There is also **cultural–familial disability**, in which the child is biologically normal but does not develop age-appropriate behaviors at the normal pace because of social isolation of one kind or another. For example, the later-born children of impoverished families may have little opportunity to interact with adults or play with stimulating toys. As a result, they may not develop sophisticated language skills or the motivation to acquire the kinds of knowledge that are valued in a technologically oriented society (Carlier & Roubertoux, 2014).

Naturally, we wish to encourage all children—including intellectually disabled children—to develop to the maximum of their capacities. As a rule of thumb, keep in mind that IQs are scores on tests. They are not perfectly reliable, which means that they can and do change somewhat from testing to testing. Thus, it is important to focus on children's current levels of achievement in the academic and self-help skills we wish to impart; by doing so, we can try to build these skills gradually and coherently, step by step.

cultural–familial disability Substandard intellectual performance that is presumed to stem from lack of opportunity to acquire the knowledge and skills considered important within a cultural setting.

Children with cultural–familial disability can change dramatically when enriched learning experiences are provided, especially at early ages. Head Start programs, for example, have enabled many children at risk for cultural–familial disability to function at above-average levels.

Giftedness

Giftedness involves more than excellence on the tasks posed by standard intelligence tests. In determining who is gifted, most educators include children who have

A Closer Look   Diversity

SOCIOECONOMIC AND ETHNIC DIFFERENCES IN IQ

What is your ethnic background? Are there any stereotypes about how people from your ethnic background perform in school or on IQ tests? If so, what is your reaction to these stereotypes? Why?

Research suggests that differences in IQ exist among socioeconomic and ethnic groups. U.S. children from lower-income families obtain IQ scores some 10–15 points lower than those obtained by children from the middle and upper classes. African American children tend to obtain IQ scores below those obtained by their European American counterparts (Saklofske et al., 2015; Nisbett, 2013). However, as noted by *Washington Post* editor Eugene Robinson (2011), "A gap has opened up between an educated middle-class Black America and a poor, undereducated Black America." In other words, we cannot lump all African Americans together. Latin American and Native American children also tend to score below the norms for European Americans (Daley & Onwuegbuzie, 2011; Nisbett, 2013).

On the other hand, youth of Asian descent frequently outscore youth of European backgrounds on achievement tests in math and science, including the math portion of the SAT (Suzuki et al., 2011). In addition, people of Asian Indian, Korean, Japanese, Filipino, and Chinese descent are more likely than European Americans, African Americans, and Latin Americans to graduate from high school and complete college (Kurtz-Costes et al., 2014). Asian Americans are highly overrepresented in competitive U.S. colleges and universities (Suzuki et al., 2011). Figure 12.13 ■ shows the extreme overrepresentation of Asian Americans at New York City's elite public high schools that specialize in science and technology (New York City Department of Education, 2015). Students are admitted to these schools on the basis of achievement tests, and Asian Americans outscore other groups on the tests.

Several studies of IQ have confused social class with ethnicity because larger proportions of African Americans, Latin Americans, and Native Americans come from lower

socioeconomic backgrounds (Nisbett, 2013). When we limit our observations to particular ethnic groups, we still find an effect for social class. That is, middle-class European Americans outscore lower-class European Americans. Middle-class African Americans, Latin Americans, and Native Americans also outscore their less affluent counterparts.

Attributions for success may also be involved. Research shows that Asian students and their mothers tend to attribute academic successes to hard work (Randel et al., 2000). American mothers, in contrast, are more likely to attribute children's academic successes to "natural" ability (Sternberg & Kaufman, 2011). Asians are more likely to believe that they can work to make good scores happen.

Because Asian Americans have suffered discrimination in blue-collar careers, they have come to emphasize the value of education (Nisbett, 2009). In Japan, emphasis on succeeding through hard work is illustrated by the increasing popularity of cram schools, or *juku*, which prepare Japanese children for entrance exams to private schools and colleges (Leung et al., 2015). More than half of Japanese schoolchildren are enrolled in these schools, which meet after

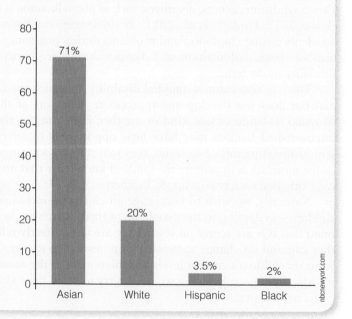

the regular school day. Parental encouragement and supervision, in combination with peer support for academic achievement, partially explain the superior performances of European Americans and Asian Americans compared with African Americans and Latin Americans (Nisbett et al., 2012).

Psychologist Richard Nisbett and his colleagues (2012) argue that the belief that European Americans are superior to African Americans in intelligence flies in the face of evidence from adoptee studies and evidence about the effects of early education on the IQ scores of African American children. Robert Sternberg and his colleagues (2005) argue that as long as there remains a dispute about what intelligence *is*, the attempt to relate intelligence to ethnicity makes no sense.

Reflect

- In my classes, many European American students are willing to believe that they are smarter than African American students for genetic reasons. However, they believe that if Asian students are smarter than they are, it is because the Asian students work harder. How would you explain that difference?

- If the members of one ethnic group are smarter, on average, than the members of another ethnic group, does that make them "better"?

- To say that one ethnic group is genetically smarter than another, do we have to be able to point to the genes that are responsible? Explain.

- Do you think we should be conducting research into the relationships between ethnicity and intelligence? Explain.

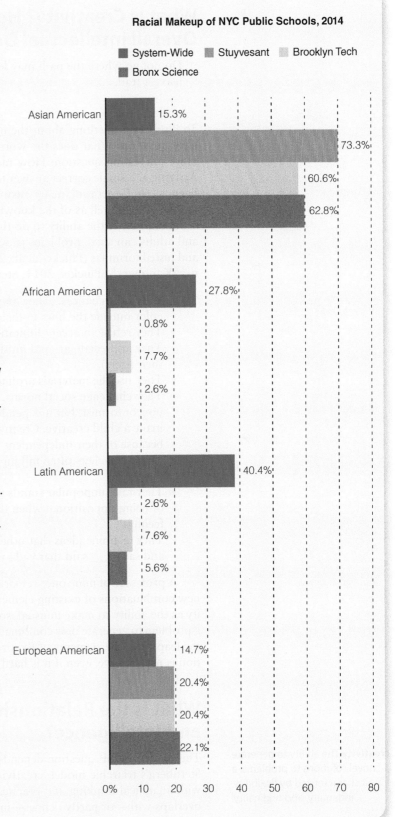

Racial Makeup of NYC Public Schools, 2014

Figure 12.13 ■ Racial Make-Up of New York City's Public Schools Overall, and at New York City's Elite Specialized High Schools, 2014

African American and Latin American students make up around 70% of the student population of New York City's public schools, but comprise a tiny percentage of the city's three elite specialized high schools. Note, too, that European American students, like Asian American students, make up about 15% of the overall student population of the city's public schools, but Asian American students outnumber European American students at the elite high schools by a ratio of about three to one.
Source: New York City Department of Education, 2015.

outstanding abilities; who are capable of high performance in a specific academic area, such as language or mathematics; or who show creativity, leadership, distinction in the visual or performing arts, or bodily talents, such as in gymnastics and dancing (Reis & Renzulli, 2011).

What Is Creativity? How Does Creativity Relate to Overall Intellectual Development?

> Do not go where the path may lead, go instead to where there is no path and leave a trail.
>
> —Ralph Waldo Emerson

To illustrate something about the nature of creativity, let me ask you a rather ordinary question: What does the word *duck* mean? Now let me ask you a somewhat more interesting question: How many meanings can you find for the word *duck*? Arriving at a single correct answer to the question might earn you points on an intelligence test. Generating many answers to the question, as we will see, may be a sign of creativity as well as of the knowledge of the meanings of words.

Creativity is the ability to do things that are novel and useful. Creative children and adults can solve problems to which there are no preexisting solutions, no tried and tested formulas (Plucker et al., 2015). Creative children share a number of qualities (Kaufman & Plucker, 2011; Sternberg, 2006):

- They take chances. (They may use sentence fragments in essays, and they may color outside the lines in their coloring books.)
- They refuse to accept limitations and try to do the impossible.
- They appreciate art and music (which sometimes leaves them out among their peers).
- They use the materials around them to make unique things.
- They challenge social norms. (Creative children are often independent and nonconformist, but independence and nonconformity do not necessarily make a child creative. Creative children may be at odds with their teachers because of their independent views. Faced with the task of managing large classes, teachers often fall into preferences for quiet, submissive, "good" children.)
- They take unpopular stands (which sometimes gives them the appearance of being oppositional when they are expressing their genuine ideas and feelings).
- They examine ideas that other people accept at face value. (They come home and say, "___ said that yada yada. What's that all about?")

A professor of mine once remarked that there is nothing new under the sun, only new combinations of existing elements. Many psychologists agree. They see creativity as the ability to make unusual, sometimes remote, associations to the elements of a problem to generate new combinations. An essential aspect of a creative response is the leap from the elements of the problem to the novel solution. A predictable solution is not creative, even if it is hard to reach.

What Is the Relationship Between Creativity and Intelligence?

creativity The ability to generate novel solutions to problems; a trait characterized by flexibility, ingenuity, and originality.

The answer to this question depends on how one defines intelligence. If one accepts Sternberg's triarchic model, creativity is one of three aspects of intelligence (along with analytical thinking and practical intelligence). From this perspective, creativity overlaps with—or partly defines—intelligence.

Some scientists argue that creativity and innovation require high levels of intelligence (Silvia & Beaty, 2012), but most of the tests we use to measure intelligence and creativity tend to show only a moderate relationship between global intelligence test scores and measures of creativity (Simonton, 2014; Sternberg, 2015). In terms of Gardner's theory of multiple intelligences, we can note that some children who have only average intellectual ability in some areas, such as logical analysis, can excel in areas that are considered more creative, such as music or art.

Considering two different kinds of thinking may help shed some light on this issue. In **convergent thinking**, thought is limited to present facts; the problem solver narrows his or her thinking to find the best solution. (A child uses convergent thinking to arrive at the right answer to a multiple-choice question or to a question on an intelligence test.)

Creative thinking tends to be divergent rather than convergent (Silvia et al., 2013). In **divergent thinking**, the child associates freely to the elements of the problem, allowing "leads" to run a nearly limitless course. (Children use divergent thinking when they are trying to generate ideas to answer an essay question or to find keywords to search on the Internet.) Tests of creativity determine how flexible, fluent, and original a person's thinking is. Here, for example, is an item from a test used by Getzels and Jackson (1962) to measure associative ability, a factor in creativity: "Write as many meanings as you can for each of the following words: (a) duck; (b) sack; (c) pitch; (d) fair." Those who write several meanings for each word, rather than only one, are rated as potentially more creative.

Another measure of creativity might ask children to produce as many words as possible that begin with *T* and end with *N* within a minute. Still another item might give people a minute to classify a list of names in as many ways as possible. In how many ways can you classify the following group of names?

Martha   Paul   Jeffry   Sally   Pablo   Joan

Sometimes arriving at the right answer involves both divergent and convergent thinking. When presented with a problem, a child—or an adult—may first use divergent thinking to generate many possible solutions to the problem. Convergent thinking may then be used to select likely solutions and reject others.

Intelligence tests such as the Stanford–Binet and Wechsler scales require children to focus in on the single right answer. On intelligence tests, ingenious responses that differ from the designated answers are marked wrong. Tests of creativity, by contrast, are oriented toward determining how flexible and fluent one's thinking can be (Plucker et al., 2015). Such tests include items such as suggesting improvements or unusual uses for a familiar toy or object, naming things that belong in the same class, producing words that are similar in meaning, and writing different endings for a story.

What Is Creativity? How is creativity related to intelligence?

convergent thinking A thought process that attempts to focus on the single best solution to a problem.

divergent thinking A thought process that attempts to generate multiple solutions to problems; free and fluent association to the elements of a problem.

What Are the Roles of Nature (Heredity) and Nurture (Environmental Influences) In the Development of Intelligence?

Let us begin this discussion with a confession: No research strategy for attempting to ferret out genetic and environmental determinants of IQ is flawless. Still, a number of ingenious approaches have been devised. The evidence provided through these approaches is instructive.

Genetic Influences

Various strategies have been devised for research into genetic factors, including kinship studies and studies of adopted children.

If heredity is involved in human intelligence, then closely related people ought to have more similar IQs than distantly related or unrelated people, even when they are reared separately. Figure 12.14 ■ shows the averaged results of more than 100 studies of IQ and heredity in humans (McGue et al., 1993; Plomin & Spinath, 2004; Plomin et al., 2008). The IQ scores of identical (monozygotic [MZ]) twins are more alike than the scores for any other pairs, even when the twins have been reared apart. The average correlation for MZ twins reared together is +0.85; for those reared apart, it is +0.67. Correlations between the IQ scores of fraternal (dizygotic [DZ]) twins, siblings, and parents and children are generally comparable, as is their degree of genetic relationship. The correlations tend to vary from about +0.40 to +0.59. Correlations between the IQ scores of

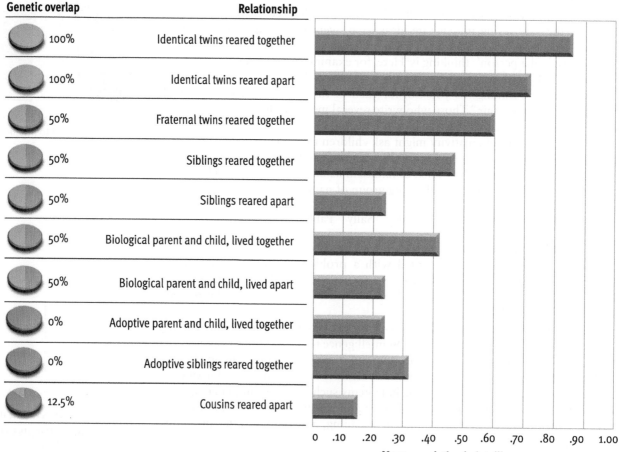

Figure 12.14 ■ **Findings of Studies of the Relationship Between IQ Scores and Heredity**

The data represent a composite of several studies. By and large, correlations are higher between people who are more closely related, yet people who are reared together have more similar IQ scores than people who are reared apart. Such findings suggest that both genetic and environmental factors contribute to IQ scores.
© Cengage Learning®

children and their natural parents (+0.48) are higher than those between children and their adoptive parents (+0.18).

> **TRUTH OR FICTION REVISITED:** Fiction! Adopted children are actually more similar in intelligence to their biological parents than to their adoptive parents. This research finding is suggestive of an important role for genetic factors in intellectual functioning.

All in all, studies suggest that the **heritability** of intelligence is between 40% and 60% (Haworth et al., 2009; Sternberg & Kaufman, 2011). Putting it another way, about half of the difference between your IQ score and the IQ scores of other people can be explained in terms of your genes and their genes.

Let us return to Figure 12.14. Note that genetic pairs (such as MZ twins) reared together show higher correlations between IQ scores than similar genetic pairs (such as other MZ twins) who were reared apart. This finding holds for MZ twins, siblings, parents, children, and unrelated people. For this reason, the same group of studies that suggests that heredity plays a role in determining IQ scores also suggests that the environment plays a role.

When children are separated from their biological parents at early ages, one can argue that strong relationships between their IQ scores and those of their natural parents reflect genetic influences. Strong relationships between their IQs and those of their adoptive parents, on the other hand, might reflect environmental influences. Classic projects involving adopted children in Colorado, Texas, and Minnesota (Scarr, 1993; Sternberg & Kaufman, 2011; Turkheimer, 1991) have found a stronger relationship between the IQ scores of adopted children and their biological parents than between the IQ scores of adopted children and their adoptive parents.

These studies, then, also point to a genetic influence on intelligence. Nevertheless, the environment also has an impact.

Environmental Influences

Psychologist Richard E. Nisbett takes what some might consider an extreme view concerning the importance of environmental factors on intellectual functioning. He writes that "environmental factors are much more important in determining intelligence than previously believed, that racial group differences owe little or nothing to genes, and that interventions, including school, influence intelligence at every level from prenatal care to college and beyond" (2013).

Let us consider the kinds of research strategies that psychologists and educators use to learn about the effects of environmental factors on the development of intelligence. These include discovering situational factors that affect IQ scores, exploring children's ability to rebound from early deprivation, and exploring the effects of positive early environments.

In some cases, we need look no further than the testing situation to explain some of the discrepancy between the IQ scores of middle-class children and those of children from economically disadvantaged backgrounds. In one study (Zigler et al., 1982), the examiner simply made children as comfortable as possible during the test. Rather than being cold and impartial, the examiner was warm and friendly, and care was taken to see that the children understood the directions. As a result, the children's test anxiety was markedly reduced and their IQ scores were 6 points higher than those for a control group treated in a more indifferent manner. Disadvantaged children made relatively greater gains from the procedure. By doing nothing more than making testing conditions more optimal for all children, we can narrow the IQ gap between low-income and middle-class children.

heritability The degree to which the variations in a trait from one person to another can be attributed to, or explained by, genetic factors.

Stereotype vulnerability is another aspect of the testing situation, and it also affects test scores. For example, African American and Latin American children may carry an extra burden on intelligence tests (Inzlicht & Good, 2006). They may worry that they risk confirming their group's negative stereotype by doing poorly. Their concern may create anxiety, which can distract them from the questions, hurting their scores.

In Chapter 7, we discussed a longitudinal study of intellectually disabled orphanage children that provided striking evidence that children can recover from early deprivation. In the orphanage, 19-month-old children were placed with surrogate mothers who provided a great deal of intellectual and social stimulation. Four years later, the children showed dramatic gains in IQ scores.

Children whose parents are responsive and provide appropriate play materials and varied experiences during the early years obtain higher IQ and achievement test scores (Bradley, 2006). Graduates of Head Start and other preschool programs show significant gains in later educational outcomes (Phillips & Styfco, 2007).

Although kinship studies and studies of adoptees suggest that there is a genetic influence on intelligence, they also suggest a role for environmental influences. For example, an analysis of a large number of twin and kinship studies showed that the older twins and other siblings become, the less alike they are on various measures of intelligence and personality (Nisbett, 2009). This appears to be due to increasing exposure to different environments and experiences outside the family.

Studies of adopted children also indicate the importance of environment. African American children who were adopted during the first year by European American parents who were above average in income and education showed IQ scores that were 15–25 points higher than those obtained by African American children reared by their biological parents (Scarr & Weinberg, 1976). The adopted children's average IQ scores, about 106, remained somewhat below those of their adoptive parents' natural children—117 (Scarr & Weinberg, 1977). Even so, the adoptive early environment closed a good deal of the IQ gap. Many psychologists believe that heredity and environment interact to influence intelligence (Daley & Onwuegbuzie, 2011; Haier, 2011). An impoverished environment may prevent some children from living up to their potential. An enriched environment may encourage other children to realize their potential, minimizing possible differences in heredity.

Perhaps we need not be concerned with how much of a person's IQ is due to heredity and how much is due to environmental influences. Psychology has traditionally supported the dignity of the individual. It might be more appropriate for us to try to identify children of all races whose environments place them at high risk for failure and to do what we can to enrich those environments.

Section Review

14. Spearman suggested that the behaviors we consider intelligent have a common factor, which he labeled _____.

15. Gardner argues for the existence of _____ intelligences, each of which is based in a different area of the brain.

16. The IQ indicates the relationship between a child's _____ age and chronological age.

17. The Wechsler scales have subtests that assess _____ tasks and performance tasks.

18. If scoring well on an IQ test requires a certain type of cultural experience, then the tests are said to have a cultural _____.

19. The first spurt in intellectual growth occurs at about the age of _____.

20. Children of lower socioeconomic status in the United States obtain IQ scores some _____ points lower than those obtained by middle- and upper-class children.

21. Children tend to use _____ (convergent or divergent?) thinking when they are thinking creatively.

22. Studies find that there is a stronger relationship between the IQ scores of adopted children and their _____ (adoptive or biological?) parents than between the IQ scores of adopted children and their _____ (adoptive or biological?) parents.

Reflect & Relate: As you look back on your own childhood, can you point to any kinds of family or educational experiences that seem to have had an impact on your intellectual development? Would you say that your background, overall, was deprived or enriched? In what ways?

Language Development

Children's ability to understand and use language becomes increasingly sophisticated in middle childhood. Children also learn to read.

How Do Children's Vocabulary and Grammar Develop in Middle Childhood?

By the age of 6, the child's vocabulary has expanded to 10,000 words, give or take a few thousand. By 7–9 years of age, most children realize that words can have different meanings, and they become entertained by riddles and jokes that require semantic sophistication. (Remember the jokes at the beginning of the chapter?) By the age of 8 or 9, children are able to form "tag questions," in which the question is tagged on to the end of a declarative sentence (Weckerly et al., 2004). "You want more ice cream, don't you?" and "You're sick, aren't you?" are examples of tag questions.

Children also make subtle advances in articulation and in their capacity to use complex grammar. For example, preschool-age children have difficulty understanding passive sentences, such as "The truck was hit by the car," but children in the middle years have less difficulty interpreting the meanings of passive sentences (Aschermann et al., 2004).

During these years, children develop the ability to use connectives, as illustrated by the sentence "I'll eat my spinach, but I don't want to." They also learn to form indirect object–direct object constructions, such as "She showed her sister the toy."

What Cognitive Skills Are Involved in Reading?

Reading is a complex activity that depends on perceptual, cognitive, and linguistic processes. Reading relies on skills in the integration of visual and auditory information. Accurate awareness of the sounds in the child's language is an extremely important factor in subsequent reading achievement. Reading also requires the ability to make basic visual discriminations. In reading, for example, children must "mind their *p*'s and *q*'s." That is, in order to recognize letters, children must be able to perceive the visual differences between letters such as *b* and *d*, and *p* and *q*.

During the preschool years, neurological maturation and experience combine to enable most children to make visual discriminations between different letters with relative ease. Those children who can recognize and name the letters of the alphabet by kindergarten age are better readers in the early school grades (Siegler & Alibali, 2005).

How do children become familiar with their own written languages? More and more today, American children are being exposed to TV programs such as *Sesame Street*, but these are relatively recent educational innovations. Children are also exposed to books, street signs, names of stores and restaurants, and the writing on packages, especially at the supermarket. Some children, of course, have more books in the home than others do. Children from affluent homes where books and other sources of stimulation are plentiful learn to read more readily than children from impoverished homes. But regardless of income level, reading storybooks with parents in the preschool years helps prepare a child for reading (Dockett et al., 2006; Raikes et al., 2006). Children who read at home during the school years also show better reading skills in school and more positive attitudes toward reading.

Methods of Teaching Reading

When they read, children integrate visual and auditory information (they associate what they see with sounds), whether they are using the whole-language approach or the phonetic method. The **whole-language approach** emphasizes the use and recognition of words in everyday situations and in books. The word-recognition method requires that children associate visual stimuli such as *cat* and *Robert* with the sound combinations that produce the spoken words "cat" and "Robert." This capacity is usually acquired by rote learning, or extensive repetition.

In the **phonetic method,** children first learn to associate written letters and letter combinations (such as *ph* or *sh*) with the sounds they are meant to indicate. Then they sound out words from left to right, decoding them. The phonetic method has the obvious advantage of giving children skills that they can use to decode (read) new words (Bastien-Toniazzo & Jullien, 2001; Murray, 2006). However, some children learn more rapidly at early ages through the word-recognition method. The phonetic method can also slow them down when it comes to familiar words. Most children and adults, in fact, tend to read familiar words by the word-recognition method (regardless of which method was used in their original training) and to make some effort to sound out new words.

Which method is superior? Controversy rages over this issue, and we cannot resolve it here. But let us note that some words in English can be read only by the word-recognition method; consider the words *one* and *two*. This method is useful when it comes to words such as *danger, stop, poison,* and the child's name, because it helps provide children with a basic **sight vocabulary**. But children must also acquire decoding skills so that they can read new words on their own.

What Does Research Reveal About the Advantages and Disadvantages of Bilingualism?

Most people throughout the world speak two or more languages. Most countries have minority populations whose languages differ from the national tongue. Many Europeans are taught English and the languages of neighboring nations. Consider the Netherlands: Dutch is the native tongue, but children are also taught French, German, and English and are expected to become fluent in them.

Even though English is the dominant language in the United States, in 2012 approximately 50 million Americans spoke a language other than English at home (U.S. Census Bureau, 2012b; see Table 12.4 ●).

A century ago, it was widely believed that children reared in homes in which a language other than English was spoken were delayed in their cognitive development. The theory was that mental capacity is limited, so people who attempted to store and use two linguistic systems were taxing their mental abilities (Barac & Bialystok, 2011). **Bilingual** children do show some confusion about which language is which from time to time, or which word is appropriate from time to time, but this difference from monolingual children may occur largely because the vocabularies used at home and in the school are not identical (Bialystok et al., 2010). However, the majority of children in the United States who speak Spanish in the home, for example, are proficient in both languages (Shin & Bruno, 2003).

whole-language approach A method for learning to read in which children come to recognize words in a variety of contexts through repeated exposure to them.

phonetic method A method for learning to read in which children decode the sounds of words via their knowledge of the sounds of letters and letter combinations.

sight vocabulary Words that are immediately recognized on the basis of familiarity with their overall shapes, rather than decoded.

bilingual Using or capable of using two languages with nearly equal or equal facility.

TRUTH OR FICTION REVISITED: It is not true that bilingual children have more academic problems than children who speak only one language (Barac & Bialystok, 2011). There is some "mixing" of languages by bilingual children (Gonzalez, 2005), but they can generally separate the two languages from an early age.

Today most linguists consider it advantageous for children to be bilingual because knowledge of more than one language contributes to the complexity of the

Languages Other Than English Most Often Spoken in the Home in the United States

Language Spoken at Home	Total Speakers
Spanish	35,468,501
Chinese	2,600,150
Tagalog	1,513,734
French	1,305,503
Vietnamese	1,251,468
German	1,109,216
Korean	1,039,021
Russian	881,723
Arabic	845,396
Italian	753,992
Portuguese	731,282
French Creole	659,053
Polish	593,598
Hindi	560,983
Japanese	445,471
Persian	396,769
Urdu	355,964
Greek	325,747
Hebrew	221,593

Source: Adapted from U.S. Census Bureau (2012b).

child's cognitive processes (Barac & Bialystok, 2011). For example, bilingual children are more likely to understand that the symbols used in language are arbitrary. Monolingual children are more likely to think, erroneously, that the word *dog* is somehow intertwined with the nature of the beast. Bilingual children therefore have somewhat more cognitive flexibility.

Section Review

23. Reading relies on skills in the integration of _____ and auditory information.

24. In using the _____ method of reading, children associate written letters and letter combinations (such as *ph* or *sh*) with the sounds they indicate.

25. Bilingual children generally _____ (can or cannot?) separate the two languages at an early age.

26. Today most linguists consider it a(n) _____ (advantage or disadvantage?) to be bilingual.

Reflect & Relate: Did you grow up speaking a language other than English in your home? If so, what special opportunities and problems were connected with the experience?

Chapter Review

12.1 How Does Children's Intellectual Functioning Develop During the Concrete-Operational Stage?

In the stage of concrete operations, children begin to show the capacity for adult logic with tangible objects. Concrete-operational thinking is characterized by reversibility, flexibility, and decentration. Concrete-operational children show understanding of conservation, transitivity, and class inclusion. Piaget believed that learning involves active discovery. Thus, teachers should not impose knowledge on the child but instead find materials to interest and stimulate the child. Instruction should be geared to the child's level of development.

12.2 What Are the Cognitive-Developmental Theories of Children's Moral Reasoning?

Piaget posited two stages of moral development: moral realism and autonomous morality. The earlier stage emerges at about the age of 5; in this stage, the child judges behavior as right when it conforms to rules. Five-year-olds see rules as embedded in the structure of things and believe in immanent justice. Preoperational children focus on one dimension at a time; for example, the amount of damage and not the intentions of the wrongdoer. Children begin to show autonomous morality in middle childhood. At that time, they view social rules as agreements that can be changed. Kohlberg believed that there are three levels of moral development and two stages within each level. In the preconventional level, children base moral judgments on the consequences of behavior. In the conventional level, right and wrong are judged in terms of conformity to conventional standards. In the postconventional level, moral reasoning is based on one's own values.

12.3 What Is the Information Processing View of Cognitive Development?

Information-processing theorists aim to learn how children store, retrieve, and manipulate information—how their "mental programs" develop. One key cognitive process is selective attention—attending to the relevant features of a task—which advances steadily through middle childhood. *Memory* refers to the storage and retrieval of information. Many psychologists divide memory functioning into three major processes: sensory memory, working memory, and long-term memory. Maintenance of information in working memory depends on cognitive strategies such as encoding and rehearsing stimuli. Older children process information more efficiently. There is no known limit to the capacity of long-term memory. Information is transferred from short-term memory to long-term memory by rehearsal and elaboration. Children organize their long-term memory into categories. Correct categorization expands knowledge and allows for efficient retrieval. Awareness and conscious control of cognitive abilities is termed *metacognition*, as evidenced by the ability to formulate problems, awareness of how to solve them, use of rules and strategies, ability to remain focused, and ability to check answers. Metamemory consists of people's awareness of the workings of their memory. By age 6 or 7, children know how to use rehearsal to remember things.

12.4 What Are the Relationships Among Intellectual Development, Creativity, and Achievement?

Intelligence provides the basis for academic achievement. It is a child's underlying competence or learning ability. Spearman suggested that the behaviors we consider intelligent have a common underlying factor: *g*. But *s*, or specific capacities, accounts for some individual abilities. Thurstone used factor analysis to define several primary mental abilities. Sternberg proposes a three-pronged theory of intelligence, including analytical intelligence (academic ability), creative intelligence, and practical intelligence ("street smarts"). Gardner believes that people have multiple "intelligences," each based in a different part of the brain. Some of these—verbal ability, logical–mathematical reasoning, and spatial intelligence—involve academic ability. Others—for example, bodily–kinesthetic intelligence, musical intelligence, interpersonal intelligence, and personal knowledge—strike other psychologists as special talents, not intelligences. The Stanford-Binet Intelligence Scale (SBIS) assumes that intelligence increases with age, so older children must answer more items correctly than younger children to obtain a comparable score, which Binet termed a *mental age (MA).* Comparing a child's MA with his or her chronological age (CA)—that is, computing MA/CA—yields an *intelligence quotient (IQ).* The average IQ score is defined as 100. Wechsler introduced the concept of the *deviation IQ,* which is based on an individual's score in relation to those of her or his agemates. The Wechsler scales group test questions into subtests that measure different types of intellectual tasks. Some tasks are mainly verbal, whereas others rely more on spatial-relations skills. Many psychologists and educational specialists believe that intelligence tests are at least somewhat biased against African Americans and members of lower social classes. In addition to underlying competence, intelligence tests reflect knowledge of the language and culture in which the test is given. During middle childhood, thought processes become more logical and abstract. Children gain the capacity to focus on two or more aspects of a problem at once. The first intellectual spurt occurs at about the age of 6 and coincides with entry into school. The second spurt occurs at age 10 or 11. Intelligence tests gain greater predictive power during middle childhood. The term *intellectual disability* refers to limitations in intellectual functioning that are characterized by an IQ score no higher than 70–75. Some causes of intellectual disability are biological, but cultural–familial disability also occurs. Giftedness involves outstanding abilities, high performance in a specific academic area (such as language or mathematics), leadership, distinction in the arts, or bodily talents. Gifted children tend to be successful as adults. Lower-socioeconomic-status U.S. children obtain lower IQ scores than more affluent children. As a group, children from most ethnic minority households score lower than European Americans, but Asian Americans tend to outscore European Americans. Creativity is the ability to do things that are novel and useful. Creative children take chances, refuse to accept limitations, and appreciate art and music. The relationship between intelligence test scores and measures of creativity are only moderate. Children use mainly convergent thinking to arrive at the correct answers on intelligence tests. Creative thinking tends to be divergent rather than convergent. The closer the genetic relationship between people, the more alike their IQ scores. The IQ scores of adopted children are more like those of their biological parents than those of their adoptive parents. Research also finds situational influences on IQ scores, including motivation, familiarity with testing materials, and the effects of enriched environments.

12.5 How Does Language Develop During Middle Childhood?

In middle childhood, language use becomes more sophisticated, including understanding that words can have multiple meanings. There are advances in articulation and use of grammar. Reading relies on skills in the integration of visual and auditory information. During the preschool years, neurological maturation and experience combine to enable most children to make visual discriminations between letters with relative ease. Research shows that bilingual children can generally separate two languages from an early age and that most Americans who first spoke another language in the home also speak English well. Knowledge of more than one language expands children's knowledge of different cultures.

Key Terms

13

Middle Childhood: Social and Emotional Development

TruthorFiction?

 Children's self-esteem rises throughout middle childhood. **p. 420**

 Parents who are in conflict should stay together "for the sake of the children." **p. 427**

 The daughters of employed women are more achievement-oriented and set higher career goals for themselves than the daughters of unemployed women. **p. 428**

In middle childhood, popular children tend to be attractive and relatively mature for their age. **p. 430**

 Teachers who have higher expectations of students may elicit greater achievements from them. **p. 435**

 Some children—like some adults—blame themselves for all the problems in their lives, whether they deserve the blame or not. **p. 440**

 It is better for children with school phobia to remain at home until the origins of the problem are uncovered and resolved. **p. 444**

A college student taking a child development course had a conversation with a 9-year-old girl named Karen:

Student: Karen, how was school today?
Karen: Oh, it was all right. I don't like it a lot.
Student: How come?
Karen: Sara and Becky won't talk to me. I told Sara I thought her dress was very pretty, and she pushed me out of the way. That made me so mad.
Student: That wasn't nice of them.
Karen: No one is nice except for Amy. At least she talks to me.

Here is part of a conversation between a different college student and her 9-year-old cousin, Sue:

Sue: My girlfriend Heather in school has the same glasses as you. My girlfriend—no, not my girlfriend, my *friend*—picked them up yesterday from the doctor, and she wore them today.
Student: What do you mean, not your girlfriend but your friend? Is there a difference?
Sue: Yeah, my friend. 'Cause Wendy is my girlfriend.

Fstop Images Gmbh/Alamy

415

Student: But what's the difference between Heather, your friend, and Wendy, your girlfriend?

Sue: Well, Wendy is my best friend, so she's my girlfriend. Heather isn't my best friend, so she's just a friend. (Adapted from Rowen, 1973).

Between the ages of 6 and 12, the child's social world expands. As illustrated by the remarks of these 9-year-old girls, peers take on greater importance and friendships deepen (Grusec, 2015). Entry into school exposes the child to the influence of teachers and to a new peer group. Relationships with parents change as children develop greater independence. Some children face adjustments resulting from the divorce and remarriage of parents. During these years, major advances occur in children's ability to understand themselves. Their knowledge of social relationships and their skill in developing such relationships increase as well (Davis, 2001; Grusec, 2015). Some children, unfortunately, develop problems during these years, although some are able to cope with life's stresses better than others.

In this chapter, we discuss each of these areas. First, we examine major theories of social and emotional development in the middle years. Next, we examine the development of self-concept and the development of relationships with parents and peers. Then we turn to the influences of the school. Finally, we look at some of the social and emotional problems that can arise in middle childhood.

13.1 Theories of Social and Emotional Development in Middle Childhood

Middle childhood is one of the least studied and yet one of the most exciting periods of life. Imagine a 5-year-old girl going to kindergarten for her first day of formal school. Now imagine this same girl at 12 years when she goes to secondary school. At 5 years, she is a cute child still anxious about separating from her parents as they leave her at the school. By 12 she will have grown into a young woman with secondary sex characteristics. In some populations she will already have begun dating, and she certainly will have begun menstruating in most American populations. In addition to starting school, she is likely to have experienced other institutional settings without her parents, settings in which she will have been exposed to a variety of peers and adults as well as many opportunities to learn new skills. Each of these new institutional settings (e.g., primary school, scouting, recreational programs, music lessons, etc.) will provide her with a series of new life experiences—experiences that will encourage the development of intellectual and interpersonal competencies, and introduce the child to new social roles in which [social approval] is based upon competence and performance.

—Jacqueline Eccles and her colleagues (2006, p. 325)

As noted by Eccles and her colleagues (2006), the major theories of personality have had less to say about this age group than about the other periods of childhood and adolescence. Nevertheless, common threads emerge. These include the development of skills, the importance of interpersonal relationships, and the expansion of self-understanding.

What Are Psychoanalytic Theory's Views on Middle Childhood?

latency stage In Freud's psychoanalytic theory, the fourth stage of psychosexual development, characterized by repression of sexual impulses and development of skills.

Is it possible that children have taken such an emotional beating from conflict over weaning in the oral stage, conflict over toilet training in the anal stage, and conflict over masturbation in the phallic stage that by the time they hit middle childhood, they repress it all and enter the **latency stage**, during which psychosexual impulses are hidden? Sigmund Freud believed that it was quite possible and that by making sexual feelings unconscious, children could focus on developing intellectual, social, and other culturally valued skills.

Erik Erikson agreed with Freud that the major developmental task of middle childhood is the acquisition of cognitive and social skills, but he did not suggest that children were sweeping 5–6 years of emotional turmoil under the rug to make it happen (Eccles et al., 2006). Erikson labeled the middle childhood years the stage of **industry versus inferiority**. Children who are able to master the various tasks and challenges of the middle years develop a sense of industry, or competence. He believed that children who have difficulties in school or with peer relationships during this period may develop a sense of inferiority.

What Is Social Cognitive Theory's View on Middle Childhood?

Social cognitive theory focuses on the continued importance of rewards and modeling in middle childhood. During these years, children depend less on external rewards and punishments and increasingly regulate their own behavior.

How do children acquire moral and social standards for judging their own behavior? One mechanism is direct reward and punishment. Parents may praise a child when she shares her toys with her younger brother. In time, she incorporates the importance of sharing into her own value system. Another mechanism is modeling. Children in the middle years are exposed to an increasing variety of models. Not only parents but also teachers, other adults, peers, TV characters, and the heroine in a story can serve as models (Grusec, 2011, 2015; Richert et al., 2011). The parents' educational level also influences children's hopes and expectations. Longitudinal research shows that the educational level of the parents when the child is 8 years old predicts the educational and occupational success of the child some 40 years later (Dubow et al., 2009).

What Is Cognitive-Developmental Theory's View on Middle Childhood?

According to Jean Piaget, middle childhood coincides with the stage of concrete operations and is partly characterized by a decline in egocentrism and an expansion of the capacity to view the world and oneself from other people's perspectives. This cognitive advance enhances the child's intellectual functioning and affects the child's social relationships (Slaughter, 2011).

Social Cognition

Social cognition consists of the development of children's knowledge about the social world. It focuses on the child's understanding of the relationship between the self and others. A key aspect of the development of social cognition is the ability to assume the role or perspective of another person (Bengtsson & Arvidsson, 2011; Killen & Smetana, 2015). Robert Selman and his colleagues (Kwok & Selman, 2013) devised a method to study the development of perspective-taking skills in childhood. Selman presented children with a social dilemma such as the following:

> Holly is an 8-year-old girl who likes to climb trees. She is the best tree climber in the neighborhood. One day while climbing down from a tall tree, she falls off the bottom branch but does not hurt herself. Her father sees her fall. He is upset and asks her to promise not to climb trees anymore. Holly promises. Later that day, Holly and her friends meet Sean. Sean's kitten is caught up in a tree and cannot get down. Something has to be done right away, or the kitten may fall. Holly is the only one who climbs trees well enough to reach the kitten and get it down, but she remembers her promise to her father.

industry versus inferiority The fourth stage of psychosocial development in Erikson's theory, occurring in middle childhood. Mastery of tasks leads to a sense of industry, whereas failure produces feelings of inferiority.

social cognition Development of children's understanding of the relationship between the self and others.

● TABLE 13.1

Levels of Perspective-Taking

Level	Approximate Age (years)ᵃ	What Happens
0	3–6	Children are egocentric and do not realize that other people have perspectives different from their own. A child of this age will typically say that Holly will save the kitten because she likes kittens and that her father will be happy because he likes kittens, too. The child assumes that everyone feels as she does.
1	5–9	Children understand that people in different situations may have different perspectives. The child still assumes that only one perspective is "right." A child might say that Holly's father would be angry if he did not know why she climbed the tree. But if she told him why, he would understand. The child recognizes that the father's perspective may differ from Holly's because of lack of information. But once he has the information, he will assume the "right" (i.e., Holly's) perspective.
2	7–12	The child understands that people may think or feel differently because they have different values or ideas. The child also recognizes that others are capable of understanding the child's own perspective. Therefore, the child is better able to anticipate the reactions of others. The typical child of this age might say that Holly knows that her father will understand why she climbed the tree and that he therefore will not punish her.
3	10–15	The child finally realizes that both she and another person can consider each other's point of view at the same time. The child may say something similar to this: Holly's father will think that Holly shouldn't have climbed the tree. But now that he has heard her side of the story, he would feel that she was doing what she thought was right. Holly realizes that her father will consider how she felt.
4	12 and above	The child realizes that mutual perspective-taking does not always lead to agreement. The perspectives of the larger social group also must be considered. A child of this age might say that society expects children to obey their parents and therefore Holly should realize why her father might punish her.

Source: Selman (1976).
ᵃAges may overlap.

The children then were asked a series of questions designed to test their ability to take the role of another person (e.g., "How will Holly's father feel if he finds out she climbed the tree?"). Based on the children's responses to these questions, Selman (1976) described five levels of perspective-taking skills in childhood (see Table 13.1 ●).

Research supports Selman's developmental progression in perspective-taking. Children with better perspective-taking skills tend to be more skilled at negotiating peer relations (Abrams et al., 2014; Kwok & Selman, 2013; Smith & Rose, 2011).

How Does the Self-Concept Develop During Middle Childhood?

In early childhood, children's self-concepts, or self-definitions, focus on concrete external traits, such as appearance, activities, and living situations. But as children undergo the cognitive developments of middle childhood, their more abstract internal traits, or personality characteristics, begin to play a role in their self-definition. Social relationships and group memberships take on significance (Bukowski & Veronneau, 2014; Rosen & Patterson, 2011).

An investigative method called the Twenty Statements Test bears out this progression and also highlights the relationships between the self-concept and general cognitive development. According to this method, children are given a sheet of paper with the question "Who am I?" and 20 spaces in which to write answers. Consider the answers of a 9-year-old boy and an 11-year-old girl:

The 9-year-old boy: "My name is Bruce C. I have brown eyes. I have brown hair. I have brown eyebrows. I'm nine years old. I LOVE! sports. I have seven people in my family. I have great! eye site. I have lots! of friends. I live on 1923 Pinecrest Dr. I'm going on 10 in September. I'm a boy. I have a uncle that is almost 7 feet tall. My school is Pinecrest. My teacher is Mrs. V. I play Hockey! I am almost the smartest boy in the class. I LOVE! food. I love fresh air. I LOVE School."

The 11-year-old girl: "My name is A. I'm a human being. I'm a girl. I'm a truthful person. I'm not pretty. I do so-so in my studies. I'm a very good cellist. I'm a very good pianist. I'm a little bit tall for my age. I like several boys. I like several girls. I'm old-fashioned. I play tennis. I am a *very* good swimmer. I try to be helpful. I'm always ready to be friends with anybody. Mostly I'm good, but I lose my temper. I'm not well-liked by some girls and boys. I don't know if I'm liked by boys or not."

—Montemayor & Eisen (1977, pp. 317–318)

Only the 9-year-old gives his age and address, discusses his family, and focuses on physical traits, such as eye color, in his self-definition. The 9-year-old mentions his likes, which can be considered rudimentary psychological traits, but they are tied to the concrete, as would be expected of a concrete-operational child.

The 9- and 11-year-olds both list their competencies. The 11-year-old's struggle to bolster her self-esteem—her insistence on her musical abilities despite her qualms about her attractiveness—shows a greater concern with internal traits, psychological characteristics, and social relationships.

Research findings suggest that females are somewhat more likely than males to define themselves in terms of the groups to which they belong (Oyserman et al., 2012). A Chinese study found that children with siblings are more likely than only children to define themselves in terms of group membership (Wang et al., 1998).

self-esteem The sense of value or worth that people attach to themselves.

Self-Esteem

One of the most critical aspects of self-concept is **self-esteem**, the value or worth that people attach to themselves. A positive self-image is crucial to psychological adjustment (Rosen & Patterson, 2011).

As children enter middle childhood, their self-concepts become more differentiated and they are able to evaluate their self-worth in many different areas (Rosen & Patterson, 2011). Preschoolers do not generally make a clear distinction between different areas of competence. They are either "good at doing things" or not. At one time, it was assumed that before age 8, children could differentiate between only two broad facets of self-concept. One involved general competence, and the other involved social acceptance (Harter, 2006). It was also believed that an overall, or general, self-concept did not emerge until the age of 8. But research indicates that even as early as 5–7 years of age, children are able to make judgments about their performance in seven different areas: physical ability, physical appearance, peer relationships, parent relationships, reading, mathematics, and general school performance. They also display an overall, or general, self-concept (Harter, 2006).

Self-Esteem in Middle Childhood Children's self-esteem tends to decline during middle childhood, in part because they come to evaluate their physical appearance and their performance in academic and social domains more realistically.

Fancy Collection/SuperStock

Do girls or boys have a more favorable self-image? The answer depends on the area. Girls tend to have more positive self-concepts regarding reading, general academics, and helping others than boys do, whereas boys tend to have more positive self-concepts in math, physical ability, and physical appearance (Tobin et al., 2010; Underwood & Rosen, 2011). Cross-cultural studies in China (Dai, 2001), Finland (Lepola et al., 2000), and Germany (Tiedemann, 2000) also find that girls tend to have higher self-concepts in writing, and boys in math.

Why do girls and boys differ in their self-concepts? Socialization and gender stereotypes appear to affect the way females and males react to their achievements. For example, girls predict that they will do better on tasks that are labeled "feminine," and boys predict better performance for themselves when tasks are labeled "masculine" (Jacobs et al., 2005; Rathus et al., 2014).

Authoritative parenting apparently contributes to children's self-esteem (Chan & Koo, 2011; Scales, 2014). Children with a favorable self-image tend to have parents who are restrictive, involved, and loving. Children with low self-esteem are more likely to have authoritarian or rejecting–neglecting parents.

Authoritative Parenting and Self-Esteem Research suggests that parental demands for mature behavior, imposition of restrictions, and warmth help children develop behavior patterns that are connected with self-esteem.

High self-esteem in children is related to their closeness to parents, especially as found in father–son and mother–daughter relationships (Fenzel, 2000). Close relationships between parents are also associated with positive self-concepts in children (DeHart et al., 2006).

Peers also play a role in children's self-esteem. Social acceptance by peers is related to self-perceived competence in academic, social, and athletic domains (Cillessen & Bellmore, 2011). Parents and classmates have an equally strong effect on children's sense of self-worth in the middle years. Friends and teachers have relatively less influence in shaping self-esteem but are also important (Harter, 2006).

Self-esteem appears to have a genetic component, which would contribute to its stability. Research evidence finds that the concordance (agreement) rate for self-esteem is higher among identical (monozygotic, MZ) twins than fraternal (dizygotic, DZ) twins (Segal, 2013). A longitudinal British study found that both genetic and environmental factors appear to contribute to the stability of children's self-esteem (Neiss et al., 2006). Most children will encounter failure, but high self-esteem may contribute to the belief that they can master adversity. Low self-esteem may become a self-fulfilling prophecy: Children with low self-esteem may not carve out much to boast about.

Learned Helplessness

One possible outcome of low self-esteem in academics is known as **learned helplessness**. Learned helplessness is an acquired belief that one is unable to obtain the rewards that one seeks. "Helpless" children tend to quit following failure, whereas children who believe in their own ability tend to persist in their efforts or change their strategies (Steca et al., 2014). One reason for this difference is that helpless children believe that success is due more to ability than to effort and they have little ability in a particular area. Consequently, persisting in the face of failure seems futile. Children

learned helplessness An acquired (hence, learned) belief that one is unable to control one's environment.

who feel helpless typically perform more poorly in school and on standardized tests of intelligence and achievement (Burnette et al., 2013; Goldstein & Brooks, 2005).

Gender Differences in Learned Helplessness

It is unclear whether girls or boys exhibit more learned helplessness in middle childhood, but a gender difference does emerge in mathematics (Else-Quest et al., 2013; Hyde, 2014). Researchers have found that even when girls are performing as well as boys in math and science, they have less confidence in their ability (Hall, 2012). Why? Parents' expectations that children will do well (or poorly) in a given area influence both the children's self-perceptions and their performance. Parents tend to hold the stereotyped view that girls have less math ability than boys, regardless of their own daughter's actual performance in math.

Section Review

1. Erikson labels middle childhood the stage of _____ versus inferiority.

2. According to Piaget, middle childhood coincides with the stage of _____ operations.

3. A key aspect of the development of social cognition is the ability to take the _____ of another person.

4. Children's self-esteem _____ (increases or decreases?) during middle childhood.

5. _____ (Authoritarian or Authoritative?) parenting contributes to high self-esteem in children.

Reflect & Relate: Are you "responsible" for your own self-esteem, or does your self-esteem pretty much vary with the opinion that others have of you? Why is this an important question?

13.2 The Family

In middle childhood, the family continues to play a key role in socializing the child, even though peers, teachers, and other outsiders begin to play a greater role (Dunn, 2015; Grusec & Davidov, 2015). In this section, we will look at developments in parent–child relationships during the middle years. We will also consider the effects of different family environments: the family environment provided by LGBT parents and the experience of living in families with varying marital arrangements. And we will consider the effects of parental employment.

What Issues Are Involved in Parent–Child Relationships During Middle Childhood?

Parent–child interactions focus on some new concerns during the middle childhood years, including school-related matters, assignment of chores, and peer activities (Grusec & Davidov, 2015).

During the middle years, parents do less monitoring of children's activities and provide less direct feedback than they did in the preschool years (Grusec, 2015). In

Ariel Skelley/Blend Images/Getty Images

Children spend less time with their parents during middle childhood than they did in early childhood, and they need fewer reminders about dos and don'ts.

LGBT PARENTS AND THEIR FAMILIES

"Where did you get that beautiful necklace?" I asked the little girl in the pediatrician's office. "From my Moms," she answered. It turned out that her family consisted of two women, each of whom had a biological child, one girl and one boy. About 23% of **lesbian** women are parents, as compared with about 68% of heterosexual women, and most lesbians become parents through prior relationships with men (Brewster et al., 2014). Yet, some lesbian mothers become pregnant via donor insemination (Bos, 2013) and others adopt (Farr & Patterson, 2013). **Gay** fathers, similarly, are most likely to have fathered children in prior relationships with women (Tornello & Patterson, 2015). However, some gay couples use surrogate mothers (Berkowitz, 2013), and, as with lesbian mothers, some adopt children (Farr & Patterson, 2013).

Research on **LGBT** parenting has fallen into two general categories: the general adjustment of children and whether the children of LGBT parents are more likely than other children to be LGBT themselves. Research by Charlotte Patterson (2006; Patterson & Farr, 2011) has generally found that the psychological adjustment of children of LGBT parents—whether conceived by intercourse or donor insemination, or adopted—is comparable to that of children of heterosexual parents. Despite the stigma attached to homosexuality, lesbians and gay men frequently create and sustain positive family relationships (Lick et al., 2011; Tasker & Granville, 2011). On the other hand, the psychological adjustment of LGBT couples and their children is to some degree related to the social climate of their locale. More specifically, the social climate is defined as the level of support for LGBT families in the area (Oswald et al., 2013). Moreover, locales in which there is greater density of LGBT populations generally offer more support. Almost needless to say, the psychological adjustment of LGBT couples and their offspring is superior is communities in which there is social support (Lick et al., 2012).

Now let us consider the sexual orientation of the children of LGBT parents. In doing so, we begin more than a generation back with the research of psychiatrist Richard Green. In a classic study, Green (1978) observed 37 children and young adults, 3–20 years old, who were being reared—or had been reared—by lesbians or **transgendered** people. All but one of the children reported or recalled preferences for toys, clothing, and friends (male or female) that were typical for their gender and age. All of the 13 older children who reported sexual fantasies or sexual behavior were heterosexually oriented. In a subsequent study, Green and his colleagues (1986) compared the children of European American mothers who were currently single, 50 of whom were lesbians and 40 of whom were heterosexual. Boys from the two groups showed no significant differences in intelligence test scores, sexual orientation, gender-role preferences, relationships with family and peer groups, or adjustment to life with a single parent. Girls showed slight differences, including somewhat more flexibility in gender roles. Green concluded that the mothers' sexual orientation had no connection with the sexual orientation of their children and general parental fitness. A study by Patterson and her colleagues (Farr et al., 2010) suggested that many adoption agencies now agree with Green's conclusions.

Another review by Patterson and her colleague Rachel Farr (Farr & Patterson, 2013) addressed the personal and social development of children who have lesbian or gay parents. Patterson found that the sexual orientation of the children was generally heterosexual, as

Research shows that being reared by lesbian or gay parents does not in and of itself influence the adjustment and sexual orientation of the children. However, the attitudes within the community play a role, such that children of lesbian or gay parents reared in intolerant social climates may experience some adjustment problems.

(Continued)

among the general population. When parents had gotten divorced and created families with same-gender partners because of their sexual orientations, their children experienced a period of adjustment that entailed some difficulties—as do children when heterosexual parents get divorced. Children who are adopted by LGBT parents tend to be well-adjusted. The point here—reinforcing Green's findings—is that wanting the child is more important to the child's adjustment than the sexual orientation of the parents.

middle childhood, children do more monitoring of their own behavior. Although the parents still retain control over the child, control is gradually transferred from parent to child, a process known as **coregulation** (Maughan, 2011). Children no longer need to be constantly reminded of dos and don'ts as they begin to internalize the standards of their parents.

Children and parents spend less time together in middle childhood than in the preschool years. But as in early childhood, children spend more of this time with their mothers than with their fathers (Grusec & Davidov, 2015). Mothers' interactions with school-age children continue to revolve around caregiving and household tasks, whereas fathers, when they are involved, are relatively more involved in recreational activities, especially with sons (Demby et al., 2015). But here, too, mothers may actually spend more time (Keown & Palmer, 2014). Fathers also appear to be relatively less available to their sons on weekdays. All in all, it does not seem surprising that mother–child attachment is found to be more important to a child's psychological adjustment than father–child attachment (Demby et al., 2015).

In the later years of middle childhood (ages 10–12), children evaluate their parents more critically than they did in the early years (Denham et al., 2011; Grusec & Davidov, 2015). This shift in perception may reflect the child's developing cognitive ability to view relationships in more complex ways (De Goede et al., 2009). Throughout middle childhood, however, children rate their parents as their best source of emotional support, rating them higher than friends (Denham et al., 2011; Dunn, 2015).

What Happens to Children Whose Parents Get Divorced?

To many in the United States, the 2000s are the period of "Generation X." However, it may be more accurate to think of our time as that of "Generation Ex"—a generation characterized by ex-wives and ex-husbands. Their children are also a part of Generation Ex, which is large and growing continuously. More than 1 million American children each year experience the divorce of their parents (U.S. Bureau of the Census, 2012a). Nearly 40% of European American children and 75% of African American children in the United States who are born to married parents will spend at least part of their childhoods in single-parent families as a result of divorce.

Although divorce may be tough on parents, it may be even tougher on children (Kim, 2011; Moon, 2011). The automatic aspects of family life cease being automatic.

lesbian A female who is interested romantically and sexually in other females.

gay A male who is interested romantically and sexually in other males. (Can also refer to lesbians.)

LGBT Descriptive of people who are either lesbian, gay, bisexual, and/or transgendered.

transgendered Descriptive of a person who sees himself or herself as a person of the other gender and who may undergo hormone treatments and/or cosmetic surgery to achieve the appearance of being a member of the other gender.

coregulation A gradual transferring of control from parent to child, beginning in middle childhood.

No longer do children eat with both parents. No longer do they go to ball games, the movies, or Disneyland with both of them. No longer do they curl up with them on the sofa to watch television. No longer do they kiss both at bedtime. The parents are now often supporting two households, which results in fewer resources for the children (Lansford et al., 2009). Children lose other things besides family life. Sometimes the losses are minor, but many children who live with their mothers scrape by—or fail to scrape by—at the poverty level or below. Some children move from spacious houses into cramped apartments or from a desirable neighborhood to one where they are afraid to walk the streets. The mother who was once available may become an occasional visitor, spending more time at work and placing the kids in day care for extended periods of time.

In considering the effects of divorce on family members—both children and adults—we must ask whether the effects are due to divorce or to "selection factors" (Amato, 2006; Lansford et al, 2009). For example, are the effects on children due to divorce per se, or are they due to marital conflict, to inadequate parental problem-solving ability, or to changes in financial status? Also, do children undergo a temporary crisis and gradually adjust, or do stressors persist indefinitely? For example, 3 years after the divorce, feelings of sadness, shock, disbelief, and desire for parental reunion tend to decline, but even 10 years later, children tend to harbor anger toward the parent they hold responsible for the breakup. Then, too, some children tend to fare better after fighting parents get divorced (Amato & Anthony, 2014).

Parents who get divorced are often in conflict about many things, and one of them typically involves how to rear the children (Amato, 2006; Lansford et al., 2009). Because the children often hear their parents fighting over child rearing, the children may come to blame themselves for the split. Young children, who are less experienced than adolescents, are more likely to blame themselves. Young children also worry more about uncharted territory—the details of life after the breakup. Adolescents

A Closer Look — Real LIFE

HOW TO ANSWER A 7-YEAR-OLD'S QUESTIONS ABOUT—GULP—SEX

Daddy, where do babies come from?

Why are you asking me? Ask your mother.

Most children do not find it easy to talk to their parents about sex. Only about one-quarter of the children in a national survey had done so (National Campaign to Prevent Teen Pregnancy, 2003). Children usually find it easier to approach their mothers than their fathers (Guttmacher Institute, 2007).

Yet, most children are curious about where babies come from, about how girls and boys differ, and the like. Adults who avoid these issues convey their own uneasiness about sex and may teach children that sex is something to be ashamed of.

Adults need not be sex experts to talk to their children about sex. They can surf the Internet to fill gaps in their knowledge or find books written for parents to read to their children. They can admit they do not know all the answers.

Here are some pointers (Rathus et al., 2014):

- Be approachable. Be willing to discuss sex.
- Provide accurate information. The 6-year-old who wants to know where babies mature within the mother should not be told "in Mommy's tummy." It's wrong and isn't cute; the "tummy" is where food is digested. The child may worry that the baby is going to be digested. The child should be told, instead, "In Mommy's uterus" and can be shown diagrams if he or she wants specifics.
- Teach children the correct names of their sex organs and that the "dirty words" others use to refer to the sex organs are not acceptable in most social settings. Avoid using silly words like *pee pee* or *private parts* to describe sex organs.

Reflect How do you feel about the advice offered in this feature? Would you follow it? Why or why not?

are relatively more independent and have some power to control their day-to-day lives.

Most children live with their mothers after a divorce (U.S. Bureau of the Census, 2012a). Some fathers remain fully devoted to their children despite the split, but others tend to spend less time with their children as time goes on. This pattern is especially common when fathers create other families, such that the children of their new partners are competing with their biological children (Angarne-Lindberg et al., 2009). Not only does the drop-off in paternal attention deprive children of activities and social interactions, but it also saps their self-esteem: "Why doesn't Daddy love me anymore? What's wrong with me?"

There is no question that divorce has challenging effects on children. Children whose parents divorce are more likely to have conduct disorders, lower self-esteem, drug abuse, and poor grades in school (Kim, 2011; Moon, 2011). Their physical health may decline, at least temporarily (Moon, 2011). There are individual differences, but by and large, the fallout for children is worst during the first year after the breakup. Children tend to rebound after a couple of years or so (Malone et al., 2004).

A parental breakup is often connected with a decline in the quality of parenting. A longitudinal study by E. Mavis Hetherington and her colleagues (Hetherington, 2006; Hetherington et al., 1989) tracked the adjustment of children who were 4 years old at the time of the divorce; the follow-ups occurred 2 months, 1 year, 2 years, and 6 years after the divorce. The investigators found that the organization of family life deteriorates. The family is more likely to eat meals pickup style, as opposed to sitting together. Children are less likely to get to school or to sleep on schedule. Divorced mothers have a more difficult time setting limits and enforcing restrictions on sons' behavior. Divorced parents are significantly less likely to show the authoritative behaviors that foster competence. They make fewer demands for mature behavior, communicate less, and show less nurturance and warmth. Their disciplinary methods become inconsistent.

Cross-cultural studies show that children of divorced parents in other cultures experience problems similar to those experienced by such children in the United States (Boey et al., 2003). A study in China matched 58 children of divorced parents with 116 children from intact families according to gender, age, and social class. Children of divorced parents were more likely than the other children to make somatic complaints ("My stomach hurts," "I feel nauseous"), demonstrate lower social competence, and behave aggressively (Liu et al., 2000a). Another Chinese study found that divorce impairs the quality of parent–child relationships, interferes with concern over the children's education, and creates financial hardships (Sun, 2001). A third Chinese study showed that divorce compromises the academic and social functioning of both Chinese and American children (Zhou et al., 2001).

A study of children and their mothers in Botswana, Africa, had similar results (Maundeni, 2000). Divorce led to economic hardship for most mothers and children. Lack of money made some children feel inferior to other children. Financial worries and feelings of resentment and betrayal led to social and emotional problems among both children and mothers.

Back to the United States: Boys seem to have a harder time than girls coping with divorce, and they take a longer time to recover (Grych, 2005; Malone et al., 2004). In the Hetherington study, boys whose parents were divorced showed more social, academic, and conduct problems than boys whose parents were married. These problems sometimes persisted for 6 years. Girls, by contrast, tended to regain normal functioning within 2 years.

K. Alison Clarke-Stewart and her colleagues (2000) compared the well-being of children in families headed by a separated or divorced mother with the well-being of about 170 children reared in intact families. As a group, the children who were

Generation Ex: Ex-Husband, Ex-Wife, Ex-Family, Ex-Security Nearly half of American marriages end in divorce, and divorce turns life topsy-turvy for children. Younger children tend to erroneously blame themselves for the dissolution of the family, but children in middle childhood come to see things more accurately. Children of divorced parents tend to develop problems, many of which fade as time passes. Should parents in conflict stay together for the sake of the children? The answer seems to be that the children will not be better off if the parents continue to fight in front of them.

being reared in two-parent families exhibited fewer problematic behaviors, more social skills, and higher IQ test scores. They were more securely attached to their mothers. But then the researchers factored in the mother's level of education, her socioeconomic status, and her psychological well-being. Somewhat surprisingly, the differences between the children in the two groups (one-parent versus intact families) almost vanished. The researchers concluded that at least in this study, it was not the parental breakup per se that caused the problems among the children. Instead, the difficulties were connected with the mother's psychological status (such as feelings of depression), income, and level of education (Hammen, 2003). The father's psychological status, of course, is frequently a factor that leads to marital conflict and divorce (Angarne-Lindberg et al., 2009; El-Sheikh et al., 2009).

By and large, research shows that the following types of support help children cope with divorce: social support from the immediate family, support from the extended family, support of friends, membership in a religious community, communication among family members, and financial security (Angarne-Lindberg et al., 2009; Greeff & Van Der Merwe, 2004).

Some children of divorced parents profit from psychological treatment (Bonkowski, 2005). Many treatment programs include parents. The usefulness of a program that includes the mother was studied with 240 children, ages 9–12 (Wolchik et al., 2000). The program addressed the quality of the mother–child relationship, ways of disciplining the child, ways of coping with interparental conflict, and the nature of the father–child relationship. Children were also helped to handle stressors (by thinking of them as difficult but not impossible) and to not blame themselves. The children showed improved adjustment at the completion of the program and at a 6-month follow-up.

Life in Stepfamilies: His, Hers, Theirs, and . . .

Most divorced people remarry, usually while the children are young. More than one in three American children will spend part of his or her childhood in a stepfamily (U.S. Bureau of the Census, 2012a).

The rule of thumb about the effects of living in stepfamilies is that there is no rule of thumb (Harvey & Fine, 2011). Living in a stepfamily may have no measurable psychological effects (Ganong & Coleman, 2003). Stepparents may claim stepchildren as their own and become intimately involved in their well-being (Marsiglio, 2004). In that case, children frequently report that they are content with the outcome of the divorce (Angarne-Lindberg et al., 2009). But there are also some risks to living in stepfamilies. Stepchildren appear to be at greater risk of being physically abused by stepparents than by biological parents (Adler-Baeder, 2006). Infanticide (killing infants) is a rarity in the United States, but the crime occurs 60 times as often in stepfamilies as in families with biological kinship (Daly & Wilson, 2000). There is a significantly higher incidence—by a factor of 8—of sexual abuse by stepparents than by natural parents. Stepparents are clearly abusing the child, which is criminal, but they may tell themselves that at least they are not breaking the incest taboo.

"All Right, We Fight—Should We Remain Married for the Sake of the Children?"

Let us have it out at once. I am going to address this issue from a psychological perspective only. Many readers believe—for moral or religious reasons—that marriage and family life must be permanent, no matter what. Readers may evaluate the moral and religious aspects of divorce in the light of their own value systems.

So—from a purely psychological perspective—what should bickering parents do? The answer seems to depend largely on how they behave in front of the children. Research shows that parental bickering—especially severe fighting—is linked to the same kinds of problems that children experience when their parents get separated or divorced (Furstenberg & Kiernan, 2001; Troxel & Matthews, 2004). Moreover, when children are exposed to adult or marital conflict, they display a biological "alarm reaction": Their heart rate, blood pressure, and sweating rise sharply (El-Sheikh et al., 2009). The bodily response is even stronger when children blame themselves for parental conflict, as is common among younger children.

One study analyzed data from 727 children, ages 4–9 years, from intact families and followed up on them 6 years later, when many of the families had gone through separation or divorce (Morrison & Coiro, 1999). Both separation and divorce were associated with increases in behavior problems in children, regardless of the amount of conflict between the parents. However, in the marriages that remained intact, high levels of marital conflict were associated with yet more behavior problems in the children. What's the message? Although separation and divorce are related to adjustment problems in children, the outcome can be worse for children when conflicted parents stay together.

Because of the stresses experienced by children caught up in marital conflict, Hetherington and her colleagues suggest that divorce can be a positive alternative to harmful family functioning (Hetherington, 1989; Wallerstein et al., 2005).

TRUTH OR FICTION REVISITED: From a psychological perspective, when parents in severe conflict stay together "for the sake of the children," the children experience chronic stress. Many psychologists, including E. Mavis Hetherington, write that divorce is sometimes a better alternative for conflicted parents than remaining together.

What Are the Effects of Parental Employment on Children?

The title of this section has undergone changes over the several editions of this book. It was initially called "The Effects of Maternal Employment." Because of the traditional stereotype of women as homemakers, when a woman went to work, some saw it as worthy of comment, and its effects on children were of great social concern. All of this history reflects social prejudice rather than scientific findings.

A half-century ago, most women remained in the home, but today, nearly three out of four married mothers of children under age 18 are employed, as are four out of five divorced, separated, or widowed mothers (U.S. Bureau of the Census, 2007). Family lifestyles have changed as more women combine maternal and occupational roles. Do problems arise when mother is not available for round-the-clock love and attention? And what about the effects of paternal employment (employment of the father)?

One common belief is that Mom's being in the workforce rather than in the home leads to delinquency. Using data on 707 adolescents, ages 12–14, from the National Longitudinal Survey of Youth, Vander Ven and colleagues (2001, 2004) examined whether the occupational status of a mother was connected with delinquent behavior. They found that maternal employment per se made relatively little or no difference, but there was a slight indirect effect in that deviant behavior was related to *lack of supervision*. The issue, then, would seem to be for the parents to ensure that children receive adequate supervision regardless of who—Mom or Dad or both—is on the job. The evidence suggests that paternal employment is potentially as harmful as maternal employment. Yet, who argues that fathers rather than mothers should remain in the home to ward off problems related to poor supervision?

Ed Bock/Flirt/Corbis

What Are the Effects of Maternal Employment? Let us be honest here. Why isn't the title of this photo "What are the effects of parental employment?" The answer is that the vestiges of sexism run rampant in society. When things go wrong with children in families where both parents must work—or both choose to work—the tendency remains to blame the mother. However, research shows that maternal employment is actually connected with few problems for children; it is also connected with more egalitarian attitudes. (Go, Mom!)

Although most of the brouhaha about maternal employment has been based on traditionalist, moralistic values that argue that the mother ought to remain in the home, some concern has been based on research findings suggesting that maternal care of children is preferable to day care (Belsky, 2006a). On the other hand, there is little evidence that maternal employment actually harms children. Elizabeth Harvey (1999) and other researchers (Han et al., 2001) have examined data from the National Longitudinal Survey of Youth on the effects of early parental employment on children. The effects were minimal. Neither the timing nor the continuity of early maternal employment was consistently related to children's development. Harvey did find that working a greater number of hours was linked with slightly lower scores on measures of cognitive development through the age of 9 and with slightly lower academic achievement scores before the age of 7. However, there was no connection between maternal employment and children's behavior problems, compliance, or self-esteem. And now for the pluses: Harvey found that early parental employment was beneficial for single mothers and lower-income families. Why? It brought in cash, and increasing family income has positive effects on children's development.

Other researchers have found other family benefits for maternal employment. Maternal employment appears to benefit school-age children, especially daughters, by fostering greater independence, greater emotional maturity, and higher achievement orientation (Hangal & Aminabhavi, 2007).

TRUTH OR FICTION REVISITED: Daughters of employed women are more achievement-oriented and do set higher career goals for themselves than daughters of nonworking women. A Canadian study found that children whose mothers were employed tended to be more prosocial and less anxious than other children (Nomaguchi, 2006). Both the sons and daughters of employed women appear to be more flexible in their gender-role stereotypes (Wright & Young, 1998). For example, sons of working women are more helpful with housework.

There are other interesting findings on maternal employment. For example, Hoffman and Youngblade (1998) studied a sample of 365 mothers of third- and fourth-graders in a midwestern city. They discovered that working-class full-time homemakers were more likely to be depressed than employed mothers. Feelings of depression were related to permissive and authoritarian parenting styles, suggesting that many financially stressed homemakers do not have the emotional resources to give their children the best possible rearing. Among middle-class mothers, employment was not related to mood or style of parenting. Greater family financial resources apparently elevate the mood.

A Japanese study of 116 urban Japanese women with children in the second grade looked at the effects of maternal employment from the perspective of the mother. It found that the most satisfied women were those who had more children but who were highly committed to their roles in the workforce and, in case that were not enough, who felt that they were doing an excellent job as mothers (Holloway et al., 2006).

Wendy Goldberg and her colleagues (2008) reviewed 68 studies on the effects of maternal employment conducted over the past four decades. They focused on child achievement outcomes: achievement tests, intelligence tests, grades, and teacher ratings of intellectual competence. They found no overall difference on any measure when they compared children whose mothers were in the workforce with children whose mothers remained in the home. However, there were interesting findings when various issues were considered. Among welfare-eligible and working-class families, the added income from maternal employment enhances financial security and the meeting of children's basic needs for food, clothing, and shelter. It increases children's material resources and opportunities for learning and lowers family stress, all of which benefit children's achievement. For example, maternal employment in low-income families was shown to increase children's reading and math scores. But when maternal employment is not financially necessary, the decreased maternal supervision and availability, along with alternative care settings that are less stimulating than the home, may lead to negative effects of maternal employment on children's achievement and to more misbehavior, especially among boys. But remember that there were no overall differences in achievement between the children of working and stay-at-home mothers. Moreover, there has not been an equivalent burst of research into the effects of maternal employment and the father's remaining in the home. Even so, the father's remaining in the home would have meaning that differed from the mother's doing so because it would run counter to societal stereotypes. For example, it would probably be assumed, by both children and outside observers, that there is something wrong with a stay-at-home dad, or at the very least that he cannot find work. These assumptions—or actualities—would also be expected to have effects on children.

Section Review

6. During the middle years, parents do _____ (more or less?) monitoring of children's activities and provide less direct feedback than they did in the preschool years.

7. The children of LGBT parents are most likely to be _____ (heterosexual or homosexual?) in their sexual orientation.

8. Children of divorced parents most often experience _____ (upward or downward?) movement in financial status.

9. Most children of divorced parents live with their _____ (mothers or fathers?).

10. _____ (Boys or Girls?) seem to have a harder time coping with divorce.

11. Research suggests that children are more likely to engage in delinquent behavior as a result of _____ (lack of supervision or maternal employment?).

Reflect & Relate: Have you known children whose families have gone through a divorce? What were the effects on the children?

13.3 Peer Relationships

Families exert the most powerful influences on a child during his or her first few years. But as children move into middle childhood, their activities and interests become directed farther away from home. Peers take on increasing importance in middle childhood (Dunn, 2015; Grusen, 2015). Let us explore the ways in which peers socialize one another. Then we will examine factors in peer acceptance and rejection. Finally, we will see how friendships develop.

What Is the Influence of Peers During Middle Childhood?

Peer relationships are a major part of growing up. Peers exert powerful socialization influences and pressures to conform (Eivers et al., 2012). Even highly involved parents can provide children only with experience relating to adults. Children profit from experience relating to peers because peers have interests and skills that reflect being part of the same generation as the child. Peers differ as individuals, however. For all these reasons, peer experiences broaden children's physical, cognitive, and social skills (Dunn, 2015).

Peers guide children and afford practice in sharing and cooperating, in relating to leaders, and in coping with aggressive impulses, including their own. Peers can be important confidants (Dunn, 2015). Peers, like parents, help children learn what types of impulses—affectionate, aggressive, and so on—they can safely express and with whom. Children who are at odds with their parents can turn to peers as sounding boards. They can compare feelings and experiences they would not bring up in the home. When children share troubling ideas and experiences with peers, they often learn that friends have similar concerns. They realize that they are normal and are not alone (Wentzel, 2014).

Peer Acceptance and Rejection

Acceptance or rejection by peers is of major importance in childhood because problems with peers affect adjustment later on (Dunn, 2015). What are the characteristics of popular and of rejected children?

Peer Rejection Few things are as painful as rejection by one's peers in middle childhood. Children may be rejected if they look unusual or unattractive, lack valued skills, or are aggressive.

TRUTH OR FICTION REVISITED: Popular children tend to be attractive, mature for their age, and successful in sports or academics. On the other hand, physical attractiveness seems to be more important for girls than boys (Rennels & Langlois, 2014).

Socially speaking, popular children are friendly, nurturant, cooperative, helpful, and socially skillful (Kornbluh & Neal, 2015; Rodkin et al., 2013). Popular children have higher self-esteem than other children, which tends to reflect success in academics or valued extracurricular activities such as sports (Chen et al., 2001). Later-born children are more likely to be popular than firstborns, perhaps because they tend to be more sociable (Beck et al., 2006).

Children who show behavioral and learning problems and who disrupt group activities are sometimes rejected by peers (Boivin et al., 2005). However, like prosocial children, aggressive children may also be highly popular and respected (Kornbluh & Neal, 2015; Ojanen & Findley-Van Nostrand, 2014; Troop-Gordon & Ranney, 2014).

Although pressure to conform to group norms and standards can be powerful, most children who are rejected by their peers do not shape up. Instead, they tend to remain lonely on the fringes of the group (Powers & Bierman, 2013; Wentzel, 2014).

How Do Children's Concepts of Friendship Develop During Middle Childhood?

In the preschool years and the early years of middle childhood, friendships are based on geographical closeness or proximity. Friendships are relatively superficial— quickly formed and easily broken. What matters are activity levels, shared activities, and who has the swing set or sandbox. Children through the age of 7 usually report that their friends are the children with whom they share activities (Berndt, 2004; Gleason et al., 2005). There is little reference to friends' traits.

Between the ages of 8 and 11, children increasingly recognize the importance of friends meeting each other's needs and possessing desirable traits (Lansford et al., 2014). Children at these ages are more likely to say that friends are nice to one

Friendship, Friendship . . . A Perfect "Blendship"? Children's concepts of friendship develop over time. In middle childhood, friendship is generally seen in terms of what children do for each other. These children are beginning to value loyalty and intimacy.

Stages in Children's Concepts of Friendship

Stage	Name	Approximate Age (Years)[a]	What Happens
0	Momentary physical interaction	3–6	Children remain egocentric and unable to take one another's point of view. Thus, their concept of a friend is one who likes to play with the same things they do and who lives nearby.
1	One-way assistance	5–9	Children realize that their friends may have different thoughts and feelings than they do, but they place their own desires first. They view a friend as someone who does what they want them to do.
2	Fair-weather cooperation	7–12	Friends are viewed as doing things for one another (reciprocity), but the focus remains on each individual's self-interest rather than on the relationship per se.
3	Intimate and mutual sharing	10–15	The focus is on the relationship itself, rather than on the individuals separately. The function of friendship is viewed as mutual support over a long period of time, rather than concern about a given activity or self-interest.
4	Autonomous interdependence	12 and above	Children (as well as adolescents and adults) understand that friendships grow and change as people change. They realize that they may need different friends to satisfy different personal and social needs.

Source: Selman (1980).
[a]Ages may overlap.

another and share interests as well as things. During these years, children increasingly pick friends who are similar to themselves in behavior and personality. Trustworthiness, mutual understanding, and a willingness to share personal information characterize friendships in middle childhood and beyond (Lansford et al., 2014). Girls tend to develop closer friendships than boys (Ellis & Zarbatany, 2007; Rodkin et al., 2013). Girls are more likely to seek confidants—girls with whom they can share their innermost feelings.

Robert Selman (1980) described five stages in children's changing concepts of friendship (see Table 13.2 ●). The stages correspond to the five levels of perspective-taking skills discussed earlier in the chapter.

Friends behave differently with each other than they do with other children. School-age friends are more verbal, attentive, expressive, relaxed, and mutually responsive to each other during play than are children who are only acquaintances (Cleary et al., 2002). Cooperation occurs more readily between friends than between other groupings, as might be expected. But intense competition can also occur among friends, especially among boys. When conflicts occur between friends, they tend to be less intense and are resolved in ways that maintain positive social interaction (Bowker et al., 2011).

In one study, 696 fourth- and fifth-grade children responded to 30 hypothetical situations involving conflict with a friend (Rose & Asher, 1999). It was found that those children who responded to conflict by seeking revenge were least likely to have friendships or close friendships. Gender differences were also found. Girls were generally more interested in resolving conflicts than boys were.

Children in middle childhood typically will tell you that they have more than one "best" friend (Bukowski et al., 2011). One study found that 9-year-olds reported having an average of four best friends (Lewis & Feiring, 1989). Best friends tend to be more alike than other friends.

In middle childhood, boys tend to play in larger groups than girls. Children's friendships are almost exclusively with others of the same gender, continuing the trend of gender segregation (Pfaff, 2010). Contact with members of the other gender is strongly discouraged by peers. For example, a study of European American, African American, Latin American, and Native American 10- and 11-year-olds found that those who crossed the "gender boundary" were especially unpopular with their peers (Sroufe et al., 1993).

Section Review

12. As children move into middle childhood, their activities and interests become directed _____ (closer to or farther away from?) the home.

13. Popular children tend to be attractive and relatively _____ (mature or immature?) for their age.

14. _____ (Firstborn or Later-born?) children are more likely to be popular.

15. During middle childhood, contact with members of the other sex is _____ (encouraged or discouraged?) by peers.

Reflect & Relate: Do you remember what your attitudes were toward playing with children of your own gender and children of the other gender? Did these attitudes change? Do you remember when? What you were thinking at the time?

 **13.4** The School

The school exerts a powerful influence on many aspects of the child's development.

What Are the Effects of the School on Children's Social and Emotional Development?

Schools, like parents, set limits on behavior, make demands for mature behavior, attempt to communicate, and are oriented toward nurturing positive physical, social, and cognitive development. Schools, like parents, have a direct influence on children's IQ scores, achievement motivation, and career aspirations (Kaplan & Owings, 2015; Wentzel, 2015). Like the family, schools influence social and moral development (Kaplan & Owings, 2015).

Schools are also competitive environments, and children who do too well—and students who do not do well enough—can suffer from the resentment or the low opinion of others. An Italian study placed 178 male and 182 female 8- to 9-year-old elementary school students in competitive situations (Tassi et al., 2001). It was found that when the students were given the task of trying to outperform one another, competition led to social rejection by students' peers. On the other hand, when the students were simply asked to do the best they could, high rates of success led to admiration by one's peers.

In this section, we will consider children's transition to school and then examine the effects of the school environment and of teachers.

What Is It Like for Children to Enter School?—Getting to Know You

An increasing number of children attend preschool. About half have had some type of formal prekindergarten experience, often part-time (Ebert & Culyer, 2011; Woolfolk, 2013). But most children first experience full-time schooling when they enter kindergarten or first grade. Children must master many new tasks when they start school. They have to meet new academic challenges, learn new school and teacher expectations, and fit into a new peer group. They must learn to accept extended separation from their parents and develop increased attention, self-control, and self-help skills.

What happens to children during the transition from home or preschool to elementary school may be critical for their eventual success or failure in their educational experience. This is particularly true for low-income children. Families of children living in poverty may be less able to supply both the material and the emotional supports that help the child adjust successfully to school (Slavin, 2012; Woolfolk, 2013).

How well prepared are children to enter school? Discussions of school readiness must consider at least three critical factors:

1. The diversity and inequity of children's early life experiences
2. Individual differences in young children's development and learning
3. The degree to which schools establish reasonable and appropriate expectations of children's capabilities when they enter school

Unfortunately, some children enter school less well prepared than others. About one U.S. child in six begins school without readiness skills needed to learn successfully (Bierman et al., 2014). More than 4 of 10 children being reared in poverty do not have adequate readiness skills. Poor health care, inadequate nutrition, and lack of adequate stimulation and support by parents place children at particular risk for academic failure even before they enter school.

The average school reports that between 10% and 20% of incoming kindergartners had difficulty adjusting to kindergarten (Buyse et al., 2011; Slavin, 2012). Adjusting to the academic demands of school was reported to be the area of greatest difficulty. Children from families with low socioeconomic status had a harder time adjusting than other children, particularly in academics. Children who enter school with deficits in language and math skills generally continue to show deficits in these areas during at least the first years of school (Ebert & Culyer, 2011; Woolfolk, 2013).

What Are the Characteristics of a Good School?

Reviews of the research (Kaplan & Owings, 2015; Woolfolk, 2013) indicate that an effective school has the following characteristics:

- An active, energetic principal
- An atmosphere that is orderly but not oppressive
- Empowerment of teachers—that is, teachers participating in decision-making
- Teachers with expectations that children will learn
- A curriculum that emphasizes academics
- Frequent assessment of student performance
- Empowerment of students—that is, students participating in setting goals, making classroom decisions, and engaging in cooperative learning activities with other students

Cheryl Casey/Shutterstock.com

BULLYING: AN EPIDEMIC OF PAIN

I was called really horrible, profane names very loudly in front of huge crowds of people, and my schoolwork suffered at one point," she said. "I didn't want to go to class. And I was a straight-A student, so there was a certain point in my high school years where I just couldn't even focus on class because I was so embarrassed all the time. I was so ashamed of who I was.

—Lady Gaga[1]

Eleven-year-old Michael Wilson committed suicide in 2011. His family found him with a plastic bag tied around his head (Nurwisah, 2011). Michael had muscular dystrophy. He struggled to walk around the block or climb the stairs. He used a walker to get by in school. At school, a 12-year-old mugged him for his iPhone. A few months before his death, Michael said, "If I have to go back to that school, I'll kill myself." And he did.

Twelve-year-old Rebecca killed herself by climbing a platform at an abandoned cement plant and jumping off. She had received a continuous stream of threatening and taunting text messages and photos—aspects of all-too-common **cyberbullying** (Alvarez, 2013).

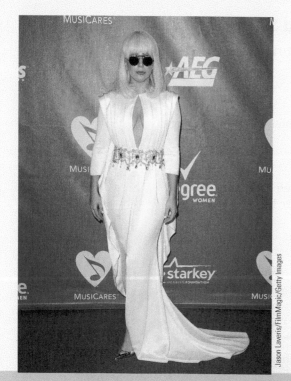

Lady Gaga may be a superstar now, but bullying led her to have serious self-doubts in school.

Bullying has devastating effects on the school atmosphere. It transforms the perception of school from a safe place into a violent place. Nine-year-old Stephanie had gotten into a disagreement with Susan, and Susan had told her she would beat her mercilessly if she showed up at school again. To highlight her warning, Susan had shoved Stephanie across the hall. Stephanie did not know it, but, ironically, Susan was also bullied from time to time by a couple of other girls at school. Stephanie's response was to refuse to go to school, not to commit suicide.

Was there something unusual about Michael, Rebecca, and Stephanie's situations? Sadly, no. Bullying is everywhere and there are all too many suicides from victims who are bullied on Facebook and in other ways on the Internet (Kowalski et al., 2014). Suicide is especially common among middle schoolers who have not yet developed a strong sense of who they are and where they are going in life (Henry et al., 2014).

Boys are more likely than girls to be bullies, but many girls engage in bullying (Juvonen & Graham, 2014). All in all, at least half of middle school students in the United States have been exposed to bullying (Baly et al., 2014).

Many, but not all, bullies have some things in common. Their achievement tends to be lower than average, such that peer approval or deference might be more important to them than academics (Batsche & Porter, 2006; Leiner et al., 2014). Bullies are more likely to come from homes of lower socioeconomic status with parental violence (Perren & Alsaker, 2006). Bullying is also associated with more frequent diagnoses of conduct disorder, oppositional defiant disorder, and attention-deficit/hyperactivity disorder (ADHD) (Leiner et al., 2014). Victims of bullies, like Michael, Rebecca, and Stephanie, are commonly anxious and depressed, and they often find that other peers avoid them to avoid getting involved (Howard et al., 2014).

Reflect

- Were you ever bullied in school? If so, how did you handle it?

- What should teachers and school officials do about bullies?

- What should parents tell their children about bullies?

[1]In Nicholas D. Kristof. (2012, March 1). Born to not get bullied. *The New York Times*, p. A31.

Jason Laveris/FilmMagic/Getty Images

Certain aspects of the school environment are important as well. One key factor is class size. Smaller classes permit students to receive more individual attention and to express their ideas more often (Ebert & Culyer, 2011). Smaller classes lead to increased achievement in mathematics and reading in the early primary grades. Smaller classes are particularly useful in teaching the "basics"—reading, writing, and arithmetic—to elementary school students who are at risk for academic failure (Ebert & Culyer, 2011; Woolfolk, 2013).

Teachers: Setting Limits, Making Demands, Communicating Values, and—Oh, Yes—Teaching

The influence of the schools is mainly due to teachers. Teachers, like parents, set limits, make demands, communicate values, and foster development. Teacher–student relationships are more limited than parent–child relationships, but teachers still have the opportunity to serve as powerful role models and dispensers of reinforcement. After all, children spend several hours each weekday in the presence of teachers.

Teacher Influences on Student Performance

Many aspects of teacher behavior are related to student achievement (Ebert & Culyer, 2011). Achievement is enhanced when teachers expect students to master the curriculum, allocate most of the available time to academic activities, and manage the classroom environment effectively. Students learn more in classes when they are actively instructed or supervised by teachers than when they work on their own. The most effective teachers ask questions, give personalized feedback, and provide opportunities for drill and practice, as opposed to straight lecturing.

Student achievement also is linked to the emotional climate of the classroom (Kaplan & Owings, 2015). Students do not do as well when teachers rely heavily on criticism, ridicule, threats, or punishment. Achievement is high in classrooms that have a pleasant, friendly atmosphere, but not in classrooms with extreme teacher warmth.

Teacher Expectations

There is a saying that "You find what you're looking for." Consider the so-called **Pygmalion effect** in education. In Greek mythology, the amorous sculptor Pygmalion breathed life into a beautiful statue he had carved. Similarly, in the musical *My Fair Lady*, a reworking of the Pygmalion legend, Henry Higgins fashions a great lady from the lower-class Eliza Doolittle. Teachers also try to bring out positive traits that they believe dwell within their students, and research by Rosenthal and Jacobson (1968) suggests that sometimes the teachers succeed.

cyberbullying The use of online media to transmit intimidating or threatening messages to a person or to spread intimidating information among the target's peers.

Pygmalion effect A self-fulfilling prophecy; an expectation that is confirmed because of the behavior of those who hold the expectation.

self-fulfilling prophecy An event that occurs because of the behavior of those who expect it to occur.

TRUTH OR FICTION REVISITED: A classic experiment by Robert Rosenthal and Lenore Jacobson suggested that teacher expectations can become **self-fulfilling prophecies**. As reported in their classic *Pygmalion in the Classroom*, Rosenthal and Jacobson (1968) first gave students a battery of psychological tests. Then they informed teachers that a handful of the students, although average in performance to date, were about to blossom forth intellectually in the current school year. In reality, the tests had indicated nothing in particular about the "chosen" children. These children had been selected at random. The purpose of the experiment was to determine whether changing teacher expectations could affect student performance. As it happened, the identified children made significant gains in intelligence test scores.

However, the outcomes of more recent research have been mixed. Some studies have found small to moderate positive outcomes for the Pygmalion effect (Friedrich et al., 2015). Others have not. A meta-analysis of many such experiments found that the Pygmalion effect was most pronounced when the procedure for informing teachers of the potential in the target student had the greatest credibility (Cohen et al., 2003). A fair conclusion seems to be that teacher expectations sometimes, but not always, affect students' motivation, self-esteem, expectations for success, and achievement.

These findings have serious implications for children from ethnic minority and low-income families. There is some indication that teachers expect less academically from children in these groups (Sorhagen, 2013). Teachers with lower expectations for certain children may spend less time encouraging and interacting with them.

What are some of the ways in which teachers can help motivate all students to do their best? Students appear to fare better when teachers (Siegle et al., 2014; Woolfolk, 2008):

- Make the classroom and the lesson interesting and inviting.
- Ensure that students can profit from social interaction.
- Make the classroom a safe and pleasant place.
- Recognize that students' backgrounds can give rise to diverse patterns of needs.
- Help students take appropriate responsibility for their successes and failures.
- Encourage students to perceive the links between their own efforts and their achievements.
- Help students set attainable short-term goals.

Sexism in the Classroom

Although girls were systematically excluded from formal education for centuries, today we might not expect to find **sexism** among teachers. Teachers, after all, are generally well-educated. They are also trained to be fair-minded and sensitive to the needs of their young charges in today's changing society.

However, we may not have heard the last of sexism in our schools. Researchers (Denmark & Williams, 2014; Sadker, 2011; Sadker et al., 2009) have recently found that:

- Many teachers pay less attention to girls than to boys, especially in math, science, and technology classes.
- Many girls are subjected to **sexual harassment**—unwelcome verbal or physical conduct of a sexual nature—from male classmates, and many teachers minimize the harmfulness of harassment and ignore it.
- Some school textbooks still stereotype or ignore women, more often portraying males as the shakers and movers in the world.

In a widely cited study, Myra and David Sadker (1994) observed students in fourth-, sixth-, and eighth-grade classes in four states and the District of Columbia. Teachers and students were European American and African American, urban, suburban, and rural. In almost all cases, the findings were depressingly similar. Boys generally dominated classroom communication, whether the subject was math (a traditionally "masculine" area) or language arts (a traditionally "feminine" area). Despite the stereotype that girls are more likely to talk or even chatter, boys were eight times more likely than girls to call out answers without raising their hands. So far, it could be said, we have evidence of a gender difference, but not of sexism. However, teachers were less than impartial in responding to boys and girls when they called out. Teachers, male and female, were significantly more likely to accept calling out from boys. Girls were significantly more likely, as the song goes, to receive "teachers' dirty looks," or to be reminded that they should raise their hands and wait to be called on. Boys, it appears, are expected to be impetuous, but impetuous girls are reprimanded for "unladylike behavior." Sad to say, until they saw tapes of themselves, the teachers generally were unaware that they were treating girls and boys differently.

sexism Discrimination or bias against people on the basis of their gender.

sexual harassment Unwelcome verbal or physical conduct of a sexual nature.

Waiting to Be Called On Who is the teacher most likely to call on? Some studies say that teachers may favor the boy and call on him before the girl, especially in math, science, and technology classes.

Other observers note that primary and secondary teachers tend to give more active teaching attention to boys than to girls, especially in math and technology courses (Friedrich et al., 2015). Math teachers call on boys more often, ask them more questions, talk to and listen to them more, give them lengthier directions, and praise and criticize them more often.

The irony is that our educational system has been responsible for lifting many generations of the downtrodden into the mainstream of American life (Sadker et al., 2009). Unfortunately, the system may be doing more to encourage the development of academic skills—especially skills needed in our technological age—in boys than in girls.

Section Review

16. Children from families with _____ (high or low?) socioeconomic status have a more difficult time adjusting to school.

17. _____ (Smaller or Larger?) classes facilitate learning during middle childhood.

18. An experiment by Rosenthal and Jacobson suggests that teacher expectations can become _____ prophecies.

19. _____ (Boys or Girls?) tend to be favored by teachers in the classroom.

Reflect & Relate: Do you remember what it was like for you to enter school at kindergarten or first grade? Did you experience some adjustment problems? What were they?

13.5 Social and Emotional Problems

Millions of children in the United States suffer from emotional or behavioral problems that could benefit from professional treatment (Denham et al., 2011). But most of them are unlikely to receive help. What are some of the more common psychological problems of middle childhood? In previous chapters, we examined attention-deficit/hyperactivity disorder (ADHD) and learning disabilities. Here, we will focus on those problems more likely to emerge during middle childhood: conduct disorders, depression, and anxiety. We use the terminology in the *Diagnostic and Statistical Manual of Mental Disorders* (DSM) of the American Psychiatric Association (2013) because it is the most widely used index of psychological disorders.

What Are Conduct Disorders?

David is a 16-year-old high school dropout. He has just been arrested for the third time in 2 years for stealing video equipment and computers from people's homes. Acting alone, David was caught in each case when he tried to sell the stolen items. In describing his actions in each crime, David expressed defiance and showed a lack of remorse. In fact, he bragged about how often he had gotten away with similar crimes.

—Adapted from Halgin & Whitbourne (1993, p. 335)

David has a **conduct disorder**. Children with conduct disorders, like David, persistently break rules or violate the rights of others. They exhibit behaviors such as lying, stealing, setting fires, truancy, cruelty to animals, and fighting (American Psychiatric Association, 2013). To receive this diagnosis, children must engage in the behavior pattern for at least 6 months. Conduct disorders typically emerge by 8 years of age and are much more prevalent in boys.

Children with conduct disorders are often involved in sexual activity before puberty and often smoke, drink, and abuse other substances (American Psychiatric Association, 2013). They have a low tolerance for frustration and may have temper flare-ups. They tend to blame other people for the trouble they get into (Schultz & Shaw, 2003). They believe that they are misunderstood and treated unfairly. Their academic achievement is usually below grade level, but intelligence is usually at least average. Many children with conduct disorders also are diagnosed with ADHD (Bendiksen et al., 2014).

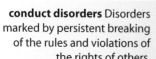

conduct disorders Disorders marked by persistent breaking of the rules and violations of the rights of others.

Jochen Tack/imageBroker/Age Fotostock

What is the connection between violent video games and conduct disorders? We cannot say that violent video games cause misconduct, because many children who play them do not engage in misconduct. May it be that more violent children are drawn to these video games? Perhaps there is an interaction between children's personalities and the games they choose to play.

Origins of Conduct Disorders

Conduct disorders may have a genetic component (Melroy et al., 2014). They are more likely to be found in the biological parents than in the adoptive parents of adopted children who have such problems (Rhee & Waldman, 2009). Other contributors include antisocial family members, deviant peers, inconsistent discipline, parental insensitivity to the child's behavior, physical punishment, and family stress (Wu et al., 2015). Involvement with violent video games may also play a role, but we must then also ask the question, why do some children choose to immerse themselves in violent video games whereas others do not?

A study of 123 African American boys and girls pointed toward relationships among parental discipline, parental monitoring, and conduct problems (Kilgore et al., 2000). The researchers found that coercive parental discipline and poor parental monitoring of children at age 4½ were reliable predictors of conduct problems for boys and girls at age 6. The families were poor, and the parents had no choice but to send the children to schools with many peers who had conduct disorders. However, once socioeconomic status and school choice were taken into account, parental discipline and monitoring were the strongest predictors of conduct disorders. These findings are consistent with research on more advantaged European American boys, which suggests that family processes are stronger predictors of conduct disorders than ethnicity.

Treatment of Conduct Disorders

The treatment of conduct disorders is challenging, but cognitive-behavioral techniques involving parent training appear to hold promise (Kapalka, 2014). Children with conduct disorders profit from interventions in which their behavior is monitored closely, there are consequences (such as time-outs) for unacceptable behavior, physical punishment is avoided, and positive social behavior is rewarded. That is, rather than just targeting noncompliant behavior, it is useful to attend to children when they are behaving properly and to reward them for doing so.

Other approaches include teaching aggressive children methods for coping with feelings of anger that will not violate the rights of others. One promising cognitive-behavioral method teaches children social skills and how to use problem solving to manage interpersonal conflicts (Burke & Loeber, 2015). Desirable social skills include asking other children to stop annoying behavior rather than hitting them. Children are also taught to "stop and think" before engaging in aggressive behavior. They are encouraged to consider the outcomes of their behavior and find acceptable ways to reach their goals.

What Is Childhood Depression? What Can We Do About It?

Kristin, an 11-year-old, feels "nothing is working out for me." For the past year, she has been failing in school, although she previously had been a B student. She has trouble sleeping, feels tired all the time, and has started refusing to go to school. She cries easily and thinks her peers are making fun of her because she is "ugly and stupid." Her mother recently found a note written by Kristin that said she wanted to jump in front of a car "to end my misery."

—Adapted from Weller & Weller (1991, p. 655)

Childhood is the happiest time of life, correct? Not necessarily. Many children are happy enough; protected by their parents and unencumbered by adult responsibilities. From the perspective of aging adults, their bodies seem made of rubber and free of aches. Their energy is apparently boundless.

Yet, many children, like Kristin, are depressed. Depressed children may feel sad, blue, or down in the dumps. They may show poor appetite, insomnia, lack of energy and inactivity, loss of self-esteem, difficulty concentrating, loss of interest in people and activities they usually enjoy, crying, feelings of hopelessness and helplessness, and thoughts of suicide (American Psychiatric Association, 2013).

But many children do not recognize depression in themselves until the age of 7 or so. Part of the problem is cognitive-developmental. The capacity for concrete operations apparently contributes to children's abilities to perceive internal feeling states (Feit et al., 2015; Glasberg & Aboud, 1982).

When children cannot report their feelings, depression is inferred from behavior. Depressed children in middle childhood engage in less social activity and have poorer social skills than peers (American Psychiatric Association, 2013). In some cases, childhood depression is "masked" by conduct disorders, physical complaints, academic problems, and anxiety.

It has been estimated that between 5% and 9% of children are seriously depressed in any given year (American Psychiatric Association, 2013). Depression occurs equally often in girls and boys during childhood but is more common among women later in life. Depressed children frequently continue to have depressive episodes as adolescents and adults.

Origins of Depression

The origins of depression are complex and varied. Psychological and biological explanations have been proposed.

Childhood Depression This mental health problem can have many origins, including feelings of failure and helplessness, losses, self-blame for problems that are not of one's own making, and, possibly, genetic factors.

Some social cognitive theorists explain depression in terms of relationships between competencies (knowledge and skills) and feelings of self-esteem. Children who gain academic, social, and other competencies usually have high self-esteem. Perceived low levels of competence are linked to helplessness, low self-esteem, and depression. Longitudinal studies of primary schoolchildren have found that problems in academics, socializing, physical appearance, and sports can predict feelings of depression (Kistner, 2006; Peterson, 2013). Conversely, self-perceived competence in these areas is negatively related to feelings of depression; that is, competence appears to "protect" children from depression. Children who have not developed competencies because of lack of opportunity, inconsistent parental reinforcement, and so on may develop feelings of helplessness and hopelessness. Stressful life events, daily hassles, and poor problem-solving ability also give rise to helplessness and hopelessness. These ideas, in turn, trigger depression (Hewitt et al., 2014; Kendler et al., 2011). In contrast, social support and self-confidence tend to protect children from depression. Some competent children might not give themselves credit because of excessive parental expectations. Or, children may be perfectionistic themselves. Perfectionistic children may be depressed because they cannot meet their own standards.

Children in elementary school are likely to be depressed because of situational stresses, such as family problems. Among middle schoolers, however, we find cognitive contributors to depression. For example, a study of 582 Chinese children from Hong Kong secondary schools found that cognitive distortions, such as minimizing accomplishments and blowing problems out of proportion, are associated with feelings of depression (Leung & Poon, 2001). A European study found that ruminating about problems (going over them again and again—and again), blaming oneself for things that are not one's fault, and blowing problems out of proportion are linked with depression (Garnefski et al., 2001).

The tendency to blame oneself (internal attribution) or others (external attribution) is called a child's **attributional style**. Certain attributional styles can contribute to helplessness and hopelessness and hence to depression (Cohen et al., 2012).

TRUTH OR FICTION REVISITED: It is true that some children blame themselves for all the problems in their lives, whether they deserve any blame or not. Research shows that children who are depressed are more likely to attribute their failures to internal, stable, and global factors—factors they are relatively helpless to change (Schacter et al., 2015; Schleider et al., 2014).

attributional style The way in which one is disposed toward interpreting outcomes (successes or failures), as in tending to place blame or responsibility on oneself or on external factors.

Feelings of helplessness trigger depression. Consider the case of two children who do poorly on a math test. John thinks, "I'm a jerk! I'm just no good in math! I'll never learn." Jim thinks, "That test was tougher than I thought it would be. I'll have to work harder next time." John is perceiving the problem as global (he's "a jerk") and stable (he'll "never learn"). Jim perceives the problem as specific rather than global (related to the type of math test the teacher makes up) and as unstable rather than stable (he can change the results by working harder). In effect, John thinks "It's me" (an internal attribution), whereas Jim thinks "It's the test" (an external attribution). Depressed children tend to explain negative events in terms of internal, stable, and global causes. As a result, they, like John, are more likely than Jim to be depressed.

There is also evidence of genetic factors in depression (Kendler et al., 2011; Rice, 2014). For example, the children of depressed parents are at greater risk for depression and other disorders. A Norwegian study of 2,794 twins estimated that the heritability of depression in females is 49% and in males is 25% (Orstavik et al., 2007). On a neurological level, evidence suggests that depressed children (and adults) "underutilize" the neurotransmitter **serotonin** (Hankin, 2015).

Treatment of Depression

Parents and teachers can do a good deal to alleviate relatively mild feelings of depression among children. They can involve children in enjoyable activities, encourage the development of skills, offer praise when appropriate, and point out when children are being too hard on themselves. But if feelings of depression persist, treatment is called for.

Psychotherapy for depression tends to be mainly cognitive-behavioral and is often straightforward. Children (and adolescents) are encouraged to do enjoyable things and build social skills. They are made aware of their tendencies to minimize their accomplishments, catastrophize their problems, and overly blame themselves for shortcomings (e.g., Kendall, 2012).

We noted that many depressed children underutilize the neurotransmitter serotonin. Antidepressant medication (selective serotonin reuptake inhibitors, or SSRIs), such as Lexapro, Prozac, and Zoloft, increase the action of serotonin in the brain and are sometimes used to treat childhood depression. Studies of their effectiveness yield a mixed review, ranging from something like "deadly dangerous" to "often effective" (Vitiello, 2006). Although SSRIs are frequently effective, the U.S. Food and Drug Administration has warned that there may be a link between their use and suicidal thinking in children (Henry et al., 2012).

Childhood depression is frequently accompanied by anxiety (Cummings et al., 2014), as we will see in the next section. Social and emotional problems that tend to emerge in middle childhood are summarized in Concept Review 13.1.

What Are the Features of Anxiety During Middle Childhood?

Children show many kinds of anxiety disorders, and these disorders are accompanied by depression in 50–60% of children (Cummings et al., 2014; Rice, 2014). Yet, many children show anxiety disorders, such as **generalized anxiety disorder (GAD)**, in the absence of depression (Rubin et al., 2011). Other anxiety disorders shown by children include **phobias** such as **separation anxiety disorder (SAD)** and stage fright (Rubin et al., 2011). Girls are more likely than boys to report feelings of anxiety.

Separation Anxiety Disorder

It is normal for children to show anxiety when they are separated from their caregivers. Separation anxiety is a normal feature of the child–caregiver relationship and begins during the first year. But the sense of security that is usually provided by bonds of attachment encourages children to explore their environments and become progressively independent of caregivers.

Separation anxiety disorder affects an estimated 4–5% of children and young adolescents (American Psychiatric Association, 2013; Shear et al., 2006). The disorder occurs most often in girls and is often associated with school refusal (Vallance & Garralda, 2011). It also frequently occurs together with social anxiety (Ferdinand et al., 2006). The disorder may persist into adulthood, leading to an exaggerated concern about the well-being of one's children and spouse and to difficulty tolerating any separation from them.

serotonin A neurotransmitter that is involved in mood disorders such as depression.

generalized anxiety disorder (GAD) An anxiety disorder in which anxiety is present continuously and is unrelated to the situation.

phobia An irrational, excessive fear that interferes with one's functioning.

separation anxiety disorder (SAD) An extreme form of normal separation anxiety that is characterized by anxiety about separating from parents; SAD often takes the form of school refusal.

Social and Emotional Problems That May Emerge During Middle Childhood

Problem	Behavior Patterns	Comments
Conduct disorders Stockbyte/Getty Images	• Precocious sexual activity and substance abuse • Truancy, stealing, lying, and aggression	• More common in boys • Child blames others for problems • Probably connected with genetic factors • Other contributors: antisocial family members, deviant peers, inconsistent discipline, physical punishment, and family stress • Tends to be stable throughout adolescence and into adulthood • Frequently accompanied by ADHD
Childhood depression Ocean Photography/Veer Images	• Feelings of sadness, poor appetite, insomnia, lack of energy and inactivity, loss of self-esteem, difficulty concentrating, loss of interest in people and activities, crying, feelings of hopelessness and helplessness, and thoughts of suicide • Can be masked by conduct disorders, physical complaints, academic problems, and anxiety	• Occurs about equally in both genders • Connected with lack of competencies (knowledge and skills) • Connected with situational stresses, such as divorce • Connected with feelings of helplessness and hopelessness • Connected with cognitive factors such as perfectionism, rumination, minimization of achievements, blowing problems out of proportion, and a negative attributional style—internal, stable, and global attributions for failures • Possibly connected with genetic factors • Connected with "underutilization" of the neurotransmitter serotonin • Frequently accompanied by anxiety
Childhood anxiety Phanie/Alamy	• Persistent, excessive worrying • Fear of the worst happening • Anxiety inappropriate for child's developmental level • Physical symptoms such as stomachaches, nausea, and vomiting • Nightmares • Concerns about death and dying	• More common in girls • Genetic factors implicated • Frequently develops after stressful life events, such as divorce, illness, death of relative or pet, or change of schools or homes • Often overlaps with—but not the same as—school refusal • Frequently accompanied by depression

442 PART 5 MIDDLE CHILDHOOD

SAD is diagnosed when separation anxiety is persistent and excessive, when it is inappropriate for the child's developmental level, and when it interferes with activities or development tasks—most important, attending school. Six-year-olds ought to be able to enter first grade without anxiety-related nausea and vomiting and without dread that they or their parents will come to harm. Children with SAD tend to cling to their parents and follow them around the house. They may voice concerns about death and dying and insist that someone stay with them while they are falling asleep. They may complain of nightmares, stomachaches, and nausea and vomiting on school days. They may plead with their parents not to leave the house, or they may throw tantrums.

SAD may occur before middle childhood, preventing adjustment to day care or nursery school. In adolescence, refusal to attend school is often connected with academic and social problems, in which case the label of SAD does not apply. SAD usually becomes a significant problem in middle childhood because that is when children are expected to adjust to school.

SAD frequently develops after a stressful life event, such as an illness, the death of a relative or pet, or a change of schools or homes. Alison's problems followed the death of her grandmother:

> Alison's grandmother died when Alison was 7 years old. Her parents decided to permit her . . . to view her grandmother in the open coffin. Alison took a tentative glance from her father's arms across the room, then asked to be taken out of the room. Her 5-year-old sister took a leisurely close-up look, with no apparent distress.
>
> Alison had been concerned about death for 2 or 3 years by this time, but her grandmother's passing brought on a new flurry of questions: "Will I die?" "Does everybody die?" and so on. Her parents tried to reassure her by saying, "Grandma was very, very old, and she also had a heart condition. You are very young and in perfect health. You have many, many years before you have to start thinking about death."
>
> Alison also could not be alone in any room in her house. She pulled one of her parents or her sister along with her everywhere she went. She also reported nightmares about her grandmother and, within a couple of days, insisted on sleeping in the same room with her parents. Fortunately, Alison's fears did not extend to school. Her teacher reported that Alison spent some time talking about her grandmother, but her academic performance was apparently unimpaired.
>
> Alison's parents decided to allow Alison time to "get over" the loss. Alison gradually talked less and less about death, and by the time 3 months had passed, she was able to go into any room in her house by herself. She wanted to continue to sleep in her parents' bedroom, however. So her parents "made a deal" with her. They would put off the return to her own bedroom until the school year had ended (a month away), if Alison would agree to return to her own bed at that time. As a further incentive, a parent would remain with her until she fell asleep for the first month. Alison overcame the anxiety problem in this fashion with no additional delays.
>
> —Author's files

Separation Anxiety Disorder, School Phobia, and School Refusal

SAD is similar to but not the same as school phobia. SAD is an extreme form of separation anxiety. It is characterized by anxiety about separating from parents and may be expressed as **school phobia**— fear of school—or refusal to go to school (which can be based on fear or other factors). Separation anxiety—fear—is not the basis of all instances of school refusal. Some children refuse school because they perceive it as unpleasant, unsatisfying, or hostile—and it certainly may be, as is clearly the case

school phobia Fear of attending school, marked by extreme anxiety at leaving parents.

School Phobia School phobia is often a form of separation anxiety. This boy imagines that something terrible will happen to him or to his mother if he goes to school. Many mornings he complains of a tummyache or of being too tired to go to school.

in bullying. Some children are concerned about doing poorly in school or being asked to answer questions in class (in which case, they might be suffering from the social phobia of stage fright). High parental expectations to perform may heighten concern. Still other children may refuse school because of problems with classmates.

Treatment of School Phobia or School Refusal

Except for extreme cases, such as the threatening and taunting of severe bullying, it is usually not better for children with school phobia to remain at home until the origins of the problem are uncovered and resolved. Most professionals agree that the first rule in the treatment of *most* cases of school phobia is to get the child back into school. The second rule: Get the child back into school. And the third rule . . . you get the idea. The disorder often diminishes once the child is back in school on a regular basis.

TRUTH OR FICTION REVISITED: It is usually not better for children with school phobia to remain at home until the origins of the problem are uncovered and resolved. Sometimes the problem is the school—or staff or other students in the school—but a phobia, by definition, is an *irrational* or *overblown* fear—a fear that is out of proportion to any danger in the situation. The current tendency in psychology is to encourage people to confront their irrational fears, whether they are adults or children in school.

There is certainly nothing wrong with trying to understand why a child refuses to attend school. Knowledge of the reasons for refusal can help parents and educators devise strategies for helping the child adjust. But should such understanding precede insistence that the child return to school? Again, depending on the apparent causes of school refusal, insisting on an early return to school might be best. Here are some things parents can do to get a child back into school:

- Do not give in to the child's demands to stay home. If the child complains of being tired or ill, tell the child that he or she may feel better at school and can rest there if necessary.
- Discuss the problem with the child's teacher, principal, and school nurse. (Gain the cooperation of school professionals.)
- If there is a specific school-related problem, such as an overly strict teacher, help the child find ways to handle the situation. (Finding ways to handle such problems can be accomplished while the child is in school. Not all such problems need to be ironed out before the child returns to school.)
- Reward the child for attending school. (Yes, parents shouldn't "have to" reward children for "normal" behavior, but do you want the child in school or not?)

What if these measures don't work? How can professionals help? A variety of therapeutic approaches have been tried, and it appears that cognitive-behavioral approaches are the most effective (Chu et al., 2014; James et al., 2015). One cognitive-behavioral method is counterconditioning to reduce the child's fear. (As described in Chapter 10, Mary Cover Jones used counterconditioning to reduce a young boy's [Peter's] fear of rabbits.) Other cognitive-behavioral methods include systematic desensitization, modeling, cognitive restructuring, and the shaping and rewarding of school attendance.

When possible, the children's parents are taught to apply cognitive-behavioral methods. One study assessed the effectiveness of family-based group cognitive-behavioral treatment (FGCBT) for anxious children (Shortt et al., 2001). It included

71 children between the ages of 6 and 10 who were diagnosed with SAD, generalized anxiety (anxiety that persisted throughout the day), or social phobia (e.g., stage fright). The children and their families were assigned at random to FGCBT or to a 10-week waiting list ("We'll get to you in 10 weeks"), which was the control group. The effectiveness of the treatment was evaluated after treatment and at a 12-month follow-up. The researchers found that nearly 70% of the children who had completed FGCBT were no longer diagnosable with anxiety disorders, compared with 6% of the children on the waiting list. Even at the 12-month follow-up, 68% of the treated children remained diagnosis-free.

Antidepressant medication has been used—often in conjunction with cognitive-behavioral methods—with a good deal of success (Mohatt et al., 2013; Warnke, 2014). Antidepressants can have side effects, however, such as abdominal discomfort. Moreover, some health professionals fear that antidepressants can trigger suicidal thoughts in children. However, drugs in themselves do not teach children how to cope with situations. Many health professionals suggest that the drugs—in this case, antidepressants—are best used only when psychological treatments, such as challenging irrational ideas as to why the child should remain out of school, have proven to be ineffective (Maric et al., 2013; Walter et al., 2014).

Daniel Pine and his colleagues (2001) reported a study on the treatment of 128 anxious children, ages 6–17 years. Like those in the Shortt study, they were diagnosed with a social phobia (such as stage fright), SAD, or GAD. All the children had received psychological treatment for 3 weeks without improvement. The children were assigned at random to receive an antidepressant (fluvoxamine) or a placebo (a "sugar pill") for 8 weeks. None of the children, their parents, their teachers, or the evaluators knew which child had received which treatment. After 8 weeks, the children's anxiety was evaluated. Forty-eight of 63 children (76%) who had received the antidepressant improved significantly, compared with 19 of 65 children (29%) who had received the placebo.

It seems unfortunate to end our study of middle childhood right after discussing social and emotional problems. Most children in developed nations come through middle childhood quite well—in good shape to take on the challenges and dramas of adolescence.

Section Review

20. Conduct disorders are more likely to be found among the _____ (biological or adoptive?) parents of adopted children who have conduct disorders.

21. Self-perceived competence appears to _____ (protect children from or make children vulnerable to?) feelings of depression.

22. Depressed children tend to _____ (underutilize or overutilize?) the neurotransmitter serotonin in the brain.

23. Separation _____ disorder is similar to but not exactly the same as school phobia.

24. Separation anxiety _____ (is or is not?) the basis of all instances of school refusal.

Reflect & Relate: Have you known children with conduct disorders, depression, or separation anxiety disorder (or school phobia)? Do you have any thoughts about the origins of the problems? Were the problems treated? What happened to the children?

Chapter Review

13.1 What Do Theories of Development Say About Social and Emotional Development in Middle Childhood?

Social development in middle childhood involves the development of skills, changes in interpersonal relationships, and the expansion of self-understanding. Freud viewed the period as the latency stage; Erikson saw it as the stage of industry versus inferiority. Social cognitive theorists note that children now depend less on external rewards and punishments and that they increasingly regulate their own behavior. Cognitive-developmental theory notes that concrete operations enhance social development. In middle childhood, children become more capable of taking the role or perspective of another person. Selman theorizes that children move from egocentricity to seeing the world through the eyes of others in five stages. In early childhood, children's self-concepts focus on concrete external traits. In middle childhood, children begin to include abstract internal traits. Social relationships and group membership assume greater importance. In middle childhood, competence and social acceptance contribute to self-esteem, but self-esteem tends to decline because the self-concept becomes more realistic. Authoritative parenting fosters self-esteem. Learned helplessness is the acquired belief that one cannot obtain rewards. "Helpless" children tend not to persist in the face of failure. Girls tend to feel more helpless in math than boys do, largely because of gender-role expectations.

13.2 How Does the Family Influence Development in Middle Childhood?

In middle childhood, the family continues to play a key role in socialization. Parent–child interactions focus on school-related issues, chores, and peers. Parents do less monitoring of children; coregulation develops. Divorce disrupts children's lives and usually lowers the family's financial status. Children are likely to greet divorce with sadness, shock, and disbelief. Children of divorced parents fare better when parents cooperate on child rearing. Children's adjustment is related to the mother's coping ability. Children appear to suffer as much from marital conflict as from divorce per se. Having both

parents in the workforce may be related to relative lack of supervision. However, there is little evidence that maternal employment harms children. Maternal employment fosters greater independence and flexibility in terms of relative freedom from gender-role stereotypes.

13.3 How Do Peers Influence Development in Middle Childhood?

Peers take on increasing importance and exert pressure to conform. Peer experiences also broaden children. Peers afford practice in developing social skills, sharing, relating to leaders, and coping with aggressive impulses. Popular children tend to be attractive and mature for their age. Early in middle childhood, friendships are based on proximity. Between the ages of 8 and 11, children become more aware of the value of friends as meeting each other's needs and having traits such as loyalty. At this age, peers tend to discourage contact with members of the other gender.

13.4 What Are the Roles and Problems Connected with the School in Middle Childhood?

Schools make demands for mature behavior and nurture positive physical, social, and cognitive development. Readiness for school is related to children's early life experiences, individual differences in development and learning, and the schools' expectations. An effective school has an energetic principal, an orderly atmosphere, empowerment of teachers and students, high expectations for children, and solid academics. Teachers' expectations can become self-fulfilling prophecies. Many girls suffer from sexism and sexual harassment in school. Math and science are generally stereotyped as masculine, and language arts as feminine.

13.5 What Kinds of Social and Emotional Problems Do Children Encounter in Middle Childhood?

Children with conduct disorders persistently break rules or violate the rights of others. There may be a genetic component to such disorders, but sociopathic models in the family, deviant peers, and inconsistent discipline all contribute. Parental training in cognitive-behavioral methods holds promise for treating these disorders. Depressed children tend to complain of poor appetite, insomnia, lack of energy, and feelings of worthlessness. Depressed children tend to blame themselves excessively for shortcomings. Psychotherapy tends to make children aware of their tendencies to minimize their accomplishments and to overly blame themselves for shortcomings. Antidepressants are sometimes helpful but remain controversial. Separation anxiety disorder (SAD) is diagnosed when separation anxiety is persistent and excessive and interferes with daily life. Children with SAD tend to cling to parents and may refuse to attend school. SAD is an extreme form of otherwise normal separation anxiety and may take the form of school phobia. But children can refuse school for other reasons, including finding school to be unpleasant or hostile. The most important aspect of treatment is to insist that the child attend school. Cognitive behavioral therapy and medication may also be useful.

Key Terms

14

Adolescence: Physical Development

Major Topics

Features

TruthorFiction?

 American adolescents are growing taller than their parents. **p. 455**

 Girls are fertile immediately after their first menstrual period. **p. 458**

 Boys and girls who mature early have higher self-esteem than those who mature late. **p. 462**

 Most adolescents in the United States are unaware of the risks of HIV/AIDS. **p. 466**

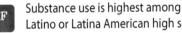 Substance use is the leading cause of death among male adolescents in the United States. **p. 471**

T | F You can never be too rich or too thin. **p. 476**

T | F Some college women control their weight by going on cycles of binge eating followed by self-induced vomiting. **p. 477**

T | F Substance use is highest among African American and Latino or Latina American high school students. **p. 482**

"When will it happen?"
"Why is my voice acting so funny?"
"How tall will I be?"
"Why do I get pimples?"
"Why am I getting hairy?"
"Why is mine not like his?"
"What's happening to me?"

Perhaps no other period of life is as exciting—and as bewildering—as adolescence. Except for infancy, more changes occur during adolescence than during any other time of life.

Photodisc Photography/Veer

14.1 Adolescence

In our society, adolescents are "neither fish nor fowl," as the saying goes—neither children nor adults. Adolescents may be old enough to reproduce and may be as large as their parents, yet they are required to remain in school through age 16, they may not be allowed to get drivers' licenses until they are 16 or 17, and they cannot attend R-rated films unless accompanied by an adult. Given the restrictions placed on adolescents, their yearning for independence, and a sex drive heightened by high levels of sex hormones, it is not surprising that adolescents occasionally are in conflict with their parents.

The capacity to think abstractly and hypothetically emerges during the teenage years. This ability gives rise to a stream of seemingly endless "Who am I?" questions, as adolescents search for a sense of identity and ponder the possible directions their adult lives may take.

How Do We Define Adolescence?

Adolescence is a transitional period between childhood and adulthood, a coming of age. A century ago, most children in the United States assumed adult responsibilities early. Adolescence began to emerge as a distinct stage of development between childhood and adulthood when the demands of an increasingly complex society required a longer period of education and delayed entry into the labor force. It is no longer easy for American adolescents to know when they have made the transition to adulthood. One legally becomes an adult at different ages, depending on whether one is enlisting in the armed services, buying a drink, driving a car, voting, or getting married.

The idea that adolescence is an important and separate developmental stage was proposed by G. Stanley Hall (1904), an early American psychologist. Hall believed that adolescence is marked by intense turmoil. He used the German phrase *Sturm und Drang* ("storm and stress") to describe the conflicts and stresses of adolescence. According to Hall, adolescents swing back and forth between happiness and sadness, overconfidence and self-doubt, dependence and independence. Hall believed that adolescent mood swings and conflicts with parents are a necessary part of growing up. He thought that children have to rebel against their parents and their parents' values to make the transition to adulthood.

Sigmund Freud (1964 [1933]) placed relatively little emphasis on adolescence because he believed that the first 5 years of life are the most critical. According to Freud, we enter the **genital stage** of psychosexual development at puberty. Sexual feelings are initially focused on the parent of the other gender, but they become transferred, or displaced, onto other adults or adolescents of the other gender. In an article titled "Adolescence as a Developmental Disturbance," Anna Freud (1969), Freud's daughter, portrayed adolescence as a turbulent period because of an increase in the sex drive. The adolescent tries to keep surging sexual impulses in check and redirects them from the parents to more acceptable outlets. The result is unpredictable behavior, defiance of parents, confusion, and mood swings. Anna Freud, like Hall, believed that adolescent turmoil is a part of normal development.

But adolescence need not be a time of "storm and stress." Contemporary theorists no longer see adolescent storm and stress as inevitable (Hollenstein & Lougheed, 2013; Smetana, 2011). Instead, they see adolescence as a period when biological changes drive certain kinds of behavior but that these behaviors are also shaped by environmental influences and adolescents' ability to regulate their emotions and behavior (Hollenstein & Lougheed, 2013). In any case, adolescents need to adapt to biological changes and social expectations.

adolescence A transitional period between childhood and adulthood, usually seen as being bounded by puberty at the lower end and by the assumption of adult responsibilities at the upper end.

genital stage In Freud's psychoanalytic theory, the fifth and final stage of psychosexual development, in which gratification is attained through sexual intercourse with a person of the other gender.

Some theorists even argue that the concept of adolescence as a period of storm and stress marginalizes adolescents (Smetana, 2011). Seeing young people as "troubled" or "troubling" encourages adults to eye them warily and to not take their problems seriously. It is more useful to try to understand adolescents' problems and find ways of helping them cope. Furthermore, a year-long longitudinal study of sixth- and seventh-graders found that adolescents who believe that adolescence is a time of storm and stress have a way of making adolescence become more stormy and stressful (Buchanan & Hughes, 2009). Perhaps our expectations of adolescents can be self-fulfilling prophecies.

Even if adolescence does not always involve storm and stress, adolescents face the challenge of adapting to numerous biological, cognitive, and social and emotional changes. These challenges, and the adolescent's ability to cope with them, vary during the phases of adolescence. Most observers divide adolescence into three phases:

1. *Early adolescence* (11 or 12 to 14 years of age)—Early adolescence is characterized by rapid biological changes, relatively high levels of stress, and relatively low coping ability (Persike & Seiffge-Krenke, 2011; Sontag et al., 2011).
2. *Middle adolescence* (approximately 14 to 16 years)—Biological changes have largely run their course. Stress diminishes somewhat and coping ability increases.
3. *Late adolescence* (16 to 18 or 19 years)—The adolescent matures so that she or he looks more like an adult. Stress usually declines, and coping ability is usually higher than in early and middle adolescence (Persike & Seiffge-Krenke, 2011; Sontag et al., 2011).

Having noted these periods, we should add that some observers (e.g., Malekoff, 2004) extend the span of adolescence to the ages of 9 through the early 20s. The earlier age may reflect the "tweeny" phenomenon, which concerns youngsters of about ages 9–12, who can seem too old to be called children and too young to be called adolescents per se. *Tweeny* is an adaptation of the word *between,* and "tweenies" may undergo a budding psychological and social sexuality prior to the onset of the key biological changes of adolescence. Many shows, such as *High School Musical* and the British *Tweenies,* are aimed at tweenies. People in their early 20s are *emerging adults* who have reached biological maturity but have not experienced some of the social milestones traditionally considered representative of adulthood. As we will see in Chapter 16, two of these milestones are financial independence and separation from parents. If adolescence is the transition between childhood and adulthood, then tweenies and emerging adults represent transitions between transitions: the transition from childhood to adolescence (tweenies) and the transition from adolescence to adulthood (emerging adulthood).

Tweenies? Because of the tweeny phenomenon, some researchers have extended the age range of adolescence— or at least the range of the transition from childhood to adolescence— downward to as young as 9 or 10.

14.2 Puberty: The Biological Eruption

Puberty is a stage of development characterized by reaching sexual maturity and the ability to reproduce. The onset of adolescence coincides with the advent of puberty. Puberty, however, is a biological concept, whereas adolescence is a psychosocial concept with biological correlates.

puberty The biological stage of development characterized by changes that lead to reproductive capacity. Puberty signals the beginning of adolescence.

What Is the Role of Hormones in Puberty?

Puberty is controlled by a complex **feedback loop** involving the **hypothalamus**, **pituitary gland**, gonads (ovaries in females and testes in males), and hormones. The hypothalamus sends signals to the pituitary gland, which, in turn, releases hormones that control physical growth and the functioning of the gonads. The gonads respond to pituitary hormones by increasing their production of sex hormones (androgens and estrogens). The sex hormones further stimulate the hypothalamus, thus perpetuating the feedback loop.

The sex hormones also trigger the development of both the primary and the secondary sex characteristics. The **primary sex characteristics** are the structures that make reproduction possible. In girls, these structures are the ovaries, vagina, uterus, and fallopian tubes. In boys, they are the penis, testes, prostate gland, and seminal vesicles. The **secondary sex characteristics** are physical indicators of sexual maturation that do not involve the reproductive structures; these include breast development, deepening of the voice, and the appearance of facial, pubic, and underarm hair. Let us now explore the physical changes of puberty, starting with the growth spurt and then examining other pubertal changes in boys and girls that involve the primary and secondary sex characteristics.

What Is the Adolescent Growth Spurt?

The stable growth patterns in height and weight that characterize early and middle childhood come to an abrupt end with the adolescent growth spurt. Girls start to spurt in height sooner than boys, at an average age of about 10. Boys start to spurt about 2 years later, at an average age of about 12. Girls and boys reach their periods of peak growth in height about 2 years after the growth spurt begins—at about 12 and 14 years, respectively (Hills & Byrne, 2011; see Figure 14.1 ■). The spurt in height for both girls and boys continues for about another 2 years at a gradually declining pace. Boys grow more than girls do during their spurt, averaging nearly 4 inches per year during the fastest year of the spurt, compared with slightly more than 3 inches per year for girls. Overall, boys add an average of 14½ inches to their height during the spurt, and girls add a little over 13 inches.

Adolescents begin to spurt in weight about half a year after they begin to spurt in height. The period of peak growth in weight occurs about a year and a half after the onset of the spurt. Like the spurt in height, the growth spurt in weight continues for a little more than 2 years for both girls and boys. As you can see in Figure 14.2 ■, girls are taller and heavier than boys from about age 9 or 10 until about age 13 or 14 because their growth spurt occurs earlier. Once boys begin their growth spurt, they catch up with girls and eventually become taller and heavier.

Because the spurt in weight lags the spurt in height, many adolescents are relatively slender compared with their preadolescent and postadolescent stature. However, adolescents tend to eat enormous quantities of food to fuel their growth spurts. Active 14- and 15-year-old boys may consume 3,000–4,000 calories a day without becoming obese. If they were to eat

feedback loop A system in which glands regulate each other's functioning through a series of hormonal messages.

hypothalamus A pea-sized structure above the pituitary gland that is involved in the regulation of body temperature, motivation (such as hunger, thirst, sexual desire), and emotion.

pituitary gland The body's "master gland," which is located in the lower central part of the brain and which secretes many hormones essential to development, such as oxytocin, prolactin, and growth hormone.

primary sex characteristics The structures that make reproduction possible.

secondary sex characteristics Physical indicators of sexual maturation—such as changes to the voice and growth of bodily hair—that do not directly involve reproductive structures.

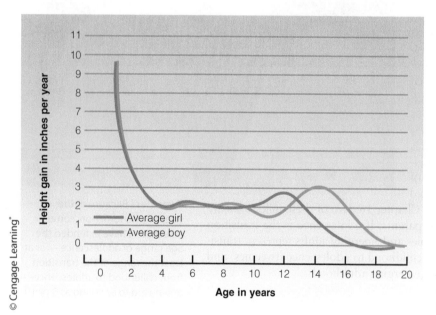

Figure 14.1 ■ Spurts in Growth
Girls begin the adolescent growth spurt about 2 years earlier than boys. Girls and boys reach their periods of peak growth about 2 years after the spurt begins, at about 12 and 14 years, respectively.

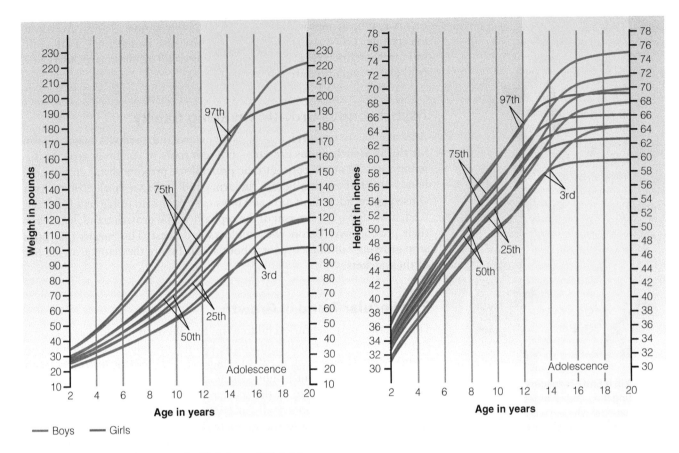

— Boys — Girls

Figure 14.2 ■ Growth Curves for Height and Weight
Girls are taller and heavier than boys from about age 9 or 10 until about age 13 because their growth spurt occurs earlier. Once boys begin their growth spurt, they catch up with girls and eventually become taller and heavier.
Source: Kuczmarski et al. (2000, Figures 9–12).

this much 20 years later, they might gain more than 100 pounds per year. Little wonder that adults fighting the dismal battle of the bulge stare at adolescents in amazement as they inhale pizza for lunch and go out later for burgers and fries!

Girls' and boys' body shapes begin to differ in adolescence. For one thing, boys' shoulders become broader than those of girls, whereas the hip dimensions of females and males do not differ much. Thus, girls have relatively broader hips compared with their shoulders, whereas the opposite is true for boys. A girl's body shape is also more rounded than that of a boy. This is because, during puberty, girls gain almost twice as much fatty tissue as boys do, whereas boys gain twice as much muscle tissue as girls. Thus, a larger proportion of a male's body weight is composed of his muscle mass, whereas a larger part of a female's body weight is composed of fatty tissue.

Individual Differences in the Growth Spurt

Figures 14.1 and 14.2 show averages. Few of us begin or end our growth spurts right on the mark. Children who spurt earlier are likely to wind up with somewhat shorter legs and longer torsos, whereas children who spurt later have somewhat longer legs (Osuch et al., 2010; Peeters et al., 2005).

Regardless of the age at which the growth spurt begins, there is a moderate to high correlation between a child's height at the onset of adolescence and her

Where Will It End? Teenagers undergoing the rapid changes of puberty wonder where it will all end and what their bodies will look like when they "grow up."

or his height at maturity (Sovio et al., 2009; Tanner, 1989). Are there exceptions? Of course. However, everything else being equal, a tall child has a reasonable expectation of becoming a tall adult, and a short child is likely to remain relatively short.

Asynchronous Growth: On Being Gawky

Adolescents are often referred to as awkward and gawky. A major reason for this is **asynchronous growth**—different parts of the body grow at different rates. In an exception to the principle of proximodistal growth, the hands and feet mature before the arms and legs (Xu et al., 2009). As a consequence, adolescent girls and boys may complain of big hands or feet. And, in an apparent reversal of the cephalocaudal growth trend, legs reach their peak growth before the shoulders and chest. This means that boys stop growing out of their pants about a year before they stop growing out of their jackets.

The Secular Trend in Growth

During the past century, children in the Western world have grown dramatically more rapidly and have wound up taller than children in earlier times (Johnson et al., 2013; Ulijaszek, 2010). This historical trend toward increasing adult height, which also has been accompanied by an earlier onset of puberty, is known as the **secular trend**. Figure 14.3 ■ shows that Swedish boys and girls grew more rapidly in 1938 and 1968 than they did in 1883 and ended up several inches taller. At the age of 15, the boys were more than 6 inches taller and the girls were more than 3 inches taller, on average, than their counterparts from the previous century (Tanner, 1989). The occurrence of a secular trend in height and also in weight has been documented in most European countries and the United States. On the other hand, it appears that children in the United States and Europe are no longer growing taller than their parents (Huang et al., 2009; Tanner, 1989).

Nutrition apparently plays an important role in reaching one's genetic potential for height (Johnson et al., 2013). U.S. government surveys have shown that children from middle- and upper-class families are taller and heavier than their agemates from lower-class families. But these data in themselves are not very convincing. For example, it could be argued that genetic factors provide advantages that increase the chances for financial gain as well as for greater height and weight. But remember that children from the middle- and upper-class portion of the socioeconomic spectrum are no longer growing taller. Perhaps Americans who have had nutritional and medical advantages have simply reached their full genetic potential in height. Continued gains among families of lower socioeconomic status suggest that poorer children are still benefiting from improved nutrition.

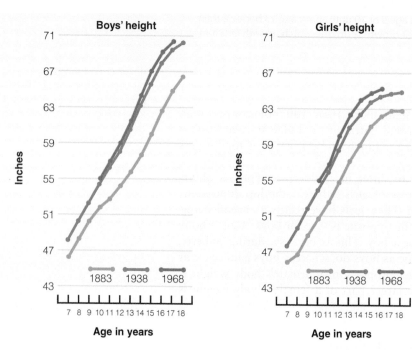

Figure 14.3 ■ Are We Still Growing Taller than Our Parents?
Twentieth-century children grew more rapidly and grew taller than children in preceding centuries.
Source: Tanner (1989).

We will now examine some of the other changes that occur during puberty. You will notice that there are wide individual differences in the timing of the events of puberty. In a group of teenagers of the same age and gender, you may well find some who have completed puberty, others who have not even started, and others who are somewhere in between.

What Pubertal Changes Occur in Boys?

At puberty, the pituitary gland stimulates the testes to increase their output of testosterone, leading to further development of the male genitals. The first visible sign of puberty is accelerated growth of the testes, which begins at an average age of about 11½, although a range of ages of plus or minus 2 years is considered perfectly normal. Testicular growth further accelerates testosterone production and other pubertal changes. The penis growth spurt begins about a year later, and still later, pubic hair develops.

Underarm hair appears at about age 15. Facial hair is at first fuzz on the upper lip. An actual beard does not develop for another 2 or 3 years; only half of American boys shave (of necessity) by age 17. The beard and chest hair continue to develop past the age of 20.

At 14 or 15, the voice deepens because of growth of the "voice box," or **larynx**, and lengthening of the vocal cords. The developmental process is gradual, and adolescent boys sometimes exhibit an embarrassing cracking of the voice.

Testosterone also triggers the development of acne, which afflicts 75–90% of adolescents—females as well as males (Bauer et al., 2009; Taylor et al., 2011). Severe acne is manifested by multiple pimples and blackheads on the face, chest, and back. Although boys are more likely to have acne, we cannot say that girls suffer less from it. In our society, a smooth complexion has a higher value for girls than for boys, and girls with acne that boys would consider mild may suffer terribly.

Males are capable of producing erections in early infancy (and some male babies are born with erections), but the phenomenon is not frequent until age 13 or 14. Adolescent males may experience unwanted and unprovoked erections. Many boys worry that they will be caught with erections when walking between classes or when asked to stand in front of the class. The organs that produce **semen** grow rapidly, and boys typically ejaculate seminal fluid by age 13 or 14—about 1½ years after the penis begins its growth spurt—although here, too, there is much individual variation. About a year later, they begin to have **nocturnal emissions**, which are also called *wet dreams* because of the myth that emissions accompany erotic dreams. However, nocturnal emissions and erotic dreams need not coincide. Mature sperm are found in ejaculatory emissions by about the age of 15. On account of this, ejaculation is not adequate evidence of reproductive capacity. Ejaculatory ability in boys usually precedes the presence of mature sperm by at least a year.

Nearly half of all boys experience enlargement of the breasts, or **gynecomastia**, which usually declines in a year or two. Gynecomastia stems from the small amount of female sex hormones secreted by the testes. When gynecomastia persists or becomes distressing, it can be treated with drugs, such as tamoxifen. Some males have surgery (Fagerlund et al., 2015).

At age 20 or 21, men stop growing taller because testosterone causes **epiphyseal closure**, which prevents the long bones from making further gains in length. And so, puberty for males draws to a close. The changes of puberty in males are summarized in Concept Review 14.1.

asynchronous growth Imbalanced growth, such as the growth that occurs during the early part of adolescence and causes many adolescents to appear gawky.

secular trend A historical trend toward increasing adult height and earlier puberty.

larynx The part of the throat that contains the vocal cords.

semen The fluid that contains sperm and substances that nourish and help transport sperm.

nocturnal emission Emission of seminal fluid while asleep.

gynecomastia Enlargement of breast tissue in males.

epiphyseal closure The process by which the cartilage that separates the long end (epiphysis) of a bone from the main part of the bone turns to bone.

Five Stages of Male Development During Puberty

Boys usually start to show the physical changes of puberty between the ages of 11 and 14, which is slightly older than when girls start puberty. The male sex hormone testosterone and other hormones cause the physical changes.

Here are the five stages and what happens:

Stage	Characteristics
Stage 1: May begin as early as age 9 and continue until age 14.	• No sign of physical development but hormone production is beginning.
Stage 2: May begin anywhere from age 11 to 13.	• Height and weight increase rapidly. • Testicles become larger and scrotum hangs lower. • Scrotum becomes darker in color. • Fine hair growth begins at the base of the penis. • Hair growth may begin on the legs and underarms.
Stage 3: May begin anywhere from age 12 to 14.	• The penis, scrotum, and testicles grow. • Pubic hair becomes darker, thicker, and curlier. • Muscles become larger and shoulders become broader. • Sweat and oil glands become more active, which can result in acne. • Sperm production may begin. • Temporary swelling and tenderness may occur around nipples. • Height and weight continue to increase. • Hair growth on the legs and underarms continues.
Stage 4: May begin anywhere from age 13 to 16.	• Sperm production has usually begun. • The larynx (Adam's apple) increases in size. Vocal chords become longer and thicker, and the voice begins to break or crack, then becomes low. • Height and weight continue to increase. • Penis and testicles continue to grow. • Pubic hair increases in amount and becomes darker, coarser, and curly.
Stage 5: May begin anywhere from age 14 to 18.	• Growth of facial hair begins. • Chest hair growth may begin (not all males get much chest hair). • Adult height is reached. • Penis and testicles have reached full adult size. • Pubic, underarm, and leg hair are adult color, texture, and distribution. • Overall look is that of a young adult man.

RubberBall Photography/Veer

Source: U.S. Department of Health and Human Services (2009). Sexual development of boys. Accessed October 26, 2009. http://www.4parents.gov/sexdevt/boysmen/boys_sexdevt/index.html.

What Pubertal Changes Occur in Girls?

In girls, the pituitary gland signals the ovaries to vastly increase estrogen production at puberty. Estrogen may stimulate the growth of breast tissue ("breast buds") as early as the age of 8 or 9, but the breasts usually begin to enlarge during the 10th year. The development of fatty tissue and ducts elevates the areas of the breasts surrounding the nipples and causes the nipples themselves to protrude. The breasts typically reach full size in about 3 years, but the **mammary glands** do not mature fully until a woman has a baby.

Estrogen also promotes the growth of the fatty and supporting tissue in the hips and buttocks, which, along with the widening of the pelvis, causes the hips to become rounded. Growth of fatty deposits and connective tissue varies considerably. For this reason, development of breasts and hips differs.

Beginning at about the age of 11, girls' adrenal glands produce small amounts of androgens, which, along with estrogen, stimulate the growth of pubic and underarm hair. Excessive androgen production can darken or increase the amount of facial hair. Androgens and estrogen have other functions as well.

Estrogen causes the **labia**, vagina, and uterus to develop during puberty, and androgens cause the **clitoris** to develop. The vaginal lining varies in thickness according to the amount of estrogen in the bloodstream.

Estrogen typically brakes the female growth spurt some years before testosterone brakes that of males. Girls deficient in estrogen during their late teens may grow quite tall, but most girls reach their heights because of normal, genetically determined variations.

Menarche

The current mean age for **menarche** (first menstruation) in the United States is the 13th year (with, for example, 12.8 years as the average for European Americans and 12.2 years as the average for African Americans) (Cabrera et al., 2014). During the past 150 years, menarche has occurred at progressively earlier ages in Western nations—an example of the secular trend in development, as shown in Figure 14.4 ■. During the past century and a half, however, the processes of puberty have occurred at progressively earlier ages in Western nations. By the 1960s, the average age of menarche in the United States had plummeted to its current figure of 12½.

No single theory of the onset of puberty has found wide acceptance. In any event, the average age of the advent of puberty for girls and boys appears to have leveled off. The precipitous drop suggested in Figure 14.4 has come to an end, at least in developed nations.

Purestock/Jupiterimages

mammary glands Glands that secrete milk.

labia The major and minor lips of the female genitalia.

clitoris A female sex organ that is highly sensitive to sexual stimulation but is not directly involved in reproduction.

menarche The onset of menstruation.

In girls, estrogen stimulates the growth of breast tissue and the development of the female genital organs.

Figure 14.4 ■ The Decline in Age at Menarche
The age at menarche has been declining since the mid-1800s among girls in Western nations, apparently because of improved nutrition and health care. Menarche may be triggered by the accumulation of a critical percentage of body fat.
Source: Tanner (1989).

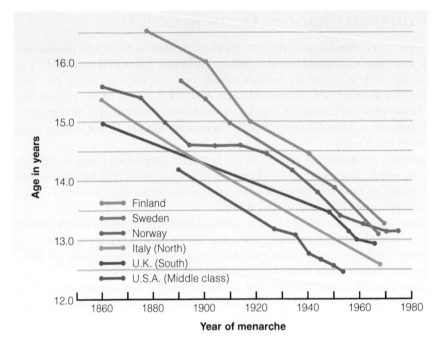

What accounts for the earlier age of puberty? One hypothesis is that girls must reach a certain body weight to trigger pubertal changes such as menarche (Crocker et al., 2014; Terasawa et al., 2012; Wagner et al., 2012). Body fat could trigger the changes because fat cells secrete the protein leptin (Terasawa et al., 2012). Leptin would then signal the brain to secrete a cascade of hormones that raise estrogen levels in the body. The average body weight for triggering menarche depends on the girl's height (Novotny et al., 2011). Today's girls are larger than those of the early 20th century because of improved nutrition and health care.

Menarche comes later to girls who have a lower percentage of body fat, such as athletes and those with eating disorders (Novotny et al., 2011). It seems that the age threshold for reaching menarche may have been attained, because the average age has leveled off in recent years.

The age at menarche has been shown to be related to adverse health outcomes later in life. For example, earlier menarche has been associated with higher risk of breast cancer and possibly with a higher risk of endometrial cancer, adult obesity, and menstrual problems (Mishra et al., 2009).

Hormonal Regulation of the Menstrual Cycle

Testosterone levels remain fairly stable in boys, although they decline gradually in adulthood. However, estrogen and progesterone levels in girls vary markedly and regulate the menstrual cycle. Following menstruation—the sloughing off of the endometrium—estrogen levels increase, leading once more to the growth of endometrial tissue.

TRUTH OR FICTION REVISITED: It is usually not true that girls can become pregnant right after they have their first menstrual period. Girls usually begin to ovulate some 12–18 months after menarche.

A ripe ovum is released by the ovary when estrogen reaches peak blood levels. Then the inner lining of the uterus thickens in response to the secretion of progesterone. In this way, it gains the capacity to support an embryo if fertilization should occur. If the ovum is not fertilized, estrogen and progesterone levels drop suddenly, triggering menstruation once again.

The average menstrual cycle is 28 days, but variation among girls and in the same girl is common. Girls' cycles are often irregular for a few years after menarche but later tend to assume patterns that are reasonably regular. Most menstrual cycles during the first 2 years or so after menarche occur without ovulation having taken place. But keep in mind that in any given individual cycle, an ovum may be produced, making pregnancy possible. So it is possible to become pregnant shortly after the onset of menarche.

The Psychological Impact of Menarche

In different times, in different places, menarche has had different meanings. The Manus of New Guinea greet menarche with an elaborate ceremony (Lohmann, 2004). The other girls of the village sleep in the menstruating girl's hut. They feast and have parties. In the West, menstruation has historically received a mixed response. The menstrual flow itself has generally been seen, erroneously, as polluting, and the frequent discomforts of menstruation have led menstruating women to be stereotyped as irrational (Hubbard, 2009). Menarche itself has generally been perceived as the event in which a girl suddenly develops into a woman, but because of taboos and prejudices against menstruating women, girls historically matured in ignorance of menarche.

Girls' attitudes toward menarche reflect their level of education as well as certain physical realities. A Hong Kong study of 1,573 Chinese high school students found a mixed response to the onset of menstruation (Tang et al., 2003). The average age of menarche was 11.67 years. Although most of the girls reported that menstruation was annoying (it involved some discomfort for them, along with the need to dispose of the menstrual flow), 2 in 3 reported feeling more "grown up," and 4 in 10 felt that they had become more feminine. Girls who felt positive about menarche were more likely to be educationally prepared to welcome it as a natural event, to have a positive body image, and to reject traditional negative attitudes. Even so, the circulating hormones connected with menarche may make the girl more vulnerable to stress (Allison & Hyde, 2013).

Most American girls currently receive advance information about menstruation, not only from family and girlfriends but also from school health classes. The old horror stories are pretty much gone, at least in mainstream society (Gillooly, 2004). However, most girls experience at least some menstrual discomfort and need to discreetly dispose of the menstrual flow (Harel, 2008). Most girls can separate pride in "becoming women" from the realities of some discomfort and the fact that menarche usually means that the girl will not be growing much taller because of the braking effects of estrogen. The changes of puberty in females are summarized in Concept Review 14.2.

Early versus Late Maturers: Does It Matter When You Arrive, as Long as You Do?

I remember Big Al from my high school days. When Al entered the ninth grade, he was all of 14, but he was also about 6 feet 3 inches tall, with broad shoulders and arms thick with muscle. His face was cut from rock, and his beard was already dark. Al paraded down the hallways with an entourage of male and female admirers. When there were shrieks of anticipation, you could bet that Al was coming around the corner. Al was given a wide berth in the boys' room. He would have to lean back when he combed his waxed hair up and back—otherwise, his head would be too high for the mirror. At that age, my friends and I liked to tell ourselves that Al was not all that bright. (This stereotype is unfounded, as we will see.) Nevertheless, my friends and I were envious of Al.

Al had arrived. Al had matured early, and he had experienced the positive aspects of maturing early. What causes some children to mature earlier or later than others? Genetic, dietary, and health factors all seem to influence the timing of puberty. And one controversial new theory suggests that childhood stress may trigger early puberty in girls.

Five Stages of Female Development During Puberty

Girls usually start to show the physical changes of puberty between the ages of 9 and 13, which is slightly sooner than boys. The female sex hormone estrogen and other hormones cause the physical changes.

Many girls are fully developed by the age of 16. Some girls will continue to develop through age 18.

Here are the five stages and what happens:

Stage	Characteristics
Stage 1: Between ages 8 and 12.	• No visible signs of physical development, but the ovaries are enlarging and hormone production is beginning.
Stage 2: May begin anywhere from age 8 to 14.	• Height and weight increase rapidly. • Fine hair growth begins close to the pubic area and underarms. • Breast buds appear; nipples become raised and this area may be tender. • Sweat and oil glands become more active which can result in acne.
Stage 3: May begin anywhere from age 9 to 15.	• Breasts become rounder and fuller. • Hips may start to widen in relation to waist. • Vagina begins secreting a clear or whitish fluid. • Pubic hair becomes darker, thicker, and curlier. • Height and weight continue to increase. • For some girls, ovulation and menstruation (periods) begin, but may be irregular.
Stage 4: May begin anywhere from age 10 to 16.	• Underarm hair becomes darker. • Pubic hair starts to form a triangular patch in front and around sides of genital area. • The nipple and the dark area around the breast (areola) may stick out from the rest of the breast. • For many girls, ovulation and menstruation (periods) begin but may be irregular.
Stage 5: May begin anywhere from age 12 to 19.	• Adult height is probably reached. • Breast development is complete. • Pubic hair forms a thick, curly, triangular patch. • Ovulation and menstruation (periods) usually occur regularly. • Overall look is that of a young adult woman.

Sean Justice/The Image Bank/Getty Images

Source: U.S. Department of Health and Human Services. (2009). Sexual development of girls. Accessed October 26, 2009.

Early and Late Maturation in Boys The effects of early maturation in boys are generally positive. Late-maturing boys may feel conspicuous because they are among the last of their peers to lose their childhood appearance. On the other hand, early-maturing boys may experience pressures to act maturely, or even aggressively, before they are ready.

Early and Late Maturation in Boys

Research findings about boys who mature early are mixed, but most of the evidence suggests that the effects of early maturation are generally positive (Teunissen et al., 2011). Late-maturing boys may feel conspicuous because they are among the last of their peers to lose their childhood appearance. The research literature is mixed as to whether the timing of maturation is related to adolescents' eventual height, but it appears that early maturers might wind up shorter and stockier than late maturers (Baker et al., 2007; Biro, 2008).

Early-maturing boys tend to be more popular than their late-maturing peers and are more likely to be leaders in school (Graber et al., 2004; Windle et al., 2008). Early-maturing boys in general are also more poised, relaxed, and good-natured. Their edge in sports and the admiration of their peers heighten their sense of self-worth. Some studies have suggested that the stereotype of the mature, tough-looking boy as dumb is just that—a stereotype.

On the negative side, early maturation is associated with greater risks of aggression and delinquency (Lynne et al., 2007), as well as abuse of alcohol and other drugs (Modecki et al., 2014). Early maturation may also hit some boys before they are psychologically prepared to live up to the expectations of those who admire their new bodies. Coaches may expect too much of them in sports, and peers may want them to fight their battles (Biro, 2008). Sexual opportunities may create demands before the boy knows how to respond to them (James et al., 2012). Some early maturers may therefore worry about living up to the expectations of others.

Late maturers have the "advantage" of avoiding these early pressures. They are not rushed into maturity. On the other hand, late-maturing boys often feel dominated by early-maturing boys. They have been found to be more dependent and insecure. Although they are smaller and weaker than early maturers, they may be more likely to get involved in disruptive behavior and substance abuse (Vroman, 2010).

But there are individual differences. Although some late maturers appear to fight their physical status and get into trouble, others adjust and find acceptance through academic achievement, music, clubs, and other activities. The benefits of early maturation appear to be greatest among lower-income adolescents because physical prowess is valued more highly among these youngsters. Middle- and upper-income adolescents also are likely to place more value on the types of achievements—academic and so on—available to late-maturing boys (Graber et al., 2004; Weichold et al., 2003).

Early and Late Maturation in Girls

The situation is somewhat reversed for girls. Whereas early maturation poses distinct advantages for boys, the picture is more mixed for girls. Adolescents tend to be concerned if they differ from their peers. Girls outgrow not only their late-maturing female counterparts but also their male agemates. With their tallness and their developing breasts, they become conspicuous (Allison & Hyde, 2013; Teunissen et al., 2011). Boys may sexually harass and tease them about their breasts and their height (Skoog et al., 2015). Tall girls of dating age frequently find that shorter boys are reluctant to approach them or be seen with them. Some tall girls walk with a slight hunch, as if trying to minimize their height. All in all, early-maturing girls are at greater risk for a host of psychological problems and substance abuse than girls who mature later (Blumenthal et al., 2011; Mrug et al., 2014).

> **TRUTH OR FICTION REVISITED:** It is true that boys who mature early often have higher self-esteem than boys who mature late, but it seems to work in the opposite way for girls. That is, late-maturing girls appear to have higher self-esteem than early-maturing girls.

Many girls who mature early have a poorer body image than those who mature later (Allison & Hyde, 2013). These negative feelings are more pronounced for girls who are in elementary school, where they are conspicuous, but are less pronounced in high school, where others are catching up.

Adolescent girls are quite concerned about their body shapes. Early maturers who are taller and heavier than other girls their age do not conform to the current cultural emphasis on thinness. Thus, they have more negative feelings about their bodies. Early maturation in girls is associated with a variety of other problems. Early-maturing girls obtain lower grades in school and have more conduct problems, a higher incidence of substance abuse, and a higher incidence of emotional disturbance, including depression (Blumenthal et al., 2011; Skoog et al., 2015). They are literally larger targets for deviant peer pressure. They initiate sexual activity earlier (Copeland et al., 2010). They become involved with older girls and boys. Their concern about their body shape also appears to heighten the risk of developing eating disorders (Allison & Hyde, 2013; Striegel-Moore et al., 2003).

The parents of early-maturing girls may increase their vigilance and restrictiveness. Increased restrictiveness can lead to new child–parent conflicts. A study of 302 African American adolescent–mother pairs found that mothers of early-maturing daughters had more heated discussions with them than with later-maturing daughters (Sagrestano et al., 1999). Girls who mature early are also at greater risk of sexual abuse (Skoog & Ozdemir, 2015; Vigil et al., 2005). The early-maturing girl can thus be a target of inappropriate parental attention and may develop severe conflicts about her body as a result.

How Do Adolescents Feel About Their Bodies?

Recall how you felt when you were undergoing the changes of puberty and beyond. How fascinated were you by what was taking place in every limb and in your torso? Was your weight stable, or were you putting on the pounds? Or, in some cases, taking them off? Did other people react to you differently as you changed? Were you fascinated by the question as to how tall you would wind up, how large your bust would be, etc., etc., etc.? And what was happening to your body image all along the way?

Our body image includes how physically attractive we perceive ourselves to be and how we feel about our body. Adolescents are quite concerned about their

How did you feel when you were undergoing the changes of puberty? Was it all a flurry of unbounded excitement and optimism, or did you have some questions and deep concerns?

Steve Prezant/Image Source/Alamy

physical appearance, particularly in early adolescence during the rapid physical changes of puberty (Bucchianeri et al., 2013).

By the age of 18, girls and boys are more satisfied with their bodies than they were in the earlier teen years (Bucchianeri et al., 2013). A 5-year longitudinal study investigated the relationship between body image and depressed mood in 645 adolescents at ages 13, 15, and 18 (Holsen et al., 2001). On average, girls reported having a more negative body image and feeling more depressed about their bodies at all three ages. Dissatisfaction with body image led to feelings of depression among both genders (Wertheim et al., 2009). Adolescent females in our society tend to be more preoccupied with body weight and slimness than are adolescent males (Tiggeman, 2014; Tiggeman & Slater, 2013). In contrast, many adolescent males want to put weight on and build their muscle mass (Field et al., 2014). Compared with adolescent boys, adolescent girls have a less positive body image and are more dissatisfied with their weight; the majority of girls are likely to be dieting or to have been on diets (Tiggeman & Slater, 2013). And girls are more likely to suffer from eating disorders, as we will see later in the chapter.

Section Review

1. G. Stanley Hall proposed that adolescence is a period of storm and _____ .

2. Puberty is controlled by a _____ loop involving hormones.

3. The gonads produce _____ hormones (androgens and estrogens).

4. Girls begin their _____ spurt in height at about 10, and boys spurt about 2 years later.

5. _____ growth may produce gawkiness in adolescents.

6. Males stop growing taller because testosterone causes _____ closure.

7. _____ brakes the female growth spurt.

8. _____ (Boys or Girls?) are more likely to benefit from early maturation.

9. _____ (Boys or Girls?) are more likely to have a positive body image.

Reflect & Relate: Was your adolescence a period of storm and stress? If so, what factors contributed to the turbulence?

Brain Development

> Unlike infants whose brain activity is completely determined by their parents and environment, [adolescents] may actually be able to control how their own brains are wired and sculpted. . . This argues for doing a lot of things as a teenager. . . You are hard-wiring your brain in adolescence. Do you want to hard-wire it for sports and playing music and doing mathematics or for lying on the couch in front of the television?
>
> —Neuroscientist Jay Giedd of the National Institute of Mental Health

What happens to the brains of adolescents who spend hours a day practicing the piano or the violin? Their learning translates physically into increases in the thickness of the parts of the cerebral cortex that are being used (Hudziak et al., 2014; Raznahan et al., 2011; see Figure 14.5 ■). The gains in thickness of the cerebral cortex represent increases in **gray matter**, which consists of associative neurons that transmit messages back and forth in the brain when we are engaged in thought and sensorimotor activities (Giedd, 2015). The neurons sprout new axon tips and dendrites, creating new synapses and increasing the flow of information.

Brain imaging studies reveal a general pattern of brain development into the teenage years related both to maturation and to the use of brain regions (Bramen et al., 2011). But even while parts of the brain gain in processing ability, there is

gray matter Neural tissue, especially of the brain and spinal cord, that contains cell bodies and their dendrites and forms most of the cortex of the brain.

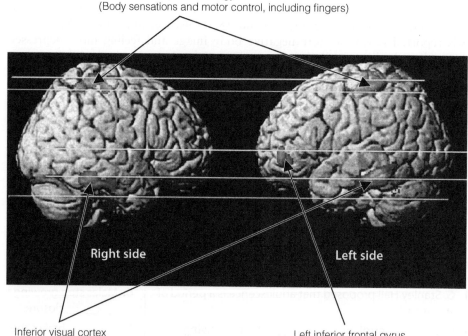

Figure 14.5 ■ **What Happens to the Brain When an Adolescent Practices the Piano Several Hours a Day?**

One result is that parts of the gray matter of the brain are likely to thicken due to the proliferation of synapses. The areas in red show thicker gray matter among professional keyboard players than in amateurs and nonmusicians. The areas in yellow show greater differences in thickness in the same direction.

Source: Gaser & Schlaug (2003). Copyright by the Society for Neuroscience. Reprinted with permission.

also a pruning process that seems to follow the principle "Use it or lose it." Neural connections, or synapses, that are used are retained, while those that lie unused are lost.

Many adolescents show poor judgment, at least from time to time, and take risks that most adults would avoid (Casey, 2015; Reyna et al., 2015). It seems that brain development or immaturity may play a role. Deborah Yurgelun-Todd and her colleagues (Sava & Yurgelun-Todd, 2008) showed pictures of people with fearful expressions to adolescents ranging in age from 11 to 17 while the adolescents' brains were scanned by functional magnetic resonance imaging (fMRI). Compared to adults, the adolescents' frontal lobes (the seat of executive functioning) were less active, and their amygdalas (a part of the limbic system that is involved in discriminating emotions, including fear) were more active. The adolescents often misread the facial expressions, with those younger than 14 more often inferring sadness, anger, or confusion rather than fear. The older adolescents responded correctly more often and also showed the more adult pattern of less activity in the amygdala and more in the frontal lobes. The researchers suggest that one reason why many adolescents fail to show the judgment, insight, and reasoning ability of adults is immaturity of the frontal lobes (Yurgelun-Todd, 2007).

Genes (heredity) and the environment interact to shape early brain development. Researchers (Lenroot et al., 2009) used magnetic resonance imaging to analyze age-related differences in the heritability of cortical thickness with 600 twins, twins' siblings, and singletons ranging in age from 5 to 19. Parts of the primary sensory and motor cortex, which develop earlier, respond to genetic influences earlier in childhood. Areas of the brain related to executive functioning (self-regulation) and language, the prefrontal cortex and the temporal lobes, show more prominent genetic influences in adolescence. It may therefore be that cognitive processes become more heritable as the brain matures. But again, there is an interaction between heredity and the environment. The experiences of adolescents also affect which parts of the cortex thicken and which are "pruned."

What Is This Teenage Girl Doing? Yes, we know that she is practicing the violin, but what is she doing to her brain? (Don't be concerned—it's all good.)

Section Review

10. The learning of adolescents who practice a musical instrument translates into increases in the thickness of the cerebral _____.

11. The risk-taking shown by many adolescents has been related to immaturity of the _____ lobes.

12. Areas of the brain related to executive functioning and language show _____ (more or less?) prominent genetic influences in adolescence.

Reflect & Relate: Does "immaturity" of the prefrontal lobes excuse adolescents who engage in risky behavior?

14.4 Emerging Sexuality and the Risks of Sexually Transmitted Infections

In an episode of a TV series, an adolescent was referred to as a "hormone with feet." Many or most adolescents are preoccupied with sex to some degree. These preoccupations are fueled by a powerful sex drive. And many or most adolescents are not quite sure about what to do with these pressing urges. Should they masturbate? Should they pet? Should they engage in sexual intercourse? Parents and sex educators often say "No," or "Wait." Yet it can seem that "Everyone's doing it." In

Chapter 16, we will discuss various sexual outlets and sexual orientation. Here, we will focus on the risks of sexually transmitted infections.

Given a body that is suddenly sexually mature, a strong sex drive, vulnerability to peer pressure, and limited experience in handling temptation, teenagers are at particular risk for sexually transmitted infections (STIs). Sexually active adolescents have higher rates of STIs than any other age group. Each year, an estimated 2.5 million adolescents—one of every six—contract a sexually transmitted infection (Gavin et al., 2009).

What Kinds of STIs Are There?

Chlamydia (a bacterial infection of the vagina or urinary tract that can result in sterility) is the most commonly occurring STI in adolescents, followed by gonorrhea, genital warts, genital herpes, syphilis, and **HIV/AIDS**. Because it is lethal, HIV/AIDS tends to capture most of the headlines. However, other STIs are more widespread, and some of them can also be deadly.

Nearly 2.8 million new chlamydia infections occur each year (Chlamydia—CDC Fact Sheet, 2011). The incidence of chlamydia infections is especially high among teenagers and college students. Chlamydia is a major cause of pelvic inflammatory disease (PID) in women, which may lead to infertility. The Centers for Disease Control and Prevention (CDC-Chlamydia statistics, 2015a) recommend that sexually active women under the age of 26 be screened for chlamydia annually.

Each year in the United States, there are about 1 million new infections with the human papillomavirus (HPV) (Genital HPV Infection—Fact Sheet, 2011), which causes genital warts and is associated with cervical cancer. A vaccine is available that prevents most young women from being infected with HPV if it is administered before they become sexually active. However, it is estimated that more than half of the sexually active adolescent women in some U.S. cities are infected with HPV. Genital warts may appear in visible areas of the skin, but most appear in areas that cannot be seen, such as on the cervix in women or in the urethra in men. Women who initiate sexual intercourse before the age of 18 and who have many sex partners are particularly susceptible to infection. Fortunately, in most healthy young people, these infections clear up on their own.

HIV/AIDS

HIV/AIDS is the most devastating STI. If left untreated, it is lethal, and the long-term prospects of those who do receive treatment remain unknown. HIV—the virus that causes AIDS—has spread rapidly around the world. According to UNICEF, more than 30 million people around the world are living with HIV/AIDS, of whom 2.1 million are youth aged 10–19 (Idele et al., 2014). The primary mode of HIV transmission worldwide is male–female sex. Anal intercourse is another mode of HIV transmission and is often practiced by gay males. Injecting drugs is another way in which HIV is spread, because sharing needles with infected individuals can transmit HIV. Among the risk factors: having sex with multiple partners, failing to use condoms, and abusing drugs and alcohol (CDC, 2015b; Patrick et al., 2012).

Women account for a minority of cases of HIV/AIDS in the United States, but in many places around the world, women are more likely than men to be infected with HIV. A United Nations study in Europe, Africa, and Southeast Asia has found that sexually active teenage girls have higher rates of HIV infection than older women or young men in these regions (Sidibe, 2015). A number of erroneous assumptions about HIV/AIDS have had a disproportionately negative effect on women. They include the false notions that HIV/AIDS is primarily a disease of gay men and people

HIV/AIDS The acronym for human immunodeficiency virus/ acquired immunodeficiency syndrome; a condition in which the virus compromises the body's immune system, making the individual vulnerable to "opportunistic" diseases.

Diagnoses of HIV Infection, by Age

Age in Years	Estimated Number of Diagnoses of HIV Infection
Under age 13	187
Ages 13–14	45
Ages 15–19	1,863
Ages 20–24	8,053
Ages 25–29	7,825
Ages 30–34	6,165
Ages 35–39	4,858
Ages 40–44	4,820
Ages 45–49	4,961
Ages 50–54	3,747
Ages 55–59	2,467
Ages 60–64	1,316
Ages 65 and older	1,045

Source: Centers for Disease Control and Prevention (2015).

who inject drugs and that it is difficult to contract HIV/AIDS through male–female intercourse. Among U.S. women, as across the globe, male–female intercourse is the major source of infection by HIV.

TRUTH OR FICTION REVISITED: Studies regarding knowledge, attitudes, and beliefs about HIV/AIDS find that even children in the early school years are aware of HIV/AIDS. About 85% of students were taught about HIV/AIDS in 2013, but adolescents often deny the threat of HIV/AIDS to them (CDC, 2015b). As one high school girl said, "I can't believe that anyone I would have sex with would be infected."

Despite the fact that most adolescents in the United States have learned about HIV/AIDS and the types of behavior that lead to infection, according to the Centers for Disease Control and Prevention, more than 1,800 U.S. adolescents aged 15–19 were diagnosed as being infected with HIV in 2013. Table 14.1 ● shows the estimated number of new cases in the United States, by age, for 2013. It is important to keep in mind that the diagnosis of HIV infection may not be made until 10 years or so after the fact. Therefore, the much higher numbers we see for ages 20–29 may at least in part reflect infection during adolescence.

What Factors Place Adolescents at Risk for Contracting STIs?

Adolescents often take risks, with harmful consequences for their health and well-being. First, and most obvious, is sexual activity itself. As you can see in Figure 14.6 ■, about half of U.S. adolescents have engaged in sexual intercourse, and significant percentages

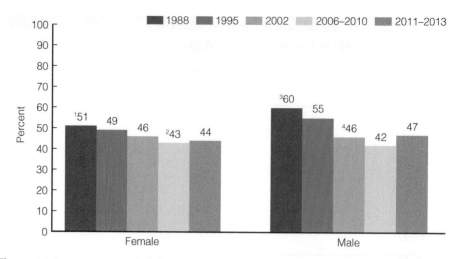

Figure 14.6 ■ Percentage of Never-Married Females and Males Aged 15-19 Who Have Ever Had Sexual Intercourse
Source: Martinez, G. M., & Abma, J. C. (2015, July). NCAS Data Brief No. 209. Sexual Activity, Contraceptive Use, and Childbearing of Teenagers Aged 15-19 in the United States. U.S. Department of Health and Human Services. Figure 1.

of these young people have not used effective means of birth control or prevention of STIs.

A second risk factor for contracting STIs is sex with multiple partners. About one in five high school students engages in sex with four or more different partners (Martinez et al., 2011).

A third factor is failure to use condoms. Many sexually active adolescents report not using condoms or using them inconsistently (National Campaign to Prevent Teen and Unplanned Pregnancy, 2012).

A fourth factor is drug abuse (Nguyen et al., 2012). Adolescents who abuse drugs are also more likely to engage in other risky behaviors, such as sex without condoms (Nguyen et al., 2012).

The causes, methods of transmission, symptoms, diagnosis, and treatment—where it exists—of major sexually transmitted infections (STIs) are described in Table 14.2 ●.

Given the Threat of HIV/AIDS and Other STIs, What Can Be Done to Prevent Them?

Prevention and education are the primary weapons against STIs (Kirby et al., 2007). Adolescents need to learn about the transmission, symptoms, and consequences of STIs. They need to learn about "safer sex" techniques, including abstinence and, if they are sexually active, the use of condoms. Educating young people to use condoms is associated with lower levels of infection (Billings et al., 2015). See the nearby "A Closer Look—Real Life" feature on preventing HIV/AIDS and other STIs.

But knowledge alone may not change behavior. For example, many female adolescents lack power in their relationships. Males are likely to pressure them into unwanted or unprotected sexual relations (Sidibe, 2015). Other goals of educational programs should include enhancing the adolescent's sense of control over the prevention of AIDS and modifying behavior associated with being infected with HIV. As with programs designed to prevent substance abuse, the development of effective decision-making and social skills may be critical in programs designed to prevent STIs (Martinez et al., 2011).

Overview of Sexually Transmitted Infections (STIs)[a]

STI and Cause	Transmission	Symptoms	Diagnosis	Treatment
Gonorrhea ("clap," "drip"): gonococcus bacterium (*Neisseria gonorrhoeae*)	Vaginal, oral, or anal sexual activity To newborns passing through the birth canal of an infected mother	In men, yellowish, thick discharge, burning urination In women, may be symptom-free or there may be increased vaginal discharge, burning urination, irregular menstruation	Clinical inspection Culture of sample discharge	Antibiotics
Syphilis: *Treponema pallidum*	Vaginal, oral, or anal sexual activity Touching an infectious chancre Can be congenital	Hard, round, painless chancre or sore appears at site of infection within 2–4 weeks May progress through additional stages if left untreated Potentially lethal	Clinical examination or examination of fluid from a chancre Blood test (the VDRL)	Antibiotics
Chlamydia and nongonococcal urethritis (NGU): *Chlamydia trachomatous* bacterium in women and several bacteria in men, including *Ureaplasma urealycticum*	Vaginal, oral, or anal sexual activity Transmitted to the eye by touching one's eyes after touching the genitals of an infected partner To newborns passing through the birth canal of an infected mother	In women, may be symptom-free or there may be frequent and painful urination, lower abdominal pain and inflammation, and vaginal discharge In men, may be symptom-free or there may be burning or painful urination, slight penile discharge Sore throat may follow oral–genital contact	The Abbott TestPack analyzes a cervical smear in women In men, an extract of fluid from the penis is analyzed	Antibiotics
Genital herpes: herpes simplex virus-type 2 (HSV-2)	Vaginal, oral, or anal sexual activity Most contagious during active outbreaks of the disease, but may be transmitted at any time	Painful, reddish bumps around the genitals, thighs, or buttocks Bumps become blisters or sores that fill with pus and break, shedding viral particles Burning urination, fever, aches and pains, swollen glands, and vaginal discharge possible	Clinical inspection of sores Culture and examination of fluid drawn from sore	Antiviral drugs may provide relief and help with healing but are not cures Counseling and support groups may be of help
HIV/AIDS: acronym for human immunodeficiency virus, the cause of acquired immunodeficiency syndrome	Vaginal or anal sexual intercourse Infusion with contaminated blood by needle sharing or from mother to baby during childbirth Breastfeeding	Usually symptom-free for many years Flulike symptoms Chronically swollen lymph nodes, fever, weight loss, fatigue, diarrhea Lethal "opportunistic infections"	Blood, saliva, or urine tests detect HIV antibodies in the bloodstream Other tests confirm the presence of the virus (HIV) itself	No cure Highly active antiretroviral therapy (HAART)—a "cocktail" of antiviral drugs—is prolonging the lives of many people with HIV/AIDS
HPV/genital warts (venereal warts): human papillomavirus (HPV)	Sexual contact Contact with infected towels or clothing	Painless warts resembling cauliflowers on the genitals or anus or in the rectum Associated with cervical cancer in women and throat cancer in men	Clinical inspection	A vaccine can prevent most adolescents from being infected with HPV Warts can be removed by freezing, podophyllin, burning, or surgery

[a]© Spencer A. Rathus. All rights reserved.

PREVENTING HIV/AIDS AND OTHER STIS: IT'S MORE THAN SAFE(R) SEX

How does one protect oneself from being infected with a sexually transmitted infection (STI)? Because discussing STIs with a partner can be such a daunting task, some people wing it. They admit that they just hope for the best. But even if they do bring up the topic, they need to recognize that many people—perhaps most people—do not know whether they are infected with an STI, especially the organisms that cause chlamydia, gonorrhea, and AIDS. In any event, putting blinders on is not the answer to STIs.

What can we do to prevent STIs? Here are some guidelines:

1. Teach sex education in schools.

2. Keep the prevalence and harmful nature of STIs in mind. Many young people try not to think about the threats posed by STIs. Don't play the dangerous game that involves pretending (especially in the heat of passion) that they do not exist.

3. Just say no—that is, remain abstinent. One way of curtailing the transmission of infections is abstinence. But what does abstinence mean? Is it limited to avoiding sexual intercourse with another person? Hugging, kissing, and petting (without contacting semen or vaginal fluids) are usually safe, although readers may argue about whether these behaviors are consistent with the definition of abstinence.

4. Limit yourself to a monogamous relationship with a partner who is not infected. It is safe to engage in sexual intercourse in a monogamous relationship with a person who does not have an STI. The question is, can you be certain that your partner is free of STIs and faithful?

5. Adolescents who are not willing to abstain from sexual intercourse or to limit themselves to one partner can still do things to make sex safer, if not perfectly safe:

6. Be picky. Limit sexual activity to people you know well. Ask yourself whether they are likely to have done things that exposed them to HIV or other disease organisms.

7. Check out your partner's genitals. Examine them for unpleasant odors, discharges, blisters, rashes, warts, and lice during foreplay. These are possible symptoms of STIs.

8. Wash the genitals. Washing yourself beforehand helps protect your partner. Washing with soap and water afterward may kill or remove some pathogens. Urinating afterward might be of some help, particularly to men, because the acidity of urine can kill some disease organisms in the urethra.

9. Use latex condoms, which protect partners from exchanging infected bodily fluids.

10. Talk to a doctor. Using antibiotics and antiviral medications after unprotected sex can guard against some bacterial and viral infections, even HIV. Check with a doctor *immediately* if you think you might have been exposed to an STI.

11. Have regular medical checkups to learn about disorders whose symptoms might go unnoticed.

Reflect How can shyness endanger your health in relation to STIs?

* Why do women need a certain degree of power in their relationships to protect themselves from STIs?

* Do some research: What is the difference between being *exposed to HIV* and being *infected by HIV*? Why should you visit a doctor as soon as possible if you suspect you might have been exposed to HIV?

Section Review

13. _____ is the most common sexually transmitted infection in adolescents.

14. Infection by _____ is linked to the development of cancer of the cervix.

15. HIV is the virus that causes _____.

16. A _____ (minority or majority?) of sexually active adolescents use condoms consistently.

Reflect & Relate: Do you—or did you—know any adolescents who contracted STIs? How? Were they aware at the time of the existence of the STIs and how these infections are transmitted? Have these STIs caused problems for those who were infected? Explain.

14.5 Health in Adolescence

Adolescents are young and growing. Most seem sturdy. Injuries tend to heal quickly.

How Healthy Are U.S. Adolescents?

The good news is that most American adolescents are healthy. Few are chronically ill or miss school. However, about 18% of the nation's adolescents have at least one serious health problem (Bloom et al., 2006). American teenagers may be less healthy than their parents were at the same age. We discussed the teen problem of sexually transmitted infections (STIs) in the preceding section. Now we will consider the causes of death in adolescence and then turn to other major health issues faced by teens: sleep, nutrition, eating disorders, and substance abuse.

What Are the Causes of Death Among Adolescents?

The reason why adolescents may be less healthy than their parents were at the same age is not an increase in the incidence of infectious diseases or other physical illnesses. Rather, the causes are external and rooted in lifestyle and risky behavior: excessive drinking, substance abuse, reckless driving, violence, disordered eating behavior, and, as we have seen, unprotected sexual activity (Schneider et al., 2012).

Death rates are low in adolescence, although they are higher for older adolescents than for younger ones. For example, each year about twice as many 15- to 17-year-olds as 12- to 14-year-olds die (Miniño, 2010). Death rates are nearly twice as high for male adolescents as for female adolescents. A major reason for this is that males are more likely to take risks that end in death as a result of accidents, suicide, or homicide (Miniño, 2010). These three causes of death account for the great majority of all adolescent deaths.

TRUTH OR FICTION REVISITED: It is not true that substance use is the leading cause of death among male adolescents in the United States. Accidents, suicide, and homicide are all more likely to be the causes of death of U.S. adolescents.

Sixty percent of adolescent deaths are due to accidents, and nearly three in four of these involve motor vehicles (Miniño, 2010). Alcohol often is involved in accidental deaths. Alcohol-related motor vehicle accidents are the leading cause of death for 15- to 24-year-olds. Alcohol frequently is implicated in other causes of accidental death or injury, including drowning and falling (Miniño, 2010).

Adolescents who are poor and who live in urban areas of high population density have the greatest risk of death by homicide (Miniño, 2010). African American adolescents are more likely than European American adolescents to live under these conditions. Therefore, it is not surprising that the homicide rate is greater among African American adolescents. Homicide is the leading cause of death in 15- to 19-year-old African American males, whereas accidents are the major cause of death for European American teens (Miniño, 2010). African American adolescents, ages 15–19, are nearly 10 times as likely as their

European American agemates to be murdered. Females are not exempt from this pattern. African American females, ages 15–19, are more than five times as likely as their European American counterparts to be victims of homicide. The figures for Latin American adolescents are lower than those for African American youth but higher than those for European Americans (Miniño, 2010).

How Much Sleep Do Adolescents Need?

It might seem that adolescents sleep around the clock, especially on weekends, but adolescents need about 8½–9¼ hours of sleep per night (National Sleep Foundation, 2012b). On weekends, therefore, many adolescents are trying to catch up on their sleep.

Research shows that many, if not most, American adolescents experience sleep deprivation, defined as 6 or fewer hours of sleep per night (Hagenauer et al., 2009; Roberts et al., 2009). Getting enough sleep is a biological need, important for coping with the rapid biological changes of puberty, but surveys show that most teenagers average less than 7 hours of sleep per school night and report feeling tired at school and during extracurricular activities (National Sleep Foundation, 2012b). Teenagers find it difficult to get enough sleep due to hectic schedules with after-school jobs and activities, homework, family obligations, and evening (or late night!) emailing, texting, and chatting with friends. Changes in the brain also tend to push back the clock for adolescents—a change called a *phase delay*—so that they prefer to go to bed later than they did as children. However, school usually begins early in the morning, so parents may push the adolescent to get to bed early. Ironically, the typical adolescent's natural time to go to sleep might be 11 P.M. or even later. Teenagers may thus feel wide awake at an imposed bedtime, even if they are exhausted. Moreover, they are compelled to wake up when their bodies are arguing that it is the middle of the night and they have not had enough sleep to feel rested and alert. As a result, many adolescents have trouble paying attention in school, solving problems, retaining information, and coping with stress. Sleep deprivation also poses a heightened risk for automobile accidents, irritability, depression, and poor impulse control.

What Are the Nutritional Needs of Adolescents? What Do Adolescents Actually Eat?

Physical growth occurs more rapidly in the adolescent years than at any other time after birth, with the exception of the first year of life. To fuel the adolescent growth spurt, the average girl, depending on her activity level, needs to consume 1,800–2,400 calories per day and the average boy needs 2,200–3,200 (Nutrition Facts, 2012). The nutritional needs of adolescents vary according to their stage of pubertal development. For example, at the peak of their growth spurt, adolescents use twice as much calcium, iron, zinc, magnesium, and nitrogen as they do during the other years of adolescence (Nutrition Facts, 2013). Calcium intake is particularly important for females to build up their bone density and help prevent **osteoporosis**, a progressive loss of bone, later in life. Osteoporosis affects millions of women, particularly after **menopause**. But most teenagers—both girls and boys—do not consume enough calcium.

Adolescents also are likely to obtain less vitamin A, thiamine, and iron but more fat, sugar, protein, and sodium than recommended (USDA, 2015). One problem is that potatoes dominate the vegetable intake of adolescents (Kimmons et al., 2009). If these were sweet potatoes or baked potatoes, the problem would not be so severe. However, adolescents—like many adults—are likely to eat French fries, which are fried in oil. Most adolescents eat few other vegetables, especially dark green and

osteoporosis A condition involving the progressive loss of bone tissue.

menopause The cessation of menstruation, typically occurring between ages 48 and 52.

SCHOOLS AND ADOLESCENT NUTRITION

The Centers for Disease Control and Prevention notes the following:

- Schools are in a unique position to promote healthy eating and help ensure appropriate food and nutrient intake among students. Schools provide students with opportunities to consume an array of foods and beverages throughout the school day and enable students to learn about and practice healthy eating behaviors.

- Schools should ensure that only nutritious and appealing foods and beverages are provided in school cafeterias, vending machines, snack bars, school stores, and other venues that offer food and beverages to students. In addition, nutrition education should be part of a comprehensive school health education curriculum.

Source: Nutrition Facts. (2012). Centers for Disease Control and Prevention. http://www.cdc.gov/healthyyouth/nutrition/facts.htm.

orange vegetables and legumes (Kimmons et al., 2009). Adolescents' intake of fruit is often limited to fruit juice, most often orange juice, which does have vitamin C but which is also high in calories.

Adolescents often skip breakfast, especially girls who are watching their weight (Wennberg et al., 2015). Teenagers are more likely to miss meals or eat away from home than they were in childhood. They may consume large amounts of fast food and junk food, which are high in fat and calories but not very nutritious (Wennberg et al., 2015). About 8% of adolescents are overweight, and another 17% are severely overweight (obese) (Ogden et al., 2014). Junk food is connected with being overweight, and being overweight in adolescence can lead to chronic illness and earlier death in adulthood, even for teens who later lose weight (Alamian & Paradis, 2012; Wang et al., 2015). Overweight adolescents are more likely than adolescents of normal weight to experience heart disease, strokes, and cancer as adults (Wang et al., 2015).

14.6 Eating Disorders: When Dieting Turns Deadly

The American ideal has slimmed down to where most American females of "average" weight (we are not talking here about those who are overweight!) are dissatisfied with the size and shape of their bodies (Miyake et al., 2010; Tiggeman, 2014; Tiggeman & Slater, 2013). The wealthier your family, the more unhappy you are likely to be with your body (Polivy et al., 2005). Sixty to 80% of college women have dieted at some time during the past 5 years (Fayet et al., 2012). In one sample of college females, 78% had a healthy body mass index, yet 43% were dieting and another 32% were struggling to avoid gaining weight (Fayet et al., 2012). It is clear, then, that dieting has become the normal way of eating for most U.S. adolescent females (Polivy et al., 2005). Plumpness has been valued in many preliterate societies, and Western paintings from earlier centuries suggest that there was a time when physically well-rounded women were the ideal. But in contemporary Western culture, slim is in (Polivy et al., 2005).

Adolescents are highly concerned about their bodies. Puberty brings rapid changes, and adolescents wonder what they will look like once the flood of hormones has ebbed. In Chapter 15, we will learn that adolescents tend to think that others are paying a great deal of attention to their appearance. Because of the cultural emphasis on slimness and the psychology of the adolescent, adolescents—especially girls—are highly vulnerable to eating disorders.

The eating disorders anorexia nervosa and bulimia nervosa are characterized by gross disturbances in patterns of eating.

What Is Anorexia Nervosa?

There's a saying, "You can never be too rich or too thin." The part about being too thin isn't true. Consider the case of Rachel:

> I wanted to be a runner. Runners were thin and I attributed this to dieting, not training. So I began restricting my diet: No butter, red meat, pork, dessert, candy, or snacking. If I ate any of the forbidden items, I obsessed about it and felt guilty for days.
>
> As a high school freshman, I wanted to run with the fastest girls so I trained hard, really hard, and ate less. Lunch was lettuce sandwiches, carrots, and an apple. By my senior year, I was number three on the team and lunch was a bagel and an orange.
>
> I maintained a rigid schedule—running cross country and track, having a seat on Student Council, volunteering, and maintaining a 3.9 GPA throughout high school—while starving myself (1,000 calories per day), trying to attain the impossible perfection I thought couldn't be far away if I only slimmed down a little bit more.
>
> Several teammates were concerned, but I shrugged them off, saying family members were tall and slender; I was a health nut; I didn't like fatty foods; I was a vegetarian; I didn't like sweets; I wasn't hungry; I wasn't starving.
>
> A psychiatrist didn't help at all. I went in, sat on the couch, and told her what she wanted to hear: I would eat more, run less, stop restricting myself, and quit obsessing about being thin. I was very good at knowing exactly what to tell others.
>
> I dropped 10 pounds my freshman year—from 125 to 115 pounds. I was 5 feet, 8 inches tall and wore a size 5. I hated my body, so I starved myself and ran like a mad woman.
>
> In quiet moments, I was sad and worried about what might be going on inside me.
>
> I was already taking birth control to regain my menstrual cycle; my weight was 15% below what was recommended for my height; I was always cold; I had chest pains and an irregular heartbeat; my hair was limp and broke off; my skin was colorless.
>
> It wasn't until I came to the University of Iowa and joined the varsity women's cross country team that I began to see what I was doing to myself. A teammate had an eating problem. Every time I saw her, I felt sick to my stomach. She had sunken cheeks, eyes so big they swallowed her face. She was an excellent student and a college-level varsity athlete. Many people wondered at her determination, but I understood. She used the same excuses I did.
>
> For one sick instant, I wondered if I would be happier if I were that thin. That is when I started to realize I was slowly killing myself.
>
> At the urging of my coach, I saw the team nutritionist, who recommended a psychiatrist who felt no pity for me and made me take a brutally honest look at who I was and why I was starving myself. She didn't accept any of my excuses. She helped me realize that there are other things to think about besides food and body image. About this time, I decided to quit the cross country team. The pressure I felt to be thin and competition at the

college level were too much when I needed to focus on getting well.

After 2 months of therapy, my weight had dropped again. I'm not sure how far because I refused to step on a scale, but my size-5 pants were falling off. My psychiatrist required weekly weigh-ins.

I wasn't putting into practice any of the things my nutritionist and counselor suggested. They told me that if I wanted to have children someday, I needed to eat. They warned me of osteoporosis at age 30. Then my psychiatrist scared me to death. She told me I needed to start eating more or I would be checked into the hospital and hooked up to an IV. That would put me on the same level as my Iowa teammate. I had looked at her with such horror and never realized that I was in the same position.

My psychiatrist asked how my family would feel if they had to visit me in the hospital because I refused to eat. It was enough to make me think hard the next time I went through the food service lines.

Of course, I didn't get better the next day. But it was a step in the right direction. It's taken me 3 years to get where I am now. At 5 foot, 8¾ inches (I even grew as I got healthier), and 145 pounds, I look and feel healthier, have better eating and exercise habits, and don't obsess about food as much as I used to. On rare occasions, I think about controlling my food intake. My eating disorder will haunt me for the rest of my life. If I'm not careful, it could creep back.

—Rachel (Ballweg, 2001)

Cultura Creative (RF)/Photostock-Israel/Alamy

Seeking Out Remaining Pockets of Fat Is this teenager at risk of developing an eating disorder? While other people, including her parents, are concerned about this teenager's weight loss, the girl herself, influenced by popular media and the ideals of her friends, is searching out remaining pockets of fat.

Rachel was diagnosed with **anorexia nervosa**, a life-threatening eating disorder characterized by extreme fear of being too heavy, dramatic weight loss, a distorted body image, and resistance to eating enough to reach or maintain a healthful weight. Rachel, like other people with anorexia nervosa, weighed less than 85% of her desirable body weight, and "desirable" body weights are already too slender for many individuals. Anorexia nervosa afflicts males as well as females, but females with eating disorders outnumber males. Most studies put the female-to-male ratio at 10 to 1 or higher, but some find a smaller gender difference (Stice et al., 2013a). By and large, anorexia nervosa afflicts women during adolescence and young adulthood (Stice et al., 2013a). The typical person with anorexia is a young European American female of higher socioeconomic status (Striegel-Moore et al, 2003). Affluent females have greater access to fitness centers and health clubs and are more likely to read the magazines that idealize slender bodies and to shop in the boutiques that cater to females with svelte figures. All in all, they are regularly confronted with unrealistically high standards of slimness that make them extremely unhappy with their own physiques (Tiggeman, 2014). Female athletes are also at risk. The *female athlete triad* describes women who have low availability of energy (as from eating poorly), menstrual problems, and lessened bone density, which usually afflicts people in late adulthood (House et al., 2013; Mountjoy & Goolsby, 2015).

Adolescents with anorexia nervosa can drop 25% or more of their weight within a year. Severe weight loss triggers abnormalities in the endocrine system (i.e., with hormones) that prevent ovulation (Dempfle et al., 2013). General health declines. Problems arise in the respiratory system and the cardiovascular system (Mehler & Brown, 2015; see Table 14.3 ●). Females with anorexia are at risk for premature development of osteoporosis (Mehler & Brown, 2015). The mortality rate for anorexic females is about 4–5%.

anorexia nervosa An eating disorder characterized by irrational fear of weight gain, distorted body image, and severe weight loss.

TABLE 14.3

Medical Complications of Anorexia Nervosa

Cardiovascular	Endocrine and Metabolic
Bradycardia and hypotension	Amenorrhea
Mitral valve prolapse	Infertility
Sudden death—arrhythmia	Osteoporosis
Dermatological	Thyroid abnormalities
Dry skin	Hypercortisolemia
Alopecia	Hypoglycemia
Lanugo hair	Diabetes
Gastrointestinal	Arrested growth
Constipation	**Neurological**
Pancreatitis	Cerebral atrophy
Hepatitis	**Pulmonary**
Dysphagia	Pneumonia
	Respiratory failure
	Emphysema

Source: Adapted from Mehler & Brown (2015). *Journal of Eating Disorders*, 3(11), Table 1.

TRUTH OR FICTION REVISITED: Most teens are not worried about the prospect of having a fat bank account, but one can certainly be too skinny, as was Rachel. Adolescents with anorexia nervosa can shed 25% of their body weight.

In one common pattern, the girl sees that she has gained some weight after menarche, and she resolves that she must lose it. But even after the weight is gone, she maintains her pattern of dieting and, in many cases, exercises at a fever pitch (Shroff et al., 2006). The patterns continue as she plunges toward her desirable weight—according to weight charts—and even after those who care about her tell her she is becoming all skin and bones. Denial is a huge part of anorexia nervosa. Anorexic girls deny that they are losing too much weight. They deny any health problems, pointing to their feverish exercise routines as evidence. Distortion of the body image is a major feature of the disorder. Others see anorexic females as skin and bones, whereas anorexic women fix their gaze in the mirror and believe they are looking at a body that is too heavy.

What Is Bulimia Nervosa?

Nicole awakens in her cold dark room and already wishes it was time to go back to bed. She dreads the thought of going through this day, which will be like so many others in her recent past. She asks herself the question every morning, "Will I be able to make it through the day without being totally obsessed by thoughts of food, or will I blow it again and spend the day [binge eating]?" She tells herself that today she will begin a new life, today she will start to live like a normal human being. However, she is not at all convinced that the choice is hers.
—Boskind-White & White (1983, p. 29)

So, does Nicole begin a new life today? No. Despite her pledge to herself, Nicole begins the day with eggs and toast—butter included. Then she downs cookies; bagels smothered with cream cheese, butter, and jelly; doughnuts; candy bars; bowlfuls of cereal and milk—all in less than an hour. When her body cries "No more!" she turns to the next step: purging. Purging also is a routine. In the bathroom, she ties back her hair. She runs the shower to mask noise, drinks some water, and makes herself throw everything up. Afterward she makes another pledge to herself: "Starting tomorrow, I'm going to change." Will she change? In truth, she doubts it.

Bulimia nervosa, Nicole's eating disorder, is characterized by recurrent cycles of binge eating and purging. Binge eating often follows on the heels of dieting (Martire et al., 2015; Osborn et al., 2013). There are various methods of purging. Vomiting is common. Other avenues include strict dieting or fasting, laxatives, and demanding exercise regimes. Individuals with eating disorders will not settle for less than their idealized body shape and weight (Chang et al., 2014; Wade et al., 2015). Bulimia, like anorexia, is connected with irregular menstrual cycles (Mendelsohn & Warren, 2010) and tends to afflict women during adolescence and young adulthood (Wade et al., 2015). Eating disorders are upsetting and dangerous in themselves, and they are also connected with depression (Erikson et al., 2014; Stice et al., 2013b).

> **TRUTH OR FICTION REVISITED:** It is true that some college women—and other young women—control their weight by going on cycles of binge eating followed by self-induced vomiting. This pattern of eating and purging describes bulimia nervosa.

What Are the Origins of Eating Disorders?

According to some psychoanalysts, anorexia nervosa may reflect a young woman's efforts to cope with sexual fears, especially the possibility of becoming pregnant. They interpret the female's behavior as an attempt to regress to prepubescence. Anorexia nervosa prevents some adolescents from separating from their families and assuming adult responsibilities. Their breasts and hips flatten once more because of the loss of fatty tissue. In the adolescent's fantasies, perhaps, she remains a sexually undifferentiated child.

Many parents are obsessed with encouraging their children—especially their infants—to eat adequately. Thus, some observers suggest that children may refuse to eat as a way of battling with their parents. ("You have to eat something!" "I'm not hungry!") It often seems that warfare does occur in the families of adolescents with eating disorders. Parents in such families are often unhappy and have their own issues with eating and dieting (Tan & Holub, 2015).

A particularly disturbing risk factor for eating disorders in adolescent females is a history of child abuse, particularly sexual abuse, although the extent to which childhood sexual abuse is connected with eating disorders is not fully clear (Leung et al., 2010). One study found the connection to be weak (Mitchell & Bulik, 2013). Another study found a history of childhood sexual abuse in about half of women with bulimia nervosa, compared to a rate of about 7% among women who do not have the disorder (Deep et al., 1999). Emily Dworkin and her colleagues (2014) investigated the relationship between childhood sexual abuse and the development of eating disorders in a sample of 649 college undergraduates. They found that the experience of sexual abuse often contributed to difficulties among the victims of regulating their control over their own behavior, leading to the development of the traits of impulsivity and compulsivity. In this sample, failure to regulate one's behavior often led to binge eating and to maladaptive methods of attempting to control one's weight, such as purging by vomiting or use of laxatives.

Certainly, young women have a very slender social ideal set before them in women who act in television and movies, and who model clothing (Prendergast

bulimia nervosa An eating disorder characterized by cycles of binge eating and vomiting as a means of controlling weight gain.

et al., 2015). Miss America, the annually renewed American role model, has also become more slender over the years. The pageant began in 1922. Over the past 80 years, the winner has added 2% in height but has lost 12 pounds. In the 1920s, Miss America's weight relative to her height yielded a body mass index (BMI) of 20–25. This is considered normal by the World Health Organization (WHO), which labels people as malnourished when their BMIs are lower than 18.5. However, recent Miss Americas come in at a BMI near 17 (Rubinstein & Caballero, 2000). So Miss America adds to the woes of "normal" young women and even to those of young women who hover near the WHO "malnourished" borderline. As the cultural ideal slenderizes, women with desirable body weights, according to the health charts, feel overweight, and overweight women feel gargantuan (Harrison, 2013; Tiggeman, 2014).

Many individuals with eating disorders, such as Rachel, are involved in activities that demand weight limits, such as dancing, acting, and modeling (Devlin & Steinglass, 2014). Gym enthusiasts and male wrestlers also feel the pressure to stay within an "acceptable" weight range. Men, like women, experience pressure to create an ideal body, one with power in the upper torso and a trim abdomen.

Eating disorders tend to run in families, which raises the possibility of genetic involvement (Dodge & Simic, 2015; Halmi et al., 2014). Genetic factors do not directly cause eating disorders, but they appear to involve obsessionistic and perfectionistic personality traits (Halmi et al., 2014). In a society in which so much attention is focused on the ideal of the slender body, these personality traits encourage dieting. Anorexia also often co-occurs with depression (Green et al., 2009). Perfectionistic people are likely to be disappointed in themselves, giving rise to feelings of depression. But it may also be that both anorexia and depression share genetic factors. Genetically inspired perfectionism, cultural emphasis on slimness, self-absorption, and family conflict may create a perfect recipe for the development of eating disorders.

How Do We Treat and Prevent Eating Disorders?

Treatment of eating disorders—particularly anorexia nervosa—is a great challenge (Stice et al., 2015). The disorders are connected with serious health problems, and the low weight of individuals with anorexia is often life-threatening. Some adolescent girls are admitted to the hospital for treatment against their will (Brunner et al., 2005). Denial is a feature of anorexia nervosa, and many girls do not recognize—or do not admit—that they have a problem. When the individual with anorexia does not—or cannot—eat adequately through the mouth, measures such as nasogastric (tube) feeding may be used.

Many different kinds of drugs have been tried in the treatment of eating disorders, and with mixed results (McElroy et al., 2015). Eating disorders are often accompanied by depression, and it may be that the common culprit in eating disorders and depression is a lower-than-normal level of the neurotransmitter serotonin. Antidepressants such as Prozac and Zoloft enhance the activity of serotonin in the brain, often increasing food intake in anorexic individuals and decreasing binge eating in bulimic people. In one study, 10 of 11 anorexic females showed significant weight gain after 14 weeks of treatment with an antidepressant, and they maintained the gain at a 64-week follow-up (Santonastaso et al., 2001). They were also evaluated as being significantly less depressed and perfectionistic. Anti-anxiety drugs and even antipsychotic drugs have been used in an effort to help people with eating disorders to control impulses (McElroy et al., 2015).

Because family problems are commonly connected with eating disorders, family therapy is often used to treat these disorders (Loeb et al., 2015). Family therapy has positive outcomes in many cases, but it is not an appropriate setting for dealing with childhood sexual abuse.

Cognitive behavioral therapy has been used to help anorexic and bulimic individuals challenge their perfectionism and distorted body images. It has also been used to systematically reinforce appropriate eating behavior. But let us remember that all of this is connected with cultural attitudes that idealize excessive thinness. "Prevention" will have to address cultural values as well as potential problems in individual adolescents.

14.7 Substance Use and Substance Use Disorders

The United States is flooded with drugs that can distort your perceptions and change your mood—drugs that can pull you up, let you down, and move you across town. Some of these drugs are legal, others illegal. Some are used recreationally, others medically. Some are safe if used correctly and dangerous if they are not. Some adolescents use drugs because their friends do or because their parents tell them not to. Some are seeking pleasure; others are seeking escape.

Adolescents often become involved with drugs that impair their ability to learn at school and are connected with reckless, or deadly, behavior (Schneider et al., 2012). Alcohol is the most popular drug on high school (and college) campuses (Johnston et al., 2014; see Table 14.4 ●). Nearly half of high school 12th-graders have smoked marijuana (Johnston et al., 2014). Two in five have tried cigarettes. Some use amphetamines or other stimulants, and of these, some use stimulants to help them focus on their studying. Cocaine was once a toy of the well-to-do, but price breaks have brought it into the lockers of high school students.

Alcohol and cigarettes are the most widely used substances by adolescents. Likelihood of use increases from 8th grade through 12th grade (see Table 14.4). Why? One reason is simply that 12th-graders have had more years of opportunity to use drugs. But note that the researchers asked whether students had ever used the drug. Therefore, many "Yes" answers reflect an incident or two of experimentation, and not regular use. Other drugs, like heroin, may be in the news, but they have been used by only about 1% of high schoolers. Johnston and his colleagues (2014) note that parental and societal warnings may be getting through to adolescents because their substance use declined steadily over the past generation. Marijuana is one of the few drugs that has seen an increase in popularity.

Figure 14.7 ■ shows trends in adolescents' self-reported use of various illicit drugs since the 1970s. When we take marijuana out of the picture, substance use dramatically falls off. Use of illicit substances appears to have peaked for 12th-graders in the late 1970s and early 1980s. Again, when we remove marijuana from the situation, it seems that we can say that there have been gradual declines in the use of illicit substances since the early 1980s. Now that marijuana use is legal (for adults) in a number of states, we will see whether adolescent use of marijuana changes.

Where does substance use end and a **substance use disorder** begin? Most health professionals use the *Diagnostic and Statistical Manual of Mental Disorders* (DSM-5) of the American Psychiatric Association (2013) in defining substance use disorders. According to the DSM-5, substance use disorders may develop with repeated use of a substance, according to the manual, leading to changes in "brain circuitry" that are connected with impaired control over use of the substance, social problems, risky behavior (such as reckless driving or "unprotected" sex), and biological factors suggestive of addiction. Some substances can lead to physical addiction; when the dosage is lowered, withdrawal symptoms, also known as **abstinence syndrome**, occur. When addicted individuals lower their intake of alcohol, for example, they may experience symptoms such as tremors (shakes), high blood pressure, rapid heart

F:online digitale Bildagentur GmbH/Alamy

Substance Use and Substance Use Disorders It is important to distinguish between the use of a substance and a substance use disorder. Many adolescents occasionally experiment with substances such as alcohol and marijuana.

substance use disorder A persistent pattern of use of a substance characterized by craving of the substance and impairment of physical, social, and/or emotional well-being.

abstinence syndrome A characteristic cluster of symptoms that results from a sudden decrease in the level of usage of a substance.

● TABLE 14.4
"Have You Ever Used . . . ?"

Drug	Grade	Percent if 8th, 10th and 12th graders saying "yes": Percent
Alcohol	8	27.8%
	10	52.1%
	12	68.2%
Amphetamines	8	4.2%
	10	8.1%
	12	12.4%
Cigarettes*	8	14.8%
	10	25.7%
	12	38.1%
Cocaine	8	1.7%
	10	3.3%
	12	4.5%
Ecstasy	8	1.8%
	10	5.7%
	12	7.1%
LSD	8	1.4%
	10	2.7%
	12	3.9%
Marijuana	8	16.5%
	10	35.8%
	12	45.5%

*Does not include e-cigarettes
Source: L.D. Johnston, P.M. O'Malley, R.A. Meich, J.G. Bachman, & J. Schulenberg (2014). *Monitoring the future. National survey results on drug use 1975–2013: Overview, key findings on adolescent drug use.* Ann Arbor: Institute for Social Research, the University of Michigan, Table 5.

and pulse rate, anxiety, restlessness, and weakness. Three of the most common types of abused substances are depressants, stimulants, and hallucinogens.

What Are the Effects of Depressants?

Depressants slow the activity of the nervous system. Depressants include alcohol, narcotics derived from the opium poppy (such as heroin, morphine, and codeine), and **sedatives** (such as barbiturates and methaqualone).

Alcohol lessens inhibitions so that drinkers may do things when drinking that they might otherwise resist (Winograd & Sher, 2015). Alcohol is also an intoxicant: It distorts perceptions, impairs concentration, hinders coordination, and slurs the speech. Alcohol use is most prevalent among 21- to 34-year-olds. More than 1 million students between the ages of 18 and 24 are accidentally injured each year

sedatives Drugs that soothe or quiet restlessness or agitation.

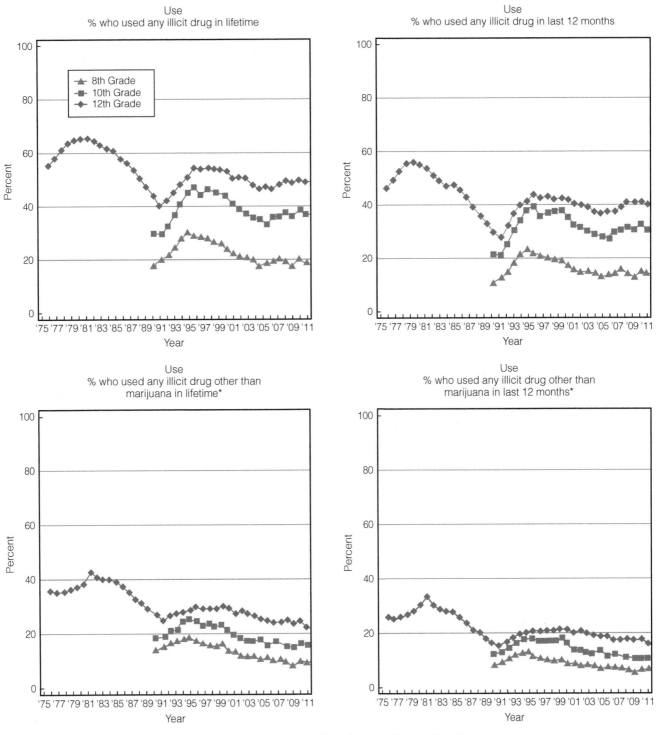

Figure 14.7 ■ **Use of Any Illicit Drug and Any Illicit Drug Other than Marijuana: Trends in Lifetime and Annual Use for 8th-, 10th-, and 12th-Graders**
Source: Johnston et al. (2015).

while under the influence, assaulted by other students who have been drinking, or raped by college men who have been drinking.

The major medical use of heroin, morphine, and other opioids is relief from pain. But they also can provide a euphoric "rush." Heroin is addictive, and regular users develop **tolerance**. *Barbiturates* are depressants with various legitimate medical uses, such as relief from pain, anxiety, and tension, but people can become rapidly dependent on them.

tolerance Habituation to a drug such that increasingly higher doses are needed to achieve similar effects.

What Are the Effects of Stimulants?

Stimulants speed up the heartbeat and other bodily functions. Nicotine, cocaine, and amphetamines are the most common stimulants. Nicotine is the addictive chemical in tobacco (Brody, 2014). Nearly 450,000 Americans die from smoking-related problems each year (American Lung Association, 2015). Cigarette smoke contains carbon monoxide, which causes shortness of breath, and hydrocarbons ("tars"). Smoking is responsible for most respiratory diseases and lung cancer. E-cigarettes contain nicotine, but not the hydrocarbons (Brody, 2014).

Cocaine

The stimulant cocaine accelerates the heart rate, spikes the blood pressure, constricts the arteries of the heart, and thickens the blood, a combination that can cause cardiovascular and respiratory collapse (Liaudet et al., 2014). Overdoses can cause restlessness, insomnia, tremors, and even death. Amphetamines can keep users awake for long periods and reduce their appetites. Tolerance for amphetamines develops rapidly. The powerful amphetamine called methamphetamine is apparently physically addictive (Shoptaw, 2014). Methamphetamine abuse can cause brain damage, leading to problems in learning and memory.

hallucinogenics Substances that giver rise to perceptual distortions.

What Are the Effects of Hallucinogenics?

Hallucinogenics give rise to perceptual distortions called hallucinations, which sometimes can be so strong as to be confused with reality. Marijuana, Ecstasy, LSD,

A Closer Look   Diversity

GENDER, COLLEGE PLANS, ETHNICITY, AND SUBSTANCE ABUSE

There is a lot of variation in the prevalence of substance abuse among adolescents. The Institute for Social Research at the University of Michigan has regularly asked high school seniors whether they have used various substances within the past year (the annual prevalence), as well as a variety of questions about alcohol and cigarettes. For every substance assessed, adolescent males are more likely than adolescent females to have used or abused the substance (L. D. Johnston et al., 2011). This finding holds for both widely abused substances, such as alcohol and marijuana, and more rarely used substances, such as heroin and crack. Plans to complete 4 years of college appear to have a restraining effect on substance abuse. Seniors who anticipate at least 4 more years of schooling are less likely to engage in substance abuse than seniors who plan no further schooling or less than 4 years of further schooling. The difference in cigarette smoking is most salient.

TRUTH OR FICTION REVISITED: Substance abuse is highest among European American 12th-graders. African American teenagers are least likely to report substance abuse.

Reflect

- Why do you think that adolescent males are more likely than adolescent females to report engaging in substance abuse?

- Why do you think that plans to attend college for 4 years might have a restraining effect on substance abuse among 12th-graders?

- Are you surprised by the relationship between substance abuse and ethnicity? Why or why not?

- Is it possible that the worst adolescent substance abusers were not in the group sampled by the Institute for Social Research? Explain.

- Can you think of any reasons why adolescents in the sample might have been motivated to misrepresent their behavior? Explain.

and PCP are hallucinogenic drugs. Marijuana, which is typically smoked, helps users relax, elevates their mood, increases sensory awareness, and can induce visual hallucinations; for example, time seeming to slow down. Marijuana carries health risks such as impairing the perceptual–motor coordination and short-term memory (Ratzan, 2014). Regular users may experience withdrawal, which is a sign of addiction (American Psychiatric Association, 2013).

Ecstasy, a popular "party" drug, provides the boost of a stimulant and mild hallucinogenic effects. The combination appears to free users from inhibitions and awareness of the consequences of risky behavior, such as unprotected sex. Ecstasy can also impair working memory, increase anxiety, and lead to depression. LSD is the acronym for lysergic acid diethylamide, another hallucinogenic drug. PCP, acronym for phencyclidine (and also known as "Angel Dust"), is another commonly used hallucinogenic drug. High doses of hallucinogenics can impair coordination and judgment (driving while using hallucinogenic drugs poses grave risks), change the mood, and cause paranoid delusions.

What Factors Are Associated with Substance Use and Substance Use Disorders?

Adolescents often become involved with substance use through experimental use (Whitbeck & Armenta, 2015). Some are conforming to peer pressure; acceptance by peers means doing what peers do. Some are rebelling against moral or social constraints. Others are in it for the experience. Of these, some are simply curious; they want to see what effects the drugs will have. Others are trying to escape from boredom or from the pressures of school or the neighborhood. Some, of course, are looking for pleasure or excitement. Some youngsters are imitating what they see their own parents doing.

Social cognitive theorists suggest that children and adolescents usually try drugs because someone has recommended them or because they have observed someone else using them. But whether or not they continue to use the drug depends on factors such as whether use is reinforced by peer approval. The drug can also be reinforcing by enhancing the user's mood or by reducing unpleasant emotions such as anxiety and tension. For individuals who are addicted, prevention of the abstinence syndrome is reinforcing. Carrying the substance and obtaining a "rainy day" supply are reinforcing because the child or adolescent does not have to worry about being caught short.

Why, you may wonder, do children and adolescents use drugs when their health education courses inform them that drugs are harmful? Don't they believe their

A Closer Look

Real LIFE

VAPING: THE ADVENT OF E-CIGARETTES

Fortunately or unfortunately, e-cigarettes have now arrived on the scene. E-cigarettes have no tobacco, and thus no hydrocarbons, or tars. Instead they have batteries and a heating element that produces a vapor that is inhaled. The vapor contains nicotine, which is as addictive as the nicotine in cigarettes. Other contents of the vapors are not always disclosed. But they come in hundreds of flavors, including milk chocolate cream and bubble gum, flavors that have an obvious appeal to youth. The *Monitoring the Future* survey (Johnston et al., 2014) reports that in the year 2014, more teenagers used e-cigarettes than cigarettes made of tobacco during the past 30 days (see Table 14.5 ●). For 8th- and 10th-graders, in fact, use of e-cigarettes was more than double the incidence of using tobacco cigarettes. Although e-cigarettes likely do not carry the cancer risk of regular cigarettes, their nicotine is just as addictive, and may serve as an entry point to smoking cigarettes made of tobacco (Nocera, 2015). Eighth- through 12th-graders consider e-cigarettes to be less risky than regular cigarettes, but given the number of users and the long-term unknowns, the accuracy of their assessment of the risk remains to be seen.

Vaping: An Adolescent with an E-Cigarette
E-cigarettes may not possess the hydrocarbons ("tars") we find in tobacco cigarettes, but they are addictive sources of nicotine.

The warnings about the dangers of smoking tobacco appear to have filtered through successfully to adolescents, because 80% to 90% of 8th- through 12th-graders see a "great risk" in smoking a pack or more of cigarettes a day. But the use of e-cigarettes is mushrooming. It seems that the warnings about the nicotine in e-cigarettes and the unknowns about the vapors have yet to be honed accurately or adequately transmitted.

● TABLE 14.5

Comparison of Incidence of Use of E-Cigarettes and Tobacco Cigarettes During Past 30 Days for 8th-, 10th-, and 12th-Graders

	8th-Graders	10th-Graders	12th-Graders
E-Cigarettes	8.7%	16.2%	17.1%
Tobacco Cigarettes	4%	7.2%	13.6%

Source: Johnston et al. (2014), p. 44.

Reflect

- Have you tried e-cigarettes? How did you pick a flavor?
- Have you heard about the addictiveness of e-cigarettes? Has it influenced your decision as to whether to try them?
- What are the laws in your locale about who can use e-cigarettes? Are they enforced?

teachers? Some do; some don't. But the reinforcement value of the substances occurs now, today. The harmful effects are frequently long-term, or theoretical.

Associating with peers who use drugs and who tolerate drug use is one of the strongest predictors of adolescent substance use and substance use disorders (Ozer et al., 2015). Children are highly vulnerable to peer pressure in the early teen years. If they are closely involved with a drug-abusing group, they may feel pressured to join in. Adolescents who are extensively involved with peers, especially to the exclusion of their families, are at greater risk for drug use.

Parenting styles play a role. Having open lines of communication with a parent helps inhibit drug use. The authoritative pattern of child rearing appears to protect children from substance abuse (Newman et al., 2008; Vermeulen-Smit et al., 2015). Heavy drug use is most likely to occur in families that have parents with permissive or neglecting–rejecting parenting styles.

Adolescent drug users often experience school problems. They do poorly in school, and their academic motivation is low (Dunn & Mezzich, 2007). Certain psychological characteristics are associated with drug use, including anxiety and depression, antisocial behavior, and low self-esteem (Ali et al., 2015; Donohue et al., 2006).

Biological factors are apparently involved in determining which experimenters will continue to use a drug and which will not. Children may inherit genetic predispositions toward abuse of specific substances, including depressants, stimulants, and hallucinogenics (Agrawal et al., 2010; Dick et al., 2009; Farrer et al., 2009; Kuo et al., 2010). For example, the biological children of alcoholics who are reared by adoptive parents are more likely to abuse alcohol than are the biological children of the adoptive parents.

How Do We Treat and Prevent Substance Abuse?

Health professionals, educators, police departments, and laypeople have devised many approaches to the prevention and treatment of substance use disorders among adolescents. However, treatment has been a frustrating endeavor, and it is not clear which approaches are most effective. In many cases, adolescents with drug dependence really do not want to discontinue the substances they are abusing. Many are referred to treatment by parents or school systems, but they deny the negative impact of drugs on their lives. They may belong to a peer group that frowns on prevention or treatment programs (Hogue et al., 2014). When addicted adolescents come for treatment, helping them through a withdrawal syndrome may be straightforward enough. But once their bodies no longer require the substance to feel "normal," they may return to the social milieu that fosters substance abuse and be unable to find strong reasons for living a life without drugs (Hogue et al., 2014). The problem of returning to abuse and dependence following treatment—that is, the problem of relapse—can thus be more troublesome than the problems involved in initial treatment.

Many adolescents with substance abuse problems also have psychological disorders or serious family problems. When treatment programs focus only on substance abuse and do little to treat the psychological disorder or relationships in the family, the outcome of treatment tends to suffer.

The ability of teenagers to deal with the physical changes of adolescence and to engage in health-promoting behaviors depends in part on their growing cognitive abilities. We will examine development in that area in Chapter 15.

Section Review

17. Death rates are higher for _____ (male or female?) adolescents.

18. Most adolescent deaths are due to _____.

19. _____ is a life-threatening eating disorder characterized by intense fear of being overweight, a distorted body image, and refusal to eat.

20. Bulimia nervosa is characterized by recurrent cycles of binge eating followed by _____.

21. Anorexia nervosa and bulimia nervosa _____ (do or do not?) tend to run in families.

22. Eating disorders are related to traits such as _____.

23. Substance _____ is the repeated use of a substance despite the fact that it is causing or compounding social, occupational, psychological, or physical problems.

24. Substance dependence is characterized by loss of control over use of the substance, tolerance, and a(n) _____ syndrome.

25. _____ is the substance most commonly used by adolescents.

26. _____ is the agent that creates physiological dependence on tobacco.

Reflect & Relate: How widespread were eating disorders and substance abuse in your own high school? Did you notice gender differences in the rates of these two problems? How did these problems begin? What are some ways in which parents and educators might help adolescents avoid them?

Chapter Review

14.1 What Is Adolescence?

Adolescence is a transitional period between childhood and adulthood. G. Stanley Hall believed that adolescence is marked by "storm and stress." Current views challenge the idea that storm and stress are normal or beneficial.

14.2 What Is Puberty?

Puberty is a stage of physical development that is characterized by reaching sexual maturity. Puberty is controlled by a feedback loop involving glands. Sex hormones trigger the development of primary and secondary sex characteristics. Girls spurt sooner than boys. Boys tend to spurt up to 4 inches per year, and girls up to 3 inches per year. During their growth spurts, boys catch up with girls and grow taller and heavier. Boys' shoulders become broader, and girls develop broader and rounder hips. More of a male's body weight is made of muscle. Adolescents may look gawky because of asynchronous growth. Boys typically ejaculate by age 13 or 14. Female sex hormones regulate the menstrual cycle. The effects of early maturation are generally positive for boys and are often negative for girls. Early-maturing boys tend to be more popular. Early-maturing girls become conspicuous, often leading them to make sexual approaches, engage in deviant behavior, and have a poor body image. Girls are generally more dissatisfied with their bodies than boys are. By age 18, dissatisfaction tends to decline.

14.3 How Does the Brain Develop During Adolescence?

Brain developments reflect genetic and environmental influences. There is general thickening of the cortex and some pruning. Cortical thickening also occurs in areas "exercised" by experience, such as practicing a musical instrument. The amygdala seems to lose "influence" as the prefrontal cortex (and executive function) increases in prominence.

14.4 What Risk Factors Are Connected with Adolescents' Contracting Sexually Transmitted Infections?

Sexually transmitted infections (STIs) include bacterial infections such as chlamydia, gonorrhea, and syphilis; viral infections such as HIV/AIDS, HPV, and genital herpes; and some others. The risk factors include sexual activity with multiple partners, sexual activity without condoms, and substance abuse. Sharing hypodermic needles with an infected person can also transmit HIV. Prevention of STIs involves education about STIs, along with advice concerning abstinence or "safer sex."

14.5 How Healthy Are Adolescents?

Most American adolescents are healthy, but about one in five has a serious health problem. Most adolescents' health problems stem from their lifestyles. Death rates are higher for older adolescents and for male adolescents. Accidents, suicides, and homicides account for about three in four deaths among adolescents. Adolescents require 8½–9¼ hours of sleep per night, but because of a phase delay in sleep and the need to rise early for school, many adolescents are sleep-deprived. The average adolescent girl needs about 2,200 calories per day, and the average boy needs about 3,000 calories. Adolescents need large amounts of elements such as calcium, iron, zinc, magnesium, and nitrogen. Adolescents usually need more vitamins than they take in but less sugar, fat, protein, and sodium.

14.6 What Are the Eating Disorders? Why Are Adolescents at Special Risk of Contracting Them?

Eating disorders include anorexia nervosa and bulimia nervosa. Anorexia nervosa is characterized by fear of being overweight, a distorted body image, and refusal to eat. Bulimia nervosa is characterized by recurrent cycles of binge eating followed by purging. Eating disorders mainly afflict females. Some psychoanalysts suggest that anorexia is an effort to remain prepubescent. One risk factor for eating disorders in adolescent females is a history of child abuse. Eating disorders may develop because of fear of gaining weight resulting from cultural idealization of the slim female. Genetic factors may connect eating disorders with perfectionistic personality styles.

14.7 Why Do Adolescents Engage in Substance Use and Develop Substance Use Disorders?

Substance abuse is the use of a substance despite the related social, occupational, psychological, or physical problems. Substance dependence is characterized by loss of control over use of the substance and is typified by tolerance and withdrawal symptoms. Depressants are addictive substances that slow the activity of the nervous system. Alcohol lowers inhibitions, relaxes, and intoxicates. Heroin can provide a strong euphoric "rush." Barbiturates relieve anxiety and tension. Stimulants accelerate the heartbeat and other bodily functions and depress the appetite. Nicotine is the stimulant in tobacco. The stimulant cocaine produces euphoria and bolsters self-confidence, but it occasionally causes respiratory and cardiovascular collapse. Adolescents use amphetamines to remain awake for cram sessions. Hallucinogenics give rise to perceptual distortions called hallucinations. Marijuana helps some adolescents relax and elevates the mood, but it impairs perceptual—motor coordination and short-term memory. LSD ("acid") produces vivid hallucinations. About half of high school seniors have tried illicit drugs. Marijuana use seems to be on the rise. Most students have tried alcohol, and many use it regularly. Substance abuse and dependence usually begin with experimental use in adolescence. Adolescents may experiment because of curiosity, conformity to peer pressure, parental use, rebelliousness, or a desire to escape from boredom or pressure and to seek excitement or pleasure. Some individuals may also have a genetic predisposition toward dependence on certain substances. It may be relatively simple to help an adolescent through an abstinence syndrome (the process is called *detoxification*); it is more difficult to prevent relapse.

Key Terms

adolescence   450
genital stage   450
puberty   451
feedback loop   452
hypothalamus   452
pituitary gland   452
primary sex characteristics   452
secondary sex characteristics   452
asynchronous growth   455
secular trend   455

larynx   455
semen   455
nocturnal emission   455
gynecomastia   455
epiphyseal closure   455
mammary glands   457
labia   457
clitoris   457
menarche   457
gray matter   464

HIV/AIDS   466
osteoporosis   472
menopause   472
anorexia nervosa   475
bulimia nervosa   477
substance use disorder   479
abstinence syndrome   479
sedatives   480
tolerance   481
hallucinogenics   482

15

Adolescence: Cognitive Development

Major Topics

Features

TruthorFiction?

 Many adolescents see themselves as being on stage. **p. 493**

It is normal for male adolescents to think of themselves as action heroes and to act as though they are made of steel. **p. 494**

Adolescent boys outperform adolescent girls in mathematics. **p. 497**

It is advisable for parents to help adolescents complete their homework. **p. 498**

 Most adolescents make moral decisions based on their own ethical principles and may choose to disobey the laws of the land if these laws conflict with their principles. **p. 502**

 The transition from elementary school is more difficult for boys than for girls. **p. 506**

 Adolescents who work after school get lower grades. **p. 512**

I am a college student of extremely modest means. Some crazy psychologist interested in something called "formal-operational thought" has just promised to pay me $200 if I can make a coherent, logical argument for the proposition that the federal government should under no circumstances ever give or lend [money] to needy college students. Now, what could people who believe that possibly say by way of supporting that argument? Well, I suppose they could offer this line of reasoning. . . .

—Flavell et al. (2002)

This "college student of extremely modest means" is thinking like an adolescent, quite differently from an elementary school child and from most middle school children. Children in the concrete-operational stage are bound by the facts as they are. They are not given to hypothetical thinking, to speculation about what might be. They are mainly stuck in what is. But the adolescent, like the adult, can ponder abstract ideas and see the world as it could be. Our "college student of extremely modest means" recognizes that a person can find arguments for causes in which he or she does not believe.

In this chapter, we learn about cognitive development in adolescence. We focus first on aspects of intellectual development, including Piaget's stage of formal operations, adolescent egocentrism, and gender differences. We then turn to moral development, focusing on the views of Kohlberg and Gilligan. We conclude with a look at some areas that are strongly tied to cognitive development: school, vocational development, and work experience.

Adrian Sherratt/Alamy

The Adolescent in Thought: My, My, How "Formal"

The growing intellectual capabilities of adolescents change the way they approach the world. The cognitive changes of adolescence influence how adolescents view themselves and their families and friends and how they deal with broader social and moral questions.

What Are Formal Operations? What Happens During Jean Piaget's Stage of Formal Operations?

According to Piaget, adolescents may—but do not always—enter the stage of **formal operations**, which is the highest level of cognitive development in his theory. Adolescents in this stage have reached cognitive maturity, even if some rough edges remain. For many children in developed nations, the stage of formal operations can begin quite early—at about the time of puberty, 11 or 12 years of age. But some children reach this stage somewhat later, and some not at all. Piaget describes the accomplishments of the stage of formal operations in terms of the individual's increased ability to classify objects and ideas, engage in logical thought, and hypothesize, just as researchers make hypotheses in their investigations. The adolescent in the stage of formal operations can think about abstract ideas and about concrete objects. The adolescent can group and classify symbols, statements, even theories—just as we classify certain views of child development as psychoanalytic theories, learning theories, or sociocultural theories, even if they differ quite a bit in their particulars. Formal operations are flexible and reversible. Adolescents are thus capable of following and formulating arguments from their premises to their conclusions and back once more, even if they do not believe in them. Hypothetical thinking, the use of symbols to represent other symbols, and deductive reasoning enable the adolescent to more fully comprehend the real world and to play with the world that dwells within the mind alone.

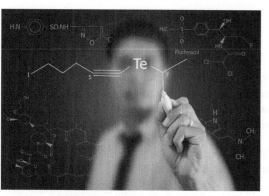

Formal Operations at Work The ability to deal with the abstract and the hypothetical and the capacity to engage in deductive reasoning are the key features of formal-operational thought. Formal-operational thinking allows adolescents to engage in scientific reasoning.

Hypothetical Thinking

In formal-operational thought, adolescents discover that they can think about "what might be" rather than just "what is." Adolescents can project themselves into situations that transcend their immediate experience, and for this reason, they may become wrapped up in lengthy fantasies (Amsel, 2011). Many adolescents can explore endless corridors of the mind, perceiving what would happen as one decision leads to another point where a choice presents itself—and then still another decision is made. Adolescents become aware that situations can have different outcomes. They can think ahead, systematically trying out various possibilities in their minds.

You may think of scientists as people in white lab coats, with advanced degrees and a devotion to exploring uncharted territory. And some are like that, of course. But many more wear blue jeans and experiment with their hair and with ways of relating to people whom they find attractive. Many adolescents in the stage of formal operations do not consider themselves interested in science, yet they conduct research daily to see whether their hypotheses about themselves and their friends and teachers are correct. These are not laboratory experiments that involve calipers or Bunsen burners. It is more common for adolescents to explore uncharted territory by trying on different clothes and "attitudes" to see which work best for them.

Adolescents who can look ahead to multiple outcomes may also see many possibilities for themselves. Some recognize that they can, to a large extent, fashion themselves according to their own images of what they are capable of becoming. In

formal operations The fourth stage in Piaget's cognitive-developmental theory, characterized by the capacity for flexible, reversible operations concerning abstract ideas and concepts, such as symbols, statements, and theories.

terms of career decisions, the wealth of possible directions leads some adolescents to experience anxiety about whether they will pick the career that really *is* them and to experience a sense of loss about the possibility that they may be able to choose only one.

This capacity to look ahead, to fashion futures, also frequently leads to **utopian** thinking. Just as adolescents can foresee many possibilities for themselves, they can also imagine different outcomes for suffering humanity. "What if" thinking enables adolescents to fashion schemes for putting an end to hunger, disease, and international strife.

Sophisticated Use of Symbols

Children in elementary school can understand what is meant by abstract symbols such as 1 and 2. They can also perform operations in which numbers are manipulated—added, subtracted, and so on. But now consider x, that unknown (and sometimes elusive) quantity in algebra. This x may be a familiar letter of the alphabet, but its designation as a symbol for an unknown quantity is a formal abstract operation. One symbol (an x) is being made to stand for something just as abstract (the unknown). Children up to the age of 11 or 12 or so usually cannot fully understand this concept, even if they can be taught the mechanics of solving for x in simple equations. But older, formal-operational children show a sophisticated grasp of the nature of symbols. They can grasp intuitively what is meant by x. Formal-operational children, or adolescents, can perform mental operations with symbols that stand for nothing in their own experience.

These symbols include those used in geometry. Adolescents work with points that have no dimensions, lines that have no width and infinite length, and circles that are perfectly round, even though they may never find them in nature. The ability to manipulate these symbols will eventually enable them to do work in theoretical physics or math or to obtain jobs in engineering or architecture. They learn to apply symbols to the world of tangible objects and materials.

Formal-operational individuals can also understand, appreciate, and sometimes produce metaphors. Metaphors are figures of speech in which words or phrases that ordinarily signify one thing are applied to another. We find metaphor in literature, but consider how everyday figures of speech also enhance our experience: *squeezing out* a living, *basking in the sunshine* of fame or glory, *hanging by a thread, jumping to conclusions,* and so on.

The moral judgments of many adolescents and adults are based on formal-operational thought. That is, they derive their judgments about what is right and wrong in specific situations by reasoning deductively from general moral principles. Their capacity for decentration also allows them to take a broad view of the situation. They can focus on many aspects of a situation at once in making judgments and solving moral dilemmas.

Enhanced cognitive abilities can backfire when adolescents adamantly advance their religious, political, and social ideas without recognizing the subtleties and practical issues that might give pause to adults. For example, let us begin with the premise "Industries should not be allowed to pollute the environment." We then discover that Industry A pollutes the environment. An adolescent may argue to shut down Industry A, at least until it stops polluting. The logic is reasonable and the goal is noble enough, but Industry A may be indispensable to the nation at large, or many thousands of people may be put out of work if it is shut down. Other people might prefer to seek some kind of compromise.

Adolescents' new intellectual powers often present them with what seem to be crystal-clear solutions to the world's problems, and they may become intolerant of the relative stodginess of their parents. Their utopian images of how to reform the world make them unsympathetic to their parents' earthbound pursuit of a livelihood and other mundane matters.

utopian Referring to an ideal vision of society.

THE PUZZLE AND THE PENDULUM

If you hang a weight from a string and set it swinging back and forth, you have a pendulum. Bärbel Inhelder and Jean Piaget (1959) used a pendulum to explore ways in which children of different ages go about solving problems. These investigators showed children several pendulums with different lengths of string and different weights at their ends, as shown in Figure 15.1 ■. They attached the strings to rods and sent the weights swinging. They dropped the weights from various heights and pushed them with different amounts of force. The question they posed—the puzzle—was: What determines how fast the pendulum will swing back and forth?

The young researchers had varied

1. The amount of weight
2. The length of the string
3. The height from which the weight was released
4. The force with which the weight was pushed

The answer lies either in one of these factors or in some combination of them. That is, one factor, two factors, three factors, or all four factors could determine the speed of the pendulum.

One can try to solve this problem by deduction based on principles of physics, and experienced physicists might prefer a deductive, mathematical approach. However, one can also solve the problem by trying out each possible combination of factors and observing the results. This is an empirical approach. Because children (and most adults) are not physicists, they usually take the empirical approach.

Of the children observed by Inhelder and Piaget, those between the ages of 8 and 13 could not arrive at the correct answer. The fault lay largely in their approach, which was only partly systematic. They made some effort to account for the various factors but did not control carefully for every possibility. For example, one child compared a pendulum with a light weight and a short string to a pendulum with a heavy weight and a long string.

The 14- and 15-year-olds generally sat back and reflected before doing anything. Then, in contrast to the younger children, who haphazardly varied several factors at once, the older children tried to exclude each factor systematically. You could say that they used the "process of elimination," as we often do with multiple-choice tests. Not all of the 14- and 15-year-olds solved the problem, but as a group, their approach was more advanced and more likely to succeed.

According to Inhelder and Piaget, the approach of the 14- and 15-year-olds typified formal-operational thought. The approach of the 8- to 13-year-olds typified concrete-operational thought. As with many other aspects of Piaget's views and methods, we have to be flexible about Piaget's age estimates for ability to solve the problem. Robert Siegler and his associates (1973), for example, were able to train 10-year-olds to approach the problem systematically and isolate the correct answer (drum roll!): the length of the string. Thus, education and training can influence the development of cognitive skills.

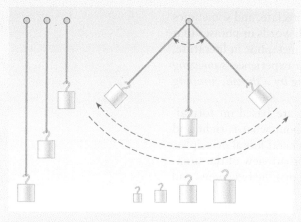

Figure 15.1 ■ The Pendulum Problem
What determines how fast the pendulum will swing back and forth? The amount of weight? The length of the string? The height from which the weight is released? The force with which the weight is pushed? Or a combination of the above? Formal-operational children attempt to exclude each factor systematically.
© Cengage Learning®

Reflect How did the adolescents in the study use an empirical approach to determine which factor controlled the speed of the pendulum?

Reevaluation of Piaget's Theory

Piaget's account of formal operations has received quite a bit of support. There appears to be little question that changes occur in the nature of reasoning between preadolescence and adolescence (Moshman, 2011, 2015). For example, research strongly supports Piaget's view that the capacity to reason deductively does not emerge until adolescence (Johnson-Laird, 2010; Moshman, 2011, 2015).

Formal-operational thought does not occur universally in cognitive development. The ability to solve abstract problems, such as those found in algebra and the pendulum problem, is more likely to be developed in adolescents in technologically oriented Western societies or in major cities than in less well-developed areas or nations (Flavell et al., 2002; Moshman, 2011, 2015). Moreover, formal-operational thought may occur later than Piaget thought, or it may not develop at all. For example, many early adolescents (ages 13–16) still perform better on concrete problems than on abstract ones (Markovits & Lortie-Forgues, 2011). Reviews of the literature suggest that formal-operational thought is found among only 40–60% of first-year college students (Flavell et al., 2002; Moshman, 2011, 2015). Also, the same individual may do well on one type of formal-operational task and poorly on another. We are more likely to use formal-operational thought in our own academic specialties. Some of us are formal-operational in math or science but not in the study of literature; for others, the opposite is true. Piaget (1972) recognized that adolescents may not always demonstrate formal-operational thought, especially when they are unfamiliar with a particular task.

Are Adolescents Egocentric? How Is Adolescent Egocentrism Related to the Imaginary Audience and the Personal Fable?

Preschool children, who have difficulty taking the perspective of other people in the three-mountains test, are not the only ones to display egocentrism. Teenagers are capable of hypothetical thinking, and they can argue for causes in which they do not believe (if you pay them enough to do so). However, they also can show a somewhat different brand of egocentrism. Adolescents comprehend the ideas of other people, but they have difficulty sorting out those things that concern other people from the things that concern themselves.

The Imaginary Audience

Many adolescents fantasize about becoming rock stars or movie stars who are adored by millions. The concept of the **imaginary audience** achieves part of that fantasy—sort of. It places the adolescent on stage, but she or he is surrounded more by critics than by admirers. An adolescent tends to assume that other people are more concerned with his or her appearance and behavior than they really are (Martin & Sokol, 2011).

The concept of the imaginary audience helps explain why teenagers are so preoccupied with their appearance. It helps explain why the mirror is the constant companion of the teenager, who grooms endlessly, searches out every facial blemish, and agonizes over every zit. The imaginary audience may also help explain why it is the adolescent who is most vulnerable to eating disorders to try to perfect her or his appearance (Fox et al., 2009). Being caught up with the mirror seems to peak sometime during eighth grade and to decline over the remainder of adolescence.

imaginary audience The belief that others around us are as concerned with our thoughts and behaviors as we are; one aspect of adolescent egocentrism.

The Imaginary Audience Adolescents tend to feel that other people are continuously scrutinizing their appearance and behavior. This may explain why so many adolescents worry about every facial blemish and spend long hours grooming.

Thomas Northcut/Stone/Getty Images

TRUTH OR FICTION REVISITED: It is true that adolescents generally see themselves as being on stage—with countless eyes peering in on them. This self-perception may account for the common adolescent intense desire for privacy.

Whereas some researchers view the emergence of the imaginary audience purely in cognitive-developmental terms, others believe that many adolescents are responding to increased social scrutiny (Bell & Bromnick, 2003). One research group attributes the imaginary audience more to social anxiety than to cognitive development (Kelly et al., 2002).

The Personal Fable

Spider-Man and Batman, stand aside! Because of the personal fable, many adolescents become action heroes, at least in their own minds. If the imaginary audience puts adolescents on stage, the personal fable justifies being there. The **personal fable**, another aspect of adolescent egocentrism, is the belief that one's thoughts and emotions are special and unique (Hill et al., 2012; Morrell et al., 2015). It also includes the common adolescent belief that one is all but invulnerable, like Superman or Superwoman.

TRUTH OR FICTION REVISITED: It is in fact normal for male adolescents to think of themselves as action heroes and to act as though they are made of steel. This self-(mis)perception is what is meant by the personal fable.

The personal fable is related to such behaviors as showing off and risk-taking (Steinberg, 2011). Many adolescents form risky online relationships with strangers (Carrier et al., 2015; McCarty et al., 2011). Many adolescents assume that they can smoke with impunity (Morrell et al., 2015). Cancer? "It can't happen to me," or, "I've got years and years to think about that." They may drive recklessly. They often engage in spontaneous, unprotected sexual activity, allowing the biological drive to rule them and possibly assuming that sexually transmitted infections (STIs) and unwanted pregnancies happen to other people, not to them. And they may mix sex and drugs—taking substances that lessen inhibitions and self-control, then engaging in risky sex (Ewing et al., 2015; Houck et al., 2014). Ronald King (2000), of the HIV Community Coalition of Metropolitan Washington, put it this way: "All youth—rich, poor, black, white—have this sense of invincibility, invulnerability." Adolescents are more likely than their parents to downplay risks (Smith et al., 2014).

The specialness and uniqueness of the adolescent experience? Many adolescents believe that their parents and other adults—even their peers—could never feel what they are feeling or know the depth of their passions. "You just don't understand me!" claims the adolescent. But, at least often enough, we do.

15.2 Gender Differences in Cognitive Abilities

Although females and males do not differ noticeably in overall intelligence, beginning in childhood gender differences appear in certain cognitive abilities (Johnson & Bouchard, 2007). Females are somewhat superior to males in verbal ability. Males, on the other hand, seem somewhat superior in visual–spatial skills. The picture for mathematics ability is more complex, with females excelling in some

Brand New Images/ Iconica/Getty Images

The Personal Fable Because of the "personal fable," many adolescent males identify with comic book and film superheroes.

personal fable The belief that our feelings and ideas are special and unique and that we are invulnerable; one aspect of adolescent egocentrism.

areas and males excelling in others. Let us take a closer look at these gender differences.

Are There Gender Differences in Verbal Abilities

Verbal abilities include reading, spelling, grammar, oral comprehension, and word fluency. As a group, females surpass males in verbal ability throughout their lives (Halpern, 2012). These differences show up early. Girls seem to acquire language faster than boys. They make more prelinguistic vocalizations, utter their first word sooner, and develop larger vocabularies. Boys in the United States are more likely than girls to have reading problems, ranging from reading below grade level to learning disorders (Brun et al., 2009).

Why do females excel in verbal abilities? For one thing, parents talk more to their infant daughters than to their infant sons (see Chapter 7). This encouragement of verbal interaction may be connected with girls' relative verbal precocity. Because of this early language advantage, girls may rely more on verbal skills to interact with people, thus furthering their abilities in this area (Halpern, 2012).

How do we account for gender differences in reading? Biological factors such as the organization of the brain may play a role, but do not discount cultural factors. One issue is whether a culture stamps reading as a gender-neutral, masculine, or feminine activity (Goldstein, 2005). Consider Nigeria and England. Reading is looked on as a masculine activity in these nations, and boys traditionally surpass girls in reading ability (and other academic skills). In the United States and Canada, however, reading tends to be stereotyped as feminine, and girls tend to excel in reading in these nations. People of all ages and all cultures tend to apply themselves more diligently to pursuits that they believe are "meant" for them—whether it is the life of the nomad, ballet, ice hockey, or reading.

Are There Gender Differences in Visual–Spatial Abilities?

Visual–spatial abilities refer to the abilities to visualize objects or shapes, to mentally manipulate and rotate them, and to find one's way by navigating the outer world. As you can imagine, these abilities are important in such fields as art, architecture, and engineering. Boys begin to outperform girls on many types of visual–spatial tasks starting at age 8 or 9, and the difference persists into adulthood (Halpern, 2012; Sneider et al., 2015; Yazzie, 2010). The gender difference is particularly notable on mental rotation tasks (see Figure 15.2 ■), which require imagining how objects will look if they are rotated in space.

What is the basis for the gender difference in visual–spatial skills? A number of biological and environmental explanations have been offered. One biological theory that has received some attention is that visual–spatial ability is influenced by sex-linked recessive genes on the X sex chromosome. But this theory has not been supported by research (Halpern, 2012).

Some researchers link visual–spatial performance to evolutionary theory and sex hormones. It may be related to a genetic tendency to create and defend a territory (Halpern, 2012; Stanyon & Bigoni, 2014). One environmental theory is that gender stereotypes influence the spatial experiences of children. Gender-stereotyped "boys' toys," such as blocks, LEGOs, and Erector sets, provide more practice with spatial skills than gender-stereotyped "girls' toys," such as baby dolls, Barbies, and play kitchens. Boys are also more likely to engage in sports, which involve moving balls and other objects through space (Ryan et al., 2015). Boys are allowed to travel farther from home than girls are, which gives them greater opportunities for exploration—and a larger "home range" (Halpern, 2012). It is no secret that participation in spatially related activities is associated with better performance on visual–spatial tasks.

Are There Gender Differences in Mathematical Ability?

The possibility—or presence—of gender differences in ability in math is as controversial a topic in psychology and education as the meaning and distribution of intelligence. Race and ethnicity are key issues in the discussion of intelligence. Gender is the source of much debate in math ability.

For half a century or more, it has been believed that male adolescents generally outperform females in mathematics, and research has tended to support that belief (Else-Quest et al., 2013; Miller & Halpern, 2014). However, research on the issue has been mixed, and gender differences are either nonexistent or not as large as has been believed.

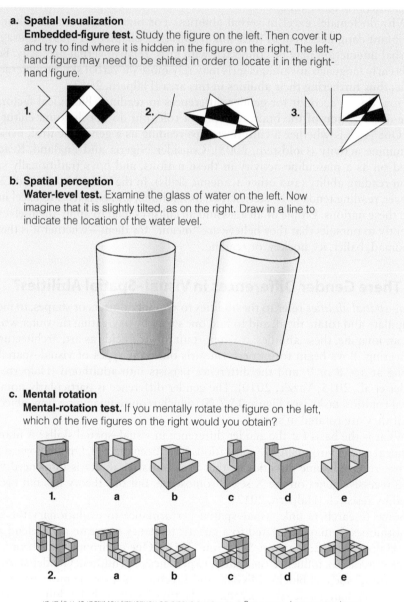

a. Spatial visualization
Embedded-figure test. Study the figure on the left. Then cover it up and try to find where it is hidden in the figure on the right. The left-hand figure may need to be shifted in order to locate it in the right-hand figure.

b. Spatial perception
Water-level test. Examine the glass of water on the left. Now imagine that it is slightly tilted, as on the right. Draw in a line to indicate the location of the water level.

c. Mental rotation
Mental-rotation test. If you mentally rotate the figure on the left, which of the five figures on the right would you obtain?

Answers: a. 1: Orient the pattern as if it were a tilted capital M, with the top left portion along the top of the white triangle. 2: This pattern fits along the right sides of the two black triangles on the left. 3: Rotate this figure about 100° to the right, so that it forms a Z, with the top line coinciding with the top line of the top white triangle. **b.** The line should be horizontal, not tilted. **c.** 1: c; 2: d.

Figure 15.2 ■ Examples of Tests Used to Measure Visual–Spatial Ability
No sex differences are found on the spatial-visualization tasks in Part A. Boys do somewhat better than girls on the task measuring spatial perception in Part B. The sex difference is greatest on the mental rotation tasks in Part C. What are some possible reasons for these differences?
© Cengage Learning®

A Closer Look

HOW PARENTS CAN HELP EARLY ADOLESCENTS IN SCHOOL

Early adolescence is often marked by declines in academic performance due to changes in developmental processes, family relationships, and the switch from a local elementary school to a more centralized middle school (Hill & Tyson, 2009). Changes in developmental processes include biological and cognitive developments, social developments, and renegotiation of family relationships, particularly the parent–adolescent relationship (Grolnick et al., 2007).

Making this transition has historically been more difficult for African American than for European American early adolescents (Hurd et al., 2012). Although African American parents and caregivers have emphasized the value and usefulness of education, many African American students experience discrimination and bias in schools, leading many students and their caregivers to mistrust the schools and teachers. These issues are heightened during adolescence, when African American students are typically trying to establish their ethnic identity (Hughes et al., 2006).

Parental involvement is one of the key factors in helping early adolescents make the transition to middle school—involvement not only with the adolescent but also with the school (Hurd et al., 2012). Hill and Tyson (2009) conducted a meta-analysis of 50 studies, highlighting various kinds of parental involvement to determine which kinds are helpful and which, if any, are not. The authors noted three kinds of parental involvement in the literature on education and academic achievement. First, *home-based involvement* includes strategies such as parent–child communication about school; involvement with school work itself—for example, helping children with their homework; taking children to places and events that encourage academic success, such as libraries and museums; and creating an environment for learning in the home, such as having books, newspapers, and educational toys around. Second, *school-based involvement* includes visiting the school for events such as PTA meetings and open houses, volunteering at school, participating in school governance, and engaging in parent–school communication, such as teacher–parent conferences about children's progress. School-based interactions increase parents' knowledge of the curriculum and teaching methods and enhance the effectiveness

David Grossman/The Image Works

The Transition from Elementary School The transition to junior high or high school is not always easy. The transition coincides with the biological forces of puberty and with concerns about how one will turn out—physically, that is. It is not surprising that some children experience a decline in grades and self-esteem.

of their involvement in the home (Hill & Taylor, 2004). Third, *academic socialization* involves communicating parental expectations about the value of education to children, making schoolwork "real" by connecting it to current events, building educational and occupational hopes and dreams, reviewing strategies for learning with children, and planning for the future.

The researchers found that parental involvement in education is generally positively correlated with children's academic progress in middle school. Among the various types of parental involvement, the most important component was communication of the value of education to students.

TRUTH OR FICTION REVISITED: There is no measurable association between parents helping children complete their homework and children's academic achievement. Does this mean that parents should avoid helping their children with homework? Not necessarily, but perhaps the best strategy is teaching children how to carry out the academic tasks at hand rather than doing their work for them. Such a strategy places children "in the zone" of proximal development.

A study by Janet Shibley Hyde and her colleagues (Hyde, 2014; Hyde et al., 2008) of some 7 million 2nd- through 11th-graders found no gender differences for performance in mathematics on standardized tests. The complexity of the test items apparently made no difference. Nevertheless, most Americans have different expectations for boys and girls, and these expectations may still dissuade girls from pursuing careers in science and math (Else-Quest et al., 2013).

Girls appear to be more vulnerable than boys to lose their self-confidence when faced with difficult math problems (Galdi et al., 2014; Dweck et al., 2007). Mathematically gifted sixth-grade girls fare poorly when they are overly perfectionistic or anxious about taking tests, especially tests that are timed (Tsui & Maziocco, 2007). Many female adolescents, especially when they are under pressure, are apparently vulnerable to feeling threatened by the stereotype that males are better than females at math. The threat is experienced as anxiety that distracts them from the tasks at hand and impairs their performance (Hyde, 2014; Passolunghi et al., 2014). On the other hand, when female adolescents' mothers strongly reject gender stereotypes concerning ability in math and science, their daughters are less likely to show stereotype vulnerability in tackling math problems (Tomasetto et al., 2011).

What, then, shall we conclude about gender differences in cognitive abilities? First, it may be that girls show greater verbal ability than boys but that boys have somewhat better visual–spatial skills (Miller & Halpern, 2014; Voyer & Voyer, 2014). However, gender differences in cognitive skills are group differences, not individual differences. That is, the difference in, say, reading skills between a male who reads well and a male who is dyslexic is greater than the average group gender difference in reading ability. Moreover, despite group differences, millions of females exceed the average American male in visual–spatial skills. Similarly, despite group differences, millions of males exceed the average American female in writing, spelling, and articulation. Hundreds of thousands of American women perform well in domains that once were considered masculine, such as medicine and law (Whitmarsh & Wentworth, 2012). Moreover, in most cases, differences in cognitive skills are small in societies in which women are empowered, including most parts of the United States, Canada, Europe, Japan, and South Korea (Else-Quest et al., 2010; Else-Quest & Grabe, 2012).

Section Review

1. The stage of _____ operations is the final stage in Piaget's scheme.

2. Adolescent _____ is connected with the concepts of the imaginary audience and the personal fable.

3. Females are somewhat _____ (superior or inferior?) to males in verbal ability.

4. Males are somewhat _____ (superior or inferior?) in visual–spatial ability.

5. Research links _____ hormones to visual–spatial performance.

Reflect & Relate: Did you have a strong need for privacy when you were an adolescent? If so, do you recall why? Can you explain this need in cognitive-developmental terms?

The Adolescent in Judgment: Moral Development

Moral development in adolescence is a complex issue, with both cognitive and behavioral aspects. Children in early childhood tend to view right and wrong in terms of rewards and punishments. Lawrence Kohlberg referred to such judgments as preconventional. In middle childhood, conventional thought tends to emerge, and children usually begin to judge right and wrong in terms of social conventions, rules, and laws (see Table 12.1 on page 379).

What Are Kohlberg's Views on Moral Reasoning in Adolescence?

In adolescence, many—though not all—individuals become capable of formal-operational thinking, which enables them to derive conclusions about what they should do in various situations by reasoning from ethical principles. And many of these individuals engage in postconventional moral reasoning. They deduce proper behavior from general principles that they apply across many different situations, just as they might deduce that whales are mammals because whales feed their young with breast milk.

What Is the the Postconventional Level of Moral Development?

In the **postconventional level,** moral reasoning is based on the person's own moral standards. Consider the case of Heinz told in Figure 15.4 ■. Moral judgments are derived from personal values, not from conventional standards or authority figures. In the contractual, legalistic orientation of Stage 5, it is recognized that laws stem from agreed-on procedures and that many rights have great value and should not be violated (see Table 15.1 ●). But under exceptional circumstances, such as in the case of Heinz, laws cannot bind the individual. A Stage 5 reason for stealing the drug might be that it is the right thing to do, even though it is illegal. Conversely, it could

Figure 15.4 ■ The Case of Heinz

In Europe, a woman was near death from a special kind of cancer. There was one drug that the doctors thought might save her. It was a form of radium that a druggist in the same town had recently discovered. The drug was expensive to make, but the druggist was charging 10 times what the drug cost him to make. He paid $200 for the radium and charged $2,000 for a small dose of the drug. The sick woman's husband, Heinz, went to everyone he knew to borrow the money, but he could only get together about $1,000 which was half of what it cost. He told the druggist that his wife was dying and asked him to sell it cheaper or let him pay later. But the druggist said: "No, I discovered the drug and I'm going to make money from it." So Heinz got desperate and broke into the man's store to steal the drug for his wife. Source: Kohlberg (1969).

● TABLE 15.1
Kohlberg's Postconventional Level of Moral Development

Stage	Moral Reasoning That Supports Heinz's Stealing the Drug	Moral Reasoning That Opposes Heinz's Stealing the Drug
Stage 5: Contractual, legalistic orientation: One must weigh pressing human needs against society's need to maintain social order.	This is complicated because society has a right to maintain law and order, but Heinz has to take the drug to save his wife.	I can see why Heinz feels he has to take the drug, but laws exist for the benefit of society as a whole and cannot simply be cast aside.
Stage 6: Universal ethical principles orientation: People must follow universal ethical principles and their own conscience, even if it means breaking the law.	In this case, the law comes into conflict with the principle of the sanctity of human life. Heinz must take the drug because his wife's life is more important than the law.	If Heinz truly believes that stealing the drug is worse than letting his wife die, he should not take it. People have to make sacrifices to do what they think is right.

Source: Adapted from Kohlberg (1963).

postconventional level
According to Kohlberg, a period during which moral judgments are derived from moral principles and people look to themselves to set moral standards.

WOMEN IN STEM FIELDS

Despite research suggesting that there is no overall gender difference in performance on standardized mathematics achievement tests, most Americans continue to have different expectations for boys and girls, and these expectations may still dissuade some math-proficient girls from entering so-called STEM (science, technology, engineering, and mathematics) fields (Leaper et al., 2012).

Thus, there is reason to believe that women have the capacity to be entering STEM fields in greater numbers. So why, in the 21st century in the United States, do women remain underrepresented in STEM fields? There are a number of possibilities (Else-Quest et al., 2013; Hyde et al., 2014):

- Women who are proficient in math are more likely than math-proficient men to prefer careers that do not require skills in math.

- More males than females obtain extremely high scores on the SAT mathematics test and the quantitative reasoning sections of the Graduate Record Exam (GRE).

- Women who are proficient in math are more likely than men with this proficiency to have high verbal competence as well, which encourages many such women to choose careers other than those in STEM fields.

- In some STEM fields, women with children find themselves penalized in terms of promotions.

Women's preferences may well be a key reason why there are more men entering and remaining in STEM fields today. However, we need to note two caveats. One caveat, as shown by Table 15.2 ● and Figure 15.3 ■, is that women are tossing these stereotypes out the window by entering STEM and other fields still dominated by men in increasing numbers. For example, women are currently receiving many more bachelor's degrees than men in biology (39 thousand versus 25 thousand) and nearly as many in chemistry (Table 15.2). Although the world of business over the centuries has "belonged" to men, the number of women now receiving degrees in business management—the most popular undergraduate degree—is very close to the number received by men. Men obtain 5 to 6 times the number of degrees in computer and information science, and about 4 times as many degrees in engineering and physics. Yet the numbers are close in numbers of bachelor degrees awarded in math: between 10 and 11 thousand for males versus 8 thousand for females. The second caveat is that women's preferences cannot be fully divorced from society's

---

● TABLE 15.2

Bachelor's Degrees Conferred by Degree-Granting U.S. Institutions, by Gender of Student

Discipline	Males	Females
Architecture	3,540	2,500
Biology	25,382	39,229
Business management	189,486	176,004
Chemistry	6,673	6,268
Computer and information science	9,143	1,636
Education	21,757	84,028
Engineering	65,829	15,553
Mathematics	10,723	8,119
Physics	4,263	1,002
Psychology	24,073	78,683

Source: National Center for Education Statistics (2013).

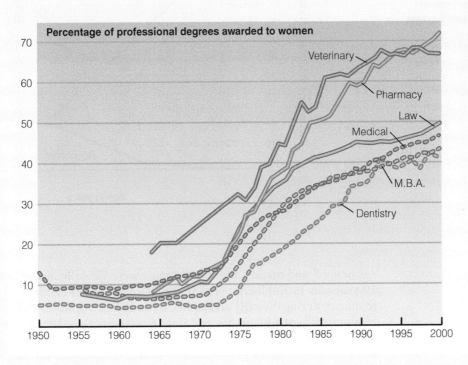

Figure 15.3 ■ **Women Flood Professions Once Populated Almost Exclusively by Men**
© Cengage Learning®

expectations. As long as gender stereotypes about who belongs in STEM fields remain, at least some women will be discouraged from entering them. Let us also note that women obtain 4 times as many degrees in education as men, and 3 to 4 times as many in psychology. Education has long been seen as the province of women especially in the lower grades, although less in high school and even less on the college campus. Women started entering the field of psychology in large numbers in the mid-twentieth century, and the great (great!) majority of clinical and developmental psychologists are now female.

Women have also achieved parity with men in medical college enrolment. In the 1960s, women accounted for some 7% of medical students in the United States. That number is now 40% (American Association of Medical Colleges, 2015). Yet specialities within medicine retain some stereotypical male–female divisions. Very few women are planning to specialize in neurological surgery, orthopaedic surgery, or thoracic surgery. Yet women are studying to make up the great majority of specialists in the fields of obstetrics and gynaecology, paediatrics, allergy and immunology, and dermatology (American Association of Medical Colleges, 2015).

be argued that if everyone in need broke the law, the legal system and the social contract would be destroyed.

Stage 6 thinking relies on supposed universal ethical principles, such as those of human life, individual dignity, justice, and **reciprocity**. Behavior that is consistent with these principles is considered right. If a law is seen as unjust or as contradicting the rights of the individual, it is wrong to obey it.

In the case of Heinz, it could be argued from the perspective of Stage 6 that the principle of preserving life takes precedence over laws prohibiting stealing. Therefore, it is morally necessary for Heinz to steal the drug, even if he must go to jail. Note that it could also be asserted, from the principled orientation, that if Heinz finds the social contract or the law to be the highest principle, he must remain within the law, despite the consequences.

reciprocity The principle that actions have mutual effects and that people depend on one another to treat each other morally.

Figure 15.5 ■ Age and Type of Moral Judgment

The incidence of preconventional reasoning declines from more than 90% of moral statements at age 7 to less than 20% of moral statements at age 16. Conventional moral statements increase with age between the ages of 7 and 13 but then level off to account for 50% to 60% of moral statements at ages 13 through 16. Postconventional moral statements are all but absent through age 10 but account for about 20% to 25% of moral statements at ages 13 through 16.
© Cengage Learning®

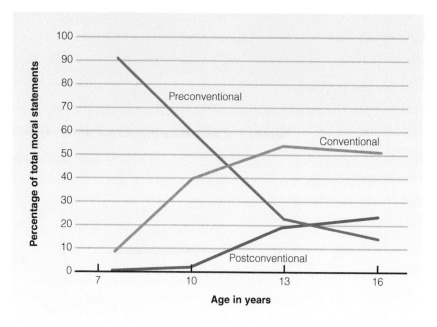

Stage 5 and Stage 6 moral judgments were virtually absent among the 7- and 10-year-olds in Kohlberg's (1963) sample of American children. They increased in frequency during the early and middle teens. By age 16, Stage 5 reasoning was shown by about 20% of adolescents, and Stage 6 reasoning was demonstrated by about 5% of adolescents. However, Stage 3 and Stage 4 judgments were made more frequently at all ages—7 through 16—studied by Kohlberg and other investigators (Commons et al., 2006; Gibbs, 2015; Rest, 1983; see Figure 15.5 ■).

TRUTH OR FICTION REVISITED: It is not true that most adolescents make moral decisions based on their own ethical principles. Although research suggests that postconventional moral reasoning, if it occurs at all, appears no earlier than in adolescence, the research also shows that most adolescents (and most adults!) actually reason at lower levels.

Are There Cross-Cultural Differences in Moral Development? What Are They?

Cultural background is a powerful shaper of moral reasoning. Kohlberg found postconventional thinking among a minority of American adolescents, and it was all but absent among adolescents in villages in Mexico, Taiwan, Turkey (Kohlberg, 1969), and the Bahamas (White et al., 1978). Reviews of the literature conclude that postconventional reasoning is more likely to be found in urban cultural groups and in middle-class populations but it is rarely seen in traditional folk cultures (Gibbs, 2015; Nucci & Gingo, 2010).

Another cross-cultural study indicates that the moral reasoning of children from Western industrialized countries such as Germany, Poland, and Italy is similar to that of American children from urban areas (Boehnke et al., 1989). On the other hand, the moral reasoning of American children and Israeli city children has been shown to be more self-oriented and less oriented toward the needs of others than the reasoning of Israeli kibbutz children (Eisenberg et al., 1990). These differences are consistent with the differences in the children's social environments. The kibbutz is a collective farm community that emphasizes cooperative relationships and a communal philosophy.

A similar pattern has been found in comparisons of middle-class American and Hindu Indian children and adults. Hindu Indians are more likely to show a caring orientation in making moral judgments, whereas Americans more often demonstrate a justice orientation. These findings are consistent with the greater emphasis that Hindu Indian culture puts on the importance of taking responsibility for others (Nucci & Gingo, 2010).

Are There Gender Differences in Moral Development?

Again, we are touching on one of the key controversial issues in psychology and education. Do females and males differ in their patterns of moral reasoning? If so, is it possible to say that females or males are "superior" in their moral reasoning?

Some researchers claim that males reason at higher levels of moral development than females in their responses to Heinz's dilemma. For example, Kohlberg and Kramer (1969) reported that the average stage of moral development for men was Stage 4, which emphasizes justice, law, and order. The average stage for women was reported to be Stage 3, which emphasizes caring and concern for others.

Because Kohlberg's cognitive-developmental theory is largely maturational, it might seem that it is "natural" for males to reason at higher levels than females. However, Carol Gilligan (Gilligan, 1977, 1982, 2011) argues that this gender difference reflects patterns of socialization that are in keeping with gender stereotypes rather than maturation. To make her point, Gilligan provides two examples of responses to Heinz's dilemma. Eleven-year-old Jake views the dilemma as a math problem. He sets up an equation showing that life has greater value than property. Heinz should thus steal the drug. Eleven-year-old Amy, on the other hand, notes that stealing the drug and letting Heinz's wife die would both be wrong. Amy searches for alternatives, such as getting a loan, stating that it would profit Heinz's wife little if he went to jail and was no longer around to help her.

Although Gilligan sees Amy's pattern of reasoning as being just as sophisticated as Jake's, it would be rated as showing a lower level of moral development in Kohlberg's system. Gilligan asserts that Amy, like other girls, has been socialized to focus on the needs of others and forgo simplistic judgments of right and wrong. Jake, by contrast, has been socialized to make judgments based on logic (Eisenberg et al., 2010; You et al., 2010). To him, clear-cut conclusions are to be derived from a set of premises. Amy was aware of the logical considerations that struck Jake, but she processed them as one source of information, not as the sole source. It is ironic that Amy's empathy, a trait that has "defined the 'goodness' of women," marks Amy "as deficient in moral development" (Gilligan, 1982, p. 18).

Kohlberg, Gilligan, and other researchers tend to agree that, in making moral judgments, females are more likely to show a caring orientation, whereas males are more likely to assume a justice orientation (Jorgensen, 2006). But there remains a dispute about whether this difference means that girls reason at a lower level than boys do (Gilligan, 2011). Kohlberg, by the way, viewed Gilligan's ideas as an extension of his own views, not as a repudiation of them, and Gilligan largely supported Kohlberg's stage theory and his claim of its universality (Gilligan, 2011; Snarey & Samuelson, 2008).

Parents Influence Children's Moral Development Parents help enhance children's moral development when they discuss moral dilemmas with them. Most adolescents respect their parents' views, but they don't always see eye to eye.

Do Boys Reason at Higher Levels of Moral Development than Girls? Not according to Carol Gilligan and many other researchers!

On Moral Behavior and Moral Reasoning: Is There a Relationship?

Is there a relationship between moral cognitive development and moral behavior? Are individuals whose moral judgments are more mature more likely to engage in moral behavior? The answer seems to be yes; many studies have found positive relationships between a person's level of moral development and his or her behavior (Bazerman & Tenbrunsel, 2011; Cheng, 2014).

Individuals whose moral reasoning is at Stage 2 cheat, steal, and engage in other problem behaviors more often than peers whose moral reasoning is at higher stages (Nucci & Gingo, 2010). Adolescents with higher levels of moral reasoning are more likely to exhibit moral behavior, including altruistic behavior (Hart et al., 2003; Maclean et al., 2004).

Experiments also have been conducted in the hope of advancing moral reasoning as a way of decreasing immoral behavior (Palmer, 2005). A number of studies have found that group discussion of moral dilemmas elevates delinquents' level of moral reasoning (Walker & Frimer, 2011). Is moral behavior affected as well? In one study, discussions of moral dilemmas improved moral reasoning and reduced incidents of, for example, school tardiness, behavior referrals, and police and court contacts among adolescents with behavioral problems (Arbuthnot & Gordon, 1988).

How, Then, Do We Evaluate Kohlberg's Theory?

Despite a number of challenges, evidence appears to continue to support Kohlberg's view that the moral judgments of children develop in an upward sequence (Boom et al., 2007), even though most children do not reach postconventional thought. Postconventional thought, when it is found, first occurs during adolescence.

Why doesn't postconventional moral reasoning appear until age 13 or so? A number of studies suggest that formal-operational thinking is a prerequisite and that education is likely to play a role (Boom et al., 2007; Patenaude et al., 2003). Postconventional reasoning appears to require the capacities to understand abstract moral principles and to empathize with the views and feelings of others. However, neither formal-operational thought nor education guarantees the development of postconventional moral judgments.

Kohlberg believed that the stages of moral development follow the unfolding of innate sequences and are therefore universal. But he may have underestimated the influence of social, cultural, and educational institutions (Dawson, 2002; Nucci & Gingo, 2010). Parents are also important. Inductive disciplinary methods, including discussions of the feelings of others, advance moral reasoning (Nucci & Gingo, 2010).

Postconventional thinking is all but absent in developing societies, and it accounts for only a minority of adolescents' judgments in the United States (Commons et al., 2006; Snarey, 1994). Perhaps postconventional reasoning reflects Kohlberg's personal ideals rather than a natural, universal stage of development (Helwig, 2006). Stage 6 reasoning is based on the acceptance of supposedly universal ethical principles. The principles of freedom, justice, equality, tolerance, integrity, and reverence for human life have high appeal for most American adolescents who are reared to idealize these principles.

As we look around the world—and at many of the horrors of the unfolding 21st century—we find that principles such as freedom and tolerance of differences are not universally admired. They may reflect Western cultural influences more than the cognitive development of the child. In many cultures, violation of the dominant religious tradition is a capital offense, and freedom to worship—or the freedom not to worship—is unheard of. In his later years, Kohlberg (1985) dropped Stage 6 reasoning from his theory in recognition of these problems.

Finally, we must recognize that Kohlberg's view of moral reasoning and moral development is not the only one; indeed, it is possible that Kohlberg's views may someday be of little more than historical interest (Krebs & Denton, 2006; Lapsley, 2006). But, as is the case with Piaget, we are not there yet.

Section Review

6. In Kohlberg's _____ level, moral reasoning is based on the person's own moral standards.

7. Many studies have found _____ (positive or negative?) relationships between the child's level of moral development and his or her moral behavior.

Reflect & Relate: What is your stage of moral development, according to Kohlberg? How do you know? How do you feel about that?

15.4 The Adolescent in School

How can we emphasize the importance of the school to the development of the adolescent? Adolescents are highly influenced by the opinions of their peers and their teachers. Their self-esteem rises or falls consistently with the levels of their skills.

How Do Adolescents Make the Transition from Elementary School to Middle, Junior High, or High School?

Most students make at least one and sometimes two transitions to a new school before they complete high school. Think back to your own school days. Did you spend the years from kindergarten to eighth grade in one building and then move on to high school? Did you instead attend elementary school through sixth grade and then go to junior high for grades 7 through 9 before starting high school? Or did you complete kindergarten through grades 4 or 5 in one school, then attend a middle school for grades 5 or 6 through 8, and then move on to high school for grades 9 through 12? (This has become the most common pattern in recent years.)

The transition to middle, junior high, or high school generally involves a shift from a smaller neighborhood elementary school with self-contained classrooms to a larger, more impersonal setting with many more students and with different teachers for different classes (Hill & Tyson, 2009). These changes may not fit very well with the developmental needs of early adolescents. For example, adolescents express a desire for increased autonomy, yet teachers in junior high typically allow less student input and exert more behavioral control than teachers in elementary school (Crosnoe, 2011). Moreover, in the shift to the new school, students move from being the "top dog" (the oldest and most experienced students) to being the "bottom dog." These changes are not the only ones facing the early adolescent. Many youngsters also are going through the early stages of pubertal development at about the same time they move to a new school.

How well do students adjust to the transition to a new school? Much of the research has examined children's experiences as they move from elementary school to junior high school. The transition to the new school setting often is accompanied by a decline in grades and in participation in school activities (Hill & Tyson, 2009). Students may also experience a drop in self-esteem and an increase in psychological distress (Crosnoe, 2011; Rudolph & Flynn, 2007). A German study (Ball et al., 2006) found a connection between an adolescent's psychological adjustment and his or her grades by the end of the first year in high school.

The gender difference in adjustment to the transition from elementary school may reflect the fact that girls are more likely to be going through puberty at about this time. Girls at this age are then also likely to attract the attention of boys in higher grades, whereas younger boys are not likely to be of much interest to older girls. Girls are experiencing major life changes, and children who experience several life changes at once find it more difficult to adjust to a new school (Tobbell & O'Donnell, 2013).

But transition need not be that stressful. Students whose elementary and middle schools and caregivers all work together to smooth out the waves make the transition more easily (Garner & Thomas, 2011; Rice et al., 2011). One longitudinal study followed the progress of students who were placed in an elementary school program in which they were given suggestions for solving social problems and making social decisions. For example, they were shown how one can handle disagreements without arguing or resorting to violence. When followed in high school 4–6 years later, these students showed higher levels of prosocial behavior and fewer conduct problems than students who had not been in the program (Elias et al., 2003). Some middle schools create a more intimate, caring atmosphere by, for instance, establishing smaller schools within the school building. Others have summer "bridge programs" between middle school and high school. These programs introduce students to the new school culture and strengthen their academic skills.

Is This Adolescent on the Path to Dropping Out of School?
The consequences of dropping out of school can be harsh. High school dropouts earn less and are more likely to be unemployed. Programs have been developed to prevent dropping out, but potential dropouts must first be identified.

What Are the Consequences of Dropping Out of School? Why Do Adolescents Drop Out?

School is a key path to success in our society, but not all adolescents complete high school.

Completing high school is one of the most critical developmental tasks facing adolescents. The consequences of dropping out can be grim indeed. High school dropouts are more likely to be unemployed (Campbell, 2015). They make lower salaries: Research suggests that each year of education, from grade school through graduate school, adds about 16% to an individual's lifetime earnings (Passell, 1992). Looking at it from another perspective, the lifetime earnings of high school dropouts are about $270,000 less than those of high school graduates (Catterall, 2011). Dropouts are also more likely to exhibit problem behaviors, including delinquency, criminal behavior, and substance abuse (Dowrick et al., 2015; Heetman et al., 2015). However, it is sometimes difficult to disentangle the consequences of dropping out from its causes. A pattern of delinquent behavior, for example, might precede as well as follow dropping out.

F:Nalinframe/Alamy

A Closer Look

WHO DROPS OUT OF SCHOOL?

It is difficult to estimate the magnitude of the school dropout problem because states use different reporting systems, and most do not track those who quit after eighth grade. Overall, about 9% of males, ages 16–24, and 7% of females in the same age group have dropped out of high school (National Center for Education Statistics, 2014–2015). However, dropout rates vary considerably from ethnic group to ethnic group. Table 15.3 ● lists the dropout rates for various racial and ethnic groups for selected years from 1981 through 2011. The reported dropout rate was highest for Latin Americans. Native Americans and African Americans had the next highest dropout rates (Chapman, 2011). The good news in all this is that over the past 40 years, dropout rates have plummeted for all racial/ethnic groups. Older students were more likely to drop out. The higher dropout rates for children from Latin American and African American minority groups are linked to the lower socioeconomic status of their families and, in the case of Latin Americans, with recency of immigration. In a number of states with strict immigration laws or practices, some Latin American children have been kept out of school for fear of deportation, although that fear appears to have diminished over the years.

Why the overall decreases? Time to put on your critical thinking caps and consider rival explanations. One possibility is that students have become smarter; remember that education can actually lead to higher IQ scores (see Chapter 10). Another possibility is grade inflation; either high school courses have become easier or teachers are more reluctant to hand out low grades. It could also be that dropout prevention programs have met with some success.

Note, too, that with the exception of African American students in 1991, male adolescents from every racial/ethnic background have been more likely than their female counterparts to drop out of school. This trend is consistent with findings that women are more likely than men to go on to college.

Reflect:

* Considering gender differences in dropout rates, are women more likely than men to work hard and study?

* Do minority women believe that they will find more acceptance than minority men in the work force?

* Does the gender difference in dropping out have something to do with the courses chosen by males and females or by their guidance counselors? Why not investigate the situation and draw your own conclusions?

● TABLE 15.3

Rates of Dropping Out of High School Among Persons 16–24 Years Old, by Gender and Race/Ethnicity: Selected Years, 1981–2011

	Male			Female		
	European American	African American	Latin American	European American	African American	Latin American
1981	12.5%	19.9%	36.0%	10.2%	17.1%	30.4%
1991	8.9%	13.5%	39.2%	8.9%	13.7%	31.1%
2001	7.9%	13.0%	31.6%	6.7%	9.0%	22.1%
2011	5.4%	8.3%	14.6%	4.6%	6.4%	12.5%

Source: Adapted from National Center for Education Statistics (2014–2015). Digest of Education Statistics: 2012. https://nces.ed.gov/programs/digest/d12/tables/dt12_128.asp?referrer=report. 128. (Accessed April 25, 2015.)

Excessive school absence and reading below grade level are two of the earliest and strongest predictors of dropping out of school (Henry et al., 2012). Other risk factors include low grades, poor problem-solving ability, low self-esteem, problems with teachers, dissatisfaction with school, substance abuse, being old for one's grade level, and being male (Archambault et al., 2009; Henry et al., 2012). Adolescents who adopt adult roles early, especially marrying at a young age or becoming a parent, are also more likely to drop out (Bohon et al., 2007). Students from low-income households, large urban areas, and the American West and South are at greater risk (National Center for Education Statistics, 2007). But not all dropouts come from low-income families. Middle-class youth who feel bored with school, alienated, or strongly pressured to succeed also are at risk (Wegner & Flisher, 2009).

How Can Psychologists and Educators Prevent Adolescents from Dropping Out of School?

Many programs have been developed to prevent school dropout. Successful programs have some characteristics in common (Hahn et al., 2015; Saxe et al., 2012):

- Early preschool interventions (such as Head Start)
- Identification and monitoring of high-risk students throughout the school years
- Small class size, individualized instruction, and counseling
- Vocational components that link learning and community work experiences
- Involvement of families or community organizations
- Positive school climate
- Clear and reasonable educational goals (if you don't know where you're going, how you get there isn't very important), student accountability for behavior, and motivational systems that involve penalties and rewards

Most intervention efforts are usually not introduced until students are on the verge of dropping out—when it is usually too late.

Section Review

8. Teachers in junior high typically exert _____ (more or less?) behavioral control than teachers in elementary school.

9. Students undergoing the transition from elementary school are more likely to experience a _____ (rise or drop?) in self-esteem.

10. _____ (Boys or Girls?) appear to be more negatively affected by the transition to junior high school.

11. High school dropouts are _____ (more or less?) likely than high school graduates to be unemployed as adults.

12. _____ (Boys or Girls?) are more likely to drop out of high school.

Reflect & Relate: Do you know people who dropped out of high school? Why did they drop out? What were the consequences of their dropping out?

15.5 The Adolescent at Work: Career Development and Work Experience

Deciding what job or career we will pursue after completion of school is one of the most important choices we make.

How Do Adolescents Make Career Choices?

When I was a child, I wanted to be an astronaut or an explorer. I became a psychologist and author. My daughter Allyn wanted to be a rock star. Now she is a drama teacher.

Children's career aspirations may not be practical at first. They become increasingly realistic—and often more conventional—as children mature and gain experience. In adolescence, ideas about the kind of work one wants to do tend to become more firmly established, or crystallized, but some people do not choose a particular occupation until the college years or even afterward (Creed & Wamelink, 2015; Rogers & Creed, 2011).

In terms of the five-factor model of personality, neuroticism (emotional instability) is connected with difficulties in career decision-making. By contrast, high scores in agreeableness, conscientiousness, extraversion, and openness apparently ease career choice (Martincin & Stead, 2015).

A Social-Cognitive Perspective

From a social-cognitive perspective, the factors that influence an adolescent's choice of a career (Creed & Wamelink, 2015; Garcia et al., 2015) include the following:

- Competencies—his or her knowledge or skills
- "Encoding strategies"—his or her way of viewing a career, or himself or herself in relation to a career
- Expectancies—his or her expectations about what will happen in a given career, including **self-efficacy expectations**; that is, his or her beliefs that he or she will be able to handle the tasks in a given career

Sometimes we plan our careers on the basis of our perceived abilities and personality traits (Garcia et al., 2015; Rottinghaus & Van Esbroeck, 2011). Sometimes our early work experiences point us in certain directions (Creed & Wamelink, 2015).

John Holland's Career Typology

Psychologists have devised approaches to matching personality traits with careers to predict adjustment in a given career. Holland's (1997) RIASEC method, as used in his Vocational Preference Inventory, matches six personality types to various kinds of careers: realistic, investigative, artistic, social, enterprising, and conventional

self-efficacy expectations One's beliefs that he or she can handle the requirements of a situation.

A Closer Look | Diversity

ETHNIC IDENTITY AND GENDER IN CAREER SELF-EFFICACY EXPECTANCIES

Our ethnic identity can play a key role in our ideas about what is available to us (Fisher et al., 2011). One study explored the effects of ethnic identity and attitudes toward gender roles on early career decision-making in a sample of ninth-grade female African American and Latina adolescents (Gushue & Whitson, 2006). It was found that girls with stronger ethnic identities and nontraditional attitudes toward gender roles had higher self-efficacy expectancies or self-confidence that they would be able to handle the tasks involved in career decision-making, such as accurately assessing their skills and abilities, gathering information about careers, selecting career and educational goals, and making appropriate plans to meet those goals.

A second study confirmed the importance of a strong ethnic identity to feelings of self-efficacy in career decision-making among female African American adolescents (Rollins & Valdez, 2006). This study also found that African American girls had higher career self-efficacy than African American boys, perhaps because they were less likely to find themselves victimized by discrimination.

Research by Albert Bandura and his colleagues (2001) suggested that adolescent girls who have more confidence in their ability to function in the business world—that is, higher self-efficacy expectations—are more likely to select nontraditional careers. Intellectually gifted girls are more likely than their less-gifted peers to throw off the shackles of traditional career expectations (Mendez, 2000).

Reflect: Why do you think ethnic identity might be related to career self-efficacy expectations among African American adolescent girls?

Conventional

These people have clerical or numerical skills. They like to work with data, to carry out other people's directions, or to carry things out in detail.

Realistic

These people have mechanical or athletic abilities. They like to work with machines and tools, to be outdoors, or to work with animals or plants.

Investigative

These people like to learn new things. They enjoy investigating and solving problems and advancing knowledge.

Enterprising

These people like to work with people. They like to lead and influence others for economic or organizational gains.

Social

This group enjoys working with people. They like to help others, including the sick. They enjoy informing and enlightening people.

Artistic

This group is highly imaginative and creative. They enjoy working in unstructured situations. They are artistic and innovative.

Figure 15.6 ■ Assessing an Adolescent's Career Type by Attending a "Job Fair"
Adolescents can gain insight into where they might fit in the career world by picturing themselves at a job fair such as the one illustrated here. Students and employers have a chat. As time passes, they discover mutual interests and begin to collect in groups accordingly. Adolescents can consider the types of people in the six groups by reading the descriptions for each. Then they can ask themselves, "Which group would I most like to join?" What does their answer suggest about the career choices that might be of greatest interest to them?
© Cengage Learning®

(see Figure 15.6 ■). Within each "type" of career, some options are more sophisticated than others and require more education and training.

- Realistic people, according to Holland, are concrete in thinking. They are mechanically oriented. They tend to be best adjusted in occupations that involve motor activity. Examples of such occupations are unskilled labor, such as attending gas stations; farming; and the skilled trades, such as auto repair, electrical work, plumbing, and construction work.
- Investigative people are abstract in their thinking. They are creative and tend to be introverted but open to new experience. They tend to do well in college and university teaching and in research positions.

- Artistic people also tend to be creative and open to new experience. As a group, they are emotional, interested in the emotional life, and intuitive. They tend to be happiest in the visual and the performing arts.
- Socially oriented people tend to be outgoing (extraverted) and concerned about social welfare. They often are agreeable and have a need for affiliation. They gravitate toward occupations in teaching (kindergarten through high school), counseling, and social work.
- Enterprising people tend to be adventurous. They tend to be outgoing and dominant. They gravitate toward industrial roles that involve leadership and planning. They climb the ladder in government and social organizations.
- Conventional people thrive on routine. They are not particularly imaginative. They have needs for order, self-control, and social approval. They gravitate toward occupations in banking, accounting, clerical work, and the military.

Many people combine vocational types. A copywriter in an advertising agency might be both artistic and enterprising. Clinical and counseling psychologists tend to be investigative, artistic, and socially oriented. Military people and beauticians tend to be realistic and conventional, but military leaders who plan major operations and form governments are also enterprising, and individuals who create new hairstyles and fashions are also artistic. Holland's Vocational Preference Inventory assesses these personality types, as do various vocational tests that are used in high schools and colleges.

All in all, more than 20,000 occupations are found in the *Dictionary of Occupational Titles,* which is compiled by the U.S. Department of Labor. But most young people choose from a relatively small range of occupations on the basis of their personalities, experiences, and opportunities (Sawitri & Creed, 2015). Many sort of fall into jobs that are offered to them or follow career paths that are blazed by parents or role models in the community (Kaziboni & Uys, 2015; Sawitri & Creed, 2015).

How Many American Adolescents Hold Jobs? What Are the Pros and Cons of Adolescents Working?

Kimberly, age 16, has a job at a fast-food restaurant in the suburb of a Midwestern city. She has already saved $1,000 toward the purchase of a car and a stereo by working at the restaurant after school and on weekends. Kimberly is worried because her state's legislature is considering regulations that would reduce the number of hours she is allowed to work.

Life experiences help shape vocational development. One life experience that is common among American teenagers is holding a job.

Prevalence of Adolescent Employment

Chances are that you held a job in high school. About half of all high school sophomores, two-thirds of juniors, and almost three-fourths of seniors have a job during the school year (Staff et al., 2015). Girls and boys are equally likely to be employed, but boys work more hours.

Millions of adolescents between the ages of 14 and 18 are legally employed. But perhaps another 2–3 million are working illegally (Staff et al., 2015). Some of these teenagers are paid in cash so that their employers can avoid paying taxes or minimum wages. Others work too many hours, work late hours on school nights, or work at hazardous jobs. Some are younger than 14, which is too young to be legally employed except on farms.

Adolescent employment rates show ethnic and social-class differences (Bachman et al., 2003). European American teenagers are twice as likely to be employed as teenagers from ethnic minority groups, for example. In past years, teenagers from poorer households were more likely to work in order to help support the family. Nowadays, adolescent employment is more common among middle-class youth. This change

may be related to the fact that middle-class families are more likely to live near locations, such as suburban shopping malls, that are fertile sources of jobs for teenagers. However, lower-income adolescents who are employed work longer hours than middle-class teens (Staff et al., 2015).

Pros and Cons of Adolescent Employment

The potential benefits of adolescent employment include developing a sense of responsibility, self-reliance, and discipline; learning to appreciate the value of money and education; acquiring positive work habits and values; and enhancing occupational aspirations (Porfeli, 2007). On the other hand, the meaning of work for adolescents—at least for middle-class adolescents—seems to have changed. Most adolescents who work do not do so to help support their families or to put money away for college. Although adolescents of lower socioeconomic status work mainly to supplement the family income, many middle-class adolescents use their income for personal purchases, such as clothing, iPads, sports gear, apps, even car payments (Staff et al., 2015). The proportion of earnings devoted to future college expenses or family expenses is small.

In addition, most employed adolescents work in service and retail jobs characterized by low pay, high turnover, little authority, and little chance for advancement. They typically perform simple, repetitive tasks requiring no special skills, minimal supervision, and little interdependence with other workers (Staff et al., 2004). Some question the benefits of such jobs.

Teenagers and Work What are the pros and cons of part-time employment during high school?

TRUTH OR FICTION REVISITED: As a group, adolescents who work after school do appear to get lower grades. Research indicates that the effects of teenage employment may be harmful for students who work long hours. Students who work more than 11–13 hours per week report lower grades, higher rates of drug and alcohol use, more delinquent behavior, lower self-esteem, and more psychological problems than students who do not work or who work only a few hours a week (Dumont et al., 2009; Holloway, 2004).

Grades and time spent on homework drop for students who work long hours. Use of drugs and alcohol increases (Ramchand et al., 2009). Adolescents who work longer hours also spend less time in family activities, are monitored less by their parents, and are granted more freedom with day-to-day decisions (Staff et al., 2015).

Perhaps the most prudent course is for parents and educators to limit the number of hours that adolescents work. Some states are tightening their regulations on the number of hours teenagers can work during the school year.

Throughout this chapter, we have seen that both parents and peers influence the intellectual, moral, and vocational development of adolescents. Adolescents' relationships with family and friends, along with other aspects of their social and emotional development, are the topic of the final chapter.

Section Review

13. Children's career aspirations become increasingly _____ as they mature and gain experience.

14. Career choices of males and females are still to some degree influenced by traditional _____-role stereotypes.

15. An adolescent's career self-_____ expectations are his or her beliefs that he or she will be able to handle the tasks in a given career.

16. The _____ (majority or minority?) of high school students have a job during the school year.

Reflect & Relate: When you were in high school, did you have a job after school and/or on weekends? What were the effects of working on your grades, your social life, and your social maturation?

Chapter Review

15.1 What Happens During Jean Piaget's Stage of Formal Operations?

In Western societies, formal-operational thought begins at about the time of puberty. The major achievements of the stage involve classification, logical thought (deductive reasoning), and the ability to hypothesize. Adolescents can project themselves into situations that transcend their experience and become wrapped up in fantasies. The imaginary audience is the belief that others around us are concerned with our thoughts and behaviors, giving rise to the desire for privacy. The personal fable is the belief that our feelings and ideas are special and that we are invulnerable, which may underlie adolescent risk-taking.

15.2 What (If Any) Are The Gender Differences in Cognitive Abilities?

Females tend to excel in verbal ability. Males tend to excel in visual–spatial ability. The literature is mixed as to whether males excel in math. Boys are more likely than girls to have reading problems. Gender differences in visual–spatial skills have been linked to biological factors and to gender stereotypes.

15.3 What Are Kohlberg's Views on Moral Reasoning in Adolescence?

At the postconventional level, according to Kohlberg, moral reasoning is based on the person's own moral standards. Not all adolescents or adults reach the postconventional level, and there is controversy over gender differences in moral reasoning.

15.4 What Are the Experiences of the Adolescent in School?

The transition to middle, junior high, or high school generally involves a shift from a smaller, neighborhood elementary school to a larger, more impersonal setting. The transition is often accompanied by a decline in grades and a drop in self-esteem. High school dropouts are more likely to be unemployed and to earn lower salaries. Dropouts are more likely to show delinquent behaviors. Truancy and reading below grade level are factors in predicting school dropout.

15.5 What Are the Influences of Work Experiences on Adolescents?

Children's career aspirations are often not practical at first but become increasingly realistic as children mature and gain experience. Two of the factors that influence the choice of a career are abilities and personality traits. More than half of high school students hold part-time jobs during the school year. The benefits of adolescent employment include developing a sense of responsibility, self-reliance, and discipline, and learning to appreciate the value of money and education. But students who work also report lower grades and other problems.

Key Terms

formal operations   490
utopian   491
imaginary audience   493

personal fable   494
postconventional level   499

reciprocity   501
self-efficacy expectations   509

16

Adolescence:
Social and Emotional
Development

TruthorFiction?

 T | F Adolescents imitate their peers' clothing, speech, hairstyles, and ideals. **p. 516**

 T | F American adolescent males are more concerned about occupational choices than American adolescent females are. **p. 521**

T | F Adolescents are in a constant state of rebellion against their parents. **p. 523**

 T | F Most adolescents' friends are "bad influences." **p. 528**

T | F Petting is practically universal among American adolescents. **p. 533**

T | F Watching sexy TV shows is a cause of teenage pregnancy. **p. 537**

T | F More than half a million U.S. teenagers become pregnant each year. **p. 538**

T | F Only a minority of American adolescents engage in delinquent behavior. **p. 544**

T | F Suicide is the leading cause of death among American adolescents. **p. 547**

T | F Adolescents reach adulthood at age 21. **p. 551**

What am I like as a person? Complicated! I'm sensitive, friendly, and outgoing, though I can also be shy, self-conscious, and even obnoxious. I'd like to be friendly and tolerant all of the time. That's the kind of person I want to be, and I'm disappointed when I'm not. I'm responsible, even studious every now and then, but on the other hand I'm a goof-off too, because if you're too studious, you won't be popular. I'm a pretty cheerful person, especially with my friends, where I can even get rowdy. But I'm usually pretty stressed-out at home, or sarcastic, since my parents are always on my case. They expect me to get all A's. It's not fair! I worry about how I probably should get better grades. But I'd be mortified in the eyes of my friends. Sometimes I feel phony, especially around boys. Say I think some guy might be interested in asking me out. I try to act different, like Madonna. I'll be flirtatious and fun-loving. And then everybody else is looking at me like they think I'm totally weird! Then I get self-conscious and embarrassed and become radically introverted, and I don't know who I really am! But I don't really care what they think anyway. I just want to know what my close friends think. I can be my true self with my close friends. I can't be my real self with my parents. They don't understand me. They treat me like I'm still a kid. That gets confusing, though. I mean, which am I, a kid or an adult? It's scary, too, because I don't have any idea what I want to be when I grow up. I mean, I have lots of ideas. My friend Sheryl and I talk about whether we'll be teachers, or lawyers, veterinarians, maybe mothers. I know I don't want to be a waitress or a secretary. But how do you decide all of this? I mean, I think about it a lot, but I can't resolve it.

—Adapted from Harter (1990, pp. 352–353)

Dean Drobot/Shutterstock.com

This self-description of a 15-year-old girl illustrates a key aspect of the adolescent years: the search for an answer to the question, who am I? She is struggling to reconcile contradictory traits and behaviors to determine the "real me." She is preoccupied not only with her present self but also with what she wants to become. What were your concerns at this age?

In this chapter, we explore social and emotional development in adolescence. We begin with the formation of identity and related changes in self-concept and self-esteem. We consider adolescents' relationships with their parents and their peers. We consider the emergence of sexual behaviors and attitudes and focus on the issue of teenage pregnancy. We address the problems of juvenile delinquency and suicide. Then, as we bring our present voyage to a close, we explore what some theorists consider to be a new stage in human development: emerging adulthood.

16.1 Development of Identity and the Self-Concept: "Who Am I?" (And Who Else?)

Adolescence is a key period in the lifelong process of defining just who we are—and who we are not. In this section, we will examine Erik Erikson's influential theory of identity development in adolescence. We will then turn to James Marcia's identity statuses. Next, we will consider sex and ethnicity in identity development. Finally, we will look at the development of self-concept and self-esteem during adolescence.

What Does Erik Erikson Have to Say About the Development of Identity During Adolescence?

Erikson's fifth stage of psychosocial development is called identity versus identity diffusion. The primary task of this stage is for adolescents to develop **ego identity**—a sense of who they are and what they stand for. Individuals are faced with making choices about their future occupation, their ideological view of the world (including political and religious beliefs), and gender roles. The ability to engage in formal-operational thinking helps adolescents make these choices. Because thought is no longer tied to concrete experience, adolescents can weigh the options available to them, even though they may not have experienced these options directly (Moshman, 2013).

An important aspect of identity development is what Erikson (1968) referred to as a **moratorium**—a sort of time-out during which adolescents experiment with different roles, values, beliefs, and relationships. During the moratorium, adolescents undergo an **identity crisis**, in which they examine their values and make decisions about their life roles. Should they attend college? What career should they pursue? Should they become sexually active? With whom? Adolescents in developed nations may feel overwhelmed by the options before them and by the need to make choices that will narrow their future alternatives (Crain, 2000).

On the other hand, as noted by Jennifer Pastor and her colleagues (2007), many adolescents, such as adolescent girls of color who live in the inner city, are not likely to have the choices that Erikson was theorizing about. They may become sexually active at early ages because of local custom and peer pressure. College may be out of the question. Occupational choices may be limited. For many indigent adolescent girls of color, the Eriksonian developmental sequence is a distant dream.

ego identity According to Erikson, one's sense of who one is and what one stands for.

moratorium An identity status that characterizes those who are actively exploring alternatives in an attempt to form an identity.

identity crisis A turning point in development during which one examines one's values and makes decisions about life roles.

TRUTH OR FICTION REVISITED: In their search for identity, many—certainly not all—adolescents join "in" groups, slavishly imitating their peers' clothing, speech, hairstyles, ideals, and MP3 players. They may become intolerant of outsiders (Erikson, 1963). Those who successfully resolve their identity crisis develop a strong sense of who they are and what they stand for. Those who fail to resolve the crisis may continue to be intolerant of people who are different and blindly follow people who adhere to convention.

What Are James Marcia's "Identity Statuses"?

Building on Erikson's approach, Marcia (2010) theorized four identity statuses, which represent the four possible combinations of the dimensions of exploration and commitment that Erikson believed were critical to the development of identity (Kroger & Marcia, 2011; Marcia, 2010; see Concept Review 16.1).

Exploration involves active questioning and searching among alternatives in the quest to establish goals, values, and beliefs. **Commitment** is a stable investment in one's goals, values, and beliefs (Kunnen & Metz, 2015).

Identity diffusion is the least developmentally advanced status. This category includes individuals who neither have commitments nor are trying to form them (Arnett, 2015; Marcia, 2014). This stage is often characteristic of primary school and early high school children. Older adolescents who remain diffused may drift

exploration Active questioning and searching among alternatives in the quest to establish goals, values, and beliefs.

commitment A stable investment in one's goals, values, and beliefs.

identity diffusion An identity status that characterizes those who have made no commitments and are not in the process of exploring alternatives.

Marcia's Identity Statuses

		Exploration	
		Yes	**No**
Commitment	**Yes**	**Identity Achievement** • Most developed in terms of identity • Has experienced a period of exploration • Has developed commitments • Has a sense of personal well-being, high self-esteem, and self-acceptance • Cognitively flexible • Sets goals and works toward achieving them	**Foreclosure** • Has commitments without considering alternatives • Commitments based on identification with parents, teachers, or other authority figures • Often authoritarian and inflexible
	No	**Moratorium** • Actively exploring alternatives • Attempting to make choices with regard to occupation, ideological beliefs, and so on • Often anxious and intense • Ambivalent feelings toward parents and authority figures	**Identity Diffusion** • Least developed in terms of identity • Lacks commitments • Not trying to form commitments • May be carefree and uninvolved or unhappy and lonely • May be angry, alienated, or rebellious

Image Source Photography/Veer

through life in a carefree, uninvolved way, or they may be unhappy and lonely. Some diffused individuals are apathetic and adopt an "I don't care" attitude. Others are angry, alienated, and rebellious and may reject socially approved goals, values, and beliefs (Marcia, 2014; Moshman, 2013).

In the **foreclosure** status, individuals make commitments without seriously considering alternatives. These commitments usually are established early in life and often are based on identification with parents, teachers, or religious leaders who have made a strong impression on the child. For example, a college student may unquestioningly prepare for a career that his parents have chosen for him. In other cases, the adolescent may uncritically adopt the lifestyle of a religious cult or an extremist political group, as in so-called closed-minded fundamentalists (Jones et al., 2012). Some foreclosed individuals are authoritarian and inflexible (Jones et al., 2012).

The moratorium status it that of a person who is actively exploring alternatives in an attempt to make choices with regard to occupation, ideological beliefs, and so on (Kunnen & Metz, 2015; Moshman, 2013). Such individuals are often anxious and intense as they struggle to work toward commitment.

Identity achievement is the status of those who have experienced a period of exploration and have developed relatively firm commitments. Individuals who have achieved a clear sense of identity show a number of strengths. They have a sense of personal well-being in the form of high self-esteem and self-acceptance. Unlike foreclosed individuals, those who achieve identity are cognitively flexible and capable of reason. They are able to set goals and work toward achieving them (Klimstra et al., 2012; Marcia, 2014).

Development of Identity Statuses

Before high school, children show little interest in questions related to identity. Most of them are in either the identity diffusion or the foreclosure status. During the high school and college years, adolescents increasingly move from the diffusion and foreclosure statuses to the moratorium and achievement statuses (Moshman, 2013; Marcia, 2014). The greatest gains in identity formation occur during college (Berzonsky, 2011). College students are exposed to a broad spectrum of lifestyles, belief systems, and career choices. These experiences spur consideration of identity issues. Are you one of the college students who has changed majors once or twice (or more)? If so, you have probably experienced the moratorium identity status, which is common among college students. You should be comforted by the results of studies showing that college seniors have a stronger sense of identity than first-year students. The identity commitments of older students are likely to result from successfully resolving crises experienced during the moratorium. Moreover, a sense of identity is associated with higher self-esteem and grades (Perez et al., 2014; Ryeng et al., 2013).

What Are the Connections Between Ethnicity and Other Sociocultural Factors—Such as Gender—and Identity?

The connection between ethnicity and identity had a special significance during journalist Don Terry's childhood:

> When I was a kid growing up in Chicago, I used to do anything I could to put off going to bed. One of my favorite delaying tactics was to engage my mother in a discussion about the important questions of the day, questions my friends and I had debated in the backyards of our neighborhood that afternoon—like Who did God root for, the Cubs or the White Sox? (The correct answer was, and still is, the White Sox.)

foreclosure An identity status that characterizes those who have made commitments without considering alternatives.

identity achievement An identity status that characterizes those who have explored alternatives and have developed commitments.

Then one night I remember asking my mother something I had been wondering for a long time. "Mom," I asked, "what am I?"

"You're my darling Donny," she said.

"I know. But what else am I?"

"You're a precious little boy who someday will grow up to be a wonderful, handsome man."

"What I mean is, you're white and Dad's black, so what does that make me?"

"Oh, I see," she said. "Well, you're half-black and you're half-white, so you're the best of both worlds."

The next day, I told my friends that I was neither black nor white. "I'm the best of both worlds," I announced proudly.

"Man, you're crazy," one of the backyard boys said. "You're not even the best of your family. Your sister is. That girl is fine."

For much of my life, I've tried to believe my mother. Having grown up in a family of blacks and whites, I'd long thought I saw race more clearly than most people. I appreciated being able to get close to both worlds, something few ever do. It was like having a secret knowledge.

And yet I've also known from an early age that things were more complicated than my mother made them out to be. Our country, from its very beginnings, has been obsessed with determining who is white and who is black. Our history has been shaped by that disheartening question. To be both black and white, then, is to do nothing less than confound national consciousness.

—Terry (2000)

To be both black and white—African American and European American—can also confound or confuse the consciousness of the individual (Arnett & Brody, 2008). Terry's mother had once been married to a European American, and Don had European American brothers. His experiences of the next several years reveal his efforts to come to grips with a nation that saw him as African American, not half and half. He chronicles his experiences with prejudice, even within his own family, and how he eventually embraced blackness—as a shield and a cause.

Being African American, Asian American, European American, Latin American, Native American, or a combination of these is part of the self-identity of the individual. So is one's gender—being male or being female. So is one's religion, whether Christian, Hindu, Jewish, Muslim, or any of the hundreds of other religions we find in the United States.

The development of self-identity is a key task for all American adolescents (Kunnen & Metz, 2015). The task is more complex for adolescents who are members of ethnic minority groups (Azmitia, 2015; Way & Rogers, 2015; Worrell, 2015). Adolescents who belong to the dominant culture—in this country, European Americans of Christian, especially Protestant, heritage—are usually faced with assimilating one set of cultural values into their identities. However, adolescents who belong to ethnic minority groups, such as African Americans and Jewish Americans, confront two sets of cultural values: the values of the dominant culture and those of their particular ethnic group (Worrell, 2015). If the cultural values conflict, the adolescent needs to sort out the values that are most meaningful to him or her and incorporate them into his or her identity (Cooper et al., 2015; Umana-Taylor et al., 2014). Some adolescents do it cafeteria style; they take a little bit of this and a little bit of that. For example, a young Catholic woman may decide to use artificial means of birth control, even though doing so conflicts with her religion's teachings. Methods of birth control are well publicized in the culture at large, and the woman may decide to use them, although she may decide not to tell her priest or her family.

How Does Ethnic Identity Develop? According to psychologist Jean S. Phinney, adolescents undergo a three-stage process of developing ethnic identity: unexamined ethnic identity, ethnic identity search, and achieved ethnic identity. Adolescents from ethnic minority groups may be faced with conflicting values: those of their ethnic group and those of the dominant culture.

Another problem in forging a sense of identity is that adolescents from ethnic minority groups often experience prejudice and discrimination. Their cultural heroes may be ignored. A relative scarcity of successful role models can be a problem, particularly for youths who live in poverty (Arnett & Brody, 2008; Way & Rogers, 2015). Identifying too strongly with the dominant culture may lead to rejection by the minority group. On the other hand, rejecting the dominant culture's values for those of the minority group may limit opportunities for advancement in the larger society. Biracial adolescents—those with parents from two different racial or ethnic groups—wrestle not only with these issues but also with issues related to their dual cultural heritage (Worrell, 2015).

Many adolescents from ethnic minority groups have fewer educational and career opportunities than those from the dominant culture (Way & Rogers, 2015). If one cannot expect a future, why explore one's options? Some adolescents from ethnic minority groups—Latin Americans, African Americans, and Native Americans—foreclose earlier on identity issues than do their European American peers. Others are actively engaged in the search for identity (Azmitia, 2015; Worrell, 2015). Adolescents from ethnic minority groups may develop strategies for handling conflicting cultural demands, such as those we find in the following comment:

> Being invited to someone's house, I have to change my ways of how I act at home, because of culture differences. I would have to follow what they do. . . . I am used to it now, switching off between the two. It is not difficult.
> —Phinney & Rosenthal (1992)

What Are the Stages in Developing an Ethnic Identity?

Some researchers hypothesize three stages in the development of **ethnic identity** (Phinney, 2006; Umaña-Taylor et al., 2004). The first is **unexamined ethnic identity**. It is similar to Marcia's identity statuses of diffusion and foreclosure. In some cases, the early adolescent has not given much thought to ethnic identity issues (diffusion). In other instances, the young adolescent may have adopted an identity either with the dominant group or with the minority group based on societal or parental values but without much exploration or thought (foreclosure). In the second stage, the adolescent embarks on an **ethnic identity search**. This stage, which is similar to Marcia's moratorium, may be based on some incident that makes the adolescent aware of her ethnicity. During this stage, the adolescent may explore her ethnic culture, intensely participating in cultural events, reading, and talking to others. In the third stage, individuals have an **achieved ethnic identity**. This involves a clear, confident acceptance of oneself as a member of one's ethnic group and helps individuals withstand the stress that comes from societal discrimination (Romero et al., 2014).

As minority youths move through adolescence, they are increasingly likely to explore their own ethnicity and to acquire an achieved ethnic identity. For example, only about one-third of African American 8th-graders were found to show evidence of ethnic identity search, compared with half of African American 10th-graders. A longitudinal study (Phinney & Chavira, 1992) found movement from lower to higher stages of ethnic identity between 16 and 19 years of age. And college undergraduates show higher levels of ethnic identity achievement than 11th-or 12th-graders (Phinney, 1992).

Does the Development of Ego Identity Differ in Males and Females?

Erikson believed that there were gender differences in the development of identity, and his views reflected the times in which he wrote. Identity development is related

ethnic identity A sense of belonging to an ethnic group.

unexamined ethnic identity The first stage of ethnic identity development; similar to the diffusion and foreclosure identity statuses.

ethnic identity search The second stage of ethnic identity development; similar to the moratorium identity status.

achieved ethnic identity The final stage of ethnic identity development; similar to the identity achievement status.

both to relationships and to occupational choice, among other matters, and Erikson (1968, 1975; Anthis et al., 2004) assumed that relationships were more important to women's development of identity, whereas occupational and ideological matters were more important to men's. He believed that a young woman's identity was intimately bound up with her roles as wife and mother. Erikson, like most thinkers of his day, saw a woman's primary roles as related to her home life. In sum, it was normal for men to develop their identities before they developed (meaningful) intimate relationships. But women might develop their identities simultaneously with the development of intimate relationships.

However, the evidence from numerous studies suggests that females approach identity formation in much the same way as males do (Murray, 1998; Phinney, 2006).

TRUTH OR FICTION REVISITED: Adolescent females and males are both concerned about occupational choices but females are more likely to integrate occupational and family plans (Berzonsky, 2011; Cinamon & Rich, 2014). This gender difference may persist because females continue to assume primary responsibility for child rearing, even though most women are employed outside the home.

Kristine Anthis and her colleagues (2004) have noted that we can think of the development of identity in terms of individuals' concept of future "possible selves"—representations of ourselves in the future (Anthis, 2006). Our possible selves are affected by cultural and personal factors, and they reflect both our hopes and our fears. Our possible selves affect our striving to become one kind of person or another. Gender-role stereotypes affect our possible selves, and men's possible selves are likely to revolve around careers, whereas women's possible selves are more likely to revolve around family life as well as careers (Anthis, 2006).

How Does the Self-Concept Develop During Adolescence?

The adolescent preoccupation with identity is part of a broader process of redefining the way adolescents view themselves. Before adolescence, children describe themselves primarily in terms of their physical characteristics and their actions. As they approach adolescence, children begin to incorporate psychological characteristics and social relationships into their self-descriptions. Adolescents tend to describe themselves in terms of distinct and enduring personality traits (Way & Rogers, 2015; Worrell, 2015).

The self-concept becomes more differentiated; adolescents add more categories to their self-descriptions (Arnett, 2015). Also, self-descriptions begin to vary according to adolescents' social roles. Like the 15-year-old at the beginning of the chapter, adolescents may describe themselves as anxious or sarcastic with parents but as caring, talkative, and cheerful with friends. Such contradictions and conflicts in self-description reach their peak at about age 14 and then begin to decline in later adolescence (Athenstaedt et al., 2008; Harter & Monsour, 1992). The more advanced formal-operational skills of older adolescents enable them to integrate the many apparently contradictory elements of the self. For example, the older adolescent might say, "I'm very adaptable. When I'm around my friends, who think that what I say is important, I'm very talkative; but around my family, I'm quiet because they're not interested enough to really listen to me" (Damon, 1991, p. 988).

What Happens to Self-Esteem During Adolescence: Bottoming? Rising?

self-esteem The sense of value or worth that people attach to themselves.

Self-esteem tends to decline as the child progresses from middle childhood to about the age of 12 or 13 (Harter & Whitesell, 2003; Kim & Cicchetti, 2009). What might account for the drop-off? The growing cognitive maturity of young adolescents makes them increasingly and painfully aware of the disparity between their ideal self and their real self. The sense of discrepancy between real self and ideal self is especially great in the area of physical appearance. Physical appearance contributes more to the development of self-esteem during adolescence than any other characteristic (Fourchard & Courtinat-Camps, 2013; Stieger et al., 2014). Boys might fantasize about having the physiques of the warriors they see in video games or other media. Most girls want to be thin, thin, thin (Daniels & Gillen, 2015).

Development of Self-Esteem During Adolescence Self-esteem tends to dip during early adolescence as young people face the differences between their real self and their ideal self. However, self-esteem tends to improve with emotional support from family and peers.

After hitting a low point at about age 12 or 13, self-esteem gradually improves throughout adolescence (Harter & Whitesell, 2003). Perhaps adolescents adjust their notions of the ideal self to better reflect reality. Also, as adolescents develop academic, physical, and social skills, they may gradually become less self-critical (Schwartz et al., 2011).

For most adolescents, low self-esteem produces temporary discomfort (Harter & Whitesell, 2003). For others, low self-esteem has serious psychological and behavioral consequences. For example, low self-esteem is often a characteristic of teenagers and adults who are depressed or suicidal (Stieger et al., 2014).

Emotional support from parents and peers is important in the development of self-esteem during adolescence. Adolescents who feel that they are highly regarded by family and friends are more likely to have positive feelings about themselves than are those who feel they are lacking such support (Boudreault-Bouchard et al., 2013; Rote & Smetana, 2015). In early adolescence, support from parents is just as important as peer support. By late adolescence, peer support carries more weight.

Section Review

1. Erikson's fifth (adolescent) stage of psychosocial development is called _____ versus identity diffusion.

2. Erikson defined a psychological _____ as a time-out during which adolescents experiment with different roles, values, beliefs, and relationships.

3. According to Marcia, identity _____ is the identity status of adolescents who have experienced a period of exploration and developed relatively firm commitments.

4. Research suggests that the most important factor in adolescent self-esteem is _____.

Reflect & Relate: Does your ethnic background play an important role in your self-identity? Explain.

16.2 Relationships with Parents and Peers

Adolescents coping with the task of establishing a sense of identity and direction in their lives are heavily influenced by both their parents and their peers.

How Do Relationships with Parents Change During Adolescence?

During adolescence, children spend much less time with their parents than they did during childhood. In one study, children ranging from 9 to 15 years old carried electronic pagers for a week and reported what they were doing each time they were signaled by the pagers (Larson & Richards, 1991). The amount of time spent with family dramatically declined as the age of the children increased. The 15-year-olds spent half as much time with their families as the 9-year-olds. For older boys, the time with family was replaced by time spent alone, whereas older girls spent more time alone or with friends.

Adolescents interact more with their mothers than with their fathers, continuing the pattern begun in childhood. Teenagers engage in more conflicts with their mothers, but they also view their mothers as being more supportive, as knowing them better, and as being more likely to accept their opinions (Rote & Smetana, 2015; Smetana et al., 2013). Adverse relationships with fathers are often associated with depression in adolescents (Sheeber et al., 2007). On the other hand, good relationships with fathers strongly contribute to the psychological well-being of adolescents (Flouri & Buchanan, 2003).

The decrease in time spent with family may reflect the adolescents' striving to become more independent of their parents. A certain degree of distancing from parents may be adaptive for adolescents as they engage in the tasks of forming relationships outside the family and entering adulthood. But greater independence does not mean that adolescents become emotionally detached from their mothers and fathers. Adolescents continue to maintain a great deal of love, loyalty, and respect for their parents (Collins & Laursen, 2006). And adolescents who feel close to their parents are more likely to show greater self-reliance and independence, higher self-esteem, better school performance, and fewer psychological and social problems (Rote & Smetana, 2015; Smetana et al., 2013).

The relationship between parents and teens is not always rosy, of course. Early adolescence, in particular, is characterized by increased bickering and disagreements and by a decrease in shared activities and expressions of affection (Rote & Smetana, 2015).

Conflict is greatest during puberty and declines in later adolescence (Rote & Smetana, 2015). Conflicts typically center on the everyday details of family life, such as chores, homework, curfews, personal appearance, finances, and dating. Conflicts may arise in these areas because adolescents believe that personal issues—such as their choices of clothes and friends—that were previously controlled by parents should now come under the control of the adolescent (Costigan et al., 2007; Rote & Smetana, 2015). But parents, especially mothers, continue to believe that they should retain control in most areas, such as encouraging adolescents to do their homework and clean their rooms. And so conflicts arise. As adolescents get older, however, they and their parents are more likely to compromise (Rote & Smetana, 2015; Smetana et al., 2013).

Despite these conflicts, parents and adolescents are usually quite similar in their values and beliefs regarding social, political, religious, and economic issues (Rote & Smetana, 2015). Even though the notion of a generation gap between adolescents and their parents may persist as a popular stereotype, there is little evidence to support it.

TRUTH OR FICTION REVISITED: Adolescents are not in a constant state of rebellion against their parents. Their values tend to be similar to those of their parents.

During adolescence, most teenagers and their parents establish a balance between adolescent independence and continued family connectedness. Although some conflict is inevitable, it usually is not severe (Rote & Smetana, 2015; Smetana et al., 2013). As adolescents grow older, parents are more likely to relax controls and less likely to use punishment (Rote & Smetana, 2015). Although parent–child relationships change, most adolescents feel that they are close to and get along with their parents, even though they may develop a less idealized view of their parents (Collins & Laursen, 2006).

Parenting Styles

Children's development is affected by the degree to which their parents show warmth and set limits on the child's behavior. Differences in parenting styles continue to influence the development of adolescents as well (Kenney et al., 2015; Vermeulen-Smit et al., 2015). Adolescents from authoritative homes—whose parents are willing to exert control and explain the reasons for doing so—show more competent behavior than any other group of teenagers. They are more self-reliant, do better in school, have better mental health, and show the lowest incidence of psychological problems and misconduct, including drug use.

How Do Relationships with Peers Change During Adolescence?

The transition from childhood to adolescence is accompanied by a shift in the relative importance of parents and peers. Although relationships with parents generally remain positive, the role of peers as a source of activities, influence, and support increases markedly during the teen years. For example, fourth-graders perceive their parents as the most frequent providers of social and emotional support. But by seventh grade, friends of the same gender are seen to be as supportive as parents. And by 10th grade, same-gender friends are viewed as providing more support than parents (Furman & Buhrmester, 1992).

Development of Friendship in Adolescence Adolescents tend to spend more time with their friends than with their families. They look for one or more close friends, or confidants. They also tend to belong to cliques and crowds. All these relationships serve different but overlapping functions.

Friendships in Adolescence

Friendships occupy an increasingly important place in the lives of adolescents. Adolescents have more friends than younger children do (Kirke, 2009). Most adolescents have one or two "best friends" and several good friends. Teenagers see their friends frequently, usually several hours a day (Hartup, 1993). And when teenagers are not with their friends, you can often find them talking with each other on the phone, texting them, or chatting with them online.

Friendships in adolescence differ in important ways from the friendships of childhood. First, adolescents are much more likely to stress the importance of acceptance, self-disclosure, and mutual understanding in their friendships (Hall, 2011). For example, one eighth-grade girl described her best friend this way: "I can tell her things and she helps me talk. And she doesn't laugh at me if I do something weird—she accepts me for who I am" (Berndt & Perry, 1990, p. 269). Second, adolescents stress loyalty and trustworthiness as important aspects of friendship more than younger children do (Hall, 2011). For example, they may say that a friend will "stick up for you in a fight" and will not "talk about you behind your back." Finally, adolescents are more likely than younger children to share with friends and are less likely to compete with them.

Adolescents and their friends are similar in many respects. They typically are the same age and the same race. They almost always are the same gender. Even though romantic attachments increase during the teen years, most adolescents still choose members of their own gender as best friends (Field et al., 2014; Van Zalk et al., 2010). Friends are likely to share certain behavioral similarities. They often are alike in their school attitudes, educational aspirations, and school achievement. Friends also tend to have similar attitudes about drinking, drug use, sexual activity, and educational plans (Kiuru et al., 2012; Mercken et al., 2012).

Friendship contributes to a positive self-concept and psychological adjustment. Adolescents who have a close friend have higher self-esteem than adolescents who do not. Teenagers who have close friendships also are more likely to show advanced stages of identity development (Brendgen et al., 2010).

And Then There Are All the Facebook Friends . . .

According to the Pew Research Center (A. Smith, 2014), Facebook is used by more than half (57%) of U.S. adults, and almost three out of four (73%) of U.S. adolescents aged 12–17. The four top dislikes of Facebook users (A. Smith, 2014) are:

- People share too much information about themselves (36%)
- Other people post information—including photos—about you without your permission (36%)
- Other people see comments or posts that you meant to keep private (27%)
- There is pressure to disclose too much information about yourself (24%)

Many adolescent Facebook users reported concerns: more and more adults are using Facebook, it is crucial to manage your self-presentation carefully, the burden of "drama" (negative social interactions), and friends sharing too much information (Madden, 2013). An overwhelming percentage (94%!) of teenagers who are social media users have Facebook profiles, as compared with 26% who report having Twitter profiles or 11% who report having Instagram profiles.

Adolescents and young adults report having more Facebook friends than all adults combined: Whereas 15% of all adults report having more than 500 friends, nearly twice that amount (27%) of users aged 18–29 report having more than 500 friends. Sixty-five-year-olds also use Facebook, but nearly three in four of them (72%) have 100 friends or fewer. This finding is consistent with research that finds that older people have fewer actual friends than younger people have, but that their friends have more in common with them and are more deeply committed to them at advanced ages.

Ethnicity, Gender, and Adolescent Friendships

I always notice one thing when I walk through the commons at my high school: The whites are on one side of the room, and the blacks are on the other. When I have to walk through the "black" side to get to class, the black students just quietly ignore me and look in the other direction, and I do the same. But there's one who sometimes catches my eye, and I can't help feeling awkward when I see him. He was a close friend from childhood. Ten years ago, we played catch in our backyards, went bike riding, and slept over at one another's houses. By the fifth grade, we went to movies and amusement parks and bunked together at summer camp. We're both juniors now at the same high school. We usually don't say anything when we see each other, except maybe a polite "Hi." Since entering high school, we haven't shared a single class or sport. It's as if fate has kept us apart, though, more likely, it's peer pressure.

—Adapted from Jarvis (1993, p. 14)

Children are more likely to choose friends from their own ethnic group than from other groups (Castelli et al., 2009). This pattern strengthens in adolescence (Hartup, 1993). Adolescents from ethnic minority groups grow aware of the differences between their culture and the dominant culture. Peers from their own ethnic group provide a sense of camaraderie that reduces their feelings of isolation from the dominant culture (Spencer et al., 1990).

One study compared friendship patterns of African American and European American adolescents who attended an integrated junior high school (DuBois & Hirsch, 1990). More than 80% of the students of both ethnic groups reported having a school friend of the other ethnicity, but only 28% of the students saw such a friend frequently outside school. African American youths were almost twice as likely as European American youths to see a friend of another ethnicity outside school. Children who lived in integrated as opposed to segregated neighborhoods were more likely to see a friend of another ethnicity outside the school setting.

Gender differences related to peer intimacy and support were found for European American students but not for African American students. European American girls reported talking more with friends about personal problems and reported that their friends were more available for help than did European American boys (Hartup, 1993; Youniss & Haynie, 1992). But African American girls and boys reported the same degree of intimacy and support in their friendships. How can these differences be explained? The researchers suggest that the African American students may have faced ethnicity-related stressors in their school, which was integrated but predominantly European American. To cope more effectively, both girls and boys may have relied heavily on the support of their peers.

Intimacy and closeness appear to be more central to the friendships of girls than of boys both in childhood and in adolescence (Gleason et al., 2009; Schraf & Hertz-Lazarowitz, 2003). Both female and male adolescents describe girls' friendships as closer than boys' friendships (Leaper, 2013). Girls spend more time with their friends than boys do (Schraf & Hertz-Lazarowitz, 2003). Adolescent girls view close friendships as more important than adolescent boys do, and they report putting more effort into improving the depth and quality of these relationships. Adolescent and adult females also are generally more likely than males to disclose secrets, personal problems, thoughts, and feelings to their friends (Leaper, 2013). Males, however, may be more likely to disclose information about their sex lives (Chiou & Wan, 2006).

Friendship networks among girls are smaller and more exclusive than friendship networks among boys (Schraf & Hertz-Lazarowitz, 2003). That is, girls tend to have one or two close friends, whereas boys tend to congregate in larger groups in which individuals are not necessarily close. The activities of girls' and boys' friendship networks differ as well. Girls are more likely to engage in unstructured activities such as talking and listening to music. Boys, on the other hand, are more likely to engage in organized group activities, games, and sports.

Peer Groups

In addition to forming close friendships, most adolescents belong to one or more larger peer groups. Peer groups include cliques and crowds (Henzi et al., 2007; Palla et al., 2007). **Cliques** consist of 5 to 10 individuals who hang around together and share activities and confidences. **Crowds** are larger groups of individuals who may or may not spend much time together and are identified by the particular activities or attitudes of the group. Crowds are usually given labels by other adolescents. Think back on your high school days. Different groups of individuals are commonly given labels such as "jocks," "brains," "druggies," "nerds," and so on. Members of the most negatively labeled groups ("druggies," "rejects," and so on) show higher levels of alcohol and drug use, delinquency, and depression than members of other groups.

Adolescent peer groups differ from childhood peer groups. For one thing, the time spent with peers increases. High school students spend more than half their

clique A group of 5 to 10 individuals who hang around together and share activities and confidences.

crowd A large, loosely organized group of people who may or may not spend much time together and who are identified by the activities of the group.

time with peers and only about 15% of their time with parents or other adults (Halpern, 2005; Staff et al., 2004). Korean and Japanese students spend significantly more time than their European and American peers doing homework and preparing for college entrance exams (Halpern, 2005).

A second difference between adolescent and childhood peer groups is that adolescent peer groups function with less adult guidance or control (Staff et al., 2004). Childhood peer groups stay closer to home, under the watchful eye of parents. Adolescent peer groups are more likely to congregate in settings where there is less adult supervision (the school) or no supervision.

A third change in adolescent peer groups is the addition of peers of the other gender. This sharply contrasts with the gender segregation of childhood peer groups (Staff et al., 2004). Association with peers of the other gender may lead to dating and romantic relationships.

Dating and Romantic Relationships

Romantic relationships begin to appear during early and middle adolescence, and most adolescents start dating or going out by the time they graduate from high school (Florsheim, 2003). Dating typically develops in the following sequence: putting oneself in situations where peers of the other gender probably will be present (e.g., hanging out at the mall), participating in group activities that include peers of the other gender (e.g., attending school dances or parties), dating in groups (e.g., joining a mixed-gender group at the movies), and then going on traditional two-person dates (Connolly et al., 2004).

Dating serves several important functions. First and foremost, people date to have fun. High school students rate time spent with a person of the other gender as the time when they are happiest (Csikszentmihalyi & Larson, 1984). Dating, especially in early adolescence, also serves to enhance prestige with one's peers. Dating gives adolescents additional experiences in learning to relate positively to different people. Finally, dating provides preparation for adult courtship activities (Florsheim, 2003).

Dating relationships tend to be casual and short-lived in early adolescence. In late adolescence, relationships tend to become more stable and committed (Connolly et al., 2000). It is therefore not surprising that 18-year-olds are more likely than 15-year-olds to mention love, trust, and commitment when describing their romantic relationships (Feiring, 1993).

Peer Influence

Parents often worry that their teenage children will fall in with the wrong crowd and be persuaded by their peers to engage in behaviors that are self-destructive or go against the parents' wishes (Brown et al., 1993). How much influence do peers have on one another? Does peer pressure cause adolescents to adopt behaviors and attitudes of which their parents disapprove? Peer pressure actually is fairly weak in early adolescence. It peaks during middle adolescence and declines in late adolescence, after about age 17 (Brown et al., 1993; Reis & Youniss, 2004).

Why does the influence of peers increase during adolescence? One suggestion is that peers provide a standard by which adolescents measure their behavior as they begin to develop independence from the family (Foster-Clark & Blyth, 1991). Another possible reason is that peers provide social, emotional, and practical support in times of trouble (Kirchler et al., 1991; Pombeni et al., 1990).

It was once the conventional wisdom that peer influence and parental influence were in conflict, with peers exerting pressure on adolescents to engage in negative behaviors such as alcohol and drug use. Research paints a more complex picture. For one thing, we have seen that adolescents often maintain close and warm relationships with their parents.

Parents and peers also seem to exert influence in somewhat different domains. Adolescents are more likely to conform to peer standards in matters pertaining to style and taste, such as clothing, hairstyles, speech patterns, and music (Camarena, 1991). They are much more likely to agree with their parents on many serious issues, such as moral principles and future educational and career goals (Savin-Williams & Berndt, 1990).

Adolescents influence each other both positively and negatively. Brown and his colleagues (1993) found that peer pressure to finish high school and achieve academically was stronger than pressure to engage in misconduct, such as drug use, sexual activity, and minor delinquency. But a 10-year longitudinal study of 20,000 9th- through 12th-graders found that more often than not, adolescents discouraged one another from doing well or from doing too well (Steinberg, 1996). One in five reported not trying to perform as well as possible for fear of incurring the disapproval of peers. Then, too, half reported that they never discussed schoolwork and grades with their friends.

It is true that adolescents who smoke, drink, use drugs, and engage in sexual activity often have friends who also engage in these behaviors. But we must keep in mind that adolescents tend to choose friends and peers who are similar to them to begin with. Peers reinforce behavior patterns and predispositions that may have existed before the individual joined the group. This is true for positive behaviors, such as academic achievement, as well as for negative behaviors, such as drug use (Allen & Antonishak, 2008).

A number of other factors affect the susceptibility of adolescents to peer influence. One of these is gender. Girls appear to be slightly more concerned with peer acceptance than boys, but boys are more likely than girls to conform to pressures to engage in misconduct (Sumter et al., 2009). Parenting style also is related to susceptibility to peer pressure. Authoritative parenting appears to discourage negative peer influence, whereas authoritarian and permissive parenting seem to encourage it (Foster-Clark & Blyth, 1991; Fuligni & Eccles, 1993).

Social Networking Online

As soon as I get home, I turn on my computer. My MySpace is always on, and when I get a message on MySpace, it sends a text message to my phone. It's not an obsession; it's a necessity.

—A 15-year-old boy

You become addicted. You can't live without it.

—A 14-year-old girl

Adolescents generally feel that peers are necessities in their lives, and they interact with them extensively—not only in the flesh and on the telephone, but also on social networking sites such as Facebook and MySpace (Ellison et al., 2007). In a scenario all too familiar to many parents, a 17-year-old couple who have been seeing each other for over a year wake up, log onto their computers between showering and doing their hair, chat on their cell phones on the way to school, send text messages back and forth throughout the school day, and finally spend time together doing homework after school. Then, in the evening, they're on the phone again and often text "I love you" before they turn in for the night. (Ito et al., 2009). "I love you" has become a ubiquitous sign-off among adolescents and young adults, but sometimes, as in this case, it actually means "I love you."

The lead author of a study on teenagers' online behavior reports: "There's been some confusion about what kids are actually doing online. Mostly, they're socializing with their friends, people they've met at school or camp or sports" (Ito, 2008). National random surveys show that at least two of three American teenagers and young adults (18- to 29-year-olds) use social networking sites (Valenzuela et al., 2009).

A study of 2,603 Texas college students focused on users of Facebook and found that about one student user in four reported having 400 or more Facebook friends (Valenzuela et al., 2009; see Table 16.1 ●). More than one student user in three (34.9%) reported using Facebook for 10–30 minutes a day, and another 41.9% reported lengthier use (see Table 16.1). Most student users agreed that:

- Facebook is part of my everyday activity.
- I am proud to tell people I am on Facebook.
- I feel out of touch when I haven't logged onto Facebook for a day.
- I would be sorry if Facebook shut down.

What are the effects of the use of social networking sites? A study of 881 Dutch tweenies and teenagers (10 to 19 years old) found that use of the sites increased the number of "friendships" created on the site (Valkenburg et al., 2006). Greater use increased the frequency with which users received feedback on their profiles. Positive feedback on their profiles increased their self-esteem and their psychological sense of well-being, whereas negative feedback had the opposite effect. A study of 500 youths with an average age of 12 found that Internet use in general, and social networking in particular, had overall positive effects on the users' self-concepts. Part of the boost derived from the sense that the youths were becoming familiar with using the technology of the day (Jackson et al., 2009). Other researchers (Ellison et al., 2007) found that using Facebook helped maintain or solidify existing offline relationships. They also found that Facebook use was apparently most beneficial for users with low self-esteem and low life satisfaction. That is, some teenagers apparently find it easier to interact with others online than in the flesh. But eventually, the social skills gained online may help them in their flesh-and-blood contacts.

David J. Green - lifestyle 2/Alamy

● TABLE 16.1

Behavior of Texas College Student Facebook Users (n = 2,603)

1. About how many total Facebook friends do you have?	Percentage
Less than 10	1.9
10–49	8.4
50–99	9.7
100–149	11.3
150–199	12.2
200–249	9.9
250–299	8.9
300–399	11.7
400 or more	26.0

2. On a typical day, how much time do you spend on Facebook?	Percentage
No time at all	4.9
Less than 10 minutes	18.2
10–30 minutes	34.9
More than 30 minutes, up to 1 hour	22.2
More than 1 hour, up to 2 hours	14.3
More than 2 hours, up to 3 hours	3.9
More than 3 hours	1.5

Source: Adapted from Valenzuela et al. (2009).

Section Review

16.3 Sexuality: When? What? (How?) Who? Where? and Why?—Not to Mention, "Should I?"

My first sexual experience occurred in a car after the high school junior prom. We were both virgins, very uncertain but very much in love. We had been going together since eighth grade. The experience was somewhat painful. I remember wondering if I would look different to my mother the next day. I guess I didn't because nothing was said.

—Morrison, 1980

Because of the flood of sex hormones, many or most adolescents experience a powerful sex drive. In addition, they are bombarded with sexual messages in the media, including scantily clad hip-grinding, crotch-grabbing pop stars; print ads for barely-there underwear; and countless articles on "How to tell if your boyfriend has been (whatever)" and "The 10 things that will drive your girlfriend wild." Teenagers are strongly motivated to follow the crowd, yet they are also influenced by the views of their parents and teachers. So what is a teen to do? What *do* U.S. teens do?

Sexual activity in adolescence can take many forms. In this section, we will consider masturbation, sexual orientation, sexual behavior, and teenage pregnancy.

How Common Is Masturbation Among Adolescents?

Masturbation—sexual self-stimulation—is the most common sexual outlet in adolescence. Even before children imagine sexual experiences with others, they may learn that touching their own genitals can produce pleasure.

Surveys indicate that about three-quarters of male adolescents and half of adolescent females masturbate (Robbins et al., 2011). Boys who masturbate may do so several times a week, on average, or even several times a day, much more frequently than most girls who masturbate. These gender differences are confirmed in nearly every survey (Kaestle & Allen, 2011; Schmitt et al., 2012). It is unclear whether this gender difference reflects a stronger sex drive in boys, greater social constraints on girls, or both. Beliefs that masturbation is harmful and guilt about masturbation tend to lessen the incidence of masturbation, although masturbation has not been shown to be physically harmful (Kaestle & Allen, 2011).

How Does One's Sexual Orientation Develop During Adolescence?

Most people, including the great majority of adolescents, have a heterosexual orientation. That is, they are sexually attracted to and interested in forming romantic relationships with people of the other gender. However, some people have a **homosexual** orientation. They are attracted to and interested in forming romantic relationships with people of their own gender. Males with a homosexual orientation are referred to as *gay males*. Females with a homosexual orientation are referred to as *lesbians*. However, males and females with a homosexual orientation are sometimes categorized together as "gay people" or "gays." Bisexual people are attracted to both females and males (Persson et al., 2015). **Transgender** individuals, such as former Olympic athlete and reality TV star Caitlyn Jenner, feel that they are actually members of the other gender, "trapped" in the body of the wrong gender (Steel, 2015). Collectively, lesbian, gay, bisexual, and transgender individuals are frequently referred to as **LGBT** people.

A person's **sexual identity** is the label that he or she adopts to inform others as to who they are as a sexual being, especially concerning sexual orientation. Most people's sexual identity is consistent with their sexual orientation. That is, most people who are attracted to members of the other gender identify themselves as "heterosexual" or "straight." Most people who are attracted to people of the same gender see themselves as being "lesbian" or "gay." However, some people's sexual orientation does not correspond to their sexual identity.

About 7% of U.S. women and men define themselves as being "other than heterosexual," but the behavior of the other 93% doesn't exactly match up with the way in which people label themselves. For example, nearly twice as many people—about 14%—say they have had oral sex with a person of the same gender (Herbenick et al., 2010a, 2010b, 2010c; Reece et al., 2010).

Former Olympic Athlete Bruce Jenner (Now Caitlyn Jenner) with His Step-Daughter Kim Kardashian (Left) and His Now Ex-Wife, Kris Jenner. Bruce Jenner—now Caitlyn Jenner—raised consciousness about sexual minorities in general, and of transgender individuals in particular, by stating that he sees himself as a woman in a 2015 interview with Diane Sawyer.

Theories of the Origins of Sexual Orientation

Theories of the origins of sexual orientation look both at nature and nurture—the biological makeup of the individual and environmental factors. Some theories bridge the two.

Social cognitive theorists look for the roles of factors such as reinforcement and observational learning. From this perspective, reinforcement of sexual behavior with members of one's own gender—as in reaching orgasm with them when members of the other gender are unavailable—might affect one's sexual orientation. Similarly, childhood sexual abuse by someone of the same gender could lead to a pattern of sexual activity with people of one's own gender and affect sexual orientation. Observation of others engaged in enjoyable male–male or female–female sexual encounters could also affect the development of sexual orientation. But critics point out that most individuals become aware of their sexual orientation before they experience sexual contacts with other people of either gender (Calzo et al., 2011; Savin-Williams, 2011). Moreover, in a society where many still frown upon the LGBT community, young people are unlikely to believe that an other-than-heterosexual orientation or identity will have positive effects for them.

There is evidence for genetic factors in sexual orientation or identity (Brakefield et al., 2014). About 52% of identical (monozygotic, MZ) twin pairs are concordant (in agreement) for a gay male sexual orientation compared with 22% for fraternal (dizygotic, DZ) twins and 11% for adoptive brothers (Dawood et al., 2009). MZ twins fully share their genetic heritage, whereas DZ twins, like other pairs of siblings, overlap 50%.

homosexual Referring to an erotic orientation toward members of one's own gender.

transgender Descriptive of people who believe that they are members of the other gender "trapped" inside the body of the wrong gender.

LGBT Acronym for lesbian, gay, bisexual, and transgender.

sexual identity A complex concept involving one's sexual orientation, one's gender role, one's gender-related preferences, and the like.

It has been demonstrated repeatedly that sex hormones predispose lower animals toward stereotypical masculine or feminine mating patterns. But can sex hormones influence the developing human embryo and fetus (Garcia-Falgueras & Swaab, 2010)? Swedish neuroscientists Ivanka Savic and her colleagues (2011) report evidence that one's gender identity as being male or being female and one's sexual orientation (heterosexual, homosexual, bisexual, or transgender) can develop during the intrauterine period. They point out that sexual differentiation of the sex organs occurs during the first 2 months of pregnancy, whereas sexual differentiation of the brain begins later, during the second half of pregnancy. Sexual differentiation of the genitals and the brain both depend on surges of testosterone, but because they happen at different times, they can occur independently. Therefore, it is possible that an individual's sex organs can develop in one direction while the biological factors that may underlie one's sexual orientation develop in another direction.

According to Ritch Savin-Williams (2011), the development of sexual orientation in gay males and lesbians involves several steps: attraction to members of the same gender, self-labeling as gay or lesbian, sexual contact with members of the same gender, and eventual disclosure of one's sexual orientation to other people. There is generally a gap of about 10 years between initial attraction to members of the same gender, which tends to occur at about the age of 8 or 9, and disclosure of one's orientation to other people, which usually occurs at about age 18. But some gay males and lesbians never disclose their sexual orientations to anyone or to certain people, such as their parents.

We have to conclude by confessing that much about the development of sexual orientation remains speculative. There are possible roles for prenatal exposure to certain hormones. Exposure to these hormones, in turn, may be related to genetic factors. Even the possibility that childhood experiences play a role has not been ruled out. But the interactions among these factors largely remain a mystery. Nor is there reason to believe that the development of sexual orientation must follow the same path in everyone.

Coming Out

The process of "coming out"—accepting one's homosexual orientation and declaring it to others—may be a long and painful struggle (Mustanski, 2015; Mustanski et al., 2014). Gay adolescents may be ostracized and rejected by family and friends. Depression and suicide rates are higher among gay youths than among heterosexual adolescents (Stone et al., 2014). It has been estimated that as many as one in three gay, lesbian, or bisexual adolescents has attempted suicide (Liu & Mustanski, 2012; Mustanski, 2015). Homosexual adolescents often engage in substance abuse, run away from home, and do poorly in school (Moskowitz et al., 2013; Russell, 2006). These factors also heighten the risk of suicide among gay, lesbian, and bisexual adolescents.

Coming out is a two-pronged process: coming out to oneself (recognizing one's sexual orientation) and coming out to others (declaring one's orientation to the world). Coming out can create a sense of pride in one's sexual orientation and foster the ability to form emotionally and sexually satisfying relationships with gay male or lesbian partners. Yet, an adolescent generally feels more comfortable telling a couple of close friends than his or her parents. Before they inform family members, gay adolescents often anticipate their family's negative reactions, including denial, anger, and rejection (Mustanski, 2015; Mustanski et al., 2014). However, some families are more accepting. Perhaps they had suspicions and prepared themselves for the news. Then, too, many families are initially rejecting but eventually come to at least grudging acceptance that an adolescent is gay.

SEXTING: ONE MORE WAY FOR ADOLESCENTS TO STAY IN TOUCH

Facebook, Instagram, Twitter, email, cell phones, and texting. These are just a handful of the ways that adolescents keep in touch—many hours per day (Saleh et al., 2014). They text in school, at home, and when out. They surf Facebook pages of their friends' friends, seeking clues as to what a face-to-face encounter might mean. There is an upside: According to the lead researcher of a MacArthur Foundation report on teenagers' electronic connections, adolescents are not just wasting time. "Their participation is giving them the technological skills and literacy they need to succeed in the contemporary world. They're learning how to get along with others, how to manage a public identity, how to create a home page" (Ito, 2008).

And some of them are learning how to titillate or shock each other by sexting—sending or receiving text messages with sexual content. The term also applies to sending nude or otherwise provocative still images or videos by cell phone. Sexting can be used to sexually excite the recipient, to highlight the intimacy of one's relationship, to humiliate someone—as in the case of "revenge porn"—or to ask or arrange for a sexual encounter.

But there are some disasters along the way. Jessica Logan was 18, and she had used her cell phone to snap and send nude photos of herself to her boyfriend. After they broke up, he forwarded the photos to other girls at their high school. The girls taunted Jessica mercilessly, calling her a whore and a slut. Jessica told her depressing tale in a local TV interview, and 2 months later—finding no peace—she hanged herself in her bedroom.

In other "case studies," a 15-year-old Pennsylvania girl has been charged with producing and sending child pornography after sending nude photos of herself to other adolescents. A 19-year-old Florida college student was expelled and ordered to register as a sex offender for the next 25 years because he shared nude photos of his girlfriend with others. These instances are anything but rare, although the penalties are high. A survey found that 20% of adolescents under age 17 have admitted to receiving revealing photos of other adolescents (Celizic, 2009).

On the *TODAY* show, attorney Larry Walters noted that the same sexting that is a crime for teenagers is legal for adults. He continued, "These teens don't see themselves as children. They see themselves as teens. They don't see what they're doing as child pornography. Teens believe it is normal. It is normal for them. To use child porn laws to punish teens for behavior the law was never designed to address is overkill, number one, and it dilutes the effectiveness of child pornography laws for everyone else" (Celizic, 2009).

How Does Male–Female Sexual Behavior Develop During Adolescence?

Adolescents today start dating and going out earlier than in past generations. Teens who date earlier are more likely to engage in sexual activity during high school (De Rosa et al., 2010). Teens who initiate sexual activity earlier are also less likely to use contraception and more likely to become pregnant. Of course, early dating does not always lead to early sex, and early sex does not always lead to unwanted pregnancies. Still, some young women find their options in adulthood restricted by a chain of events that began in early adolescence.

TRUTH OR FICTION REVISITED: It is true that petting is practically universal among American adolescents and has been for many generations. Adolescents use petting to express affection, satisfy their curiosities, heighten their sexual arousal, and reach orgasm while avoiding pregnancy and maintaining virginity.

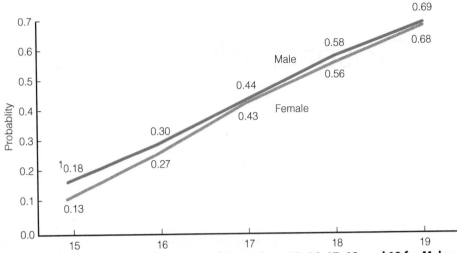

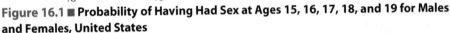

Figure 16.1 ■ Probability of Having Had Sex at Ages 15, 16, 17, 18, and 19 for Males and Females, United States

Source: Martinez, G. M., & Abma, J. C. (2015, July). NCAS Data Brief No. 209. Sexual Activity, Contraceptive Use, and Childbearing of Teenagers Aged 15–19 in the United States. U.S. Department of Health and Human Services. Figure 2.

Many adolescents do not think that they have had sex if they stop short of vaginal intercourse. Girls are more likely than boys to be pushed into petting and to feel guilty about it (Slotboom et al., 2011).

Since the 1980s, the percentage of teenagers aged 15 to 19 who have had sexual intercourse has gradually descended from 51% for females and 60% for males to the low 40s between 2006–2010, and has more recently risen slightly to the mid 40s (NCHS Data Brief 209, 2015; see Figure 14.6 on page 468). Figure 16.1 ■ shows that the probability of having had sex increases steeply between the ages of 15 to 19. Note from Figure 16.2 ■ that in recent years, teenagers have become more careful to use contraception, even the first time they are having

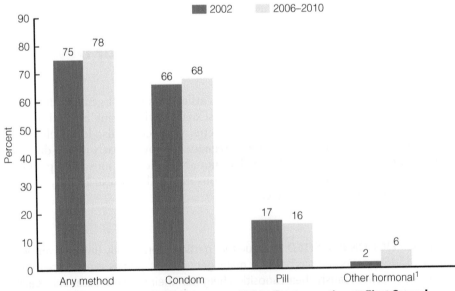

Figure 16.2 ■ Percentage of U.S. Teenagers Using Contraception at First Sexual Intercourse

Source: Martinez et al. (2011), Figure 2.

TABLE 16.2

Attitudes of Teenagers Ages 15–19 Toward Their First Sexual Experience

	Didn't Want It to Happen	Had Mixed Feelings	Really Wanted It to Happen
Females	10.8%	48.0%	41.2%
Males	5.0%	32.5%	62.5%

Source: Martinez et al. (2011).

sex. Some two out of three used a condom and about one out of six females were using birth control pills. That does not mean that these girls were using the pill to prevent pregnancy. You have to plan ahead to use the pill for that purpose. Many teenage females use the pill to regularize their menstrual periods or to help them cope with menstrual discomfort.

Some teenagers do not intend for their first sexual experience to happen. Rather, they perceive it as simply happening to them (Martinez et al., 2011). According to the National Survey of Family Growth, females were more likely than males to say they didn't want it to happen (see Table 16.2 ●). In fact, the largest number of females had mixed feelings about it. But the great majority of males were likely to report that they really wanted it to happen (Martinez et al., 2011).

Table 16.3 ● shows the reasons that teenagers give for having abstained from having sex. Overall, the main reason for females abstaining is that having sex is against their religious beliefs or moral values. For males, religious or moral beliefs and not having found the right person are mentioned about equally often. European Americans are much less likely than Latin Americans or African Americans to be worried about pregnancy or sexually transmitted infections (STIs). In terms of socioeconomic status, it is possible that European Americans have greater access to preventive measures.

The incidences of kissing, petting, oral sex, and sexual intercourse all increase with age (McLeod & Knight, 2010). For example, according to a Centers for Disease Control and Prevention (CDC) survey, 42% of girls aged 15–17 reported engaging in oral sex, compared to 72% of girls aged 18–19 (Mosher et al., 2005). Among adolescents who have not engaged in sexual intercourse, the lowest rates of oral sex—about 19%—were for adolescents who cited moral or religious reasons for abstaining from sexual intercourse. Some adolescent couples use oral sex as a means of maintaining virginity and preventing pregnancy.

What Are the Effects of Puberty on Adolescent Sexual Behavior?

The hormonal changes of puberty probably are partly responsible for the onset of sexual activity. In boys, levels of testosterone are associated with sexual behavior. In girls, however, testosterone levels are linked to sexual interests but not to sexual behavior. Social factors may therefore play a greater role in regulating sexual behavior in girls than in boys (De Rosa et al., 2010).

The physical changes associated with puberty also may serve as a trigger for the onset of sexual activity. For example, the development of secondary sex characteristics such as breasts in girls and muscles and deep voices in boys may make them more sexually attractive. Early-maturing girls are more likely to have older friends, which may draw them into early sexual relationships.

Main Reason for Never Having Had Sex, Ages 15–19

Gender and Reason	Latin American	European American	African American
Female			
Against religion or moral values	28.2%	48.3%	28.7%
Don't want to get pregnant	22.4%	13.6%	21.5%
Don't want to get a sexually transmitted infection	10.1%	5.5%	13.9%
Haven't found the right person yet	20.6%	20.2%	15.4%
In a relationship, but waiting for the right time	8.1%	4.7%	7.4%
Other reason	10.7%	7.6%	13.2%
Male			
Against religion or moral values	27.2%	33.3%	20.9%
Don't want to get (a female) pregnant	16.8%	11.1%	13.4%
Don't want to get a sexually transmitted infection	7.0%	4.7%	16.3%
Haven't found the right person yet	31.8%	29.0%	25.9%
In a relationship, but waiting for the right time	7.5%	12.0%	12.7%
Other reason	9.7%	9.8%	10.6%

Source: Martinez et al. (2011), Table 15.

How Do Relationships with Parents Influence Adolescent Sexual Behavior?

Teenagers who have close relationships with their parents are less likely to initiate sexual activity at an early age (Bynum, 2007; DiIorio et al., 2007; Ohalete, 2007). If these youngsters do have sexual intercourse, they are more likely to use birth control and to have fewer sexual partners (Aspy et al., 2007; National Campaign to Prevent Teen and Unplanned Pregnancy, 2012a).

The double standard of sexuality in our society—that premarital sexual activity is acceptable for boys but not for girls—seems to influence the way in which parental communication affects sexual behavior in teenagers. The message for daughters appears to be "Don't do it," whereas the message for sons is "It's okay to do it as long as you take precautions."

How Do Relationships with Peers Influence Adolescent Sexual Behavior?

Peers also play an important role in determining the sexual behavior of adolescents. One of the most powerful predictors of sexual activity for female and male adolescents is the sexual activity of their best friends (Ali & Dwyer, 2011; Lansford et al., 2009). When teenagers are asked why they do not wait to have sexual intercourse until they are older, the main reason reported is usually peer pressure (Ali & Dwyer, 2011).

Peers, especially those of the same gender, also serve as a key source of sex education for adolescents. Adolescents report that they are somewhat more likely

A Closer Look | Research

DO SEXY TV SHOWS ENCOURAGE SEXUAL BEHAVIOR IN TEENAGERS AND LEAD TO TEENAGE PREGNANCY?

What happens when teenagers watch *Girls, Gossip Girl, The Secret Life of the American Teenager,* and other TV shows with sexual content? Does it roll off their backs or encourage them to go for a roll in the hay?

A study reported in *Pediatrics* (Collins et al., 2004) found an association between watching sexual content on television and initiation into sexual intercourse. The study included more than 1,700 teenagers aged 12–17. In a longitudinal study, the researchers followed up the same cohort of adolescents after 3 years to determine whether watching sex on television led to a higher incidence of pregnancy (Chandra et al., 2008).

The 718 adolescents (43% female) who reported having engaged in sexual intercourse, and who provided information about pregnancy, were included in the data analysis. The researchers controlled for other variables connected with teenage pregnancy, such as school grades and conduct problems. They found that teenage

What effects does viewing sexy TV scenes have on adolescents?

PhotoAlto sas /Katarina Sundelin/Alamy

pregnancy, like initiation into sex, was significantly correlated with exposure to sexual content on television. Teenagers categorized as having high levels of exposure (that is, being in the 90th percentile on the variable) were two to three times more likely to report having pregnancies—or, in the case of males, being responsible for pregnancies—than teenagers in the 10th percentile. The total number of hours of watching television was not significantly correlated with pregnancy.

Reflect It might seem at first glance that we can conclude that watching sexual content on television is a *cause* of sexual initiation and teenage pregnancy. However, the study showed a *correlation* between what teenagers watched and sexual outcomes.

TRUTH OR FICTION REVISITED: Correlational studies may reveal relationships, but they do not show cause and effect. Because the researchers in the *Pediatrics* study did not run an experiment in which some randomly selected teens were shown TV shows with sexual content and others were not, rival explanations for the sexual variables associated with TV-watching patterns are possible. Could the outcomes reported in this research be due to a *selection factor?* Is it possible that teenagers who had greater interest in sex, who came from more permissive homes, or who had friends who touted sexy shows were more likely to watch sexy TV shows and *also* more likely to have sex and get pregnant? In these cases, sexual interest, home atmosphere, and peer influence would be more likely to be "causal."

Why, by the way, cannot researchers run experiments in which they select teens at random and have the treatment group watch sexy TV shows while the control group does not? What ethical issues would be involved in showing racy TV shows to teens? And could the researchers prevent teens in the control group from watching racy TV shows on their own?

to receive information about sex from friends and media sources—TV shows, films, magazines, and the Internet—than from sex education classes or their parents (Kaiser Family Foundation et al., 2003).

What Are the Causes and Effects of Teenage Pregnancy in Our Society?

The title of this section is "loaded": It suggests that there is a problem with teenage pregnancy. So let us toss in a couple of caveats at the beginning. First, throughout most of history, even most of the history of the United States, girls first became pregnant in their teens. Second, throughout most cultures in the world today, girls are first becoming pregnant in their teens. Why, then, do we bother with a section

on this topic? The answer is that in the United States today, the great majority of adolescents who become pregnant do so accidentally and without committed partners (Guttmacher Institute, 2013). Most young women in developed nations defer pregnancy until after they have completed some or all of their education. Many defer pregnancy until they are well into their careers—in their late 20s, their 30s, or even their 40s. So it is in our place and time that we have a topic called "Teenage Pregnancy," implying that there might be a problem with it.

In our culture, today, why do teenage girls become pregnant? For one thing, adolescent girls typically get little advice in school or at home about how to deal with boys' sexual advances. Another reason is failure to use contraception. Some initiate sex at very early ages, when they are least likely to use contraception (Ali & Dwyer, 2011). Many adolescent girls, especially younger adolescents, do not have access to contraceptive devices. Among those who do, fewer than half use them reliably (Teen pregnancy prevention and United States students, 2011).

Some teenage girls purposefully get pregnant to try to force their partners to make a commitment to them. Some are rebelling against their parents or the moral standards of their communities. But most girls are impregnated because they and their partners do not know as much about reproduction and contraception as they think they do, or because they miscalculate the odds of getting pregnant (National Campaign to Prevent Teen and Unplanned Pregnancy, 2012a). Even those who have been to all the sex education classes and who have access to family planning clinics slip up now and then, especially if their partners push them or do not want to use condoms.

TRUTH OR FICTION REVISITED: For reasons discussed in this section, it is true that more than half a million teenage girls in the United States become pregnant each year. However, as you can see in Figure 16.3 ■, it is also true that the number of teenage pregnancies has declined by 50% since 1990. About two in three of these pregnancies result in a live birth. The other third end in abortion.

The recent drop-off in teenage pregnancies may reflect findings that sexual activity among teenagers has leveled off and that relatively more adolescents are using condoms (Guttmacher Institute, 2012; Martinez et al., 2011). Researchers at the

US teenage pregnancy

Rates per 1,000 women aged 15-19 years

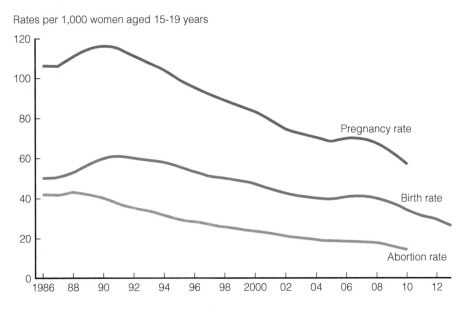

Figure 16.3 ■ Pregnancy, Birth, and Abortion Rates for U.S. Women Aged 15–19, 1986–2012
Source: US Department of Health and Human Services (2014).

CDC also attribute the drop-off in careless sex to educational efforts by schools, the media, religious institutions, and communities (National Campaign to Prevent Teen and Unplanned Pregnancy, 2012a).

Let us now consider the ethnic/racial breakdown of these numbers. Figure 16.4 ■ compares the teenage pregnancy rates from 4 years: 1991, 2005, 2007, and 2010. The figure shows that Latin American teenagers currently have the highest pregnancy rates (55.7 per 1,000 girls aged 15–19), and Asian Americans have the lowest teenage pregnancy rates (10.9 per 1,000 girls of the same age range). How do we interpret these findings? We could say that Latin American and African American teenagers have the highest pregnancy rates, and that would be accurate (Khurana et al., 2011). On the other hand, we can focus on the fact that the overall teenage pregnancy rate for all races has dropped by about half since 1991. We can also note that the teenage pregnancy rate from African Americans has dropped by more than half since 1991 (from 118.2 per 1,000 women to 51.5 per 1,000 women) and that the rate for Latin Americans has dropped by nearly half (from 104.6 per 1,000 women to 55.7 per 1,000 women)! According to the National Center for Health Statistics (Hamilton & Ventura, 2012), if the overall birth rates for teenagers had remained

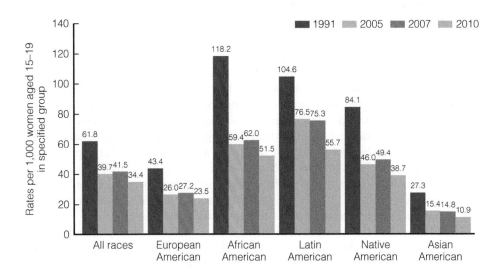

Figure 16.4 ■ Birth Rates for U.S. Women Aged 15–19, by Race and Ethnicity
Source: Hamilton & Ventura (2012), Figure 3.

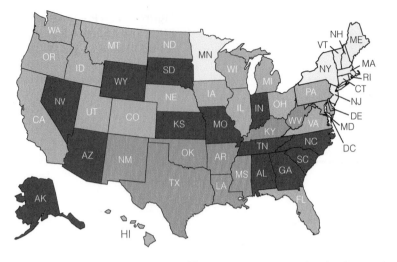

Figure 16.5 ■ Birth Rates for U.S. Women Aged 15–19, by State, 2012

Source: CDC Vital Statistics Reports, "Birth: Final Data for 2012," 62(9);2013.

☐ <20 births per 1,000 females (9 states)

☐ 20–29.9 births per 1,000 females (20 states)

■ 30–39.9 births per 1,000 females (13 states + DC)

☐ ≥ 40 births per 1,000 females (8 states)

as they were in 1991, we would have had another *3.4 million* children born to them by today.

Now let us consider differences in teenage birth rates among the states, as shown in Figure 16.5 ■. If we look at broad regions of the United States, we see that teenage birth rates are lowest in the Northeast and in Minnesota. The birth rates are generally highest in the South and the Southwest. According to 2013 CDC Vital Statistics Reports, there are a number of factors to consider. First is the racial and ethnic makeup of the various states. New England, for example, is one of the areas of the country most densely populated by European Americans. The South and the Southwest tend to have higher percentages of Latin Americans and African Americans in the population, and these groups continue to have the highest teenage birth rates, although, as noted earlier, the numbers have dropped by half over the past couple of decades. Second is the general level of education. Americans in the northern states and on the West Coast tend to have more years of education, on average, than people in the South and Southwest. But these levels of education are intertwined with race, ethnicity, and socioeconomic status; that is, European Americans in these areas tend to have higher incomes and to spend more years in school. Third is the extent to which the various states invest in sex education, and what kind of sex education they offer. For example, areas that stress the importance of contraception, and that teach students how to use contraceptives, tend to have lower teenage pregnancy rates than areas that do not have sex education or that teach abstinence-only education (Guttmacher Institute, 2013; Martinez et al., 2011).

In the contemporary United States, most pregnant teenagers will become single mothers. Pregnancy rates are higher among adolescents of lower socioeconomic status and among those from ethnic minority groups (Hamilton & Ventura, 2012).

Consequences of Teenage Pregnancy

Again, some caveats: The outcomes of teenage pregnancies for young women who want their babies and have the resources to nurture them are generally good (Rathus et al., 2014). Females tend to be healthy in late adolescence, and again—historically speaking—people might wonder why we raise this issue at all.

We raise it because the medical, social, and economic costs of unplanned or unwanted pregnancies among adolescents are enormous both to the mothers and to the children. The problems begin with the pregnancy itself. Adolescent mothers are more likely to experience medical complications during the months of pregnancy, and their labor is likely to be prolonged. The babies are at greater risk of being premature and of low birth weight (Mathews & MacDorman, 2007). These medical problems are not necessarily due to the age of the mother but rather to the fact that teenage mothers—especially those at the lower end of the socioeconomic spectrum—are less likely to have access to prenatal care or to obtain adequate nutrition.

The education of the teenage mother also suffers. She is less likely than her peers to graduate from high school or move on to college. Her deficit in education means that she earns less and is in greater need of public assistance. Few teenage mothers obtain reliable assistance—financial or emotional—from the babies' fathers. The fathers typically cannot support themselves, much less a family. Their marriages—if they are married—are more likely to be unstable, and they often have more children than they intended (Bunting & McAuley, 2004).

Although the most attention has been directed toward teenage mothers, young fathers bear an equal responsibility for teenage pregnancies. The consequences of parenthood for adolescent fathers are similar to those for adolescent mothers (Kalil et al., 2005; Quinlivan & Condon, 2005). Teenage fathers tend to have lower grades in school than their peers, and they enter the work force at an earlier age.

Children born to teenage mothers also are at a disadvantage. As early as the preschool years, they show lower levels of cognitive functioning and more behavioral and emotional problems. Boys appear to be more affected than girls. By adolescence, offspring of teenage mothers are doing more poorly in school, and they are more likely to become teenage parents themselves (Gavin et al., 2009). Again, these problems seem to result not from the mother's age but from the socially and economically deprived environments in which teen mothers and their children often live.

Preventing Teenage Pregnancy

The past several decades have seen a dramatic increase in programs to help prevent teenage pregnancies. Prevention efforts include educating teenagers about sexuality and contraception and providing contraception and family planning services (Guttmacher Institute, 2013). An overwhelming majority of American parents want their children to have sex education in the public schools.

How successful are sex education programs? The better programs increase students' knowledge about sexuality. Despite fears that sex education will increase sexual activity in teenagers, some programs seem to delay the onset of sexual activity (Martinez et al., 2011). Among teenagers who already are sexually active, sex education is associated with the increased use of effective contraception.

School-based clinics that distribute contraceptives and contraceptive information to students have been established in some school districts, and not without controversy. In high schools that have such clinics, birth rates often drop significantly (Blake et al., 2003). Whether or not school-based programs distribute contraceptives or contraceptive information, a federally funded multi-year study by the nonpartisan Mathematica Policy Research, Inc., of Princeton, New Jersey, found that abstinence-only programs have no effect on teenage pregnancy rates (Trenholm et al., 2007). Put it this way: Abstinence itself works, but teaching nothing but abstinence in sex education has not been shown to cut the rate of teenage pregnancy (Khurana et al., 2011).

Section Review

9. _____ is the most common sexual outlet in adolescents.

10. A _____ orientation is defined as being attracted to, and interested in forming romantic relationships with, people of one's own gender.

11. It is believed that prenatal exposure to sex _____ may play a key role in sexual orientation.

12. Teenagers who have close relationships with their parents are _____ (more or less?) likely to initiate sexual activity at an early age.

13. The top reason adolescents usually give for why they did not wait to have sexual intercourse is _____ pressure.

Reflect & Relate: How important a part of your adolescence (or that of your peers) was sexuality? Did any of your peers experience problems related to their sexuality during adolescence? Did they resolve these problems? If so, how?

SEX EDUCATION, U.S.A.

Sixty or 70 years ago in the United States, people did not generally talk openly about sex. Sure, there were dirty jokes. Friends confided in one another, or asked for opinions. Mothers may have "warned" their daughters about the onset of menstruation or about the aggressive "advances" of boys, but there was little, if any, formal discussion about human anatomy, STIs, or methods of preventing unwanted pregnancies. In fact, many young

What Parents Want in Sex Education Courses U.S. parents overwhelmingly favor sex education. Nearly all want these courses to educate teens about sexually transmitted infections, and majorities want the courses to cover abortion and sexual orientation. However, there are concerns about how these topics are covered.

people weren't sure exactly how females got pregnant, and there were myths such as the (wrong!) belief that a female cannot get pregnant the first time she has sex. The message from mother and church was simply "Don't." And hundreds of thousands of teenage girls became pregnant each year, and many youngsters wound up infected with the STIs of the day, such as gonorrhea and syphilis.

In the decades since that time, the numbers of teenagers getting pregnant showed some increase and the threat of HIV/AIDS emerged. Even so, many parents felt that sex education should not be taught outside the home or the church, and some still felt that sex should not be discussed at all.

It is interesting, then, that some kind of formal sex education for children or adolescents is nearly universal in the United States today (Figure 16.6 ■). There is more than discussion; adolescents practice unrolling condoms on bananas and the like. There is more than warnings about pregnancy and illness; some adolescents are told how to engage in oral sex and other sexual activities.

Figure 16.6 shows the results of the National Survey of Family Growth, conducted by the National Center for Health Statistics division of the CDC (Martinez et al., 2010), that recruited some 7,000 females and 6,000 males. The question answered in Figure 16.6 was whether they had received—or were receiving—any formal sex education between the ages of 15 and 19. "Formal" meant at a school, church, community center, or a similar setting, rather than from parents, friends,

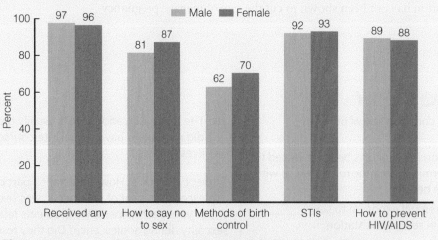

Figure 16.6 ■ Percentage of U.S. Adolescents Aged 15–19 Who Reported Receiving Formal Sex Education Before the Age of 18
Source: Martinez et al. (2010), Figure 1.

books, or the Internet. Ninety-seven percent of males and 96% of females had received at least some formal sex education. That information was most likely to be about the nature and prevention of STIs. A strong runner-up was learning "how to say no to sex." The teenagers were less likely to be taught about methods of birth control, but even so, 70% of females and 62% of males received that information. Of course, the primary method of preventing disease is by using condoms, so recognizing their usefulness to prevent pregnancy would be a "side effect."

Figure 16.7 ■ shows that the majority of teenagers aged 15–19 actually have talked with a parent about sex. Females were more likely to do so than males, and nearly four out of five (79%) reported doing so. Therefore, in the United States today, parent–child communication about sex is quite common. *What* they talk about is suggested in Figure 16.8 ■.

Generally speaking, parents were most likely to talk to their children and adolescents about abstinence—how to say no to sex—although females (63%) were much more likely than males (42%) to discuss that issue. About half of the children and adolescents (55% of females and 50% of males) reported discussing STIs with their parents. More than half of females (51%) were told about birth control, compared with fewer than one-third (31%) of males, and nearly twice as many females (38%) as males (20%) were told where to get birth control. In other words, many youngsters were told, "Don't get pregnant" and "Don't get sick," but not

all of them were given the specifics of ways to avoid these problems.

Reflect: What is your view concerning each of the following topics in high school sex education programs? Explain why you feel as you do.

- Methods of abortion
- How to obtain methods of contraception without parental knowledge or permission
- How to use condoms

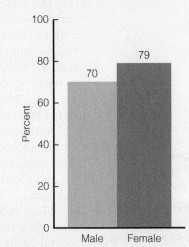

Figure 16.7 ■ Percentage of U.S. Teenagers Aged 15–19 Who Have Talked with a Parent About Sex
Source: Martinez et al. (2010), Figure 3.

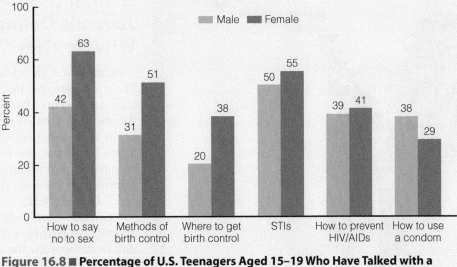

Figure 16.8 ■ Percentage of U.S. Teenagers Aged 15–19 Who Have Talked with a Parent About Sex, by Topic and Gender
Source: Martinez et al. (2010), Figure 4.

16.4 Juvenile Delinquency

Did you ever commit a delinquent act in your teen years? If you answer yes, then you are like most adolescents. The great majority of adolescents have done something against the law, whether it is underage smoking, underage drinking, or something like petty theft.

> **TRUTH OR FICTION REVISITED:** Therefore, it is not true that only a minority of American adolescents engage in delinquent behavior. However, much delinquent behavior, such as underage drinking, is not violent and is no longer delinquent once the adolescent reaches the age of 18 or 21.

The term **juvenile delinquency** tends to be used specifically in reference to children or adolescents who engage in illegal activities and come into contact with the criminal justice system (Whitehead & Lab, 2013). At the most extreme end, juvenile delinquency includes serious behaviors such as homicide, rape, and robbery, which are considered criminal acts at any age. Less serious offenses, such as truancy, underage drinking, running away from home, and sexual promiscuity, are considered illegal only when performed by minors. Hence, these are termed **status offenses**.

Antisocial and criminal behaviors show a dramatic increase in many societies during adolescence and then taper off during adulthood. For example, about 4 in 10 serious crimes in the United States are committed by individuals under the age of 21, and about 3 in 10 are committed by adolescents under the age of 18 (Snyder & Sickmund, 2006).

Many delinquent acts do not result in arrest or conviction. And when adolescents are arrested, their cases may be disposed of informally, such as by referral to a mental health agency, without the juvenile being formally declared delinquent in a juvenile court (Snyder & Sickmund, 2006).

juvenile delinquency Conduct in a child or adolescent characterized by illegal activities.

status offenses Offenses considered illegal only when performed by minors, such as truancy and underage drinking.

What Are the Ethnic and Gender Differences in Juvenile Delinquency? Why Do They Occur?

African American adolescents are more likely to be arrested than European American adolescents. For example, African American youths constitute about 13% of the adolescent population in the United States but about one-fourth of the juvenile arrests and about one-half of those arrested for violent crimes (Andersen, 2015; Bishop, 2012).

Criminologists believe that there are at least two possible explanations for the difference between the delinquency rates for European Americans and African Americans (Andersen, 2015; Whitehead & Lab, 2013). The *differential offending hypothesis* suggests that there are actual racial differences in the incidence and seriousness of delinquent behavior. The *differential treatment hypothesis* suggests that African American and European American youths probably do not behave all that differently but that they are treated differently—intentionally or accidentally—by the juvenile justice system. In other words, "the system" expects worse behavior from African American youngsters, so it polices them more actively and cracks down on them more harshly. One result of differential treatment is that African American adolescents are likely to have much more interaction with the juvenile justice system and thus are more likely to develop the self-concept of being offenders or criminals—outside the system, outside the mainstream.

Economic and family factors are also connected with racial and ethnic differences in juvenile offending. African American (and Latin American) children and adolescents are three times as likely as European American youths to be living in poverty (Felson & Kreager, 2015; Snyder & Sickmund, 2006). Moreover, African American children are less likely than European American (or Latin American) children to be living with both of their biological parents, regardless of whether their parents are married. We cannot say that poverty *causes* delinquency or that a broken family *causes* delinquency, but statistically speaking, poverty and broken families are risk factors.

Boys are much more likely than girls to engage in delinquent behavior, especially in crimes of violence (see Table 16.4 ●). On the other hand, girls are more likely to commit status offenses, such as truancy and running away (not shown in the table; Snyder & Sickmund, 2006).

Who Are the Delinquents? What Are They Like?

Many risk factors are associated with juvenile delinquency, but the direction and timing of these factors are not always clear-cut. For example, poor school performance is related to delinquency (Andersen, 2015; Felson & Kreager, 2015). But does school failure lead to delinquency, or is delinquency the cause of the school failure?

Even if the causal paths are less than clear, a number of factors are associated with delinquency. Children who show aggressive, antisocial, and hyperactive behavior at an early age are more likely to show delinquent behavior in adolescence (Siegel & Welsh, 2011). Delinquency also is associated with having a lower verbal IQ, immature moral reasoning, low self-esteem, feelings of alienation, and impulsivity (Andersen, 2015; Felson & Kreager, 2015). Other personal factors include little interest in school, early substance abuse, early sexuality, and delinquent friends (Whitehead & Lab, 2013). On a cognitive level, aggressive delinquents tend to approve of violence as a way of dealing with social provocations and to misinterpret other people's intentions as hostile when they are not (Calvete, 2007).

Family factors also are powerful predictors of delinquent behavior. The families of juvenile delinquents often are characterized by lax and ineffective discipline, low levels of affection, and high levels of family conflict, physical abuse, severe parental punishment, and neglect (Siegel & Welsh, 2011). The parents and siblings of juvenile delinquents frequently have engaged in antisocial, deviant, or criminal behavior themselves (Whitehead & Lab, 2013).

● TABLE 16.4

Proportion of Juvenile Offenses Committed by Females

Offense	Percentage
Crimes against people	28
Homicide	13
Forcible rape	3
Robbery	9
Assault	26–32
Crimes against property	26
Burglary	10
Larceny (theft)	38
Motor vehicle theft	23
Arson	13
Vandalism	16
Trespassing	19
Drug law violation	18
Public order offense	28
Obstruction of justice	29
Disorderly conduct	33
Weapons offense	14
Liquor law violation	32
Nonviolent sex offense	19
TOTAL DELINQUENCY	**26**

Source: Adapted from Snyder & Sickmund (2006), p. 160.

Delinquents are also more likely to live in neighborhoods in which they themselves are likely to have been victimized, giving rise to the belief that crime is "normal" in a statistical sense, and giving rise to feelings of anger (Hay & Evans, 2006). Moreover, when youths in such situations are tempted by opportunities to victimize others, they are unlikely to be restrained by considerations such as what a criminal record might do to their chances of being admitted to Yale and to their career aspirations of becoming physicians or attorneys (Siegel & Welsh, 2011). These constraints are as unlikely to enter their minds as the realities are to enter their lives.

Prenatal smoking (by the mother!) is another interesting risk factor for juvenile delinquency. Lauren Wakschlag and her colleagues (2006) compared boys in the Pittsburgh Youth Study whose mothers had smoked when the boys were in utero with boys whose mothers had not smoked. When compared with the other boys, the sons of the smokers were significantly more likely to develop a combination of conduct disorder and attention-deficit/hyperactivity disorder (ADHD) in early grades and to have an earlier onset of delinquent behavior. The authors admit that they cannot precisely define the role of prenatal smoking in children's behavioral problems, but it seems to be another risk factor or marker.

How Can We Prevent and Treat Juvenile Delinquency?

Many approaches have been tried to prevent delinquent behavior or to deal with it early. One type of approach focuses on the individual adolescent offender. Such programs may provide training in moral reasoning, social skills, problem-solving skills, or a combination of these. These programs focus on individual offenders rather than on the larger social systems in which juvenile delinquents are embedded, and the results are mixed at best (Manchak & Cullen, 2015). Moreover, delinquents are individuals with individual problems and situations, and it is not possible to meaningfully generalize the effects of a treatment method to delinquency per se (Zonnevylle-Bender et al., 2007). Also, delinquency is crime, not illness. Therefore, the concept of treatment may very well be misplaced.

Another approach tries to deal with various social systems, such as the family, peer groups, school, or community (Whitehead & Lab, 2013). Examples of such interventions include family therapy approaches; school-based strategies involving teams of students, parents, teachers, and staff; and various community- and neighborhood-based programs. These broader, multisystem approaches appear to be more successful in reducing problem behaviors and improving the family relations of delinquent adolescents (Siegel & Welsh, 2011).

One other promising approach starts with the very young child and is aimed at promoting a host of positive child outcomes, not just delinquency prevention. This approach consists of early childhood intervention programs, such as Head Start. Preschoolers who participated in several of these programs have been tracked longitudinally through adolescence. These follow-ups show several encouraging outcomes, including reductions in aggressive and delinquent behavior (Aber et al., 2007).

Section Review

14. Offenses that are illegal only when performed by minors are called _____ offenses.

15. Boys are _____ (more or less?) likely than girls to engage in most delinquent behaviors.

16. Children who show aggressive, antisocial, and hyperactive behavior at an early age are _____ (more or less?) likely to show delinquent behavior in adolescence.

Reflect & Relate: Were there any juvenile delinquents in your high school? What behavior patterns led to the label? What happened to them? Do you know what they are doing now?

Suicide: When the Adolescent Has Nothing—Except Everything—to Lose

How Many Adolescents Commit Suicide?

Adolescence is such an exciting time of life. For many, the future is filled with promise. Many count the days until they graduate from high school, until they enter college. Many enjoy thrilling fantasies of what might be.

And then there are those who take their own lives. There are 7–8 adolescent suicides per 100,000 population (Miniño, 2010). About 46% of these are by firearms, and another 39% are hangings. Yet even more adolescents attempt suicide, and still more think about it. In a nationwide survey of high school students, 15% reported seriously considering suicide, 11% had created a plan, and 7% had tried to take their lives during the year preceding the survey (Miniño, 2010).

TRUTH OR FICTION REVISITED: Suicide is the third leading cause of death among adolescents (Miniño, 2010). Since 1960, the suicide rate has more than tripled for young people aged 15–24.

What Prompts Adolescents to Take Their Own Lives? Who Is Most at Risk?

Most suicides among adolescents and adults are linked to feelings of depression and hopelessness (Effinger & Stewart, 2012; Miranda & Shaffer, 2013). Suicidal adolescents experience four areas of psychological problems: (1) confusion about the self, (2) impulsiveness, (3) emotional instability, and (4) interpersonal problems. Some suicidal teenagers are high-achieving, rigid perfectionists who have set impossibly high expectations for themselves (Roxborough et al., 2012). Many teenagers throw themselves into feelings of depression and hopelessness by comparing themselves negatively with others, even when the comparisons are inappropriate. ("OK, you didn't get into Harvard, but you did get into the University of California at Irvine, and it's a great school.")

Adolescent suicide attempts are more common after traumatic events, especially events that entail a loss of social support, as in the death of a parent or friend, a breakup with a boyfriend or girlfriend, or a family member leaving home (Chehil & Kutcher, 2012; Nock et al., 2013). Another traumatic event that contributes to suicidal thinking is childhood sexual abuse (Wilcox et al., 2009). Other contributors to suicidal behavior include concerns about sexuality, pressures to achieve in school, problems at home, and substance abuse (Chehil & Kutcher, 2012; Nock et al., 2013). It is not always a stressful event itself that precipitates suicide but the adolescent's anxiety or fear of being "found out" for something, such as failing a course or getting arrested. Young people contemplating suicide are less likely to find productive ways of changing the stressful situation.

Suicide tends to run in families (Centers for Disease Control and Prevention, 2014a; Strauss et al., 2012). Many suicide attempters have family members with serious psychological problems, and many have family members who have taken their own lives. How do we account for the correlation? Do genetic factors play a role, possibly leading to psychological disorders, such as depression, that are connected with suicide? Could it be that a socially impoverished family environment infuses several family members with feelings of hopelessness? Or does the suicide of one family member simply give others the idea that suicide is the way to manage problems? Perhaps these possibilities and others—such as poor problem-solving ability—form a complex web of contributing factors.

A Closer Look

Diversity

ETHNICITY, GENDER, AND SUICIDE

Rates of suicide and suicide attempts vary among different ethnic groups. Native American and Latin American teenagers have the highest suicide rates, in part because of the stressors to which they are exposed and in part because of their lack of access to health care (Miniño, 2010). European Americans are next. African American teens are least likely to attempt suicide or to think about it. However, African American adolescents are only 65% as likely as European American adolescents to contact health professionals when they are considering suicide (Miniño, 2010).

About three times as many adolescent females as males attempt suicide, but five out of six completed suicides are by males (Chehil & Kutcher, 2012; Tucker et al., 2015). Males are apparently more likely to "succeed" because of the methods they choose. Males are more likely to use more rapid and lethal methods, such as shooting themselves, whereas females are more likely to overdose on drugs such as tranquilizers or sleeping pills (McLoughlin et al., 2015; Miniño, 2010). Females often do not take enough of these chemicals to kill themselves. It also takes time for the chemicals to work, which provides an opportunity for other people to intervene before the suicide attempter dies.

Andrew Bret Wallis/The Image Bank/Getty Images

Suicide Why are women more likely than men to attempt suicide? Why are men more likely to "succeed"?

Reflect: How do gender differences in suicide rates fit (or fail to fit) with gender-role stereotypes?

Here is a summary of risk factors for suicide:

- Belief that it is acceptable to kill oneself
- Drug abuse and other kinds of delinquency
- Victimization by bullying
- Extensive body piercing
- Stress
- Hostility
- Depression and other psychological disorders
- Heavy smoking
- Low self-esteem

The nearby "A Closer Look—Real Life" feature describes some of the warning signs of suicide and some things you can do if you notice them in a friend or family member.

We began our discussion of adolescence by noting that no other period of life is as exciting—and bewildering—as adolescence. Adolescence is a period when we form much of our sense of who we are and where we are going. For many, perhaps most, it's a time of discovery and self-invention. These are excellent, but in this section on suicide, we have come to realize that not all discoveries are pleasant and not all inventions actually work. On the other hand, the majority of adolescents come through just fine and flower into well-adjusted and productive adults.

A Closer Look

REAL LIFE

WARNING SIGNS OF SUICIDE

Most young people who commit suicide signal their intentions (Chehil & Kutcher, 2012; Tucker et al., 2015). Sad to say, their signals often go unrecognized. Adolescents may not receive help until they attempt suicide, and sometimes not even then. Here are some signals that a teenager may be at risk:

- Changes in eating and sleeping patterns
- Difficulty concentrating on schoolwork; poor grades and attendance
- Loss of interest in previously enjoyed activities and relationships
- Giving away prized possessions
- Complaints about physical problems with no basis
- Personality or mood changes
- Talking or writing about death or dying
- Abuse of drugs or alcohol
- Availability of a handgun
- A precipitating event such as an argument with parents, a broken romantic relationship, academic difficulties, loss of a friend, or trouble with the law
- Knowing or hearing about another teenager who has committed suicide
- Threatening or attempting suicide

Here are some things you can do if you notice one or more of these (Chehil & Kutcher, 2012; Tucker et al., 2015):

- Make an appointment for the adolescent with a helping professional, or suggest that the adolescent go with you right now to get professional help.
- Draw the adolescent out. Ask questions: What's going on? Where do you hurt? What would you like to see happen? Questions like these may encourage the expression of frustrated needs and provide some relief.
- Be empathic. Show that you understand how upset the adolescent is.

Mary Kate Denny/PhotoEdit

- Suggest that actions other than suicide might solve the problem, even if they are not apparent at the time.
- Ask how the adolescent intends to commit suicide. Adolescents with concrete plans and an available weapon are at greater risk. Ask if you might hold on to the weapon for a while. Sometimes the adolescent says yes.
- Extract a promise that the adolescent will not commit suicide before seeing you again.
- Arrange a concrete time and place to meet. Get professional help as soon as you are apart.

Reflect

- Would you feel flustered or resentful if an adolescent told you he or she is thinking about committing suicide? (Many people do.) Explain.
- Do you know anybody right now who is thinking about committing suicide? Do you think you should do anything about it? Explain.
- Do you think people have the right to commit suicide? Why or why not?

Section Review

17. Suicide is a _____ (rare or common?) cause of death among older teenagers.

18. Most suicides among adolescents and adults are linked to feelings of _____.

19. Suicide _____ (does or does not?) tend to run in families.

Reflect & Relate: Do you know anyone who has committed suicide or thought about committing suicide? What pressures or disappointments was the person experiencing at the time? Did anybody intervene? How?

16.6 Epilogue: Emerging Adulthood—Bridge Between Adolescence and the Life Beyond

When our mothers were our age, they were engaged. They at least had some idea what they were going to do with their lives. I, on the other hand, will have a dual degree in majors that are ambiguous at best and impractical at worst (English and political science), no ring on my finger and no idea who I am, much less what I want to do. Under duress, I will admit that this is a pretty exciting time. Sometimes, when I look out across the wide expanse that is my future, I can see beyond the void. I realize that having nothing ahead to count on means I now have to count on myself; that having no direction means forging one of my own.

—Kristen, age 22 (Cited in Arnett, 2000)

Well, Kristen has some work to do; she needs to forge her own direction. Just think: What if Kristen had been born into the caste system of old England or India, into a traditional Islamic society, or into the United States of the 1950s, where the TV sitcom *Father Knows Best* was perennially in the top 10? Kristen would have had a sense of direction, that's certain. But, of course, it would have been the sense of direction that society or tradition had created for her, not her own.

What Is Emerging Adulthood?

But Kristen was not born into any of these societies. She was born into the open and challenging United States of the current generation. She has the freedom to become whatever the interaction of her genetic heritage and her educational and social opportunities enables her to become—and the opportunities are many. With freedom comes the need to make choices. When we need to make choices, we profit from information. Kristen is in the process of accumulating information about herself and about the world outside. According to psychologist Jeffrey Arnett (2007, 2012), she is in emerging adulthood. In earlier days, adolescents made a transition, for better or worse, directly into adulthood. Now, many of them—especially those in affluent nations with abundant opportunities—spend time in what some theorists think of as a new period of development roughly spanning the ages of 18–25, although we also see the age of 29 mentioned as the upper limit.

Adulthood itself has been divided into stages, and the first of these, young adulthood, has been seen largely as the period of life when people focus on establishing their careers or pathways in life. It has been acknowledged that the transition to adulthood can be slow or piecemeal, with many individuals in their late teens and early 20s remaining dependent on their parents and reluctant or unable to make enduring commitments, in terms of either identity formation or the development of intimate relationships. The question is whether another stage of development exists, one that bridges adolescence and young adulthood. A number of developmental theorists, including Arnett (2011, 2012) and Labouvie-Vief (2006), believe there is another stage.

Michele Constantini/PhotoAlto/Alamy

"Emerging Adulthood": A New Stage of Development in Developed Nations Some researchers suggest that affluent societies like ours have spawned a new stage of development, emerging adulthood, which involves an extended period of self-exploration, during which one remains financially dependent.

By and large, adulthood is usually defined in terms of what people do rather than how old they are. Over the years, marriage has been a key criterion for adulthood, according to people who write about human development (Carroll et al., 2007). Other criteria include holding a full-time job and living independently (not with one's parents). Today, the transition to adulthood is mainly marked by adjustment issues, such as deciding on one's values and beliefs, accepting self-responsibility, becoming financially independent, and establishing an equal relationship with one's parents (Arnett, 2011, 2012; Gottlieb et al., 2007). Marriage or being in a committed relationship is no longer a crucial marker for entering adulthood (Gottlieb et al., 2007).

Traditional guidelines have been shattered. Half a century ago, by their late teens or early 20s, most young people had begun reasonably stable adult lives in terms of romantic relationships and work. Not too many undertook advanced training or education beyond the level of high school. In 1960, the median age for marriage for women was 20. For men, it was 22. By 1970, a decade later, the ages had risen to 21 for women and 23 for men. But by the year 2000, there was a dramatic 4-year rise, to 25 for women and 27 for men. And now, the median ages are 26 for women and 28 for men. Something has changed.

One factor is sex—sexual behavior, that is. Because of the advent of the birth control pill, sex, for millions, became divorced from pregnancy—despite the fact that many adolescents become pregnant because they do not use birth control reliably. The sexual revolution of the 1960s and 1970s was another reason why most young people decided that they did not have to wait until marriage to enter into sexual relationships. On the other hand, most young people are not promiscuous. They tend to enter into a series of sexually monogamous relationships (termed serial monogamy) until they are ready to form more lasting unions. There is also wide acceptance today of multiple premarital sexual relationships—for women as well as men—so long as they occur within the context of committed relationships.

Fifty years ago, couples tended to have their first child about a year after getting married. Nowadays, many couples delay childbearing because of college and graduate school and in order to devote much of their 20s to establishing a career. As noted by Arnett (2011, 2012), through much of their 20s, many emerging adults do not see having children as an achievement to be sought, but rather as a pitfall or, worse, as a threat to the good life.

Gender roles have also changed over the past half-century. Fifty to 60 years ago, very few women entered college. The occupations open to women were secretarial work, waiting tables, cleaning, and, at the professional level, teaching and nursing. Even these were largely viewed as temporary positions until a woman could find a husband and have children. Today, however, women occupy about 56% of the undergraduate seats in colleges across the nation (National Center for Education Statistics, 2010). Today's women, as we have seen, also enter careers once considered the preserve of men, such as law, medicine, and the STEM fields of science, technology, engineering, and math. It takes time to prepare for and become established in these fields. Once there, women are unlikely to leave them for a family. Many women do take maternity leaves when necessary, but men are also becoming likely to take paternity leaves.

For both women and men, the changes from a manufacturing-based economy to an information-based economy increased the need for advanced education and training over the past half-century (Arnett, 2011, 2012). Now, about 60% of young people undergo advanced training and education (National Center for Education Statistics, 2010) to prepare themselves.

What Are the Features of Emerging Adulthood?

Emerging adulthood is postulated to be a distinct period of development found in societies that offer young people an extended opportunity to explore their roles in life. These tend to be affluent societies, such as those found in industrialized nations, our own among them. Many parents in the United States are affluent enough to continue to support their children throughout college and in graduate school. When parents cannot do the job, the government often steps in to help; for example, through student loans. These supports give young people the luxury of sorting out identity issues and creating meaningful life plans—even if some still do not know where they are going after they graduate from college. Should they know who they are and what they are doing by the age of 21 or 22? Are they spoiled? These are value judgments that may or may not be on the mark. But let us note that many adults change their careers several times, partly because they did not sort out who they were and where they were going at an early age. On the other hand, even in the United States, many people lack the supports needed for successfully emerging into adulthood.

Arnett (2007, 2011) hypothesizes that five features characterize the stage of emerging adulthood that is sandwiched between the stage of adolescence, which precedes it, and young adulthood, which follows it. Let us look briefly at each of these features.

The Age of Identity Explorations

Many people of the ages discussed by Arnett and Labouvie-Vief—from 18 or 20 to about 25 or 30—are on the path to making vital choices in terms of their love lives and their career lives. As noted in the following section, they are experimenting with romantic partners and career possibilities.

The Age of Instability

In times past, it might be the case that adolescents would obtain jobs fresh out of high school—if they completed high school—and keep them for many years, sometimes for a lifetime. Today, Arnett notes, Americans have an average of about seven different jobs during the years between 20 and 29. Over this period, they also frequently change their romantic partners—sometimes by choice, sometimes because the partner decides to move on. They also switch their living arrangements, often moving from place to place with little, if any, furniture. And they frequently change educational directions, finding what they like, finding what they can actually do, and finding what is available to them.

The Age of Self-Focus

People are exceptionally self-focused during emerging adulthood. This does not mean that they are egocentric as in childhood or adolescence (Arnett, 2011, 2012; Labouvie-Vief, 2006), or selfish. It means, simply, that they are freer to make decisions than they were as children or adolescents; they are more mature, they are more independent of parental influences, and they usually have more resources. They are also free of the constraints of trying to mesh their lives with those of life partners.

The Age of Self-Focus Emerging adults tend to be self-focused, meaning that they are freer to make decisions than they were as children or adolescents.

PhotoAlto/Odilon Dimier/Alamy

The Age of Feeling In-Between

Emerging adults are similar to adolescents in one way: Whereas adolescents may feel that they exist somewhere between childhood and adulthood, emerging adults are likely to think that they are swimming between adolescence and "real" adulthood. They are likely to be out of school—that is, high school or undergraduate college—but obtaining further training or education. They are beyond the sometimes silly flirtations of adolescence but not yet in permanent, or at least long-term, relationships. They may not be completely dependent on caregivers, but they are just as unlikely to be self-supporting. They may be between roommates or apartments.

Where are they? In transit. Emerging adults seem to be well aware of the issues involved in defining the transition from adolescence to adulthood. Arnett (2000) reported what people say when they are asked whether they think they have become adults. The most common answer of 18- to 25-year-olds was something like "In some respects yes and in other respects no" (see Figure 16.9 ■). Many think that they have developed beyond the conflicts and exploratory voyages of adolescence, but they may not yet have the ability—or desire—to assume the financial and interpersonal responsibilities they associate with adulthood.

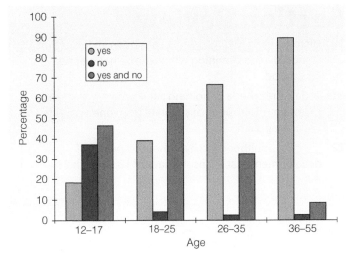

Figure 16.9 ■ Subjective Conceptions of Adult Status in Response to the Question "Do You Feel That You Have Reached Adulthood?"
Source: Arnett (2000), Figure 2.

The Age of Possibilities

> I take a very practical view of raising children. I put a sign in each of their rooms: "Checkout Time is 18 years."
>
> —Erma Bombeck

Emerging adults typically feel that the world lies open before them. Like the majority of adults, they have what Arnett (2011, 2012) and Labouvie-Vief (2006) term an optimistic bias. The majority believe that things will work out.

In this age of possibilities, emerging adults have the feeling that they have the opportunity to make dramatic changes in their lives. Unlike children and adolescents, they are, to a large degree, independent of their parents. Many of them leave home for good; others return home for financial reasons. Some lead a "revolving door" existence: They leave home and then come back, according to the ebb and flow of financial and emotional resources.

What Are Erik Erikson's Views on Emerging Adulthood?

Erikson (1968) did not use the term *emerging adulthood,* but he did recognize that developed nations tend to elongate the period of adolescence. Erikson used the term *moratorium* to describe the extended quest for identity among people who dwell in adolescence. Erikson and other theorists also believed that it was more meaningful for the individual to take the voyage to identity than to foreclose it by adopting the viewpoints of other people. Yet, even though there are pluses to taking time to formulate one's identity, there are downsides. For example, remaining dependent on parents can compromise an individual's self-esteem. Taking out loans for graduate school means that there is more to pay back; many individuals mortgage their own lives as they invest in their futures. Women who focus on their educations and their careers may bear children later. Many people appreciate children more when they bear them later in life, but they also become less fertile as the years pass, and they may find themselves in a race with their "biological clock."

And then, of course, there are those who remain adolescents forever.

Section Review

20. Historically speaking, _____ has been an important standard in determining whether one has reached adulthood.

21. Today, the criteria of holding a full-time _____ and maintaining a residence separate from one's parents are also applied.

22. _____ adulthood is a hypothesized period of development that spans the ages of 18 through 25

and exists in societies that permit young people extended periods of independent role exploration.

Reflect & Relate: Do you see yourself as an adolescent, an emerging adult, or an adult? What standards are you using in defining yourself?

Chapter Review

16.1 Development of Identity and the Self-Concept: "Who Am I?" (And Who Else?)

Erikson's adolescent stage of psychosocial development is identity versus identity diffusion. The primary task of this stage is for adolescents to develop a sense of who they are and what they stand for. The identity statuses represent the four combinations of the dimensions of exploration and commitment: identity diffusion, foreclosure, moratorium, and identity achievement. Development of identity is more complicated for adolescents who belong to ethnic minority groups. Youths from minority groups are faced with two sets of cultural values and may need to reconcile and incorporate elements of both. Researchers propose a three-stage model of the development of ethnic identity: unexamined ethnic identity, ethnic identity search, and achieved ethnic identity. As minority youths move through adolescence, they are increasingly likely to explore and achieve ethnic identity. Females and males approach identity formation in much the same way. Both are concerned about occupational choices, although females are more likely to integrate occupational and family plans.

Adolescents become increasingly likely to describe themselves in terms of psychological traits and social relationships, and the self-concept becomes more differentiated. Self-esteem tends to decline as the child progresses from middle childhood into early adolescence, perhaps because of increasing recognition of the disparity between the ideal self and the real self. Then, self-esteem gradually improves.

16.2 Relationships with Parents and Peers

Children spend much less time with their parents during adolescence than during childhood. Although adolescents become more independent of their parents, they generally continue to love and respect them. The role of peers increases markedly during the teen years. Adolescents are more likely than younger children to stress self-disclosure and mutual understanding in friendships. The two major types of peer groups are cliques and crowds. Unlike younger peer groups, adolescent peer groups include peers of the other gender. Romantic relationships begin to appear during early and middle adolescence. Dating is a source of fun, it enhances prestige, and it provides experience in relationships. Dating is also a preparation for adult courtship.

16.3 Sexuality: When? What? (How?) Who? Where? and Why?—Not to Mention, "Should I?"

Masturbation is the most common sexual outlet in adolescence. Some adolescents have a homosexual orientation. The process of "coming out" may be a long and painful struggle. From a learning-theory point of view, early reinforcement of sexual behavior influences sexual orientation. Researchers have found evidence for genetic and hormonal factors in sexual orientation. Early onset of puberty is connected with earlier sexual activity. Adolescents who have close relationships with their parents are less likely to initiate sexual activity early. Peer pressure is a powerful contributor to sexual activity. Many girls who become pregnant receive little advice about how to resist sexual advances. Most of them do not have access to contraception. Most misunderstand reproduction or miscalculate the odds of conception. Teenage mothers are more likely to have medical complications during pregnancy and birth, largely because of inadequate medical care. Their babies are more likely to be premature and to have low birth weight. Teenage mothers have a lower standard of living and a greater need for public assistance. Their children have more academic and emotional problems.

16.4 Juvenile Delinquency

Juvenile delinquency refers to illegal activities committed by a child or adolescent. Behaviors, such as drinking, that are considered illegal only when performed by minors are called status offenses. Boys are more likely than girls to engage in most delinquent behaviors. Boys are more apt to commit crimes of violence, whereas girls are more likely to commit status offenses. Risk factors associated with juvenile delinquency include poor school performance, delinquent friends, early aggressive or hyperactive behavior, substance abuse, low verbal IQ scores, low self-esteem, impulsivity, and immature moral reasoning. The parents and siblings of delinquents have frequently engaged in antisocial behavior themselves.

16.5 Suicide: When the Adolescent Has Nothing—Except Everything—to Lose

How many adolescents commit suicide? Why do they do so?

Suicide is the third leading cause of death among teenagers. Most suicides among adolescents and adults are linked to stress, feelings of depression, identity problems, impulsivity, and social problems. Girls are more likely to attempt suicide, whereas boys are more likely to "succeed."

16.6 Epilogue: Emerging Adulthood—Bridge Between Adolescence and the Life Beyond

Historically, marriage has been an important criterion in defining adulthood. Today, the focus is more on holding a full-time job and maintaining a separate residence. Emerging adulthood is a period of development, spanning the ages of 18–25, in which young people engage in extended role exploration. Emerging adulthood can occur in affluent societies that grant young people the luxury of developing their identities and their life plans.

Key Terms

Answers to Active Reviews

CHAPTER 1

1. Puberty
2. Development
3. Development
4. Theories
5. Freud
6. Eight
7. Operant
8. Piaget
9. Processing
10. Ecological
11. Sociocultural
12. Nature
13. Discontinuous
14. Hypothesis
15. Naturalistic
16. Case
17. Cause
18. Control
19. Longitudinal
20. Sectional

CHAPTER 2

1. Chromosomes
2. Deoxyribonucleic
3. Mitosis
4. Meiosis
5. Monozygotic, identical
6. Dizygotic, fraternal
7. Carriers
8. Down syndrome
9. Recessive
10. Sickle-cell
11. Amniocentesis
12. Ultrasound
13. Genotype
14. Phenotype
15. 50
16. Monozygotic, identical
17. Dizygotic, fraternal
18. Conception, fertilization
19. Fallopian
20. Sperm
21. Ovulate

CHAPTER 3

1. Blastocyst
2. Trophoblast
3. Implantation
4. Amniotic
5. Proximodistal
6. Outer
7. Females
8. Placenta
9. Umbilical cord
10. Maturation
11. Third
12. Fourth
13. Neural
14. Teratogens
15. Can
16. Blood
17. Rh
18. DES
19. Marijuana
20. Fetal
21. Oxygen
22. Slow

CHAPTER 4

1. Braxton-Hicks
2. Amniotic
3. Dilated
4. Transition
5. Umbilical
6. Placenta
7. General
8. Epidural, spinal
9. Lamaze
10. Cesarean section, C-section
11. Oxygen
12. Preterm
13. Birth weight
14. Helpful
15. Majority
16. Estrogen
17. Does not
18. Apgar
19. Rooting
20. Nearsighted
21. Do
22. Smaller
23. Sudden infant death syndrome (SIDS)

CHAPTER 5

1. Head, brain
2. Proximodistal
3. Five
4. Positive
5. Canalization
6. Antibodies
7. Neurons
8. Axon
9. 70
10. Cerebellum
11. One
12. Ulnar
13. Visual
14. Sit up, crawl
15. Increase
16. Experience, practice, nurture
17. Did not
18. Real
19. Edges
20. Cliff
21. 2–3
22. Greater
23. Capture
24. Nurture

CHAPTER 6

1. Schemes
2. Assimilate
3. Sensorimotor
4. Circular
5. Secondary
6. Tertiary
7. Permanence
8. Information
9. Memory
10. Deferred
11. Internalizing
12. Motor
13. Neurological
14. Visual
15. Babbling
16. Referential
17. Overextension
18. Holophrases
19. The same
20. Learning
21. Psycholinguistic
22. Acquisition
23. Left
24. Wernicke's

CHAPTER 7

1. Attachment
2. Strange situation
3. Insecure
4. Explore
5. Indiscriminate
6. Behavioral, behaviorist, learning
7. Contact
8. Fixed
9. Avoided
10. Withdrawal
11. Neglect
12. Autism, autism spectrum disorders
13. Majority
14. Higher
15. More
16. Majority
17. Referencing
18. Regulation
19. Concept
20. Temperament
21. Slow
22. 12 to 18

CHAPTER 8

1. 2 to 3
2. 4 to 6
3. Brain
4. Myelination
5. Cerebellum
6. Right
7. Right
8. Plasticity
9. Girls
10. Boys
11. Decrease
12. Boys
13. Higher
14. Decreases
15. Unintentional injuries, accidents
16. Lead
17. 10
18. Sleep terrors
19. Sleep walking
20. Does
21. Boys
22. Constipation

CHAPTER 9

1. Symbolic, pretend
2. Operations
3. Egocentric
4. Animistic
5. Transductive
6. Conservation
7. One
8. Scaffolding
9. Responsive
10. Home environment
11. Can
12. Less
13. More
14. False
15. Senses
16. Recognition
17. Autobiographical, episodic
18. Better
19. Positively
20. Rehearsal, rote rehearsal, rote learning
21. Mapping
22. Whole
23. One
24. Contrast
25. Inner

CHAPTER 10

1. Restrictiveness–permissiveness
2. Inductive
3. Authoritative
4. Authoritarian
5. First
6. Solitary
7. Associative
8. Same
9. Altruism
10. Reject
11. Testosterone
12. Social cognitive, social learning
13. Disinhibit
14. Categorical
15. Esteem
16. Securely
17. Initiative
18. Safety
19. Girls
20. Roles, role stereotypes
21. Males
22. Fathers
23. Constancy
24. Schema

CHAPTER 11

1. Steady
2. 2
3. 5 to 7
4. Boys
5. 11
6. 25
7. Do not
8. Does
9. Steady
10. 8 to 10
11. Decreases
12. Boys
13. Girls
14. Unfit
15. Attention-deficit/hyperactivity disorder
16. Boys
17. Does
18. Stimulants
19. Disabilities, disorders
20. Dyslexia
21. Neurological
22. Does

CHAPTER 12

1. Less
2. Transitivity
3. Inclusion
4. Autonomous
5. The amount of damage done
6. Preconventional
7. Conventional
8. Increases
9. Working, short-term
10. Encode, rehearse
11. Rote
12. Elaborative
13. Metamemory

14. g
15. Multiple
16. Mental
17. Verbal
18. Bias
19. 6
20. to 15
21. Divergent
22. Biological, Adoptive
23. Visual
24. Phonetic
25. Can
26. Advantage

CHAPTER 13

1. Industry
2. Concrete
3. Perspective, viewpoint
4. Decreases
5. Authoritative
6. Less
7. Heterosexual
8. Downward
9. Mothers
10. Boys
11. Lack of supervision
12. Farther away from
13. Mature
14. Later-born
15. Discouraged
16. Low
17. Smaller
18. Self-fulfilling
19. Boys
20. Biological
21. Protect children from
22. Underutilize
23. Anxiety
24. Is not

CHAPTER 14

1. Stress
2. Feedback
3. Sex
4. Growth
5. Asynchronous
6. Epiphyseal
7. Estrogen
8. Boys
9. Boys
10. Cortex
11. Frontal
12. More
13. Chlamydia
14. Human papillomavirus (HPV or genital warts)
15. Acquired immunodeficiency syndrome, AIDS
16. Minority
17. Male
18. Accidents
19. Anorexia nervosa
20. Purging
21. Do
22. Perfectionism, obsessiveness, depression
23. Abuse
24. Abstinence, withdrawal
25. Alcohol
26. Nicotine
27. Regular

CHAPTER 15

1. Formal
2. Egocentrism
3. Superior
4. Superior
5. Sex
6. Postconventional

7. Positive
8. More
9. Drop
10. Girls
11. More
12. Boys
13. Realistic, practical, conventional
14. Gender
15. Efficacy
16. Majority

CHAPTER 16

1. Identity, ego identity
2. Moratorium
3. Achievement
4. Physical attractiveness, appearance
5. Mothers
6. Do
7. Increases
8. Their own
9. Masturbation
10. Homosexual, gay male or lesbian
11. Hormones
12. Less
13. Peer
14. Status
15. More
16. More
17. Common
18. Depression, helplessness, hopelessness
19. Does
20. Marriage
21. Job
22. Emerging

Glossary

abstinence syndrome A characteristic cluster of symptoms that results from a sudden decrease in the level of usage of a substance.

accommodation According to Piaget, the modification of existing schemes to permit the incorporation of new events or knowledge.

achieved ethnic identity The final stage of ethnic identity development; similar to the identity achievement status.

achievement That which is attained by one's efforts and presumed to be made possible by one's abilities.

active genetic–environmental correlation The correlation between the child's genetic endowment and the choices the child makes about which environments they will seek.

adaptation According to Piaget, an interaction between the organism and the environment that consists of two processes: assimilation and accommodation.

adolescence A transitional period between childhood and adulthood, usually seen as being bounded by puberty at the lower end and by the assumption of adult responsibilities at the upper end.

allele A member of a pair of genes.

alpha-fetoprotein (AFP) assay A blood test that assesses the mother's blood level of alphafetoprotein, a substance that is linked to fetal neural tube defects.

ambivalent/resistant attachment A type of insecure attachment characterized by severe distress at the leave-takings of, and ambivalent behavior at reunions with, an attachment figure.

American Sign Language (ASL) The communication of meaning through the use of symbols that are formed by moving the hands and arms; the language used by some deaf people.

amniocentesis A procedure for drawing out and examining fetal cells sloughed off into amniotic fluid to determine whether various disorders are present.

amniotic fluid Fluid within the amniotic sac that suspends and protects the fetus.

amniotic sac The sac containing the fetus.

amplitude The maximum vibration of a sound wave. The higher the amplitude of sound waves, the louder they are.

androgens Male sex hormones.

anesthesia A method that produces partial or total loss of the sense of pain.

animism The attribution of life and intentionality to inanimate objects.

anorexia nervosa An eating disorder characterized by irrational fear of weight gain, distorted body image, and severe weight loss.

anoxia A condition characterized by lack of oxygen.

Apgar scale A measure of a newborn's health that assesses appearance, pulse, grimace, activity level, and respiratory effort.

aphasia A disruption in the ability to understand or produce language.

appearance–reality distinction The difference between real events and mental events, fantasies, and misleading appearances.

artificial insemination Injection of sperm into the uterus to fertilize an ovum.

artificialism The belief that environmental features were made by people.

assimilation According to Piaget, the incorporation of new events or knowledge into existing schemes.

asynchronous growth Imbalanced growth, such as the growth that occurs during the early part of adolescence and causes many adolescents to appear gawky.

attachment An affectional bond between individuals characterized by a seeking of closeness or contact and a show of distress upon separation.

attachment-in-the-making phase The second phase in the development of attachment, occurring at 3 or 4 months of age and characterized by preference for familiar figures.

attention-deficit/hyperactivity disorder (ADHD) A behavior disorder characterized by excessive inattention, impulsiveness, and hyperactivity.

attributional style The way in which one is disposed toward interpreting outcomes (successes or failures), as in tending to place blame or responsibility on oneself or on external factors.

authoritarian A child-rearing style in which parents demand submission and obedience from their children but are not very communicative and warm.

authoritative A child-rearing style in which parents are restrictive and demanding, yet communicative and warm.

autism An autism spectrum disorder characterized by extreme aloneness, communication problems, intolerance of change, and ritualistic behavior.

autism spectrum disorders (ASDs) Developmental disorders—including autism, Asperger's syndrome, Rett's disorder, and childhood disintegrative disorder—that are characterized by impaired communication skills, poor social interactions, and repetitive, stereotyped behavior.

autobiographical memory The memory of specific episodes or events.

autonomous morality The second stage in Piaget's cognitive-developmental theory of moral development. In this stage, children base moral judgments on the intentions of the wrongdoer more so than on the amount of damage done. Social rules are viewed as agreements that can be changed.

autosome A member of a pair of chromosomes (with the exception of sex chromosomes).

avoidant attachment A type of insecure attachment characterized by apparent indifference to the leave-takings of, and reunions with, an attachment figure.

axon A long, thin part of a neuron that transmits impulses to other neurons through small branching structures called axon terminals.

babbling The child's first vocalizations that have the sounds of speech.

Babinski reflex A reflex in which infants fan their toes when the undersides of their feet are stroked.

bedwetting Failure to control the bladder during the night.

behaviorism John B. Watson's view that a science or theory of development must study observable behavior only and investigate relationships between stimuli and responses.

bilingual Using or capable of using two languages with nearly equal or equal facility.

blastocyst A stage within the germinal period of prenatal development in which the zygote has the form of a sphere of cells surrounding a cavity of fluid.

bonding The process of forming bonds of attachment between parent and child.

Braxton-Hicks contractions The first (usually painless) contractions of childbirth.

breech presentation A position in which the fetus enters the birth canal buttocks first.

Broca's aphasia A form of aphasia caused by damage to Broca's area and characterized by slow, laborious speech.

bulimia nervosa An eating disorder characterized by cycles of binge eating and vomiting as a means of controlling weight gain.

canalization The tendency of growth rates to return to genetically determined patterns after undergoing environmentally induced change.

carrier A person who carries and transmits characteristics but does not exhibit them.

case study A carefully drawn biography of the life of an individual.

categorical self Definitions of the self that refer to concrete external traits.

centration Focusing on one dimension of a situation while ignoring others.

cephalocaudal From head to tail.

cerebellum The part of the hindbrain involved in muscle coordination and balance.

cerebrum The large mass of the forebrain, which consists of two hemispheres.

cesarean section A method of childbirth in which the neonate is delivered through a surgical incision in the abdomen. (Also spelled *Caesarean*.)

child A person undergoing the period of development from infancy through puberty.

chorionic villus sampling (CVS) A method for the prenatal detection of genetic abnormalities that samples the membrane enveloping the amniotic sac and fetus.

chromosomes Rod-shaped structures that are composed of genes and found within the nuclei of cells.

chronological age (CA) A person's age.

chronosystem The environmental changes that occur over time and have an impact on the child (from the Greek chronos, meaning "time").

class inclusion The principle that one category or class of things can include several subclasses.

classical conditioning A simple form of learning in which one stimulus comes to bring forth the response usually elicited by a second stimulus by being paired repeatedly with the second stimulus.

clear-cut attachment phase The third phase in the development of attachment, occurring at 6 or 7 months of age and characterized by intensified dependence on the primary caregiver.

clique A group of 5 to 10 individuals who hang around together and share activities and confidences.

clitoris A female sex organ that is highly sensitive to sexual stimulation but is not directly involved in reproduction.

cognitive-developmental theory The stage theory that holds that the child's abilities to mentally represent the world and solve problems unfold as a result of the interaction of experience and the maturation of neurological structures.

cohort effect Similarities in behavior among a group of peers that stem from the fact that group members are approximately the same age.

collectivist A person who defines herself or himself in terms of relationships to other people and groups and gives priority to group goals.

commitment A stable investment in one's goals, values, and beliefs.

communication disorders Persistent problems in understanding or producing language.

conception The union of a sperm cell and an ovum that occurs when the chromosomes of each of these cells combine to form 23 new pairs.

concrete operations The third stage in Piaget's cognitive-developmental theory of moral development, characterized by flexible, reversible thought concerning tangible objects and events.

conduct disorders Disorders marked by persistent breaking of the rules and violations of the rights of others.

cones In the eye, cone-shaped receptors of light that transmit sensations of color.

congenital Present at birth; resulting from the prenatal environment.

conservation In cognitive psychology, the principle that properties of substances, such as weight and mass, remain the same (are conserved) when superficial

characteristics such as their shapes or arrangement are changed.

contact comfort The pleasure derived from physical contact with another; a hypothesized need or drive for physical contact with another.

contrast assumption The assumption that objects have only one label. Also known as the mutual exclusivity assumption (if a word means one thing, then it cannot mean another).

control group A group made up of subjects in an experiment who do not receive the treatment, but for whom all other conditions are comparable to those of subjects in the experimental group.

conventional level According to Kohlberg, a period during which moral judgments largely reflect social rules and conventions.

convergence The inward movement of the eyes as they focus on an object that is drawing nearer.

convergent thinking A thought process that attempts to focus on the single best solution to a problem.

cooing Prelinguistic, articulated vowel-like sounds that appear to reflect feelings of positive excitement.

coregulation A gradual transferring of control from parent to child, beginning in middle childhood.

corpus callosum The thick bundle of nerve fibers that connects the hemispheres of the brain.

correlation A relationship between variables in which one variable increases as a second variable also increases (a positive correlation) or decreases (a negative correlation).

correlation coefficient A number ranging from $+1.00$ to -1.00 that expresses the direction (positive or negative) and strength of the relationship between two variables.

creativity The ability to generate novel solutions to problems; a trait characterized by flexibility, ingenuity, and originality.

critical period In this context, a period during which an embryo is particularly vulnerable to a certain teratogen.

cross-sectional research The study of developmental processes by taking measures of children of different age groups at the same time.

cross-sequential research An approach that combines the longitudinal and cross-sectional methods by following individuals of different ages for abbreviated periods of time.

crowd A large, loosely organized group of people who may or may not spend much time together and who are identified by the activities of the group.

cultural bias A factor hypothesized to be present in intelligence tests that bestows an advantage on test takers from certain cultural or ethnic backgrounds but that does not reflect true intelligence.

cultural–familial disability Substandard intellectual performance that is presumed to stem from lack of opportunity to acquire the knowledge and skills considered important within a cultural setting.

culture-free Descriptive of a test in which cultural biases have been removed. On

such a test, test takers from different cultural backgrounds would have an equal opportunity to earn scores that reflect their true abilities.

cyberbullying The use of online media to transmit intimidating or threatening messages to a person or to spread intimidating information among the target's peers.

cystic fibrosis A fatal genetic disorder in which mucus obstructs the lungs and pancreas.

decentration Simultaneous focusing (centering) on more than one aspect or dimension of a problem or situation.

deep structure The underlying meaning of a sentence.

deferred imitation The imitation of people and events that were encountered or experienced hours, days, or weeks in the past.

dendrites The rootlike parts of a neuron that receive impulses from other neurons.

deoxyribonucleic acid (DNA) Genetic material that takes the form of a double helix made up of phosphates, sugars, and bases.

dependent variable In a scientific study, a measure of an assumed effect of an independent variable.

DES Abbreviation for diethylstilbestrol, an estrogen that has been linked to cancer in the reproductive organs of children of women who used it when pregnant.

development The processes by which organisms unfold features and traits, grow, and become more complex and specialized in structure and function.

differential emotions theory Izard's view that the major emotions are distinct at birth but emerge gradually in accord with maturation and the child's developing needs.

differentiation The process by which behaviors and physical structures become more specialized.

dilate To widen or enlarge.

disinhibit To stimulate a response that has been suppressed (inhibited) by showing a model engaging in that response without aversive consequences.

disorganized–disoriented attachment A type of insecure attachment characterized by dazed and contradictory behaviors toward an attachment figure.

divergent thinking A thought process that attempts to generate multiple solutions to problems; free and fluent association to the elements of a problem.

dizygotic (DZ) twins Twins that derive from two zygotes; fraternal twins.

dominant trait A trait that is expressed.

donor IVF The transfer of a donor's ovum, fertilized in a laboratory dish, to the uterus of another woman.

double-deficit hypothesis The theory of dyslexia that suggests that dyslexic children have biological deficits in two areas: *phonological processing* (interpreting sounds) and *naming speed* (for example, identifying letters, such as *b* versus *d*, or *w* versus *m*).

Down syndrome A chromosomal abnormality characterized by intellectual disability and caused by an extra chromosome in the 21st pair.

dramatic play Play in which children enact social roles; made possible by the attainment of symbolic thought. A form of pretend play.

dyslexia A reading disorder characterized by problems such as letter reversals, mirror reading, slow reading, and reduced comprehension (from the Greek roots *dys*, meaning "bad," and *lexikon*, meaning "of words").

echolalia The automatic repetition of sounds or words.

ecological systems theory The view that explains child development in terms of the reciprocal influences between children and the settings that make up their environment.

ecology The branch of biology that deals with the relationships between living organisms and their environment.

ectoderm The outermost cell layer of the newly formed embryo from which the skin and nervous system develop.

efface To thin.

ego identity According to Erikson, one's sense of who one is and what one stands for.

egocentrism Putting oneself at the center of things such that one is unable to perceive the world from another person's point of view. Egocentrism is normal in early childhood, but is a matter of choice, and rather intolerable, in adults. (Okay, I sneaked an editorial comment into a definition. No apologies.)

elaborative strategy A method for increasing retention of new information by relating it to well-known information.

electroencephalograph (EEG) An instrument that measures electrical activity of the brain.

embryonic disk The platelike inner part of the blastocyst that differentiates into the ectoderm, mesoderm, and endoderm of the embryo.

embryonic stage The stage of prenatal development that lasts from implantation through the eighth week of pregnancy. It is characterized by the development of the major organ systems.

embryonic transplant The transfer of an embryo from the uterus of one woman to that of another.

emergentist theory of language development The view that the child's complex abilities to understand and produce language emerge from simpler processes that are biological, cognitive, and social in nature.

emotion A state of feeling that has physiological, situational, and cognitive components.

emotional regulation Techniques for controlling one's emotional states.

empathy Ability to share another person's feelings.

empirical Based on observation and experimentation.

encode To transform sensory input into a form that is more readily processed.

encopresis Failure to control the bowels after the normal age for bowel control has been reached. Also called *soiling*.

endoderm The inner layer of the embryo from which the lungs and digestive system develop.

endometriosis Inflammation of endometrial tissue sloughed off into the abdominal cavity rather than out of the body during menstruation; the condition is characterized by abdominal pain and sometimes by infertility.

endometrium The inner lining of the uterus.

enuresis Failure to control the bladder (urination) after the normal age for control has been reached.

epigenesis The view that development reflects continual bidirectional exchanges between one's genotype and one's environmental conditions.

epiphyseal closure The process by which the cartilage that separates the long end (epiphysis) of a bone from the main part of the bone turns to bone.

episiotomy A surgical incision in the area between the birth canal and the anus that widens the vaginal opening, preventing random tearing during childbirth.

equilibration The creation of an equilibrium, or balance, between assimilation and accommodation as a way of incorporating new events or knowledge.

estrogen A female sex hormone produced mainly by the ovaries.

ethnic groups Groups of people distinguished by their cultural heritage, race, language, and common history.

ethnic identity A sense of belonging to an ethnic group.

ethnic identity search The second stage of ethnic identity development; similar to the moratorium identity status.

ethology The study of behaviors that are specific to a species—how these behaviors evolved, help the organism adapt, and develop during critical periods.

evocative genetic–environmental correlation The correlation between the child's genetic endowment and the responses the child elicits from other people.

exosystem Community institutions and settings that indirectly influence the child, such as the school board and the parents' workplaces (from the Greek exo, meaning "outside").

experiment A method of scientific investigation that seeks to discover cause-and-effect relationships by introducing independent variables and observing their effects on dependent variables.

experimental group A group made up of subjects who receive a treatment in an experiment.

exploration Active questioning and searching among alternatives in the quest to establish goals, values, and beliefs.

expressive language style Use of language primarily as a means for engaging in social interaction.

expressive vocabulary The sum total of the words that one can use in the production of language.

extinction The decrease and eventual disappearance of a response in the absence of reinforcement.

factor A condition or quality that brings about a result—in this case, "intelligent" behavior. A cluster of related items, such as those found on an intelligence or personality test.

factor analysis A statistical technique that enables researchers to determine the relationships among a large number of items, such as test items.

failure to thrive (FTT) A disorder of impaired growth in infancy and early childhood characterized by failure to gain weight within normal limits.

fallopian tube A tube through which ova travel from an ovary to the uterus.

fast mapping A process of quickly determining a word's meaning, which facilitates children's vocabulary development.

feedback loop A system in which glands regulate each other's functioning through a series of hormonal messages.

fetal alcohol effect (FAE) A cluster of symptoms, less severe than those of fetal alcohol syndrome, shown by children of women who drank moderately during pregnancy.

fetal alcohol syndrome (FAS) A cluster of symptoms shown by children of women who drank during pregnancy, including characteristic facial features and intellectual disability.

fetal stage The stage of development that lasts from the beginning of the ninth week of pregnancy through birth.

fine motor skills Skills that employ the small muscles used in manipulation, such as those in the fingers.

foreclosure An identity status that characterizes those who have made commitments without considering alternatives.

formal operations The fourth stage in Piaget's cognitive-developmental theory, characterized by the capacity for flexible, reversible operations concerning abstract ideas and concepts, such as symbols, statements, and theories.

gay A male who is interested romantically and sexually in other males. (Can also refer to lesbians.)

gender constancy The concept that one's gender remains the same despite superficial changes in appearance or behavior.

gender identity Knowledge that one is female or male. Also, the name of the first stage in Kohlberg's cognitive-developmental theory of the assumption of gender roles.

gender role A complex cluster of traits and behaviors that are considered stereotypical of females or of males.

gender stability The concept that one's gender is a permanent feature.

gender-schema theory The view that one's knowledge of the gender schema in one's society (the behavior patterns that are considered appropriate for men and women) guides one's assumption of gender-typed preferences and behavior patterns.

gene The basic unit of heredity. Genes are composed of deoxyribonucleic acid (DNA).

generalized anxiety disorder (GAD) An anxiety disorder in which anxiety is present continuously and is unrelated to the situation.

genetic counseling Advice concerning the probabilities that a couple's children will show genetic abnormalities.

genetics The branch of biology that studies heredity.

genital stage In Freud's psychoanalytic theory, the fifth and final stage of psychosexual development, in which gratification is attained through sexual intercourse with a person of the other gender.

genotype The genetic form, or constitution, of a person as determined by heredity.

germinal stage The period of development between conception and the implantation of the embryo.

goodness of fit Agreement between the parents' expectations of, or demands on, the child and the child's temperamental characteristics.

grasping reflex A reflex in which infants grasp objects that cause pressure against their palms.

gray matter Neural tissue, especially of the brain and spinal cord, that contains cell bodies and their dendrites and forms most of the cortex of the brain.

gross motor skills Skills that employ the large muscles used in locomotion.

growth The processes by which organisms increase in size, weight, strength, and other traits as they develop.

growth spurt A period during which growth advances at a dramatically rapid rate compared with other periods.

gynecomastia Enlargement of breast tissue in males.

habituation A process in which one becomes used to a repeated stimulus and therefore pays less attention to it.

hallucinogenics Substances that giver rise to perceptual distortions.

hemophilia A genetic disorder in which blood does not clot properly.

heredity The transmission of traits and characteristics from parent to child by means of genes.

heritability The degree to which the variations in a trait from one person to another can be attributed to, or explained by, genetic factors.

heterozygous Having two different alleles.

HIV/AIDS HIV stands for human immunodeficiency virus, which cripples the body's immune system. AIDS stands for acquired immunodeficiency syndrome— the body's state when the immune system is weakened to the point where it is vulnerable to diseases that would otherwise be fought off.

holophrase A single word that is used to express complex meanings.

homosexual Referring to an erotic orientation toward members of one's own gender.

homozygous Having two identical alleles.

hue Color.

Huntington disease (HD) A fatal genetic neurological disorder whose onset is in middle age.

hyperactivity Excessive restlessness and overactivity; one of the primary characteristics of attention-deficit/hyperactivity disorder (ADHD). Not to be confused with misbehavior or with high activity levels that are normal during childhood.

hypothalamus A pea-sized structure above the pituitary gland that is involved in the regulation of body temperature, motivation (such as hunger, thirst, sexual desire), and emotion.

hypothesis A specific statement about behavior that is tested by research.

hypoxia A condition characterized by less oxygen than is required.

identity achievement An identity status that characterizes those who have explored alternatives and have developed commitments.

identity crisis According to Erikson, an adolescent period of inner conflict during which one examines one's values and makes decisions about one's life roles.

identity diffusion An identity status that characterizes those who have made no commitments and are not in the process of exploring alternatives.

imaginary audience The belief that others around us are as concerned with our thoughts and behaviors as we are; one aspect of adolescent egocentrism.

immanent justice The view that a negative experience is a direct consequence of wrongdoing, reflecting the belief that morality is embedded within the structure of the universe.

imprinting The process by which some animals exhibit the fixed action pattern (FAP) of attachment in response to a releasing stimulus. The FAP occurs during a critical period and is difficult to modify.

in vitro fertilization (IVF) Fertilization of an ovum in a laboratory dish.

incubator A heated, protective container in which premature infants are kept.

independent variable In a scientific study, the condition that is manipulated (changed) so that its effects can be observed.

indiscriminate attachment The display of attachment behaviors toward any person.

individualist A person who defines herself or himself in terms of personal traits and gives priority to her or his own goals.

inductive Characteristic of disciplinary methods, such as reasoning, that try to teach an understanding of the principles behind parental demands

industry versus inferiority The fourth stage of psychosocial development in Erikson's theory, occurring in middle childhood. Mastery of tasks leads to a sense of industry, whereas failure produces feelings of inferiority.

infancy The period of very early childhood, characterized by lack of complex speech; the first 2 years after birth.

information processing The view in which cognitive processes are compared to the functions of computers. The theory deals with the input, storage, retrieval, manipulation, and output of information. The focus is on the development of children's strategies for solving problems— their "mental programs."

initial pre-attachment phase The first phase in the formation of bonds of attachment, lasting from birth to about 3 months of age and characterized by indiscriminate attachment.

insomnia A sleep disorder characterized by difficulty falling asleep, difficulty remaining asleep during the night, and waking early.

intelligence A complex and controversial concept, defined by David Wechsler as "[the] capacity . . . to understand the world [and the] resourcefulness to cope with its challenges." Intelligence implies the capacity to make adaptive choices (from the Latin *inter*, meaning "among," and *legere*, meaning "to choose").

intelligence quotient (IQ) Originally, a ratio obtained by dividing a child's score (or "mental age") on an intelligence test by his or her chronological age. In general, a score on an intelligence test.

intensity Brightness.

intonation The use of pitches of varying levels to help communicate meaning.

irreversibility Lack of recognition that actions can be reversed.

juvenile delinquency Conduct in a child or adolescent characterized by illegal activities.

Klinefelter syndrome A chromosomal disorder found among males that is caused by an extra X sex chromosome and is characterized by infertility and mild intellectual disability.

kwashiorkor A form of protein–energy malnutrition in which the body may break down its own reserves of protein, resulting in enlargement of the stomach, swollen feet, and other symptoms.

labia The major and minor lips of the female genitalia.

Lamaze method A method of childbirth in which women are educated about childbirth, learn to relax and breathe in patterns that conserve energy and lessen pain, and have a coach (usually the father) present during childbirth. Also termed *prepared childbirth*.

language acquisition device (LAD) In psycholinguistic theory, neural "prewiring" that facilitates the child's learning of grammar.

lanugo Fine, downy hair that covers much of the body of neonates, especially preterm babies.

larynx The part of the throat that contains the vocal cords.

latency stage In Freud's psychoanalytic theory, the fourth stage of psychosexual development, characterized by repression of sexual impulses and development of skills.

learned helplessness An acquired (hence, learned) belief that one is unable to control one's environment.

learning disabilities A group of disorders characterized by inadequate development of specific academic, language, and speech skills.

lesbian A female who is interested romantically and sexually in other females.

LGBT Acronym for lesbian, gay, bisexual, and transgender.

life crisis An internal conflict that attends each stage of psychosocial development. Positive resolution of early life crises sets the stage for positive resolution of subsequent life crises.

locomotion Movement from one place to another.

longitudinal research The study of developmental processes by taking repeated measures of the same group of children at various stages of development.

long-term memory The memory structure capable of relatively permanent storage of information.

macrosystem The basic institutions and ideologies that influence the child, such as the American ideals of freedom of expression and equality under the law (from the Greek makros, meaning "long" or "enlarged").

mainstreaming Placing children with disabilities in classrooms of children without disabilities. Today, most students with mild disabilities spend at least part of their school day in regular classrooms. The goals of mainstreaming include providing broader educational opportunities for students with disabilities and fostering interactions with children without disabilities.

mammary glands Glands that secrete milk.

marasmus A wasted, potentially lethal body condition caused by inadequate nutrition and characterized by painful thinness.

mean length of utterance (MLU) The average number of morphemes used in an utterance.

medulla A part of the brain stem that regulates vital and automatic functions such as breathing and the sleep–wake cycle.

meiosis The form of cell division in which each pair of chromosomes splits and one member of each pair moves to the new cell. As a result, each new cell has 23 chromosomes.

memory The processes by which we store and retrieve information.

menarche The onset of menstruation.

menopause The cessation of menstruation, typically occurring between ages 48 and 52.

mental age (MA) The accumulated months of credit that a person earns on the Stanford–Binet Intelligence Scale.

mental representations The mental forms that a real object or event can take.

mesoderm The central layer of the embryo from which the bones and muscles develop.

mesosystem The interlocking settings that influence the child, such as the interaction of the school and the larger community when children are taken on field trips (from the Greek mesos, meaning "middle").

metacognition Awareness of and control of one's cognitive abilities, as shown by the intentional use of cognitive strategies in solving problems.

metamemory Knowledge of the functions and processes involved in one's storage and retrieval of information (memory), as shown by the use of cognitive strategies to retain information.

microsystem The immediate settings with which the child interacts, such as the home, the school, and the child's peers (from the Greek mikros, meaning "small").

midwife An individual who helps women in childbirth.

mitosis The form of cell division in which each chromosome splits lengthwise to double in number. Half of each chromosome combines with chemicals to retake its original form and then moves to the new cell.

models In learning theory, those whose behaviors are imitated by others.

monozygotic (MZ) twins Twins that derive from a single zygote that has split into two; identical twins. Each MZ twin carries the same genetic code.

moral realism The first stage in Piaget's cognitive-developmental theory of moral development. In this stage, children judge acts as moral when they conform to authority or to the rules of the game. Morality is perceived as embedded in the structure of the universe.

moratorium An identity status that characterizes those who are actively exploring alternatives in an attempt to form an identity.

Moro reflex A reflex in which infants arch their back, fling out their arms and legs, and draw them back toward the chest in response to a sudden change in position.

morpheme The smallest unit of meaning in a language.

motility Self-propulsion.

multifactorial problems Problems that stem from the interaction of heredity and environmental factors.

multiple sclerosis A disorder in which myelin is replaced by hard, fibrous tissue that impedes neural transmission.

muscular dystrophy A chronic disease characterized by a progressive wasting away of the muscles.

mutation A sudden variation in a heritable characteristic, caused by an accident that affects the composition of genes.

mutism Inability or refusal to speak.

myelin sheath A fatty, white substance that encases and insulates neurons, permitting more rapid transmission of neural impulses.

myelination The process by which axons are coated with myelin.

natural childbirth A method of childbirth in which women use no anesthesia and are educated about childbirth and strategies for coping with discomfort.

naturalistic observation A method of scientific observation in which children (and others) are observed in their natural environments.

nature The processes within an organism that guide that organism to develop according to its genetic code.

NBAS Brazelton Neonatal Behavioral Assessment Scale.

negative correlation A relationship between two variables in which one variable decreases as the other variable increases.

negative reinforcer A reinforcer that, when removed, increases the frequency of a behavior.

neonate A newborn child.

nerves Bundles of axons from many neurons.

neural Of the nervous system.

neural tube A hollowed-out area in the blastocyst from which the nervous system develops.

neurons Nerve cells; cells found in the nervous system that transmit messages.

neurotransmitter A chemical substance that makes possible the transmission of neural impulses from one neuron to another.

niche-picking Choosing environmental conditions that foster one's genetically transmitted abilities and interests.

nightmares Frightening dreams that occur during REM sleep, often in the morning hours.

NNNS Neonatal Intensive Care Unit Network Neurobehavioral Scale.

nocturnal emission Emission of seminal fluid while asleep.

non–rapid eye movement (non-REM) sleep Periods of sleep during which we are unlikely to dream.

nonsocial play Forms of play (solitary play or onlooker play) in which play is not influenced by the play of nearby children.

nurture The processes external to an organism that nourish it as it develops according to its genetic code or that cause it to swerve from its genetically programmed course. Environmental factors that influence development.

object permanence Recognition that objects continue to exist even when they are not seen.

objective morality The perception of morality as objective, or as existing outside the cognitive functioning of people; a characteristic of Piaget's stage of moral realism.

operant conditioning A simple form of learning in which an organism learns to engage in behavior that is reinforced.

operations Flexible, reversible mental manipulations of objects, in which objects can be mentally transformed and then returned to their original states.

oral rehydration therapy A treatment involving the administration of a salt and sugar solution to a child who is dehydrated from diarrhea.

osteoporosis A condition involving the progressive loss of bone tissue.

overextension Use of words in situations in which their meanings become extended or inappropriate.

overregularization The application of regular grammatical rules (e.g., to create past tense and plurals) to irregular verbs and nouns.

ovulation The release of an ovum from an ovary.

oxytocin A pituitary hormone that stimulates labor contractions.

passive genetic–environmental correlation The correlation between the genetic endowment parents give their children and the environments in which they place their children.

peers Children of the same age. (More generally, people of similar background and social standing.)

pelvic inflammatory disease (PID) An infection of the abdominal region that may have various causes and may impair fertility.

perception The process by which sensations are organized into a mental map of the world.

perceptual constancy The tendency to perceive objects as the same even though the sensations produced by them may differ when, for example, they differ in position or distance.

permissive–indulgent A child-rearing style in which parents are not controlling and restrictive but are warm.

personal fable The belief that our feelings and ideas are special and unique and that we are invulnerable; one aspect of adolescent egocentrism.

personality An individual's distinctive ways of responding to people and events.

phenotype The actual form, or constitution, of a person as determined by heredity and environmental factors.

phenylketonuria (PKU) A genetic abnormality in which phenylalanine builds up and causes intellectual disability.

phobia An irrational, excessive fear that interferes with one's functioning.

phonetic method A method for learning to read in which children decode the sounds of words via their knowledge of the sounds of letters and letter combinations.

pincer grasp The use of the opposing thumb to grasp objects between the thumb and other fingers.

pitch The highness or lowness of a sound, as determined by the frequency of sound waves.

pituitary gland The body's "master gland," which is located in the lower central part of the brain and which secretes many hormones essential to development, such as oxytocin, prolactin, and growth hormone.

placenta An organ connected to the uterine wall and to the fetus by the umbilical cord. The placenta serves as a relay station between mother and fetus for the exchange of nutrients and wastes.

plasticity The tendency of new parts of the brain to take up the functions of injured parts.

polygenic Resulting from many genes.

positive correlation A relationship between two variables in which one variable increases as the other variable increases.

positive reinforcer A reinforcer that, when applied, increases the frequency of a behavior.

postconventional level According to Kohlberg, a period during which moral judgments are derived from moral principles and people look to themselves to set moral standards.

postpartum depression (PPD) Severe, prolonged depression that afflicts 10–20% of women after delivery and that is characterized by sadness, apathy, and feelings of worthlessness.

postpartum period The time that immediately follows childbirth.

pragmatics The practical aspects of communication, such as adaptation of language to fit the social situation.

precausal A type of thought in which natural cause-and-effect relationships are attributed to will and other preoperational concepts, as in thinking that the sun sets because it is tired.

preconventional level According to Kohlberg, a period during which moral judgments are based largely on expectations of rewards or punishments.

pre-eclampsia A life-threatening disease that can afflict pregnant women. It is characterized by high blood pressure.

prelinguistic Referring to vocalizations made by the infant before the development of language. (In language, words symbolize objects and events.)

premature Born before the full term of gestation. (Also referred to as preterm.)

prenatal Before birth.

preoperational stage The second stage in Piaget's scheme, characterized by inflexible and irreversible mental manipulation of symbols.

preterm Born at or before completion of 37 weeks of gestation.

primary circular reactions The repetition of actions that first occurred by chance and that focus on the infant's own body.

primary sex characteristics The structures that make reproduction possible.

private speech Vygotsky's concept of the ultimate binding of language and thought. Private speech originates in vocalizations that may regulate the child's behavior and become internalized by age 6 or 7.

progestin A hormone that is used to maintain pregnancy and can also cause masculinization of the fetus.

prosocial behavior Behavior intended to benefit another without expectation of reward.

prostaglandins Hormones that stimulate uterine contractions.

proximodistal From the inner part (or axis) of the body outward.

psycholinguistic theory The view that language learning involves an interaction between environmental influences and an inborn tendency to acquire language. The emphasis is on the inborn tendency.

psychosexual development Freud's view that as children develop, they find sexual gratification through stimulating different parts of their bodies.

psychosocial development Erikson's theory, which emphasizes the importance of social relationships and conscious choice throughout the eight stages of development.

puberty The biological stage of development characterized by changes that lead to reproductive capacity. Puberty signals the beginning of adolescence.

punishment An unpleasant stimulus that suppresses behavior.

Pygmalion effect A self-fulfilling prophecy; an expectation that is confirmed because of the behavior of those who hold the expectation.

rapid eye movement (REM) sleep Periods of sleep during which we are likely to dream, as indicated by rapid eye movements.

reaction range The variability in the expression of inherited traits as they are influenced by environmental factors.

reaction time The amount of time required to respond to a stimulus.

receptive vocabulary The sum total of the words whose meanings one understands.

recessive trait A trait that is not expressed when the gene or genes involved have been paired with dominant genes. Recessive traits are transmitted to future generations and expressed if they are paired with other recessive genes.

reciprocity The principle that actions have mutual effects and that people depend on one another to treat each other morally.

referential language style Use of language primarily as a means for labeling objects.

reflex An unlearned, stereotypical response to a stimulus.

regression A return to behaviors characteristic of earlier stages of development.

rehearsal Repetition—mental, behavioral, or both.

rehearse Repeat.

reinforcement The process of providing stimuli following a behavior, which has the effect of increasing the frequency of the behavior.

rejecting–neglecting A child-rearing style in which parents are neither restrictive and controlling nor supportive and responsive.

respiratory distress syndrome A cluster of breathing problems, including weak and irregular breathing, to which preterm babies are particularly prone.

reversibility According to Piaget, recognition that processes can be undone, leaving things as they were before. Reversibility is a factor in conservation of the properties of substances.

Rh incompatibility A condition in which antibodies produced by the mother are transmitted to the child, possibly causing brain damage or death.

rods In the eye, rod-shaped receptors of light that are sensitive to intensity only. Rods permit black-and-white vision.

rooting reflex A reflex in which infants turn their mouths and heads in the direction of a stroking of the cheek or corner of the mouth.

rote learning A memorization technique based on repetition.

rubella A viral infection that can cause retardation and heart disease in the embryo. Also called German measles.

saturation Richness or purity of a color.

scaffolding Vygotsky's term for temporary cognitive structures or methods of solving problems that help the child as he or she learns to function independently.

scheme According to Piaget, an action pattern (such as a reflex) or mental structure that is involved in the acquisition or organization of knowledge.

schizophrenia A severe psychological disorder that is characterized by disturbances in thought and language, perception and attention, motor activity, and mood, and by withdrawal and absorption into daydreams or fantasy.

school phobia Fear of attending school, marked by extreme anxiety at leaving parents.

scripts Abstract generalized accounts of familiar repeated events.

secondary circular reactions The repetition of actions that produce an effect on the environment.

secondary sex characteristics Physical indicators of sexual maturation—such as changes to the voice and growth of bodily hair—that do not directly involve reproductive structures.

secular trend A historical trend toward increasing adult height and earlier puberty.

secure attachment A type of attachment characterized by showing mild distress at leave-takings, seeking nearness to an attachment figure, and being readily soothed by this figure.

sedatives Drugs that soothe or quiet restlessness or agitation.

self-concept One's impression of oneself; self-awareness.

self-efficacy expectations One's beliefs that he or she can handle the requirements of a situation.

self-esteem The sense of value or worth that people attach to themselves.

self-fulfilling prophecy An event that occurs because of the behavior of those who expect it to occur.

semantic code A code based on the meaning of information.

semen The fluid that contains sperm and substances that nourish and help transport sperm.

sensation The stimulation of sensory organs, such as the eyes, ears, and skin, and the transmission of sensory information to the brain.

sensitive period In linguistic theory, the period from about 18 months to puberty when the brain is thought to be especially capable of learning language because of its plasticity.

sensory memory The structure of memory that is first encountered by sensory input. Information is maintained in sensory memory for only a fraction of a second.

sensory register Another term for sensory memory.

separation anxiety Fear of being separated from a target of attachment, usually a primary caregiver.

separation anxiety disorder (SAD) An extreme form of normal separation anxiety that is characterized by anxiety about separating from parents; SAD often takes the form of school refusal.

seriation Placing objects in an order or series according to a property or trait.

serotonin A neurotransmitter that is involved in the responsiveness of the medulla, emotional responses such as depression, and motivational responses such as hunger.

sex chromosome A chromosome in the shape of a Y (male) or an X (female) that determines the sex of the child.

sexism Discrimination or bias against people on the basis of their gender.

sex-linked chromosomal abnormalities Abnormalities that are transmitted from generation to generation, carried by a sex chromosome, usually an X sex chromosome.

sex-linked genetic abnormalities Abnormalities resulting from genes that are found on the X sex chromosome.

sexual harassment Unwelcome verbal or physical conduct of a sexual nature.

sexual identity A complex concept involving one's sexual orientation, one's gender role, one's gender-related preferences, and the like.

shape constancy The tendency to perceive objects as being the same shape even though the shapes of their images on the retina may differ when the objects are viewed from different positions.

shaping In learning theory, the gradual building of complex behavior patterns through reinforcement of successive approximations of the target behavior.

sibling rivalry Jealousy or rivalry among brothers and sisters.

sickle-cell anemia A genetic disorder that decreases the blood's capacity to carry oxygen.

sight vocabulary Words that are immediately recognized on the basis of familiarity with their overall shapes, rather than decoded.

size constancy The tendency to perceive objects as being the same size even though the sizes of their images on the retina may differ as a result of distance.

sleep terrors Frightening dreamlike experiences that occur during the deepest stage of non-REM sleep, shortly after the child has gone to sleep.

small for dates A description of neonates who are unusually small for their age.

social cognition Development of children's understanding of the relationship between the self and others.

social cognitive theory A cognitively oriented learning theory that emphasizes the role of observational learning in determining behavior.

social play Play in which children interact with others and are influenced by their play. Examples include parallel play, associative play, and cooperative play.

social referencing Using another person's reaction to a situation to form one's own assessment of it.

social smile A smile that occurs in response to a human voice or face.

socioeconomic status (SES) Social position as determined mainly by level of income.

somnambulism Sleepwalking.

sonogram A procedure for using ultrasonic sound waves to create a picture of an embryo or fetus.

spina bifida A neural tube defect that causes abnormalities of the brain and spine.

spontaneous abortion Unplanned, accidental abortion.

stage theory A theory of development characterized by hypothesizing the existence of distinct periods of life. Stages follow one another in an orderly sequence.

standardized test A test of some ability or trait in which an individual's score is compared to the scores of a group of similar individuals.

status offenses Offenses considered illegal only when performed by minors, such as truancy and underage drinking.

stepping reflex A reflex in which infants take steps when held under the arms by leaning forward so that their feet press against the ground.

stillbirth The birth of a dead fetus.

stimulants Drugs that increase the activity of the nervous system.

stimulus A change in the environment that leads to a change in behavior.

stranger anxiety A fear of unfamiliar people that emerges between 6 and 9 months of age. Also called *fear of strangers*.

substance use disorder A persistent pattern of use of a substance characterized by craving of the substance and impairment of physical, social, and/or emotional well-being.

sudden infant death syndrome (SIDS) The death, while sleeping, of apparently healthy babies who stop breathing for unknown medical reasons. Also called crib death.

surface structure The superficial grammatical construction of a sentence.

surrogate mother A woman who is artificially inseminated and carries to term a child who is then given to another woman, typically the spouse of the sperm donor.

symbolic play Play in which children make believe that objects and toys are other than what they are. Also termed *pretend play*.

syntax The rules in a language for placing words in the proper order to form meaningful sentences.

syphilis A sexually transmitted infection that can attack major organ systems.

Tay-Sachs disease A fatal genetic neurological disorder in which nerve cells in the brain and spinal cord are progressively destroyed.

telegraphic speech Type of speech in which only the essential words are used.

temperament Individual differences in styles of reaction that are present early in life.

teratogens Environmental influences or agents that can damage the embryo or fetus.

term The typical period of time between conception and the birth of a baby.

tertiary circular reactions The purposeful adaptation of established schemes to new situations.

testosterone A male sex hormone produced by the testes that promotes the development of male sexual characteristics and sperm.

thalidomide A sedative linked to birth defects, especially deformed or absent limbs.

theory A formulation of relationships underlying observed events. A theory involves assumptions and logically derived explanations and predictions.

theory of mind A common sense understanding of how the mind works.

time-lag comparison The study of developmental processes by taking measures of children of the same age group at different times.

time-out A behavior-modification technique in which a child who misbehaves is temporarily removed from positive reinforcement.

toddler A child who walks with short, uncertain steps. Toddlerhood lasts from about 12 months to 30 months of age, thereby bridging infancy and early childhood.

tolerance Habituation to a drug such that increasingly higher doses are needed to achieve similar effects.

tonic-neck reflex A reflex in which infants turn their head to one side, extend the arm and leg on that side, and flex the limbs on the opposite side. Also known as the fencing position.

transductive reasoning Reasoning from the specific to the specific. (In deductive reasoning, one reasons from the general to the specific; in inductive reasoning, one reasons from the specific to the general.)

transgendered Descriptive of a person who sees himself or herself as a person of the other gender and who may undergo hormone treatments and/or cosmetic surgery to achieve the appearance of being a member of the other gender.

transition The initial movement of the head of the fetus into the birth canal.

transitional object A soft, cuddly object often carried to bed by a child to ease the separation from parents.

transitivity The principle that if A is greater than B in a property and B is greater than C, then A is greater than C.

treatment In an experiment, a condition received by subjects so that its effects may be observed.

triarchic Governed by three. Descriptive of Sternberg's view that intellectual functioning has three aspects: analytical intelligence, creative intelligence, and practical intelligence.

trophoblast The outer part of the blastocyst from which the amniotic sac, placenta, and umbilical cord develop.

Turner syndrome A chromosomal disorder found among females that is caused by having a single X sex chromosome and is characterized by infertility.

ulnar grasp A method of grasping objects in which the fingers close somewhat clumsily against the palm.

ultrasound Sound waves too high in pitch to be sensed by the human ear.

umbilical cord A tube that connects the fetus to the placenta.

unexamined ethnic identity The first stage of ethnic identity development; similar to the diffusion and foreclosure identity statuses.

uterus The hollow organ within females in which the embryo and fetus develop.

utopian Referring to an ideal vision of society.

variables Quantities that can vary from child to child or from occasion to occasion, such as height, weight, intelligence, and attention span.

vernix An oily, white substance that coats the skin of neonates, especially preterm babies.

visual accommodation The automatic adjustments made by the lenses of the eyes to bring objects into focus.

visual acuity Keenness or sharpness of vision.

visual recognition memory The kind of memory shown in an infant's ability to discriminate previously seen objects from novel objects.

Wernicke's aphasia A form of aphasia caused by damage to Wernicke's area and characterized by impaired comprehension of speech and difficulty in attempting to produce the right word.

whole-language approach A method for learning to read in which children come to recognize words in a variety of contexts through repeated exposure to them.

whole-object assumption The assumption that words refer to whole objects and not to their component parts or characteristics.

working memory The structure of memory that can hold a sensory stimulus for up to 30 seconds after the trace decays. Also called short-term memory.

zone of proximal development (ZPD) Vygotsky's term for the range of tasks that a child can carry out with the help of someone who is more skilled, frequently an adult who represents the culture in which the child develops.

zygote A new cell formed from the union of a sperm and an ovum (egg cell); a fertilized egg.

References

Abdelaziz, Y. E., Harb, A. H., & Hisham, N. (2001). *Textbook of Clinical Pediatrics*. Philadelphia: Lippincott Williams & Wilkins.

Aber, J. L., Bishop-Josef, S. J., Jones, S. M., McLearn, K. T., & Phillips, D. A. (Eds.). (2007). *Child development and social policy: Knowledge for action. APA Decade of Behavior volumes*. Washington, DC: American Psychological Association.

Abrams, D., et al. (2014). The role of cognitive abilities in children's inferences about social atypicality and peer exclusion and inclusion in intergroup contexts. *British Journal of Developmental Psychology*, DOI10.1111/bjdp.12034.

Abravanel, E., & DeYong, N. G. (1991). Does object modeling elicit imitative-like gestures from young infants? *Journal of Experimental Child -Psychology, 52*, 22–40.

Academy of Nutrition and Dietetics. (2012). *Getting Started on Eating Right*. Retrieved from http://www.eatright.org/Public /content.aspx?id=8044. Accessed February 17, 2012.

Addy, S., & Wight, V. R. (2012, February). *Basic facts about low-income children, 2010*. National Center for Children in Poverty. Retrieved from http://www.nccp .org/publications/pub_1049.html. Accessed February 17, 2012.

Adhikari, D., & Liu, K. (2013). Regulation of quiescence and activation of oocyte growth in primordial follicles. In G. Coticchio et al. (Eds.). *Oogenesis* (pp. 49–62). London: Springer-Verlag.

Adler-Baeder, F. (2006). What do we know about the physical abuse of stepchildren? A review of the literature. *Journal of Divorce & Remarriage, 44*(3–4), 67–81.

Adolph, K. E., & Berger, S. E. (2005). Physical and motor development. In M. H. Bornstein & M. E. Lamb (Eds.), *Developmental science: An advanced textbook* (5th ed.) (pp. 223–281). Hillsdale, NJ: Erlbaum.

Adolph, K. E., & Tamis-LeMonda, C. S. (2014). The costs and benefits of development: The transition from crawling to walking. *Child Development Perspectives, 8*(4), 187–192.

Agency for Healthcare Research and Quality. (2004, April). Chronic illnesses. In *Child Health Research Findings*, Program Brief, AHRQ Publication 04-P011. Rockville, MD: Agency for Healthcare Research and Quality. Available at http://www.ahrq.gov /research/childfind/chfchrn.htm.

Agrawal, A., Silberg, J. L., Lynskey, M. T., Maes, H. H., & Eaves, L. J. (2010). Mechanisms underlying the lifetime co-occurrence of tobacco and cannabis use in adolescent and young adult twins. *Drug and Alcohol Dependence, 108*(1-2), 49–55.

Aguiar, A., & Baillargeon, R. (1999). 2.5-month-old infants' reasoning about when objects should and should not be occluded. *Cognitive Psychology, 39*(2), 116–157.

Aguiar, N. R., & Taylor, M. (2015). Children's concepts of the social affordances of a virtual dog and a stuffed dog. *Cognitive Development, 34*, 16–27.

Ainsworth, M. D. S. (1967). *Infancy in Uganda: Infant care and the growth of love*. Baltimore, MD: Johns Hopkins University Press.

Ainsworth, M. D. S. (1989). Attachments beyond infancy. *American Psychologist, 44*, 709–716.

Ainsworth, M. D. S., Blehar, M. C., Waters, E., & Wall, S. (1978). *Patterns of attachment: A psychological study of the Strange Situation*. Hillsdale, NJ: Erlbaum.

Ainsworth, M. D. S., & Bowlby, J. (1991). An ethological approach to personality development. *American Psychologist, 46*(4), 333–341.

Ajulo, M. O., Omole, M. K., & Moody, J. O. (2014). Impact of highly active antiretroviral therapy (HAART) on organs of HIV infected children in Abia State, Nigeria. *British Journal of Pharmaceutical Research, 4*(7), 837–848.

Akolekar, R., et al. (2014). Procedure-related risk of miscarriage following amniocentesis and chorionic villus sampling: A systematic review and meta-analysis. *Ultrasound in Obstetrics & Gynecology*, DOI10.1002/uog.14636.

Alamian, A., & Paradis, G. (2012). Individual and social determinants of multiple chronic disease behavioral risk factors among youth. *BMC Public Health, 12*, 224.

Alexander, G. M., Wilcox, T., & Woods, R. (2009). Sex differences in infants' visual interest in toys. *Archives of Sexual Behavior, 38*(3), 427–433.

Ali, B., Seitz-Brown, C. J., & Daughters, S. B. (2015). The interacting effect of depressive symptoms, gender, and distress tolerance on substance use problems among residential treatment-seeking substance users. *Drug and Alcohol Dependence, 148*, 21–26.

Ali, M. M., & Dwyer, D. S. (2011). Estimating peer effects in sexual behavior among adolescents. *Journal of Adolescence, 34*(1), 183–190.

Alink, L. R. A., et al. (2008). Maternal sensitivity moderates the relation between negative discipline and -aggression in early childhood. *Social Development, 18*(1), 99–120.

Allen, G., et al. (2011). Functional neuroanatomy of the cerebellum. In A. S. Davis (Ed.). *Handbook of pediatric neuropsychology*. New York: Springer.

Allen, J. P., & Antonishak, J. (2008). Adolescent peer influences: Beyond the dark side. In M. J. Prinstein & K. A. Dodge (Eds.). *Understanding peer influence in children and adolescents* (pp. 141–160). New York: Guilford.

Allison, C. M., & Hyde, J. S. (2013). Early menarche: Confluence of biological and contextual factors. *Sex Roles, 68*(1), 55–64.

Alloway, R. G., & Alloway, T. P. (2013). Working memory in development. In T. P. Alloway, & R. G. Alloway (Eds.). *Working memory: The connected intelligence* (pp. 63–82). New York: Psychology Press.

Alm, P. A. (2014). Stuttering in relation to anxiety, temperament, and personality: Systematic review and analysis with focus on causality. *Journal of Fluency Disorders, 40*, 5–21.

Aloi, J. A. (2009). Nursing the disenfranchised: Women who have relinquished an infant for adoption. *Journal of Psychiatric and Mental Health Nursing, 16*(1), 27–31.

Als, H., et al. (2003). A three-center, randomized, controlled trial of individualized developmental care for very low birth weight preterm infants: Medical, neurodevelopmental, parenting, and caregiving effects. *Journal of Developmental and Behavioral Pediatrics, 24*(6), 399–408.

Alvarez, L. (2013, September 14). Girl's suicide points to rise in apps used by cyberbullies. *The New York Times*, p. A1.

Amanatullah, E. T., & Morris, M. W. (2010). Negotiating gender roles: Gender differences in assertive negotiating are mediated by women's fear of backlash and attenuated when negotiating on behalf of others. *Journal of Personality and Social Psychology, 98*(2), 256–267.

Amato, P. R. (2006). Marital discord, divorce, and children's well-being: Results from a 20-year longitudinal study of two generations. In A. Clarke-Stewart & J. Dunn (Eds.), *Families count: Effects on child and adolescent development. The Jacobs Foundation series on adolescence* (pp. 179–202). New York: Cambridge University Press.

Amato, P. R., & Anthony, C. J. (2014). Estimating the effects of parental divorce and death with fixed effects models. *Journal of Marriage and Family, 76*(2), 370–386.

Ambridge, B., Pine, J. M., Rowland, C. F., Chang, F., & Bidgod, A. (2013). The retreat from overgeneralization in child language acquisition: Word learning, morphology, and verb argument structure.

Wiley Interdisciplinary Reviews: Cognitive Science, 4(1), 47–62.

American Academy of Pediatrics. (2012). Breastfeeding initiatives. Retrieved from http://www2.aap.org/breastfeeding/faqsbreastfeeding.html. Accessed July 28, 2012.

American Academy of Pediatrics. (2012). Safe sleep and your baby: How parents can reduce the risk of SIDS and suffocation. Available at http://www.healthychildren.org/English/ages-stages/baby/sleep/pages/Preventing-SIDS.aspx.

American Academy of Pediatrics. (2015). Benefits of breastfeeding for mothers. Available at https://www.healthychildren.org/English/ages-stages/baby/breastfeeding/Pages/Benefits-of-Breastfeeding-for-Mom.aspx.

American Association of Intellectual and Developmental Disabilities. (2015). Retrieved from http://aaidd.org/intellectual-disability/definition#.VczMKM5idLk. Accessed August 13, 2015.

American Association of Medical Colleges. (2015). The State of Women in Academic Medicine, 2013–2014. Retrived from https://www.aamc.org/members/gwims/statistics/#tables. Accessed August 16, 2015.

American Fertility Association. (2012a). Infertility: Causes and treatments. Available at http://www.theafa.org/family-building/infertility-causes-treatments.

American Fertility Association. (2012b). *LGBT Family Building.* Available at http://www.theafa.org/family-building/lgbt-family-building.

American Fertility Association. (2014). *Infertility: Causes and treatments.* Available at http://www.theafa.org.

American Heart Association. (2009). Retrieved from http://www.americaheart.org/presenter.jhtml?identifier=1200000. Accessed July 27, 2009.

American Lung Association. (2015). State of tobacco control 2014. Retrieved from http://www.stateoftobaccocontrol.org. Accessed April 24, 2015.

American Pregnancy Association. (2011). Alcohol and pregnancy: What you should know. Retrieved from http://www.americanpregnancy.org/pregnancyhealth/alcohol.html. Accessed February 14, 2012.

American Psychiatric Association. (2013). Diagnostic and Statistical Manual of the Mental Disorders–5th edition (DSM-5). Washington, DC: American Psychiatric Association.

American Psychiatric Association. (2014). Postpartum depression. Available at http://www.psychiatry.org/postpartum-depression.

Ammaniti, M., Speranza, A. M., & Fedele, S. (2005). Attachment in infancy and in early and late childhood: A longitudinal study. In K. A. Kerns & R. A. Richardson (Eds.), *Attachment in middle childhood* (pp. 115–136). New York: Guilford.

Amsel, E. (2011). Hypothetical thinking in adolescence: Its nature, development, and applications. In E. Amsel, & J. Smetana (Eds.), *Adolescent vulnerabilities and opportunities* (pp. 86–116). New York: Cambridge University Press.

Anastasiou, L., et al. (2015). The construction of scientific knowledge at an early age. *Creative Education, 6*(2), DOI10.4236/ce.2015.62025.

Anblagen, D., et al. (2013). Maternal smoking during pregnancy and fetal organ growth: A magnetic resonance imaging study. *PLOS ONE,* DOI10.1371/journal/pone.0067223.

Andersen, T. S. (2015). Race, ethnicity, and structural variations in youth risk of arrest: Evidence from a national longitudinal sample. *Criminal Justice and Behavior,* DOI10.1177/0093854815570963.

Anderson, B. J. (2011). Plasticity of gray matter volume: The cellular and synaptic plasticity that underlies volumetric change. *Developmental Psychobiology, 53*(5), 456–465.

Anderson, C. A., et al. (2010). Violent video game effects on aggression, empathy, and prosocial behavior in Eastern and Western countries: A meta-analytic review. *Psychological Bulletin, 136*(2), 151–173.

Andersen, N. E., Dahmani, L., Konishi, K., & Dohbot, V. D. (2012). Eye tracking, strategies, and sex differences in virtual navigation. *Neurobiology of Learning and Memory, 97*(1), 81–89.

Anderson, P. (2002). Assessment and development of executive function (EF) during childhood. *Child Neuropsychology, 8*(2), 71–82.

Angarne-Lindberg, T., Wadsby, M., & Bertero, C. (2009). Young adults with childhood experience of divorce: Disappointment and contentment. *Journal of Divorce & Remarriage, 50*(3), 172–184.

Anthis, K. (2006). Possible selves in the lives of adult women: A short-term longitudinal study. In C. Dunkel & J. Kerpelman (Eds.), *Possible selves: Theory, research and applications* (pp. 123–140). Hauppauge, NY: Nova Science Publishers.

Anthis, K. S., Dunkel, C. S., & Anderson, B. (2004). Gender and identity status differences in late adolescents' possible selves. *Journal of Adolescence, 27*(2), 147–152.

Arbib, M. A. (2015). Language evolution: An emergentist perspective. In B. MacWinney, & W. O'Grady (Eds.). *The handbook of language emergence* (pp. 600–623). West Sussex, UK: Wiley.

Arbuthnot, J., & Gordon, D. A. (1988). Crime and cognition: Community applications of sociomoral reasoning development. *Criminal Justice and Behavior, 15*(3), 379–393.

Archambault, I., Janosz, M., Fallu, J-S., & Pagani, L. S. (2009). Student engagement and its relationship with early high school dropout. *Journal of Adolescence, 32*(3), 651–670.

Archer, L. R. (2014). Harms of hedging in scientific discourse: Andrew Wakefield and the origins of the autism vaccine controversy. *Technical Communication Quarterly, 23*(3), 165–183.

Armstrong, K. H., Hangauer, J., Agazzi, H., Nunez, A., & Gieron-Korthals, M. (2013). Psychopathology of intellectual and developmental disabilities. In A. S. Davis (Ed.). *Psychopathology of childhood and adolescence: A neuropsychological approach* (pp. 27–44). New York: Springer.

Arnett, J. J. (2000). Emerging adulthood: A theory of development from the late teens through the twenties. *American Psychologist, 55*(5), 469–480.

Arnett, J. J. (2007). Socialization in emerging adulthood: From the family to the wider world, from socialization to self-socialization. In J. E. Grusec & P. D. Hastings (Eds.), *Handbook of socialization: Theory and research* (pp. 208–231). New York: Guilford.

Arnett, J. J. (2011). Emerging adulthood. In L. A. Jensen (Ed.), *Bridging cultural and developmental approaches to psychology: New syntheses in theory, research and policy* (pp. 255–275). New York: Oxford University Press.

Arnett, J. J. (2012). New horizons in research on emerging and young adulthood. *Early Adulthood in a Family Context: National Symposium on Family Issues, 2*(5), 231–244.

Arnett, J. J. (2015). Identity development from adolescence to emerging adulthood: What we know and (especially) don't know. In K. C. McLean, & M. Syed (Eds.). *The Oxford handbook of identity development* (pp. 53–64). New York: Oxford University Press.

Arnett, J. J., & Brody, G. H. (2008). A fraught passage: The identity challenges of African American emerging adults. *Human Development, 51*(5–6), 291–293.

Aschermann, E., Gülzow, I., & Wendt, D. (2004). Differences in the comprehension of passive voice in German- and English-speaking children. *Swiss Journal of Psychology, 63*(4), 235–245.

Aslin, R. N. (2012). Infant eyes: A window on cognitive development. *Infancy: Special Issue: Advances in Eye Tracking in Infancy Research, 17*(1), 126–140.

Aspy, C. B., et al. (2007). Parental communication and youth sexual behaviour. *Journal of Adolescence, 30*(3), 449–466.

Athanasopoulou, E., & Fox, J. R. E. (2014). Effects of kangaroo mother care on maternal mood and interaction patterns between parents and their preterm, low birth weight infants: A systematic review. *Infant Mental Health Journal, 35*(3), 245–262.

Athenstaedt, U., Mikula, G., & Bredt, C. (2008). Gender role self-concept and leisure activities of adolescents. *Sex Roles, 60*(5–6), 399–409.

August, D., Carlo, M., Dressler, C., & Snow, C. (2005). The critical role of vocabulary development for English language learners. *Learning Disabilities Research & Practice, 20*(1), 50–57.

Auyeung, B., et al. (2009). Fetal testosterone predicts sexually differentiated childhood behavior in girls and in boys. *Psychological Science, 20*(2), 144–148.

Avinum, R., & Knafo-Noam, A. (2015). Socialization, genetics, and their interplay in development. In J. E. Grusec & P. D. Hastings (Eds.). *Handbook of* socialization: Theory and Research (pp. 347–371). New York. Guilford.

Axelin, A., & Salanterä, S. (2008). Ethics in neonatal pain research. *Nursing Ethics*, 15(4), 492–499.

Ayyash-Abdo, H. (2001). Individualism and collectivism: The case of Lebanon. *Social Behavior and Personality*, 29(5), 503–518.

Azar, B. (1998). What predicts which foods we eat? A genetic disposition for certain tastes may affect people's food preferences. *APA Monitor*, 29, 1.

Azmitia, M. (2015). Reflections on the cultural lenses of identity development. In K. C. McLean, & M. Syed (Eds.). *The Oxford handbook of identity development* (pp. 286–298). New York: Oxford University Press.

Babic, M. J., et al. (2014). Physical activity and physical self-concept in youth: Systematic review and meta-analysis. *Sports Medicine*, 44(11), 1589–1601.

Bachman, J. G., Johnston, L. D., & O'Malley, P. M. (2014). *Monitoring the future: Questionnaire responses from the nation's high school seniors 2012*. Survey Research Center. Institute for Social Research. Ann Arbor, MI: The University of Michigan.

Bachman, J. G., Safron, D. J., Sy, S. R., & Schulenberg, J. E. (2003). Wishing to work: New perspectives on how adolescents' part-time work intensity is linked to educational disengagement, substance use, and other problem behaviours. *International Journal of Behavioral Development*, 27(4), 301–315.

Bailey, R. K., & Owens, D. L. (2005). Overcoming challenges in the diagnosis and treatment of attention-deficit /hyperactivity disorder in African Americans. *Journal of the National Medical Association*, 97(10, Suppl), S5–S10.

Baillargeon, R. (1987). Object permanence in 3½- and 4½-month-old infants. *Developmental Psychology*, 23, 655–664.

Baillargeon, R., Li, J., Gertner, Y., & Wu, D. (2010). In U. Goswami (Ed.), *The Wiley–Blackwell handbook of childhood cognitive development*. (2nd ed.) (pp. 11–48). Chichester, West Sussex, UK: Wiley–Blackwell.

Bakalar, N. (2014, March 4). Is breast-feeding really better? *The New York Times*. Retrieved from http://well.blogs.nytimes.com/2014/03/04/is-breast-feeding-really-better/?_r=0. Accessed February 26, 2015.

Baker, B., Birch, L., Trost, S., & Davison, K. (2007). Advanced pubertal status at age 11 and lower physical activity in adolescent girls. *The Journal of Pediatrics*, 151(5), 488–493.

Baker, J. L., et al. (2008). Breastfeeding reduces postpartum weight retention. *American Journal of Clinical Nutrition*, 88(6), 1543–1551.

Bakker, D. J. (2006). Treatment of developmental dyslexia: A review. *Pediatric Rehabilitation*, 9(1), 3–13.

Bakker, R., et al. (2010). Maternal caffeine intake from coffee and tea, fetal growth, and the risks of adverse birth outcomes: The Generation R Study. *The American Journal of Clinical Nutrition*, 91(6), 1691–1698.

Bales, J. E., et al. (2013). Origins of externalizing behavior problems at eight years of age. In K. H. Rubin, & D. J. Pepler (Eds.). *The development and treatment of childhood depression* (pp. 93–120). New York: Psychology Press.

Ball, J., Lohaus, A., & Miebach, C. (2006). Psychological adjustment and school achievement during transition from elementary to secondary school. *Zeitschrift für Entwicklungs-psychologie und Pädagogische Psychologie*, 38(3), 101–109.

Ballweg, Rachel. (2001). *Can you be too rich or too thin? Well and Good*, no. 3. Retrieved from http://www.uihealthcare.com/wellandgood/ 2001issue3/eating disorders.htm

Baltazar, N. C., Shutts, K., & Kinzler, K. D. (2012). Children show heightened memory for threatening social actions. *Journal of Experimental Child Psychology*, http://dx.doi.org/10.1016/j.jecp.2011.11.003.

Baly, M., Cornell, D. G., & Lovegrove, P. (2014). A longitudinal investigation of self- and peer reports of bullying victimization across middle school. *Psychology in the Schools*, 51(3), 217–240.

Bandura, A. (1986). *Social foundations of thought and action: A social-cognitive theory*. Englewood Cliffs, NJ: Prentice Hall.

Bandura, A. (2006a). Going global with social cognitive theory: From prospect to paydirt. In S. I. Donaldson, D. E. Berger & K. Pezdek (Eds.), *Applied psychology: New frontiers and rewarding careers* (pp. 53–79). Hillsdale, NJ: Erlbaum.

Bandura, A. (2006b). Toward a psychology of human agency. *Perspectives on Psychological Science*, 1(2), 164–180.

Bandura, A. (2011). The social and policy impact of social cognitive theory. In M. M. Mark, S. I. Donaldson, & B. Campbell (Eds.). *Social psychology and evaluation*. (pp. 33–71). New York: Guilford Press.

Bandura, A. (2012). On the functional properties of perceived self-efficacy revisited. *Journal of Management*, 38(1), 9–44.

Bandura, A., Barbaranelli, C., Vittorio Caprara, G., & Pastorelli, C. (2001). Self-efficacy beliefs as shapers of children's aspirations and career trajec-tories. *Child Development*, 72(1), 187–206.

Bandura, A., Blanchard, E. B., & Ritter, B. (1969). The relative efficacy of desensitization and modeling approaches for inducing behavioral, affective, and cognitive changes. *Journal of Personality and Social Psychology*, 13, 173–199.

Bandura, A., Ross, S. A., & Ross, D. (1963). Imitation of film-mediated aggressive models. *Journal of Abnormal and Social Psychology*, 66, 3–11.

Bangal, V. B., Giri, P. A., & Mahajan, A. S. (2012). Maternal and foetal outcome in pregnancy induced hypertension: A study from rural tertiary care teaching hospital in India. *International Journal of Biomedical Research*, 2(12), 595–599.

Bangs, R., & Davis, L. E. (2015). America's racial realities. In R. Bangs, & L. E. Davis (Eds.). *Race and social problems: Restructuring inequality* (pp. 3–14). New York: Springer Science+Business Media.

Barac, R., & Bialystok, E. (2011). Cognitive development in bilingual children. *Language Teaching*, 44, 36–54.

Barnett, L. M., Ridgers, N. D., & Salmon, J. (2014). Associations between young children's perceived and actual ball skill competence and physical activity. *Journal of Science and Medicine in Sport*, 18(2), 167–171.

Barni, D., Roccato, M., Vieno, A., & Alfieri, S. (2014). Birth order and conservatism: A multilevel test of Sulloway's "Born to rebel" thesis. *Personality and Individual Differences*, 66, 58–63.

Barr, R., Walker, J., Gross, J., & Hayne, H. (2014). Age-related changes in spreading activation during infancy. *Child Development*, 85(2), 549–563.

Barr, R. G., et al. (2015). Education about crying in normal infants is associated with a reduction in pediatric emergency room visits for crying complaints. *Journal of Developmental and Behavioral Pediatrics*, 36(4), 252–257.

Barr, R. G., Paterson, J. A., MacMartin, L. M., Lehtonen, L., & Young, S. N. (2005). Prolonged and unsoothable crying bouts in infants with and without colic. *Journal of Developmental & Behavioral Pediatrics*, 26(1), 14–23.

Barrile, M., Armstrong, E. S., & Bower, T. G. R. (1999). Novelty and frequency as determinants of newborn preference. *Developmental Science*, 2(1), 47–52.

Barrouillet, P. (2015). Theories of cognitive development: From Piaget to today. *Developmental Review*, DOI:10.1016/j.dr.2015.07.004.

Barth, J., & Call, J. (2006). Tracking the displacement of objects: A series of tasks with great apes (Pan troglodytes, Pan paniscus, Gorilla, and Pongo pygmaeus) and young children (Homo sapiens). *Journal of Experimental Psychology: Animal Behavior Processes*, 32(3), 239–252.

Bartzokis, G., et al. (2010). Lifespan trajectory of myelin integrity and maximum motor speed. *Neurobiology of Aging*, 31(9), 1554–1562.

Bastien-Toniazzo, M., & Jullien, S. (2001). Nature and importance of the logographic phase in learning to read. *Reading and Writing*, 14(1–2), 119–143.

Bates, E. (2001). Plasticity, localization and language development. In S. T. Parker, J. Langer & C. Milbrath (Eds.), *Biology and knowledge revisited* (pp. 205–254). London: Routledge.

Bates, J. E., & Pettit, G. S. (2015). Temperament, parenting, and socialization. In J. E. Grusec & P. D. Hastings (Eds.). *Handbook of socialization: Theory and research* (pp. 372–397). New York: Guilford.

Batsche, G. M., & Porter, L. J. (2006). Bullying. In G. G. Bear & K. M. Minke (Eds.), *Children's needs III: Development, prevention, and intervention* (pp. 135–148). Washington, DC: National Association of School Psychologists.

Bauer, K. A., et al. (2009). Acne vulgaris and steroid acne. In R. Fife, S. Schrager & S. B. Schrager (Eds.), *The ACP handbook of women's health* (pp. 337ff.). Philadelphia: ACP Press.

Bauer, P. J., & Fivush, R. (2010). Context and consequences of autobiographical memory development. *Cognitive Development, 25*(4), 303–308.

Bauer, P. J., & Fivush, R. (2013). *The Wiley handbook on the development of children's memory.* Hoboken, NJ: Wiley.

Baum, N., Weidberg, Z., Osher, Y., & Kohelet, D. (2012). No longer pregnant, not yet a mother: Giving birth prematurely to a very low birth weight baby. *Qualitative Health Research, 22*(5), 595–606.

Bauman, M. L., Anderson, G., Perry, E., & Ray, M. (2006). Neuroanatomical and neurochemical studies of the autistic brain: Current thought and future directions. In S. O. Moldin & J. L. R. Rubenstein (Eds.), *Understanding autism: From basic neuroscience to treatment* (pp. 303–322). Boca Raton, FL: CRC Press.

Baumrind, D. (1989). Rearing competent children. In W. Damon (Ed.), *Child development today and tomorrow.* San Francisco: Jossey-Bass.

Baumrind, D. (2013). Authoritative parenting revisited: History and current status. In R. E. Larzelere, A. S. Morris, & A. W. Harrist (Eds.). *Authoritative parenting: Synthesizing nurturance and discipline for optimal child development* (pp. 11–34). Washington, DC: American Psychological Association.

Baxter-Jones, A. D. G., & Faulkner, R. A. (2012). Exercise and skeletal growth. In J. J. B. Anderson et al. (Eds.). Diet, nutrients, and bone health (pp. 369–380). Boca Raton, FL: CRC Press.

Bazerman, M. H., & Tenbrunsel, A. A. (2011). *Blind spots: Why we fail to do what's right and what to do about it.* Princeton, NJ: Princeton University Press.

Bearce, K. H., & Rovee-Collier, C. (2006). Repeated priming increases memory accessibility in infants. *Journal of Experimental Child Psychology, 93*(4), 357–376.

Beauchamp, G. K., & Mennella, J. A. (2011). Flavor perception in human infants: Development and functional significance. *Digestion, 83*(Suppl. 1), 1–6.

Bebko, J. M., McMorris, C. A., Metcalfe, A., Ricciuti, C., & Goldstein, G. (2014). Language proficiency and metacognition as predictors of spontaneous rehearsal in children. *Canadian Journal of Experimental Psychology, 68*(1), 46–58.

Beck, E., Burnet, K. L., & Vosper, J. (2006). Birth-order effects on facets of extraversion. *Personality and Individual Differences, 40*(5), 953–959.

Becker, M., et al. (2012). Culture and the distinctiveness motive: Constructing identity in individualistic and collectivistic contexts. *Journal of Personality and Social Psychology, 102*(4), 833–855.

Beckwith, A. M., & Burke, S. A. (2015). Identification of early developmental deficits in infants with prenatal heroin, methadone, and other opioid exposure. *Clinical Pediatrics, 54*(4), 328–335.

Bedny, M., Pascual-Leone, A., Dravida, S., & Saxe, R. (2012). A sensitive period for language in the visual cortex: Distinct patterns of plasticity in congenitally versus late blind adults. *Brain and Language,* in press.

Beebe, B., et al. (2010). The origins of 12-month attachment: A microanalysis of 4-month mother-infant interaction. *Attachment & Human Development, 12*(1–2), 3–141.

Beer, J. M., & Horn, J. M. (2000). The influence of rearing order on personality development within two adoption cohorts. *Journal of Personality, 68*(4), 789–819.

Begum, K. S., Khan, N. U., & Akter, F. (2014). Factors affecting the pregnancy outcome in patients with previous one Caesarean section. *Medicine Today, 26*(1), 1–3.

Behrman, R. E., Kliegman, R. M., & Jenson, H. B. (2000). *Nelson review of pediatrics* (2nd ed.). Philadelphia: Saunders.

Beilei, L., Lei, L., Qi, D., & von Hofsten, C. (2002). The development of fine motor skills and their relations to children's academic achievement. *Acta Psychologica Sinica, 34*(5), 494–499.

Bekkhus, M., Rutter, M., Maughan, B., & Borge, A. I. H. (2011). The effects of group daycare in the context of paid maternal leave and high-quality provision. *European Journal of Developmental Psychology, 8*(6), 681–696.

Belkin, L. (2009, April 5). Your old man. *The New York Times Magazine.*

Bell, J. H., & Bromnick, R. D. (2003). The social reality of the imaginary audience: A ground theory approach. *Adolescence, 38*(150), 205–219.

Bell, S. M., & Ainsworth, M. D. S. (1972). Infant crying and maternal responsiveness. *Child Development, 43*(4), 1171–1190.

Belsky, J. (2001). Emanuel Miller Lecture: Developmental risks (still) associated with early child care. *Journal of Child Psychology and Psychiatry and Allied Disciplines, 42*(7), 845–859.

Belsky, J. (2006a). Determinants and consequences of infant–parent attachment. In L. Balter & C. S. Tamis-LeMonda (Eds.), *Child psychology: A handbook of contemporary issues* (2nd ed.) (pp. 53–77). New York: Psychology Press.

Belsky, J. (2009). Classroom composition, childcare history and social development: Are childcare effects disappearing or spreading? *Social Development, 18*(1), 230–238.

Bem, S. L. (1989). Genital knowledge and gender constancy in preschool children. *Child Development, 60,* 649–662.

Bendiksen, B., et al. (2014). Impairment in young preschool children with symptoms of attention-deficit/hyperactivity disorder and co-occurring oppositional defiant disorder and conduct disorder. *Scandinavian Journal of Child and Adolescent Psychiatry and Psychology, 2*(3).

Bengtsson, H., & Arvidsson, A. (2011). The impact of developing social perspective-taking skills on emotionality in middle and late childhood. *Social Development, 20*(2), 353–375.

Bennett, T. A., et al. (2014). Language impairment and early social competence in preschoolers with autism spectrum disorders: A comparison of DSM-5 profiles. *Journal of Autism and Developmental Disorders, 44,* 2797–2808.

Benoit, D., & Coolbear, J. (2004). Disorders of attachment and failure to thrive. In L. Atkinson & S. Goldberg (Eds.), *Attachment issues in psychopathology and intervention* (pp. 49–64). Hillsdale, NJ: Erlbaum.

Beratis, I. O., et al. (2013). Investigation of the link between higher order cognitive functions and handedness. *Journal of Clinical and Experimental Neuropsychology, 35*(4), 393–403.

Berenbaum, S. A., Martin, C. L., Hanish, L. D., Briggs, P. T., & Fabes, R. A. (2008). Sex differences in children's play. In J. B. Becker et al. (Eds.). *Sex differences in the brain* (pp. 275–290). New York: Oxford University Press.

Berg, C. J., Chang, J., Callaghan, W. M., & Whitehead, S. J. (2003). Pregnancy-related mortality in the United States, 1991–1997. *Obstetrics and Gynecology, 101,* 289–296.

Berge, J. M., et al. (2015). All in the family: Correlations between parents' and adolescent siblings' weight and weight-related behaviors. *Obesity, 23*(4), 833–839.

Bergen, D. (2015). Psychological approaches to the study of play. In J. E. Johnson et al. (Eds.). *The handbook of the study of play, Vol. 2* (pp. 51–70). Lanham, MD: Rowman & Littlefield.

Berko, J. (1958). The child's learning of English morphology. *Word, 14,* 150–177.

Berkowitz, D. (2013). Gay men and surrogacy. In A. E Goldberg, & K. R. Allen (Eds.). *LGBT-parent families: Innovations in research and implications for practice* (pp. 71–85). New York: Springer Science+Business Media.

Berndt, T. J. (2004). Friendship and three A's (aggression, adjustment, and attachment). *Journal of Experimental Child Psychology, 88*(1), 1–4.

Berndt, T. J., & Perry, T. B. (1990). Distinctive features and effects of early adolescent friendships. In R. Montemayor, G. R. Adams & T. P. Gullotta (Eds.), *From childhood to adolescence: A transitional period?* Newbury Park, CA: Sage.

Berry, J. W., & Triandis, H. C. (2006). Culture. In K. Pawlik & G. d'Ydewalle (Eds.), *Psychological concepts: An international historical perspective* (pp. 47–62). Hove, England: Psychology Press/Taylor & Francis.

Bersoff, D. N. (Ed.) (2008). *Ethical conflicts in psychology* (4th ed.). Washington, DC: American Psychological Association.

Bersoff, D. N. (2014). Protecting victims of violent parents while protecting confidentiality. *American Psychologist, 69*(5), 461–467.

Berzenski, S. R., Yates, T. M., & Egeland, B. (2014). A multidimensional view of continuity in intergenerational transmission of child maltreatment. In J. E. Korbin, & R. D. Krugman (Eds.).

Handbook of child maltreatment, 2, 115–129. New York: Springer.

Berzonsky, M. D. (2011). A social-cognitive perspective on identity construction. In S. J. Schwatrz, K. Luyckx, & V. L. Vignoles (Eds.). Handbook of identity theory and research (pp. 55–76). New York: Springer Science+Business Media.

Bezdjian, S., Tuvblad, C., Raine, A., & Baker, L. A. (2011). The genetic and environmental covariation among psychopathic personality traits, and reactive and proactive aggression in children. *Child Development*, 82(4), 1267–1281.

Bhat, S., Acharya, U. R., Adeli, H., Bairy, G. M., & Adeli, A. (2014). Autism: Cause factors, early diagnosis and therapies. *Reviews in the Neurosciences*, 25(6), 841–850.

Bialystok, E., Luk, G., Peets, K. F., & Yang, S. (2010). Receptive vocabulary differences in monolingual and bilingual children. *Bilingualism: Language and Cognition*, 13, 525–531.

Bierman, K. L., et al. (2014). Effects of Head Sart REDI on children's outcomes 1 year later in different kindergarten contexts. *Child Development*, 85(1), 140–159).

Bierman, K. L., Nix, R. L., Domitrovich, C. E., Welsh, J. A., & Gest, S. D. (2014). The Head Start REDI Project and school readiness. In A. J. Reynolds, A. J. Rolnick, & J. A. Temple (Eds.). *Health and education in early childhood* (pp. 208–233). Cambridge, UK: Cambridge University Press.

Bigelow, A. E., et al. (2010). Maternal sensitivity throughout infancy: Continuity and relation to attachment security. *Infant Behavior and Development*, 33(1), 50–60.

Billings, D. W., et al. (2015). A randomized trial to evaluate the efficacy of a web-based HIV behavioral intervention for high-risk African American women. *AIDS and Behavior*, 19(7), 1263–1274.

Birch, L. L., Gunder, L., Grimm-Thomas, K., & Laing, D. G. (1998). Infants' consumption of a new food enhances acceptance of similar foods. *Appetite*, 30(3), 283–295.

Biro, F. M. (2008). Normal growth and development. In G. B. Slap (Ed.), *Adolescent Medicine* (pp. 3ff.). Philadelphia: Elsevier Health Sciences.

Bishop, D. M. (2012). Evidence-based practice and juvenile justice. *Criminology & Public Policy*, 11(3), 483–489.

Black breast-feeding gatherings battle troubling health gaps. (2015, January 29). Associated Press. Retrieved from http:// www.nytimes.com/aponline/2015/01/29 /health/ap-us-med-blacks-breast-feeding .html. Accessed February 26, 2015.

Black, M. M., et al. (2007). Early intervention and recovery among children with failure to thrive. *Pediatrics*, 120(1), 59–69.

Blair, C., & Raver, C. C. (2012). Child development in the context of adversity: Experiential canalization of brain and behavior. *American Psychologist*, 67(4), 309–318.

Blake, S. M., Ledsky, R., Goodenow, C., Sawyer, R., Lohrmann, D., & Windsor, R. (2003). Condom availability programs in Massachusetts high schools: Relationships with condom use and sexual behavior. *American Journal of Public Health*, 93, 955–962.

Blakemore, J. E. O., & Hill, C. A. (2008). The Child Gender Socialization Scale: A measure to compare traditional and feminist parents. *Sex Roles*, 58(3–4), 192–207.

Blanchette, N., Smith, M. L., Fernandes-Penney, A., King, S., & Read, S. (2001). Cognitive and motor development in children with vertically transmitted HIV infection. *Brain and Cognition*, 46(1–2), 50–53.

Bloom, B., Dey, A. N., & Freeman, G. (2006). Summary health statistics for U.S. children: National Health Interview Survey, 2005. *National Center for Health Statistics, Vital Health Stat 10*(231).

Bloom, L. (1998). Language acquisition in its developmental context. In W. Damon (Ed.), *Handbook of child psychology* (5th ed.), Vol. 2. New York: Wiley.

Blow, C. M. (2014, September 17). On spanking and abuse. The New York Times. Retrieved from http://www.nytimes.com.

Blumberg, M. S., & Seelke, A. M. H. (2010). The form and function of infant sleep: From muscle to neocortex. In M. S. Blumberg, J. H. Freeman, & S. R. Robinson (Eds.), *Oxford handbook of developmental behavioral neuroscience* (pp. 391–423). New York: Oxford University Press.

Blumenthal, H., et al. (2011). Elevated social anxiety among early maturing girls. *Developmental Psychology*, 47(4), 1133–1140.

Boccia, M., & Campos, J. J. (1989). Maternal emotional signals, social referencing, and infants' reactions to strangers. In N. Eisenberg (Ed.), *New directions for child development*, No. 44, *Empathy and related emotional responses*. San Francisco: Jossey-Bass.

Boccia, M. L., Campbell, F. A., Goldman, B. D., & Skinner, M. (2009). Differential recall of consent information and parental decisions about enrolling children in research studies. *Journal of General Psychology*, 136(1), 91–108.

Boden, C., & Giaschi, D. (2007). M-stream deficits and reading-related visual processes in developmental dyslexia. *Psychological Bulletin*, 133(2), 346–366.

Boehnke, K., Silbereisen, R. K., Eisenberg, N., Reykowski, J., & Palmonari, A. (1989). The development of prosocial motivation: A cross-national study. *Journal of Cross-Cultural Psychology*, 20, 219–243.

Boey, C. C. M., Omar, A., & Phillips, J. A. (2003). Correlation among academic performance, recurrent abdominal pain and other factors in year-6 urban primary-school children in Malaysia. *Journal of Paediatrics and Child Health*, 39(5), 352–357.

Bohon, C., Garber, J., & Horowitz, J. L. (2007). Predicting school dropout and adolescent sexual behavior in offspring of depressed and nondepressed mothers. *Journal of the American Academy of Child & Adolescent Psychiatry*, 46(1), 15–24.

Boisvert, S. (2014). Evolutionary theories of criminal behaviors. In G. Bruinsma, & D. Weisburd (Eds.). *Encyclopedia of Criminology and Criminal Justice* (pp. 1454–1463). New York: Springer Science+Business Media.

Boivin, M., Vitaro, F., & Poulin, F. (2005). Peer relationships and the development of aggressive behavior in early childhood. In R. E. Tremblay, W. W. Hartup & J. Archer (Eds.), *Developmental origins of aggression* (pp. 376–397). New York: Guilford.

Boman, U. W., Hanson, C., Hjelmquist, E., & Möller, A. (2006). Personality traits in women with Turner syndrome. *Scandinavian Journal of Psychology*, 47(3), 219–223.

Bonkowski, S. (2005). Group work with children of divorce. In G. L. Greif & P. H. Ephross (Eds.), *Group work with populations at risk* (2nd ed.) (pp. 135–145). New York: Oxford University Press.

Boom, J., Wouters, H., & Keller, M. (2007). A cross-cultural validation of stage development: A Rasch re-analysis of longitudinal socio-moral reasoning data. *Cognitive Development*, 22(2), 213–229.

Booth, A., Johnson, D. R., Granger, D. A., Crouter, A. C., & McHale, S. (2003). Testosterone and child and adolescent adjustment: The moderating role of parent–child relationships. *Developmental Psychology*, 39(1), 85–98.

Borelli, J., et al. (2010). Attachment and emotion in school-aged children. *Emotion*, 10(4). 475–485.

Bornstein, M. C., & Colombo, J. (2012). Infant cognitive functioning and mental development. In S. M. Pauen (Ed.). *Early childhood development and later outcome* (pp. 118–147). New York: Cambridge University Press.

Borghese, M. M., et al. (2015). Television viewing and food intake during television viewing in normal-weight, overweight and obese 9- to 11-year-old Canadian children: a cross-sectional analysis. *Journal of Nutritional Science*, 4, http://dx.doi .org/10.1017/jns.2014.72.

Bos, H. (2013). Lesbian-mother families formed through donor insemination. In A. E Goldberg, & K. R. Allen (Eds.). *LGBT-parent families: Innovations in research and implications for practice* (pp. 21–37). New York: Springer Science+Business Media.

Boskind-White, M., & White, W. C. (1983). *Bulimarexia: The binge/purge cycle*. New York: Norton.

Bouchard, T. J., Jr., & Loehlin, J. C. (2001). Genes, evolution, and personality. *Behavior Genetics*, 31(3), 243–273.

Boudreault-Bouchard, A., et al. (2013). Impact of parental emotional support and coercive control on adolescents' self-esteem and psychological distress: Results of a four-year longitudinal study. *Journal of Adolescence*, 36(4), 695–704.

Boukydis, C. F. Z., & Lester, B. M. (2008). Mother–infant consultation during drug treatment: Research and innovative clinical practice. *Harm Reduction Journal*, 5, 6. doi:10.1186/1477-7517-5-6.

Bouldin, P., & Pratt, C. (1999). Characteristics of preschool and school-age children with imaginary companions. *Journal of Genetic Psychology, 160*(4), 397–410.

Bower, T. G. R. (1974). *Development in infancy.* San Francisco: Freeman.

Bowker, J. C., Thomas, K. K., Norman, K. E., & Spencer, S. V. (2011). Mutual best friend involvement. *Journal of Youth and Adolescence, 40*(5), 545–555.

Bowlby, J. (1988). *A secure base.* New York: Basic Books.

Boyatzis, R. E., Gaskin, J., & Wei, H. (2015). Emotional and social intelligence and behavior. In S. Goldstein, D. Princiotta, & J. A. Naglieri (Eds.). *Handbook of intelligence: Evolutionary theory, historical perspective, and current concepts* (pp. 243–262). New York: Springer Science+Business Media.

Boyden, J., Crivello, G., & Morrow, V. (2015). Gender, development, children, and young people. In A. Coles, L., Gray, & J. Momsen (Eds.). *The Routledge handbook of gender and development.* New York: Routledge.

Boysson-Bardies, B. de, & Halle, P. A. (1994). Speech development: Contributions of cross-linguistic studies. In A. Vyt et al. (Eds.), *Early child development in the French tradition: Contributions from current research.* Hillsdale, NJ: Erlbaum.

Braddick, O., & Atkinson, J. (2011). Development of human visual function. *Vision Research, 51*(13), 1588–1609.

Bradley, R. H. (2006). The home environment. In N. F. Watt et al. (Eds.), *The crisis in youth mental health: Critical issues and effective programs,* Vol. 4, *Early intervention programs and policies, Child psychology and mental health* (pp. 89–120). Westport, CT: Praeger/Greenwood.

Bradley, R. H., Caldwell, B. M., & Corwyn, R. F. (2003). The child care HOME inventories: Assessing the quality of family child care homes. *Early Childhood Research Quarterly, 18*(3), 294–309.

Bradley, R. H., & Corwyn, R. F. (2006). The family environment. In L. Balter & C. S. Tamis-LeMonda (Eds.), *Child psychology: A handbook of contemporary issues* (2nd ed.) (pp. 493–520). New York: Psychology Press.

Brakefield, T. A. et al. (2014). Same-sex sexual attraction does not spread in adolescent social networks. *Archives of Sexual Behavior, 43,* 335–344.

Bramen, J. E., et al. (2011). Puberty influences medial temporal lobe and cortical gray matter maturation differently in boys than girls matched for sexual maturity. *Cerebral Cortex, 21*(3), 636–646.

Braun, K., & Champagne, F. A. (2014). Paternal influences on off spring development: Behavioural and epigenetic pathways. *Journal of Neuroendocrinology, 26*(10), 697–706.

Bray, G., & Bouchard, C. (2014). *Handbook of obesity: Epidemiology, etiology, and physiopathology (4th ed.).* CRC Press.

Bray, S., Dunkin, B., Hong, D. S., & Reiss, A. L. (2011). Reduced functional connectivity during working memory in Turner syndrome. *Cerebral Cortex, 21*(11), 2471–2481.

Brazelton, T. B., & Nugent, J. K. (2011). *The Neonatal Behavioral Assessment Scale.* Cambridge, UK: Mac Keith Press.

Breastfeeding. (2006). Centers for Disease Control and Prevention. Department of Health and Human Services. Retrieved from http://www.cdc.gov/breastfeeding/faq/index.htm. Accessed July 16, 2007.

Breastfeeding report card. (2014). Centers for Disease Control and Prevention. Retrieved from http://www.cdc.gov/breastfeeding/pdf/2014breastfeedingreportcard.pdf. Accessed October 1, 2015.

Bremner, J. G., Wachs, T. D., Ross, H., Vickar, M., & Perlman, M. (2010). Early social cognitive skills at play in toddlers' peer interactions. In J. G. Bremner & T. D. Wachs (Eds.), *Wiley-Blackwell handbook of infant development,* Vol. 1 (2nd ed.) (pp. 510–531). Chichester, West Sussex, UK: Wiley-Blackwell.

Brendgen, M., et al. (2010). Link between friendship relations and early adolescents' trajectories of depressed mood. *Developmental Psychology, 46*(2), 491–501.

Brewster, K. L., Tillman, K. H., & Jokinen-Gordon, H. (2014). Demographic characteristics of lesbian parents in the United States. *Population Research and Policy Review, 33,* 503–526.

Bridges, M. A., Justice, L. M., Hogan, T. P., & Gray, S. (2012). Promoting lower- and higher-level language skills. In R. C. Pianta (Ed.). *Early childhood education* (pp. 177–193). New York: Guilford.

Brigham, N. B., Yoder, P. J., Jarzynka, M. A., & Tapp, J. (2011). The sequential relationship between parent attentional cues and attention to objects in young children with autism. *Journal of Autism and Developmental Disorders, 40*(2), 200–208).

Brockington, I. (2011). Maternal rejection of the young child: Present status of the clinical syndrome. *Psychopathology, 44*(5), 329–336.

Brody, J. S. (2014). The promise and problems of e-cigarettes. *American Journal of Respiratory and Critical Care Medicine, 189*(4), 379–380.

Bronfenbrenner, U., & Morris, P. A. (2006). The bioecological model of human development. In R. M. Lerner & W. Damon (Eds.), *Handbook of child psychology* (6th ed.), Vol. 1, *Theoretical models of human development* (pp. 793–828). Hoboken, NJ: Wiley.

Brook, J. S., et al. (2009). Psychosocial antecedents and adverse health consequences related to substance use. *American Journal of Public Health, 99*(3), 563–568.

Brooker, R. J., et al. (2013). The development of stranger fear in infancy and toddlerhood: Normative development, individual differences, antecedents, and outcomes. *Developmental Science, 16*(6), 864–878.

Brower, T., & Wilcox, T. (2012). Shaking things up: Young infants' use of sound information for object individuation. *Infant Behavior and Development, 35*(2), 323–327.

Brown, B. B., Mounts, N., Lamborn, S. D., & Steinberg, L. (1993). Parenting practices and peer group affiliation in adolescence. *Child Development, 64,* 467–482.

Brown, R. (1973). *A first language: The early stages.* Cambridge, MA: Harvard University Press.

Brown, R. (1977). Introduction. In C. A. Snow & C. Ferguson (Eds.), *Talking to children.* New York: Cambridge University Press.

Brown, W. H., et al. (2009). Social and environmental factors associated with preschoolers' nonsedentary physical activity. *Child Development, 80*(1), 45–58.

Bruchmüller, K., Margraf, J., & Schneider, S. (2012). Is ADHD diagnosed in accord with diagnostic criteria? Overdiagnosis and influence of client gender on diagnosis. *Journal of Consulting and Clinical Psychology, 80*(1), 128–138.

Bruck, M., Ceci, S. J., & Principe, G. F. (2006). The child and the law. In K. Renninger, I. E. Sigel, W. Damon & R. M. Lerner (Eds.), *Handbook of child psychology* (6th ed.), Vol. 4, *Child psychology in practice* (pp. 776–816). Hoboken, NJ: Wiley.

Brucker, B., et al. (2015). Watching corresponding gestures facilitates learning with animations by activating human mirror-neurons: An fNIRS study. *Learning and Instruction, 36*(1), 27–37.

Brun, C. C., et al. (2009). Sex differences in brain structure in auditory and cingulate regions. *NeuroReport: For Rapid Communication of Neuroscience Research, 20*(10), 930.

Brunner, R., Parzer, P., & Resch, F. (2005). Involuntary hospitalization of patients with anorexia nervosa: Clinical issues and empirical findings. *Fortschritte der Neurologie, Psychiatrie, 73*(1), 9–15.

Bucchianeri, M. M., et al. (2013). Body dissatisfaction from adolescence to young adulthood: Findings from a 10-year longitudinal study. *Body Image, 10*(1), 1–7.

Buchanan, C. M., & Hughes, J. (2009). Construction of social reality during early adolescence: Can expecting storm and stress increase real or perceived storm and stress? *Journal of Research on Adolescence, 19*(2), 261–285.

Bucholz, E. M., Desai, M. M., & Rosenthal, M. S. (2011). Dietary intake in Head Start vs non-Head Start preschool-aged children: Results from the 1999–2004 National Health and Nutrition Examination Survey. *Journal of the American Dietetic Association, 111*(7), 1021–1030.

Buckley, C. (2013, November 15). China to ease longtime policy of 1-child limit. *The New York Times,* p. A1.

Bugental, D. B., Corpuz, R., & Beaulieu, D. A. (2015). An evolutionary approach to socialization. In J. E. Grusec & P. D. Hastings (Eds.). *Handbook of socialization: Theory and Research* (pp. 325–346). New York. Guilford.

Bugental, D. B., Corpuz, R., & Samec, R. (2013). Outcomes of parental investment in high-risk children. *Journal of Experimental Child Psychiatry, 116*(1), 59–67.

Bugental, D. B., et al. (2010). A cognitive approach to child abuse prevention. *Psychology of Violence*, 1(Suppl.), 84–106.

Bukowski, W. M., Buhrmeister, D., & Underwood, M. K. (2011). Peer relations as a developmental context. In M. K. Underwood & L. H. Rosen (Eds.), *Social development: Relationships in infancy, childhood, and adolescence* (pp. 153–179). New York: Guilford.

Bukowski, W. M., Castellanos, M., Vitaro, F., & Brendgen, M. (2015). Socialization and experiences with peers. In J. E. Grusec & P. D. Hastings (Eds.). *Handbook of socialization: Theory and Research* (pp. 228–250). New York: Guilford.

Bukowski, W, M., & Veronneau, M. (2014). Studying withdrawal and isolation in the peer group. pp. 14–33. In R. J. Coplan, & J. C. Bowker (Eds.). *The handbook of solitude: Psychological perspectives on social isolation* (pp. 14–33). Hoboken, NJ: Wiley.

Bull, R., Espy, K. A., Wiebe, S. A., Sheffield, T. D., & Nelson, J. M. (2011). Using confirmatory factor analysis to understand executive control in preschool children: Sources of variation in emergent mathematics achievement. *Developmental Science*, 14(4), 679–692.

Bunting, L., & McAuley, C. (2004). Teenage pregnancy and motherhood: The contribution of support. *Child and Family Social Work*, 9(2), 207–215.

Burgess, J., & Fleet, A. (2009). Frameworks for change: Four recurrent themes for quality in early childhood education initiatives. *Asia-Pacific Journal of Teacher Education*, 37(1), 45–61.

Burghardt, G. M. (2015). Integrative approaches to the biological study of play. In J. E. Johnson et al. (Eds.). *The handbook of the study of play*, Vol. 2 (pp. 21–40). Lanham, MD: Rowman & Littlefield.

Burke, J. D., & Loeber, R. (2015). Mechanisms of behavioral and affective treatment outcomes in a cognitive behavioral intervention for boys. *Journal of Abnormal Child Psychology*, 1–11.

Burnett, A., et al. (2014). Extremely preterm birth and adolescent mental health in a geographical cohort born in the 1990s. *Psychological Medicine*, 44(7), 1533–1544.

Burnette, J. L., O'Boyle, E. H., VanEpps, E. M., Pollack, J. M., & Finkel, E. J. (2013). Mind-sets matter: A meta-analytic review of implicit theories and self-regulation. *Psychological Bulletin*, 139(3), 655–701.

Burnham, D., and Mattock, K. (2010). Auditory development. In J. G. Bremner & T. D. Wachs (Eds.). *The Wiley-Blackwell handbook of infant development*, Vol. 1 (2nd ed.) (Chapter 3). Wiley-Blackwell, Oxford, UK.

Bushman, B. J., & Anderson, C. A. (2009). Comfortably numb: Desensitizing effects of violent media on helping others. *Psychological Science*, 20(3), 273–277.

Bushnell, E. W. (1993, June). *A dual-processing approach to cross-modal matching: Implications for development.* Paper presented at the Society for Research in Child Development, New Orleans, LA.

Bushnell, I. W. R. (2001). Mother's face recognition in newborn infants: Learning and memory. *Infant and Child Development*, 10(1–2), 67–74.

Bussey, K., & Bandura, A. (1984). Influence of gender constancy and social power on sex-linked modeling. *Journal of Personality and Social Psychology*, 47, 1292–1302.

Bussey, K., & Bandura, A. (1999). Social cognitive theory of gender development and differentiation. *Psychological Review*, 106(4), 676–713.

Butterfield, S. A., & Loovis, E. M. (1993). Influence of age, sex, balance, and sport participation on development of throwing by children in grades K–8. *Perceptual and Motor Skills*, 76, 459–464.

Buyse, E., Verschueren, K., & Doumen, S. (2011). Preschoolers' attachment to mother and risk for adjustment problems in kindergarten: Can teachers make a difference? *Social Development*, 20(1), 33–50.

Bynum, M. S. (2007). African American mother–daughter communication about sex and daughters' sexual behavior: Does college racial composition make a difference? *Cultural Diversity & Ethnic Minority Psychology*, 13(2), 151–160.

Cabrera, S. M., et al. (2014). Age of thelarche and menarche in contemporary US females: A cross-sectional analysis. *Journal of Pediatric Endocrinology and Metabolism*, 27(1–2), 47–51.

Call, J. (2001). Object permanence in orangutans (Pongo pygmaeus), chimpanzees (Pan troglodytes), and children (Homo sapiens). *Journal of Comparative Psychology*, 115(2), 159–171.

Callaghan, T., & Corbit, J. (2015). The development of symbolic representation. In R. M. Lerner, L. S. Liben, & U. Mueller (Eds.). *Handbook of child psychology and developmental science*, Vol. 2: Cognitive processes (7th ed.) (pp. 250–295). Hoboken, NJ: Wiley.

Callahan, R., et al. (2015). Pregnancy and contraceptive use among women participating in the FEM-PrEP Trial. *Journal of Acquired Immune Deficiency Syndrome*, 68(2), 196–203.

Callan, M. J., Sutton, R. M., Harvey, A. J., & Dawtry, R. J. (2014). Immanent justice reasoning: Theory, research, and current directions. *Advances in experimental social psychology*, Vo. 49 (pp. 106–162). San Diego: Academic Press.

Calvete, E. (2007). Justification of violence beliefs and social problem-solving as mediators between maltreatment and behavior problems in adolescents. *The Spanish Journal of Psychology*, 10(1), 131–140.

Calvete, E., & Orue, I. (2012). Social information processing as a mediator between cognitive schemas and aggressive behavior in adolescents. *Journal of Abnormal Child Psychology*, 40(1), 105–117.

Calzo, J. P., Antonucci, T. C., Mays, V. M., & Cochran, S. D. (2011). Retrospective recall of sexual orientation identity among, gay, lesbian, and bisexual adults. *Developmental Psychology*, 47(6), 1658–1673.

Camann, W. (2014). In E. I. Eger. *The wondrous story of anesthesia* (pp. 847–858). New York: Springer.

Camarena, P. M. (1991). Conformity in adolescence. In R. M. Lerner, A. C. Petersen & J. Brooks-Gunn (Eds.), *Encyclopedia of adolesence*. New York: Garland.

Camos, V., & Barrouillet, P. (2011). Developmental change in working memory strategies: From passive maintenance to active refreshing. *Developmental Psychology*, 47(3), 898–904.

Campanella, J., & Rovee-Collier, C. (2005). Latent learning and deferred imitation at 3 months. *Infancy*, 7(3), 243–262.

Campbell, A., Shirley, L., & Caygill, L. (2002). Sex-typed preferences in three domains: Do two-year-olds need cognitive variables? *British Journal of Psychology*, 93(2), 203–217.

Campbell, C. (2015). The socioeconomic consequences of dropping out of high school: Evidence from an analysis of siblings. *Social Science Research*, 51, 108–118.

Campbell, D. W., Eaton, W. O., & McKeen, N. A. (2002). Motor activity level and behavioural control in young children. *International Journal of Behavioral Development*, 26(4), 289–296.

Campbell, J. O., Bliven, T. D., Silver, M. M., Snyder, K. J., & Spear, L. P. (2000). Effects of prenatal cocaine on behavioral adaptation to chronic stress in adult rats. *Neurotoxicology and Teratology*, 22(6), 845–850.

Campbell, S. B., et al. (2004). The course of maternal depressive symptoms and maternal sensitivity as predictors of attachment security at 36 months. *Development and Psychopathology*, 16(2), 231–252.

Campos, J. J., Hiatt, S., Ramsey, D., Henderson, C., & Svejda, M. (1978). The emergence of fear on the visual cliff. In M. Lewis & L. Rosenblum (Eds.), *The origins of affect*. New York: Plenum.

Campos, J. J., Langer, A., & Krowitz, A. (1970). Cardiac responses on the visual cliff in prelocomotor human infants. *Science*, 170, 196–197.

Candy, T. R., Crowell, J. A., & Banks, M. S. (1998). Optical, receptoral, and retinal constraints on foveal and peripheral vision in the human neonate. *Vision Research*, 38(24), 3857–3870.

Cannizzaro, E., et al. (2014). Exposure to ototoxic agents and hearing loss: A review of current knowledge. *Hearing, Balance and Communication*, 12(4), 166–175.

Caplan, M., Vespo, J., Pedersen, J., & Hale, D. F. (1991). Conflict and its resolution in small groups of one- and two-year-olds. *Child Development*, 62, 1513–1524.

Carlier, M., & Roubertoux, P. L. (2014). Genetic and environmental influences on intellectual ability in childhood. In D. Finkel, & C. A. Reynolds (Eds.). Behavior genetics of cognition across the lifespan (pp. 69–104). New York: Springer.

Caron, A. J., Caron, R. F., & Carlson, V. R. (1979). Infant perception of the invariant shape of objects varying in slant. *Child Development, 50,* 716–721.

Carre, J. M., & Olmstead, N. A. (2015). Social neuroendocrinology of human aggression: Examining the role of competition-induced testosterone dynamics. *Neuroscience, 286,* 171–186.

Carrier, L. M., et al. (2015). Executive function in risky online behaviors by adolescents and young adults. In L. D. Rosen, N. Cheever, & L. M. Carrier (Eds.) *The Wiley Blackwell handbook of psychology, technology and society* (pp. 119–141). Hoboken, NJ: Wiley.

Carroll, J. S., et al. (2007). So close, yet so far away: The impact of varying marital horizons on emerging adulthood. *Journal of Adolescent Research, 22*(3), 219–247.

Carver, L. J., & Vaccaro, B. G. (2007). 12-month-old infants allocate increased neural resources to stimuli associated with negative adult emotion. *Developmental Psychology, 43*(1), 54–69.

Cascio, C. J. (2010). Somatosensory processing in neurodevelopmental disorders. *Journal of Neuro-developmental Disorders, 2*(2), 62–69.

Casey, B. J. (2015). Beyond simple models of self-control to circuit-based accounts of adolescent behavior. *Annual Review of Psychology, 66,* 295–319.

Casey, L. (2013). Caring for children with phenylketonuria. *Canadian Family Physician, 59*(8), 837–840.

Casselman, R. B., & McKenzie, M. D. (2015). Young adults' recollections of parental rejection and self-reported aggression: The mediating roles of insecure adult attachment and emotional dysregulation. *Journal of Child & Adolescent Trauma, 8*(1), 61–71.

Cassia, V. M., Simion, F., & Umilta, C. (2001). Face preference at birth: The role of an orienting mechanism. *Developmental Science, 4*(1), 101–108.

Castelli, L., De Amicis, L., & Sherman, S. J. (2007). The loyal member effect: On the preference for ingroup members who engage in exclusive relations with the ingroup. *Developmental Psychology, 43,* 1347–1359.

Castelli, L., De Dea, C., & Nesdale, D. (2008). Learning social attitudes: Children's sensitivity to the nonverbal behaviors of adult models during interracial interactions. *Personality and Social Psychology Bulletin, 34,* 1504–1513.

Castelli, L., Zogmaister, C., & Tomelleri, S. (2009). The transmission of racial attitudes within the family. *Developmental Psychology, 45*(2), 586–591.

Cattaneo, L., Sandrini, M., & Schwarzbach, J. (2010). State-dependent TMS reveals a hierarchical representation of observed acts in the temporal, parietal, and premotor cortices. *Cerebral Cortex, 20*(9), 2252–2258.

Cattell, R. B. (1949). *The culture-fair intelligence test.* Champaign, IL: Institute for Personality and Ability Testing.

Catterall, J. (2011). The societal benefits and costs of school dropout recovery.

Education Research International, Article ID 957303. DOI:10.1155/2011/957303.

Ceci, S. J. (1993, August). *Cognitive and social factors in children's testimony.* Master lecture presented at the meeting of the American Psychological Association, Toronto.

Celizic, M. (2009, March 10). *With child porn charges being leveled, some say laws are behind the times.* Retrieved from www.todayshow.com.

Centers for Disease Control and Prevention. (2002). Cited in J. E. Brody (2002, January 1), What women must know about fertility, *The New York Times,* p. F6.

Centers for Disease Control and Prevention. (2011). Coverage Estimates for School Entry Vaccinations: 2009–2010 School Year. National Center for Immunization and Respiratory Diseases. Retrieved from http://www2.cdc.gov/nip/schoolsurv/nationalavg.asp. Accessed August 4, 2012.

Centers for Disease Control and Prevention. (2013). Sexually transmitted diseases. Available at http://www.cdc.gov/std/pregnancy/stdfact-pregnancy.htm.

Centers for Disease Control and Prevention. (2014a). Suicide prevention; Youth suicide. Available at http://www.cdc.gov/violenceprevention/pub/youth_suicide.html.

Centers for Disease Control and Prevention. (2014b). U.S. Department of Health and Human Services. *10 Things You Need to Know about Childhood Immunizations.* Retrieved from http://www.cdc.gov/vaccines/vac-gen/10-shouldknow.htm. Accessed March 26, 2015.

Centers for Disease Control and Prevention. (2015a). Chlamydia. Retrieved from http://www.cdc.gov/std/stats13/chlamydia.htm. Accessed August 14, 2015.

Centers for Disease Control and Prevention. (2015b). HIV among youth. Retrieved from http://www.cdc.gov/hiv/risk/age/youth/index.html?s_cid=tw_std0141316. Accessed April 25, 2015.

Cernoch, J., & Porter, R. (1985). Recognition of maternal axillary odors by infants. *Child Development, 56,* 1593–1598.

Chaillet, N., et al. (2014). Nonpharmalogic approaches for pain management during labor compared with usual care: A meta-analysis. *Birth, 41*(2), 122–137.

Chambers, S. A., Freeman, R., Anderson, A. S., & MacGillivray, S. (2015). Reducing the volume, exposure and negative impacts of advertising for foods high in fat, sugar and salt to children: A systematic review of the evidence from statutory and self-regulatory actions and educational measures. *Preventive Medicine,* in press. Available at http://www.sciencedirect.com/science/article/pii/S0091743515000626.

Chamness, J. A. (2008). Taking a pediatric sleep history. *Pediatric Annals, 37*(7), 502–508.

Chan, T. W., & Koo, A. (2011). Parenting style and youth outcomes in the UK. *European Sociological Review, 27*(3), 385–399.

Chance, S. E., Brown, R. T., Dabbs, J. M., Jr., & Casey, R. (2000). Testosterone, intelligence and behavior disorders in

young boys. *Personality and Individual Differences, 28*(3), 437–445.

Chandra, A., et al. (2008). Does watching sex on television predict teen pregnancy? Findings from a national longitudinal survey of youth. *Pediatrics, 122*(5), 1047–1054.

Chang, E. C., Yu, E. A., & Lin, E. Y. (2014). An examination of ethnic variations in perfectionism and interpersonal influences as predictors of eating disturbances: A look at Asian and European American females. *Asian American Journal of Psychology, 5*(3), 243–251.

Chapman, C., Laird, J., Ifill, N., & KewalRamani, A. (2011). *Trends in high school dropout and completion rates in the United States: 1972–2009* (NCES 2012-006). U.S. Department of Education, Washington, DC.

Chapman, M., & McBride, M. C. (1992). Beyond competence and performance: Children's class inclusion strategies, superordinate class cues, and verbal justifications. *Developmental Psychology, 28,* 319–327.

Chatham, M. L. (2008). Early predictors of disinhibited attachment behaviors among internationally adopted children. *Dissertation Abstracts International: Section B: The Sciences and Engineering, 69*(3-B), 1985.

Chehab, M., Madala, A., & Trussell, J. C. (2015). On-label and off-label drugs used in treatment of male infertility. *Fertility and Sterility, 103*(3), 595–604.

Chehil, S., & Kutcher, S. (2012). Suicide risk assessment. In *Suicide risk management* (pp. 56–87). Hoboken, NJ: Wiley.

Chen, H., & Wang, Y. (2015). Do weight status and television viewing influence children's subsequent dietary changes? A National Longitudinal Study in the United States. *International Journal of Obesity,* DOI:10.1038/ijo. 2015.16.

Chen, X., Chen, H., & Kaspar, V. (2001). Group social functioning and individual socioemotional and school adjustment in Chinese children. *Merrill-Palmer Quarterly, 47*(2), 264–299.

Chen, X., & Eisenberg, N. (2012). Understanding cultural issues in child development: Introduction. *Child Development Perspectives, 6*(1), 1–4.

Chen, Z., & Hancock, J. E. (2011). Cognitive development. In A. S. Davis (Ed.). *Handbook of pediatric neuropsychology.* New York: Springer.

Chen, Z., et al. (2014). Placental transfer and concentrations of cadmium, mercury, lead, and selenium in mothers, newborns, ad young children. *Journal of Exposure Science & Environmental Epidemiology, 24,* 537–544.

Cheng, C. (2014). Predictive effects of self-esteem, moral self, and moral reasoning on delinquent behaviors of Hong Kong young people. *International Journal of Criminology and Sociology, 3,* 133–145.

Cherney, I. D., Harper, H. J., & Winter, J. A. (2006). Nouveaux jouets: Ce que les enfants identifient comme "jouets de garcons" et "jouets de filles." *Enfance, 58*(3), 266–282.

Chess, S., & Thomas, A. (1984). *Origins and evolution of behavior disorders: From infancy to early adult life.* New York: Brunner/Mazel.

Chess, S., & Thomas, A. (1991). Temperament. In M. Lewis (Ed.), *Child and adolescent psychiatry: A comprehensive textbook.* Baltimore: Williams & Wilkins.

Chetty, R., Friedman, J. N., & Rockoff, J. E. (2012). The long-term impacts of teachers: Teacher value-added and student outcomes in adulthood. Available at http://obs.rc.fas.harvard.edu/chetty/value_added.pdf.

Child Care. (2011). *America's children: Key national indicators of well-being, 2011.* ChildStats.gov. Indicator FAM3.A: Primary Care Arrangements for Children Ages 0–4 with Employed Mothers, Selected Years 1985–2010. Retrieved from http://www.childstats.gov/americaschildren/famsoc3.asp. Accessed February 20, 2012.

Child Trends Data Bank (2012). *Attitudes toward spanking.* Available at http://www.childtrends.org/wp-content/uploads/2012/10/51_Attitudes_Toward_Spanking.pdf.

Childhood obesity facts. (2011). Centers for Disease Control and Prevention. Retrieved from http://www.cdc.gov/healthyyouth/obesity/facts.htm. Accessed March 1, 2012.

Child Maltreatment. (2010). See U.S. Department of Health and Human Services, Administration for Children and Families, Administration on Children, Youth and Families, Children's Bureau. (2011). *Child Maltreatment 2010.* Available at http://www.acf.hhs.gov/programs/cb/stats_research/index.htm#can.

Chiou, W-B., & Wan, C-S. (2006). Sexual self-disclosure in cyberspace among Taiwanese adolescents: Gender differences and the interplay of cyberspace and real life. *CyberPsychology & Behavior, 9*(1), 46–53.

Chlamydia—CDC Fact Sheet. (2011). Centers for Disease Control and Prevention. Available at http://www.cdc.gov/std/Chlamydia/STDFact-Chlamydia.htm.

Chmielewski, W. X., & Beste, C. (2015). Action control processes in autism spectrum disorder–Insights from a neurobiological and neuroanatomical perspective. *Progress in Neurobiology, 124,* 49–83.

Chomsky, N. (1988). *Language and problems of knowledge.* Cambridge, MA: MIT Press.

Chomsky, N. (1990). On the nature, use, and acquisition of language. In W. G. Lycan (Ed.), *Mind and cognition.* Oxford: Blackwell.

Chonchaiya, W., et al. (2012). Increased prevalence of seizures in boys who were probands with the fMRI premutation and co-morbid autism spectrum disorder. *Human Genetics, 131*(4), 581–589.

Christie, J. F., & Roskos, K. A. (2015). How does play contribute to literacy? In J. E. Johnson et al. (Eds.). *The handbook of the study of play, Vol. 2* (pp. 417–424). Lanham, MD: Rowman & Littlefield.

Chu, B. C., Skriner, L. C., & Zandberg, L. J. (2014). Trajectory and predictors of alliance in cognitive behavioral therapy for youth anxiety. *Journal of Clinical Child and Adolescent Psychology, 43*(5), 721–734.

Cicchetti, D., Rogosch, F. A., & Toth, S. L. (2006). Fostering secure attachment in infants in maltreating families through preventive interventions. *Development and Psychopathology, 18*(3), 623–649.

Cillessen, A. H. N., & Bellmore, A. D. (2010) Social skills and social competence in interactions with peers. In P. K. Smith, & C. H. Hart (Eds.). *The Wiley-Blackwell handbook of childhood social development* (2nd ed.). Oxford, UK: Wiley-Blackwell. DOI:10.1002/9781444390933.ch21.

Cinamon, R. G., & Rich, Y. (2014). Work and family plans among at-risk Israeli adolescents: A mixed-methods study. *Journal of Career Development, 41*(3), 163–184.

Clancy, B., & Finlay, B. (2001). Neural correlates of early language learning. In M. Tomasello & E. Bates (Eds.), *Language development: The essential readings.* Malden, MA: Blackwell.

Clark, C., et al. (2013). Relation of neural structure to persistently low academic achievement: A longitudinal study of children with differing birth weights. *Neuropsychology, 27*(3), 364–377.

Clark, E. B. (1950). Leading causes of childhood death. Palo Alto, CA: The Palo Alto Clinic, Department of Pediatrics. Retrieved from http://www.ncbi.nlm.nih.gov/pmc/articles/PMC1520569/pdf/califmed00241-0024.pdf. Accessed August 4, 2012.

Clark, E. V. (1973). What's in a word? On the child's acquisition of semantics in his first language. In E. Moore (Ed.), *Cognitive development and the acquisition of language.* New York: Academic Press.

Clark, E. V. (1975). Knowledge, context, and strategy in the acquisition of meaning. In D. P. Date (Ed.), *Georgetown University roundtable on language and linguistics.* Washington, DC: Georgetown University Press.

Clark, J. C. (2014). Towards a cultural historical theory of knowledge mapping: Collaboration and activity in the zone of proximal development. In D. Ifenthaler, & R. Hanewld (Eds.). *Digital knowledge maps in education* (pp. 161–174). New York: Springer Science+Business Media.

Clark, J. J. (2010). Life as a source of theory: Erik Erikson's contributions, boundaries, and marginalities. In T. W. Miller (Ed.). *Handbook of stressful transitions across the lifespan, Part 1* (pp. 59–83). New York: Springer Science+Business Media, LLC.

Clarke-Stewart, K. A., & Beck, R. J. (1999). Maternal scaffolding and children's narrative retelling of a movie story. *Early Childhood Research Quarterly, 14*(3), 409–434.

Clarke-Stewart, K. A., Vandell, D. L., McCartney, K., Owen, M. T., & Booth, C. (2000). Effects of parental separation and divorce on very young children. *Journal of Family Psychology, 14*(2), 304–326.

Clayton, R., & Crosby, R. A. (2006) Measurement in health promotion. In R. A. Crosby, R. J. DiClemente & L. F. Salazar (Eds.), *Research methods in health promotion* (pp. 229–259). San Francisco: Jossey-Bass.

Cleary, D. J., Ray, G. E., LoBello, S. G., & Zachar, P. (2002). Children's perceptions of close peer relationships: Quality, congruence and meta-perceptions. *Child Study Journal, 32*(3), 179–192.

Coelho, D. P. (2011). Encopresis: A medical and family approach. *Pediatric Nursing, 37*(3), 107–112.

Coffee, G., & Kratochwill, T. R. (2013). Examining teacher use of praise taught during behavioral consultation: Implementation and generalization considerations. *Journal of Educational and Psychological Consultation, 23*(1), 1–35.

Cohen, D. K., Raudenbush, S. W., & Ball, D. L. (2003). Resources, instruction, and research. *Educational Evaluation and Policy Analysis, 25*(2), 119–142.

Cohen, J. R., Young, J. F., & Abela, J. R. Z. (2012). Cognitive vulnerability to depression in children. *Cognitive Therapy and Research, 36*(6), 643–654.

Cohen, L. B., & Brunt, J. (2009). Early word learning and categorization: Methodological issues and recent empirical evidence. In J. Colombo, P. McCardle & L. Freud (Eds.), *Infant pathways to language: Methods, models, and research disorders* (pp. 245–266). New York: Psychology Press.

Cohen-Bendahan, C. C. C., Buitelaar, J. K., van Goozen, S. H. M., Orlebeke, J. F., & Cohen-Kettenis, P. T. (2005). Is there an effect of prenatal testosterone on aggression and other behavioral traits? A study comparing same-sex and opposite-sex twin girls. *Hormones and Behavior, 47*(2), 230–237.

Cole, C., et al. (2003). The educational impact of Rechov Sumsum/Shara'a Simsim: A Sesame Street television series to promote respect and understanding among children living in Israel, the West Bank, and Gaza. *International Journal of Behavioral Development, 27*(5), 409–422.

Coleman, P. K. (2003). Perceptions of parent–child attachment, social self-efficacy, and peer relationships in middle childhood. *Infant and Child Development, 12*(4), 351–368.

Collins, R. L., et al. (2004). Watching sex on television predicts adolescent initiation of sexual behavior. *Pediatrics, 114*(3), e280–e289.

Collins, W. A. (1984). Conclusion: The status of basic research on middle childhood. In W. A. Collins (Ed.), *Development during middle childhood: The years from six to twelve.* Washington, DC: National Academy Press.

Collins, W. A., & Laursen, B. (2006). Parent–adolescent relationships. In P. Noller & J. A. Feeney (Eds.), *Close relationships: Functions, forms and processes* (pp. 111–125). Hove, England: Psychology Press/Taylor & Francis.

Commons, M. L., Galaz-Fontes, J. F., & Morse, S. J. (2006). Leadership, cross-cultural contact, socio-economic status, and formal operational reasoning about moral dilemmas among Mexican non-literate adults and high school students. *Journal of Moral Education*, 35(2), 247–267.

Comtois, K. A., Schiff, M. A., & Grossman, D. C. (2008). Psychiatric risk factors associated with postpartum suicide attempt in Washington State, 1992–2001. *American Journal of Obstetrics and Gynecology*, 199(2), 120.e1–120.e5.

Condon, J. (2006). What about dad? Psychosocial and mental health issues for new fathers. *Australian Family Physician*, 35(9), 657–752.

Conel, J. L. (1959). *The postnatal development of the human cerebral-cortex*, Vol. VI, *The cortex of the twenty-four month infant*. Cambridge, MA: Harvard University Press.

Cong, X., et al. (2013). Neonatal nurses' perceptions of pain assessment and management in NICUs: A national survey. *Advances in Neonatal Care*, 13(5), 353–360.

Connolly, J., Craig, W., Goldberg, A., & Pepler, D. (2004). Mixed-gender groups, dating, and romantic relationships in early adolescence. *Journal of Research on Adolescence*, 14(2), 185–207.

Connolly, J., Furman, W., & Konarski, R. (2000). The role of peers in the emergence of heterosexual romantic relationships in adolescence. *Child Development*, 71(5), 1395–1408.

Connor, P. D., Sampson, P. D., Streissguth, A. P., Bookstein, F. L., & Barr, H. M. (2006). Effects of prenatal alcohol exposure on fine motor coordination and balance: A study of two adult samples. *Neuropsychologia*, 44(5), 744–751.

Conrad, N. J., Walsh, J. A., Allen, J. M., & Tsang, C. D. (2011). Examining infants' preferences for tempo in lullabies and playsongs. *Canadian Journal of Experimental Psychology/Revue canadienne de psychologie expérimentale*, 65(3), 168–172.

Cooper, C. R., Gonzalez, E., & Wilson, A. R. (2015). Identities, cultures, and schooling: How students navigate racial-ethnic, indigenous, immigrant, social class, and gender identities on their pathways through school. In K. C. McLean, & M. Syed (Eds.). *The Oxford handbook of identity development* (pp. 299–318). New York: Oxford University Press.

Coovadia, H. (2004). Antiretroviral agents: How best to protect infants from HIV and save their mothers from AIDS. *New England Journal of Medicine*, 351(3), 289–292.

Copeland, W., et al. (2010). Do the negative effects of early pubertal timing on adolescent girls continue into young adulthood? *American Journal of Psychiatry*, 167(10), 1218–1225.

Corriveau, K. H., & Harris, P. L. (2015). Children's developing realization that some stories are true: Links to the understanding of beliefs and signs. *Cognitive Development*, 34, 76–87.

Costigan, C. L., Cauce, A. M., & Etchison, K. (2007). Changes in African American mother–daughter relationships during adolescence: Conflict, autonomy, and warmth. In B. J. R. Leadbeater & N. Way (Eds.), *Urban girls revisited: Building strengths* (pp. 177–201). New York: New York University Press.

Cowan, N. (2014). Working memory underpins cognitive development, learning, and education. *Educational Psychology Review*, 26, 197–223.

Cowan, N. (2015, March 9). George Miller's magical number of immediate memory in retrospect: Observations on the faltering progression of science. *Psychological Review*.

Cowan, N., et al. (2010). With development, list recall includes more chunks, not just larger ones. *Developmental Psychology*, 46(5), 1119–1131.

Cozolino, L. (2014). *The neuroscience of human relationships* (2nd Ed.). New York: W. W. Norton.

Crain, W. C. (2000). *Theories of development: Concepts and applications* (4th ed.). Englewood Cliffs, NJ: Prentice Hall.

Crane, J. M., Murphy, P., Burrage, L., & Hutchens, D. (2013). Maternal and perinatal outcomes of extreme obesity in pregnancy. *Journal of Obstetrics and Gynaecology Canada*, 35(7), 606–611.

Cratty, B. (1986). *Perceptual and motor development in infants and children* (3rd ed.). Englewood Cliffs, NJ: Prentice Hall.

Creed, P. A., & Wamelink, S. H. (2015). Antecedents and consequences to perceived career goal-progress discrepancies. *Journal of Vocational Behavior*, 87, 43–53.

Crisp, R. J., & Turner, R. N. (2011). Cognitive adaptation to the experience of social and cultural diversity. *Psychological Bulletin*, 137(2), 242–266.

Crocker, M. K., et al. (2014). Sexual dimorphisms in the associations of BMI and body fat with indices of pubertal development in girls and boys. *The Journal of Clinical Endocrinology & Metabolism*, 99(8), DOI: 10.1210/jc.2014-1384.

Crook, C. K., & Lipsitt, L. P. (1976). Neonatal nutritive sucking: Effects of taste stimulation upon sucking rhythm and heart rate. *Child Development*, 47, 518–522.

Crosnoe, R. (2011). Schools, peers, and the big picture of adolescent development. In E. Amsel, & J. Smetana (Eds.), *Adolescent vulnerabilities and opportunities* (pp. 182–204). New York: Cambridge University Press.

Csikszentmihalyi, M., & Larson, R. (1984). *Being adolescent*. New York: Basic Books.

Cummings, C. M., Caporino, N. E., & Kendall, P. C. (2014). Comorbidity of anxiety and depression in children and adolescents: 20 years after. *Psychological Bulletin*, 140(3), 816–845.

Currie, J., DellaVigna, S., Moretti, E., & Pathania, V. (2009). *The effect of fast food restaurants on obesity*. National Bureau of Economic Research (NBER). NBER Working Paper No. W14721.

Cystic Fibrosis Foundation (2014). Retrieved from http://www.cff.org/AboutCF/. Accessed January 9, 2014.

Dai, D. Y. (2001). A comparison of gender differences in academic self-concept and motivation between high-ability and average Chinese adolescents. *Journal of Secondary Gifted Education*, 13(1), 22–32.

Dağlioğlu, H. E., et al. (2010). Examination of human figure drawings by gifted and normally developed children at preschool period. *Elementary Education Online*, 9(1), 31–43.

Daley, C. E., & Onwuegbuzie, A. J. (2011). Race and intelligence. In R. J. Sternberg & S. J. Kaufman (Eds.), *The Cambridge handbook of intelligence* (pp. 293–308). New York: Cambridge University Press.

Dalla-Bona, D., et al. (2015). Unilateral ear fullness and temporary hearing loss diagnosed and successfully managed as a temporomandibular disorder. *The Journal of the American Dental Association*, 146(3), 192–194.

Daly, M., & Wilson, M. (2000). Genetic ties may be factor in violence in stepfamilies. *American Psychologist*, 55(6), 679–680.

Damon, W. (1991). Adolescent self-concept. In R. M. Lerner, A. C. Petersen & J. Brooks-Gunn (Eds.), *Encyclopedia of adolescence*. New York: Garland.

Daniels, E. A., & Gillen, M. M. (2015). Body image and identity: A call for new research. In S. J. Schwarz, K. Luyckx, & V. L. Vignoles (Eds.). *Handbook of identity theory and research* (pp. 406–422). New York: Springer Science+Business Media.

Daniels, H. (2010). Vygotsky and psychology. In U. Goswami (Ed.), *The Wiley–Blackwell handbook of childhood cognitive development*. (2nd ed.) (pp. 673–696). Chichester, West Sussex, UK: Wiley-Blackwell.

Daniels, H., et al. (Eds.). (2007). *The Cambridge companion to Vygotsky*. New York: Cambridge University Press.

Daniels, S. R. (2006). The consequences of childhood overweight and obesity. *The Future of Children*, 16(1), 47–67.

Daoud, Y., et al. (2009). Refractive surgery in children: Treatment options, outcomes, and controversies. *American Journal of Ophthalmology*, 147(4), 573–582.

Daugherty, A. M., & Ofen, N. (2015). That's a good one! Belief in efficacy of mnemonic strategies contributes to age-related increase in associative memory. *Journal of Experimental Child Psychology*, 136, 17–29.

Daum, M. M., Ulber, J., & Gredeback, G. (2013). The development of pointing perception in infancy. *Developmental Psychology*, 49(10), 1898–1908.

Davies, M. J., et al. (2012). Reproductive technologies and the risk of birth defects. *New England Journal of Medicine*, 366, 1803–1813.

Davies, W., et al. (2014). Genetic and pharmacological modulation of the steroid sulfatase axis improves response control; Comparison with drugs used in ADHD. *Neurophychopharmacology*, 39, 2622–2632.

Davis, H. A. (2001). The quality and impact of relationships between elementary school students and teachers. *Contemporary Educational Psychology*, 26(4), 431–453.

Davis, P. E., Meins, E., & Femyhough, C. (2013). Individual differences in children's private speech: The role of imaginary companions. *Journal of Experimental Child Psychology*, 116(3), 561–571.

Davis, S. R. (2013). Androgen therapy in women, beyond libido. *Climacteric*, 16(S1), 18–24.

Dawood, K., Bailey, J. M., & Martin, N. G. (2009). Genetic and environmental influences on sexual orientation. In Y-K. Kim (Ed.), *Handbook of behavior genetics* (pp. 269–279). New York: Springer.

Dawson, C., et al. (2011). Dietary treatment of phenylketonuria: The effect of phenylalanine on reaction time. *Journal of Inherited Metabolic Disease*, 34(2), 449–454.

Dawson, T. L. (2002). New tools, new insights: Kohlberg's moral judgement stages revisited. *International Journal of Behavioral Development*, 26(2), 154–166.

Day, N. L., Goldschmidt, L., & Thomas, C. A. (2006). Prenatal marijuana exposure contributes to the prediction of marijuana use at age 14. *Addiction*, 101(9), 1313–1322.

Dean III, D. C., et al. (2015). Characterizing longitudinal white matter development during early childhood. *Brain Structure and Function*, 220(4), 1921–1933.

Deary, I. J., Whiteman, M. C., Starr, J. M., Whalley, L. J., & Fox, H. C. (2004). The impact of childhood intelligence on later life: Following up the Scottish mental surveys of 1932 and 1947. *Journal of Personality and Social Psychology*, 86(1), 130–147.

DeCasper, A. J., & Fifer, W. P. (1980). Of human bonding: Newborns prefer their mothers' voices. *Science*, 208, 1174–1176.

DeCasper, A. J., & Prescott, P. A. (1984). Human newborns' perception of male voices: Preference, discrimination, and reinforcing value. *Developmental Psychobiology*, 17, 481–491.

DeCasper, A. J., & Spence, M. J. (1986). Prenatal maternal speech influences newborns' perception of speech sounds. *Infant Behavior and Development*, 9, 133–150.

DeCasper, A. J., & Spence, M. J. (1991). Auditorially mediated behavior during the perinatal period: A cognitive view. In M. J. Weiss & P. R. Zelazo (Eds.), *Infant attention* (pp. 142–176). Norwood, NJ: Ablex.

DeCasper, A. J., Granier-Deferre, C., Fifer, W. P., & Moon, C. M. (2011). Measuring fetal cognitive development: When methods and conclusions don't match. *Developmental Science*, 14(2), 224–225.

Deep, A. L., et al. (1999). Sexual abuse in eating disorder subtypes and control women: The role of comorbid substance dependence in bulimia nervosa. *International Journal of Eating Disorders*, 25(1), 1–10.

De Goede, I. H. A., Branje, S. J. T., & Meeus, W. H. J. (2009). Developmental changes and gender differences in adolescents' perceptions of friendships. *Journal of Adolescence*, 38(1), 75–88.

De Haan, M., & Groen, M. (2006). Neural bases of infants' processing of social information in faces. In P. J. Marshall & N. A. Fox (Eds.), *The development of social engagement: Neurobiological perspectives. Series in affective science* (pp. 46–80). New York: Oxford University Press.

DeHart, T., Pelham, B. W., & Tennen, H. (2006). What lies beneath: Parenting style and implicit self-esteem. *Journal of Experimental Social Psychology*, 42(1), 1–17.

Delaney-Black, V., et al. (2004). Prenatal cocaine: Quantity of exposure and gender influences on school-age behavior. *Developmental and Behavioral Pediatrics*, 25(4), 254–263.

De Leeuw, E., Borgers, N., & Smits, A. (2004). Pretesting questionnaires for children and adolescents. In S. Presser et al. (Eds.), *Methods for testing and evaluating survey questionnaires*. Hoboken, NJ: Wiley.

De Leonibus, C., et al. (2014). Distinct gene expression is associated with growth-related network modules in relation to gender differences in the timing of the pubertal growth spurt. *Endocrine Abstracts*, 34, 164.

De Lisi, R. (2015). Piaget's sympathetic but unromantic account of children's play. In J. E. Johnson et al. (Eds.). *The handbook of the study of play, Vol. 2* (pp. 227–238). Lanham, MD: Rowman & Littlefield.

De Lisi, M., Vaughn, M. G., Gentiel, D. A., Anderson, C. A., & Shook, J. J. (2013). Violent video games, delinquency, and youth violence: New evidence. *Youth Violence and Juvenile Justice*, 11(2), 132–142.

DeLoache, J. S., Cassidy, D. J., & Brown, A. L. (1985). Precursors of mnemonic strategies in very young children's memory. *Child Development*, 56, 125–137.

Delorme-Axford, E., Sadovsky, Y., & Coyne, C. B. (2014). The placenta as a barrier to viral infections. *Annual Review of Virology*, 1, 133–146.

Demby, K. P., Riggs, S. A., & Kaminski, P. L. (2015). Attachment and family processes in children's psychological adjustment in middle childhood. *Family Process*, DOI:10.1111/famp.12145.

Dempfle, A., et al. (2013). Predictors of the resumption of menses in adolescent anorexia nervosa. *BMC Psychiatry*, 13, 308.

De Medina, P. G. R., Visser, G. H. A., & Huizink, J. K. (2003). Fetal behaviour does not differ between boys and girls. *Early Human Development*, 73(2), 17.

Deneault, J., & Ricard, M. (2006). The assessment of children's understanding of inclusion relations: Transitivity, asymmetry, and quanitification. *Journal of Cognition and Development*, 7(4), 551–570.

Denham, S., et al. (2011). Emotions and social development in childhood. In P. K. Smith, & C. H. Hart (Eds.). *The Wiley-Blackwell handbook of childhood social development* (pp. 413–433). Chichester, West Sussex, UK: Wiley-Blackwell.

den Hoed, M., & Loos, R. J. F. (2014). Genes and the predisposition to obesity. In G. Bray, & C. Bouchard (Eds.). *Handbook of obesity: Epidemiology, etiology, and physiopathology* (4th ed.) (pp. 105–120). CRC Press.

Deniz, C. B. (2004). Early childhood teachers' beliefs about and self-reported practices toward children's private speech. *Dissertation Abstracts International Section A: Humanities and Social Sciences*, 64(9-A), 3185.

Denmark, F. L., & Williams, D. (2014). Gender bias, overview. In T. Teo (Ed.). *Encyclopedia or Critical Psychology* (pp. 761–762). New York: Springer Science+Business Media.

Dennis, W. (1960). Causes of retardation among institutional children: Iran. *Journal of Genetic Psychology*, 96, 47–59.

Dennis, W., & Dennis, M. G. (1940). The effect of cradling practices upon the onset of walking in Hopi children. *Journal of Genetic Psychology*, 56, 77–86.

de Oliveira, F. S., Viana, M. R., Antoniolli, A. R., & Marchioro, M. (2001). Differential effects of lead and zinc on inhibitory avoidance learning in mice. *Brazilian Journal of Medical and Biological Research*, 34(1), 117–120.

De Rosa, C. J., et al. (2010). Sexual intercourse and oral sex among public middle school students: Prevalence and correlates. *Perspectives on Sexual and Reproductive Health*, 42(3), 197–205.

Desai, K. S., et al. (2013). Study of effect of advanced maternal age related risks for Down syndrome & other trisomies. *International Journal of Biomedical and Advance Research*, 4(2), DOI:10.7439/ijbar.v4i2.301.

de Souza, A. S., Fernandes, F. S., & do Carmo, M. (2011). Effects of maternal malnutrition and postnatal nutritional rehabilitation on brain fatty acids, learning, and memory. *Nutrition Reviews*, 69(3), 132–144.

Devaney, S. A., Palomaki, G. E., Scott, J. A., & Bianchi, D. W. (2011). Noninvasive fetal sex determination using cell-free fetal DNA: A systematic review and analysis. *New England Journal of Medicine*, 306(6), 627–636.

De Villiers, J. G., & de Villiers, P. A. (1999). Language development. In M. H. Bornstein & M. E. Lamb (Eds.), *Developmental psychology: An advanced textbook* (4th ed.) (pp. 313–373). Mahwah, NJ: Erlbaum.

Devlin, M. J., & Steinglass, J. E. (2014). Feeding and eating disorders. In J. Cutler (Ed.). *Psychiatry*, 3rd ed. (pp. 291–322). New York: Oxford University Press.

de Vries, J. I. P., & Hopkins, B. (2005). Fetal movements and postures: What do they mean for postnatal development? In B. Hopkins & S. P. Johnson (Eds.), *Prenatal development of postnatal functions. Advances in infancy research* (pp. 177–219). Westport, CT: Praeger/Greenwood.

Dezoete, J. A., MacArthur, B. A., & Tuck, B. (2003). Prediction of Bayley and Stanford–Binet scores with a group of very low birth-weight children. *Child: Care, Health and Development*, 29(5), 367–372.

Dick, D. M., Prescott, C., & McGue, M. (2009). The genetics of substance use and substance use disorders. In Y-K. Kim (Ed.), *Handbook of behavior genetics* (pp. 433–453). New York: Springer.

DiIorio, C., McCarty, F., Denzmore, P., & Landis, A. (2007). The moderating influence of mother–adolescent discussion on early and middle African-American adolescent sexual behavior. *Research in Nursing & Health*, 30(2), 193–202.

Ding, Q. J., & Hesketh, T. (2006). Family size, fertility preferences, and sex ratio in China in the era of the one child family policy: Results from National Family Planning and Reproductive Health Survey. *British Medical Journal*, 333(7564), 371–373.

Dixon, G., & Clarke, C. (2013). The effect of falsely balanced reporting of the autism–vaccine controversy on vaccine safety perceptions and behavioral intentions. *Health Education Research*, 28(2), 352–359.

Dockett, S., Perry, B., & Whitton, D. (2006). Picture storybooks and starting school. *Early Child Development and Care*, 76(8), 835–848.

Dodd, B., & Crosbie, S. (2010). Language and cognition. In U. Goswami (Ed.), *The Wiley–Blackwell handbook of childhood cognitive development.* (2nd ed.) (pp. 604–625). Chichester, West Sussex, UK: Wiley–Blackwell.

Dodge, E., & Simic, M. (2015). Anorexia runs in families: does this make the families responsible? A commentary on 'Anorexia runs in families: is this due to genes or the family environment?' (Dring, 2014). *Journal of Family Therapy*, 37(1), 93–102.

Dodge, K. A., Laird, R., Lochman, J. E., Zelli, A., & Conduct Problems Prevention Research Group U.S. (2002). Multidimensional latent-construct analysis of children's social information processing patterns: Correlations with aggressive behavior problems. *Psychological Assessment*, 14(1), 60–73.

Donner, M. B., VandeCreek, L., Gonsiorek, J. C., & Fisher, C. B. (2008). Balancing confidentiality: Protecting privacy and protecting the public. *Professional Psychology: Research and Practice*, 39(3), 369–376.

Donohue, B. C., Karmely, J., & Strada, M. J. (2006). Alcohol and drug abuse. In M. Hersen (Ed.), *Clinician's handbook of child behavioral assessment* (pp. 337–375). San Diego, CA: Elsevier Academic Press.

Dorfberger, S., Adi-Japha, E., & Karni, A. (2009). Sex differences in motor performance and motor learning in children and adolescents: An increasing male advantage in motor learning and consolidation phase gains. *Behavioural Brain Research*, 198(1), 165–171.

Douglas, E. M., & Mohn, B. L. (2014). Fatal and non-fatal child maltreatment in the US: An analysis of child, caregiver, and service utilization with the National Child Abuse and Neglect Data Set. *Child Abuse & Neglect*, 38(1), 42–51.

Douglas, P. S., & Hill, P. S. (2011). The crying baby: What approach? *Current Opinion in Pediatrics*, 23(5), 523–529.

Dowrick, P. W., Back, L. T., & Mills, N. C. (2015). School failure and school success. In T. P. Gullotta, R. W. Plant, & M. A. Evans (Eds.). Handbook of adolescent behavioral problems (pp. 395ff). New York: Springer Science+Business Media.

Doyle, O., et al. (2009). Investing in early human development. *Economics & Human Biology*, 7(1), 1–6.

Drasgow, E., Halle, J. W., & Phillips, B. (2001). Effects of different social partners on the discriminated requesting of a young child with autism and severe language delays. *Research in Developmental Disabilities*, 22(2), 125–139.

Drewett, R. F., Corbett, S. S., & Wright, C. M. (2006). Physical and emotional development, appetite and body image in adolescents who failed to thrive as infants. *Journal of Child Psychology and Psychiatry*, 47(5), 524–531.

DuBois, D. L., & Hirsch, B. J. (1990). School and neighborhood friendship patterns of blacks and whites in early adolescence. *Child Development*, 61, 524–536.

Dubois, L., et al. (2012). Genetic and environmental contributions to weight, height, and BMI from birth to 19 years of age: An international study of over 12,000 twin pairs. *PLoS ONE*, 7(2): e30153. doi:10.1371/journal.pone.0030153.

Dubow, E. F., Boxer, P., & Huesmann, L. R. (2009). Long-term effects of parents' education on children's educational and occupational success: Mediation by family interactions, child aggression, and teenage aspirations. *Merrill-Palmer Quarterly*, 55(3), 224–249.

Dubow, E. F., et al. (2010). Exposure to conflict and violence across contexts: Relations to adjustment among Palestinian children. *Journal of Clinical Child and Adolescent Psychology*, 39(1), 103–116.

Duggan, A., et al. (2004). Evaluating a statewide home visiting program to prevent child abuse in at-risk families of newborns: Fathers' participation and outcomes. *Child Maltreatment: Journal of the American Professional Society on the Abuse of Children*, 9(1), 3–17.

Dumont, M., Leclerc, D., & McKinnon, S. (2009). Consequences of part-time work on the academic and psychosocial adaptation of adolescents. *Canadian Journal of School Psychology*, 24(1), 58–75.

Dunn, J., (2015). Siblings. In J. E. Grusec & P. D. Hastings (Eds.). *Handbook of socialization: Theory and Research* (pp. 182–201). New York: Guilford.

Dunn, M. G., & Mezzich, A. C. (2007). Development in childhood and adolescence: Implications for prevention research and practice. In P. Tolan, J. Szapocznik & S. Sambrano (Eds.), *Preventing youth substance abuse: Science-based programs for children and adolescents* (pp. 21–40). Washington, DC: American Psychological Association.

Durdiakova, J., et al. (2015). Differences in salivary testosterone, digit ratio and empathy between intellectually gifted and control boys. *Intelligence*, 48, 76–84.

Du Rocher Schudlich, T. D., Shamir, H., & Cummings, E. M. (2004). Marital conflict, children's representations of family relationships, and children's dispositions towards peer conflict strategies. *Social Development*, 13(2), 171–192.

Dvorak, R. D., & Day, A. M. (2014). Marijuana and self-regulation: Examining likelihood and intensity of use and problems. *Addictive Behaviors*, 39(3), 709–712.

Dweck, C. S. (2007). Is math a gift? Beliefs that put females at risk. In S. J. Ceci & W. M. Williams (Eds.), *Why aren't more women in science: Top researchers debate the evidence* (pp. 47–55). Washington, DC: American Psychological Association.

Dworkin, E., Javdani, S., Verona, E., & Campbell, R. (2014). Child sexual abuse and disordered eating: The mediating role of impulsive and compulsive tendencies. *Psychology of Violence*, 4(1), 21–36.

Dykman, R. A., Casey, P. H., Ackerman, P. T., & McPherson, W. B. (2001). Behavioral and cognitive status in school-aged children with a history of failure to thrive during early childhood. *Clinical Pediatrics*, 40(2), 63–70.

Dyson, J. C. (2015). Play in America: A historical overview. In J. E. Johnson et al. (Eds.). *The handbook of the study of play*, Vol. 2 (pp. 41–50). Lanham, MD: Rowman & Littlefield.

Dyson, M. E. (2014, September 18). Punishment or child abuse? *The New York Times*, p. A33.

Eaton, W. O., McKeen, N. A., & Campbell, D. W. (2001). The waxing and waning of movement: Implications for psychological development. *Developmental Review*, 21(2), 205–223.

Eberhardy, F. (1967). The view from "the couch." *Journal of Child Psychological Psychiatry*, 8, 257–263.

Ebert, E. S., & Culyer, R. C. (2011). *School: An introduction to education* (2nd ed.). Belmont, CA: Cengage.

Ebstein, R., Israel, S., Chew, S., Zhong, S., & Knafo, A. (2010). Genetics of human social behavior. *Neuron*, 65(6), 831–844.

Eccles, J. S., Roeser, R., Vida, M., Fredricks, J., & Wigfield, A. (2006). Motivational and achievement pathways through middle childhood. In L. Balter & C. S. Tamis-LeMonda (Eds.), *Child psychology: A handbook of contemporary issues* (2nd ed.) (pp. 325ff). New York: Psychology Press.

Eddy, J. M., Leve, L. D., & Fagot, B. I. (2001). Coercive family processes: A replication and extension of Patterson's Coercion Model. *Aggressive Behavior*, 27(1), 14–25.

Eder, R. A. (1989). The emergent persono-lo-gist: The structure and content of 3½-, 5½-, and 7½-year-olds' concepts of themselves and other persons. *Child Development*, 60, 1218–1228.

Eder, S., & Borzi, P. (2014, September 13). N.F.L. rocked again as Adrian Peterson faces a child abuse charge. *The New York Times*, p. A1.

Edwards, J., et al. (2011). Developmental coordination disorder in school-aged children born very preterm and/or at very low birth weight: A systematic review. *Journal of Developmental Behavioral Pediatrics*, 32(9), 678–687.

Effinger, J. M., & Stewart, D. G. (2012). Classification of co-occurring depression and substance abuse symptoms predicts suicide attempts in adolescents. *Suicide and Life-Threatening Behavior, 42*(4), 353–358.

Egeland, B., & Sroufe, L. A. (1981). Attachment and early maltreatment. *Child Development, 52,* 44–52.

Eger II , E. I., Saidman, L. J., & Westhorpe, R. N. (Eds.) (2014). *The wondrous story of anesthesia* (pp. 847–858). New York: Springer.

Eimas, P. D., Sigueland, E. R., Juscyk, P., & Vigorito, J. (1971). Speech perception in infants. *Science, 171,* 303–306.

Eisenberg, N., Eggum, N. D., & Edwards, A. (2010). Emotions, aggression, and morality in children. In W. F. Arsenio, & E. A. Lemerise (Eds.), *Emotions, aggression, and morality in children: Bridging development and psychopathology* (pp. 115–135). Washington, DC: American Psychological Association.

Eisenberg, N., Hertz-Lazarowitz, R., & Fuchs, I. (1990). Prosocial moral judgment in Israeli kibbutz and city children: A longitudinal study. *Merrill-Palmer Quarterly, 36,* 273–285.

Eivers, A. R., Brendgen, M., Vitaro, F., & Borge, A. I. H. (2012). Concurrent and longitudinal links between children's and their friends' antisocial and prosocial behavior in preschool. *Early Childhood Research Quarterly, 27*(1), 137–146.

Elfayomy, A. K., & Almasry, S. M. (2014). Effects of a single course versus repeated courses of antenatal corticosteroids on fetal growth, placental morphometry and the differential regulation of vascular endothelial growth factor. *The Journal of Obstetrics and Gynaecology Research, 40*(11), 2135–2145.

Elias, M. J., Zins, J. E., Graczyk, P. A., & Weissberg, R. P. (2003). Implementation, sustainability, and scaling of social-emotional and academic innovations in public schools. *School Psychology Quarterly, 32,* 303–319.

Elkind, D. (2007). *The power of play: How spontaneous imaginative activities lead to happier, healthier children.* Cambridge, MA: Da Capo Press.

Ellis, W., & Zarbatany, L. (2007). Explaining friendship formation and friendship stability. *Merrill-Palmer Quarterly, 53*(1), 79–104.

Ellison, N. B., Steinfield, C., & Lampe, C. (2007). The benefits of Facebook "friends": Social capital and college students' use of online social network sites. *Journal of Computer-Mediated Communication, 12*(4), 1143–1168.

Elman, J. L. (2009). The emergence of language: A conspiracy theory. In B. MacWhinney (Ed.). *The emergence of language* (pp. 1–27). New York: Taylor & Francis e-Library.

Else-Quest, N. M., & Grabe, S. (2012). The political is personal: Measurement and application of nation-level indicators of gender equity in psychological research. *Psychology of Women Quarterly, 36*(2), 131–144.

Else-Quest, N. M., Hyde, J. S., & Linn, M. C. (2010). Cross-national patterns of gender differences in mathematics: A meta-analysis. *Psychological Bulletin, 136*(1), 103–127.

Else-Quest, N. M., Mineo, C. C., & Higgins, A. (2013). Math and science attitudes at the intersection of gender and ethnicity. *Psychology of Women Quarterly, 37*(3), 293–309.

El-Sheikh, M., et al. (2009). Marital conflict and children's externalizing behavior: Interactions between parasympathetic and sympathetic nervous system activity: V. Discussion. *Monographs of the Society for Research in Child Development, 74*(1), 56–69.

Emde, R. N., Gaensbauer, T. J., & Harmon, R. J. (1976). *Emotional expression in infancy: A biobehavioral study.* New York: International Universities Press.

Environmental Protection Agency. (2015). Abridged from Lead Poisoning Prevention. Retrieved from http://www.epa.gov/region07/citizens/lead.htm. Accessed March 26, 2015.

Erikson, E. H. (1963). *Childhood and society.* New York: Norton.

Erikson, E. H. (1968). *Identity: Youth and crisis.* New York: Norton.

Erikson, E. H. (1975). *Life history and the historical moment.* New York: Norton.

Erikson, M. G., Hansson, B., & Lundblad, S. (2014). Desirable possible selves and depression in adult women with eating disorders. *Eating and Weight Disorders: Studies on Anorexia, Bulimia and Obesity, 19*(2), 145–151.

Erlandson, M. C., et al. (2008). Growth and maturation of adolescent female gymnasts, swimmers, and tennis players. *Medicine & Science in Sports & Exercise, 40*(1), 34–42.

Eron, L. D., Huesmann, L. R., & Zelli, A. (1991). The role of parental variables in the learning of aggression. In D. J. Pepler & K. H. Rubin (Eds.), *The development and treatment of childhood aggression.* Hillsdale, NJ: Erlbaum.

Erwin, H., Fedewa, A., Belghle, A., & Ahn, S. (2012). A quantitative review of physical activity, health, and learning outcomes associated with classroom-based physical activity interventions. *Journal of Applied School Psychology, 28*(1), 14–36.

Esposito, E. A., & Gunnar, M. R. (2014). Early deprivation and developmental psychopathology. In M. Lewis & K. D. Rudolph (Eds.). *Handbook of developmental psychopathology* (pp. 371–388). New York: Springer Science + Business Media.

Estes, A., et al. (2011). Basal ganglia morphometry and repetitive behavior in young children with autism spectrum disorder. *Autism Research, 4*(3), 212–220.

Etchell, A. C., Johnson, B. W., & Sowman, P. F. (2014). Beta oscillations, timing, and stuttering. *Frontiers in Human Neuroscience, 8,* 1036.

Evans, S. W., et al. (2001). Dose–response effects of methylphenidate on ecolo-gically valid measures of academic performance and classroom behavior in adolescents with ADHD. *Experimental and Clinical Psychopharmacology, 9*(2), 163–175.

Evlampidou, I., et al. (2015). Prenatal second-hand smoke exposure measured with urine cotinine may reduce gross motor development at 18 months of age. *The Journal of Pediatrics, 167*(2), 246–252.

Ewing, S. W. F., Houck, J. M., & Bryan, A. D. (2015). Neural activation during response inhibition is associated with adolescents' frequency of risky sex and substance use. *Addictive Behaviors, 44,* 80–87.

Fagan, J., Day, R., Lamb, M.E., & Cabrare, N. J. (2014). Should researchers conceptualize differently the dimensions of parenting for fathers and mothers? *Journal of Family Theory & Review, 6*(4), 390–405.

Fagan, M. K. (2015). Why repetition? Repetitive babbling, auditory feedback, and cochlear implantation. *Journal of Experimental Child Psychology, 137,* 125–136.

Fagerlund, A., et al. (2015). Gynecomastia: A systematic review. *Journal of Plastic Surgery and Hand Surgery,* DOI:10.3109/2000656X.2015.1053398.

Fantz, R. L. (1961). The origin of form perception. *Scientific American, 204,* 66–72.

Fantz, R. L., Fagan, J. F., III, & Miranda, S. B. (1975). Early visual selectivity. In L. B. Cohen & P. Salapatek (Eds.), *Infant perception: From sensation to cognition,* Vol. 1. New York: Academic Press.

Farr, R. H., Forssell, S. L., & Patterson, C. J. (2010). Parenting and child development in adoptive families: Does parental sexual orientation matter? *Applied Developmental Science, 14*(3), 164–178.

Farr, R. H., & Patterson, C. J. (2013). Lesbian and gay adoptive parents and their children. In A. E Goldberg, & K. R. Allen (Eds.). *LGBT-parent families: Innovations in research and implications for practice* (pp. 39–55). New York: Springer Science+Business Media.

Farrer, L. A., et al. (2009). Association of variants in MANEA with cocaine-related behaviors. *Archives of General Psychiatry, 66*(3), 267–274.

Farrow, C. V., Haycraft, E., & Blissett, J. M. (2015).Teaching our children when to eat: How parental feeding practices inform the development of emotional eating—a longitudinal experimental design. *The American Journal of Clinical Nutrition, 101*(5), 908–913.

Fayet, F., Petocz, P. & Samman, S. (2012). Prevalence and correlates of dieting in college women: A cross sectional study. *International Journal of Women's Health, 4,* 405–411.

Fehr, K. K., & Russ, S. W. (2014). Assessment of pretend play in preschool-aged children: Validation and factor analysis of the Affect in Play Scale—Preschool version. *Journal of Personality Assessment, 96*(3), 350–357.

Feijó, L., et al. (2006). Mothers' depressed mood and anxiety levels are reduced after massaging their preterm infants. *Infant Behavior & Development, 29*(3), 476–480.

Feinberg, M. E., Neiderhiser, J. M., Howe, G., & Hetherington, E. M. (2001). Adolescent, parent, and observer perceptions of parenting: Genetic and environmental influences on shared and distinct perceptions. *Child Development, 72*(4), 1266–1284.

Feiring, C. (1993, March). *Developing concepts of romance from 15 to 18 years.* Paper presented at the meeting of the Society for Research in Child Development, New Orleans, LA.

Feit, M. D., Holmes, J., Minor, J., Strong, R., & Murphy, K. (2015). Preventative services for children and adolescents. In J. S. Wodarski, M. J. Holosko, & M. D. Feit (Eds.). *Evidence-informed assessment and practice in child welfare* (pp. 279–293). Switzerland: Springer International Publishing.

Feldman, R., Rosenthal, Z., & Eidelman, A. I. (2014). Maternal-preterm skin-to-skin contact enhances child physiologic organization and cognitive control across the first 10 years of life. *Biological Psychiatry, 75*(1), 56–64.

Fellman, J. (2013). Statistical analyses of monozygotic and dizygotic twinning rates. *Twin Research and Human Genetics, 16*(6), 1107–1111.

Felson, R. B., & Kreager, D. A. (2015). Group differences in delinquency: What is there to explain? *Race and Justice, 5*(1), 58–87.

Fenzel, L. M. (2000). Prospective study of changes in global self-worth and strain during the transition to middle school. *Journal of Early Adolescence, 20*(1), 93–116.

Ferdinand, R. F., Bongersa, I. L., van der Ende, J., van Gastela, W., Tick, N., Utens, E., et al. (2006). Distinctions between separation anxiety and social anxiety in children and adolescents. *Behaviour Research and Therapy, 44*, 1523–1535.

Fergusson, A. (2007). What successful teachers do in inclusive classrooms: Research-based teaching strategies that help special learners succeed. *European Journal of Special Needs Education, 22*(1), 108–110.

Fergusson, D. M., McLeod, G. F. H., & Horwood, L. J. (2014). Breast feeding, infant growth, and body mass index at 30 and 35 years. *Paediatric and Perinatal Epidemiology, 28*(6), 545-552.

Fernandes, A., Campbell-Yeo, M., & Johnston, C. C. (2011). Procedural pain management for neonates using nonpharmacological strategies: Part 1: Sensorial interventions. *Advances in Neonatal Care, 11*(4), 235–241.

Féron, J., Gentaz, E., & Streri, A. (2006). Evidence of amodal representation of small numbers across visuo-tactile modalities in 5-month-old infants. *Cognitive Development, 21*(2), 81–92.

Ferre, C. L., Babik, I., & Michel, G. F. (2010). Development of infant prehension handedness: A longitudinal analysis during the 6- to 14-month age period. *Infant Behavior and Development, 33*(4), 492–502.

Ferrer, E., O'Hare, E. D., & Bunge, S. A. (2009). Fluid reasoning and the developing brain. *Frontiers in Neuroscience, 3*(1), 46–51.

Field, A. E., et al. (2014). Prospective associations of concerns about physique and the development of obesity, binge drinking, and drug use among adolescent boys and adult young men. *JAMA Pediatrics, 168*(1), 34–39.

Field, T., Orozco, A., Corbin, J., Dominguez, G., & Frost, P. (2014). Face-to-face interaction behaviors of preadolescent same-sex and opposite-sex friends and acquaintances. *Journal of Child and Adolescent Behavior*, DOI:10.4172/jcalb.1000134.

Fillo, J., Simpson, J. A., Rholes, W. S., & Kohn, J. L. (2015). Dads doing diapers: Individual and relational outcomes associated with the division of childcare across the transition to parenthood. *Journal of Personality and Social Psychology, 108*(2), 298–316.

Finkelhor, D., Turner, H. A., Shattuck, A., & Hamby, S. L. (2013). Violence, crime, and abuse exposure in a national sample of children and youth: An update. *JAMA Pediatrics, 167*(7), 614–621.

Finkelhor, D., Vanderminden, J., Turner, H., Hamby, S., & Shattuck, A. (2014). Child maltreatment rates assessed in a national household survey of caregivers and youth. *Child Abuse & Neglect, 38*(9), 1421–1435.

Finn, E. S., et al. (2014). Disruption of functional networks in dyslexia: A whole-brain, data-driven analysis of connectivity. *Biological Psychiatry, 76*(5), 397–404.

Fisher, B., Rose, N. C., & Carey, J. C. (2008). Principles and practice of teratology for the obstetrician. *Clinical Obstetrics and Gynecology, 51*(1), 106–118.

Fisher, L. D., Gushue, G. V., & Cerrone, M. T. (2011). The influences of career support and sexual identity on sexual minority women's career aspirations. *Career Development Quarterly, 59*(5), 441–454.

Fitzgerald, H. E., et al. (1991). The organization of lateralized behavior during infancy. In H. E. Fitzgerald, B. M. Lester & M. W. Yogman (Eds.), *Theory and research in behavioral pediatrics.* New York: Plenum.

Fivush, R., & Hammond, N. R. (1990). Autobiographical memory across the preschool years: Toward reconceptualizing childhood amnesia. In R. Fivush & J. A. Hudson (Eds.), *Knowing and remembering in young children.* Cambridge: Cambridge University Press.

Flavell, J. H. (1993). Young children's understanding of thinking and consciousness. *Current Directions in Psychological Science, 2*, 40–43.

Flavell, J. H., Miller, P. H., & Miller, S. A. (2002). *Cognitive development* (4th ed.). Upper Saddle River, NJ: Prentice Hall.

Fleisher, D. R. (2014). Management of functional gastrointestinal disorders in children: Biopsychosocial concepts for clinical practice, New York: Springer Science+Business Media. DOI:10.1007/978-1-4939-1089-2_7.

Fletcher, K. L. (2011). Neuropsychology of early childhood (3 to 5 years old). In A. S. Davis (Ed.). *Handbook of pediatric neuropsychology.* New York: Springer.

Fletcher, R., et al. (2008). The evaluation of tailored and web-based information for new fathers. *Child: Care, Health & Development, 34*(4), 439–446.

Florsheim, P. (Ed.). (2003). *Adolescent romantic relations and sexual behavior: Theory, research, and practical implications.* Mahwah, NJ: Erlbaum.

Flouri, E., & Buchanan, A. (2003). The role of father involvement and mother involvement in adolescents' psychological well-being. *British Journal of Social Work, 33*(3), 399–406.

Fogassi, L., & Rizzolatti, G. (2013). The mirror mechanism as neurophysiological basis for action and intention understanding. In A. Suarez, & P. Adams (Eds.). *Is science compatible with free will?* (pp. 117–134). New York: Springer.

Foley, G. M. (2006). Self and social–emotional development in infancy: A descriptive synthesis. In G. M. Foley & J. D. Hochman (Eds.), *Mental health in early intervention: Achieving unity in principles and practice* (pp. 139–173). Baltimore, MD: Paul H. Brookes.

Food and Drug Administration. (2004, July 20). *Decreasing the chance of birth defects.* Available at http://www.fda.gov/fdac/features/996_bd.html.

Foster-Clark, F. S., & Blyth, D. A. (1991). Peer relations and influences. In R. M. Lerner, A. C. Petersen & J. Brooks-Gunn (Eds.), *Encyclopedia of adolescence.* New York: Garland.

Fourchard, F., & Courtinat-Camps, A. (2013). L'estime de soi globale et physique à l'adolescence. *Neuropsychiatrie de l'Enfance et de l'Adolescence, 61*(6), 333-339.

Fournier, K. A., Hass, C. J., Naik, S. K., Lodha, N., & Cauraugh, J. H. (2010). Motor coordination in autism spectrum disorder: A synthesis and meta-analysis. *Journal of Autism and Developmental Disorders, 40*(10), 1227–1240.

Fox, A., Harrop, C., Trower, P., & Leung, N. (2009). A consideration of developmental egocentrism in anorexia nervosa. *Eating Behaviors, 10*(1), 10–15.

Franchak, J. M., & Adolph, K. E. (2012). What infants know and what they do: Perceiving possibilities for walking through openings. *Developmental Psychology, 48*(5), 1254–1261.

Frazier, T. W., Georgiades, S., Bishop, S. L., & Hardan, A. Y. (2014). Behavioral and cognitive characteristics of females and males with autism in the Simons Simplex Collection. *Journal of the American Academy of Child & Adolescent Psychiatry, 53*(3), 329–340.

Freeman, M. S., Spence, M. J., and Oliphant, C. M. (1993, June). *Newborns prefer their mothers' low-pass filtered voices over other female filtered voices.* Paper presented at the meeting of the American Psychological Society, Chicago.

Frenkel, T. I., & Fox, N. A. (2015). Caregiver socialization factors influencing socioemotional development in infancy and childhood: A neuroscience perspective. In J. E. Grusec & P. D. Hastings (Eds.). *Handbook of socialization: Theory and research* (pp. 419–447). New York: Guilford.

Frethelm, A., et al. (2013). The impact of an intervention program employing a hands-on technique to reduce the incidence of anal sphincter tears: Interrupted time-series analysis. *British Medical Journal Open, 3*(10), DOI:10.1136/bmjopen-2013-003355.

Freud, A. (1969). Adolescence as a developmental disturbance. In G. Caplan & S. Lebovici (Eds.), *Adolescence, Psychosocial perspectives* (pp. 5–10). New York: Basic Books.

Freud, S. (1964 [1933]). *The standard edition of the complete psychological works of Sigmund Freud.* James Strachy (trans.). Oxford: Macmillan.

Frieden, T. R. (2013, April 1). Cited in Schwartz, A., & Cohen, S. (2013, March 31). ADHD seen in 11% of U.S. children as diagnoses rise. *The New York Times*, p. A1.

Friedman, L. A., & Rapoport, J. L. (2015). Brain development in ADHD. *Current Opinion in Neurobiology, 30*, 106–111.

Friedrich, A., Flunger, B., Nagengast, B., Jonkmann, K., & Trautwein, U. (2015). Pygmalion effects in the classroom: Teacher expectancy effects on students' math achievement. *Contemporary Educational Psychology, 41*, 1–12.

Frieze, I. H., & Li, M. Y. (2010). Gender, aggression, and prosocial behavior. *Handbook of Gender Research in Psychology, 4*, 311–335.

Frith, U. (2001). What framework should we use for understanding developmental disorders? *Developmental Neuropsychology, 20*(2), 555–563.

Frostad, P., & Pijl, S. J. (2007). Does being friendly help in making friends? The relation between the social position and social skills of pupils with special needs in mainstream education. *European Journal of Special Needs Education, 22*(1), 15–30.

Frühmesser, A., & Kotzot, D. (2011). Chromosomal variants in Klinefelter syndrome. *Sexual Development, 5*(3), 109–123.

Fuhs, M. W., & Day, J. D. (2011). Verbal ability and executive functioning development in preschoolers at Head Start. *Developmental Psychology, 47*(2), 404–416.

Fuligni, A. J., & Eccles, J. S. (1993). Perceived parent–child relationships and early adolescents' orientation toward peers. *Developmental Psychology, 29*, 622–632.

Fuller, T. (2012). Is scientific theory change similar to early cognitive development? Gopnik on science and childhood. *Philosophical Psychology, 16*(1), 109–128.

Fulton, A. B., et al. (2014). Normal and abnormal visual development. In C. S. Hoyt, & D. Taylor (Eds.). *Pediatric ophthalmology and strabismus* (4th ed.) (pp. 23–30). New York: Elsevier Saunders.

Funatogawa, K., Funatogawa, T., & Yano, E. (2008). Do overweight children necessarily make overweight adults? Repeated cross sectional annual nationwide survey of Japanese girls and women over nearly six decades. *British Medical Journal, 337*, a802. doi:10.1136/bmj.a802.

Furman, W., & Buhrmester, D. (1992). Age and sex differences in perceptions of networks of personal relationships. *Child Development, 63*, 103–115.

Furman, W., Rahe, D., & Hartup, W. W. (1979). Social rehabilitation of low-interactive preschool children by peer intervention. *Child Development, 50*, 915–922.

Furstenberg, F. F., & Kiernan, K. E. (2001). Delayed parental divorce: How much do children benefit? *Journal of Marriage and the Family, 63*(2), 446–457.

Galdi, S., Cadinu, M., & Tomasetto, C. (2014). The root of stereotype threat: When automatic associations disrupt girls' math performance. *Child Development, 85*(1), 250–263.

Gallese, V., Fadiga, L., Fogassi, L., & Rizzolatti, G. (1996). Action recognition in the premotor cortex. *Brain, 119*(2), 593–609.

Ganong, L. H., & Coleman, M. (2003). Studying stepfamilies. In L. H. Ganong & M. Coleman (Eds.), *Stepfamily relationships: Development, dynamics, and interventions* (pp. 1–24). New York: Springer.

Garber, H. L. (1988). *The Milwaukee Project: Preventing mental retardation in children at risk.* Washington, DC: American Association on Mental Retardation.

Garcia, P. R. J. M., et al. (2015). Career optimism: The roles of contextual support and career decision-making self-efficacy. *Journal of Vocational Behavior, 88*, 10–18.

Garcia-Falgueras, A., & Swaab, D. F. (2010). Sex hormones and the brain: An essential alliance for sexual identity and sexual orientation. In S. Loche et al. (Eds.), Pediatric neuroendocrinology (Vol. 17, pp. 22–35). Basel, Switzerland: Karger.

Gardner, H. (1983). *Frames of mind: The theory of multiple intelligences.* New York: Basic Books.

Garland, A. F., et al. (2015). Does patient race/ethnicity influence physician decision-making for diagnosis and treatment of childhood disruptive behavior problems? *Journal of Racial and Ethnic Health Disparities, 2*(2), 219–230.

Garnefski, N., Kraaij, V., & Spinhoven, P. (2001). De relatie tussen cognitieve copingstrategieen en symptomen van depressie, angst en suiecidaliteit. *Gedrag and Gezondheid: Tijdschrift voor Psychologie and Gezondheid, 29*(3), 148–158.

Garner, J., & Thomas, M. (2011). The role and contribution of nurture groups in secondary schools: Perceptions of children, parents, and staff. *Emotional and Behavioural Difficulties, 16*(2), 207–224.

Gartstein, M. A., Slobodskaya, H. R., & Kinsht, I. A. (2003). Cross-cultural differences in temperament in the first year of life: United States of America (U.S.) and Russia. *International Journal of Behavioral Development, 27*(4), 316–328.

Gaser, C., & Schlaug, G. (2003). Brain structures differ between musicians and nonmusicians. *Journal of Neuroscience, 23*(27), 9240–9245.

Gathercole, S. E., & Alloway, T. P. (2008). *Working memory and learning.* Thousand Oaks, CA: Sage Publications.

Gauthier, J. L., et al. (2009). Uniform signal redundancy of parasol and midget ganglion cells in primate retina. *Journal of Neuroscience, 29*(14), 4675–4680.

Gauthier, K., Genesee, F., Dubois, M. E., & Kasparian, K. (2011). Communication patterns between internationally adopted children and their mothers: A special case of early second language learning. *Child Development, 82*(3), 887–901.

Gauvain, M., Perez, S. M., & Beebe, H. (2013). Authoritative parenting and parental suppor for children's cognitive development. In R. E. Larzelere, A. S. Morris, & A. W. Harrist (Eds.). *Authoritative parenting: Synthesizing nurturance and discipline for optimal child development* (pp. 211–233). Washington, DC: American Psychological Association.

Gavin, L., et al. (2009, July 17). Sexual and reproductive health of persons aged 10–24 years—United States, 2002–2007. *Morbidity and Mortality Weekly Report, 58*(27), 1–58. Available at http://www.cdc.gov/mmwr/preview/mmwrhtml/ss5806a1.htm.

Gee, R. E., Wood, S. F., & Schubert, K. G. (2014). Women's health, pregnancy, and the U.S. Food and Drug Administration. *Obstetrics & Gynecology, 123*(1), 161–165.

Gelman, S. (2010). Modules, theories, or islands of expertise? Domain specificity in socialization. *Child Development, 81*(3), 715–719.

Genital HPV Infection—Fact Sheet. (2011). Centers for Disease Control and Prevention. Available at http://www.cdc.gov/std/HPV/STDFact-HPV.htm.

George, M. R. W., Koss, K. J., McCoy, K. P., Cummings, E. M., & Davies, P. T. (2010). *Advances in School Mental Health Promotion, 3*(4), 51–62.

Georgiades, S., et al. (2010). Phenotypic overlap between core diagnostic features and emotional/behavioral problems in preschool children with autism spectrum disorder. *Journal of Autism and Developmental Disorders, 41*(10), 1321–1329.

Geraghty, K., Waxman, S. R., & Gelman, S. A. (2014). Learning words from pictures: 15- and 17-month-old infants appreciate the referential and symbolic links among words, pictures, and objects. *Cognitive Development, 32*, 1–11.

Gervain, J., Berent, I., & Werker, J. F. (2012). Binding at birth: The newborn brain detects identity relations and sequential position in speech. *Journal of Cognitive Neuroscience, 24*(3), 564–574.

Gesell, A. (1928). *Infancy and human growth.* New York: Macmillan.

Gesell, A. (1929). Maturation and infant behavior patterns. *Psychological Review, 36*, 307–319.

Getzels, J. W., & Jackson, P. W. (1962). *Creativity and intelligence.* New York: Wiley.

Gibbs, J. C. (2015). *Moral development and reality,* 3rd ed. New York: Oxford.

Gibson, E. J. (1969). *Principles of perceptual learning and development.* New York: Appleton-Century-Crofts.

Gibson, E. J. (1991). *An odyssey in learning and perception.* Cambridge, MA: MIT Press.

Gibson, E. J., & Walk, R. D. (1960). The visual cliff. *Scientific American, 202,* 64–71.

Gidding, S. S., et al. (2006). Dietary recommendations for children and adolescents: A guide for practitioners. *Pediatrics, 117*(2), 544–559.

Giedd, J. N., et al. (2015). Child Psychiatry Branch of the National Institute of Mental Health Longitudinal Structural Magnetic Resonance Imaging Study of Human Brain Development. *Neuropsychopharmacology Reviews, 40,* 43–49.

Gignac, G. E., & Weiss, L. G. (2015). Digit span is (mostly) related linearly to general intelligence: Every extra bit of span counts. *Psychological Assessment,* http://dx.doi.org/10.1037/pas0000105.

Gilbert-Barness, E., Spicer, D. E., & Steffensen, T. S. (2014). Congenital abnormalities. *Handbook of Pediatric Autopsy Pathology* (pp. 197–227). New York: Springer.

Giles, A., & Rovee-Collier, C. (2011). Infant long-term memory for associations formed during mere exposure. *Infant Behavior and Development, 34*(2), 327–338.

Gilligan, C. (1977). In a different voice: Women's conceptions of self and morality. *Harvard Educational Review, 47,* 481–517.

Gilligan, C. (1982). *In a different voice.* Cambridge, MA: Harvard University Press.

Gilligan, C. (2011). *Resistance refined, patriarchy defined: Carol Gilligan reflects on her journey from difference to resistance.* Malden, MA: Polity Press.

Gillooly, J. B. (2004). Making menarche positive and powerful for both mother and daughter. *Women & Therapy, 27*(3–4), 23–35.

Gilmore, K. (2008). Birth mother, adoptive mother, dying mother, dead mother. In E. L. Jurist et al. (Eds.), *Mind to mind: Infant research, neuroscience, and psychoanalysis* (pp. 373–397). New York: Other Press.

Gini, G., Pozzoli, T., & Hymel, S. (2014). Moral disengagement among children and youth: A meta-analytic review of links to aggressive behavior. *Aggressive Behavior, 40*(1), 56–68.

Giussani, D. A. (2011). The vulnerable developing brain. *Proceedings of the National Academy of Sciences, 108*(7), 2641–2642.

Glasberg, R., & Aboud, F. (1982). Keeping one's distance from sadness: Children's self-reports of emotional experience. *Developmental Psychology, 18,* 287–293.

Gleason, K. A., Jensen-Campbell, L. A., & Ickes, W. (2009). The role of empathic accuracy in adolescents' peer relations and adjustment. *Personality and Social Psychology Bulletin, 35*(8), 997–1011.

Gleason, T. R. (2013). Imaginary relationships. In M. Taylor (Ed.). *The Oxford handbook on the development of imagination* (pp. 251–271). New York: Oxford University Press.

Gleason, T. R., Gower, A. L., Hohmann, L. M., & Gleason, T. C. (2005). Temperament and friendship in preschool-aged children. *International Journal of Behavioral Development, 29*(4), 336–344.

Gleason, T. R., & Hohmann, L. M. (2006). Concepts of real and imaginary friendships in early childhood. *Social Development, 15*(1), 128–144.

Goble, P., Martin, C. L., Hanish, L. D., & Fabes, R. A. (2012). Children's gender-typed activity choices across preschool social contexts. *Sex Roles, 67*(7–8), 435–451.

Goessaert, A., et al. (2015). Nocturnal enuresis and nocturia, differences and similarities—lessons to learn? *Acta Clinica Belgica, 70*(2), 81–86.

Goldberg, W. A., & Keller, M. A. (2007). Co-sleeping during infancy and early childhood: Key findings and future directions. *Infant and Child Development, 16*(4), 457–469.

Goldberg, W. A., Kelly, E., Matthews, N. L., Kang, H., Weilin, L., & Sumaroka, M. (2012). The more things change, the more they stay the same: Gender, culture, and college students' views about work and family. *Journal of Social Issues, 68*(4), 814–837.

Goldberg, W. A., Prause, J., Lucas-Thompson, R., & Himsel, A. (2008). Maternal employment and children's achievement in context: A meta-analysis of four decades of research. *Psychological Bulletin, 134*(1), 77–108.

Golden, C., & McHugh, M. (2015). Sandra Lipsitz Bem (1944–2014). *American Psychologist, 70*(3), 280.

Goldschmidt, L., Day, N. L., & Richardson, G. A. (2000). Effects of prenatal marijuana exposure on child behavior problems at age 10. *Neurotoxicology and Teratology, 22*(3), 325–336.

Goldstein, S., & Brooks, R. B. (2005). *Handbook of resilience in children.* New York: Kluwer Academic/Plenum.

Goleman, D. (2006). *Social intelligence.* New York: Bantam Books.

Gomez, A. M. (2011). Testing the cycle of violence hypotheses: Child abuse and adolescent dating violence as predictors of intimate partner violence in young adulthood. *Youth & Society, 43*(1), 171–192.

Gonzaga-Jauregui, C., Lupski, J. R., & Gibbs, R. A. (2012). Human genome sequencing in health and disease. *Annual Review of Medicine, 63,* 35–61.

Gonzalez, V. (2005). Cultural, linguistic, and socioeconomic factors influencing monolingual and bilingual children's cognitive development. In V. Gonzalez & J. Tinajero (Eds.), *Review of research and practice,* Vol. 3 (pp. 67–104). Mahwah, NJ: Erlbaum.

Goodman, G. S., & Clarke-Stewart, A. (1991). Suggestibility in children's testimony: Implications for sexual abuse investigations. In J. Doris (Ed.), *The suggestibility of children's recollections.* Washington, DC: American Psychological Association.

Goodman, G. S., Pipe, M-E., & McWilliams, K. (2011). Children's eyewitness testimony: Methodological issues. In B. Rosenfeld & S. D. Penrod (Eds.), *Research methods in forensic psychology* (pp. 257–282). Hoboken, NJ: Wiley.

Gopnik, A., & Slaughter, V. (1991). Young children's understanding of changes in their mental states. *Child Development, 62,* 98–110.

Gordon, J., King, N. J., Gullone, E., Muris, P., & Ollendick, T. H. (2007). Treatment of children's nighttime fears: The need for a modern randomised controlled trial. *Clinical Psychology Review, 27*(1), 98–113.

Gorin, S., Hooper, C., Dyson, C., & Cabral, C. (2008). Ethical challenges in conducting research with hard-to-reach families. *Child Abuse Review, 17*(4), 275–287.

Gorini, F., Muratori, F., & Morales, M. A. (2014). The role of heavy metal pollution in neurobehavioral disorders: A focus on autism. *Review Journal of Autism and Developmental Disorders, 1*(4), 354–372.

Goskan, S., et al. (2015). fMRI reveals neural activity overlap between adult and infant pain. eLife, doi:10.7554/eLife.06356.

Gottlieb, B. H., Still, E., & Newby-Clark, I. R. (2007). Types and precipitants of growth and decline in emerging adulthood. *Journal of Adolescent Research, 22*(2), 132–155.

Gottfried, G. M., Hickling, A. K., Totten, L. R., Mkroyan, A., & Reisz, A. (2003). To be or not to be a galaprock: Preschoolers' intuitions about the importance of knowledge and action for pretending. *British Journal of Developmental Psychology, 21*(3), 397–414.

Gower, A. L., Lingras, K. A., Mathieson, L. C., Kawabata, Y., & Crick, N. R. (2014). The role of preschool relational and physical rejection in the transition to kindergarten: Links with social-psychological adjustment. *Early Education and Development, 25*(5), 619–640.

Gowers, S. G., & Bryan, C. (2005). Families of children with a mental disorder. In N. Sartorius et al. (Eds.), *Families and mental disorders: From burden to empowerment* (pp. 127–159). Hoboken, NJ: Wiley.

Graber, J. A., Seeley, J. R., Brooks-Gunn, J., & Lewinsohn, P. M. (2004). Is pubertal timing associated with psychopathology in young adulthood? *Journal of the American Academy of Child and Adolescent Psychiatry, 43*(6), 718–726.

Granot, D., & Mayseless, O. (2001). Attachment security and adjustment to school in middle childhood. *International Journal of Behavioral Development, 25*(6), 530–541.

Greeff, A. P., & Van Der Merwe, S. (2004). Variables associated with resilience in divorced families. *Social Indicators Research, 68*(1), 59–75.

Green, M. A., et al. (2009). Eating disorder behaviors and depression: A minimal relationship beyond social comparison, self-esteem, and body dissatisfaction. *Journal of Clinical Psychology, 65*(9), 989–999.

Green, R. (1978). Sexual identity of 37 children raised by homosexual or transsexual parents. *American Journal of Psychiatry, 135,* 692–697.

Green, R., Mandel, J. B., Hotvedt, M. E., Gray, J., & Smith, L. (1986). Lesbian mothers and their children: A comparison with solo parent heterosexual mothers and their children. *Archives of Sexual Behavior, 15*, 167–184.

Greene, F. J., Han, L., & Marlow, S. (2013). Like mother, like daughter? Analyzing maternal influences upon women's entrepreneurial propensity. *Entrepreneurship: Theory and Practice, 37*(4), 687–711.

Greene, R. W., & Ablon, J. S. (2001). What does the MTA study tell us about effective psychosocial treatment for ADHD? *Journal of Clinical Child Psychology, 30*(1), 114–121.

Greenwood, J. D. (2015). Intelligence defined: Wundt, James, Cattell, Thorndike, Goddard, and Yerkes. In S. Goldstein, D. Princiotta, & J. A. Naglieri (Eds.). *Handbook of intelligence: Evolutionary theory, historical perspective, and current concepts* (pp. 123–135). New York: Springer Science+Business Media.

Gregory, A. M., Light-Häusermann, J. H., Rijsdijk, F., & Eley, T. C. (2009). Behavioral genetic analyses of prosocial behavior in adolescents. *Developmental Science, 12*(1), 165–174.

Griffin, I. J., Lee, H. C., Profit, J., & Tancedi, D. J. (2015). The smallest of the small: Short-term outcomes of profoundly growth restricted and profoundly low birth weight preterm infants. *Journal of Perinatology, 35*, 503–510.

Grigorenko, E. L. (2009). Speaking genes or genes for speaking? Deciphering the genetics of speech and language. *Journal of Child Psychology and Psychiatry, 50*(1–2), 116–125.

Groenman, A. P., et al. (2015). Dopamine and serotonin genetic risk scores predicting substance and nicotine use in attention deficit/hyperactivity disorder. *Addiction Biology*, DOI:10.1111/adb.12230.

Grolnick, W. S., Price, C. E., Beiswenger, K. L., & Sauck, C. C. (2007). Evaluative pressure in mothers. *Developmental Psychology, 43*(4), 991–1002.

Groothuis, T. G. G., & Trillmich, F. (2011). Unfolding personalities: The importance of studying ontogeny. *Developmental Psychobiology, 53*(6), 641–655.

Grön, G., Wunderlich, A. P., Spitzer, M., Tomczak, R., & Riepe, M. W. (2000). Brain activation during human navigation: Gender-different neural networks as substrate of performance. *Nature Neuroscience, 3*(4), 404–408.

Gross, L. (2006). Evolution of neonatal imitation. *PLoS Biol, 4*(9): e311. DOI:10.1371journal.pbio.0040311.

Grossmann, K., et al. (2002). The uniqueness of the child–father attachment relationship: Fathers' sensitive and challenging play as a pivotal variable in a 16-year longitudinal study. *Social Development, 11*(3), 307–331.

Grusec, J. E. (1991). Socializing concern for others in the home. *Developmental Psychology, 27*, 338–342.

Grusec, J. E. (2006). The development of moral behavior and conscience from a socialization perspective. In M. Killen & J. G. Smetana (Eds.), *Handbook of moral development* (pp. 243–265). Mahwah, NJ: Erlbaum.

Grusec, J. E. (2011). Socialization processes in the family: Social and emotional development. *Annual Review of Psychology, 62*, 243–269.

Grusec, J. E. (2014). Parent–child conversations from the perspective of socialization theory. In C. Wainryb, & H. E. Recchie (Eds.). *Talking about right and wrong*. Cambridge, UK: Cambridge University Press.

Grusec, J. E. (2015). Family relationships and development. In R. A. Scott, & S. M. Kosslyn (Eds.). *Emerging Trends in the Social and Behavioral Sciences*, DOI:10.1002/9781118900772.etrds0130. Hoboken, NJ: Wiley.

Grusec, J. E., & Davidov, M. (2015). Analyzing socialization from a domain-specific perspective. In J. E. Grusec, & P. D. Hastings (Eds.). *Handbook of socialization: Theory and research* (pp. 158–181). New York: Guilford.

Grusec, J. E., & Hastings, P. D. (2015). *Handbook of socialization: Theory and research*. New York: Guilford.

Grych, J. H. (2005). Interparental conflict as a risk factor for child maladjustment: Implications for the development of prevention programs. *Family Court Review, 43*(1), 97–108.

Gudmundsson, G. (2010). Infantile colic is a pain syndrome. *Medical Hypotheses, 75*(6), 528–529.

Guerdjikova, A. I., McElroy, S. L., Kotwal, R., Stanford, K., & Keck, P. E., Jr. (2007). Psychiatric and metabolic characteristics of childhood versus adult-onset obesity in patients seeking weight management. *Eating Behaviors, 8*(2), 266–276.

Guerin, D. W., Gottfried, A. W., & Thomas, C. W. (1997). Difficult temperament and behaviour problems: A longitudinal study from 1.5 to 12 years. *International Journal of Behavioral Development, 21*(1), 71–90.

Guerrero, M. C. M., & Villamil, O. S. (2000). Activating the ZPD: Mutual scaffolding in L2 peer revision. *Modern Language Journal, 84*(1), 51–68.

Guerrini, I., Thomson, A. D., & Gurling, H. D. (2007). The importance of alcohol misuse, malnutrition and genetic susceptibility on brain growth and plasticity. *Neuroscience & Biobehavioral Reviews, 31*(2), 212–220.

Guerrini, R., & Dobyns, W. B. (2014). Malformations of cortical development. *The Lancet: Neurology, 13*(7), 710–726.

Gushue, G. V., & Whitson, M. L. (2006). The relationship of ethnic identity and gender role attitudes to the development of career choice goals among black and Latina girls. *Journal of Counseling Psychology, 53*(3), 379–385.

Guttmacher Institute. (2007, June 8). Available at http://www.guttmacher.org.

Guttmacher Institute. (2012). Facts on American teens' sources of information about sex. Retrieved from http://www.guttmacher.org/pubs/FB-Teen-Sex-Ed.html. Accessed May 6, 2012.

Guttmacher Institute. (2013, June). In brief: fact sheet: Facts on American teens' sexual and reproductive health. Retrieved from http://www.guttmacher.org/pubs/FB-ATSRH.html. Accessed February 27, 2014.

Guzzetti, B. J. (2010). Feminist perspectives on the new literacies. In E. A. Baker & D. J. Leu (Eds.), *The new literacies* (pp. 242–264). New York: Guilford.

Habersaat, S., et al. (2014). Posttraumatic stress symptoms and cortisol regulation in mothers of very preterm infants. *Stress & Health, 30*(2), 131–141.

Hackman, D. A., Gallop, R., Evans, G. W., & Farah, M. J. (2015). Socioeconomic status and executive function: Developmental trajectories and mediation. *Developmental Science, 18*(5), 686–702.

Haden, C. A., Ornstein, P. A., Eckerman, C. O., & Didow, S. M. (2001). Mother–child conversational interactions as events unfold: Linkages to subsequent remembering. *Child Development, 72*(4), 1016–1031.

Hagenauer, M. H., Perryman, J. I., Lee, T. M., & Carskadon, M. A. (2009). Adolescent changes in the homeostatic and circadian regulation of sleep. *Developmental Neuroscience, 31*(4), 276–284.

Hahn, R. A., et al. (2015). Programs to increase high school completion: A community guide systematic health equity review. *American Journal of Preventive Medicine, 48*(5), 599–608.

Haier, R. J. (2011). Biological basis of intelligence. In R. J. Sternberg & S. J. Kaufman (Eds.), *The Cambridge handbook of intelligence* (pp. 351–370). New York: Cambridge University Press.

Haith, M. M. (1979). Visual cognition in early infancy. In R. B. Kearsly & I. E. Sigel (Eds.), *Infants at risk: Assessment of cognitive functioning*. Hillsdale, NJ: Erlbaum.

Haith, M. M. (1990). Progress in the understanding of sensory and perceptual processes in early infancy. *Merrill-Palmer Quarterly, 36*, 1–26.

Haith, M. M. (1998). Who put the cog in infant cognition? Is rich interpretation too costly? *Infant Behavior and Development, 21*(2), 167–179.

Halgin, R. P., & Whitbourne, S. K. (1993). *Abnormal psychology*. Fort Worth, TX: Harcourt Brace Jovanovich.

Halim, M. L., Ruble, D. N., Tamis-LeMonda, C. S., & Shrout, P. E. (2013). Rigidity in gender-typed behaviors in early childhood. *Child Development, 84*(4), 1269–1284.

Halim, M. L., Ruble, D. N., Tamis-LeMonda, C. S., Zosuls, K. M., Lurye, L. E., & Greulich, F. K. (2014). *Developmental Psychology, 50*(4), 1091–1101.

Hall, G. S. (1904). *Adolescence: Its psychology and its relations to physiology, anthropology, sociology, sex, crime, religion, and education*, Vol. I. New York: D. Appleton & Company.

Hall, J. (2012). Gender issues in mathematics. *Journal of Teaching and Learning, 8*(1), 59–72.

Hall, J. A. (2011). Sex differences in friendship expectations: A meta-analysis. *Journal of Social and Personal Relationships, 28*(6), 723–747.

Halmi, K. A., et al. (2014). Perfectionism in anorexia nervosa: Variation by clinical subtype, obsessionality, and pathological eating behavior. *The American Journal of Psychiatry, 157*(11), 1799–1805.

Halpern, D. (2012). *Sex differences in cognitive abilities* (4th ed.). New York: Psychology Press.

Halpern, R. (2005). Book review: Examining adolescent leisure time across cultures: New Directions for child and adolescent development, No. 99. *Journal of Adolescent Research*, 20(4), 524–525.

Hamm, J. V. (2000). Do birds of a feather flock together? The variable bases for African American, Asian American, and European American adolescents' selection of similar friends. *Developmental Psychology*, 36(2), 209–219.

Hammen, C. (2003). Social stress and women's risk for recurrent depression. *Archives of Women's Mental Health*, 6(1), 9–13.

Hamilton, B. E., & Ventura, S. J. (2012). *Birth rates for U.S. teenagers reach historic lows for all age and ethnic groups*. NCHS data brief no. 89. Hyattsville, MD. National Center for Health Statistics.

Han, W., Waldfogel, J., & Brooks-Gunn, J. (2001). The effects of early maternal employment on later cognitive and behavioral outcomes. *Journal of Marriage and the Family*, 63(2), 336–354.

Hane, A. A., et al. (2015). Family nurture intervention improves the quality of maternal caregiving in the NICU: Evidence from a randomized controlled trial. *Journal of Developmental and Behavioral Pediatrics*, 36(3), 188–196.

Hangal, S., & Aminabhavi, V. A. (2007). Self-concept, emotional maturity, and achievement motivation of the adolescent children of employed mothers and homemakers. *Journal of the Indian Academy of Applied Psychology*, 33(1), 103–110.

Hankin, B. L. (2015). Depression from childhood through adolescence: Risk mechanisms across multiple systems and levels of analysis. *Current Opinion in Psychology*, 4, 13–20.

Hannon, P., Bowen, D. J., Moinpour, C. M., & McLerran, D. F. (2003). Correlations in perceived food use between the family food preparer and their spouses and children. *Appetite*, 40(1), 77–83.

Hannon, P., Willis, S. K., Bishop-Townsend, V., Martinez, I. M., & Scrimshaw, S. C. (2000). African-American and Latina adolescent mothers' infant feeding decisions and breastfeeding practices: A qualitative study. *Journal of Adolescent Health*, 26(6), 399–407.

Harel, Z. (2008). Dysmenorrhea in adolescents. *Annals of the New York Academy of Sciences*, 1135, 185–195.

Harkonen, J. (2014). Birth order effects on educational attainment and educational transitions in West Germany. *European Sociological Review*, 30(2), 166–179.

Harlow, H. F., & Harlow, M. K. (1966). Learning to love. *American Scientist*, 54, 244–272.

Harlow, H. F., Harlow, M. K., & Suomi, S. J. (1971). From thought to therapy: Lessons from a primate laboratory. *American Scientist*, 59, 538–549.

Harlow, H. F., & Zimmermann, R. R. (1959). Affectional responses in the infant monkey. *Science*, 130(3373), 421–432.

Harris, S. R., Megens, A. M., Backman, C. L., & Hayes, V. E. (2005). Stability of the Bayley II Scales of Infant Development in a sample of low-risk and high-risk infants. *Developmental Medicine & Child Neurology*, 47(12), 820–823.

Harrison, K. (2013). Media, body image, and eating disorders. In D. Lemish (Ed.). *The Routledge international handbook of children, adolescents, and media* (pp. 224–231). New York: Routledge.

Hart, D., Burock, D., London, B., & Atkins, R. (2003). Prosocial tendencies, antisocial behavior, and moral development. In A. Slater & G. Bremner (Eds.), *An introduction to developmental psychology* (pp. 334–356). Malden, MA: Blackwell.

Hartocollis, A. (2015, February 10). Doulas, a growing force in maternity culture, are organizing for more recognition. *The New York Times*. Retrived from http://www.nytimes.com.

Harter, S. (1990). Self and identity development. In S. S. Feldman & G. R. Elliott (Eds.), *At the threshold: The developing adolescent*. Cambridge, MA: Harvard University Press.

Harter, S. (2006). The Self. In K. A. Renninger, I. E. Sigel, W. Damon & R. M. Lerner (Eds.), Handbook of child psychology (6th ed.), Vol. 4, *Child psychology in practice* (pp. 505–570). Hoboken, NJ: Wiley.

Harter, S. (2012). *The construction of the self: Developmental and sociocultural foundations* (2nd ed). New York: Guilford.

Harter, S., & Monsour, A. (1992). Developmental analysis of conflict caused by opposing attributes in the adolescent self-portrait. *Developmental Psychology*, 28, 251–260.

Harter, S., & Whitesell, N. R. (2003). Beyond the debate: Why some adolescents report stable self-worth over time and situation, whereas others report changes in self-worth. *Journal of Personality*, 71(6), 1027–1058.

Hartung, P. J., Fouad, N. A., Leong, F. T. L., & Hardin, E. E. (2010). Individualism–collectivism. *Journal of Career Assessment*, 18(1), 34–45.

Hartup, W. W. (1993). Adolescents and their friends. In B. Laursen (Ed.), *Close friendships in adolescence* (pp. 3–22). San Francisco: Jossey-Bass.

Harvey, E. (1999). Short-term and long-term effects of early parental employment on children of the National Longitudinal Survey of Youth. *Developmental Psychology*, 35(2), 445–459.

Harvey, J. H., & Fine, M. A. (2011). *Children of divorce*. New York: Routledge, Taylor & Francis Group.

Hasan, Y., Begue, L., Scharkow, M., & Bushman, B. J. (2013). The more you play, the more aggressive you become: A long-term experimental study of cumulative violent video game effects on hostile expectations and aggressive behavior. *Journal of Experimental Social Psychology*, 49(2), 224–227.

Hasselhorn, M. (1992). Task dependency and the role of typicality and metamemory in the development of an organizational strategy. *Child Development*, 63, 202–214.

Hassett, J. M., Siebert, E. R., & Wallen, K. (2008). Sex differences in rhesus monkey toy preferences parallel those of children. *Hormones and Behavior*, 54(3), 359–364.

Hauck, F. R., et al. (2011). Breastfeeding and reduced risk of sudden infant death syndrome: A meta-analysis. *Pediatrics*, 128(1), 103–110.

Haushofer, J., & Fehr, E. (2014). On the psychology of poverty. *Science*, 23(6186), 862–867.

Haworth, C. M. A., et al. (2009). A twin study of the genetics of high cognitive ability selected from 11,000 twin pairs in six studies from four countries. *Behavior Genetics*, 39(4), 359–370.

Hay, C., & Evans, M. M. (2006). Violent victimization and involvement in delinquency: Examining predictions from general strain theory. *Journal of Criminal Justice*, 34(3), 261–274.

Hay, D. F., Payne, A., & Chadwick, A. (2004). Peer relations in childhood. *Journal of Child Psychology and Psychiatry*, 45(1), 84–108.

Hayatbakhsh, M. R., et al. (2012). Birth outcomes associated with cannabis use before and during pregnancy. *Pediatric Research*, 71(2), 215–219.

Haywood, K. M., & Getchell, N. (2008). *Life span motor development* (5th ed.). Champaign, IL: Human Kinetics.

Haywood, K. M., & Getchell, N. (2014). *Life span motor development* (6th ed.). Champaign, IL: Human Kinetics.

Healy, M. D., & Ellis, B. J. (2007). Birth order, conscientiousness, and openness to experience: Tests of the family-niche model of personality using a within-family methodology. *Evolution and Human Behavior*, 28(1), 55–59.

Heard, E., & Turner, J. (2011). Function of the sex chromosomes in mammalian fertility. *Cold Spring Harbor Perspectives in Biology*, DOI:10.1101/cshperspect.a002675.

Hebebrand, J., & Hinney, A. (2009). Environmental and genetic risk factors in obesity. *Child and Adolescent Psychiatric Clinics of North America*, 18(1), 83–94.

Hediger, M. L. (2011). Pregnancy, prenatal care, weight, and maternal age. In G. B. Louis & R. W. Platt (Eds.). *Reproductive and perinatal epidemiology* (pp. 85–100). New York: Oxford University Press.

Heetman, I., Bosma, H., Kulper, G., & Feron, F. (2015). Preventive healthcare surveillance can detect emerging behavioural problems that are related to later school dropouts. *Acta Paediarica*, 104(1), e27–e31.

Heimann, M., et al. (2006). Exploring the relation between memory, gestural communication, and the emergence of language in infancy: A longitudinal study. *Infant and Child Development*, 15(3), 233–249.

Heindel, J. J., & Lawler, C. (2006). Role of exposure to environmental chemicals in developmental origins of health and disease. In P. Gluckman & M. Hanson (Eds.), *Developmental origins of health and disease* (pp. 82–97). New York: Cambridge University Press.

Heinonen, K., et al. (2011). Trajectories of growth and symptoms of attention-deficit/hyperactivity disorder in children: A longitudinal study. *BMC Pediatrics*, 11(84). DOI:10.1186/1471-2431-11-84.

Helwig, C. C. (2006). Rights, civil liberties, and democracy across cultures. In M. Killen & J. G. Smetana (Eds.), *Handbook of moral development* (pp. 185–210). Mahwah, NJ: Erlbaum.

Henricks, T. S. (2015). Classic theories of play. In J. E. Johnson et al. (Eds.). *The handbook of the study of play, Vol. 2* (pp. 163–180). Lanham, MD: Rowman & Littlefield.

Henry, A., Kisicki, M. D., & Varley, C. (2012). Efficacy and safety of antidepressant drug treatment in children and adolescents. *Molecular Psychiatry, 17,* 1186–1193.

Henry, K. L., et al. (2014). The potential role of meaning in life in the relationship between victimization and suicidal ideation. *Journal of Youth and Adolescence, 43,* 221–232.

Henry, K. L., Knight, K. E., & Thornberry, T. P. (2012). School disengagement as a predictor of dropout, delinquency, and problem substance abuse during adolescence and early adulthood. *Journal of Youth and Adolescence, 41*(2), 156–166.

Henzi, S. P., et al. (2007). Look who's talking: Developmental trends in the size of conversational cliques. *Evolution and Human Behavior, 28*(1), 66–74.

Herbenick, D., et al. (2010a). Sexual behavior in the United States: Results from a national probability sample of males and females ages 14 to 94. *Journal of Sexual Medicine, 7*(Suppl. 5), 255–265.

Herbenick, D., et al. (2010b). Sexual behaviors, relationships, and perceived health among adult women in the United States: Results from a national probability sample. *Journal of Sexual Medicine, 7*(Suppl. 5), 277–290.

Herbenick, D., et al. (2010c). An event-level analysis of the sexual characteristics and composition among adults ages 18 to 59: Results from a national probability sample in the United States. *Journal of Sexual Medicine, 7*(Suppl. 5), 346–361.

Hergenhahn, B.R., & Henley, T. (2014). *An introduction to the history of psychology* (7th ed). San Francisco, CA: Cengage Learning.

Herrera-Marschitz, M., et al. (2014). Perinatal asphyxia: CNS development and deficits with delayed onset. *Frontiers in Neuroscience, 8,* 47.

Hervey-Jumper, H., Douyon, K., & Franco, K. N. (2006). Deficits in diagnosis, treatment and continuity of care in African-American children and adolescents with ADHD. *Journal of the National Medical Association, 98*(2), 233–238.

Hetherington, E. M. (1989). Coping with family transition: Winners, losers, and survivors. *Child Development, 60,* 1–14.

Hetherington, E. M. (2006). The influence of conflict, marital problem solving and parenting on children's adjustment in nondivorced, divorced and remarried families. In A. Clarke-Stewart & J. Dunn (Eds.), *Families count: Effects on child and adolescent development, The Jacobs Foundation series on adolescence* (pp. 203–237). Cambridge, UK: Cambridge University Press.

Hetherington, E. M., Stanley-Hagan, M., & Anderson, E. R. (1989). Marital transitions: A child's perspective. *American Psychologist, 44,* 303–312.

Hewitt, P. L., Caelian, C. F., Chen, C., & Flett, G. L. (2014). Perfectionism, stress, daily hassles, hopelessness, and suicide potential in depressed psychiatric adolescents. *Journal of Psychopathology and Behavioral Assessment, 36*(4), 663–674.

Hill, N. E., & Taylor, L. C. (2004). Parental school involvement and children's academic achievement: Pragmatics and issues. *Current Directions in Psychological Science, 13,* 161–164.

Hill, N. E., & Tyson, D. F. (2009). Parental involvement in middle school: A meta-analytic assessment of the strategies that promote achievement. *Developmental Psychology, 45*(3), 740–763.

Hill, P. L., Duggan, P. M., & Lapsley, D. K. (2012). Subjective invulnerability, risk behavior, and adjustment in early adolescence. *The Journal of Early Adolescence, 32*(4), 489–501.

Hill, S. E., & Flom, R. (2007). 18- and 24-month-olds' discrimination of gender-consistent and inconsistent activities. *Infant Behavior & Development, 30*(1), 168–173.

Hillerer, K. M., Jacobs, V. R., Fischer, T., & Aigner, L. (2014). The maternal brain: An organ with peripartal plasticity. *Neural Plasticity,* http://dx.doi.org/10.1155/2014/574159.

Hilliard, L. J., & Liben, L. S. (2010). Differing levels of gender salience in preschool classrooms: Effects on children's gender attitudes and intergroup bias. *Child Development, 81*(6), 1787–1798.

Hills, A. P., & Byrne, N. M. (2011). An overview of physical growth and maturation. In J. Jürimäe, A. P. Hills, & T. Jürimäe (Eds.), *Cytokines, growth mediators and physical activity in children during puberty* (pp. 1–13). Basel, Switzerland: S. Karger.

Hindley, C. B., Filliozat, A. M., Klackenberg, G., Nicolet-Neister, D., & Sand, E. A. (1966). Differences in age of walking for five European longitudinal samples. *Human Biology, 38,* 364–379.

Hines, M. (2011a). Prenatal endocrine influences on sexual orientation and on sexually differentiated childhood behavior. *Frontiers in Neuroendocrinology, 32*(2), 170–182.

Hines, M. (2011b). Gender development and the human brain. *Annual Review of Neuroscience, 34,* 69–88.

Hines, M. (2013). Sex and sex differences. In P. D. Zelazo (Ed.). *The Oxford handbook of developmental psychology,* Vol. 1: Body and mind (pp. 164–201). New York: Oxford University Press.

Hodapp, R. M., Griffin, M. M., Burke, M. M., & Fisher, M. H. (2011). Intellectual disabilities. In R. J. Sternberg & S. J. Kaufman (Eds.), *The Cambridge handbook of intelligence* (pp. 193–209). New York: Cambridge University Press.

Hoff, E. (2014). *Language development* (5th Ed.). San Francisco: Cengage Learning.

Hoff, E. V. (2013). The relationship between pretend play and creativity. In M. Taylor (Ed.). *The Oxford handbook on the development of imagination* (pp. 251–271). New York: Oxford University Press.

Hoffmann, J., & Russ, S. (2012). Pretend play, creativity, and emotion regulation in children. *Psychology of Aesthetics, Creativity, and the Arts, 6*(2), 175–184.

Hoffman, K. L., & Edwards, J. N. (2004). An integrated theoretical model of sibling violence and abuse. *Journal of Family Violence, 19*(3), 185–200.

Hoffman, L. W., & Youngblade, L. M. (1998). Maternal employment, morale, and parenting style: Social class comparisons. *Journal of Applied Developmental Psychology, 19*(3), 389–413.

Hofmann, W., Gschwendner, T., Castelli, L., & Schmitt, M. (2008). Impulsive and reflective determinants of interracial interaction behavior: The moderating role of situationally available control resources. *Group Processes and Intergroup Behaviors, 11,* 69–87.

Hogue, A., Henderson, C. E., Ozechowski, T. J., & Robbins, M. S. (2014). Evidence base on outpatient behavioral treatment for adolescent substance use: Updates and recommendations 2007–2013. *Journal of Clinical Child & Adolescent Psychology, 43*(5), 695–720.

Holden, G. W., Vittrup, B., & Rosen, L. H. (2011). Families, parenting and discipline. In M. K. Underwood & L. H. Rosen (Eds.), *Social development: Relationships in infancy, childhood, and adolescence* (pp. 127–152). New York: Guilford.

Holditch-Davis, D., et al. (2014). Maternally administered interventions for preterm infants in the NICU: Effects on maternal psychological distress and mother–infant relationship. *Infant Behavior and Development, 37*(4), 695–710.

Holland, A., Simpson, A., & Riggs, K. J. (2015). Young children retain fast mapped object labels better than shape, color, and texture words. *Journal of Experimental Child Psychology, 134,* 1–11.

Holland, J. L. (1997). *Making vocational choices: A theory of vocational personalities and work environments* (3rd ed.). Odessa, FL: Psychological Assessment Resources.

Hollen, L. I., et al. (2014). Are diet and feeding behaviours associated with the onset and recovery from slow weight gain in early infancy? *British Journal of Nutrition, 111*(9), 1696–1704.

Hollenstein, T., & Lougheed, J. P. (2013). Beyond storm and stress: Typicality, transactions, timing, and temperament to account for adolescent change. *American Psychologist, 68*(6), 444–454.

Hollich, G. J. et al. (2000). Breaking the language barrier: An emergentist coalition model for the origins of word learning. *Monographs of the Society for Research in Child Development,* Serial No. 262, *Vol.* 65, No. 3.

Holloway, J. H. (2004). *Part-time work and student achievement.* Alexandria VA: Association for Supervision and Curriculum Development. Available at http://www.ascd.org/publications /ed_lead/200104/ holloway.html.

Holloway, S. D., Suzuki, S., Yamamoto, Y., & Mindnich, J. D. (2006). Relation of maternal role concepts to parenting, employment choices, and life satisfaction among Japanese women. *Sex Roles, 54*(3–4), 235–249.

Holmes, S. A. (2014, September 18). *Is corporal punishment acceptable?* CNN News.

Holsen, I., Kraft, P., & Roysamb, E. (2001). The relationship between body image and depressed mood in adolescence: A 5-year longitudinal panel study. *Journal of Health Psychology, 6*(6), 613–627.

Homae, F., Watanabe, H., Nakano, T., & Taga, G. (2011). Functional development in the human brain for auditory pitch processing. *Human Brain Mapping, 33*(3), 596–608.

Hong, D. S., Dunkin, B., & Reiss, A. L. (2011). Psychosocial functioning and social cognitive processing in girls with Turner syndrome. *Journal of Developmental & Behavioral Pediatrics, 32*(7), 512–520.

Hong, J. S., & Eamon, M. K. (2012). Students' perceptions of unsafe schools: An ecological systems analysis. *Journal of Child and Family Studies, 21*(3), 428–438.

Honig, A. S., & Nealls, A. L. (2011). What do young children dream about? *Early Child Development and Care, 182*(6), 771–795.

Honzik, M. P., Macfarlane, J. W., & Allen, L. (1948). The stability of mental test performance between two and eighteen years. *Journal of Experimental Education, 17,* 309–324.

Hoover, J. R., Sterling, A. M., & Storkel. (2011). Speech and language development. In A. S. Davis (Ed.). *Handbook of pediatric neuropsychology.* New York: Springer.

Horst, J. S., et al. (2009). Toddlers can adaptively change how they categorize: Same objects, same session, two different categorical distinctions. *Developmental Science, 12*(1), 96–105.

Hossain, M., Chetana, M., & Devi, P. U. (2005). Late effect of prenatal irradiation on the hippocampal histology and brain weight in adult mice. *International Journal of Developmental Neuroscience, 23*(4), 307–313.

Houck, C., et al. (2014). Adolescents' emotions prior to sexual activity and associations with sexual risk factors. *AIDS and Behavior, 18*(8), 1615–1623.

House, S., Loud, K., & Shubkin, C. (2013). Female athlete triad for the primary care pediatrician. *Current Opinion in Pediatrics, 25*(6), 755–761.

Howard, A. M., Landau, S., & Pryor, J. B. (2014). Peer bystanders to bullying: Who wants to play with the victim? *Journal of Abnormal Child Psychology, 42,* 265–276.

Howe, M. L. (2015). Memory development. *Cognitive Processes, 2; Handbook of child psychology and developmental science.* Hoboken, NJ: Wiley. DOI:10.1002/9781118963418. childpsy206.

Hoy, E. A., & McClure, B. G. (2000). Preschool experience: A facilitator of very low birthweight infants' development? *Infant Mental Health Journal, 21*(6), 481–494.

Huang, B., Biro, F. M., & Dorn, L. D. (2009). Determination of relative timing of pubertal maturation through ordinal logistic modeling. *Journal of Adolescent Health,* in press.

Huang, X-N., et al. (2010). Co-sleeping and children's sleep in China. *Biological Rhythm Research, 41*(3), 169–181.

Hubbard, T. K. (2009). The paradox of "natural" heterosexuality with "unnatural" women. *Classical World, 102*(3), 249–258.

Huber, J., Darling, S., Park, K., & Soliman, K. F. A. (2001). Altered responsiveness to stress and NMDA following prenatal exposure to cocaine. *Physiology and Behavior, 72*(1–2), 181–188.

Hudak, M. L., & Tan, R. C. (2012). Neonatal drug withdrawal. *Pediatrics, 129*(2), e540–e560.

Hudson, J. A. (1990). The emergence of autobiographical memory in mother–child conversation. In R. Fivush & J. A. Hudson (Eds.), *Knowing and remembering in young children.* Cambridge: Cambridge University Press.

Hudziak, J. J., et al. (2014). Cortical thickness maturation and duration of music training: Health-promoting activities shape brain development. *Journal of the American Academy of Child & Adolescent Psychiatry, 53*(11), 1153–1161.

Huesmann, L. R., Dubow, E. F., Eron, L. D., & Boxer, P. (2006). Middle childhood family contextual factors as predictors of adult outcomes. In A. C. Huston & M. N. Ripke (Eds.), *Middle childhood: Contexts of development.* Cambridge, UK: Cambridge University Press.

Huesmann, L. R., Dubow, E. F., & Yang, G. (2013). Why is it hard to believe that media violence causes aggression? In K. E. Dill (Ed.). *The Oxford handbook of media psychology* (pp. 159–171). New York: Oxford University Press.

Huesmann, L. R., Moise-Titus, J., Podolski, C., & Eron, L. D. (2003). Longitudinal relations between children's exposure to TV violence and their aggressive and violent behavior in young adulthood: 1977–1992. *Developmental Psychology, 39*(2), 201–221.

Hughes, D., Rodriguez, J., Smith, E. P., Johnson, D. J., Stevenson, H. C., & Spicer, P. (2006). Parents' ethnic–racial socialization practices: A review of research and directions for future study. *Developmental Psychology, 42,* 747–770.

Huizink, A. C. (2013). Prenatal cannabis exposure and infant outcomes: Overview of studies. *Progress in Neuro-Psychopharmacology and Biological Psychiatry,* DOI:10.1016/j.pnpbp.2013.09.014.

Hunter, T., & Cattelona, G. (2014). Breastfeeding initiation and duration in first-time mothers: Exploring the impact of father involvement in the early post-partum period. *Health Promotion Perspectives, 4*(2), 132–136.

Hur, Y. (2005). Genetic and environmental influences on self-concept in female pre-adolescent twins: Comparison of Minnesota and Seoul data. *Twin Research and Human Genetics, 8*(4), 291–299.

Hurd, N. M., Sanchez, B., Zimmerman, M. A., & Caldwell, C. H. (2012). Natural mentors, racial identity, and educational attainment among African American adolescents: Exploring pathways to success. *Child Development, 83*(4), 1196–1212.

Hurd, Y. L., Michaelides, M., Miller, M. L., & Jutras-Aswad, D. (2014). Trajectory of cannabis use on addiction vulnerability. *Neuropharmacology, 76*(Part B), 416–424.

Hyde, J. S. (2014). Gender similarities and differences. *Annual Review of Psychology, 65,* 373–398.

Hyde, J. S., Lindberg, S. M., Linn, M. C., Ellis, A. B., & Williams, C. C. (2008). Gender similarities characterize math performance. *Science, 321,* 494–495.

Idele, P., et al. (2014). Epidemiology of HIV and AIDS among adolescents: Current status, inequities, and data gaps. Retrieved from http://data.unicef.org/corecode/uploads/document6/uploaded_pdfs/corecode/Epidemiology_of_HIV_and_AIDS_Among_Adolescents_169.pdf. Accessed April 25, 2015.

IJzendoorn, M. H. van, & Hubbard, F. O. A. (2000). Are infant crying and maternal responsiveness during the first year related to infant–mother attachment at 15 months? *Attachment and Human Development, 2*(3), 371–391.

IJzendoorn, M. H. van, Moran, G., Belsky, J., Pederson, D., Bakermans-Kranenburg, M. J., & Kneppers, K. (2000). The similarity of siblings' attachments to their mother. *Child Development, 71*(4), 1086–1098.

Inhelder, B., & Piaget, J. (1959). *The early growth of logic in the child: Classification and seriation.* New York: Harper & Row.

Inzlicht, M., & Good, C. (2006). How environments can threaten academic performance, self-knowledge, and sense of belonging. In S. Levin & C. van Laar (Eds.), *Stigma and group inequality: Social psychological perspectives. The Claremont symposium on Applied Social Psychology* (pp. 129–150). Mahwah, NJ: Erlbaum.

Israel, S., Hasenfratz, L., & Knafo-Noam, A. (2015). The genetics of morality and prosociality. *Current Opinion in Psychology,6,* 55–59.

Ito, M. (2008). Cited in T. Lewin (2008, November 19). Study finds teenagers' Internet socializing isn't such a bad thing. *The New York Times.* Retrived from http://www.nytimes.com.

Ito, M., Robinson, L., Horst, H. A., Pascoe, C. J., & Bittanti, M. (2009). *Living and learning with new media: Summary of findings from the Digital Youth Project.* Cambridge, MA: MIT Press.

Izard, C. E. (1983). *Maximally discriminative facial movement scoring system.* Newark: University of Delaware Instructional Resources Center.

Izard, C. E. (2004). The generality–specificity issue in infants' emotion responses: A comment on Bennett, Bendersky, and Lewis (2002). *Infancy, 6*(3), 417–423.

Izard, C. E., & Malatesta, C. Z. (1987). Perspectives on emotional development.

I. Differential emotions theory of early emotional development. In J. D. Osofsky (Ed.), *Handbook of infant development* (2nd ed.). New York: Wiley.

Izard, C. E., Youngstrom, E. A., Fine, S. E., Mostow, A. J., & Trentacosta, C. J. (2006). Emotions and developmental psychopathology. In D. Cicchetti & D. J. Cohen (Eds.), *Developmental psychopathology*, Vol. 1, *Theory and method* (2nd ed.) (pp. 244–292). Hoboken, NJ: Wiley.

Jack, F., & Zajac, R. (2014). The effect of age and reminders on witnesses' responses to cross-examination-style questioning. *Journal of Applied Research in Memory and Cognition*, 3(1), 1–6.

Jackson, D. N., & Rushton, J. P. (2006). Males have greater g: Sex differences in general mental ability from 100,000 17- to 18-year-olds on the Scholastic Assessment Test. *Intelligence*, 34(5), 479–486.

Jackson, L. A., et al. (2009). Self-concept, self-esteem, gender, race, and information technology use. *CyberPsychology & Behavior*, 12(4), 437–440.

Jacobs, J. E., Davis-Kean, P., Bleeker, M., Eccles, J. S., & Malanchuk, O. (2005). "I can, but I don't want to": The impact of parents, interests, and activities on gender differences in math. In A. M. Gallagher & J. C. Kaufman (Eds.), *Gender differences in mathematics: An integrative psychological approach* (pp. 246–263). New York: Cambridge University Press.

Jacobson, J. L., Jacobson, S. W., Padgett, R. J., Brumitt, G. A., & Billings, R. L. (1992). Effects of prenatal PCB exposure on cognitive processing efficiency and sustained attention. *Developmental Psychology*, 28, 297–306.

Jaffe, A. C. (2011). Failure to thrive: Current clinical concepts. *Pediatrics in Review*, 32(3), 100–108.

James, A. C., James, G., Cowdrey, F. A., Soler, A., & Choke, A. (2015). Cognitive behavioural therapy for anxiety disorders in children and adolescents. *Cochrane Library*, DOI:10.1002/14651858. CD004690.pub4.

James, J., Ellis, B. J., Schlomer, G. L., & Garber, J. (2012). Sex-specific pathways to early puberty, sexual debut, and sexual risk taking: Tests of an integrated evolutionary–developmental model. *Developmental Psychology*, 48(3), 687–702.

James, W. H. (2014). Hypothesis: High levels of maternal adrenal androgens are a major cause of miscarriage and other forms of reproductive suboptimality. *Journal of Theoretical Biology*, DOI:10.1016/j.jtbi.2014.09.027.

Jamieson, S., & Marshall, W. L. (2000). Attachment styles and violence in child molesters. *Journal of Sexual Aggression*, 5(2), 88–98.

Javo, C., Ronning, J. A., & Heyerdahl, S. (2004). Child-rearing in an indigenous Sami population in Norway: A cross-cultural comparison of parental attitudes and expectations. *Scandinavian Journal of Psychology*, 45(1), 67–78.

Jeng, S-F., Yau, K-I. T., Liao, H-F., Chen, L-C., & Chen, P-S. (2000). Prognostic factors for walking attainment in very low-birthweight preterm infants. *Early Human Development*, 59(3), 159–173.

Jian, M. (2013, May 21). China's brutal one-child policy. *The New York Times*, p. A27.

Johansson, M., Forssman, L., & Bohlin, G. (2014). Individual differences in 10-month-olds' performance on the A-not-B task. *Scandinavian Journal of Psychology*, 55(2), 130–135.

John, A., Halliburton, A., & Humphrey, J. (2013). Child-mother and child-father play interaction with preschoolers. *Early Child Development and Care*, 183(3–4), 483–497.

Johnson, K. L., Lurye, L. E., & Tassinary, L. G. (2010). Sex categorization among preschool children: Increasing utilization of sexually dimorphic cues. *Child Development*, 81(5), 1346–1355.

Johnson, M. H. (2011). *Developmental cognitive neuroscience* (3rd ed.). Chichester, West Sussex, UK: Wiley-Blackwell.

Johnson, N. B., et al. (2014). CDC National Health Report: Leading causes of morbidity and mortality and associated risk and protective factors—United States, 2005 – 2013. Centers for Disease Control and Prevention. Available at http://www.cdc.gov/mmwr/preview/mmwrhtml/su6304a2.htm.

Johnson, S. P. (2011). Development of visual perception. *WIREs Cognitive Science*, 2, 515–528. DOI:10.1002/wcs.128.

Johnson, W., & Bouchard, T. J., Jr. (2007). Sex differences in mental abilities: g masks the dimensions on which they lie. *Intelligence*, 35(1), 23–39.

Johnson, W., Chumlea, W. C., Czerwinski, S. A., & Demerath, E. W. (2013). Secular trends in the fat and fat-free components of body mass index in children ages 8–18 years born 1958–1995. *Annals of Human Biology*, 40(1), 107–110.

Johnson, W., et al. (2012). A changing pattern of childhood BMI growth during the 20th century: 70 years of data from the Fels Longitudinal Study. *The American Journal of Clinical Nutrition*, 95(5), 1136–1143.

Johnson, W., McGue, M., Krueger, R. F., & Bouchard, T. J., Jr. (2004). Marriage and personality: A genetic analysis. *Journal of Personality and Social Psychology*, 86(2), 285–294.

Johnson-Laird, P. (2010). Deductive reasoning. *Wiley Interdisciplinary Reviews: Cognitive Science*, 1(1), 8–17.

John-Steiner, V. P. (2007). Vygotsky on thinking and speaking. In H. Daniels et al. (Eds.), *The Cambridge companion to Vygotsky* (pp. 136–152). New York: Cambridge University Press.

Johnston, C. C., Campbell-Yeo, M., & Fillon, F. (2011). Paternal vs maternal kangaroo care for procedural pain in preterm neonates: A randomized crossover trial. *Archives of Pediatrics and Adolescent Medicine*, 165(9), 792–796.

Johnston, D. W., Nicholls, M. E. R., Shah, M., & Shields, M. A. (2013). Handedness, health and cognitive development: Evidence from children in the National Longitudinal Survey of Youth. *Journal of the Royal Statistical Society*, 176(4), 841–860.

Johnston, L. D., O'Malley, P. M., Bachman, J. G., & Schulenberg, J. E. (December 14, 2011). Marijuana use continues to rise among U.S. teens, while alcohol use hits historic lows. University of Michigan News Service: Ann Arbor, MI. Retrieved from http://www.monitoringthefuture.org. Accessed March 14, 2012.

Johnston, L. D., O'Malley, P. M., Meich, R. A., Bachman, J. G., & Schulenberg, J. E. (2014). *Monitoring the future: National survey results on drug use 1975–2013: Overview, key findings on adolescent drug use.* Ann Arbor: Institute for Social Research, The University of Michigan.

Johnston, L. D., O'Malley, P. M., Miech, R. A., Bachman, J. G., & Schulenberg, J. E. (2015). *Monitoring the Future national survey results on drug use: 1975-2014: Overview, key findings on adolescent drug use.* Ann Arbor: Institute for Social Research, The University of Michigan.

Johnston, M. V., et al. (2009). Plasticity and injury in the developing brain. *Brain and Development*, 31(1), 1–10.

Jolley, R. P. (2010). *Children and pictures: Drawing and understanding.* Chichester, West Sussex, UK: Wiley-Blackwell.

Jones, D. C., Swift, D. J., & Johnson, M. A. (1988). Nondeliberate memory for a novel event among preschoolers. *Developmental Psychology*, 24, 641–645.

Jones, M. C. (1924). Elimination of children's fears. *Journal of Experimental Psychology*, 7, 381–390.

Jones, R. M., Dick, A. J., Coyl-Shepherd, D. D., & Ogletree, M. (2012). Antecedents of the male adolescent identity crisis. *Youth and Society*, DOI:10.1177/0044118X12438904.

Jordan, N. C., Kaplan, D., Ramineni, C., & Locuniak, M. N. (2009). Early math matters: Kindergarten number competence and later mathematics outcomes. *Developmental Psychology*, 45(3), 850–867.

Jorgensen, G. (2006). Kohlberg and Gilligan: Duet or duel? *Journal of Moral Education*, 35(2), 179–196.

Joshi, P. T., Salpekar, J. A., & Daniolos, P. T. (2006). Physical and sexual abuse of children. In M. K. Dulcan & J. M. Wiener (Eds.), *Essentials of child and adolescent psychiatry* (pp. 595–620). Washington, DC: American Psychiatric Publishing.

Junod, A. F. (2008). Overweight children do not necessarily become overweight adults. *Swiss Medical Review*, 4(174), 2175.

Juvonen, J., & Graham, S. (2014). Bullying in schools: The power of bullies and the plight of victims. *Annual Review of Psychology*, 65, 159–185.

Kaestle, C. E., & Allen, K. R. (2011). The role of masturbation in healthy sexual development: Perceptions of young adults. *Archives of Sexual Behavior*, 40(5), 983–994.

Kagan, J., & Klein, R. E. (1973). Cross-cultural perspectives on early development. *American Psychologist*, 28, 947–961.

Kaiser Family Foundation, Holt, T., Greene, L., & Davis, J. (2003). *National Survey of Adolescents and Young Adults: Sexual health knowledge, attitudes, and experiences*. Menlo Park, CA: Henry J. Kaiser Family Foundation.

Kalat, J. (2015). *Biological psychology, 12th edition*. San Francisco: Cengage Learning.

Kalil, A., Ziol-Guest, K. M., & Coley, R. L. (2005). Perceptions of father involvement patterns in teenage-mother families: Predictors and links to mothers' psychological adjustment. *Family Relations, 54*(2), 197–211.

Käll, A., & Lagercrantz, H. (2012). Highlights in this issue. *Acta Paediatrica, 101*(1). DOI:10.1111/j .1651-2227.2011.02524.x.

Kaminski, R. A., & Stormshak, E. A. (2007). Project STAR: Early intervention with preschool children and families for the prevention of substance abuse. In P. Tolan, J. Szapocznik & S. Sambrano (Eds.), *Preventing youth substance abuse: Science-based programs for children and adolescents* (pp. 89–109). Washington, DC: American Psychological Association.

Kapalka, M. (2014). *Treating disruptive disorders*. New York: Routledge.

Kaplan, L., & Owings, W. (2015). *Educational foundations* (2nd ed.). San Francisco: Cengage.

Karavasilis, L., Doyle, A. B., & Markiewicz, D. (2003). Associations between parenting style and attachment to mother in middle childhood and adolescence. *International Journal of Behavioral Development, 27*(2), 153–164.

Kaufman, J. C., & Plucker, J. A. (2011). Intelligence and creativity. In R. J. Sternberg & S. J. Kaufman (Eds.), *The Cambridge handbook of intelligence* (pp. 771–783). New York: Cambridge University Press.

Kaufman, S. B., Reynolds, M. R., Liu, X., Kaufman, A. S., & McGrew, K. S. (2012). Are intelligence g and academic achievement g one and the same g? *Intelligence*. http://dx.doi.org/10.1016/j.intell.2012 .01.009.

Kavcic, T., & Zupancic, M. (2005). Sibling relationship in early/middle childhood: Trait- and dyad-centered approach. *Studia Psychologica, 47*(3), 179–197.

Kavšek, M., Yonas, A., & Granrud, C. E. (2012). Infants' sensitivity to pictorial depth cues: A review and meta-analysis of looking studies. *Infant Behavior and Development, 35*(1), 109–128.

Kawamura, Y., et al. (2014). Effects of thalidomide on Fgf8, Bmp4 and Hoxa11 expression in the limb bud in Kbl.JW rabbit embryos. *Congenital Abnormalities, 54*(1), 54–62.

Kaye, D. A., & Shah, R. V. (2015). *Case studies in pain management*. Cambridge, UK: Cambridge University Press.

Kaziboni, A., & Uys, T. (2015). The selection of academic role models by first year university students. *Journal of Sociology and Social Anthropology, 6*(1), 77–86.

Keebaugh, A. C., et al. (2015). RNAi knockdown of oxytocin receptor in the nucleus accumbens inhibits social attachment and parental care in monogamous prairie voles. *Social Neuroscience*, DOI:10.1080/17470919 .2015.1040893.

Keitel, A., Prinz, W., & Daum, M. M. (2014). Perception of individual and joint action

in infants and adults. *PLOS ONE*, DOI:10.1371/journal.pone.0107450.

Keller, H., Kärtner, J., Borke, J., Yovsi, R., & Kleis, A. (2005). Parenting styles and the development of the categorical self: A longitudinal study on mirror self-recognition in Cameroonian Nso and German families. *International Journal of Behavioral Development, 29*(6), 496–504.

Kellman, P. J., & Arterberry, M. E. (2006). Infant visual perception. In D. Kuhn et al. (Eds.), *Handbook of child psychology*, Vol. 2, *Cognition, perception, and language* (6th ed.) (pp. 109–160). Hoboken, NJ: Wiley.

Kellogg, R. (1959). *What children scribble and why*. Oxford: National Press.

Kellogg, R. (1970). Understanding children's art. In P. Cramer (Ed.), *Readings in developmental psychology today*. Del Mar, CA: CRM.

Kelly, K. M., Jones, W. H., & Adams, J. M. (2002). Using the Imaginary Audience Scale as a measure of social anxiety in young adults. *Educational and Psychological Measurement, 62*(5), 896–914.

Kelly, Y., et al. (2013). Light drinking versus abstinence in pregnancy—behavioural and cognitive outcomes in 7-year-old children: A longitudinal cohort study. *British Journal of Gynecology, 120*(11), 1340–1347.

Kempes, M., Matthys, W., de Vries, H., & van Engeland, H. (2005). Reactive and proactive aggression in children: A review of theory, findings and the relevance for child and adolescent psychiatry. *European Child & Adolescent Psychiatry, 14*(1), 11–19.

Kendall, P. C. (2011). *Child and adolescent therapy: Cognitive-behavioral prodecures* (4th ed.). New York: Guilford.

Kendler, K. S. (2010). Advances in our understanding of genetic risk factors for autism spectrum disorders. *American Journal of Psychiatry, 167*(11), 1291–1293.

Kendler, K. S., et al. (2011). The impact of environmental experiences on symptoms of anxiety and depression across the life span. *Psychological Science, 22*(1), 1343–1352.

Kendler, K. S., et al. (2012). Recent advances in the genetic epidemiology and molecular genetics of substance use disorders. *Nature Neuroscience, 15*, 181–189.

Kenney, S. R., et al. (2015). Pathways of parenting style on adolescents' college adjustment, academic achievement, and alcohol risk. *Journal of College Student Retention*, DOI:10.1177/1521025115578232.

Keown, L. J., & Palmer, M. (2014). Comparisons between paternal and maternal involvement with sons: Early to middle childhood. *Early Child Development and Care, 184*(1), 99–117.

Khurana, A., Cooksey, E. C., & Gavazzi, S. M. (2011). Juvenile delinquency and teenage pregnancy. *Psychology of Women Quarterly, 35*(2), 282–289.

Kibbe, M. M., & Leslie, A. M. (2013). What's the object of object working memory in infancy? Unraveling "what" and "how many." *Cognitive Psychology, 66*(4), 380–404.

Kilgore, K., Snyder, J., & Lentz, C. (2000). The contribution of parental discipline, parental monitoring, and school risk to early-onset conduct problems in African American boys and girls. *Developmental Psychology, 36*(6), 835–845.

Killen, M., & Smetana, J. G. (2010). Future directions: Social development in the context of social justice. *Social Development, 19*(3), 642–657.

Killen, M., & Smetana, J. G. (2015). Origins and development of morality. In M. E. Lamb (Ed.). *Handbook of child psychology and developmental science*, Vol. 3 (pp. 701-749). New York: Wiley Blackwell.

Kim, H. I., & Johnson, S. P. (2014). Detecting "infact-directedness" in face and voice. *Developmental Science, 17*(4), 621-627.

Kim, H. S. (2011). Consequences of parental divorce for child development. *American Sociological Review, 76*(3), 487–511.

Kim, J., & Cicchetti, D. (2009). Mean-level change and intraindividual variability in self-esteem and depression among high-risk children. *International Journal of Behavioral Development, 33*(3), 202–214.

Kimmons, J., et al. (2009). Fruit and vegetable intake among adolescents and adults in the United States: Percentage meeting individualized recommendations. *The Medscape Journal of Medicine, 11*(1), 26.

Kimura, et al. (2010). Infants' recognition of objects using canonical color. *Journal of Experimental Child Psychology, 105*(3), 256–263.

King, R. (2000). Interview comments in L. Frazier (2000, July 16), The new face of HIV is young, black. *Washington Post*, p. C01.

Kirby, D. B., et al. (2007). Sex and HIV education programs: Their impact on sexual behaviors of young people throughout the world. *Journal of Adolescent Health, 40*(3), 206–217.

Kirchler, E., Pombeni, M. L., & Palmonari, A. (1991). Sweet sixteen . . . Adolescents' problems and the peer group as source of support. *European Journal of Psychology of Education, 6*, 393–410.

Kirke, D. M. (2009). Gender clustering in friendship networks. *Methodological Innovations Online, 4*, 23–36.

Kistner, J. (2006). Children's peer acceptance, perceived acceptance, and risk for depression. In T. E. Joiner, J. S. Brown & J. Kistner (Eds.), *The interpersonal, cognitive, and social nature of depression* (pp. 1–21). Mahwah, NJ: Erlbaum.

Kiuru, N., et al. (2012). Best friends in adolescence show similar educational careers in early adulthood. *Journal of Applied Developmental Psychology, 33*(2), 102–111.

Klahr, A. M., McGue, M., Iacono, W. G., & Burt, S. A. (2011). The association between parent–child conflict and adolescent conduct problems over time: Results from a longitudinal adoption study. *Journal of Abnormal Psychology, 120*(1), 46–56.

Klaus, M. H., & Kennell, J. H. (1978). Parent-to-infant attachment. In J. H. Stevens, Jr. & M. Mathews (Eds.), *Mother/child, father/child relationships*. Washington, DC: National Association for the Education of Young Children.

Klee, T., & Stokes, S. F. (2011). Language development. In D. Skuse et al. (Eds.). *Child psychology and psychiatry: Frameworks for practice* (2nd ed.) (pp. 45–50). Chichester, UK: John Wiley.

Klein, P. J., & Meltzoff, A. N. (1999). Long-term memory, forgetting and deferred imitation in 12-month-old infants. *Developmental Science*, 2(1), 102–113.

Klemfuss, J. Z, & Ceci, S. J. (2012). Legal and psychological perspectives on children's competence to testify in court. *Developmental Review*, 32(3), 268–286.

Klier, C. M. (2006). Mother–infant bonding disorders in patients with postnatal depression: The Postpartum Bonding Questionnaire in clinical practice. *Archives of Women's Mental Health*, 9(5), 289–291.

Klimstra, T. A., et al. (2012). Associations of identity dimensions with Big Five personality domains and facets. *European Journal of Personality*, DOI:10.1002/per.1853.

Knickmeyer, R., et al. (2005). Gender-typed play and amniotic testosterone. *Developmental Psychology*, 41, 517–528.

Kobayashi-Winata, H., & Power, T. G. (1989). Childrearing and compliance: Japanese and American families in Houston. *Journal of Cross-Cultural Psychology*, 20, 333–356.

Kochanek, K. D., et al. (2011). Deaths: Preliminary data for 2009. *National Vital Statistics Reports*, 59(4), Table 7. Hyattsville, MD: National Center for Health Statistics.

Kochanska, G. (2001). Emotional development in children with different attachment histories: The first three years. *Child Development*, 72(2), 474–490.

Kochanska, G., Coy, K. C., & Murray, K. T. (2001). The development of self-regulation in the first four years of life. *Child Development*, 72(4), 1091–1111.

Kohlberg, L. (1963). Moral development and identification. In H. W. Stevenson (Ed.), *Child psychology: 62nd yearbook of the National Society for the Study of Education*. Chicago: University of Chicago Press.

Kohlberg, L. (1966). Cognitive stages and preschool education. *Human Development*, 9, 5–17.

Kohlberg, L. (1969). Stage and sequence: The cognitive-developmental approach to socialization. In D. A. Goslin (Ed.), *Handbook of socialization theory and research*. Chicago: Rand McNally.

Kohlberg, L. (1981). *The meaning and measurement of moral development*. Worcester, MA: Clark University Press.

Kohlberg, L. (1985). *The psychology of moral development*. San Francisco: Harper & Row.

Kohlberg, L., & Kramer, R. (1969). Continuities and discontinuities in childhood and adult moral development. *Human Development*, 12, 93–120.

Kohyama, J., Shiiki, T., Ohinata-Sugimoto, J., & Hasegawa, T. (2002). Potentially harmful sleep habits of 3-year-old children in Japan. *Journal of Developmental and Behavioral Pediatrics*, 23(2), 67–70.

Kokko, K., et al. (2014). Country, sex, and parent occupational status: Moderators of the continuity of aggression from childhood to adulthood. *Aggressive Behavior*, 40(6), 552–567.

Kolb, B., & Gibb, R. (2007). Brain plasticity and recovery from early cortical injury. *Developmental Psychobiology*, 49(2), 107–118.

Kooistra, L., et al. (2010). Differentiating attention deficit in child with fetal alcohol spectrum disorder or attention-deficit-hyperactivity disorder. *Developmental Medicine & Child Neurology*, 52(2), 205–211.

Koopmans-van Beinum, F. J., Clement, C. J., & van den Dikkenberg-Pot, I. (2001). Babbling and the lack of auditory speech perception: A matter of coordination? *Developmental Science*, 4(1), 61–70.

Kopp, C. B. (1989). Regulation of distress and negative emotions: A developmental view. *Developmental Psychology*, 25, 343–354.

Kopp, C. B. (2011). Development in the early years: Socialization, motor development, and consciousness. *Annual Review of Psychology*, 62, 165–187.

Korja, R., Latva, R., & Lehtonen, L. (2011). The effects of preterm birth on mother-infant interaction and attachment during the infant's first two years. *ACTA Obstetrica et Gynecologica Scandinavica*, DOI:10.1111/j.1600-0412 .2011.01304.x.

Kornbluh, M., & Neal, J. W. (2015). Examining the many dimensions of children's popularity: Interactions between aggression, prosocial behaviors, and gender. *Journal of Social and Personal Relationships*, DOI:10.1177/0265407514562562.

Koss, K. J., Hostinar, C. E., Donzella, B., & Gunnar, M. R. (2014). Social deprivation and the HPA axis in early development. *Psychoneuroendocrinology*, 50, 1–13.

Kotlicka-Antczak, M., Pawelczyk, A., Rabe-Jablonska, J., Smigielski, J., & Pawelczyk, T. (2014). Obstetrical complications and Apgar scores in subjects at risk for psychosis. *Journal of Psychiatric Research*, 48(1), 79–85.

Kowalski, R. M., Giumetti, G. W., Schroeder, A. N., & Lattanner, M. R. (2014). Bullying in the digital age: A critical review and meta-analysis of cyberbullying research among youth. *Psychological Bulletin*, DOI:10.1037/a0035618.

Krebs, D. L., & Denton, K. (2006). Explanatory limitations of cognitive-developmental approaches to morality. *Psychological Review*, 113(3), 672–675.

Krebs, J. (2013). Moral dilemmas in serious games. *International Conference on Advanced Information and Communication Technology for Education* (pp. 232–236). Atlantis Press.

Kristof, N. D. (2012a, January 11). The value of teachers. *The New York Times*, p. A7.

Kroeger, K. A., & Nelson, W. M., III. (2006). A language programme to increase the verbal production of a child dually diagnosed with Down syndrome and autism. *Journal of Intellectual Disability Research*, 50(2), 101–108.

Kroger, J., & Marcia, J. E. (2011). The identity statuses: Origins, meanings, and interpretations. In S. J. Schwartz et al. (Eds.), Handbook of identity theory and research (Part 1, pp. 31–53). New York, NY: Springer.

Krueger, P. M., et al. (2015). Family structure and multiple domains of child well-being in the United States: A cross-sectional study. *Population Health Metrics*, 13(6). DOI:10.1186/s12963-015-0038-0.

Kuczaj, S. A., II. (1982). On the nature of syntactic development. In S. A. Kuczaj, II (Ed.), *Language development*, Vol. 1, *Syntax and semantics*. Hillsdale, NJ: Erlbaum.

Kuczmarski, R. J., et al. (2000, December 4). *CDC growth charts: United States. Advance Data from Vital and Health Statistics*, No. 314. Hyattsville, MD: National Center for Health Statistics.

Kuhl, P. K., et al. (1997). Cross-language analysis of phonetic units in language addressed to infants. *Science*, 277(5326), 684–686.

Kuhl, P. K., et al. (2006). Infants show a facilitation effect for native language phonetic perception between 6 and 12 months. *Developmental Science*, 9(2), F13–F21.

Kuja-Halkola, R., D'Onofrio, B. M., Larsson, H., & Lichtenstein, P. (2014). Maternal smoking during pregnancy and adverse outcomes in offspring. *Behavior Genetics*, 44(5), 456–467.

Kunnen, S. E., & Metz, M. (2015). Commitment and exploration: The need for a developmental approach. In K. C. McLean, & M. Syed (Eds.). *The Oxford handbook of identity development* (pp. 115–131). New York: Oxford University Press.

Kuo, P-H., et al. (2010). Genome-wide linkage scans for major depression in individuals with alcohol dependence. *Journal of Psychiatric Research*, 44(9), 616–619.

Kurosawa, K., Masuno, M., & Kuroki, Y. (2012). Trends in occurrence of twin births in Japan. *American Journal of Medical Genetics Part A*, 158A(1), 75–77.

Kurtz-Costes, B., Swinton, A. D., Skinner, O. D. (2014). Racial and ethnic gaps in the school performance of Latino, African American, and white students. In F. T. L. Leong, et al. (Eds.). *APA handbook of multicultural psychology, Vol. 1*: Theory and research (pp. 231–146). Washington, DC: American Psychological Association.

Kwok, J., & Selman, R. (2013). Moral reasoning, moral motivation and informed social reflection. *Handbook of Moral Motivation: Moral Development and Citizenship Education, Vol. 1*, 551–565.

Kyser, K. L., Morris, F. H., Bell, E. F., Klein, J. M., & Dagle, J. M. (2013). Improving survival of extremely premature infants born between 22 and 25 weeks of gestation. *Obstetric Anesthesia Digest*, 33(3), 159–159.

Labouvie-Vief, G. (2006). Emerging structures of adult thought. In J. J. Arnett & J. L. Tanner (Eds.), *Emerging adults in America* (pp. 59–84). Washington, DC: American Psychological Association.

Labouvie-Vief, G. (2015). Cognitive-emotional development in infants. In G. Labouvie-Vief (Ed.). *Integrating emotions and cognition throughout the lifespan* (pp. 45–66). New York: Springer International Publishing.

Lagattuta, K. H., et al. (2015). Beyond Sally's missing marble: Further development in children's understanding of mind and emotion in middle childhood. *Advances in Child Development and Behavior, 48,* 185–217.

Lagercrantz, H. (2010). Basic consciousness of a newborn. *Seminars in Perinatology, 34*(3), 201–206.

Lai, C. K., et al. (2009). Global variation in the prevalence and severity of asthma symptoms: Phase three of the International Study of Asthma and Allergies in Childhood (ISAAC). *Thorax, 64*(6), 476–483.

Lai, T. J., Guo, Y. I., Guo, N-W., & Hsu, C. C. (2001). Effect of prenatal exposure to polychlorinated biphenyls on cognitive development in children: A longitudinal study in Taiwan. *British Journal of Psychiatry, 178*(Suppl. 40), S49–S52.

Laible, D., Thompson, R. A., & Froimson, J. (2015). Early socialization: The influence of close relationships. In J. E. Grusec & P. D. Hastings (Eds.). *Handbook of socialization: Theory and Research* (pp. 35–59). New York: Guilford.

Lamaze, F. (1981). *Painless childbirth.* New York: Simon & Schuster.

Lampel, J., & Honig, B. (2006). Let the children play: Muppets in the middle of the Middle East. In J. Lampel, J. Shamsie & T. K. Lant (Eds.), *Strategic perspectives on entertainment and media.* Mahwah, NJ: Erlbaum.

Lampl, M. (2012). Limitation of growth chart curves in terms of individual growth biology. In V. R. Preedy (Ed.). *Handbook of growth and growth monitoring in health and disease* (pp. 3013–3027). New York: Springer Science+Business Media.

Lamy, C. (2012). Poverty is a knot, and preschool is an untangler. In R. C. Pianta (Ed.). *Early childhood education* (pp. 158–176). New York: Guilford.

Landolt, A. S., & Milling, L. S. (2011). The efficacy of hypnosis as an intervention for labor and delivery pain: A comprehensive methodological review. *Clinical Psychology Review, 31*(6), 1022–1031.

Landrigan, P. J. (2010). What causes autism? Exploring the environmental contribution. *Current Opinion in Pediatrics, 22*(2), 219–225.

Lansford, J. E., et al. (2009). Social network centrality and leadership status: Links with problem behaviors and tests of gender differences. *Merrill-Palmer Quarterly, 55*(1), 1–25.

Lansford, J. E., Yu, T., Petit, G. S., Bates, J. E., & Dodge, K. A. (2014). Pathways of peer relationships from childhood to young adulthood. *Journal of Applied Developmental Psychology, 35*(2), 111–117.

Lapsley, D. K. (2006). Moral stage theory. In K. Killen & J. G. Smetana (Eds.), *Handbook of moral development* (pp. 37–66). Mahwah, NJ: Erlbaum.

Lapsley, D. K., & Carlo, G. (2014). Moral development at the crossroads: New trends and possible futures. *Developmental Psychology, 50*(1), 1–7.

Largo, R. H., et al. (2001). Neuromotor development from 5 to 18 years. Part 1: Timed performance. *Developmental Medicine and Child Neurology, 43*(7), 436–443.

Larson, R., & Richards, M. H. (1991). Daily companionship in late childhood and early adolescence: Changing developmental contexts. *Child Development, 62,* 284–300.

Larzelere, R. E., Morris, A. S., & Harrist, A. W. (2013). *Authoritative parenting: Synthesizing nurturance and discipline for optimal child development.* Washington, DC: American Psychological Association.

Latkin, C. A., German, D., Vlahov, D., & Galea, S. (2013). Neighborhoods and HIV: A social ecological approach to prevention and care. *American Psychologist, 68*(4), 210–224.

Laturi, C. A., et al. (2010). Treatment of adolescent gynecomastia. *Journal of Pediatric Surgery, 45*(3), 650–654.

Laurendeau, M., & Pinard, A. (1970). *The development of the concept of space in the child.* New York: International Universities Press.

Laxman, D. J., et al. (2013). Stability and antecedents of coparenting quality: The parent personality and child temperament. *Infant Behavior and Development, 36*(2), 210–222.

Leaper, C. (2011). More similarities than differences in contemporary theories of social development? A plea for theory bridging. *Advances in Child Development and Behavior, 40,* 337–378.

Leaper, C. (2013). Gender development during childhood. In P. D. Zalazo (Ed.). *The Oxford handbook of developmental psychology,* Vol. 2: Self and other (pp. 326–377). New York: Oxford University Press.

Leaper, C., & Bigler, R. S. (2011). Gender. In M. K. Underwood & L. H. Rosen (Eds.), *Social development: Relationships in infancy, childhood, and adolescence* (pp. 289–315). New York: Guilford.

Leaper, C., & Farkas, T. (2015). The socialization of gender during childhood and adolescence. In J. E. Grusec & P. D. Hastings (Eds.). *Handbook of socialization: Theory and Research* (pp. 541–565). New York: Guilford.

Leaper, C., Farkas, T., & Brown, C. S. (2012). Adolescent girls' experiences and gender-related beliefs in relation to their motivation in math/science and English. *Journal of Youth and Adolescence, 41*(3), 268–282.

Lecce, S., Bianco, F., Demicheli, P., & Cavvalini, E. (2014). Training preschoolers on first-order false belief understanding: Transfer on advanced ToM skills and metamemory. *Child Development, 85*(6), 2404–2418.

Lecce, S., Demicheli, P., Zocchi, A., & Palladino, P. (2015). The origins of children's metamemory: The role of theory of mind. *Journal of Experimental Child Psychology, 131,* 56–72.

Lee, A., & Hankin, B. L. (2009). Insecure attachment, dysfunctional attitudes, and low self-esteem predicting prospective symptoms of depression and anxiety during adolescence. *Journal of Clinical Child and Adolescent Psychology, 38*(2), 219–231.

Lee, A. C., He, J., & Ma, M. (2011). Olfactory marker protein is crucial for functional maturation of olfactory sensory neurons and development of mother preference. *The Journal of Neuroscience, 31*(8), 2974–2982.

Lee, N. R., Lopez, K. C., Adeyemi, E. I., & Giedd, J. N. (2011). Sex chromosome aneuploidies: A window for examining the effects of the X and Y chromosomes on speech, language, and social development. In D. J. Fidler (Ed.). *Early development in neurogenetic disorders* (pp. 141–171). New York: Elsevier.

Lee, S. A. S., & Davis, B. L. (2010). Segmental distribution patterns of English infant- and adult-directed speech. *Journal of Child Language, 37,* 767–791.

Leech, R. M., McNaughton, S. A., & Timperio, A. (2014). The clustering of diet, physical activity and sedentary behavior in children and adolescents: A review. *International Journal of Behavioral Nutrition and Physical Activity, 11*(4). Available at http://www.ijbnpa.org /content/11/1/4.

Leerkes, E. M., Paradise, M. J., O'Brien, M., Calkins, S. D., & Lange, G. (2008). Emotion and cognition processes in preschool children. *Merrill-Palmer Quarterly, 54*(1), 102–124.

Leiner, M., et al. (2014). Psychosocial profile of bullies, victims, and bully-victims: A cross-sectional study. *Frontiers in Pediatrics,* DOI:10.3389/fped.2014.00001.

Lenneberg, E. H. (1967). *Biological foundations of language.* New York: Wiley.

Lenroot, R. K., et al. (2009). Differences in genetic and environmental influences on the human cerebral cortex associated with development during childhood and adolescence. *Human Brain Mapping, 30*(1), 163–173.

Lepola, J., Vaurus, M., & Maeki, H. (2000). Gender differences in the development of academic self-concept of attainment from the 2nd to the 6th grade: Relations with achievement and perceived motivational orientation. *Psychology: The Journal of the Hellenic Psychological Society, 7*(3), 290–308.

Lerner, R. M., & Benson, B. J. (Eds.). (2013). *Advances in child development and behavior: Embodiment and epigenesist,* Vol. 44. Waltham, MA: Elsevier.

Lester, B. M., & Tronick, E. Z. (2004). *NICU Network Neurobehavioral Scale (NNNS) manual.* Baltimore, MD: Brookes.

Leung, F. K. S., Park, K., Shimizu, Y., & Xu, B. (2015). Mathematics education in East Asia. In S. J. Cho (Ed.). *The Proceedings of the 12*th *International Congress on Mathematical Education* (pp. 123–143). SpringerLink.

Leung, P., Curtis, R. L., Jr., & Mapp, S. C. (2010). Incidences of sexual contacts of children: Impacts of family characteristics and family structure from a national sample. *Children and Youth Services Review, 32*(5), 650–656.

Leung, P. W. L., & Poon, M. W. L. (2001). Dysfunctional schemas and cognitive distortions in psychopathology. *The Journal of Child Psychology and Psychiatry and Allied Disciplines, 42,* 755–765.

Levendosky, A. A., Bogat, G. A., - Huth-Bocks, A. C., Rosenblum, K., & von Eye, A. (2011). *Journal of Clinical Child & Adolescent Psychology, 40*(3), 398–410.

Levitt, M. J., Weber, R. A., Clark, M. C., & McDonnell, P. (1985). Reciprocity of exchange in toddler sharing behavior. *Developmental Psychology, 21,* 122–123.

Levy, G. D., Sadovsky, A. L., & Troseth, G. L. (2000). Aspects of young children's perceptions of gender-typed occupations. *Sex Roles, 42*(11–12), 993–1006.

Lewin, T. (2014, September 17). Surrogates and couples face a maze of laws, state by state. *The New York Times.* Retrived from http://www.nytimes.com.

Lewis, B. A., et al. (2004). Four-year language outcomes of children exposed to cocaine in utero. *Neurotoxicology and Teratology, 26*(5), 617–627.

Lewis, B. A., et al. (2011). The effects of prenatal cocaine on language development at 10 years of age. *Neurotoxicology and Teratology, 33*(1), 17–24.

Lewis, M., & Feiring, C. (1989). Early predictors of childhood friendship. In T. J. Berndt & G. W. Ladd (Eds.), *Peer relationships in child development.* New York: Wiley.

Lewis, M. D. (2013). The development of emotion regulation: Integrating normative and individual differences through developmental neuroscience. In P. D. Zelazo (Ed.). *The Oxford handbook of developmental psychology,* Vol. 2: Personality and emotional development (pp. 81–97). New York: Oxford University Press.

Lewis, S. (2011). Development: Pruning the dendritic tree. *Nature Reviews Neuroscience, 12,* 493. DOI:10.1038/nrn3099.

Li, X., et al. (2015). Pathological changes of the inner ear cochlea in different time windows of murine cytomegalovirus-induced hearing loss in a mouse model. *Acta Oto-laryngologica,* DOI:10.3109/00016489.2014.995830.

Liaudet, L., Calderari, B., & Pacher, P. (2014). Pathophysiological mechanisms of catecholamine and cocaine-mediated cardiotoxicity. *Heart Failure Reviews,* DOI:10.1007/s10741-014-9418-y.

Liben, L. S., Bigler, R. S., & Hilliard, L. J. (2014). Gender development: From universality to individuality. In E. T. Gershoff, R. G. Mistry, & D. A. Crosby (Eds.). *Societal contexts of child development: Pathways of influence and implications for practice and policy* (pp. 3–18). New York: Oxford University Press.

Lick, D. J., Schmidt, K. M., & Patterson, C. J. (2011). The Rainbow Families Scale (RFS): A measure of experiences among individuals with lesbian and gay parents. *Journal of Applied Measurement, 12*(3), 222–241.

Lick, D. J., Tornello, S. L., Riskind, R. G., Schmidt, K. M., & Patterson, C. J. (2012). Social climate for sexual minorities predicts well-being among heterosexual offspring of lesbian and gay parents. *Sexuality Research and Social Policy, 9*(2), 99–112.

Lickenbrock, D. M., et al. (2013). Early temperament and attachment security with mothers and fathers as predictors of toddler compliance and noncompliance. *Infant and Child Development, 22*(6), 580–602.

Lillard, A. S., Li, H., & Boguszewski, K. (2015). Chapter 7—Television and children's executive function. *Advances in Child Development and Behavior, 48,* 219–248.

Lim, L., et al. (2015). Disorder-specific grey matter deficits in attention deficit hyperactivity disorder relative to autism spectrum disorder. *Psychological Medicine, 45*(5), 965–976.

Limin Shi, N. T., & Patterson, P. H. (2005). Maternal influenza infection is likely to alter fetal brain development indirectly: The virus is not detected in the fetus. *International Journal of Developmental Neuroscience, 23*(2–3), 299–305.

Lin, J-H. (2013). Do video games exert stronger effects on aggression than film? The role of media interactivity and identification on the association of violent content and aggressive outcomes. *Computers in Human Behavior, 29*(3), 535–543.

Lindsay, A. R., et al. (2014). Field assessments for obesity prevention in children and adults: Physical activity, fitness, and body composition. *Journal of Nutrition Education and Behavior, 46*(1), 43–53.

Lipman, E. L., et al. (2006). Testing effectiveness of a community-based aggression management program for children 7 to 11 years old and their families. *Journal of the American Academy of Child & Adolescent Psychiatry, 45*(9), 1085–1093.

Lipsitt, L. P. (2002). Early experience and behavior in the baby of the twenty-first century. In J. Gomes-Pedro et al. (Eds.), *The infant and family in the twenty-first century* (pp. 55–78). London: Brunner-Routledge.

Lipsitt, L. P. (2003). Crib death: A biobehavioral phenomenon? *Current Directions in Psychological Science, 12*(5), 164–170.

Liu, J., et al. (2008). The role of antenatal corticosteroids for improving the maturation of choroid plexus capillaries in fetal mice. *Pediatrics, 167*(10), 1209–1212.

Liu, R. T., & Mustanski, B. (2012). Suicidal ideation and self-harm in lesbian, gay, bisexual, and transgender youth. *American Journal of Preventive Medicine, 42*(3), 221–228.

Liu, X., et al. (2000a). Behavioral and emotional problems in Chinese children of divorced parents. *Journal of the American Academy of Child and Adolescent Psychiatry, 39*(7), 896–903.

Liu, X., Sun, Z., Uchiyama, M., Li, Y., & Okawa, M. (2000b). Attaining nocturnal urinary control, nocturnal enuresis, and behavioral problems in Chinese children aged 6 through 16 years. *Journal of the American Academy of Child and Adolescent Psychiatry, 39*(12), 1557–1564.

Llewellyn, C. H. (2011). Genetic influences on appetite and weight in infancy. Doctoral thesis, UCL (University College London).

Loeb, K. L., Le Grange, D., & Lock, J. (2015). *Family therapy for adolescent eating and weight disorders.* New York: Routledge.

Logue, D. D., Logue, R. T., Kaufmann, W. E., & Belcher, H. M. E. (2015). Psychiatric disorders and left-handedness in children living in an urban environment. *Laterality: Asymmetries of Body, Brain and Cognition, 20*(2), 249–256.

Lohmann, R. I. (2004). Sex and sensibility: Margaret Mead's descriptive and rhetorical ethnography. *Reviews in Anthropology, 33*(2), 111–130.

Lorenz, K. (1962). *King Solomon's ring.* London: Methuen.

Lorenz, K. (1981). *The foundations of ethology.* New York: Springer-Verlag.

Lovaas, O. I., Smith, T., & McEachin, J. J. (1989). Clarifying comments on the young autism study: Reply to Schapler, Short, and Mesibov. *Journal of Consulting and Clinical Psychology, 57,* 165–167.

Lowrey A. (2012, January 6). Big study links good teachers to lasting gain. *The New York Times,* p. A1.

Lubinski, D. (2004). Introduction to the special section on cognitive abilities: 100 years after Spearman's (1904) "'General Intelligence,' Objectively Determined and Measured." *Journal of Personality and Social Psychology, 86*(1), 96–111.

Lucas, C. P., Hazen, E. P., and Shaffer, D. (2015). Childhood elimination disorders. In A. Tasman, J. Kay, J. A. Lieberman, M. B. First, & M. B. Riba (Eds.) *Psychiatry* (4th ed.). Chichester, UK: John Wiley. DOI:10.1002/9781118753378.ch65.

Lucassen, N., et al. (2011). The association between paternal sensitivity and infant–father attachment security: A meta-analysis of three decades of research. *Journal of Family Psychology, 25*(6), 986–992.

Luciano, M., Kirk, K. M., Heath, A. C., & Martin, N. G. (2005). The genetics of tea and coffee drinking and preference for source of caffeine in a large community sample of Australian twins. *Addiction, 100*(10), 1510–1517.

Luders, E., Thompson, P. M., & Toga, A. W. (2010). The development of the corpus callosum in the healthy human brain. *The Journal of Neuroscience, 30*(33), 10985–10990.

Lundborg, G. (2014). Right hand or left hand? In G. Lundborg (Ed.) *The Hand and the Brain* (pp. 145–153). London: Springer-Verlag.

Lundstrom, S., et al. (2012). Autism spectrum disorders and autisticlike traits. *Archives of General Psychiatry, 69*(1), 46–52.

Lustig, S. L. (2011). Chaos and its influence on children's development: An ecological perspective. In G. W. Evans & T. D. Wachs (Eds.). *Decade of behavior (science conference)* (pp. 239–251). Washington, DC: American Psychological Association.

Lykken, D. T., & Csikszentmihalyi, M. (2001). Happiness: Stuck with what you've got? *Psychologist, 14*(9), 470–472.

Lynch, J. B., et al. (2011). The breadth and potency of passively acquired human immunodeficiency virus Type 1- Specific neutralizing antibodies do not correlate with the risk of infant infection. *Journal of Virology, 85*(11), 5252–5261.

Lynne, S. D., Graber, J. A., Nichols, T. R., Brooks-Gunn, J., & Botvin, G. J. (2007). Links between pubertal timing, peer influences, and externalizing behaviors among urban students followed through middle school. *Journal of Adolescent Health, 40*(2), 181.e7–181.e13.

Lyon, G. R., Shaywitz, S. E., & Shaywitz, B. A. (2003). A definition of dyslexia. *Annals of Dyslexia, 53*, 1–14.

Maccoby, E. E. (2015). Historical overview of socialization research and theory. In J. E. Grusec & P. D. Hastings (Eds.). *Handbook of socialization: Theory and Research* (pp. 3–34). New York: Guilford.

Maccoby, E. E., & Jacklin, C. N. (1974). *The psychology of sex differences.* Stanford, CA: Stanford University Press.

Macfarlane, A. (1975). Olfaction in the development of social preferences in the human neonate. In M. A. Hofer (Ed.), *Parent–infant interaction.* Amsterdam: Elsevier.

Macfarlane, A. (1977). The psychology of childbirth. Cambridge, MA: Harvard University Press.

Mackner, L. M., Black, M. M., & Starr, R. H., Jr. (2003). Cognitive development of children in poverty with failure to thrive: A prospective study through age 6. *Journal of Child Psychology and Psychiatry and Allied Disciplines, 44*(5), 743–751.

Maclean, A. M., Walker, L. J., & Matsuba, M. K. (2004). Transcendence and the moral self: Identity integration, religion, and moral life. *Journal for the Scientific Study of Religion, 43*(3), 429–437.

MacWhinney, B. (1998). Models of the emergence of language. *Annual Review of Psychology, 49*, 199–227.

MacWhinney, B., & O'Grady, W. (2015). *The handbook of language emergence* (pp. 600–623). West Sussex, UK: Wiley.

Madden, M. (2013). Teens haven't abandoned Facebook (yet). Available at http://www .pewinternet.org/2013/08/15/teens-havent-abandoned-facebook-yet/.

Madkour, A. S., Harville, E. W., & Xie, Y. (2014). Neighborhood disadvantage, racial concentration, and the birthweight of infants born to adolescent mothers. *Maternal and Child Health Journal, 18*(3), 663–671.

Malaspina, D. (2009). Cited in L. Belkin (2009, April 5), Your old man, *The New York Times Magazine.*

Malekoff, A. (2004). *Group work with adolescents* (2nd ed.). New York: Guilford.

Malone, P. S., et al. (2004). Divorce and child behavior problems: Applying latent change score models to life event data. *Structural Equation Modeling, 11*(3), 401–423.

Manchak, S. M., & Cullen, F. T. (2015). Intervening effectively with juvenile offenders: Answers from meta-analysis. In J. Morizot, & L. Kazemian (Eds.). *The development of criminal and antisocial behavior* (pp. 477–490). New York: Springer International Publishing.

Marchant, M., & Anderson, D. H. (2012). Improving social and academic outcomes for all learners through the use of teacher praise. *Beyond Behavior, 21*(3), 22–28.

Marcia, J. E. (2010). Life transitions and stress in the context of psychosocial development. In T. W. Miller (Ed.). *Handbook of stressful transitions across the lifespan, Part 1* (pp. 19–34). New York: Springer Science+Business Media, LLC.

Marcia, J. E. (2014). From industry to integrity. *Identity: An International Journal of Theory and Research, 14*(3), 165–176.

Marcovitch, S., et al. (2015). A longitudinal assessment of the relation between executive function and theory of mind at 3, 4, and 5 years. *Cognitive Development, 33*, 40–55.

Marean, G. C., Werner, L. A., & Kuhl, P. K. (1992). Vowel categorization by very young infants. *Developmental Psychology, 28*, 396–405.

Mares, M., & Pan, Z. (2013). Effects of Sesame Street: A meta-analysis of children's learning in 15 countries. *Journal of Applied Developmental Psychology, 34*(3), 140–151.

Maric, M., et al. (2013). Cognitive mediation of cognitive-behavioural therapy outcomes for anxiety-based school refusal. *Behavioural and Cognitive Psychotherapy, 41*(5), 549–564.

Maric, M., van Steensel, F. J. A., & Bogels, S. M. (2015). Parental involvement in CBT for anxiety-disordered youth revisited: Family CBT outperforms child CBT in the long term for children with comorbid ADHD symptoms. *Journal of Attention Disorders,* DOI:10.1177/1087054715573991.

Markova, G., & Legerstee, M. (2006). Contingency, imitation, and affect sharing: Foundations of infants' social awareness. *Developmental Psychology, 42*(1), 132–141.

Markovits, H., & Lortie-Forgues, H. (2011). Conditional reasoning with false premises facilitates the transition between familiar and abstract reasoning. *Child Development, 82*(2), 646–660.

Markus, H., & Kitayama, S. (1991). Culture and the self. *Psychological Review, 98*(2), 224–253.

Marlier, L., & Schaal, B. (2005). Human newborns prefer human milk: Conspecific milk odor is attractive without postnatal exposure. *Child Development, 76*(1), 155–168.

Marsiglio, W. (2004). When stepfathers claim stepchildren: A conceptual analysis. *Journal of Marriage and Family, 66*(1), 22–39.

Martel, M-J., et al. (2008). Determinants of the incidence of childhood asthma: A two-stage case-control study. *American Journal of Epidemiology,* DOI:10.1093/aje/kwn309.

Martel, M. M., et al. (2011). The dopamine receptor D4 gene (DRD4) moderates family environmental effects on ADHD. (2011). *Journal of Abnormal Child Psychology, 39*(1), 1–10.

Martin, C. L., & Dinella, L. M. (2012). Congruence between gender stereotypes and activity preference in self-identified tomboys and non-tomboys. *Archives of Sexual Behavior, 41*(3), 599–610.

Martin, C. L., & Ruble, D. (2004). Children's search for gender cues: Cognitive perspectives on gender development. *Current Directions in Psychological Science, 13*(2), 67–70.

Martin, J., & Sokol, B. (2011). Generalized others and imaginary audience: A neo-Meadian approach to adolescent egocentrism. *New Ideas in Psychology, 29*(3), 364–375.

Martincin, K. M., & Stead, G. B. (2015). Five-factor model and difficulties in career decision making: A meta-analysis. *Journal of Career Assessment, 23*(1), 3–19.

Martinez, G., Abma, J., & Copen, C. (2010). *Educating teenagers about sex in the United States.* NCHS data brief no. 44. Hyattsville, MD: National Center for Health Statistics.

Martinez, G., Copen, C. E., & Abma, J. C. (2011). Teenagers in the United States: Sexual activity, contraceptive use, and childbearing, 2006–2010. National Survey of Family Growth. National Center for Health Statistics. *Vital and Health Statistics, 23*(31).

Martínez, I., Musitu, G., Garcia, J. F., & Camino, L. (2003). A cross-cultural analysis of the effects of family socialization on self-concept: Spain and Brazil. *Psicologia Educação Cultura, 7*(2), 239–259.

Martire, S. I., Westbrook, R. F., & Morris, M. J. (2015). Effects of long-term cycling between palatable cafeteria diet and regular chow on intake, eating patterns, and response to saccharin and sucrose. *Physiology & Behavior, 139*, 80–88.

Massaro, A. N., et al. (2014). Biomarkers S100B and neuron-specific enolase predict outcome in hypothermia-treated encephalopathic newborns. *Pediatric Critical Care Medicine, 15*(7), 615–622.

Mathews, T. J., & MacDorman, M. F. (2007). Infant mortality statistics from the 2004 period linked birth/infant death data set. *National Vital Statistics Reports, 55*(14). Hyattsville, MD: National Center for Health Statistics.

Maughan, B. (2011). Family and systemic influences. In D. Skuse, H. Bruce, L. Dowdney, & D. Mrazek (Eds.). *Child psychology and psychiatry: Frameworks for practice* (2nd ed.) (pp. 1–7). Hoboken, NJ: Wiley.

Maundeni, T. (2000). The consequences of parental separation and divorce for the economic, social and emotional circumstances of children in Botswana. *Childhood: A Global Journal of Child Research, 7*(2), 213–223.

Maurer, D. M., Lewis, T. L., Brent, H. P., & Levin, A. V. (1999). Rapid improvement in the acuity of infants after visual input. *Science, 286*(5437), 108–110.

Maurer, D. M., & Maurer, C. E. (1976, October). Newborn babies see better than you think. *Psychology Today,* pp. 85–88.

Mayer, S. J. (2008). Dewey's dynamic integration of Vygotsky and Piaget. *Education and Culture, 24*(2), Article 3.

Available at http://docs.lib.purdue.edu/eandc/vol24/iss2/art3.

Mayes, L. C., & Ward, A. (2003). Principles of neurobehavioral teratology. In D. Cicchetti & E. Walker (Eds.), *Neurodevelopmental mechanisms in psychopathology* (pp. 3–33). New York: Cambridge University Press.

Mayor, J., & Plunkett, K. (2010). A neurocomputational account of taxonomic responding and fast mapping in early word learning. *Psychological Review*, *117*(1), 1–31.

Maynard, A. E., Subrahmanyam, K., & Greenfield, P. M. (2005). Technology and the development of intelligence: From the loom to the computer. In R. J. Sternberg & D. D. Preiss (Eds.), *Intelligence and technology: The impact of tools on the nature and development of human abilities. The educational psychology series* (pp. 29–53). Mahwah, NJ: Erlbaum.

McAweeney, M., et al. (2010). Symptom prevalence of ADHD in a community residential substance abuse treatment program. *Journal of Attention Disorders*, *13*(6), 601–608.

McCall, R. B. (1977). Childhood IQ's as predictors of adult educational and occupational status. *Science, 197*(4302), 482–483.

McCall, R. B., Applebaum, M. I., & Hogarty, P. S. (1973). *Developmental changes in mental performance*. Monographs of the Society for Research in Child Development, 38(3, ser. 150).

McCardle, P., Colombo, J., & Freud, L. (2009). Measuring language in infancy. In J. Colombo, P. McCardle & L. Freud (Eds.), *Infant pathways to language: Methods, models, and research disorders* (pp. 1–12). New York: Psychology Press.

McCartney, K., Owen, M. T., Booth, C. L., Clarke-Stewart, K. A., & Vandell, D. L. (2004). Testing a maternal attachment model of behavior problems in early childhood. *Journal of Child Psychology and Psychiatry, 45*(4), 765–778.

McCarty, C., Prawitz, A. D., Derscheid, L. E., & Montgomery, B. (2011). Perceived safety and teen risk taking in online chat sites. *Cyberpsychology, Behavior, and Social Networking, 14*(3), 169–174.

McGlaughlin, A., & Grayson, A. (2001). Crying in the first year of infancy: Patterns and prevalence. *Journal of Reproductive and Infant Psychology, 19*(1), 47–59.

McGue, M., Bouchard, T. J., Jr., Iacono, W. G., & Lykken, D. T. (1993). Behavioral genetics of cognitive ability: A life-span perspective. In R. Plomin & G. E. McClearn (Eds.), *Nature, nurture & psychology* (pp. 59–76). Washington, DC: American Psychological Association.

McGue, M., & Christensen, K. (2013). Growing old but not growing apart: Twin similarity in the latter half of the lifespan. *Behavior Genetics, 43*(1), 1–12.

McLafferty, C. L., Jr. (2006). Examining unproven assumptions of Galton's nature–nurture paradigm. *American Psychologist, 61*(2), 177–178.

McLeod, J. D., & Knight, S. (2010). The association of socioemotional problems with early sexual initiation. *Perspectives on Sexual and Reproductive Health, 42*(2), 93–101.

McLoughlin, A. B., Gould, M. S., & Malone, K. M. (2015). Global trends in teenage suicide: 2003–2014. *QJM*, DOI:10.1093/qjmed/hcv026.

McMurray, B., Kovack-Lesh, K. A., Goodwin, D., & McEchron, W. (2013). Infant directed speech and the development of speech perception: Enhancing development or an unintended consequence? *Cognition, 129*(2), 362–378.

McElroy, S. L., Guerdjikova, A. I., Mori, N., & Keck, P. E. (2015). Psychopharmacologic treatment of eating disorders: Emerging findings. *Current Psychiatry Reports, 17*(35). DOI:10.1007/s11920-015-0573-1.

Medland, S. E., et al. (2009). Genetic influences on handedness: Data from 25,732 Australian and Dutch twin families. *Neuropsychologia, 47*(2), 330–337.

Medline Plus. (2014, October 9). Miscarriage. U.S. National Library of Medicine, National Institutes of Health. Available at http://www.nlm.nih.gov/medlineplus/ency/article/001488.htm.

Meek, J. Y. (Ed.). (2011). *American Academy of Pediatrics New Mother's Guide to Breastfeeding* (2nd ed.). New York: Bantam Books.

Mehler, P. S., & Brown, C. (2015). Anorexia nervosa—Medical complications. *Journal of Eating Disorders, 3*(11). DOI:10.1186/s40337-015-0040-8.

Melegari, M. G., et al. (2015). Temperamental and character profiles of preschool children with ODD, ADHD, and anxiety disorders. *Comprehensive Psychiatry, 58*, 94–101.

Mellet, E. et al. (2014). Relationships between hand laterality and verbal and spatial skills in 436 healthy adults balanced for handedness. *Laterality: Asymmetries of Body, Brain and Cognition, 19*(4), 383–404.

Melroy, W. E., et al. (2014). Examination of genetic variation in GABRA2 with conduct disorder and alcohol abuse and dependence in a longitudinal study. *Behavior Genetics, 44*, 356–367.

Meltzoff, A. N. (2010). Social cognition and the origins of imitation, empathy, and theory of mind. In U. Goswami (Ed.), *The Wiley–Blackwell handbook of childhood cognitive development*. (2nd ed.) (pp. 49–75). Chichester, West Sussex, UK: Wiley–Blackwell.

Meltzoff, A. N., & Moore, M. K. (1977). "Imitation of facial and manual gestures by human neonates," *Science*, 198 (1977), 75–78.

Meltzoff, A. N., & Moore, M. K. (2002). Imitation, memory, and the representation of persons. *Infant Behavior and Development, 25*(1), 39–61.

Meltzoff, A. N., Williamson, R. A., & Marshall, P. J. (2013). Developmental perspectives on action science: Lessons from infant imitation and cognitive neuroscience. In W. Prinz, M. Beisert, & A. Herwig (Eds.), *Action science: Foundations of an emerging discipline* (pp. 281–306). Cambridge, MA: MIT Press.

Mendelsohn, F., & Warren, M. (2010). Anorexia, bulimia, and the female athlete triad: Evaluation and management. *Endocrinology and Metabolism Clinics of North America, 39*(1), 155–167.

Mendez, L. M. R. (2000). Gender roles and achievement-related choices: A comparison of early adolescent girls in gifted and general education programs. *Journal for the Education of the Gifted, 24*(2), 149–169.

Mennella, J., Turnbull, B., Ziegler, P., & Martinez. H. (2005). Infant feeding practices and early flavor experiences in Mexican infants. *Journal of the American Dietetic Association, 105*(6), 908–915.

Mennella, J. A. (2001). Regulation of milk intake after exposure to alcohol in mothers' milk. *Alcoholism: Clinical and Experimental Research, 25*(4), 590–593.

Mennella, J. A. (2014). Ontogeny of taste preferences: Basic biology and implications for health. *The American Journal of Clinical Nutrition, 99*(3), 7045–7115.

Mennella, J. A., & Garcia, P. L. (2000). Children's hedonic response to the smell of alcohol: Effects of parental drinking habits. *Alcoholism: Clinical & Experimental Research, 24*(8), 1167–1171.

Mercken, L., Steglich, C., Knibbe, R., & Vries, H. (2012). Dynamics of friendship networks and alcohol use in early and mid-adolescence. *Journal of Studies in Alcohol and Drugs, 73*(1), 99–110.

Mesman, J., Bongers, I. L., & Koot, H. M. (2001). Preschool developmental pathways to preadolescent internalizing and externalizing problems. *Journal of Child Psychology and Psychiatry and Allied Disciplines, 42*(5), 679–689.

Meyer, P. (2009). Evaluation and management of gynecomastia. *Revue Médicale Suisse, 5*(198), 783–787.

Mezzacappa, E. S., Kelsey, R. M., & Katkin, E. S. (2005). Breast feeding, bottle feeding, and maternal autonomic responses to stress. *Journal of Psychosomatic Research, 58*(4), 351–365.

Michels, N., et al. (2015). Longitudinal association between child stress and lifestyle. *Health Psychology, 34*(1), 40–50.

Miklos, E. A., Brahler, C. J., Baer, J. T., & Dolan, P. (2004). Dietary deficiencies and excesses: A sample of African American mothers and daughters eligible for nutrition assistance programs. *Family and Community Health, 27*(2), 123–129.

Mikulincer, M., & Shaver, P. R. (2001). Attachment theory and intergroup bias: Evidence that priming the secure base schema attenuates negative reactions to out-groups. *Journal of Personality and Social Psychology, 81*(1), 97–115.

Miljkovitch, R., Danet, M., & Bernier, A. (2012). Intergenerational transmission of attachment representations in the context of single parenthood in France. *Journal of Family Psychology, 26*(5), 784–792.

Millar, W. S. (1990). Span of integration for delayed-reward contingency learning in 6- to 8-month-old infants. In A. Diamond (Ed.), *The development and neural bases of higher cognitive functions*. New York: New York Academy of Sciences.

Miller, D. I., & Halpern, D. F. (2014). The new science of cognitive sex differences. *Trends in Cognitive Sciences*, 18(1), 37–45.

Miller, F. A., Christensen, R., Giacomini, M., & Robert, J. S. (2008). Duty to disclose what? Querying the putative obligation to return research results to participants. *Journal of Medical Ethics*, 34(3), 210–213.

Miller, G. A. (1956). The magical number seven, plus or minus two: Some limits on our capacity to process information. *Psychological Review*, 63, 81–97.

Miller, P. H. (2010). In U. Goswami (Ed.), *The Wiley–Blackwell handbook of childhood cognitive development*. (2nd ed.) (pp. 649–672). Chichester, West Sussex, UK: Wiley–Blackwell.

Miniño, A. M. (2010). Mortality among teenagers aged 12–19 years: United States, 1999–2006. Centers for Disease Control and Prevention. NCHS data brief. Number 37, May 2010. Retrieved from http://www.cdc.gov/nchs/data/databriefs/db37.htm. Accessed September 19, 2012.

Minnes, S., Lang, A., & Singer, L. (2011). Prenatal tobacco, marijuana, stimulant, and opiate exposure: Outcomes and practice implications. *Addiction Science & Clinical Practice*, 6(1), 57–70.

Miranda, A., & Presentacion, M. J. (2000). Efectos de un tratamiento cognitivo-conductual en niños con trastorno por déficit de atención con hiperactividad, agresivos y no agresivos: Cambio clínicamente significativo. *Infancia y Aprendizaje*, 92, 51–70.

Miranda, R., & Shaffer, D. (2013). Understanding the suicidal moment in adolescence. *Annals of the New York Academy of Sciences*, 1304, 14–21.

Mirkovic, K. R., Perrine, C. G., Scanlon, K. S., & Grummer-Strawn, L. M. (2014). In the United States, a mother's plans for infant feeding are associated with her plans for employment. *Journal of Human Lactation*, 30(3), 292–297.

Mishra, G. D., Cooper, R., Tom, S. E., & Kuh, D. (2009). Early life circumstances and their impact on menarche and menopause. *Women's Health*, 5(2), 175–190.

Misra, D. P., Caldwell, C., Young, A. A., & Abelson, S. (2010). Do fathers matter? Paternal contributions to birth outcomes and racial disparities. *American Journal of Obstetrics & Gynecology*, 202(2), 99–100.

Mitchell, K. S., & Bulik, C. M. (2013). Life course epidemiology of eating disorders. In K. C. Koenen, et al. (Eds.). *A life course approach to mental disorders* (pp. 148–155). New York: Oxford.

Miyake, Y., et al. (2010). Neural processing of negative word stimuli concerning body image in patients with eating disorders: An fMRI study. *NeuroImage*, 50(3), 1333–1339.

Modecki, K. L., Barber, B. L., & Eccles, J. S. (2014). Binge drinking trajectories across adolescence: For early maturing youth, extra-curricular activities are protective. *Journal of Adolescent Health*, 54(1), 61–66.

Mohatt, J. W., Keller, E. K., & Walkup, J. T. (2013). Psychopharmacology of pediatric anxiety disorders. *Current Clinical Psychiatry*, 289–314.

Molfese, V. J., DiLalla, L. F., & Bunce, D. (1997). Prediction of the intelligence test scores of 3- to 8-year-old children by home environment, socioeconomic status, and biomedical risks. *Merrill-Palmer Quarterly*, 43(2), 219–234.

Monk, C., Georgieff, M. K., & Osterholm, E. A. (2013). Research review: Maternal prenatal distress and poor nutrition—mutually influencing risk factors affecting infant neurocognitive development. *The Journal of Child Psychology and Psychiatry*, 54(2), 115–130.

Montemayor, R., & Eisen, M. (1977). The development of self-conceptions from childhood to adolescence. *Developmental Psychology*, 13, 314–319.

Montero, I., & De Dios, M. J. (2006). Vygotsky was right. An experimental approach to the relationship between private speech and task performance. *Estudios de Psicología*, 27(2), 175–189.

Montoya, E. R., Terburg, D., Bos, P. A., & van Honk, J. (2012). Testosterone, cortisol, and serotonin as key regulators of social aggression: A review and theoretical perspective. *Motivation and Emotion*, 36(1), 65–73.

Moon, M. (2011). The effects of divorce on children: Married and divorced parents' perspectives. *Journal of Divorce & Remarriage*, 52(5), 344–349.

Moon, R. Y., et al. (2011). Pacifier use and SIDS: Evidence for a consistently reduced risk. *Maternal and Child Health Journal*, DOI:10.1007/s10995-011-0793-x.

Moore, D. S. (2007). A very little bit of knowledge: Re-evaluating the meaning of the heritability of IQ. *Human Development*, 49(6), 347–353.

Moore, L. L., et al. (1991). Influence of parents' physical activity levels on activity levels of young children. *Journal of Pediatrics*, 118, 215–219.

Moreno-Briseño, P., et al. (2010). Sex-related differences in motor learning and performance. *Brain and Behavioral Functions*, 6, 74.

Morgenstern, A., Leroy-Collombel, M., & Caet, S. (2013). Self- and other-repairs in child–adult interaction at the intersection of pragmatic abilities and language acquisition. *Journal of Pragmatics*, 56, 151–167.

Morine, K. A., et al. (2011). Relational aggression in preschool students: An exploration of the variables of sex, age, and siblings. *Child Development Research*, DOI:10.1155/2011/931720.

Morrell, H. E. R., Lapsley, D. K., & Halpern-Felsher, B. L. (2015). Subjective invulnerability and perceptions of tobacco-related benefits predict adolescent smoking behavior. *The Journal of Early Adolescence*, DOI:10.1177/0272431615578274.

Morrell, J., & Steele, H. (2003). The role of attachment security, temperament, maternal perception, and care-giving behavior in persistent infant sleeping problems. *Infant Mental Health Journal*, 24(5), 447–468.

Morrison, D. R., & Coiro, M. J. (1999). Parental conflict and marital disruption: Do children benefit when high-conflict marriages are dissolved? *Journal of Marriage and the Family*, 61(3), 626–637.

Morrison, E. S. (1980). Growing up sexual. New York: Van Nostrand Co.

Morrison, K. M., Shin, S., Tarnopolsky, M., & Taylor, V. H. (2015). Association of depression & health related quality of life with body composition in children and youth with obesity. *Journal of Affective Disorders*, 172, 18–23.

Morton, S. M. B. (2006). Maternal nutrition and fetal growth and development. In P. Gluckman & M. Hanson (Eds.), *Developmental origins of health and disease* (pp. 98–129). New York: Cambridge University Press.

Moses, L. J., & Flavell, J. H. (1990). Inferring false beliefs from actions and reactions. *Child Development*, 61, 929–945.

Mosher, W. D., Chandra, A., & Jones, J. (2005). *Sexual behavior and selected health measures: Men and women 15–44 years of age, United States, 2002. Advance data from vital and health statistics.* Centers for Disease Control and Prevention. National Center for Health Statistics, Number 362, Figures 2 and 3.

Moshman, D. (2011). *Adolescent rationality and development: Cognition, morality, and identity* (3rd ed.). New York: Psychology Press.

Moshman, D. (2013). Epistemic cognition and development. In P. Barrouillet, & C. Gauffroy (Eds.). *The development of thinking and reasoning* (pp. 13–33). New York: Psychology Press.

Moshman, D. (2015). *Epistemic cognition and development: The psychology of justification and truth.* New York: Psychology Press.

Moskowitz, A., Stein, J. A., & Lightfoot, M. (2013). The mediating roles of stress and maladaptive behaviors on self-harm and suicide attempts among runaway and homeless youth. *Journal of Youth and Adolescence*, 42(7), 1015–1027.

Mottweiler, C. M., & Taylor, M. (2014). Elaborated role play and creativity in preschool age children. *Psychology of Aesthetics, Creativity, and the Arts*, 8(3), 277–286.

Mountjoy, M. L., & Goolsby, M. (2015). Female athlete triad. *Handbook of sports medicine and science: The female athlete.* Hoboken, NJ: Wiley.

Mowrer, O. H., & Mowrer, W. M. (1938). Enuresis—A method for its study and treatment. *American Journal of Orthopsychiatry*, 8, 436–459.

Moyal, W. N., Lord, C., & Walkup, J. T. (2014). Quality of life in children and adolescents with autism spectrum disorders: What is known about the effects of pharmacotherapy? *Pediatric Drugs*, 16, 123–128.

Moylan, C. A., et al. (2010). The effects of child abuse and exposure to domestic violence on adolescent internalizing and externalizing behavior problems. *Journal of Family Violence*, 25(1), 53–63.

Mrug, S., et al. (2014). Early puberty, negative peer influence, and problem behaviors in adolescent girls. *Pediatrics, 133*(1), 7–14.

Muir, D. W., & Hains, S. M. J. (1993). Infant sensitivity to perturbations in adult facial, vocal, tactile, and contingent stimulation during face-to-face interactions. In B. de Boysson-Bardies, S. de Schonen, P. W. Jusczyk, P. F. MacNeilage & J. Morton (Eds.), *Changes in speech and face processing in infancy: A glimpse at developmental mechanisms of cognition.* Dordrecht, Netherlands: Kluwer Academic.

Muller, U., Ten Eycke, K., & Baker, L. (2015). Piaget's theory of intelligence. In S. Goldstein, D. Princiotta, & J. A. Naglieri (Eds.). *Handbook of intelligence* (pp. 137–151). New York: Springer Science+Business Media.

Munck, P., et al. (2010). Cognitive outcome at 2 years of age in Finnish infants with very low birth weight born between 2001 and 2006. *Acta Paediatrica, 99*(3), 359–366.

Muris, P., & Field, A. P. (2011). The "normal" development of fear. In W. K. Silverman, & A. P. Field (Eds.), *Anxiety disorders in children and adolescents* (pp. 76–89). New York: Cambridge University Press.

Murk, W., Risnes, K. R., & Bracken, M. B. (2011). Prenatal or early-life exposure to antibiotics and risk of childhood asthma: A systematic review. *Pediatrics, 127*(6), 1125–1138.

Murphy, K. E., et al. (2011). Maternal side-effects after multiple courses of antenatal corticosteroids (MACS): The three-month follow-up of women in the Randomized Controlled Trial of MACS for Preterm Birth Study. *Journal of Obstetrics and Gynecology, Canada, 33*(9), 909–921.

Murray, B. (1998). Survey reveals concerns of today's girls. *APA Monitor, 29*(10).

Murray, B. A. (2006). Hunting the elusive phoneme: A phoneme-direct model for learning phoneme awareness. In K. A. Dougherty Stahl & M. C. McKenna (Eds.), *Reading research at work: Foundations of effective practice* (pp. 114–125). New York: Guilford.

Murry, V. M. (2014). Evaluating the contributions of culture and cultural fit in evidence-based programs. *Journal of Clinical Child & Adolescent Psychology, 43*(3), 454–458.

Mustanski, B. (2015). Future directions in research on sexual minority adolescent mental, behavioral, and sexual health. *Journal of Clinical Child & Adolescent Psychology, 44*(1), 204–219.

Mustanski, B., Birkett, M., Greene, G. J., Hatzenbuehler, M. L., & Newcomb, M. E. (2014). Envisioning an America without sexual orientation inequities in adolescent health. *American Journal of Public Health, 104*(2), 218–225.

Nagin, D. S., & Tremblay, R. E. (2001). Parental and early childhood predictors of persistent physical aggression in boys from kindergarten to high school. *Archives of General Psychiatry, 58*(4), 389–394.

National Campaign to Prevent Teen and Unplanned Pregnancy. (2012). Preventing unplanned and teen pregnancy: Why it matters. Retrieved from http://www .thenationalcampaign.org/why-it-matters/default.aspx. Accessed September 17, 2012.

National Campaign to Prevent Teen Pregnancy. (2003, September 30). *Teens say parents most influence their sexual decisions: New polling data and "Tips for Parents"* released. Available at http://www .teenpregnancy.org/about/announcements /pr/2003/release9_30_03.asp.

National Center for Children in Poverty. (2012, February). *Basic facts about low-income children, 2010.* The Trustees of Columbia University in the City of New York. Retrieved from http://www.nccp .org/publications/pub_1049.html. Accessed February 17, 2012.

National Center for Education Statistics. (2007, June). *Dropout rates in the United States: 2005.* Retrieved from http://nces .ed.gov/pubs2007/dropout05. Accessed July 20, 2007.

National Center for Education Statistics. (2010). *The condition of education 2010.* Washington, DC: Author. Retrieved from http://nces.ed.gov/pubsearch/pubsinfo .asp?pubid=2010028. Accessed September 26, 2012.

National Center for Education Statistics (2011). Digest of Education Statistics. Bachelor's, master's, and doctor's degrees conferred by degree-granting institutions, by sex of student, 2009–2010. Retrieved from http://nces.ed.gov/programs/digest /d11/tables/dt11_290.asp. Accessed September 18, 2012.

National Center for Education Statistics (2013). Digest of Education Statistics. Table 318.30. Retrieved from https:// nces.ed.gov/programs/digest/d13/tables /dt13_318.30.asp. Accessed August 15, 2015.

National Center for Education Statistics (2014–2015). Digest of Education Statistics. Retrieved from https://nces. ed.gov/programs/digest/d12/tables/ dt12_128.asp?referrer=report. Accessed April 25, 2015.

NHLBI (National Heart Lung and Blood Institute). (2011). http://www.nhlbi.nih .gov/health/health-topics/topics/asthma. Accessed August 18, 2012.

National Mathematics Advisory Panel. (2008). *Foundations for success: The final report of the National Mathematics Advisory Panel.* Washington, DC: U.S. Department of Education.

National Sleep Foundation. (2012a). Children and sleep. Retrieved from http://www .sleep foundation.org/article/sleep-topics /children-and-sleep. Accessed December 10, 2012.

National Sleep Foundation. (2012b). Adolescent sleep needs and patterns. Retrieved from http://www.sleep foundation.org/article/hot-topics /adolescent-sleep-needs-and-patterns. Accessed December 10, 2012.

National Sleep Foundation. (2014). Nightmares and sleep. Available at http:// sleepfoundation.org/sleep-disorders-problems/abnormal-sleep-behaviors /nightmares-and-sleep.

National Sleep Foundation. (2015a). Children and sleep. Available at http:// sleepfoundation.org/sleep-topics/children-and-sleep.

National Sleep Foundation. (2015b). Everything you need to know about co-sleeping. Available at https://sleep. org/articles/everything-to-know-about-cosleeping.

Nazzi, T., & Gopnik, A. (2000). A shift in children's use of perceptual and causal cues to categorization. *Developmental Science, 3*(4), 389–396.

Ndekha, M. (2008). Kwashiorkor and severe acute malnutrition in childhood. *The Lancet, 371*(9626), 1748.

Nduati, R., et al. (2000). Effect of breastfeeding and formula feeding on transmission of HIV-1. *Journal of the American Medical Association, 283,* 1167–1174.

Neiss, M. B., Sedikides, C., & Stevenson, J. (2006). Genetic influences on level and stability of self-esteem. *Self and Identity, 5*(3), 247–266.

Neisser, U., et al. (1996). Intelligence: Knowns and unknowns. *American Psychologist, 51,* 77–101.

Nelson, C. A., de Haan, M., & Thomas, K. M. (2006). *Neuroscience of cognitive development: The role of experience and the developing brain.* Hoboken, NJ: Wiley.

Nelson, C. A., & Luciana, M. (Eds.). (2001). *Handbook of developmental cognitive neuroscience.* Cambridge, MA: MIT Press.

Nelson, K. (1973). *Structure and strategy in learning to talk.* Monographs for the Society for Research in Child Development, 38(1–2, ser. 149).

Nelson, K. (2006). Advances in pragmatic developmental theory: The case of language acquisition. *Human Development, 49*(3), 184–188.

Nelson, K., & Fivush, R. (2004). The emergence of autobiographical memory: A social cultural developmental theory. *Psychological Review, 111*(2), 486–511.

Nelson, L. J., Hart, C. H., & Evans, C. A. (2008). Solitary-functional play and solitary-pretend play: Another look at the construct of solitary-active behavior using playground observations. *Social Development, 17*(4), 812–831.

Newman, K., Harrison, L., Dashiff, C., & Davies, S. (2008). Relationships between parenting styles and risk behaviors in adolescent health: An integrative literature review. *Revista Latino-Americana de Enfermagem, 16*(1). DOI:10.1590/S0104-11692008000100022.

Newman, R., Ratner, N. B., Jusczyk, A. M., Jusczyk, P. W., & Dow, K. A. (2006). Infants' early ability to segment the conversational speech signal predicts later language development: A retrospective analysis. *Developmental Psychology, 42*(4), 643–655.

Newport, E. L. (1992, June). *Critical periods and creolization: Effects of maturational state and input on the acquisition of language.* Paper presented at the meeting of American Psychological Society, San Diego, CA.

Newton, K. N. (2009). Factors associated with exclusive breastfeeding among Latina women giving birth at an inner-city baby-friendly hospital. *Journal of Human Lactation, 25*(1), 28–33.

Nguyen, H. V., et al. (2012). Risky sex: Interactions among ethnicity, sexual sensation seeking, sexual inhibition, and sexual excitation. *Archives of Sexual Behavior*, DOI:10.1007/s10508-012-9904-z.

Niemann, S., & Weiss, S. (2011). Attachment behavior and children adopted internationally at six months post adoption. *Adoption Quarterly, 14*(4), 246–267.

Nigg, J. T. & Holton, K. (2014). Restriction and elimination diets in ADHD treatment. *Child and Adolescent Psychiatric Clinics of North America, 23*(4), 937–953.

Nisbett, R. E. (2009). *Intelligence and how to get it*. New York: Norton.

Nisbett, R. E. (2013). Schooling makes you smarter: What teachers need to know about IQ. *American Educator, 37*(1), 10–19, 38–39.

Nisbett, R. E., Aronson, J., Blair, C., Dickens, W., Flynn, J., Halpern, D. T., & Turkheimer, E. (2012). Group differences in IQ are best understood as environmental in origin. *American Psychologist, 67*(6), 503–504.

Niu, Z., et al. (2015). Placenta mediates the association between maternal second-hand smoke exposure during pregnancy and small for gestational age. *Placenta*, DOI:10.1016/j.placenta.2015.05.005.

Nocera, J. (2015, May 26). Smoking, vaping, and nicotine. *The New York Times*, p. A19.

Nock, M. K., et al. (2013). Prevalence, correlates, and treatment of lifetime suicidal behavior among adolescents. *JAMA Psychiatry, 70*(3), 300–310.

Nomaguchi, K. M. (2006). Maternal employment, nonparental care, mother–child interactions, and child outcomes during preschool years. *Journal of Marriage and Family, 68*(5), 1341–1369.

Nordhov, S. M., et al. (2012). Early intervention improves behavioral outcomes for preterm infants: Randomized controlled trial. *Pediatrics, 129*(1), e9–e16.

Norton, A., & D'Ambrosio, B. S. (2008). ZPC and ZPD: Zones of teaching and learning. *Journal for Research in Mathematics Education, 39*(3), 220–246.

Novotny, R., et al. (2011). Puberty, body fat, and breast density in girls of several ethnic groups. *American Journal of Human Biology, 23*(3), 359–365.

Nucci, L. P. & Gingo, M. (2010). The development of moral reasoning. In U. Goswami (Ed.), *The Wiley-Blackwell handbook of childhood cognitive development* (2nd ed.) (pp. 420–455). Hoboken, NJ: Wiley.

Nucci, L. P., Narvaez, D., & Krettenauer, T. (2014). *Moral and character education* (2nd Ed.). New York: Routledge.

Nurwisah, R. (2011, September 29). Mitchell Wilson suicide: Disabled boy's death raises bullying concerns. *Huffington Post Canada*.

Nutrition Facts. (2012). Centers for Disease Control and Prevention. Available at http://www.cdc.gov/healthyyouth/nutrition/facts.htm.

O'Brien, M., Weaver, J. M., Burchinal, M., Clarke-Stewart, K. A., & Vandell, D. L. (2014). Women's work and child care. In E. T. Gershoff, R. S. Mistry, & D. A. Crosby (Eds.). *Societal contexts of child development: Pathways of influence and implications for practice and policy* (pp. 37–53). New York: Oxford University Press.

O'Connor, K. A., et al. (2011). The puzzle of sibling attachment non-concordance. *Psychology Presentations*, Paper 32. Available at http://ir.lib.uwo.ca/psychologypres/32.

O'Hara, M. W., & McCabe, J. E. (2013). Postpartum depression: Current status and future directions. *Annual Review of Clinical Psychology, 9*, 379–407.

Ohri-Vachaspati, P., et al. (2015). Child-directed marketing inside and on the exterior of fast food restaurants. *American Journal of Preventive Medicine, 48*(1) 22–30.

Office of Minority Health & Health Disparities. (2010). Eliminate disparities in HIV and AIDS. Retrieved from http://www.cdc.gov/omhd/amh/factsheets/hiv.htm. Accessed February 14, 2012.

Ogden, C. L., Carroll, M. D., Kit, B. K., & Flegal, K. M. (2014). Prevalence of childhood and adult obesity in the United States, 2011–2012. *Journal of the American Medical Association, 311*(8), 806–814.

Ogilvie, C. M., & Akolekar, R. (2013). Procedure-related pregnancy loss following invasive prenatal sampling: Time for a new approach to risk assessment and counseling. *Expert Review of Obstetrics & Gynecology, 8*(2), 135–142.

Ohalete, N. (2007). Adolescent sexual debut: A case for studying African American father–adolescent reproductive health communication. *Journal of Black Studies, 37*(5), 737–752.

Ohnishi, T., Matsuda, H., Hirakata, M., & Ugawa, Y. (2006). Navigation ability dependent neural activation in the human brain: An fMRI study. *Neuroscience Research, 55*(4), 361–369.

Ojanen, T., & Findley-Van Nostrand, D. (2014). Social, goals, aggression, peer preference, and popularity: Longitudinal links during middle school. *Developmental Psychology, 50*(8), 2134–2143.

O'Leary, C. M., et al. (2010). Prenatal alcohol exposure and risk of birth defects. *Pediatrics, 126*(4), e843–e850.

Ollendick, T. H., & Seligman, L. D. (2006). Anxiety disorders. In C. Gillberg, R. Harrington & H-C. Steinhausen (Eds.), *A clinician's handbook of child and adolescent psychiatry* (pp. 144–187). New York: Cambridge University Press.

Olsen, E. M., et al. (2007). Failure to thrive: The prevalence and concurrence of anthropometric criteria in a general infant population. *Archives of Disease in Childhood, 92*, 109–114.

Olson, S. D., Fauci, L. J., & Suarez, S. S. (2011). Mathematical modeling of calcium signaling during sperm hyperactivation. *Molecular Human Reproduction, 17*(8), 500–510.

Olson, S. L., Bates, J. E., Sandy, J. M., & Lanthier, R. (2000). Early developmental precursors of externalizing behavior in middle childhood and adolescence. *Journal of Abnormal Child Psychology, 28*(2), 119–133.

Olson, S. L., Kashiwagi, K., & Crystal, D. (2001). Concepts of adaptive and maladaptive child behavior: A comparison of U.S. and Japanese mothers of preschool-age children. *Journal of Cross-Cultural Psychology, 32*(1), 43–57.

O'Neill, D. K., & Gopnik, A. (1991). Young children's ability to identify the sources of their beliefs. *Developmental Psychology, 27*, 390–397.

O'Neill, D. K., & Chong, S. C. F. (2001). Preschool children's difficulty understanding the types of information obtained through the five senses. *Child Development, 72*(3), 803–815.

Örnkloo, H., & von Hofsten, C. (2007). Fitting objects into holes: On the development of spatial cognition skills. *Developmental Psychology, 43*(2), 404–416.

Orstavik, R. E., Kendler, K. S., Czajkowski, N., Tambs, K., & Reichborn-Kjennerud, T. (2007). Genetic and environmental contributions to depressive personality disorder in a population-based sample of Norwegian twins. *Journal of Affective Disorders, 99*(1–3), 181–189.

Osborn, R., et al. (2013). Loss of control and binge eating in children and adolescents. In J. Alexander, A. B. Goldschmidt, & D. Le Grange (Eds.). A clinician's guide to binge eating disorder (pp. 170–181). New York: Routledge.

Osterman, M. J. K., & Martin, J. A. (2013, June). Changes in cesarean delivery rates by gestational age: 1996–2011. U.S.D.H.H.S.: NCHS Data Brief, No. 124. Available at http://www.cdc.gov/nchs/data/databriefs/db124.pdf.

Osuch, J. R., et al. (2010). Association of age at menarche with adult leg length and trunk height: Speculations in relation to breast cancer risk. *Annals of Human Biology, 37*(1), 76–85.

Oswald, R. F., et al. (2013). LGB families in community context. In A. E Goldberg, & K. R. Allen (Eds.). *LGBT-parent families: Innovations in research and implications for practice* (pp. 193–208). New York: Springer Science+Business Media.

Otero, T. M. (2015). Intelligence: Defined as neurocognitive processing In S. Goldstein, D. Princiotta, & J. A. Naglieri (Eds.). *Handbook of intelligence: Evolutionary theory, historical perspective, and current concepts* (pp. 193–208). New York: Springer Science+Business Media.

Out, D., et al. (2010). Intended sensitive and harsh caregiving responses to infant crying: The role of cry pitch and perceived urgency in an adult twin sample. *Child Abuse & Neglect, 34*(11), 863–873.

Overweight and obesity. (2011). Retrieved from http://www.cdc.gov/obesity/childhood/problem.html. Accessed August 18, 2012.

Oyserman, D., Elmore, K., & Smith, G. (2012). Self, self-concept, and identity. In M. R. Leary, & J. P. Tangney (Eds.). *Handbook of self and identity*, 2nd ed (pp. 69–104). New York: Guilford.

Ozer, B. U., LeBlanc, S., & Essau, C. A. (2015). Substance-related disorders. *The encyclopedia of clinical psychology*, DOI:10.1002/9781118625392.wbecp563. Hoboken, NJ: Wiley.

Oztop, E., Kawato, M., & Arbib, M. (2006). Mirror neurons and imitation: A computationally guided review. *Neural Networks*, 19(3), 254–271.

Pace, C. S., Cavanna, D., Velotti, P., & Zavattini, G. S. (2014). Attachment representations in late-adopted children. *Adoption & Fostering*, 38(3), 255–270.

Palla, G., Barabási, A-L., & Vicsek, T. (2007). Quantifying social group evolution. *Nature*, 446(7136), 664–667.

Pallanti, S., & Salerno, L. (2015). Raising attention to attention deficit hyperactivity disorder in schizophrenia. *World Journal of Psychiatry*, 5(1), 47–55.

Palmer, E. J. (2005). The relationship between moral reasoning and aggression, and the implications for practice. *Psychology, Crime & Law*, 11(4), 353–361.

Palmer, E. L. (2003). Realities and challenges in the rapidly changing televisual media landscape. In E. L. Palmer & B. M. Young (Eds.), *The faces of televisual media: Teaching, violence, selling to children* (2nd ed.) (pp. 361–377). Mahwah, NJ: Erlbaum.

Paquette, D., & Dumont, C. (2013). Is father-child rough-and-tumble play associated with attachment or activation relationships? *Early Child Development and Care*, 183(6), 760–773.

Park, J. S. (2008). Is diagnostic ultrasound harmful to the fetus? *Journal of the Korean Medical Association*, 51(9), 823–830.

Park, Y., Kwon, J. Y., Kim, Y. H., Kim, M., & Shin, J. C. (2010). Maternal age-specific rates of fetal chromosomal abnormalities at 16–20 weeks' gestation in Korean pregnant women greater than or equal to 35 years of age. *Fetal Diagnosis and Therapy*, 27(4), 214–221.

Parker-Pope, T. (2009, May 28). Study urges weight gain be curbed in pregnancy. *The New York Times*. Retrieved from http://www.nytimes.com.

Parks, P., & Bradley, R. (1991). The interaction of home environment features and their relation to infant competence. *Infant Mental Health Journal*, 12, 3–16.

Parsons, H. G., George, M. A., & Innis, S. M. (2011). Growth assessment in clinical practice: Whose growth curve? *Current Gastroenterology Reports*, 13(3), 286–292.

Partanen, E., Kujala, T., Tervaniemi, M., & Huotilainen, M. (2013). Prenatal music exposure induces long-term neural effects. *PLOS ONE*, DOI:10.1371/journal.pone.0078946.

Passell, P. (1992, August 9). Twins study shows school is a sound investment. *The New York Times*, p. A14.

Passolunghi, M. C., Ferreira, T. I. R., & Tomasetto, C. (2014). Math-gender stereotypes and math-related beliefs in childhood and early adolescence. *Learning and Individual Differences*, 34, 70–76.

Pastor, J., et al. (2007). Makin' homes: An urban girl thing. In B. J. R. Leadbeater & N. Way (Eds.), *Urban girls revisited: Building strengths* (pp. 75–96). New York: New York University Press.

Patel, S., Gaylord, S., & Fagen, J. (2013). Generalization of deferred imitation in 6-, 9-, and 12-month-old infants using visual and auditory contexts. *Infant Behavior and Development*, 36(1), 25–31.

Patenaude, J., Niyonsenga, T., & Fafard, D. (2003). Changes in students' moral development during medical school: A cohort study. *Canadian Medical Association Journal*, 168(7), 840–844.

Paterson, D. S., et al. (2006). Multiple serotonergic brainstem abnormalities in sudden infant death syndrome. *Journal of the American Medical Association*, 296, 2124–2132.

Patrick, M. E., O'Malley, P. M., Johnston, L. D., Terry-McElrath, Y. M., & Schulenberg, J. E. (2012). HIV/AIDS risk behaviors and substance abuse by young adults in the United States. *Prevention Science*, 13(5), 532–538.

Patterson, C. J. (2006). Children of lesbian and gay parents. *Current Directions in Psychological Science*, 15(5), 241–244.

Patterson, C. J., & Farr, R. H. (2011). Coparenting among lesbian and gay couples. In J. P. McHale, & K. M. Lindahl (Eds.). *Coparenting: A conceptual and clinical examination of family systems* (pp. 127–146). Washington, DC: American Psychological Association.

Patterson, G. R. (2005). The next generation of PMTO models. *The Behavior Therapist*, 28(2), 27–33.

Peeters, M. W., et al. (2005). Genetic and environmental causes of tracking in explosive strength during adolescence. *Behavior Genetics*, 35(5), 551–563.

Pellis, S. M., & Pellis, V. V. (2007), Rough-and-tumble play and the development of the social brain. *Current Directions in Psychological Science*, 16(2), 95–98.

Pelphrey, K. A., et al. (2004). Development of visuospatial short-term memory in the second half of the first year. *Developmental Psychology*, 40(5), 836–851.

Perez, T., Cromley, J. G., & Kaplan, A. (2014). The role of identity development, values, and costs in college STEM retention. *Journal of Educational Psychology*, 106(1), 315–329.

Perren, S., & Alsaker, F. D. (2006). Social behavior and peer relationships of victims, bully-victims, and bullies in kindergarten. *Journal of Child Psychology and Psychiatry*, 47(1), 45–57.

Perrin, M. C., Brown, A. S., & Malaspina, D. (2007, August 21). Aberrant epigenetic regulation could explain the relationship of paternal age to schizophrenia. *Schizophrenia Bulletin online*. Available at http://schizophreniabulletin.oxfordjournals.org/cgi/content/abstract/sbm093v1.

Perrin, N., Sayer, L., & While, A. (2015). The efficacy of alarm therapy versus desmopressin therapy in the treatment of primary mono-symptomatic nocturnal enuresis: A systematic review. *Primary Health Care Research & Development*, 16(1), 21–31.

Persike, M., & Seiffge-Krenke, I. (2011). Competence in coping with stress in adolescents from three regions of the world. *Journal of Youth and Adolescence*, DOI:10.1007/s10964-011-9719-6.

Persson, G. E. B. (2005). Developmental perspectives on prosocial and aggressive motives in preschoolers' peer interactions. *International Journal of Behavioral Development*, 29(1), 80–91.

Persson, T. J., Ryder, A. G., & Pfaus, J. G. (2015). Comparing subjective ratings of sexual arousal and desire in partnered sexual activities from women of different sexual orientations. *Archives of Sexual Behavior*, DOI:10.1007/s10508-014-0468-y.

Perusse, L., Rice, T. K., & Bouchard, C. (2014). Genetic component to obesity: Evidence from genetic epidemiology. In G. Bray, & C. Bouchard (Eds.). *Handbook of obesity: Epidemiology, etiology, and physiopathology* (4th ed.) (pp. 91–104). CRC Press.

Peterka, M., Likovsky, Z., & Peterkova, R. (2007). Environmental risk and sex ratio in newborns. *Congenital Diseases and the Environment*, 23, 295–319.

Peterson, B. S. (2013). From correlations to causation: The value of preventive interventions in studying pathogenic mechanisms in childhood psychiatric disorders. *Journal of Child Psychology and Psychiatry*, 54(8), 813–815).

Pfaff, N. (2010). Gender segregation in pre-adolescent peer groups as a matter of class. *Childhood*, 17(1), 43–60.

Pfiffner, L. J. (2014). Meta-analysis supprts efficacy of behavioral intervention for attention deficit/hyperactivity disorder-related problems. *Journal of the American Academy of Child & Adolescent Psychiatry*, 53(8), 830–832.

Phillips, A. S., & Phillips, C. R. (2000). Birth-order differences in self-attributions for achievement. *Journal of Individual Psychology*, 56(4), 474–480.

Phillips, D. A., & Styfco, S. J. (2007). Child development research and public policy: Triumphs and setbacks on the way to maturity. In J. L. Aber et al. (Eds.), *Child development and social policy: Knowledge for action. APA Decade of Behavior volumes* (pp. 11–27). Washington, DC: American Psychological Association.

Phinney, J. S. (1992). The multigroup ethnic identity measure: A new scale for use with adolescents and young adults with diverse groups. *Journal of Adolescent Research*, 12, 156–176.

Phinney, J. S. (2006). Ethnic identity exploration in emerging adulthood. In J. J. Arnett & J. L. Tanner (Eds.), *Emerging adults in America: Coming of age in the 21st century* (pp. 117–134). Washington, DC: American Psychological Association.

Phinney, J. S., & Chavira, P. (1992). Ethnic identity and self-esteem: An exploratory longitudinal study. *Journal of Adolescence*, 15, 1–11.

Phinney, J. S., & Rosenthal, D. A. (1992). Ethnic identity in adolescence: Process, context, and outcome. In G. R. Adams, T. P. Gullotta & R. Montemayor (Eds.),

Adolescent identity formation. Newbury Park, CA: Sage.

Physical activity and health. (2011). Centers for Disease Control and Prevention. Retrieved from http://www.cdc.gov /physicalactivity/everyone/health/index .html. Accessed August 18, 2012.

Piaget, J. (1932). *The moral judgment of the child.* London: Kegan Paul.

Piaget, J. (1962). *Play, dreams, and imitation in childhood.* New York: Norton. (Originally published in 1946.)

Piaget, J. (1963). *The origins of intelligence in children.* New York: Norton. (Originally published in 1936.)

Piaget, J. (1967). In D. Elkind (Ed.), *Six psychological studies.* New York: Random House. (Originally published in 1964.)

Piaget, J. (1972). Intellectual evolution from adolescence to adulthood. *Human Development, 15,* 1–12.

Piaget, J. (1976). *The grasp of consciousness: Action and concept in the young child.* Cambridge, MA: Harvard University Press.

Pianta, R. C. (2012). *Early childhood education.* New York: Guilford.

Pickren, W. E., Marsella, A. J., Leong, F. T. L., & Leach, M. M. (2012). Playing our part: Crafting a vision for a psychology curriculum marked by multiplicity. In F. T. L. Leong, W. E. Pickren, M. M. Leach, & A. J. Marsella (Eds.). *Internationalizing the psychology curriculum in the United States* (pp. 307–322). New York: Springer.

Piek, J. P., Baynam, G. B., & Barrett, N. C. (2006). The relationship between fine and gross motor ability, self-perceptions and self-worth in children and adolescents. *Human Movement Science, 25(1),* 65–75.

Pine, D. S., et al. (2001). Fluvoxamine for the treatment of anxiety disorders in children and adolescents. *New England Journal of Medicine, 344(17),* 1279–1285.

Pinker, S. (2007). *The stuff of thought: Language as a window into human nature.* New York: Viking.

Pinker, S., & Jackendoff, R. (2005). The faculty of language: What's special about it? *Cognition, 95(2),* 201–236.

Platje, E., et al. (2015). Testosterone and cortisol in relation to a nonclinical sample of boys and girls. *Aggressive Behavior,* DOI:10.1002/ab.21585.

Plomin, R., DeFries, J. C., Knopik, V. S., & Nelderheiser, J. M. (2013). *Behavioral genetics, 6th edition.* New York: Worth Publishers.

Plomin, R., DeFries, J. C., McClearn, G. E., & McGuffin, P. (2008). *Behavioral genetics.* New York: Worth Publishers.

Plomin, R., Owen, M. J., & McGuffin, P. (1994). The genetic basis of complex human behaviors. *Science, 264,* 1733–1739.

Plomin, R., & Spinath, F. M. (2004). Intelligence: Genetics, genes, and genomics. *Journal of Personality and Social Psychology, 86(1),* 112–129.

Plourde, V., et al. (2015). Phenotypic and genetic associations between reading comprehension, decoding skills, and ADHD dimensions: evidence from two population-based studies. *The Journal*

of Child Psychology and Psychiatry, DOI:10.1111/jcpp. 12394.

Plucker, J. A., Esping, A., Kaufman, J. C., & Avitia, M. J. (2015). Creativity and intelligence. In S. Goldstein, D. Princiotta, & J. A. Naglieri (Eds.). *Handbook of intelligence: Evolutionary theory, historical perspective, and current concepts* (pp. 283–291). New York: Springer Science+Business Media.

Plunkett, J., et al. (2011). An evolutionary genomic approach to identify genes involved in human birth timing. *PLoS Genetics, 7(4):* e1001365. DOI:10.1371 /journal.pgen.1001365.

Poehner, M. E. (2012). The zone of proximal development and the genesis of self-assessment. *The Modern Language Journal, 96(4),* 610–622.

Polivy, J., Herman, C. P., & Boivin, M. (2005). Eating disorders. In J. E. Maddux & B. A. Winstead (Eds.), *Psychopathology: Foundations for a contemporary understanding* (pp. 229–254). Mahwah, NJ: Erlbaum.

Pollock, B., Prior, H., & Güntürkün, O. (2000). Development of object permanence in food-storing magpies *(Pica pica). Journal of Comparative Psychology, 114(2),* 148–157.

Pombeni, M. L., Kirchler, E., & Palmonari, A. (1990). Identification with peers as a strategy to muddle through the troubles of the adolescent years. *Journal of Adolescence, 13,* 351–369.

Poorthuis, A. M. G., et al. (2014). Dashed hopes, dashed selves? A sociometer perspective on self-esteem change across the transition to secondary school. *Social Development, 23(4),* 770 783.

Porfeli, E. J. (2007). Work values system development during adolescence. *Journal of Vocational Behavior, 70(1),* 42–60.

Porter, R. H., Makin, J. W., Davis, L. B., & Christensen, K. M. (1992). Breast-fed infants respond to olfactory cues from their own mother and unfamiliar lactating females. *Infant Behavior and Development, 15,* 85–93.

Portnoy, J., Chen, F. R., Gao, Y., Niv, S., Schug, R. A., Yang, Y., & Raine, A. (2014). Biological perspectives on sex differences in crime and antisocial behavior. In R. Gartner & B. McCarthy (Eds.). *The Oxford handbook of gender, sex, and crime* (pp. 260–285). New York: Oxford University Press.

Posner, M. I., Rothbart, M. K., Sheese, B. E., & Voelker, P. (2014). Developing attention: Behavioral and Brain Mechanisms. *Advances in Neuroscience,* DOI:10.1155/2014/405094.

Posner, M. I., Rothbart, M. K., & Tang, Y. (2013). Developing self-regulation in early childhood. *Trends in Neuroscience and Education, 2(3–4),* 107–110.

Potter, D. (2010). Psychosocial well-being and the relationship between divorce and children's academic achievement. *Journal of Marriage and the Family, 72(4),* 933–946.

Powers, C. J., & Bierman, K. L. (2013). The multifaceted impact of peer relations on aggressive-disruptive behavior in

early elementary school. *Developmental Psychology, 49(6),* 1174–1186.

Powrie, R. O., et al. (2010). Special concerns for patients with advanced maternal age. In *de Swiet's Medical disorders in obstetric practice,* 5th ed. Hoboken, NJ: Wiley.

Premberg, A., Hellström, A-L., & Berg, M. (2008). Experiences of the first year as father. *Scandinavian Journal of Caring Sciences, 22(1),* 56–63.

Prendergast, G., West, D. C., & Yan, L. K. (2015). Eating disorders: The role of advertising and editorial. In H. E. Spotts (Ed.). *Developments in marketing science: Proceedings of the Academy of Marketing Science* (pp. 175 – 178). New York: Springer International Publishing.

President's Council on Fitness, Sports & Nutrition. (2015). Retrieved from www .fitness.gov. Accessed April 5, 2015.

Priest, N., et al. (2014). Understanding the complexities of ethnic-racial socialization processes for both minority and majority groups: A 30-year systematic review. *International Journal of Intercultural Relations,* DOI:10.1016/j. jijintrel.2014.08.003.

Principe, C. P., & Langlois, J. H. (2012). Shifting the prototype: Experience with faces influences affective and attractiveness preferences. *Social Cognition, 30(1),* 109–120.

Provence, S., & Lipton, R. C. (1962). *Infants in institutions.* New York: International Universities Press.

Pulverman, R., Hirsh-Pasek, K., Golinkoff, R. M., Pruden, S., & Salkind, S. J. (2006). Conceptual foundations for verb learning: Celebrating the event. In K. Hirsh-Pasek & R. M. Golinkoff (Eds.), *Action meets word: How children learn verbs* (pp. 134–159). New York: Oxford University Press.

Quick, V., et al. (2014). Body image and weight control in youth: 9-year international trends from 24 countries. *The FASEB Journal, 28(1),* Suppl. 811.5.

Quinlivan, J. A., & Condon, J. (2005). Anxiety and depression in fathers in teenage pregnancy. *Australian and New Zealand Journal of Psychiatry, 39(10),* 915–920.

Quinn, P. C. (2010). Born to categorize. In U. Goswami (Ed.), *The Wiley–Blackwell handbook of childhood cognitive development.* (2nd ed.) (pp. 129–152). Chichester, West Sussex, UK: Wiley–Blackwell.

Quintana, S. (2011). Ethnicity, race, and children's social development. In P. K. Smith & C. H. Hart (Eds.), *The Wiley-Blackwell handbook of childhood social development* (2nd ed.) (pp. 299–316). Chichester, West Sussex, UK: Wiley–Blackwell

Quintana, S. M. (1998). Children's developmental understanding of ethnicity and race. *Applied and Preventive Psychology, 7(1),* 27–45.

Quintana, S. M., et al. (2006). Race, ethnicity, and culture in child development: Contemporary research and future directions. *Child Development, 77(5),* 1129–1141.

Rabasca, L. (2000). Pre-empting racism. *Monitor on Psychology, 31*(11), 60.

Raby, K. L., Cicchetti, D., Carlson, E. A., Egeland, B., & Collins, W. A. (2013). Genetic contributions to continuity and change in attachment security: a prospective, longitudinal investigation from infancy to young adulthood. *The Journal of Child Psychology and Psychiatry, 54*(11), 1223–1230.

Raikes, H., et al. (2006). Mother–child bookreading in low-income families: Correlates and outcomes during the first three years of life. *Child Development, 77*(4), 924–953.

Ramani, G. B., & Siegler, R. S. (2008). Promoting broad and stable improvements in low-income children's numerical knowledge through playing number board games. *Child Development, 79*, 375–394.

Ramchand, R., et al. (2009). Substance use and delinquency among fifth graders who have jobs. *American Journal of Preventive Medicine, 36*(4), 297–303.

Ramey, C. T., Campbell, F. A., & Ramey, S. L. (1999). Early intervention: Successful pathways to improving intellectual development. *Developmental Neuropsychology, 16*(3), 385–392.

Ramsey, J. L., Langlois, J. H., Hoss, R. A., Rubenstein, A. J., & Griffin, A. M. (2004). Origins of a stereotype: Categorization of facial attractiveness by 6-month-old infants. *Developmental Science, 7*(2), 201–211.

Randel, B., Stevenson, H. W., & Witruk, E. (2000). Attitudes, beliefs, and mathematics achievement of German and Japanese high school students. *International Journal of Behavioral Development, 24*(2), 190–198.

Rapee, R. M. (2012). Family factors in the development and management of anxiety disorders. *Clinical Child and Family Psychology Review, 15*(1), 69–80.

Rasmussen, K. M., et al. (2009, May 27). Institute of Medicine report. In T. Parker-Pope (2009, May 28), Study urges weight gain be curbed in pregnancy, *The New York Times*. Retrived from http://www.nytimes.com.

Rathus, S. A., Nevid, J. S., & Fichner-Rathus, L. (2014). *Human sexuality in a world of diversity* (9th ed.). Upper Saddle River, NJ: Pearson Education.

Ratzan, S. C. (2014). The tyranny of marijuana: Legislation, science, and evidence? *Journal of Health Communication: International Perspectives, 19*(2), 133–135.

Ray, W. J. (2012). *Evolutionary psychology.* Thousand Oaks, CA: Sage.

Raynes-Greenough, C. H., Gordon, A., Li, Q., & Hyett, J. A. (2013). A cross-sectional study of maternal perception of fetal movements and antenatal advice in a general pregnant population, using a qualitative framework. *BMC Pregnancy and Childbirth, 13*, 32.

Raznahan, A., et al. (2011). How does your cortex grow? *Journal of Neuroscience, 31*(19), 7174–7177.

Reece, M., et al. (2010). Sexual behaviors, relationships, and perceived health among adult men in the United States: Results from a national probability sample. *Journal of Sexual Medicine, 7*(Suppl. 5), 291–304.

Reed, S. K. (2013). *Cognition: Theories and applications* (9th ed.). San Francisco, CA: Cengage Learning.

Reichenberg, A., et al. (2006). Advancing paternal age and autism. *Archives of General Psychiatry, 63*(9), 1026–1032.

Reichman, D. E., White, P. C., New, M. I., & Rosenwaks, Z. (2014). Fertility in patients with congenital adrenal hyperplasia. *Fertility and Sterility, 101*(2), 301–309.

Reiersen, A. M., & Handen, B. (2011), Commentary on "Selective serotonin reuptake inhibitors (SSRIs) for autism spectrum disorders (ASDs)." *Evidence-Based Child Health: A Cochrane Review Journal, 6*, 1082–1085.

Reijneveld, S. A., et al. (2004). Infant crying and abuse. *Lancet, 364*(9442), 1340–1342.

Reis, O., & Youniss, J. (2004). Patterns in identity change and development in relationships with mothers and friends. *Journal of Adolescent Research, 19*(1), 31–44.

Reis, S. M., & Renzulli, J. S. (2011). Intellectual giftedness. In R. J. Sternberg & S. J. Kaufman (Eds.), *The Cambridge handbook of intelligence* (pp. 235–252). New York: Cambridge University Press.

Remington, A., et al. (2012). Accepting food acceptance in the home setting; A randomized controlled trial of parent-administered taste exposure with incentives. *The American Journal of Clinical Nutrition, 95*(1), 72–77.

Rennels, J. L., & Langlois, J. H. (2014). Children's attractiveness, gender, and race biases: A comparison of their strength and generality. *Child Development, 85*(4), 1401–1418.

Renzaho, A. M. N., McCabe, M., & Sainsbury, W. J. (2011). Parenting, role reversals, and the preservation of cultural values among Arabic speaking migrant families in Melbourne, Australia. *International Journal of Intercultural Relations, 35*(4), 416–424.

Rest, J. R. (1983). Morality. In P. H. Mussen (Ed.), *Handbook of child psychology*, Vol. 3, *Cognitive development*. New York: Wiley.

Reyna, V. F., Wilhelms, E. A., McCormick, M. J., & Weldon, R. B. (2015). Dvelopment of risky decision making: Fuzzy-trace theory and neurobiological perspectives. *Child Development Perspectives*, DOI:10.1111/cdep.12117.

Reynolds, A. J., Temple, J. A., Ou, S-R., Arteaga, I. A., & White, B. A. B. (2011). School-based early childhood education and age-28 well-being: Effects by timing, dosage, and subgroups. *Science, 333*(6040), 360–364.

Rezael, Z., Haghighi, Z., Haeri, G., & Hekmatdoust, A. (2014). A comparative study on relieving post-episiotomy pain with diclofenac and indomethacin suppositories or placebo. *Journal of Obstetrics & Gynaecology, 34*(4), 293-296.

Rhee, S. H., & Waldman, I. D. (2009). Genetic analysis of conduct disorder and antisocial behavior. In Y-K. Kim (Ed.), *Handbook of behavior genetics* (pp. 455–471). New York: Springer.

Rheingold, H. L., Gewirtz, J. L., & Ross, H. W. (1959). Social conditioning of vocalizations in the infant. *Journal of Comparative and Physiological Psychology, 52*, 68–73.

Rice, C. (2007). Prevalence of autism spectrum disorders—Autism and Developmental Disabilities Monitoring Network, 14 Sites, United States. *Morbidity and Mortality Weekly Report, 56*(SS01), 12–28.

Rice, F. (2014). Genetic influences on depression and anxiety in childhood and adolescence. *Behavior genetics of psychopathology, 2*, 67–97.

Rice, F., Frederickson, N., & Seymour, J. (2011). Assessing pupil concerns about transition to secondary school. *British Journal of Educational Psychology, 81*(2), 244–263.

Rice, T. R., & Sher, L. (2013). Testosterone, emotion regulation and childhood aggression. *Neuropsychiatry, 3*(3), 267–270.

Richardson, G. A., Goldschmidt, L., Larkby, C., & Day, N. L. (2013). Effects of prenatal cocaine exposure on child behavior and growth at 10 years of age. *Neurotoxicology and Teratology, 40*(1), 1–8.

Richert, R. A., Robb, M. B., & Smith, E. I. (2011). Media as social partners: The social nature of young children's learning from screen media. *Child Development, 82*(1), 82–95.

Ricketts, S., Tolliver, R., & Schwalberg, R. (2014). Short-lived success: Assessment of an intervention to improve pregnancy weight gain in Colorado. *Maternal and Child Health Journal, 18*(4), 772–777.

Rizzolatti, G., & Fabbri-Destro, M. (2011). Mirror neurons: From discovery to autism. *Experimental Brain Research, 200*(3–4), 223–237.

Robbins, C. L., et al. (2011). Prevalence, frequency, and associations of masturbation with partnered sexual behaviors among US adolescents. *JAMA Pediatrics, 165*(12), 1087–1093.

Robbins, T., Stagman, S., & Smith, S. (2012). Young children at risk. National Center for Children in Poverty. Available at http://www.nccp.org/publications/pub_1073.html.

Roberts, C. L., et al. (2015). Association of prelabor cesarean delivery with reduced mortality in twins born near term. *Obstetrics & Gynecology, 125*(1), 103–110.

Roberts, R. E., Roberts, C. R., & Duong, H. T. (2009). Sleepless in adolescence: Prospective data on sleep deprivation, health and functioning. *Journal of Adolescence, 32*(5): 1045–1057.

Roberts, W., Strayer, J., & Denham, S. (2014). Empathy, anger, guilt: Emotions and prosocial behavior. *Canadian Journal of Behavioural Science, 46*(4), 465–474.

Robertson, L., McAnally, H. M., & Hancox, R. J. (2013). Child and adolescent television viewing and antisocial behavior in early adulthood. *Pediatrics, 131*(3), 439–446.

Robinson, E. (2011). *Disintegration: The splintering of Black America.* New York: Random House.

Robinson, J. B., Burns, B. M., & Davis, D. W. (2008). Maternal scaffolding and attention regulation in children living in poverty. *Journal of Applied Developmental Psychology, 30*(2), 82–91.

Robinson, J. R., Drotar, D., & Boutry, M. (2001). Problem-solving abilities among mothers of infants with failure to thrive. *Journal of Pediatric Psychology, 26*(1), 21–32.

Robson, W. L. M. (2009). Evaluation and management of enuresis. *New England Journal of Medicine, 360*(14), 1429–1436.

Rodkin, P. C., Ryan, A. M., Jamison, R., & Wilson, T. (2013). Social goals, social behavior, and social status in middle childhood. *Developmental Psychology, 49*(6), 1139–1150.

Roebers, C. M., Krebs, S. S., & Roderer, T. (2014). Metacognitive monitoring and control in elementary school children: Their interrelations and their role for test performance. *Learning and Individual Differences, 29*, 141–149.

Roffwarg, H. P., Muzio, J. N., & Dement, W. C. (1966). Ontogenetic development of the human sleep-dream cycle. *Science, 152*, 604–619.

Rogers, M. A., & Creed, P. A. (2011). A longitudinal investigation of adolescent career planning and exploration using a social cognitive career theory framework. *Journal of Adolescence, 34*(1), 163–172.

Roisman, G. I., & Groh, A. M. (2011). Attachment theory and research in developmental psychology: An overview and appreciative critique. In M. K. Underwood & L. H. Rosen (Eds.), *Social development: Relationships in infancy, childhood, and adolescence* (pp. 101–126). New York: Guilford.

Rollins, V. B., & Valdez, J. N. (2006). Perceived racism and career self-efficacy in African American adolescents. *Journal of Black Psychology, 32*(2), 176–198.

Romans, S. E., Gendall, K. A., Martin, J. L., & Mullen, P. E. (2001). Child sexual abuse and later disordered eating: A New Zealand epidemiological study. *International Journal of Eating Disorders, 29*(4), 380–392.

Romero, A. J., Edwards, L. M., Fryberg, S. A., & Orduna, M. (2014). Resilience to discrimination distress across ethnic identity stages of development. *Journal of Applied Social Psychology, 44*(1), 1–11.

Rose, A. J., & Asher, S. R. (1999). Children's goals and strategies in response to conflicts within a friendship. *Developmental Psychology, 35*(1), 69–79.

Rose, A. M., Hall, C. S., & Martinez-Adler, N. (2014). Aetiology and management of malnutrition in HIV-positive children. *Archives of Disease in Childhood,* DOI:10.1136/archdischild-2012-303348.

Rose, L. Y., & Fischer, K. W. (2011). Intelligence in childhood. In R. J. Sternberg & S. J. Kaufman (Eds.), *The Cambridge handbook of intelligence* (pp. 144–173). New York: Cambridge University Press.

Rose, S. A., Feldman, J. F., & Jankowski, J. J. (2001). Visual short-term memory in the first year of life: Capacity and recency effects. *Developmental Psychology, 37*(4), 539–549.

Rose, S. A., Feldman, J. F., Jankowski, J. J., & Van Rossem, R. (2011). The structure of memory in infants and toddlers: An SEM study with full-terms and pre-terms. *Developmental Science, 14*(1), 83–91.

Rose, S. A., Feldman, J. F., Jankowski, J. J., & Van Rossem, R. V. (2012). Information processing from infancy to 11 years. *Intelligence, 40*(5), 445–457.

Rose, S. A., Feldman, J. F., & Wallace, I. F. (1992). Infant information processing in relation to six-year cognitive outcomes. *Child Development, 63*, 1126–1141.

Rosen, L. H., & Patterson, M. M. (2011). The self and identity. In M. K. Underwood & L. H. Rosen (Eds.), *Social development: Relationships in infancy, childhood, and adolescence* (pp. 73–100). New York: Guilford.

Rosenstein, D., & Oster, H. (1988). Differential facial responses to four basic tastes. *Child Development, 59*, 1555–1568.

Rosenthal, R., & Jacobson, L. (1968). *Pygmalion in the classroom.* New York: Holt, Rinehart & Winston.

Ross, G., Kagan, J., Zelazo, P. R., & Kotelchuck, M. (1975). Separation protest in infants in home and laboratory. *Developmental Psychology, 11*, 256–257.

Ross, H., Ross, M., Stein, N., & Trabasso, T. (2006). How siblings resolve their conflicts: The importance of first offers, planning, and limited opposition. *Child Development, 77*(6), 1730–1745.

Rote, W. M., & Smetana, J. G. (2015). Parenting, adolescent–parent relationships, and social domain theory: Implications for identity development. In S. J. Schwatrz, K. Luyckx, & V. L. Vignoles (Eds.). Handbook of identity theory and research (pp. 437–453). New York: Springer Science+Business Media.

Rothbart, M. K., & Sheese, B. E. (2007). Temperament and emotion regulation. In J. J. Gross (Ed.), *Handbook of emotion regulation* (pp. 331–350). New York: Guilford.

Rothrauff, T., Middlemiss, W., & Jacobson, L. (2004). Comparison of American and Austrian infants' and toddlers' sleep habits: A retrospective, exploratory study. *North American Journal of Psychology, 6*(1), 125–144.

Rottinghaus, P. J., & Van Esbroeck, R. (2011). Improving person–environment fit and self-knowledge. In P. J. Hartung & L. M. Subich (Eds.), *Developing self in work and career: Concepts, cases, and contexts* (pp. 35–52). Washington, DC: American Psychological Association.

Rovee-Collier, C. (1993). The capacity for long-term memory in infancy. *Current Directions in Psychological Science, 2*, 130–135.

Rowen, B. (1973). *The children we see.* New York: Holt, Rinehart & Winston.

Roy, A. L., McCoy, D. C., & Raver, C. C. (2014). Instability versus quality: Residential mobility, neighborhood poverty, and children's self-regulation. *Developmental Psychology, 50*(7), 1891–1896.

Roxborough, H. M., et al. (2012). Perfectionistic self-presentation, socially prescribed perfectionism, and suicide in youth. *Suicide and Life-Threatening Behavior, 42*(2), 217–233.

Rübeling, H., Schwarzer, S., Keller, H., & Lenk, M. (2011). Young children's nonfigurative drawings of themselves and their families in two different cultures. *Journal of Cognitive Education and Psychology, 10*(1), 63–76.

Rubella. (2009, March 2). *The New York Times Health Guide.* Available at http://health.nytimes.com/health/guides/disease/rubella/overview.html.

Rubin, K. H., Bukowski, W. M., & Parker, J. G. (2006). Peer interactions, relationships, and groups. In N. Eisenberg, W. Damon & R. M. Lerner (Eds.), *Handbook of child psychology* (6th ed.), Vol. 3, *Social, emotional, and personality development* (pp. 571–645). Hoboken, NJ: Wiley.

Rubin, K. H., & Coplan, R. J. (Eds.). (2010). *The development of shyness and social withdrawal.* New York: Guilford.

Rubin, K. H., Coplan, R. J., Bowker, J. C., & Menzer, M. (2011). Social withdrawal and shyness. In P. K. Smith, & C. H. Hart (Eds.). *The Wiley–Blackwell handbook of childhood social development* (pp. 434–452). Chichester, West Sussex, UK: Wiley-Blackwell.

Rubinstein, S., & Caballero, B. (2000). Is Miss America an undernourished role model? *Journal of the American Medical Association, 283*(12), 1569.

Rudolph, K. D., & Flynn, M. (2007). Childhood adversity and youth depression: Influence of gender and pubertal status. *Development and Psychopathology, 19*(2), 497–521.

Russell, S. T. (2006). Substance use and abuse and mental health among sexual-minority. In A. M. Omoto & H. S. Kurtzman (Eds.), *Sexual orientation and mental health: Examining identity and development in lesbian, gay, and bisexual people* (pp. 13–35). Washington, DC: American Psychological Association.

Russo, N. F., Pirlott, A. G., & Cohen, A. B. (2012). The psychology of women and gender in international perspective: Issues and challenges. In F. T. L. Leong, W. E. Pickren, M. M. Leach, & A. J. Marsella (Eds.). *Internationalizing the psychology curriculum in the United States* (pp. 157–178). New York: Springer.

Rutter, M. (2006). The psychological effects of early institutional rearing. In P. J. Marshall & N. A. Fox (Eds.) *The development of social engagement: Neurobiological perspectives. Series in affective science* (pp. 355–391). New York: Oxford University Press.

Ryan, L. R., Brownlow, S., & Patterson, B. (2015). Women's mental rotation abilities as a function of priming. *Psychology, 6*(3), DOI:10.4236/psych.2015.63021.

Ryeng, M. S., Kroger, J., & Martinussen, M. (2013). Identity status and self-esteem: A meta-analysis. *Identity: An International Journal of Theory and Research, 13*(3), 201–213.

Rysavy, M. A., et al. (2015). Between-hospital variation in treatment and outcomes in extremely preterm infants. *The New England Journal of Medicine, 372*, 1801–1811.

Rytter, M. J. H., et al. (2015). Diet in the treatment of ADHD in children—A systematic review of the literature. *Nordic Journal of Psychiatry, 69*(1), 1–18.

Sadker, D. (2011). More than Title IX: How equity in education has shaped the nation. *Journal of Women, Politics, and Policy, (32)*2, 167–169.

Sadker, D., Sadker, M., & Zittleman, K. (2009). *Still failing at fairness: How gender bias cheats girls and boys in school and what we can do about it.* New York: Scribner.

Sadker, M., & Sadker, D. (1994). *Failing at fairness: How America's schools cheat girls.* New York: Scribners.

Sadler, T. W. (Ed.). (2005). Abstracts of papers presented at the thirty-fifth annual meeting of the Japanese Teratology Society, Tokyo, Japan. *Teratology, 52*(4), b1–b51.

Saffran, J. R. (2009). Acquiring grammatical patterns: Constraints on learning. In J. Colombo, P. McCardle & L. Freud (Eds.), *Infant pathways to language: Methods, models, and research disorders* (pp. 31–47). New York: Psychology Press.

Sagrestano, L. M., McCormick, S. H., Paikoff, R. L., & Holmbeck, G. N. (1999). Pubertal development and parent–child conflict in low-income, urban, African American adolescents. *Journal of Research on Adolescence 9*(1), 85–107.

Saklofske, D. H., van de Vijver, F. J. R., Oakland, T., Mpofu, E., & Suzuki, L. A. (2015). Intelligence and culture: History and assessment. In S. Goldstein, D. Princiotta, & J. A. Naglieri (Eds.). *Handbook of intelligence: Evolutionary theory, historical perspective, and current concepts* (pp. 341–365). New York: Springer Science+Business Media.

Salapatek, P. (1975). Pattern perception in early infancy. In L. B. Cohen & P. Salapatek (Eds.), *Infant perception: From sensation to cognition.* New York: Academic Press.

Salas, H. S., Aziz, Z., Villareale, N., & Diekema, D. S. (2008). The research and family liaison: Enhancing informed consent. *IRB: Ethics & Human Research, 30*(4), 1–8.

Saleh, F. M., Grudzinskas, A., & Judge, A. (2014). *Adolescent sexual behavior in the digital age: Considerations for clinicians, legal professionals, and educators.* New York: Oxford University Press.

Salvy, S-J., et al. (2008). Peer influence on children's physical activity: An experience sampling study. *Journal of Pediatric Psychology, 33*(1), 39–49.

Salzarulo, P., & Ficca, G. (Eds.). (2002). *Awakening and sleep-wake cycle across development.* Amsterdam: John Benjamins.

Salzburger, W., et al. (2008). Annotation of expressed sequence tags for the East African cichlid fish *Astatotilapia burtoni* and evolutionary analyses of cichlid ORFs. *BMC Genomics, 9,* 96. Published online February 25, 2008.

Sanchez-Gomez, M. V., Perez-Cerda, F., & Matute, C. (2014). White matter damage in multiple sclerosis. *Springer Series in Translational Stroke Research, 4,* 405–429.

Sandin, S., et al. (2012). Advancing maternal age is associated with risk for autism: A review and meta-analysis. *Journal of the American Academy of Child & Adolescent Psychiatry, 51*(5), 477–486.

Santonastaso, P., Friederici, S., & Favaro, A. (2001). Sertraline in the treatment of restricting anorexia nervosa: An open controlled trial. *Journal of Child and Adolescent Psychopharmacology, 11*(2), 143–150.

Santos, J., Pearce, S. E., & Stroustrup, A. (2015). Impact of hospital-based environmental exposures on neurodevelopmental outcomes of preterm infants. *Current Opinion in Pediatrics,* DOI:10.1097/MOP.0000000000000190.

Saudino, K. J. (2012). Sources of continuity and change in activity level in early childhood. *Child Development, 83*(1), 266–281.

Sava, S., & Yurgelun-Todd, D. A. (2008). Functional magnetic resonance in psychiatry. *Topics in Magnetic Resonance Imaging, 19*(2), 71–79.

Save the Children. (2013). *State of the world's mothers 2013.* Westport, CT: Save the Children. Available at www.savethechildren.org.

Save the Children. (2014). *State of the world's mothers 2014.* Westport, CT: Save the Children. Available at www.savethechildren.org.

Savic, I., Garcia-Falgueras, A., & Swaab, D. F. (2011). Sexual differentiation of the human brain in relation to gender identity and sexual orientation. In I. Savic (Ed.). *Sex differences in the human brain, their underpinnings and implications: Progress in brain research, 186* (pp. 41–64). New York: Elsevier.

Savin-Williams, R. C. (2011). Identity development among sexual-minority youth. In S. J. Schwartz et al. (Eds.). *Handbook of identity theory and research* (pp. 671–689). New York: Springer.

Savin-Williams, R. C., & Berndt, T. (1990). Friendship and peer relations. In S. S. Feldman & G. R. Elliott (Eds.), *At the threshold: The developing adolescent.* Cambridge, MA: Harvard University Press.

Sawitri, D. R., & Creed, P. A. (2015). Perceived career congruence between adolescents and their parents as a moderator between goal orientation and career aspirations. *Personality and Individual Differences, 81,* 29–34.

Saxe, G. N., Ellis, B. H., Fogler, J., & Navalta, C. P. (2012). Innovations in practice: Preliminary evidence for effective family engagement in treatment for child traumatic stress—Trauma systems therapy approach to preventing school dropout. *Child and Adolescent Mental Health, 17*(1), 58–61.

Sayal, K., Heron, J., Maughan, B., Rowe, R., & Ramchandani, P. (2013). Infant temperament and childhood psychiatric disorder: Longitudinal study. *Child: Care, Health and Development,* DOI:10.1111/cch.12054.

Sayegh, Y., & Dennis, W. (1965). The effect of supplementary experience upon the behavioral development of infants in institutions. *Child Development, 36*(1), 81–90.

Scales, P. C. (2014). Developmental assets and the promotion of well-being in middle childhood. In A. Ben-Arieh et al., (Eds.). *Handbook of child well-being* (pp. 1649–1678). New York: Springer.

Scarr, S. (1993, March). *IQ correlations among members of transracial adoptive families.* Paper presented at the meeting of the Society for Research in Child Development, New Orleans, LA.

Scarr, S. (1998). How do families affect intelligence? Social environmental and behavior genetic predictions. In J. J. McArdle & R. W. Woodcock (Eds.), *Human cognitive abilities in theory and practice* (pp. 113–136). Mahwah, NJ: Erlbaum.

Scarr, S., & Weinberg, R. A. (1976). IQ test performance of black children adopted by white families. *American Psychologist, 31,* 726–739.

Scarr, S., & Weinburg, R. A. (1977). Intellectual similarities within families of both adopted and biological children. *Intelligence, 1,* 170–191.

Schachner, A., & Hannon, E. E. (2011). Infant-directed speech drives social preferences in 5-month-old infants. *Developmental Psychology, 47*(1), 19–25.

Schacter, H. L., White, S. J., Chang, V. Y., & Juvonen, J. (2015). "Why me?": Characterological self-blame and continued victimization in the first year of middle school. *Journal of Clinical Child & Adolescent Psychology, 44*(3), 446–455.

Schaffer, H. R., & Emerson, P. E. (1964). The development of social attachments in infancy. *Monographs of the Society for Research in Child Development, 29*(94).

Schein, S. S., & Langlois, J. H. (2015). Unattractive infant faces elicit negative affect from adults. *Infant Behavior and Development, 38,* 130–134.

Scherf, K. S., Behrmann, M., Kimchi, R., & Luna, B. (2009). Emergence of global shape processing continues through adolescence. *Child Development, 80*(1), 162–177.

Schieve, L. A., Clayton, H. B., Durkin, M. S., Wingate, M. S., & Drews-Botsch, C. (2015). Comparison of perinatal risk factors associated with autism spectrum disorder (ASD), intellectual disability (ID), and co-occurring ASD and ID. *Journal of Autism and Developmental Disorders,* DOI:10.1007/s10803-015-2402-0.

Schleider, J. L., Velez, E., Krause, E. D., & Gillham, J. (2014). Perceived psychological control and anxiety in early adolescents: The mediating role of attributional style. *Cognitive Therapy and Research, 38*(1), 71–81.

Schmidt, M. E., et al. (2009). Television viewing in infancy and child cognition at 3 years of age in a US cohort. *Pediatrics, 123*(3), e370–e375.

Schmidt, M. E., & Anderson, D. R. (2007). The impact of television on cognitive development and educational achievement. In N. Pecora et al. (Eds.), *Children and television: Fifty years of research.* Mahwah, NJ: Erlbaum.

Schmitow, C., & Stenberg, G. (2013). Social referencing in 10-month-old infants. *European Journal of Developmental Psychology, 10*(5), 533–545.

Schmitt, D. P., et al. (2012). A reexamination of sex differences in sexuality: New studies reveal old truths. *Current Directions in Psychological Science, 21*(2), 135–139.

Schneider, S., et al. (2012). Risk taking and adolescent reward system: A potential common link to substance abuse. *American Journal of Psychiatry, 169*(1), 39–46.

Schneider, W. (2010). Memory development in childhood. In U. Goswami (Ed.), *The Wiley–Blackwell handbook of childhood cognitive development.* (2nd ed.) (pp. 347–376). Chichester, West Sussex, UK: Wiley–Blackwell.

Schneider, W. (2015). Memory development during the infant and toddler years. Motor Development from Early Childhood Through Emerging Adulthood (pp. 39 -74). Switzerland: Springer International Publishing.

Schoenmaker, C., et al. (2015). From maternal sensitivity in infancy to adult attachment representations: A longitudinal adoption study with secure base scripts. *Attachment & Human Development, 17*(3), 241–256.

Schoenmaker, C., Juffer, F., van IJzendoorn, M. H., & Bakermans-Kranenburg, M. J. (2014). Does family matter? The well-being of children growing up in institutions, foster care and adoption. In A. Ben-Arieh et al., (Eds.). *Handbook of child well-being* (pp. 2197–2228). New York: Springer.

Schonfeld, A. M., Mattson, S. N., & Riley, E. P. (2005). Moral maturity and delinquency after prenatal alcohol exposure. *Journal of Studies on Alcohol, 66*(4), 545–554.

Schraf, M., & Hertz-Lazarowitz, R. (2003). Social networks in the school context: Effects of culture and gender. *Journal of Social and Personal Relationships, 20*(6), 843–858.

Schuetze, P., Zeskind, P. S., & Eiden, R. D. (2003). The perceptions of infant distress signals varying in pitch by cocaine-using mothers. *Infancy, 4*(1), 65–83.

Schultz, D., & Shaw, D. S. (2003). Boys' maladaptive social information processing, family emotional climate, and pathways to early conduct problems. *Social Development, 12*(3), 440–460.

Schultz, D. P., & Schultz, S. E. (2012). *A history of modern psychology* (10th ed.). Belmont, CA: Cengage.

Schumacher, D., & Queen, J. A. (2007). *Overcoming obesity in childhood and adolescence: A guide for school leaders.* Thousand Oaks, CA: Corwin Press.

Schwartz, A., & Cohen, S. (2013, March 31). ADHD seen in 11% of U.S. children as diagnoses rise. *The New York Times.* Retrieved from http://www.nytimes.com/2013/04/01/health/more-diagnoses-of-hyperactivity-causing-concern.html?pagewanted=all&_r=0. Accessed April 5, 2015.

Schwartz, D., Lansford, J. E., Dodge, K. E., Pettit, G. S., & Bates, J. E. (2013). The link between harsh home environments and negative academic trajectories is exacerbated by victimization in the elementary school peer group. *Developmental Psychology, 49*(2), 305–316.

Schwartz, S. J., et al. (2011). Daily dynamics of personal identity and self-concept clarity. *European Journal of Personality, 25*(5), 373–385.

Scull, A. (2010). Left brain, right brain: One brain, two brains. *Brain, 133*(10), 3153–3156.

Sears, J. (2009). *Signs of being ready for solid foods.* Retrieved from http://www.wholesomebabyfood.com/readyforsolids.htm. Accessed March 18, 2009.

Segal, N. L. (2013). Personality similarity in unrelated look-alike pairs: Addressing a twin study challenge. *Personality and Individual Differences, 54*(1), 23–28.

Seiler, C. B., Jones, K. E., Shera, D., & Armstrong, C. L. (2011). Brain region white matter associations with visual selective attention. *Brain Imaging and Behavior, 5*(4), 262–273.

Selman, R. L. (1976). Social-cognitive understanding. In T. Lickona (Ed.), *Moral development and behavior: Theory, research, and social issues.* New York: Holt, Rinehart & Winston.

Selman, R. L. (1980). *The growth of interpersonal understanding: Developmental and clinical analysis.* New York: Academic Press.

Sengpiel, V., et al. (2013). Maternal caffeine intake during pregnancy is associated with birth weight but not with gestational length: results from a large prospective observational cohort study. *BMC Medicine, 11,* 42.

Sengsavang, S., & Krettenauer, T. (2015). Children's moral self-concept: The role of aggression and parent–child relationships. *Merrill-Palmer Quarterly, 61*(2), 213–235.

Serbin, L. A., Poulin-Dubois, D., Colburne, K. A., Sen, M. G., & Eichstedt, J. A. (2001). Gender stereotyping in infancy: Visual preferences for and knowledge of gender-stereotyped toys in the second year. *International Journal of Behavioral Development, 25*(1), 7–15.

Shaw, D. S., & Shelleby, E. C. (2014). Early-starting conduct problems: Intersection of conduct problems and poverty. *Annual Review of Clinical Psychology, 10,* 503–528.

Shaw, G. M., Velie, E. M., & Schaffer, D. (1996). Risk of neural tube defect–affected pregnancies among obese women. *Journal of the American Medical Association, 275,* 1093–1096.

Shaw, P., Stringaris, A., Nigg, J., & Leibenluft, E. (2014). Emotion dysregulation in attention deficit/hyperactivity disorder. *The American Journal of Psychiatry, 171*(3), 276–293.

Shaw, R. J., et al. (2014). Prevention of traumatic stress in mothers of preterms: 6-month outcomes. *Pediatrics, 134*(2), e481–e488.

Shaywitz, S. E., & Shaywitz, B. A. (2003). Neurobiological indices of dyslexia. In H. L. Swanson et al. (Eds.), *Handbook of learning disabilities* (pp. 514–531). New York: Guilford.

Shaywitz, S. E., & Shaywitz, B. A. (2013). Psychopathology of dyslexia and reading disorders. In A. S. Davis (Ed.). *Psychopathology of childhood and adolescence: A neuropsychological approach* (pp. 109–126). New York: Springer.

Shear, K., Jin, R., Ruscio, A. M., Walters, E. E., & Kessler, R. C. (2006). Prevalence and correlates of estimated DSM-IV child and adult separation anxiety disorder in the National Comorbidity Survey Replication. *American Journal of Psychiatry 163,* 1074–1083.

Sheeber, L. B., Davis, B., Leve, C., Hops, H., & Tildesley, E. (2007). Adolescents' relationships with their mothers and fathers: Associations with depressive disorder and subdiagnostic symptomatology. *Journal of Abnormal Psychology, 116*(1), 144–154.

Shin, H. B., & Bruno, R. (2003, October). *Language use and English speaking ability: 2000.* Washington, DC: U.S. Bureau of the Census.

Shiner, R. L. (2012). What is temperament now? Assessing Progress in Temperament Research on the Twenty-Fifth Anniversary of Goldsmith et al. *Child Development Perspectives, 6*(4), 436 – 444.

Shiner, R. L., & DeYoung, C. G. (2013). The structure of temperament and personality traits: A developmental perspective. In P. D. Zelazo (Ed.). *The Oxford handbook of developmental psychology,* Vol. 2: Personality and emotional development (pp. 113–141). New York: Oxford University Press.

Shiozaki, A., et al. (2014). Multiple pregnancy, short cervix, part-time worker, steroid use, low educational level and male fetus are risk factors for preterm birth in Japan: A multicenter, prospective study. *The Journal of Obstetrics and Gynaecology Research, 40*(1), 53–61.

Shoptaw, S. (2014). Brain is behavior—methamphetamine dependence and recovery. *Addiction, 109*(2), 248–249.

Shortt, A. L., Barrett, P. M., & Fox, T. L. (2001). Evaluating the FRIENDS Program: A cognitive-behavioral group treatment for anxious children and their parents. *Journal of Clinical Child Psychology, 30*(4), 525–535.

Shroff, H., et al. (2006). Features associated with excessive exercise in women with eating disorders. *International Journal of Eating Disorders, 39*(6), 454–461.

Shuster, M. M., Li, Y., Shi, J. (2012). Maternal cultural values and parenting practices: Longitudinal associations with Chinese adolescents' aggression. *Journal of Adolescence, 35*(2), 345–355.

Sidibe, M. (2015). Empowering women is critical to ending the AIDS epidemic. UNAIDS. Retrieved from http://www.unaids.org/en/resources/presscentre/pressreleaseandstatementarchive/2015/march/20150308_IWD. Accessed August 14, 2015.

Siegal, M., & Surian, L. (2012). *Access to language and cognitive development.* New York: Oxford University Press.

Siegel, L. J., & Welsh, B. C. (2011). *Juvenile delinquency: Theory, practice, and law* (11th ed.). Belmont. CA: Cengage.

Siegel, L. S. (1992). Infant motor, cognitive, and language behaviors as predictors of achievement at school age. In C. Rovee-Collier & L. P. Lipsitt (Eds.), *Advances in infancy research,* Vol. 7. Norwood, NJ: Ablex.

Siegle, D., Rubenstein, L. D., & Mitchell, M. S. (2014). Honors students' perceptions of their high school experiences: The influence of teachers on student motivation. *Gifted Child Quarterly*, 58(1), 35–50.

Siegler, R. S., & Alibali, M. W. (2005). *Children's thinking* (4th ed.). Upper Saddle River, NJ: Prentice Hall.

Siegler, R. S., Liebert, D. E., & Liebert, R. M. (1973). Inhelder and Piaget's pendulum problem: Teaching pre-adolescents to act as scientists. *Developmental Psychology*, 9, 97–101.

Sigafoos, J., Green, V. A., Payne, D., O'Reilly, M. F., & Lancioni, G. E. (2009). A classroom-based antecedent intervention reduces obsessive-repetitive behavior in an adolescent with autism. *Clinical Case Studies*, 8(1), 3–13.

Silk, T. J., & Wood, A. G. (2011). Lessons about neurodevelopment from anatomical magnetic resonance imaging. *Journal of Developmental Behavioral Pediatrics*, 32(2), 158–168.

Silles, M. (2010). The implications of family size and birth order for test scores and behavioral development. *Economics of Education Review*, 29(5), 795–803.

Silva, C., et al. (2012). Literacy: Exploring working memory systems. *Journal of Clinical and Experimental Neuropsychology*, 26(2), 266–277.

Silverman, J. C. (2007). Epistemological beliefs and attitudes toward inclusion in pre-service teachers. *Teacher Education and Special Education: The Journal of the Teacher Education Division of the Council for Exceptional Children*, 30(1), 42–51.

Silvia, P. J., & Beaty, R. E. (2012). Making creative metaphors: The importance of fluid intelligence for creative thought. *Intelligence*, 40(4), 343–351.

Silvia, P. J., Beaty, R. E., & Nusbaum, E. C. (2013). Verbal fluency and creativity: General and specific contributions of broad retrieval ability (Gr) factors to divergent thinking. *Intelligence*, 41(5), 328–340.

Sim, T. N., & Ong, L. P. (2005). Parent physical punishment and child aggression in a Singapore Chinese preschool. *Journal of Marriage and Family*, 67(1), 85–99.

Simion, F., Cassia, V. M., Turati, C., & Valenza, E. (2001). The origins of face perception: Specific versus nonspecific mechanisms. *Infant and Child Development*, 10(1–2), 59–65.

Simonelli, A., Monti, F., & Magalotti, D. (2005). The complex phenomenon of failure to thrive: Medical, psychological and relational-affective aspects. *Psicologia Clinica dello Sviluppo*, 9(2), 183–212.

Simonton, D. K. (2014). Creative performance, expertise acquisition, individual differences, and developmental antecedents: An integrative research agenda. *Intelligence*, 45(1), 66–73.

Sinclair, S., Dunn, E., & Lowery, B. S. (2005). The relationship between parental racial attitudes and children's implicit prejudice. *Journal of Experimental Social Psychology*, 41, 283–289.

Singh, A., et al. (2012). Physical activity and performance at school. *Archives of Pediatrics and Adolescent Medicine*, 166(1), 49–55.

Singh, L., Nestor, S., Parikh, C., & Yull, A. (2009). Influences of infant-directed speech on early word recognition. *Infancy*, 14(6), 654–666.

Sinno, S. M., & Killen, M. (2009). Moms at work and dads at home: Children's evaluations of parental roles. *Applied Developmental Science*, 13(1), 16–29.

Sirgy, M. J. (2012). Effects of genetics, health, biology, the environment, and drugs on subjective QOL. *The Psychology of the Quality of Life*, 50, 123–138.

Skeels, H. M. (1966). Adult status of children with contrasting early life experiences: A follow-up study. *Monographs of the Society for Research in Child Development*, 31(3, ser. 105).

Skinner, B. F. (1957). *Verbal behavior*. New York: Appleton.

Skoog, T., & Ozdemir, S. B. (2015). Explaining why early-maturing girls are more exposed to sexual harassment in early adolescence. *The Journal of Early Adolescence*, DOI:10.1177/0272431614568198.

Skoog, T., Ozdemir, S. B., & Stattin, H. (2015). Understanding the link between pubertal timing in girls and the development of depressive symptoms: The role of sexual harassment. *Journal of Youth and Adolescence*, DOI:10.1007/s10964-015-0292-2.

Slane, J. D., Burt, A., & Klump, K. L. (2012). Bulimic behaviors and alcohol use: Shared genetic influences. *Behavior Genetics*, 42(4), 603–613.

Slater, A., et al. (2010) Visual perception. In J. G. Bremner & T. D. Wachs (Eds.). *The Wiley-Blackwell handbook of infant development*, Vol. 1 (2nd ed.). Wiley-Blackwell, Oxford, UK. DOI:10.1002/9781444327564.ch2.

Slaughter, V. (2011). Development of social cognition. In D. Skuse, H. Bruce, L. Dowdney, & D. Mrazek (Eds.). *Child psychology and psychiatry: Frameworks for practice* (2nd ed.) (pp. 51–55). Hoboken, NJ: Wiley.

Slavin, R. E. (2012). *Educational psychology: Theory and practice* (10th ed.). Upper Saddle River, NJ: Pearson.

Sloan, S., Sneddon, H., Stewart, M., & Iwaniec, D. (2006). Breast is best? Reasons why mothers decide to breastfeed or bottlefeed their babies and factors influencing the duration of breastfeeding. *Child Care in Practice*, 12(3), 283–297.

Slobin, D. I. (2001). Form/function relations: How do children find out what they are? In M. Tomasello & E. Bates (Eds.), *Language development: The essential readings*. Malden, MA: Blackwell.

Slotboom, A., Hendriks, J., & Verbruggen, J. (2011). Contrasting adolescent female and male sexual aggression. *Journal of Sexual Aggression*, 17(1), 15–33.

Smetana, J. G. (2011). *Adolescents, families, and social development*. Chichester, West Sussex, UK: Wiley-Blackwell.

Smetana, J. G., Jambon, M., & Ball, C. (2013). The social domain approach to children's moral and social judgments. In M. Killen, & J. G. Smetana (Eds.). *Handbook of moral development*, 2nd ed. (pages 23–45). New York: Psychology Press.

Smiley, P. A., & Johnson, R. S. (2006). Self-referring terms, event transitivity and development of self. *Cognitive Development*, 21(3), 266–284.

Smith, A. (2014). 6 new facts about Facebook. Available at http://www.pewresearch.org/fact-tank/2014/02/03/6-new-facts-about-facebook/.

Smith, A. R., Chein, J., & Steinberg, L. (2014). Peers increase adolescent risk taking even when the probabilities of negative outcomes are known. *Developmental Psychology*, 50(5), 1564–1568.

Smith, K. E., Patterson, C. A., Szabo, M. M., Tarazi, R. A., & Barakat, L. P. (2013). Predictors of academic achievement for school-age children with sickle-cell disease. *Advances in School Mental Health Promotion*, 6(1), 5–20.

Smith, R. L., & Rose, A. J. (2011). The "cost of caring" in youths' friendships: Considering associations among social perspective taking, co-rumination, and empathetic distress. *Developmental Psychology*, 47(6), 1792–1803.

Snarey, J., & Samuelson, P. L. (2008). Moral education in the cognitive developmental tradition: Lawrence Kohlberg's revolutionary ideas. In L. P. Nucci & D. Narváez (Eds.), *Handbook of moral and character education* (pp. 53–79). London: Routledge.

Snarey, J., & Samuelson, P. L. (2014). Lawrence Kohlberg's revolutionary ideas: Moral education in the cognitive-developmental tradition. In L. Nucci, T. Krettenauer, & D. Narvaez. *Handbook of moral and character education* (pp. 61–83). New York: Routledge.

Snarey, J. R. (1994). Cross-cultural universality of social-moral development: A critical review of Kohlbergian research. In B. Puka (Ed.), *New research in moral development* (pp. 268–298). New York: Garland.

Snegovskikh, V., Park, J. S., & Norwitz, E. R. (2006). Endocrinology of parturition. *Endocrinology and Metabolism Clinics of North America*, 35(1), 173–191.

Snegovskikh, V. V., et al. (2011). Surfactant protein-A (SP-A) selectively inhibits prostaglandin F2α (PGF2α) production in term decidua: Implications for the onset of labor. *The Journal of Clinical Endocrinology & Metabolism*, 96,(4), E624–E632.

Sneider, J. T., et al. (2015). Sex differences in spatial navigation and perception in human adolescents and emerging adults. *Behavioural Processes*, 111, 42–50.

Snyder, H. M., & Sickmund, M. (2006). *Juvenile offenders and victims: 2006 national report*. Washington, DC: U.S. Department of Justice, Office of Justice Programs, Office of Juvenile Justice and Delinquency Prevention.

Soan, S., & Tod, J. (2006). Review of dyslexia. *European Journal of Special Needs Education*, 21(3), 354–356.

Sobel, D. M., & Legare, C. H. (2014). Causal learning in children. *Wiley*

Interdisciplinary Reviews: Cognitive Science, 5(4), 423–427.

Sodian, B., Taylor, C., Harris, P. L., & Perner, J. (1991). Early deception and the child's theory of mind: False trails and genuine markers. *Child Development, 62,* 468–483.

Solmeyer, A. R., & Feinberg, M. E. (2011). Mother and father adjustment during early parenthood: The roles of infant temperament and coparenting relationship quality. *Infant Behavior and Development, 34*(4), 504–514.

Solmeyer, A. R., McHale, S. M., & Crouter, A. C. (2014). Longitudinal associations between sibling relationship qualities and risky behavior across adolescence. *Developmental Psychology, 50*(2), 600–610.

Somers, M., Shields, L. S., Boks, M. P., Kahn, R. S., & Sommer, I. E. (2015). Cognitive benefits of right-handedness: A meta-analysis. *Neuroscience & Biobehavioral Reviews, 51,* 48–63.

Sommer, I. E. C., Ramsey, N. F., Mandl, R. C. W., & Kahn, R. S. (2002). Language lateralization in monozygotic twin pairs concordant and discordant for handedness. *Brain, 125*(12), 2710–2718.

Sontag, L. M., Graber, J. A., & Clemans, K. H. (2011). The role of peer stress and pubertal timing on symptoms of psychopathology during early adolescence. *Journal of Youth and Adolescence, 40*(10), 1371–1382.

Sontag, L. W., & Richards, T. W. (1938). Studies in fetal behavior: Fetal heart rate as a behavioral indicator. *Child Development Monographs, 3*(4).

Sorce, J., Emde, R. N., Campos, J. J., & Klinnert, M. D. (2000). Maternal emotional signaling: Its effect on the visual cliff behavior of 1-year-olds. In D. Muir & A. Slater (Eds.), *Infant development: The essential readings. Essential readings in developmental psychology* (pp. 282–292). Malden, MA: Blackwell.

Sorhagen, N. S. (2013). Early teacher expectations disproportionately affect poor children's high school performance. *Journal of Educational Psychology, 105*(2), 465–477.

Sousa, C., et al. (2011). Longitudinal study of the effects of child abuse and children's exposure to domestic violence, parent-child attachments, and antisocial behavior in adolescence. *Journal of Interpersonal Violence, 26*(1), 111–136.

Sovio, U., et al. (2009). Genetic determinants of height growth assessed longitudinally from infancy to adulthood in the Northern Finland Birth Cohort 1966. *PLoS Genetics, 5*(3), e1000409.

Sozener, Z. C., et al. (2015). Prognosis of adult asthma: A 7-year follow-up study. *Annals of Allergy, Asthma and Immunology,* DOI:10.1016/j.anai.2015.02.010.

Spelke, E. S., & Owsley, C. (1979). Inter-modal exploration and knowledge in infancy. *Infant Behavior and Development, 2,* 13–27.

Spencer, M. B., Dornbusch, S. M., & Mont-Reynaud, R. (1990). Challenges in studying minority youth. In S. S. Feldman & G. R. Elliott (Eds.), *At the threshold: The developing adolescent.* Cambridge, MA: Harvard University Press.

Sperry, D. M., & Widom, C. S. (2013). Child abuse and neglect, social support, and psychopathology in adulthood: A prospective investigation. *Child Abuse & Neglect, 37*(6), 415–425.

Spieker, S., Nelson, D., DeKlyen, M., & Staerkel, F. (2005). Enhancing early attachments in the context of Early Head Start: Can programs emphasizing family support improve rates of secure infant–mother attachments in low-income families? In L. J. Berlin, Y. Ziv, L. Amaya-Jackson & M. T. Greenberg (Eds.), *Enhancing early attachments: Theory, research, intervention, and policy. Duke series in child development and public policy* (pp. 250–275). New York: Guilford.

Spitz, R. A. (1965). *The first year of life: A psychoanalytic study of normal and deviant object relations.* New York: International Universities Press.

Spitzer, R. L., Gibbon, M., Skodol, A. E., Williams, J. B. W., & First, M. B. (2002). *DSM–IV–TR casebook.* Washington, DC: American Psychiatric Press.

Sroufe, L. A., Bennett, C., Englund, M., Urban, J., & Shulman, S. (1993). The significance of gender boundaries in pre-adolescence: Contemporary correlates and antecedents of boundary violation and maintenance. *Child Development, 64,* 455–466.

Staff, J., Mont'Alvao, A., & Mortimer, J. T. (2015). Children at work. In R. M. Lerner (Ed.). *Handbook of child psychology and developmental science, Vol. 4.* DOI:10.1002/9781118963418.childpsy409.

Staff, J., Mortimer, J. T., & Uggen, C. (2004). Work and leisure in adolescence. In R. M. Lerner & L. Steinberg (Eds.), *Handbook of adolescent psychology* (2nd ed.) (pp. 429–450). Hoboken, NJ: Wiley.

Stahmer, A. C., Ingersoll, B., & Koegel, R. L. (2004). Inclusive programming for toddlers autism spectrum disorders: Outcomes from the Children's Toddler School. *Journal of Positive Behavior Interventions, 6*(2), 67–82.

Stanford University School of Medicine. (2012). Sibling preparation classes. Palo Alto, CA: Lucille Packard Children's Hospital at Stanford.

Stanyon, R., & Bigoni, F. (2014). Sexual selection and the evolution of behavior, morphology, neuroanatomy and genes in humans and other primates. *Neuroscience & Biobehavioral Reviews, 46*(4), 579–590.

State of the World's Mothers. (2014). Save the Children. Save the Children: Westport, CT.

Stauffacher, K., & DeHart, G. B. (2006). Crossing social contexts: Relational aggression between siblings and friends during early and middle childhood. *Journal of Applied Developmental Psychology, 27*(3), 228–240.

Steca, P., et al. (2014). Cognitive vulnerability to depressive symptoms in children: The protective role of self-efficacy beliefs in a multi-wave longitudinal study. *Journal of Abnormal Child Psychology, 42*(1), 137–148.

Steel, E. (2015, April 25). Bruce Jenner's transgender announcement draws 16.8 million on ABC News. *The New York Times,* p. A20.

Steele, H. (2005). Editorial. *Attachment & Human Development, 7*(4), 345.

Steele, M., Hodges, J., Kaniuk, J., Hillman, S., & Henderson, K. (2003). Attachment representations and adoption: Associations between maternal states of mind and emotion narratives in previously maltreated children. *Journal of Child Psychotherapy, 29*(2), 187–205.

Stein, S. J., & Deonarine, J. M. (2015). Current concepts in the assessment of emotional intelligence. In S. Goldstein, D. Princiotta, & J. A. Naglieri (Eds.). *Handbook of intelligence: Evolutionary theory, historical perspective, and current concepts* (pp. 381–402). New York: Springer Science+Business Media.

Steinberg, L. (1996). *Beyond the classroom: Why school reform has failed and what parents need to do.* New York: Simon & Schuster.

Steinberg, L. (2011). Adolescent risk taking: A social neuroscience perspective. In E. Amsel, & J. Smetana (Eds.), *Adolescent vulnerabilities and opportunities* (pp. 41–64). New York: Cambridge University Press.

Stephenson, R. H., & Banet-Weiser, S. (2007). Super-sized kids: Obesity, children, moral panic, and the media. In J. A. Bryant (Ed.), *The children's television community* (pp. 277–291). Mahwah, NJ: Erlbaum.

Sternberg, R. J. (2006). The nature of creativity. *Creativity Research Journal, 18*(1), 87–98.

Sternberg, R. J. (2015). Multiple intelligences in the new age of thinking. In S. Goldstein, D. Princiotta, & J. A. Naglieri (Eds.). *Handbook of intelligence: Evolutionary theory, historical perspective, and current concepts* (pp. 229–241). New York: Springer Science+Business Media.

Sternberg, R. J., Grigorenko, E. L., & Kidd, K. K. (2005). Intelligence, race, and genetics. *American Psychologist, 60*(1), 46–59.

Sternberg, R. J., & Kaufman, S. J. (Eds.). (2011). *The Cambridge handbook of intelligence.* New York: Cambridge University Press.

Stevens, B., et al. (2005). Consistent management of repeated procedural pain with sucrose in preterm neonates: Is it effective and safe for repeated use over time? *Clinical Journal of Pain, 21*(6), 543–548.

Stevenson, J., et al. (2014). Research Review: The role of diet in the treatment of attention-deficit/hyperactivity disorder—an appraisal of the evidence on efficacy and recommendations on the design of future studies. *The Journal of Child Psychology and Psychiatry, 55*(5), 416-427.

Steward, D. K. (2001). Behavioral characteristics of infants with nonorganic failure to thrive during a play interaction. *American Journal of Maternal/Child Nursing, 26*(2), 79–85.

Stice, E., Martti, C. N., & Rohde, P. (2013a). Prevalence, incidence, impairment, and course of the proposed DSM-5 eating disorder diagnoses in an 8-year prospective community study of young women. *Journal of Abnormal Psychology, 122*(2), 445–457.

Stice, E., Rohde, P., Butryn, M., Menke, K. S., & Marti, C. N. (2015). Randomized controlled pilot trial of a novel dissonance-based group treatment for eating disorders. *Behaviour Research and Therapy, 65*, 67–75.

Stice, E., Rohde, P., Shaw, H., & Marti, C. N. (2013b). Efficacy trial of a selective prevention program targeting both eating disorders and obesity among female college students: 1- and 2-year follow-up effects. *Journal of Consulting and Clinical Psychology, 81*(1), 183–189.

Stillbirth Collaborative Research Network Writing Group. (2011). Association between stillbirth and risk factors known at pregnancy confirmation. *The Journal of the American Medical Association, 306*(22), 2469–2479.

Stipek, D., & Hakuta, K. (2007). Strategies to ensure that no child starts from behind. In J. L. Aber et al. (Eds.), *Child development and social policy: Knowledge for action, APA Decade of Behavior* (pp. 129–145). Washington, DC: American Psychological Association.

Stipek, D., Recchia, S., & McClintic, S. (1992). Self-evaluation in young children. *Monographs of the Society for Research in Child Development, 57*(1, ser. 226).

Stockdale, L., Morrison, R., Kmiecik, M., Garbarino, J. & Silton, R. (2015). Emotionally anesthetized: Media violent induces neural changes during emotional face processing. *Social Cognitive and Affective Neuroscience*, DOI:10.1093/scan/nsv025.

Stone, D. M., et al. (2014). Sexual orientation and suicide ideation: Plans, attempts, and medically serious attempts; Evidence from local youth risk behavior surveys, 2001–2009. *American Journal of Public Health*.

Strategies and solutions. (2011). Retrieved from http://www.cdc.gov/obesity/childhood/solutions.html. Accessed August 18, 2012.

Straus, M. A. (1995). Cited in C. Collins (1995, May 11), Spanking is becoming the new don't. *The New York Times*, p. C8.

Strauss, J., et al. (2012). Association study of early-immediate genes in childhood-onset mood disorders and suicide attempt. *Psychiatry Research, 197*(1), 49–54.

Strenze, T. (2015). Intelligence and success. In S. Goldstein, D. Princiotta, & J. A. Naglieri (Eds.). *Handbook of intelligence: Evolutionary theory, historical perspective, and current concepts* (pp. 405–413). New York: Springer Science+Business Media.

Streri, A. (2002). Hand preference in 4-month-old infants: Global or local processing of objects in the haptic mode. *Current Psychology Letters: Behaviour, Brain and Cognition, 7*, 39–50.

Striegel-Moore, R. H., et al. (2003). Eating disorders in White and Black women. *American Journal of Psychiatry, 160*(7), 1326–1331.

Stieger, A. E., Allemand, M., Robins, R. W., & Fend, H. A. (2014). Low and decreasing self-esteem during adolescence predict adult depression two decades later. *Journal of Personality and Social Psychology, 106*(2), 325–338.

Strock, M. (2004). *Autism spectrum disorders (pervasive developmental disorders).* NIH Publication NIH-04-5511. Bethesda, MD: National Institute of Mental Health, National Institutes of Health, U.S. Department of Health and Human Services. Available at http://www.nimh.nih.gov/publicat/autism.cfm.

Strohner, H., & Nelson, K. E. (1974). The young child's development of sentence comprehension: Influence of event probability, nonverbal context, syntactic form, and strategies. *Child Development, 45*, 567–576.

Strunk, T., Simmer, K., & Burgner, D. (2012). Prematurity and mortality in childhood and early adulthood. *Journal of the American Medical Association, 307*(1). DOI:10.1001/jama.2011.1952.

Strutt, G. F., Anderson, D. R., & Well, A. D. (1975). A developmental study of the effects of irrelevant information on speeded classification. *Journal of Experimental Child Psychology, 20*, 127–135.

Stupica, B., Sherman, L. J., & Cassidy, J. (2011). Newborn irritability moderates the association between infant attachment security and toddler exploration and sociability. *Child Development, 82*(5), 1381–1389.

Subiaul, F., Anderson, S., Brandt, J., & Elkins, J. (2012). Multiple imitation mechanisms in children. *Developmental Psychology, 48*(4), 1165–1179.

Subramaniam, A., et al. (2013). Effect of corticosteroid interval on markers of inflammation in spontaneous preterm birth. *American Journal of Obstetrics and Gynecology, 209*(4), 379.e1–379.e6.

Sugiura-Ogasawara, M., et al. (2013). Frequency of recurrent spontaneous abortion and its influence on further marital relationship and illness. *The Journal of Obstetrics and Gynecology Research, 39*(1), 126–131.

Sullivan, R., et al. (2011). Infant bonding and attachment to the caregiver: Insights from basic and clinical science. *Clinics in Perinatology, 38*(4), 643–655.

Sulloway, F. J. (2011). Why siblings are like Darwin's finches: Birth order, sibling competition, and adaptive divergence within the family. In D. M. Buss, & P. H Hawley (Eds.). *The evolution of personality and individual differences* (pp. 86–120). New York: Oxford University Press.

Sumter, S. R., Bokhorst, C. L., Steinberg, L., & Westenberg, P. M. (2009). The developmental pattern of resistance to peer influence in adolescence: Will the teenager ever be able to resist? *Journal of Adolescence, 32*(4), 1009–1021.

Sun, Y. (2001). Family environment and adolescents' well-being before and after parents' marital disruption: A longitudinal analysis. *Journal of Marriage and Family, 63*(3), 697–713.

Suomi, S. J. (2005). Mother–infant attachment, peer relationships, and the development of social networks in rhesus monkeys. *Human Development, 48*(1–2), 67–79.

Suomi, S. J., Harlow, H. F., & McKinney, W. T. (1972). Monkey psychiatrists. *American Journal of Psychiatry, 128*, 927–932.

Suzuki, L. A., Short, E. L., & Lee, C. S. (2011). Racial and ethnic group differences in intelligence in the United States. In R. J. Sternberg & S. J. Kaufman (Eds.), *The Cambridge handbook of intelligence* (pp. 273–292). New York: Cambridge University Press.

Swaggart, K. A., Pavlicev, M., & Muglia, L. J. (2015). Genomics of preterm birth. Coldspring Harbor Perspectives in Medicine, DOI:10.1101/cshperspect.a023127.

Swanson, H. L., & Alloway, T. P. (2012). Working memory, learning, and academic achievement. In K. R. Harris et al. (Eds.), *APA educational psychology handbook,* Vol 1: Theories, constructs, and critical issues (pp. 327–366). Washington, DC: American Psychological Association.

Syed, E. C. J., et al. (2010). Effect of sensory stimulation in rat barrel cortex, dorsolateral striatum and on corticostriatal functional connectivity. *European Journal of Neuroscience, 33*(3), 461–470.

Takahashi, K. (1990). Are the key assumptions of the "Strange Situation" procedure universal? A view from Japanese research. *Human Development, 33*, 23–30.

Talaei, S. A., & Salami, M. (2013). Sensory experience differentially underlies developmental alterations of LTP in CA1 area and dentate gyrus. *Brain Research, 1537*, 1–8.

Tallandini, M. A., & Valentini, P. (1991). Symbolic prototypes in children's drawings of schools. *Journal of Genetic Psychology, 152*, 179–190.

Tamis-LeMonda, C. S., Cristofaro, T. N., Rodriguez, E. T., & Bornstein, M. H. (2006). Early language development: Social influences in the first years of life. In L. Balter & C. S. Tamis-LeMonda (Eds.), *Child psychology: A handbook of contemporary issues* (2nd ed.) (pp. 79–108). New York: Psychology Press.

Tamis-LeMonda, C. S., et al. (2014a). Children's vocabulary growth in English and Spanish across early development and associations with school readiness skills. *Developmental Neuropsychology, 39*(2), 69–87.

Tamis-LeMonda, C. S., Kuchirko, Y., & Song, L. (2014b). Why is infant language learning facilitated by parental responsiveness? *Current Directions in Psychological Science, 23*(2), 121–126.

Tan, C. C., & Holub, S. C. (2015). Emotional regulation feeding practices link parents' emotional eating to children's emotional eating: A moderated mediation study. *Journal of Pediatric Psychology*, DOI:10.1093/jpepsy/jsv015.

Tan, G. (1999). Perceptions of multiculturalism and intent to stay in school among Mexican American students. *Journal of*

Research and Development in Education, 33(1), 1–14.

Tang, C. S., Yeung, D. Y., & Lee, A. M. (2003). Psychosocial correlates of emotional responses to menarche among Chinese adolescent girls. *Journal of Adolescent Health, 33*(3), 193–201.

Tang, G., et al. (2014). Loss of mTOR-dependent macroautophagy causes autistic-like synaptic pruning deficits, *Neuron, 83*(5), 1131–1143.

Tanner, J. M. (1989). *Fetus into man: Physical growth from conception to maturity.* Cambridge, MA: Harvard University Press.

Tansey, K. E., et al. (2014). Genetic susceptibility for bipolar disorder and response to antidepressants in major depressive disorder. *American Journal of Medical Genetics, 165*(1), 77–83.

Tasker, F., & Granville, J. (2011). Children's views of family relationships in lesbian-led families. *Journal of GLBT Studies, 7*(1–2), 182–199.

Tassi, F., Schneider, B. H., & Richard, J. F. (2001). Competitive behavior at school in relation to social competence and incompetence in middle childhood. *Revue Internationale de Psychologie Sociale, 14*(2), 165–184.

Taumoepeau, M., & Reese, E. (2014). Understanding the self through siblings: Self-awareness mediates the sibling effect on social understanding. *Social Development, 23*(1), 1–18.

Taylor, H. G., Minich, N. M., Klein, N., & Hack, M. (2004). Longitudinal outcomes of very low birth weight: Neuropsychological findings. *Journal of the International Neuropsychological Society, 10*(2), 149–163.

Taylor, M. (2013). *The Oxford handbook on the development of imagination* (pp. 251–271). New York: Oxford University Press.

Taylor, M., Gonzalez, M., & Porter, R. (2011). Pathways to inflammation: Acne pathophysiology. *European Journal of Dermatology, 21*(3), 323–333.

Taylor, M., & Hort, B. (1990). Can children be trained in making the distinction between appearance and reality? *Cognitive Development, 5*, 89–99.

Teen pregnancy prevention and United States students. (2011, July 12). Centers for Disease Control and Prevention. Retrieved from http://www.cdc.gov/healthyyouth/yrbs/pdf/us_pregnancy_combo.pdf. Accessed September 25, 2012.

Tehrani, J. A., & Mednick, S. A. (2000). Genetic factors and criminal behavior. *Federal Probation, 64*(2), 24–27.

Tennant, P. W. G., Rankin, J., & Bell, R. (2011). Impact of maternal obesity on stillbirth and infant death: Absolute risk and temporal trends. *Journal of Epidemiology and Community Health, 65*, DOI:10.1136/jech.2011.142976a.79.

Terasawa, E., et al. (2012). Body weight impact on puberty: Effects of high-calorie diet on puberty onset in female rhesus monkeys. *Endocrinology*, DOI:10.1210/en.2011-1970.

Terry, D. (2000, July 16). *Getting under my skin.* Retrieved from http://www.nytimes.com.

Teunissen, H. A., et al. (2011). The interaction between pubertal timing and peer popularity for boys and girls. *Journal of Abnormal Child Psychology, 39*(3), 413–423.

Thaler, N. S., et al. (2013). Neuropsychological profiles of six children with anoxic brain injury. *Child Neuropsychology: A Journal on Normal and Abnormal Development in Childhood and Adolescence, 19*(5), 479–494.

Tharner, A., et al. (2012). Maternal lifetime history of depression and depressive symptoms in the prenatal and early postnatal period do not predict infant–mother attachment quality in a large, population-based Dutch cohort study. *Attachment & Human Development, 14*(1), 63–81.

Thomas, A., & Chess, S. (1989). Temperament and personality. In G. A. Kohnstamm, J. E. Bates & M. K. Rothbart (Eds.), *Temperament in childhood.* Chichester, England: Wiley.

Thompson, K. M., Simons, E. A., Badizadegan, K., Reef, S. E., & Cooper, L. Z. (2014). Characterization of the risks of adverse outcomes following rubella infection in pregnancy. *Risk Analysis*, DOI:10.1111/risa.12264.

Thompson, R. A. (2008). Measure twice, cut once: Attachment theory and the NICHD Study of Early Child Care and Youth Development. *Attachment and Human Development, 10*(3), 287–297.

Thompson, R. A., Easterbrooks, M. A., & Padilla-Walker, L. M. (2003). Social and emotional development in infancy. In R. M. Lerner et al. (Eds.), *Handbook of psychology: Developmental psychology.* New York: Wiley.

Thompson, R. A., & Meyer, S. (2007). Socialization of emotion regulation in the family. In J. J. Gross (Ed.), *Handbook of emotion regulation* (pp. 249–268). New York: Guilford.

Thompson, V. J., et al. (2003). Influences on diet and physical activity among middle-class African-American 8- to 10-year old girls at risk of becoming obese. *Journal of Nutrition Education and Behavior, 35*(3), 115–123.

Thurstone, L. L. (1938). *Primary mental abilities.* Psychometric Monographs, 1.

Tiedemann, J. (2000). Parents' gender stereotypes and teachers' beliefs as predictors of children's concept of their mathematical ability in elementary school. *Journal of Educational Psychology, 92*(1), 144–151.

Tiggeman, M. (2014). The status of media effects on body image research. *Media Psychology, 17*(2), 127–133.

Tiggemann, M., & Slater, A. (2013). NetGirls: The Internet, Facebook, and body image concern in adolescent girls. *International Journal of Eating Disorders, 46*(6), 630–633.

Tijms, J. (2007). The development of reading accuracy and reading rate during treatment of dyslexia. *Educational Psychology, 27*(2), 273–294.

Tisdale, S., & Pitt-Catsuphes, M. (2012). Linking social environments with the well-being of adolescents in dual-earner and single working parent families. *Youth & Society, 44*(1), 118–140.

Tobbell, J., & O'Donnell, V. L. (2013). The formation of interpersonal and learning relationships in the transition from primary to secondary school: Students, teachers, and school context. *International Journal of Educational Research, 59*, 11–23.

Tobin, D. D., et al. (2010). The intrapsychics of gender: A model of self-socialization. *Psychological Review, 117*(2), 601–622.

Tomasello, M. (2010). Language development. In U. Goswami (Ed.), *The Wiley–Blackwell handbook of childhood cognitive development.* (2nd ed.) (pp. 239–257). Chichester, West Sussex, UK: Wiley–Blackwell.

Tomasetto, C., Alparone, F. M., & Cadinu, M. (2011). Girls' math performance under stereotype threat: The moderating role of mothers' gender stereotypes. *Developmental Psychology, 47*(4), 943–949.

Tong, J. H. S., et al. (2015). An association between a dopamine transporter gene (SLC6A3) haplotype and ADHD symptom measures in nonclinical adults. *American Journal of Medical Genetics: Neuropsychiatric genetics, 168*(2), 89–96.

Tornello, S. L., & Patterson, C. J. (2015). Timing of parenthood and experiences of gay fathers: A life course perspective. *Journal of GLBT Family Studies, 11*(1), 35–56.

Townsend, C. L., et al. (2014). Earlier initiation of ART and further decline in mother-to-child HIV transmission rates. *AIDS, 28*(7), 1049–1057.

Towse, J. N., Hitch, G. J., Hamilton, Z., & Pirrie, S. (2008). The endurance of children's working memory: A recall time analysis. *Journal of Experimental Child Psychology, 101*(2), 156–163.

Trenholm, C., et al. (2007). *Impacts of four Title V, Section 510 abstinence education programs. Final report.* Submitted to USDHHS, Office of the Assistant Secretary for Planning and Evaluation. Submitted by Mathematica Policy Research, Inc., Contract No.: HHS 100-98-0010. Available at http://www.mathematica-mpr.com/publications/PDFs/impactabstinence.pdf.

Trent, K. (2011). Too many men? Sex ratios and women's partnering behavior in China. *Social Forces, 90*(1), 247–267.

Trevarthen, C. (2003). Conversations with a two-month-old. In J. Raphael-Leff (Ed.), *Parent–infant psychodynamics: Wild things, mirrors, and ghosts.* London: Whurr.

Triandis, H. C. (2005). Issues in individualism and collectivism research. In R. M. Sorrentino, D. Cohen, J. M. Olson & M. P. Zanna (Eds.), *Cultural and social behavior: The Ontario Symposium,* Vol. 10 (pp. 207–225). Mahwah, NJ: Erlbaum.

Troop-Gordon, W., & Ranney, J. D. (2014). Popularity among same-sex and cross-sex peers: A process-oriented examination of links to aggressive behaviors and depressive affect. *Developmental Psychology, 50*(6), 1721–1733.

Troxel, W. M., & Matthews, K. A. (2004). What are the costs of marital conflict and dissolution to children's physical health? *Clinical Child and Family Psychology Review*, 7(1), 29–57.

Trzaskowski, M., Shakeshaft, N. G., & Plomin, R. (2013). Intelligence indexes generalist genes for cognitive abilities. *Intelligence*, 41(5), 560–565.

Tsui, J. M., & Maziocco, M. M. M. (2007). Effects of math anxiety and perfectionism on timed versus untimed math testing in mathematically gifted sixth graders. *Roeper Review*, 29(2), 132–139.

Tucker, R. P., et al. (2015). Risk factors, warning signs, and drivers of suicide: What are they, how do they differ, and why does it matter? *Suicide and Life-Threatening Behavior*, DOI:10.1111/sltb.12161.

Tulp, M. J., & Paech, M. J. (2014). Analgesia for childbirth: Insights into an age-old challenge and the quest for an ideal approach. *Pain Management*, 4(1), 69–78.

Turkheimer, E. (1991). Individual and group differences in adoption studies of IQ. *Psychological Bulletin*, 110, 392–405.

Turrell, G., & Vandevijvere, S. (2015). Socio-economic inequalities in diet and body weight: Evidence, causes, and intervention options. *Public Health Nutrition*, 18(5), 759–763.

Tzuriel, D., & Egozi, G. (2010). Gender differences in spatial ability of young children: The effects of training and processing strategies. *Child Development*, 81(5), 1417–1430.

Ulijaszek, S. J. (2010). Variation in human growth patterns due to environmental factors. In M. P. Muehlenbein, *Human evolutionary biology* (pp. 396–404). New York: Cambridge University Press.

Ullal-Gupta, S., et al. (2013). Linking prenatal experience to the emerging musical mind. *Frontiers in Systems Neuroscience*, 7, 48.

Ullman, S. E. (2007). Relationship to perpetrator, disclosure, social reactions, and PTSD symptoms in child sexual abuse survivors. *Journal of Child Sexual Abuse*, 16(1), 19–36.

Umaña-Taylor, A. J., et al. (2014). Ethnic and racial identity during adolescence and into young adulthood: An integrated conceptualization. *Child Development*, 85(1), 21–39.

Umaña-Taylor, A. J., Yazedjian, A., & Bámaca-G√≥mez, M. (2004). Developing the ethnic identity scale using Eriksonian and social identity perspectives. *Identity*, 4(1), 9–38.

Underwood, M. K. (2011). Aggression. In M. K. Underwood & L. H. Rosen (Eds.), *Social development: Relationships in infancy, childhood, and adolescence* (pp. 207–234). New York: Guilford.

Underwood, M. K., & Rosen, L. H. (Eds.). (2011). *Social development: Relationships in infancy, childhood, and adolescence* (pp. 289–315). New York: Guilford.

UNICEF. (2012). HIV and Infant Feeding. Retrieved from http://www.unicef.org/programme/breastfeeding/hiv.htm. Accessed January 15, 2012.

United States Department of Agriculture. (2015). ChooseMyPlate.gov. Available at http://www.choosemyplate.gov/food-groups/downloads/results/MyDailyFoodPlan_1600_4and5yr.pdf.

Uno, Y., et al. (2015). Early exposure to the combined measles–mumps–rubella vaccine and thimerosal-containing vaccines and risk of autism spectrum disorder. *Vaccine*, DOI:10.1016/j.vaccine.2014.12.036.

Upton, K. J., & Sullivan, R. M. (2010). Defining age limits of the sensitive period for attachment learning in rat pups. *Developmental Psychobiology*, 52(5), 453–464.

U.S. Bureau of the Census. (2007). *Statistical abstract of the United States* (127th ed.). Washington, DC: U.S. Government Printing Office.

U.S. Bureau of the Census. (2010). Statistical abstract of the United States (130th ed.). Washington, DC: U.S. Government Printing Office.

U.S. Bureau of the Census. (2012a). *Children characteristics: 2010 American Community Survey*. Available at http://factfinder2.census.gov/faces/tableservices/jsf/pages/productview.xhtml?pid=ACS_10_1YR_S0901&prodType=table.

U.S. Bureau of the Census. (2012b). Available at http://www.census.gov/compendia/statab/2012/tables/12s0053.pdf.

U.S. Bureau of the Census. (2014). America's Families and Living Arrangements: 2014: Unmarried Couples. Table UC3. Available at www.census.gov/hhes/families/data/cps2014UC.html.

U.S. Department of Health and Human Services. (2009). Sexual development of boys. Retrieved from http://www.4parents.gov/sexdevt/boysmen/boys_sexdevt/index.html. Accessed October 26, 2009.

U.S. Department of Health and Human Services. (2009). Sexual development of girls. Accessed October 26, 2009.

U.S. Department of Health and Human Services. (2013). Administration on Children, Youth and Families, Children's Bureau. Child maltreatment 2012. Available at http://www.acf.hhs.gov/programs/cb/research-data-technology/statistics-research/child-maltreatment. Accessed October 1, 2015.

Uylings, H. B. M. (2006). Development of the human cortex and the concept of "critical" or "sensitive" periods. *Language Learning*, 56(Suppl. 1), 59–90.

Valenzuela, S., Park, N., & Kee, K. F. (2009). Is there social capital in a social network site? Facebook use and college students' life satisfaction, trust, and participation. *Journal of Computer-Mediated Communication*, 14(4), 875–901.

Valkenburg, P. M., Peter, J., & Schouten, A. P. (2006). Friend networking sites and their relationship to adolescents' well-being and social self-esteem. *CyberPsychology & Behavior*, 9(5), 584–590.

Vallance, A., & Garralda, E. (2011). Anxiety disorders in children and adolescents. In D. Skuse, H. Bruce, L. Dowdney, & D. Mrazek (Eds.). *Child psychology and psychiatry: Frameworks for practice* (2nd ed.) (pp. 169–174). Hoboken, NJ: Wiley.

van de Beek, C., van Goozen, S. H. M., Buitelaar, J. K., & Cohen-Kettenis, P. T. (2009). Prenatal sex hormones (maternal and amniotic fluid) and gender-related play behavior in 13-month-old infants. *Archives of Sexual Behavior*, 38(1), 6–15.

Van den Bergh, B. R. H., Mulder, E. J. H., Mennes, M., & Glover, V. (2005). Antenatal maternal anxiety and stress and the neurobehavioural development of the fetus and child: Links and possible mechanisms. *A review. Neuroscience & Biobehavioral Reviews*, 29(2), 237–258.

van Dujin, E., et al. (2014). Course of irritability, depression and apathy in Huntington's disease in relation to motor symptoms during a two-year follow-up period. *Neuro-degenerative diseases*, 13(1), DOI:10.1159/000343210.

van Gameren-Oosterom, H. B. M., et al. (2013). Problem behavior of individuals with Down syndrome in a nationwide cohort assessed in late adolescence. *The Journal of Pediatrics*, 163(5), 1396–1401.

Vander Ven, T., & Cullen, F. T. (2004). The impact of maternal employment on serious youth crime: Does the quality of working conditions matter? *Crime & Delinquency*, 50(2), 272–291.

Vander Ven, T. M., Cullen, F. T., Carrozza, M. A., & Wright, J. P. (2001). Home alone: The impact of maternal employment on delinquency. *Social Problems*, 48(2), 236–257.

Vando, J., Rhule-Louie, D. M., McMahon, R. J., & Spieker, S. J. (2008). Examining the link between infant attachment and child conduct problems in grade 1. *Journal of Child and Family Studies*, 17(5), 615–628.

Van Zalk, M. H. W., et al. (2010). It takes three: Selection, influence, and de-selection processes of depression in adolescent friendship networks. *Developmental Psychology*, 46(4), 927–938.

Vélez, C. E., Wolchik, S. A., Tein, J-Y., & Sandler, I. (2011). Protecting children from the consequences of divorce: A longitudinal study of the effects of parenting on children's coping processes. *Child Development*, 82(1), 244–257.

Vellutino, F. R., Fletcher, J. M., Snowling, M. J., & Scanlon, D. M. (2004). Specific reading disability (dyslexia): What have we learned in the past four decades? *Journal of Child Psychology and Psychiatry*, 45(1), 2–40.

Velumian, A., & Samoilova, M. (2014). White matter: Basic principles of axonal organization and function. *Springer Series in Translational Stroke Research*, 4, 3–38.

Vennila, V., et al. (2014). Tetracycline-induced discoloration of deciduous teeth: Case series. *Journal of International Oral Health*, 6(3), 115–119.

Verlohren, S., Stepan, H., & Dechend, R. (2012). Angiogenic growth factors in the diagnosis and prediction of pre-eclampsia. *Clinical Science*, 122, 43–52.

Vermeulen-Smit, E., Verdurmen, J. E. E., Engels, R. C. M. E., & Vollebergh, W. A. M. (2015). The role of general parenting and cannabis-specific parenting practices in adolescent cannabis and other illicit drug use. *Drug and Alcohol Dependence*, 147, 222–228.

Versace, E., & Vallortigara, G. (2015). Forelimb preferences in human beings and other species: Multiple models for testing hypotheses on lateralization. *Frontiers in Psychology, 6*, 233. DOI:10.3339/fpsyg.2015.00233.

Vigil, J. M., Geary, D. C., & Byrd-Craven, J. (2005). A life history assessment of early childhood sexual abuse in women. *Developmental Psychology, 41*(3), 553–561.

Vigod, S. N., Villegas, L., Dennis, C-L., & Ross, L. E. (2010). Prevalence and risk factors for postpartum depression among women with preterm and low-birth-weight infants: A systematic review. *BJOG: An International Journal of Obstetrics & Gynaecology, 117*(5), 540–550.

Virji-Babul, N., Kerns, K., Zhou, E., Kapur, A., & Shiffrar, M. (2006). Perceptual-motor deficits in children with Down syndrome: Implications for intervention. *Down Syndrome: Research & Practice, 10*(2), 74–82.

Visser, G. H. A. (2015). Women are designed to deliver vaginally and not by cesarean section: An obstetrician's view. *Neonatology, 107*(1), 8–13.

Vitiello, B. (Ed.). (2006). Guest editorial: Selective serotonin reuptake inhibitors (SSRIs) in children and adolescents. *Journal of Child and Adolescent Psychopharmacology, 16*(1–2), 7–9.

Voineskos, A. N. (2015). Genetic underpinnings of white matter "connectivity": Heritability, risk, and heterogeneity in schizophrenia. *Schizophrenia Research, 161*(1), 50–60.

Volkova, A., Trehub, S. E., & Schellenberg, E. G. (2006). Infants' memory for musical performances. *Developmental Science, 9*(6), 583–589.

Volling, B. L. (2001). Early attachment relationships as predictors of preschool children's emotion regulation with a distressed sibling. *Early Education and Development, 12*(2), 185–207.

Volterra, M. C., Caselli, O., Capirci, E., & Pizzuto, E. (2004). Gesture and the emergence and development of language. In M. Tomasello & D. I. Slobin (Eds.), *Beyond nature–nurture*. Mahwah, NJ: Erlbaum.

Vorstman, J. A. S., & Burbach, J. P. H. (2014). Autism and schizophrenia: Genetic and phenotypic relationships. In V. B. Patel et al. (Eds.). *Comprehensive guide to autism* (pp. 1645–1662). New York: Springer.

Voyer, D., & Voyer, S. D. (2014). Gender differences in scholastic achievement: A meta-analysis. *Psychological Bulletin, 140*(4), 1174–1204.

Vroman, K. (2010). In transition to adulthood: The occupations and performance skills of adolescents. In J. Case-Smith, & J. C. O'Brien (Eds.). *Occupational therapy for children* (pp. 84–107). Mosby/Elsevier, Maryland Heights, Missouri.

Vuoksimaa, E., Eriksson, C. J. P., Pulkkinen, L., Rose, R. J., & Kaprio, J. (2010). Decreased prevalence of left-handedness among females with male co-twins: Evidence suggesting prenatal testosterone transfer in humans? *Psychoneuroendocrinology, 35*(10), 1462–1472.

Vurpillot, E. (1968). The development of scanning strategies and their relation to visual differentiation. *Journal of Experimental Child Psychology, 6*, 632–650.

Vygotsky, L. S. (1962). *Thought and language.* Cambridge, MA: MIT Press.

Vygotsky, L. S. (1978). *Mind in society: The development of higher psychological processes.* Cambridge, MA: Harvard University Press.

Wade, T. D., Wilksch, S. M., Paxton, S. J., Byrne, S. M., & Austin, S. B. (2015). How perfectionism and ineffectiveness influence growth of eating disorder risk in young adolescent girls. *Behaviour Research and Therapy, 66*, 56–63.

Wagner, A., Pimentel, V. M., & Eckardt, M. J. (2014). Maternal health. In N. Gupta et al. (Eds.). *The MassGeneral Hospital for Children Handbook of Pediatric Global Health* (pp. 73–86). New York: Springer Science+Business Media.

Wagner, I. V., et al. (2012). Effects of obesity on human sexual development. *Nature Reviews: Endocrinology, 8*, 246–254.

Wakschlag, L. S., Pickett, K. E., Kasza, K. E., & Loeber, R. (2006). Is prenatal smoking associated with a developmental pattern of conduct problems in young boys? *Journal of the American Academy of Child & Adolescent Psychiatry, 45*(4), 461–467.

Walker, A. (2010). Breast milk as the gold standard for protective nutrients. *Journal of Pediatrics, 156*(Suppl. 2), S3–S7.

Walker, L. J., & Frimer, J. A. (2011). The science of moral development. In M. K. Underwood & L. H. Rosen (Eds.), *Social development* (pp. 235–263). New York, NY: Guilford.

Walker, R. F., & Murachver, T. (2012). Representation and theory of mind development. *Developmental Psychology, 48*(2), 509–520.

Wallen, K., & Hassett, J. M. (2009). Sexual differentiation of behaviour in monkeys: Role of prenatal hormones. *Journal of Neuroendocrinology, 21*(4), 421–426.

Wallerstein, J., Lewis, J., Blakeslee, S., Hetherington, E. M., & Kelly, J. (2005). Issue 17: Is divorce always detrimental to children? In R. P. Halgin (Ed.), *Taking sides: Clashing views on controversial issues in abnormal psychology* (3rd ed.) (pp. 298–321). New York: McGraw-Hill.

Walline, J. J., et al. (2009). Randomized trial of the effect of contact lens wear on self-perception in children. *Optometry & Vision Science, 86*(3), 222–232.

Walter, D., et al. (2014). Short- and long-term effects of inpatient cognitive-behavioral treatment of adolescents with anxious-depressed school absenteeism: A within-subject comparison of changes. *Child & Family Behavior Therapy, 36*(3), 171–190.

Walter, J. L., & LaFreniere, P. J. (2000). A naturalistic study of affective expression, social competence, and sociometric status in preschoolers. *Early Education and Development, 11*(1), 109–122.

Walther, F. J., Ouden, A. L. den, & Verloove-Vanhorick, S. P. (2000). Looking back in time: Outcome of a national cohort of very preterm infants born in The Netherlands in 1983. *Early Human Development, 59*(3), 175–191.

Wang, J., et al. (2015). Associations between added sugar (solid vs. liquid) intakes, diet quality, and adipose indicators in Canadian children. *Applied Physiology, Nutrition, and Metabolism*, DOI:10.1139/apnm-2014-0447.

Wang, Q., Leichtman, M. D., & White, S. H. (1998). Childhood memory and self-description in young Chinese adults: The impact of growing up an only child. *Cognition, 69*(1), 73–103.

Wang, S-H., Baillargeon, R., & Paterson, S. (2005). Detecting continuity violations in infancy: A new account and new evidence from covering and tube events. *Cognition, 95*(2), 129–173.

Wang, X., Dow-Edwards, D., Anderson, V., Minkoff, H., & Hurd, Y. L. (2004). In utero marijuana exposure associated with abnormal amygdala dopamine d-sub-2 gene expression in the human fetus. *Biological Psychiatry, 56*(12), 909–915.

Warnke, A. (2014). Anxiety disorders and phobias. *Psychiatric Drugs in Children and Adolescents*, 359–368.

Washburn, D. A. (Ed.). (2007). *Primate perspectives on behavior and cognition.* Washington, DC: American Psychological Association.

Wass, R., Harland, T., & Mercer, A. (2011). Scaffolding critical thinking in the zone of critical development. *Higher Education Research & Development, 30*(3), 317–328.

Wasserman, G. A., et al. (2000). Yugoslavia Prospective Lead Study: Contributions of prenatal and postnatal lead exposure to early intelligence. *Neurotoxicology and Teratology, 22*(6), 811–818.

Watson, J. B. (1924). *Behaviorism.* New York: Norton.

Watson, J. B., & Rayner, R. (1920). Conditioned emotional reactions. *Journal of Experimental Psychology, 3*(1), 1–14.

Waxman, S. R., & Goswami, U. (2012). Learning about language: Acquiring the spoken and written word. In S. M. Pauen (Ed.). *Early childhood development and later outcome* (pp. 89–117). New York: Cambridge University Press.

Waxmonsky, J. G. (2005). Nonstimulant therapies for attention-deficit hyperactivity disorder (ADHD) in children and adults. *Essential Psychopharmacology, 6*(5), 262–276.

Way, N., & Rogers, O. (2015). "They say black men won't make it, but I know I'm gonna make it": Ethnic and racial identity development in the context of cultural stereotypes. In In K. C. McLean, & M. Syed (Eds.). *The Oxford handbook of identity development* (pp. 269–285). New York: Oxford University Press.

Weber, M. A., et al. (2011). Autopsy findings of co-sleeping-associated sudden unexpected deaths in infancy: Relationship between pathological features and asphyxial mode of death. *Journal of Paediatrics and Child Health, 48*(4), 335–341.

Wechsler, D. (1975). Intelligence defined and undefined: A relativistic appraisal. *American Psychologist, 30*, 135–139.

Weckerly, J., Wulfeck, B., & Reilly, J. (2004). The development of morphosyntactic ability in atypical populations: The acquisition of tag questions in children with early focal lesions and children with specific-language impairment. *Brain and Language, 88*(2), 190–201.

Wegner, L., & Flisher, A. J. (2009). Leisure boredom and adolescent risk behaviour: A systematic literature review. *Journal of Child and Adolescent Mental Health, 21*(1), 1–28.

Weichold, K., Silbereisen, R. K., & Schmitt-Rodermund, E. (2003). Short-term and long-term consequences of early versus late physical maturation in adolescents. In C. Hayward (Ed.), *Gender differences at puberty* (pp. 241–276). New York: Cambridge University Press.

Weller, E. B., & Weller, R. A. (1991). Mood disorders. In M. Lewis (Ed.), *Child and adolescent psychiatry: A comprehensive textbook*. Baltimore: Williams & Wilkins.

Wellman, H. M., Cross, D., & Bartsch, K. (1986). Infant search and object permanence: A meta-analysis of the A-not-B error. *Monographs of the Society for Research in Child Development, 5*(3, ser. 214).

Wennberg, M., Gustafsson, P. E., Wennberg, P., & Hammarstrom, A. (2015). Poor breakfast habits in adolescence predict the metabolic syndrome in adulthood. *Public Health Nutrition, 18*(1), 122 – 129.

Wentzel, K. R. (2014). Prosocial behavior and peer relations in adolescence. In L. M. Padilla-Walker, & G. Carlo (Eds.). *Prosocial development: A multidimensional approach* (pp. 178–200). New York: Oxford University Press.

Wentzel, K. R. (2015). Socialization in school settings. In J. E. Grusec, & P. D. Hastings (Eds.) *Handbook of socialization: Theory and research*, 2nd ed. (pp. 251–275). New York: Guilford.

Werker, J. F. (1989). Becoming a native listener. *American Scientist, 77*, 54–59.

Werker, J. F., et al. (2007). Infant-directed speech supports phonetic category learning in English and Japanese. *Cognition, 103*(1), 147–162.

Werker, J. F., & Hensch, T. K. (2015). Critical periods in speech perception: New directions. *Annual Review of Psychology, 66*, 173–196.

Werner, E. E. (1988). A cross-cultural perspective on infancy. *Journal of Cross-Cultural Psychology, 19*, 96–113.

Werner, L. A., & Bernstein, I. L. (2001). Development of the auditory, gustatory, olfactory, and somatosensory systems. In E. B. Goldstein (Ed.), *Blackwell handbook of perception, Handbook of experimental psychology series* (pp. 669–708). Boston: Blackwell.

Wertheim, E. H., Paxton, S. J., & Blaney, S. (2009). Body image in girls. In L. Smolak & J. K. Thompson (Eds.), *Body image, eating disorders, and obesity in youth: Assessment, prevention, and treatment* (2nd ed.) (pp. 47–76). Washington, DC: American Psychological Association.

Whalen, C. K. (2001). ADHD treatment in the 21st century: Pushing the envelope. *Journal of Clinical Child Psychology, 30*(1), 136–140.

Whitbeck, L. B., & Armenta, B. E. (2015). Patterns of substance use initiation among indigenous adolescents. *Addictive Behaviors, 45*, 172–179.

White, C. B., Bushnell, N., & Regnemer, J. L. (1978). Moral development in Bahamian school children: A three-year examination of Kohlberg's stages of moral development. *Developmental Psychology, 14*, 58–65.

Whitehead, J. T., & Lab, S. P. (2013). *Juvenile justice*. Waltham, MA: Anderson Publishing.

Whiting, B. B., & Edwards, C. P. (1988). *Children of different worlds*. Cambridge, MA: Harvard University Press.

Whitmarsh, L., & Wentworth, D. K. (2012). Gender similarity or gender difference? Contemporary women's and men's career patterns. *Career Development Quarterly, 60*(1), 47–64.

Wilcox, H. C., Storr, C. L., & Breslau, N. (2009). Posttraumatic stress disorder and suicide attempts in a community sample of urban American young adults. *Archives of General Psychiatry, 66*(3), 305–311.

Wilcox, W. B., & Marquardt, E. (Eds.). (2011). *The state of our unions: Marriage in America 2011*. Institute for American Values. Charlottesville, VA: University of Virginia: The National Marriage Project.

Williams, N. A., et al. (2013). Body esteem, peer difficulties and perceptions of physical health in overweight and obese urban children aged 5 to 7 years. *Child: Care, Health and Development, 39*(6), 825–834.

Williams, R. L. (1974, May). Scientific racism and IQ: The silent mugging of the black community. *Psychology Today*, p. 32.

Williamson, K. E., & Jakobson, L. S. (2014). Social perception in children born at very low birthweight and its relationship with social/behavioral outcomes. *The Journal of Child Psychology and Psychiatry, 55*(9), 990–998.

Willis, J. O., Dumont, R., & Kaufman, A. S. (2011). Factor-analytic models of intelligence. In R. J. Sternberg & S. J. Kaufman (Eds.), *The Cambridge handbook of intelligence* (pp. 39–57). New York: Cambridge University Press.

Wilson, A. R., & Leaper, C. (2015). Bridging multidimensional models of ethnic–racial and gender identity among ethnically diverse emerging adults. *Journal of Youth and Adolescence*, DOI:10.1007/s10964-015-0323-z.

Wilson, C., Kline, E., Reeves, G. M., Anthony, L., & Schiffman, J. (2014). Blurred edges: Evolving concepts of autism spectrum disorders and schizophrenia. *Adolescent Psychiatry, 4*(3), 133–146.

Windle, M., et al. (2008). Transitions into underage and problem drinking: Developmental processes and mechanisms between 10 and 15 years of age. *Pediatrics, 121*(Suppl. April 2008), S273–S289.

Wingood, G. M., et al. (2006). Efficacy of an HIV prevention program among female adolescents experiencing gender-based violence. *American Journal of Public Health, 96*(6), 1085–1090.

Winograd, R. P., & Sher, K. J. (2015). *Binge drinking and alcohol misuse: Advances in psychotherapy*. Boston: The Hogrefe Group Publishing.

Wismer Fries, A. B., Shirtcliff, E. A., & Pollak, S. D. (2008). Neuroendocrine dysregulation following early social deprivation in children. *Developmental Psychobiology, 50*(6), 588–599.

Witherington, D. C., Campos, J. J., Harriger, J. A., Bryan, C., and Margett, T. E. (2010). Emotion and its development in infancy. In J. G. Bremner & T. D. Wachs (Eds.). *The Wiley-Blackwell handbook of infant development*, Vol. 1 (2nd ed.). Wiley-Blackwell, Oxford, UK. DOI:10.1002/9781444327564.ch19.

Witt, W. P., et al. (2014). Determinants of cesarean delivery in the US: A lifecourse approach. *Maternal and Child Health Journal*, DOI:10.1007/s10995-014-1498-8.

Wolchik, S. A., et al. (2000). An experimental evaluation of theory-based mother and mother–child programs for children of divorce. *Journal of Consulting and Clinical Psychology, 68*(5), 853–856.

Wolfe, D. A. (2011). Violence against women and children. In J. W. White, M. P. Koss, & A. E. Kazdin (Eds.). *Violence against women and children*, Vol. 1: *Mapping the terrain* (pp. 31–53). Washington, DC: American Psychological Association.

Wong, F. Y., et al. (2011). Cerebral oxygenation is depressed during sleep in healthy term infants when they sleep prone. *Pediatrics, 127*(3), e558–e565.

Wong, W. I., & Hines, M. (2015). Preferences for pink and blue: The development of color preferences as a distinct gender-typed behavior in toddlers. *Archives of Sexual Behavior*, DOI:10.1007/s10508-015-0489-1.

Wood, A. C., et al. (2008). High heritability for a composite index of children's activity level measures. *Behavior Genetics, 38*(3), 266–276.

Woolfolk, A. (2008). *Educational psychology, Active learning edition* (10th ed.). Boston: Allyn & Bacon.

Woolfolk, A. (2013). *Educational psychology* (12th ed.). Upper Saddle River, NJ: Pearson.

Worell, J., & Goodheart, C. D. (Eds.). (2006). *Handbook of girls' and women's psychological health: Gender and well-being across the lifespan*. New York: Oxford University Press.

World Health Organization. (2010a). Centers for Disease Control and Prevention. Birth to 24 months: Girls. Length-for-age and weight-for-age percentiles. From WHO Child Growth Standards. Available at http://www.cdc.gov/growthcharts/data/who/grchrt_girls_24lw_9210.pdf.

World Health Organization. (2010b). Centers for Disease Control and Prevention. Birth to 24 months: Boys. Length-for-age and weight-for-age percentiles. From WHO Child Growth Standards. Available at http://www.cdc.gov/growthcharts/data/who/grchrt_boys_24lw_100611.pdf.

World Health Organization. (2011, March 16). WHO, nutrition experts take action

on malnutrition. Retrieved from http://
www.who.int/nutrition/pressnote_action_
on_malnutrition/en. Accessed February
20, 2012.

World Hunger Organization. (2012). 2012
World hunger and poverty facts and
statistics. World Hunger Organization
Service. Retrieved from http://www
.worldhunger.org/articles/Learn/world%20
hunger%20facts%202002.htm. Accessed
February 20, 2012.

Worrell, F. C. (2015). Culture as race/
ethnicity. In K. C. McLean, & M. Syed
(Eds.). *The Oxford handbook of identity
development* (pp. 249–268). New York:
Oxford University Press.

Wright, D. W., & Young, R. (1998). The
effects of family structure and maternal
employment on the development of
gender-related attitudes among men and
women. *Journal of Family Issues, 19*(3),
300–314.

Wright, P., Stamatakis, E. A., & Tyler, L. K.
(2012). Differentiating hemispheric
contributions to syntax and semantics
in patients with left-hemisphere lesions.
The Journal of Neuroscience, 32(24),
8149–8157.

Wu, T., et al. (2014). Conduct disorder. In
G. M. Kapalka (Ed.). *Treating disruptive
disorders*. New York: Routledge.

Xu, L., et al. (2009). Bone and muscle
development during puberty in girls—A
7-year longitudinal study. *Journal of Bone
and Mineral Research,* DOI:10.1359/
jbmr.090405.

Xu, N., Burnham, D., Kitamura, C., &
Vollmer-Conna, U. (2013). Vowel
hyperarticulation in parrot-, dog-, and
infant-directed speech. *Anthrozoos:
A Multidisciplinary Journal of the
Interactions of People and Animals, 26*(3),
373–380.

Xue, Y. F., Moran, G., Pederson, D. R., &
Bento, S. (2010, March). The continuity
of attachment development from infancy
to toddlerhood: The role of maternal
sensitivity. International Conference on
Infant Studies. Baltimore, MD.

Yaros, A., Lochman, J. E., Rosenbaum, J., &
Jimenez-Camargo, L. A. (2014). Real-
time hostile attribution measurement
and aggression in children. *Aggressive
Behavior, 40*(5), 409–420.

Yarrow, L. J., & Goodwin, M. S. (1973). The
immediate impact of separation: Reactions
of infants to a change in mother figures.
In L. J. Stone, H. T. Smith & L. B. Murphy
(Eds.), *The competent infant: Research
and commentary*. New York: Basic Books.

Yarrow, L. J., Goodwin, M. S., Manheimer,
H., & Milowe, I. D. (1971, March).
*Infant experiences and cognitive and
personality development at ten years.*
Paper presented at the meeting of the
American Orthopsychiatric Association,
Washington, DC.

Yazzie, A. (2010). Visual-spatial thinking
and academic achievement: A concurrent

and predictive validity study. Dissertation
Abstracts International: Section A,
Humanities and Social Sciences, 70(8-A),
2897.

Yee, G. L., & Kisilevsky, B. S. (2014). Fetuses
respond to father's voice but prefer
mother's voice after birth. *Developmental
Psychobiology, 56*(1), 1–11.

Yermolayeva, Y., & Rakison, D. H.
(2014). Connectionist modeling of
developmental changes in Infancy:
Approaches, challenges, and contributions.
Psychological Bulletin, 140(1), 224–255.

You, D., Maeda, Y., & Bebeau, M. J. (2011).
Gender differences in moral sensitivity: A
meta-analysis. *Ethics & Behavior, 21*(4),
263–282.

Young, D. (2006). Review of breastfeeding
handbook for physicians. *Birth: Issues in
Perinatal Care, 33*(3), 260–261.

Young, L. J. (2015). Oxytocin,
social cognition and psychiatry.
Neuropsychopharmacology, 40, 243–244.

Youniss, J., & Haynie, D. L. (1992).
Friendship in adolescence. *Developmental
and Behavioral Pediatrics, 13*, 59–66.

Yurgelun-Todd, D. A. (2007). Emotional and
cognitive changes during adolescence.
Current Opinion in Neurobiology, 17(2),
251–257.

Zachrisson, H. D., & Dearing, E. (2015).
Family income dynamics, early childhood
education and care, and early child
behavior problems in Norway. *Child
Development, 86*(2), 425–440.

Zajonc, R. B. (2001). The family dynamics
of intellectual development. *American
Psychologist, 56*(6/7), 490–496.

Zeanah, C. H., Berlin, L. J., & Boris, N.
W. (2011). Practitioner review: Clinical
applications of attachment theory and
research for infants and young children.
*The Journal of Child Psychology &
Psychiatry, 52*(8), 819–833.

Zeifman, D. M. (2004). Acoustic features
of infant crying related to intended
caregiving intervention. *Infant and Child
Development, 13*(2), 111–122.

Zelazo, P. D. (Ed.). (2013). *The Oxford
handbook of developmental psychology,*
Vol. 1: Body and mind. New York: Oxford
University Press.

Zelazo, P. D., and Müller, U. (2010).
Executive function in typical and
atypical development. In U. Goswami
(Ed.). *The Wiley-Blackwell handbook
of childhood cognitive development*
(2nd ed.). Wiley-Blackwell, Oxford, UK.
DOI:10.1002/9781444325485.ch22.

Zhai, F., Brooks-Gunn, J., & Waldfogel, J.
(2011). Head Start and urban children's
school readiness: A birth cohort study
in 18 cities. *Developmental Psychology,
47*(1), 134–152.

Zheng, L., Lippa, R. A., & Zheng, Y. (2011).
Sex and sexual orientation differences in
personality in China. *Archives of Sexual
Behavior, 40*(3), 533–541.

Zhiqi, L., Kun, Y., & Zhiwu, H. (2010).
Tympanometry in infants with middle ear

effusion having been identified using spiral
computerized tomography. *American
Journal of Otolaryngology, 31*(2),
96–103.

Zhou, Z., Bray, M. A., Kehle, T. J., & Xin,
T. (2001). Similarity of deleterious effects
of divorce on Chinese and American
children. *School Psychology International,
22*(3), 357–363.

Zigler, E., Abelson, W. D., Trickett, P. K.,
& Seitz, V. (1982). Is an intervention
program necessary in order to improve
economically disadvantaged children's IQ
scores? *Child Development, 53*, 340–348.

Zilioli, S., Ponzi, D., Henry, A., &
Maestripieri, D. (2014). Testosterone,
cortisol, and empathy: Evidence for the
dual-hormone hypothesis. *Adaptive
Human Behavior and Physiology,*
DOI:10.1007/s40750-014-0017-x.

Zimmerman, A. W. (Ed.). (2008). *Autism:
Current theories and evidence.* Totowa,
NJ: Humana Press.

Zimmerman, F. J., Christakis, D. A., &
Meltzoff, A. N. (2007). Associations
between media viewing and language
development in children under age 2 years.
Journal of Pediatrics, 151, 364–368.

Zimmerman, P., Maier, M. A., Winter, M.,
& Grossmann, K. E. (2001). Attachment
and adolescents' emotion regulation
during a joint problem-solving task with a
friend. *International Journal of Behavioral
Development, 25*(4), 331–343.

Zonnevylle-Bender, M. J. S., Matthys,
W., Van De Wiel, N. M. H., & Lochman,
J. E. (2007). Preventive effects of
treatment of disruptive behavior disorder
in middle childhood on substance use
and delinquent behavior. *Journal of the
American Academy of Child & Adolescent
Psychiatry, 46*(1), 33–39.

Zosuls, K. M., Martin, C. L., Ruble, D. N.,
Miller, C. F., Gaertner, B. M., England,
D. E., & Hill, A. P. (2011). "It's not that
we hate you": Understanding children's
gender attitudes and expectancies about
peer relationships. *British Journal of
Developmental Psychology, 29*(2),
288–304.

Zosuls, K. M., Miller, C. F., Ruble, D. N.,
Martin, C. L., & Fabes, R. A. (2011).
Gender development research in sex roles:
Historical trends and future directions.
Sex Roles, 64(11–12), 826–842.

Zuckerman, K. E., et al. (2014). Racial, ethnic,
and language disparities in early childhood
developmental/behavioral evaluations: A
narrative review. *Clinical Pediatrics, 53*(7),
619–631.

Zuckerman, M. (2011). Personality science:
Three approaches and their applications
to the causes and treatment of depression.
In M. Zuckerman (Ed.). *Three approaches
and their applications to the causes and
treatment of depression* (pp. 47–77).
Washington, DC: American Psychological
Association.

Name Index

Abdelaziz, Y. E., 355
Aber, J. L., 546
Ablon, J. S., 361
Abma, J. C., 534
Aboud, F., 439
Abrams, D., 418
Abravanel, E., 193
Academy of Nutrition and Dietetics, 157
Addy, S., 156
Adhikari, D., 66
Adler-Baeder, F., 426
Adolph, K. E., 87, 168, 173, 174
Agrawal, A., 485
Aguiar, A., 188
Aguiar, N. R., 279
Ainsworth, M. D. S., 22, 42, 142, 216, 219, 220, 222–223, 224
Ajulo, M. O., 97
Akolekar, R., 59
Alamian, A., 473
Alexander, G. M., 323, 335, 338, 340
Ali, B., 485
Ali, M. M., 536, 538
Alibali, M. W., 374, 409
Alink, L. R. A., 218
Allen, G., 253, 255
Allen, J. P., 528
Allen, K. R., 530
Allison, C. M., 459, 462
Alloway, R. G., 387
Alloway, T. P., 383, 387
Alm, P. A., 366
Almasry, S. M., 108
Aloi, J. A., 73
Als, H., 124
Alsaker, F. D., 434
Alvarez, L., 434
Amanatullah, E. T., 335
Amato, P. R., 424
Ambridge, B., 302
American Academy of Pediatrics, 145, 156, 158, 160, 264, 265
American Association of Intellectual and Developmental Disabilities (AAIDD), 401
American Association of Medical Colleges, 500
American Fertility Association, 53, 68, 69, 70
American Heart Association, 349
American Lung Association, 482
American Pregnancy Association, 102
American Psychiatric Association, 127, 128, 233, 234, 271, 275, 360, 438, 439, 441, 479, 483
Aminabhavi, V. A., 428
Ammaniti, M., 219
Amsel, E., 490
Anastasiou, L., 280
Andersen, N. E., 337
Andersen, T. S., 544, 545
Anderson, B. J., 166
Anderson, C. A., 330
Anderson, D. H., 17
Anderson, D. R., 292
Anderson, P., 347
Angarne-Lindberg, T., 425, 426

Anthis, K. S., 521
Anthony, C. J., 424
Antonishak, J., 528
Arbib, M. A., 193
Arbuthnot, J., 504
Archambault, I., 507
Archer, L. R., 235
Armenta, B. E., 484
Armstrong, K. H., 363, 364
Arnett, J. J., 517, 519, 520, 521, 550–553
Arterberry, M. E., 134, 136
Arvidsson, A., 417
Aschermann, E., 409
Asher, S. R., 431
Aslin, R. N., 172, 173
Aspy, C. B., 536
Athanasopoulou, E., 124
Athenstaedt, U., 521
Atkinson, J., 136, 137
August, D., 205
Auyeung, B., 338
Avinum, R., 337
Axelin, A., 42
Ayyash-Abdo, H., 317
Azmitia, M., 519, 520

Babic, M. J., 357
Bachman, J. G., 36, 480, 511
Bailey, R. K., 362
Baillargeon, R., 188, 189, 281
Bakalar, N., 157
Baker, B., 461
Bakker, D. J., 364
Bakker, R., 102
Bales, J. E., 244
Ball, J., 506
Ballweg, Rachel, 475
Baltazar, N. C., 388
Baly, M., 434
Bandura, A., 17, 28, 32, 44, 45, 323, 328, 329, 333, 338, 509
Banet-Weiser, S., 350
Bangal, V. B., 97
Bangs, R., 97
Barac, R., 410, 411
Barnett, L. M., 356, 357
Barni, D., 318
Barr, R., 192
Barr, R. G., 142, 143
Barrile, M., 175
Barrouillet, P., 184, 376, 388
Barth, J., 191
Bartzokis, G., 165
Bastien-Toniazzo, M., 410
Bates, E., 208
Bates, J. E., 217
Batsche, G. M., 434
Bauer, K. A., 455
Bauer, P. J., 297, 298, 300
Baum, N., 124
Bauman, M. L., 235
Baumrind, D., 310, 312, 313, 314
Baxter-Jones, A. D. G., 347
Bazerman, M. H., 504

Bearce, K. H., 192
Beaty, R. E., 405
Beauchamp, G. K., 138
Bebko, J. M., 299
Beck, E., 318, 430
Beck, R. J., 287
Becker, M., 316
Beckwith, A. M., 100
Bedny, M., 208
Beebe, B., 216, 219
Beer, J. M., 318
Begum, K. S., 120
Behrman, R. E., 105
Beilei, L., 355
Bekkhus, M., 237
Belkin, L., 105
Bell, J. H., 494
Bell, S. M., 142
Bellmore, A. D., 256, 420
Belsky, J., 217, 218, 237, 428
Bem, S. L., 339, 340
Bendiksen, B., 438
Bengtsson, H., 417
Bennett, T. A., 234
Benoit, D., 155
Benson, B. J., 62
Beratis, I. O., 259
Berenbaum, S. A., 246
Berg, C. J., 105
Berge, J. M., 350
Bergen, D., 320
Berger, S. E., 87
Berko, J., 303
Berkowitz, D., 422
Berndt, T. J., 430, 524, 528
Bernstein, I. L., 137, 138
Berry, J. W., 317
Bersoff, D. N., 42, 43
Berzenski, S. R., 217
Berzonsky, M. D., 518, 521
Beste, C., 235
Bezdjian, S., 326
Bhat, S., 233, 235
Bialystok, E., 410, 411
Bierman, K. L., 290, 430, 433
Bigelow, A. E., 217
Bigler, R. S., 246
Bigoni, F., 495
Billings, D. W., 469
Birch, L. L., 178
Biro, F. M., 461
Bishop, D. M., 544
Black, M. M., 155
Blair, C., 61
Blake, S. M., 541
Blakemore, J. E. O., 246
Blanchette, N., 163
Bloom, B., 471
Bloom, L., 201
Blow, C. M., 230
Blumberg, M. S., 142
Blumenthal, H., 462
Blyth, D. A., 527, 528
Boccia, M., 241

Frimer, J. A., 504
Frith, U., 364
Frostad, P., 367
Frühmesser, A., 54
Fuhs, M. W., 291
Fuligni, A. J., 528
Fuller, T., 189
Fulton, A. B., 171
Funatogawa, K., 349
Furman, W., 226, 524
Furstenberg, F. F., 426

Galdi, S., 497
Gallese, V., 193
Ganong, L. H., 426
Garber, H. L., 290
Garcia, P. L., 178
Garcia, P. R. J. M., 509
Garcia-Falgueras, A., 532
Gardner, H., 392–393, 394, 405
Garland, A. F., 362
Garnefski, N., 440
Garner, J., 506
Garralda, E., 441
Gartstein, M. A., 243
Gaser, C., 464
Gathercole, S. E., 387
Gauthier, J. L., 254
Gauthier, K., 73
Gauvain, M., 310
Gavin, L., 465, 541
Gee, R. E., 99
Gelman, S., 386
George, M. R. W., 217
Georgiades, S., 234
Geraghty, K., 305
Gervain, J., 137
Gesell, A., 7, 8, 169
Getchell, N., 169, 170, 255, 257
Getzels, J. W., 405
Giaschi, D., 365
Gibb, R., 254
Gibbs, J. C., 502
Gibson, E. J., 173, 177
Gidding, S. S., 347
Giedd, J. N., 464
Gignac, G. E., 383, 387
Gilbert-Barness, E., 99
Giles, A., 192
Gillen, M. M., 522
Gilligan, C., 380, 489, 503
Gillooly, J. B., 459
Gilmore, K., 73
Gingo, M., 502–504
Gini, G., 327
Giussani, D. A., 93, 100, 102
Glasberg, R., 439
Gleason, K. A., 526
Gleason, T. R., 279, 319, 430
Goble, P., 247, 298
Goessaert, A., 272
Goldberg, W. A., 268, 270, 339, 428
Golden, C., 340
Goldschmidt, L., 100
Goldstein, S., 421, 495
Goleman, D., 393
Gomez, A. M., 230
Gonzaga-Jaurequi, C., 48
Gonzalez, V., 410
Good, C., 408
Goodheart, C. D., 246, 247
Goodman, G. S., 389
Goodwin, M. S., 226, 227
Goolsby, M., 475
Gopnik, A., 295, 296, 305

Gordon, A., 87
Gordon, D. A., 504
Gordon, J., 333
Gorin, S., 43
Gorini, F., 103
Goskan, S., 139
Goswami, U., 300, 301, 304, 305
Gottfried, G. M., 282
Gottlieb, B. H., 551
Gower, A. L., 325
Gowers, S. G., 53
Grabe, S., 497
Graber, J. A., 461
Graham, S., 434
Granot, D., 217
Granville, J., 422
Grayson, A., 143
Greeff, A. P., 426
Green, M. A., 478
Green, R., 422
Greene, F. J., 339
Greene, R. W., 361
Greenwood, J. D., 395
Gregory, A. M., 48
Griffin, I. J., 123
Grigorenko, E. L., 366
Groen, M., 172
Groenman, A. P., 360
Groh, A. M., 332
Grolnick, W. S., 498
Grön, G., 337
Groothuis, T. G. G., 62
Gross, L., 193
Grossmann, K., 218
Grusec, J. E., 310–314, 324, 327, 332, 416, 417, 421, 423
Grych, J. H., 425
Gudmundsson, G., 143
Guerdjikova, A. I., 350
Guerin, D. W., 244
Guerrero, M. C. M., 25
Guerrini, I., 102
Guerrini, R., 166
Gunnar, M. R., 226
Gushue, G. V., 509
Guzzetti, B. J., 335

Habersaat, S., 123
Hackman, D. A., 347
Haden, C. A., 287
Hagenauer, M. H., 472
Hahn, R. A., 508
Haier, R. J., 401, 408
Hains, S. M. J., 172
Haith, M. M., 167, 173, 177
Hakuta, K., 291
Halgin, R. P., 438
Halim, M. L., 336, 340
Hall, J., 421
Hall, J. A., 524
Hall, S. G., 7, 450
Halle, P. A., 201
Halmi, K. A., 478
Halpern, D., 495
Halpern, D. F., 496, 497
Halpern, R., 527
Hamilton, B. E., 539, 540
Hammen, C., 426
Hammond, N. R., 299
Han, W., 428
Hancock, J. E., 189
Handen, B., 236
Hane, A. A., 143
Hangal, S., 428
Hankin, B. L., 217, 441

Hannon, E. E., 207
Hannon, P., 158, 260
Harel, Z., 459
Harkonen, J., 318
Harlow, H. F., 221–222, 224–226
Harris, P. L., 296
Harris, S. R., 196
Harrison, K., 478
Hart, D., 504
Harter, S., 332, 419, 420, 515, 521, 522
Hartocollis, A., 118, 119
Hartung, P. J., 316, 317
Hartup, W. W., 524, 526
Harvey, E., 428
Harvey, J. H., 426
Hasan, Y., 36
Hasselhorn, M., 388
Hassett, J. M., 338
Hastings, P. D., 324, 327
Hauck, F. R., 144
Haushofer, J., 27
Haworth, C. M. A., 407
Hay, C., 546
Hay, D. F., 323
Hayatbakhsh, M. R., 100
Haynie, D. L., 526
Haywood, K. M., 169, 170, 255, 257
Healy, M. D., 318
Heard, E., 54
Hebebrand, J., 63
Hediger, M. L., 50
Heetman, I., 506
Heimann, M., 197
Heindel, J. J., 103, 104
Heinonen, K., 122
Helwig, C. C., 504
Henley, T., 8, 18
Henricks, T. S., 321
Henry, A., 441
Henry, K. L., 434, 507
Hensch, T. K., 179
Henzi, S. P., 526
Herbenick, D., 531
Hergenhahn, B.R., 8, 18
Herrera-Marschitz, M., 121
Hertz-Lazarowitz, R., 526
Hervey-Jumper, H., 362
Hesketh, T., 67
Hetherington, E. M., 39, 310, 425, 427
Hewitt, P. L., 440
Higgins, H., 435
Hill, C. A., 246
Hill, N. E., 498, 505
Hill, P. L., 494
Hill, P. S., 142, 143
Hill, S. E., 246
Hillerer, K. M., 128
Hilliard, L. J., 336
Hills, A. P., 452
Hindley, C. B., 169
Hines, M., 21, 99, 246, 247, 323, 340
Hinney, A., 63
Hirsch, B. J., 526
Hodapp, R. M., 401
Hoff, E., 200, 201, 207, 209
Hoff, E. V., 278, 279
Hoffman, K. L., 330
Hoffman, L. W., 428
Hoffmann, J., 278
Hofmann, W., 326
Hogue, A., 485
Hohmann, L. M., 319
Holden, G. W., 310
Holditch-Davis, D., 124
Holland, A., 301

cerebellum
    defined, 164
    functions, 253
cerebral cortex
    autism and, 235
    brain development in adolescence, 464
    Broca's and Wernicke's areas of, 209f
cerebrum, 164
cervix, in labor, 113
Cesarean section, childbirth, 119–120, 119f
    hypoxia, reducing risk of, 120
    indications for, 119
    preventing HIV/AIDS, 119–120
Charles (Prince of England), 259
child abuse and neglect
    causes of, 230–231
    eating disorders and, 477
    effects of, 230
    incidence of, 228–229, 228f, 229f
    sexual abuse, 230
    solutions/prevention, 232–233
    types of neglect, 230t
Child and Adult Care Food Program, 155
childbirth. See birth
child-centered programs, 290
child development
    active–passive controversy, 32
    birth order and, 317–319
    continuity–discontinuity controversy,
        31–32
    defined, 4–5
    history of study of, 6–7
    nature–nurture controversy, 31
    peer relationships and, 319
    pioneers in study of, 7
    play and, 320–323. See also play
    reasons for studying, 5–6
    theories of. See theories of child
        development
child development study. See study of child
    development
Childhood and Society (Erikson), 219
Childhood anxiety, 441–442
childhood asthma, 351–354
childhood depression, 439–441, 442
    origins of, 439–441
    treatment for, 441
childhood disintegrative disorder, 233
childhood immunizations, 263–264,
    264t, 265f
childhood memory, 298
child labor, 6, 7p
child pornography, sexting as, 533
child rearing, 310–311. See also
    parenting styles
children
    African American, ADHD and, 362
    coping with fear, 333
    day care, attachment and, 236–237
    defined, 4
    divorce and, 423–426
    drawings, motor skills and, 258
    eyewitness testimony of, 389
    friendship, five stages of, 431–432, 431t
    obesity in, 348–351. See also obesity, in
        children
    parental age and, 105
    parental employment and, 427–429
    parental relationship and, 421–423,
        426–427
    questions about sex, 424
    social deprivation studies and, 225–227
Children's Television Act, 291
chlamydia infections, 466, 468t
chorionic villus sampling (CVS), 58–59

chromosomal abnormalities
    amniocentesis and, 57–58, 58f
    Down syndrome, 53, 53f, 55t
    genetic disorders and, 55t
    sex-linked, 54, 55t
chromosomes
    defined, 48
    genes and, 48–49
    ova and, 66
    sex differentiation and, 82
    23 pairs of, 50f
chronological age (CA), 395–396
chronosystems, 23f, 24
cigarettes, prenatal use of, 102–103
classical conditioning, 13–17
    bedwetting, 13f
    in neonates, 139
class inclusion, 283, 283f
    concrete operations and, 374
clear-cut attachment phase, 220
Clinical Evaluation of Language
    Fundamentals–Preschool (CELF-P), 101
cliques, 526
clitoris, 457
Clomiphene, fertility drug, 69
cocaine, 100–101, 479, 483
cognitive behavioral therapy
    ADHD and, 361
    eating disorders and, 478
    separation anxiety and, 444–445
cognitive development
    commercials and, 292
    couch-potato effect, 292–293
    day care and, 237
    educational television and, 291–292
    gender differences and, 339–340
    home environment and, 288–289
    individual differences among infants,
        195–197
    information processing, 20–21, 29,
        192–193
    language development and. See language
        development
    Piaget's theory of, 18–19, 29, 184–191,
        278–286
    play and, 320–321
    preschool education and, 290–291
    social influences on early, 194
    stages of (Piaget), 19–20
    Vygotsky's views on, 287–288
cognitive-developmental theory, 339–340, 417
cognitive factors theory, aggression and,
    327–328
cognitive functioning
    individual differences among infants,
        195–197
    preterm low birth weight infants and, 122
    testing infants, 196
cognitive scaffolding, 25
cognitive view of attachment, 220, 224
cohort effect, 40
cold parents, 310
collectivist, 316, 317
colors, neonates' vision and, 136–137
colostrum, 158
"coming out," adolescent sexual orientation
    and, 532
commercials, children and, 292, 293
commitment, 517
communication disorders, 365–366
conception, odds against, 64–68
concrete operational stage (Piaget), 19, 20
    application to education, 374–375
    aspects of, 375
    class inclusion, 374

conservation, 372–373, 372f
    defined, 372
    evaluation of theory, 376
    transitivity, 373–374, 374f
condoms, STIs and, 469
conduct disorders
    about, 438, 442
    bullying and, 434
    origins of, 438
    treatment of, 439
cones, 137
confidential information, in studies, 43
conflict in adolescence, 523
congenital syphilis, 96
consent, research and, 42
conservation
    concrete operations and, 372–373, 372f
    defined, 375
    preoperational children and,
        282–283, 282f
constructive play, 320
contact comfort, 221–222, 224
continuity–discontinuity controversy, 31–32
contraception
    teenager use of, 533–534, 535f
contrast assumption, 301
control group, 38
conventional career typology, 510f, 511
conventional level, of moral development,
    379t, 379–380
convergence, vision and, 136, 136f
convergent thinking, 405
cooing, infants and, 198
cooperative play, 321, 322
coordination
    of secondary schemes, 186
    of senses, 177
coregulation, 423
corpus callosum, 254
correlation, 35
correlational information, 35–37
correlation coefficient, 35
correlation study method, 35–37
corticosteroids, prenatal exposure to,
    104, 108
co-sleeping, 270
couch-potato effect, 292–293
cradle boards, motor development and,
    169–170, 170f
crawling, motor development, 168, 168f
creative intelligence, 391–392
creativity, intelligence and, 404–405
creeping, motor development, 168
crib death. See Sudden infant death syndrome
    (SIDS)
critical periods, in prenatal development,
    94, 96f
cross-role activities, play, 323
cross-sectional research, 39–40
cross-sequential research, 40–41
crowds, 526
crying, in neonates, 142–144
C-sections, childbirth, 119–120
cultural bias, intelligence testing and, 399
cultural–familial disability, 401
culture
    adolescent death and, 471–472
    anxiety in children and, 441–443
    asthma, childhood and, 351, 354
    authoritarian parenting and, 313
    bilingualism and, 410
    Cattel's Culture-Fair intelligence test, 399f
    child development and, 5
    childhood depression and, 440
    child rearing in U.S. and Japan, 316t

age of instability, 552
age of possibilities, 553
age of self-focus, 552
gender roles and, 551–552
emotion
  defined, 239
  overeating and, 351
  self-conscious, 242
  stuttering and, 366
emotional development
  conduct disorders and. *See* conduct disorders
  day care and, 237
  defined, 239
  depression and, 439–441. *See also* depression
  emotional regulation, 241
  fear of strangers, 240
  fears and, 332–334
  initiative *vs.* guilt, 332
  patterns of attachment, 239–240
  psychoanalytical theory of, 416–417
  self and, 331–332
  siblings and, 314–317
  social cognitive theory, 417
  social referencing, 240–241
emotional intelligence, 393
emotional learning, 13
emotional regulation, 241
empathy, 324
empirical approach, 32
employment
  adolescent, 511–512
  parental, effects on children, 427–429
  See also career development
encode, 383
encopresis, 272
  risk factors for, 274*t*
endoderm, 80
endometriosis, 69
endometrium, 66, 69
enterprising career typology, 510*f*, 511
enuresis, 271–272
environment
  goodness of fit, temperament and, 245
  intelligence and, 407–408
environment, prenatal development and
  drugs, parental use, 98–103
  hazards, 103–104
  maternal stress, 104, 108
  nutrition, 91–94
  risks to embryo and fetus, 106–107
  teratogens, maternal health and, 94–98
environment *vs.* heredity. *See* nature *vs.* nurture
epidural anesthesia kit, 116
epigenesis, 62
epigenetic framework, 62
epiphyseal closure, 455
episiotomy, 113–114
episodic memory, 298
equilibration, 19
Erikson, Erik
  attachment, 221
  Childhood and Society, 219
  emerging adulthood, 553
  identity development, 516
  psychosocial development, 10–12, 28, 417
estrogen, 54, 457
ethics, research and, 42
ethnic groups
  breast feeding and, 158
  IQ and, 402–403
  motor development and, 169
  sociocultural perspective and, 26

ethnic identity, 520
ethnic identity search, 520
ethnicity
  birth rate of teens and, 539–540*f*. *See also* teenage pregnancy
  career self-efficacy expectancies and, 509
  friendships, 525–526
  college plans, substance abuse and, 482
  hate and, 326
  identity development and, 518–520
  juvenile delinquency and, 544–545
  race and, developmental concepts of, 285
  suicide and, 548
ethological view of attachment, 222, 224
ethology
  Ainsworth/Bowlby attachment and, 222–223
  evolution and, biological perspective, 21–22
Eustachian tube, 348
evocative genetic–environmental correlation, 62
evolution
  ethology and, biological perspective, 21–22
  heredity, gender differences and, 337, 341
evolutionary theory of aggression, 326
exercise
  motor development and, 357
  overweight children and, 352
  in pregnancy, 117
existential intelligence, 392*f*, 393
exosystem, ecological perspective, 22, 23*f*, 24
experiment (method of study)
  advantages over correlation, 37
  control groups, 38
  defined, 37
  experimental group, 38
  independent and dependent variables, 37–38
  random assignment, 38
experimental group, 38
exploration, 517
expressive language
  disorder, 365, 366
  style, 201
expressive vocabulary, 200
extinction, 205

F

facial expressions, 239
Facebook, 525, 529*t*, 533
factor, 391
factor analysis, 391
factor theories of intelligence, 391
failure to thrive (FTT), 154–155
fair-weather cooperation, 431*t*
fallopian tubes, 65
false beliefs, theory mind and, 294–295, 295*f*
family
  about, 421
  divorce, generation X and, 423–427
  influence in middle childhood, 421–429
  lesbian and gay parents, 422–423
  parental employment, effects on children, 427–429
  parent–child relationship, 421–423
  stepfamilies, 426
family-based group cognitive–behavioral treatment (FGCBT), 444
Fantz, Robert, 135, 172
fast food
  growth and, 347
  obesity and, 347

fast-mapping, vocabulary development and, 300–301
Father Knows Best, 550
fathers
  attachment and, 218–219
  behavior toward infant boys/girls, 246–247
  expectant, 95
  Lamaze method of childbirth and, 118
  newborn bonding and, 130–131
  older, risks, 105
  See also parents
fear
  coping with, 333
  development of, 332–334
  of strangers, emotional development and, 240
  See also anxiety
feedback loop, of puberty, 452
feeling in-between, age of, 553
Feingold, Benjamin, 360
Feingold diet, 360
Fels Longitudinal Study, 39, 400, 400*f*
fertility rates, worldwide, 92*t*
fetal activity, 87
fetal alcohol effect (FAE), 102
fetal alcohol syndrome, 5, 101–102
fetal malnutrition, 92–93
fetal monitoring, in childbirth, 121
fetal movement, first, 87*f*
fetal perception, 88
fetal stage, prenatal development, 85–87, 87*f*
fetus, stages of development, 80*f*, 85*p*, 86*p*
fine motor skills, 257, 257*t*, 355
firstborn children, birth order and, 318–319
fitness, motor development and, 357
fixed action pattern (FAP), 22, 44
flu, pregnancy and, 97
folic acid, prenatal, 93
food
  additives, ADHD and, 360
  early exposure to different, 178
  making healthy choices, 353
  See also eating disorders; fast food; nutrition
Food Stamp Program, 155
food timeline (first 2 years), 157
foreclosure (identity), 518, 520
formal games, play and, 320
formal operational stage, 19, 20
  defined, 490
  hypothetical thinking, 490–491
  reevaluation of theory, 493
  symbols, sophisticated use of, 491
fraternal twins. *See* dizygotic (DZ) twins; twins
Freud, Anna, 450
Freud, Sigmund, 7
  genital stage, 450
  latency stage, 9, 10, 416
  oral activities, attachment and, 221
  psychosexual development theory, 9–12, 28
friendships
  adolescent, 524–525. *See also* peer relationships
  development of, 430–432, 431*t*
  interethnic among children, 285
  peer relationships, child development and, 319
fruit, adolescent intake of, 473
functional magnetic resonance imaging (fMRI), 465
functional play, 320

hormones
  menstrual cycle regulation and, 458–459
  prenatal parental use of, 99
Horney, Karen, 12
hue, 136
human development
  contexts of, 23f
  See also development
human diversity, sociocultural perspective
  and, 26–27, 30
human nature, child development and, 5
human papillomavirus (HPV), 466, 469t
hunger
  child poverty and, 155–156
  wasting away from, 159–160
Huntington disease (HD), 55t, 56
hyperactivity, ADHD and, 359
HypnoBirthing, 117
hypnosis, childbirth and, 117
hypothalamus, 350, 452
hypothesis, 33
hypothetical thinking, 490–491
hypoxia, 121

I

id, 9
ideal self, 522
identity achievement, 517, 518
identity crisis, 12, 13, 516
identity development
  Erikson's view of, 516
  ethnicity and, 518–520
  gender and, 520–521
  identity statuses, 517–518
  self-concept, 521
  self-esteem, 521–522
identity diffusion, 516, 517
identity exploration, 552
identity statuses, 517–518
identity *vs.* role diffusion stage, 11
illness, minor/major, ages 2–6, 262–266
imaginary audience, 493–494
imaginary friends, pretend play, 279
imitation
  infants and, 192, 193f
  language development and, 203–204
immanent justice, 377, 378
immunizations, 263–264, 264t, 265f
imprinting, 22, 222
increased arousal, 330
incubator, preterm and low birth weight
  infants, 123
independent variable, 37
indiscriminate attachment, 219–220
individualist, 316, 317
inductive techniques, of enforcing
  restrictions, 311
Industrial Revolution, child development
  and, 6
industry *vs.* inferiority, 10, 417
infancy, 4
  body proportions, changes in, 152–154,
    153f
  catch-up growth, 155
  cephalocaudal development, 150
  differentiation, 152
  failure to thrive, 154–155
  growth patterns, height/weight, 152–154,
    153f
  proximodistal development, 150–152
  sequences of, 151
  See also infants
infant-directed speech, 206–207
infanticide, 426

infants
  brain development. *See* brain development
  differences in functioning among, 195
  first words, 200–201. *See also* vocabulary
    development
  food timeline, first two years, 157
  heroin/methadone addiction, 100
  imitation, 192, 193f
  maternal mortality and, around the world,
    125, 126t
  memory and, 192, 192f
  motor development. *See* motor
    development
  nervous system development. *See* nervous
    system development
  nutrition, growth, 155–157, 156f
  operant conditioning and vocalization
    in, 16
  premature, 97
  preterm low birth weight infants, 121–124
  See also infancy; neonates
inferior visual cortex, 464f
infertility, assisted reproductive technology
  and
  adoption, 72–73
  artificial insemination, 70–71
  causes of, 68–69
  defined, 68
  donor IVF, 71
  in vitro fertilization, 71
  surrogate mothers, 71–72
information-processing theory, 20–21, 29
  defined, 380
  imitation, infant, 192, 193f
  infants memory, 192, 192f
  long-term memory, 385–386, 386f.
    See also long-term memory
  selective attention, development of,
    381, 381f
  sensory memory, 382
  storage and retrieval of information,
    382–388
  working memory (short-term), 382–383
informed consent, 42
Inhelder, Bärbel, 492
inhibition, 361
initial pre-attachment phase, 220
initiative *vs.* guilt
  emotional development and, 332
  psychosocial stage of development, 10
inner speech. *See* private speech
insecure attachment, 216–217
insomnia, 269
instability, age of, 552
intellectual development
  creativity and, 404–405
  differences in, 401–402, 404
  environmental influences, 407–408
  genetic influences, 406–407, 406f
  giftedness, 402, 404
  intellectual disability, 401–402
  measures of, 393–397
  nature and nurture in, 405–408
  patterns of, 400–401, 400f
  Stanford-Binet Intelligence Scale (SBIS),
    395–396, 396t
  Wechsler Scales, 397, 397t, 398f
intellectual disability, 401–402
intelligence
  Cattel's Culture-Fair test of, 399f
  creativity and, 404–405
  defined, 390
  emotional, 393
  factor theories of, 391
  items on test, 398f

multiple, 392–393
  social, 393
  tests, cultural bias, 397–399, 399f
  theories of, 394
  triarchic theory of, 391–392, 391f
  variations in scores, 398f
intelligence quotients, 394. *See also* IQ scores
intensity, 136
interest level, memory and, 298
intergenerational transmission of
  attachment, 217
Internet
  cyberbullying and, 434
  social networking, of adolescents,
    528–529
interpersonal intelligence, 392f
intervention, for preterm low birth weight
  infants, 124
intimacy *vs.* isolation, psychosocial stage of
  development, 11
intimate and mutual sharing, 431t
intonation, 200
intrapersonal intelligence, 392f
intrauterine insemination (IUI), 70
investigative career typology, 510f, 510
in vitro fertilization (IVF), 71
IQ scores
  home environment and, 288–289
  individual differences in, of infant, 196
  intellectual disability and, 401
  patterns of change in, 400f
  preschool programs and, 290
  testing, cultural bias, 397–399, 399f
  variations in, 398f
  See also intelligence; intelligence quotients
irreversibility, preoperational, 283
Izard, Carroll, 239

J

job fair, 510f
Jolie, Angelina, 73
Jones, Mary Cover, 333
*Journal of the American Medical Association,
  The*, 93
judgment
  moral development and, 500–505
junk food, 473
juvenile delinquency
  characteristics of, 545–546
  defined, 544
  delinquents, 551
  ethnicity, gender and, 544–545
  prevention and treatment of, 546

K

Kellogg, Rhoda, 258
kinesthetic intelligence, 392f
kinship studies, 63
Klinefelter syndrome, 54
knowledge, origins of, 295
Kohlberg, Lawrence
  gender constancy, 339–340
  theory of moral development, 378–380,
    379t, 499–505
kwashiorkor (malnutrition), 158, 159

L

labia, 457
labor. *See* birth
Lady Gaga, 434
Lamaze method of childbirth, 118
language

gross motor skills, 254–255, 255t, 354–355
handedness, right or left, 258–260. *See also* handedness, right or left
hands, control of, 167
infant, 151
lifting and holding torso and head, 167
locomotion, 168–169
nature and nurture in, 169–170
physical activity, 256, 357. *See also* physical activity
preterm low birth weight infants, 122
Müllerian ducts, 82–83
multiculturalism, children and, 24
multifactorial problems, 52
multiple intelligences, 392–393, 392f
multiple sclerosis, 163
muscular dystrophy, 57
music
brain development and, 464f
fetal perception and, 88
musical intelligence, 392f
mutations, 49
mutism, 234
My Daily Food Plan, 261
myelination, 163
myelin, 163
myelin sheaths, nervous system development and, 163
My Fair Lady (movie), 435
MySpace, 528
MZ twins. *See* monozygotic (MZ) twins

N

naming speed, 365
National Longitudinal Survey of Youth, 427–428
National School Lunch and School Breakfast programs, 155
nativist view of language development, 207–208
natural childbirth, 117
naturalistic observation, 33, 34
naturalist intelligence, 392f
nature, 31
nature *vs.* nurture
brain development and, 165–166
controversy, 31
debate, 8
in motor development, 169–170
roles in perceptual development, 179–180
See also heredity and environment
negative correlations, 35, 36, 37f
negative reinforcers, 14, 15, 15f
neglect. *See* child abuse and neglect
Neonatal Intensive Care Unit Network Neurobehavioral Scale (NNNS), 132, 132t
neonate(s)
classical conditioning in, 139
crying in, 142–144
defined, 112
health of, assessing, 131–133
learning ability, 139–140
operant conditioning of, 139–140, 140f
reflexes of, 133–134
sensory capabilities of, 134–139
shape constancy and, 174
sleep and waking, 140–142, 141t
sudden infant death syndrome (SIDS) and, 144–145
visual preferences, developing, 172–174, 172f, 173f

nerves, development of, 162
nervous system development
myelin, 163
neurons, development of, 162–163
neural, 133
neural connections, increase in brain, 165f
neural tube, 80
neural tube defects, maternal obesity and, 93
neurological development
depression and, 441
preterm low birth weight infants, 122
reading skills, 409
neuron(s), 81
anatomy of, 163f
development of, 464
nervous system development, 162
neurotransmitters, 82
autism and, 235–236
nervous system development, 162
niche-picking, 62
nicotine, 482
nightmares, 269
nocturnal emissions, 455
nonorganic FTT, 154
non-rapid eye movement sleep (non-REM), 141–142, 141f
nonsocial play, 321
nurture
defined, 31
gender typing and, 341
language development and, 203–205
nutrition
in adolescence, 472–473
breastfeeding *vs.* bottle, 157–162
growth patterns and, 347
growth spurts and, 454
infant growth and, 155–157, 156f
maternal weight gain and, 92, 93
menarche and, 458f
needs, ages 2–6, 260
patterns of eating, ages 2–6, 260–261
prenatal, 91–93
See also fast food; obesity

O

obesity
in adolescents, 472
breast feeding and, 158
causes of, 350–351
in children, 348–349, 349f
healthy food choices, 353
managing weight and, 352
prenatal, 93
objective morality, 377
object permanence, 187–189, 188f, 189f, 191
observation, methods of, 34–35
observational learning, 17, 330
obstetrician, selecting, 81
one-way assistance, 431t
onlooker play, 321, 322
operant conditioning, 13–16
coping with fear and, 333
in neonates, 139–140
vocalization in infants, 16
operations, 279
oral rehydration therapy, 262
oral sex, 535
oral stage, of psychosexual development, 9, 10
organic FTT, 154
organization of brain, gender differences and, 337–338
orphans, social deprivation study and, 227. *See also* adoption

osteoporosis, 472
ova
conception and, 65, 68, 68f
infertility and, 69
overextension, vocabulary development, 201–202
overregularization, language development and, 302–303
overweight. *See* obesity
ovulation, 50
oxygen deprivation, childbirth and, 121
oxytocin, 112, 130
breast milk production and, 161

P

pacifiers, infant crying and, 143
pain, neonates and, 139
paradoxical sleep, 141
parallel play, 321
parent behavior, toward infant boys/girls, 246–247
parent–child bonding, post birth, 129
parent–child relationship, middle childhood, 421–423
parenting styles
adolescent development and, 524
adolescent drug use and, 485
authoritarian, 313
authoritative, 312
patterns of, 312t
permissive, 313
siblings, influence of, 314–317
situation, effects of on child and, 314, 314t
parents
adolescent relationship with, 523–524
child abuse, stress and, 230–231
conduct disorder of children and, 438–439
divorce, 423–427
influence on adolescent sexual behavior, 536
juvenile delinquency and, 545
lesbian and gay, 422–423
moral development, influence on child, 503
restrictive/permissive, 310–311
sex education and, 542–543
teaching hate, 326
warmth/coldness of, 310
See also family, influence in middle childhood
participant modeling, coping with fear and, 333
passive genetic–environmental correlation, 61
passive sentences, vocabulary development and, 303–304
patterns, of infant cries, 142–143
Pediatrics journal, 537
peer groups, friendships and, 526–527
peer influence, 527–528
peer relationships
acceptance and rejection, 430
adolescent drug use and, 485
adolescent relationship with, 524–525
child development and, 319
dating and romantic, 527
friendships, adolescent, 525–526
friendships, development of, 430–432, 431t
peer groups, 526–527
peer influence, 527–528
self-esteem and, 420
sexual behavior, influences, 537
as socialization influences, 429
social networking online, 528–529

psychotherapy, for depression, 441
psychotic features, postpartum, 128
puberty
    body image in, 462–463
    defined, 451
    female development, 457–459, 460
    growth spurt in adolescence, 452–455, 452f
    hormones, role of, 452
    male development, 455–456
    maturation, early *vs.* late, 459–462
    menarche, 457–458. *See also* menarche
    sexual behavior, effects on adolescents, 536
pudendal block, childbirth, 117
punishments, 15
    behavior and, 14–16
    encopresis and, 272
    negative reinforcers *vs.*, 15f
Pygmalion effect, 436
Pygmalion in the Classroom, 436

Q

questions, vocabulary development and, 303

R

race
    adoption, intelligence and, 406
    African Americans, ADHD and, 362
    birth rate of teens, 539–540f. *See also* teenage pregnancy
    conduct disorders and, 438–439
    death rates, adolescence and, 471–472
    divorce and, 423
    employment, adolescent, 511–512
    environmental influences, IQ and, 407
    ethnic identity, career and, 509
    ethnicity and, 285, 544–545
    gender, friendships ethnicity and, 525–526
    genetic abnormalities and, 56
    hate and, 326
    identity development and, 518–520
    intelligence quotients and, 395
    IQ and, 397–399, 402–403
    obesity in children and, 348–349
    school dropout rates and, 507
    substance abuse, college plans, ethnicity and, 482
    suicide and, 548
radiation, prenatal exposure to, 104
random assignment, 38
rapid eye movement sleep (REM), 141–142
reaction time, 355
reactive-attachment disorder, 155
reading
    disability, 363. *See also* dyslexia
    gender differences in, 494
    methods of teaching, 409–410
    skills, middle childhood, 409
realistic career typology, 510f, 510
reality distinction, appearance and, 295–296
real self, 522
reasoning, moral, 504
recall, recognition and, memory tasks, 296, 297
recall memory, development of, 387–388
receptive vocabulary, 200
recessive traits, 50–52, 51f, 52t
reciprocal in vitro fertilization (RIVF), 70
reciprocity, 501
recognition and recall memory, 296–297, 297f
reduction division, 49
referential language style, 201

reflexes, of neonates, 19, 133–134
regression, 316
rehearsal, memory and, 299
rehearsal strategies, 385
rehearse, 383
reinforcement, 15
    behavior, 14
    role of, in language development, 204–205
rejecting–neglecting parents, 313
rejection, peer, 430
religion, identity development and, 519
REM sleep, 141–142, 141f, 269
reproductive organs, female, 65f
reproductive technology, infertility and. *See* infertility, assisted reproductive technology
research
    attitudes toward living together before marriage, 36
    bedwetting treatment, 14
    bullying, epidemic of pain, 434–435
    children's storytelling ability, 287
    cross-cultural differences in sleeping arrangements, 270
    daddy hormones, 130
    early math, importance of, 387
    effects of scaffolding on children's abilities, 287
    eyewitness testimony of children, 389
    fetal perception, 88
    hate, teaching to, 326
    Little Albert study, 42
    mirror neurons, infant imitation and, 193, 193f
    object permanence in animals, 191
    operant conditioning for vocalization in infants, 16
    puzzle and pendulum, 492
    sex selection, 72
    shape constancy, 175
    teaching, long-term effects of good, 384
    visual acuity in neonates, 135
research, ethical considerations, 42–43
respiratory distress syndrome, preterm and lowbirthweight infants, 123
restrictions
    inductive technique, 311
    power-assertive methods of enforcing, 311–312
    withdrawal of love, 312
restrictive parents, 310–311
retrieval cues, memory and, 298–299
Rett's disorder, 233
Rheingold, Harriet, 16
reversibility, 372
Rh incompatibility, 98
Rh-positive antibodies, 94
RIASEC method (career typology), 509–511
right brain development, 253–254
risk factor(s)
    asthma, childhood, 354
    delinquency, 545–546
    drug use, 484–485
    eating disorders, 477
    encopresis, 274t
    STI contraction, 467
ritual, autism and, 234
Rockefeller, Nelson, 363
rods, 137
roll over (motor development), 168
rooting reflex, of neonates, 133
rote learning, 383
rough-and-tumble play, 256
Rousseau, Jean-Jacques, 6
rubella, pregnancy and, 97

S

SAD. *See* separation anxiety
Salovey, Peter, 393
saturation, 136
SBIS (Stanford-Binet Intelligence Scales), 395–396, 396t
scaffolding
    early childhood cognitive development and, 287–288
    social influences, on cognitive development, 194
    sociocultural theory and, 25
Scarr, Sandra, 61
schemes, in cognitive development, 19, 184
schizophrenia
    birth, oxygen deprivation and, 121
    risk factors, 365
school, adolescents in
    dropping out of, 506–508
    elementary school, transition from, 505–506
    nutrition and, 472–473
    working students, effects of, 512
school, influence on development
    bullying, 434–435
    depression in children and, 440
    environment, 433–435
    first experiences, 432–433
    influence of teachers, 435
    social and emotional development, 432
    teacher expectations, 435–436
school phobia, 443–445
school refusal, 443–445
scripts, 297
secondary circular reactions, 185
secondary sex characteristics, 452
Secret Life of the American Teenager, The, 537
secular trend, in growth, 454–455, 454f
secure attachment, 216–217, 218
sedatives, 482
selection factor, 101, 537
selective attention, 381, 381f
selective serotonin reuptake inhibitors (SSRIs), 236, 441
self
    development of, 331–332
    in relation to others, 317f
self-awareness, 242
self-concept
    defined, 242
    development of, 242, 418–419, 521
self-efficiency expectations, 509
self-esteem
    authoritative parenting and, 420
    in adolescence, 521–522
    depression and, 440
    social development and, 419–420
self-focus, age of, 552
self-fulfilling prophecies, 436
self-mutilation, autism and, 235
Selman, Robert, 417, 431
semantic code, 385–386
semen production, 455
sensations, 171
senses, coordination of, 177
sensitive period, language development and, 208–210
sensorimotor stage (Piaget's theory of cognitive development), 19, 20
    mental combinations, 186–187
    primary circular reactions, 184–185
    secondary circular reactions, 185
    secondary schemes, 186